barbri®

BAR REVIEW

Constitutional Law

celebrating **35** **YEARS** *of preparing law students for the bar exam*

BAR REVIEW

A Thomson Company

Director
Professor Richard J. Conviser

BAR/BRI Multistate Board
Coordinator
Richard F. Duffy, Esq.

Editors
Elizabeth L. Snyder, Esq.
Roger W. Meslar, Esq.
Steven J. Levin, Esq.
Deborah A. Grimm, Esq.
Lisa D. Senter, Esq.
Michelle M. Oberts, Esq.
Paul T. Phillips, Esq.

Multistate

Table of Contents

At BAR/BRI We Take The Multistate Every Time—
So You Only Have To Take It Once.
That's Why Our Multistate Program Has No Equal!

celebrating
35 YEARS
of preparing
law students
for the bar exam

CONSTITUTIONAL LAW

TABLE OF CONTENTS

PART ONE: POWERS OF THE FEDERAL GOVERNMENT

I. THE JUDICIAL POWER

A. ARTICLE III
The federal government is a government of limited powers, which means that for federal action to be legitimate, it must be authorized. The Constitution is the instrument that authorizes the federal government to act. Thus, whenever a question involves action by an entity of the federal government, the action will be valid only if it is authorized by the Constitution. The Constitution authorizes a federal court system in Article III, which provides that federal courts shall have judicial power over all "*cases and controversies*":

1. Arising under the Constitution, laws, or treaties of the United States;

2. Of admiralty and maritime jurisdiction;

3. In which the United States is a party;

4. Between two or more states;

5. Between a state and citizens of another state;

6. Between citizens of different states;

7. Between citizens of the same state claiming lands under grants of different states; and

8. Between a state or citizens thereof and foreign states, citizens, or subjects.

B. POWER OF JUDICIAL REVIEW

1. Review of Other Branches of Federal Government
The Constitution does not explicitly state that the Supreme Court may determine the constitutionality of acts of other branches of government. However, judicial review of other branches of the federal government was established in *Marbury v. Madison*, 5 U.S. 137 (1803) (per Marshall, C.J.); the Constitution is "law" and it is the province and duty of the judiciary to declare what the law is.

a. Separation of Powers and Finality of Court Decisions
The Constitution separates governmental powers among the branches of government. This separation of powers doctrine prohibits the legislature from interfering with the courts' final judgments.
Example: The Supreme Court inferred a limitations period under an ambiguous federal securities law. Because new Supreme Court rulings generally apply to all pending cases, the limitations period imposed by the Court resulted in the dismissal of many pending cases as time-barred. Congress amended the securities law to provide (i) a different limitations period and (ii) a special motion for reinstating the cases dismissed as time-barred by the Supreme Court's ruling. The Supreme Court held that the statute providing for the reinstatement of the dismissed cases violated the separation of powers doctrine under the Constitution. [Plaut v. Spendthrift Farm, Inc., 514 U.S. 211 (1995)]

2. Federal Review of State Acts
Federal review of state acts (executive, legislative, or judicial) was established by the Marshall Court in a series of decisions. Clear basis exists here in the Supremacy Clause of Article VI, which states that the Constitution, Laws, and Treaties of the United States take precedence over state laws and that the judges of the state courts must follow federal law, anything in the constitution or laws of any state to the contrary notwithstanding. [Fletcher v. Peck, 10 U.S. 87 (1810)]

C. FEDERAL COURTS
Only the actions of Article III courts are the subject of our outline, but you should know that there are two types of federal courts.

1. Article III Courts
Article III courts are those established by Congress pursuant to the provisions of Article III,

Section 1. Although Congress has plenary power to delineate the jurisdictional limits, both original and appellate, of these courts, it is bound by the standards of judicial power set forth in Article III as to subject matter, parties, and the requirement of "case or controversy." Thus, Congress cannot require these courts to render advisory opinions or perform administrative or nonjudicial functions.

2. Article I Courts
Congress has created certain other courts, however, by way of implementing its various legislative powers; *e.g.,* United States Tax Court, courts of the District of Columbia. Judges of such Article I courts do not have life tenure or protection from salary decrease as do Article III court judges. Article I courts are sometimes vested with ***administrative as well as judicial*** functions, and the congressional power to create such "hybrid" courts has been sustained by the Supreme Court. [Glidden v. Zdanok, 370 U.S. 530 (1962)]

a. Limitation
Congress may not take cases of the type traditionally heard by Article III courts and assign jurisdiction over them to Article I courts. [Northern Pipeline Construction Co. v. Marathon Pipeline Co., 458 U.S. 50 (1982)—broad grant of jurisdiction to bankruptcy courts, including jurisdiction over contract claims, violates Article III]

D. JURISDICTION OF THE SUPREME COURT

1. Original (Trial) Jurisdiction
Under Article III, Section 2, the Supreme Court has original jurisdiction "in all cases affecting Ambassadors, other public Ministers and Consuls, and those in which a State shall be a Party." This provision is self-executing: Congress may ***neither restrict nor enlarge*** the Supreme Court's original jurisdiction, but Congress may give concurrent jurisdiction to lower federal courts and has done so regarding all cases except those between states.

2. Appellate Jurisdiction
Article III, Section 2 further provides that "in all other Cases before mentioned [*i.e.,* arising under the Constitution, Act of Congress, or treaty], the Supreme Court shall have appellate jurisdiction, both as to Law and Fact, with such Exceptions, and under such Regulations as the Congress shall make."

a. Statutory Application of Appellate Jurisdiction
Congress has provided two methods for invoking Supreme Court appellate jurisdiction: ***appeal*** (where jurisdiction is mandatory), and ***certiorari*** (where jurisdiction is within the Court's discretion). Very few cases fall within the Court's mandatory appeal jurisdiction; thus, appellate jurisdiction is almost completely discretionary.

1) Writ of Certiorari (Discretionary)
The Supreme Court has complete discretion to hear cases that come to it by writ of certiorari. A case will be heard if four justices agree to hear it. The following cases may be heard by certiorari:

a) Cases from the ***highest state courts*** where (i) the constitutionality of a federal statute, federal treaty, or state statute is called into question; or (ii) a state statute allegedly violates federal law [28 U.S.C. §1257]; and

b) All cases from ***federal courts of appeals*** [28 U.S.C. §1254].

2) Appeal (Mandatory)
The Supreme Court must hear those few cases that come to it by appeal. Appeal is available only as to decisions made by three-judge federal district court panels that grant or deny injunctive relief. [28 U.S.C. §1253]

b. Limitations on Statutory Regulation
Ex parte McCardle, 74 U.S. 506 (1868), has been read as giving Congress full power to regulate and limit the Supreme Court's appellate jurisdiction. However, ***possible*** limitations on such congressional power have been suggested:

1) Congress may eliminate certain avenues for Supreme Court review as long as it does not eliminate all avenues. For example, in *McCardle,* two statutes had allowed the Supreme Court to grant habeas corpus to federal prisoners. The Supreme Court upheld the constitutionality of the repeal of one of the statutes

because the other statute remained as an avenue for Supreme Court habeas corpus review.

2) Although Congress may eliminate Supreme Court review of certain cases within the federal judicial power, it must permit jurisdiction to remain in *some* lower federal court.

3) If Congress were to deny *all* Supreme Court review of an alleged violation of constitutional rights—or go even further and deny a hearing before any federal judge on such a claim—this would violate due process of law.

E. **CONSTITUTIONAL AND SELF-IMPOSED LIMITATIONS ON EXERCISE OF FEDERAL JURISDICTION—POLICY OF "STRICT NECESSITY"**
Even if a federal court has jurisdiction over the subject matter of a case, it still might refuse to hear the case. Whether the court will hear the case (*i.e.,* whether the case is justiciable) depends on whether a "case or controversy" is involved, and on whether other limitations on jurisdiction are present.

1. **No Advisory Opinions**
The Supreme Court's interpretation of the "case and controversy" requirement in Article III bars rendition of "advisory" opinions. Thus, federal courts will not render decisions in *moot* cases, *collusive* suits, or cases involving challenges to governmental legislation or policy whose enforcement is neither actual nor threatened.

   a. **Compare—Declaratory Judgments**
   Federal courts can hear actions for declaratory relief. A case or controversy will exist if there is an actual dispute between parties having adverse legal interest. Complainants must show that they have engaged in (or wish to engage in) specific conduct and that the challenged action poses a *real and immediate danger* to their interests. However, the federal courts will not determine the constitutionality of a statute if it has never been enforced and there is no real fear that it ever will be. [Poe v. Ulman, 367 U.S. 497 (1961)—anticontraceptive law not enforced for 80 years despite open public sales]

2. **Ripeness—Immediate Threat of Harm**
A plaintiff generally is not entitled to review of a state law before it is enforced (*i.e.,* may not obtain a declaratory judgment). Thus, a federal court will not hear a case unless the plaintiff has been harmed or there is an immediate threat of harm.

3. **Mootness**
A federal court will not hear a case that has become moot; a *real, live controversy* must exist *at all stages of review*, not merely when the complaint is filed. [*See, e.g.,* De Funis v. Odegaard, 416 U.S. 312 (1974)—dismissing as moot a white law student's challenge to state's affirmative action program, since the student, although originally passed over for minority applicants with allegedly poorer records, had been admitted to law school while litigation was pending, was about to graduate by the time the case reached the Supreme Court, and would receive the same law degree whether or not the affirmative action program was invalidated]

   a. **Exception—Capable of Repetition But Evading Review**
   Where there is a reasonable expectation that the same complaining party will be subjected to the same action again and would again be unable to resolve the issue because of the short duration of the action (*i.e.,* where the controversy is capable of repetition yet evading review), the controversy will not be deemed moot. [*See* Weinstein v. Bradford, 423 U.S. 147 (1975)]
   Examples: 1) Issue concerns events of short duration (*e.g.,* pregnancy, elections, divorce actions); and

   2) Defendant voluntarily stops the offending practice, but is free to resume it.

   b. **Class Actions**
   A class representative may continue to pursue a class action even though the representative's controversy has become moot, as long as the claims of others in the class are still viable. [United States Parole Commission v. Geraghty, 445 U.S. 388 (1980)]

   c. **Distinguish Ripeness**
   Ripeness and mootness are related concepts in that the court will not hear a case unless

there is a live controversy. Ripeness bars consideration of claims *before* they have been developed; mootness bars their consideration *after* they have been resolved.

4. Standing

The Supreme Court will not decide a constitutional challenge to a government action unless the person who is challenging the government action has "standing" to raise the constitutional issue. A person has standing only if she can demonstrate a concrete stake in the outcome of the controversy.

a. Components

A plaintiff will be able to show a sufficient stake in the controversy only if she can show an *injury in fact*—caused by the government—that will be *remedied* by a decision in her favor (*i.e.,* causation and redressability).

1) Injury

To have standing, a person must be able to assert that she is injured by a government action or that the government has made a clear threat to cause injury to her if she fails to comply with a government law, regulation, or order. Some *specific injury* must be alleged, and it *must be more* than the merely theoretical injury that all persons suffer by seeing their government engage in unconstitutional actions.

Example: A Communist Party member would have standing to challenge a statute making it a crime to be a member of the Communist Party because the member's freedom of association is directly infringed, but a non-Party member would have no standing.

a) Injury Need Not Be Economic

The injury does not always have to be economic. In some cases the Court has found that an individual is harmed because the alleged illegal act or unconstitutional action has an impact on the person's well-being.

Example: Law students were allowed to challenge an Interstate Commerce Commission rate-setting policy on the ground that such policies discouraged recycling and thereby diminished the quality of each student's physical environment. If the ICC rate-setting policy violated congressional statutes, the elimination of those rate-setting policies would have an impact on the students' physical environment. [United States v. SCRAP, 412 U.S. 669 (1973)]

2) Causation

There must be a causal connection between the injury and the conduct complained of—*i.e.,* the injury must be traceable to the challenged conduct of the defendant and not be attributable to some independent third party not before the court.

Example: Plaintiffs claiming that a municipality's zoning policies prevented low income persons from finding housing in the municipality were denied standing because they failed to show a substantial probability that they would be able to afford housing in the municipality even absent the zoning policies. [Warth v. Seldin, 422 U.S. 490 (1975)]

3) Redressability

In determining whether a litigant has a sufficient injury to establish standing, courts ask whether a ruling favorable to the litigant would eliminate the harm to him. If a court order declaring a government action to be illegal or unconstitutional (and ending that government action) would not eliminate the harm to the litigant, then that individual does not have the type of specific injury that would grant him standing to challenge the government action.

Examples: 1) The Supreme Court held that mothers do not have standing to challenge the government's refusal to enforce criminal laws that would require the fathers of their children to pay child support. The enforcement of the criminal laws against a father who is guilty of nonsupport would not necessarily result in the father's providing support to the mother and her children.

2) Indigents have no standing to challenge an Internal Revenue Service policy that allows hospitals to receive favorable tax treatment

even though they refuse to provide free or subsidized care for indigents. The indigents could not demonstrate that a different IRS policy would cause hospitals to provide them with free care.

b. Common Standing Issues

1) Congressional Conferral of Standing
Congress has no power to eliminate the case or controversy requirement, because the requirement is based in the Constitution. [*See* United Food & Commercial Workers Union Local 751 v. Brown Group, Inc., 517 U.S. 544 (1996)]

Example: Congress passes a law prohibiting kite flying on Sundays. The law provides that ***anyone*** who disagrees with it may challenge the law in the Federal District Court for the District of Columbia. This jurisdictional grant violates the case or controversy requirement since it purports to grant standing to persons who have not suffered an "injury in fact." Of course, one arrested for flying a kite on Sundays would have standing.

Compare: Congress passes a law requiring political committees to disclose to voters certain information and providing that ***anyone*** who believes the law has been violated may file a complaint with the Federal Election Commission ("FEC"). The law further provides that any complainant aggrieved by the FEC's dismissal of such a complaint may seek judicial review in district court. This statute is sufficient to give any voter standing. *Rationale:* Although the injury from a failure to disclose is widely shared, it is sufficiently concrete—the law gives voters a right to information, and any voter denied such information has suffered an injury. [Federal Election Commission v. Akins, 524 U.S. 11 (1998)]

2) Standing to Enforce Government Statutes—Zone of Interests
In some instances a plaintiff may bring suit to force government actors to conform their conduct to the requirements of a specific federal statute. Even in such cases, the person must have an "injury in fact." Often, the Court asks whether the injury caused to the individual or group seeking to enforce the federal statute is within the "zone of interests" that Congress meant to protect with the statute. If Congress intended the statute to protect such persons, and intended to allow private persons to bring federal court actions to enforce the statute, the courts are likely to be lenient in granting standing to those persons.

Example: Persons who sold data processing services to private businesses had standing to challenge a ruling by the Comptroller of Currency that allowed national banks to make data processing services available to other banks and bank customers. These plaintiffs had an injury in fact because the Comptroller's ruling would hurt their future profits. The plaintiffs were determined to be within the "zone of interests" protected by the federal statutes limiting the authority of the Comptroller and national banks.

3) Standing to Assert Rights of Others
To have standing, the claimant must have suffered or may presently suffer a direct impairment of his ***own*** constitutional rights. A plaintiff may, however, ***assert third-party rights*** where he himself has suffered injury and:

a) ***Third parties find it difficult to assert their own rights*** (the NAACP was permitted to assert the freedom of association rights of its members in attacking a state law requiring disclosure of membership lists because its members could not file suit without disclosing their identities) [NAACP v. Alabama, 357 U.S. 449 (1958)]; or

b) ***The injury suffered by the plaintiff adversely affects his relationship with third parties***, resulting in an indirect violation of their rights (a vendor of beer was granted standing to assert the constitutional rights of males under 21 in attacking a state law prohibiting sale of beer to them but not to females under 21) [Craig v. Boren, 429 U.S. 190 (1976)].

4) Standing of Organizations

An organization (unincorporated association, corporation, union, etc.) has standing to challenge government action that causes injury to *the organization itself*. An organization also has standing to challenge government actions that cause an injury in fact to *its members if* the organization can demonstrate the following three facts:

(i)   There must be an injury in fact to the members of the organization that would give individual members a right to sue on their own behalf;

(ii) The injury to the members must be related to the organization's purpose; *and*

(iii) Neither the nature of the claim nor the relief requested requires participation of the individual members in the lawsuit.

Example: The All Dentist Association ("ADA") is composed entirely of dentists; its purpose is to promote the professional well-being of dentists. Assume that most ADA members make between $100,000 and $200,000 per year. The ADA would not have standing to challenge a change in the federal income tax rates that will disadvantage all persons making between $100,000 and $200,000 on the basis that the statute deprives all persons (in the income category) of property without due process, because that claim is not related to the organization's purpose—the representation of dentists as such. But the ADA probably could bring a lawsuit challenging a state regulation of dental practices if the regulation injures ADA members, as long as the injury to ADA members does not vary.

Note: Only the first prong of the above three-part test is constitutionally required. Thus, Congress can adopt a statute giving organizations standing even though the nature of the claim asserted or the relief sought would require participation of the individual members in the lawsuit. [United Food & Commercial Workers Union Local 751 v. Brown Group, Inc., *supra*]

5) No Citizenship Standing

As stated above, if an injury is too generalized, there can be no standing. Thus, people have no standing merely "as citizens" to claim that government action violates federal law or the Constitution. Congress cannot change this rule by adopting a statute that would allow persons to have standing merely as citizens (where they otherwise have no direct, personal claim) to bring suit to force the government to observe the Constitution or federal laws. [Lujan v. Defenders of Wildlife, 504 U.S. 555 (1992)]

6) Taxpayer Standing

a) Generally No Standing to Litigate Government Expenditures

A taxpayer, of course, has standing to litigate her tax bill (*e.g.,* whether she really owes X dollars). However, people generally do not have standing as taxpayers to challenge the way tax dollars are spent by the state or federal government, because their interest is too remote.

b) Exception—Measures Under Taxing and Spending Power that Violate Establishment Clause

There is an exception to the general rule: A federal taxpayer has standing to challenge federal appropriation and spending measures if she can establish that the challenged measure:

(i)   Was enacted under Congress's taxing and spending power (*see* II.A.2., 3., *infra*); and

(ii) Exceeds some specific limitation on the power.

To date, the only limit that the Supreme Court has found on the taxing power is the Establishment Clause. (*See* XXII.D., *infra.*)

Note: The measure challenged must arise under the taxing and spending power. Thus, there was no standing to challenge a federal government transfer of surplus property under the Property Clause that allegedly violated the Establishment Clause. [Valley Forge Christian College v. Americans United for Separation of Church and State, 454 U.S. 464 (1982)]

7) Legislators' Standing

Legislators may have standing to challenge the constitutionality of government action if they have a sufficient "personal stake" in the dispute and suffer sufficient "concrete injury." [Raines v. Byrd, 521 U.S. 811 (1997)]

Example: A state's lieutenant governor cast the deciding vote to break a tie in the state senate. Legislators who had voted against the prevailing position had standing to challenge the right of the lieutenant governor to vote because his vote completely nullified theirs and caused the specific legislative enactment to go into effect. [Coleman v. Miller, 307 U.S. 433 (1939)]

Compare: Members of Congress had *no* standing to challenge the Line Item Veto Act authorizing the President to cancel (veto) certain spending and tax law measures that are part of a bill that he signs into law. *Rationale:* Rather than causing a "personal" and "concrete" injury, the challenged statute caused only a type of "institutional" injury to all members of Congress equally. [Raines v. Byrd, *supra*]

5. Adequate and Independent State Grounds

The Supreme Court will hear a case from a state court only if the state court judgment turned on federal grounds. The Court will refuse jurisdiction if it finds *adequate and independent* nonfederal grounds to support the state decision.

a. "Adequate"

The nonfederal grounds must be "adequate" in that they are fully dispositive of the case, so that even if the federal grounds are wrongly decided, it would not affect the outcome of the case. Where that is the case, the Supreme Court's review of the federal law grounds for the state court's decision would have no effect on the judgment rendered by the state court, so that the Supreme Court, in effect, would be rendering an advisory opinion.

b. "Independent"

The nonfederal grounds must also be "independent": If the state court's interpretation of its state provision was based on federal case law interpreting an identical federal provision, the state law grounds for the decision are not independent.

c. Where Basis Is Unclear

If it is unclear whether the state court decision turned on federal or state law, the Supreme Court may dismiss the case or remand it to the state court for clarification. However, the Court will usually assume that there is no adequate state ground unless the state court expressly stated that its decision rests on state law. [*See* Michigan v. Long, 463 U.S. 1032 (1983)]

6. Abstention

a. Unsettled State Law

When a federal constitutional claim is premised on an *unsettled question of state law*, the federal court should stay its hand ("abstain" temporarily), so as to give state courts a chance to settle the underlying state law question and thus potentially avoid the needless resolution of a federal constitutional issue. [Railroad Commission of Texas v. Pullman, 312 U.S. 496 (1941)]

b. Pending State Proceedings

Generally, federal courts will *not enjoin pending state criminal proceedings*. [Younger v. Harris, 401 U.S. 37 (1971)]

1) Pending

State court proceedings are pending if begun before the federal court begins proceedings on the merits. Hence, order of filing charges is irrelevant. "Proceedings of substance" must occur first in federal court before an injunction will issue. [Hicks v. Miranda, 422 U.S. 332 (1975)]

2) Civil and Administrative Proceedings

Federal courts should abstain from enjoining pending state administrative or civil proceedings when those proceedings involve an important state interest.

Examples: 1) A federal court should not enjoin a pending state civil action to remove a child from the child's parents due to alleged child abuse.

2) A federal court should not enjoin: (i) a state court order holding a person or corporation in contempt for failing to pay a civil judgment; or (ii) a state court judgment that permits a plaintiff to execute a lien against a defendant's property. [Judice v. Vail, 430 U.S. 327 (1977); Pennzoil Co. v. Texaco, Inc., 481 U.S. 1 (1987)]

3) Exception

An order enjoining state proceedings will be issued in cases of *proven harassment* or *prosecutions taken in bad faith* (without hope of a valid conviction).

7. Political Questions

The Court will not decide political questions.

a. Definition

Political questions are:

(i) Those issues committed by the Constitution to another branch of government; or

(ii) Those inherently incapable of resolution and enforcement by the judicial process.

Examples: Political questions include:

1) What constitutes a "republican form of government" guaranteed to the states by Article IV, Section 4 [Pacific States Telephone & Telegraph Co. v. Oregon, 223 U.S. 118 (1912)];

2) Questions regarding the conduct of foreign relations; or issues as to when hostilities have stopped;

3) Questions relating to which group of delegates should be seated at the Democratic National Convention [O'Brien v. Brown, 409 U.S. 1 (1972)]; and

4) The procedures used by the Senate to "try" impeachments. Thus, the Court refused to rule on the constitutionality of the Senate's delegation of the duty to take evidence and testimony to a committee of senators prior to the Senate deciding whether to vote for conviction on an impeachment of a federal judge [Nixon v. United States, 506 U.S. 224 (1993)].

b. Compare—"Nonpolitical Controversies"

1) Legislative Apportionment

Legislative apportionment was considered to be "political" until *Baker v. Carr,* 369 U.S. 186 (1962). The numerous court decisions requiring "one person-one vote" make clear that this is no longer true. [Reynolds v. Sims, 377 U.S. 533 (1964)]

2) Congressional Membership

The Constitution prescribes the minimum requirements of membership in both houses and further provides that each house shall be the judge of election returns and the qualifications of its members. Generally, the question of which of two candidates is entitled to be seated in the Senate is political. But an *arbitrary exclusion of a delegate is reviewable*. [Powell v. McCormack, 395 U.S. 486 (1969)]

3) Presidential Papers and Communications

These are generally considered to be privileged and protected against disclosure in the exercise of the executive power. But where these documents are necessary to the continuation of criminal proceedings, the question of production is *justiciable and not political*. [United States v. Nixon, 418 U.S. 683 (1974)]

4) **"Origination Clause" Cases**
The "Origination Clause" [Art. 1, §7] provides that bills for raising revenue must originate in the House of Representatives. The determination of whether a federal statute is one for raising revenue (as opposed to a statute with an incidental effect of producing such income, which may originate in the Senate) is *not* a political question. [United States v. Munoz-Flores, 495 U.S. 385 (1990)—federal statute requiring monetary assessment to be imposed on persons convicted of some federal misdemeanors is not a revenue measure]

8. **Eleventh Amendment Limits on Federal Courts**
The Eleventh Amendment is a jurisdictional bar that modifies the judicial power by prohibiting a federal court from hearing a private party's or foreign government's claims against a state government. [*See* Hans v. Louisiana, 134 U.S. 1 (1890)]

a. **What Is Barred?**
The Eleventh Amendment's jurisdictional bar extends to the following:

(i) Actions against state governments *for damages*;

(ii) Actions against state governments for injunctive or declaratory relief *where the state is named as a party*;

(iii) Actions against state government officers where the effect of the suit will be that *retroactive damages* will be paid from the state treasury or where the action is the functional equivalent of a *quiet title action* that would divest the state of ownership of land; and

(iv) Actions against state government officers *for violating state law*.

1) **Compare—Sovereign Immunity**
The Court has also held that the following are barred by the doctrine of *sovereign immunity:*

a) Suits against a state government in state court, even on federal claims, without the defendant state's consent [Alden v. Maine, 527 U.S. 706 (1999)—provision in federal Fair Labor Standards Act creating a private cause of action in state courts against state employers who violate the Act violates sovereign immunity]; and

b) Adjudicative actions against states and state agencies before federal administrative agencies [Federal Maritime Commission v. South Carolina State Ports Authority, 122 S. Ct. 1864 (2002)].

b. **What Is Not Barred?**

1) **Actions Against Local Governments**
The Eleventh Amendment protects only state governments. Local governments (*e.g.,* cities or counties) are not protected.

2) **Actions by the United States Government or Other State Governments**
Actions by the United States Government or other state governments are not barred.

Note: Native American tribes are treated as other private parties, and so they are barred from bringing an action against a state government in federal court. [Blatchford v. Native Village of Noatak, 501 U.S. 775 (1991)]

c. **Exceptions to Eleventh Amendment**

1) **Certain Actions Against State Officers**
The Supreme Court allows the following actions to be brought against *state officials* despite the Eleventh Amendment:

a) Actions Against State Officers for Injunctions

A federal court may enjoin a state officer to refrain from future actions that violate federal law or to take prospective actions to comply with constitutional mandates. [*Ex parte* Young, 209 U.S. 123 (1908)]

b) Actions Against State Officers for Monetary Damages from Officer

A federal court may hear an action for damages against a state officer for violations of *federal law if* the monetary damages are to be paid out of the officer's own pocket. *Rationale:* By acting outside the scope of federal law, the officer is stripped of his representative capacity—the action is not one against a state, but rather is against an individual.

c) Actions Against State Officers for Prospective Payments from State

A federal court may hear an action for damages against a state officer where the effect of the action will be to force the state to pay money in the future to comply with the court order. [*Ex parte* Young, *supra*] However, federal court jurisdiction is barred if the action will result in retroactive damages to be paid from the state treasury. [Edelman v. Jordan, 415 U.S. 651 (1984)]

Example: P sues the State Commissioner of the Department of Public Welfare for failing to comply with federal welfare regulations. The federal court can order future compliance with the federal regulations, even if this will result in costing the state a large amount of money in the future. However, the federal court cannot award back payments of amounts previously improperly withheld, because the order would require payment from the state treasury for retroactive relief. [Edelman v. Jordan, *supra*]

2) State Consents

A state may consent to suit in federal court. However, no consent will be found unless the state clearly waives its Eleventh Amendment immunity. A state may only waive its Eleventh Amendment immunity *expressly and unequivocally* (or by voluntarily invoking a federal court's jurisdiction, such as by its removal of a state law claim from state to federal court [Lapides v. Board of Regents of the University System of Georgia, 122 S. Ct. 1640 (2002)]). A state will *not* be held to have impliedly or constructively waived its immunity simply because Congress provides that a state will be subject to private suit if it engages in certain federally regulated conduct (such as infringing a federally granted patent) and the state voluntarily elects to engage in that conduct. [College Savings Bank v. Florida Prepaid Postsecondary Education Expense Board, 527 U.S. 666 (1999), *overruling* Parden v. Terminal Railway, 377 U.S. 184 (1964)]

3) Congressional Removal of Immunity Under the Fourteenth Amendment

Congress can remove the states' Eleventh Amendment immunity under its power to *prevent discrimination under the Fourteenth Amendment.* For example, the Equal Pay Act—based on the Fourteenth Amendment—can serve as a basis for federal suits against a state by its employees. [Fitzpatrick v. Bitzer, 427 U.S. 445 (1976)]

a) Compare—Article I Powers

Unlike its power under the Fourteenth Amendment, Congress's legislative powers under Article I (*see* II., *infra*) do *not* include the power to abrogate state immunity under the Eleventh Amendment. [Seminole Tribe of Florida v. Florida, 517 U.S. 114 (1996), *overruling* Pennsylvania v. Union Gas Co., 491 U.S. 1 (1989)—Congress has no power to abrogate state immunity under the Commerce Clause; Florida Prepaid Postsecondary Education Expense Board v. College Savings Bank, 527 U.S. 627 (1999)—Congress has no power to abrogate state immunity under the Patent Clause]

d. Summary

For most bar exam questions, a key principle to remember is this: The Eleventh Amendment will prohibit a federal court from hearing a claim for damages against a state government (although not against state officers) unless:

1) The state has consented to allow the lawsuit in federal court;

2) The plaintiff is the United States or another state; or

3) Congress has clearly granted federal courts the authority to hear a specific type of damage action under the Fourteenth Amendment (*e.g.*, under a civil rights statute).

II. LEGISLATIVE POWER

A. ENUMERATED AND IMPLIED POWERS
The Constitution grants Congress a number of specific powers, many of which are enumerated in Article I, Section 8. It also grants Congress auxiliary power under the Necessary and Proper Clause.

1. **Necessary and Proper "Power"**
   The Necessary and Proper Clause grants Congress the power to make all laws necessary and proper (*i.e.*, appropriate) for carrying into execution *any* power granted to *any* branch of the federal government.
   Example: Congress has the power to charter banks since that power is appropriate to executing Congress's enumerated powers to tax, borrow money, regulate commerce, etc. [McCulloch v. Maryland, 17 U.S. 316 (1819)]

   Note: The Necessary and Proper Clause is not itself a basis of power; it merely gives Congress power to execute specifically granted powers. Thus, if a bar exam question asks what is the best source of power for a particular act of Congress, the answer should not be the Necessary and Proper Clause, standing alone.

   a. **Limitation**
      Congress cannot adopt a law that is expressly prohibited by another provision of the Constitution.

2. **Taxing Power**
   Congress has the power to lay and collect taxes, imposts, and excises, but they must be uniform throughout the United States. [Art. I, §8] Capitation or other direct taxes must be laid in proportion to the census [Art. I, §9, cl. 4], and direct taxes must be apportioned among the states [Art. I, §2, cl. 3].

   a. **Uniformity**
      Requirement of uniformity in the levy of indirect taxes (generally, this means any kind of "privilege" tax, including duties and excises) has been interpreted by the Court to mean *geographical uniformity* only—*i.e.*, identical taxation of the taxed Article in every state where it is found. [Fernandez v. Wiener, 326 U.S. 340 (1945)]

   b. **Direct Taxes—Must Be Apportioned**
      A "direct" tax (imposed directly on property or on the person) has seldom been employed by Congress because of the cumbersome *apportionment requirement*; taxes on income from real or personal property were initially held "direct" by the Court, but the resulting need for apportioning such taxes was obviated by the Sixteenth Amendment (income tax amendment).

   c. **Export Taxes Not Permitted**
      Neither Congress nor the state can tax exports to foreign countries.

   d. **Taxes Are Generally Valid**
      Absent a specific restriction such as those above, be very hesitant to rule against a tax measure on the exam. A tax measure will be upheld if it bears some *reasonable relationship to revenue production* or if Congress has the *power to regulate* the taxed activity.
      Example: Special excise tax levied on dealers in illegal narcotics is valid because it raises revenue. [United States v. Doremus, 249 U.S. 86 (1919)]

3. **Spending Power**
   Congress may spend to "provide for the common defense and general welfare." [Art. I, §8]

This spending may be for **any public purpose**—not merely the accomplishment of other enumerated powers. However, nonspending regulations are not authorized. Remember that the Bill of Rights still applies to this power; *i.e.*, the federal government could not condition welfare payments on an agreement not to criticize government policies.

a. Regulation Through Spending

Note that Congress can use its spending power to "regulate" areas, even where it otherwise has no power to regulate the area, by requiring entities that accept government money to act in a certain manner (*i.e.*, attaching "strings" to government grants). (*See* VI.A.2.b., *infra.*)

4. Commerce Power

Article I, Section 8, Clause 3 empowers Congress to "regulate commerce with foreign nations and among the several states, and with the Indian tribes."

a. Definition of Commerce

1) Includes Basically All Activity Affecting Two or More States

Chief Justice Marshall in *Gibbons v. Ogden,* 22 U.S. 1 (1824), defined commerce as "every species of commercial intercourse . . . which concerns more states than one" and included within the concept virtually every form of activity involving or affecting two or more states.

2) Includes Transportation or Traffic

The Court has consistently regarded transportation or traffic as commerce whether or not a commercial activity is involved.

Example: Interstate transportation of liquor for personal consumption, women for immoral purposes (not necessarily prostitution), and interstate transportation of stolen motor vehicles are all interstate commerce.

a) Vehicular Transportation Not Required

Any *transmission across state lines*, such as electricity, gas, telegraph, telephone, TV, radio, and mail transmission (including educational materials and sale of insurance), will constitute interstate commerce.

b. "Substantial Economic Effect"

The Supreme Court has sustained congressional power to regulate any activity, local or interstate, that either in itself *or in combination with other activities* has a *"substantial economic effect upon,"* or *"effect on movement in,"* interstate commerce.

Example: The classic case is the Court's holding that Congress can control a farmer's *production* of wheat *for home consumption*. [Wickard v. Filburn, 317 U.S. 111 (1942)] *Rationale:* Cumulative effect of many instances of such production could be felt on the supply and demand of the interstate commodity market.

1) Power Not Unlimited

The Supreme Court has recently made clear that the power of Congress to regulate commerce, although very broad, does have limits so as not to obliterate the distinction between what is national and what is local. To be within Congress's power under the Commerce Clause, a federal law must either:

(i) *Regulate the channels* of interstate commerce;

(ii) *Regulate the instrumentalities* of interstate commerce and persons and things in interstate commerce; or

(iii) *Regulate activities that have a substantial effect* on interstate commerce.

If Congress attempts to regulate noneconomic (*i.e.*, noncommercial) *intrastate* activity, the federal government must prove to the Court that the activity in fact *affects interstate* commerce. It is unlikely that the Court will allow Congress to use its commerce power to regulate a noneconomic activity occurring in a single state, particularly if the activity has historically been regulated by local law. [*See* United States v. Lopez, 514 U.S. 549 (1995)—federal statute barring possession of a gun in a school zone is invalid; United States v. Morrison, 529 U.S. 598 (2000)—federal civil remedy for victims of gender-motivated violence is invalid]

5. **War and Related Powers**
Article I, Section 8 gives Congress the power to declare war, raise and support armies, provide for and maintain a navy, make rules for the government and regulation of the armed forces, and organize, arm, discipline, and call up the militia. Of course, several other congressional powers may have direct or indirect application to military purposes: tax and spending power, commerce power, Senate's treaty consent power, maritime power, investigatory power, etc.

a. **Economic Regulation**

1) **During War**
Regulatory power of Congress, especially in economic matters and mobilization of troops, in support of war effort is *pervasive* (although theoretically limited by the Bill of Rights); thus, the Court has sustained national price and rent control, as well as conscription and regulation of civilian/military production and services.

2) **Postwar**
To a considerable extent, this pervasive regulatory power may be validly extended into post-wartime periods both to *remedy wartime disruptions* [*e.g.,* Woods v. Miller, 333 U.S. 138 (1948)—rent controls] and to cope with *"cold war" exigencies*. Legislation in the field of veterans' rights and limitations thereon may be extended indefinitely as long as veterans or their relatives may survive.

b. **Military Courts and Tribunals**
The constitutional basis of courts of military justice (trial and review of offenses by military personnel, including courts-martial and reviewing agencies and tribunals) is not Article III, but rather Article I, Section 8, Clause 14 (congressional power to make rules for government and regulation of armed forces), buttressed by the Necessary and Proper Clause.

1) **Judicial Review**
The regular federal (or state) courts have *no general power of review* over court-martial proceedings. However, in habeas corpus cases, the Article III courts, including the Supreme Court, may make a limited inquiry into the military court's jurisdiction of the person and offense or the validity of the court's legislative creation.

2) **Court-Martial of Enemy Civilians and Soldiers Permitted**
Military courts may try enemy civilians as well as enemy military personnel, at least during wartime, with only the basic jurisdictional review by the Article III courts.

3) **Court-Martial of American Soldiers Permitted**
Military courts have jurisdiction over *all* offenses (not just service connected offenses) committed by persons who are members of the armed services both when charged and at the time of the offense. [Solorio v. United States, 483 U.S. 435 (1987), *overruling* O'Callahan v. Parker, 395 U.S. 258 (1969)]

4) **Court-Martial of American Civilians Generally Prohibited**
The Supreme Court has denied Congress the power to authorize the court-martial trial of American civilians as long as actual warfare has not forced courts to shut down, even though martial law has been declared [*Ex parte* Milligan, 71 U.S. 2 (1866)]; even though the civilians accused may have been members of the armed forces when committing the alleged offense [Toth v. Quarles, 350 U.S. 11 (1955)] or are dependents of military personnel accompanying the latter overseas [Reid v. Covert, 354 U.S. 1 (1957)] or are civilian employees of the military forces at overseas bases and installations; such trials by court-martial violate the Fifth and Sixth Amendments, particularly the right to trial by jury.

c. **Curfew and Exclusion of Civilians from Sensitive Areas**
Both of these powers have been upheld (as jointly exercised by Congress and the President) as implied war powers during World War II, even as to exclusion and confinement elsewhere of United States citizens (of Japanese ancestry). [Korematsu v.

United States, 319 U.S. 432 (1944)] However, to avoid violation of due process under the Fifth Amendment, the area of exclusion must be very sensitive militarily; *i.e.,* there must be a reasonable belief that the excluded persons, if allowed to remain, would pose a high risk of assistance to the enemy (by way of invasion, sabotage, or espionage).

d. **Calling Forth the Militia**
By statute, Congress has authorized the President to order members of National Guard units into federal service in circumstances that do not involve a national emergency (*e.g.,* for training outside of the United States). This statute is constitutional under the Militia Clauses [Art. I, §8, cl. 15, 16], and the President need not obtain the consent of the governor of a unit's home state to call it into such service. [Perpich v. Department of Defense, 496 U.S. 334 (1990)]

6. **Investigatory Power**
The power to investigate to secure information as a basis for potential legislation or other official action (such as impeachment or trying impeachments) is a well-established implied power. It is a *very broad power*, in that an investigation need not be directed toward enactment of particular legislation, but the following limitations on its use do exist.

a. **Authorized Investigation**
The investigatory inquiry must be expressly or impliedly authorized by the congressional house concerned, *i.e.,* by statute or resolution creating or directing the investigating committee or subcommittee.

b. **Witnesses' Rights**

1) **Fifth Amendment**
The privilege against compulsory self-incrimination (the Fifth Amendment) is available to witnesses, whether formal or informal, unless a statutory immunity co-extensive with the constitutional immunity is granted.

2) **Relevance**
Written or oral information elicited by the investigative body must be "pertinent" to the subject of the inquiry.

3) **Procedural Due Process**
Witnesses are generally entitled to procedural due process, such as presence of counsel and right of cross-examination; but it is not yet clear whether such rights are constitutionally required or whether some of them are required merely by house rule or statute.

c. **Enforcement of Investigatory Powers**
Congress can hold a subpoenaed witness in contempt for refusing to appear or answer before Congress.

7. **Property Power**
Congress has the power to "dispose of and make all needful rules and regulations respecting the territory or other property belonging to the United States." [Art. IV, §3] Many other congressional powers (war, commerce, postal, fiscal, etc.) obviously would be unworkable if the ancillary *power to acquire and dispose of property of all kinds*—real, personal, and intangible—were not also implied from the main grants.
Example: The Property Clause empowers Congress to even protect wildlife wandering onto federally owned lands. [Kleppe v. New Mexico, 426 U.S. 529 (1976)]

a. **No Limits on Disposition of Property**
There is no express limitation on Congress's power to dispose of property owned by the United States. The power extends to all species of property, such as leasehold interests and electrical energy, as well as ordinary realty and personalty. Moreover, disposal may involve direct competition with private enterprise and has never been invalidated on that ground.

b. **Eminent Domain**
Acquisition of property for a public purpose by eminent domain is indirectly recognized by the Fifth Amendment: ". . . nor shall private property be taken for public use,

without just compensation." Federal taking must be for the purpose of *effectuating an enumerated power* under some other provision of the Constitution.

8. **No Federal Police Power**
Congress has no general police power (*i.e.*, power to legislate for the health, welfare, morals, etc., of the citizens). Thus, on the bar exam the validity of a federal statute cannot rely on "the police power." However, Congress can exercise police power-type powers as to the District of Columbia pursuant to its power to legislate over the capitol [Art. I, §8, cl. 17] and over all United States possessions (*e.g.*, territories, military bases, Indian reservations) pursuant to the property power.

9. **Bankruptcy Power**
Article I, Section 8, Clause 4 empowers Congress "to establish uniform laws on the subject of bankruptcies throughout the United States." This power has been interpreted by the Supreme Court as nonexclusive; *i.e.*, state legislation in the field is superseded only to the extent that it conflicts with federal legislation therein.

10. **Postal Power**
Article I, Section 8, Clause 7 empowers Congress "to establish post offices and post roads."

    a. **Exclusive**
    The postal power has been interpreted as granting Congress a postal monopoly. Neither private business nor the states may compete with the Federal Postal Service absent Congress's consent. [Air Courier Conference of America v. American Postal Workers Union, 498 U.S. 517 (1991)]

    b. **Scope of Power**
    Congress may validly classify and place *reasonable restrictions* on use of the mails, *but may not deprive* any citizen or group of citizens of the general mail "privilege" or regulate the mail in such a way as to abridge freedom of speech or press (except under valid standards, such as "obscenity") or violate the ban of the Fourth Amendment against unreasonable search and seizure.

11. **Power Over Citizenship**
Article I, Section 8, Clause 4 empowers Congress "to establish a uniform rule of naturalization."

    a. **Exclusion of Aliens**
    Congress's power to exclude aliens is broad.

        1) **Nonresident Aliens**
        Aliens have no right to enter the United States and *can be refused entry* because of their political beliefs. [Kleindienst v. Mandel, 408 U.S. 753 (1972)]

        2) **Resident Aliens**
        Resident aliens are entitled to *notice and hearing* before they can be deported.

    b. **Naturalization and Denaturalization—Exclusive Control of Congress**
    Congress has exclusive power over naturalization and denaturalization. The Supreme Court has held that this grant gives Congress plenary power over aliens (*see* XVIII.D.2.a., *infra*).

        1) **No Loss of Citizenship Without Consent**
        Under the Fourteenth Amendment, Congress may not take away the citizenship of any citizen—native-born or naturalized—without his consent.
        Example: The Court held unconstitutional a statute that provided for loss of citizenship upon voting in a foreign election. [Afroyim v. Rusk, 387 U.S. 253 (1967)]

            a) **Proof of Intent**
            A citizen's intent to relinquish citizenship may be expressed by words or conduct—and Congress may provide that such intent may be proven by a preponderance of the evidence. [Vance v. Terrazas, 444 U.S. 252 (1980)]

        2) **Rights of Children of Citizens**
        A person born in another country to United States citizen parents does not have a

constitutional right to become a United States citizen. Congress can grant citizenship to children born abroad conditioned on their return to live in the United States within a specified period of time or for a specified number of years. Such a child who fails to return to the United States loses his grant of citizenship because he has failed to meet the statutory condition precedent to his final grant of citizenship.

12. Admiralty Power

Although congressional power to legislate in maritime matters is not expressed in the Constitution, the Supreme Court has implied it from the exclusive jurisdiction given the federal courts in this field by Article III, Section 2, supported by the Necessary and Proper Clause of Article I, Section 8.

a. Exclusive Power

The congressional power is plenary and exclusive, except to the extent that Congress may leave (and has left) some maritime matters to state jurisdiction.

b. Navigable Waterways

The federal admiralty power attaches to all navigable waterways—actually or potentially navigable—and to small tributaries that affect navigable waterways. The federal maritime power is not limited to tidewaters or interstate waters.

13. Power to Coin Money and Fix Weights and Measures

Congress has the power to coin money and fix the standard of weights and measures under Article I, Section 8, Clause 5.

14. Patent/Copyright Power

Congress has the power to control the issuance of patents and copyrights under Article I, Section 8, Clause 8.

B. DELEGATION OF LEGISLATIVE POWER

1. Broad Delegation Allowed

Congress has broad discretion to delegate its legislative power to executive officers and/or administrative agencies [Schechter Poultry Corp. v. United States, 295 U.S. 495 (1935)], and even delegation of rulemaking power to the courts has been upheld [Mistretta v. United States, 488 U.S. 361 (1989)].

Example: Congress can delegate the power to establish sentencing guidelines for criminal cases to a sentencing commission located in the federal courts and made up, in part, of federal judges, as long as the tasks delegated do not undermine the integrity of the judiciary or usurp the powers of the other branches. [Mistretta v. United States, *supra*]

2. Limitations on Delegation

a. Power Cannot Be Uniquely Confined to Congress

To be delegable, the power must not be uniquely confined to Congress; *e.g.*, the power to declare war cannot be delegated, nor the power to impeach.

b. Clear Standard

It is said that delegation will be upheld only if it includes intelligible standards for the delegate to follow. However, as a practical matter almost anything will pass as an "intelligible standard" (*e.g.*, "upholding public interest, convenience, or necessity").

c. Separation of Powers Limitations

While Congress has broad power to delegate, the separation of powers doctrine restricts Congress from keeping certain controls over certain delegates. For example, Congress cannot give itself the power to remove an officer of the executive branch by any means other than impeachment (*e.g.*, if Congress delegates rulemaking power to an executive branch agency (*e.g.*, the FCC), it may not retain the power to fire the agency head). (*See* III.B.1.b.2)a), *infra*.) Similarly, Congress cannot give a government employee who is subject to removal by Congress (other than by impeachment) purely executive powers. (*See* III.B.1.b.2)b), *infra*.)

Example: A federal statute transferred the authority to control two D.C. area airports from the federal government to a local authority. However, the statute reserved to a review board a veto power over the local authority's decisions. The review board was comprised of nine members of Congress. The statute violates the separation of powers doctrine in one of two ways: (i) If the review board's power is considered to be legislative, the statute created an unconstitutional legislative veto (*see* D., *infra*). (ii) If the review board's power is considered to be executive, the separation of powers doctrine prohibits members of Congress from exercising it. [Metropolitan Washington Airports Authority v. Citizens for Abatement of Aircraft Noise, 501 U.S. 252 (1991)]

d. Important Liberty Interests

If the delegate interferes with the exercise of a fundamental liberty or right, the burden falls upon the delegate to show that she has the power to prevent the exercise of the right and her decision was in furtherance of that particular policy.

Example: In *Kent v. Dulles,* 357 U.S. 116 (1958), the secretary of state was required to issue a passport to a communist because he could not show that Congress gave him the power to encroach upon the fundamental right to travel simply because the applicant was a communist.

e. Criminal vs. Civil Punishment

The legislature may delegate its authority to enact regulations, the violation of which are crimes, but prosecution for such violations must be left to the executive and judicial branches. [*See* United States v. Grimaud, 220 U.S. 506 (1911)] However, agencies may enact and impose civil penalties (*i.e.,* fines labeled as civil fines) without prosecution in court. [Helvering v. Mitchell, 303 U.S. 391 (1938)]

C. THE SPEECH OR DEBATE CLAUSE—SPECIAL IMMUNITY FOR FEDERAL LEGISLATORS

Article I, Section 6 provides that "For any speech or debate in either House [members of Congress] shall not be questioned in any other place."

1. Persons Covered

The immunity extends to aides who engage in acts that would be immune if performed by a legislator. [Gravel v. United States, 408 U.S. 606 (1972)]

Note: The Speech or Debate Clause does *not extend to state legislators* who are prosecuted for violation of federal law. [United States v. Gillock, 445 U.S. 360 (1980)]

2. Scope of Immunity

Conduct that occurs in the regular course of the legislative process and the motivation behind that conduct are immune from prosecution.

a. Bribes Excluded

Taking of a bribe is not an act in the regular course of the legislative process and is therefore actionable. [United States v. Brewster, 408 U.S. 501 (1972)]

b. Speeches Outside Congress

Speeches and publications made outside Congress are not protected.

c. Defamatory Statements

Republication in a press release or newsletter of a defamatory statement originally made in Congress is not immune. [Hutchinson v. Proxmire, 443 U.S. 111 (1979)]

D. CONGRESSIONAL "VETO" OF EXECUTIVE ACTIONS INVALID

A legislative veto is an attempt by Congress to overturn an executive agency action *without* bicameralism (*i.e.,* passage by both houses of Congress) or presentment (*i.e.,* giving the bill to the President for his signature or veto). Legislative vetoes of executive actions are invalid. [Immigration & Naturalization Service v. Chadha, 462 U.S. 919 (1983)] The legislative veto usually arises where Congress delegates discretionary power to the President or an executive agency. In an attempt to control the delegation, Congress requires the President or agency to present any action taken under the discretionary power to certain members of Congress for approval. If they disapprove, they veto the action and that is the final decision on the action. This is unconstitutional because to be valid, legislative action (the veto) must be approved by both houses and presented to the President for his approval (*see* III.B.3., *infra*). In *Chadha,* the Court also noted that the legislative veto violates the implied separation of powers requirements of the Constitution.

Examples: 1) Congress granted to the Immigration & Naturalization Service ("INS") the power to deport or suspend from deportation illegal aliens. INS decisions to suspend deportations had to be submitted to Congress. Either house could pass a resolution overriding the decision. This legislative veto provision is unconstitutional. [Immigration & Naturalization Service v. Chadha, *supra*]

2) By statute, Congress grants to the President the power to send military troops into combat, without Congress's prior approval, whenever the United States or its territories are attacked. The statute, however, reserves in Congress the power to force the President to withdraw the troops. The statute does not provide for presidential veto of Congress's decision to withdraw. The decision in *Chadha* suggests that this statute is unconstitutional.

III. THE EXECUTIVE POWER

A. VESTED IN PRESIDENT

The entire "executive power" is vested in the President by Article II, Section 1 of the Constitution. Various executive functions may be and are delegated within the "executive branch" by the President or by Congress.

B. DOMESTIC POWERS

1. Appointment and Removal of Officers

a. Appointment

Under Article II, Section 2, the President is empowered "with the advice and consent of the Senate" to appoint "all *ambassadors*, other *public ministers* and consuls, *judges of the Supreme Court*, and all *other officers of the United States*, whose appointments are not herein otherwise provided for . . . but the Congress may by law vest the appointment of such inferior officers, as they think proper, in the President alone, in the courts of law, or in the heads of departments."

1) Appointment of "Independent Counsel" (Special Prosecutor)

Under the Ethics in Government Act of 1978, a special prosecutor (*i.e.,* a prosecutor appointed by the federal court upon the attorney general's recommendation that alleged government employee misconduct be investigated) is an "inferior officer," since the prosecutor has limited duties (to investigate and prosecute a narrow range of persons and subjects). Therefore, the Appointment Clause of Article II, Section 2 allows Congress to vest the power to appoint a special prosecutor in the judiciary. Moreover, the Ethics in Government Act scheme does not give executive powers to the judiciary, since the Act gives the executive branch control of the decision to investigate and the power to dismiss the independent counsel for good cause. [Morrison v. Olson, 487 U.S. 654 (1988)]

2) No Appointments by Congress

Although Congress may appoint its own officers to carry on *internal legislative tasks* (*i.e.,* its staff), it may not appoint members of a body with administrative or enforcement powers; such persons are "officers of the United States" and must, pursuant to Article II, Section 2, be appointed by the President with senatorial confirmation unless Congress has vested their appointment in the President alone, in federal courts, or in heads of departments. [Buckley v. Valeo, 424 U.S. 1 (1976)]

b. Removal

As to removal of appointees, the *Constitution is silent* except for ensuring tenure of all Article III judges "during good behavior."

1) By President

Under the Court's decisions, the President probably can remove high level, purely executive officers (*e.g.,* Cabinet members) at will, without any interference from Congress. However, after *Morrison v. Olson, supra,* it appears that Congress may provide statutory limitations (*e.g.,* removal for good cause) on the President's power to remove all other executive appointees.

2) By Congress

a)   **Limitation on Removal Power**
Congress cannot give itself the power to remove an officer charged with the execution of laws except through impeachment. A congressional attempt through legislation to remove from government employment specifically named government employees is likely to be held invalid as a bill of attainder.

b)   **Limitation on Powers of Removable Officers**
Congress cannot give a government employee who is subject to removal from office by Congress any powers that are truly executive in nature. For this reason, Congress could not give to the Comptroller General (who could be removed from office not only by impeachment but also by a joint resolution of Congress) the function of establishing the amount of automatic budget reductions that would be required if Congress failed to make budget reductions necessary to insure that the federal budget deficit did not exceed a legislatively established maximum amount. [Bowsher v. Synar, 478 U.S. 714 (1986)]

2.   **Pardons**
The President is empowered by Article II, Section 2, "to grant reprieves and pardons for offenses against the United States, *except in cases of impeachment*." This power has been held to apply before, during, or after trial, and to extend to the offense of criminal contempt, but not to civil contempt, inasmuch as the latter involves the rights of third parties. The pardon power *cannot be limited by Congress*, and includes power to commute a sentence on any conditions the President chooses, as long as they are not independently unconstitutional. [Schick v. Reed, 419 U.S. 256 (1974)]

3.   **Veto Power**

a.   **Congress May Override Veto by Two-Thirds Vote**
Every act of Congress must be approved by the President before taking effect, unless passed over his disapproval by two-thirds vote of *each house*. [Art. I, §7]

b.   **President Has Ten Days to Veto**
The President has 10 days (excepting Sundays) to exercise his veto power. If he fails to act within that time:

(i)   The bill becomes law if Congress is still in session; or

(ii)   The bill is automatically vetoed if Congress is not in session (a "*pocket veto*"). [Pocket Veto Case, 279 U.S. 655 (1929)]

Note: Brief recesses during an annual session create no pocket veto opportunity. [Wright v. United States, 302 U.S. 583 (1938)]

c.   **Line Item Veto Unconstitutional**
The veto power allows the President only to approve or reject a bill in toto; he cannot cancel part (through a line item veto) and approve other parts. *Rationale:* The President's veto power does not authorize him to amend or repeal laws passed by Congress. [Clinton v. City of New York, 524 U.S. 417 (1998)]

4.   **Power as Chief Executive**
The President's power over internal (*i.e.*, within the United States) affairs as the chief executive is unclear. Clearly the President has some power to direct subordinate executive officers, and there is a long history of presidents issuing executive orders. Perhaps the best guide for determining the validity of presidential actions regarding internal affairs can be based on Justice Jackson's opinion in *Youngstown Sheet & Tube v. Sawyer*, 343 U.S. 579 (1952):

(i)   Where the President acts with the express or implied authority of Congress, his authority is at its maximum and his actions likely are valid;

(ii)   Where the President acts where Congress is silent, his action will be upheld as long as the act does not take over the powers of another branch of the government or prevent another branch from carrying out its tasks [*see, e.g.,* United States v. Nixon, 418 U.S.

683 (1974)—President's invocation of executive privilege was invalidated because it kept federal courts from having evidence they needed to conduct a fair criminal trial];

(iii) Where the President acts against the express will of Congress, he has little authority and his action likely is invalid.

a. No Power to Impound

It follows from the above that the President has no power to refuse to spend appropriated funds when Congress has expressly mandated that they be spent. [Kendall v. United States, 37 U.S. 524 (1838)]

C. POWER OVER EXTERNAL AFFAIRS

1. War

Although lacking the power to declare or initiate a "formal" war, the President has extensive military powers (essentially an external field, although applicable to civil war as well and to many domestic affairs caught up in military necessities).

a. Actual Hostilities

The President may act militarily under his power as *commander in chief* of the armed forces and militia (when federalized), under Article II, Section 2, in actual hostilities against the United States without a congressional declaration of war. But *Congress* may limit the President under its power to enact a *military appropriation every two years*. (A military appropriation may not be for more than two years.)

b. Military Government

This power includes the establishment of military governments in occupied territories, including military tribunals.

2. Foreign Relations

The President's power to represent and act for the United States in day-to-day foreign relations is paramount. He has the power to appoint and receive ambassadors and make treaties (with the advice and consent of the Senate), and to enter into executive agreements. His power is broad even as to foreign affairs that require congressional consent. No significant judicial control has been exercised over this power.

3. Treaty Power

The treaty power is granted to the President "by and with the advice and consent of the Senate, provided *two-thirds of the Senators* present concur." [Art. II, §2, cl. 2]

a. Supreme Law

All treaties "which shall be made under the authority of the United States" are the "supreme law of the land" (along with the Constitution itself and laws of the United States made in pursuance thereof) under Article VI, Paragraph 2. Thus, it is clear that any state action or law in conflict with a United States treaty is invalid (regardless of whether it is a state law or a state constitutional provision).

1) Self-Executing

No treaty has this supremacy status, however, unless it is expressly or impliedly self-executing, *i.e.,* without necessity for congressional implementation.

2) Non-Self-Executing Treaties

Some treaties require the signatory nations to *pass legislation* to effectuate their ends. This serves as an independent source of congressional power. (Thus, the implementing statute need not be connected to commerce power, etc.)

3) Conflict with Congressional Acts

Valid treaties are clearly on a "supremacy parity" with acts of Congress; assuming that an act of Congress is within its powers, a conflict between such act and a valid treaty is resolved by order of adoption—*the last in time prevails*.

4) Conflict with Constitution

Treaties are not co-equal with the Constitution. For example, no treaty (or executive agreement) could confer on Congress authority to act in a manner inconsistent with any specific provision of the Constitution. [Reid v. Covert, 354 U.S. 1

(1957)] However, a treaty *can broaden* the scope of Congress's affirmative authority—as was the case in *Missouri v. Holland,* 252 U.S. 416 (1920), sustaining the Migratory Bird Act after a treaty with Canada, despite an earlier decision that the Commerce Clause alone did not suffice to support the act.

b.   Other Limitations
Other substantive limitations on the treaty power have not been judicially established; but in one case the Court expressed in dictum the view that a treaty could not upset the basic structure of the United States's federalism, or wield a power barred to the national government by the Constitution, or cede any part of a state to a foreign nation without the state's consent. The Court has *never held a treaty unconstitutional* (*Reid v. Covert, supra,* invalidated an executive agreement for violating the Fifth Amendment), but it is conceivable that the treaty power extends only to subjects plausibly bearing on our relations with other countries.

4.   Executive Agreements
The President's power to enter into agreements (*i.e.,* executive agreements) with the heads of foreign countries is not expressly provided for in the Constitution; nevertheless, the power has become institutionalized. Executive agreements can probably be on any subject as long as they do not violate the Constitution. They are very similar to treaties, except that they do not require the consent of the Senate.

a.   Conflicts with Other Governmental Action
Executive agreements that are not consented to by the Senate are not the "supreme law of the land." Thus, conflicting federal statutes and treaties will prevail over an executive agreement, regardless of which was adopted first. However, executive agreements prevail over conflicting state laws.

b.   Example—Power to Settle Claims of United States Citizens
The President, with the implicit approval of Congress, has power to settle claims of United States citizens against foreign governments through an executive agreement. [Dames & Moore v. Regan, 453 U.S. 654 (1981)]

D.   EXECUTIVE PRIVILEGE/IMMUNITY

1.   Executive Privilege
The executive privilege is not a constitutional power, but an inherent privilege necessary to protect the confidentiality of presidential communications.

a.   Extent of the Privilege
Presidential *documents and conversations* are *presumptively privileged*, but the privilege must yield to the need for such materials as evidence in a criminal case to which they are relevant and otherwise admissible. This determination must be made by the trial judge after hearing the evidence.

   1)   National Security Secrets
   Military, diplomatic, or sensitive national security secrets are given great deference by the courts.

   2)   Criminal Proceedings
   In criminal proceedings, presidential communiques will be available to the prosecution, where a need for such information is demonstrated. [United States v. Nixon, 418 U.S. 683 (1974)]

   3)   Screening Papers and Recordings of Former President
   A federal statute requiring the Administrator of General Services to screen the presidential papers is valid, notwithstanding the privilege. [Nixon v. Administrator of General Services, 433 U.S. 425 (1977)]

   4)   Screening by Judge in Chambers
   The court will determine in an in-camera inspection which communications are protected and which are subject to disclosure.

2.   Executive Immunity

a. **Absolute Immunity for President**
The President has *absolute immunity from civil damages* based on any action that the President took within his *official responsibilities* (even if the action was only arguably within the "outer perimeter" of presidential responsibility). [Nixon v. Fitzgerald, 457 U.S. 731 (1982)] However, the President has *no* immunity from private suits in federal courts based on *conduct that allegedly occurred before taking office*. [Clinton v. Jones, 520 U.S. 681 (1997)] *Rationale:* The immunity is intended only to enable the President to perform his *designated functions* without fear of personal liability.

b. **Immunity May Extend to Presidential Aides**
Presidential aides share in this immunity only if they are exercising discretionary authority for the President in "sensitive" areas of national concern, such as foreign affairs. Other aides are entitled only to a qualified immunity (a "good faith" defense). [Harlow v. Fitzgerald, 457 U.S. 800 (1982)]
Example: The Attorney General does not share the President's absolute immunity for authorizing a warrantless wiretap on "national security" grounds. The Attorney General would have a defense to a lawsuit regarding such a wiretap if it was shown that he was able to act in good faith because his actions were not violating clearly established or well-settled statutory or constitutional rights. [Mitchell v. Forsyth, 472 U.S. 511 (1985)]

E. IMPEACHMENT

1. **Persons Subject to Impeachment**
The President, Vice President, and all civil officers of the United States are subject to impeachment.

2. **Grounds**
The grounds for impeachment are treason, bribery, high crimes, and misdemeanors.

3. **Impeachment by the House**
A *majority vote* in the House is necessary to invoke the charges of impeachment.

4. **Conviction by the Senate**
A *two-thirds vote* in the Senate is necessary to convict.

PART TWO: THE FEDERAL SYSTEM

IV. RELATIVE SPHERES OF FEDERAL AND STATE POWER

A. EXCLUSIVE FEDERAL POWERS

1. **Power of States Expressly Limited**
Some powers are exclusively federal because of express constitutional limitation on or prohibition of the states' exercise thereof—such as the treaty power, coinage of money, and duty on imports.

2. **Inherent Federal Powers**
Others are exclusively federal in view of their nature—such as declaration of war, federal citizenship, naturalization, and borrowing money on the credit of the United States. Any state exercise of these powers would basically subvert the federal system. On the exam, *do not* allow states to take actions that might touch upon *foreign relations*.
Example: In *Zschernig v. Miller*, 389 U.S. 429 (1968), the Court held invalid state statutes that sought to withhold the proceeds of local decedents' estates from heirs living in nations that (i) discriminate against Americans in their probate laws, (ii) impede the transmission of funds to the United States, or (iii) confiscate property inherited by their citizens. The Court concluded that such laws are so potentially disruptive of a nationally conducted foreign policy that they are invalid notwithstanding the traditional commitment of probate law to the states.

B. EXCLUSIVE STATE POWERS
Whereas the federal government has only those powers granted to it by the Constitution, the state governments are governments of "unlimited" powers, having all powers not prohibited to them by the Constitution. This is recognized by the Tenth Amendment, which provides that all powers

not delegated to the federal government by the Constitution are reserved to the states (or to the people). However, given the expansive interpretation of federal powers (*e.g.,* the commerce power; *see* II.A.4., *supra*), little state power is exclusive.

C. CONCURRENT FEDERAL AND STATE POWER—SUPREMACY CLAUSE

Most governmental power is concurrent, belonging to both the states and the federal government. Thus, it is possible for states and the federal government to pass legislation on the same subject matter. When this occurs, the Supremacy Clause provides that the federal law is supreme, and the conflicting state law is rendered void.

1. Actual Conflict Between State and Federal Laws

A valid act of Congress or federal regulation supersedes any state or local action that actually conflicts with the federal rule—whether by commanding conduct inconsistent with that required by the federal rule, or by forbidding conduct that the federal rule is designed to foster.

2. State Prevents Achievement of Federal Objective

The conflict need not relate to conduct; it is sufficient if the state or local law interferes with achievement of a federal objective. This is true even if the state or local law was enacted for some valid purpose and not merely to frustrate the federal law.

Example: A purpose of the federal bankruptcy laws is to give bankrupts a fresh start, free of their old debts. A state law providing for suspension of the driver's license of persons who have failed to pay off auto accident judgments, regardless of the judgment debtor's discharge in bankruptcy, interferes with the federal objective and will fail. [Perez v. Campbell, 402 U.S. 637 (1971)]

3. Preemption

A state or local law may fail under the Supremacy Clause, even if it does not conflict with federally regulated conduct or objectives, if it appears that Congress intended to "occupy" the entire field, thus precluding *any* state or local regulation. If the federal law does not explicitly indicate whether state law shall be preempted, the courts will consider a number of factors, including the following:

a. Comprehensiveness

The more a federal scheme leaves uncovered, the less likely a finding of implied preemption.

b. Agency to Administer

When a federal statute creates an agency (like the NLRB) to enforce the law, all matters arguably in the agency's jurisdiction are ordinarily deemed preempted; such matters must hence be regulated by the federal agency or not at all.

D. ABSENCE OF FEDERAL AND STATE POWERS

Some powers are denied to both Congress and the states. For example, the Supreme Court has held that the Qualifications Clauses [Art. I, §2, cl. 2; §3, cl. 3], setting the qualifications to serve in Congress, are exclusive and cannot be altered by Congress or the states. [United States Term Limits, Inc. v. Thornton, 514 U.S. 779 (1995)—state-imposed term limit for members of Congress invalidated; *and see* Cook v. Gralike, 531 U.S. 510 (2001)—state law instructing each member of its congressional delegation to support a constitutional amendment for term limits, and providing that failure to do so be noted on the ballot, was held invalid because it imposes a substantive qualification rather than regulates the "manner" in which elections are held]

E. INTERSTATE COMPACT CLAUSE

The Constitution provides that states may enter into agreements or compacts with other states upon the consent of Congress. [Art. I, §10, cl. 3] However, not all agreements between states are "compacts" requiring congressional consent. The Compact Clause reaches only interstate agreements that *increase the political power* of the states at the expense of federal supremacy (*e.g.,* an agreement whereby one state cedes territory to another state). [*See* United States Steel Corp. v. Multistate Tax Commission, 434 U.S. 552 (1978)—congressional consent not required for multistate tax compact because the compact does not give member states any powers they could not exercise in its absence] The Supreme Court has the power to interpret such compacts—the member states do not have final authority over interpretation. [West Virginia *ex rel.* Dyer v. Sims, 341 U.S. 22 (1951)]

F. FULL FAITH AND CREDIT CLAUSE

The Full Faith and Credit Clause provides that "full faith and credit shall be given in each state to the public acts, records, and judicial proceedings of every other state." By virtue of the Clause, if a judgment is entitled to full faith and credit, it must be recognized in sister states (*i.e.*, a party who loses a case in New York generally may not relitigate it in New Jersey; the New Jersey courts are bound by the New York ruling). However, not every decision is entitled to full faith and credit. There are three requirements:

1. The court that rendered the judgment must have had *jurisdiction over the parties and the subject matter*;

2. The judgment must have been *on the merits*; *i.e.,* on the substance of the plaintiff's claim rather than on a procedural issue, such as improper venue or running of the statute of limitations; and

3. The judgment must be *final*.

V. INTERSOVEREIGN LITIGATION

A. SUITS BY THE UNITED STATES AGAINST A STATE

1. State Need Not Consent
The United States may sue a state without its consent.

2. Original Jurisdiction in Supreme Court
Congress has restated the scope of original jurisdiction in 28 U.S.C. section 1251. The Supreme Court has *nonexclusive* original jurisdiction in all controversies between the United States and a state. This means that the Supreme Court may take original jurisdiction of such a case if it so chooses or it can allow the case to be heard originally in a lower federal court. The jurisdictional system complies with Article III.

B. SUITS BY STATE AGAINST UNITED STATES—UNITED STATES MUST CONSENT
Public policy forbids a state from suing the United States without its consent. Congress can pass legislation that permits the United States to be sued by a state in given situations.

C. FEDERAL OFFICER AS DEFENDANT

1. Limitation
Suits against a federal officer are *deemed to be brought against the United States* itself *if* the judgment sought would be satisfied out of the public treasury or would interfere with public administration and therefore are not permitted.

2. Specific Relief Against the Individual Officer
Specific relief against an officer as an individual will be granted if the officer acted ultra vires:

a. Beyond his statutory powers; or

b. The valid power was exercised in an unconstitutional manner.

D. SUITS BY ONE STATE AGAINST ANOTHER
One state may sue another state without the latter's consent. The Supreme Court has *exclusive original jurisdiction*.

VI. INTERGOVERNMENTAL TAX AND REGULATION IMMUNITIES

A. FEDERAL TAXATION AND REGULATION OF STATE OR LOCAL GOVERNMENTS
The Tenth Amendment provides that powers not delegated to the United States by the Constitution, nor prohibited to the states, are reserved to the states. This reservation of power is often cited as a restriction on Congress's power to regulate the states.

1. Tax or Regulation Applying to State and Private Entities—Valid
The Supreme Court will not likely strike down on Tenth Amendment grounds a tax or regulation that subjects states or local governments to regulations or taxes that apply to *both*

the public sector and the private sector. It has held that in such cases, the states' interests are best protected by the states' representation in Congress. [Garcia v. San Antonio Metropolitan Transit Authority, 469 U.S. 528 (1985)]

Example: Congress can require state and local governments to follow the provisions of the Federal Fair Labor and Standards Act requiring minimum wages for all employees. [Garcia v. San Antonio Metropolitan Transit Authority, *supra*]

2. Tax or Regulation that Applies Only to States

However, the Tenth Amendment does limit Congress's power to regulate the states alone by requiring the states to act in a particular way. Congress may not compel states to enact or enforce a regulatory program. [New York v. United States, 504 U.S. 144 (1992)—federal statute requiring states to either regulate radioactive waste or take title to it is beyond Congress's power] Similarly, if Congress passes a tax that does not apply to private businesses but merely taxes state government entities, there is a possibility that the Court would use the Tenth Amendment to prohibit the tax.

a. Exception—Civil Rights

Congress *may* use its power under the Fourteenth and Fifteenth Amendments to restrict state activities that it determines would violate the civil liberties of persons within the state.

Examples: 1) Congress may invalidate state laws establishing a literacy test as a prerequisite to voting in state elections. [Oregon v. Mitchell, 400 U.S. 112 (1970)]

2) Congress may restrict changes in state voting laws that have the effect of diminishing the voting power of racial minorities even though the change in state law was not purposeful racial discrimination that would violate Section 1 of the Fifteenth Amendment. [Rome v. United States, 446 U.S. 156 (1980)]

b. Exception—Spending Power Conditions

Congress may also "regulate" states through the spending power by imposing explicit conditions on the grant of money to state or local governments. Such conditions will not violate the Tenth Amendment merely because Congress lacked the power to directly regulate the activity that is the subject of the spending program.

Example: A federal law that would withhold 5% of the federal highway funds otherwise allocable to a state if the state did not set a 21 years' minimum age for the drinking of alcohol has been upheld. [South Dakota v. Dole, 483 U.S. 203 (1987)]

3. Commandeering State Officials

The Supreme Court has held that the Tenth Amendment prohibits Congress from adopting a statute that "commandeers" state officials by *requiring states to regulate their own citizens*. [Printz v. United States, 521 U.S. 898 (1997)—striking portions of a federal gun law that required state law enforcement officers to collect from gun dealers reports regarding prospective handgun purchasers and to conduct background checks on them] However, the Court has allowed Congress to *regulate the states by prohibiting them from performing certain acts*. [*See* Reno v. Condon, 528 U.S. 141 (2000)—upholding federal act that bars states (as well as private resellers) from disclosing personal information required on drivers' license applications]

B. STATE TAXATION AND REGULATION OF FEDERAL GOVERNMENT

1. No Direct Tax on Federal Instrumentalities

A state tax levied directly against the property or operation of the federal government without the consent of Congress is invalid.

2. Nondiscriminatory, Indirect Taxes

Nondiscriminatory, indirect taxes on the federal government or its property are permissible if they *do not unreasonably burden* federal government.

Examples: 1) State income taxes on salaries of federal employees are valid. However, a state tax that imposes a higher tax on federal employees (or retired federal employees) than on state or local government employees (or retired employees) would violate the principle of intergovernmental tax immunity, unless Congress had approved this discriminatory tax. [Davis v. Michigan Department of Treasury, 489 U.S. 803 (1989)]

2) Private contractors, acting as purchasing agents for the federal government, cannot be compelled to pay state sales or use taxes on materials purchased on behalf of the federal government. State sales or use taxes are valid where the contractor is working for the federal government on a "cost-plus" basis. These extra costs are not characterized as direct taxes.

3. State Regulation of Federal Government

The states have no power to regulate the activities of the federal government unless Congress consents to the regulation. Thus, instrumentalities and agents of the federal government are immune from state regulations relating to performance of their federal functions.

Examples: 1) A state may not require a post office employee to obtain a state driver's license in order to drive a mail truck. [Johnson v. Maryland, 254 U.S. 51 (1920)]

2) A state may not require a contractor to obtain a state license to build facilities on an Air Force base, located within the state, pursuant to a government contract. [Leslie Miller, Inc. v. Arkansas, 352 U.S. 187 (1956)]

VII.   PRIVILEGES AND IMMUNITIES CLAUSES

A.   INTRODUCTION

There are two Privileges and Immunities Clauses: the Fourteenth Amendment Privileges and Immunities Clause and the Interstate Privileges and Immunities Clause of Article IV. The Fourteenth Amendment clause protects attributes of United States citizenship and is rarely applicable. The Article IV provision prevents some discrimination by states against nonresidents, and is usually more relevant on the bar exam.

B.   ARTICLE IV—PRIVILEGES OF STATE CITIZENSHIP

Article IV, Section 2, the Interstate Privileges and Immunities Clause, provides that "[t]he Citizens of each state shall be entitled to all Privileges and Immunities of citizens in the several states." Thus, it prohibits discrimination by a state against nonresidents.

1. Corporations and Aliens Not Protected

Corporations and aliens are *not citizens* of a state for purposes of the Privileges and Immunities Clause.

2. Only "Fundamental Rights" Protected

The Interstate Privileges and Immunities Clause does not prohibit all discrimination by a state in favor of its own citizens, but only when the denial concerns "fundamental rights"—*i.e.*, those involving important *commercial activities* (such as pursuit of a livelihood) or *civil liberties*. For example, the following have been struck down:

a. *Statute charging nonresident commercial fishermen substantially more for commercial fishing license* than resident commercial fishermen ($2,500 vs. $25) [Toomer v. Witsell, 334 U.S. 385 (1948); *cf.* Baldwin v. Montana Fish & Game Commission, 436 U.S. 371 (1978)—vast difference between resident and nonresident *recreational* hunting license constitutional since no essential commercial activity involved];

b. *Statute giving resident creditors priority* over nonresident creditors as to assets of foreign corporations in receivership proceedings [Blake v. McClung, 172 U.S. 239 (1898)];

c. *Statute or court rule requiring state residency to be licensed* to practice law within the state [Supreme Court of Virginia v. Friedman, 487 U.S. 59 (1988)];

d. *State income tax only on nonresidents* who earn money within the state [Austin v. New Hampshire, 420 U.S. 656 (1975)]; and

e. *State law requiring private sector employers to give hiring preference to residents* absent a closely related substantial justification (*see* below) [Hicklin v. Orbeck, 437 U.S. 518 (1978)], but states *may* require a person to be a resident to hold *government employment* [McCarthy v. Philadelphia Civil Service Commission, 424 U.S. 645 (1976) (per curiam)].

3. **Substantial Justification Exception**

A state law discriminating against nonresidents may be valid if the state has a substantial justification for the different treatment. In effect, it must show that nonresidents either cause or are part of the problem it is attempting to solve, and that there are *no less restrictive means* to solve the problem.

Example: The Court held that a city ordinance requiring 40% of employees of contractors and subcontractors working on city construction projects to be city residents was an apparent violation of the Article IV Privileges and Immunities Clause because it gave a preference in private sector employment to city residents. However, the Court found that it could not make a final determination as to *whether the preference was justified* in this case because the record from the lower courts did not allow it to evaluate the city's argument that the preference was necessary *to counteract grave economic and social ills* in urban environments caused by spiraling unemployment and declines in the population base of such cities. [United Building & Construction Trades Council v. Mayor of Camden, 465 U.S. 208 (1984)]

4. **Note—Relationship to Commerce Clause**

Although the Article IV Privileges and Immunities Clause and the Commerce Clause may apply different standards and produce different results, they tend to mutually reinforce each other. Consequently, they both have to be considered in analyzing bar exam questions.

C. **FOURTEENTH AMENDMENT—PRIVILEGES OF NATIONAL CITIZENSHIP**

The Fourteenth Amendment Privileges and Immunities Clause prohibits states from denying their citizens the privileges and immunities of national citizenship, such as the right to petition Congress for redress of grievances, the right to vote for federal officers, the right to enter public lands, the right to interstate travel, and any other right flowing from the distinct relation of a citizen to the United States Government.

1. **Corporations Not Protected**

Corporations are *not citizens* of the United States and are *not protected*.

2. **Bill of Rights Not Included**

The *Slaughterhouse Cases,* 83 U.S. 36 (1873), held that the fundamental rights protected against federal abuse (first 10 amendments) are *not privileges and immunities of national citizenship* within the meaning of the Fourteenth Amendment; nor are such other basic rights as the right to live, work, and eat. Thus, the guarantees of the Bill of Rights are protected from state action only by the Due Process and Equal Protection Clauses of the Fourteenth Amendment.

3. **Right to Travel and the Privileges and Immunities Clause**

The right to travel, which is protected by the Fourteenth Amendment, includes the right of newly arrived citizens to enjoy the same privileges and immunities as are enjoyed by other citizens of the state.

Example: A California statute limiting the welfare benefits of first year residents was held unconstitutional under the Fourteenth Amendment Privileges and Immunities Clause. The statute provided that citizens who had lived in California for less than one year could receive only the benefits they would have received in their prior state of residence. The Court noted that the right to travel includes the right to be treated equally in a new state of residence. [Saenz v. Roe, 526 U.S. 489 (1999)]

PART THREE: STATE REGULATION OR TAXATION OF COMMERCE

VIII. REGULATION OF FOREIGN COMMERCE

A. **LIES EXCLUSIVELY WITH CONGRESS**

For all practical purposes, the power to regulate foreign commerce lies exclusively with Congress. "Foreign" commerce has been held to include traffic on the high seas, even though both terminal ports are within the United States. [Japan Line, Ltd. v. County of Los Angeles, 441 U.S. 434 (1979)]

B. MINOR EXCEPTIONS WHERE STATE REGULATION PERMITTED

The Supreme Court, however, has recognized a few minor exceptions; thus, the states are free to regulate local aspects of port pilotage and navigation of ships in foreign commerce (*e.g.,* aspects such as safety of handling); and in one case the Court permitted state regulation of excursion boat traffic between Detroit and a Canadian island (state barred racial discrimination among boat passengers) since no Canadians or Canadian products or services were involved. [Bob-Lo Excursion Co. v. Michigan, 333 U.S. 28 (1948)]

IX. REGULATION OF INTERSTATE COMMERCE

A. REGULATION OF COMMERCE BY CONGRESS

As already seen, Congress's power over interstate commerce is "plenary" and pervasive. However, the power is *nonexclusive*—it is shared with the states to some degree.

1. Power of Congress to Supersede or Preempt State Regulation

Recall that the Supremacy Clause makes federal law supreme. (*See* IV.C., *supra.*) Thus, if a state law regulating commerce conflicts with a federal law, the state law will be void. Moreover, if Congress desires, it may preempt an entire area of regulation, thus preventing states from making any laws concerning the area preempted. (*See* IV.C.3., *supra.*)

2. Power of Congress to Permit or Prohibit State Regulation

Although Congress's commerce power is nonexclusive, the states' power to regulate interstate commerce is restricted by the negative implications of the Commerce Clause, even absent federal legislation—the states generally may *not* discriminate against interstate commerce. (*See* below.) Nevertheless, Congress is not so restricted; it may allow the states to adopt legislation that would otherwise violate the Commerce Clause.

Example: A state imposed a 3% tax on out-of-state insurance companies for all premiums received from insuring residents of the state. No similar tax was placed on in-state insurance companies. Although such a tax would ordinarily be held invalid under the Commerce Clause—because it discriminates against interstate commerce—the tax here was upheld because Congress had adopted an act permitting the states to regulate insurance in any manner, as long as the state regulation did not conflict with a federal statute specifically regulating insurance. [Prudential Insurance Co. v. Benjamin, 328 U.S. 408 (1946); *and see* Northeast Bancorp, Inc. v. Board of Governors, 472 U.S. 159 (1985)]

Note: As indicated above, Congress may also prohibit the states from adopting legislation that would otherwise be permitted under the Commerce Clause.

a. Limitation

While Congress may permit states to adopt regulations that would otherwise violate the Commerce Clause, such consent will not obviate other constitutional objections to the regulation. Thus, Congress may not give states the power to restrict civil liberties. (*See* X.A.1.b.2)a), *infra.*)

B. STATE REGULATION OF COMMERCE IN THE ABSENCE OF CONGRESSIONAL ACTION

If Congress has not enacted laws regarding the subject, a state or local government may regulate local aspects of interstate commerce if the regulation:

(i) Does *not discriminate* against out-of-state competition to benefit local economic interests; and

(ii) Is *not unduly burdensome* (*i.e.,* the incidental burden on interstate commerce does not outweigh the legitimate local benefits produced by the regulation).

If either test is not met, the regulation will be held void for violating the Commerce Clause (sometimes called the *"Dormant Commerce Clause"* or *"Negative Commerce Clause"* under such circumstances).

1. Discriminatory Regulations

a. Generally Invalid

State or local regulations that discriminate against interstate commerce to protect local economic interests are almost always invalid.

b. **Examples**

1) **Regulations Protecting Local Businesses**
Laws designed to protect local businesses against interstate competition generally will be invalidated.

Examples: 1) A state cannot place a surcharge on out-of-state milk to make that milk as (or more) expensive as milk produced in the state.

2) A state cannot exempt local business or products from taxation or regulation that it seeks to apply to out-of-state businesses or products that come into the state.

3) A law requiring all locally produced solid waste to be processed at a local waste processing business was held to violate the Commerce Clause because it was a trade barrier against competition from out-of-state waste processors. [C&A Carbone, Inc. v. Town of Clarkstown, 511 U.S. 383 (1994)]

2) **Regulations Requiring Local Operations**
If a state law requires a business to perform specific business operations in the state to engage in other business activity within the state, the law will normally be held invalid as an attempt to discriminate against other states where the business operations could be performed more efficiently.

Example: If a state required all businesses that produce melons in the state and all businesses that purchase melons from local producers to wrap or package the melons in the state (before the melons were exported from the state), the law would be invalid as an attempt to force businesses to locate their packaging operations in the state.

3) **Regulations Limiting Access to In-State Products**
A state law that makes it difficult or impossible for out-of-state purchasers to have access to in-state products (other than products owned by the state itself) is likely to be held invalid.

Examples: 1) A state cannot prohibit in-state owners of "ground water" from selling and exporting the water they own to persons in other states.

2) A state cannot require in-state companies to sell products at a lower price to in-state residents than to out-of-state residents.

4) **Regulations Prohibiting Out-of-State Wastes**
A state may not prohibit private landfill or waste disposal facilities from accepting out-of-state garbage or waste or surcharge such waste [Philadelphia v. New Jersey, 437 U.S. 617 (1978); Chemical Waste Management v. Hunt, 504 U.S. 334 (1992)] unless Congress authorizes such discrimination [New York v. United States, VI.A.2., *supra*—federal statute allowing states to impose surcharge on certain out-of-state nuclear wastes upheld]. This rule applies even to hazardous wastes. [Oregon Waste Systems, Inc. v. Department of Environmental Quality, 511 U.S. 93 (1994)]

c. **Exceptions**

1) **Necessary to Important State Interest**
A discriminatory state or local law may be valid if it furthers an important, non-economic state interest (*e.g.,* health or safety) and there are *no reasonable alternatives* available.

Example: A state could prohibit the importation of live baitfish (such as minnows) into the state because the state could demonstrate that it had no other way of effectively avoiding the possibility that such baitfish might bring certain parasites into the state or, in other ways, have a detrimental effect on the state's wild fish population. [Maine v. Taylor, 476 U.S. 1138 (1986)] However, a state could not prohibit the export of live baitfish to out-of-state purchasers because the sale of such fish to out-of-state purchasers would not impair any interest of the state, except the interest of protecting local purchasers of baitfish from competition by out-of-state purchasers. [Hughes v. Oklahoma, 441 U.S. 322 (1979)]

2) State as Market Participant

The Commerce Clause does not prevent a state from preferring its own citizens when the state is acting as a market participant (*e.g.,* buying or selling products, hiring labor, giving subsidies).

Examples: 1) A state may purchase scrap automobiles from its citizens at a higher-than-market rate and refuse to pay nonresidents the same amount. [Hughes v. Alexandria Scrap Corp., 426 U.S. 794 (1976)]

2) Under the market participant exception to the Commerce Clause, a city may require that all construction *projects funded by the city* be performed by contractors using a workforce composed of at least 50% bona fide residents of the city. [White v. Massachusetts Council of Construction Employers, 460 U.S. 204 (1983)]

a) Limitation—Interstate Privileges and Immunities Clause

While a state or local government does not violate the *Commerce Clause* by preferring its own citizens while acting as a market participant, there is no market participant exception to the Interstate Privileges and Immunities Clause. Thus, a regulation that interferes with private sector employment, such as the one in example 2), above, may violate the Privileges and Immunities Clause unless the regulating entity can show a substantial justification for the regulation. (*See* VII.B.3., *supra.*)

b) Limitation—"Downstream" Restrictions

While a state may choose to sell only to state residents, it may not attach conditions to a sale that would discriminate against interstate commerce.

Example: Alaska violated the Commerce Clause when it imposed a contractual requirement on purchasers of state-owned timber that the timber be processed in Alaska before being shipped out of state. [South-Central Timber Development, Inc. v. Wunnicke, 467 U.S. 82 (1984)—plurality opinion]

2. Nondiscriminatory Laws—Balancing Test

Sometimes a nondiscriminatory state or local law that regulates commerce may impose a burden on interstate commerce; *e.g.,* a state law regulating the size of trucks within that state may burden interstate commerce because interstate trucking operations will be subject to the law when their trucks enter the state. A nondiscriminatory law will be invalidated only if the burden on interstate commerce outweighs the promotion of legitimate (not discriminatory) local interests. This is a case-by-case balancing test. Thus, some regulations of trucks will be upheld, because they do not impose an undue burden on interstate commerce, whereas other truck regulations will be invalidated, because they would make it extremely difficult for interstate trucking operators to have their trucks travel into or through the state.

a. Less Restrictive Alternatives

In determining whether a nondiscriminatory state regulation of interstate commerce violates the Commerce Clause, a court will sometimes consider whether less restrictive alternatives are available.

Example: Although it is legitimate for a city to pass laws designed to ensure that milk products sold within the city are safe, a city cannot require those businesses that wish to sell milk in the city to have the milk processed (purified and placed in bottles) at a processing site close to the city. *Rationale:* The city has a variety of alternatives that impose less burden on interstate commerce.

b. Absence of Conflict with Other States

State and local laws regulating commerce are more likely to be upheld when there is little chance that states would have conflicting regulations of the same subject matter.

Example: A state could validly apply a state law prohibiting racial or gender discrimination in the hiring of personnel to an airline doing business in the state because the law was not discriminatory against out-of-state businesses, it promoted a legitimate interest, and no other state could validly require or permit racial or gender discrimination by airlines.

c. State Control of Corporations

A different standard may apply to statutes regulating the internal governance of a corporation adopted by the state of incorporation. Because of the states' long history of regulating the internal governance of corporations that they create, and because of their strong interest in doing so, even a statute that heavily impacts interstate commerce may be upheld.

Example: To protect shareholders of corporations incorporated in Indiana from hostile takeovers, the Indiana legislature adopted a "control share acquisition statute." The statute provided that once a person acquires shares that take him across a specified ownership threshold (*e.g.*, one-third ownership of all voting shares), he may not vote those shares unless the other shareholders consent. Even though most hostile take-over bids originate from outside the state, the Supreme Court found that the statute did not violate the Commerce Clause because its aim was to protect current shareholders, it did not discriminate between takeover bidders based on their state of origin, and there is no chance that the state law would conflict with the laws of other states because the internal governance of a corporation is regulated only by the state in which the corporation is incorporated. [CTS Corp. v. Dynamics Corp. of America, 481 U.S. 69 (1987)]

C. TWENTY-FIRST AMENDMENT—STATE CONTROL OVER INTOXICATING LIQUOR

1. Intrastate Regulations

The Twenty-First Amendment, which repealed prohibition, gives state governments wide latitude over the importation of liquor and the conditions under which liquor is sold or used within the state. However, state liquor regulations that constitute only an economic preference for local liquor manufacturers may violate the Commerce Clause. The Commerce Clause prohibits both outright economic favoritism for local businesses and attempts to regulate out-of-state transactions in order to guarantee the competitive position of in-state businesses.

Examples: 1) A state sales tax on liquor produced in other states that does not tax sales of locally produced alcoholic beverages violates the Commerce Clause.

2) A state law that requires out-of-state distillers or sellers of alcoholic beverages to affirm that the price the distiller/seller is charging liquor retailers or wholesalers in the state is no greater than the price the distiller/seller is charging in other states violates the Commerce Clause. Such a price affirmation law directly interferes with and burdens interstate commerce. The Twenty-First Amendment does not authorize this type of state interference with commerce. [Brown-Forman Distillers Corp. v. New York State Liquor Authority, 476 U.S. 573 (1986); Healy v. The Beer Institute, Inc., 491 U.S. 324 (1989)]

2. Interstate Regulations

Transitory liquor (liquor bound for out-of-state destinations) is subject to the Commerce Clause. Thus, a state prohibition on transporting liquor through the state would probably be held unconstitutional as violating the Commerce Clause.

3. Conflicts Between State Liquor Laws and Individual Rights

a. General Rule—Individual Rights Paramount
Individual rights guaranteed by the Bill of Rights and the Fourteenth Amendment outweigh state liquor control laws.

b. "Excessive Drinkers"
"Excessive drinkers" are entitled to procedural due process before the state can post their names in liquor stores. [Wisconsin v. Constantineau, 400 U.S. 433 (1971)]

c. Equal Protection Clause
The Equal Protection Clause prohibits different age minimums based on sex in the sale of liquor. A state cannot permit 18-year-old females to buy beer and prohibit 18- to 21-year-old males from doing so. [Craig v. Boren, 429 U.S. 190 (1976)]

4. Federal Power
The Twenty-First Amendment does not prohibit Congress from controlling economic

transactions involving alcoholic beverages under the federal commerce power. Thus, federal antitrust law can prohibit a practice of liquor dealers that has the effect of fixing minimum prices. [324 Liquor Corp. v. Duffy, 479 U.S. 335 (1987)] Similarly, as mentioned above, Congress may, without violating the Twenty-First Amendment, "regulate" liquor distribution by imposing conditions on the grant of federal funds given under the spending power. [South Dakota v. Dole, VI.A.2.b., *supra*]

D. BAR EXAM APPROACH

Whenever a bar exam question involves a state regulation that affects the free flow of interstate commerce, you should proceed as follows:

First, see if the question refers to *any federal legislation* that might be held either to: (i) *supersede* the state regulation or *preempt* the field, or (ii) *authorize* state regulation otherwise impermissible.

Second, if neither of these possibilities is dispositive of the question, ask if the state legislation either *discriminates* against interstate or out-of-state commerce or places an *undue burden* on the free flow of interstate commerce. If the legislation is discriminatory, it will be invalid unless (i) it furthers an important state interest *and* there are no reasonable nondiscriminatory alternatives, or (ii) the state is a market participant. If the legislation does not discriminate but burdens interstate commerce, it will be invalid if the burden on commerce outweighs the state's interest. Consider whether there are less restrictive alternatives.

X. POWER OF STATES TO TAX INTERSTATE COMMERCE

A. GENERAL CONSIDERATIONS

The same general considerations applicable to state regulation of commerce (*supra*) apply to taxation. Pursuant to the Commerce Clause, Congress has complete power to authorize or forbid state taxation affecting interstate commerce. If Congress has not acted, look to see whether the tax *discriminates* against interstate commerce. If it does, it is invalid. If it does not, assess whether the burden on interstate commerce outweighs the benefit to the state. Three tests must be met: (i) there must be a *substantial nexus* between the taxpayer and the state; (ii) the tax must be *fairly apportioned*; and (iii) there must be a *fair relationship* between the tax and the services or benefits provided by the state.

1. Discriminatory Taxes

Unless authorized by Congress, state taxes that discriminate against interstate commerce violate the Commerce Clause. Such taxes may also be held to violate the Interstate Privileges and Immunities Clause (*see* VII.B., *supra*) if they also discriminate against nonresidents of the state [Austin v. New Hampshire, 420 U.S. 656 (1975)], as well as the Equal Protection Clause if the discrimination is not rationally related to a legitimate state purpose [WHYY, Inc. v. Borough of Glassboro, 393 U.S. 117 (1968)—denial of tax exemption solely because taxpayer was incorporated in another state is invalid].

a. Finding Discrimination

1) Tax Singles Out Interstate Commerce

If a state tax singles out interstate commerce for taxation, the Court ordinarily will not "save" the tax by finding other state taxes imposed only on local commerce (which might arguably eliminate the "apparent" discrimination against interstate commerce).

Example: The Supreme Court invalidated an Ohio statute that gave a tax credit against the Ohio motor vehicle fuel sales tax (paid by fuel dealers) for each gallon of ethanol sold as a component of gasohol if, but only if, the ethanol was produced in Ohio or in a state that granted a similar tax advantage to ethanol produced in Ohio. The Supreme Court found that this tax credit system constituted discrimination against interstate commerce. [New Energy Co. of Indiana v. Limbach, 486 U.S. 269 (1988)]

Note: However, state taxes that single out interstate commerce are considered *nondiscriminatory* if the particular statutory section or scheme *also* imposes the same type of tax on *local* commerce (*e.g.,* sales and use taxes, discussed *infra*).

2) Tax with In-State Subsidy

A seemingly uniform tax may be ruled to be discriminatory if the proceeds from the tax are "earmarked" for subsidies to in-state businesses.

Example: A state imposed a tax on all milk dealers, but the tax law provided that revenue from the tax would be put into a fund that would be used to pay subsidies to in-state dairy farmers. This assessment-subsidy system violates the Commerce Clause because it operates identically to a tax placed only on sales of milk produced outside the state. [West Lynn Creamery, Inc. v. Healy, 512 U.S. 186 (1994)]

b. Choosing the Proper Clause

While a state or local tax that discriminates against interstate commerce generally violates the Commerce Clause, the Clause is not always the strongest argument against the tax.

1) Interstate Privileges and Immunities Clause

If a state or local tax discriminates against a *natural person who is a nonresident*, the Article IV Interstate Privileges and Immunities Clause is the strongest argument against the tax's validity, because it is more direct than a Commerce Clause argument.

2) Equal Protection

a) Where Congress Approves the Discrimination

Although the Supreme Court normally uses the Commerce Clause to invalidate discriminatory legislation, it may also find that such discrimination violates the Equal Protection Clause. This is important where Congress has given the states the power to do something that would otherwise violate the Commerce Clause: Congress can give states the power to take actions that otherwise would violate the Commerce Clause, but it *cannot* approve state actions that would violate equal protection. Thus, if Congress has approved a type of state tax that discriminates against out-of-state businesses, that state tax will not be in violation of the Commerce Clause, but it might be found to be a violation of equal protection.

Example: In *Metropolitan Life Insurance Co. v. Ward,* 470 U.S. 869 (1985), the Court invalidated a state tax on insurance companies that imposed a higher tax on out-of-state insurance companies than was paid by in-state companies. The Court found that federal statutes exempted state regulation of insurance businesses from Commerce Clause restrictions but found that the tax violated equal protection because it did not relate to a legitimate interest of government (*i.e.,* the state does not have a legitimate interest in discriminating against out-of-state businesses simply to protect local economic interests from competition).

b) Taxes Based on Suspect Classifications or Infringing on Fundamental Rights

The Court may use equal protection analysis rather than Commerce Clause analysis to strike state taxes that are imposed on the basis of a *suspect classification* or that burden a *fundamental right*. A state tax system giving tax exemptions only to long-time residents of the state and denying a similar tax exemption to newer residents will be held to violate the Equal Protection Clause.

Example: The Court invalidated a state property tax provision that gave an exemption from the property tax only to those Vietnam era veterans who had been residents of the state before May 1976. [Hooper v. Bernalillo County Assessor, 472 U.S. 612 (1985)]

2. Nondiscriminatory Taxes

The Court reviews nondiscriminatory state and local taxes affecting interstate commerce and balances the state need to obtain the revenue against the burden the tax imposes on the free flow of commerce—an approach similar to the one used for examining nondiscriminatory regulations to see whether they impose an undue burden on interstate commerce (*see* IX.B.2., *supra*).

a. Factors

The Court generally considers three factors in determining whether the nondiscriminatory tax is valid:

1) Substantial Nexus

A state tax will be valid under the Commerce Clause only if there is a substantial nexus between the activity or property taxed and the taxing state.

Example: A state in which a sale is made may force the seller to pay a sales tax if the seller has some significant contact with the state (*e.g.,* carries on business in the state). However, the state may not force the seller to pay a sales tax if its only contact with the state is the receipt of orders from sales representatives that may be accepted or rejected by the seller.

a) More than "Minimum Contacts" Under Due Process Clause

The substantial nexus requirement is not necessarily satisfied by establishing the "minimum contacts" between the taxed party and the state necessary to satisfy the Due Process Clause. Minimum contacts only requires there to be sufficient contacts with the forum such that it is reasonable for the taxed party to expect to be subject to the taxing state's jurisdiction. Substantial nexus requires significant or substantial activity within the taxing state. Thus, substantial nexus is not (necessarily) established by showing minimum contacts.

Example: If an interstate seller solicits sales in a state by mail only with orders shipped to the state by mail or common carrier, minimum contacts are present. However, the substantial nexus required by the Commerce Clause is not present—the mere mailing of catalogs to the state and shipment by mail or common carrier is not significant activity within the state. [Quill Corp. v. North Dakota, 504 U.S. 298 (1992)]

2) Fair Apportionment

A state or local tax affecting interstate commerce will be valid under the Commerce Clause only if it is fairly apportioned according to a rational formula (*i.e.,* the tax should be based on the extent of the taxable activity or property in the state). Otherwise the activity or property would be subject to cumulative tax burdens.

Examples: 1) State A imposes a 1% tax on gross receipts of all businesses within the state. Harvester is located in State A but makes a number of sales out-of-state. The tax is invalid as to Harvester's out-of-state sales since it potentially subjects those sales to cumulative burdens—the tax by the seller's state and a similar tax by the buyer's state—without apportioning the tax.

2) Chooch is a resident of State A. It owns railroad cars used in interstate commerce. The cars are in State A three months each year and State B three months each year. For a State B property tax on the railroad cars to be valid, it must fairly apportion the tax, so that the cars will not be subjected to a similar tax by State A, thus cumulating Chooch's tax burden.

Note: The taxpayer has the burden of proving an unfair apportionment.

a) Equal Protection Clause

If a tax is not fairly apportioned, it may also violate the Equal Protection Clause. Equal protection requires state or local government tax classifications to have a rational relationship to a legitimate government interest. The state may divide property into different classifications, and impose different levels of tax on each classification, if the classification system meets the rational relationship test. [Lehnhausen v. Lake Shore Auto Parts Co., 410 U.S. 356 (1973)—state personal property tax only on property owned by corporations is valid]

> *Example:* If a government tax assessment system results in identical pieces of property being valued and taxed at different rates for no reason other than the government assessor's refusal to adopt a more evenhanded valuation system, the resulting difference in the taxes imposed on the similar pieces of property will violate the Equal Protection Clause. [Allegheny Pittsburgh Coal Co. v. County Commission, 488 U.S. 336 (1989)]

3) Fair Relationship

A state or local tax affecting interstate commerce will be valid under the Commerce Clause only if the tax is fairly related to the services or benefits provided by the state.

> *Example:* A state may levy a tax on passengers enplaning at a state airport if the tax is related to the benefits that the passengers receive from the state (*e.g.,* the airport facilities). [*See* Evansville-Vanderburg Airport Authority District v. Delta Airlines, Inc., 405 U.S. 707 (1972)]

B. USE TAX

Use taxes are taxes imposed on the users of goods purchased out of state.

1. Permissible in Buyer's State

Use taxes are not considered to discriminate against interstate commerce even though they single out interstate commerce for taxation (*i.e.,* they are imposed only on goods purchased outside the state), as long as the use tax rate is not higher than the sales tax rate. *Rationale:* The purpose of such a tax is to *equalize* the tax on in-state and out-of-state goods rather than to give in-state goods an advantage. [*See* Henneford v. Silas Mason Co., 300 U.S. 577 (1937)]

2. Credit for Sales Tax Paid in Seller's State

It has been argued that if the sale is consummated outside the state and is subjected *there* to a *sales tax*, a use tax by the buyer's state must give a credit for the sales tax already paid in the seller's state; *i.e., if no credit* is given, the transaction is subjected to *two taxes* (a multiple burden) simply because the transaction involved interstate commerce.

3. State May Force Seller to Collect Use Tax

Often, states force the user to come forward and pay the state the use tax owed. However, a state may force the nonresident, interstate seller to *collect* the use tax from the local buyer and remit it to the state *if* the seller has the substantial nexus required by the Commerce Clause. The substantial nexus requirement can be met if the seller engages in some *significant activity* in the buyer's state, *e.g.,* maintains offices there.

a. Drummers Sufficient

The use of "drummers" (*i.e.,* persons who solicit orders locally, but who must submit all orders to the out-of-state seller's offices for approval and shipment) in the buyer's state *is* significant activity and can subject the out-of-state seller to the duty of collecting a use tax for the buyer's state. [General Trading Co. v. Iowa Tax Commission, 322 U.S. 335 (1944)]

Note: The use of "drummers" is *not* sufficient to force an out-of-state seller to collect a sales tax for the buyer's state. (*See* C.2.b., *infra.*)

b. Mail Solicitation Insufficient

If the interstate seller solicits sales by mail, with orders to be shipped by mail or common carrier, the interstate seller lacks the substantial nexus required by the Commerce Clause, and thus the buyer's state may *not* impose a duty on the interstate seller to collect a use tax on sales to local residents. [Quill Corp. v. North Dakota, A.2.a.1)a), *supra*]

C. SALES TAXES

Sales taxes are taxes imposed on the seller of goods for sales consummated within the state. They generally do not discriminate against interstate commerce; rather the issue usually involves whether there is a substantial nexus (*see* A.2.a.1), *supra*) between the taxpayer and the taxing state, or whether the tax is properly apportioned.

1. **Sales Tax by Seller's State**

   a. **Sale Consummated Within the State**
   If the sale is consummated within the state (*i.e.,* buyer takes possession within the state), there is a substantial nexus between the taxing state and the taxpayer; thus, the tax is valid under the Commerce Clause—even if the buyer immediately takes the goods outside the state for use. [International Harvester Co. v. Department of Treasury, 322 U.S. 340 (1944)] Also, there is no need to apportion the sales tax, even if the sale includes services to be performed in another state. [Oklahoma Tax Commission v. Jefferson Lines, Inc., 517 U.S. 1 (1995)—sale of bus ticket for transportation beginning in one state and ending in another]

   b. **Sale Made to a Buyer Outside the State**
   If the sale is made to a buyer outside the state (*i.e.,* goods delivered there by the seller or a common carrier), the tax will not be invalid for lack of a substantial nexus, because the relationship between the seller and the state is sufficient. However, all such laws to date have been found to violate the Commerce Clause because they were not fairly apportioned (*i.e.,* they did not provide for apportionment when the transaction could be taxed by other states, such as the buyer's state). [*See* J.D. Adams Manufacturing Co. v. Storen, 304 U.S. 307 (1938)]

2. **Sales Tax by Buyer's State**

   a. **Tax Permitted If Seller Has Substantial Contacts**
   If the interstate seller has **substantial contacts** with the consumer state (*e.g.,* office, salesroom, property, etc.), the substantial nexus requirement is satisfied and the Commerce Clause does not prohibit a sales tax by the consumer state—even though the goods are delivered from outside the state. [McGoldrick v. Berwind-White Coal Mining Co., 309 U.S. 33 (1940)]

   b. **"Drummers" Insufficient**
   However, if the only contact between the interstate seller and the consumer state consists of "drummers," the Commerce Clause **prohibits any sales tax** by the consumer state—because there is no substantial nexus. [McLeod v. J.E. Dilworth Co., 322 U.S. 327 (1944)] Note, however, that the buyer's state could force the seller to collect a use tax. (*See* B.3., *supra.*)

   c. **Tax on Telephone Calls**
   A state may impose a tax on the amount paid for a telephone call (in lieu of a sales or use tax on the transaction) if: (i) one of the parties to the telephone call (the caller or the recipient of the call) was in the taxing state; (ii) the call is charged to an address billed within the taxing state or paid within the taxing state; and (iii) the state tax minimizes the chance of a single call being subject to multiple state taxes by granting some form of credit against its tax for taxes paid to another state. [Goldberg v. Sweet, 488 U.S. 252 (1989)]

D. **AD VALOREM PROPERTY TAXES**
Ad valorem property taxes are taxes based on a percentage of the assessed value of the property in question. Such taxes are generally valid. However, a Commerce Clause issue arises when the property taxed moves in interstate commerce. Goods in transit are **totally exempt** from taxation. Once the goods come to a halt in a state (*i.e.,* obtain a **taxable situs**), they may be taxed. Then, the issue usually revolves around whether the tax imposes an undue cumulative burden (*i.e.,* apportionment).

1. **No Tax on Commodities in the Course of Interstate Commerce**
   Commodities in the course of interstate commerce are **entirely exempt** from local taxation—since each state could otherwise exact a toll as the goods passed through, imposing an intolerable burden on interstate commerce. [Standard Oil v. Peck, 342 U.S. 382 (1952)] Thus, states may not levy an ad valorem property tax on commodities being shipped in interstate commerce, even if the goods happen to be in the state on tax day.

   a. **When Is Property "in the Course of" Interstate Commerce?**
   Only property "in the course of" interstate commerce is immune from local property taxation.

1) **When Does Interstate Transportation Begin?**
Interstate transportation begins when (i) the cargo is delivered to an interstate carrier (the shipper thereby relinquishing further control), *or* (ii) the cargo actually starts its interstate journey. Goods merely being prepared for transit are *not* in the course of interstate commerce.

   a) **Severance Taxes Are Permissible**
   A nondiscriminatory state tax on *extraction of minerals* from the state, measured by a percentage of the value of the minerals, is valid even though most of the minerals are *sold in interstate commerce*. [Commonwealth Edison Co. v. Montana, 453 U.S. 609 (1981)]

2) **Effect of a "Break" in Transit**
Once started, a shipment remains in the course of interstate commerce unless actually diverted. Breaks in the continuity of transit will not destroy the interstate character of the shipment, unless the break was *intended to end or suspend* (rather than temporarily interrupt) the shipment.

3) **When Does Interstate Shipment End?**
The interstate shipment usually ends when it *reaches its destination*, and thereafter the goods are *subject to local tax*. However, a few cases have held that goods are still in transit where further acts are necessary after arrival to make an effective delivery. [York v. Colley, 247 U.S. 21 (1917)—shipment of complex industrial machinery, which vendor had to erect and install before effective delivery to purchaser] But there are limits to this doctrine. Thus, the Court has refused to find goods still in transit after the arrival of machinery that was simple to install and could be assembled by the purchaser as well as the vendor. [Browning v. City of Waycross, 233 U.S. 16 (1914)]

b. **No Apportionment Required**
The validity of state taxes on goods in interstate commerce is strictly a Commerce Clause question; *i.e.,* either the goods are "in the course of" interstate commerce and exempt from tax or they are not. There is no need for apportionment.

2. **Tax on Instrumentalities Used to Transport Goods Interstate**
The validity of ad valorem property taxes on instrumentalities of commerce (airplanes, railroad cars, etc.) depends on (i) whether the instrumentality has acquired a *"taxable situs"* in the taxing state (*i.e.,* whether there are *sufficient "contacts" with the taxing state* to justify the tax), and (ii) since the physical situs of the instrumentalities may change from state to state during the year, whether the *value* of the instrumentality has been properly *apportioned according to the amount of "contacts"* with each taxing state. (The taxable situs ("nexus") is required by the Due Process Clause to establish the state's power to tax at all, and apportionment is required by the Commerce Clause to prevent an intolerable burden on interstate commerce.)

   a. **Taxable Situs ("Nexus")**

   1) **Property Receiving Benefits or Protection from Taxing State**
   In general, an instrumentality has a taxable situs in a state if it receives *benefits or protection* from the state. [Braniff Airways v. Nebraska Board of Equalization and Assessment, 347 U.S. 490 (1954)—airplanes have taxable situs in non-domiciliary state where airline company owned no property but made 18 regularly scheduled flights per day from rented depot space, even though same aircraft did not land every day]

   2) **May Be More than One Taxable Situs**
   An instrumentality may have more than one taxable situs, upon each of which states can impose a tax subject to the required apportionment (*infra*).

   3) **Exception for Ships in International Waters—"Home-Port Doctrine"**
   An exception to the general rule prohibits taxation of ships sailing international waters by any state other than that in which the owner of the ship (or the ship itself) is domiciled. The domiciliary state may tax the ship at *full value*.

   Note: The "home-port doctrine" was developed prior to the concept of apportioned taxation, and its validity today is questionable. It has been expressly *repudiated* as to ships sailing inland or on interstate waters. [Ott v. Mississippi Valley Barge Line Co., 336 U.S. 169 (1949)]

b. Apportionment Requirement
Where an instrumentality has only one situs, the domiciliary state can tax at full value. Where the instrumentality has more than one taxable situs, a tax apportioned on the value of the instrumentality will be upheld if it fairly approximates the average physical presence of the instrumentality within the taxing state. [Union Tank Line Co. v. Wright, 249 U.S. 275 (1919)]

1) Proper Apportionment
The following methods have been upheld:

(i) Using the proportion of *miles traveled* within the taxing state to the total number of miles traveled by the instrumentalities in the entire operation. [Ott v. Mississippi Valley Barge Line Co., *supra*]

(ii) Computing the *average number of instrumentalities* (tank cars) *physically present* in the taxing state on any one day during the tax year and taxing that portion at full value—*i.e.,* as if in the state all year. [Johnson Oil Refining Co. v. Oklahoma, 290 U.S. 158 (1933)]

Note: Since different states may use different apportionment formulas to tax the same property, there may still be some double taxation of the same instrumentalities. However, the double taxation should be minimal if proper apportionment formulas have been used.

2) Improper Apportionment
The apportionment formula used must be *rational*, both on its face and as applied to property values connected with the taxing state. A state is not permitted to use imprecise formulas resulting in totally unrealistic assessments, since this would violate both the Due Process and Commerce Clauses. However, the taxpayer has a heavy burden of showing "gross overreaching." [Norfolk & Western Railroad v. Missouri Tax Commission, 390 U.S. 317 (1968)]

3) Domiciliary State Can Tax Full Value Unless Taxpayer Proves Taxable Situs Elsewhere
The taxpayer's domiciliary state can tax the full value of instrumentalities used in interstate commerce unless the taxpayer can prove that a defined part thereof has acquired a taxable "situs" elsewhere. [Northwest Airlines, Inc. v. Minnesota, 322 U.S. 292 (1944)]

a) Taxpayer's Required Proof
In this regard, mere proof that some determinable fraction of the instrumentalities was absent from the domiciliary state for part of the tax year is not enough. The taxpayer must prove either (i) that the instrumentalities were *permanently* located in some other state, or (ii) that they were *habitually employed* in interstate commerce in some other state or states, thus acquiring a "taxable situs" outside the domiciliary state. But the taxpayer need not prove that the instrumentalities are actually being taxed by a nondomiciliary state. [Central Railroad v. Pennsylvania, 370 U.S. 607 (1962)]

c. Tax on Value of Entire Interstate Enterprise
As an alternative to taxing each separate piece of property, a state may tax the value of an interstate business as a whole. Again, however, such a tax will be upheld only if the value of the total business is *apportioned* so as to reflect fairly that portion of the business property attributable to the taxing state. [Nashville, Chattanooga & St. Louis Railway v. Browning, 310 U.S. 362 (1940)—apportionment of value of railroad by local track mileage as compared to its total track]

E. PRIVILEGE, LICENSE, FRANCHISE, OR OCCUPATION TAXES
These taxes (cumulatively known as "doing business" taxes) may be measured by a flat amount or by a proportional rate based on revenue derived from the taxing state.

1. **General Rule—Such Taxes Are Permitted**

    States generally can impose such taxes—on companies engaged exclusively in interstate commerce, as well as on interstate companies engaged in local commerce—for the privilege of doing business within the state. However, the tax must meet the basic requirements—the activity taxed must have a *substantial nexus to the taxing state*; and the tax must be *fairly apportioned*, must *not discriminate* against interstate commerce, and must *fairly relate to services provided* by the state. [Complete Auto Transit, Inc. v. Brady, 430 U.S. 274 (1977)— *overruling* Spector Motor Service v. O'Connor, 340 U.S. 602 (1951)]

    Examples: 1) A privilege tax for doing business, based on the gross income derived from transporting goods within the state, can be applied to a trucking company that delivers goods coming from outside the state. [Complete Auto Transit, Inc. v. Brady, *supra*]

    2) An occupation tax on all businesses, based on gross income derived within the state, can be applied to a stevedoring company operating within the state that loads and unloads ships carrying goods in interstate commerce. [Department of Revenue v. Association of Washington Stevedoring Cos., 435 U.S. 734 (1978)—*overruling* Joseph v. Carter & Weekes Stevedoring Co., 330 U.S. 442 (1947)]

    a. **Taxpayer Has Burden of Proof**

    The taxpayer has the burden of showing that the state's apportionment formula is unfair. However, a state tax that discriminates against interstate commerce will be held invalid regardless of whether the taxpayer can show that an actual, unfair multiple burden is imposed on his business.

2. **Flat License Taxes on "Drummers" Prohibited**

    Flat license fees may not be levied upon "drummers" (solicitors) who seek local orders to be filled from goods shipped interstate, even if the same fee is levied on those selling intrastate goods. [Nippert v. Richmond, 327 U.S. 416 (1946)] Otherwise each municipality visited by the drummer could impose such a tax (resulting in a tremendous cumulative burden), while the local retail merchant would be subject to only one local tax—thereby constituting an unreasonable burden upon interstate commerce.

    a. **Compare—License Tax on Peddler Selling and Delivering Wares Within State**

    However, the state *may* impose a license tax on a peddler (itinerant salesperson) who *actually sells and delivers* her wares within a state (regardless of the fact that the goods are shipped into the state by interstate commerce), provided the tax rates are *nondiscriminatory*. [Dunbar Stanley Studios v. Alabama, 393 U.S. 537 (1969)]

3. **Taxes on Interstate Carriers**

    a. **In General**

    Interstate carriers (such as trucking companies) can be made to pay taxes that compensate the state for the use of its roads and the cost of administering traffic regulations. If a tax is fairly related to the use of the roads it is valid even though the proceeds are used for purposes unrelated to road use or road maintenance. However, a tax must not discriminate against interstate commerce or interstate carriers.

    b. **Flat Taxes**

    A "flat tax" on an interstate carrier is one that establishes a single fee to use the roads of the state (such as a fixed fee or a fee based on the size of the vehicle); it is not related to the amount of time that a vehicle spends in the state. Such a tax will violate the Commerce Clause whenever it has the effect of discriminating against out-of-state carriers by exposing a multistate carrier to a higher tax burden than would be borne by a solely in-state carrier. The Supreme Court has indicated that flat taxes on trucks may be inherently discriminatory unless either: (i) the state grants out-of-state carriers a credit against the flat tax for license fees (or similar taxes) paid to other states (so that the interstate carrier is not subject to multiple or discriminatory tax burdens); or (ii) the particular flat tax is nondiscriminatory and a reasonable charge for the use of the roads, and administrative difficulties make the collection of a more carefully apportioned tax (based on actual road use) impracticable. [American Trucking Associations, Inc. v. Scheiner, 483 U.S. 266 (1987)]

4. **Taxes on Interstate Passengers**

    A $1 state or municipal tax, imposed on enplaning commercial airline passengers to help defray airport construction costs, does not violate the Commerce Clause (or the Equal Protection Clause, or the "right to travel"). As long as (i) the amount of the tax is based on some *fair approximation of use* and is not excessive in comparison with the government benefit conferred, and (ii) the tax *does not discriminate* against interstate commerce, it is valid even though some other formula might better reflect the relative use of airports by individual users. [Evansville-Vanderburg Airport Authority District v. Delta Airlines, Inc., 405 U.S. 707 (1972)]

F. NET INCOME TAXES

States may impose fairly apportioned, nondiscriminatory net income taxes on interstate firms that conduct business within their borders. [Northwestern States Portland Cement Co. v. Minnesota, 358 U.S. 450 (1959)]

1. Adequate Contacts

In *Portland Cement,* the taxpayer had several sales representatives and a rented office in the taxing state, and the Court found this a sufficient "nexus" for the tax. (*Note:* Congress subsequently enacted 15 U.S.C. sections 381-384, *prohibiting* state net income taxes, irrespective of fair apportionment, on out-of-state businesses whose only contacts with the taxing state are salespeople.)

2. Fair Apportionment

a. Three-Factor Formula

The state in *Portland Cement* used a "three-factor" apportionment formula (ratio of property, payroll, and sales within state to taxpayer's total property, payroll, and sales). The taxpayer could not show that this was unfair, given state protection and services for the taxpayer's local activities; and there was no showing of "multiple burden."

b. Single-Factor Formula

A "single-factor" formula (ratio of sales within state to taxpayer's total sales) has also been *upheld* as "presumptively valid"—the taxpayer being unable to prove by "clear and cogent evidence" that it "led to a grossly distorted result." The fact that some income may be subject to overlapping taxes because other states (even a majority) use a different formula (the "three-factor" formula) does not prove that the single-factor formula is arbitrary. [Moorman Manufacturing Co. v. Bair, 437 U.S. 267 (1978)]

3. Income Includible in Tax Base

Income from separate corporate divisions or from subsidiary corporations operating in other states or foreign countries may be included in the tax base—unless the taxpayer proves that the divisions or subsidiaries were not part of its "single unitary business."

Examples: 1) The Court has applied the *unitary business tax* principle to allow California to include both *domestic and foreign subsidiary income* in the tax base of a corporation for purposes of applying the state income tax to the domestic corporation.

2) A substantial flow of value from the foreign subsidiary to the domestic parent company and a substantial degree of mutual interdependence justified including the foreign subsidiary income in the domestic parent corporation's tax base. [Container Corp. of America v. Franchise Tax Board, 463 U.S. 159 (1983)]

G. VALUE ADDED TAX

A value added tax is a tax on the value added at each stage of production or distribution. A state may impose such a tax on value added to products by businesses in the state. Like other state taxes, to be valid the tax must: (i) not discriminate against interstate commerce; (ii) tax an activity with a substantial nexus to the state; (iii) be fairly apportioned; and (iv) be fairly related to the services provided by the state.

1. Apportionment

The state is not required to measure precisely the value added to each product by each business in the state. It may use an apportionment formula to fairly determine the share of value added to the business's products attributable to its in-state activities. Thus, a three-part test based on the business's property, payroll, and sales, as is used for apportioning state income taxes (*see* F.2.a., *supra*), is proper. [Trinova Corp. v. Michigan Department of Treasury, 498 U.S. 358 (1991)]

H. TAXES ON FOREIGN CORPORATIONS

1. **State May Impose Tax as a Condition of Doing Business**
   A state may impose a tax or fee as a condition of allowing a foreign corporation (one incorporated in another state) to do business in the state. [Atlantic Refining Co. v. Virginia, 302 U.S. 22 (1937)]

2. **State Cannot Discriminate Against Foreign Corporation Once Admitted to Do Business**
   Once a foreign corporation *is* admitted to do business, the state cannot impose discriminatory rates as to business done locally. This would constitute an unreasonable burden on interstate commerce and deprive the corporation of the equal protection to which it is entitled. [Western Union v. Kansas, 216 U.S. 1 (1910)] Under the *Equal Protection Clause*, a state may *not* impose more onerous taxes or other burdens on foreign corporations than on domestic corporations unless the discrimination is *rationally* related to a *legitimate* state purpose. [Western & Southern Life Insurance Co. v. State Board of Equalization, 451 U.S. 648 (1981)]

XI. POWER OF STATES TO TAX FOREIGN COMMERCE

A. IMPORT-EXPORT CLAUSE
Article I, Section 10, Clause 2 provides: "No state shall, without the Consent of the Congress, lay any Imposts or Duties on Imports or Exports, except what may be absolutely necessary for executing its inspection Laws. . . ."

1. **State Taxation of "Imports" Prohibited Absent Congressional Consent**
   The Import-Export Clause prohibits the states from imposing any tax on imported goods as such or on commercial activity connected with imported goods *as such* (*i.e.*, taxes discriminating against imports), except with congressional consent. [Brown v. Maryland, 25 U.S. 419 (1827)]

   a. **Nondiscriminatory Ad Valorem Property Taxes on Goods in State—Permissible**
      A nondiscriminatory ad valorem property tax on all goods located in the state (including imported goods) is not prohibited. [Michelin Tire Corp. v. Wages, 423 U.S. 276 (1976)] *Rationale:* Such taxes merely apportion the cost of state services among all beneficiaries, and imports must bear their fair share.
      Example: It is permissible for a state to impose a nondiscriminatory property tax on imported goods stored under bond in a warehouse and destined for domestic manufacture and sale. [R.J. Reynolds Tobacco Co. v. Durham County, 479 U.S. 130 (1986)]

      1) **Goods in Transit**

         a) **Property Tax**
            The Court has left as an *open question* whether a nondiscriminatory property tax may be imposed on imported goods still in transit.

         b) **Occupation Tax**
            But a nondiscriminatory occupation tax on all businesses operating within the state may be applied to a company that *services* imported (or exported) goods, even when the goods are still in transit. [Department of Revenue v. Association of Washington Stevedoring Cos., X.E.1., *supra*]

2. **Inspection Fees for Imports and Exports**
   Such fees are permitted if "absolutely necessary," and are presumed reasonable (and upheld) unless the fees are so excessive that the state purpose is deemed to be revenue-raising rather than reimbursement of inspection costs. [Red "C" Oil Manufacturing Co. v. Board of Agriculture, 222 U.S. 380 (1912)]

3. **State Taxation of "Exports" Prohibited**
   The Import-Export Clause prohibits the states from imposing any tax on goods after they have entered the "export stream."

a. "Export Stream" Defined

Commodities sold to foreign purchasers enter the "export stream" (and hence are exempt from tax) only after it is *certain* that they are headed for their foreign destination and will not be diverted to domestic use.

B. COMMERCE CLAUSE

The Commerce Clause gives Congress the exclusive power to regulate foreign commerce and thus inherently limits a state's power to tax that commerce. Therefore, a state tax applied to foreign commerce must meet all of the Commerce Clause tests that apply to state taxation of interstate commerce. (*See* X.A., *supra.*) And even if a state tax meets those tests, the tax is invalid if it would (i) create a substantial risk of international multiple taxation or (ii) prevent the federal government from "speaking with one voice" regarding international trade or foreign affairs issues. [Barclays Bank PLC v. Franchise Tax Board, 512 U.S. 298 (1994)]

1. Instrumentalities of Foreign Commerce

A state may *not* impose an ad valorem property tax on instrumentalities that are *foreign owned* and used *exclusively in international commerce*. This is true even if the property has a situs in the taxing state and the tax is nondiscriminatory and fairly apportioned. [Japan Line, Ltd. v. County of Los Angeles, 441 U.S. 434 (1979)] In the absence of congressional authorization, there are stricter limits on state taxation of foreign commerce than of interstate commerce because there is greater need for federal uniformity and a lesser opportunity for the court to prevent multiple taxation.

2. Compare—Domestically Owned Instrumentalities of Foreign Commerce

A state may impose a fairly apportioned sales tax on a lease of domestically owned cargo containers that will be used in foreign commerce. Such a tax does not interfere with the federal interest in international commerce or present a substantial possibility of international multiple taxation. [Itel Containers International Corp. v. Huddleston, 507 U.S. 60 (1993)]

3. Income Tax—Apportioned Share of Unitary Business Income

A state may apply its income tax to a share of a multinational corporation's unitary (total) business income attributable to its activity in the state. The state tax must meet the same nexus (contacts), fair apportionment, and nondiscrimination requirements that are applied to determine whether the state can tax the unitary business of a multistate business. [Container Corp. of America v. Franchise Board, 463 U.S. 159 (1983); Barclays Bank PLC v. Franchise Tax Board, *supra*]

**PART FOUR: INDIVIDUAL GUARANTEES
AGAINST GOVERNMENTAL OR PRIVATE ACTION**

XII. LIMITATIONS ON POWER AND STATE ACTION REQUIREMENT

A. CONSTITUTIONAL RESTRICTIONS ON POWER OVER INDIVIDUALS

The Constitution provides individuals with a number of rights that restrict the power of the government (*e.g.*, the right to speak freely). Some rights/restrictions are applicable only to the federal government, some are applicable only to state and local governments, and some are applicable to all governmental bodies. A few even apply to private action. Several constitutional provisions also give Congress the power to adopt legislation to protect individual rights.

1. Bill of Rights

The Bill of Rights (first 10 Amendments to the Constitution) is the most important source of limitations on the federal government's power. By its terms, the Bill is not applicable to the states, although most of its safeguards have been held to be applicable to the states through the Fourteenth Amendment Due Process Clause.

a. Rights Applicable to States

The Supreme Court has stated that only those safeguards in the Bill of Rights that are "essential to liberty" are applicable to the states through the Fourteenth Amendment. Included in this concept are: *all the First Amendment* guarantees (speech, press, assembly, right to petition, free exercise, and nonestablishment of religion); the *Fourth Amendment* (unreasonable search and seizure); some *elements of the Fifth Amendment* (privilege against self-incrimination; compensation for taking of private property for public use); the *Sixth Amendment* (speedy and public trial by impartial jury, notice and right of confrontation, compulsory process, and right to legal counsel in all serious criminal proceedings); and the *Eighth Amendment* (cruel and unusual punishment, excessive bail, and excessive fine provisions are *assumed* to be incorporated but there is no precise ruling).

b. **Rights Not Applicable to States**
The Supreme Court has refused to "incorporate" (make applicable to the states) the following:

(i) *Second Amendment*—arms;

(ii) *Grand Jury Clause* of the Fifth Amendment;

(iii) *Seventh Amendment*—jury in civil cases; and

(iv) It is not clear whether the *Ninth Amendment* (regarding the existence of un-enumerated individual rights) applies to the states, but in any event, the Ninth Amendment has not been the primary basis for Supreme Court invalidation of a federal, state, or local law.

There has never been a Supreme Court decision on the Third Amendment (quartering of soldiers). The *Tenth Amendment,* by its terms, limits the federal government's power over states, and so is inapplicable to the states.

2. **Thirteenth Amendment**
The Thirteenth Amendment provides that slavery shall not exist in the United States.

a. **No Requirement of State Action**
The amendment contains no language limiting its effect to governmental action (*e.g.,* "no *state* shall . . . "); thus, it is applicable even to *private action*.

b. **Congressional Power**
The enabling clause of the amendment gives Congress the power to adopt appropriate legislation, and the Supreme Court apparently will uphold legislation proscribing almost any private racially discriminatory act that can be characterized as a "badge or incident of slavery."
Examples: The Supreme Court has upheld legislation:

1) Prohibiting private parties from refusing to rent or sell housing to a person because of race [Jones v. Alfred H. Mayer Co., 392 U.S. 409 (1968)];

2) Prohibiting private, nonsectarian schools from refusing to admit nonwhite children [Runyon v. McCrary, 427 U.S. 160 (1967)]; and

3) Prohibiting a private employer from discriminating in hiring on the basis of race [Patterson v. McLean Credit Union, 491 U.S. 164 (1989)].

Note: The above are examples of where Congress used its power to adopt statutes prohibiting "badges of slavery"; the proscribed activities would not necessarily be held to violate the Thirteenth Amendment absent the legislation.

3. **Fourteenth Amendment**
The Fourteenth Amendment *prohibits states* (not the federal government or private persons) from depriving any person of life, liberty, or property without due process and equal protection of the law. As discussed above, this amendment is a most important source of limitations on the states' power over individuals, since through the Due Process Clause, most of the protections of the Bill of Rights are applicable to the states.

Note: The meaning of due process and equal protection will be discussed later in this outline.

a. Requirement of State Action
The Fourteenth Amendment applies only if there is action by a state or local government, government officer, or private individual whose behavior meets the requirements for state action (*see* B., below).

b. Scope of Congressional Power
Section 5 of the Fourteenth Amendment is an enabling clause giving Congress the power to adopt *appropriate legislation* to enforce the rights and guarantees provided by the Fourteenth Amendment. Under Section 5, Congress may *not* expand existing constitutional rights or create new ones—it may only enact laws to prevent or remedy violations of rights already recognized by the courts. To adopt a valid law, Congress must point to a history or pattern of state violation of such rights and adopt legislation that is *congruent and proportional* (*i.e.*, narrowly tailored) to solving the identified violation.

Examples: 1) The Americans With Disabilities Act ("ADA") includes provisions that, among other things, prohibit states from discriminating against disabled persons in hiring practices and requires states to make reasonable accommodations for disabled employees. Under the Fourteenth Amendment Equal Protection Clause, the Court has recognized a right of disabled people to be free from irrational state discrimination. In adopting the ADA, Congress did not identify a history or pattern of irrational employment practices by the states. Even if there were such a pattern, the provisions here were not congruent and proportional to remedying irrational discrimination; they are overinclusive, because they prohibit states from making employment decisions that are constitutional under the rational basis test. [Board of Trustees of University of Alabama v. Garrett, 531 U.S. 356 (2001)]

2) Under similar reasoning, the Supreme Court has held that Congress has no power under Section 5 to broadly restrict age discrimination by state employers. [Kimel v. Florida Board of Regents, 528 U.S. 62 (2000)—the federal law is not congruent and proportional because it would forbid many employment decisions based on age that have a "rational basis," which the Court has held is the standard for judgment under the Equal Protection Clause for age-based discrimination]

3) The Supreme Court held that there is no violation of the First Amendment, applicable to the states through the Fourteenth Amendment, where a state law incidentally burdens a religious practice. [Employment Division v. Smith, XXII.C.3., *infra*] In response, Congress adopted a statute, purportedly under Section 5, providing that a state may not burden religious practices absent a compelling interest. The statute was held unconstitutional because it sought to expand substantive First Amendment rights beyond those recognized by the Supreme Court. [City of Boerne v. Flores, 521 U.S. 507 (1997)]

4. Fifteenth Amendment
The Fifteenth Amendment is a limitation on both the *states and the federal government*. It prohibits them from denying any citizen the right to vote on account of race or color. As indicated above, the amendment contains an enabling clause that allows Congress to adopt legislation protecting the right to vote from discrimination.

5. Commerce Clause
The Supreme Court has allowed Congress to use the Commerce Clause to limit the power of individuals over other individuals—by adopting legislation barring private racial discrimination in activities "connected with" interstate commerce. Recall that under the affectation

doctrine, almost any activity can be said to be connected with interstate commerce. (*See* II.A.4.a.1), *supra.*)

a.   **Civil Rights Act**
Provisions of the Civil Rights Act of 1964 *barring discrimination in places of public accommodation* are proper and valid exercises of commerce power.

b.   **Extent of Commerce Power**
The reach of the commerce power is broad. Any business which is *open to interstate travelers* or *uses products shipped in interstate commerce* is covered. [Daniel v. Paul, 395 U.S. 298 (1969)—private resort held to be a public place of accommodation encompassed within the Act because drinks and entertainment facilities had been purchased and shipped through interstate commerce]

6.   **Rights of National Citizenship**
The Supreme Court has also allowed Congress to limit the power of private individuals to infringe upon others' rights of national citizenship (*e.g.,* the right of interstate travel, the right to assemble to petition Congress for redress), without pointing to any specific constitutional source for the power. [Griffin v. Breckenridge, 403 U.S. 88 (1971)]

B.   **STATE ACTION REQUIREMENT**
As indicated above, the Constitution generally prohibits only governmental infringement of constitutional rights. Thus, to find some action unconstitutional, it is generally necessary to attribute the action to the state, which includes government agencies and officials acting under the color of state law. However, this does not mean that the act must be directly by a government actor; "state action" can be found in the actions of seemingly private individuals who (i) perform exclusive public functions, or (ii) have significant state involvement in their activities.

1.   **Exclusive Public Functions**
The Supreme Court has found that certain activities are so *traditionally* the *exclusive* prerogative of the state that they constitute state action even when undertaken by a private individual or organization. To date, only running a town and running an election for public office have been found to be such exclusive public functions.
Examples: 1) The owner of a "company town" with *all* of the attributes of a public town (*e.g.,* homes, sidewalks, streets, police and fire protection, etc.) cannot deny a person's First Amendment right to distribute religious literature in the town, since the company town is equivalent to a town. [Marsh v. Alabama, 326 U.S. 501 (1946)] However, the owner of a shopping mall can deny people their First Amendment right to picket, since a mall does not have all of the attributes of a town. [Hudgens v. NLRB, 424 U.S. 507 (1976)]

2) Running elections is an exclusive public function, so if a private organization runs a preprimary that has a substantial effect on who is ultimately elected, its actions will be state action. [Terry v. Adams, 345 U.S. 461 (1953)—county political group whose candidate almost always runs unopposed in primary and general election cannot discriminate]

a.   **Must Be Traditional *and* Exclusive Function**
To be state action, the activity must be *both* a *traditional* and *exclusive* government function. Thus, the Court has held that a warehouseman authorized by statute to sell goods stored with him for unpaid charges is not exercising state action when he makes the sale, because while resolution of private disputes is a traditional public function, it is not exclusive—the bailor had state law remedies to check abuses by the warehouseman. [Flagg Brothers v. Brooks, 436 U.S. 149 (1978)] State action exists, and due process guarantees apply, *only if* the creditor uses judicial or executive agencies to secure properties in the possession of the debtor.

2.   **Significant State Involvement—Facilitating Private Action**
"State action" also exists whenever a state *affirmatively* facilitates, encourages, or authorizes acts of discrimination by its citizens. Note, however, that there must be some sort of affirmative act by the state approving the private action; it is not enough that the state permits the conduct to occur.

a. **Instances of Significant State Involvement**

1) **Official Encouragement**
Purportedly private action will be given state action status if the action is encouraged or sanctioned by the state.

a) **Judicial Approval**
State court enforcement of *restrictive covenants prohibiting sale or lease of property to blacks* constitutes state action even in civil proceedings between private parties. [Shelley v. Kraemer, 334 U.S. 1 (1948)]

(1) **Peremptory Challenges**
The use of peremptory challenges, even by a private party, constitutes state action both because jury selection is a traditional public function and because there is overt, significant participation by the government (the judge) in the jury selection process. Thus, private litigants and defendants are prohibited from using peremptory challenges in a discriminatory manner. [*See* Edmonson v. Leesville Concrete, 500 U.S. 614 (1992); Georgia v. McCollum, 505 U.S. 42 (1992)]

b) **Official Acts**
State action may be found in the absence of an unconstitutional statute or ordinance if it appears that the state sanctions constitutional violations by its own officers.

(1) **Discriminatory Law Enforcement**
The Court reversed a conviction of sit-in demonstrators where no statute or ordinance required segregation but the mayor and police had announced publicly that they would invoke trespass and breach of the peace laws to enforce a local custom of racial separation in eating places. [Lombard v. Louisiana, 373 U.S. 267 (1963)]

(2) **Apparent Legal Authority**
Even if a state forbids officers from acting in a certain way (*e.g.,* depriving constitutional rights), the forbidden action may still constitute state action if the state puts the actor in a position to commit the unconstitutional act.
Example: A sheriff beat a prisoner to death in an effort to secure a confession. Both the state and the sheriff were held liable. The actions of the sheriff involved "state action" because the sheriff *acted under "the color of state law—* the state in effect cloaked him with the apparent legal authority." [Screws v. United States, 325 U.S. 91 (1945)]

(3) **Public Defenders**
A public defender does *not act for the state* when he represents an indigent client. Negligence or malpractice by the public defender is not a denial of due process because his actions are not "state actions." [Polk County v. Dodson, 454 U.S. 312 (1982)]

2) **State Authorization**
In *Reitman v. Mulkey,* 387 U.S. 369 (1967), the Court invalidated a state constitutional provision that *repealed* all existing *state laws banning discrimination* in the sale or lease of property and prohibited reenactment of such laws in the future because such laws "authorize" private discrimination.

3) **The State as Lessor for a Racially Discriminatory Lessee**
In *Burton v. Wilmington Parking Authority,* 365 U.S. 715 (1961), Delaware was held responsible under the Fourteenth Amendment Equal Protection Clause for the exclusion of blacks from a coffee shop which was located in a public building. The shop was constructed by and leased from the state. The *maintenance* of the facility was *paid for with public funds* and Delaware was able to charge a higher rent because it allowed the restaurant owner to cater to the prejudices of its white customers.

4) Administration of Private Discriminatory Trust by Public Officials
State action exists where city personnel maintain a park, "open to all except blacks," under a private trust. [Evans v. Newton, 382 U.S. 296 (1966)]

5) Entwinement of State and Private Entities
The fact that a state entity helps formulate and adopts the rules of a private entity, and chooses to follow the order of the private entity pursuant to those rules, does not convert the private entity's action into state action. However, a state may be so entwined with a private organization that the organization's actions will be considered state action. [Brentwood Academy v. Tennessee Secondary School Athletic Association, 531 U.S. 288 (2001)]

Example: The National Collegiate Athletic Association ("NCAA") is a voluntary association of public and private universities that establishes rules for its members regarding collegiate sports. Pursuant to its rules, the NCAA urged a member college to suspend its coach for recruiting violations. The coach cannot successfully sue the NCAA for violating his constitutional rights because there is no state action. [National Collegiate Athletic Association v. Tarkanian, 488 U.S. 179 (1988)]

Compare: An association that regulates high school sports within a single state: (i) to which most public high schools belong; (ii) whose governing body is made up mostly of public school officials; (iii) whose meetings are held during regular school hours; (iv) whose employees may join the state retirement system; and (v) which is funded by gate receipts from the regulated sports is so entwined with the state that its action can be considered state action. [Brentwood Academy v. Tennessee Secondary School Athletic Association, *supra*]

b. Instances of Insignificant State Involvement

1) Heavily Regulated Businesses and/or Granting of a Monopoly to a Utility

a) Electric Company
State action will not be found merely because the state has granted a monopoly to a business or heavily regulates it.
Example: In *Jackson v. Metropolitan Edison*, 419 U.S. 345 (1974), **no state action** was found where an electric company terminated the user's service without notice and hearing. The state had not directed or ordered the termination and the fact that the company was heavily regulated and the state commission had approved private utility regulations authorizing such termination was not enough.

b) Nursing Home
A nursing home operated by a private corporation did **not exercise state action** when it discharged Medicaid patients, even though its operation was extensively regulated by the government. [Blum v. Yaretsky, 457 U.S. 991 (1982)]

c) School
A school operated by a private corporation did **not** exercise state action when it discharged teachers (allegedly in violation of their First Amendment rights) even though the school had contracts with the state to educate or care for many of its students and it received almost all of its operating funds from the government. [Rendell-Baker v. Kohn, 457 U.S. 830 (1982)]

2) Licensing and Provision of Essential Services
Granting a liquor license and providing essential services (police, fire, water, power, etc.) to a **private club** that imposes racial restrictions on its members and guests are **not** sufficient to constitute state action. [Moose Lodge v. Irvis, 407 U.S. 163 (1972)]

3) Congressional Grant of Corporate Charter and Exclusive Name
Congressional grant of a corporate charter and exclusive use of a name is not

sufficient to constitute state action. [San Francisco Arts & Athletics, Inc. v. United States Olympic Committee, 483 U.S. 522 (1987)—congressional charter and grant of exclusive name "Olympic" does not clothe United States Olympic Committee with state action]

4) No Government Duty to Protect Individuals from Harm by Private Persons
The mere refusal of government agents to protect a victim from harm by a private person will not result in a finding that the harm was attributable to "state action," at least when state law does not give the victim a right to government protection. [DeShaney v. Winnebago County Department of Social Services, 489 U.S. 189 (1989)—government not responsible for harm inflicted on a child by his father, even though government social worker had reason to believe the child was being abused and did nothing to protect the child] However, if government employees enter into an agreement or conspiracy with private persons to cause harm to a victim, the victim's injuries are the result of state action; the private persons, as well as the government employees with whom they conspired, will have violated the victim's constitutional rights. [Screws v. United States, 325 U.S. 91 (1945); Dennis v. Sparks, 449 U.S. 24 (1980)]

C. TIPS FOR BAR EXAM

1. State Must Be "Significantly Involved" in Private Entity
The state must be "significantly involved" in the private entity. Merely granting a license or providing essential services is insufficient.

2. No Constitutional Mandate to Outlaw Discrimination
States are not constitutionally required to outlaw discrimination. The Constitution forbids only their encouraging or authorizing it.

XIII. RETROACTIVE LEGISLATION

A. CONTRACT CLAUSE—IMPAIRMENT OF CONTRACT
The Contract Clause prohibits *states* from enacting any law that *retroactively* impairs contract rights. It does not affect contracts not yet entered into.

1. Not Applicable to Federal Government
There is no comparable clause applicable to the federal government, although a flagrant contract impairment would be forbidden by the Due Process Clause of the Fifth Amendment.

2. Only Applicable to State Legislation
The provision applies only to state *legislation*, not court decisions. [*See* Tidal Oil v. Flanagan, 263 U.S. 444 (1924)]

3. Basic Impairment Rules

a. Private Contracts
The Contract Clause prevents only *substantial impairments* of contract (*i.e.,* destruction of most or all of a party's rights under a contract). However, not all substantial impairments are invalid. In determining whether legislation is valid under the Contract Clause, use a three-part test:

(i) Does the legislation substantially impair a party's rights under an existing contract? If it does not, the legislation is valid under the Contract Clause. If it does, it will be valid *only if* it:

(ii) Serves an important and legitimate public interest; and

(iii) Is a reasonable and narrowly tailored means of promoting that interest.

Examples: 1) A Minnesota statute that imposed a moratorium on mortgage foreclosures during a severe depression did not violate the Contract Clause. [Home Building & Loan Association v. Blaisdell, 290 U.S. 398 (1934)]

2) A state statute that restricted underground coal mining to protect a variety of public and private uses of surface land (and buildings) and that left the owners of subsurface mining rights with some reasonable value in, or return from, their investment does not violate the Contract Clause. [Keystone Bituminous Coal Association v. DeBenedictis, 480 U.S. 470 (1987)]

b. **Public Contracts—Stricter Scrutiny**
Public contracts (*i.e.,* those in which the state or political subdivision is a party) are tested by the same basic test detailed above; however, they will likely receive stricter scrutiny, especially if the legislation reduces the contractual burdens on the state. When applying the three-part test, note the following:

1) There is no substantial impairment if the state has reserved the power to *revoke*, *alter*, *or amend* either in the contract itself or in a statute or law the terms of which should be considered to be incorporated into the contract [Dartmouth College v. Woodward, 17 U.S. 518 (1819)];

2) In determining whether the law serves as a legitimate public interest, note that the state cannot be obligated by contract to refrain from exercising its police powers necessary to protect the health and safety of its residents; and

3) To be narrowly tailored, the law should not constitute an unnecessarily broad repudiation of contract obligations.

4. **Important Decisions**

a. **Covenant to Private Bondholders Violated**
In the past few decades, the Supreme Court allowed states to statutorily modify many contracts for a public purpose, including the termination of redemption rights to state lands when oil was discovered there. However, the Court subsequently invalidated such an action. In *United States Trust Co. v. New Jersey,* 431 U.S. 1 (1977), the Court held that New York and New Jersey violated the Contract Clause by enacting legislation to allow the Port Authority to use port income to subsidize rail passenger transportation in violation of a previous statutory covenant to private bondholders. The state had agreed to certain terms that the bondholders might have relied upon—the public interest in improved rail service could be pursued without violating their contract rights.

b. **State Pension Reform Legislation Violated**
In *Allied Structural Steel Co. v. Spannaus,* 438 U.S. 234 (1978), the Court invalidated state pension reform legislation which increased the obligation of companies under preexisting pension plans to employees who previously had terminated their work for the company or who previously had retired from employment with the company. Because the legislation constituted a substantial impairment of contract by changing the compensation for work already completed and because it was not necessary to remedy an important social problem in the nature of an emergency, it was held to be a violation of the Contract Clause.

c. **Regulation of Future Pricing Conduct Permissible**
In *Exxon Corp. v. Eagerton,* 462 U.S. 176 (1983), the Court upheld a state law that increased the state severance tax on oil and gas taken from property in the state and prohibited oil or gas producers from "passing on" that tax increase to their customers. This statute was not a Contract Clause violation even though it effectively limited price increases under preexisting contracts. The law regulated future pricing conduct (conduct after the effective date of the legislation); it was not merely a repeal or impairment of preexisting contracts.

B. EX POST FACTO LAWS

1. **Two Ex Post Facto Clauses**
Neither the state nor the federal government may pass an ex post facto law. [Art. I, §9—federal prohibition; Art. I, §10—state prohibition] An ex post facto law is *legislation* that *retroactively* alters the *criminal law* (not civil regulations such as denial of professional licenses) as to offenses or punishments in a *substantially prejudicial* manner. Thus, within the definition are the following:

a. Create New Crime
Statutes that make criminally punishable an act that was not a crime when it was committed.

b. Increase Punishment
Statutes that increase the severity of punishment for a crime after its commission.

Example: Florida has sentencing guidelines that restrict judicial discretion by creating a presumptive sentence for certain types of crimes. On the day D committed a "sexual battery," the guidelines created a presumptive 3½-4½ year sentence for that crime. The guidelines were subsequently modified to provide for a 5½-7 year presumptive sentence. The Ex Post Facto Clause prohibits imposition of the new guidelines on D since the guidelines establish a higher presumptive sentence than existed on the date D committed the crime. [Miller v. Florida, 482 U.S. 423 (1987)]

c. Reduce Required Evidence
Statutes that reduce the quantum of evidence or burden of proof required for conviction below what was required at the time of commission.

Example: A law that raises the age of a sexual abuse victim whose testimony need not be corroborated for a conviction *is* an ex post facto law. [Carmell v. Texas, 529 U.S. 513 (2000)]

2. Procedural Changes that Do Not Affect Substantive Elements Are Not Ex Post Facto
Mere procedural changes in state law will not necessarily trigger the Ex Post Facto Clause. A modified law can be applied to a crime committed before the law's modification if the defendant had notice of the possible penalty and the modified law does not increase the burden on the defendant.

Example: Florida had a death penalty statute that was invalidated by the Supreme Court because the statute restricted discretion in sentencing. Before a new statute was enacted, D committed a murder. Florida then passed a new death penalty provision that complied with Supreme Court criteria. The new provision was applied at D's trial, and he was sentenced to death. This was not a prohibited ex post facto law, since the earlier statute (although unconstitutional) gave D notice of the possible penalty and the new provision made it *less likely* that the death penalty would be imposed in a given case. [Dobbert v. Florida, 432 U.S. 282 (1977)]

3. Indirect "Application" to Courts
Although the Ex Post Facto Clauses prohibit only retroactive *legislation*, the Supreme Court has held that due process prohibits courts from retroactively interpreting criminal law in an unexpected and indefensible way. [Rogers v. Tennessee, 532 U.S. 451 (2001)—state supreme court's abolition of common law "year and a day rule" (which prohibits prosecution for murder if the victim dies more than a year after an attack) was not unexpected and indefensible because medical science has undermined the rule's usefulness and the rule has already been abolished in most jurisdictions]

C. BILLS OF ATTAINDER
A bill of attainder is a legislative act that *inflicts punishment without a judicial trial* upon individuals who are designated either by name or in terms of past conduct. Past conduct acts to define who those particular persons are.

1. Two Clauses
Both the *federal and state governments* are prohibited from passing bills of attainder.

2. Two Requirements Preclude Finding of Bill of Attainder
These provisions *require both judicial machinery* for trial and punishment of crime and *definition of criminal conduct in such general terms* as not to ensnare within the definition a single individual or small group for punishment because of past behavior.

Example: The Court found a provision in the Landrum-Griffin Act, making it a crime for a member of the Communist Party to act as an officer or employee of a labor union, to be legislative punishment for a party membership, and hence a bill of attainder. [United States v. Brown, 381 U.S. 437 (1965)]

3. *Nixon* Case
In *Nixon v. Administrator of General Services,* 433 U.S. 425 (1977), Congress passed

legislation to authorize government control of the presidential papers and tape recordings of former President Nixon. The Supreme Court held that this was *not a bill of attainder*. The circumstances of the Nixon resignation made him a unique "class of one" as to the need to control his papers. The act was held "*nonpunitive*" and in pursuance of *important public policy*.

4. Draft Registration Case

In *Selective Service System v. Minnesota Public Interest Research Group,* 468 U.S. 841 (1984), the Court upheld a federal statute denying financial aid for higher education to male students between the ages of 18 and 26 who had failed to register for the draft. The law required applicants for the aid to file a statement with their institutions of higher learning certifying their compliance. Failure to register within 30 days of one's 18th birthday was a felony, but the regulations allowed men who failed to register in a timely manner to qualify for aid by registering late. The Court found that this was *not a bill of attainder*. The law reasonably *promoted nonpunitive goals* and was *not a legislative punishment* taken on the basis of any irreversible act, since aid was awarded to those who registered late. The Court also found that the statute did not violate the Fifth Amendment privilege against self-incrimination.

D.   DUE PROCESS CONSIDERATIONS

Under the Due Process Clauses of the Fifth and Fourteenth Amendments, retroactive legislation or other governmental action may be, but is not necessarily, a violation of the Constitution. The question of whether a retroactive law (that does not violate the Contracts, Ex Post Facto, or Bill of Attainder Clauses) violates due process is a *substantive due process* issue. If the law does not relate to a fundamental civil right, the retroactive law should be upheld if it is rationally related to a legitimate government interest.

Examples: 1) A retroactive tax law will be upheld as long as the retroactive aspects of the law are rationally related to legitimate government interests. [United States v. Carlton, 512 U.S. 26 (1994)—upholding retroactive modification of the estate tax]

2) Retroactive legislation affecting *merely a remedy* does not violate due process (*e.g.,* repealing or extending a statute of limitations), unless it would oust an already vested property interest. [Chase Securities Corp. v. Donaldson, 325 U.S. 304 (1945)—permissible to revive a previously dead cause of action]

3) Employers may be compelled to compensate former employees for work-connected diseases even if the employment terminated before the compensation statute was passed. [Usery v. Elkhorn Mining Co., 428 U.S. 1 (1976)]

XIV.   PROCEDURAL DUE PROCESS

A.   BASIC PRINCIPLE

The Due Process Clauses of the Fifth Amendment (applicable to the federal government) and the Fourteenth Amendment (applicable to the states) provide that the government shall not take a person's life, liberty, or property without due process of law. Due process contemplates fair process/procedure, which requires at least an opportunity to present objections to the proposed action to a fair, neutral decisionmaker (not necessarily a judge).

1. When Is Individualized Adjudication Required?

There is a right to procedural due process only when the government acts to deprive an *individual* of life, liberty, or property (*see* below). There is no right to individualized adjudication when the government acts generally, even if the action will result in burdening individuals' life, liberty, or property interests.

Example: A state legislature need not provide individuals with an opportunity for a hearing when adopting the general requirements for obtaining a driver's license (*e.g.,* age, residence, ability, etc.), but it must provide individualized process to determine whether a particular person meets the requirements.

2. Intentional Deprivation vs. Negligent Deprivation

Fair process is required for *intentional* acts of the government or its employees. If an injury is caused to a person through the mere *negligence* of a government employee, there is no violation of the Due Process Clause. [Daniels v. Williams, 474 U.S. 327 (1986); Davidson v. Cannon, 474 U.S. 344 (1986)]

a. **"Deprivation"**
A "deprivation" of life, liberty, or property requires more than a mere denial of certain kinds of remedies. Only when the government affords *no* remedy or *inadequate* remedies may a deprivation of life, liberty, or property result. [Florida Prepaid Postsecondary Education Expense Board v. College Savings Bank, 527 U.S. 627 (1999)]

3. **Protection vs. Creation**
The due process provisions do not create property or liberty interests; their purpose is to provide *procedural safeguards against arbitrary deprivation*. Hence, the Fourteenth Amendment Due Process Clause does not, for example, give out-of-state attorneys the right to appear in state courts without meeting a state's bar admission requirements. [Leis v. Flynt, 439 U.S. 438 (1979)]

B. **IS LIFE, LIBERTY, OR PROPERTY BEING TAKEN?**
Older Supreme Court cases indicated that due process protects "rights," but not "privileges." This approach is no longer followed; rather the Court will determine whether a *legitimate* liberty or property interest is being taken.

1. **Liberty**
The term "liberty" is not specifically defined. It includes more than just freedom from bodily restraints (*e.g.,* it includes the right to contract and to engage in gainful employment). A deprivation of liberty occurs if a person:

(i) Loses significant freedom of action; *or*

(ii) Is denied a freedom provided by the Constitution or a statute.

Examples of liberty interests include:

a. **Commitment to Mental Institution**

1) **Adults**
Adults are entitled to an *adversary hearing* before they are indefinitely committed to a mental institution against their will. The state must prove the basis for commitment by "clear and convincing" evidence. However, after a person has been acquitted of criminal charges on the basis of an insanity defense, the acquitted defendant can be committed if a court finds by a "preponderance of the evidence" that the person should be committed to a mental health care facility. [Jones v. United States, 463 U.S. 354 (1983)]

2) **Minor Children**
Minor children have a substantial liberty interest in not being confined unnecessarily for medical treatment. Thus, they are entitled to a *screening by a "neutral factfinder"* before commitment to a mental institution. Mere parental consent to commitment is not enough. [Parham v. J.R., 442 U.S. 584 (1979)]

b. **Injury to Reputation**
Injury to reputation in itself is not a deprivation of liberty or property. [Paul v. Davis, 424 U.S. 693 (1976)] However, if governmental acts (such as a statement of reasons given for termination of public employment) so injure a person's reputation that he will have *lost significant employment or associational opportunities*, there is a loss of liberty.

c. **Exercise of Fundamental Constitutional Rights**
The Due Process Clause protects a person's freedom to engage in activities that involve fundamental constitutional rights, such as the right to speak and associate, the right to travel, and the right to vote.

1) **Application—Government Employee's Freedom of Speech**
A public employee may not be discharged for engaging in constitutionally protected speech. If a government employee is discharged for her speech or writing, a hearing must be held to determine whether the speech was protected. If so, the employee cannot be fired. [*See* Girhan v. Western Line Consolidated School District, 439 U.S. 410 (1979)—Court held that teacher could not be fired for privately communicating her grievances about working conditions or opinions concerning public issues to her employer]

2. **Property**
"Property" includes more than personal belongings and realty, chattels, or money, but an abstract need or desire for (or a unilateral expectation of) the benefit is not enough. There must be a *legitimate claim* or "*entitlement*" to the benefit under state or federal law. [Board of Regents v. Roth, 408 U.S. 564 (1972); Leis v. Flynt, *supra*] Examples of property interests include:

a. **Public Education**
There is a property interest in public education when school attendance is required. Thus, a significant suspension (*e.g.,* 10 days) requires procedural due process. [Goss v. Lopez, 419 U.S. 565 (1975)]

b. **Welfare Benefits**
One has a property interest in welfare benefits if she has previously been determined to meet the statutory criteria. [Goldberg v. Kelly, 397 U.S. 254 (1970)]

c. **Continued Public Employment**
If there is a state statute or ordinance that creates a public employment contract, or there is some clear practice or mutual understanding that an employee can be terminated only for "cause," then there is a property interest [Arnett v. Kennedy, 416 U.S. 134 (1974)]; but if the employee holds his position only at the "will" of the employer, there is no property interest in continued employment [Bishop v. Wood, 426 U.S. 341 (1976)].

C. **WHAT TYPE OF PROCESS IS REQUIRED?**
While all intentional governmental deprivations of life, liberty, or property require fair process, what constitutes fair process in terms of the timing and scope of the hearing varies according to the circumstances of the deprivation. The Court will weigh:

(i) The importance of the *individual interest* involved;

(ii) The value of specific *procedural safeguards* to that interest; and

(iii) The *governmental interest* in fiscal and administrative efficiency.

[Mathews v. Eldridge, 424 U.S. 319 (1976)] In all situations, the Court will probably require *fair procedures* and an *unbiased decisionmaker*. Normally, the person whose interest is being deprived should also receive *notice* of the government's action and have an *opportunity to respond before* termination of the interest. However, the court may allow a post-termination hearing in situations where a pre-termination hearing is highly impracticable. The Court has made the following rulings with regard to specific types of deprivations:

1. **Welfare Benefits**
Due process requires an *evidentiary hearing prior to termination* of welfare benefits. It need not be a judicial or quasi-judicial trial if there is adequate post-termination review; but the recipient must have timely and adequate *notice* of the reasons for the proposed termination, the right to confront adverse witnesses, and the right to present his own arguments and evidence orally. Counsel need not be provided, but must be permitted. Finally, the decision must be based solely on evidence adduced at the hearing and must be rendered by an impartial decisionmaker (thus disqualifying any participant in the termination proposal under review). [Goldberg v. Kelly, *supra*]

2. **Disability Benefits**
No prior evidentiary hearing is required for termination of disability benefits, as long as there is *prior notice* to the recipient, an opportunity to respond in writing, and a *subsequent evidentiary hearing* (with retroactive payment if the recipient prevails). *Rationale*: Disability benefits (unlike welfare benefits) are not based on financial need and hence are not vital. [Mathews v. Eldridge, *supra*]

3. **Public Employment**
A public employee who is subject to removal only for "cause" (and who, therefore, has a property interest in his job) generally must be given *notice* of charges against him that are to be the basis for his job termination, and a *pre-termination opportunity to respond* to those charges. The employee does not have to be given a full, formal hearing before his termination, as long as there is a fair system of pre-termination notice, an opportunity to respond (to

the person making the termination decision), and a *subsequent evidentiary hearing* regarding the termination (with reinstatement if the employee prevails). [Cleveland Board of Education v. Loudermill, 470 U.S. 532 (1985)] *But note:* If there is a *significant reason* for not keeping the employee on the job, he may be suspended without pay and without an opportunity to respond as long as there is a prompt post-suspension hearing with reinstatement and back pay if the employee prevails. [Gilbert v. Homar, 520 U.S. 924 (1997)—police officer suspended after being arrested and formally charged with a felony]

4. Public Education—Disciplinary Suspension
Although no formal evidentiary hearing is required before a student may be temporarily suspended (for 10 days or less), due process usually requires *notice* of the charges and an *opportunity to explain*. However, if the student's presence poses a danger to persons or property, or threatens to disrupt the academic process, such notice and hearing may *follow* removal as soon as practicable. [Goss v. Lopez, *supra*]

a. Corporal Punishment in Public School
This may involve constitutionally protected "liberty." However, the traditional common law tort remedies for excessive punishment satisfy procedural due process, and a prior hearing is not required. [Ingraham v. Wright, 430 U.S. 651 (1977)]

5. Public Education—Academic Dismissal
No prior evidentiary hearing is required when a student is dismissed for "academic" deficiencies rather than for "disciplinary" reasons. Due process is satisfied if the student is adequately informed of the deficiency and given an opportunity to respond. [Board of Curators v. Horowitz, 435 U.S. 78 (1978)]

6. Creditors' Remedies
Pretrial remedies, such as attachment of property or garnishment of wages, that are merely designed to provide a plaintiff with some guarantee that there will be assets to satisfy a judgment against the defendant if the plaintiff eventually wins the case *should not be issued by a court without notice* to the defendant and a *hearing prior to the issuance* of the order. A court may issue a temporary order of this type if there are exigent circumstances that justify the order and the defendant is given a hearing after the order is issued but prior to trial. [Sniadach v. Family Finance Corp., 395 U.S. 337 (1969); Connecticut v. Doehr, 501 U.S. 1 (1991)] However, laws authorizing creditors to garnish assets, or a conditional seller to seize or sequester property, will be upheld *without prior notice* to the debtor *if*:

a. The creditor posts a security bond;

b. The application is made to a judge, is not conclusory, and documents narrowly confined facts susceptible of summary disposition; *and*

c. Provision is made for an early hearing at which the creditor must show probable cause.

7. Driver's License
The state generally must afford a *prior hearing* before a driver's license is suspended or terminated. [Bell v. Burson, 402 U.S. 535 (1971)] However, a post-suspension hearing satisfies due process where a statute mandates suspension of a driver's license for refusing to take a breathalyzer test upon arrest for drunk driving. [Mackey v. Montrym, 443 U.S. 1 (1979)]

8. Parental Status Litigation and Hearing

a. Termination of Parental Status
Due process does *not require the appointment of counsel* for indigent parents in every case in which the state seeks to terminate parental status (*i.e.,* take children from their parents), *but* only when "fundamental fairness" requires the appointment. [Lassiter v. Department of Social Services, 452 U.S. 18 (1981)] To terminate parental rights, the state must prove its allegations of parental neglect or misconduct by "clear and convincing evidence." [Santosky v. Kramer, 455 U.S. 745 (1982)]

b. Paternity Actions
A state may allow paternity to be established in a support proceeding brought by a mother or child by a *preponderance of evidence*—no greater burden of proof is required by the Due Process Clause. [Rivera v. Minnich, 483 U.S. 574 (1987)] However, due process requires the state to *pay for blood tests* that might exculpate an indigent

defendant in a paternity action if the *state is responsible for the lawsuit* (the suit is brought by a state agency or the state requires the mother to bring the civil paternity suit). [Little v. Streater, 452 U.S. 1 (1981)]

c.   Hearings for Men Who Seek to Establish Paternity

1)   Unmarried Father Living with Mother
If the father of an illegitimate child is a part of a "family unit" that includes the child, the relationship between the father and child will be protected by due process. [Stanley v. Illinois, 405 U.S. 645 (1972)—state cannot take child from father after mother dies, unless state has a fair process to determine whether the parental relationship should be severed]

2)   Father Who Never Tried to Establish Paternity
The father of an illegitimate child who has never attempted to establish a legal or personal relationship with the child has no right to notice prior to the adoption of the child by other persons. [Lehr v. Robertson, 463 U.S. 248 (1983)]

3)   Mother Married to Another Man
The Supreme Court has upheld a statute that presumed that a child born during wedlock was the husband's child where the statute allowed an alleged biological father to have a hearing regarding visitation rights, but the Court did not rule on whether a biological father could be denied visitation under these circumstances without a hearing. [Michael H. v. Gerald D., 491 U.S. 110 (1989)]

9.   Treatment of Patients in Mental Health Care Facilities
Persons who have been involuntarily committed to a state mental health care facility have a *liberty interest* in reasonably *safe conditions and treatment*. Patients have a due process right to determination by a "professional" in the health care field as to the proper treatment of the patient. [Youngberg v. Romeo, 457 U.S. 307 (1982)]

10.   Notice of Adversary Proceedings
When the government seeks to use a judicial or administrative process to take or terminate property interests, it *must give notice* to those persons whose property interests may be taken by that process. The form of notice must be reasonably designed to insure that those persons will in fact be notified of the proceedings.
Example: Personal notice or notice by mail must be given to both mortgagor and mortgagee before a "tax sale" of property for unpaid taxes. [Mennonite Board of Missions v. Adams, 462 U.S. 791 (1983)]

11.   Limitation of Attorneys' Fees for Veterans' Benefit Hearings
Persons applying for veterans' benefits for service related disabilities apparently have little due process right to be represented by an attorney at hearings before a Veterans Administration Board. The Supreme Court has upheld a statute that limited payments to attorneys in such cases to $10. [Walters v. National Association of Radiation Survivors, 468 U.S. 1323 (1985)]

12.   Civil Forfeitures
Procedural due process limits the government's ability to seize property allegedly subject to forfeiture (which most often occurs when the government claims that the property was connected to, or was the product of, criminal activity). Absent exceptional circumstances, the government must provide the owner of *real property* notice and an opportunity for some type of hearing *prior* to seizing real property. [United States v. James Daniel Good Real Property, 510 U.S. 43 (1993)] However, the government might be able to seize *personal property prior* to providing the owner a hearing, since personal property can be hidden or destroyed. [Calero-Toledo v. Pearson Yacht Leasing Co., 416 U.S. 663 (1974)]

13.   Punitive Damages
Substantive due process might require that punitive damages be reasonable under the circumstances of the case. There must be a *fair process for awarding* punitive damages, and the states may not eliminate all judicial review of the amount of punitive damages awarded—there must be a *fair opportunity to appeal* punitive damage awards to an appellate court. [Honda Motor Corp., Ltd. v. Oberg, 512 U.S. 415 (1994)]

D. DUE PROCESS RIGHTS ARE SUBJECT TO WAIVER

Due process rights are subject to waiver. However, the Supreme Court has not clearly defined the standard for determining whether someone has validly waived the right to a hearing before governmental deprivation of liberty or property. Presumably, any such waiver must be **voluntary**. Additionally, it is possible that a waiver will be valid only if it is made **knowingly** (with an understanding of the nature of the rights being waived).

E. ACCESS TO COURTS—INDIGENT PLAINTIFFS

There may often be a fee for government services, including a fee for use of courts (*e.g.*, a filing fee). Whether the government must waive such fees for indigents depends on the nature of the rights involved.

1. Fundamental Rights—Waiver Required

The Supreme Court has required a waiver of government fees when the imposition of a fee would deny a fundamental right to the indigent. (Fundamental rights are examined in the substantive due process and equal protection sections of this outline.)

Examples: 1) The government cannot deny an indigent the right to marry or divorce because of the indigent's inability to pay a marriage license fee or a divorce court filing fee.

      2) The government must waive even a reasonable filing fee for candidates for electoral office if it can be shown that the candidate cannot afford to pay the filing fee. The right to be a candidate is connected to the fundamental right of individuals to vote for candidates of their choice.

      3) The government may not require an indigent to pay the cost of a transcript in order to appeal from termination of her parental rights. [M.L.B. v. S.L.J., 519 U.S. 102 (1997)]

2. Nonfundamental Rights—Waiver Not Required

When there is no fundamental right regulated by the imposition of a fee, the government can refuse to grant the service to those persons who cannot pay the required fee.

Examples: 1) The federal government can refuse to grant access to bankruptcy courts to persons who cannot pay a filing fee. There is no fundamental right to receive a bankruptcy discharge from debts.

      2) A state can limit judicial review of welfare termination hearings to those persons who pay a $25 fee.

XV. THE "TAKING" CLAUSE

A. IN GENERAL

The Fifth Amendment prohibits governmental taking of private property "for public use without just compensation." The prohibition is applicable to the states through the Fourteenth Amendment [Chicago Burlington & Quincy Railroad v. Chicago, 166 U.S. 226 (1897)], and taking questions often arise in connection with states' exercise of their police power (*i.e.*, the power to legislate for the health, welfare, safety, etc., of the people).

1. Not a Grant of Power

The Fifth Amendment is not a grant of power, but rather is a limitation on power (*i.e.*, a taking must be for a public purpose and compensation must be paid). The power for a taking must arise out of some other source (*e.g.*, the police power).

2. Scope of Taking

The concept of a governmental taking probably originally contemplated only physical appropriations of property. Today, however, the term also encompasses some governmental action that significantly damages property or impairs its use (*e.g.*, frequent flyovers by airplanes near airport [United States v. Causby, 328 U.S. 256 (1946)]). Moreover, even intangibles may be the subject of a taking. [*See* Ruckelshaus v. Monsanto Co., 467 U.S. 986 (1984)—government requirement that trade secret be disclosed may be a taking where government takes and discloses the secret in such a way that it diminishes the secret's economic value and interferes with reasonable, investment-backed expectations of its holders]

3. **Scope of Property**

Whether an item is property is determined by state law, but in any case, there is no constitutional requirement that an item have positive economic or market value to constitute property; *i.e.,* "worthless" property is still property. [*See* Phillips v. Washington Legal Foundation, 524 U.S. 156 (1998)—even if interest attributable to a particular client in an attorney's trust fund account is economically worthless to the client—because the costs of accounting and crediting the interest would eat up all the interest earned—the interest still is the client's property and so is subject to the Takings Clause]

B. **"PUBLIC USE" LIMITATION LIBERALLY CONSTRUED**

The Court will not review underlying policy decisions, such as general desirability for a particular public use or the extent to which property must be taken therefor. A use will be held to be "public" as long as it is rationally related to a legitimate public purpose, *e.g.,* health, welfare, safety, moral, social, economic, political, or aesthetic ends. The government may even authorize a taking by private enterprise, as long as the taking will redound to the public advantage (*e.g.,* railroads and public utilities).

Example: The Supreme Court upheld a state program under which the fee simple interest in land would be condemned and the fee owner paid a *fair market value* for that property interest, which the state would then transfer for value to tenants on the land. The state's asserted interest in ending social problems caused by "land oligopoly" was sufficient public use. [Hawaii Housing Authority v. Midkiff, 467 U.S. 229 (1984)]

C. **"TAKING" VS. "REGULATION"**

While the government must fairly compensate an owner when her property is taken for public use, it need not pay compensation for mere regulation of property. Thus, whether government action amounts to a taking or is merely regulation is a crucial issue. The question is one of degree; there is no clear cut formula for determining whether there has been a taking. The following guidelines have emerged.

1. **Actual Appropriation or Physical Invasion**

A taking will almost always be found if there is an actual appropriation or destruction of a person's property or a permanent physical invasion by the government or by authorization of law.

Examples: A taking was found in the following situations:

1) Ordinance requiring landlords to allow installation of cable TV in their rental units but limiting to $1 the fee landlords could charge for this access. [Loretto v. Teleprompter Manhattan CATV Corp., 455 U.S. 904 (1982)]

2) Statute *abolishing* rights of descent and devise of property (although government has broad authority to regulate this area). [Hodel v. Irving, 481 U.S. 704 (1987)]

3) Requirement that public be given free access to a privately developed waterway. [Kaiser Aetna v. United States, 444 U.S. 164 (1980)]

a. **Exception—Emergencies**

A taking is less likely to be found in emergency situations, even where there is destruction or actual occupation of private property.

Examples: 1) No compensation was required when the state ordered the destruction of cedar trees that threatened to spread disease to apple orchards. [Miller v. Schoene, 276 U.S. 272 (1928)]

2) No compensation was required when federal troops destroyed oil facilities to prevent them from falling into enemy hands. [United States v. Caltex, Inc., 344 U.S. 149 (1952)]

2. **Use Restrictions**

a. **Denial of *All* Economic Value of Land—Taking**

If a government regulation denies a landowner *all* economic use of his land, the regulation is equivalent to a physical appropriation and is thus a taking unless principles of nuisance or property law that existed when the owner acquired the land make the use prohibited. [Lucas v. South Carolina Coastal Council, 505 U.S. 1003 (1992)—state's zoning ordinance, adopted after owner purchased lots, amounted to a taking because the ordinance prohibited owner from erecting any permanent structures on his lots]

1) **Temporary Denials of All Economic Use**
Temporarily denying an owner of all economic use of property does not constitute a per se taking. Instead, the Court will carefully examine and weigh all the relevant circumstances—the planners' good faith, the reasonable expectations of the owners, the length of the delay, the delay's actual effect on the value of the property, etc.—in order to determine whether "fairness and justice" require just compensation. [Tahoe-Sierra Preservation Council, Inc. v. Tahoe Regional Planning Agency, 122 S. Ct. 1465 (2002)—finding no taking where there was a 32-month moratorium on land development in the Lake Tahoe Basin while a comprehensive land-use plan was being developed for the area]

b. **Decreasing Economic Value—Balancing Test**
Regulations that merely decrease the value of property (*e.g.,* prohibit its most beneficial use) do not necessarily result in a taking, *as long as they leave an economically viable use for the property*. The Court balances:

(i)   The social goals sought to be promoted;

(ii) The diminution in value to the owner; *and*

(iii) The owner's reasonable expectations regarding use of the property.

Generally, the regulation will be found to be a taking only if it *unjustly* reduces the economic value of the property (*e.g.,* greatly reduces property value and only slightly promotes public welfare).

Examples: The Supreme Court has considered two cases where statutes prohibited coal companies from mining under property, even though the mining company had previously entered into contract for, or received a deed for, subsurface mineral rights. If the statutory prohibition is designed to protect only the economic interests of a *limited group* of building owners and the reduction in the value of the mining company's mineral rights is *almost 100%*, a court might be authorized in finding that the prohibition of subsurface mining constitutes a taking of property for which compensation is due. [Pennsylvania Coal Co. v. Mahon, 260 U.S. 393 (1922)] If the statute promotes a *public purpose* because a danger of subsidence threatens a variety of public and nonpublic buildings, and *diminution in the value of the mining company's rights is not extreme*, the statute restricting the mining activities may be a permissible regulation for which no compensation is due. [Keystone Bituminous Coal Association v. DeBenedictis, XIII.A.3.a., *supra*]

1) **Zoning Ordinances**
The Court has long held that governments may adopt zoning ordinances that regulate the way real property may be used, pursuant to the police power (*e.g.,* limiting development in a particular area to single family homes, restricting buildings to a particular height, etc.). Such regulations do not amount to a taking—even if they deny an owner the highest and best use of her property—as long as they "substantially advance legitimate state interests" and do not "extinguish a fundamental attribute of ownership." [Agins v. Tiburon, 447 U.S. 255 (1980)—ordinance permitting only five houses on five-acre tract upheld]

Example: The Court upheld a "landmark" zoning ordinance that prohibited altering the external appearance of Grand Central Station. It found historic preservation to be an important government interest and that certain rights granted to the landmark owners mitigated their loss. [Penn Central Transportation Co. v. New York, 438 U.S. 104 (1978)]

2) **Building/Development Permits—Transfer of Occupation Rights**
Municipalities often attempt to condition building or development permits on a landowner's (i) conveying title to part, or all, of the property to the government or (ii) granting the public access to the property (*e.g.,* an easement across the property). Such conditions constitute an uncompensated taking unless (i) the government can show that the condition relates to a legitimate government interest and

(ii) the adverse impact of the proposed building/development on the area is roughly proportional to the loss caused to the property owner from the forced transfer of occupation rights. [Nollan v. California Coastal Commission, 483 U.S. 825 (1987); Dolan v. City of Tigard, 512 U.S. 374 (1994)]

> *Example:* City agreed to approve a permit to expand plaintiff's retail store and pave a parking lot on the condition that plaintiff dedicate land for (i) a public greenway and (ii) a bike path. The Supreme Court found that City did not show a sufficient relationship between the dedications and the impact that the expansion would have on the area. [Dolan v. City of Tigard, *supra*]

3) Utility Rate Regulation

There is no taking where the government sets rates that utility companies can charge, as long as the rates are not set so low that they are unjust and confiscatory. [Duquesne Light Co. v. Barash, 488 U.S. 299 (1989)]

3. Remedy

If a property owner challenges a regulation and the court determines that there was a taking, the government will be required to either:

(i) *Pay the property owner compensation* for the taking (*see* below); or

(ii) *Terminate the regulation and pay the owner for damages* that occurred while the regulation was in effect (*i.e.,* temporary taking damages).

[First English Evangelical Church v. County of Los Angeles, 482 U.S. 304 (1987)]

a. Who May Sue

The right to claim a "taking" is *not* limited to persons who held title to the property at the time a challenged use restriction was imposed. A person who purchases property after a regulation is in place still may bring a taking claim. [Palazzolo v. Rhode Island, 533 U.S. 606 (2001)]

D. "JUST COMPENSATION"

The owner is entitled to the *reasonable value* of her property *at the time of the taking*—fair market value. The test is ordinarily a *loss to the owner*, not a gain to the taker. Due process guarantees notice and hearing, administrative or judicial, on the amount of compensation, but the hearing need not precede the taking.

XVI. INTRODUCTION TO SUBSTANTIVE DUE PROCESS AND EQUAL PROTECTION

A. RELATIONSHIP BETWEEN SUBSTANTIVE DUE PROCESS AND EQUAL PROTECTION

The Due Process Clauses and the Equal Protection Clause guarantee the fairness of laws—substantive due process guarantees that laws will be reasonable and not arbitrary, and equal protection guarantees that similarly situated persons will be treated alike. Both guarantees require the Court to review the *substance of the law* rather than the procedures employed.

1. Substantive Due Process

Generally where a law limits the liberty of *all* persons to engage in some activity, it is a due process question.

2. Equal Protection

Where a law treats a person or class of persons differently from others, it is an equal protection question. [*See* Village of Willowbrook v. Grace, 528 U.S. 562 (2000)—equal protection claims may be brought by a class with as few as one member]

3. Examples

If a law prohibits all persons from purchasing contraceptive devices, there is a due process issue; if the law prohibits only purchases by unmarried persons, there is an equal protection issue. A state's refusal to have any publicly funded schools raises a due process issue; a state law that establishes separate schools for children of different races raises an equal protection issue.

4. Note—Clauses Not Necessarily Mutually Exclusive
Since both clauses protect against unfairness, both may be appropriate challenges to the same governmental act, and a discussion of both may be appropriate in an essay answer. On the MBE, however, the examiners will probably not include both as alternatives in the same question. The above approaches can be used as a rough guideline of when each clause applies.

B. WHAT STANDARD OF REVIEW WILL THE COURT APPLY?
The Court employs one of three tests in reviewing laws under these clauses, depending on the circumstances.

1. Strict Scrutiny (Maximum Scrutiny)
The Court uses the strict scrutiny standard when a suspect classification or fundamental right (these terms will be discussed *infra*) is involved. Under the strict scrutiny standard, a law will be upheld only if it is *necessary* to achieve a *compelling* or *overriding* government purpose. The Court will always consider whether less burdensome means for accomplishing the legislative goal are available. Most governmental action examined under this test fails.

    a. Burden of Proof on Government
When the strict scrutiny standard is applied, the *government* will have the burden of proving that the law is necessary. The Court will not allow a loose fitting law (*i.e.,* if a law reaches more people or conduct than is necessary (overinclusive) or does not reach all of the people or conduct sought to be regulated (underinclusive), it will likely be struck down).

2. Intermediate Scrutiny
The Court uses intermediate scrutiny when a classification based on gender or legitimacy is involved. Under the intermediate scrutiny standard, a law will be upheld if it is *substantially* related to an *important* government purpose.

    a. Burden of Proof Probably on Government
It is unclear who has the burden of proof when the Court uses the intermediate standard, but in most cases, it appears to be the government.

3. Rational Basis (Minimal Scrutiny)
The rational basis standard is used whenever the other two standards are not applicable (*i.e.,* most legislation). Under the rational basis standard, a law will be upheld if it is *rationally related to a legitimate* interest. It is difficult to fail this test; so most governmental action examined under this standard is upheld unless it is *arbitrary* or *irrational*.

    a. Burden of Proof on Challenger
Under the rational basis standard, laws are presumed valid. Therefore, the challenger has the burden of proof. This is a very difficult burden to meet, given the deference the Court gives to legislatures under the rational basis standard. (*See* below.)

    b. Deference to Legislature
Under the rational basis standard, the Court will usually defer to a legislature's decision that a law is rational. Loose fitting laws are permissible here: The law need not be the best law that could have been written to achieve the legislative goal. Indeed, it need not go far at all toward a conceivable legislative goal; the Court will uphold a law taking a "first step" toward any legitimate goal, even if the Court thinks the law is unwise.
    Example: City decided that advertisements on motor vehicles are traffic hazards; so it banned such advertisements except for those on vehicles advertising the owner's own product. Even though the excepted advertisements were no less distracting than the banned ones, the Court upheld the "first step" law. [Railway Express Agency v. New York, 336 U.S. 106 (1949)]

XVII. SUBSTANTIVE DUE PROCESS

A. CONSTITUTIONAL SOURCE—TWO CLAUSES
There are two separate clauses protecting substantive due process:

(i) The Due Process Clause of the Fifth Amendment (applies to the federal government); and

(ii) The Due Process Clause of the Fourteenth Amendment (applies to state and local governments).

As indicated above, *the same tests* are employed under each clause.

B. APPLICABLE STANDARDS

1. **Fundamental Right—Strict Scrutiny**
   Where a law limits a fundamental right, strict scrutiny will be applied, and the law (or other governmental action) will be upheld only if it is necessary to promote a *compelling or overriding interest*. Fundamental rights include:

   a. Right to travel;

   b. Privacy;

   c. Voting; and

   d. All First Amendment rights.

2. **All Other Cases—Mere Rationality**
   In all other cases, the mere rationality test is applied, and the law will be upheld if it is *rationally related to any conceivable legitimate end of government*. Examples include the following:

   a. **Business and Labor Regulations**
      The Court will sustain all varieties of business regulation; *e.g.,* "blue sky" laws, bank controls, insurance regulation, price and wage controls, unfair competition and trade practice controls, etc.

   b. **Taxation**
      Taxation is also invariably *sustained*. However, discriminatory taxes might still be invalidated.

   c. **Lifestyle**
      There is, as yet, *no recognized right* to lead a certain lifestyle. Thus, the Supreme Court will uphold laws: prohibiting drugs ("hard" or "soft"), requiring motorcyclists to wear helmets, or requiring police officers to wear short hair. [Kelley v. Johnson, 425 U.S. 238 (1976)]

   d. **Zoning**
      Regulation of the ownership or use of property has also been liberally tolerated by the Court.

      1) **Statutes Forbidding Nuisances or Promoting Community's Preferred Lifestyle**
         Statutes forbidding certain uses as nuisances have been sustained, as have all kinds of statutes designed to promote the public's enjoyment of space and safety or to promote a community's preferred lifestyle and character. For example, the Supreme Court held that a Long Island suburb could zone out all groups of three or more persons unrelated by blood, adoption, or marriage. [Village of Belle Terre v. Boraas, 416 U.S. 1 (1974)]

      2) **Cannot Prohibit Traditionally Related Families from Living Together**
         However, you should know that the Supreme Court held that zoning regulations that prohibit members of traditional families from living together (*i.e.,* zoning excluding cousins or grandchildren) violate due process. [Moore v. City of East Cleveland, 431 U.S. 494 (1977)]

   e. **Punitive Damages**
      The Supreme Court has held that punitive damages—even large punitive awards—do

not necessarily violate substantive due process. [Pacific Mutual Life Insurance Co. v. Haslip, 499 U.S. 1 (1991)—upholding punitive damages 200 times greater than compensatory damages] However, "grossly excessive" damages—those that are unreasonably high to vindicate the state's interest in punishment—are invalid. [TXO Production Corp. v. Alliance Resources Corp., 509 U.S. 443 (1993)] Although there is no bright line marking the limits on punitive awards, a person must receive fair notice of their possible magnitude. The Court has indicated that it will look to the following factors: (i) the degree of reprehensibility of the defendant's conduct, (ii) the disparity between the actual or potential harm suffered by the plaintiff and the punitive award, and (iii) the difference between the punitive damages awarded and the criminal and civil penalties authorized for comparable misconduct. [BMW of North America, Inc. v. Gore, 517 U.S. 559 (1996)]

f.   High Speed Chases
A high speed police chase that results in a death violates due process only when the chase is arbitrary (or irrational) in the constitutional sense. Only a chase that shocks the conscience of the court (*i.e.,* where the police intend to cause harm) will be found to be sufficiently arbitrary to be unconstitutional. [County of Sacramento v. Lewis, 523 U.S. 833 (1998)—no due process violation where officers chased motorcycle that sped by the officers for no apparent reason and a passenger on the motorcycle fell off and was killed when struck by an officer's car]

g.   Compare—Vagueness Doctrine
Under the Due Process Clause of the Fourteenth Amendment, a law can be held unconstitutional if it fails to provide minimal guidelines to govern law enforcement officers so as to encourage arbitrary and discriminatory enforcement. [Kolender v. Lawson, 461 U.S. 352 (1983); City of Chicago v. Morales, 527 U.S. 41 (1999)—holding unconstitutional on vagueness grounds an ordinance that allowed officers to disperse suspected gang members when they were "loitering," which was defined as remaining in any one place with no *apparent purpose*]

C.   A FEW IRREBUTTABLE PRESUMPTIONS MAY BE INVALID

If the government "presumes facts" against a person so that she is not qualified for some important benefit or right, the irrebuttable presumption may be unconstitutional. Although the Court often characterizes this as a due process question, it is more accurately an equal protection question because the government is creating an arbitrary classification. In any case, if the presumption affects a fundamental right (*e.g.,* right to travel) or a suspect or quasi-suspect classification (*e.g.,* gender), it will likely be invalid under strict scrutiny or intermediate scrutiny analysis, because the administrative convenience created by the presumption is not an important enough interest to justify the burden on the right or class. If some other classification or right is involved, the presumption will likely be upheld under the rational basis standard.

Examples: 1) A state may not presume a teacher incapable of continuous service in the classroom merely because she is four or five months pregnant or has a child under age three. [Cleveland Board of Education v. LaFleur, 414 U.S. 632 (1974)]

2) The government may presume that a marriage entered into within nine months of a wage earner's death was simply to secure Social Security benefits. [Weinberger v. Salfi, 422 U.S. 749 (1975)]

XVIII.   EQUAL PROTECTION

A.   CONSTITUTIONAL SOURCE
The Equal Protection Clause of the Fourteenth Amendment has *no counterpart in the Constitution applicable to the federal government*; it is limited to state action. Nevertheless, it is clear that grossly unreasonable discrimination by the federal government violates the *Due Process Clause of the Fifth Amendment*. [Bolling v. Sharpe, 347 U.S. 497 (1954)—racial discrimination in the public schools of the District of Columbia held a violation of due process] Thus, there are really two equal protection guarantees. The Court applies the same standards under either constitutional provision.

B.   APPLICABLE STANDARDS
As indicated above, the Court will apply one of three standards when examining governmental action involving classifications of persons. If a *suspect classification or fundamental right* is involved, the strict scrutiny standard will be applied and the action will be struck down unless

the government proves that it is necessary to achieve a compelling interest. If a *quasi-suspect classification* is involved, the Court will likely require the government to prove that the action is substantially related to an important government interest. If *any other classification* is involved, the action will be upheld unless the challenger proves that the action is not rationally related to a legitimate government interest.

C. PROVING DISCRIMINATORY CLASSIFICATION

The mere fact that legislation or governmental action has a discriminatory effect is not sufficient to trigger strict scrutiny or intermediate scrutiny. There must be *intent* to discriminate on the part of the government. Intent can be shown in three ways: (i) facial discrimination; (ii) discriminatory application; or (iii) discriminatory motive.

1. Facial Discrimination

A law may include a classification on its face. This type of law, by its own terms, makes an explicit distinction between classes of persons (perhaps by race or gender; *e.g.,* all white males 21 or older may serve as jurors [*see* Strauder v. West Virginia, 100 U.S. 303 (1880)]). In such cases the courts merely have to apply the appropriate standard of review for that classification. (The standards for racial classifications and gender classifications are described below.)

a. Facial Discrimination Absent Racial Language

In a few cases the Supreme Court has held that a law used a racial classification "on its face" even though the language of the law did not include racial language. In these cases, the Supreme Court found that the law could not be explained except in racial terms.

Example: The Court found that a state law establishing districts for the election of Representatives to the United States Congress should be deemed to use a racial classification on its face because one bizarrely shaped district could not be explained except in terms of establishing a district where minority race voters would control the outcome of the election. The Court did not rule on the question of whether this racial classification was narrowly tailored to a compelling interest, such as remedying proven past discrimination, because that question had not been addressed in the lower courts. [Shaw v. Reno, 509 U.S. 630 (1993)]

Note: If a legislative districting map could be explained in terms other than race, the Court would not find that the law constituted racial discrimination on its face. In such a case, the persons attacking legislative districts as being based on racial classification would have to show that district lines were drawn for a racially discriminatory purpose. [Hunt v. Cromartie, 532 U.S. 234 (2001)—"Hunt II"]

2. Discriminatory Application

In some instances, a law that appears to be neutral on its face will be applied in a different manner to different classes of persons. If the persons challenging the governmental action can prove that the government officials applying the law had a discriminatory purpose (and used discriminatory standards based on traits such as race or gender), the law will be invalidated.

Examples: 1) A law prohibited operating a laundry in wooden buildings, but gave a government agency discretion to grant exemptions. It was shown that most such laundries were owned by people of Chinese descent, but the agency granted exemptions only to non-Asian applicants. The law was deemed to involve racial or national origin classification and was invalidated as applied. [Yick Wo v. Hopkins, 118 U.S. 356 (1886)]

2) Laws allow attorneys to move to strike potential jurors from a jury either for cause or without cause (a peremptory strike). In either case, there is an equal protection violation when it is proved that an attorney excluded a person from a jury on account of the person's race or sex. [*See* Batson v. Kentucky, 476 U.S. 79 (1986); J.E.B. v. Alabama *ex rel.* T.B., 511 U.S. 127 (1994)] Note that because striking potential jurors from a jury significantly involves the state, even attorneys representing private parties are prohibited from discriminatory strikes. (*See* XII.B.2.a.1)a)(1), *supra.*)

3. Discriminatory Motive

Sometimes a government action will appear to be neutral on its face and in its application, but will have disproportionate impact on a particular class of persons (such as a racial minority or women). Such a law will be found to involve a classification (and be subject to the level of scrutiny appropriate to that classification) only if a court finds that the lawmaking body enacted or maintained the law for a *discriminatory purpose*. In such cases, the court should admit into evidence statistical proof that the law has a disproportionate impact on one class of persons. However, mere statistical evidence will rarely be sufficient in itself to prove that the government had a discriminatory purpose in passing a law. Statistical evidence may be combined with other evidence of legislative or administrative intent to show that a law or regulation is the product of a discriminatory purpose.

Examples: 1) A police department used results from a written test as a criterion for hiring police officers. Members of identifiable racial minorities consistently got low scores on the test, although there was no proof that the test was written or otherwise employed for the purpose of disadvantaging minority applicants. Because of the absence of nonstatistical proof of discriminatory purpose, there was no equal protection violation. [Washington v. Davis, 426 U.S. 229 (1976)]

2) A state law gave a preference in the hiring and promotion of civil service employees to persons who were honorably discharged from the United States military. The foreseeable and actual impact of this law was to disadvantage the female population of job applicants, because the majority of veterans are men. Because there was no proof (other than the statistical impact of the law) that the legislature enacted the law for the purpose of hurting women (as opposed to the purpose of aiding veterans), the law was upheld.

3) A statistical study showing that black defendants in capital cases are much more likely to receive the death penalty than are white defendants in a state will not in itself establish that a particular black defendant was denied equal protection by being sentenced to death for murder in that state. The statistical study is insufficient to prove purposeful discrimination. [McCleskey v. Kemp, 481 U.S. 279 (1987)]

D. SUSPECT CLASSIFICATIONS

1. Race and National Origin

If governmental action classifies persons based on exercise of a fundamental right or involves a suspect classification (race, national origin, or alienage), strict scrutiny is applied. The result is invalidation of almost every case where the classification would burden a person because of her status as a member of a racial or national origin minority. The only explicit race discrimination upheld despite strict scrutiny was the wartime incarceration of United States citizens of Japanese ancestry on the West Coast. [Korematsu v. United States, 323 U.S. 214 (1944)—found to be necessary to achieve compelling interest of national security]

Example: A state could not deny custody of a child from a previous marriage to a white mother merely because her new husband was black, where the mother was otherwise found to be an appropriate parent. Racial prejudice against mixed race couples does not justify taking a child from his mother. [Palmore v. Sidoti, 466 U.S. 429 (1984)]

a. School Integration

Recall that only intentional discrimination will be found to create discriminatory classifications calling for strict scrutiny (*see* C., *supra*); thus, only intentional segregation in schools will be invalidated under equal protection.

Example: No equal protection violation was found where a school system established attendance zones in a racially neutral manner, but racial imbalance occurred because of housing patterns. [Keyes v. School District No. 1, 413 U.S. 189 (1973)]

1) Remedying Intentional School Segregation

If it is proven that a school board has engaged in the racial districting of schools, the board must take steps to eliminate the effects of that discrimination. If the school board refuses to do so, a court may order the school district to take all appropriate steps to eliminate the discrimination.

a) **Busing**

To remedy past discrimination, a court may order the "busing" of students. A federal court order requiring the transfer or busing of students must be tailored to eliminate proven racial discrimination in the school system.

(1) **Limitation—Interdistrict Busing**

A court may order busing between two independent school districts only if it has been proven that both districts cooperated in the purposeful discriminatory scheme.

(2) **Limitation—Voter Initiatives**

While citizens of a state may vote to prohibit state judges from ordering busing to remedy past discrimination, they may not prohibit the transfer of students to other attendance zones if such transfers are allowed for other reasons. [Washington v. Seattle School District No. 1, 458 U.S. 457 (1982); Crawford v. Board of Education, 458 U.S. 527 (1982)]

b) **Order Limited**

A court may not impose a remedy that goes beyond the purpose of remedying the vestiges of past segregation. Thus, it is impermissible for a court to impose a remedy whose purpose is to attract nonminority students from outside the school district when there is no evidence of past segregation outside the district (*see* a.1)a), *supra*). [Missouri v. Jenkins, 515 U.S. 70 (1995)—state not required to fund salary increases and remedial programs to create magnet schools to attract suburban students to urban schools]

c) **Termination of Order**

When a school district subject to a federal court-ordered integration plan has eliminated "the vestiges of past discrimination," the federal court should terminate its integration decree. [Board of Education v. Dowell, 498 U.S. 237 (1991)] If the district has eliminated discrimination only over certain aspects of school administration (*e.g.,* student assignments), the court *may* withdraw supervision over this aspect even though vestiges of discrimination remain with respect to other aspects. [Freeman v. Pitts, 503 U.S. 467 (1992)]

b. **"Benign" Government Discrimination—Affirmative Action**

Government action—whether by federal, state, or local governmental bodies—that *favors* racial or ethnic minorities is subject to strict scrutiny, as is government action discriminating *against* racial or ethnic minorities. [Adarand Constructors, Inc. v. Pena, 515 U.S. 200 (1995)—*overruling* Metro Broadcasting, Inc. v. Federal Communications Commission, 497 U.S. 547 (1990), which applied intermediate standard to federal discrimination]

Note: Prior to its ruling in *Adarand, supra*, the Supreme Court upheld a federal requirement that 10% of federal grants for public works be set aside for minority businesses. [Fullilove v. Klutznick, 448 U.S. 448 (1980)] In *Adarand*, the Court reserved judgment on whether a *Fullilove*-type program would survive strict scrutiny. Some commentators have suggested that it might, because the Court might give Congress more deference than the states based on Congress's power under the Enabling Clause of the Fourteenth Amendment (*see* XII.A.3., *supra*), but the continued validity of *Fullilove* is, at best, uncertain.

1) **Remedying Past Discrimination**

The government has a compelling interest in remedying past discrimination against a racial or ethnic minority. Thus, if a court finds that a governmental agency has engaged in racial discrimination, it may employ a race conscious remedy tailored to end the discrimination and eliminate its effects. A remedy of this type is permissible under the Equal Protection Clause because it is narrowly tailored to further a compelling interest (the elimination of the illegal or unconstitutional discrimination).

Example: When it has been proven that a public employer engaged in persistent racial discrimination, a court may order relief that establishes a goal for the hiring or promotion of minority persons so as to eliminate the effects of the past discrimination. [United States v. Paradise, 480 U.S. 149 (1987)]

2) Where There Has Been No Past Discrimination by Government

Even where a state or local government has not engaged in past discrimination, it may have a compelling interest in affirmative action. However, the governmental action must be *narrowly tailored* to that interest. [City of Richmond v. J.A. Croson Co., 488 U.S. 469 (1989)]

a) Remedial Justifications

(1) Local Private Discrimination

Remedying past private discrimination *within* the governmental agency's jurisdiction is a compelling interest, but there is no compelling interest in remedying the general effects of societal discrimination. Thus, for a city to give a preference to minority race applicants for city construction contracts, it must identify the past unconstitutional or illegal discrimination against minority-owned construction businesses that it is now attempting to correct. [City of Richmond v. J.A. Croson Co., *supra*]

Example: In *United Jewish Organizations v. Carey,* 430 U.S. 144 (1977), the Court upheld New York's revised voting district plan, based solely on racial statistics, because the revisions were made to insure that minorities that had previously been discriminated against in New York would be represented in the legislature.

(2) Diversity in Public Education

The government appears to have a "compelling interest" in promoting racial diversity in public school student bodies and faculties (although a majority of the Justices have not accepted this principle in a majority opinion). However, this interest will not support a program that attempts to achieve or maintain a mathematical balance in student bodies or faculties (*i.e.,* quota systems will not be found to be necessary to promote educational diversity).

Examples: 1) A state university may consider race or ethnic origin when admitting students, in an attempt to have a diverse student body. [University of California Regents v. Bakke, 438 U.S. 265 (1978)]

2) A school board may not fire or lay off white teachers with greater seniority than minority race teachers for the sole purpose of maintaining racial balance in a faculty during a period when teacher layoffs are necessary. [Wygant v. Jackson Board of Education, 476 U.S. 267 (1989)]

c. Discriminatory Legislative Apportionment

Race can be considered in drawing up new voting districts, but it *cannot be the predominant factor*. If a plaintiff can show that a redistricting plan was drawn up predominantly on the basis of racial considerations (as opposed to the more traditional factors, such as compactness, contiguity, and community interest), the plan will violate the Equal Protection Clause *unless* the government can show that the plan is *narrowly tailored* to serve a *compelling state interest*. [Miller v. Johnson, 515 U.S. 900 (1995)—while eradicating the effects of past discrimination would be a compelling state interest, the redistricting here was driven by the Justice Department's policy of maximizing the number of districts where racial minority members are the majority, which is not a compelling interest]

d. Private Affirmative Action

Private employers, of course, are not restricted by the Equal Protection Clause, since the Clause applies only to the government, and private employers lack state action. Nevertheless, Congress has adopted statutes regulating private discrimination by employers pursuant to its power under the enabling provisions of the Thirteenth and Fourteenth Amendments and the Commerce Clause. Thus, if an exam question asks whether private employer discrimination is valid, the answer generally cannot be based on equal protection.

2. Alienage Classifications

a. Federal Classifications
The standard for review of federal government classifications based on alienage is not clear, but they never seem to be subject to strict scrutiny. Because of Congress's plenary power over aliens, these classifications are valid if they are **not arbitrary and unreasonable**. Thus, federal Medicare regulations could establish a five-year residency requirement for benefits that eliminated many resident aliens. [Mathews v. Diaz, 426 U.S. 67 (1976)]

b. State and Local Classifications
State/local laws are **subject to strict scrutiny** if based on alienage. A "compelling state interest" must be shown to justify disparate treatment. For example, a state law requiring United States citizenship for welfare benefits, civil service jobs, or a license to practice law will be struck down because there is no compelling interest justifying the requirement.

1) Exception—Participation in Self-Government Process
If a law discriminates against alien participation in the functioning of the state government, the **rational basis** standard is applied.

Examples: 1) A state cannot require a notary public to be a citizen. A notary's responsibilities are essentially clerical and do not fall within the exception for positions related to participation in the governmental process, and there is no compelling government interest justifying such a requirement. [Bernal v. Fainter, 467 U.S. 216 (1984)]

2) A state can validly refuse to hire aliens as police officers and teachers and for all other positions that have a direct effect on the functioning of government. [Ambach v. Norwick, 441 U.S. 68 (1979); Cabell v. Chavez-Salido, 454 U.S. 432 (1982)]

c. Undocumented Aliens

1) Punitive Laws Against "Illegal" Alien Adults
The Supreme Court has **not** held that undocumented ("illegal") aliens are a suspect classification. Thus, a state law that denies benefits to (or imposes burdens on) persons who are in the United States without the permission of the federal government might be upheld under the rational basis test as long as the law was not totally arbitrary.

2) Education Rights of Alien Children
In *Plyler v. Doe,* 457 U.S. 202 (1982), the Court held that a state denied equal protection to undocumented alien children when it denied them state supported primary or secondary education. However, the Supreme Court upheld a state statute that permitted a school district to deny tuition-free education to any child (whether or not he was a United States citizen) who lived apart from his parent or lawful guardian if the child's presence in the school district was for the "primary purpose" of attending school in the district. The state does not have to consider such a child to be a bona fide resident of the school district. [Martinez v. Bynum, 461 U.S. 321 (1983)]

E. QUASI-SUSPECT CLASSIFICATIONS
Classifications based on gender or legitimacy are almost always suspect. When analyzing government action based on such classifications, the Court will apply the intermediate standard and strike the action unless it is **substantially related** to an **important** government interest.

1. Gender
The Court has expressly held that the **government** bears the burden of proof in gender discrimination cases and that an **"exceedingly persuasive justification"** is required in order to show that gender discrimination is substantially related to an important government interest. [United States v. Virginia, 518 U.S. 515 (1996)]

a. Intentional Discrimination Against Women
Gender classifications that **intentionally** discriminate against women will generally be invalid under the intermediate standard, because the government is unable to show the "exceedingly persuasive justification" that is required.

Examples: 1) A statute giving the husband, as head of the household, the right to unilaterally dispose of property jointly owned with his wife violates equal protection. [Kirchberg v. Feenstra, 450 U.S. 455 (1981)]

2) A statute giving preference to males over females to act as administrator of an estate violates equal protection. [Reed v. Reed, 404 U.S. 71 (1971)—ease in determining who should serve is not an important interest]

Compare: 1) A state law that excluded from state disability insurance benefits "disabilities" arising from normal pregnancy and childbirth was upheld on a holding that it did not constitute a gender classification and so did not constitute intentional discrimination. [Geduldig v. Aiello, 417 U.S. 484 (1974)]

2) A state statute granting a hiring preference to veterans was upheld even though the result would disadvantage women since most veterans are men. The Court found that the purpose of the statute was to help veterans, not to discriminate against women. [Personnel Administrator of Massachusetts v. Feeney, 442 U.S. 256 (1979)]

1) Government Interest Must Be Genuine

The "important government interest" advanced to justify categorization on the basis of gender must be *genuine*—not hypothesized for the purpose of litigation defense. Neither may the government's justification rely on *overbroad generalizations* about males and females that will create or perpetuate the legal, social, and economic inferiority of women. [United States v. Virginia, *supra*]

Example: When a state military school's policy of admitting only men was challenged, the state justified the policy claiming that: (i) offering a diversity of educational approaches within the state (*e.g.,* some schools having men only, some having women only, and some having both) yields important educational benefits, and (ii) females *generally* would not be able to meet the school's physical requirements and would not do well under the school's adversative approach to education. The Supreme Court found these arguments unavailing. There was no evidence that the single-sex school in question was established or had been maintained with a view toward fostering a diversity of educational opportunities, and there was some evidence that *some* women could meet the school's physical requirements and thrive under the school's adversative approach. [United States v. Virginia, *supra*]

b. Affirmative Action Benefiting Women

Classifications benefiting women that are designed to *remedy past discrimination* against women will generally be upheld.

Examples: 1) Social Security and tax exemptions that entitle women to greater benefits to make up for past discrimination in the workplace are valid. [Califano v. Webster, 430 U.S. 313 (1977)]

2) A Navy rule granting female officers longer tenure than males before mandatory discharge for nonproduction is valid to make up for past discrimination against females in the Navy. [Schlesinger v. Ballard, 419 U.S. 498 (1975)]

c. Intentional Discrimination Against Men

Intentional discrimination against men generally is invalid. However, a number of laws have been held valid as being substantially related to an important government interest.

1) Invalid Discrimination

The following have been held invalid under the Equal Protection Clause:

a) Denial to admit males to a state university or nursing school [Mississippi University for Women v. Hogan, 458 U.S. 718 (1982)];

b) Law that provides that only wives are eligible for alimony [Orr v. Orr, 40 U.S. 268 (1979)];

c) Law that permits unwed mother but not unwed father to stop adoption of offspring [Caban v. Mohammed, 441 U.S. 380 (1979)]; and

d) Law providing a higher minimum drinking age for men than for women [Craig v. Boren, 429 U.S. 190 (1976)].

2) Valid Discrimination
The following have been upheld under the Equal Protection Clause despite their discriminatory intent:

a) Law punishing males but not females for statutory rape (sexual intercourse with a minor) [Michael M. v. Superior Court, 450 U.S. 464 (1981)—classification was found to be substantially related to important interest of preventing pregnancy of minors];

b) Male only draft registration [Rostker v. Goldberg, 453 U.S. 57 (1981)—classification was found to be substantially related to important interest of preparing combat troops]; and

c) A law granting automatic United States citizenship to nonmarital children born abroad to American mothers, but requiring American fathers of children born abroad to take specific steps to establish paternity in order to make such children United States citizens. [Nguyen v. Immigration and Naturalization Service, 533 U.S. 53 (2001)—promotes the important governmental interest of avoiding proof of paternity problems, which are more difficult to resolve for fathers]

2. Legitimacy Classifications

Distinctions drawn between legitimate and illegitimate children are also reviewed under the intermediate scrutiny standard. Such classifications "must be **substantially related** to an **important** governmental objective." [Clark v. Jeter, 486 U.S. 456 (1988)]

a. No Punitive Purpose
When the Court examines a classification based on illegitimacy, it gives greater attention to the purpose behind the distinction. It will not uphold discriminatory legislation intended to punish the offspring of illicit relationships.

1) Inheritance from Father
A state statute cannot absolutely exclude illegitimate children from inheriting from their intestate fathers. [Trimble v. Gordon, 430 U.S. 762 (1977)]

Note: However, to promote efficient disposition of property at death (an important government interest), a state can require that the paternity of the father be proved before his death, since the requirement is substantially related to the important interest. [Lalli v. Lalli, 439 U.S. 259 (1978)]

2) Statute of Limitations on Paternity Suits May Be Discriminatory
The Supreme Court struck down a state statute that required illegitimate children to bring paternity suits within six years of their birth while allowing legitimate children to seek support from parents at any time. The Court found that the law was not related to the state interest of preventing stale or fraudulent claims. [Clark v. Jeter, *supra*]

b. Immigration Preference to Legitimate Children—Permissible
Due to the plenary power over immigration, the Court upheld a federal law granting immigration preferences to legitimate children. [Fiallo v. Bell, 430 U.S. 787 (1977)]

F. OTHER CLASSIFICATIONS

All other classifications are reviewed under the rational basis standard and will be upheld unless they bear no rational relationship to any conceivable legitimate government interest. Nevertheless, if the government has no interest in denying a benefit or imposing a burden on a group of persons other than a societal fear or dislike of them, the classification will not meet the standard.
Examples: 1) The Court struck down a zoning ordinance that allowed denial of a special use permit to a group of unrelated, mentally retarded persons who wished to share a residential home or apartment building. Retarded persons are not a suspect or quasi-suspect class and the right to housing is not a fundamental right; thus the

Court applied the rational basis standard. It found that the sole reason the permit was denied was the applicants' mental condition and that the government has no legitimate interest in prohibiting mentally retarded persons from living together. [Cleburne v. Cleburne Living Center, Inc., 470 U.S. 1002 (1985)]

2) Several municipalities passed ordinances banning discrimination in housing, employment, etc., based on sexual orientation. In response, the state voters adopted a state constitutional amendment prohibiting any state or local action protecting the status of persons based on their homosexual, lesbian, or bisexual orientation. *Held:* A state constitutional provision that identifies persons by a single trait and then denies them the right to seek *any* specific protections from the law—no matter how local or widespread the injury—is so unprecedented as to imply animosity toward such persons and is thus not related to any legitimate state interest. [Romer v. Evans, 517 U.S. 620 (1996)]

1. Age Not Suspect

Age is not a suspect class. Thus, government action based on age will be upheld if there is a conceivable rational basis for the classification. [*See, e.g.,* Massachusetts Board of Retirement v. Murgia, 427 U.S. 307 (1976)—police officer can be forced to retire at age 50, even though he is as physically fit as a younger officer; Gregory v. Ashcroft, 501 U.S. 452 (1991)—a state constitution that requires state judges to retire at age 70 does not violate the Equal Protection Clause]

2. Wealth Not Suspect

The Court has never held that wealth alone is a "suspect classification." However, the lack of wealth, or the inability to pay a governmentally required fee, cannot be the sole basis upon which a person is deprived of a *fundamental* constitutional right.

Example: The government will be required to waive a marriage license fee or divorce court fee for a person who cannot afford to pay that fee. Marriage and divorce rights are part of the right of privacy.

a. Abortions

The Supreme Court upheld the governmental refusal to pay for abortions. The Court found that a woman did not have a fundamental constitutional right to obtain abortion services, but only a fundamental right to make her decision to have an abortion without government interference.

b. Education

The Supreme Court has not yet held education to be a fundamental right. The Court has not found that children are denied equal protection when the government provides greater educational opportunities for children who can afford to pay for access to the best state operated schools. In fact, the Court has upheld the use of a property tax to fund local schools where the tax system resulted in children in districts with a high tax base getting a significantly better education than children in tax districts that could not afford significant taxes for education. [San Antonio Independent School District v. Rodriguez, 411 U.S. 1 (1973)] The Court has also upheld a statute that authorizes some school districts in the state to charge user fees for bus transportation to the local public schools. [Kadrmas v. Dickinson Public Schools, 487 U.S. 450 (1988)]

XIX. FUNDAMENTAL RIGHTS

A. INTRODUCTION

Certain fundamental rights are protected under the Constitution. If they are denied to everyone, it is a substantive due process problem. If they are denied to some individuals but not to others, it is an equal protection problem. The applicable standard in either case is strict scrutiny. Thus, to be valid the governmental action must be *necessary* to protect a *compelling interest*.

B. RIGHT OF PRIVACY

Various privacy rights, including marriage, sexual relations, abortion, and childrearing, are fundamental rights. Thus, regulations affecting these rights are reviewed under the *strict scrutiny* standard and will be upheld only if they are *necessary* to a *compelling interest*.

1. Marriage

The right of a male and female to enter into (and, probably, to dissolve) a marriage relationship is a fundamental right. Although not all cases examining marriage regulations clearly use the compelling interest standard, a law prohibiting a class of adults from marrying is likely to be invalidated unless the government can demonstrate that the law is narrowly tailored to promote a compelling or overriding or, at least, important interest.

Note: The Court has indicated that there is a "marital zone of privacy" [*see* Griswold v. Connecticut, 381 U.S. 479 (1965)], so it will likely grant broader protection to private sexual relations between married persons than it does concerning nonmarried persons.

a. Special Test in Prisoners' Rights Cases

A statute or regulation that restricts the constitutional rights of prison inmates will be upheld as long as the statute or regulation "is reasonably related to legitimate penological interests."

Example: Even under this lenient standard, a prison regulation that prohibited an adult prisoner from establishing a legal marriage relationship with another adult unless the prison superintendent approved the marriage was held invalid, because the regulation was not reasonably related to any asserted penological interest. [Turner v. Safley, 482 U.S. 78 (1987)]

2. Use of Contraceptives

A state cannot prohibit distribution of nonmedical contraceptives to adults except through licensed pharmacists, nor prohibit sales of such contraceptives to persons under 16 who do not have approval of a licensed physician. [Carey v. Population Services International, 431 U.S. 678 (1977)]

3. Abortion

The Supreme Court has held that the right of privacy includes the right of a woman to have an abortion under certain circumstances without undue interference from the state. [Roe v. Wade, 410 U.S. 113 (1973)] However, because the Court has held that the states have a compelling interest in protecting the health of both the woman and the fetus that may become a child, it is difficult to apply the normal "strict scrutiny" analysis to abortion regulations (since these two compelling interests may conflict with each other and with the woman's privacy right). Moreover, the Supreme Court has actively been changing the rules regarding abortions and the Justices have not come to agreement on any applicable standard. In the Court's latest announcement, the plurality opinion adopted two rules: a pre-viability rule and a post-viability rule.

a. Pre-Viability Rule—No Undue Burdens

Before viability (*i.e.,* a realistic possibility of maintaining the fetus's life outside the womb), a state may adopt regulations protecting the mother's health and the life of the fetus only if the regulation does not impose an "undue burden" or substantial obstacle to the woman's right to have an abortion. The Court has not specifically defined what will constitute an undue burden, stating that a state can adopt a statute designed to persuade a woman to choose childbirth over abortion as long as the statute is reasonably related to that purpose and does not put a *substantial* obstacle to abortion in the woman's path. A statute will not impose a substantial obstacle or an undue burden simply because it has the incidental effect of making it more difficult or more expensive to obtain an abortion. [Planned Parenthood of Southeastern Pennsylvania v. Casey, 505 U.S. 833 (1992)]

1) Informed Consent—No Undue Burden

States can require abortions to be performed by licensed physicians, and it is not an "undue burden" to require the *physician* to provide the woman with truthful information about the nature of the abortion procedure, the health risks of abortion and childbirth, and the probable gestational age of the fetus. [Planned Parenthood of Southeastern Pennsylvania v. Casey, *supra*]

2) Waiting Period—No Undue Burden

Requiring a 24-hour waiting period between the time the woman gives her informed consent and the time of the abortion does not amount to an undue burden. [Planned Parenthood of Southeastern Pennsylvania v. Casey, *supra*]

3) Parental Consent—No Undue Burden

A state may require a minor to obtain her parents' (one or both) consent to have an abortion (or give notice to them even if their consent is not required) if there is a "bypass procedure" whereby the minor may obtain the abortion (without notice to or consent of her parents) with the consent of a judge. The judge is required to make a prompt decision as to (i) whether the minor is sufficiently mature to make her own abortion decision, and (ii) if she is not sufficiently mature, whether having an abortion without notice to her parents is in her best interests. [Hodgson v. Minnesota, 497 U.S. 417 (1990); Ohio v. Akron Center for Reproductive Health, 497 U.S. 502 (1990); Planned Parenthood of Southeastern Pennsylvania v. Casey, *supra;* Lambert v. Wicklund, 520 U.S. 292 (1997)]

4) **Compare—Spousal Consent Is Undue Burden**
It is an undue burden to require a woman to sign a statement that she has notified her spouse that she is about to undergo an abortion. [Planned Parenthood of Southeastern Pennsylvania v. Casey, *supra*]

5) **"Physician Only" Requirement—No Undue Burden**
A law restricting the performance of abortions to licensed physicians does not impose an undue burden on a woman seeking an abortion. [Mazurek v. Armstrong, 520 U.S. 968 (1997)—*per curiam*]

6) **"Partial-Birth Abortion"**
A state may *not* completely proscribe so-called partial-birth abortion procedures since they are the *most commonly* used methods for pre-viability, second-trimester abortions. Such a ban would impose an undue burden on a woman's right to choose a pre-viability abortion. [Stenberg v. Carhart, 530 U.S. 793 (2000)] However, a state could bar one type of partial-birth abortion if there are other adequate, safe methods of abortion available *and* the law provides an exception for those instances when the banned procedure is necessary to preserve the life or *health* of the mother. [Stenberg v. Carhart, *supra*]

7) **Other Regulations Uncertain**
Prior to *Planned Parenthood of Southeastern Pennsylvania v. Casey, supra,* the Supreme Court upheld a requirement that abortions be performed in a clinic or medical facility with all of the basic medical equipment that would be found in a hospital surgery room. The Court also upheld a requirement that tissue from an aborted fetus be sent to a pathologist. These holdings surely are still valid. But the Court struck down certain other regulations (*e.g.*, requiring early term abortions to be approved by another doctor or hospital committee). Whether these regulations would be found to be undue burdens is uncertain.

b. **Post-Viability Rule—May Prohibit Abortion Unless Woman's Health Threatened**
Once the fetus has become viable, the state's interest in the fetus's life can override the woman's right to choose an abortion, but it does not override the state's interest in the woman's health. Thus, after viability the state can prohibit a woman from obtaining an abortion unless an abortion is necessary to protect the mother's life or health. However, viability is itself a medical question, and a state cannot unduly interfere with the attending physician's judgment as to the reasonable likelihood that the fetus can survive outside the womb. [Colautti v. Franklin, 439 U.S. 379 (1979)]

c. **Financing Abortions**
Neither federal nor local governments are required to grant medical benefit payments for abortions to indigent women, even if they grant benefits to indigent women for childbirth services. [Maher v. Roe, 432 U.S. 464 (1977); Harris v. McRae, 448 U.S. 297 (1980)] Moreover, a state may prohibit the public funding of abortions by prohibiting the use of public facilities for abortions and prohibiting any public employee acting within the scope of her public employment from performing or assisting in the performance of abortions. [Webster v. Reproductive Health Services, 486 U.S. 592 (1989)] The Court has not addressed the question of whether a state could prohibit public employees from performing abortions at times and places not a part of their public employment.

4. **Obscene Reading Material**
The right of privacy encompasses the freedom to read obscene material in your home, except for child pornography. [Stanley v. Georgia, 394 U.S. 557 (1969); Osborne v. Ohio, 495 U.S. 103 (1990)] It does not, however, include the right to sell, purchase, receive, or transport obscene material. [Paris Adult Theatre v. Slayton, 413 U.S. 49 (1973)]

5. Keeping Extended Family Together

The right of privacy includes the right of family members—even extended ones—to live together. Thus, a zoning ordinance cannot prohibit extended families from living in a single household since there is no compelling interest to justify such a rule. [Moore v. City of East Cleveland, 431 U.S. 494 (1977)]

6. Rights of Parents

Parents have a fundamental right to make decisions concerning the care, custody, and control of their children. [Troxel v. Granville, 530 U.S. 57 (2000)]

a. Education

Although the state may prescribe reasonable educational standards, it may *not* require that all children be educated in public schools. [Pierce v. Society of Sisters, 268 U.S. 510 (1925)] Neither may the state forbid education in a language other than English. [Meyer v. Nebraska, 262 U.S. 390 (1923)]

b. Visitation

A state law was found to be overbroad and in violation of parents' rights where it (i) authorized the courts to grant "any person" (including grandparents) a right to visit a child upon finding that this would be in the child's best interests and (ii) did not allow the judge to give significant weight to the parent's offer of meaningful visitation opportunity and the traditional presumption that a fit parent will act in the child's best interests. [Troxel v. Granville, *supra*]

7. Sodomy—No Privacy Right

The right of privacy does not include the right of consenting adults to engage in sodomy. [Bowers v. Hardwick, 478 U.S. 186 (1986)] It should be noted that the Supreme Court did not determine whether a significant prison sentence for private, consensual homosexual acts would violate the Eighth Amendment prohibition of cruel and unusual punishment.

8. Freedom from Collection and Distribution of Personal Data

The right of privacy does not prevent the state from accumulating and computerizing the names and addresses of patients for whom dangerous drugs are prescribed. [Whalen v. Roe, 429 U.S. 589 (1977)] And the state can republish the recording of an official act, such as an arrest. [Paul v. Davis, 424 U.S. 693 (1976)]

C. RIGHT TO VOTE

The right of all United States citizens over 18 years of age to vote is mentioned in the Fourteenth, Fifteenth, Nineteenth, Twenty-Fourth, and Twenty-Sixth Amendments. It extends to all national and state government elections, including primaries. The right is fundamental; thus, restrictions on voting, other than on the basis of age, residency, or citizenship, are *invalid* unless they can pass strict scrutiny.

1. Restrictions on Right to Vote

a. Residency Requirements

Relatively short residency requirements restricting the right to vote (*e.g.,* 30 days) are valid because there is a compelling interest in ensuring that only bona fide residents vote. However, longer residency requirements will probably be held invalid (*e.g.,* one year) because they discriminate against newer residents without a compelling reason, and thus violate the Equal Protection Clause. Such residency requirements might also violate the right to travel interstate. (*See* D.1.b.1), *infra.*) Note also that Congress may override state residency requirements in *presidential* elections. [Oregon v. Mitchell, 400 U.S. 112 (1970)]

1) Members of Armed Forces

The right to vote cannot automatically be denied to members of the armed forces stationed at a particular locality. They must be given an opportunity to prove their bona fide residency. [Carrington v. Rash, 380 U.S. 89 (1965)]

2) Compare—Nonresidents

Laws that prohibit nonresidents from voting are generally valid as long as they have a rational basis. [*See* Holt Civic Club v. City of Tuscaloosa, 439 U.S. 60 (1978)—upholding denial of right to vote in city elections to persons outside of city limits, but within the city's police and licensing jurisdiction]

b. Property Ownership

Conditioning the right to vote, to be a candidate, or to hold office on property owner-ship is usually invalid under the Equal Protection Clause, since property ownership is not necessary to any compelling governmental interest related to voting. [*See, e.g.,* Kramer v. Union Free School District, 395 U.S. 622 (1969)—requirement of owning property or having children in schools to vote in school board elections struck] How-ever, certain special purpose elections (*e.g.,* water storage district elections) can be based on property ownership. (*See* below.)

c. Poll Taxes

Poll taxes are prohibited under the Twenty-Fourth Amendment, and the Supreme Court has held that they also violate equal protection because wealth is not related to the government's interest in having voters vote intelligently. [Harper v. Virginia Board of Elections, 383 U.S. 663 (1966)]

d. Primary Elections

1) State Regulation of Party Primaries

States may exercise some control over primary elections, but such regulation is subject to restrictions under the First Amendment (freedom of political associa-tion) and the Fourteenth Amendment (Equal Protection Clause). Thus, to prevent interparty "raiding," the Supreme Court has held that states can require a person to have been registered with a party for a reasonable time before that party's primary election in order to be eligible to vote in the primary. [Rosario v. Rockefeller, 410 U.S. 752 (1973)—11 months registration upheld; Kusper v. Pontikes, 414 U.S. 51 (1973)—23 months not upheld] However, if a political party wishes to open its primary elections to anyone, whether or not registered with the party, the state cannot prohibit this because the state interest here is overridden by the right of political association. [Tashjian v. Republican Party of Connecticut, 479 U.S. 208 (1986)]

2) States May Subsidize Primaries of Major Parties

States may subsidize the primaries of major parties without similarly defraying the costs of mechanisms through which minor parties qualify candidates for the general election [American Party of Texas v. White, 415 U.S. 767 (1974)—upholding law requiring new or small parties to proceed by petition or convention at their own expense rather than by publicly funded primary], as long as new or small parties are given some effective way to qualify for the general election [Williams v. Rhodes, 393 U.S. 23 (1968)—unduly burdensome petition require-ments for new or small parties struck down as not justified].

2. Dilution of Right to Vote

a. One Person, One Vote Principle

The Equal Protection Clause of the Fourteenth Amendment has been interpreted to prohibit state dilution of the right to vote, and Article I has been interpreted to place the same type of restriction on the federal government.

1) Establishing Voting Districts

Whenever a governmental body establishes voting districts for the election of representatives, the number of persons in each district may not vary significantly. This is commonly referred to as the one person, one vote principle.

a) Congressional Elections—Almost Exactly Equal

States establish the districts for congressional elections. However, the Su-preme Court requires *almost exact mathematical equality* between the *congressional* districts within a state; thus, deviations of even a few percent-age points between the congressional districts within a state may result in the invalidation of the congressional district plan.

(1) Compare—Apportionment Among the States

Congress apportions representatives among the states "according to their respective number." [Art. I, §2] Congress's good faith choice of method in so apportioning the representatives commands far more deference than state districting decisions and is *not* subject to the same precise mathematical standard as state plans. [United States Department of Commerce v. Montana, 503 U.S. 442 (1992)]

b) State and Local Elections—Variance Not Unjustifiably Large
The variance in the number of persons included in districts for the purpose of electing representatives to a ***state or local governmental body*** must not be unjustifiably large, but the districts need not be within a few percentage points of each other: If a state can show that the deviation from mathematical equality between districts is reasonable and tailored to promote a legitimate state interest, the law establishing the districts may be upheld. [Mahan v. Howell, 410 U.S. 315 (1973)—16% variance in district populations was upheld in light of state's interest in preserving political subdivisions, although 30% variance would be excessive]

c) Scope
The one person, one vote principle applies to almost every election where a person is being elected to perform normal governmental functions. [Hadley v. Junior College District, 397 U.S. 50 (1970)—trustees for junior college district] However, there are a few exceptions to note:

(1) Exception—Appointed Officials and Officials Elected "At-Large"
The apportionment requirement is inapplicable to appointed officials. Neither is it applicable in at-large systems of election, because in such a system there are no electoral districts to violate the one person, one vote principle. However, if an at-large voting system were established or maintained for the purpose of suppressing the voting power of minority race voters, it would be unconstitutional.

(2) Exception—Special Purpose Government Units (Water Storage Districts)
The government can limit the class of persons who are allowed to vote in an election of persons to serve on a special purpose government unit ***if*** the government unit has a special impact on the class of enfranchised voters. To date, the Supreme Court has found only "water storage districts" to be so specialized that their governing boards are not subject to the one person, one vote principle. [Salyer Land Co. v. Tulane Water District, 410 U.S. 719 (1973); Ball v. James, 451 U.S. 355 (1981)—apportionment rules do not apply to water district even if the district is major supplier of electricity in the state]

2) Standardless Recount
Counting uncounted ballots in a presidential election without standards to guide ballot examiners in determining the intent of the voter violates the Fourteenth Amendment Equal Protection Clause. [Bush v. Gore, 531 U.S. 98 (2000)]

b. Gerrymandering

1) Racial Gerrymandering
As indicated above, race (and presumably other suspect classifications) cannot be the predominate factor in drawing the boundaries of a voting district unless the district plan can pass muster under strict scrutiny. [*See* Miller v. Johnson, XVIII.D.1.c., *supra*] Moreover, a district's bizarre shape can be used to show that race was the predominate factor in drawing the district's boundaries [*see* Shaw v. Reno, XVIII.C.1.a., *supra*], although a bizarre shape is not necessary to such a finding. Note that the person challenging the reapportionment has the burden of proving the race-based motive. [Shaw v. Hunt, 517 U.S. 899 (1996)]

2) Political Gerrymandering
It is also unconstitutional to gerrymander based on political-group membership, but to prove unconstitutional ***political*** gerrymandering, a plaintiff would have to show that the district lines were drawn to suppress voting power of a political party ***and*** that (through one or more elections) the districting system consistently diluted the voting power of a particular group of voters. [Davis v. Bandemer, 478 U.S. 109 (1986)]

c. **Multi-Member Districts**

A state is generally free to have some multi-member districts together with some single-member districts, as long as the number of members representing a district is proportional to its population. However, single-member or multi-member districts will be held to violate equal protection (even though they meet the one person, one vote principle) if the district lines were drawn on the basis of unconstitutional criteria, such as to suppress the voting power of racial minorities or an identifiable political group.

3. **Candidates and Campaigns**

a. **Candidate Qualifications**

1) **Fee Must Not Preclude Indigents as Candidates**

States may not charge candidates a fee that results in making it impossible for indigents to run for office. An unreasonably high filing fee (which was not tailored to promote a substantial or overriding state interest) might be held totally invalid so that no candidate would have to pay the fee. A reasonable, valid fee would have to be waived for an indigent candidate who could not pay the fee.

2) **Restrictions on Ability of Person to Be a Candidate**

Restrictions on the ability of persons to be candidates must be examined to see if they violate either the First Amendment right of political association or the Fourteenth Amendment Equal Protection Clause. Such regulations are judged on a sliding scale of scrutiny. (*See* XXI.B., *infra.*)

Example: The Court invalidated a March deadline for filing a nominating petition for independent candidates for a November election where the state allowed the major political parties to name their candidates later in the year. [Anderson v. Celebrezze, 460 U.S. 780 (1983)]

Note: A state may require candidates to show reasonable support (signatures or votes) to qualify to have their names placed on the ballot. [Munro v. Socialist Workers Party, 479 U.S. 189 (1986)—upholding requirement of receipt of at least 1% of the votes cast in the primary election]

3) **Required Resignation of Office Is Permissible**

A state may require state officials to resign their office if they enter an election for another government office. [Clements v. Fashing, 457 U.S. 957 (1982)]

b. **Campaign Funding, Contributions, and Expenditures**

Government *may* allocate more public funds to the two "major" parties than to "minor" parties for political campaigns, and may withhold public funding from candidates who do not accept reciprocal limits on their total campaign expenses; but such expenses cannot otherwise be limited, unlike campaign contributions to political candidates, which may be limited if government chooses. (XXI.B., *infra.*)

4. **Extraordinary Majorities—Referendum Elections**

The government may require a supermajority vote for voter referendums, even though such a requirement might give a minority disproportionate power. [Gordon v. Lance, 403 U.S. 1 (1971)—upholding 60% requirement for referendum approval; Town of Lockport v. Citizens for Community Action, 430 U.S. 259 (1977)—upholding requirement that new county charter be approved by separate majorities of city and noncity voters]

5. **Absentee Ballots**

The state has no duty to provide absentee ballots to persons otherwise unable to vote in some manner. However, if it does provide for absentee ballots, it may not deny the ballots in a discriminatory manner. [*See* McDonald v. Board of Election Officials, 394 U.S. 802 (1969)—striking law that granted absentee ballots to those incarcerated outside of their home county but denied them to those incarcerated within their home county]

6. **Replacement of Incumbent Legislators**

A state may validly give to a political party the right to name an interim appointee to the legislature to fill out the unexpired term of a legislator from that political party who left office. No voter is denied equal protection by this system. [Rodriguez v. Popular Democratic Party, 457 U.S. 1 (1982)]

D. RIGHT TO TRAVEL

1. Interstate Travel

a. Nature of the Right
Individuals have a fundamental right to travel from state to state, which encompasses the right: (i) to leave and enter another state, and (ii) to be treated equally if they become permanent residents of that state. [Saenz v. Roe, VII.C.3., *supra*—striking California law that limited welfare benefits for new residents to what they would have received in their prior state of residence]

b. Standard of Review
When a state uses a durational residency requirement (a waiting period) for dispensing benefits, that requirement normally should be subject to the "strict scrutiny" test. This means that the government must show that the waiting period requirement is tailored to promote a compelling or overriding interest. However, in some right to travel cases, the Court has not been clear as to whether it is using this strict scrutiny-compelling interest standard of review. The important point to note for the bar exam is that state residency requirements should not be upheld merely because they have some theoretical rational relationship to an arguably legitimate end of government.

1) Examples
Because of the ad hoc nature of these rulings, we will list four examples of Supreme Court decisions in this area:

a) A one-year waiting period before a person may receive subsistence welfare payments is *invalid*. Similarly, a law providing that persons residing in the state for less than a year may receive welfare benefits no greater than those paid in the state of prior residence is also invalid. [Saenz v. Roe, *supra*]

b) A one-year waiting period for state subsidized medical care is *invalid*.

c) A one-year waiting period to get a divorce is *valid*.

d) A state may require a voter to register to vote in a party primary 10 months before the primary election (to avoid interparty "raiding"). However, a 23-month registration period would be *invalid*.

c. Distinctions Between Old and New Residents
Some state laws that have an adverse impact on new residents do not involve a waiting period. For example, a state may attempt to dispense state benefits on the basis of the length of time a person has resided in the state. A state law that distinguishes between residents of the state on the sole basis of their length of residency will serve no legitimate state interest. This type of law should be *stricken* under the rational basis test because it has *no rational relationship* to any legitimate state interest.

Examples: 1) A state statute that dispensed differing amounts of state money to residents of the state based on each resident's length of residence was held invalid.

2) A state statute that grants an annual property tax exemption to a veteran of military service only if he resided in the state before a specific date (May 1976) is invalid.

3) A state law that grants a hiring preference (for civil service employment) to a veteran only if he was a resident of the state prior to joining the armed services is invalid.

2. International Travel
The Supreme Court has not yet declared that the right to international travel is fundamental, although the right appears to be *protected from arbitrary federal interference* by the Due Process Clause of the Fifth Amendment. The Court has held that this right is not violated when the federal government refuses to pay social security benefits to persons who leave the country. The test here is "mere rationality, not strict scrutiny." [Califano v. Aznavorian, 439 U.S. 170 (1978)] Congress may give the executive branch the power to revoke the passport of a person whose conduct in another country presents a danger to United States foreign policy. [Haig v. Agee, 453 U.S. 280 (1981)] The Treasury Department, with congressional

authorization, could restrict travel to and from Cuba without violating the Fifth Amendment. [Regan v. Wald, 468 U.S. 222 (1984)]

E. RIGHT TO REFUSE MEDICAL TREATMENT

The Supreme Court had held that the right to refuse medical treatment is a part of an individual's "liberty" that is protected by the Fifth and Fourteenth Amendment Due Process Clauses. However, the Supreme Court has not ruled that this aspect of liberty is a "fundamental right" and **has not** explained which standard of review should be used. Nevertheless, the Court has ruled on the validity of several types of legislation.

1. Vaccination

An individual can be made to submit to vaccination against contagious diseases because of the governmental and societal interest in preventing the spread of disease. [Jacobsen v. Massachusetts, 197 U.S. 11 (1905)]

2. Refusal of Medical Treatment

The Supreme Court has assumed (without deciding) that a mentally competent adult has the right to refuse lifesaving medical treatment (including lifesaving nutrition). [Cruzan v. Director, Missouri Department of Health, 497 U.S. 261 (1990)]

a. Compare—No Right to Assisted Suicide

There is no general right to commit suicide; thus, a state may ban persons from giving individuals assistance in committing suicide. [Washington v. Glucksberg, 521 U.S. 702 (1997)] It is not irrational to permit competent persons to refuse life-sustaining treatment but prohibit physicians to assist in suicide because there is a logical, rational, and well-established distinction between letting someone die and making someone die. [Vacco v. Quill, 521 U.S. 793 (1997)]

3. Family or Guardian Decisions for Comatose Adult

A state may give relatives or the guardian of an individual the power to decide whether to refuse lifesaving medical treatment if the individual is incapable of making or expressing the decision (*e.g.,* if the individual is in a coma), but the state does not have to grant this power. If the state chooses to grant the power, it can condition the power on proof, by clear and convincing evidence, that the comatose adult would have chosen to refuse medical treatment if she were capable of making the decision and expressing herself. [Cruzan v. Director, Missouri Department of Health, *supra*]

PART FIVE: FIRST AMENDMENT FREEDOMS

The First Amendment prohibits Congress from establishing a religion or interfering with the exercise of religion, abridging the freedom of speech or the press, or interfering with the right of the people to assemble. These prohibitions have been made applicable to the states through the Fourteenth Amendment. The freedoms, however, are not absolute, and exam questions often focus on their boundaries. The following material will outline the scope of each freedom.

XX. FREEDOM OF SPEECH AND ASSEMBLY

A. GENERAL PRINCIPLES

The freedoms of speech and assembly protect the free flow of ideas, a most important function in a democratic society. Thus, whenever the government seeks to regulate these freedoms, the Court will weigh the importance of these rights against the interests or policies sought to be served by the regulation. When analyzing regulations on speech and press, keep the following guidelines in mind:

1. Content vs. Conduct

A regulation seeking to forbid communication of specific ideas (*i.e.,* a **content** regulation) is less likely to be upheld than a regulation of the **conduct** incidental to speech.

a. Content

It is presumptively unconstitutional for the government to place burdens on speech because of its content. To justify such content-based regulation of speech, the government must show that the regulation (or tax) is **necessary** to serve a **compelling** state interest and is narrowly drawn to achieve that end. [Simon & Schuster, Inc. v. Members of the New York State Crime Victims Board, 502 U.S. 105 (1991)—striking a law requiring that proceeds to criminals from books and other productions describing their crimes be placed in escrow for five years to pay claims of victims of the crimes]

1) **Exception—Unprotected Categories of Speech**
   The Supreme Court has previously determined that certain categories of speech (*e.g.,* obscenity, defamation, and "fighting words"; *see* C., *infra*) generally are proscribable despite the First Amendment. Even in these cases, however, the Court is less likely to uphold a prior restraint (*i.e.,* a regulation prohibiting speech before it occurs) than a punishment for speech that has already occurred.

2) **Content-Neutral Speech Regulations**
   While content-based regulation of speech is subject to strict scrutiny, content-neutral speech regulations generally are subject to *intermediate scrutiny*—they will be upheld if the government can show that: (i) they advance *important* interests unrelated to the suppression of speech, and (ii) they *do not burden substantially more speech than necessary* to further those interests. [Turner Broadcasting System, Inc. v. FCC, 512 U.S. 622 (1994)]

b. **Conduct**
   The Court has allowed the government more leeway in regulating the conduct related to speech, allowing it to adopt content-neutral, *time, place, and manner* regulations. Regulations involving public forums (*i.e.,* forums historically linked with the exercise of First Amendment freedoms) must be *narrowly tailored* to achieve an *important* government interest (*e.g.,* a prohibition against holding a demonstration in a hospital zone). Regulations involving nonpublic forums must have a reasonable relationship to a legitimate regulatory purpose (*e.g.,* a law prohibiting billboards for purposes of traffic safety).

2. **Reasonableness of Regulation**

a. **Overbroad Regulation Invalid**
   Since the purpose of the freedoms of speech and assembly is to encourage the free flow of ideas, a regulation will not be upheld if it is overbroad (*i.e.,* prohibits *substantially* more speech than is necessary). Thus, if a regulation bans a broad range of speech at a particular location or under a particular circumstance, it will likely be held invalid for overbreadth.

   Examples:
   1) The Supreme Court struck down as overbroad an ordinance that prohibited speech that *"in any manner"* interrupts a police officer in the performance of her duties. [Houston v. Hill, 482 U.S. 451 (1987)]

   2) An airport authority rule that bans *"all* First Amendment activities" within the "central terminal area" is invalid as being substantially overbroad. [Board of Airport Commissioners v. Jews for Jesus, 482 U.S. 569 (1987)]

   3) A law banning *all* door-to-door solicitations will be struck as being overbroad [Martin v. City of Struthers, 319 U.S. 141 (1943)], but a law requiring solicitors to obtain a homeowner's consent to solicit is valid [Breard v. City of Alexandria, 341 U.S. 622 (1951)].

   4) An ordinance that prohibited *all* canvassers from going onto private residential property to promote *any* cause without first obtaining a permit was overbroad. While the government may have an interest in preventing fraud from door-to-door solicitation, the permit requirement here went beyond cases where fraud was likely to occur, and applied to religious proselytization, advocacy of political speech, and enlisting support for unpopular causes. [Watchtower Bible and Tract Society of New York, Inc. v. Village of Stratton, 122 S. Ct. 2080 (2002)]

   5) A city ordinance that prohibits homeowners from displaying *any sign* on their property except "residence identification" or "for sale" signs is invalid because the ordinance bans virtually all residential signs. [Ladue v. Gilleo, 512 U.S. 43 (1994)]

b. **Vague Regulations Invalid—Void for Vagueness Doctrine**

If a criminal law or regulation fails to give persons reasonable notice as to what is prohibited, it violates the Due Process Clause. This principle is applied strictly when First Amendment activity is involved to avoid the chilling effect a vague law might have on speech (*i.e.,* if it is unclear what speech is regulated, people might refrain from speech that is permissible for fear that they will be violating the law). Vagueness issues most often arise in relation to content regulations, but the same principles would apply to time, place, and manner restrictions.

Examples: 1) A municipal ordinance that prohibited vagrants was held void for vagueness when it defined vagrants as "rogues and vagabonds . . . lewd, wanton, and lascivious persons . . . persons wandering or straying around from place to place without any lawful purpose or object . . . ." [Papachristou v. City of Jacksonville, 405 U.S. 156 (1972)]

2) A statute that prohibits attorneys representing clients in a pending case from making statements that would have a substantial likelihood of prejudicing a trial, but that also allows attorneys to make public statements regarding the "general nature of the defense" they will present at trial, is void for vagueness, because it does not give fair notice of the types of trial-related statements that are punishable. [Gentile v. State Bar, 501 U.S. 1030 (1991)]

1) **Funding Speech Activity**

Greater imprecision is allowed when the government acts as a patron in funding speech activity than when enacting criminal statutes or regulatory schemes, because speakers are less likely to steer clear of forbidden areas when only a subsidy is at stake. [National Endowment for the Arts v. Finley, 524 U.S. 569 (1998)—requirement that NEA consider standards of "decency" and "respect for values of American people" is not invalid on its face]

c. **Cannot Give Officials Unfettered Discretion**

A regulation cannot give officials broad discretion over speech issues; there must be *defined standards* for applying the law. The fear, of course, is that the officials will use their discretionary power to prohibit dissemination of ideas that they do not agree with. This issue usually arises under licensing schemes established to regulate the time, place, and manner of speech. To be valid, such licensing schemes must be related to an important government interest, contain procedural safeguards (*see* D.2., *infra*), and not grant officials unbridled discretion.

Example: County required persons desiring to hold a parade, march, or rally to first obtain a permit from the county administrator. The administrator was empowered to charge up to $1,000 for the permit, but could adjust the fee to meet the necessary expenses of administration and police protection. This scheme is invalid because it gives the administrator unbridled discretion despite the $1,000 limit. It also is unconstitutional because it is a content-based restriction (the administrator theoretically would adjust the costs based on the popularity of the subject at issue— an unpopular subject would require greater police protection). [Forsyth County, Georgia v. Nationalist Movement, 505 U.S. 123 (1992)]

1) **Unlimited Discretion—Void on Face**

If a statute gives licensing officials unbridled discretion, it is *void on its face*, and speakers need not even apply for a permit. They may exercise their First Amendment rights even if they could have been denied a permit under a valid law, and they may not be punished for violating the licensing statute. [Lovell v. City of Griffin, 303 U.S. 444 (1938)]

Examples: 1) An ordinance vesting officials with the power to grant or deny parade permits based on their judgment as to the effect of the parade on community "welfare" or "morals" is unconstitutional on its face. [Shuttlesworth v. Birmingham, 394 U.S. 147 (1969)] Similarly, ordinances giving officials broad discretion as to who may place magazine racks on public property or who may obtain licenses to solicit door to door are invalid. [City of Lakewood v. Plain Dealer Publishing Co., 486 U.S. 750 (1988); Lovell v. City of Griffin, *supra*]

2) A statute prohibiting excessively loud sound trucks is valid [Kovacs v. Cooper, 336 U.S. 77 (1949)], but an ordinance giving officials discretion as to who may use sound trucks is invalid [Saia v. New York, 334 U.S. 558 (1948)].

2) Statutes Valid on Face

If the licensing statute is valid on its face because it contains adequate standards, a speaker may not ignore the statute, but must seek a permit. If he is denied a permit, even if he believes the denial was incorrect, he must then seek reasonably available administrative or judicial relief. Failure to do so precludes later assertion that his actions were protected by the First Amendment. [Poulos v. New Hampshire, 345 U.S. 395 (1953)]

3. Scope of Speech

a. Includes Freedom Not to Speak

The freedom of speech includes not only the right to speak, but also the right to refrain from speaking or endorsing beliefs with which one does not agree.

Examples: 1) A state *cannot force school children to salute* or say a pledge to the flag. [West Virginia State Board of Education v. Barnette, 319 U.S. 624 (1943)]

2) A motorist *could not be punished* for blocking out the portion of his automobile license plate bearing the motto "Live Free or Die"; as long as he left the license plate in a condition that served its auto identification purpose, he did not have to display a slogan endorsed by the state. [Wooley v. Maynard, 430 U.S. 705 (1977)]

3) A state may not require private parade organizers to include in their parade groups with messages with which the organizers disagree. [Hurley v. Irish-American Gay, Lesbian & Bisexual Group of Boston, 515 U.S. 557 (1995)]

1) Mandatory Financial Support

The government may require a person to pay fees to support a *comprehensive program* that is benefiting the person, even if some of the money is being used to support ideas offensive to the person. However, mandatory financial support will violate the First Amendment if the primary purpose of the program is to require individuals to pay subsidies for speech to which they object. [United States v. United Foods, Inc., 533 U.S. 405 (2001)]

Examples: 1) Public university students can be required to pay a student fee to attend a public university even if the fee is used to support political and ideological speech by student groups whose beliefs are offensive to the student, as long as the program is *viewpoint neutral* (*see* B.2.a., *infra*). [Board of Regents of University of Wisconsin v. Southworth, 529 U.S. 217 (2000)]

2) Government employees can be made to pay dues to a union even if they refuse to technically join it, because the government may allow the unions to negotiate benefits for all and impose a reasonable "service charge." However, government employees cannot be required to pay an amount above the service fee that would be used by the union to contribute to political candidates or express social or political views. [Abood v. Detroit Board of Education, 431 U.S. 209 (1977); Lehnert v. Ferris Faculty Association, 500 U.S. 507 (1991)]

3) Attorneys can be required to pay mandatory bar dues, as long as the money is used for activities related to regulating the legal profession. [Keller v. State Bar of California, 496 U.S. 1 (1990)]

Compare: Mushroom handlers objected to paying subsidies that were used solely to generically advertise mushrooms. [United States v. United Foods, Inc., *supra*] The Court differentiated *United Foods* from prior cases because in the prior cases required fees were used to support a comprehensive program that incidentally impacted speech; in *United Foods* the fee was used primarily to fund advertising that the plaintiff objected to.

2) State Can Require Shopping Center to Permit Persons to Exercise Speech Rights

Note that the freedom not to speak does not prohibit a state's requiring a large shopping center (that is open to the public) to permit persons to exercise their speech rights on shopping center property—at least as long as the particular message is not dictated by the state and is not likely to be identified with the owner of the shopping center. [Pruneyard Shopping Center v. Robins, 447 U.S. 74 (1980)]

b. Includes Symbolic Conduct

Speech includes not only verbal communication, but also conduct that is undertaken to communicate an idea. Of course, not all regulation of symbolic conduct is prohibited. The Court will uphold a conduct regulation if: (i) the regulation is within the constitutional power of the government; (ii) it furthers an important governmental interest; (iii) the governmental interest is *unrelated to suppression of speech*; and (iv) the incidental burden on speech is no greater than necessary. [United States v. O'Brien, 391 U.S. 367 (1968)—upholding a prohibition against burning draft cards to protect the government's important interest in facilitating the smooth functioning of the draft system]

Examples: 1) A state may prohibit public nudity, even as applied to nude dancing at bars and places of adult entertainment. Although nude dancing is marginally within the protections of the First Amendment—because it involves the communication of an erotic message—the government has a "substantial" interest in combating crime and other "secondary effects" caused by the presence of adult entertainment establishments that is unrelated to the suppression of free expression. [Barnes v. Glen Theatre, Inc., 501 U.S. 560 (1991); City of Erie v. Pap's A.M., 529 U.S. 277 (2000)—city council made findings regarding secondary effects]

2) To protect the smooth operation of the draft system, the government may selectively prosecute for draft registration violations only those persons who have been brought to the government's attention, *e.g.,* because they sent protest letters or participated in rallies. [Wayte v. United States, 470 U.S. 598 (1985)]

Compare: 1) A prohibition against students wearing armbands to protest the war in Vietnam was struck because it had no regulatory interest other than prohibiting the communicative impact of the conduct. [Tinker v. Des Moines Independent Community School District, 393 U.S. 503 (1969)]

2) A prohibition against mutilating a United States flag (except in cases of proper disposal of a soiled flag) was held invalid as an attempt to restrain speech; the Court found that no imminent breach of the peace was likely to result, and the government has no other interest in prohibiting such burnings. [United States v. Eichman, 496 U.S. 310 (1990)]

4. Prison Speech

A regulation concerning the activities of prison inmates, including *any* First Amendment activities, is governed by a different standard to facilitate prison order: they will be upheld if they are *reasonably related to legitimate penological interests.* [Shaw v. Murphy, 532 U.S. 223 (2001)] Thus, a restriction on *incoming* mail will be upheld if it is rational; a restriction on *outgoing* mail must be narrowly tailored because there is less of a penological interest involved. [*See* Thornburgh v. Abbott, 490 U.S. 401 (1989)]

5. Funding vs. Regulation

In contrast to direct regulation of speech, government *funding* of speech may be based on content-based criteria as long as the criteria are viewpoint neutral (*see* B.2.a., *infra*). Congress may selectively fund programs to encourage activities it believes to be in the public interest while denying funding to alternative programs.

Examples: 1) The government may prohibit organizations receiving government funds for "family planning services" from providing abortion information as part of the federally funded service. The government is not required to subsidize abortion (*see* XIX.B.3.c., *supra*), and this prohibition is merely a viewpoint neutral means of ensuring that government funds are spent only on the family planning services for which they were granted. [Rust v. Sullivan, 500 U.S. 173 (1991)]

2) The government cannot fund all artists, and choosing among those it will fund and those it will not inevitably must be based on the content of the art. [National Endowment for the Arts v. Finley, 2.b.1), *supra*]

    a.   Government Encouragement of Private Speech

In contrast to government funding of speech for the purpose of promoting its own policies (such as the family planning program in *Rust v. Sullivan, supra*), viewpoint restrictions are ordinarily invalid when government funds *private* speech. [Rosenberger v. Rector and Visitors of the University of Virginia, 515 U.S. 819 (1995)—state university exclusion of religious magazine from program financially supporting student publications violates First Amendment]

Example: A federal statute funding legal assistance to indigents, but forbidding assisting lawyers from challenging the validity of welfare regulations, violates the First Amendment. [Legal Services Corp. v. Velazquez, 531 U.S. 533 (2001)—federal program was designed to promote private (not government) speech, and prohibition would substantially distort traditional role of lawyers]

B.   TIME, PLACE, AND MANNER RESTRICTIONS—REGULATION OF CONDUCT

All speech is conveyed through physical action (*e.g.*, talking, writing, distributing pamphlets, etc.), and while the freedom of belief is absolute, the freedom to convey beliefs cannot be. The extent to which governments may regulate speech-related conduct depends on whether the forum involved is a public forum, a designated public forum (sometimes called a limited public forum), or nonpublic forum.

1.   Public Forums and Designated Public Forums

Public property that has historically been open to speech-related activities (*e.g.*, **streets, sidewalks,** and **public parks**) is called a public forum. Public property that has not historically been open to speech-related activities, but which the government has thrown open for such activities on a permanent or limited basis, by practice or policy (*e.g.*, school rooms that are open for after school use by social, civic, or recreation groups) is called a designated or limited public forum. The government may regulate speech in public forums and designated public forums with reasonable time, place, and manner regulations.

    a.   Test

To be valid, government regulations on speech and assembly in public forums and designated public forums must:

    (i)   Be *content neutral* (*i.e.,* subject matter neutral and viewpoint neutral);

    (ii)   Be *narrowly tailored* to serve a *significant* government interest; and

    (iii)   Leave open *alternative channels* of communication.

Remember: Even if a regulation meets the above conditions, it might still be struck down on other grounds (*e.g.,* overbreadth, vagueness, unfettered discretion; *see* A.2., *supra*).

        1)   Content Neutral

The regulation cannot be based on the content of the speech, absent substantial justification (*see* C., *infra*).

Examples: 1) The Court held invalid an ordinance allowing peaceful *labor* picketing near schools, but prohibiting all other picketing, since it was a content-based restriction. [Chicago Police Department v. Mosely, 408 U.S. 92 (1972)]

2) A law may not forbid only those signs within 500 feet of a foreign embassy that are critical of the foreign government. [Boos v. Barry, 485 U.S. 312 (1988)]

        2)   Narrowly Tailored

The regulation must be narrowly tailored (*i.e.,* it may not burden *substantially* more speech than is necessary to further the significant government interest). However, the regulation need not be the *least restrictive* means of accomplishing the goal.

Example: A law requiring persons performing at a city's theater to use the city's sound equipment is narrowly tailored to the city's interest in preventing excessive noise. [Ward v. Rock Against Racism, 491 U.S. 781 (1989)]

Compare: An ordinance that prohibited *all* canvassers from going onto private residential property to promote *any* cause without first obtaining a permit was not narrowly tailored to the interest of preventing fraud because it included too much speech that was not likely to give rise to fraud (*e.g.*, religious proselytization, advocacy of political speech, and enlisting support for unpopular causes). [Watchtower Bible and Tract Society of New York, Inc. v. Village of Stratton, A.2.a., *supra*]

Note: A regulation that is not narrowly tailored might also fail on overbreadth grounds. (*See* A.2.a., *supra.*)

3) Significant Interest
The regulation must further an important government interest. Such interests include: traffic safety, orderly crowd movement, personal privacy, noise control, litter control, aesthetics, etc.

Example: The Court upheld the constitutionality of a state law prohibiting persons within 100 feet of a health care facility from approaching within eight feet of those seeking access to the health care facility for purposes of oral protest, education, or counseling. The Court found that the law was a content-neutral regulation of speech and a reasonable time, place, and manner restriction that served the important interest of preserving access to health care facilities. [Hill v. Colorado, 530 U.S. 703 (2000)—statute upheld against challenge by petitioners who wished to "counsel" women as they enter abortion clinics]

4) Alternative Channels Open
The law must leave open alternative channels of communication; *i.e.,* other reasonable means for communicating the idea must be available.

b. Examples—Residential Areas

1) Targeted Picketing
The Supreme Court upheld a statute that prevented focused residential picketing (*i.e.*, picketing in front of a single residence). The street/sidewalk involved was a public forum, but the ordinance passed the three-part test: (i) it was content neutral since it regulated the location and manner of picketing rather than its message; (ii) it was narrowly tailored (since it applied only to focused picketing) to the important interest of protecting a homeowner's privacy; and (iii) alternative means of communications were available since the protesters could march *through* the neighborhood in protest. [Frisby v. Schultz, 487 U.S. 474 (1988)]

2) Charitable Solicitations
Charitable solicitations for funds in residential areas are within the protection of the First Amendment. However, they are subject to reasonable regulation.

Example: A state cannot require professional fundraisers (before making an appeal for funds) to disclose to potential donors the percentage of contributions collected over the previous year that were actually turned over to the charity. The disclosure is not necessary to promote the state interest of protecting the public from fraud. However, the state can require a fundraiser to disclose her professional status. [Riley v. National Federation of the Blind of North Carolina, 487 U.S. 781 (1988)] In *Riley,* the Court also invalidated a restriction on the fees that professional fundraisers could charge a charity, because the particular statute was not narrowly tailored to protect either the public or the charities.

3) Permits
A state may not require persons to obtain permits in order to canvass door-to-door for noncommercial or nonfundraising purposes. [Watchtower Bible and Tract Society of New York, Inc. v. Village of Stratton, *supra*]

c. **Example—Designated Public Forum**
Schools generally are not public forums. However, if a public school or university allows private organizations and members of the public to use school property for meetings when school programs or classes are not in session, the property is a designated public forum for that time, and the school cannot deny a religious organization permission to use the property for meetings merely because religious topics will be discussed. Such a restriction would be content discrimination. [Widmar v. Vincent, 454 U.S. 263 (1981); Lamb's Chapel v. Center Moriches Union Free School District, 508 U.S. 384 (1993)]

d. **Injunctions**
Injunctions that restrict First Amendment activity in public forums are treated differently from generally applicable ordinances because injunctions present a greater risk of censorship and discriminatory application. The test to be used to determine whether an injunction that restricts speech or protest is constitutional depends on whether the injunction is content neutral.

1) **Content Based—Necessary to a Compelling Interest**
If the injunction is content based, it will be upheld only if it is necessary to achieve a compelling government interest.

2) **Content Neutral—Burdens No More Speech than Necessary**
If the injunction is content neutral, it will be upheld only if it burdens no more speech than is necessary to achieve a *significant* government purpose.
Example: Parts of an injunction establishing a 36-foot buffer zone between protesters and abortion clinic entrances were upheld. [Madsen v. Women's Health Center, 512 U.S. 753 (1994)]

Compare: An injunction providing for a "floating buffer zone" of 15 feet between protesters and persons entering and leaving an abortion clinic was held to violate the First Amendment. The floating zone barred all verbal and written communication from a normal conversational distance on public sidewalks, and thus burdened more speech than necessary to ensure ingress and egress from the clinic. [Schneck v. Pro-Choice Network of Western New York, 510 U.S. 357 (1997)]

2. **Nonpublic Forums**
Other than streets, sidewalks, parks, and designated public forums, most public property is considered to be a nonpublic forum. The government can regulate speech in such a forum to reserve the forum for its intended use. Regulations will be upheld if they are:

(i) *Viewpoint neutral*; and

(ii) *Reasonably related to a legitimate government purpose.*

a. **Viewpoint Neutral**
Regulations on speech in nonpublic forums need not be content neutral; *i.e.,* the government may allow speech regarding some subjects but not others. However, such regulations must be *viewpoint* neutral; *i.e.,* if the government allows an issue to be presented in a nonpublic forum, it may not limit the presentation to only one view.
Example: If a high school newspaper is a nonpublic forum, a school board could decide to prohibit articles in the paper regarding nuclear power. However, it may not allow an article in favor of nuclear power and prohibit an article against nuclear power.

Similarly, the government may discriminate based on the identity of the speaker in nonpublic forums (*e.g.,* a school board might limit speakers to licensed teachers).

b. **Reasonableness**
Regulation of speech and assembly in nonpublic forums need only be rationally related to a legitimate governmental objective.
Example: A city bus is not a public forum. The city, therefore, may constitutionally sell space for signs on the public buses for commercial and public

service advertising while refusing to sell space for political or public issue advertising in order to minimize the appearance of favoritism and the risk of imposing on a captive audience. [Lehman v. Shaker Heights, 418 U.S. 298 (1974)]

c. Significant Cases

1) Military Bases
Military bases are not public forums; thus, on-base speech and assembly may be regulated, even during open houses where the public is invited to visit. [*See* United States v. Albertini, 472 U.S. 675 (1985)] However, if the military leaves its streets open as thoroughfares, they will be treated as public forums. [Flower v. United States, 407 U.S. 197 (1972)]

2) Schools
Generally, schools and curriculum-based school activities are not public forums. Thus, speech in schools may be reasonably regulated.

Examples: Schools can control the content of student speeches or student newspapers for legitimate pedagogical concerns. [*See, e.g.,* Bethel School District No. 403 v. Fraser, 478 U.S. 675 (1986)—student suspended for sexually explicit speech at school assembly] However, a school was forbidden to prohibit the wearing of black armbands in the school (to protest government policies), because that prohibition was designed to suppress communication, *i.e.,* not related to regulatory interest. [Tinker v. Des Moines Independent Community School District, A.3.b., *supra*]

3) Government Workplace or Charity
Neither a government workplace (including a court building and its grounds) nor a government controlled charity drive constitutes a public forum.

Examples: 1) The government may conduct an annual fundraising drive which includes some charities but excludes others on some ideologically neutral basis (*e.g.,* all charities that lobby). However, it cannot exclude a charity merely because it disagrees with the organization's political views. [Cornelius v. NAACP Legal Defense and Education Fund, Inc., 473 U.S. 788 (1985)]

2) A state may develop a system for meeting with and hearing the views of a select group of its employees (*e.g.,* union representatives) while denying the ability to voice opinions at such restricted meetings to other government employees. [Minnesota State Board v. Knight, 465 U.S. 271 (1984)]

Compare: In a public forum, the government cannot restrict the ability to participate in public speech on the basis of union membership. Thus, the Court has held that a teacher cannot be constitutionally prohibited from speaking at a meeting of the school board that was open to the public. [City of Madison Joint School District No. 8 v. Wisconsin Employment Relations Commission, 429 U.S. 167 (1976)]

4) Postal Service Property
Although sidewalks generally are public forums, sidewalks on postal service property are not public forums. [United States v. Kokinda, 497 U.S. 720 (1990)]

5) Signs on Public Property
The Supreme Court has upheld a city ordinance prohibiting posting signs on public property (including sidewalks, crosswalks, street lamp posts, fire hydrants, and telephone poles), even if the sign is temporary in nature and could be removed without damage to the public property. [Members of City Council v. Taxpayers for Vincent, 466 U.S. 789 (1984)]

6) Airport Terminals
Airport terminals operated by a public authority are *not* public forums. Thus, it is reasonable to ban *solicitation* within airport terminals, since it presents a risk of fraud to hurrying passengers. [International Society of Krishna Consciousness v.

Lee, 505 U.S. 672 (1992)] However, it is *not* reasonable to ban *leafletting* within multipurpose terminals having qualities similar to a shopping mall [Lee v. International Society of Krishna Consciousness, 505 U.S. 830 (1992)]; although such leafletting can still be subject to reasonable time, place, and manner regulations (*see* B.1., *supra*).

7) Candidate Debates on Public Television

A public television station debate for congressional candidates from major parties or who have strong popular support is not a "public forum" because such debates are not open to a class of speakers (*e.g.*, all candidates), but rather to selected members of the class. Exclusion of candidates not from a major party and lacking popular support is permissible because these criteria are (i) viewpoint neutral and (ii) reasonable in light of the logistics for an educationally valuable debate. [Arkansas Educational Television Commission v. Forbes, 523 U.S. 666 (1998)]

8) Mailboxes

A letter/mailbox at a business or residence is *not* a public forum. Thus, the government may prohibit the placing of unstamped items in post boxes to promote efficient mail service. [United States Postal Service v. Council of Greenburgh Civic Association, 453 U.S. 114 (1981)]

C. UNPROTECTED SPEECH—REGULATION OR PUNISHMENT BECAUSE OF CONTENT

Restrictions on the content of speech must be narrowly tailored to achieve a compelling government interest. As indicated above, very few restrictions on the content of speech are tolerated. The Court allows them only to prevent grave injury. The following is a list of the only reasons for which the Court has allowed content-based restrictions on speech (*i.e., the following are categories of unprotected speech):

(i) It creates a *clear and present danger* of imminent lawless action.

(ii) It constitutes *"fighting words"* as defined by a narrow, precise statute.

(iii) The speech, film, etc., is *obscene*. (This category includes "child pornography.")

(iv) The speech constitutes *defamation*, which may be the subject of a civil "penalty" through a tort action brought by the injured party in conformity with the rules set out *infra*.

(v) The speech violates regulations against *false or deceptive advertising—commercial speech is protected* by the First Amendment and it cannot be proscribed simply to help certain private interests.

(vi) The government can demonstrate a *"compelling interest"* in limitation of the First Amendment activity.

Recall that even if a regulation falls within one of the above categories, it will not necessarily be held valid; it might still be held to be void for vagueness or overbreadth. (*See* A.2., *supra*.)

1. Clear and Present Danger of Imminent Lawlessness

A state cannot forbid advocating the use of force or of law violation unless such advocacy (i) *is directed to producing or inciting imminent lawless action,* and (ii) *is likely to produce or incite such action*. [Brandenberg v. Ohio, 395 U.S. 444 (1969)]

Example: The "clear and present danger" test has been applied to hold that a state may not punish as contempt out-of-court utterances critical of a judge, absent special circumstances showing an extremely high likelihood of serious interference with the administration of justice. [*See* Wood v. Georgia, 370 U.S. 375 (1962)]

a. Allows for Sanctions Against Speech

The test allows for sanctions against speech causing demonstrable danger to important government interests. Disclosure of United States intelligence operations and personnel is "clearly not protected" speech. [Haig v. Agee, 453 U.S. 280 (1981)]

b. Compelling Justification Test

A similar test—one of "compelling justification"—was employed to hold unconstitutional the Georgia legislature's refusal to seat Julian Bond, an elected black representative, where Bond's speeches, critical of United States policy on Vietnam and the draft, led the legislature to doubt his fitness and his ability to take the oath of office in good faith. [Bond v. Floyd, 385 U.S. 116 (1966)]

2. Fighting Words

a. States May Ban Words Likely to Incite Physical Retaliation

States are free to ban the use of "fighting words," *i.e.,* those personally abusive epithets that, when addressed to the ordinary citizen, are inherently likely to incite immediate physical retaliation. [Chaplinsky v. New Hampshire, 315 U.S. 568 (1942)] *Chaplinsky* has, however, been narrowly read. Thus, in *Cohen v. California,* 403 U.S. 15 (1971), the Court held that the state may not punish the defendant for wearing a jacket bearing the words "Fuck the Draft," pointing out that "while the four-letter word displayed by Cohen in relation to the draft is commonly employed in a personally provocative fashion, in this instance, it was clearly not directed to the person of the hearer."

b. Statutes Regulating Fighting Words Tend to Be Overbroad or Vague

While this classification of punishable speech continues to exist *in theory*, the Court rarely upholds punishments for the use of such words. Statutes that attempt to punish fighting words will tend to be overbroad or vague; the statute will define the punishable speech as "opprobrious words," "annoying conduct," or "abusive language." Such statutes will fail, as their imprecise terms could be applied to protected (nonfighting words) speech. Such a statute could not be used to punish a person for saying to a police officer, "White son of a bitch, I'll kill you." [Gooding v. Wilson, 405 U.S. 518 (1972); Lewis v. City of New Orleans, 415 U.S. 130 (1974)]

c. Statutes Cannot Be Content-Based—Limits Hate Crime Legislation

Although the general class of "fighting words" is proscribable under the First Amendment, the Supreme Court will not tolerate in fighting words statutes restrictions that are designed to punish only certain viewpoints (*i.e.,* proscribing fighting words only if they convey a particular message). [R.A.V. v. City of St. Paul, 505 U.S. 377 (1992)— ordinance that applies only to those fighting words that insult or provoke violence on the basis of race, religion, or gender is invalid]

1) Compare—Punishing Racially Motivated Conduct

The First Amendment does not protect conduct simply because it happens to be motivated by a person's views or beliefs. Thus, a state can increase a convicted defendant's sentence for aggravated battery based on the fact that the defendant selected the victim of his crime because of the victim's race. [Wisconsin v. Mitchell, 508 U.S. 476 (1993)] However, punishment may not be increased merely because of the defendant's abstract beliefs. [Dawson v. Delaware, 503 U.S. 159 (1992)— unconstitutional to increase defendant's sentence merely because it was proved that he belongs to an organization that advocates racism]

3. Obscenity

Obscenity is *not protected* speech. [Roth v. United States, 354 U.S. 476 (1957)] The Court has defined "obscenity" as a description or depiction of sexual conduct that, taken *as a whole*, by the *average person*, applying *contemporary community standards*:

(i) Appeals to the *prurient interest* in sex;

(ii) Portrays sex in a *patently offensive* way; and

(iii) Does not have serious literary, artistic, political, or scientific value—using a national, reasonable person standard, rather than the contemporary community standard. [Miller v. California, 413 U.S. 15 (1973); Pope v. Illinois, 481 U.S. 497 (1987)]

a. Elements

1) Appeal to Prurient Interest

The dominant theme of the material considered as a *whole* must appeal to the prurient interest in sex of the average person. The Supreme Court has found this to include that which appeals to *shameful or morbid interests* in sex, but not that which incites *lust* (insofar as lust may include a *normal* interest in sex). [Brockett v. Spokane Arcades, Inc., 472 U.S. 491 (1985)] For exam purposes, it is probably sufficient merely to know the standard (since its application is a fact determination).

a) **Average Person**
Both sensitive and insensitive adults may be included in determining contemporary community standards, but children may not be considered part of the relevant audience.

b) **Material Designed for Deviant Group**
Where the allegedly obscene material is designed for and primarily disseminated to a clearly defined deviant sexual group (*e.g.*, sadists), rather than to the public at large, the prurient appeal requirement is satisfied if the ***dominant theme*** of the material, taken as a whole, ***appeals to the prurient interest of that group***. [Mishkin v. New York, 383 U.S. 502 (1966)]

2) **Patently Offensive**

a) **Community Standard**
The material must be patently offensive in affronting contemporary community standards regarding the description or portrayal of sexual matters.

b) **National Standard Not Required**
A statewide standard is permissible but not mandatory. A juror may draw on knowledge of the community or vicinity from which he comes, and the court may either direct the jury to apply "community standards" without specifying what "community," or to define the standard in more precise geographic terms. [Hamling v. United States, 418 U.S. 87 (1974); Jenkins v. Georgia, 418 U.S. 153 (1974)]

3) **Lacking in Serious Social Value**
The fact that the material may have some redeeming social value will not necessarily immunize it from a finding of obscenity. It must have serious literary, artistic, political, or scientific value, using a national standard. [Pope v. Illinois, *supra*]

4) **Standard May Be Different for Minors**
The state can adopt a specific definition of obscenity applying to materials sold to minors, even though the material might not be obscene in terms of an adult audience. [Ginsberg v. New York, 390 U.S. 629 (1968)] However, government may not prohibit the sale or distribution of material to adults merely because it is inappropriate for children.

Example: Because of the present lack of "gateway" technology that would permit speakers on the Internet to block their communications, a federal statute's bar on transmitting "indecent" or "patently offensive" messages to minors effectively amounts to a total ban and thus violates the First Amendment right of adults to receive such materials. [Reno v. American Civil Liberties Union, 521 U.S. 844 (1997)]

a) **Pictures of Minors**
To protect minors from exploitation, the government may prohibit the sale or distribution of ***visual*** depictions of sexual conduct involving minors, even if the material would not be found obscene if it did not involve children. [New York v. Ferber, 456 U.S. 942 (1982)]

b) **Compare—Simulated Pictures of Minors**
The government may not bar visual material that only appears to depict minors engaged in sexually explicit conduct, but that in fact uses young-looking adults or computer generated images. [Ashcroft v. Free Speech Coalition, 122 S. Ct. 1389 (2002)] A holding otherwise would bar speech that is not obscene under the *Miller* test and that does not involve the exploitation of children as in *Ferber*.

b. **Question of Fact and Law**

1) Jury Question
The determination of whether material is obscene is a question of fact for the jury. Of course, the judge can grant a directed verdict if the evidence is such that a reasonable, unprejudiced jury could not find that all parts of the test have been met.

2) Independent Review by Appellate Court
Appellate courts will conduct an independent review of constitutional claims, when necessary, to assure that the proscribed materials "depict or describe patently offensive 'hard core' sexual conduct." [Jenkins v. Georgia, *supra*]

3) Evidence of Pandering
In close cases, evidence of "pandering"—commercial exploitation for the sake of prurient appeal—by the defendant may be probative on whether the material is obscene. Such evidence may be found in the defendant's advertising, his instructions to authors and illustrators of the material, or his intended audience. In effect, this simply accepts the purveyor's own estimation of the material as relevant. [Ginzburg v. United States, 383 U.S. 463 (1966)]

4) Evidence—Similar Published Materials Not Automatically Admissible
The state need not produce expert testimony. Evidence that similar materials are available on community newsstands, or that the publication has acquired a second-class mailing privilege, does not necessarily show that the material is not obscene and hence is not automatically admissible. Nor is there any automatic right to have other materials held not to be obscene admitted into evidence. [Hamling v. United States, *supra*]

c. Statutes Must Not Be Vague

1) Sweeping Language
Attempts to define obscenity broadly have encountered difficulties before the Court.

Examples: 1) A statute banning publication of news or stories of "bloodshed or lust so massed as to become vehicle for inciting crime" is unconstitutionally vague and uncertain. [Winters v. New York, 333 U.S. 507 (1948)]

2) The Court held invalid a statute prohibiting the sale of any book "tending to the corruption of the morals of youth." [Butler v. Michigan, 352 U.S. 380 (1957)]

2) Construction May Save Vague Statute
A state statute will be upheld if it meets the tests as construed by the courts of the state. Thus, a seemingly vague obscenity statute may be saved by a state supreme court opinion that limits it to a proscription of depictions of specific types of sexual conduct. [Ward v. Illinois, 430 U.S. 983 (1977)]

d. Land Use Regulations
A land use (or zoning) regulation may limit the location or size of adult entertainment establishments (*i.e.*, businesses that focus on sexual activities) if the regulation is designed to reduce the secondary effects of such businesses (*e.g.*, rise in crime rates, drop in property values and neighborhood quality, etc.). However, regulations may not ban such establishments altogether. [City of Los Angeles v. Alameda Books, Inc., 122 S. Ct. 1728 (2002)]

Example: A city ordinance limiting adult entertainment establishments to one corner of the city occupying less than 5% of the city's area was deemed constitutional. [City of Renton v. Playtime Theatres, Inc., 475 U.S. 41 (1986)]

e. Liquor Regulation
The Twenty-First Amendment grants states more than the usual regulatory authority with respect to intoxicating beverages. Therefore, regulations prohibiting explicit live sexual entertainment and films in establishments licensed to sell liquor by the drink, even though proscribing some forms of visual presentation that would not be obscene under *Miller,* do not violate the First Amendment as long as they are not "irrational."

f. Display

The Court has suggested that the state *may regulate* the display of certain material, to prevent it from being so obtrusive that an unwilling viewer cannot avoid exposure to it. [Redup v. New York, 386 U.S. 767 (1967)]

g. Private Possession of Obscenity

Private possession of obscenity at home cannot be made a crime because of the constitutional right of personal privacy. [Stanley v. Georgia, 394 U.S. 557 (1969)] However, the protection does not extend beyond the home. Thus, importation, distribution, and exhibition of obscene materials can be prohibited.

1) Exception—Child Pornography

The state may make private possession of child pornography a crime, even private possession for personal viewing in a residence. [Osborne v. Ohio, 495 U.S. 103 (1990)]

4. Defamatory Speech

When a person is sued for making a defamatory statement, the First Amendment places restrictions on the ability of the government (through its tort law and courts) to grant a recovery where the person suing is a *public official or public figure*, or where the defamatory statement involves an issue of *public concern*. In these cases the plaintiff must prove not only the elements of defamation required by state law, but also that the statement was *false* and that the person making the statement was at *fault* to some degree in not ascertaining the truth of the statement.

a. Falsity

At common law, a defamatory statement was presumed to be false; to avoid liability for an otherwise defamatory statement on the ground that it was true, the defendant had to assert truth as an affirmative defense. The Supreme Court has rejected this presumption in all public figure or public concern cases. In these cases, the plaintiff must prove by clear and convincing evidence that the statement was false. [Philadelphia Newspapers, Inc. v. Hepps, 475 U.S. 767 (1986)]

1) Requirement of Factual Statement

To be defamatory, the false statement must be viewed by a reasonable person as a statement of fact, rather than as a statement of opinion or a parody. Furthermore, a public figure cannot circumvent the First Amendment restrictions by using a different tort theory to collect damages for a published statement about him that is not a false statement of fact.

Example: Even though a publisher may have intended to cause psychological distress to a public figure by publishing statements about him that were derogatory, the public figure cannot receive a judgment for "emotional distress" damages if a reasonable person who read or viewed the publication would not understand it to contain a statement of fact about that public figure. [Hustler Magazine Inc. v. Falwell, 485 U.S. 46 (1988)]

Note: The fact that a publisher labels a statement as "opinion" will not provide First Amendment protection if the statement would reasonably be understood to be a statement of fact. [Milkovich v. Lorain Journal Co., 497 U.S. 1 (1990)]

b. Fault

At common law, a defendant who had no reason to know that the statement he was making was false and defamatory could still be liable for defamation. Now, however, a plaintiff in a public figure or public concern case must prove fault on the part of the defendant. The degree of fault required is higher when the plaintiff is a public official or public figure than when the plaintiff is a private person suing on a matter of public concern.

1) Public Official or Public Figure—Malice Required

A public official may not recover for defamatory words relating to his official conduct or a matter of public concern without clear and convincing evidence that the statement was made with "malice" (defined below). [New York Times v. Sullivan, 376 U.S. 254 (1964)] This rule has since been extended to public figure plaintiffs. (Note that while the Supreme Court has not specifically held that all statements regarding public officials or public figures necessarily involve matters of public concern, a case to the contrary should be rare.)

a) Malice Defined
Malice was defined by the Supreme Court in *New York Times v. Sullivan* as:

(i) *Knowledge* that the statement was false, *or*

(ii) *Reckless disregard* as to its truth or falsity.

The plaintiff must show that the defendant was subjectively aware that the statement he published was false or that he subjectively *entertained serious doubts* as to its truthfulness.

(1) Malice in False Quotation Cases
Proof that a defamation plaintiff was inaccurately quoted does not, by itself, prove actual malice, even if the quotation was intentionally altered by the defendant. If the published "quotation" is substantially accurate, the plaintiff may not collect damages. To show malice, the public figure plaintiff must prove that the defendant's alteration of the quotation materially changed the meaning of the actual statements made by the plaintiff. [Masson v. New Yorker Magazine, Inc., 501 U.S. 496 (1991)]

(2) Permitted Inquiries by Plaintiff
In attempting to prove knowing or reckless disregard of the truth, the plaintiff may inquire into the state of mind of those who edit, produce, or publish (*i.e.,* conversations with editorial colleagues). [Herbert v. Lando, 441 U.S. 153 (1979)]

(3) Petition Clause Does Not Protect Defamatory Statement Made with Malice
The First Amendment guarantees individuals the right to "petition government for a redress of grievances." However, this right to petition the government does not grant absolute immunity to persons who make defamatory statements about public officials or public figures in their communications with government officials. The defamed individual may prevail by meeting the *New York Times* requirements. [McDonald v. Smith, 472 U.S. 479 (1985)]

b) Two Ways to Become a Public Figure

(1) General Fame or Notoriety
A person may be a public figure for all purposes and all contexts if he achieves "*general fame or notoriety* in the community and pervasive involvement in the affairs of society," although "a citizen's participation in community and professional affairs" does not render him a public figure for all purposes.

(2) Involvement in Particular Controversy
A person may "*voluntarily inject* himself or be drawn into a particular controversy to influence the resolution of the issues involved" and thereby become a public figure for a limited range of issues. [Gertz v. Robert Welch, Inc., 418 U.S. 323 (1974)]

Note that *Gertz* appears to allow for the possibility of a person's being an involuntary public figure for a limited range of issues, although such a case would be "exceedingly rare."

c) Examples of Persons Not Deemed Public Figures

(1) Spouse of Wealthy Person
Marriage to an extremely wealthy person and divorcing such a person does not amount to voluntarily entering the public arena, even though press conferences are held by the plaintiff, because going to court is the

only way she could dissolve her marriage. [Time, Inc. v. Firestone, 424 U.S. 448 (1976)]

(2) Person Engaging in Criminal Conduct
A person who engages in *criminal conduct* does not automatically become a public figure even when the defamatory statements relate solely to his conviction. [Wolston v. Reader's Digest Association, 443 U.S. 157 (1979)]

(3) Scientist in Federally Funded Program
A behavioral scientist engaged in *federally funded* animal research studies is not a public figure because he applies for federal grants and *publishes* in professional journals. [Hutchinson v. Proxmire, 443 U.S. 111 (1979)]

2) Private Individual Suing on Matter of Public Concern—At Least Negligence Required
When a private individual is defamed, there is less of a need to protect freedom of speech and press and more of a need to protect private individuals from injury from defamation because they do not have opportunities as effective for rebuttal as public figures. Accordingly, defamation actions brought by private individuals are subject to constitutional limitations only when the defamatory statement involves a matter of public concern. And even in those cases, the limitations are not as great as those established for public officials and public figures. [Gertz v. Robert Welch, Inc., *supra*] When the defamatory statement involves a matter of public concern, *Gertz* imposes two restrictions on private plaintiffs: (i) it prohibits liability without fault, and (ii) it restricts the recovery of presumed or punitive damages.

a) No Liability Without Proof of at Least Negligence
The plaintiff must show that the defendant was negligent in failing to ascertain the truth of the statement. If plaintiff establishes negligence but not malice, which is a higher degree of fault, he also has to provide competent evidence of "actual" damages. (This changes the common law rule that damages would be presumed by law for injury to reputation and did not need to be proved by plaintiff.) Actual damages may be awarded not only for economic losses but also for injury to plaintiff's reputation in the community and for personal humiliation and distress.

b) Presumed or Punitive Damages Allowed Only If Malice Established
If plaintiff establishes that the defendant made the statement with malice, the actual damage requirement is extinguished. Plaintiff can recover whatever damages are permitted under state law (usually presumed damages and even punitive damages in appropriate cases). In other words, there is no constitutional protection for statements made with malice, even though a matter of public concern is involved.

c) What Is a Matter of Public Concern?
The courts decide on a case-by-case basis whether the defamatory statement involves a matter of public concern, looking at the content, form, and context of the publication. [Dun & Bradstreet, Inc. v. Greenmoss Builders, Inc., 472 U.S. 749 (1985)]

Example: In *Dun & Bradstreet,* the Court determined that a credit agency's erroneous report of plaintiff's bankruptcy, distributed to five subscribers, was speech solely in the private interest of the speaker and its specific business audience. Therefore, because a matter of public concern was not involved, the First Amendment restrictions did not apply and the state court award of presumed and punitive damages was upheld.

3) Private Individual Suing on Matter Not of Public Concern
The Supreme Court has not imposed constitutional restrictions on defamation actions brought by private individuals that do not involve a matter of public concern. Hence, presumed and punitive damages can be recovered even if malice is not established.

c. **Procedural Issues**

1) **Federal Summary Judgment Standard**
    When ruling on a motion for summary judgment in a federal court defamation action in a case involving an issue of public concern, a judge must apply the clear and convincing evidence standard (*i.e.,* the judge should grant the motion **unless** it appears that the plaintiff could meet his burdens of proving falsity and actual malice at trial by clear and convincing evidence). However, the Supreme Court has not clearly held that state courts must follow this practice under similar circumstances.

2) **Judicial Review**
    An appellate court must review a defamation case by conducting an independent review of the record to determine if the finder of fact (the jury) could have found that the malice standard was met in the case. [Harte-Hanks Communications, Inc. v. Connaughton, 491 U.S. 657 (1989)]

d. **Recovery for Depiction in a False Light**
    To recover damages for depiction in a false light (as opposed to a defamatory injury to reputation) arising out of comments directed at activities of public interest, an individual must establish *falsity* and *actual malice* whether or not he qualifies as a public figure under *Time, Inc. v. Hill,* 385 U.S. 374 (1967). However, it is *assumed* that the Court would now modify this to mirror the *Gertz* negligence rule for private plaintiffs.

e. **True Privacy Actions**

1) **Publishing True Fact of Public Record**
    A newspaper or broadcaster cannot be sued for publishing a true fact once it is lawfully obtained from the public record or otherwise released to the public. [Cox Broadcasting Corp. v. Cohn, 420 U.S. 469 (1975)—rape victim's name already in court records open to the public; The Florida Star v. B.J.F., 491 U.S. 524 (1989)— rape victim's name inadvertently given to the press by police]

2) **Publishing Name of Juvenile Charged with Crime**
    A state cannot require judicial approval before the media can print the name of a juvenile charged with murder where the name of the juvenile was obtained through legal means (reporter heard name of defendant over police frequency radio and questioned witnesses to the crime). [Smith v. Daily Mail Publishing Co., 442 U.S. 97 (1979)]

3) **Publishing Information on Judge's Competency**
    A state cannot make it a crime to publish information, released in a confidential proceeding, concerning the competency of members of the state judiciary. [Landmark Communications v. Virginia, 435 U.S. 829 (1978)]

f. **Commercial Privacy—Disclosing a Private Performance Can Violate "Right to Publicity"**
    In *Zacchini v. Scripps-Howard Broadcasting Co.,* 433 U.S. 562 (1977), the Court held that state law could award damages to an entertainer who attempted to restrict the showing of his act to those who paid admission, when a television station broadcast his entire act. Here the "human cannonball" had his entire 15-second act broadcast over his objection.

g. **Copyright Infringement**
    The First Amendment does not require an exception to copyright protection for material written by a former President or other public figures. Magazines have no right to publish such copyrighted material beyond the statutory fair use exception. [Harper & Row Publishers v. Nation Enterprises, 471 U.S. 539 (1985)]

5. **Some Commercial Speech**
    False advertising is not protected by the First Amendment, although commercial speech in general does have some First Amendment protection. In determining whether a regulation on commercial speech is valid, the Supreme Court asserts that it uses a four-step process.

However, it may be easiest to think about this as an initial question followed by a three-step inquiry. *First,* determine whether the commercial speech concerns a lawful activity and is not misleading or fraudulent. Speech proposing an unlawful transaction (*e.g.,* "I will sell you this pound of heroin for X dollars") and fraudulent speech may be outlawed. If the speech regulated concerns a *lawful activity* and is *not misleading or fraudulent*, the regulation will be valid only if it:

(i)   Serves a *"substantial"* government interest;

(ii) *"Directly advances"* the asserted interest; and

(iii) Is *narrowly tailored* to serve the substantial interest. This part of the test does *not* require that the "least restrictive means" be used. Rather, there must be a *reasonable fit* between the legislation's end and the means chosen. [Board of Trustees of State University of New York v. Fox, 492 U.S. 469 (1989)]

[Central Hudson Gas v. Public Service Commission, 447 U.S. 557 (1980)]

Examples: 1) Under the above rules, the Court has stricken statutes prohibiting truthful advertisements for: (i) legal abortions; (ii) contraceptives; and (iii) drug prices.

2) A city could not prohibit the use of newsracks on sidewalks for the distribution for commercial publications (such as free publications advertising products or real estate for sale) if the city allowed sidewalk newsracks for the distribution of newspapers. This city law failed the commercial speech test because there was no "reasonable fit" between the category of commercial speech and any substantial interest. Commercial newsracks did not cause any physical or aesthetic harm different from that caused by newspaper newsracks. [Cincinnati v. Discovery Network, Inc., 507 U.S. 410 (1993)] Similarly, a law prohibiting beer bottle labels from displaying alcohol content was held invalid because, although the government has a substantial interest in preventing "strength wars," the government did not show that the label prohibition advanced this interest in a material way. [Rubin v. Coors Brewing Co., 514 U.S. 476 (1995)]

3) A law prohibiting advertising of smokeless tobacco and cigars within 1,000 feet of a school or playground, which amounted to a complete ban in many areas, was held invalid. Even though such a ban directly advances the substantial government interest in preventing underage use of those products, its geographic reach demonstrates a *"lack of tailoring,"* thus unduly affecting use of tobacco products by adults (which is a legal activity). [Lorillard Tobacco Co. v. Reilly, 533 U.S. 525 (2001)]

a.   Liquor Price Regulation
The Court has stricken a ban prohibiting *all* advertisement of liquor prices. [44 Liquormart, Inc. v. Rhode Island, 517 U.S. 484 (1996)] In *44 Liquormart,* five Justices in separate opinions found that a complete ban on truthful, nonmisleading commercial speech in order to protect the public (*i.e.,* people will drink less if liquor prices are not advertised because the advertising ban makes it difficult to comparison shop, which keeps the price of liquor artificially high) will rarely be upheld. Note also that the *Twenty-First Amendment*—giving states power to regulate liquor commerce within their borders—*does not give states power to override First Amendment protections*.

Note: After *44 Liquormart,* it seems unlikely that the government can *completely ban* truthful advertising of any lawful product or service.

b.   Commercial Sign Regulation
It is unclear whether billboards may be totally banned from a city. However, they can be regulated for purposes of traffic safety and aesthetics.

1)   Blockbusting
A town could not prohibit the use of outdoor "for sale" signs by owners of private homes as a way of reducing the effect of "blockbusting" real estate agents. [Linmark Associates v. Willingboro Township, 431 U.S. 85 (1977)]

c. **Attorney Advertising**
The Court applies the general three-part *Central Hudson Gas* commercial speech standard to attorney advertisement. Thus, the Court has struck down absolute bans against attorney advertising. [Bates v. State Bar of Arizona, 433 U.S. 350 (1977)—ban against advertising nature and price of attorneys' professional services; Peel v. Illinois Attorney Registration & Disciplinary Commission, 496 U.S. 91 (1990)—ban against advertising status as "certified" or a "specialist" by or of a legitimate attorney organization] However, the Court has upheld prohibitions against in-person solicitation for pecuniary gain [Ohralik v. Ohio State Bar, 436 U.S. 447 (1978)—state interest in protecting lay persons from fraud and overreaching is substantial, and prohibition here is narrowly tailored and directly advances that interest] and sending mail solicitations to accident victims and their relatives within 30 days following an accident [Florida Bar v. Went For It, Inc., 515 U.S. 618 (1995)—state interest in protecting lawyers' reputation is substantial, and ban here is narrowly tailored and directly advances that interest].

d. **Certified Public Accountants' Services**
A state may not ban uninvited in-person or telephone soliciting, and advertising for business, by certified public accountants ("CPAs"). The Court held that the ban on CPA solicitation was not reasonably tailored to protecting consumers because the state failed to demonstrate that this type of solicitation by CPAs presented potential danger to consumers (as would in-person solicitation by attorneys). [Edenfield v. Fane, 507 U.S. 761 (1993)] Similarly, a CPA cannot be prevented from truthfully indicating that she is a "certified financial planner" and an attorney, because these terms are neither false nor misleading. [Ibanez v. Florida Department of Business and Professional Regulation, 512 U.S. 136 (1994)]

D. PRIOR RESTRAINTS

A prior restraint is any governmental action that would prevent a communication from reaching the public (*e.g.,* a licensing system, a prohibition against using mails, an injunction, etc.). Prior restraints are not favored in our political system; the Court would rather allow speech and then punish it if it was unprotected. However, the Court will uphold prior restraints if some special harm would otherwise result. As with other restrictions on speech, a prior restraint must be narrowly tailored to achieve some compelling or, at least, significant governmental interest. The Court has also required that certain procedural safeguards be included in any system of prior restraint.

1. **Sufficiency of Governmental Interest**
The Supreme Court has not adopted a brightline standard for determining when a prior restraint is justified, but it has said that the government's burden is heavy. For exam purposes, you should ask whether there is some *special societal harm* that justifies the restraint.

a. **National Security**
National security is certainly a sufficient harm justifying prior restraint. Thus, a newspaper could be prohibited from publishing troop movements in times of war. [Near v. Minnesota, 283 U.S. 697 (1931)] However, the harm must be more than theoretical. Thus, the Court refused to enjoin publication of *The Pentagon Papers* on the basis that publication might possibly have a detrimental effect on the Vietnam War. [New York Times v. United States, 403 U.S. 713 (1971)]

b. **Preserving Fair Trial**
Preserving a fair trial for an accused might be a sufficient basis for prior restraint. However, the restraint will be upheld only if it is the only sure way of preserving a fair trial. [Nebraska Press Association v. Stewart, 427 U.S. 539 (1976)]

1) **Compare—Grand Jury Prior Restraint**
A state law prohibiting a grand jury witness from ever disclosing the testimony he gave to the grand jury (even after the grand jury term had ended) violates the First Amendment. Such a law is not narrowly tailored to a compelling interest, since any such interest that the government may have in protecting the grand jury process can be protected by a nonpermanent prohibition. [Butterworth v. Smith, 494 U.S. 624 (1990)]

c. **Contractual Agreements**
The Supreme Court has held that prior restraint is permissible where the parties have

contractually agreed to the restraint. [Snepp v. United States, 444 U.S. 507 (1980)—CIA agent contractually agreed to give agency a prepublication review of any item related to his employment]

d.   Military Circumstances
The Supreme Court has held that the interests of maintaining discipline among troops and efficiency of operations on a military base justify a requirement that persons on a military base obtain the commander's permission before circulating petitions.

e.   Obscenity
The Court has held in a number of cases that the government's interest in preventing the dissemination of obscenity is sufficient to justify a system of prior restraint.

2.   Procedural Safeguards
The Supreme Court has held that no system of prior restraint will be upheld unless it provides the persons whose speech is being restrained certain procedural safeguards. The safeguards arose in the context of movie censorship for obscenity, but the court has held that similar safeguards must be provided in all prior restraint cases:

(i)   The standards must be "*narrowly drawn, reasonable, and definite*," so as to include only prohibitable speech (*e.g.,* improper to permanently enjoin witness from disclosing grand jury testimony; government interest can be protected by nonpermanent injunction [Butterworth v. Smith, *supra*]);

(ii)   If the restraining body wishes to restrain dissemination of an item, it must *promptly seek an injunction* (*e.g.,* improper to allow 50 days before seeking injunction [Tietel Film Corp. v. Cusack, 390 U.S. 676 (1968)]); and

(iii)   There must be a *prompt and final judicial determination* of the validity of the restraint (*e.g.,* improper to leave an injunction in place pending an appeal that could take up to a year; government must either lift the injunction or expedite the appeal [National Socialist Party v. Village of Skokie, 432 U.S. 43 (1977)]).

A number of other cases, especially in the area of movie censorship, also provide that the *government bears the burden* of proving that the speech involved is unprotected. [Freedman v. Maryland, 380 U.S. 51 (1965)]

a.   Example—Denial of Use of Mails
A federal statute authorized the Postmaster General (i) to deny use of the mails and postal money orders for materials found to be obscene in an administrative hearing, and (ii) to obtain a court order, upon a showing of probable cause, to detain incoming mail pending completion of the administrative hearing. The Court found that this denial of use of the mails violated the First Amendment: The procedures did not require the government to initiate proceedings to obtain a final judicial determination of obscenity, failed to assure prompt judicial review, and failed to limit any restraint in advance of a final judicial determination to preserving the status quo for "the shortest fixed period compatible with sound judicial resolution." [Blount v. Rizzi, 400 U.S. 410 (1971)]

b.   "Informal" Blacklists
"Informal" sanctions by a state agency that have the *effect* of a prior restraint without adequate procedural and judicial safeguards are unconstitutional.
Example: In *Bantam Books, Inc. v. Sullivan,* 372 U.S. 58 (1963), a state juvenile delinquency commission made "informal" recommendations to book distributors as to which publications were objectionable for sale to youths; and the recommendations were followed by threats of court action, visits from police, etc. Distributors were given no notice or hearing before their publications were listed as objectionable. The Court held that compliance with the commission's directives by distributors was not voluntary and represented unconstitutional censorship.

c.   Adversary Hearing Usually Required
An adversary hearing, upon notice to all interested parties, is usually essential to any injunction procedure—especially when *political* speech is involved and timing is important. [Carroll v. Princess Anne Co., 393 U.S. 175 (1969)—invalidating an ex parte court order restraining members of a political party from holding rallies that would tend to "disturb or endanger" local residents]

3. Obscenity Cases

Much of the case law in the area of prior restraint has arisen in connection with banning obscenity.

a. Seizure of Books and Films

As with any seizure by the government, seizures of books and films may be made only upon probable cause that they contain obscenity or are otherwise unlawful. (*See* Criminal Procedure outline.)

1) Single Seizures

Seizures of a single book or film (to preserve it as evidence) may be made only with a warrant issued by a neutral and detached magistrate. And even here, a prompt post-seizure determination of obscenity must be available. If other copies of a seized film are not available to the exhibitor, he must be allowed to make a copy so that he may continue showing the film until a final determination has been made. [Heller v. New York, 413 U.S. 483 (1973)] Of course, if the materials are available for sale to the general public, an officer may enter into the establishment and purchase the book or film to use it as evidence in a later prosecution without obtaining a warrant. [Maryland v. Macon, 472 U.S. 463 (1985)]

2) Large Scale Seizures

"Large scale" seizures of allegedly obscene books and films—"to destroy them or block their distribution or exhibition"—must be *preceded* by a *full adversary hearing* and a judicial determination of obscenity. [Fort Wayne Books, Inc. v. Indiana, 489 U.S. 46 (1989)]

3) Forfeiture of Business

The First Amendment does not prohibit forfeiture of a defendant's adult entertainment business after the defendant has been found guilty of violating the Racketeer Influenced and Corrupt Organizations Act and criminal obscenity laws, even though the business assets included nonobscene books and magazines, where the entire business was found to be part of the defendant's racketeering activity. [Alexander v. United States, 509 U.S. 544 (1993)]

b. Injunction

After seizing material, the government may enjoin its further publication only after it is determined to be obscene in a *full judicial hearing*. [Kingsley Books, Inc. v. Brown, 354 U.S. 346 (1957)]

c. Movie Censorship

The Court has noted that movies are different from other forms of expression, and that time delays incident to censorship are less burdensome for movies than for other forms of expression. Thus, the Court allows governments to establish censorship boards to screen movies *before* they are released in the community, as long as the procedural safeguards mentioned above are followed. The censor bears the burden of proving that the movie is unprotected speech.

E. FREEDOM OF THE PRESS

As a general rule, the press has no greater freedom to speak than does the public. However, a number of issues have arisen in the freedom of press context.

1. Publication of Truthful Information

Generally, the press has a right to publish information about a matter of public concern, and this right can be restricted only by a sanction that is narrowly tailored to further a state interest of the highest order. The right applies even if the information has been unlawfully obtained in the first instance, as long as (i) the speech relates to a matter of public concern, (ii) the publisher did not obtain it unlawfully nor know who did, and (iii) the original speaker's privacy expectations are low. [Bartnicki v. Vopper, 532 U.S. 514 (2001)]

Example: During heated collective bargaining negotiations between a teachers' union and a school board, an unknown person intercepted a cell phone call between a union negotiator and the union's president. The tape was forwarded to a radio commentator, who played it on the radio. The commentator was sued for damages under civil liability provisions of state and federal wiretap laws that prohibited intentional disclosure of the contents of an electronically transmitted conversation when one has reason to know that the conversation was intercepted unlawfully. The Supreme Court held that the statute violated the First Amendment as applied under these circumstances. [Bartnicki v. Vopper, *supra*]

2. Access to Trials

The First Amendment guarantees the public and press a right to attend criminal trials. But the right may be outweighed by an overriding interest articulated in findings by the trial judge. [Richmond Newspapers v. Virginia, 448 U.S. 555 (1980)—no majority opinion] The right probably applies to civil trials, although the Supreme Court has not conclusively resolved that issue.

a. Access to Voir Dire Examination

The First Amendment guarantee of public and press access to criminal trials also includes access to proceedings involving the voir dire examination of potential jurors. In *Press-Enterprise Co. v. Superior Court,* 464 U.S. 501 (1984), the Court found that a trial court could not constitutionally close voir dire examination of potential jurors without consideration of alternatives to closure even though, in some circumstances, there may be a compelling interest in restricting access to such proceedings to protect the privacy of potential jurors or the fairness of the trial.

b. Access to Other Pretrial Proceedings

Pretrial proceedings are presumptively subject to a First Amendment right of access for the press and public. Thus, a law requiring that all preliminary hearings be closed to the press and public violates the First Amendment. [El Vocero de Puerto Rico (Caribbean International News Corp.) v. Puerto Rico, 508 U.S. 147 (1993)—per curiam] If the prosecution and defense counsel seek to have a judge close pretrial proceedings, the judge would have to make specific findings on the record demonstrating (i) that closure was essential to preserve "higher" or "overriding" values, and (ii) that the closure order was narrowly tailored to serve the higher or overriding value. [Press-Enterprise Co. v. Superior Court, 478 U.S. 1 (1986)]

If the prosecution seeks to have a pretrial hearing or trial closed to the public and the defendant objects to the closure, there will be a Sixth Amendment violation if the judge excludes the public and the press from the hearing or trial without a clear finding that a closure order was necessary to protect an overriding interest.

c. Compelling Interest in Protecting Children

The government has a compelling interest in protecting children who are victims of sex offenses. Portions of trials wherein such children testify may be closed to the public and press, but only if the trial court makes a finding that such closure is necessary to protect the child in the individual case. A state statute, however, violates the First Amendment if it requires closure of the trial during testimony of a child victim of a sex offense without a finding of necessity by the trial judge. [Globe Newspaper Co. v. Superior Court, 457 U.S. 596 (1982)]

d. Protective Order in Publishing Information Gained in Pretrial Discovery

The Supreme Court has upheld a state trial court "protective order" prohibiting a newspaper defendant in a defamation suit from publishing, disseminating, or using information gained through pretrial discovery from the plaintiff in any way except where necessary for preparation for trial. [*See* Seattle Times Co. v. Rhinehart, 467 U.S. 20 (1984)]

3. Requiring Members of the Press to Testify Before Grand Juries

In *Branzburg v. Hayes,* 408 U.S. 665 (1972), the Court held that requiring a journalist to appear and testify before state or federal grand juries ***does not abridge freedom of speech or press***, despite the claim that such a requirement would so deter the flow of news from confidential sources as to place an unconstitutionally heavy burden on the First Amendment interest in the free flow of information to the public. The Court's opinion refused to create—and even rejected—a conditional privilege not to reveal confidential sources to a grand jury conducting a good faith inquiry. This position was affirmed in *New York Times v. Jascalevich,* 439 U.S. 1331 (1978).

4. Interviewing Prisoners

Although the First Amendment protects prisoners, and especially those corresponding with them by mail, from a sweeping program of censorship [Procunier v. Martinez, 416 U.S. 396 (1974)], it does not permit journalists to insist upon either interviewing specified prisoners of their choice [Pell v. Procunier, 417 U.S. 817 (1974)] or inspecting prison grounds [Houchins v. KQED, Inc., 438 U.S. 1 (1978)].

5. Business Regulations or Taxes

Press and broadcasting companies can be subject to general business regulations (*e.g.,* antitrust laws) or taxes (*e.g.,* federal or state income taxes). Thus, a tax or regulation applicable to both press and non-press businesses will be upheld, even if it has a special impact on a portion of the press or broadcast media, as long as it is not an attempt to interfere with First Amendment activities. However, no tax or regulation impacting on the press or subpart of the press may be based on the content of the publication absent a compelling justification.

Examples: 1) State tax on publisher's use of more than $100,000 of paper and ink products annually violates the First Amendment. [Minneapolis Star & Tribune v. Minnesota Commissioner of Revenue, 460 U.S. 575 (1983)]

2) State sales tax or "receipts tax" on the sale of general interest magazines that exempts newspapers and religious, professional, trade, and sports journals from the tax violates the First Amendment. [Arkansas Writers' Project, Inc. v. Ragland, 481 U.S. 221 (1987)]

3) A state sales tax that exempted the sales of newspapers and magazines from the tax but did not give a similar exemption to the sale of broadcast services (cable or subscription television) did not violate the First Amendment. The tax was not based on the content of broadcasts and did not target a small category of publishers. The tax was applicable to all cable or satellite television sales. (There is no comparable sale of "free T.V." such as network broadcasts.) [Leathers v. Medlock, 499 U.S. 439 (1991)]

6. Monetary Damages for Failure to Keep Identity Confidential

When a reporter or publisher promises a "source person" to keep his identity confidential and then publishes the source person's name, state contract law or promissory estoppel law may allow the source person to recover from the reporter or publisher any damages caused by the publication of his identity. [Cohen v. Cowles Media Co., 501 U.S. 663 (1991)]

7. Broadcasting Regulations

Radio and television broadcasting may be more closely regulated than the press. *Rationale:* Due to the limited number of frequencies available, broadcasters have a special privilege—and, consequently, a special responsibility to give suitable time to matters of public interest and to present a suitable range of programs. The paramount right is the ***right of viewers and listeners*** to receive information of public concern, rather than the right of broadcasters to broadcast what they please.

a. Fairness Doctrine

Accordingly, the Court has upheld, under a regulatory "fairness doctrine" (which is no longer enforced), FCC orders requiring a radio station to offer free broadcasting time (i) to opponents of political candidates or views endorsed by the station, and (ii) to any person who has been personally attacked in the course of a broadcast, for a reply to the attack. [Red Lion Broadcasting Co. v. FCC, 395 U.S. 367 (1969)]

1) Compare—Grant of Equal Newspaper Space

A statute granting political candidates a right to equal space to reply to criticism by the newspaper ***violates*** First Amendment freedom of the press. Decisions respecting size and content of newspaper are forbidden to government. [Miami Herald Publishing Co. v. Tornillo, 418 U.S. 241 (1974)]

b. Newspaper Ownership of Radio or TV Station

Similarly, to promote the diversity of information received by the public, the FCC may forbid ownership of a radio or television station by a daily newspaper located in the same community. [FCC v. National Citizens Committee, 436 U.S. 765 (1978)]

c. Prohibiting Indecent Speech

Because of a broadcast's ability to invade the privacy of the home, the First Amendment does not forbid imposing civil sanctions on a broadcaster for airing a full monologue (in contrast to isolated use of a few such words) of "patently offensive sexual and excretory speech," even though it is not "obscene"—at least at those times when children are likely to be listening. [FCC v. Pacifica Foundation, 438 U.S. 726 (1978)]

d. Political Advertisements
The First Amendment does *not* require broadcasters to accept political advertisements. Congress and the FCC, in seeking to assure balanced coverage of public issues, could appropriately conclude that licensed broadcasters subject to the "fairness doctrine" should generally determine what should be broadcast, rather than having affluent persons monopolize air time. [CBS, Inc. v. Democratic National Committee, 412 U.S. 94 (1973)] However, *under a statutory right of access*, the FCC may require licensed broadcasters to sell reasonable amounts of time to legally qualified candidates for federal office. [CBS, Inc. v. FCC, 453 U.S. 367 (1981)]

e. Elimination of Editorial Speech from Stations Receiving Public Grants
Congress violated the First Amendment when it forbade any noncommercial educational station receiving a grant from the Corporation for Public Broadcasting from engaging in "editorializing." [FCC v. League of Women Voters, 468 U.S. 364 (1984)] This was the *suppression of speech* because of its content; the elimination of editorial speech from stations receiving public grants of this type was not narrowly tailored to promote an overriding government purpose regarding the regulation of broadcasting in general or noncommercial broadcasters in particular. Congress could deny persons receiving the federal funds the right to use those funds for editorial activities, but it could not condition the receipt of those funds upon a promise not to engage in any such speech.

8. Cable Television Regulation
While generally regulations of newspapers are subject to strict scrutiny, and regulations of the broadcast media are subject to less critical review, regulations of cable television transmissions are subject to review by a standard somewhere between these two. *Rationale:* The physical connection to a viewer's television set makes the cable subscriber a more captive audience than a newspaper reader and distinguishes cable from newspapers, which cannot prevent access to competing newspapers. On the other hand, unlike broadcast media, which is limited to a small number of frequencies (*see* 7., *supra*), there is no practical limitation on the number of cable channels; thus, the government's interest in protecting viewers' rights is weaker with regard to cable. [Turner Broadcasting System v. FCC, A.1.a.2), *supra*]
Example: A law requiring cable operators to carry local stations is subject to "intermediate scrutiny" since it is content-neutral (*see* A.1.a.2), *supra*). Since a "must carry" provision directly serves the important interest of preserving economic viability of local broadcasters and promotes the dissemination of information to noncable viewers, it is constitutional. [Turner Broadcasting System v. FCC, *supra*]

a. Compare—Content-Based Cable Broadcast Regulations
A content-based cable broadcast regulation will be upheld only if it passes muster under the strict scrutiny test. [United States v. Playboy Entertainment Group, Inc., 529 U.S. 803 (2000)—law requiring cable operators to limit "sexually oriented" programs to after 10 p.m. is invalid because of the less restrictive alternative of enabling each household to block undesired channels]

9. Internet Regulation
The strict standard of First Amendment scrutiny, rather than the more relaxed standard applicable to broadcast regulation, applies to regulation of the Internet. *Rationale*: In contrast to broadcasting, there is no scarcity of frequencies (*see* 7., *supra*) on the Internet and little likelihood that the Internet will unexpectedly invade the privacy of the home (*see* 7.c., *supra*). [Reno v. American Civil Liberties Union, C.3.a.4), *supra*]

XXI. FREEDOM OF ASSOCIATION AND BELIEF

A. NATURE OF THE RIGHT
Although the First Amendment does not mention a right of freedom of association, the right to join together with other persons for expressive or political activity is protected by the First Amendment. However, the right to associate for expressive purposes is *not absolute*. Infringements on the right may be justified by *compelling state interests*, unrelated to the suppression of ideas, that cannot be achieved through means significantly less restrictive of associational freedoms.
Example: A state's interest in ending invidious discrimination justifies prohibiting private

clubs that are large and basically unselective in their membership, or that are often used for business contacts, from discriminating on the basis of race, creed, color, national origin, or sex—at least when it is not shown that this would impede the individual members' ability to engage in First Amendment activity. [New York State Club Association, Inc. v. New York City, 487 U.S. 1 (1988); Board of Directors of Rotary Club International v. Rotary Club of Duarte, 481 U.S. 537 (1987); Roberts v. United States Jaycees, 468 U.S. 609 (1984)]

Compare: 1) A state antidiscrimination law may not bar the Boy Scouts from excluding an openly gay assistant scoutmaster from membership. Forced inclusion would **significantly burden** the right of expressive association of the Boy Scouts, since one of the **sincerely held** purposes of the Scouts is to instill certain moral values in young people, including the value that "homosexual conduct is not morally straight." [Boy Scouts of America v. Dale, 530 U.S. 640 (2000)]

2) A city ordinance that restricted admission to certain dance halls to persons between the ages of 14 and 18 was constitutional; it did not have to be justified with a compelling interest because the associational activity of meeting in a dance hall is not an activity within the protection of the First Amendment. [Dallas v. Stanglin, 490 U.S. 19 (1989)]

B. ELECTORAL PROCESS

Laws regulating the electoral process might impact on First Amendment rights of speech, assembly, and association. The Supreme Court uses a balancing test in determining whether a regulation of the electoral process is valid: if the restriction on First Amendment activities is severe, it will be upheld only if it is narrowly tailored to achieve a compelling interest, but if the restriction is reasonable and nondiscriminatory, it generally will be upheld on the basis of the states' important regulatory interests. [Burdick v. Takushi, 504 U.S. 428 (1992)—upholding prohibition against write-in candidates]

1. Ballot Regulation

a. Signature Requirements
The Court has found that the interest of running an efficient election supports a requirement that candidates obtain a reasonable number of signatures to get on the ballot [Munro v. Socialist Workers Party, 479 U.S. 189 (1986)—1%], but the Court struck down a severe ballot restriction requiring new political parties to collect twice as many signatures to run for county office as for state office [Norman v. Reed, 502 U.S. 279 (1992)].

b. Primary Voting Regulations
A state may enforce a party rule requiring that a person be registered as a member of the party within a reasonable amount of time prior to a primary to be able to vote. [Rosario v. Rockefeller, 410 U.S. 752 (1973)] However, such a state law is invalid if it is contrary to the party's rules (*e.g.,* the party would allow unregistered independent voters to vote). [Tashjan v. Republican Party of Connecticut, 479 U.S. 208 (1986)]

c. Single Party Limitation
A state law that prohibits an individual from appearing on the ballot as the candidate of more than one party does **not** impose a severe burden on the association rights of political parties. The state's interest in ballot integrity and political stability are "sufficiently weighty" to justify the law. [Timmons v. Twin Cities Area New Party, 520 U.S. 35 (1997)]

2. Party Regulation
The state has less interest in governing party activities than in governing elections in general. Thus, the Court has held invalid a statute prohibiting the governing committee of a political party from endorsing or opposing candidates in primary elections. [Eu v. San Francisco County Democratic Central Committee, 489 U.S. 214 (1989); *and see* California Democratic Party v. Jones, 530 U.S. 567 (2000)—state cannot require political parties to allow nonparty members to vote in the party's primary election] Similarly, it has held invalid state regulations concerning the selection of delegates to a national party convention and the selection of candidates at such elections. [Cousins v. Wigoda, 419 U.S. 477 (1975); Democratic Party v. LaFolette, 450 U.S. 107 (1981)]

3. Limits on Contributions

a. To Political Candidate

Laws limiting the amount of money that a person or group may contribute to a political candidate are *valid*, since the government has a sufficiently important interest in stopping the fact (or appearance) of corruption that may result from large contributions. Moreover, such laws do not substantially restrict freedom of expression or freedom of association (as long as the contributor may spend his money directly to discuss candidates and issues). [Buckley v. Valeo, 424 U.S. 1 (1976)]

b. To Ballot Referendum Committee

The government may *not* limit contributions to a political committee that supports or opposes a ballot referendum (as opposed to one that supports a political candidate). Such a limitation on contributions to influence referendum elections violates the freedoms of speech and association. [Citizens Against Rent Control v. Berkeley, 454 U.S. 290 (1982)]

c. Disclosure of Contributors or Recipients of Money

The government may require a political party or committee to disclose the names of contributors or recipients of money to or from the party or committee. However, if the party or committee can show a "reasonable probability" that disclosure will cause harm to the party, committee, or private individuals, they have a First Amendment right to refuse to make such disclosures. [Brown v. Socialist Workers '74 Campaign Committee, 454 U.S. 1122 (1982)]

4. Limits on Expenditures

Laws limiting the amount that an individual or group (including a candidate) may spend on a political campaign are *invalid*. Such laws impose "direct and substantial restraints" on political speech and do not satisfy the "exacting scrutiny applicable to limitations on core First Amendment rights of political expression." Government may not restrict the speech of wealthy persons to enhance the voice of others. [Buckley v. Valeo, *supra*]

Examples: 1) The Supreme Court invalidated a state statute that prohibited paying individuals to circulate initiative or referendum petitions. The prohibition against the use of paid circulators was not necessary to the promotion of any state interest that might override the freedom to engage in political speech. [Meyer v. Grant, 486 U.S. 414 (1988)]

2) The federal government *cannot* make it a crime for a "political committee" to expend more than $1,000 to further the nomination or election of a presidential candidate who is receiving federal financing. [Federal Election Commission v. National Conservative Political Action Committee, 470 U.S. 480 (1985)]

a. Corporations

1) Limiting Contributions to Political Candidates—Permissible

Laws limiting the amount that a corporation or unincorporated association may contribute to a political candidate have been upheld. [California Medical Association v. Federal Election Commission, 453 U.S. 182 (1981)] Corporations or unions can be prohibited from making contributions to political candidates from funds that are not contributed by corporate or union members but, instead, solicited from nonmembers. [Federal Election Commission v. National Right to Work Committee, 456 U.S. 914 (1982)]

a) Exception—Ideological Corporations

Although contributions to political candidates by ordinary corporations may be limited, contributions by *ideological corporations* (*i.e.,* voluntary political associations that have incorporated; *e.g.,* a corporation formed to oppose abortion) may not be limited. [Federal Election Commission v. Massachusetts Citizens for Life, Inc., 479 U.S. 238 (1986)] To be exempt from the independent campaign expenditure limitations placed on corporations, a nonprofit corporation must: (i) be formed to promote ideas and not business activity; (ii) not have shareholders who have a claim on its assets; and (iii) not be tied to business interests or business corporations. Thus, even though a "Chamber of Commerce" is a nonprofit corporation, its campaign spending can be limited in the same way as other corporations. [Austin v. Michigan Chamber of Commerce, 494 U.S. 652 (1990)]

2) Expenditures to Influence Vote on Referendum—Permissible
The Court has left open the broad question of whether corporations have the full measure of rights that individuals have under the First Amendment. But laws prohibiting corporate expenditures to influence the vote on a *referendum* violate the First Amendment. Such speech is "indispensable to decisionmaking in a democracy."

Examples: 1) A law limiting corporate expenditures to referenda that "materially affect" corporate business or property was held invalid. [First National Bank v. Bellotti, 435 U.S. 765 (1978)]

2) A law forbidding a corporation from using bill inserts to express its views on controversial issues of public policy also violates the First Amendment. [Consolidated Edison Co. v. Public Service Commission, 447 U.S. 530 (1980)]

b. "Coordinated" Expenditures
If political parties, like others, make expenditures "in cooperation, consultation, or concert" with a candidate, the expenditures are treated like "contributions" and may be limited accordingly. *Rationale*: The opposite rule would induce individuals to circumvent contribution limits by simply giving money to the party with the understanding that it should go to the candidate, thus furthering corruption or its appearance. [Federal Election Commission v. Colorado Republican Federal Campaign Committee, 533 U.S. 431 (2001)]

5. Compare—Regulations of Core Political Speech
Regulation of "core political speech" must be distinguished from regulation of the process surrounding elections. Regulation of "core political speech" will be upheld only if it passes muster under strict scrutiny. [McIntyre v. Ohio Elections Commission, 514 U.S. 334 (1995)]

a. Prohibiting Any Election Day Campaigning
A state law prohibiting *any* campaigning on election day has been held *invalid* as applied to a newspaper urging people to vote in a certain way. The right to comment on political issues is one of the most essential elements of free speech, and such conduct by newspapers would pose little danger to conducting elections. [Mills v. Alabama, 384 U.S. 214 (1966)]

1) Compare—Hundred-Foot Limit
A law prohibiting campaign activity within 100 feet of a polling place is *valid*. Even though the law is content based and concerns an essential element of free speech, it is *necessary* to serve the *compelling* interest of preventing voter intimidation and election fraud. [Burson v. Freeman, 504 U.S. 191 (1992)]

b. Prohibiting Anonymous Campaign Literature
Laws prohibiting distribution of anonymous campaign literature involve core political speech and have been stricken because they were not narrowly tailored to a compelling state interest. [McIntyre v. Ohio Elections Commission, *supra*; Buckley v. American Constitutional Law Foundation, 525 U.S. 182 (1999)]

c. Prohibiting Judge Candidates from Announcing Their Views
A rule prohibiting candidates for judicial election from announcing their views on disputed legal and political issues violates the First Amendment. This is both a content-based restriction and a restriction on core political speech. In either case, it can be justified only if it is necessary to a compelling state interest. Two state interests were suggested to support the rule here: It is necessary to maintain an impartial judiciary and it is necessary to preserve the appearance of impartiality. The Court found that the rule is "woefully underinclusive" and so is not tailored at all toward achieving these goals. For example, it allows candidates to show bias toward political parties while it prohibits them from stating an opinion about political issues. The Court also found that finding judges without any preconceptions in favor of particular legal views is not a compelling interest because it would be both impossible to find such a person and undesirable. [Republican Party of Minnesota v. White, 122 S. Ct. 2528 (2002)]

C. BAR MEMBERSHIP AND PUBLIC EMPLOYMENT

The government often requires persons who accept government jobs to submit to loyalty oaths and refrain from certain conduct (*e.g.,* campaigning). Such regulations often impact upon the freedom of speech and association.

1. Restraints on Conduct

If a government employer seeks to fire an employee for speech-related conduct, one of two tests will apply depending on whether the speech involved a matter of public concern. If a matter of public concern is involved, courts must carefully balance the employee's rights as a citizen to comment on a matter of public concern against the government's interest as an employer in efficient performance of public service. If the speech did not involve a matter of public concern, the courts should give a wide degree of deference to the government employer's judgment concerning whether the speech was disruptive.

Examples: 1) A teacher cannot be fired for writing a letter to a newspaper attacking school board policies. [Pickering v. Board of Education, 391 U.S. 563 (1968)]

2) The Court held invalid the firing of a clerical employee from a constable's office for expressing her disappointment that an assassination attempt on President Reagan did not succeed, because in context the statement could not be understood to be an actual threat or an action that would interfere with the running of the office; rather, the Court viewed it as a commentary on the public issue of the President's policies. [Rankin v. McPherson, 483 U.S. 378 (1987)]

Compare: The Court upheld the firing of an attorney for circulating in the office a petition regarding transfer policies. [Connick v. Myers, 461 U.S. 138 (1983)]

a. Independent Contractors Have Similar Rights

With regard to government projects, an independent contractor has speech rights similar to those of a government employee—the contractor cannot be discharged or have a contract not renewed merely because the government disagrees with something the contractor says. [*See* Board of County Commissioners v. Umbehr, 518 U.S. 668 (1996); *and see* O'Hare Truck Service Inc. v. City of Northlake, 518 U.S. 712 (1996)]

b. Participation in Political Campaigns

A provision of the Hatch Act making it unlawful for employees in the federal executive branch to take an active part in political campaigns has been sustained. The rationale is twofold: to further nonpartisanship in administration and to protect employees from being coerced to work for the election of their employers. [United Public Workers v. Mitchell, 330 U.S. 75 (1947)]

c. Bans on Receiving Honoraria

A provision of the Ethics in Government Act banning government employees from accepting an honorarium for making speeches, writing articles, or making appearances was held to violate the First Amendment when applied to "rank and file" employees. Such a rule deters speech within a broad category of expression by a massive number of potential speakers and thus can be justified only if the government can show that the employees' and their potential audiences' rights are outweighed by the necessary impact the speech would have on actual operation of the government. The government failed to cite any evidence of misconduct related to honoraria by the rank and file employees, and so failed to meet the burden here. [United States v. National Treasury Employees Union, 513 U.S. 454 (1995)]

d. Patronage

The First Amendment freedoms of political belief and association forbid the hiring, promotion, transfer, firing, or recall of a public employee because of political party affiliation unless the hiring authority demonstrates that party affiliation is an appropriate requirement for the effective performance of the public office involved, *e.g.,* "policymaking" or "confidential" nature of work. [Rutan v. Republican Party of Illinois, 497 U.S. 62 (1990)]

e. Bill of Attainder

Legislative punishment without judicial trial by discharging a public employee for political activity is invalid as a bill of attainder. [United States v. Lovett, 328 U.S. 303 (1946)]

f. Must Not Be Vague
A standard for conduct may not be vague.

Example: A statute providing for removal of public school teachers for "treasonable or seditious" utterances is void for vagueness. [Keyishian v. Board of Regents, 385 U.S. 589 (1967)]

2. Loyalty Oaths
It is permissible for the federal government to require employees and other public officers to take loyalty oaths. However, such oaths will not be upheld if they are overbroad (*i.e.,* prohibit constitutionally protected activities) or are vague so that they have a chilling effect on First Amendment activities.

a. Overbreadth

1) Knowledge of Organization's Aim Required
Public employment cannot be denied to persons who are simply members of the Communist Party because only knowing membership with "specific intent to further unlawful aims" is unprotected by the First Amendment. [Keyishian v. Board of Regents, *supra*]

2) Advocacy of Doctrine Protected
A political party may not be denied a place on the ballot for refusing to take a loyalty oath that it does not advocate violent overthrow of the government as an abstract doctrine. The First Amendment forbids "statutes regulating advocacy that are not limited to advocacy of action." [Communist Party v. Whitcomb, 414 U.S. 441 (1974)]

b. Vagueness

1) Oaths Upheld
Compare the following oaths that have been upheld:

a) To Support the Constitution
An oath that required public employees and bar applicants to "support the Constitution of the United States" and the state constitution has been upheld. [Connell v. Higgenbotham, 403 U.S. 207 (1971)]

b) To Oppose the Overthrow of the Government
An oath required of all state employees "to oppose the overthrow of the government . . . by force, violence, or by an illegal or unconstitutional method" has also been upheld. The Court read this oath as akin to those requiring the taker simply to "support" the Constitution, "to commit themselves to live by the constitutional processes of our system." Moreover, the oath provided fair notice, because its violation could be punished only by a prosecution for perjury, which required proof of knowing falsity. [Cole v. Richardson, 405 U.S. 676 (1972)]

2) Oath Not Upheld
A loyalty oath for public employees that they "promote respect for the flag and . . . reverence for law and order" is void for vagueness, since a refusal to salute the flag on religious grounds might be found in breach thereof. [Baggett v. Bullitt, 377 U.S. 360 (1964)]

3. Disclosure of Associations
Forcing disclosure of First Amendment activities as a condition of public employment, bar membership, or other public benefits may have a chilling effect. Thus, the state cannot force every prospective government employee to disclose *every* organizational membership. Such a broad disclosure has **insufficient relation** to loyalty and professional competence, and the state has available **less drastic means** to achieve its purpose. [Shelton v. Tucker, 364 U.S. 479 (1960)] The state may inquire only into those activities that are relevant to the position. If the candidate fails to answer relevant questions, employment may be denied. [Konigsberg v. State Bar of California, 366 U.S. 36 (1961)]

a. Fifth Amendment Limitation
If the job candidate refuses to answer on a claim of the privilege against self-incrimination, denial of the job violates the Fifth and Fourteenth Amendments. [Spevack v.

Klein, 385 U.S. 511 (1967)] However, if individuals are ordered by appropriate authorities to answer questions "specifically, directly, and narrowly relating to their official duties," and they refuse to do so by claiming the privilege against self-incrimination, they may be denied the job or discharged without violating the Fifth Amendment, if they were given immunity from the use of their answers or the fruits thereof in a criminal prosecution. [Lefkowitz v. Turley, 414 U.S. 70 (1973); Gardner v. Broderick, 392 U.S. 273 (1968)]

4. Practice of Law

Regulation of the legal profession may conflict with the freedom of association rights of certain groups since it may impair their ability to band together to advise each other and utilize counsel in their common interest.

a. Countervailing State Interest Required

To overcome a group's right to exercise its First Amendment rights, the state must show a substantial interest, such as evidence of objectionable practices occurring or an actual or clearly threatened conflict of interest between lawyer and client.

Examples: 1) NAACP encouraged, instructed, and offered to represent parents of black children to litigate against school segregation. This was held to be protected political expression. The state's ban on solicitation of legal business was inapplicable because the NAACP sought no monetary gain. [NAACP v. Button, 371 U.S. 415 (1963)]

2) Railroad labor union recommended a specific lawyer to pursue rights of members injured on the job, and also obtained a fee from a lawyer for performing investigative services. This was held protected. [Brotherhood of Railroad Trainmen v. Virginia, 377 U.S. 1 (1964)]

D. SOCIAL ISSUE BOYCOTTS

A state may not impose civil or criminal liability on those persons who engage in a nonviolent boycott of commercial enterprises to influence governmental and private decisions on social issues. Imposition of liability in such circumstances would violate the freedoms of speech and association. [NAACP v. Claiborne Hardware Co., 458 U.S. 886 (1982)] However, courts may regulate or punish labor organizations that engage in "secondary boycotts." [International Longshoreman's Association v. Allied International, Inc., 456 U.S. 212 (1982)]

1. Compare—Economic Boycotts

Economic boycotts can be restricted.

Example: A group of attorneys in the District of Columbia agreed not to represent indigent criminal defendants until the District raised the compensation for such cases. The Federal Trade Commission charged the attorneys with conspiracy to fix prices. The Supreme Court held that the attorneys had no First Amendment right to engage in the boycott because it involved economic, rather than social, issues. Further, the FTC found that the boycott could be a *per se* violation of federal law. [FTC v. Superior Court Trial Lawyers Association, 493 U.S. 411 (1990)]

E. TAX EXEMPT ORGANIZATIONS LIMITED IN LOBBYING ACTIVITIES

Tax exempt charitable organizations (ones to which contributions are tax deductible) are prohibited by the Internal Revenue Code from "substantial" lobbying activities. This prohibition is permissible even though certain military veterans' organizations are eligible for tax exempt status despite their lobbying activities. The Congress does not have to subsidize First Amendment activity, but it may choose to give a special subsidy to military veterans' organizations. [Regan v. Taxation With Representation of Washington, 461 U.S. 540 (1983)]

XXII. FREEDOM OF RELIGION

A. CONSTITUTIONAL PROVISION

The First Amendment provides "Congress shall make no law respecting an establishment of religion, or prohibiting the free exercise thereof."

B. APPLICABILITY TO THE STATES

Both the Establishment and Free Exercise Clauses of the First Amendment apply to the states under the Fourteenth Amendment.

C. FREE EXERCISE CLAUSE

1. No Punishment of Beliefs

The Free Exercise Clause prohibits the government from punishing (denying benefits to, or imposing burdens on) someone on the basis of the person's *religious beliefs*. It is sometimes said that the government can engage in such activity only if it is necessary to achieve a compelling interest; sometimes the rule is stated as a total prohibition of such government actions. In any case, the Supreme Court has never found an interest that was so "compelling" that it would justify punishing a religious belief.

a. What Constitutes Religious Belief?

The Supreme Court has not defined what constitutes a religious belief. However, it has made clear that religious belief does not require recognition of a supreme being [Torcaso v. Watkins, 367 U.S. 488 (1961)], and need not arise from a traditional, or even an organized, religion [*see* Frazee v. Illinois Department of Employment Security, 489 U.S. 829 (1989)]. One possible definition is that the "belief must occupy a place in the believer's life parallel to that occupied by orthodox religious beliefs." [United States v. Seeger, 380 U.S. 163 (1965)—interpreting statutory, rather than constitutional, provision] In any case, the Court has never held an asserted religious belief to be not religious for First Amendment purposes.

1) Courts May Not Find Religious Beliefs to Be False

The courts may not declare a religious belief to be "false." For example, if a person says he talked to God and that God said the person should solicit money, he cannot be found guilty of fraud on the basis that God never made such a statement. However, the court may determine whether the person is sincerely asserting a belief in the divine statement. [United States v. Ballard, 322 U.S. 78 (1944), *as described in* Employment Division v. Smith, 494 U.S. 872 (1990)]

b. Religious Oaths for Governmental Jobs Prohibited

The *federal* government may not require any federal office holder or employee to take an oath based on a religious belief as a condition for receiving the federal office or job, because such a requirement is prohibited by Article VI of the Constitution. State and local governments are prohibited from requiring such oaths by the Free Exercise Clause. [Toccaso v. Watkins, 367 U.S. 488 (1961)]

c. States May Not Exclude Clerics from Public Office

A state may not exclude clerics (persons who hold an office or official position in a religious organization) from being elected to the state legislature, or from other governmental positions, because that exclusion would impose a disability on these persons based upon the nature of their religious views and their religious status. [McDaniel v. Paty, 435 U.S. 618 (1978)]

2. No Punishment of Religious Conduct Solely Because It Is Religious

The Supreme Court has stated that the Free Exercise Clause prohibits the government from punishing conduct merely because it is religious or displays religious belief (*e.g.*, the state cannot ban the use of peyote only when used in religious ceremonies). [Employment Division v. Smith, *supra*—dicta] A law that is designed to suppress actions only because the actions are religiously motivated is not a neutral law of general applicability. Such a law will be invalid unless it is necessary to promote a compelling interest.

Example: A city law that prohibited the precise type of animal slaughter used in the ritual of a particular religious sect violated the Free Exercise Clause because the Court found that the law was designed solely to exclude the religious sect from the city. The law was not a neutral law of general applicability; nor was the law necessary to promote a compelling interest. [Church of the Lukumi Babalu Aye, Inc. v. Hialeah, 508 U.S. 520 (1993)]

3. States Can Regulate General Conduct—Criminal Laws and Other Regulations

Of course, states may prohibit or regulate conduct in general, and this is true even if the prohibition or regulation happens to interfere with a person's religious practices. The Free Exercise Clause cannot be used to challenge a law of general applicability unless it can be shown that the law was motivated by a desire to interfere with religion. [Employment Division v. Smith, *supra*]

a. **Generally No Exemptions Required**
The Free Exercise Clause does not require exemptions from criminal laws or other governmental regulations for a person whose religious beliefs prevent him from conforming his behavior to the requirements of the law. In other words, a law that regulates the conduct of all persons can be applied to prohibit the conduct of a person despite the fact that his religious beliefs prevent him from complying with the law.

b. **Examples**
The Supreme Court has held that no religious exemption was required from the following religiously neutral regulations, even though certain groups objected because the regulation interfered with conduct inspired by sincerely held religious beliefs:

1) Prohibition against *use of peyote* [Employment Division v. Smith, *supra*—challenged by person whose religious beliefs require use of peyote during religious ceremony];

2) *Denial of tax exempt status to schools that discriminate* on the basis of race [Bob Jones University v. United States, 461 U.S. 574 (1983)—challenged by religious school whose tenets require certain separations of races];

3) Requirement that employers comply with *federal minimum wage laws* [Tony and Susan Alamo Foundation v. Secretary of Labor, 471 U.S. 290 (1985)—challenged by employer that argued minimum wages interfere with members' religious desires to work without compensation];

4) Requirement that employers pay *Social Security taxes* [United States v. Lee, 455 U.S. 252 (1982)—challenged by person whose religious beliefs prohibited payment and receipt of Social Security type payments]; and

5) *Sales and use taxes* [Jimmy Swaggart Ministries v. Board of Equalization of California, 493 U.S. 378 (1990)—challenged as applied to sales of goods and literature by religious group].

4. **Unemployment Compensation Cases—Some Exemptions Required**
Many state unemployment compensation programs make payments only to persons who are involuntarily unemployed (*i.e.,* were fired or laid off rather than resigned), and who are available for work (*i.e.,* willing to accept offered employment). Here, however, unlike other areas of regulation, the Supreme Court has held that the states must grant religious exemptions. Thus, if a person resigns from a job or refuses to accept a job because it conflicts with her religious beliefs, the state must pay her unemployment compensation if she is otherwise entitled.

Examples: 1) A state cannot deny unemployment compensation merely because the applicant quit a job rather than work on a "holy day" on which religious beliefs forbid work. [Sherbert v. Verner, 374 U.S. 398 (1963)]

2) A state cannot deny unemployment compensation merely because the applicant quit his job rather than work on production of military equipment after his factory converted from nonmilitary to military production. [Thomas v. Review Board, 450 U.S. 707 (1981)]

a. **Need Not Belong to Formal Religious Organization**
A person does not have to be a member of a formal religious organization to receive the above exemptions from unemployment compensation requirements. All that is required is that the person *sincerely hold* religious beliefs that prevent him from working on a certain day or on military products. [Frazee v. Illinois Department of Employment Security, 1.a., *supra*]

b. **Limitation—Criminal Prohibitions**
The unemployment compensation cases do not give individuals a right to disregard criminal laws due to their religious beliefs. Thus, unemployment compensation laws may disqualify persons fired for "misconduct" (which includes any violation of criminal law).

Example: A person was fired from his job as a counselor at a private drug abuse clinic when it was discovered that he used peyote (at times when he was not at work) for religious reasons. All use of peyote was illegal in the state (even if the use was part of a religious ceremony). The Supreme Court held that unemployment compensation could properly be denied here. [Employment Division v. Smith, *supra*]

5. Right of Amish Not to Educate Children

The Supreme Court has required an exemption for the Amish from a neutral law that required school attendance until age 16, because a fundamental tenet of Amish religion forbids secondary education. The Court found that the Amish are productive and law-abiding, and ruled that the right to educate one's children (*see* XIX.B.6., *supra*) and the Free Exercise Clause outweighed the state's interest here. [Wisconsin v. Yoder, 406 U.S. 205 (1972)]

6. Special Rule for Prison Regulations

A prison regulation restricting inmates' constitutional rights (including First Amendment rights) will be upheld if the regulation is "reasonably related to legitimate penological interests." Applying this standard, the Supreme Court has upheld a prison regulation regarding the work duties of inmates that precluded Islamic inmates from attending a religious service held on Friday afternoons. [O'Lone v. Estate of Shabazz, 482 U.S. 342 (1987)]

D. ESTABLISHMENT CLAUSE

The Establishment Clause prohibits laws respecting the establishment of religion.

1. Sect Preference

If a law or government program includes a preference for some religious sects over others, the law will be held invalid unless it is *narrowly tailored* to promote a *compelling interest*.

Example: A state law created a public school district whose boundaries were intentionally set to match the boundaries of a particular Jewish neighborhood (so that several handicapped students would not have to be sent outside their neighborhood to attend special education classes that the state required and which the students' private school could not adequately provide). The Supreme Court found the law unconstitutional. [Board of Education v. Grumet, 512 U.S. 687 (1994)]

2. No Sect Preference

Where there is no "sect preference," the compelling interest test is not used; instead the governmental program will be valid under the Establishment Clause if it:

(i) Has *secular purpose*;

(ii) Has a *primary effect* that neither advances nor inhibits religion; *and*

(iii) Does not produce *excessive government entanglement* with religion.

The Establishment Clause cases can be grouped into three categories: (i) a limited group of cases unconnected to financial aid or education; (ii) cases involving financial aid to religiously affiliated institutions; and (iii) cases concerning religious activities in public schools. The details regarding the Supreme Court rulings are given below.

a. Cases Unconnected to Financial Aid or Education

In cases unconnected to financial aid or education, a good rule of thumb is that a law favoring or burdening religion or a specific religious group in particular will be invalid, but a law favoring or burdening a larger segment of society that happens to include religious groups will be upheld.

Example: The government may not delegate governmental power to religious organizations because such action would involve excessive governmental entanglement. [Larkin v. Grendel's Den, Inc., 456 U.S. 913 (1982)— statute gave church-affiliated schools power to veto nearby liquor licenses]

Compare: The IRS may deny tax exemptions claimed for religious donations when the sums were paid to the church *in exchange for services* (*e.g.*, classes) since this is a general rule that applies to all charities. [Hernandez v. Commissioner of Internal Revenue, 490 U.S. 680 (1989)]

1) **State Legislature Can Employ a Chaplain**
Despite the principle of separation of church and state, the Court has held that a state legislature could employ a chaplain and begin each legislative day with a prayer. [Marsh v. Chambers, 463 U.S. 783 (1983)] This decision was based on the history of legislative prayer in America; it does not modify the "Religious Activities in Public Schools" rulings examined below.

2) **Some Holiday Displays Are Permissible**
If the *government* maintains a holiday-Christmastime display that does not appear to endorse religion, the display will survive review under the three-part Establishment Clause test. If a government's holiday display includes religious symbols (*e.g.*, a nativity scene or a menorah) as well as other holiday decorations (*e.g.*, a Christmas tree or a Santa Claus figure), the courts will hold that the display: (i) has a secular purpose (based on the history of government recognition of holidays); (ii) has a primary nonreligious effect (it does not endorse religion); and (iii) does not create excessive entanglement between government and religion. If the display includes only the religious symbols (*e.g.*, only a nativity scene), it will violate the Establishment Clause because it has a religious effect (it "endorses" religion). [County of Allegheny v. A.C.L.U., 492 U.S. 573 (1989)]

3) **Absolute Right Not to Work on a Sabbath Impermissible**
The state may not force employers to grant all employees an absolute right to refrain from working on their sabbath, since the primary effect of such a law is to advance religion. [Estate of Thornton v. Caldor, 472 U.S. 703 (1985)] However, a state may require employers to make reasonable efforts to accommodate employee religious practices.

4) **Exemptions from Antidiscrimination Laws**
The federal government may exempt religious organizations from the federal statutory prohibition against discrimination in employment on the basis of religion, at least regarding their nonprofit activities. Thus, a janitor can be discharged from his employment at a gymnasium owned by a religious organization (which was open to the public and run as a nonprofit facility) because he was not a member of that religious organization. [Corporation of the Presiding Bishop of the Church of Jesus Christ of Latter-Day Saints v. Amos, 483 U.S. 327 (1987)]

b. **Cases Involving Financial Benefits to Church-Related Institutions**
A statute authorizing governmental aid to a religiously affiliated institution (hospital, school, etc.) must be tested under the general test detailed above (secular purpose, primary effect, and excessive entanglement). However, the Supreme Court applies these tests with greater strictness when the government aid is going to a religiously affiliated grade school or high school than it does when the aid is going to another type of religiously affiliated institution (such as a college or hospital).

1) **Recipient-Based Aid**
The government may give aid in the form of financial assistance to a defined class of persons as long as the class is defined without reference to religion or religious criteria. Such a program is valid even if persons who receive the financial assistance are thereby enabled to attend a religiously affiliated school.
Examples: 1) The Supreme Court upheld a state program that made education subsidy payments directly to a blind or disabled student even though a student used his aid to study at a Christian college for the purpose of becoming a pastor or missionary. The class of persons who received the aid was defined without reference to any religious criteria; only an incidental benefit would go to the religiously affiliated college or vocational training institution. The aid program thus passed review under the purpose, effect, and entanglement tests. [Witters v. Washington Department of Services, 474 U.S. 481 (1986)]

2) The Court held that the Establishment Clause would not prevent a public school district from paying for a sign language interpreter

for a deaf student at a religious high school under a religiously neutral program of aid to all handicapped school children in both public and private schools [Zobrest v. Catalina Foothills School District, 509 U.S. 1 (1993)].

3) The Supreme Court upheld a program that provided tuition vouchers to parents of poor children in kindergarten through the eighth grade which could be used to pay for attending participating public or private schools of their parents' choice, even though a very high percentage of the recipients chose to attend religiously affiliated schools. The program was part of a larger program that also created publicly funded magnet schools and community schools that were independent from the local school district. The Court found that the program did not have the purpose or effect of advancing religion. Its purpose was secular—to provide educational assistance to poor children in a failing public school system. Its primary effect was to provide poor children with funds to attend other schools. Any benefit to the religious schools resulted from parents choosing to send their children to those schools and was not attributable to the government. [Zelman v. Simmons-Harris, 122 S. Ct. 2460 (2002)]

a) **Compare—Tuition Tax Deductions or Credits Limited to Religious School Tuition**
A state may not use a system of statutory grants, tax credits, or tax deductions to reimburse parents or students for tuition paid *only to religiously affiliated schools*. However, a tax deduction to all students or parents based on the actual expenditures for attending any public or private school (including religious schools) has been upheld. [Mueller v. Allen, 463 U.S. 388 (1983)]

It would appear that a valid tax deduction statute must allow a deduction for: (i) expenditures for public as well as private schools; and (ii) some expenditures other than tuition (such as expenditures for school supplies or books) so that public school students or their parents may benefit from the deduction.

2) **Aid to Colleges, Hospitals, Etc.**
The Court will uphold a government grant of aid to the secular activity of a religiously affiliated hospital or college (such as grant to build a new hospital ward or a laboratory-classroom building) as long as the government program requires that the aid be used only for *nonreligious purposes*, and the recipient so agrees in good faith. [Tilton v. Richardson, 403 U.S. 672 (1971); Bradfield v. Roberts, 175 U.S. 291 (1899)]

Example: The Adolescent Family Life Act—which provides for grants of government funds to a variety of public and private (including religiously affiliated) agencies to provide counseling and educational services to young people regarding sexual activity—has been upheld. The Act has a secular purpose (dealing with problems of teenage pregnancy). The Act does not on its face advance religion because a religiously affiliated organization could contractually be required to use the funds for nonreligious counseling. And the Act does not give rise to excessive entanglement because there is no reason to assume that a significant percentage of the funds would be granted to pervasively sectarian institutions. [Bowen v. Kendrick, 487 U.S. 589 (1988)]

3) **Aid to Religiously Affiliated Grade Schools or High Schools**
Programs of aid to these institutions are subject to the same three-part test as are all other laws under the Establishment Clause. All government programs examined by the Supreme Court which provide aid for religiously affiliated grade schools or high schools have been found to have a "secular purpose." However, if significant aid is given to the religious school, the program may be deemed to have a primary effect that advances religion. If the government program has detailed administrative or legislative regulations that are designed to ensure that the aid does not result in a primary effect of advancing religion, the law may be

stricken as giving rise to an excessive entanglement between government and religion.

a) **Aid Upheld**
The Supreme Court has upheld state programs that:

(1) Provide state-approved *textbooks* to *all* students [Board of Education v. Allen, 392 U.S. 236 (1968)] (but note that the state may not loan textbooks to students attending schools that discriminate on the basis of race, since this would violate the Fourteenth Amendment [Norwood v. Harrison, 413 U.S. 455 (1973)]);

(2) Lend religiously neutral instructional materials (*e.g.*, library books, computers) to parochial schools as well as to public and other nonprofit private schools, where the program did not define recipients by reference to religion and the *challenger did not prove* that the neutral aid was used for religious indoctrination. [Mitchell v. Helms, 530 U.S. 793 (2000), *overruling* Meek v. Pittenger, 421 U.S. 349 (1975)];

(3) Provide *transportation to and from school* to *all* students [Everson v. Board of Education, 330 U.S. 1 (1947)];

(4) Reimburse private schools for the expenses of *compiling state required data*, such as student attendance records, or administering and grading *standardized* state educational achievement tests [Committee for Public Education and Religious Liberty v. Regan, 444 U.S. 646 (1980)];

(5) Provide government employees to perform *diagnostic tests* for health and learning problems at private schools [Wolman v. Walter, 443 U.S. 229 (1977)]; and

(6) Provide *"auxiliary services"* (*e.g.*, remedial education, guidance, or job counseling) to all disadvantaged children at their school, including children at parochial schools [Agostini v. Felton, 521 U.S. 203 (1997)].

b) **Aid Invalidated**
The Supreme Court has struck down the following state programs, either because they had a primary effect that advanced religion or because they involved excessive entanglement between government and religion:

(1) Programs paying for *field trip transportation* for private school students (goes too far; primary effect aids religion) [Wolman v. Walter, *supra*];

(2) Programs paying a portion of private school *teachers' salaries* (for their secular classes), since the primary effect would be to advance religion and a system to ensure that the money/teachers not be used for religious purposes would involve excessive entanglements. [Grand Rapids School District v. Ball, 473 U.S. 373 (1985); Lemon v. Kurtzman, 403 U.S. 602 (1971)]; and

(3) Programs reimbursing private schools for *writing achievement tests* (this would have the primary effect of advancing religion since the schools could write tests advancing their religious mission) [Levitt v. Community for Public Education, 413 U.S. 472 (1973)].

4) **Tax Exemption for Religious, Charitable, or Educational Property**
An exemption from property taxation for "real or personal property used exclusively for religious, educational, or charitable purposes" does not violate the Establishment Clause. Neither the purpose nor the effect of such an exemption is the advancement or the inhibition of religion; and it constitutes neither sponsorship nor hostility, nor excessive government entanglement with religion. The "government does not transfer part of its revenue to churches but simply abstains from demanding that the church support the state. . . ." [Walz v. Tax Commission, 397 U.S. 664 (1970)]

5) **Tax Exemption Available Only to Religions**
Although religious schools or religious associations may be included in tax

exemptions available to a variety of secular and religious organizations, a tax exemption that is available only for religious organizations or religious activities violates the Establishment Clause. [Texas Monthly, Inc. v. Bullock, 489 U.S. 1 (1989)—an exemption from the sales and use tax for religious magazines or books (but no other publications) violates the Establishment Clause]

c. Religious Activities in Public Schools

1) Prayer and Bible Reading

Prayer and Bible reading in school are invalid as establishments of religion. [Engel v. Vitale, 370 U.S. 421 (1962); Abington School District v. Schempp, 374 U.S. 203 (1963)] It does not matter whether participation is voluntary or involuntary, and neither does it matter that the prayer period is designated as a period of silent prayer or meditation. [Wallace v. Jaffree, 472 U.S. 38 (1985)] This rule extends to prohibit public school officials from having clerics give invocation and benediction prayers at graduation ceremonies. [Lee v. Weisman, 505 U.S. 577 (1992)] Similarly, a school policy authorizing students to elect whether to have a student invocation before varsity games, to select a student to deliver it, and to decide its content *violates* the Establishment Clause. Unlike student speeches at an open public forum (*see* 4), below), this policy's purpose is to encourage religious messages. [Santa Fe Independent School District v. Doe, 530 U.S. 290 (2000)]

2) Posting Ten Commandments in Classroom Is Invalid

Posting the Ten Commandments on the walls of public school classrooms plainly serves a religious purpose and is invalid despite the legislature's statement that it was for a secular purpose. [Stone v. Graham, 449 U.S. 39 (1980)]

3) Released-Time Programs

a) In Public School Building

Programs in which regular classes end an hour early one day a week and religious instruction is given in public school classrooms to students who request it are invalid. [McCollum v. Board of Education, 333 U.S. 203 (1948)]

b) Nonpublic Building Used

Programs in which participating children go to religious classes conducted at religious centers away from the public school do not violate the Establishment Clause. [Zorach v. Clauson, 343 U.S. 306 (1952)]

4) Accommodation of Religious Students—On Campus Meetings

As discussed at XX.B.1.c., *supra*, under the Free Speech Clause, if a public school allows members of the public and private organizations to use school property when classes are not in session, it cannot deny a religious organization permission to use the property for meetings merely because religious topics will be discussed. Such an "equal access rule" does not violate the Establishment Clause because the primary purpose of such programs is secular (to accommodate all interests), people are not likely to assume that the government endorses the religious ideas discussed, and there is no excessive government entanglement, at least where the meetings are not run by school personnel. [Good News Club v. Milford Central School, 533 U.S. 98 (2001)]

5) Curriculum Controls

A government statute or regulation that modifies a public school curriculum will violate the Establishment Clause if it fails the secular purpose test, primary effect test, or excessive government entanglement test.

Example: A state statute that prohibited the teaching of human biological evolution in the state's public schools was held to violate the Establishment Clause because the Supreme Court found that the legislature had a religious purpose for enacting the statute. [Epperson v. Arkansas, 393 U.S. 97 (1968)] Similarly, the Court invalidated a state statute that prohibited instruction regarding "evolution science" (the theory of human biological evolution) in the public schools unless that instruction was accompanied by instruction regarding "creation science" because the Court found that the legislature enacted this statute for the purpose of promoting religion. [Edwards v. Aguillard, 482 U.S. 578 (1987)]

BAR REVIEW

Contracts

celebrating
35 YEARS
*of preparing
law students
for the bar exam*

CONTRACTS

TABLE OF CONTENTS

I. WHAT IS A CONTRACT?

A. GENERAL DEFINITION
A contract is a promise or set of promises, for breach of which the law gives a remedy, or the performance of which the law in some way recognizes as a duty.

B. LAW GOVERNING CONTRACTS
Generally, the common law governs contracts. However, contracts for the sale of *goods* (*i.e.,* things that are movable) are governed by special rules found in Article 2 of the Uniform Commercial Code ("U.C.C."). The common law still applies to contracts for the sale of goods, but any rules in the U.C.C. that conflict with the common law replace the common law. The differences between Article 2 and the common law are often pointed out in this outline, but are explained in more detail in the Sales outline.

C. TYPES OF CONTRACTS

1. Types of Contracts as to Formation
Contracts are frequently described as express, implied, or quasi. Only the first two are actually contracts, and they differ in no way other than the manner in which they are formed.

a. Express Contract
Express contracts are formed *by language*, oral or written.

b. Implied Contract
Implied contracts are formed by manifestations of assent other than oral or written language, *i.e., by conduct*.

c. Quasi-Contract
Quasi-contracts are *not contracts* at all. They are constructed by courts to *avoid unjust enrichment* by permitting the plaintiff to bring an action in restitution to recover the amount of the benefit conferred on the defendant. Their only relationship to genuine contracts is historical.

2. Types of Contracts as to Acceptance

a. Traditional Bilateral/Unilateral Contracts

1) Bilateral Contracts—Exchange of Mutual Promises
The traditional bilateral contract was one consisting of the exchange of mutual promises, *i.e.,* a promise for a promise, in which each party is both a promisor and a promisee.
Example: Sidney promises to sell Blackacre to Bertram for $6,000, and Bertram promises to purchase Blackacre at that price.

2) Unilateral Contracts—Acceptance by Performance
The traditional unilateral contract was one in which the offer requested performance rather than a promise. Here, the offeror-promisor would promise to pay upon the *completion of the requested act* by the promisee. Once the act was completed, a contract was formed. In such contracts, there is one promisor and one promisee.
Example: Susan promises to pay Charles $5 if he will deliver a textbook to Rick. Charles is not obligated to deliver the book, but if he does in fact deliver it, Susan is obligated to pay him the $5.

b. Modern View—Most Contracts Are Bilateral

1) Acceptance by Promise or Start of Performance
Under the U.C.C. and the Restatement (Second) of Contracts, it is possible to form a bilateral contract by starting performance. *All* offers are "doubtful" or "indifferent" offers, which may be accepted by promising or by performing, unless clearly indicated otherwise by the language or circumstances. In this typical situation, an offer that is accepted by the beginning of performance constitutes a bilateral contract. Therefore, it is no longer accurate to suggest that bilateral contracts are relegated to an exchange of promises.

> *Example:* Acme Co. orders specifically manufactured goods from Barnes Manufacturing Co. Recognizing the speed with which the order must be filled, Barnes begins to manufacture the ordered item shortly after the order is received. This constitutes an acceptance of the offer and creates an implied promise on the part of Barnes to complete manufacture. *Note:* Notification within a reasonable time is essential in such cases as a condition to the duty of Acme Co. to pay once the goods are completed.

2) Unilateral Contracts Limited to Two Circumstances

Neither the U.C.C. nor the Second Restatement employs the term "unilateral contract." In fact, under the U.C.C. and Second Restatement, a traditional unilateral contract occurs in only two situations: (i) where the offeror clearly (unambiguously) indicates that ***completion of performance is the only manner of acceptance***—the offeror is the master of the offer and may create the offer in this fashion; and (ii) where there is an ***offer to the public***, such as a reward offer, which so clearly contemplates acceptance by performance rather than a promise (not to mention the total ineffectiveness of a promise in such a situation), that only the performance requested in the offer will manifest acceptance.

Note: While the U.C.C. and Second Restatement are clear along these lines, you should remember the traditional distinctions between bilateral and unilateral contracts until the new usage is firmly entrenched.

3) Test for Determining Bilateral vs. Unilateral Contracts

Under the old view of the bilateral/unilateral dichotomy *or* the Second Restatement/U.C.C. view, the only workable test to decide whether the contract is bilateral or unilateral is whether, at the time the contract is formed, ***each party has a right and a duty*** (bilateral) or ***one party only has a right and the other party only has a duty*** (unilateral). (*See* II.E., *infra,* for further discussion of unilateral vs. bilateral contracts.)

3. Types of Contracts as to Validity

a. Void Contract

A void contract is one that is totally ***without any legal effect*** from the beginning (*e.g.,* an agreement to commit a crime).

b. Voidable Contract

A voidable contract is one that one or both parties may ***elect to avoid*** or to ratify (*e.g.,* contracts of infants or mentally ill parties).

c. Unenforceable Contract

An unenforceable contract is an agreement that is otherwise valid, but that may not be enforceable due to ***various defenses*** extraneous to contract formation, such as the statute of limitations or Statute of Frauds.

D. CREATION OF A CONTRACT

When a suit is brought in which one party seeks to enforce a contract or to obtain damages for breach of contract, a court must first decide whether there was in fact a contract. In making this determination, a court will ask the following three basic questions:

1. Was there ***mutual assent***?

2. Was there ***consideration*** or some substitute therefor?

3. Are there any ***defenses*** to creation of the contract?

II. MUTUAL ASSENT—OFFER AND ACCEPTANCE

A. IN GENERAL

Mutual assent is often said to be an agreement on the "same bargain at the same time"—"a meeting of the minds." The process by which parties reach this meeting of the minds generally is some form of negotiation, during which, at some point, one party makes a proposal (an offer) and the other agrees to it (an acceptance). An actual subjective meeting of the minds is not necessary. Rather, courts use an *objective measure*, by which each party is bound to the *apparent intention* that he manifested to the other(s).

B. THE OFFER

An offer creates a power of acceptance in the offeree and a corresponding liability on the part of the offeror. For a communication to be an offer, it must create a *reasonable expectation* in the offeree that the offeror is willing to enter into a contract on the basis of the offered terms. In deciding whether a communication creates this reasonable expectation, you should ask the following three questions:

(i)   Was there an expression of a *promise*, *undertaking*, *or commitment* to enter into a contract?

(ii) Were there *certainty and definiteness* in the essential terms?

(iii) Was there *communication* of the above to the offeree?

1. Promise, Undertaking, or Commitment

For a communication to be an offer, it must contain a promise, undertaking, or commitment to enter into a contract, rather than a mere invitation to begin preliminary negotiations (*i.e.,* there must be an *intent* to enter into a contract). The criteria used to determine whether a communication is an offer include the following:

a. Language

The language used may show that an offer was or was not intended. Technical language such as "I offer" or "I promise" is useful to show that an offer was made, but not necessary. Certain language is generally construed as contemplating an invitation to deal, preliminary negotiations, or "feelers," rather than an offer. This includes phrases such as "I quote," "I am asking $30 for," and "I would consider selling for." No mechanical formula is available.

Example: "I quote you . . . for immediate acceptance" will probably be construed as an offer. By coupling words of invitation with words of offer, the offeror has at least created an *ambiguity*, which will be *construed in favor of the offeree*.

b. Surrounding Circumstances

The surrounding circumstances will be considered by courts in determining whether an offer exists. For example, where the statement is made in jest, anger, or by way of bragging, and the statement is reasonably understood in this context, it will have no legal effect. However, where the statement is subjectively intended to be in jest but reasonably understood by the hearer to have been made seriously, the statement is an offer because it is interpreted objectively (*i.e.,* according to a reasonable person's expectations).

c. Prior Practice and Relationship of the Parties

In determining whether certain remarks constitute an offer rather than preliminary negotiations, the court will look to the prior relationship and practice of the parties involved.

d. Method of Communication

1) Use of Broad Communications Media

The broader the communicating media, *e.g.,* publications, the more likely it is that the courts will view the communication as merely the *solicitation of an offer*. (Note, herein, an exception as to reward offers.)

2) Advertisements, Etc.

Advertisements, catalogs, circular letters, and the like containing price quotations are *usually* construed as mere *invitations for offers*. They are announcements of prices at which the seller is willing to receive offers. In certain situations, courts have treated advertisements as *offers* where the language of the advertisement can be construed as containing a promise, where the terms are certain and definite, and where the offeree(s) is clearly identified.

Example: Defendant store advertised a particular coat worth $140 for $1 on a "first come, first served" basis. *Held:* Valid offer to first person accepting on this basis as nothing was left open for negotiation.

e. Industry Custom
The courts will also look to generally accepted custom in the industry in determining whether the proposal qualifies as an offer.

f. Certainty and Definiteness of Terms
Certainty and definiteness of terms is a separate element of an offer. This also bears on intention, however. The more definite and certain the terms of a communication are, the more reasonable the receiver's expectation that the sender has expressed an intention to contract. Thus, a court will look at whether the communication calls for a simple "yes" or "no" answer. The *more inquiries* that are required, the more likely it is that the court will view the communication as merely part of *preliminary negotiations* not amounting to an offer.

2. Terms Must Be Definite and Certain
An offer must be definite and certain in its terms. The basic inquiry is whether enough of the essential terms have been provided so that a contract including them would be *capable of being enforced*. The principle is that the parties make their own contract; the courts do not make it for them. What is essential for the requisite certainty in an offer will, of course, depend upon the kind of contract contemplated. "Essential" elements include: (i) the *identity of the offeree* and the *subject matter*; (ii) the *price* to be paid; (iii) the *time* of payment, delivery, or performance; (iv) the *quantity* involved; and (v) the *nature of the work* to be performed. However, if the parties fail to explicitly state one or more of these essential elements, the court may in certain circumstances attempt to supply the missing term(s). (*See* b.2), *infra*.)

a. Identification of the Offeree
To be considered an offer, a statement must sufficiently identify the offeree or a class to which she belongs to justify the inference that the offeror intended to create a power of acceptance.

Examples: 1) In the example above with the $140 coat selling for $1, the "first come, first served" language eliminates any identification problem.

2) Harvey promises a reward to the person who captures a wanted fugitive. Although the offeree is unidentified and indeed unidentifiable at the time the offer is made, the performance of the requested act constitutes both an identification of the offeree and an acceptance.

b. Definiteness of Subject Matter
The subject matter of the deal must be certain, since a court can enforce a promise only if it can tell with reasonable accuracy what the promise is. A promise generally will be enforceable even if it does not spell out every material term, as long as it contains some *objective standard* to supply the missing terms.

1) Requirements for Specific Types of Contracts

a) Real Estate Transactions
An offer involving realty must identify the *land* and the *price* terms. The land must be identified with some particularity, and the courts will not supply reasonable prices or reasonable mortgage terms.

b) Sale of Goods
In a contract for the sale of goods, the *quantity* being offered must be certain or capable of being made certain.

(1) "Requirements" and "Output" Contracts
In a requirements contract, a buyer promises to buy from a certain seller all the goods she requires, and the seller agrees to sell that amount to the buyer. In an output contract, a seller promises to sell to a certain buyer all the goods the seller produces, and the buyer agrees to buy that amount from the seller. Although no specific quantity is mentioned in offers to make these contracts, the offers are sufficiently definite because the quantity is *capable* of being made certain by reference to objective, extrinsic facts (*i.e.,* the buyer's actual requirements or the seller's actual output).

> **(a) Quantity Cannot Be Unreasonably Disproportionate**
> It is assumed that the parties will act in good faith; hence, there may not be a tender of or a demand for a quantity unreasonably disproportionate to a stated estimate or to prior output or requirements.

> **(b) Going Business vs. New Business**
> Some courts draw a distinction between a going business and a new business. These courts will not enforce a requirements contract with a new business because the requirements of a new business are uncertain.

(2) Reasonable Range of Choices
An offer allowing one to specify an item within a reasonable range of choices may be sufficiently definite to result in a contract if accepted.

Example: Seller states to Buyer: "I will sell you any of these motorcycles for $1,000. Pick one." These words will result in a contract when Buyer's choice is made and manifested.

c) Employment Contracts
In contracts for employment, the ***duration*** of the employment must be specified. If not, the offer, if accepted, is construed as creating a contract terminable at the will of either party. Some courts hold that if the offer states a rate of pay, *e.g.,* $800 per month, a contract is created for the minimum period stated.

2) Inference of Reasonable Terms
Not every term need be spelled out completely. The majority of jurisdictions and the U.C.C. have provided that uncertainty as to some terms is not fatal; *i.e.,* reasonable terms will be supplied by the court. These terms will be supplied, however, only where they are consistent with the parties' intent as otherwise expressed. The terms that can be supplied by a "reasonableness" standard include the following:

a) Price Term
Unless the parties have shown at the time of contracting that they do not want a contract until they have agreed on price, a ***reasonable price*** will be supplied. [U.C.C. §2-305]

b) Specific Time Provision
Courts will hold that performance within a ***reasonable time*** was implied. [U.C.C. §2-309]

3) Vague Terms
The presumption that the parties' intent was to include a reasonable term goes to supplying ***missing*** terms. The presumption ***cannot*** be made if the parties have ***included*** a term that makes the contract too vague to be enforced. The problem then is that the parties have manifested an intent that cannot be determined.

Examples: 1) An agreement to divide profits "on a liberal basis" is too vague to be enforced.

2) An agreement to purchase a parcel of land for "$8,000 or less" is also too vague.

a) Vagueness Can Be Cured by Part Performance
Where part performance supplies the needed clarification of the terms, it can be used to cure vagueness.

b) Uncertainty Can Be Cured by Acceptance
If uncertainty results because the offeree is given a choice of alternative performances, the offer becomes definite when the offeree communicates her choice. (*See* above example about choice of motorcycle for $1,000.)

c) Focus on Contract
In short, the ***contract*** (as distinguished from the offer) must be definite and certain in its terms—hence, even if the offer lacks certainty, the problem can

be cured if there is some way in which the offer is capable of being made certain, *e.g.,* by part performance or acceptance.

4) Terms to Be Agreed On
Often, an offer will state that some term is to be agreed on at a future date. If the term is a *material* term, the offer is *too uncertain*. The courts will not supply a reasonable term, as the parties have provided otherwise. However, the U.C.C. permits a reasonable *price* term to be supplied by the court under these circumstances if the other evidence indicates that the parties intended to form a contract.

3. Communication to Offeree
To have the power to accept, the offeree must have *knowledge* of the offer. Therefore, the proposal must be communicated to her.

Example:　　Chauncey returned Bowater's lost briefcase unaware that Bowater had placed an advertisement offering a $20 reward for its return. Since the offer had not been communicated, there could not be mutual assent. Hence, there is no contract.

C. TERMINATION OF OFFER
The power of acceptance created by an offer ends when the offer is terminated. The mutual assent requirement obviously cannot be met where the termination occurs before acceptance is effective. Thus, you must establish whether the offer has been terminated, and if so, in what fashion.

1. Termination by Acts of Parties

a. Termination by Offeror—Revocation
A revocation is the retraction of an offer by the offeror. A revocation terminates the offeree's power of acceptance if it is communicated to her *before she accepts*.

1) Methods of Communication

a) Revocation by Direct Communication
Revocation directly communicated to the offeree by the offeror terminates the offer.

(1) Revocation by Publication
Offers made by publication may be terminated by publication of revocation *through comparable means*.

Example:　　An offer published in *The New York Times* may be revoked by publication in *The New York Times*. It may not be revoked by publication in *Readers' Digest* or by a TV spot.

b) Revocation by Indirect Communication
The offer may be effectively terminated if the offeree *indirectly* receives: (i) correct information, (ii) from a reliable source, (iii) of acts of the offeror that would indicate to a reasonable person that the offeror no longer wishes to make the offer.

Example:　　Offeree, before attempting to accept Offeror's offer to sell Greenacre, was informed by a reliable third party that Offeror had sold Greenacre to another. *Held:* Offeror revoked the offer.

2) Effective When Received
A revocation is generally effective when *received* by the offeree. Where revocation is by publication, it is effective when *published*.

3) Limitations on Offeror's Power to Revoke
Offers not supported by consideration or detrimental reliance can be revoked at will by the offeror, even if he has promised not to revoke for a certain period. There are, however, certain situations where the offeror's power to terminate the offer is limited.

a) Options
An option is a distinct contract in which the *offeree gives consideration* for a promise by the offeror not to revoke an outstanding offer.

b) **Firm Offers Under the U.C.C.**

An offer by a *merchant* to buy or sell goods in a *signed writing* that, by its terms, gives assurances that it will be held open is not revocable for lack of consideration during the time stated, or if no time is stated, for a reasonable time (but in no event may such period exceed three months). If the term assuring the offer will be held open is on a form supplied by the offeree, it must be separately signed by the offeror. [U.C.C. §2-205]

Note: Under U.C.C. Article 2, a "merchant" is one who deals in the type of goods involved in the transaction, or who through his occupation has specialized knowledge of the business practices involved.

c) **Detrimental Reliance**

Where the offeror could reasonably expect that the offeree would rely to her detriment on the offer, it will be held *irrevocable as an option contract for a reasonable length of time*. At the very least, the offeree would be entitled to relief measured by the extent of any detrimental reliance. [Rest. 2d §87] The case law indicates that this may be limited to those situations in which the offeror would *reasonably contemplate reliance* by the offeree in using the offer before it is accepted.

Example: A general contractor solicited bids from various subcontractors before making its own irrevocable offer on a construction project. For the subcontractor to be held to its offer, the subcontractor must reasonably have foreseen the possible use of its subcontracting bid in the making of the general contractor's irrevocable offer.

d) **Part Performance—True Unilateral Contract Offers**

If the offer is clearly one for a unilateral contract (*i.e.,* clearly requiring acceptance by complete performance rather than a promise), the problem is whether the offer may be revoked after the offeree has begun performance in reliance on the offer. Traditionally, a unilateral contract could be revoked at any time before acceptance, *i.e.,* before performance of the requested act was completed. Thus, under the traditional rule, the offeree would be at the offeror's mercy until she completed performance. However, modern courts usually avoid this harsh result by applying the following concepts:

(1) **Implied Contract for Reasonable Time**

Under the First and Second Restatements, as well as the U.C.C., an offer becomes *irrevocable once performance has begun*. Note that the unilateral contract will not be formed until the total act is complete. However, once the offeree begins to perform, she is given a *reasonable time to complete performance* during which time the offer is irrevocable. Note also that the offeree is *not bound* to complete performance—she may withdraw at any time prior to completion of performance.

Example: Matt offers Lisa $500 if she will paint his house, insisting that the acceptance occur only by the act of painting the house rather than through Lisa's promise. Lisa begins to paint the house. Matt attempts to revoke the offer. Matt's attempt at revocation is ineffective since Lisa must have a reasonable time in which to complete the act of painting. If Matt refuses to allow Lisa to continue to paint, Matt will be in breach of contract and will be liable for damages.

(a) **First Restatement**

The First Restatement reaches the above result by holding that a contract is formed at the moment performance is begun, but the offeror's duty of performance is conditional upon completion of the requested act within a reasonable time or within the time stated in the offer. [Rest. §45]

(b) **Second Restatement**

Under the Second Restatement, an *option contract* is formed upon the start of performance by the offeree, making the offer irrevocable for a reasonable time. It is as if the offeree had paid consideration to keep the offer open for a reasonable time. [Rest. 2d §45]

(2) Series of Acts—Divisibility
Where the consideration on both sides may be broken into clear segments, the court may find that the proposed "unilateral" contract is, in reality, several distinct contracts. In this case, performance of one severable part of the offeree's consideration will bind the offeror to some specific severable duty. The offeror could, of course, withdraw the offer at any time with respect to *future acts* of the series.

(3) Offeree Compensated to Extent of Performance
The court could allow the offeror to revoke, provided that he pays the offeree to the extent of her performance in reliance on the offer. The amount of compensation would, of course, depend on how reasonable the reliance was, *e.g.,* did the offeree reasonably expect the offeror to keep the offer open until she had performed? Note that the "reliance" interest of the offeree could very well exceed the value of the benefit received by the offeror.

(4) What Is Part Performance?

(a) Preparations to Perform
The rules limiting the offeror's power to revoke an offer for a unilateral contract only apply where the offeree has *embarked* on performance. They do not apply where she is only preparing to perform. Note, however, that preparations to perform *may constitute detrimental reliance* sufficient to make the offeror's promise binding. [Rest. 2d §90]

(b) Offeror Refuses to Accept Performance
What happens if performance is tendered by the offeree but refused by the offeror? If the offeror's cooperation is necessary for performance, his withholding of it upon the tender of part performance is the equivalent of part performance. [Rest. 2d §45]

e) Part Performance—Offer Indifferent as to Manner of Acceptance
As noted above, most offers are indifferent as to the manner of acceptance, and thus, a bilateral contract may be formed upon the start of performance by the offeree. (*See* I.C.2.b., *supra.*) Therefore, once the offeree *begins performance,* the contract is complete and *revocation* becomes *impossible. But note:* Notification of the start of performance may be necessary. (*See* E.4.b., *infra.*)

b. Termination by Offeree

1) Rejection

a) Express Rejection
An express rejection is a statement by the offeree that she does not intend to accept the offer. Such a rejection will terminate the offer. [Rest. 2d §36]

b) Counteroffer as Rejection
A counteroffer is an offer made by the *offeree* to the offeror that contains the same subject matter as the original offer, but differs in its terms. A counteroffer serves as a rejection of the original offer *as well as a new offer*. [Rest. 2d §39] This usually happens in two situations:

(i) Counteroffer combined with express rejection, *e.g.,* "Not at that price, but I'll take it at $200."

(ii) Acceptance conditional upon additional terms, *e.g.,* "I'll take it at that price, but only if it is also equipped with air conditioning."

Note: The U.C.C. provides for exceptions to the above general treatment in the "battle of forms" provision. (*See* D.2.b., *infra.*)

(1) Distinguish Mere Inquiry

Distinguish between a counteroffer (which constitutes a rejection) and a mere inquiry. The latter will not terminate the offer when it is consistent with the idea that the offeree is still keeping the original proposal under consideration.

Example: "I am still thinking, but can give you an answer right away if you want to lower the price now." This is merely an inquiry, not a rejection.

Indeed, the offeree may be accepting the offer—thus creating a contract—and merely inquiring about additional matters, or merely restating the duties imposed by the contract. The test is whether a *reasonable person* would believe that the original offer had been rejected.

Example: Even though the offeree suggests a time for performance in her acceptance of the offer, her otherwise valid acceptance is not converted into a counteroffer.

c) Effective When Received

The rejection is effective when *received* by the offeror.

d) Revival of Offer

If an offer is rejected, the offeror may restate the same offer and create a new power of acceptance. Some courts refer to this as the revival of the original offer. It is more precise to suggest that a new offer, although the same as the original offer, has been made.

2) Lapse of Time

a) Must Accept Within Specified or Reasonable Time

The offeree must accept the offer within the time period specified, or if no time period is specified, within a reasonable time. If she does not do so, then she will have allowed the offer to terminate. (*Note:* Where the offer's terms are unclear as to time, *e.g.,* "by return mail," the time limit is what a reasonable person in the offeree's position would have assumed.)

b) Look to When Offer Is Received by Offeree

If the offer provides that it will expire within a particular time period, that period commences when the offer is received by the offeree. If the offer is delayed in transmission and this fact *is or should have been apparent to the offeree*, the offer terminates at the time it would have expired had there been no delay. All relevant facts must be considered in determining whether this knowledge is present. These include, *e.g.,* date of letter, postmark, postal strike, and any subsequent statements made by the offeror.

2. Termination by Operation of Law

a. Termination by Death or Insanity of Parties

If either of the parties dies or is adjudicated insane prior to acceptance, the offer is terminated. It is *not* necessary that the death or insanity be *communicated* to the other party. [Rest. 2d §48] (*Compare:* Supervening mental incapacity of the offeror without an adjudication thereof will terminate an offer only if the offeree is aware of the incapacity.) Note, however, that the offer will *not* terminate in this fashion if the rules limiting an offeror's power to terminate are applicable (*e.g.,* in an option contract, the offer becomes irrevocable because the offeree gives consideration to keep it open).

b. Termination by Destruction of Subject Matter

Destruction of the subject matter terminates the offeree's power of acceptance. [Rest. 2d §36]

c. Termination by Supervening Legal Prohibition of Proposed Contract

If the subject matter of the proposed contract becomes illegal, the offer will terminate. [Rest. 2d §36]

Example: Lucky Lou offers Vegas Vernon a share in his casino business. Prior to acceptance, a law is passed banning casinos. The offer is automatically terminated.

D. THE ACCEPTANCE

An acceptance is a manifestation of assent to the terms of an offer in the manner prescribed or authorized in the offer. Through this manifestation of assent, the offeree exercises the power given her by the offeror to create a contract.

1. Who May Accept

a. Party to Whom Offer Is Addressed or Directed
Generally, only the person to whom an offer is addressed has the power of acceptance. This is so even though the offer does not call for personal performance or special financial responsibility on the part of the offeree. One may also have the power of acceptance if she is a member of a class to which an offer has been directed. If the offer is made to the general public, anyone may qualify as an offeree. If the offer requests performance from an unlimited number of persons, performance by anyone knowing of the offer will cut off the power of every other person to accept, provided that the offeror desires only one performance and there is no indication that he is willing to pay more than once.

b. Assignment of Offeree's Power of Acceptance
Unlike rights under an existing contract, the offeree's power of acceptance *cannot be assigned.* An exception exists for option contracts since the power to accept is itself a contract right in these contracts.

2. Acceptance Must Be Unequivocal
Traditional contract law insisted on an absolute and unequivocal acceptance of each and every term of the offer.

a. Common Law Rule
At common law, any different or additional terms in the acceptance make the response a *rejection and counteroffer.* Distinguish the following:

1) Statements that Make Implicit Terms Explicit
Statements by the offeree that make implicit terms explicit do not prevent acceptance. For example, the statement by an offeree, "I accept provided you convey marketable title," is a valid acceptance because the obligation to convey marketable title is implicit in the offer to sell.

2) "Grumbling Acceptance"
A "grumbling acceptance" (*i.e.,* an acceptance accompanied by an expression of dissatisfaction) is an effective acceptance as long as it stops short of actual dissent.

3) Request for Clarification
A request for clarification does not necessarily amount to a rejection and counteroffer.

b. U.C.C. Rule
In contracts for the sale of goods, the U.C.C. substantially alters the common law rules on acceptance. The proposal of additional or different terms by the offeree in a definite and timely acceptance does *not* constitute a rejection and counteroffer. Rather, the acceptance is effective unless it is *expressly* made conditional on assent to the additional terms. Whether the additional or different terms become part of the contract depends on the status of the parties.

1) Party Not a Merchant—Terms of Offer Govern
If one (or both) of the parties to the contract is not a merchant, the additional or different terms are considered to be mere proposals to modify the contract that do not become part of the contract unless the offeror agrees.

2) Both Parties Merchants—Acceptance Terms Usually Included
If both parties to the contract are merchants, *additional* terms automatically become part of the contract unless:

(i) They *materially alter* the original terms of the offer (*e.g.,* they change a party's risk or the remedies available);

(ii) The offer *expressly limits acceptance* to the terms of the offer; or

(iii) The *offeror has already objected* to the particular terms, or *objects within a reasonable time* after notice of them is received.

Note: There is a split of authority over whether terms in the acceptance that are *different* from (as opposed to additional to) the terms in the offer will become part of the contract. Some courts treat different terms *like additional terms*, and follow the test set out above in determining whether the terms should be part of the contract. Other courts follow the *"knockout rule,"* which states that conflicting terms in the offer and acceptance are knocked out of the contract because each party is assumed to object to the inclusion of such terms in the contract. Under the knockout rule, gaps left by knocked out terms are filled by the U.C.C. (*e.g.,* when the date of delivery differs in the offer and the acceptance, the U.C.C. provides that delivery must be made within a reasonable time).

3. Generally, Acceptance Must Be Communicated
The general rule is that the acceptance must be communicated to the offeror. (The few exceptions to this rule are discussed in c., *infra*.)

a. Objective Manifestation of Assent
An acceptance, like an offer, is judged on an objective standard. The offeree's subjective state of mind is irrelevant.

b. When Effective

1) Common Law Rule
Under traditional common law rules, whether an acceptance became effective upon dispatch or receipt depended on whether the offeree used an authorized mode of communication. Ordinarily, the mode used by the offeror to transmit the offer was impliedly authorized for transmittal of the acceptance.

2) Modern Rule (U.C.C. and Second Restatement)
Today most courts ignore the technical common law rule. The U.C.C. states that an offer may be accepted by any "medium reasonable in the circumstances." [U.C.C. §2-206] The offeror may still limit acceptance to a particular means, but he must do so unambiguously since any ambiguity will allow the offeree to use any reasonable means.

3) The Mailbox Rule
Acceptance by mail or similar means creates a contract at the *moment of dispatch*, provided that the mail is properly addressed and stamped, *unless:*

(i) The *offer stipulates* that acceptance is not effective until received; or

(ii) An *option contract* is involved (an acceptance under an option contract is effective only upon *receipt* [Rest. 2d §63]).

Note: Since in most states a revocation is effective only upon receipt (*see* C.1.a.2), *supra*), under the mailbox rule if the offeree dispatches an acceptance *before he receives a revocation* sent by the offeror, a contract is formed. This is true even though the acceptance is dispatched after the revocation is dispatched and received after the revocation is received.

a) Effect of Offeree Sending Both Acceptance and Rejection
Because a rejection is effective only when received, an offeree sending both an acceptance and rejection could create problems for the offeror if the mailbox rule were applicable; *e.g.,* a contract would be created when the acceptance was dispatched even if the offeror received the rejection and relied on it before receiving the acceptance.

(1) Offeree Sends Rejection, Then Acceptance—Mailbox Rule Does Not Apply
If the offeree sends a rejection and then sends an acceptance, the mailbox rule does not apply. Whichever one is *received first* is effective.

(2) Offeree Sends Acceptance, Then Rejection—Mailbox Rule Generally Applies

If the offeree sends the acceptance first, the mailbox rule applies; *i.e.,* a contract is created upon dispatch of the acceptance. However, if the offeror received the rejection first and *changed his position in reliance* on it, the offeree will be *estopped* from enforcing the contract.

4) Acceptance by Unauthorized Means

An acceptance transmitted by unauthorized means or improperly transmitted by authorized means may still be *effective if it is actually received* by the offeror while the offer is still in existence.

Examples: 1) Bailey makes an offer to Janet specifying that acceptance should be by telegram. Janet mails Bailey her acceptance. The acceptance will not be effective upon dispatch of the letter but only upon receipt by Bailey, if the offer is still open.

2) Janet, in a situation where the mailbox rule otherwise applies, incorrectly addressed the envelope in mailing back the acceptance. It will be effective upon receipt if the offer is still open.

5) "Crossing" Offers

If offers stating precisely the same terms cross in the mail, they do *not* give rise to a contract despite the apparent meeting of the minds. An offer cannot be accepted if there is no knowledge of it.

c. Exception—Acceptance Without Communication

Under a few circumstances, an executory bilateral contract may be formed without any communication of acceptance.

1) Express Waiver in Offer

The terms of an offer may expressly waive any communication of acceptance. An example of this type of offer is a mail order form that states, "Your order is an offer only, pending acceptance by our home office." In such a situation, the party making the order becomes the offeror and his response constitutes an offer that incorporates the term regarding approval by the home office. Absent a prior course of dealing or trade practices to the contrary (*see* 3), *infra*), a contract is formed without the offeree's communication of acceptance.

2) Act as Acceptance

The offer may require some act to signify acceptance such as wearing a yellow carnation in one's lapel. When the offeree performs the act requested with the intent of accepting, a contract is formed.

Caution: Do not confuse this means of forming a bilateral contract—doing an act to manifest a promise—with a unilateral contract, where the offeree's acceptance is by performance of the act specified by the offeror.

3) Silence as Acceptance

Although the offeree cannot be forced to speak under penalty of having her silence treated as an acceptance, if the offeree silently takes offered benefits, the courts will often find an acceptance. This is especially true if prior dealings between the parties, or trade practices known to both, create a commercially reasonable expectation by the offeror that silence represents an acceptance. In such a case, the offeree is under a duty to notify the offeror if she does not intend to accept. [Rest. 2d §69]

E. UNILATERAL OR BILATERAL CONTRACT—A CRITICAL DISTINCTION AT THE FORMATION STAGE

If an offer makes acceptance possible only by performing a stipulated act, a unilateral contract is contemplated. By contrast, if the offeror promises contractual liability in exchange for a counter-promise by the offeree to do a stipulated act, the exchange of promises creates a bilateral contract.

1. Unilateral Contracts

A unilateral contract is advantageous for the offeror since his offer can be accepted only by the contract performance he desires.

a. **Test**
There is a unilateral contract if at the time the contract is formed only the *offeror has executory* (unperformed) *duties.*
Example: Kay offers to pay $10 for the return of a lost ring. Kay's contractual liability to pay the reward does not arise unless the specified article is returned. Once the offeree tenders the ring, a contract is formed, and, at that time, only the offeror's duty to pay remains undischarged.

b. **Risk to Offeree**
To protect the offeree who has commenced but not completed performance, the courts have developed the various limitations on revocation previously discussed.

2. Bilateral Contract
If the offeree need only *promise to do an act*, a bilateral contract is contemplated. The offer is accepted by communicating the required promise to the offeror. Some jurisdictions hold that performing the specified act without making the promise will also suffice.
Example: Bill writes Linda, "I will pay you $1,000 if you agree to deliver 500 gallons of #2 heating oil to my residence before November 1." Linda can form an executory bilateral contract by communicating her promise to make the requested delivery. The contract is bilateral since, at the moment of contract formation, both parties have executory duties (Linda to deliver the oil and Bill to pay for it).

3. Interpreting Contracts as Unilateral or Bilateral
In many cases, it is difficult to tell whether a given offer proposes a unilateral or bilateral contract. For example, "I'll pay you $1,000 to landscape my lot," appears to contemplate acceptance by doing the act of landscaping. Yet this interpretation would place all the risk on the offeree. Accordingly, modern courts generally interpret an offer as *unilateral only if its terms clearly warn* the offeree that an act is required for acceptance. They reach this result by using one of the following methods.

a. **Construe Ambiguous Offers as Bilateral**
If the offer could be interpreted as one for either a unilateral or bilateral contract, many courts automatically construe it as an offer for a bilateral contract. They reason that bilateral contracts afford immediate rights and protection for both parties.

b. **Allow Acceptance by Act or Promise**
Unless an offer expressly limits acceptance to an act, the U.C.C. and Second Restatement provide that it may be accepted either by performing the requested act or by a timely promise to do so. [U.C.C. §2-206(1)(b); Rest. 2d §32]

1) **Shipment of Nonconforming Goods**
While at common law a tender of nonconforming goods does not constitute an acceptance, under U.C.C. section 2-206(1)(b), the shipment of nonconforming goods results in both an acceptance and a breach of the newly formed contract unless the shipper precedes or accompanies the tender with notice that the shipment is offered only as an *accommodation*. The buyer is not required to accept accommodation goods and may reject them. If he does, the shipper is not in breach and may reclaim the accommodation goods because her tender does not constitute an acceptance of the buyer's original offer.

4. Formation Problems Peculiar to Unilateral Contracts

a. **Acceptance of Unilateral Contract**
In acting as requested by an offer for a unilateral contract, the offeree must act with *knowledge* of the offer and be *motivated* by it.
Examples: 1) Peter offers a reward in a local newspaper for return of a lost watch. Paula, who has not seen the newspaper and is otherwise unaware of the offer, finds the watch and returns it to Peter. Paula has no contractual right to the reward.

2) Paula reads the advertisement and realizes that the watch that she had purchased earlier that day is stolen. Fearing criminal prosecution, Paula returns the watch to Peter. Paula has no contractual right to the reward because she lacks the requisite motivation.

3) A *minority* of jurisdictions would give Paula a contractual right to the reward, even without knowledge or motivation, on the theory that Peter has gained the benefit of his bargain and should therefore be obliged to perform.

b. Duty to Give Notice of Performance
Acceptance of an offer to form a unilateral contract is generally accomplished by performance of the requested act without notice to the offeror. In some situations, there is a duty to notify.

1) Offeror Requests Notice
If the offeror requests notice of the acceptance, the offeree is under a duty to notify him.

2) Act Would Not Normally Come to Offeror's Attention
Where the requested performance would not normally come to the offeror's attention within a reasonable time, the offeree has a duty to give notice within a reasonable time after performance. Otherwise, the offeror might make a duplicate offer to another party who might perform the same act.

Example: In an offer of guaranty, Joe writes to Susan, "Loan Tim $1,000; if he fails to repay you when due, I will repay you." When Susan lends the money to Tim, Joe is liable to Susan as guarantor, but that liability may be discharged unless Susan gives notice of acceptance to Joe.

5. Formation Problems Peculiar to Bilateral Contracts

a. Acceptance of Bilateral Contract
Any objective manifestation of the offeree's counterpromise, whether by words or acts, is usually sufficient for acceptance and the formation of a bilateral contract.

Example: Jennifer offers to purchase Steve's automobile for $1,000, specifying that Steve accept the offer by wearing a yellow shirt to lunch next Tuesday. Steve can accept the offer only by acting as requested. But note that Jennifer has only bargained for Steve's promise to sell the car; the act required for acceptance manifests Steve's counterpromise, but does not form a unilateral contract.

If Steve simply tenders the automobile, some courts would find a valid unilateral contract. Most, however, would construe Steve's tender of the car as a rejection and counteroffer since Jennifer bargained for a promise rather than an act.

Steve must know of the offer to accept. If he simply wears a yellow shirt without knowing of Jennifer's offer, there is no acceptance and no bilateral contract.

1) Subjective Intent Is Irrelevant
A bilateral contract is formed when an offeree with knowledge takes steps that a reasonable person would consider an acceptance. Subjective reservations in the offeree's mind are irrelevant.

2) Performance as Acceptance
Recall that under the U.C.C. and the Second Restatement, offers that are ambiguous or indifferent as to whether a unilateral or bilateral contract is intended may be accepted in any reasonable manner under the circumstances. In these situations, a bilateral contract is formed even if acceptance is by performance. (*See* I.C.2.b., *supra.*)

a) U.C.C.—Notice Required Within Reasonable Time
U.C.C. section 2-206(2) provides that "[w]here the beginning of a requested performance is a reasonable mode of acceptance, an offeror who is not notified of acceptance within a reasonable time may treat the offer as having lapsed before acceptance."

b) Restatement—Notice Required If Offeror Unaware of Performance
The Second Restatement clearly indicates that the beginning of performance constitutes acceptance, and notice is a condition that must occur to activate the offeror's duty in a situation where the offeror would not normally become aware of the beginning of performance.

Note: U.C.C. section 2-206 and section 62 of the Second Restatement deal with *bilateral* contracts. The beginning of performance operates as an implied promise. Do not confuse this with the unilateral contract situation.

b. Knowledge of Contractual Terms
The offeree's ignorance of certain contractual terms may be a defense to the formation of a bilateral contract.

1) Knowledge Judged by an Objective Standard
If the offeree objectively manifests her assent, she is bound by all contract terms that a reasonable person would have noted and understood. This rule of construction is frequently used in consumer protection cases.

a) Oppressive Terms
If the contract contains oppressive terms, the court may declare a contract wholly voidable at the option of the innocent party or it may "blue pencil" the agreement and enforce it without the offending provisions. [U.C.C. §2-302]

b) Blanket Form Recitals
Blanket form recitals stating that the offeree has read and understood every provision and agrees to be bound thereby will not prevent a court from applying the objective standard.

c) Provisions Contrary to Public Policy
Provisions that are contrary to public policy, such as usurious interest rates, may be set aside even if they could be understood by a reasonable person.

III. CONSIDERATION

A. INTRODUCTION
The majority of agreements that qualify as legally enforceable contracts contain a bargained-for change in legal position between the parties, *i.e.,* valuable consideration. While substitute doctrines may permit enforcement of an agreement, only the presence of *valuable consideration on both sides* of the bargain will make an executory bilateral contract fully enforceable from the moment of formation. Simply stated, consideration is the price for enforceability in the courts.

B. ELEMENTS OF CONSIDERATION
Basically, two elements are necessary to constitute consideration: (i) there must be a *bargained-for exchange* between the parties; and (ii) that which is bargained for must be considered of *legal value* or, as it is traditionally stated, it must constitute a benefit to the promisor *or* a detriment to the promisee. At the present time, the *detriment* element is emphasized in determining whether an exchange contains legal value.

Example: Jeff promises to sell his used television to Kristen for $100 in exchange for Kristen's promise to pay $100. Both elements of consideration are found in this example. First, Jeff's promise was bargained for. Jeff's promise induced a detriment in the promisee, Kristen. Kristen's detriment induced Jeff to make the promise. Second, both parties suffered detriments. The detriment to Jeff was the transfer of ownership of the television, and the detriment to Kristen was the payment of $100 to Jeff.

1. Bargained-for Exchange
This element of consideration requires that the promise induce the detriment *and* the detriment induce the promise (*see* preceding example). Unless both of these elements are present, the "bargained-for exchange" element of consideration is not present.

a. Gift
If either of the parties intended to make a gift, he was not bargaining for consideration, and this requirement will not be met.

1) **Act or Forbearance by Promisee Must Be of Benefit to Promisor**
It is not enough that the promisee incurs detriment; the detriment must be the *price* of the exchange, and not merely fulfillment of certain conditions for making the gift. The test is whether the act or forbearance by the promisee would be of any benefit to the promisor. In other words, if the promisor's motive was to induce the detriment, it will be treated as consideration; if the motive was no more than to state a condition of a promise to make a gift, there is no consideration.

Example: "Come to my house and I will give you my old television." The promisee suffers a detriment by going to promisor's house, as she did not have to go there at all. However, the promise of the television was probably not made to induce the promisee to come to promisor's house. Hence, there is no consideration.

2) **Economic Benefit Not Required**
The benefit to the promisor need not have economic value. Peace of mind or the gratification of influencing the mind of another may be sufficient to establish bargained-for consideration, provided that the promisee is not already legally obligated to perform the requested act.

Example: Father tells Daughter, "I'll give you $1,000 if you stop smoking." Father's emotional gratification from influencing his daughter's health suffices as consideration.

b. **"Past" or "Moral" Consideration**

1) **General Rule—Not Sufficient Consideration**
If something was already given or performed before the promise was made, it will not satisfy the "bargain" requirement. The courts reason that it was not given in exchange for the promise when made.

Example: A loose piece of molding fell from a building and was about to hit Sam. Sherry, seeing this, pushed Sam out of the molding's path and was herself struck by it and seriously injured. Sam later promised Sherry that he would pay her $100 per month for life. There is no consideration because Sherry did not bargain for Sam's promise.

2) **Exceptions**
There is substantial disagreement with the general rule. Thus, the courts have sought to avoid its application by creating exceptions.

a) **Debt Barred by a Technical Defense**
If a past obligation would be enforceable except for the fact that a technical defense to enforcement stands in the way (*e.g.,* statute of limitations), the courts will enforce a new promise if it is *in writing* or has been *partially performed*.

b) **Promise to Pay for Past Requested Act**
Under the modern trend, if acts have been previously performed by the promisee at the promisor's *request,* a new promise will be enforceable. A number of states and the Second Restatement have even extended this rule to cover *"unrequested"* acts, if they were rendered during an emergency. (*See* the falling molding example, *supra.*)

c) **Terms of New Promise Binding**
Most courts applying these exceptions will enforce the new promise according to *its* terms, rather than the terms of any prior understanding.

2. **Legal Value**

a. **Adequacy of Consideration**
Courts of law normally will *not* inquire into the adequacy of consideration (*i.e.,* the relative values exchanged). If a party wishes to contract to sell an item of high market value for a relatively low price, courts of law will not inquire into the relative values. However, courts of equity may inquire into the relative values and deny an equitable remedy where they find a contract to be unconscionable.

1) **Token Consideration**
Where the consideration is only token (*i.e.,* something entirely devoid of value), it

will usually not be legally sufficient. The courts reason that this indicates a gift rather than bargained-for consideration.

2) Sham Consideration

Parties to a written agreement often recite that it was made in consideration of $1 or some other insignificant sum. Frequently, this recited sum was not in fact paid and, indeed, it was never intended to be paid. Most courts hold that evidence may be introduced to show that the consideration was not paid and no other consideration was given in its stead.

3) Possibility of Value

Where there is a possibility of value in the bargained-for act, adequacy of consideration will be found even though the value never comes into existence.

Example: Harry promises to convey upon his death certain land by quitclaim deed in consideration for a promise to bequeath him money. Consideration will be found even though Harry has already conveyed the land, as there is a possibility of a future interest in his favor coming into effect.

b. Legal Benefit and Legal Detriment Theories

1) Majority Rule

The majority of courts still adhere to the view that *detriment to the promisee* in performing an act or making a promise is the exclusive test of consideration. The fact that this act or promise may confer a legal benefit on the other party, taken alone, is not sufficient consideration.

2) Minority and First Restatement

The minority and First Restatement view is stated in the alternative (although the Restatement does not use the benefit/detriment terminology): Either *detriment or benefit* to the other party will suffice.

3) Second Restatement

The Second Restatement departs from the use of the benefit/detriment test. The only question it would ask about consideration is whether something was *bargained for and given* (or promised to be given) in exchange.

4) Detriment and Benefit Defined

a) Legal Detriment to Promisee

Legal detriment will result if the promisee does something he is under no legal obligation to do or refrains from doing something that he has a legal right to do. It is important to remember that the detriment to the promisee need not involve any actual loss to the promisee or benefit to the promisor.

Example: Uncle promises Nephew $5,000 if he will refrain from drinking, smoking, swearing, and gambling until he reaches age 21. Nephew's refraining is a legal detriment, and since it was bargained for, Uncle must pay the $5,000 if Nephew so refrains. Note that it makes no difference that Uncle, the promisor, received no benefit. [*See* Hamer v. Sidway, 124 N.Y. 538 (1891)]

Note: Remember that the promisor must have primarily sought to induce the detrimental act by his promise. (*See* television set example under B.1.a.1), *supra.*)

b) Legal Benefit to Promisor

A legal benefit to the promisor is simply the reverse side of legal detriment. In other words, it is a forbearance or performance of an act by the promisee which the promisor was not legally entitled to expect or demand, but which confers a benefit on the promisor.

c. Specific Situations

1) Preexisting Legal Duty

a) General Rule

It has traditionally been said that the promise to perform or the performance of an existing legal duty will *not be sufficient consideration*.

Examples: 1) Mike contracts to build a garage for Richard for $5,000. Mike discovers that he cannot make a profit at that price and tells Richard that he will not build the garage unless Richard promises to pay him $6,000. Since Richard does not have time to find a new contractor before winter and he does not want his new car exposed to snow, he agrees to pay Mike the $6,000. When Mike finishes the garage, Richard pays Mike $5,000. Mike cannot enforce the promise for the additional $1,000 because he was under a preexisting duty to build the garage.

2) Smith offers a $10,000 reward for recovery of his kidnapped daughter. Jones, a police officer assigned to this case, recovers the daughter. Jones's performance of her official duty is not sufficient consideration.

b) Exceptions

The preexisting legal duty rule has become riddled with exceptions.

(1) New or Different Consideration Promised

If the promisee has given something in addition to what she already owes in return for the promise she now seeks to enforce, or has in some way agreed to vary her preexisting duty, such as by accelerating performance, there is consideration. It is important to note that it is usually immaterial how slight the change is, since courts are anxious to avoid the preexisting duty rule.

(a) Modification

If the parties agree to modify their contract, consideration is usually found to exist where the obligations of both parties are *varied*. However, a modification solely for the benefit of one of the parties is unenforceable (except in a contract under the U.C.C., where the modification is sought in good faith; *see* (6), *infra*).

(2) Voidable Obligation

A promise to perform a voidable obligation (*i.e.,* ratification) is enforceable despite the absence of new consideration. Thus, an infant's ratification of a contract upon reaching majority is enforceable without new consideration, as is a defrauded person's promise to go through with the tainted contract after learning of the fraud.

(3) Preexisting Duty Owed to Third Party

Traditionally, when a preexisting duty was owed to a third party, courts held that the new promise did not constitute consideration. However, the modern view adopted by the Second Restatement and the majority of jurisdictions states that the new promise *constitutes consideration*. [*See* Rest. 2d §73]

Example: Saul Pimon contracts with Pam Promotor to sing at a concert in New York for $25,000. Later, when Pimon threatens to cancel, Dud Dooright, president of a New York environmental group, Greenprice, offers to pay Pimon an additional $5,000 if he sings at the concert. Dooright knows that whenever Pimon sings in New York, donations to Greenprice increase. Pimon appears and sings as agreed. Under the traditional view, Pimon cannot enforce Dooright's promise to pay the additional $5,000, but under the majority view Pimon can enforce the promise because Pimon did not owe a duty to Dooright under the original contract.

(4) Honest Dispute as to Duty

If the scope of the legal duty owed is the subject of honest dispute, then a modifying agreement relating to it will ordinarily be given effect.

(5) Unforeseen Circumstances

Under the majority view, mere unforeseen difficulty in performing is *not* a substitute for consideration. But where the unforeseen difficulty *rises to the level of impracticability*, such that the duty of performance would be discharged (*see* VII.C.5.b., *infra*), most states will hold that the unforeseen difficulty is an exception to the preexisting legal duty rule.

(6) U.C.C. Provision

U.C.C. section 2-209(1) states that an agreement modifying a contract subject to the U.C.C. *needs no consideration to be binding*. However, this rule operates only where both parties are acting in *good faith*.

c) Existing Debts

One of the recurring problems in the preexisting duty area concerns promises regarding existing debts. Generally, *payment of a smaller sum* than due will *not* be sufficient consideration for a promise by the creditor to discharge the debt. Neither a legal detriment nor a benefit would be present.

But again, bear in mind that courts will attempt to avoid this result by application of the above exceptions. Thus, for example, if the consideration is in any way *new or different* (*e.g.,* payment before maturity or to one other than the creditor; payment in a different medium, *e.g.,* stock instead of cash; or payment of a debt that is subject to an honest dispute), then sufficient consideration may be found. (*See* "Discharge by Accord and Satisfaction," VII.C.12., *infra.*)

2) Forbearance to Sue

The promise to refrain from suing on a claim may constitute consideration. If the claim is *valid*, the forbearance to sue is, of course, sufficient consideration.

If the claim is *invalid* and the claimant is aware of this fact, he has no such right; his suit is no more than the wrongful exercise of a power. But even if the claim is invalid, in law or in fact, if the claimant reasonably and in good faith believes his claim to be valid, forbearance of the legal right to have his claim adjudicated constitutes detriment and consideration.

C. MUTUAL AND ILLUSORY PROMISES—THE REQUIREMENT OF MUTUALITY

Consideration must exist on both sides of the contract; that is, promises must be mutually obligatory. There are many agreements in which one party has become bound but the other has not. Such agreements lack mutuality, *i.e.,* at least one of the promises is "illusory." If so, consideration fails.

Example: Acme Co. promises to buy from Batcher, Inc. "such ice cream as I may wish to order from Batcher, Inc." Acme's promise is illusory, since it is still free to buy from anyone else it chooses, or not to buy at all.

However, the requisite mutuality will be found to exist in certain situations even though the promisor has some choice or discretion. Notable among these are the following:

1. Requirements and Output Contracts

"Requirements" contracts (promises to buy "all that I will require") and "output" contracts (promises to sell "all that I manufacture") are enforceable. Consideration exists, as the promisor is suffering a legal detriment; he has parted with the legal right to buy (or sell) the goods he may need (or manufacture) from (or to) another source. [U.C.C. §2-306]

a. No Unreasonably Disproportionate Quantities

The U.C.C. provides that any quantities subject to such contracts may not be unreasonably disproportionate (i) to any stated estimate, or (ii) in the absence of any stated estimate, to any normal or otherwise comparable prior output or requirements. The promisee is thus protected when the promisor alters quantity in such an unforeseeable fashion, *even if this change in demand was made in good faith*.

b. "Going Out of Business" Problem

Does the fact that a party to a requirements or output contract might go out of business make the promise illusory? It appears well settled that the answer is no.

c. **No Previously Established Business**
A number of courts have sometimes refused to enforce such agreements where the promisor did not have an established business. The courts in these cases reason that due to the lack of any basis for estimating quantity, the agreement is illusory or the damages too speculative. The U.C.C. avoids this problem by reading a "good faith" agreement into the contract; *i.e.,* the promisor must operate his plant or conduct his business in good faith and according to commercial standards of fair dealing in the trade so that his output or requirements will approximate a reasonably foreseeable figure.

2. **Conditional Promises**
Conditional promises are *enforceable*, no matter how remote the contingency, *unless* the "condition" is entirely within the promisor's control.
Example: Alice promises to deliver goods to Charles "only if her son comes into the business." Valid consideration exists. If the promise were "only if I decide to take my son into the business," a court might find no consideration.

a. **Promise Conditioned on Satisfaction**
A promise to buy if satisfied with goods is *not illusory* since one cannot reject them unless dissatisfied. The courts have assumed that the party would exercise his rights under such a condition in good faith. The U.C.C. is in accord. [U.C.C. §1-304]

3. **Right to Cancel or Withdraw**
Although reservation of an unqualified right to cancel or withdraw at any time may be an illusory promise, the consideration is valid if this right is in *any way restricted*, *e.g.,* the right to cancel upon 60 days' notice. The U.C.C. will imply a requirement of reasonable notice even if it is not specified in the contract. [U.C.C. §2-309(3)]

4. **Best Efforts Implied**
A court may find an implied promise furnishing mutuality in appropriate circumstances (such as exclusive marketing agreements). The courts generally will find an implied promise to use best efforts and sustain agreements that might otherwise appear illusory.
Example: Y Corp. was granted exclusive rights to sell Dominick's dresses in return for one-half the profit. The agreement was silent as to any obligation on the part of Y Corp. *Held:* Y Corp. impliedly promised to use its best efforts to sell. [*See* U.C.C. §2-306(2)]

5. **Voidable Promises**
Voidable promises are not held objectionable on "mutuality" grounds. [Rest. 2d §78]
Example: Victor entered into a contract with Baby Jane, an infant. Baby Jane's power to disaffirm her contractual obligation will not prevent her promise from serving as consideration.

6. **Unilateral/Option Contracts**
Unilateral contracts, enforceable because one has begun performance, or option contracts, enforceable because one has purchased time to decide (*e.g.,* whether to purchase land), are not held objectionable on "mutuality" grounds.

7. **Suretyship Promises**
A suretyship contract involves a promise to pay the debt of another. The usual type of suretyship transaction occurs where one person (the debtor or principal) wishes to borrow money from a creditor, but the creditor will not grant credit unless the debtor finds another person who will also be liable on the debt. The debtor then asks a friend or relative to sign a note promising to pay. Such promises to act as surety are enforceable as long as the promise is made *before* the consideration flows from the creditor to the debtor. *Rationale:* Mutuality does not require that the consideration flow to the promisor; it is sufficient that consideration in exchange for the promisor's promise flows to a third party.
Example: Buyer negotiates with Seller to purchase a car from Seller on credit. Seller and Buyer agree on a price, but Seller tells Buyer that he will not extend her credit unless she obtains a surety who will sign a promissory note with Buyer. Buyer asks Father to sign the note with her, and he does so. Even though Father did not receive the car, he will be liable on the note along with Buyer.

If the surety makes his promise *after* the consideration from the creditor already has been given, he is not bound unless: (i) the contract between the debtor and creditor makes the debtor's obtaining a surety a condition precedent to the creditor's performance; or (ii) the surety signs a negotiable instrument.

Examples: 1) Buyer and Seller mention in their negotiations that Seller would like Buyer to provide a surety. However, when the contract is reduced to writing and signed, there is no mention of a surety. After the contract has been signed, Buyer obtains the written promise of her friend Sam to be a surety on the contract. Sam's promise is not binding because he made his promise after the Buyer and Seller executed their contract and none of the applicable exceptions applies.

2) Buyer and Seller enter into a written contract that provides: "Buyer will provide a surety acceptable to Seller and Seller is not obligated to perform until such a surety has been provided." After the contract has been signed, Buyer obtains the written promise of her friend Sam to be a surety on the contract. Seller approves of Sam, and in reliance on Sam's promise, ships goods under the contract. Sam's promise is binding because the promise was a condition precedent to Seller's performance.

3) Buyer and Seller enter into a sales contract. Seller delivers the goods, but Buyer fails to pay. Seller threatens to bring suit. Buyer tells Seller that if Seller will give her a six-month extension on the amount due, she will obtain the promise of her friend Sam to guarantee payment. Seller agrees, and Buyer obtains the written promise of Sam to guarantee payment. Sam's promise is binding because it was given in exchange for the six-month extension.

8. Right to Choose Among Alternative Courses

A promise to choose one of several alternative means of performance is illusory unless *every alternative* involves *some legal detriment* to the promisor. However, if the power to choose rests with the *promisee* or some *third party* not under the control of the promisor, the promise is enforceable as long as *at least one alternative* involves some legal detriment.

Example: Smith, an English professor, tells Jack that in return for Jack's promise to pay $250, Smith will either (i) give Jack swimming lessons, (ii) paint Jack's portrait, or (iii) teach his English class (of which Jack is a member) on a regular basis during the next term, the choice to be entirely Smith's. Since alternative (iii) represents a *preexisting duty* owed by Smith to the university under his contract of employment, it involves no legal detriment, and Smith's promise does not constitute valuable consideration for Jack's promise to pay $250.

Compare: Had Smith allowed Jack's mother (or Jack) to select the performance, there would be a legal detriment and valuable consideration—even if alternative (iii) were selected.

a. Selection of Valuable Alternative Cures Illusory Promise

Even if a promisor retains the power to select an alternative without legal detriment, his *actual* selection of an alternative involving legal detriment would cure the illusory promise.

Example: In the above example (in which Smith was allowed to select a means of performance), if Smith had *actually* chosen alternative (i) or (ii), his illusory promise would have been cured.

D. NO REQUIREMENT THAT ALL CONSIDERATION BE VALID

There is no requirement that all of the promises given as consideration necessarily be sufficient as consideration.

Example: Father tells Daughter: "In consideration of your past law school performance and in consideration of your promise to refrain from drinking while studying for the bar exam, I will pay you $1,000." If Daughter gives the requested counterpromise, a contract will be formed. The fact that a portion of the consideration is defective, *i.e.,* past consideration, does not render the agreement invalid for lack of consideration.

E. SUBSTITUTES FOR CONSIDERATION

While valuable consideration is necessary to make an executory bilateral agreement fully enforceable, certain substitutes for consideration can make an agreement at least partially enforceable.

1. **Promissory Estoppel or Detrimental Reliance**

   a. **Majority View**
   Under what is now probably the majority view, *consideration is not necessary* where the facts indicate that the promisor should be estopped from not performing.

   b. **Elements of Promissory Estoppel**
   Under section 90 of the First Restatement, a promise is enforceable to the extent necessary to prevent injustice if:

   (i) The promisor should reasonably expect to induce action or forbearance;

   (ii) Of a definite and substantial character;

   (iii) And such action or forbearance is in fact induced.

   In the Second Restatement, section 90 no longer requires that the action or forbearance be "of a definite and substantial character." It also provides that the remedy "may be limited as justice requires."

   Examples: 1) Albert Alum promises to bequeath State University $5 million for a new School of Management building. State University puts up a plaque announcing the new building and otherwise relies on the promise. It may recover $5 million.

   2) Tom offers to give Betty $15,000 if she will buy herself a new car. Betty buys a car for $13,000. Tom is liable for at least $13,000.

2. **Promises in Writing**

   a. **The U.C.C. and Written Promises**

      1) **Modification of a Contract**
      Consideration is *not necessary* to a good faith written modification of a contract. Note that oral modifications are also valid without consideration except when prohibited by the contract. Generally, modifications have to be in writing only if the contract *as modified* is within the Statute of Frauds ($500 or more). [U.C.C. §2-209]

      2) **Firm Offers by Merchants**
      Merchants may bind themselves to keep an offer open for a period not to exceed three months if the offer so states in its terms and is in a signed writing. If the offer form is supplied by the offeree, the clause promising to make the offer irrevocable must be separately signed by the offeror. [U.C.C. §2-205]

      3) **Claim Arising Out of an Alleged Breach of Sales Contract**
      Any money claim or other claim arising out of an alleged breach of a sales contract can be discharged in whole or in part by agreement of the aggrieved party in an authenticated record (*e.g.,* signed writing). [U.C.C. §1-306]

   b. **Common Law Minority Rule**
   In a few jurisdictions, a promise in writing may be enforced, despite the absence of consideration, simply because it is in writing. Except to the extent that this rule is adopted by the U.C.C., most states do not follow this rule.

3. **Promises to Pay Legal Obligations Barred by Law**
   As noted above, a promise to pay a legal obligation barred by law is *enforceable*. Usually, it is required that this *new promise* be *in writing*, *or* that there have been some *part performance*. Further, it is important to remember that the "new" promise will be enforceable only according to its terms, not the terms of the original obligation.
   Example: Acme Sales Corp. owes Jones $30,000. This claim is barred by the statute of limitations. Acme agrees in writing to pay Jones $22,000. Jones can enforce this agreement without further consideration on her part (but only to the extent of $22,000).

4. **Reaffirmation of Voidable Promise**
   Most contracts made by persons without capacity are not enforceable against them. However, if the incapacitated person affirms the contract upon attaining capacity, her promise at that time will be binding. (*See* IV.C., *infra.*)

5. Promises Under Seal

a. Common Law
At common law, the seal is a substitute for consideration. A sealed promise is enforceable without more. The requirements of a sealed contract are threefold: (i) a writing, (ii) the seal, and (iii) delivery (although delivery may be in escrow, *i.e.,* to a third person to be redelivered). In addition to those formalities, it must appear that the parties to the agreement *intended* it to be a sealed instrument.

b. Distinction Abolished in Many States
Statutes in many states have abolished all distinctions between sealed and unsealed contracts. In other states, the seal will raise only a presumption of consideration.

c. U.C.C. Does Not Recognize
The U.C.C. has eliminated the seal as consideration for *sales* contracts. [U.C.C. §2-203]

IV. REQUIREMENT THAT NO DEFENSES EXIST

A. INTRODUCTION
Even where an agreement is supported by valuable consideration or a recognized substitute, contract rights may still be unenforceable because there is a defense to formation of the contract, because there is a defect in capacity (making the obligations voidable by one of the parties), or because a defense to enforcement of certain terms exists.

B. DEFENSES TO FORMATION
There are three categories of defenses to formation of a contract: (i) absence of mutual assent; (ii) absence of consideration; and (iii) public policy considerations that deny contractual status to the agreement.

1. Absence of Mutual Assent

a. Mutual Mistake
When both parties entering into a contract are mistaken about facts relating to the agreement, the contract may be voidable by the adversely affected party if:

(i) The mistake concerns a *basic assumption* on which the contract is made (*e.g.,* the parties think they are contracting for the sale of a diamond but in reality the stone is a cubic zirconia);

(ii) The mistake has a *material effect* on the agreed-upon exchange (*e.g.,* the cubic zirconia is worth only a hundredth of what a diamond is worth); and

(iii) The party seeking avoidance *did not assume the risk* of the mistake.

1) Assumption of Risk
Mutual mistake is not a defense if the adversely affected party bore the risk that the assumption was mistaken. This commonly occurs where the parties knew that their assumption was doubtful (*i.e.,* where the parties were consciously aware of their ignorance).

Example: Roger finds a stone that appears to be valuable and shows it to his friend Betsy. The two do not know what the stone is, but think it is a topaz. Roger agrees to sell the stone to Betsy for $100. The parties subsequently discover that the stone is a diamond worth $1,000. Roger cannot void the contract on mutual mistake grounds because the parties knew that their assumption about the stone was doubtful.

Compare: Roger finds a stone that appears to be valuable. Since Roger is not an expert as to gems, he takes it to Jeweler. Jeweler, in good faith, tells Roger that the stone is a topaz worth very little and offers to buy it for $100. Roger accepts, but subsequently discovers that the stone actually is a diamond worth $1,000. Roger can rescind the contract on mutual mistake grounds. Roger's reliance on an expert's opinion shows that Roger did not intend to assume the risk of not knowing about the stone.

a) Mistake in Value Generally Not a Defense

If the parties to a contract make assumptions as to the value of the subject matter, mistakes in those assumptions will generally not be remedied—even though the value of the subject matter is generally a basic assumption and the mistake creates a material imbalance—because both parties usually assume the risk that their assumption as to value is wrong. However, it is possible for the facts to show that the adversely affected party did not assume the risk in determining value.

Example: Roger finds a stone that appears to be valuable and shows it to his friend Betsy. The two properly determine that the stone is a topaz. Roger believes the topaz is worth $500, and Betsy believes the topaz is worth $50, but Roger agrees to sell it to Betsy for $200. The parties subsequently discover that the topaz is worth $600. Roger cannot void the contract because he knew that the parties did not know the true value of the stone, and so assumed the risk that their valuation was incorrect.

Compare: Same facts as above, but because Roger and Betsy did not know the value of a topaz, they took it to Jeweler, who told them the stone was worth $200. Subsequently Roger discovers that Jeweler knows nothing about topaz stones and determines that the stone was worth $600. Roger can void the contract for mutual mistake and force Betsy to return the stone because here the facts show that the parties did not intend to assume the risk of determining value (since they sought out an expert to determine the true value).

b. Compare—Unilateral Mistake

Where only one of the parties is mistaken about facts relating to the agreement, the mistake will *not* prevent formation of a contract. However, if the nonmistaken party *knew or had reason to know of the mistake* made by the other party, he will not be permitted to snap up the offer.

Examples: 1) Customer contracts to purchase an expensive ring from Jeweler on credit. Jeweler mistakenly believes that Customer is another party with a similar name who is wealthy. Customer did nothing to cause this mistaken belief on the part of Jeweler, and Customer, in good faith, is *unaware* of Jeweler's mistake. The contract is not voidable by Jeweler since Jeweler's unilateral mistake of identity was not known to Customer nor should it have been known.

2) Seller advertises a particular dredge for sale. After an employee of Buyer inspects the dredge, Buyer offers $35,000 for it, which Seller accepts. Prior to the delivery of the dredge, Buyer discovers that the dredge will not perform certain operations in shallow water, which was the central purpose Buyer intended for the dredge. Seller was unaware of Buyer's belief and in no way created the belief that the dredge would perform the particular operation that Buyer had in mind. The contract is not voidable by Buyer since Buyer's unilateral mistake about the contract's subject matter was not known by Seller nor should it have been known.

3) Seller agrees to sell Buyer a number of different items of hardware. Seller computes the total price at $15,000, and Buyer agrees to pay this amount. Subsequently, Seller discovers that he made an error in computation and the price should be $17,000. In this situation, the preferred analysis is that there *is* a contract at $15,000, assuming that Buyer was *reasonably unaware of the unilateral computation error*. Note also that the error was not an error in the offer; the mistake was *antecedent* to the offer by Seller. When Seller stated the offer at $15,000, he meant $15,000.

1) Unilateral Mistake May Be Canceled in Equity

There is authority in a number of cases that contracts with errors such as mistakes in *computation* may be canceled in equity assuming that the nonmistaken party has *not relied* on the contract. There is also modern authority indicating that a unilateral mistake that is *so extreme* that it outweighs the other party's expectations under the agreement will be a ground for cancellation of the contract.

c. Mistake by the Intermediary (Transmission)

Where there is a mistake in the transmission of an offer or acceptance by an intermediary, *e.g.,* the telegraph company makes a mistake in the transmission of a message, the prevailing view is that the message *as transmitted* is operative unless the other party knew or should have known of the mistake.

Example: Harry sought bids to have a sign made. Sally sent her $910 bid by telegram. The telegraph company made a mistake, transmitting the price at $901. Harry received two other bids: $925 and $950. If Harry accepts Sally's bid, there will be a contract for $901. However, if the telegraph company mistakenly sent a $91 bid, there would be no contract because Harry should have known of the error.

d. Latent Ambiguity Mistakes—Mutual Misunderstanding

1) Three Situations

A latent ambiguity occurs where the expression of the parties' agreement appears perfectly clear at the time the contract is formed, but because of subsequently discovered facts, the expression may be reasonably interpreted in either of two ways. In this situation, the following possibilities are present.

a) Neither Party Aware of Ambiguity—No Contract

If neither party was aware of the ambiguity at the time of contracting, there is *no contract unless* both parties happened to intend the same meaning.

Example: Buyer agrees to purchase cotton from Seller when the cotton is delivered by a ship named Peerless. This is the total expression of agreement. It is subsequently determined that Buyer contemplated a ship named Peerless that was to dock in September while Seller contemplated a ship named Peerless that was to dock in December. Neither party was aware that there were two ships named Peerless. Their subsequent expression of the ship each intended indicates that they did not intend the same ship at the time of contracting. Therefore, there is no contract. [*See* Raffles v. Wichelhaus, 159 Eng. Rep. 375 (1864)]

b) Both Parties Aware of Ambiguity—No Contract

If both parties were aware of the ambiguity at the time of contracting, there is *no contract unless* both parties in fact intended the same meaning.

c) One Party Aware of Ambiguity—Contract

If one party was aware of the ambiguity and the other party was not at the time of contracting, a *contract* will be enforced according to the intention of the party who was unaware of the ambiguity.

Example: Collector agrees to purchase a Picasso sketch from Gallery. It is subsequently determined that Gallery has two sketches and that Gallery intended to sell one of these to Collector while Collector intended to buy the other one. Collector did not know that Gallery owned two sketches; Gallery, of course, knew that it did. Here, there is a contract for the sketch that Collector had in mind since this is a situation in which one party knew of the ambiguity (Gallery) while the other party did not (Collector).

2) Subjective Intention of Parties Controls

While the objective test is used in contract law generally, the latent ambiguity situation is unique in that the courts look to the subjective intention of the parties. This is because the objective test simply does not work in this situation. The objective manifestations of the parties appear to be perfectly clear but subsequent facts indicate the latent ambiguity. It is then necessary to receive evidence of what each party subjectively thought at the time of contracting.

e. Misrepresentation

1) Fraudulent Misrepresentation Voidable

If a party induces another to enter into a contract by using *fraudulent misrepresentation* (*e.g.*, by asserting information she knows is untrue), the contract is *voidable* by the innocent party if she *justifiably relied* on the fraudulent misrepresentation. This is a type of *fraud in the inducement.*

Example: Buyer agreed to buy a painting from Seller because Seller told her that the painting previously had been owned by Bubbles Springfield, a famous rock star. In fact, Seller knew that Springfield had never owned the painting. Buyer's promise is voidable if she justifiably relied on Seller's misrepresentation.

a) Distinguish—Fraud in the Factum

If one of the parties was tricked into giving assent to the agreement under circumstances that prevented her from appreciating the significance of her action, the agreement cannot be enforced; it is *void*.

Example: Joe Rocket, a famous football player, signs autographs after each game. After one game, a fan handed him a paper to sign that was in reality the last page of a contract. The contract is void due to fraud in the factum because Rocket was tricked into signing it.

2) Nonfraudulent Misrepresentation Voidable If Material

Even if a misrepresentation is *not* fraudulent, it is *voidable* by the innocent party if the innocent party *justifiably relied* on the misrepresentation and the misrepresentation was *material.* A misrepresentation is material if either: (i) the information asserted would induce a reasonable person to agree; or (ii) the maker of the misrepresentation knew the information asserted would cause a particular person to agree.

Example: Same facts as in the painting example in 1), above, except that Seller truly believed that the painting had once belonged to Springfield. Because a famous prior owner would likely make a reasonable person agree to buy a painting, the misrepresentation is material. Therefore, Buyer's promise is voidable if she justifiably relied on Seller's misrepresentation.

3) Innocent Party May Rescind Agreement

Note that the innocent party need not wait until she is sued on the contract, but may take affirmative action in equity to *rescind* the agreement. This right to void or rescind such a contract may be lost, however, if the party so induced affirms the contract in question.

2. Absence of Consideration

If the promises exchanged at the formation stage lack the elements of bargain or legal detriment, *no contract* exists. In this situation, one of the promises is always illusory.

3. Public Policy Defenses to Contract Formation—Illegality

If either the *consideration or the subject matter* of a contract is illegal, this will serve as a defense to enforcement. Contracts may be illegal because they are inconsistent with the Constitution, violate a statute, or are against public policy as declared by the courts.

a. Some Typical Cases of Illegality

Some of the most common areas in which problems of illegality have arisen are:

1) Agreements in restraint of trade;

2) Gambling contracts;

3) Usurious contracts;

4) Agreements obstructing administration of justice;

5) Agreements inducing breach of public fiduciary duties; and

6) Agreements relating to torts or crimes.

b. Effect of Illegality

1) Generally Contract Is Void
Illegal consideration or subject matter renders a contract void and unenforceable. In a close case, a court may sever an illegal clause from the contract rather than striking down the entire contract.

2) Effect Depends on Timing of Illegality
If the subject matter or consideration was illegal at the time of the offer, there was *no valid offer*. If it became illegal after the offer but before acceptance, the supervening illegality operates to *revoke the offer*. If it became illegal after a valid contract was formed, the supervening illegality operates to *discharge the contract* because performance has become impossible (*see* VII.C.5.a., *infra*).

3) Compare—Illegal Purpose
If the contract was formed for an illegal *purpose* but neither the consideration nor the subject matter is illegal (*e.g.,* a contract to rent a plane when the purpose is to smuggle drugs out of Colombia), the contract is only *voidable* (rather than void) by the party who (i) did not know of the purpose; or (ii) knew but did not facilitate the purpose *and* the purpose does not involve "serious moral turpitude." If both parties knew of the illegal purpose and facilitated it, or knew and the purpose involves serious moral turpitude, the contract is *void* and unenforceable. [Rest. 2d §182]

c. Limitations on Illegality Defense

1) Plaintiff Unaware of Illegality
If the plaintiff contracted without knowledge that the agreement was illegal and the defendant acted with knowledge of the illegality, the innocent plaintiff may recover on the contract.

2) Parties Not in Pari Delicto
A person may successfully seek relief if he was not as culpable as the other.
Example: Punter, a casual bettor, may recover against Dimitri, a professional bookie. (Some courts reach this result on the theory that the criminal proscription was designed to protect a class to which Punter belongs.)

3) Licensing—Revenue Raising vs. Protection
If a contract is illegal solely because a party does not have a required license, whether the contract will be enforceable depends on the reason for the license:

a) Revenue Raising—Contract Enforceable
If the license is required merely to raise revenue (*e.g.,* a city requires all vendors at a fair to pay a $25 license fee), the contract generally is enforceable.

b) Protection of Public—Contract Not Enforceable
If the license is required to ensure that the licensee meets minimum requirements to protect the public welfare (*e.g.,* a license to practice law, medicine, accounting, etc.), the contract is void. This means that even if the unlicensed party performs perfectly under the contract, the party cannot collect any damages.

C. DEFENSES BASED ON LACK OF CAPACITY

1. Legal Incapacity to Contract
Individuals in certain protected classes are legally incapable of incurring binding contractual obligations. Timely assertion of this defense by a promisor makes the contract *voidable* at his election.

a. Contracts of Infants

1) Who Is an Infant?
The age of majority in most jurisdictions is 18. However, an increasing number of states are passing legislation terminating infancy for some or all contractual purposes at a younger age. Further, in many states, married persons under 18 are considered adults.

2) Effect of Infant's Contract
Infants generally lack capacity to enter into a contract binding on themselves. However, contractual promises of an adult made to an infant are binding on the adult. In other words, a contract entered into between an infant and an adult is *voidable by the infant but binding on the adult*.

3) Affirmance upon Majority
An infant may affirm, *i.e.,* choose to be bound by his contract, upon reaching majority. He affirms either expressly or by conduct, *e.g.,* failing to disaffirm the contract within a reasonable time after reaching majority.

4) Exceptions
There are, however, certain situations where the infant cannot choose to avoid the contract entered into by him. These are:

a) Necessities
An infant is bound to pay the reasonable value of necessities. What a necessity is depends on the infant's station in life.

b) Statutory Exceptions
Some states have statutory exceptions. Such statutes usually encompass insurance contracts, student loan contracts, and the like.

b. Mental Incapacity
One whose mental capacity is so deficient that he is incapable of understanding the nature and significance of a contract may disaffirm when lucid or by his legal representative. He may likewise affirm during a lucid interval or upon complete recovery even without formal restoration by judicial action. In other words, the contract is *voidable*. As in the case of infants, mental incompetents are liable in quasi-contract for necessities furnished to them.

c. Intoxicated Persons
One who is so intoxicated as not to understand the nature and significance of his promise may be held to have made only a *voidable* promise if the other party had reason to know of the intoxication. The intoxicated person may affirm the contract upon recovery. Once again, there may be quasi-contractual recovery for necessities furnished during the period of incapacity.

2. Lack of Volitional Consent
Even where a person has the legal capacity to contract, morally offensive pressure or artifice exerted by one party against the other may make "consent" to the bargain ineffective. As with other defects in capacity, the innocent party may elect to ratify the voidable contract or to rescind the obligation.

a. Duress and Coercion
Contracts induced by duress and coercion, like those induced by fraud or misrepresentation, are *voidable* and may be rescinded as long as not affirmed. Duress will usually *not* be found, however, where one party takes economic advantage of the other's pressing need to enter the contract.

b. Fraud in the Inducement
Unlike fraud in the execution of an agreement (fraud in the factum), which precludes formation because the victim is not aware that any contract was contemplated, the victim of fraud in the inducement realizes that a bargain is being made but consents with a false impression of the terms or obligations engendered by the other party. Such a contract is *voidable* at the election of the innocent party.

D. DEFENSES TO ENFORCEMENT

Defects in the subject matter of a bargain or in the capacity of one party to contract arise at the formation stage and make the agreement void or voidable. Other defenses, however, involve failure of the agreement to qualify for judicial relief and may arise at the formation stage or later.

1. Statute of Frauds

In most instances, an oral contract is valid. However, certain agreements, by statute, must be evidenced by a *writing signed by the parties sought to be bound.*

a. Agreements Covered

1) Executor or Administrator Promises Personally to Pay Estate Debts

A promise by an executor or administrator to pay the estate's debts out of his own funds must be in writing.

2) Promises to Pay Debt of Another (Suretyship Promises)

a) Must Be a Collateral Promise

A promise to answer for the debt or default of another must be in writing. The promise may arise as a result of a tort or contract, but it must be collateral to another person's promise to pay, and not a primary promise to pay.

Example: "Give him the goods, and if he does not pay, I will." This promise is a collateral promise and must be in writing. But if the promise is, "Give him the goods, and I will pay for them," the promise is a primary promise and need not be in writing.

b) Main Purpose Must Not Be Pecuniary Interest of Promisor

Where the main purpose or leading object of the promisor is to serve a pecuniary interest of his own, the contract is *not within the Statute of Frauds* even though the effect is still to pay the debt of another.

Example: Ernie contracted with ABC Co. to have some machines custom-made for his factory. He promised ABC Co.'s supplier that if it would continue to deliver materials to ABC, Ernie would guarantee ABC Co.'s payment to the supplier. This promise need not be in writing because Ernie's main purpose in guaranteeing payment was to assure that ABC Co. had adequate supplies to build his machines.

3) Promises in Consideration of Marriage

A promise made in consideration of marriage must be in writing. This applies to promises that induce marriage by offering something of value (other than a return promise to marry).

4) Interest in Land

A promise creating an interest in land must be in writing. This includes not only agreements for the sale of real property or an interest therein, but other agreements pertaining to land.

a) What Is an Interest in Land?

A problem may exist as to whether the subject matter of a given contract constitutes an interest in land. In addition to agreements for the *sale of real property* or an interest therein, the following items are among the more important interests in land generally covered by the Statute:

(1) *Leases for more than one year;*

(2) *Easements of more than one year;*

(3) *Fixtures;*

(4) *Minerals (or the like) or structures* if they are to be severed by the *buyer.* If they are to be severed by the seller, they are not an interest in land but rather goods. If the subject matter is growing crops, timber to be cut, or other things attached to realty capable of severance without material harm thereto, this is a contract for the sale of goods (*see* 6), *infra*) [U.C.C. §2-107]; and

(5) *Mortgages* and most other security liens.

b) Items Not Within the Statute
Even though the end result of some contracts may be an interest in land, they still do not come within the Statute. For example, a contract to build a building or a contract to buy and sell real estate and divide the profits does not come within the Statute.

c) Effect of Performance on Contracts
If the seller conveys to the purchaser (*i.e.,* fully performs), the seller can enforce the buyer's oral promise to pay.

Similarly, the purchaser may be able to specifically enforce a land contract if the "*part performance doctrine*" is applicable. Under the doctrine, conduct (*i.e.,* part performance) that **unequivocally indicates** that the parties have contracted for the sale of the land will take the contract out of the Statute of Frauds. What constitutes sufficient part performance varies among the jurisdictions. Most require **at least two** of the following: payment (in whole or in part), possession, and/or valuable improvements.

5) Performance Not Within One Year
A promise that by its terms *cannot* be performed within a year is subject to the Statute of Frauds.

a) Effective Date
The date runs from the **date of the agreement** and not from the date of performance.

Example: Maria entered into an employment agreement whereby she was to perform services from April 1, 2003, until March 31, 2004. The agreement was entered into on March 15, 2003. It must be in writing.

b) Contracts Not Within the Statute
The following contracts do not fall within this provision of the Statute.

(1) Possibility of Completion Within One Year
If the contract is possible to complete within one year, it is not within this provision, even though actual performance may extend beyond the one-year period.

Example: Crotchet makes the following oral statement to Nellie: "Be my nurse until I recover and I will pay you a small salary now, but leave you a large estate in my will." The contract need not be in writing since Crotchet could recover within one year.

(2) Right to Terminate Within Year
If a contract that cannot be performed within one year allows both parties the right to terminate within a year, there is a *split* as to whether the right to terminate takes the contract out of the one-year provision of the Statute of Frauds. The majority view is that nonperformance is not performance within one year, and so the contract is still within the Statute of Frauds. The minority Second Restatement view suggests that since the contract is terminable by either party within a year, it is outside the Statute.

Example: Susan contracts to employ Linda for two years. Part of their agreement allows either party to terminate on 30 days' notice. Under one view, this contract would be within the Statute of Frauds (excusable nonperformance is still not performance within a year). The Second Restatement view makes this contract enforceable because giving the 30 days' notice is an alternative form of performance that can occur within one year.

(3) Lifetime Contracts
A contract measured by a lifetime (*e.g.,* a promise to "employ until I

die" or "work until I die") is not within the Statute because it is capable of performance within a year since a person can die at any time.

6) Goods Priced at $500 or More

Generally, a promise for the *sale of goods of $500 or more* is not enforceable unless evidenced by a writing signed by the party to be charged. [U.C.C. §2-201(1)]

a) Enforceable Oral Contracts

The Code permits enforcement of an oral contract for the sale of goods of $500 or more in the following situations:

(1) Specially Manufactured Goods

If goods are to be specially manufactured for the buyer and are not suitable for sale to others by the seller in the ordinary course of his business, and the seller has made either a substantial beginning on their manufacture or commitments for their procurement before notice of repudiation is received, the oral contract may be enforced.

(2) Written Confirmation Between Merchants

Between merchants, a writing in confirmation of the contract that is sufficient against the sender and received by the other merchant who has reason to know of its contents satisfies the requirements of the Statute of Frauds against the recipient *unless* written notice of objection to the writing's contents is given within *10 days* after the writing is received. [U.C.C. §2-201(2)]

(3) Admissions in Pleadings or Court

If the party against whom enforcement is sought admits in pleadings, testimony, or otherwise in court that the contract for sale was made, the contract is enforceable (but in such a case the contract is not enforced beyond the quantity of goods admitted).

(4) Partial Payment or Delivery

When payment has been made and accepted, the contract is enforceable *to the extent of the payment* received and accepted. Similarly, when delivery has been made and accepted, the contract is enforceable *to the extent of the goods* received and accepted.

b) Defining "Goods"

Applying this section of the U.C.C., there may be some problems as to the definition of "goods." Generally, "goods" include all things that are movable at the time of identification to the contract of sale (tangible, movable property in general). The Code contains a different Statute of Frauds for security agreements. [U.C.C. §9-203]

c) Oral Modification Clause

The Code contains a "private" Statute of Frauds in section 2-209(2) that expressly makes a "no oral modification" clause enforceable. However, such a clause can be waived [U.C.C. §2-209(4)], and if the waiver is relied on, it is irrevocable [U.C.C. §2-209(5)].

b. Requirements

Under the Statute of Frauds, any writing will suffice (*e.g.,* printed form, handwritten note, faxed copy, etc.), as long as it contains *every essential term* of the oral or implied agreement that it memorializes. The Statute will be satisfied if the memorandum contains the following:

(i) The *identity of the party* sought to be charged;

(ii) Identification of the *contract's subject matter*;

(iii) *Terms and conditions* of the agreement;

(iv) Recital of *consideration* (in most states); and

(v) *Signature of the party to be charged* or of his agent.

Note: The U.C.C. requires only three things of the memorandum: (i) quantity, (ii) signature of party to be charged, and (iii) a writing "sufficient to indicate" that a contract was formed. [U.C.C. §2-201]

c. **Effect of Noncompliance with the Statute**
Under the majority rule, noncompliance with the Statute of Frauds renders the contract unenforceable at the option of the party to be charged (*i.e.,* the party being charged may raise the lack of a sufficient writing as an affirmative defense). If the Statute is not raised as a defense, it is waived.

d. **Situations Where Statute Not Applicable**
In addition to the nonapplicability of the Statute under the specific provisions as spelled out in subsection a., above, the following should also be noted:

1) **Admission**
Where the party sought to be charged admits in his pleadings, testimony, or otherwise in court that the contract was formed, the Statute does not apply, at least to the extent of the admission.

2) **Performance**

   a) **Sale of Goods**
   As noted above, performance (part payment or acceptance and receipt of part of the goods) takes the contract out of the Statute to the extent of such part payment or partial acceptance and receipt of the goods.

   b) **Sale of Land**
   What constitutes performance sufficient to take a contract for the sale of land out of the Statute of Frauds varies from state to state. As indicated *supra,* most states require at least two of the following: payment (in whole or in part), possession, and/or valuable improvements.

   c) **Full Performance of Contract Not Performable Within One Year**
   Generally, full performance will remove the bar of the Statute.

3) **Promissory Estoppel**
Promissory estoppel is sometimes applied in cases where it would be inequitable to allow the Statute of Frauds to defeat a meritorious claim. When a defendant falsely and intentionally tells a plaintiff that the contract is not within the Statute or that a writing will subsequently be executed, or when his conduct foreseeably induces a plaintiff to change his position in reliance on an oral agreement, courts may use the doctrine to remove the contract completely from the Statute of Frauds.

e. **Remedies If Contract Is Within Statute**
Even if a contract is within the Statute of Frauds, in almost all cases a party can sue for the *reasonable value* of the services or part performance rendered, *or* the *restitution* of any other benefit that has been conferred. This recovery would be in *quantum meruit* rather than a suit on the contract.

f. **Contract Made by Agent**
The problem: A given contract is required under state law to be in writing. An agent now purports to enter into such a contract on behalf of her principal. Must the agent's authority also be in writing? Most states would answer no, except for contracts involving interests in real property. A few states would answer yes as to all such contracts pursuant to the states' *equal dignities* statutes. However, even where written authority would otherwise be required, written authority may be dispensed with if the agent contracted in the presence and under the direction of the principal or if the principal later ratified the contract in writing.

2. **Unconscionability**
The concept of unconscionability was given significance through U.C.C. section 2-302,

which allows a court to *refuse to enforce a provision or an entire contract* (or to modify the contract) to avoid unconscionable terms. The drafters of the Code did not define "unconscionable," but the principle behind the provision is the prevention of oppression and unfair surprise. The basic test is whether, in light of the general commercial background and needs of the particular parties, the clauses involved are so one-sided as to be unconscionable *under the circumstances existing at the time the contract was formed.* [U.C.C. §2-302, comment 1] The unconscionability concept is often applied to one-sided bargains where one of the parties to the contract has *substantially superior bargaining power* and can dictate the terms of the contract to the other party with inferior bargaining power. An analysis of the case law suggests the following elements of unconscionability:

a. **Inconspicuous Risk-Shifting Provisions**
    Standardized printed form contracts often contain a material provision that seeks to shift a risk normally borne by one party to the other. Examples of such provisions are:

    (i)   Confession of judgment clauses, which are illegal in most states and have been attacked on a constitutional basis;

    (ii) Disclaimer of warranty provisions; and

    (iii) "Add-on" clauses that subject all of the property purchased from a seller to repossession if a newly purchased item is not paid for.

    Typically, such clauses are found in the fine print ("boilerplate") in printed form contracts. Courts have invalidated these provisions because they are *inconspicuous* or *incomprehensible* to the average person, even if brought to his actual attention.

b. **Contracts of Adhesion—"Take It or Leave It"**
    Courts will deem a clause unconscionable and unenforceable if the signer is unable to procure necessary goods, such as an automobile, from any seller without agreeing to a similar provision. The buyer has no choice.

c. **Price Unconscionability**
    A few cases have invalidated the price term of a contract because the buyer was being charged more than the goods were actually worth. However, courts are generally reluctant to determine the fairness of pricing, at least where the parties have reached an agreement on a price. Thus, the price unconscionability analysis relates primarily to consumer transactions in which the buyer is unaware of the actual price he was agreeing to pay.

V. RIGHTS AND DUTIES OF NONPARTIES TO THE CONTRACT

A. INTRODUCTION
Once it is determined that a valid contract has been formed, ascertain whether nonparties to the contract have rights or duties in connection with it. The general rule is that a contract operates to confer rights and impose duties only on the parties thereto and on no other person. Two important exceptions to this general rule exist: (i) contractual rights involving third-party beneficiaries, and (ii) contractual rights or duties that are transferred to third parties. In the first situation, the original contract will confer the rights and duties on the third party; in the second situation, the original contract does not confer any rights or obligations on the third party, but subsequently one of the parties has sought to transfer his rights and/or duties under the contract to a third party (*i.e.,* assignment of rights, delegation of duties).

B. THIRD-PARTY BENEFICIARIES
The basic situation to be dealt with here is: A enters into a valid contract with B that provides that B will render some performance to C. A is the promisee, B is the promisor, and C is a third party. Three main problems must be focused on:

(i)   Is C a third-party beneficiary?

(ii) Can A and B alter the contract's terms to deprive C of her rights? That is, when do C's rights vest?

(iii) What are the rights of A and C against B; of C against A?

1. **Which Third-Party Beneficiaries Can Sue?**

   a. **Categories of Beneficiaries**

      1) **Intended vs. Incidental Beneficiaries**
         The first line of demarcation to be drawn is between intended beneficiaries, who can recover, and mere incidental beneficiaries, who cannot.

         a) **Test**
            The best test for determining whether someone is an intended beneficiary is to pose the following question: "To whom is performance to be given according to the language of the contract?" In other words, was the purpose of the promisee, according to the language of the contract, to get the benefit for herself primarily or to confer a right on another directly?
            Example: General Motors cannot recover on Dan's broken promise to buy a Cadillac for Alicia because General Motors is not an intended beneficiary of Dan and Alicia's contract.

         b) **Determining Promisee's Intention**
            The courts generally look at the following *factors* in resolving this question of intention:

            (1) Is the third party expressly *designated* in the contract? If so, it is more likely that it is primarily for her benefit. But note that it is not necessary that the third-party beneficiary be named, or even identifiable, at the time the contract is made; she need only be identifiable at the time performance is due.

            (2) Is *performance to be made directly* to the third party? If so, it is more likely that the contract is primarily for her benefit.

            (3) Does the third party have any *rights* under the contract (*e.g.,* the right to designate when and where performance is to be made)? If so, it is more likely that the contract is primarily for her benefit.

            (4) Does the third party stand in such a *relationship* to the promisee that one could infer that the promisee wished to make an agreement for the third party's benefit? If so, it is more likely that the contract is primarily for her benefit.

      2) **Creditor or Donee Beneficiary**
         There are two basic categories of "intended" beneficiaries who may sue on the promise: creditor and donee beneficiaries. The distinction between the two is based on the purpose of the promisee in extracting the promisor's commitment to render a performance to the third party.

         a) **Creditor Beneficiary**
            A third party is a creditor beneficiary if the promisee's primary intent in contracting was to *discharge an obligation* he owed to the third party. Under the *majority view*, it is sufficient if the obligation is real or merely supposed.

         b) **Donee Beneficiary**
            A third party is a donee beneficiary if the promisee's primary intent in contracting was to confer a *gift* on the third party or *create a right* in the third party irrespective of motive.

         c) **No Distinction in Second Restatement**
            Many of the decisions use the creditor/donee beneficiary terminology. The Second Restatement has dispensed with these terms; it uses only the term "intended" beneficiary and makes no distinction between the two types.

2. **When Do the Rights of the Beneficiary Vest?**
   An "intended" beneficiary can enforce a contract only after his rights have vested. This becomes important when the original parties to the contract take actions (*e.g.,* rescission, modification, etc.) that affect the third-party beneficiary. The general rule for *both* creditor and donee beneficiaries is that their rights vest when the beneficiary:

(i) Manifests *assent* to the promise in a manner invited or requested by the parties;

(ii) Brings *suit* to enforce the promise; or

(iii) Materially *changes position* in justifiable reliance on the promise.

[Rest. 2d §311]

3. What Are the Rights of the Promisee and Third-Party Beneficiary?

a. Third-Party Beneficiary vs. Promisor
The third-party beneficiary may sue the promisor on the contract.

1) Promisor's Defenses

a) All of Promisor's Defenses Against Promisee
Because the third-party beneficiary's rights are derivative, the promisor may raise any defense against the third-party beneficiary that he would have against the promisee, including: lack of assent, lack of consideration, illegality, impossibility, and failure of a condition.

b) May Raise Promisee's Defenses Against Third-Party Beneficiary If Promise Not Absolute
Whether the promisor can use any of the defenses that the promisee would have against the third-party beneficiary depends on whether the promisor made an absolute promise to pay (*e.g.,* "I will pay T $500 in exchange for your services") or only a promise to pay what the promisee owes the beneficiary (*e.g.,* "I will pay T whatever you owe him in exchange for your services"). In the former case, the promisor *cannot* assert the promisee's defenses; in the latter case, the promisor *can* assert the promisee's defenses.

b. Third-Party Beneficiary vs. Promisee

1) Creditor Beneficiary
A third-party creditor beneficiary may sue the promisee on the existing obligation between them. The contract between the promisor and promisee does not act to discharge the promisee's obligation to the third party.

The rights of a creditor beneficiary are cumulative. She need not elect between the promisor and her own debtor (*i.e.,* the promisee). She may *sue both*. Of course, she may obtain but *one satisfaction*.

2) Donee Beneficiary
A third-party donee beneficiary *may not sue the promisee* because the promisee's act is gratuitous.

But note: If the *promisee tells* the beneficiary of the contract and should *foresee reliance* by the beneficiary, and the beneficiary *reasonably relies* to her detriment, the beneficiary can sue the promisee directly under a promissory estoppel/detrimental reliance theory (*see* III.E.1., *supra*), even though the beneficiary cannot sue the promisee as a third-party beneficiary.

Example: Alex contracts to rent his house to Ben for one year, but the contract provides that Ben is to make the first three payments to Alex's daughter Carla. Alex then calls Carla and tells her that she will be able to buy the new furniture that she has wanted because Ben will be making his first three payments to Carla. Carla rushes out and buys new furniture. Alex decides not to rent the house to Ben. Carla can sue Alex under a promissory estoppel/detrimental reliance theory but not as a third-party beneficiary under the contract.

c. Promisee vs. Promisor

1) Donee Beneficiary Situation
Where the contract involves a donee beneficiary, it was once said that the promisee could not sue the promisor at law. The rationale was that since the donee

beneficiary had no cause of action against the promisee, there was no damage suffered. Today, however, the *majority view* is that the *promisee has a cause of action*. Since the promisee hardly ever suffers any actual damage, however, she will usually receive only nominal damages. Hence, most courts have resolved this problem by allowing *specific performance* in this situation.

2) Creditor Beneficiary Situation
Where a creditor beneficiary is involved and a promisee has had to pay the beneficiary on the existing debt, the promisee *may recover* against the promisor. If the debt has not yet been paid by the promisee to the third party, the promisee can compel the promisor to pay in a *specific performance* action.

C. ASSIGNMENT OF RIGHTS AND DELEGATION OF DUTIES
The basic fact situation to be dealt with here is: X enters into a valid contract with Y. This contract does not contemplate performance to or by a third party. Subsequently, one of the parties seeks to transfer her rights and/or duties under the contract to a third party.

1. Assignment of Rights
A transfer of a right under a contract is called an "assignment." The main issues regarding assignments are:

(i) What rights may be assigned?

(ii) What is necessary for an effective assignment?

(iii) Is the assignment revocable or irrevocable?

(iv) What are the rights and liabilities of the various parties?

(v) What problems exist if there have been successive assignments of the same rights?

a. Terminology
X and Y have a contract. Y assigns her rights thereunder to Z. Y is the assignor, Z is the assignee, and X is the obligor.

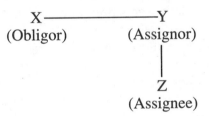

b. What Rights May Be Assigned?
Generally, *all* contractual rights may be assigned. Several *exceptions* to this rule exist, however.

1) Assigned Rights Would Substantially Change Obligor's Duty
If an assignment of rights would substantially change the obligor's duty, the assignment will be barred.

a) Personal Service Contracts
Where the assignment of rights would result in the obligor having to perform personal services for someone other than the original obligee, the attempted assignment will be invalid. This will usually apply, however, only where the nature of personal services is *unique* (*e.g.,* services involving lawyers, doctors, authors, etc.) rather than routine.

b) Requirements and Output Contracts
At common law, the right to receive goods under a requirements contract or to sell goods under an output contract generally was not assignable, because the assignment could change the obligation.
Example: Small Ice Cream Co., a small company located in one city, had a requirements contract with Glacier Ice Co. to purchase

all of the ice it needed to make ice cream from Glacier. Small sold out to Big Ice Cream Co., a large, multi-city ice cream manufacturer, and assigned its rights under the requirements contract to Big. The court held that the rights under the requirements contract were not assignable, because Big might require a significantly greater amount of ice from Glacier, thus changing Glacier's obligation. [*See* Crane Ice Cream Co. v. Terminal Freezing & Heating Co., 128 A. 280 (Md. 1925)]

(1) Assignments May Be Valid Under Code's Good Faith Requirement
U.C.C. section 2-306 might allow the assignment in the example above if Big does not alter the quantity required in an unreasonably disproportionate way. The common law rule prohibiting assignment of output and requirements contracts was based on the notion that the assignment would vary the obligor's risk. The Code has eliminated this concern by providing that quantity under such contracts must be measured by good faith output or requirements and cannot be unreasonably disproportionate to a stated estimate or, if there is no stated estimate, prior output or requirements. Thus, it would appear that output and requirements contracts are assignable under the Code as long as the assignee does not disproportionately alter the contemplated quantity. Therefore, in the example above, if Big continued to run Small's facilities, it probably could force Glacier to provide it with all of the ice it needed for those facilities. Big could not force Glacier to provide it with all of the ice that it needs nationally.

(2) Compare—Duties Under Output and Requirements Contracts
The buyer's duty to purchase goods under an output contract and the seller's duty to sell goods under a requirements contract can always be delegated, unless they fall within the general restrictions on delegation listed at 2.b., *infra,* because the other party's rights are not affected.
Example: In the example in b), *supra*, if Small Ice Cream Co. stayed in business, but Glacier Ice Co. no longer wished to supply Small under the contract, it probably could delegate the duty to supply Small with ice to Vanilla Ice Co.

2) Rights Assigned Would Substantially Alter Obligor's Risk
When the obligor's risk would be substantially altered by any attempted assignment, the assignment will fail.
Example: John owns a summer home that is insured by Acme Insurance Co. against loss due to fire. John sells the building to Joanna, who intends to convert it into a restaurant. John may not, without the consent of Acme, assign his rights under the policy to Joanna.

3) Assignment of Future Rights
The assignment of a *right expected to arise* under a contract of employment not then existing operates only as a promise to assign the right when it arises, *i.e.,* when the expected future contract is in fact entered into.

Contrast this with *future rights in existing contracts*, which are generally *assignable* even though the right might not yet have vested.

4) Assignment Prohibited by Law
A right may not be assigned if the assignment is prohibited by law. Such public policy against assignment may be embodied either in statute or in case precedent. For example, many states have laws prohibiting, or at least limiting, wage assignments.

5) Express Contractual Provision Against Assignment

a) Assignment of "the Contract"
Absent circumstances suggesting otherwise, a clause prohibiting the assignment of "the contract" will be construed as barring *only the delegation* of the assignor's *duties*. [Rest. 2d §322; U.C.C. §2-210(4)]

> *Example:* Sam and Betty enter into a contract wherein Betty will purchase 100 books from Sam, a book collector, for $5,000. The contract provides that "this contract shall not be assigned." Subsequently, Sam assigns to Charlie his right to receive the $5,000 from the contract. Sam has not breached the contract because he merely assigned his right to receive payment; he did not delegate his duty to deliver the books.

b) Assignment of Rights Under the Contract

A clause prohibiting the assignment of *contractual rights* generally does not bar assignment, but merely gives the obligor the right to sue for breach if an assignment is made. [Rest. 2d §322] In other words, the assignor has the *power but not the right* to assign.

(1) Factors that Make Assignment Ineffective

Notwithstanding the general rule, if the clause provides that any attempt to assign will be *"void,"* assignment will be ineffective (*i.e.,* the assignor has neither the power nor the right to assign). Also, if the assignee has *notice* of the nonassignment clause, assignment will be ineffective.

c. What Is Necessary for an Effective Assignment?

1) Requirement of Writing

A writing is usually *not required* to have an effective assignment, so an oral assignment is generally effective. However, there are situations where an assignment *must* be in writing:

a) Wage assignments;

b) Assignments of an interest in land;

c) Assignments of choses in action worth more than $5,000; and

d) Assignments intended as security interests under Article 9 of the U.C.C.

2) Requirement of Adequate Description

The right being assigned must be adequately described in the manifestation of assignment.

3) Requirement of Present Words of Assignment

The assignor must also manifest an intent to transfer his rights under the contract *completely and immediately* to the assignee. Whether such intent is present will be determined by looking to the terms of the transfer itself, *i.e.,* the test is objective, not subjective. It is not necessary to use the word "assign"; any generally accepted words of transfer will suffice (*e.g.,* "convey," "sell," "transfer," etc.).

4) No Requirement of Consideration

Consideration is *not required*; a gratuitous assignment is effective.

Note: It is important to remember, however, that even though neither a writing nor consideration is generally required, the lack thereof will affect revocability. (*See* e., *infra.*)

d. Partial Assignments

Contract rights may be transferred to one assignee or split up and transferred to two or more. Similarly, the assignor may transfer some rights under the contract and retain others.

e. Is the Assignment Revocable or Irrevocable?

When, if ever, do the rights of the assignee "vest" so that the assignment becomes irrevocable?

1) Assignment for Consideration

If an assignment has been given for consideration, it is *irrevocable*.

2) Assignment Not for Consideration
An assignment not supported by consideration, *i.e.,* a "gratuitous" assignment, is generally *revocable*.

a) Exceptions to Rule of Revocability
In certain situations, however, a gratuitous assignment will be held irrevocable.

(1) Performance by Obligor
If the obligor has already performed, the assignment will be irrevocable.

(2) Delivery of Token Chose
If a token chose (tangible claim) involving the rights to be assigned (*e.g.,* stock certificates, savings account passbook, etc.) has been delivered, the assignment will be irrevocable.

(3) Assignment of Simple Chose in Writing
If the assignment involves a simple chose, *i.e.,* an intangible claim not embodied by any token (or the great majority of ordinary contract rights), setting it forth in a writing will make the assignment irrevocable.

(4) Estoppel
The theory of estoppel may prevent the assignor from revoking a gratuitous assignment. This occurs where the assignor should reasonably foresee that the assignee will change her position in reliance on the assignment and such detrimental reliance does in fact occur.

b) Methods of Revocation
A gratuitous revocable assignment may be terminated in a number of ways:

(1) *Death* of the assignor;

(2) *Bankruptcy* of the assignor;

(3) *Notice* of revocation communicated by the assignor to either the assignee or the obligor;

(4) The *assignor takes performance* directly from the obligor; and

(5) *Subsequent assignment* of the same right by the assignor to another.

3) Effect of Assignment—Real Party in Interest
The effect of an assignment is to establish privity of contract between the obligor and the assignee while extinguishing privity between the obligor and assignor. The assignee then replaces the assignor as the real party in interest and she alone is entitled to performance under the contract.

4) Effect of "Irrevocable" Assignment
One should note that the term "irrevocable" as applied to an assignment may be misleading. The effect of such irrevocability is to remove from the assignor the right to revoke or make a subsequent assignment of the same right to a third party. However, in many situations, even though the assignor no longer has this *right*, he still has the *power* to do so. He would, of course, be liable for a breach of contract. *Exception:* An exception exists for assignments accompanied by *delivery of a token chose*. In this case, the assignor loses both the right *and* the power to revoke or further assign.

f. What Are the Rights and Liabilities of the Various Parties?

1) Assignee vs. Obligor
As the assignee is the real party in interest, she may enforce her rights against the obligor *directly*.

a) What Defenses Does Obligor Have Against Assignee?
As noted above with respect to third-party beneficiary situations, the promisor may usually assert against a third-party beneficiary any defense that he

can assert against the promisee. A similar rule prevails here. In other words, the assignee's rights against the obligor may be subject to any defenses that the obligor had against the assignor.

(1) Exception—Personal Defenses Arising After Assignment
If the obligor's defense is unrelated to the contract itself (*i.e.,* it is a personal defense against the assignor, such as a setoff or counterclaim), the defense is not available against the assignee if it arose *after* the obligor had notice of the assignment.

(a) Test
Is the defense *inherent* in the contract itself (*e.g.,* failure of consideration) *or* is it a defense *unrelated* to the contract, the right of which has been assigned? As to defenses inherent in the contract itself, these defenses are always available against the assignee because they came into existence when the contract was made. As to setoffs, counterclaims, and the like, such defenses are good against the assignee only if they came into existence before the obligor had notice or knowledge of the assignment.

(2) Estoppel
The estoppel doctrine may operate to prevent the obligor from asserting a defense that might otherwise exist against the assignor.

Example: Jim and Harold entered into a contract. Subsequently, Harold sought to assign his rights thereunder to Zorba. Zorba inquired of Jim whether he had any defenses against Harold. Jim replied in the negative. Thereupon, Zorba paid Harold valuable consideration for the assigned rights. Jim may be estopped to raise any defenses existing at the time of his statement to Zorba.

b) Modification of the Contract
Suppose that after the obligor has received *notice* of the assignment, the obligor and assignor attempt to *modify* the contract. Will the modification affect the assignee's rights?

(1) No Effect on Rights of Assignee
Generally, such a modification of the contract will *not* affect the rights of the assignee. This is so even when the modification is undertaken in good faith.

(2) U.C.C. Position
The U.C.C. provides that such a modification of an assigned right to payment that *has not yet been fully earned by performance* is effective against the assignee if made in *good faith*. However, the modification will cause a breach of an assignment contract that prohibits such modifications. [U.C.C. §9-405]

c) Defenses of Assignor Not Available
The obligor will not be able to raise by way of defense any defenses that the assignor might have against the assignee.

2) Assignee vs. Assignor

a) Implied Warranties
The assignor is deemed to give several implied warranties to the assignee, the breach of which will give rise to a cause of action.

(1) Warranty Not to Defeat Assigned Right
If the assignment is irrevocable, the assignee has the right to enforce the obligation and may proceed against the assignor if he wrongfully exercises his *power* to revoke.

(2) Warranty that Right Is Not Subject to Defenses
The assignee may also have a cause of action against the assignor where the obligor successfully asserts the defense she had against the assignor

in an action brought by the assignee to enforce the obligation, thereby defeating the assigned right. This is so only if the assignee was without notice of the defense at the time of the assignment.

b) Obligor Incapable of Performance
The assignor will *not* be liable to the assignee if the obligor is incapable of performing, *e.g.,* is insolvent.

c) Rights of Sub-Assignees
Sub-assignees do not have any rights against the original assignor. The courts reason that there is no privity of contract. However, the assignee who "sub-assigns" becomes the assignor with respect to that assignment and can be held liable thereon.

3) Do Third Parties Have Any Equities Relating to Assignment?
If third parties have any equities in the subject matter of the assignment, the assignee will take subject to them if she has notice; she will not be subject to such equities if she is a bona fide purchaser without notice of the assigned interest.

g. What Problems Exist If There Have Been Successive Assignments of the Same Rights?
The problem: X assigns to Y a right to the payment of $500 owed him by Smith. Subsequently, X assigns this same right to Z. Who prevails—Y or Z?

1) Revocable Assignments
Where the first assignment made is *revocable*, a subsequent assignment will serve to *revoke* it (*i.e.,* the subsequent assignee prevails).

2) Irrevocable Assignments

a) First Assignee Has Priority
The general rule is that where the assignor makes two assignments of the same right and the first assignment is *irrevocable*, the *first* assignee has priority.

b) Exceptions
In certain situations, a second assignee who *pays value* and takes *without notice* of the earlier irrevocable assignment will prevail.

(1) Judgment Against Obligor
If the subsequent assignee gets the *first judgment* against the obligor, she will prevail.

(2) Payment of Claim
If the later assignee gets *first payment* from the obligor on the assigned claim, her rights will be superior.

(3) Delivery of Token Chose
If the subsequent assignee gets the *first delivery of a token chose* from the assignor, she will prevail.

(4) Novation
The second assignee will prevail if she obtains a novation that supersedes the obligation running to the assignor in favor of the new one running to her. This assumes that the obligor had *no knowledge* of the prior assignment at the time of the novation.

(5) Estoppel
If the subsequent assignee is able to set up an estoppel against the first assignee, she will have priority, *e.g.,* the first assignee permits the assignor to retain a document that would indicate to a reasonable person that the assignor was sole owner of the right. (Estoppel could, of course, operate the other way as well. Thus, if the subsequent assignee has actual knowledge of the earlier assignment, she will be estopped to assert her claim as against the earlier assignee even though she would, under any of the other rules above, normally succeed.)

3) U.C.C. Rules
There have been considerable changes under the U.C.C. concerning the priority of competing assignments of contract rights subject to the Code. Basically, the U.C.C. has approached this problem by imposing *filing requirements*. [U.C.C. §9-310] If the filing provision is applicable to the transaction, generally the assignee who is the first to file will prevail. [U.C.C. §9-322]

2. Delegation of Duties
A transfer of contractual duties is called a "delegation." The main issues regarding delegations are:

(i) What duties may be delegated?

(ii) How does one make a valid delegation?

(iii) What are the rights and liabilities of the various parties where there has been a valid delegation?

a. Terminology
X and Y have a contract. Y delegates duties thereunder to Z. Y is the *obligor* since Y is the one with the duty to perform the obligation. Y also is the *delegator* (sometimes called the delegant) since Y delegated the duty. Z is the *delegate* (sometimes called the delegatee) since Z is the one to whom the duty was delegated. X is called the *obligee*, since X is the one for whom Y or Z is obligated to perform.

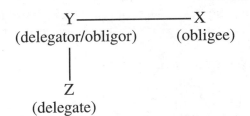

b. What Duties May Be Delegated?

1) General Rule
As a general rule, *all contractual duties* may be delegated to a third person.

2) Exceptions
There are several exceptions to the general rule.

a) Duties Involving Personal Judgment and Skill
If the duties involve personal judgment and skill, they may not be delegated.
Example: A talent agency cannot delegate its duty to select performers for a certain show to some other agency. It is immaterial that the other agency may have a better reputation and may have more performers under contract than the delegator. A court will not make such inquiries at all.

b) "Special Trust" in Delegator
Where a special trust has been reposed in the delegator, he may not delegate his duties (*e.g.*, relationship of attorney and client, physician and patient, etc.).

c) Change of Obligee's Expectancy
If performance by the delegate will materially change the obligee's expectancy under the contract, the duty may not be delegated (*e.g.*, "requirements" and "output" contracts).

d) Contractual Restriction on Delegation
Where a contract restricts either party's right to delegate duties, such a provision will usually be given *strict effect*.

c. What Is Necessary for Effective Delegation?
In general, no special formalities are required to have a valid delegation. The delegation may be either *written or oral*. However, the delegator must manifest a *present*

intention to make the delegation. There is no need that the word "delegate" be used; any generally accepted words of transfer may be used.

d. What Are Rights and Liabilities of Parties?

1) Obligee
The obligee must accept performance from the delegate of all duties that may be delegated. She need not accept performance from the delegate of those duties that may not be delegated.

2) Delegator
The delegator will *remain liable* on his contract. This is so even if the delegate expressly assumes the duties. There may be a different result if the obligee expressly consents to this transfer of duties. This could be construed as an offer of novation.

3) Delegate
The liability of a delegate turns largely on the question of whether there is a mere "delegation" or that plus an "assumption of duty."

a) Delegation
Delegation is the creation of a *power* in another to perform the delegator's contract duty. The nondelegating party to the contract (the obligee) cannot compel the delegate to perform, as the latter has not promised to perform.

b) Assumption
An assumption occurs where the delegate promises that she will perform the duty delegated and the *promise* is *supported by consideration* or its equivalent. This creates a third-party beneficiary situation in which the nondelegating party to the contract can compel performance or bring suit for nonperformance.

c) Result When Duties Delegated with Assignment of Rights
What happens if a delegation of duties is made in connection with an assignment of rights under the same contract out of which the duties arise, but the delegate has nonetheless not expressly assumed the duties? The majority of courts, the Restatement, and the U.C.C. hold that unless a contrary intention appears, words assigning "the contract" or "all my rights under the contract" are to be construed as including an *assumption* of the duties; *i.e.,* they imply a promise by the assignee to assume the duties of performance.

D. NOVATION DISTINGUISHED FROM OTHER THIRD-PARTY SITUATIONS
Note the difference between novation and the other third-party situations discussed above. Novation *substitutes a new party* for an original party to the contract. It requires the *assent of all parties* and *completely releases* the original party. (*See* VII.C.8., *infra.*) The consent of the remaining party may be express or by implication of the acceptance of performance by the new party with knowledge that a novation is intended.

VI. RULES OF CONTRACT CONSTRUCTION AND THE PAROL EVIDENCE RULE

A. INTRODUCTION
Commencing with the next section, we will be dealing with contract interpretation and enforcement questions. In making the analysis required there, one should always bear in mind the general rules of contract construction as well as ramifications of the parol evidence rule.

B. RULES OF CONTRACT CONSTRUCTION
There are a number of general rules of construction applied by the courts when interpreting contracts. The following are among the more frequently invoked:

1. Construed as a Whole
Contracts will be construed as a "whole"; specific clauses will be subordinated to the contract's general intent.

2. Ordinary Meaning of Words

The courts will construe words according to their "ordinary" meaning unless it is clearly shown that they were meant to be used in a technical sense.

3. Inconsistency Between Provisions

If provisions appear to be inconsistent, written or typed provisions will prevail over printed provisions (which indicate a form contract).

4. Custom and Usage

The courts will generally look to see what custom and usage is in the particular business and in the particular locale where the contract is either made or to be performed. [*See also* U.C.C. §1-303]

5. Preference to Construe Contract as Valid and Enforceable

It is important to note that the courts generally will try to reach a determination that a contract is valid and enforceable. Hence, they will be inclined to construe provisions in such a fashion as to make them operative. Obviously, this general policy will not be carried so far as to contravene the intention of the parties.

6. Ambiguities Construed Against Party Preparing Contract

Ambiguities in a contract are construed against the party preparing the contract, absent evidence of the intention of the parties. This is particularly true when there is no evidence of fraud, mutual mistake, duress, or knowledge by one party of unilateral mistake; and both parties are represented by counsel.

C. PAROL EVIDENCE RULE

In interpreting and enforcing a contract, questions often arise as to whether the written instrument is the complete embodiment of the parties' intention. Where the parties to a contract express their agreement in a *writing* with the *intent* that it embody the full and final expression of their bargain (*i.e.,* the writing is an *"integration"*), any other expressions—written or oral—made *prior to* the writing, as well as any oral expressions *contemporaneous with* the writing, are *inadmissible to vary* the terms of the writing.

1. Purpose

Its name notwithstanding, the parol evidence rule is not generally regarded as a rule of evidence but rather as a rule of *substantive contract law*. It is designed to carry out the apparent intention of the parties and to facilitate judicial interpretation by having a single clean source of proof (the writing) on the terms of the bargain.

2. Is the Writing an "Integration"?

The question of whether a writing is an "integration" of all agreements between the parties can be broken down into two further subquestions:

(i)   Is the writing intended as a *final* expression?

(ii) Is the writing a *complete* or *partial* integration?

a. Is the Writing Intended as a Final Expression?

Writings that evidence a purported contract are not necessarily the "final" expression of that contract. Thus, for example, the parties might only have intended such writings to be preliminary to a final draft. If so, the parol evidence rule will not bar introduction of further evidence. One should note that the *more complete* the agreement appears to be on its face, the more likely it is that it was intended as an *integration*.

b. Is the Writing a Complete or Partial Integration?

After establishing that the writing was "final," one should determine if the integration was "complete" or only "partial." In the former case, it may not be contradicted or supplemented; in the latter it cannot be contradicted, but may be supplemented by proving up consistent additional terms.

Where the agreement contains a *merger clause* reciting that the agreement is complete on its face, this clause strengthens the *presumption* that all negotiations were merged in the written document.

c. Who Makes Decision?

The *majority view* is that the question as to whether an agreement is an integration is one of fact. However, this fact question, unlike others, is decided by the *judge*, not the jury. If the judge decides that the writing was an integration of all agreements between the parties, he will exclude any offered evidence. Otherwise, he may admit the offered extrinsic evidence. Then, if there is a jury, it will make its own determination as to whether this extrinsic evidence was part of the agreement.

d. How Is This Determination Made?

The prevailing test is the *Williston test:* Would parties situated as were these parties to this contract *naturally and normally include the extrinsic matter* in the writing? If such reasonable parties would have included the matter in the writing, evidence of the extrinsic matter will not be admitted. On the other hand, if the judge determines as a matter of fact that normal parties, such as the parties to this contract, would not have included the extrinsic matter in the writing, evidence of the matter may be introduced. Other tests include the Wigmore "aid," which asks whether the extrinsic matter was mentioned or dealt with at all in the writing. If it was mentioned or dealt with in the writing, presumably the writing states all that the parties intended to say as to that matter and the evidence is excluded. Some courts also suggest another test: an examination of the writing itself to determine whether it appears to be complete on its face.

3. Extrinsic Evidence Outside Scope of Rule

Since the rule prohibits admissibility only of extrinsic evidence that seeks to vary, contradict, or add to an "integration," other forms of extrinsic evidence may be admitted where they will not bring about this result, *i.e.,* they will fall outside the scope of the parol evidence rule.

a. Attacking Validity

A party to a written contract can attack the agreement's validity. The party acknowledges (concedes) that the writing reflects the agreement but asserts, most frequently, that the *agreement never came into being* because of any of the following:

1) Formation Defects

Formation defects (*e.g.,* fraud, duress, mistake, and illegality) may be shown by extrinsic evidence.

2) Conditions Precedent

Where a party asserts that there was an oral agreement that the written contract would not become *effective* until a condition occurred, all evidence of the understanding may be offered and received. This would be a condition precedent to effectiveness. The rationale is that you are not altering a written agreement by means of parol evidence if the written agreement never came into being. It should be borne in mind that parol evidence of such a condition precedent will not be admitted if it contradicts the express language of the written contract.

Example: Jane and Susan sign what appears to be a complete contract, but agree orally that the agreement is not to become binding unless Susan can secure financing, or until her home office approves, or the like. The nonhappening of the stipulated event may be shown because the parol evidence rule does not come into play until a binding contract exists.

a) Distinguish from Condition Subsequent

Parol evidence is inadmissible as to conditions subsequent, *i.e.,* an oral agreement that the party would not be obliged to *perform* until the happening of an event. This latter type of condition limits or modifies a duty under an existing or formed contract.

b. Interpretation

If there is uncertainty or ambiguity in the written agreement's terms or a dispute as to the *meaning* of those terms, parol evidence can be received to aid the fact-finder in reaching a correct interpretation of the agreement. If the meaning of the agreement is plain, parol evidence is inadmissible.

c. Showing of "True Consideration"

The parol evidence rule will not bar extrinsic evidence showing the "true consideration" paid.

Example: A contract states that $10 has been given as full and complete consideration. Extrinsic evidence will be admitted, by way of a defense, to show that this sum has never been paid.

d. Reformation
Where a party to a written agreement alleges facts (*e.g.*, mistake) entitling him to reformation of the agreement, the parol evidence rule is inapplicable. Why? Because the plaintiff is asserting as a cause of action that despite the apparently unambiguous terms of the written agreement, those terms do not in fact constitute the agreement between the parties. For the plaintiff to obtain reformation, he must show:

(i) There was an *antecedent valid agreement* that

(ii) Is *incorrectly reflected* in the writing (*e.g.*, by mistake).

Note that the variance must be established by *clear and convincing evidence* rather than by merely a preponderance of the evidence.

4. Collateral Agreements
In certain well-known cases, courts have suggested that extrinsic evidence is admissible to show agreements between the parties that are "collateral" to the transaction otherwise evidenced by an apparently integrated writing. Note that the determination that an agreement is "collateral" is nothing more than a conclusion. If it is "collateral," it obviously must be an agreement that parties situated as are the parties to this contract would *naturally and normally not include* in the apparently integrated writing. Thus, if under the application of the prevailing Williston test, a court decides that evidence of the extrinsic matter may be introduced, it may characterize that extrinsic agreement as "collateral." It is submitted that this characterization adds nothing to the parol evidence rule analysis.

5. Parol Evidence Rule Applicable Only to Prior or Contemporaneous Negotiations
Parol evidence can be offered to show *subsequent* modifications of a written contract, since the parol evidence rule applies only to prior or contemporaneous negotiations. In short, the parties may show that they have altered the integrated writing after its making.

6. U.C.C. Rule
Under the U.C.C., a party cannot contradict the writing but he may add *consistent additional terms* unless: (i) there is a merger clause, or (ii) the courts find from all the circumstances that the writing was intended as a complete and exclusive statement of the terms of the agreement. [U.C.C. §2-202] This Code section also provides that a written contract's terms may be explained or supplemented by: (i) course of dealing or usage in the trade, or (ii) the course of performance to date, even if the terms appear to be unambiguous.

VII. INTERPRETATION AND ENFORCEMENT OF THE CONTRACT

A. INTRODUCTION
We now turn to the question of contract breach. To establish a breach, one must be able to prove that a party under a present duty to perform has not done so. The two basic questions are:

1. Has a present duty to perform arisen?

2. Has the duty to perform been discharged?

B. WHEN HAS A CONTRACTING PARTY'S DUTY TO PERFORM BECOME ABSOLUTE?

1. Distinction Between Promise and Condition
In looking at the terms of a contract, a distinction has to be drawn between an absolute promise on the one hand and a condition on the other.

a. Definitions

1) Promise
A promise is a commitment to do or refrain from doing something. The promise in the contract may be unconditional or conditional. An unconditional promise is absolute; a conditional promise may become absolute by the occurrence of the condition. If the promise is unconditional, the failure to perform according to its terms is a breach of contract.

2) Condition

A condition is an event, other than the passage of time, the occurrence or non-occurrence of which will create, limit, or extinguish the other contracting party's absolute duty to perform. A condition is a *"promise modifier."* There can be no breach of promise until the promisor is under an immediate duty to perform. He may insert conditions on his promise to prevent that duty of immediate performance from arising until the conditions are met. The failure of a contractual provision that is only a condition is *not a breach of contract*, but it discharges the liability of the promisor whose obligations on the conditional promise never mature.

Example: Gene agrees to sell his horse to Roy, the contract providing that delivery of possession will take place on June 1. On May 25, the horse dies. Was delivery of possession of the horse a condition? If so, its failure to occur will discharge Roy's duty to pay; however, Roy will not have a cause of action against Gene for nondelivery. Or was it a promise by Gene, the breach of which will give to Roy both an action against Gene for breach of contract and release him from his duty to pay?

b. Interpretation of Provision as Promise or Condition

As the above example indicates, it is of considerable importance whether any given contractual provision is to be interpreted as a promise or condition. The basic test is one of *"intent of the parties."* The courts employ several basic criteria in reaching a determination as to intent.

1) Words of Agreement

Both the specific words of the phrase and the words of the rest of the agreement (thus the context of the entire contract) will be examined by the courts in drawing a conclusion.

2) Prior Practices

The prior practices of the contracting parties, particularly with one another, will be taken into consideration.

3) Custom

The custom with respect to that business in the community will be examined.

4) Third-Party Performance

If performance is to be rendered by a third party, it is more likely to be a condition than an absolute promise.

5) Courts Prefer Promise in Doubtful Situations

In doubtful situations, most courts will hold that the provision in question is a *promise*. The underlying rationale is that this result will serve to support the contract, thereby preserving the expectancy of the parties. This preference is particularly significant in situations where the breaching party has *substantially performed*, because if the provision is treated as a *condition*, the nonbreaching party is completely discharged from her obligation; whereas, if the provision is treated as a *promise*, the nonbreaching party must perform, although she may recover for the damage she has suffered as a result of the breach.

Example: Stan contracts to build a house for Nancy using pipe of Reading manufacture. In return, Nancy agrees to pay Stan $100,000. Without Stan's knowledge, a subcontractor mistakenly uses pipe of Cohoes manufacture, which is identical in quality and is virtually indistinguishable from Reading pipe. The substitution is not discovered until the house is completed, when replacement of the pipe would require substantial destruction of the house. Nancy refuses to pay Stan. The installation of Reading pipe was a promise, not a condition, of the contract; therefore, Stan has a claim against Nancy for $100,000, subject to her claim against him for breach of duty to use Reading pipe. To treat it as a condition would be unfair to Stan, because he would be penalized in an amount far greater than the amount of the damage suffered by Nancy.

Note: When seeking to establish the reasonable expectations of the parties, one should determine whether the performance of the stipulation goes to the "very root" of the contract's consideration. If so, it is probably a condition rather than a promise.

c. Condition and Promise

A particular contractual provision may serve as a promise for one party *and* a condition for the other. These are frequently called constructive conditions of exchange.

Example: Sally agrees to type Joe's moot court brief by April 15 if Joe will agree to pay Sally $45 on that date for the typing. Joe agrees to these terms. Sally's promise to type Joe's brief by April 15 is an absolute promise and her performance of this promise is a condition to Joe's duty to pay $45 on April 15.

d. Promissory Conditions

A term may be both a promise and a condition for the same party.

Example: David agrees to buy Peter's house if David obtains sufficient financing. David tries, but is unable to obtain financing. Was obtaining financing a condition or was it a promise? In this case, it was probably both a promise and a condition. (Condition: to obtain financing first. Promise: to reasonably attempt to secure it.) David will satisfy his promissory obligation by making reasonable efforts to obtain financing, in which case his failure to obtain it discharges any further duty on either side of the contract.

2. Classification of Conditions

a. According to Time of Occurrence

1) Condition Precedent

A condition precedent is one that must occur *before* an absolute duty of immediate performance arises in the other party.

Example: Sal and Mary agree that "in consideration of Mary's promise to repay principal plus 8% interest, Sal hereby promises to loan Mary $50,000 for one year, provided that on July 1, the market value of Mary's country home is not less than $100,000." On July 1, Mary's country home is appraised at a market value of $80,000. Sal refuses to make the loan, and Mary sues. Sal wins because his duty to loan the $50,000 is subject to an express condition precedent. Since the condition was not satisfied, Sal's contingent liability never matured.

a) Party's Satisfaction as Condition Precedent

If a party has no duty to perform unless she is "satisfied" with another party's performance, the level of satisfaction required depends on the subject matter of the contract. If the contract involves mechanical fitness, utility, or marketability (*e.g.*, a construction or manufacturing contract), the party's performance is judged objectively, and thus it must satisfy a *reasonable person*. However, if the contract involves personal taste or judgment (*e.g.*, a contract to paint a portrait), the party's performance is judged subjectively, and thus it must satisfy the *particular party* receiving performance. *Note:* If a particular party's satisfaction is required, the party must act *honestly* and in *good faith*.

2) Conditions Concurrent

Conditions concurrent are those that are capable of occurring *together*, and that the parties are bound to perform at the same time (*e.g.*, tender of deed for cash). Thus, in effect, each is a condition "precedent" to the other.

Example: Smith and Jones agree that "in consideration of Jones's promise to pay the sum of $500, Smith promises to convey his 1970 Buick." Having signed this agreement, Jones never tenders the $500 and Smith does not tender the car. Neither party is in breach of contract. The contract is silent regarding time and place of performance, but the promises exchanged as consideration can obviously be performed at the same time and place. Hence, tender of the promised performance by each party is a constructive condition concurrent to liability of the other. Since both parties failed to tender performance, neither obligation matured.

3) Condition Subsequent

A condition subsequent is one the occurrence of which **cuts off** an already existing absolute duty of performance.

Example: Will and Grace enter the following contract: In consideration of Will's conveying his painting to her, Grace promises to pay Will $5,000 on July 1. Grace further promises to permit Will to retain the painting for purposes of exhibition during the months of July and August, provided security precautions for the safety of the painting are approved by Captain Smith. On July 1, Grace pays Will $5,000, and Will begins to exhibit the painting. On July 10, Captain Smith inspects security at the exhibition and declares it to be inadequate. Grace immediately asserts her right to possession, but Will refuses to surrender the painting. Grace is entitled to immediate possession of the painting. Her allowing Will to retain the painting for exhibition was subject to an express condition subsequent based on Captain Smith's approval of security precautions. Since the condition subsequent has ripened, Grace's conditional obligation to allow Will to retain the painting is extinguished.

4) Condition Precedent vs. Condition Subsequent

As a practical matter, there is **no substantive difference** between conditions precedent and conditions subsequent. When somebody brings a suit, the question is not whether she had a cause of action in the past, but whether she has one now. Thus, the distinction between a condition precedent and a condition subsequent is important only in regard to burdens of pleading and proof.

a) Condition Precedent—Plaintiff's Burden

The plaintiff must usually plead and prove the condition precedent because she claims there is a duty to be performed. (*Note:* Many local pleading rules require the plaintiff to plead generally performance of all conditions precedent and require the defendant to plead specifically those not performed.)

b) Condition Subsequent—Defendant's Burden

The defendant must usually plead and prove a condition subsequent because he claims the duty that existed no longer exists.

c) Other Factors Affecting Burden of Proof

Although the distinction between conditions precedent and subsequent is relevant to burden of proof issues, it is not necessarily determinative, because who bears the burden of proof may turn on many factors. Thus, for example, if the facts are specially within the knowledge of one party, the court may shift the burden of proof as justice requires. In other cases, the law establishes certain presumptions that will, in effect, shift the burden of proof notwithstanding any distinctions between conditions precedent and subsequent.

Example: While an insurance policy on Smith's life may provide that the beneficiary has the burden of proving that the cause of Smith's death was not suicide, the legal presumption against suicide will shift the burden of proof to the insurance company.

b. Express, Implied, and Constructive Conditions

1) Express Conditions

Express conditions are those expressed in the contract.

2) Implied Conditions

Implied conditions are those fairly to be inferred from evidence of the parties' intention; *i.e.,* their existence is determined by the process of contract interpretation. These are usually referred to as "implied in fact" conditions.

3) Constructive Conditions

a) In General

These are conditions **read into** a contract by the court without regard to or even despite the parties' intention. This is done in the interest of fairness to ensure that both parties receive the performance for which they bargained. These are usually referred to as "implied in law" conditions.

Example: Brother contracts to sell his stereo to Sister. The courts generally *infer* that Brother cannot demand payment of the money before he gives Sister the stereo (unless otherwise provided in the contract).

As the above example shows, whether a court finds a condition as a matter of interpretation (*i.e.,* implied in fact) or imposes it as a matter of construction (*i.e.,* implied in law) may be difficult to discern. Thus, in this example, the court might have gone either way.

b) The "Time Test"
The courts will also imply constructive conditions relating to the time for performing under the contract.

(1) Constructive Conditions Concurrent
Where both performances can be rendered at the same time, they are constructively concurrent; thus, each is a condition "precedent" to the other. Hence, absent excuse, each party must first tender his own performance if he wishes to put the other under a duty of immediate performance resulting in breach if he fails to perform.

(2) Constructive Conditions Precedent
Where one performance will take a period of time to complete while the other can be rendered in an instant, completion of the longer performance is a constructive condition precedent to execution of the shorter performance.

Example: Lulu agrees to paint Hank's barn for $400. In absence of a contract provision to the contrary, Lulu must paint the barn before Hank must pay.

4) Effect of Condition—Equitable Remedy
If a contract is not enforceable due to the failure or occurrence of a condition, the party who provided benefits to the other party can usually recover under unjust enrichment theories, although the measure of damages in that case may be less advantageous than the contract price.

3. Have the Conditions Been Excused?
A duty of immediate performance with respect to a conditional promise does not become *absolute* until the conditions (i) have been *performed*, or (ii) have been *legally excused*. Thus, in analyzing a question, if the facts do not reveal performance of the applicable condition precedent or concurrent, look to see whether the condition has been excused. Excuse of conditions can arise in a variety of ways.

a. Excuse of Condition by Hindrance or Failure to Cooperate
If a party having a duty of performance that is subject to a condition prevents the condition from occurring, she no longer has the benefit of the condition if the prevention is *wrongful*. Note, however, that it is not necessary to prove bad faith or malice. Courts construe the requirement simply to mean that the other party would not have reasonably contemplated or assumed the risk of this type of conduct.

Example: Franz agrees to paint Worthington's portrait. Worthington's promise to pay for the portrait is conditional upon her being satisfied with it. Worthington refuses to even look at the portrait. Her promise to pay becomes absolute.

Note: It appears fairly well settled today that a condition will be excused not only by "active" noncooperation but by "passive" noncooperation as well.

b. Excuse of Condition by Actual Breach
An actual breach of the contract when performance is due will excuse the duty of counterperformance. Note, however, that counterperformance will be excused *only* if the **breach is material**. A minor breach may suspend this duty, but it will not excuse it. Even if the minor breach may be cured, it will not suffice to excuse conditions. Rather, the courts will make the nonbreaching party whole by either giving him damages or otherwise mitigating his promised performance so as to account for the breach. (As to rules determining materiality of breaches, *see* VIII.B., *infra.*)

c. Excuse of Condition by Anticipatory Repudiation

Anticipatory repudiation occurs where a promisor, prior to the time set for performance of his promise, indicates that he will not perform when the time comes. If the requirements set forth below are met, this anticipatory repudiation will serve to excuse conditions.

1) Executory Bilateral Contract Requirement

Anticipatory repudiation will apply only where there is a bilateral contract with *executory (unperformed) duties on both sides*. Where the nonrepudiating party has nothing further to do at the moment of repudiation, as in the case of a unilateral contract or a bilateral contract fully performed by the nonrepudiator, the doctrine of anticipatory repudiation does not apply. The nonrepudiator must wait until the time originally set for performance by the repudiating party. Until such time, the repudiator has the option to change his mind and withdraw the repudiation and perform in accordance with the contract. [*Accord:* U.C.C. §2-611]

Example: Winston promises to pay Salem $2,000 on November 15 as consideration for Salem's car, the latter to be delivered on October 20. Salem delivers the car to Winston on October 20; on November 3, Winston repudiates. Salem will not have a cause of action until November 15.

2) Requirement that Anticipatory Repudiation Be Unequivocal

An anticipatory repudiation stems from the words or conduct of the promisor *unequivocally* indicating that he cannot or will not perform when the time comes. This statement must be positive.

Example: Wright states to Jones, "Business has not been going well and I have doubts about whether I will be able to perform my contract with you." This is *not* an anticipatory repudiation; mere expressions of doubt or fear will not suffice (although such expressions may establish prospective inability to perform, discussed below).

3) Effect of Anticipatory Repudiation

In the case of an anticipatory repudiation, the nonrepudiating party has four alternatives:

(i) Treat the anticipatory repudiation as a total repudiation and sue immediately;

(ii) Suspend performance and wait to sue until the performance date;

(iii) Treat the repudiation as an offer to rescind and treat the contract as discharged; or

(iv) Ignore the repudiation and urge the promisor to perform (but note that by urging the promisor to perform, the nonrepudiating party is not waiving the repudiation—she can still sue for breach and is excused from performing unless the promisor retracts the repudiation).

Note: U.C.C. section 2-610 provides substantially identical alternatives to a nonrepudiating party when there is an anticipatory repudiation in the case of the sale of goods.

4) Retraction of Repudiation

A repudiation may be retracted until the nonrepudiating party has accepted the repudiation or detrimentally relied on it.

d. Excuse of Condition by Prospective Inability or Unwillingness to Perform

Prospective failure of consideration occurs when a party has reasonable grounds to believe that the other party will be unable or unwilling to perform when performance is due.

Example: John contracts with Barbara to buy her house for $150,000. Payment is due on August 1. On July 10, John goes into bankruptcy (or Barbara transfers title to the house to Emily). Prospective inability to perform has occurred.

1) Distinguish from Actual and Anticipatory Repudiation

Prospective inability or unwillingness to perform is not an actual repudiation because it occurs prior to the time set for performance. It is not an anticipatory repudiation because such a repudiation must be *unequivocal*, whereas prospective failure to perform involves conduct or words that merely raise doubts that the party will perform. (In short, the distinction between anticipatory repudiation and prospective inability to perform is one of degree.)

2) What Conduct Will Suffice?
Any conduct may suffice for a finding that there is prospective inability or unwillingness to perform. Note that in judging this conduct, a *reasonable person* standard will be applied.

3) Effect of Prospective Failure
The effect of this prospective failure is to allow the innocent party to suspend further performance on her side until she receives *adequate assurances* that performance will be forthcoming. If she fails to obtain adequate assurances, she may be excused from her own performance and may treat the failure to provide assurances as a repudiation. (This same basic right is provided in U.C.C. section 2-609.)

4) Retraction
As with anticipatory repudiation, retraction is possible if the defaulting party regains his ability or willingness to perform. However, this fact must be communicated to the other party in order to be effective. If the other party has already changed her position in reliance on the prospective failure, an attempted retraction may be ineffective.

e. Excuse of Condition by Substantial Performance
The performance of one contractual promise is sometimes a condition precedent to the duty of immediate performance of the return promise. Technically, where the promise has not been performed, the other performance is not yet due. This can cause forfeiture if the breach is minor, because the promisee can receive almost complete performance with no duty to perform in return. To avoid this harsh result, the courts have adopted the "substantial performance" and "divisibility" concepts.

1) The Rule of Substantial Performance
Generally, the condition of complete performance may be excused if the party has rendered substantial performance. In this case, the other party's duty of counter-performance becomes absolute. It should be noted, however, that courts generally apply this doctrine only where a *constructive* (implied in law) condition is involved. They will not apply it where there is an *express* condition for fear this would defeat the express intent of the parties.

2) Substantial Performance Arises If Breach Is Minor
Rules for determining substantiality of performance are the same as those for determining materiality of breach. (*See* VIII.B.2., *infra.*) In other words, the test is whether the breach of contract by the performing party is material or minor. If it is material, then performance *has not* been substantial; if it is minor, performance *has* been substantial.

3) Inapplicable Where Breach "Willful"
Most courts will not apply the substantial performance doctrine where the breach has been "willful." (This is so even though willfulness is only one of the six factors usually relied on in determining materiality of a breach. *See* VIII.B.2., *infra.*) Trivial defects, however, even if they are willful, will be ignored by the courts as de minimis.

4) Damages Offset
Even though the party who has substantially performed is able to enforce the contract, the other party will be able to mitigate by deducting damages suffered due to the first party's incomplete performance.

5) Applicability of Substantial Performance to Sale of Goods
The doctrine of substantial performance was developed in construction contracts cases, and there is considerable doubt as to the application of the doctrine beyond such cases. As to contracts for the sale of goods, the U.C.C. "*perfect tender rule*" gives the buyer the right to reject goods that do not conform to the contract in any manner. [U.C.C. §2-601] However, the perfect tender rule is *subject to six exceptions:*

(i) The parties may otherwise agree;

(ii) Rejection of the goods under an installment contract may occur only if there is a substantial impairment of value (*see* f.3)b), *infra*);

(iii) The failure of the seller to make a reasonable contract with a carrier or the failure of the seller to notify the buyer, promptly, of shipment gives the buyer the right to reject only if material delay or loss ensues;

(iv) If the buyer has "accepted" the goods, he no longer has the right to reject;

(v) A bad faith rejection by the buyer in relation to an immaterial defect may preclude his right of rejection; and

(vi) Though the buyer has the right to reject for *any* defect in general, if contract time remains, the seller has the right to *cure*.

Thus, the buyer does not have an absolute right to reject under the Code, and the so-called perfect tender rule is misleading under the U.C.C. If the seller has substantially performed and if one of the exceptions or limitations to the buyer's absolute right to reject is involved, one may conclude that the doctrine of substantial performance, to this extent, applies under the Code as to contracts for the sale of goods. (*See also* Sales outline.)

f. **Excuse of Condition by "Divisibility" of Contract**
Divisibility, like the doctrine of substantial performance, is a concept designed to mitigate the harsh result of a potential forfeiture.

1) **Rule of "Divisibility"**
Where a party performs one of the units of a divisible contract, he is entitled to the agreed-on equivalent for that unit even though he fails to perform the other units. It is not a condition precedent to the other's liability that the whole contract be performed. The other has a cause of action for failure to perform the other units and may withhold his counterperformance for those units.
Example: Cambridge Construction Co. is to build 10 houses for $800,000 at $80,000 per house for Beth. Since the building takes a long time and payment can be rendered in one instant, the substantial completion of 10 houses would normally be a constructive condition precedent to payment. Completion of seven houses would leave Cambridge without any remedy on the contract itself (whatever rights it might have as a defaulting party would be by way of quasi-contractual relief). The divisibility doctrine allows Cambridge to sue for the pro rata price each time it completes a house.

2) **What Is a "Divisible" Contract?**
Obviously, the rule applies only where there is a finding that the contract is "divisible" (as compared to "entire"). *Three tests* must be *concurrently* satisfied in order to make this finding.

(i) The performance of each party is divided into two or more parts under the contract; and

(ii) The number of parts due from each party is the same; and

(iii) The performance of each part by one party is agreed on as the equivalent of the corresponding part from the other party, *i.e.,* each performance is the quid pro quo of the other.

[Rest. 2d §240]

a) **Interpretation**
Decisions on divisibility are questions of interpretation. The underlying consideration is one of fairness. Generally, the courts will construe contracts as divisible so as to avoid hardships and forfeitures that might otherwise result.

b) **Contract Expressly Indivisible**
Where the contract by its own terms is expressly indivisible, the court may not construe it as otherwise.

3) **Installment Contracts**
The U.C.C. assumes that all goods called for by a single contract must be tendered in a single delivery unless circumstances clearly point to a contrary intent, *e.g.*, there are not enough railroad cars on any one date. [U.C.C. §2-307] Where the contract authorizes or requires *deliveries in separate lots*, it is an installment contract. If an installment contract is involved, note the following [U.C.C. §§2-307, 2-612]:

a) The price, if it can be apportioned, may be demanded for *each lot* unless a contrary intent appears;

b) The buyer may reject an installment only if the defect *substantially impairs* the value of that *installment* and *cannot be cured*. Otherwise, she must accept the installment. *Note:* If the buyer gets *adequate assurance* of cure from the seller, the buyer must accept that installment; and

c) The buyer may declare a total breach only if the defects are such as to *substantially impair* the value of the *entire contract*. Note that even a material breach is easily waived and the duties reinstated if the buyer, *e.g.*, demands further performance or sues only for past installments.

g. **Excuse of Condition by Waiver or Estoppel**
One having the benefit of a condition may indicate by words or conduct that she will not insist on it. The courts, in certain circumstances, will enforce this expression on the basis that the party has "waived" the condition or is "estopped" from asserting it.

1) **Estoppel Waiver**
Whenever a party indicates that she is "waiving" a condition before it is to happen, or she is "waiving" some performance before it is to be rendered, and the person addressed *detrimentally relies* on such an indication, the courts will hold this to be a binding (estoppel) waiver. Note, however, that the promise to waive a condition may be retracted at any time *before* the other party has changed his position to his detriment.

2) **Election Waiver**
When a condition or a duty of performance is broken, the beneficiary of the condition or duty must make an election; she may: (i) terminate her liability, *or* (ii) continue under the contract. If she chooses the latter course, she will be deemed to have waived the condition or duty. This election waiver requires neither consideration nor estoppel (although estoppel elements are often present).
Example: Frederick contracted with Karen to sell her a new CD player in "perfect working order." In fact, the player when delivered had some minor mechanical troubles that Karen was apprised of at the time. Karen, nonetheless, elects to accept the player. She will be deemed to have waived the "perfect working order" condition.

3) **Conditions that May Be Waived**
If *no consideration* is given for the waiver, the condition must be *ancillary or collateral* to the main subject and purpose of the contract for the waiver to be effective. In other words, one cannot "waive" entitlement to the entire or substantially entire return performance. This would amount to a new undertaking that is really a gift in the disguise of a waiver.
Example: Robinson, a contractor, breaches a promise to build a garage for Hortense at a price of $6,000. Hortense says, "Even though you have not built the garage, I shall pay you the $6,000, waiving the constructive condition of performance." This waiver will not be enforceable; Robinson did not give consideration for the waiver, and the condition concerned the main subject and purpose of the contract.

4) **Right to Damages for Failure of Condition**
It is important to note that a waiver severs only the right to treat the failure of the

condition as a total breach excusing counterperformance. However, the waiving party does **not** thereby waive her right to damages. Thus, for instance, in the example above involving delivery of the CD player in "perfect working order," the waiving party still has her right to damages for the defects in the player—she merely waived her right to treat the failure to meet the condition as a total breach excusing counterperformance.

h. Excuse of Condition by Impossibility, Impracticability, or Frustration
Conditions may be excused by impossibility, impracticability, or frustration of purpose. (*See* discussion of these tests, *infra*.)

C. HAS THE ABSOLUTE DUTY TO PERFORM BEEN DISCHARGED?
Once it is determined that a party is under an immediate duty to perform, the duty to perform must be discharged.

1. Discharge by Performance
The most obvious way to discharge a contractual duty is, of course, by full and complete performance.

2. Discharge by Tender of Performance
Good faith tender of performance made in accordance with contractual terms will also discharge contractual duties. Note that the tendering party must possess the **present ability** to perform; a mere promise of performance will not suffice.

3. Discharge by Occurrence of Condition Subsequent
The occurrence of a condition subsequent will serve to discharge contractual duties.

4. Discharge by Illegality
If the subject matter of the contract has become illegal due to a subsequently enacted law or other governmental act, performance will be discharged. This is often referred to as "supervening illegality."

Example: Jim and Beam enter into a partnership contract to operate a tavern in the city of Clover. Subsequently, the Clover legislature enacts a prohibition law. The contract is discharged.

5. Discharge by Impossibility, Impracticability, or Frustration
The occurrence of an unanticipated or extraordinary event may make contractual duties impossible or impracticable to perform or may frustrate the purpose of the contract. Where the nonoccurrence of the event was a **basic assumption** of the parties in making the contract and **neither** party has expressly or impliedly **assumed the risk** of the event occurring, contractual duties may be discharged.

a. Discharge by Impossibility
Contractual duties will be discharged where it has become impossible to perform them.

1) Impossibility Must Be "Objective"
For this rule to operate, the impossibility must be "objective"; *i.e.,* the duties could not be performed by anyone. "Subjective" impossibility will not suffice, *i.e.,* where the duties could be performed by someone but not the promisor.

2) Timing of Impossibility
The impossibility must arise **after** the contract has been entered into. If the facts giving rise to impossibility already existed when the contract was formed, the question is not really one of "discharge of contractual duties." Rather, it is a "contract formation" problem, namely, whether the contract is voidable because of mistake.

3) Effect of Impossibility
Where a contract is discharged because of impossibility, each party is excused from duties arising under the contract that are yet to be fulfilled. Either party may sue for rescission and receive restitution of any goods delivered, payments made, etc.

4) Partial Impossibility
If the performance to be rendered under the contract becomes only partially impossible, the duty may be discharged **only to that extent**. The remainder of the

performance may be required according to the contractual terms. This is so even though this remaining performance might involve added expense or difficulty.

5) Temporary Impossibility
Temporary impossibility *suspends* contractual duties; it does not discharge them. When performance once more becomes possible, the duty "springs back" into existence. Note, however, that a duty will not "spring back" into existence if the burden on either party to the contract would be substantially increased or different from that originally contemplated.

6) Part Performance Prior to Impossibility—Quasi-Contractual Recovery
If part performance has been rendered by either party prior to the existence of the facts leading to impossibility, that party will have a right to recover in quasi-contract at the contract rate or for the reasonable value of his performance if that is a more convenient mode of valuation. (Note that such recovery will also be available where contract duties are discharged by impracticability or frustration, discussed below.)

7) Specific Situations

a) Death or Physical Incapacity
Death or the physical incapacity of a person *necessary* to effectuate the contract serves to discharge it.

Example: Helmut agrees to teach German to Max. Helmut's death or physical incapacity would discharge the contract. Max's death or physical incapacity would similarly discharge the contract. (The death or physical incapacity may also be that of a third person. Thus, for example, if Helmut had contracted with Max to teach German to Max's son, the death or physical incapacity of the son would also serve to discharge the contract.)

Note: Most fact situations on this point involve personal service contracts. Check to see whether the services involved are *"unique."* If the services are the kind that could be delegated (*see* "Delegation of Duties," V.C.2., *supra*), the contract is *not* discharged by the incapacity of the person who was to perform them.

b) Supervening Illegality
As we have seen, supervening illegality may serve to discharge a contract. Many courts treat such supervening illegality as a form of impossibility.

c) Subsequent Destruction of Contract's Subject Matter or Means of Performance
If the contract's subject matter is destroyed or the designated means for performing the contract are destroyed, contractual duties will be discharged. Note, however, that this destruction must not have been the fault of the promisor. Substantial damage to the subject matter will generally be construed by the courts as the equivalent of "destruction."

Example: Olivia hires Charlie to replace the shingles on the roof of her house. When Charlie has completed 90% of the work, the house is hit by lightning and is destroyed by fire. The contract will be discharged for impossibility since there no longer is a house needing reshingling. Charlie will be able to recover for the work done in quasi-contract. (*See* VIII.D.4.b., *infra*.)

(1) Compare—Contracts to Build
A contractor's duty to *construct* a building is *not* discharged by destruction of the work in progress. *Rationale:* Construction is not rendered impossible; the contractor can still rebuild. However, if the destruction was not caused by the contractor, most courts will excuse the contractor from meeting the original deadline.

Example: Olivia hires Charlie to build her a garage. When Charlie has completed 90% of the work, the garage is hit by lightning and is destroyed by fire. Charlie will not be discharged from his contractual duty to build the garage because it is not impossible to rebuild the garage.

(2) Specificity Required

(a) Subject Matter
Note that destruction of the subject matter will render a contract impossible only if the very thing destroyed is necessary to fulfill the contract. If the thing destroyed is not actually necessary, impossibility is not a defense.

Example: Linda contracts to sell her car to John. Subsequently, the car is destroyed through no fault of either party. The contract will be discharged because of impossibility because the only car that could fulfill the obligation no longer exists.

Compare: John orders a new car from his local Kia dealer. While the car that the dealer ordered for John is being delivered from the factory, it is destroyed in a crash. The contract is not discharged for impossibility because it is not impossible for the dealer to get another Kia that will satisfy the contract.

(b) Specificity of Source
As with the destruction of the subject matter, destruction of a source for fulfilling the contract will render the contract impossible only if the source is the one source specified by the parties.

Example: Jackson contracts to sell Daley 100 tons of iron ore from the Blarney Iron Mine, which Jackson owns. A nearby dam breaks and floods the mine. Jackson will be discharged from the contract for impossibility.

Compare: Jackson, who owns the Blarney Iron Mine, contracts to sell Daley 100 tons of iron ore. A nearby dam breaks and floods Jackson's mine. Jackson will not be discharged from the contract because the contract did not specify that the iron ore was to come from Jackson's mine. Thus, iron ore from any other mine can fulfill the contract.

(3) Where Risk of Loss Has Already Passed to Buyer
The rules relating to discharge because of destruction of the subject matter *will not apply* where the risk of loss has already passed to the buyer. The usual situations involve contracts for the sale of goods under the U.C.C. and contracts for the sale of land where equitable conversion has taken place.

b. Discharge by Impracticability
Modern courts will also discharge contractual duties where performance has become impracticable.

1) Test for Impracticability
The test for a finding of impracticability is that the party to perform has encountered:

(i) *Extreme and unreasonable* difficulty and/or expense; and

(ii) This difficulty was *not anticipated*.

In effect, these courts will allow relief against performance where subjective impossibility is found. It should be noted, however, that a mere change in the degree of difficulty or expense due to such causes as increased wages, prices of raw materials, or costs of construction, unless well beyond the normal range, does *not* amount to impracticability, because these are the types of risks that a fixed-price contract is intended to cover. [Rest. 2d §261]

2) Contracts for Sale of Goods

In contracts for the sale of goods under the U.C.C., the seller's duty to perform may be discharged where performance would be impracticable. The facts giving rise to impracticability must be such that their nonoccurrence was a basic assumption on which the contract was made. Typical examples of conditions giving rise to "commercial impracticability" under the U.C.C. would include embargoes, crop failure, currency devaluation, war, labor strikes, or the like entailing substantial unforeseen cost increases. [U.C.C. §2-615]

3) Temporary or Partial Impracticability

The rules spelled out above for temporary and partial impossibility are equally applicable to temporary and partial impracticability.

c. Discharge by Frustration

Has there been a frustration of the contract's purpose? Frustration will exist if the purpose has become valueless by virtue of some supervening event not the fault of the party seeking discharge. If the purpose has been frustrated, a number of courts will discharge contractual duties even though performance of these duties is still possible. The elements necessary to establish frustration are as follows:

(i)   There is some *supervening act* or event leading to the frustration;

(ii) At the time of entering into the contract, the parties *did not reasonably foresee* the act or event occurring;

(iii) The *purpose* of the contract has been completely or almost completely *destroyed* by this act or event; and

(iv) The purpose of the contract was realized by *both parties* at the time of making the contract.

Example: Sports, Inc. contracted to rent a sports stadium for a boxing match to be held on August 1 in the town of Greensville. On July 31, a sudden hurricane resulted in tremendous damage in Greensville, causing it to be classified as a "disaster area." Sports, Inc.'s promise to rent the stadium (which was still intact) was discharged by frustration of purpose (a hurricane was not anticipated by the parties and it completely destroyed the value of the contract).

In cases dealing with the sale of goods, U.C.C. section 2-615 (as described above) would apply in frustration cases the same as in the case of impracticability.

Remember that the promisor's duties to perform serve as a condition precedent to the other party's duty to perform. Hence, if these duties should be excused by impossibility, impracticability, or frustration, the other party's contractual duties will also be discharged.

6. Discharge by Rescission

Rescission will serve to discharge contractual duties. This rescission may be either mutual or unilateral.

a. Mutual Rescission

The contract may be discharged by an *express agreement* between the parties to rescind. The agreement to rescind is itself a binding contract supported by consideration, namely, the giving up by each party of his right to counterperformance from the other. The reasons for entering into such an agreement are immaterial absent duress or fraud.

1) Contract Must Be Executory

For a contract to be effectively discharged by rescission, the duties must be executory on *both* sides.

a) Unilateral Contracts

Where the contract is unilateral (*i.e.,* only one party owes an absolute duty), a contract to mutually rescind where one party still has a duty to perform will be ineffective. The courts reason that the original promisor, who has not suffered a legal detriment, has not given consideration. Thus, for an effective rescission in a unilateral contract situation where the offeree has already performed, the rescission promise must be supported by one of the following:

(1) An offer of *new consideration* by the nonperforming party;

(2) Elements of *promissory estoppel*, *i.e.,* detrimental reliance; or

(3) Manifestation of an *intent* by the original offeree to make a *gift* of the obligation owed her.

b) Partially Performed Bilateral Contracts

A mutual agreement to rescind will usually be enforced where a bilateral contract has been partially performed. Whether the party who has partially performed will be entitled to compensation will depend on the terms of the rescission agreement. The party seeking such compensation must affirmatively prove his right thereto in order to recover.

2) Formalities

Mutual rescission may be made *orally*. This is so even though the contract to be rescinded expressly states that it can be rescinded only by a written document. Several *exceptions* should be noted, however:

a) Subject Matter Within Statute of Frauds

If the subject matter of the contract to be rescinded falls within the Statute of Frauds (*e.g.,* transfer of land), then the rescission should generally be in writing. Some courts, however, hold that even where the Statute of Frauds comes into play, the oral rescission will still be enforceable where it is "executed" or promissory estoppel is present.

b) Contracts for the Sale of Goods

In addition to the Statute of Frauds requirement with respect to contracts for the sale of goods, the U.C.C. requires a written rescission or modification where the original contract to be rescinded or modified expressly requires a written rescission. [U.C.C. §2-209(2)]

3) Contracts Involving Third-Party Beneficiary Rights

Where the rights of third-party beneficiaries have already *vested*, the contract may *not* be discharged by mutual rescission.

b. Unilateral Rescission

Unilateral rescission results where one of the parties to the contract desires to rescind it but the other party desires that the contract be performed according to its terms. For unilateral rescission to be granted, the party desiring rescission must have adequate legal grounds. Most common among these are mistake, misrepresentation, duress, and failure of consideration. Where the nonassenting party refuses to voluntarily grant rescission, the other party may file an action in equity to obtain it.

7. Partial Discharge by Modification of Contract

If a contract is subsequently modified by the parties, this will serve to discharge those terms of the original contract that are the subject of the modification. It will *not* serve to discharge the *entire contract*. To have such a partial discharge, the following requirements must usually be met.

a. Mutual Assent

The modifying agreement must have been mutually assented to. Note, however, that under the doctrine of *reformation,* either of the parties to the contract may bring an equity action to have its terms modified where the writing, through mistake or misrepresentation, does not incorporate the terms orally agreed on.

b. Consideration

Generally, consideration is necessary to modify a contract. However, the courts usually find consideration to be present because each party has limited his right to enforce the original contract as is. Check the facts to see whether the modification would operate to the benefit of one of the parties only. If so, it may be unenforceable without some consideration being given to the other party. (*See* discussion of the preexisting legal duty rule, III.B.2.c.1), *supra.*)

    1)   Requirement Where Modification Is Only "Correction"
No consideration is necessary where the effect of the modification is merely to correct an error in the original contract.

    2)   Contracts for the Sale of Goods
No consideration is needed for the modification of a contract for the sale of goods under the U.C.C. [U.C.C. §2-209(1)]

8. Discharge by Novation
A novation occurs where a new contract substitutes a new party to receive benefits and assume duties that had originally belonged to one of the original parties under the terms of the old contract. A novation will serve to discharge the old contract. The elements for a valid novation are as follows:

(i)   A *previous* valid contract;

(ii) An *agreement* among all parties, including the new party (or parties) to the new contract;

(iii) The *immediate extinguishment* of contractual duties as between the original contracting parties; and

(iv) A valid and enforceable *new* contract.

Example: John contracts to sell his house to Jane for $150,000. Before the closing date, John, Jane, and Joanna execute a new agreement wherein all rights and duties in connection with the transaction are transferred by Jane to Joanna. The original John-Jane contract will be discharged by novation.

9. Discharge by Cancellation
The destruction or surrender of a written contract will not usually by itself discharge the contract. If, however, the parties manifest their *intent* to have these acts serve as a discharge, it will usually have this effect if consideration or one of its alternatives is present.

10. Discharge by Release
A release and/or contract not to sue will serve to discharge contractual duties. The release or contract not to sue usually must be in *writing* and supported by *new consideration* or *promissory estoppel* elements. [*Compare* U.C.C. §1-306—governing the sale of goods and requiring an authenticated record (such as a writing) but *not* requiring consideration]

11. Discharge by Substituted Contract
A contract may be discharged by a substituted contract. This occurs where the parties to a contract enter into a second contract that *immediately revokes* the first contract.

    a. Revocation May Be Express or Implied
The second contract may revoke the first contract either expressly or impliedly. The first contract will be impliedly revoked if the second contract's terms are inconsistent with the terms of the first contract.

    b. Intent Governs
Whether a second contract will constitute a substituted contract depends on whether the parties intend an immediate discharge or a discharge only after performance of the second contract. If an immediate discharge is intended, there is a substituted contract. If the parties intend the first contract to be discharged only after performance of the second contract, there is an executory accord (*see* 12.a., *infra*) rather than a substituted contract.

12. Discharge by Accord and Satisfaction
A contract may be discharged by an accord and satisfaction.

    a. Accord
An accord is an agreement in which one party to an existing contract agrees to accept, in lieu of the performance that she is supposed to receive from the other party to the existing contract, some other, different performance.

Example: Mel owes Alice $1,000 under a contract. Mel promises to give his car to Alice in settlement of the debt, and Alice agrees to accept the car in settlement of the debt. This agreement is an accord.

1) Requirement of Consideration

In general, an accord must be supported by consideration. Where the consideration is of a lesser value than the originally bargained-for consideration in the prior contract, it will be sufficient if the new consideration is of a *different type* or if the claim is to be paid to a *third party*.

Example: Fred owes Barney $700 under an existing contract. Fred offers Barney a new TV set worth $500 in lieu of the existing debt. Barney accepts. This new consideration is sufficient to form a valid accord, even though it is worth less than the consideration originally owed, because it is of a different type.

a) Partial Payment of Original Debt

One often-encountered problem involves the offer of a smaller amount than the amount due under an existing obligation in satisfaction of the claim, *i.e.,* partial payment of an original debt. The *majority view* is that this will suffice for an *accord and satisfaction* if there is a *"bona fide dispute"* as to the claim or there is otherwise some alteration, even if slight, in the debtor's consideration. (*See* discussion of the preexisting legal duty rule, III.B.2.c.1), *supra.*)

2) Effect of Accord

The accord, taken alone, will not discharge the prior contract. It merely *suspends* the right to enforce it in accordance with the terms of the accord contract.

b. Satisfaction

Satisfaction is the performance of the accord agreement. Its effect is to discharge not only the original contract but the accord contract as well.

c. Effect of Breach of Accord Agreement Before Satisfaction

What happens when the accord agreement is not followed by an immediate satisfaction, and one of the parties breaches the accord agreement?

1) Breach by Debtor

Where the breach is by the debtor, the creditor may sue either on the original undischarged contract *or* for breach of the accord agreement.

2) Breach by Creditor

Where the accord agreement is breached by the creditor, *i.e.,* he sues on the *original* contract, the debtor has two courses of action available:

a) She may raise the accord agreement as an equitable defense and ask that the contract action be dismissed.

b) As an alternative, she may *wait until she is damaged*, *i.e.,* the creditor is successful in his action on the original contract, and then bring an action at law for damages for breach of the accord contract.

d. Checks Tendered as "Payment in Full"

If a monetary claim is *uncertain* or is subject to a *bona fide dispute*, an accord and satisfaction may be accomplished by a *good faith* tender and acceptance of a check when that check (or an accompanying document) *conspicuously states* that the check is tendered in *full satisfaction* of the debt. [U.C.C. §3-311]

13. Discharge by Account Stated

An account stated is a contract between parties whereby they agree to an amount as a *final balance due* from one to the other. This final balance encompasses a number of transactions between the parties and serves to merge all of these transactions by discharging all claims owed thereon. In other words, all rights as to the individual, original transactions are discharged and the new agreement is enforceable. It is necessary, in order for the agreement to qualify as an account stated, that the parties have had *more than one prior transaction* between them.

  a. **Writing Generally Not Required**
   It is not necessary that the account stated be in writing. However, if one or more of the original transactions was subject to the Statute of Frauds, a writing will usually be required.

  b. **Account May Be Implied**
   It is also not required that an account stated be "express." It may be implied.
   Example: Becky and Dave have entered into a number of transactions. Becky presents Dave with a bill for $1,000 covering all of these previous transactions. Dave does not object to this amount within a reasonable period of time. It will be held that there is an account stated.

14. **Discharge by Lapse**
Where the duty of each party is a condition concurrent to the other's duty, it is possible that on the day set for performance, neither party is in breach and their contractual obligations lapse.

  a. **Time When Lapse Becomes Effective**
   If the contract states that time is "of the essence," the lapse will occur immediately; otherwise the contract will lapse after a reasonable time.
   Example: Sally contracts with Susan to sell 100 widgets to her for $1,000 on November 15. On November 15, Sally does not tender the widgets and Susan does not tender the $1,000. Ten months afterward, Sally attempts to put Susan in breach by tendering the widgets. Sally will not have a claim, as the contractual obligations of both parties have been discharged by lapse.

15. **Discharge by Operation of Law**
Where one party to a contract obtains a judgment against the other for breach of contractual duties, the contractual duty of performance is *merged* in the judgment, thereby discharging it. Note, however, that the judgment debtor is still obligated under the terms of the judgment for any new performance, *i.e.,* damages. Similarly, contractual duties will be discharged by merger where an award is made pursuant to properly provided-for arbitration. Also, a discharge in bankruptcy bars any right of action on the contract.

16. **Effect of Running of Statute of Limitations**
Where the statute of limitations on an action has run, it is generally held that an action for breach of contract may be barred. Note, however, that only *judicial remedies* are barred; the running of the statute *does not discharge the duties*. (Hence, if the party who has the advantage of the statute of limitations subsequently agrees to perform, new consideration will not be required.)

VIII. BREACH OF THE CONTRACT AND AVAILABLE REMEDIES

A. **WHEN DOES A BREACH OCCUR?**
If it is found that (i) the promisor is under an absolute duty to perform, and (ii) this absolute duty of performance has not been discharged, then this failure to perform in accordance with contractual terms will amount to a breach of the contract.

B. **MATERIAL OR MINOR BREACH?**
Once you have determined that there is a breach of contract, the next determination to be made is whether that breach is material or minor.

 1. **Effect of Breaches**

  a. **Minor Breach**
   A breach of contract is minor if the obligee gains the substantial benefit of her bargain despite the obligor's defective performance. Examples would be insignificant delays in completing performance or small deficiencies in the quality or quantity of performance where precision is not critical. The effect of a minor (immaterial) breach is to provide a remedy for the immaterial breach to the aggrieved party. The aggrieved party is *not relieved* of her duty of performance under the contract.

  b. **Material Breach**
   If the obligee does not receive the substantial benefit of her bargain as a result of

failure to perform or defective performance, the breach is considered material. If the breach is material, the consequences are more severe. The nonbreaching party (i) may treat the contract as at an end, *i.e.,* any duty of counterperformance owed by her will be discharged, and (ii) will have an ***immediate right*** to all remedies for breach of the entire contract, including total damages.

c.   Minor Breach Coupled with Anticipatory Repudiation
If a minor breach is coupled with an anticipatory repudiation, the nonbreaching party may treat it as a material breach; *i.e.,* she may sue immediately for total damages and is permanently discharged from any duty of further performance. Indeed, the courts hold that the aggrieved party must not continue on, because to do so would be a failure to mitigate damages. The U.C.C. modifies this to permit a party to complete the manufacture of goods to avoid having to sell unfinished goods at the lower salvage value. (*See infra.*)

2.   Determining Materiality of Breach

a.   General Rule
In determining whether a breach is material or minor, the courts generally apply the following six criteria [Rest. §275]:

1)   Amount of Benefit Received
Look to the extent to which the nonbreaching party will receive substantially the benefit she could have anticipated from full performance. The greater the extent, the less material the breach.

2)   Adequacy of Damages
Look to the extent to which the injured party may be adequately compensated in damages. The greater the extent, the less material the breach.

3)   Extent of Part Performance
Look to the extent the party failing to perform completely has already performed or made preparations to perform. The greater the extent, the less material the breach.

4)   Hardship to Breaching Party
Look to the extent of hardship on the breaching party should the contract be terminated. The greater the extent, the less material the breach.

5)   Negligent or Willful Behavior
Look to the extent of negligent or willful behavior of the party failing to perform. The greater the extent, the more material the breach.

6)   Likelihood of Full Performance
Look to the extent of likelihood the party who has failed to perform will perform the remainder of his contract. The greater the extent, the less material the breach.

b.   Failure of Timely Performance
The basic question here is whether the parties to the contract must perform on time. Assuming that the defaulting party had a duty of immediate performance when his failure to perform occurred, then his failure to perform on time will always be a breach of contract. There are, however, additional specific rules for determining the materiality of breach by failure of timely performance.

1)   As Specified by Nature of Contract
Unless the nature of the contract is such as to make performance on the exact day agreed upon of vital importance, or the contract by its terms provides that time is of the essence, failure by a promisor to perform at the stated time will not be material.

2)   When Delay Occurs
Delay at the onset of performance before the delaying party has rendered any part of his agreed-on performance is more likely to be considered material than delay where there has been part performance.

3) Mercantile Contracts
In mercantile contracts, timely performance as agreed is important, and unjustified delay is material.

4) Land Contracts
More delay in land contracts is required for materiality than in mercantile contracts.

5) Availability of Equitable Remedy
In equity, the courts generally are much more lenient in tolerating considerable delay. Hence, they will tend to find the breach immaterial and award compensation for the delay where possible.

C. NONBREACHING PARTY'S ABILITY TO PERFORM
The nonbreaching party who sues for breach of contract must show that she is *willing and able* to perform but for the breaching party's failure to perform.

D. REMEDIES FOR BREACH
Where the plaintiff can prove a breach and that she herself is not in material breach, she will have available to her a choice of remedies. Whether more than one remedy will be available in any given case will depend on the facts and applicable rules.

1. Damages
The most frequently sought remedy for breach of contract is an action at law for damages. In cases of willful breach, courts are more likely to be flexible in determining the plaintiff's damages alternatives.

a. Types of Damages

1) Compensatory (Contract) Damages
The purpose of contract damages based on affirmance of the contract is to give compensation for the breach; that is, to *put the nonbreaching party where she would have been had the promise been performed* so far as money can do this. If the breach is minor, the remedy is an award of damages sufficient to compensate for defective performance. Since the nonbreaching party is under a duty to tender counterperformance, her claim is usually asserted as a setoff against her liability to the obligor.

a) "Standard Measure" of Damages—Expectation Damages
In most cases, the plaintiff's standard measure of damages will be based on an "expectation" measure, *i.e.,* sufficient damages for her to buy a *substitute performance*. This is also known as "benefit of the bargain" damages.

(1) Reliance Damages Alternative
In other cases, the plaintiff's expectation damages will be too speculative to measure (*e.g.,* the plaintiff cannot show with sufficient certainty the profits she would have made if the defendant had performed the contract). In these cases, the plaintiff may elect to recover damages based on a "reliance" measure rather than an expectation measure. Reliance damages award the plaintiff the cost of her performance; *i.e.,* they are designed to *put the plaintiff in the position she would have been in had the contract never been formed.*
Example: J-Mart gives Sam a "dealer franchise" to sell J-Mart's products in a stated area for one year. In preparation for performance, Sam spends money on advertising, hiring sales personnel, and acquiring premises that cannot be used for other purposes. J-Mart then repudiates before performance begins. If it cannot be established with reasonable certainty what profit Sam would have made if the contract had been performed (*i.e.,* Sam's expectation damages), Sam can recover as reliance damages his expenditures in preparation for performance.

b) Consequential Damages

(1) Reasonable Person Standard

In addition to the standard measure of damages imposed on the breaching party, the courts will hold him liable for any further losses resulting from the breach that any *reasonable person* would have *foreseen* would occur from a breach at the time of entry into the contract. Requiring that damages be foreseeable helps to promote commercially viable agreements since it prompts parties to reflect on the risks inherent in the bargain and to disclose any nonobvious elements of risk from nonperformance. [*See also* U.C.C. §2-715]

(2) Plaintiff Has Burden of Proof

For the plaintiff to prevail, she must show that both parties were aware of the special circumstances that existed at the time of contract formation. The parties, as reasonable people, must have realized that these special circumstances would involve a substantial amount of risk and resulting damage if the contract were to be breached.

2) Punitive Damages

Punitive or exemplary damages are generally *not* awarded in commercial contract cases; they may be awarded under limited circumstances in a noncommercial type of contract.

3) Nominal Damages

Nominal (token) damages (*e.g.*, $1) may be awarded where a breach is shown but no actual loss is proven.

4) Liquidated Damages

Liquidated damages that have been agreed to by both parties at the time of the contract, and that are not punitive, are enforceable. (*See* e., *infra.*)

b. "Standard Measure"—Specific Situations

1) Contracts for Sale of Goods

The damage remedies for breach of a contract for the sale of goods are found in the Uniform Commercial Code. Section 2-703 lists the remedies of the seller when the buyer breaches; section 2-711 lists the remedies of the buyer when the seller breaches. (To aid in structuring the material and for review purposes, *all* Article 2 remedies are listed below.)

a) Remedies of the Seller

When the buyer wrongfully rejects or revokes acceptance of goods, fails to make a payment due on or before delivery, or repudiates, the seller may:

(1) *Withhold delivery* of the goods;

(2) *Stop delivery* by the carrier;

(3) *Resell the goods and recover the difference* between the resale price and the contract price;

(4) *Cancel the contract*;

(5) *Recover the price* if: (i) the goods have been accepted or conforming goods were lost or damaged within a reasonable time after risk of loss passed to the buyer; or (ii) the goods have been identified to the contract and the seller is unable to resell; or

(6) *Recover ordinary contract damages* for nonacceptance, and the measure here is the difference between the market price at the time and place for tender and the contract price, together with any incidental damages.

b) Remedies of the Buyer for Breach by the Seller

If the seller fails to deliver or repudiates or the buyer rightfully rejects or revokes acceptance with respect to the goods, the buyer may:

(i) *Cancel*;

(ii) *"Cover,"* i.e., buy substitute goods and recover the difference between the price of the substitute goods and the contract price;

(iii) *Recover goods identified to the contract* if the buyer has paid a part or all of the price;

(iv) *Recover the goods contracted for* if the buyer is unable to cover *and* the goods were either in existence when the contract was made or were later identified to the contract;

(v) *Obtain specific performance* if appropriate (e.g., if the goods are *unique*); or

(vi) *Recover damages for nondelivery*, and the measure is the difference between the market price at the time when the buyer learned of the breach and the contract price plus incidental and consequential damages.

(1) Anticipatory Repudiation by Seller
The buyer's damage formula for recovery is different from pre-Code law. There is a significant problem with the use of this formula in relation to anticipatory repudiation. If there is an anticipatory repudiation by the seller, the buyer may await the seller's performance for a commercially reasonable time. In most cases, this would allow the buyer to await the seller's performance until the time for performance arrived.

(a) Problem—Contract Formed Far in Advance of Shipment
It is possible for a contract to be formed long in advance of the time for shipment of the goods. For example, a contract formed on January 5 might not be performable by the seller until December 20. If the subject matter of the contract is fluctuating greatly in value, particularly if the market price is rapidly ascending, the question is what is a commercially reasonable time during which the buyer may await the seller's performance. If, in the unusual case, the buyer's action based on anticipatory repudiation came to trial before the time for performance, the market price would be determined as of the time when the aggrieved party learned of the repudiation. [U.C.C. §2-723] However, in the typical case, the action will not be started until after the time for performance has arrived. Therefore, by negative implication, the time of repudiation is not the time of breach and there is a gap or hole in the Code as to how to measure the damages.

(b) Computation of Damages Under Code
Under section 2-713, the measure is the difference between the market price at the time the buyer learned of the breach and the contract price. *Query:* In this situation, when did the buyer "learn of the breach"? Since an anticipatory repudiation is not a breach until treated as such by the aggrieved party, the breach cannot be said to have occurred until it was so treated by the purchaser in this situation. Using the Code concept that the buyer could await performance for a commercially reasonable time, it is submitted that the probable result will be the courts' construing the breach as having occurred at the *end of the "commercially reasonable time"* and using that date as the time the "buyer learned of the breach" so as to allow the computation of the buyer's damages under section 2-713.

(2) Remedy of Buyer Who Keeps Nonconforming Goods
If the seller delivers goods breaching one of his warranties (e.g., he breaches his warranty to deliver conforming goods) and the buyer decides to *keep* the goods, the buyer may recover the *difference* between the

value the goods would have had if they had been as warranted and the *actual value* of the goods. [U.C.C. §2-714(2)]

2) Contracts for Sale of Land
The standard measure of damages for breach of land sale contracts will be the difference between the contract price and the fair market value of the land.

3) Employment Contracts
In employment contracts, check to see whether the breach was by the employer or the employee.

a) Breach by Employer
Irrespective of when the breach occurs—*i.e.,* before performance, after part performance, or after full performance, the standard measure of the employee's damages will be the *full contract price*.

b) Breach by Employee
If the employee is the breaching party, check to see whether the breach is intentional or unintentional.

(1) Intentional Breach
If the employee's breach is intentional, the employer will be entitled to a standard measure of damages computed according to what it *costs to replace* the employee, *i.e.,* the difference between the cost incurred to get a second employee to do the work and the cost to the employer had the first breaching employee done the work. The modern view allows the employee to offset any monies due from work done to date.

(2) Unintentional Breach
The standard measure of damages for unintentional breach is the same as for intentional breach. However, where the breach is unintentional, *e.g.,* personal illness, the employee may have a right to quasi-contractual recovery for work done to date.

4) Construction Contracts
Where construction contracts are involved, check to see whether the owner or the builder is breaching.

a) Breach by Owner
If the owner has breached, check to see when the breach occurred.

(1) Breach Before Construction Started
If the breach occurred before construction started, the builder will be entitled to the *profits* he would have derived from the contract.

(2) Breach During Construction
If the breach occurs during construction, the builder will be entitled to any *profit* he would have derived from the contract *plus* any *costs* he has incurred to date. The formula is also stated as the contract price minus the cost of completion. Either formula will give the same result.

(3) Breach After Construction Completed
Where the breach occurs after construction has been completed, the builder is entitled to the full *contract price plus interest* thereon.

b) Breach by Builder
If the breach is by the builder, check to see when it occurred.

(1) Breach Before Construction Started
Where the builder breaches before construction, the owner's measure of damages is the *cost of completion*, *i.e.,* the amount above the contract price that it will cost to get the building completed *plus* reasonable compensation for any delay in performance.

(2) Breach During Construction
Where the builder breaches after partially performing, the owner is

entitled to the *cost of completion plus reasonable compensation for any delay* in performance. If, however, completion would involve undue economic waste, the measure of damages will be the difference between the value of what the owner *would have received* if the builder had properly performed the contract and the value of what the owner *actually received*.

(3) Breach by Late Performance
Where the builder completes performance, but it is late, the owner has a right to damages for any loss incurred by not being able to use the property when performance was due, *e.g.,* loss of reasonable rental value where property could have been leased. However, if damages for this "lost use" are not easily determined or were not foreseeable at the time the contract was entered into, the owner can recover only the *interest* on the value of the building as a capital investment.

5) Contracts Calling for Installment Payments
If a contract calls for payments in installments and a payment is not made, there is only a partial breach. The aggrieved party is limited to recovering only the missed payment, not the entire contract price. However, the contract may include an *acceleration clause* making the entire amount due on any late payment, in which case the aggrieved party may recover the entire amount. [Rest. 2d §243(3)]

6) Duty to Mitigate—All Contracts
When computing the standard measure of damages for any of the above situations, one should always keep in mind the duty to mitigate (*see infra*).

c. Certainty Rule
The plaintiff must prove that the losses suffered were certain in their nature and *not speculative*.

1) Profits from New Business
Traditionally, if the breaching party prevented the nonbreaching party from setting up a new business, courts would not award lost profits from the prospective business as damages because they were too speculative. However, modern courts may allow lost profits as damages if they can be made more certain by observing similar businesses in the area or other businesses previously owned by the same party.

d. Duty to Mitigate Damages
The nonbreaching party has a duty to mitigate damages. Thus, she must refrain from piling up losses after she receives notice of the breach; she must not incur further expenditures or costs, and she must make reasonable efforts to cut down her losses by procuring a substitute performance at a fair price. Should she not do so, she will not be allowed to recover those damages that might have been avoided by such mitigation after the breach. Generally, a party may *recover the expenses of mitigation*. Note the following specific contract situations:

1) Employment Contracts
Where the employer breaches, the employee is under a duty to use *reasonable care* in finding a position of the same kind, rank, and grade in the same locale (although it does not necessarily have to be at the same exact pay level). However, note that the burden is on the employer to show that such jobs were available.

2) Contracts for Sale of Goods

a) Buyer Is in Breach
If the buyer is in breach, the seller has a right to *resell the goods* in a commercially reasonable manner. If he does this, he may recover the difference between the resale price (which need not be the "market value") and the contract price. [U.C.C. §2-706] Should he not resell, his damages will be limited to the difference between the contract price and the market value at the time set for performance. Note that if the seller should resell and derive a profit, he will not be able to collect resale damages from the buyer because the resale price is higher than the contract price, and he also will not be accountable to the buyer for the profit.

b) **Seller Is in Breach**
If the seller is in breach, the buyer has the right to *purchase substitute goods* at a reasonable price. If she does buy substitute goods, she may recover the difference between the contract price and the cost of the substitute goods (not necessarily "market value"). This is the U.C.C. concept of "cover." [U.C.C. §2-712] Should the buyer not "cover," she will be limited to recovery of the difference between the contract price and market value and cannot recover any consequential damages that could have been avoided by covering. [U.C.C. §2-715]

3) **Manufacturing Contracts**
Generally, in a contract to manufacture goods, if the person for whom the goods are being manufactured breaches, the manufacturer is under a duty to mitigate by *not continuing work* after the breach. However, if the facts are such that completion of the manufacturing project will decrease rather than increase damages, the manufacturer has a right to continue.

Example: Partly manufactured goods may be without value because they cannot be sold. The nonbreaching manufacturer may complete production and recover for his expenses in doing so, because finished goods usually can be resold, and the damages will be decreased as a result.

4) **Construction Contracts**
A builder does not owe a duty to avoid the consequences of an owner's breach, *e.g.,* by securing other work, but does have a duty to mitigate by *not continuing work* after the breach. Again, however, if completion will decrease damages, it will be allowed.

e. **Effect of Liquidated Damages Provision**

1) **Requirements for Enforcement**
The parties to a contract may stipulate what damages are to be paid in the event of a breach. These liquidated damage clauses will be enforceable if the following two requirements are met:

(i) Damages for contractual breach must have been *difficult to ascertain* or estimate *at the time the contract was formed*.

(ii) The amount agreed on must have been a *reasonable forecast* of compensatory damages in the case of breach. The test for reasonableness is a comparison between the amount of damages prospectively probable at the time of contract formation and the liquidated damages figure. If the liquidated damages amount is unreasonable, the courts will construe this as a *penalty* and will not enforce the provision.

a) **U.C.C. Rule**
The U.C.C. allows a court to consider actual damages to validate a liquidated damages clause. Even if the clause was not a reasonable forecast of damages at the time of the contract formation, it will be valid if it was reasonable in light of the subsequent actual damages. [U.C.C. §2-718(1)]

2) **Recoverable Even If No Actual Damages**
If both of the above requirements are met, the plaintiff will receive the liquidated damages amount. Most courts hold this is so even when no actual money or pecuniary damages have been suffered. Should one or both of the above requirements not be met, the provision fails and the plaintiff will recover only those damages that she can *prove*.

3) **Effect of Electing Liquidated or Actual Damages**
Should a contract stipulate that the plaintiff may elect to recover liquidated damages set by a clause or actual damages, the liquidated damage clause may be unenforceable.

2. **Suit in Equity for Specific Performance**
If the *legal remedy is inadequate*, the nonbreaching party may seek specific performance,

which is essentially an order from the court to the breaching party to perform or face contempt of court charges. The legal remedy (damages) generally is inadequate when the *subject matter of the contract is rare or unique*. The rationale is that if the subject matter is rare or unique, damages will not put the nonbreaching party in as good a position as performance would have, because even with the damages the nonbreaching party would not be able to purchase substitute performance.

a. **Available for Land and Rare or Unique Goods**
Specific performance is always available for land sale contracts because all land is considered to be unique. It is also available for goods that are rare or unique at the time performance is due (*e.g.*, rare paintings, gasoline in short supply because of oil embargoes, etc.).

b. **Not Available for Service Contracts**
Specific performance is not available for breach of a contract to provide services, even if the services are rare or unique. This is because of problems of enforcement (it would be difficult for the court to supervise the performance) and because the courts feel it is tantamount to involuntary servitude, which is prohibited by the Constitution.

1) **Injunction as Alternate Remedy**
In contrast, a court may *enjoin* a breaching employee from working for a competitor throughout the duration of the contract if the services contracted for are rare or unique. This is allowed because less court supervision is required for a negative injunction than for a specific performance decree, and the prohibition against working (as opposed to the requirement of working) does not run afoul of the Constitution. The rationale for this approach is that an employee providing rare or unique services expressly or impliedly covenants that she will not work for a competitor during the contract term.

c. **Equitable Defenses Available**
Because specific performance is an equitable remedy, it is subject to equitable defenses. The most frequently claimed equitable defenses are laches, unclean hands, and sale to a bona fide purchaser.

1) **Laches**
The equitable defense of laches arises when a party delays in bringing an equitable action and the delay prejudices the defendant (*e.g.*, the delay has substantially increased the cost or difficulty of performance). Note that mere delay itself is not a ground for this defense.

2) **Unclean Hands**
The unclean hands defense arises when the party seeking specific performance is guilty of some wrongdoing in the transaction being sued upon (*e.g.*, the defendant entered into the contract because of the plaintiff's lies). Note that the wrongdoing must be related to the transaction being sued upon; it is not sufficient that the plaintiff has defrauded other persons in similar transactions.

3) **Sale to a Bona Fide Purchaser**
If the subject matter of a goods or land contract has already been sold to another who purchased for value and in good faith (*i.e.*, a bona fide purchaser), the right to specific performance is cut off.
Example: Store contracts to sell a specific van Gogh painting to Ben. Before Store delivers the painting to Ben, Carla, who is unaware of Ben's contract with Store, offers to buy the same van Gogh from Store. Store accepts Carla's offer and gives the painting to Carla. Ben may not obtain specific performance.

3. **Rescission and Restitution**
The nonbreacher may rescind (*i.e.*, cancel) and sue for restitution at law or in equity. Where the nonbreacher has transferred a "benefit" to the breacher in an attempt to perform on her side, she is entitled to restitution of that benefit. This may be accomplished by giving her "value" restitution, *i.e.*, the fair market value of the benefit transferred. This amount may be greater than the contract price in certain cases (*see* 4.b.2)b), *infra*).

4. **Other Forms of Relief Arising Out of "Contractual" Situations**

a. Tort Actions

Courts have increasingly shown a tendency to impose a tort duty as well as a contractual duty with respect to contractual performance where there is a *reasonably foreseeable risk of harm* in connection with that performance. Thus, the improper performance of a contract may also give rise to a tort action by the injured party. In particular, the situation arises in the area of products liability.

b. Quasi-Contract

A quasi-contract is *not really a contract* at all; rather it is a legal fiction designed to *avoid injustice* by preventing unjust enrichment of the defendant to the detriment of the plaintiff. As such, there is no requirement that the formalities necessary for the formation of a contract (*e.g.,* mutual assent) be present for quasi-contractual relief. Note further that although quasi-contractual relief is a remedy at law, the principles of equity govern.

1) Requirements for Quasi-Contractual Relief

a) Failed Contract

Where quasi-contractual relief is used to remedy a failed contract, the failed contract must result in *unjust enrichment* of one of the parties.

Examples: 1) Ann hires Ben to sign autographs in Ann's sporting goods store one day next month and gives Ben half of his $1,000 fee upon making the contract. Ben then dies and so is discharged from his obligation to perform. Ann can recover the $500 from Ben's estate in quasi-contract.

2) Owner hires Builder to repair Owner's house. After Builder has completed half of the repair work, the house is destroyed by a tornado. Although the parties will be discharged for impossibility, Builder will be able to recover in quasi-contract for the valuable improvements made to the house before it was destroyed.

3) Landlord promises to sell Tenant five acres of a 1,000-acre tract that Tenant is leasing, but the contract fails to state which five acres. Tenant plants fruit trees on the five acres that he thinks were intended. Tenant cannot enforce the promise because it does not specify which five acres were intended, but he can recover in quasi-contract for the value of the fruit trees.

(1) Breaching Party May Recover in Quasi-Contract

Even a party who has breached a contract might be able to recover in quasi-contract as long as the breach did not involve seriously wrongful or unconscionable conduct.

Example: Alex agrees to reshingle Beth's roof for $1,000. Alex does the work at a cost to him of $800 but inadvertently uses the wrong type of shingles so that there is no substantial performance. Nevertheless, the reshingling increased the value of Beth's house by $600. The defects cannot be corrected without pulling off the new shingles and completely reshingling the roof. Some courts would allow Alex to recover $600—the benefit conferred on Beth.

(2) Equitable Principles Apply

Although an action based on quasi-contract lies in law, the principles of equity apply. Thus, the equitable defense of "unclean hands" may come into play if the plaintiff's "unclean hands" are directly related to the transaction at issue.

b) Where No Contract Involved

Where there is no contractual relationship between the parties, the courts require the following to establish a right to quasi-contractual relief:

(i) The plaintiff has **conferred a benefit** on the defendant by rendering services or expending properties;

(ii) The plaintiff had a **reasonable expectation** of being compensated;

(iii) The benefits were conferred at the express or implied request of the defendant—*i.e.,* the plaintiff was **not a "volunteer"**; and

(iv) If the defendant is allowed to retain the benefits without compensating the plaintiff, he will be **unjustly enriched**.

Example: Doctor witnesses an automobile accident and rushes to aid a victim. Doctor can recover the reasonable value of his services.

Note: Where the parties are in a **close relationship** to one another, it is usually presumed that the benefits were given gratuitously and the party claiming relief bears the burden of showing that they were conferred with an expectation of being paid therefor.

2) Measure of Quasi-Contractual Recovery

a) Defendant's Benefit or Plaintiff's Detriment
Although the usual measure of quasi-contractual relief is the **benefit** received by the defendant, the prevailing modern rule allows recovery measured by the **detriment** suffered by the plaintiff if the benefits are difficult to measure or if the "benefit" measure would achieve an unfair result.

Example: Painter agrees to paint Owner's house. In expectation of performing this task, Painter spends $1,000 on materials. Before performance, Owner sells the house. Painter may recover $1,000 in quasi-contract even though Owner will not receive any real benefit.

b) Relief May Exceed Contract Price
Most courts will not allow recovery in quasi-contract to exceed the contract price. However, if the plaintiff has not breached the contract, some courts allow the plaintiff to recover the full value of the benefit received by the defendant or the detriment incurred by the plaintiff, even if it exceeds the contract price. This is useful if the plaintiff has made a losing contract; he may prefer to proceed on a quasi-contractual basis rather than pursue the standard breach of contract remedy (expectation damages).

3) Exam Tactic
In analyzing bar examination questions in the contracts area, one should always keep quasi-contractual relief in mind. For even if the facts indicate that a party is not entitled to relief under a contract, it is still possible that she may be entitled to quasi-contractual relief if she has suffered a loss or rendered services.

BAR REVIEW

Sales

celebrating
35 YEARS
*of preparing
law students
for the bar exam*

SALES

TABLE OF CONTENTS

I. INTRODUCTION

A. UNIFORM COMMERCIAL CODE GOVERNS TRANSACTIONS IN GOODS

The preceding Contracts outline sets out the general law of contracts, and the rules discussed in that outline apply in most contractual situations. However, special rules have been developed for contracts involving transactions in *goods*, and those rules are contained in Article 2 of the Uniform Commercial Code ("U.C.C."). Article 2 has adopted much of the common law of contracts, but where the common law and Article 2 differ, Article 2 prevails.

B. SUBJECT MATTER OF ARTICLE 2

1. Applies to All Contracts for the Sale of Goods

Article 2 applies to transactions in goods, including all contracts *involving the sale of goods*.

a. "Sale" Defined

A sale is a contract in which title to goods passes from the seller to the buyer for a price. [U.C.C. §2-106]

b. "Goods" Defined

The Code defines "goods" as all *things movable* at the time they are identified as the goods to be sold under the contract. [U.C.C. §2-105(1)] Thus, Article 2 applies to sales of most tangible things (*e.g.,* cars, horses, hamburgers), but does not apply to the sale of real estate, services (*e.g.,* a health club membership), or intangibles (*e.g.,* a patent). If a sale involves both goods and services (*e.g.,* a contract to paint a portrait), a court will determine which aspect is dominant and apply the law governing that aspect to the whole contract.

c. Goods Associated with Real Estate

"Goods associated with real estate" *may* fall under Article 2. The U.C.C. applies the following rules in determining whether Article 2 applies to such goods:

1) Sales of Structures to Be Removed from Land, Minerals, or the Like

Sales of "structures to be removed from land," "minerals," "or the like" fall under Article 2 *if severance is to be made by the seller.* Until severance, a purported present sale, not effective as a transfer of an interest in land, is effective only as a contract to sell.

2) Growing Crops and Uncut Timber

Sales of growing crops or timber to be cut, made separate from a sale of the land on which the crops or timber are growing, fall under Article 2 *regardless of who severs*. The parties can, by identification, effect a present sale before severance.

3) "Other Things" (Mostly "Fixtures")

Other things (except those described in 1) and 2), above) that can be removed from the land *without material harm to the land* are within Article 2. This is so regardless of who severs.

2. Merchants vs. Nonmerchants

A number of the rules in Article 2 depend on whether the seller and/or buyer are merchants. The Code defines "merchant" as one who regularly deals in goods of the kind sold or who otherwise by his profession holds himself out as having special knowledge of the goods sold. [U.C.C. §2-104(1)]

3. Good Faith Requirement

The Code requires all parties to act in good faith. Good faith is defined as "honesty in fact and the observance of reasonable commercial standards of fair dealing." [U.C.C. §1-201(20)]

II. FORMATION OF THE CONTRACT

A. IN GENERAL

A contract for the sale of goods can be made in any manner sufficient to show agreement. Thus, the contract can be oral, written, or established through any conduct of the parties that indicates a contract was formed. [U.C.C. §2-204]

B. OFFER AND ACCEPTANCE

1. Offer—Merchants' Firm Offers

Article 2 includes one important modification of the common law concerning offers. Recall that under the common law, offers generally are revocable unless the offeror receives consideration to keep the offer open, in which case an option contract (*i.e.,* a contract to keep the offer open) is formed. Article 2 follows the general rule *except for certain offers made by merchants*. If a merchant signs a written offer giving assurances that it will be held open (*e.g.,* "this offer will be held open for 10 days," "this offer is firm for 10 days," "I shall not revoke this offer for 10 days"), the offer is *irrevocable* for the stated period or for a reasonable time if no period is stated. [U.C.C. §2-205]

a. Three-Month Limit

In no event may the period of irrevocability exceed *three months*. If the stated period extends beyond three months, the firm offer will stand, but it will only last for the three-month maximum.

b. Formalities

No consideration is necessary to make the offer irrevocable as long as the offer: (i) gives *words of firmness*; (ii) is in *writing*; and (iii) is *signed* by the *merchant*.

2. Methods of Acceptance

Unless otherwise indicated by language or circumstances, an offer may be accepted using the following methods:

a. Any Reasonable Manner

An offer is construed as inviting acceptance in *any reasonable manner* and by any medium reasonable under the circumstances. [U.C.C. §2-206]

Example: Nikki *telephones* an offer to Skip that is to remain open for five days. Two days later, Skip *wires* an acceptance, or two days later Skip *mails* an acceptance. Whether there has been a proper acceptance depends on whether the use of the telegraph or mail was reasonable under the circumstances.

b. Shipment or Promise to Ship

An offer to buy goods for current or prompt shipment is construed as inviting acceptance either by a *promise to ship* or by *current or prompt shipment* of conforming or nonconforming goods.

1) Shipment of Nonconforming Goods

The shipment of nonconforming goods is an acceptance creating a bilateral contract as well as a *breach* of the contract. However, if the seller seasonably notifies the buyer that a shipment of nonconforming goods is offered only as an *accommodation* to the buyer, the shipment is a *counteroffer* rather than an acceptance.

Examples: 1) Craig orders 1,500 blue widgets from Susy. Susy ships 1,500 black widgets but does not notify Craig that the goods are offered only as accommodation. Susy's shipment is both an acceptance of Craig's offer and a breach of the resulting contract. Craig may sue for any appropriate damages.

2) In the example above, Susy, before the goods arrive, notifies Craig that black widgets have been sent as an accommodation. The shipment is a counteroffer and, if Craig accepts delivery, there will be a contract for the purchase of black widgets.

2) Acceptance by Performance

An offer that may be construed as inviting acceptance by the seller's beginning performance may be accepted by such performance if the offeror is *notified* of acceptance within a reasonable time.

3. Mirror Image Rule Abandoned—Battle of the Forms

Recall that under the common law, a contract can be formed only if the acceptance mirrors the offer. Article 2 has abandoned this rule. Under Article 2, any acceptance or written confirmation sent within a reasonable time that indicates an intention to enter into a contract will be effective as an acceptance, even if it states additional or different terms for the contract, *unless* the acceptance is expressly made conditional on assent to the acceptance terms. Whether the acceptance terms will be included in the contract depends on whether **both** parties are merchants. [U.C.C. §2-207]

Example:　Harry offers to sell Sally 1,000 cases of soda at $5 each plus freight. Sally replies, "I accept on the condition that you make the price $5.05 including freight." There is no contract. The reply was merely a counteroffer since the acceptance was expressly conditioned on assent to the new terms.

a.　Contracts Involving a Nonmerchant—Terms of Offer Govern

If one of the parties to the contract is not a merchant, the contract will include only the terms of the offer. The additional or different terms in the acceptance will be ignored unless specifically accepted.

Example:　Paul sends a letter offering to sell his car to Stephanie for $1,200. Stephanie sends Paul a letter stating: "I accept and want you to put new tires on it." This is a contract, but Paul is not bound to put new tires on the car. However, if Stephanie had said, "I accept on the condition that you put new tires on," there would be no contract unless Paul agreed to put on the new tires.

b.　Contracts Between Merchants—Acceptance Containing Additional Terms

If *both* parties to the contract are merchants, *additional* terms in the acceptance will be included in the contract *unless*:

(i)　They *materially alter* the original contract (an alteration is material if it changes either party's risk or available remedies);

(ii)　The offer *expressly limits acceptance* to the terms of the offer; or

(iii)　The *offeror has already objected* to the particular terms, or objects within a reasonable time after notice of them is received.

If any of the above three circumstances is present, the offeror's terms will control.

Example:　Widgetco offers to sell Machineco 1,500 widgets at $10 each. Machineco replies, "We accept. Any disputes will be settled by arbitration." The parties have formed a contract. However, the arbitration provision will be construed by most courts as a material alteration that will not be included in the terms of the contract.

c.　Contracts Between Merchants—Acceptance Containing Different Terms

There is a split of authority over whether terms in the acceptance that are *different* from (as opposed to additional to) the terms in the offer will become part of the contract. Some courts treat different terms like additional terms, and follow the test set out above in determining whether the terms should be part of the contract. Other courts follow the *"knockout rule,"* which states that conflicting terms in the offer and acceptance are knocked out of the contract because each party is assumed to object to the inclusion of such terms in the contract. Under the knockout rule, gaps left by knocked out terms are filled by the U.C.C. (*e.g.,* when the date of delivery differs in the offer and the acceptance, the U.C.C. provides that delivery must be made within a reasonable time).

Example:　Seller offers to sell to Buyer 1,500 widgets at $10 each plus freight. Buyer replies: "I accept. Price is $10.10 each including freight." There is a contract. Under the approach treating different terms like additional terms, since the difference in total cost is only $150 out of a $15,150 contract, the change is probably not material (in that it does not substantially vary Seller's price term or risk) and becomes part of the contract unless Seller objects. If Seller does object, there is a contract on Seller's original terms. However, under the knockout rule, the different price terms will be knocked out. The price will be a "reasonable price at the time of delivery" according to the U.C.C. (*see infra*).

4.　Open Terms

The fact that one or more terms are left open does not prevent the formation of a contract if it appears the parties intended to make a contract and there is a reasonably certain basis for giving a remedy; *i.e.,* the **court can supply reasonable terms** for those that are missing. [*See* U.C.C. §§2-204, 2-305] The more terms the parties leave open, the less likely it is that the parties intended to enter into a binding agreement.

    a.   **Price**
The failure to state the price does not prevent the formation of a contract if the parties intended to form a contract without the price being settled.

        1)   **Reasonable Price**
In such a case, the price is a *reasonable price at the time of delivery* if:

            (i)   Nothing is said as to price; or

            (ii)   The price is left to be agreed to by the parties and they fail to agree; or

            (iii)   The price is to be fixed by some external factor or third party and it is not so set.

[U.C.C. §2-305]

        2)   **Price Fixed by Party**
A contract will be formed even if the parties agree that one of the parties will fix the price in the future (*e.g.,* "price to be set by seller at time of delivery"). However, the party to whom the contract gives the right to fix the price must act in *good faith*. If that party does not fix the price in good faith, the other party may either cancel the contract or fix a reasonable price herself. [U.C.C. §2-305(3)]

        3)   **C.I.F. and C. & F. Contracts**
A C.I.F. price term means that the price includes the cost of the goods, insurance, and freight. A C. & F. price term means that the price term includes the cost of the goods and the freight.

    b.   **Quantity**

        1)   **Term Must Be Included**
Under the Code, unlike price, the quantity term is a necessary term, and *without it there can be no contract*. Therefore, the quantity term in a sale of goods contract must be certain (stated) or capable of being made certain (as in a requirements or output contract).

        2)   **Requirements and Output Contracts**
Offers that define the quantity term as the buyer's requirements or the seller's output satisfy the quantity requirement because requirements and output can usually be determined objectively and therefore are capable of being made certain. In addition to requiring that the output or requirements quantity be set in good faith, the U.C.C. also provides that the quantity ultimately required or produced may not be *unreasonably disproportionate* to (i) any stated estimate, or (ii) any normal or otherwise comparable prior output or requirements (in the absence of a stated estimate).

C. AUCTION CONTRACTS
The U.C.C. contains some special rules regulating auction sales. [*See* U.C.C. §2-328] They are:

    1.   **Goods Auctioned in Lots**
In a sale by auction, if goods are put up in lots, each lot is the subject of a separate sale.

    2.   **When Sale Is Complete**
A sale by auction is complete when the auctioneer so announces by the *fall of the hammer* or in another customary manner. Where a bid is made while the hammer is falling in acceptance of a prior bid, the auctioneer may, in his discretion, reopen the bidding or declare the goods sold under the bid on which the hammer was falling.

    3.   **Auction With Reserve or Without Reserve**
An auction sale is with reserve unless the goods are explicitly put up without reserve. "*With reserve*" means the *auctioneer may withdraw the goods* at any time until he announces completion of the sale. In an auction without reserve, once the auctioneer calls for bids on an article or lot, that article or lot cannot be withdrawn unless no bid is made within a reasonable time. In either case, a bidder may retract his bid until the auctioneer announces completion of the sale, but a bidder's retraction does not revive any previous bid.

    4.   **A Bid on Seller's Behalf**
Except at a forced sale, if the auctioneer knowingly receives a bid on the seller's behalf, or

the seller makes or procures such a bid (in order to drive up the price of the goods), and notice has not been given that liberty for such bidding is reserved, the winning bidder may at his option avoid the sale or take the goods at the price of the *last good faith bid* prior to the completion of the sale.

D. DEFENSES TO THE FORMATION OF A CONTRACT

1. Statute of Frauds

a. General Rule—Writing Required for Sale of Goods of $500 or More
Except as indicated below, contracts for the sale of goods for $500 or more are not enforceable unless there is some writing made that is *signed by the party to be charged* or such party's agent. [U.C.C. §2-201] The writing need not be a contract or a memorandum of a contract, but only some writing. A writing is sufficient even though it omits or incorrectly states a term, but the contract is *not enforceable beyond the quantity of goods shown in the writing*.

1) Writing Requirement
The writing need not be a single document, and it is probably sufficient even if it is made in lead pencil on a scratch pad. [U.C.C. §2-201, comment 1]

2) Signature Requirement
A signature includes any symbol executed or adopted with a present intention to adopt or accept a writing. The symbol may be on any part of the document, and in an appropriate case, may be found in a billhead or letterhead (*e.g.,* where it appears that the writing was made to serve as a memorandum of an agreement). [U.C.C. §1-201(37)]

Example: Buyer offers as meeting the Statute of Frauds requirement a notation in pencil on the office pads of Seller reading: "Sold to Buyer, 1,500 widgets. RXW." RXW are the initials of Seller's president. The memorandum is likely sufficient. Even absent the initials, the memorandum may be sufficient if the firm's name appears on the office pads.

3) Requirement of $500 or More—Applied as Modified
In determining whether a contract is for $500 or more, Article 2 gives effect to any modification—if the contract *as modified* is for $500 or more, it must be evidenced by a writing; if the contract *as modified* is for less than $500, no writing is necessary. [U.C.C. §2-209]

Examples: 1) Seller agrees to sell Buyer his car for $525 and the parties put the contract in writing to satisfy the Statute of Frauds. Subsequently, Buyer discovers that he can afford to spend only $475 on a car. Buyer calls Seller and tells Seller of his trouble. Seller agrees to lower the price to $475. A writing is no longer necessary and either party can enforce the oral modification.

2) Mary phones Paul and asks Paul for his price on widgets. Paul informs Mary that he currently is selling widgets for $3 each. Mary asks Paul to send her 150 widgets. Paul agrees, and tells Mary that he will ship them the next day. The contract is enforceable without a writing. A few hours later, Mary phones Paul back and asks Paul whether he could send her 200 widgets instead of 150. Paul agrees. The contract no longer is enforceable absent a written memorandum satisfying the Statute of Frauds.

4) Quantity Key Factor
The quantity term is the key to the sufficiency of a memorandum. The contract will not be enforceable beyond the extent of the quantity shown in the writing. All other terms of the contract can be proven through parol evidence. [U.C.C. §2-201(1)]

Examples: 1) To meet the Statute of Frauds requirement, Constructo offers a notation made on Widgetco's office pad and signed by Widgetco's president reading: "Sold to Constructo, widgets." The writing is probably not sufficient because no quantity term is given.

2) Facts the same as above, but the memorandum reads: "Sold to Constructo, 1,500 widgets." The memorandum is sufficient to support a contract for up to 1,500 widgets. If the actual agreement was for 15,000 widgets, the agreement would be enforceable only to the extent of 1,500 widgets. However, if the actual agreement was for only 150 widgets, the actual agreement may be shown.

b. Merchants—Confirmatory Memo Rule
In contracts between merchants, if one party, within a reasonable time after an oral agreement has been made, sends to the other party a *written* confirmation of the understanding that is sufficient under the Statute of Frauds to bind the sender, it will also bind the recipient if: (i) he has reason to know of the confirmation's contents; and (ii) he does not object to it in writing within 10 days of receipt. [U.C.C. §2-201(2)]

c. When Writing Not Required
There are three situations described in U.C.C. section 2-201(3) in which contracts are enforceable without the writing described above:

1) Specially Manufactured Goods
If the goods are to be specially made for the buyer and are not suitable for sale to others in the ordinary course of the seller's business, the contract is enforceable if the seller has, under circumstances that reasonably indicate that the goods are for the buyer, made *substantial beginnings* in their manufacture or *commitments* for their purchase before notice of repudiation is received.

2) Admission in Pleadings
If the party admits in her pleadings, testimony, or otherwise in court that a contract of sale was made, the contract is enforceable without the writing. *But note:* The contract is not enforceable beyond the quantity of goods admitted.

3) Performance
If goods are either received and accepted or paid for, the contract is enforceable. However, the contract is not enforceable beyond the quantity of goods accepted or paid for. Thus, if only part of the goods called for in the oral contract are accepted or paid for, the contract is only partially enforceable. If an indivisible item is partially paid for, most courts hold the Statute of Frauds is satisfied for the whole item.

Examples: 1) Kay and Lydia orally agree that Lydia will purchase 150 widgets from Kay at a price of $10 each. Lydia gives Kay a check for $70. The contract is enforceable for seven widgets only.

2) Joe orally contracts to buy a car from Susan for $15,000. Joe gives Susan a $1,000 down payment. Although Joe has only partially paid for the car, most courts would hold that the contract is enforceable.

2. Unconscionability
Unconscionability is determined on a case-by-case basis. The test is whether, *at the time of execution*, the contract or one of its provisions could result in unfair surprise and was oppressive to a disadvantaged party.

a. Effect If Court Finds Unconscionable Clause
If a court finds as a matter of law that a sales contract or any clause of the contract was unconscionable *when made*, the court may: (i) refuse to enforce the contract; (ii) enforce the remainder of the contract *without* the unconscionable clause; or (iii) *limit the application of any clause* so as to avoid an unconscionable result. [U.C.C. §2-302]

b. Application
This provision has been used in some states to strike oppressive clauses from *consumer* sales contracts. For example, these states would strike down a clause stating that New York law will apply to a contract involving a Wisconsin consumer and a clause waiving defenses against an assignee. This provision has also been used to void or reduce the buyer's obligation on contracts where the goods were *grossly overpriced*.

III. CONTRACT MODIFICATION

A. BY AGREEMENT OF THE PARTIES

At common law, a contract modification generally is unenforceable unless it is supported by new consideration. Article 2 does not follow this rule.

1. Modification Without Consideration

Under Article 2, contract modifications sought in *good faith* are binding without consideration. Modifications extorted from the other party are in bad faith and are unenforceable. [*See* U.C.C. §2-209, comment 2]

Example: Jenny has agreed to sell to Bill 15,000 gallons of paint at a price of $5 per gallon, the paint deliverable 500 gallons each month for 30 months. After 15 months, the price of materials rises so that Jenny is losing 50¢ per gallon. Jenny had at the inception of the contract made a profit of 25¢ per gallon. Jenny tells Bill the circumstances and asks if Bill will agree to pay $5.75 per gallon for the remaining deliveries. Bill agrees and the proper writing is executed. The modification was no doubt sought in good faith and is binding even though Jenny gave Bill no new consideration. If Jenny had asked for an increased price because she believed that it was too late for Bill to purchase elsewhere and Bill would pay the higher price to get the paint, the modification would be in bad faith and would be unenforceable.

Note: Remember that contract modifications must meet the Statute of Frauds requirement of Article 2 if the contract *as modified* falls within the Statute of Frauds provisions. (*See* II.D.1.a.3), *supra.*)

2. Writing Prohibiting Oral Modification

A provision that a written contract cannot be modified or rescinded except by a signed writing is *valid* and binding. Except as between merchants, such a term in a form supplied by a merchant must be separately signed by the other party.

3. Waiver of Writing Requirement

Even though an oral modification may itself be invalid because the contract provides that modifications must be in writing or the modification brings the contract within the Statute of Frauds, the oral modification may serve as a *waiver* of a party's right to enforce the contract as written. However, the modification will serve as a waiver only if it would be unjust to retract the modification because one of the parties *relied* on it. Thus, until one of the parties relies to his detriment on the prohibited oral modification, it may be retracted.

B. BY OPERATION OF LAW

1. Destruction or Injury to Identified Goods

If the contract requires for its performance particular goods identified when the contract is made, and, *before risk passes to the buyer*, the goods are destroyed or damaged without the fault of either party:

(i) If the goods are *completely destroyed*, the contract is *avoided*; and

(ii) If the goods are *damaged*, the contract is *avoided unless* the *buyer elects* to take the goods with a reduction in price for the damages but without any other claim against the seller.

[U.C.C. §2-613] *Compare:* If the goods are destroyed or damaged *after risk of loss has passed to the buyer*, the contract is not avoided. Rather, the seller may enforce the contract and the buyer will bear the loss.

2. Failure of Agreed-Upon Method of Transportation

If the agreed-upon delivery facilities become unavailable or commercially impractical, then any *commercially reasonable* transportation *must* be tendered and *must* be accepted. [U.C.C. §2-614]

3. Failure of Presupposed Conditions—Impracticability

Sometimes, an event will occur or a circumstance will arise that causes a seller's performance of a contract to become more difficult than expected. Generally, a seller assumes the risk of the occurrence of such events and must continue to perform. However, if performance has become "commercially impracticable," the seller will be discharged to the extent of the impracticability. [U.C.C. §2-615]

a. When Performance Is Impracticable
Performance is deemed to be impracticable when it becomes extremely more difficult than expected because of the occurrence of a circumstance the nonoccurrence of which was a *basic assumption* of the parties. The nonoccurrence of a circumstance is a basic assumption when: (i) the parties did not discuss the circumstance, but it can fairly be said that *both* parties assumed that it would not occur; and (ii) occurrence of the circumstance would have a *material effect* on a party's ability to perform.

The rule is intended to fairly allocate risk where the contract is silent. Although ordinarily the seller will be held liable for the occurrence of most unforeseen circumstances, if it is fair to say that the parties would not have placed the risk on the seller for the occurrence of an extraordinary circumstance, the seller will be discharged.

b. Events Sufficient for Discharge
Events sufficient to excuse performance include a *shortage of raw materials* or the inability to convert them into the seller's product because of contingencies such as war, strike, embargo, or unforeseen shutdown of a major supplier. Catastrophic local crop failure (as opposed to a mere shortage) also is sufficient for discharge. However, mere increases in costs are rarely sufficient for discharge unless they change the nature of the contract.

Example: Assume StoneOil contracted with Manuco to sell Manuco one million gallons of Persian Gulf crude oil. If a war subsequently breaks out in the Gulf, and supplies of Gulf oil are interrupted, StoneOil is discharged. However, if instead a war breaks out between Israel and Egypt and the Suez Canal is blocked, thus forcing StoneOil to ship the oil around the Cape of Good Hope, StoneOil will probably not be discharged merely because of the increase in the cost of shipping. [*See* Transatlantic Financing Co. v. United States, 363 F.2d 312 (D.C. Cir. 1966)]

Note: There is no bright line test for determining when a rise in price changes the nature of the contract, but increases in costs of more than 50% have been held to be insufficient. [*See, e.g.,* Iowa Light and Power Co. v. Atlas Corp., 467 F. Supp. 129 (N.D. Iowa 1978)]

1) Failure of a Particular Source
If the parties to the contract have contemplated the use of a particular source of supply, the failure of that source is sufficient for discharge, even if other sources are readily available. Note, however, that many courts require that the parties explicitly designate the source for the rule to apply.

Example: Assume that Burns owns a gold mine and that Homer contracts with Burns to purchase 100 pounds of gold from him. If the mine is closed by a cave-in, Burns may be discharged, but many courts will discharge Burns only if the contract specified that the gold would come from Burns's mine. If the contract was silent, these courts would hold that Burns must obtain the gold from some other source, on the rationale that Homer did not care about the source of the gold. If the contract was for produce from a farmer, however, most courts will hold that the parties intended that the particular farm be the sole source of goods, even where the contract is silent.

c. Seller's Partial Inability to Perform
If the seller's inability to perform as a result of the unforeseen circumstance is only partial, he *must allocate deliveries* among his customers and, at his option, may include in the allocation regular customers not then under contract. The seller must reasonably notify his buyers of any delay or reduction in deliveries because of unforeseen circumstances. A buyer who receives such a notification may refuse any particular delivery affected, and if the deficiency substantially impairs the whole contract, she may treat the contract as at an end.

IV. PAROL EVIDENCE RULE— RULES OF INTERPRETATION

A. PAROL EVIDENCE RULE
The terms of a contract that are set forth in the confirmatory memoranda of the parties or that are

set forth in a writing intended as a final expression of the parties' agreement cannot be contradicted by evidence of any **prior agreement** or **contemporaneous oral agreement**. [U.C.C. §2-202] (Note, however, that parol evidence may be offered to show **subsequent** modifications of a written contract.)

B. EXPLANATION OR SUPPLEMENTATION

Although the parol evidence rule prohibits contradicting the terms of a contract, the terms may be *explained* or *supplemented* by the following:

1. Consistent Additional Terms

Unless the court finds the writing to be the complete and exclusive statement of the agreement of the parties, the court may accept evidence of consistent additional terms.

2. Course of Dealing

The parties' course of dealing may be used to explain a contract. A course of dealing is a sequence of conduct concerning **previous transactions** between the parties to a particular transaction that may be regarded as establishing a common basis of their understanding. [U.C.C. §1-303(b), (d)]

3. Usage of Trade

A usage of trade may also be used to explain a contract. A usage of trade is a **practice or method of dealing**, regularly observed in a particular business setting so as to justify an expectation that it will be followed in the transaction in question. [U.C.C. §1-303(c), (d)]

4. Course of Performance

Where a contract involves **repeated occasions for performance** by either party and the other party has the opportunity to object to such performance, any course of performance accepted or acquiesced to is relevant in determining the meaning of the contract. [U.C.C. §1-303(a), (d)]

Note: There is no requirement that an ambiguity be found in the writing before allowing an explanation by course of dealing, usage of trade, or course of performance.

V. PERFORMANCE OF THE CONTRACT

A. SELLER'S OBLIGATION OF TENDER AND DELIVERY

1. Noncarrier Cases

Noncarrier cases are instances in which it appears that the parties did not intend that the goods be moved by carrier.

a. Tender of Delivery

In a proper tender of delivery, the seller must put and hold conforming goods at the buyer's disposition for a time sufficient for the buyer to take possession. The seller must give the buyer notice reasonably necessary to enable her to take possession of the goods. The tender must be at a reasonable hour. [U.C.C. §2-503]

b. Place of Delivery

In the absence of agreement otherwise, the place of delivery is the **seller's place of business**, or if he has none, his residence. However, if at the time of contracting, the goods are, to the knowledge of both parties, at some other place, that place is the place of delivery. [U.C.C. §2-308]

2. Carrier Cases

Carrier cases are instances where, due either to the circumstances or to the express terms of the agreement, it appears that the parties intended that a carrier be used to move the goods.

a. Shipment Contracts—Where Seller Has Not Agreed to Tender at Particular Destination

In the absence of agreement otherwise, the seller need not see that the goods reach the buyer, but need only:

(i) Put the goods into the hands of a reasonable carrier and make a reasonable contract for their transportation to the buyer;

(ii) Obtain and promptly tender any documents required by the contract or usage of trade or otherwise necessary to enable the buyer to take possession; and

(iii) Promptly notify the buyer of the shipment.

Failure to make the contract called for in (i) or to notify the buyer under (iii) is a ground for rejection only if a material loss or delay occurs as a result. [U.C.C. §2-504; *see* VII.A.2.b.2), *infra*]

b. Destination Contracts—Where Seller Has Agreed to Tender at Particular Destination
If the contract requires the seller to tender delivery of the goods at a particular destination, the seller must, at the destination, put and hold conforming goods at the buyer's disposition. He must also give the buyer any notice of tender that is reasonably necessary and provide her with any documents of title necessary to obtain delivery. Tender of documents through ordinary banking channels is sufficient. [U.C.C. §2-503]

c. F.O.B. Contracts
In contracts that specify that delivery is F.O.B. (free on board) a particular point, the *F.O.B. point is the delivery point*. If the contract is F.O.B. the seller's place of shipment, the seller need only, at his expense and risk, put the goods in the hands of such carrier as is described in a., above. If the contract is F.O.B. destination, the seller must, at his expense and risk, tender delivery of the goods at the destination as described in b., above. [U.C.C. §2-319]

d. F.A.S. Contracts
In contracts that specify that delivery is F.A.S. (free alongside), the seller must *deliver the goods alongside the vessel* in the manner usual in the port of delivery or on a dock designated by the buyer and obtain and tender a receipt for the goods.

B. BUYER'S OBLIGATION TO PAY—RIGHT TO INSPECT

1. Delivery and Payment Concurrent Conditions
In *noncarrier cases*, unless the contract provides otherwise, a sale is for cash and the price is due concurrently with tender of delivery. However, unless otherwise agreed, when goods are shipped *by carrier*, the price is due only at the time and place at which the buyer receives the goods. Therefore, in a shipment case in which the seller "delivers" when he places the goods in the hands of a carrier at his plant (*e.g.*, an F.O.B. seller's plant contract), the price is not due until the goods arrive at the destination.

2. Shipment Under Reservation—Buyer Pays Prior to Receipt of Goods
In cases where there is no express provision as to payment or the contract specifies cash, and the contract is one for shipment by carrier, the seller may send the goods "under reservation" so that the buyer will be unable to get the goods from the carrier until she pays. Goods are shipped under reservation either by having a negotiable bill of lading issued that is given to the buyer only after she has paid the price or by consigning the goods under a straight (nonnegotiable) bill to someone other than the buyer who will turn the goods over to the buyer only after the buyer has paid the price. [U.C.C. §2-505] This procedure prevents a buyer from getting goods on credit where no credit was intended (by the seller) under the contract.

Example: Seller in New York and Buyer in California make a contract for the sale of steel F.O.B. New York, the steel to be moved to California by rail. Under such a contract, the price is not due until the goods arrive in California even though the seller's delivery obligations ended when he placed the goods in the possession of a carrier in New York. In this case, Seller may ship the goods under a negotiable bill of lading made out to Seller or order and forward to a California bank the bill of lading properly indorsed to the bank. The bank will notify Buyer, and when Buyer pays, will indorse the bill of lading over to her. Only with the bill of lading can Buyer get the goods from the carrier. The same result could be achieved by making a straight (nonnegotiable) bill of lading out to the bank as consignee. In this case, the railroad would surrender the goods without surrender of the bill of lading, but only on the instructions of the bank.

3. Payment by Check
Tender of payment by check is sufficient unless the seller demands legal tender and gives

the buyer time to get cash. Where a check is given, the buyer's duty to pay is suspended until the check is either paid or dishonored. If the check is paid, the buyer's duty to pay is discharged. If the check is dishonored, the seller may sue for the price or recover the goods. [U.C.C. §3-310]

4. Installment Contracts
In an installment contract (*i.e.,* one that requires or authorizes delivery in separate installments), the seller may demand payment for each installment if the price can be so apportioned, unless a contrary intent appears. [U.C.C. §2-307]

5. Buyer's Right of Inspection
Unless the contract provides otherwise, the buyer has a right to inspect the goods before she pays. Expenses of inspection must be borne by the buyer but may be recovered from the seller if the goods do not conform and are rejected. A buyer may inspect at any reasonable time and in any reasonable manner. [U.C.C. §2-513]

Note: The right to inspect exists even though the seller has properly shipped under reservation. However, if the contract between the parties provides for payment C.O.D. or against documents or otherwise indicates that the buyer has promised to pay without inspecting the goods, there is no right of inspection prior to payment. If payment is due before inspection, the fact that the goods are defective does not excuse nonpayment unless the defect appears without inspection or there is fraud in the transaction. [U.C.C. §§2-512, 2-513]

Examples: 1) Buyer in California and Seller in New York contract for sale of steel to be shipped to California. Nothing is said as to payment. Seller may ship the goods under reservation, but Buyer has a right to inspect the goods before payment.

2) Same situation as above, except that the contract provides for payment "against order bill of lading." Buyer must pay when the bank or other agent of Seller in California notifies her that the bill of lading is ready for her, and she does not have a right of inspection prior to payment.

3) Same situation as last example, except that the goods are defective. To put Seller in breach, Buyer must pay, unless the defect appears without inspection.

VI.   ALLOCATION OF INTEREST AND RISK OF LOSS

A.   IN GENERAL
Under pre-U.C.C. law, title was a central concept in sales law controlling risk of loss, the seller's right to the sales price, and the buyer's right to the goods. Under the U.C.C., the importance of title has been substantially reduced. It controls none of the above questions, and the drafters of the U.C.C. tried to divorce the question of title as completely as possible from the question of the rights and remedies of the parties to a sales contract. Section 2-401 provides: "[E]ach provision of this Article with respect to the rights, obligations, and remedies of the seller, the buyer, purchasers or other third parties applies irrespective of title to the goods except where the provisions refer to such title."

Under the U.C.C. scheme, *several concepts replace title*. They are: (i) identification, (ii) insurable interest, and (iii) the risk of loss. [U.C.C. §§2-501, 2-509, 2-510]

B.   IDENTIFICATION
Identification is a *designation of specific goods* as ones to be delivered under the contract of sale. The significance of identification is that it gives the buyer an insurable interest in the goods, and, in certain circumstances, the right to get the goods from the seller and the right to sue third parties for injury to the goods. [U.C.C. §2-501] The parties may contract as to when identification takes place, but if they do not, the following rules apply:

1. Specific, Ascertained, and Existing Goods
Identification takes place at the time the contract is made if it calls for the sale of specific and ascertained goods already existing.

2. Crops and Unborn Animals
If the sale is of unborn animals to be born within 12 months after the contract is made, or is of crops to be harvested within 12 months or the next harvest season after contracting,

whichever is longer, identification takes place **when the young are conceived** or when the **crops are planted** or otherwise become growing crops.

3. Other Goods

In other cases, identification takes place when the goods are shipped, marked, or otherwise designated by the seller as the goods to pass under the contract. The seller may delegate to the buyer the right to identify goods.

C. INSURABLE INTEREST

The buyer has an insurable interest in identified goods and may procure insurance covering the goods even before the risk of loss has passed to her. This insurance could cover any actual loss to the buyer arising out of the loss or injury. The seller also has an insurable interest in goods as long as the seller has title to or a security interest in them.

D. RISK OF LOSS

Risk of loss is a concept that denotes which party will pay for goods that are lost, stolen, damaged, or destroyed. Risk of loss always originates with the seller, but at some point in a transaction the risk shifts to the buyer. The central issue is when the risk of loss shifts from the seller to the buyer. It is important to note that the risk may shift from the seller to the buyer even before the buyer takes physical possession of the goods. Thus, while possession is important, it is not dispositive as to who bears the risk of loss.

1. Risk in the Absence of Breach

a. Noncarrier Cases

Except as hereafter noted, if the **seller is a merchant**, risk of loss passes to the buyer only when she **takes physical possession** of the goods. If the **seller is not a merchant**, risk of loss passes to the buyer upon **tender of delivery**. [*See* U.C.C. §2-509(3)]

Examples: 1) Merchant Seller in California sells goods to Buyer who is to pick them up. Risk of loss does not pass to Buyer until she actually picks them up.

2) Nonmerchant Seller in California sells goods to Buyer and the parties agree that the goods will be picked up by Buyer at noon on Monday. Seller has the goods ready for Buyer at that time, but Buyer does not arrive. The goods are destroyed at 1:30 p.m. that day. Risk of loss falls on Buyer since Seller tendered delivery at noon when he had the goods ready for pick-up by Buyer.

b. Carrier Cases

1) Contracts Not Requiring Delivery at Particular Destination

If the contract authorizes or requires the seller to ship the goods by carrier but does not require him to deliver them at a particular destination, risk of loss passes to the buyer when the goods are duly **delivered to the carrier**. [U.C.C. §2-509(1)(a)]

Example: Seller in New York sells 10,000 tons of steel to Buyer in California, F.O.B. New York. The contract authorizes shipment by carrier but does not require Seller to tender the goods in California. Risk passes to Buyer when the goods are placed in possession of the carrier. If the goods are damaged in transit, the loss falls on Buyer.

2) Destination Contracts

If the contract requires the seller to deliver the goods at a particular destination, the risk of loss passes to the buyer when the goods are **tendered to the buyer at the destination**. [U.C.C. §2-509(1)(b)]

Example: If in the last example, the contract had been F.O.B. California, risk of loss during transit to California would have been on Seller.

c. Goods Held by Bailee to Be Delivered Without Being Moved

If the goods are in the hands of a warehouser or other bailee and are not to be shipped or moved as a part of the contract, **risk passes to the buyer** upon occurrence of **one** of the following:

(i) The buyer's **receipt** of a negotiable **document of title** covering the goods;

(ii) An **acknowledgment** by the bailee of the **buyer's rights** to the goods; or

(iii) The *lapse of reasonable time* for the buyer to notify the bailee of the buyer's rights in the goods after the buyer's receipt of a nonnegotiable document of title or other written direction to the bailee to deliver.

[U.C.C. §2-509(2)]

2. Effect of Breach on Risk of Loss

a. Defective Goods
If goods are so defective that the buyer has a right to reject them, the risk of loss does not pass to her until the defects are *cured* or she *accepts* the goods in spite of their defects. [U.C.C. §2-510(1)]
Example: Buyer has ordered blue widgets from Seller, F.O.B. Seller's plant. Seller ships blue-black widgets, giving Buyer a right to reject. The widgets are damaged in transit. The risk of loss falls on Seller, though the risk would have been on Buyer if blue widgets had been shipped.

b. Revocation of Acceptance
Where the buyer rightfully revokes acceptance, the *risk of loss* is treated as having rested *on the seller from the beginning* to the extent of any deficiency in the buyer's insurance coverage, the risk of loss at issue being that between the time of acceptance and the time of revocation of acceptance. [U.C.C. §2-510(2)] However, revocation of acceptance is rightful only if it occurs "before any substantial change in condition of the goods which is not caused by their own defects." [U.C.C. §2-608(2)] Thus, there can be no revocation of acceptance after a casualty loss to the goods.

c. Breach by Buyer
Where the seller has identified conforming goods to the contract and the buyer repudiates or otherwise breaches the contract *before* the risk of loss has passed to her under the contract, *any loss* occurring within a commercially reasonable time after the seller learns of the breach *falls on the buyer* to the extent of any deficiency in the seller's insurance coverage. [U.C.C. §2-510(3)]
Example: Seller in New York and Buyer in Chicago make a contract for the sale of widgets, F.O.B. New York. Seller marks and labels the goods preparatory to shipment, but before he puts them in possession of a carrier, Buyer repudiates the contract. One day after the repudiation the goods are destroyed. If Seller's insurance does not completely cover the loss, he may recover any balance of the loss from Buyer if one day is within a commercially reasonable time after the repudiation.

3. Risk in Sale or Return and Sale on Approval Contracts

a. Sale or Return
For the purpose of determining the risk of loss, a sale or return contract (*i.e.,* the buyer takes goods for resale but may return them if she is unable to resell them) is treated as an ordinary sale and the above rules apply. If the goods are returned to the seller, the *risk remains on the buyer* while the goods are in transit. [U.C.C. §2-327(2)]

b. Sale on Approval
In a sale on approval (*i.e.,* the buyer takes goods for use but may return them even if they conform to the contract), the risk of loss does not pass to the buyer until she *accepts*. Acceptance may take place by failure to return or notify the seller of an intention to return within the required time. If the buyer decides not to take the goods, return is *at the seller's risk*. [U.C.C. §2-327(1)]

E. RULES FOR PASSAGE OF TITLE

1. Agreement by the Parties
While title is not a central concept under the U.C.C., it does state rules as to when title passes. The parties may by contract fix the time for passage of title except that: (i) it is logically impossible to pass title prior to identification, and (ii) a reservation by the seller of title after the goods have been delivered to the buyer is limited in effect to the reservation of a security interest in the goods. [*See* U.C.C. §2-401]

2. In the Absence of Agreement—Title Passes on Delivery
The general rule is that title passes when the *seller completes his performance* with respect to the physical delivery of the goods.

a. **Carrier Cases**
In carrier contracts, title passes to the buyer at the time and place of shipment if the contract does not require the seller to tender delivery at a particular destination. If the contract requires delivery at a particular destination, title passes when the goods are tendered at the destination. Observe that these rules are the same as the passage of risk rules in such cases.

b. **Noncarrier Cases**
If delivery is to be made without moving the goods and the seller is to deliver a document of title, title passes when and where the document is delivered. Where delivery is to be made without moving the goods and they are already identified and no document is to be delivered, title passes at the time and place of contract.

VII. REMEDIES

A. BUYER'S REMEDIES

1. **When Acceptance Occurs**
The remedies available to a buyer vary depending on whether the buyer has already accepted the goods. A buyer's remedies are the broadest prior to acceptance. Therefore, it is necessary to understand when acceptance occurs. Under the U.C.C., the buyer accepts goods:

   (i) When she, after a reasonable opportunity to inspect them, indicates to the seller that they conform to requirements or that she will keep them even though they fail to conform; or

   (ii) When she fails to reject within a reasonable time after tender or delivery of the goods or fails to seasonably notify the seller of her rejection; or

   (iii) When she does any act inconsistent with the seller's ownership.

   [U.C.C. §2-606]

2. **Buyer's Right of Rejection Prior to Acceptance of Goods—Seller's Right to Cure**

   a. **Right of Rejection Generally**
   When goods that *do not conform* to the contract are tendered to a buyer, the buyer may either keep them and sue for damages or, under some circumstances, reject the goods and either cancel the contract or sue for damages under the contract. The right of the buyer to reject differs substantially depending on whether the contract calls for only one or more than one delivery. (In the absence of an express or implied agreement to the contrary, sales contracts call for a single delivery.) [U.C.C. §2-307]

   b. **Right of Rejection in Single Delivery Contracts**

      1) **Generally**
      Except as stated in 3.a., *infra,* in single delivery contracts, if the *goods or the tender* "fail in any respect to conform to the contract," the *buyer may reject all or accept all*, *or accept any commercial units* and reject the rest. The test for "commercial unit" is "not only what unit has been the basis of contract, but whether the partial acceptance produces so materially an adverse effect upon the remainder as to constitute bad faith." [U.C.C. §2-601, comment 1]
      Example: Widgets are always sold in units of 100. Buyer orders 500 widgets. They arrive but are found to be defective. Buyer keeps 25 and rejects 475. Buyer is probably required to reject in units of 100 and the rejection of the 75 above 400 is probably wrongful.

      2) **Failure to Make Reasonable Contract with Carrier or to Notify Buyer of Shipment**
      The seller's failure to make a reasonable contract with a carrier when the seller is required to send the goods to the buyer or his failure to notify the buyer that the goods have been shipped (both of which are defects in tender) are grounds for rejection *only if material loss or delay* results. [U.C.C. §2-504]
      Example: Seller, under a contract specifying delivery F.O.B. Buyer's store, ships widgets worth $1 per pound under a freight classification

under which the carrier's liability for loss or damages is limited to $0.50 per pound. This probably is improper tender, but is a ground for rejection only if the goods are, as a matter of fact, damaged or destroyed and the carrier will not pay the full amount of loss.

c. Right of Rejection in Installment Contracts

In an installment contract (*see* V.B.4., *supra*), an *installment* can be rejected only if the nonconformity *substantially impairs* the value of *that installment* and *cannot be cured*. (*See* f., *infra*, on cure.) In addition, the *whole contract* is breached if the nonconformity *substantially impairs* the value of the *entire contract*. [U.C.C. §2-612]

d. Formal Requirements for Rejection

Rejection must be *within a reasonable time* after delivery or tender and before acceptance. It is ineffective unless the buyer *seasonably notifies* the seller. If in connection with rejection the buyer fails to state that the goods have a particular defect that is ascertainable by reasonable inspection, she *cannot rely on that defect* to justify rejection or to show seller's breach *if*:

(i) The *seller could have cured* the defect if he had been told about it; or

(ii) *Between merchants* when the *seller has*, after rejection, *made a request* in writing for a full and final written statement of all defects upon which the buyer proposes to rely.

[U.C.C. §2-605]

Example: Buyer has ordered blue widgets. Buyer rejects because the shipment did not contain the widget wrench that, under the contract, went with each widget. Buyer does not give the reason for rejection. If Seller had known the reason, he could have had the necessary number of widget wrenches at Buyer's business within hours. That probably would have constituted adequate cure. If so, Buyer's rejection is unjustified; she will not be able to rely on the absence of the wrenches as a reason for rejection or as the basis for a claim for damages.

e. Buyer's Responsibility for Goods After Rejection

1) Buyer Must Hold Goods with Reasonable Care

After rejecting goods in her physical possession, the buyer has an obligation to hold them with reasonable care at the seller's disposition for a time sufficient to permit the seller to remove them. If the seller has no agent or place of business within the market area where the goods are rejected, a *merchant* buyer has an obligation to obey any reasonable instructions as to the rejected goods (*i.e.,* she must arrange to reship the goods to a destination designated by the seller or resell on request of the seller, if reasonable). [U.C.C. §2-602]

2) Seller Gives No Instructions on Disposal of Goods

If a seller gives no instructions within a reasonable time after notification of rejection, the buyer may *reship* the goods to the seller, *store* them for the seller's account, or *resell* them for the seller's account. The buyer has a *security interest* in rejected goods in her possession for *any part of the price already paid* and for expenses reasonably incurred in connection with handling them after rejection. [U.C.C. §2-604]

3) Where Buyer Resells Goods

If the buyer does resell rejected goods, she is entitled to have her expenses of selling and any commission ordinarily paid in the trade or, if there is none, a reasonable commission not exceeding 10%. [U.C.C. §2-603(2)]

f. Seller's Right to Cure

1) Single Delivery Contracts

a) Buyer May Reject Goods for Any Defect

As indicated, in single delivery contracts, with very limited exceptions, the buyer can reject goods for "any defect" in the goods or tender. This is the Code's *"perfect tender" rule*, which does not require material breach to allow a party to reject goods. However, the perfect tender rule is substantially softened by the Code cure rules.

b) Seller Can Cure by Notice and New Tender Within Time for Performance

Where a buyer has rejected goods because of defects, the seller may within the time originally provided for performance "cure" by giving *reasonable notice* of her intention to do so and making a *new tender of conforming goods* that the buyer must then accept. [U.C.C. §2-508]

Example: Buyer ordered blue widgets for delivery during the first 15 days of June. The widgets are delivered on June 9, but the widget wrenches required by the contract are missing. Seller can cure this defect by giving reasonable notice of his intention to provide and subsequently providing wrenches for the widgets by June 15. If he does, Buyer must accept, or Buyer will breach the contract.

c) Seller's Right to Cure Beyond Original Contract Time

Ordinarily, the seller has no right to cure beyond the original contract time. However, in cases where the buyer rejects a tender that the seller reasonably believed would be acceptable "with or without money allowance," the seller, upon a reasonable notification to the buyer, has a *further reasonable time* beyond the original contract time within which to make a conforming tender. A seller will probably be found to have had reasonable cause to believe that the tender would be acceptable where the seller can show that (i) trade practices or prior dealings with the buyer led him to believe that the goods would be acceptable, or (ii) the seller could not have known of the defect despite proper business conduct (*e.g.,* packaged goods purchased from a supplier).

Examples: 1) In the last example above, widgets are delivered without wrenches on June 15. Seller and Buyer have had a number of contracts over the years for the sale of widgets in which the wrench was a part of the contract. On several occasions, Seller has not been able to deliver the wrenches, and on each occasion, Buyer has accepted the widgets with a reduction in price and purchased the wrenches from another source. This time Buyer rejects the widgets. Seller will have a reasonable time after June 15 within which to cure by furnishing the wrenches.

2) Barry ordered 100 barrels of grade A oil from Sandy to be delivered on or before January 1. On January 1, Sandy delivered to Barry 100 barrels of oil that Sandy had purchased from her supplier, Refineco. Upon delivery, Barry opened a barrel and found that the oil was grade B oil. Barry rejected the delivery immediately. Sandy checked with Refineco and discovered that Refineco had made a packaging error and could replace the oil within two days. Assuming two days is a reasonable time under the circumstances (*e.g.,* if Barry does not need the oil immediately), Sandy will have a right to cure even though the time for performance has passed.

2) Installment Contracts

In installment contracts, the seller has the *same right to cure* as to rejected goods as he has in the single delivery contracts just discussed. Additionally, the Code provides that a defective shipment in an installment contract cannot be rejected *if the defect can be cured*. Ordinarily, defects in the particular goods themselves cannot be cured, so the buyer can reject them, but then might be required to accept substitute goods under the provisions discussed above. Note that a deficiency in quantity may be cured by an additional delivery, and a delivery of too much may be cured by acceptance or return of a part. [U.C.C. §2-612]

3. Revocation of Acceptance

a. Importance of Acceptance

The time of acceptance (*see* A.1., *supra*) is important because it terminates the buyer's power to reject goods and obligates her to pay the price less any damages resulting from the seller's breach. There are limited situations in which a buyer may revoke an acceptance already made.

b. Revocation of Acceptance

1) When Acceptance May Be Revoked
The buyer may revoke her acceptance of goods if the goods have a defect that *substantially impairs* their *value* to her *and*:

(i) She accepted them on the reasonable belief that the defect would be cured and it has not been; or

(ii) She accepted them because of the difficulty of discovering defects or because of the seller's assurance that the goods conformed to the contract.

[U.C.C. §2-608]

2) Other Requirements for Revocation of Acceptance
Revocation of acceptance must occur:

a) *Within a reasonable time* after the buyer discovers or should have discovered the defects; and

b) *Before any substantial change in the goods occurs* that is not caused by a defect present at the time the seller relinquished possession. [U.C.C. §2-608(2)]

> *Example:* If the buyer receives defective goods and due to her own fault damages the goods in some other way, she can no longer revoke acceptance, because the damage is a substantial change in the goods not caused by the seller. Similarly, if the buyer receives damaged goods and then resells the goods, she cannot revoke acceptance and her only remedy is to recover damages for the defect (*see* 6.b.1), *infra*). If the buyer sells some but not all of the defective units, she can revoke acceptance (within a reasonable time) of any unsold unit.

3) Effect of Revocation of Acceptance
A proper revocation of acceptance has the effect of a rejection.

4. Buyer's Right to Replevy Identified Goods

a. On Buyer's Prepayment
If a buyer has made at least *part payment* of the purchase price of goods that have been identified under a contract and the seller *has not delivered* the goods, the buyer may *replevy* the goods from the seller in two circumstances:

(i) The seller becomes *insolvent* within 10 days after receiving the buyer's first payment; or

(ii) The goods were purchased for *personal, family, or household purposes.*

In either case, the buyer must *tender* any unpaid portion of the purchase price to the seller. [U.C.C. §2-502]

b. On Buyer's Inability to Cover
In addition, the buyer may replevy undelivered identified goods from the seller if the buyer, after reasonable effort, is *unable to secure adequate substitute goods*. [U.C.C. §2-716]

> *Example:* Buyer and Seller enter into a contract for the delivery of 10,000 widgets on December 31. Seller, who has identified goods to the contract, refuses to deliver. Buyer makes reasonable efforts to find widgets from another source, but the earliest delivery date he can arrange is March 15. The widgets are needed for Buyer's manufacturing operations in February and March. Buyer can replevy the goods from Seller. However, if the widgets were not to be used by Buyer until June, widgets for March 15 delivery would probably be reasonable substitute goods and Buyer could not recover the widgets from Seller.

c. **Replevy Not Dependent on Title**
The replevy rights just discussed *do not depend on title*; the buyer can replevy in situations where title has not passed to her. Can the buyer replevy goods if title has passed to her even though the seller's insolvency, repudiation, or failure to deliver or the buyer's inability to cover are not present? Under pre-Code law, the buyer could have replevied on the strength of title. However, section 2-401 states that rights and remedies apply irrespective of title, which suggests that even after title has passed to the buyer, she cannot replevy goods from the seller except on the *seller's insolvency, repudiation, or failure to deliver* or upon the *buyer's inability to cover*. There are no cases on this point and the question must be considered an open one.

5. **Buyer's Right to Specific Performance**
A right closely related to the buyer's right to replevy is her right to specific performance "where the goods are unique or in other proper circumstances." [U.C.C. §2-716] The court may order specific performance *even where the goods have not yet been identified* to the contract by the seller. An interesting question is whether inability to cover is an "other circumstance" in which the court may give specific performance. The comments to section 2-716 say that inability to cover is "strong evidence of other circumstances." If this suggestion is followed by the courts, buyers in inability-to-cover situations would have their choice of replevin or specific performance remedies. Of course, a specific performance remedy is always discretionary with the court, and unclean hands, laches, etc., might bar an equity action but would not affect a replevin recovery. As pointed out, *replevin will lie only for identified goods* (*see* 4.b., *supra*), while specific performance may be decreed even though the goods have not previously been identified.

6. **Buyer's Damages**

a. **For Nondelivery or upon Rejection or Revocation of Acceptance**
The buyer's basic remedy where the seller does not deliver or the buyer properly rejects or revokes her acceptance of tendered goods is the difference between the contract price and either the market price (*i.e., benefit of the bargain* damages) or the cost of buying replacement goods (*i.e., cover*).

1) **Difference Between Contract Price and Market Price**
If the buyer measures damages by the difference between contract price and market price, market price is determined as of the time the buyer learns of the breach and at the place of tender, except in cases of rejection after arrival, when market price is measured at the place of arrival. [U.C.C. §2-713] Note that the *buyer's damages* are measured as of the *time she learns of the breach*, while the *seller's damages* (*see* B.4.a., *infra*) are measured as of the *time for delivery*.

a) **Anticipatory Breach by Buyer or Seller**
In the case of anticipatory breach by the buyer, the seller's damages are measured as of the actual time for performance, unless the suit comes to trial before the time for performance, in which case damages are measured at the time the seller learns of the breach. In the case of a seller's anticipatory breach, the buyer's damages are always measured as of the time she learns of the breach. (*See* Contracts outline for more detail.)

2) **Difference Between Contract Price and Cost of Replacement Goods— "Cover"**
If the buyer chooses to "cover," she may measure her damages by the difference between contract price and the amount she actually has to pay for replacement goods. If the buyer intends to fix damages in this manner, she must make a *reasonable contract* for substitute goods *in good faith* and *without unreasonable delay.* [U.C.C. §2-712]
Example: Seller and Buyer have a contract for the sale of 10,000 widgets at $1 per widget. Seller does not deliver. At the time and place for determining market price, the average price is $1.05. However, Buyer made a replacement contract within a reasonable time and in good faith at a price of $1.07. Buyer can recover $700 based on her replacement costs. If, on the other hand, Buyer could have bought substitute widgets for $1.03 while the general market price was $1.05, but she chose not to cover, she could recover $500 based on the difference between contract and market prices, rather than being limited to her cover costs.

3) Incidental and Consequential Damages

In either case, the buyer is also entitled to incidental and consequential damages less expenses saved as a result of the seller's breach. *Incidental damages* include expenses reasonably incurred by the buyer in inspection, receipt, transportation, care, and custody of goods rightfully rejected and other expenses reasonably incident to the breach. *Consequential damages* include any loss resulting from the buyer's general or particular requirements and needs of which the seller had reason to know at the time of contracting (the rule of *Hadley v. Baxendale*) and which could not be prevented by buying substitute goods or otherwise (mitigation of damages rules apply). [U.C.C. §§2-712, 2-713, 2-715]

b. Buyer's Damages as to Accepted Goods

1) Measure of Damages

When the buyer accepts goods that breach one of the seller's warranties, the buyer may recover as damages "loss resulting in the normal course of events from the breach." The basic measure of damages in such a case is the difference between the value of the goods delivered and the value they would have had if they had been according to contract plus incidental and consequential damages. [U.C.C. §2-714]

2) Notice Requirement

To recover damages for any defect as to accepted goods, the buyer must, *within a reasonable time after she discovers or should have discovered the breach,* notify the seller of the defect. If she does not notify the seller within a reasonable time, she loses her right to sue. "Reasonable time" is, of course, a flexible standard. It is apt to be somewhat shorter in the case of merchant buyers to prevent the buyer from acting in bad faith, and somewhat longer in the case of consumer buyers to prevent them from being barred from a remedy because of a technical notice requirement.

3) Vouching In—Where Buyer Resells Goods and Is Sued

If a buyer is sued on a breach of warranty or other obligation and she in turn will be able to recover from the person who sold her the goods if damages are assessed against her in the suit, the buyer may notify the seller that he may come in and defend the suit or be bound by any determination of fact which is common to both litigations. If the seller does not come in and defend after this notice, he is bound by the litigation's outcome. [U.C.C. §2-607]

B. SELLER'S REMEDIES

1. Seller's Right to Withhold Goods

When the buyer fails to make a payment due on or before delivery, the seller may withhold delivery of the goods. The seller may also withhold goods when the goods are sold on credit and, before the goods are delivered, the seller discovers that the buyer is insolvent. However, in such a case, the seller must deliver the goods if the buyer tenders cash for their payment. [U.C.C. §2-702]

2. Seller's Right to Recover Goods

a. Right to Recover from Buyer on Buyer's Insolvency

When a seller learns that a buyer has received delivery of goods on credit while insolvent, he may reclaim the goods upon demand made within 10 days after the buyer's receipt of the goods. However, the 10-day limitation does not apply if a misrepresentation of solvency has been made in writing to the particular seller within three months before delivery. The seller's right to reclaim the goods is subject to the rights of a buyer in the ordinary course or any other good faith purchaser. (*See* the discussion of third-party rights, IX., *infra*.) [U.C.C. §2-702]

b. Right to Recover Shipped or Stored Goods from Bailee

1) On Buyer's Insolvency

The seller may stop delivery of goods in the possession of a carrier or other bailee when he discovers the buyer to be insolvent. Of course, the seller must deliver the goods if the buyer tenders cash for their payment. [U.C.C. §2-705(1)]

2) On Buyer's Breach
The seller may stop delivery of carload, truckload, planeload, or larger shipments of goods when the buyer breaches the contract or when the seller has a right to withhold performance pending receipt of assurances. (*See* C.1., *infra,* on the right to demand assurances.) [U.C.C. §2-705(1)]

3) When Goods May Not Be Stopped
The seller may stop delivery of the goods to the buyer *until:*

(i) Receipt of the goods by the buyer;

(ii) Acknowledgment to the buyer by a bailee other than a carrier that the bailee holds the goods for the buyer;

(iii) Such acknowledgment to the buyer by a carrier by reshipment or as warehouser; or

(iv) Negotiation to the buyer of any negotiable document of title covering the goods.

[U.C.C. §2-705(2)]

4) Obligation of Carrier or Bailee
The seller's notification must come in time to give the person in possession a *reasonable time to stop delivery*. If a negotiable document covers the goods, the carrier or bailee is not obligated to obey a stop order until the document is surrendered.

3. Seller's Right to Force Goods on Buyer and Recover Full Price—Limited
Under the pre-Code law, the seller could recover the full price of goods if title had passed to the buyer. Under the U.C.C., however, the seller has a right to force goods on a buyer who has not accepted them only if the seller is *unable to resell* the goods to others at a reasonable price *or* if the goods have been *lost or damaged* within a reasonable time after the risk of loss passed to the buyer. [U.C.C. §2-709]

4. Seller's Damages
When the buyer repudiates or refuses to accept goods, the seller is entitled to recover incidental damages plus either the difference between the contract price and the market price or the difference between the contract price and the resale price of the particular goods. If damages based on the difference between the contract price and market or resale price do not put the seller in as good a position as performance would have, then the seller may recover lost profits plus incidental damages. [U.C.C. §§2-706, 2-708, 2-710]

a. Difference Between Contract Price and Market Price
If the seller chooses this measure of damages, market price is measured as of the time and at the place for *delivery*.

b. Difference Between Contract Price and Resale Price
If the seller chooses this measure of damages, he must resell under the provisions of section 2-706. This section requires a *good faith, commercially reasonable sale* that may be either private or public (auction).

1) Private Sale
In the case of a private sale, the breaching buyer must be given reasonable notice of intention to resell.

2) Auction Sale
In the case of an auction sale, the sale must be at a usual market for such goods if such a market is reasonably available. Notice of the sale must be given to the breaching buyer unless the goods are perishable or threaten to decline rapidly in value. Only existing and identified goods may be sold unless there is a market in futures for the particular goods. The seller may buy the goods at an auction sale.

c. Damages Based on Lost Profits
The previous two measures of damages do not give adequate compensation for the buyer's breach in situations where the seller has an unlimited supply of the goods and

the demand is limited (*e.g.,* a car dealership). In such a case, the seller is known as a *lost volume seller*, because although he is able to resell the goods for the same or similar price as the initial contract, he loses *volume* of business: But for the buyer's breach, the seller would have made *two* sales instead of one.

Generally, lost profit is measured by list price less cost to the dealer, or list price less manufacturing cost to the manufacturer.

Examples: 1) Seller, a distributor of widgets, can get all the widgets he needs for sale. He makes a contract to sell 10,000 widgets to Buyer at a price of $1 per widget. Buyer repudiates the contract. Seller resells the widgets he had identified to Buyer's contract to Z for $1 per widget. If damages are measured by the difference between the contract price and resale price, Seller will be denied recovery. However, assuming Seller paid 85¢ per widget for these widgets, his lost profit on the Buyer deal is $1,500 ($10,000 less $8,500), because even if Buyer had not breached, Seller would have been able to supply Z with widgets. Since Buyer's breach did not *enable* Seller to make the sale to Z, and since the sale to Z would have been made in any event, the only way to make Seller whole is to allow him to recover his lost profits, *i.e.,* $1,500. If Seller would have incurred sales commissions of $500 and delivery expenses of $100 if Buyer had taken the goods, but does not now incur those expenses, the saved expenses reduce the recovery. Therefore, the recovery would be $900 ($1,500 less saved expenses of $600).

                   2) Seller and Buyer enter into a contract for the sale of a particular painting by van Gogh at a price of $25,000. Buyer repudiates. Seller resells to Z at $24,000. The measure of damages is $1,000 plus incidental damages. Lost profit (difference between what Seller paid for the painting and the contract price) is not appropriate because there is only one painting, and Seller could not have made the sale to Z but for Buyer's repudiation.

d. Incidental Damages
No matter which measure of damages is used—contract-market, contract-resale, or lost profits—the seller is also entitled to incidental damages, which include such expenses as costs of storing, shipping, returning, and reselling the goods, which are incurred as a result of the buyer's breach.

C. REMEDIES AVAILABLE TO BOTH BUYER AND SELLER

1. Right to Demand Assurances

a. May Not Immediately Repudiate
Under general contract law, intentional or unintentional actions or situations that make it unlikely that the party will be able to carry out his contract may sometimes be treated as an anticipatory breach. However, under Article 2 of the U.C.C., actions or circumstances that increase the risk of nonperformance by the other party to the contract, but that do not clearly indicate that performance will not be forthcoming, may not be treated immediately as a repudiation. The protection given by the U.C.C. to the party who reasonably fears that the other party will not perform is that he may demand assurances that the performance will be forthcoming at the proper time.

b. Repudiation May Follow Failure to Give Assurances
In U.C.C. terms, if "reasonable grounds for insecurity arise with respect to the performance of either party, the other party may in writing demand adequate assurance of due performance." [U.C.C. §2-609] Until he receives adequate assurances, he may suspend his own performance. If the proper assurances are not given within a reasonable time (within 30 days after a justified demand for assurances), the party seeking assurances can treat the contract as repudiated. What constitutes an adequate assurance depends on the facts of the case.

Examples: 1) Seller hears a rumor, in fact false, that Buyer is in financial trouble. Seller reasonably believes that the rumor may have foundation in fact. He is justified in making a demand for assurances and withholding any goods for which he has not been paid. Buyer, within a reasonable time, sends a financial report from her banker showing good financial condition. This is adequate assurance and Seller must resume performance.

2) Same facts as above except that Buyer *is* in bad financial condition. Adequate assurance may require a third party of good credit to back up Buyer.

3) Same facts as above. Buyer does not give any assurances. Seller may treat the failure to give assurances as a repudiation of the contract.

2. Anticipatory Repudiation
In cases where the other party's words, actions, or circumstances make it *clear* that she is unwilling or unable to perform, the aggrieved party may:

(i) For a commercially reasonable time *await performance* by the other party;

(ii) Resort to *any remedy for breach* even though he has also urged the other party to perform; or

(iii) *Suspend his own performance.*

[U.C.C. §2-610]

3. Retraction of Repudiation
A repudiating party may at any time before his next performance is due withdraw his repudiation unless the other party has *canceled, materially changed* her *position* in reliance on the repudiation, or otherwise indicated that she considers the *repudiation final.* Withdrawal of the repudiation may be in any manner that clearly indicates intention to perform, but must include any assurances justifiably demanded. [U.C.C. §2-611]

4. Right to Sue Third Parties
Where a third party so deals with goods identified to a contract for sale as to injure a party to the contract, the *seller may sue* if he has either title or a security interest in the goods, and the *buyer may sue* if the goods have been identified to the contract. If the party suing did not have the risk of loss, she sues, subject to her own interest, as a fiduciary for the other party. [U.C.C. §2-722]

5. Liquidated Damages—Other Contractual Modification of Remedy

a. Liquidated Damages
The parties may liquidate damages at any amount that is reasonable in view of the actual or anticipated harm caused by the breach, the difficulties of proof of loss, and the inconvenience or infeasibility of otherwise obtaining an adequate remedy. *Unreasonably large* liquidated damages are considered penalties and are *void*. [U.C.C. §2-718]

b. Other Contractual Modification of Remedy
Parties may provide for remedies in addition to or in substitution for those provided by the U.C.C., provided that such limitations *are not unconscionable*. [U.C.C. §2-719]

D. PROOF OF MARKET PRICE AND STATUTE OF LIMITATIONS

1. Proof of Market Price
If evidence is not available as to market price at the time and place used for computing damages under the U.C.C., evidence of market price prevailing within any reasonable time before or after the time fixed and at any other place that, in commercial judgment or usage of trade, would serve as a reasonable substitute may be used. If an action for anticipatory repudiation comes to trial before the time for performance, damages based on market price are based on market price prevailing when the aggrieved party learned of the repudiation. [U.C.C. §2-723]

2. Statute of Limitations—Four Years
The statute of limitations for actions for breach of a sales contract is four years from the time of breach. An action for breach of warranty accrues when the goods are tendered except that, if the warranty explicitly extends to future performance of goods and the breach cannot be discovered until such performance, the cause of action accrues when the breach is or should have been discovered. The parties may, by contract, reduce the period of limitations to not less than one year, but cannot extend it. [U.C.C. §2-725]

VIII. WARRANTIES

A. TYPES OF WARRANTIES

Under the U.C.C., there are four types of warranties: (i) the warranty of *title* and against infringement, (ii) the implied warranty of *merchantability*, (iii) the implied warranty of *fitness* for a particular purpose, and (iv) *express* warranties.

B. THE WARRANTY OF TITLE AND AGAINST INFRINGEMENT

1. The Warranty of Title

Any seller of goods warrants that the title transferred is good, that the transfer is rightful, and that there are no liens or encumbrances against the title of which the buyer is unaware at the time of contracting. [U.C.C. §2-312]

2. The Warranty Against Infringement

A *merchant seller* regularly dealing in goods of the kind sold also warrants that the goods are delivered free of any patent, trademark, copyright, or similar claims. But a *buyer who furnishes specifications* for the goods to the seller must hold the seller harmless against such claims. If this warranty is breached and the buyer is sued, she must give the seller notice of the litigation within a reasonable time or lose her right to any remedy. In such a case, the seller can give the buyer notice of his wish to defend the lawsuit and, if the seller agrees to bear all expenses and satisfy any adverse judgment, the buyer must let him defend or lose any rights against him arising out of the breach. [U.C.C. §2-607(3), (5)]

3. Disclaimer of the Title Warranty

The title warranty can be disclaimed or modified only by specific language or by circumstances which give the buyer notice that the seller does not claim title or that he is selling only such rights as he or a third party may have (*e.g.,* a sheriff's sale).

C. IMPLIED WARRANTY OF MERCHANTABILITY

1. When Given

In every *sale by a merchant* who deals in goods of the kind sold, there is an implied warranty that the goods are merchantable. The serving of food or drink for consumption on the premises is a sale of goods subject to the warranty of merchantability. [U.C.C. §2-314]

2. Elements of the Warranty of Merchantability

Goods to be merchantable must at least:

(i) Pass without objection in the trade under the contract description;

(ii) In the case of fungible goods, be of fair average quality within the description;

(iii) Be fit for the ordinary purposes for which such goods are used;

(iv) Run, within the variations permitted by the agreement, of even kind, quality, and quantity within each unit and among all units involved;

(v) Be adequately contained, packaged, or labeled according to the contract; and

(vi) Conform to any promises or affirmations of fact made on the label. Other warranties of merchantability may arise from the course of dealing or usage of trade.

[U.C.C. §2-314(2)] The most important test is "*fit for the ordinary purposes for which such goods are used*," and a failure to live up to this test is the usual claim in a merchantability suit.

As in all implied warranty cases, it makes no difference that the seller himself did not know of the defect or that he could not have discovered it. Implied warranties are not based on negligence but on *absolute liability* that is imposed on certain sellers.

D. IMPLIED WARRANTY OF FITNESS FOR A PARTICULAR PURPOSE

This warranty arises whenever (i) *any seller*, merchant or not, *has reason to know the particular purpose* for which the goods are to be used and that the *buyer is relying* on the seller's skill and judgment to select suitable goods, and (ii) the *buyer in fact relies* on the seller's skill or judgment. [U.C.C. §2-315] The comment to section 2-315 says, "A particular purpose differs from the ordinary purpose for which goods are used in that it envisages a specific use by the buyer which is peculiar to the nature of his business whereas the ordinary purposes for which goods are used are those envisaged in the concept of merchantability."

Examples: 1) Seller, who as a hobby prepared an automobile for dirt track racing, sold it to Buyer for racing purposes. Buyer was a novice in racing. The steering mechanism collapsed in a turn during a race. The mechanism would not have collapsed in ordinary driving. There was a breach of warranty of fitness for "particular purposes" if the seller had reason to know that the buyer was relying on him to provide a suitable racing vehicle.

2) Seller, a law student, sells his used automobile to Buyer. The steering mechanism collapses during an ordinary Sunday afternoon drive. There is no breach of warranty of merchantability since Seller is not a merchant who ordinarily deals in goods of that kind. There probably is no breach of a warranty of fitness for particular purposes because the element of selection based on Seller's purported skill is not present.

3) Note that in both of the above examples, if the seller knew that the automobile had a particular defect and did not disclose this fact to the buyer, he might be subject to liability because of a lack of good faith. Section 1-203 provides: "Every contract or duty within this Act imposes an obligation of good faith in its performance or enforcement."

E.   EXPRESS WARRANTIES

Any affirmation of fact or promise made by the seller to the buyer, any description of the goods, and any sample or model creates an express warranty if the statement, description, sample, or model is part of the *basis of the bargain*. For the statement, description, sample, or model to be a part of the basis of the bargain, it need only come at such a time that the *buyer could have relied* on it when she entered into the contract. The buyer does not need to prove that she actually did rely, though the seller may negate the warranty by proving that the buyer as a matter of fact did not rely. It is not necessary that the seller intended the affirmation of fact, description, model, or sample to create a warranty. [U.C.C. §2-313]

A statement relating merely to the value of the goods, or a statement purporting to be only the seller's opinion or commendation of the goods, does not create an express warranty.

Examples: 1) "Chevrolet cars are better." No warranty.

2) "You will like this." No warranty.

3) A number of courts have held that such statements as "this tractor is in A-1 condition" or "this automobile is in top mechanical condition" do create express warranties that are breached if the statement is not a proper characterization of the condition of the thing sold.

F.   DISCLAIMER OF WARRANTIES

1.   Express Warranties

a.   In General

Any affirmation of fact or promise, description of the goods, model, or sample will create an express warranty. If there are also words or conduct negating the express warranty, problems of interpretation will arise. The U.C.C. provides that words or conduct relevant to the creation of express warranties and words or conduct tending to negate such warranties shall wherever possible be construed as consistent with each other, but "*negation or limitation is inoperative to the extent that such construction is unreasonable*." [U.C.C. §2-316] Practically every sale will involve some description of the goods, and the comment to section 2-313 suggests that the *basic obligation* created by this description cannot be read out of the contract by a disclaimer clause.

Example: Seller sells to Buyer something that Seller describes as an "automobile" being sold "as is," and with sufficient disclaimers of all implied warranties. The thing delivered is an automobile body without an engine, a transmission, or wheels. While an automobile with very substantial defects would have fulfilled this contract, what was delivered was not an "automobile" at all. Seller's description "automobile" created an express warranty that an automobile would be delivered, and the disclaimer did not negate this basic obligation.

Of course, the language of disclaimer in the example would substantially reduce the quality of the automobile that must be delivered.

b.   The Parol Evidence Rule
The parol evidence rule might be an obstacle to a buyer to whom an express warranty was made when the contract contains a broad disclaimer of warranties. In a typical situation, the seller makes an express warranty verbally, but the written contract contains no such warranty and instead contains a clause disclaiming all warranties not set forth in the contract. Here, the parol evidence rule could prevent the buyer from introducing evidence of the verbal warranty. *But note:* The buyer can often avoid the rule by a showing that he did not intend that the writing be the complete and exclusive expression of the parties' agreement (*see* IV.B.1., *supra*) or that the disclaimer is unconscionable under the circumstances (*see* 3., *infra*).

2.   Implied Warranties
The implied warranties of merchantability and fitness for a particular purpose can be disclaimed by either specific disclaimers or general methods of disclaimer.

a.   Specific Disclaimers
The U.C.C. provides specific methods for disclaiming the implied warranties of merchantability and fitness. Use of these methods is the best way for a seller to ensure that a disclaimer is effective.

1)   Disclaimer of Warranty of Merchantability
The warranty of merchantability can specifically be disclaimed or modified only by *mentioning merchantability*. If the sale contract is in writing, the disclaimer must be *conspicuous*. [U.C.C. §2-316(2)]

2)   Disclaimer of Warranty of Fitness for a Particular Purpose
The warranty of fitness for a particular purpose can specifically be disclaimed only by a *conspicuous writing*. A written disclaimer, according to the statute, is sufficient if it says, for example, "[t]here are no warranties which extend beyond the description on the face hereof." [U.C.C. §2-316(2)]

3)   "Conspicuous" Defined
A term is conspicuous when it is "so written, displayed, or presented that a reasonable person against whom it is to operate ought to have noticed it." A printed heading in capital letters at least equal in size to the surrounding text, or in a contrasting type, font, or color, is conspicuous. Language in the body of a record or display is conspicuous if: (i) it is in larger type than surrounding text; (ii) it is in a contrasting type, font, or color; or (iii) it is set off from the text by marks that call attention to it. [U.C.C. §1-201(10)] The court, not the jury, decides any fact question as to conspicuousness.

b.   General Disclaimer Methods
The U.C.C. also provides several general methods for disclaiming implied warranties. These methods are more dependent on the circumstances than the specific methods, and so are less certain to be effective than specific disclaimers.

1)   By General Disclaimer Language
Unless the circumstances indicate otherwise, the implied warranties of merchantability and fitness can be disclaimed by expressions such as "*as is*," "with all faults," or other expressions that in common understanding call the buyer's attention to the fact that there are no implied warranties.

2)   By Inspection or Refusal to Inspect
When the buyer, before entering into the contract, has examined the goods or a sample or model as fully as she desires or has refused to examine, there is no warranty as to defects that a reasonable examination would have revealed to her.

3)   By Course of Dealing, Etc.
Implied warranties may also be disclaimed by the course of dealing, course of performance, or usage of trade.

3.   Unconscionability and Warranty Disclaimers
Some courts will, in addition to determining whether disclaimers have met the formal requirements discussed above, test warranty disclaimers by the conscionability standards of U.C.C. section 2-302. Such things as lack of bargaining position, lack of choice, and failure to understand would be relevant in determining whether a disclaimer is unconscionable. (*See* II.D.2., *supra*.)

4. Federal Consumer Product Warranties Law of 1975 ("Magnuson-Moss")
Under this act, if a consumer product manufacturer or marketer issues any written warranties, it must comply with several requirements. [*See* 15 U.S.C. §§2301-2312]

a. Classification of Warranties
Warranties must be described as "full" (meeting rigid federal standards regarding content and performance) or "limited." If a seller uses a full warranty, he must provide reasonable repair facilities. The seller must also allow refund or replacement if the product is defective and the seller is unable to repair it after several attempts.

b. Effect of Classification

1) Full Warranties
If there is a full *written* warranty, implied warranties *cannot* be disclaimed.

2) Limited Warranties
If the *written* warranty is described as a limited warranty, implied warranties cannot be disclaimed or modified, but they may be limited to the duration of the written warranty.

c. Informal Dispute Settlement Encouraged
Informal dispute settlement procedures with customers are encouraged, such encouragement being motivated by the creation of a federal class action contingent upon the consumer first resorting to the informal procedures.

d. Successful Consumer Recovers Costs and Attorneys' Fees
Consumers may sue sellers violating the Act for legal or equitable relief. A successful plaintiff may recover costs and expenses, including attorneys' fees.

G. LIMITATION OF DAMAGES FOR BREACH OF WARRANTY

1. In General
In contrast to the U.C.C. sections dealing with complete warranty disclaimer, the U.C.C. sections dealing with enforceability of contractual provisions limiting damages for breach of warranty apply a basic unconscionability test.

2. Consequential Damages

a. May Be Limited or Extended If Not Unconscionable
Consequential damages recoverable for breach of warranty may be limited or excluded only if the limitation or exclusion is not unconscionable. [U.C.C. §2-719(3)] A buyer is entitled to consequential damages if there is "(a) any loss resulting from general or particular requirements and needs of which the seller at the time of contracting had reason to know and which could not reasonably be prevented by cover or otherwise, and (b) injury to person or property proximately resulting from any breach of warranty." [U.C.C. §2-715(2)]

b. Personal Injury or Commercial Loss
The Code provides that limitation of damages for injury to the person in the case of *consumer goods* is prima facie unconscionable, but limitation of damages where the loss is *commercial* is not.

3. Liquidated Damages
The Code also provides that damages for breach of warranty may be liquidated, but only at an amount that is reasonable in light of anticipated or actual harm, the difficulties of proof, and the inconvenience or infeasibility of other remedies. [U.C.C. §2-718]

Examples: 1) Business Seller sells Consumer Buyer a new snowblower and properly disclaims all warranties by using the proper words in a conspicuous writing. A defect in the blade causes it to break and strike Buyer, resulting in serious bodily injury. There is no warranty liability. (However, this may be insignificant since there may be *strict tort liability* that cannot be disclaimed. Strict tort liability is no longer thought to be "grounded in warranty." *See* I., *infra*.)

2) However, if Seller does not disclaim warranties but instead provides that "damages for breach of warranty are limited to repair or replacement of the

snowblower or any defective part," the limitation is prima facie **unconscionable** and ineffective. Unless Seller overcomes the presumption, Buyer would be able to recover her damages in a warranty action.

H. WARRANTY AND THIRD PARTIES

Most states have adopted **Alternative A** of U.C.C. section 2-318, which provides that the seller's warranty liability extends to any natural person who is in the **family** or **household** of the buyer or who is a **guest** in the buyer's home if it is reasonable to expect that the person may use, consume, or be affected by the goods and that person suffers **personal injury** because of a breach of warranty. The seller cannot escape the effect of this section by contract. (The comments say that beyond this, the section is neutral and is not intended to enlarge or restrict the developing case law on whether the seller's warranties given to his buyer who resells extend to other persons in the distributive chain.)

Alternative B to section 2-318 extends a seller's express or implied warranty liability to **any natural person** who may reasonably be expected to use, consume, or be affected by the goods and who is **injured in person** by breach of the warranty. A seller may not exclude or limit the operation of this section. **Alternative C** is even broader, extending the warranty to **any person** who may reasonably be expected to use, consume, or be affected by the goods and who is **injured** by breach of the warranty (this includes property damage). The seller may not exclude or limit the operation of the section with respect to **personal injury**.

I. STRICT TORT LIABILITY

Many states have adopted a strict tort liability theory to make a manufacturer or seller of goods liable for injuries to person or property caused by unreasonably dangerous defects in goods sold. The theory allows a purchaser to recover from all sellers in the distributive chain **without regard to privity** of contract. It also allows an injured person who is not a purchaser to recover from the same parties. Strict tort liability has also been applied to make a manufacturer or seller liable even though there is no defect in the product if the product is likely to cause injury when used in a way within the range of ordinarily anticipated uses and the manufacturer/seller does not give notice of the danger. Contributory negligence is not a defense to a strict tort action. However, **assumption of the risk**, i.e., use of the product after becoming aware of the potential danger, **is a defense**. In a strict tort liability action, the seller may not use warranty defenses such as disclaimers or modification of warranty, or failure to give proper notice of the defect.

IX. THIRD-PARTY RIGHTS

A. POWER OF PERSON OTHER THAN OWNER TO TRANSFER GOOD TITLE TO A PURCHASER

1. Entrusting

Entrusting goods to a merchant **who deals in goods of that kind** gives him the power (but not the right) to transfer all rights of the entruster to a **buyer in the ordinary course of business**. [U.C.C. §2-403] Entrusting includes both delivering goods to the merchant and leaving purchased goods with the merchant for later pick-up or delivery. Buying in the ordinary course means buying in good faith from a person who deals in goods of the kind without knowledge that the sale is in violation of the ownership rights of third parties.

Examples: 1) Amy leaves her watch with Jeweler for repairs. Jeweler sells the watch to Zoe, who does not know that Jeweler has no right to sell. Zoe gets good title as against Amy. Amy's only remedy is to sue Jeweler for damages.

2) Amy leaves her watch with Jeweler for repairs. Jeweler borrows money from the bank, giving specific items of inventory, including Amy's watch, as pledged collateral. Amy can recover the watch from the bank. The bank is not a **buyer**.

2. Voidable Title Concept

The U.C.C. continues the pre-Code concept of voidable title. [*See* U.C.C. §2-403] That is, if a sale is induced by fraud, the seller can rescind the sale and recover the goods from the fraudulent buyer. However, the defrauded seller may not recover the goods from a **good faith purchaser for value** who bought from the fraudulent buyer. The U.C.C. specifies four particular situations in which the bona fide purchaser for value cuts off the rights of the true owner; in several of these instances the result under pre-Code law is changed.

Under the U.C.C., the ***good faith purchaser for value cuts off the defrauded seller's rights***, even though:

(i) The seller was deceived as to the identity of the buyer (this rule obliterates the pre-Code distinction between face-to-face impersonations and impersonations by mail and provides that in both cases the bona fide purchaser cuts off the true owner's rights);

(ii) The delivery was in exchange for a check later dishonored;

(iii) The sale was a "cash sale"; or

(iv) The fraudulent conduct of the buyer is punishable as larceny.

The rights of a defrauded seller are cut off both by a buyer and by a person who takes a ***security interest*** in the goods.

3. Thief Generally Cannot Pass Title

If a thief steals goods from the true owner and then sells them to a buyer, the thief is ***unable*** to pass title to the buyer (because his title is ***void***). *Rationale:* A seller can transfer only the title he has or has power to transfer. Therefore, even a good faith purchaser for value generally cannot cut off the rights of the true owner if the seller's title was void. [U.C.C. §2-403(1)]

Example: Thief stole a painting from Owner and sold it to Buyer. Later, Owner discovered that Buyer had her painting. Owner may recover the painting from Buyer, even if Buyer purchased the painting in good faith and for value.

a. Exceptions

A thief may pass title in limited circumstances, such as where:

1) The goods are ***money***;

2) The goods are ***negotiable instruments*** that were transferred to a holder in due course;

3) The buyer has made ***accessions*** (*i.e.,* valuable improvements) to the goods; or

4) The true owner is ***estopped*** from asserting title (*e.g.,* if the true owner expressly or impliedly represented that the thief had title).

B. FRAUDULENT RETENTION OF POSSESSION RULES

1. Pre-Code Law

All states under non-Code law have rules making retention of possession in certain cases by a seller of sold goods either presumptively or conclusively fraudulent (as against the seller's creditors). The result of these rules under pre-Code law was that in certain cases the seller's creditors could levy on the goods still in the hands of the seller even though title had passed to the buyer.

2. U.C.C.

The U.C.C. continues the state pre-Code rules with some modification. It provides that the seller's creditors may treat a sale or identification as ***void if*** the retention of possession is ***fraudulent under state law except*** that retention of possession in ***good faith*** and current course of trade by a merchant seller for a ***commercially reasonable time*** after sale or identification is not fraudulent. [U.C.C. §2-402] Under this exception, retentions by merchants in good faith and for bona fide reasons of business will not be considered fraudulent regardless of state law.

3. Effect on Buyer's Right to Goods

As has been pointed out, under the U.C.C., the buyer has the right in certain cases to get goods from the seller even though ***title has not passed***. This right apparently exists as against the ***seller's creditors*** as well, unless the fraudulent possession rules prevent it. Also, as pointed out above, it is not clear whether a buyer can ***replevy*** goods from a seller based on title alone and, if she cannot, it would seem she also cannot recover goods as against a levying creditor of the seller, even in the absence of fraudulent retention of possession.

C. SALE OR RETURN

Where a buyer takes goods for resale and has a right to return them if they are not sold, the goods are subject to the claims of the buyer's creditors while they are in her possession. [U.C.C. §2-326]

BAR REVIEW

Criminal Law

celebrating
35 *YEARS*
of preparing
law students
for the bar exam

CRIMINAL LAW

TABEL OF CONTENTS

INTRODUCTION: GENERAL APPROACH

The Multistate Examination directs examinees to answer questions according to "the generally accepted view" unless otherwise noted. In Criminal Law, this usually means the common law rule, which is the general rule stated in the outline. However, examination fact patterns may also set out statutes defining crimes or defenses and ask questions based upon those statutes. The statutes are usually similar or identical to statutory provisions found in modern criminal codes. To help you better analyze these questions, the outline discusses typical statutes on a variety of topics that may be the subject of examination questions.

best defense = most complete defense. unconstitutional ans. in crim law & crim pro questions are usually wrong ans.

I. JURISDICTION AND GENERAL MATTERS

conduct & result

A. JURISDICTION

As used in this section, jurisdiction means the authority of a sovereign to *create* substantive criminal law. The authority of a court to *enforce* criminal laws is also an aspect of jurisdiction, but is more properly treated as a matter of criminal procedure.

1. Federal Criminal Jurisdiction

The power of the federal government to create crimes falls into the following broad categories:

a. Power over Federally Owned or Controlled Territory

The federal government has extensive power to enact general criminal codes governing conduct in the District of Columbia, the territories, and federal enclaves (*e.g.,* naval yards, federal courthouses, national parks, etc.).

b. Power over Conduct Occurring Within a State

In contrast, federal power to criminalize conduct within a state is limited by the requirement that each statute be founded upon an express or implied constitutional grant of authority.

c. Power over United States Nationals Abroad

Federal criminal statutes may, by express provision, reach conduct by citizens while on foreign soil.

d. Power over Conduct on Ships or Airplanes

Federal "maritime jurisdiction" extends to conduct by all persons aboard American ships or aircraft when on or over the high seas or even in foreign waters or ports.

2. State Criminal Jurisdiction

Unlike the federal government, every state has inherent authority by virtue of its "police power" to regulate its internal affairs for the protection or promotion of the health, safety, welfare, and morals of its citizens.

a. Situs of the Crime

At common law, and in those states that have not expanded jurisdiction by statute, only the state in which the situs of the crime is located has jurisdiction over the crime. "Situs" is generally defined as the place where the proscribed act (or omission) takes place, if the crime is defined in these terms; or the place of the harmful result, if the crime includes a result as a material element.

Example: A libelous statement may be made a crime where it is published, not where it is written, because the crime of libel proscribes the act of publication rather than the act of writing the libelous statement.

b. Modern Bases for Jurisdiction

A person is subject to prosecution in a state for an offense that he commits within or outside that state, by his own conduct or that of another for which he is legally accountable, under the following conditions:

1) When the *offense is committed wholly or partly within the state* ("partly within the state" includes occurrences within the state of either (i) conduct that is an element of the offense, or (ii) a result constituting such an element—*e.g.,* in homicide, the "result" is either the physical contact causing death or the death itself); or

2) When there is ***conduct outside the state that constitutes an attempt or conspiracy*** to commit an offense within the state ***plus an act inside the state***; or

3) When there is ***conduct within the state constituting an attempt, solicitation, or conspiracy to commit, in another jurisdiction, an offense*** under the laws of both the state and such other jurisdiction; or

4) When an offense based on the ***omission of performance of a duty*** imposed by the law of a state is committed within that state, regardless of the location of the offender at the time of the omission.

B. SOURCES OF CRIMINAL LAW

1. Common Law Crimes
A common law crime is one created and enforced by the judiciary in the absence of a statute defining the offense.

a. No Federal Common Law Crimes
Federal criminal law is governed entirely by statute. Although there are no federal common law crimes, Congress has provided for common law crimes in the District of Columbia.

b. Majority View—Common Law Crimes Retained
A majority of the states retain common law crimes either implicitly or by express "retention statutes."

c. Minority View (Modern Trend)—Common Law Crimes Abolished
A minority of the states (about 20) have abolished common law crimes either expressly by statute or impliedly by the enactment of comprehensive criminal codes. These states nevertheless retain the various common law defenses such as insanity and self-defense.

2. Statutory Crimes
Today, state legislative statutes are the primary source of criminal law. Many states have adopted or are in the process of drafting comprehensive criminal codes.

3. Constitutional Crimes
The Constitution defines treason as levying war against the United States, adhering to enemies of the United States, or giving them aid and comfort. No person can be convicted of treason unless two witnesses testify to the same overt act, or unless the defendant confesses.

4. Administrative Crimes
A legislature may delegate to an administrative agency the power to prescribe rules, the violation of which may be punishable as a crime. Note, however, that the legislature may not delegate the power to determine which regulations shall carry criminal penalties; nor may it delegate the power of adjudication (*i.e.,* the determination of guilt or innocence). With the proliferation of administrative agencies, this source of criminal law is becoming increasingly important.
Example: Violation of the antifraud rules adopted by the Securities and Exchange Commission may result in severe criminal liability.

5. The Model Penal Code
Although not a source of law, the Model Penal Code ("M.P.C.") was a scholarly endeavor to compile a comprehensive and coherent body of criminal law. Since its publication in 1962, the M.P.C. has greatly influenced the drafting of state criminal statutes. Due to its enlightened position on many different issues, the M.P.C. may be the single most important source of general criminal law.

C. THEORIES OF PUNISHMENT
Historically, several theories have been advanced to justify criminal punishment.

1. Incapacitation (Restraint)
While imprisoned, a criminal has fewer opportunities to commit acts causing harm to society.

2. Special Deterrence
Punishment may *deter the criminal* from committing future crimes.

3. General Deterrence
Punishment may *deter persons other than the criminal* from committing similar crimes for fear of incurring the same punishment.

4. Retribution
Punishment is imposed to vent society's sense of outrage and need for revenge.

5. Rehabilitation
Imprisonment provides the opportunity to mold or reform the criminal into a person who, upon return to society, will conform her behavior to societal norms.

6. Education
The publicity attending the trial, conviction, and punishment of some criminals serves to educate the public to distinguish good and bad conduct and to develop respect for the law.

D. CLASSIFICATION OF CRIMES
At common law, all crimes were divided into three classes: treason, felonies, and misdemeanors. Several additional means of classifying crimes are now frequently employed either by the courts or by state statutory schemes.

1. Felonies and Misdemeanors
Most states now classify as *felonies* all crimes punishable by *death or imprisonment exceeding one year*. Under such modern schemes, *misdemeanors* are crimes punishable by *imprisonment for less than one year or by a fine* only. At common law, the only felonies were murder, manslaughter, rape, sodomy, mayhem, robbery, larceny, arson, and burglary; all other crimes were considered misdemeanors.

2. Malum In Se and Malum Prohibitum
A crime *malum in se* (wrong in itself) is one that is *inherently evil*, either because criminal intent is an element of the offense, or because the crime involves "moral turpitude." By contrast, a crime *malum prohibitum* is one that is wrong only because it is *prohibited by legislation*.
Example: Battery, larceny, and drunken driving are mala in se, whereas hunting without a license, failure to comply with the Federal Drug Labeling Act, and driving in excess of the speed limit are mala prohibita.

3. Infamous Crimes
At common law, infamous crimes are all crimes involving fraud, dishonesty, or the obstruction of justice. Under modern law, this concept has been expanded to include most felonies.

4. Crimes Involving Moral Turpitude
The concept of moral turpitude—committing a base or vile act—is often equated with the concept of malum in se. Conviction of a crime involving moral turpitude may result in the deportation of an alien, the disbarment of an attorney, or the impeachment of a trial witness.

E. PRINCIPLE OF LEGALITY—VOID-FOR-VAGUENESS DOCTRINE
The Due Process Clause of the federal Constitution, found in the Fifth and Fourteenth Amendments, has been interpreted by the Supreme Court to require that no criminal penalty be imposed without fair notice that the conduct is forbidden. The "void-for-vagueness" doctrine, which has been held to require particular scrutiny of criminal statutes capable of reaching speech protected by the First Amendment, incorporates two considerations:

1. Fair Warning
A statute must give a person of ordinary intelligence fair notice that his contemplated conduct is forbidden by the statute.

2. Arbitrary and Discriminatory Enforcement Must Be Avoided
A statute must not encourage arbitrary and erratic arrests and convictions.

F. CONSTITUTIONAL LIMITATIONS ON CRIME CREATION
In addition to the constitutional requirement that a criminal statute be sufficiently specific to

provide fair warning and prevent arbitrary enforcement, Article I of the federal Constitution places two substantive limitations on both federal and state legislatures.

1. **No Ex Post Facto Laws**
   The Constitution expressly prohibits ex post facto laws. The Supreme Court has defined an ex post facto law as one that operates retroactively to:

   (i) *Make criminal an act* that when done was not criminal;

   (ii) *Aggravate a crime or increase the punishment* therefor;

   (iii) *Change the rules of evidence* to the detriment of criminal defendants as a class; or

   (iv) *Alter the law of criminal procedure* to deprive criminal defendants of a substantive right.

   [Calder v. Bull, 3 U.S. (3 Dall.) 386 (1798)]

2. **No Bills of Attainder**
   Bills of attainder are also constitutionally prohibited. A bill of attainder is a legislative act that inflicts punishment or denies a privilege *without a judicial trial*. Although a bill of attainder may also be an ex post facto law, a distinction can be drawn in that an ex post facto law does not deprive the offender of a judicial trial.

G. INTERPRETATIONS OF CRIMINAL STATUTES

1. **Plain Meaning Rule**
   When the statutory language is plain and its meaning clear, the court must give effect to it even if the court feels that the law is unwise or undesirable. An exception to this rule exists if the court believes that applying the plain meaning of a statute will lead to injustice, oppression, or an absurd consequence.

2. **Ambiguous Statutes Strictly Construed in Favor of Defendant**
   The rule of lenity requires that an ambiguous criminal statute must be strictly construed in favor of the defendant. Ambiguity should be distinguished from vagueness. An ambiguous statute is one susceptible to two or more equally reasonable interpretations. A vague statute is one that is so unclear as to be susceptible to no reasonable interpretation.

3. ***Expressio Unius, Exclusio Alterius***
   According to this maxim, the expression of one thing impliedly indicates an intention to exclude another.
   Example: A criminal statute defines bigamy as the act of remarriage by one who has a living spouse. The statute expressly provides an exception for one whose spouse disappeared more than seven years before. Can a person remarry if the spouse has been gone for less than seven years provided he or she believes in good faith that the spouse is dead? Most jurisdictions answer no. The fact that the statute provides one exception impliedly excludes all others.

4. **The Specific Controls the General, the More Recent Controls the Earlier**
   If two statutes address the same subject matter but dictate different conclusions, the more specific statute will be applied rather than the more general. The more recently enacted statute will control an older statute.
   Examples: 1) If one statute prohibits all forms of gambling and another permits charity-sponsored raffles, the latter will control a church raffle.

   2) A 1980 statute banning advertising of cigarettes will govern a 1975 statute providing a limit on advertising expenditure by cigarette manufacturers.

5. **Effect of Repeal**
   At common law, in the absence of a saving provision, the repeal or invalidation of a statute operates to bar prosecutions for earlier violations, provided the prosecution is pending or not yet under way at the time of the repeal. However, a repeal will not operate to set free a person who has been prosecuted and convicted and as to whom the judgment has become final.

   a. **Saving Provision**
      Many of the new comprehensive codes include a provision to the effect that crimes

committed prior to the effective date of the new code are subject to prosecution and punishment under the law as it existed at the time the offense was committed.

H. MERGER

[handwritten: Solicitation & attempt merge into the substantive offense]

1. Common Law Rule

a. Merger of Misdemeanor into Felony
At common law, if a person engaged in conduct constituting both a felony and a misdemeanor, she could be convicted only of the felony. The misdemeanor was regarded as merged into the felony.

b. No Merger Among Offenses of Same Degree
If the same act or a series of acts that were all part of the same transaction constituted several felonies (or several misdemeanors), there was no merger of any of the offenses into any of the others.

2. Current American Rule—No Merger
[handwritten: conspiracy doesn't merge w substantive offense]

There is generally no merger in American law, with the following limited *exceptions*:

a. "Merger" of Solicitation or Attempt into Completed Crime
One who solicits another to commit a crime (where solicitation itself is a crime) cannot be convicted of both the solicitation and the completed crime (if the person solicited does complete it). Similarly, a person who completes a crime after attempting it may not be convicted of both the attempt and the completed crime. Conspiracy, however, does not merge with the completed offense (*e.g.,* one can be convicted of robbery and conspiracy to commit robbery).

b. "Merger" of Lesser Included Offenses into Greater Offenses
Lesser included offenses "merge" into greater offenses, in the sense that one placed in jeopardy for either offense may not later be retried for the other. Nor may one be convicted of both the greater offense and a lesser included offense. A lesser included offense is one that consists entirely of some, but not all, elements of the greater crime. This rule is sometimes labeled a rule of merger, but it is also clearly required by the constitutional prohibition against double jeopardy.

Examples: 1) D allegedly possessed certain narcotics. On the basis of this, she is charged with (i) illegal possession of narcotics, (ii) illegal possession of narcotics for sale, and (iii) possession of a drug not in a properly stamped container. May she be convicted of all three offenses? *Held:* No. She may not be convicted of simple possession and possession for sale. She may be convicted of possession for sale and possession in an improper container, because neither is a lesser included offense of the other. Each requires proof of something the other does not, *i.e.,* intent to sell and use of an improper container.

2) D is convicted of operating a motor vehicle without the owner's consent. She is then charged with stealing the vehicle based upon the same incident. Operating the vehicle without the owner's consent is a lesser included offense of theft, because theft requires proof of everything necessary to prove operation of a vehicle without consent of the owner *plus* the intent to steal. May D be prosecuted for theft? *Held:* No. Conviction for a lesser included offense bars prosecution for the greater offense. [Brown v. Ohio, 432 U.S. 161 (1977)]

3) D is convicted of felony murder based on proof that his accomplice shot and killed a store clerk during an armed robbery. He is then charged and convicted of armed robbery based on the same incident. *Held:* Because the armed robbery was the underlying felony for the felony murder conviction, it is a lesser included offense of the felony murder and the subsequent prosecution is barred. [Harris v. Oklahoma, 433 U.S. 682 (1977)]

3. Developing Rules Against Multiple Convictions for Parts of Same "Transaction"
Many jurisdictions are developing prohibitions against convicting a defendant for more than one offense where the multiple offenses were all part of the same "criminal transaction." In some states, this is prohibited by statute. In others, courts adopt a rule of merger or of double jeopardy to prohibit it.

a. **No Double Jeopardy If Statute Provides Multiple Punishments for Single Act**
Imposition of cumulative punishments for two or more statutorily defined offenses, specifically intended by the legislature to carry ***separate punishments***, arising from the same transaction, and constituting the same crime, does not violate the Double Jeopardy Clause prohibition against multiple punishments for the same offense when the punishments are imposed at a single trial. [Missouri v. Hunter, 459 U.S. 359 (1983)]
Example: D robs a store at gunpoint. D can be sentenced to cumulative punishments for armed robbery and "armed criminal action" under a "use a gun, go to jail" statute.

II. ESSENTIAL ELEMENTS OF CRIME

A. ELEMENTS OF A CRIME
Culpability under Anglo-American criminal law is founded upon certain basic premises that are more or less strictly observed by legislatures and courts when formulating the substantive law of crimes. Consequently, the prosecution is generally required to prove the following elements of a criminal offense:

(i) ***Actus Reus*** (guilty act): A physical act (or unlawful omission) by the defendant;

(ii) ***Mens Rea*** (guilty mind): The state of mind or intent of the defendant at the time of his act;

(iii) ***Concurrence***: The physical act and the mental state existed at the same time; and

(iv) ***Harmful Result and Causation***: A harmful result caused (both factually and proximately) by the defendant's act.

Virtually all crimes require a physical act and may require some sort of intent. Many crimes also require proof of certain ***attendant circumstances*** without which the same act and intent would not be criminal. For example, the crime of receipt of stolen property requires that the property received has in fact been stolen. If the defendant receives property (the act) that he believes to have been stolen (the mental element), when in fact the property has not been stolen, the absence of this required circumstance renders the defendant not liable for receipt of stolen property. Other crimes require result and causation. Homicide, for example, requires that the victim die and that the defendant's act be the cause of death.

B. PHYSICAL ACT
For there to be criminal liability, the defendant must have either performed a voluntary physical act or failed to act under circumstances imposing a legal duty to act. For this purpose, an act is defined as a ***bodily movement***. A thought is not an act. Therefore, bad thoughts alone cannot constitute a crime. Note, however, that speech, unlike thought, is an act that can cause liability (*e.g.*, perjury, solicitation).

1. **The Act Must Be Voluntary**
The defendant's act must be voluntary in the sense that it must be a ***conscious exercise of the will***. *Rationale:* An involuntary act will not be deterred by punishment. The following acts are ***not*** considered "voluntary" and therefore cannot be the basis for criminal liability:

not own volition

a. Conduct that is ***not the product of the actor's determination***.
Example: A shoves B into C, with the result that C falls to his death. Can B be held criminally liable for C's death? No.

b. ***Reflexive or convulsive*** acts. *ex: seizures*

sleep walking

c. Acts performed while the defendant was either ***unconscious or asleep unless*** the defendant knew that she might fall asleep or become unconscious and engaged in dangerous behavior.

2. **Omission as an "Act"**
Although most crimes are committed by affirmative action rather than by nonaction, a defendant's ***failure to act*** will result in criminal liability provided ***three requirements*** are satisfied.

a. **Legal Duty to Act**
The defendant must have a legal duty to act under the circumstances. A legal duty to act can arise from the following sources:

1) A *statute* (*e.g.,* filing an income tax return or reporting an accident).

2) A *contract* obligating the defendant to act, such as one entered into by a lifeguard or a nurse.

3) The *relationship* between the defendant and the victim, which may be sufficiently close to create a duty.
Examples: 1) A parent has the duty to prevent physical harm to his or her children.

2) A spouse has the duty to prevent harm to his or her spouse.

4) The *voluntary assumption of care* by the defendant of the victim. Although in general there is no common law duty to help someone in distress, once aid is rendered, the good Samaritan may be held criminally liable for not satisfying a reasonable standard of care.
Examples: 1) A, while hiking, sees B drowning in a river. Although A is a good swimmer, he takes no steps to save B, who drowns. Was A's failure to act an "act" upon which liability could be based? No, because A had no duty to act. Note that the answer would be the same even if A recognized B as a person whom he disliked and took great pleasure in watching B drown.

2) If A began to swim out toward B and only after reaching B decided that B was someone not worth saving, A would have violated his duty to act by unreasonably abandoning a rescue effort that was voluntarily undertaken.

5) The *creation of peril* by the defendant.
Example: Believing that B can swim, A pushes B into a pool. It becomes apparent that B cannot swim, but A takes no steps to help B. B drowns. Was A's failure to attempt a rescue an "act" on which liability can be based? Yes.

b. **Knowledge of Facts Giving Rise to Duty**
As a general rule, the duty to act arises when the defendant is aware of the facts creating the duty to act (*e.g.,* the parent must know that his child is drowning before his failure to rescue the child will make him liable). However, in some situations the law will impose a duty to learn the facts (*e.g.,* a lifeguard asleep at his post would still have a legal duty to aid a drowning swimmer).

c. **Reasonably Possible to Perform**
It must be reasonably possible for the defendant to perform the duty or to obtain the help of others in performing it.
Example: A parent who is unable to swim is under no duty to jump in the water to attempt to save his drowning child.

3. **Possession as an "Act"**
Criminal statutes that penalize the possession of contraband generally require only that the defendant have *control* of the item for a long enough period to have had an opportunity to terminate the possession. The defendant must be aware of his possession of the object but need not be aware of its illegality.

C. **MENTAL STATE** *big area for test*
A mental state

1. **Purpose of Mens Rea Requirement**
The reason that mens rea is normally required is to distinguish between inadvertent or accidental acts and acts performed by one with a "guilty mind." The latter type of act is more blameworthy and, arguably, can be deterred. However, in some cases (strict liability crimes), mens rea is not required.

2. **Specific Intent**
If the definition of a crime requires not only the doing of an act, but the doing of it with a specific intent or objective, the crime is a "specific intent" crime.

a. **Significance**
It is necessary to identify specific intent for two reasons:

1) **Need for Proof**
The existence of a specific intent cannot be inferred from the doing of the act. The prosecution must produce evidence tending to prove the existence of the specific intent.

2) **Applicability of Certain Defenses**
Some defenses, such as voluntary intoxication and unreasonable mistake of fact, apply only to specific intent crimes.

b. **Enumeration of Specific Intent Crimes**
The major specific intent crimes and the intent they require are as follows:

1) *Solicitation*: Intent to have the person solicited commit the crime;

2) *Attempt*: Intent to complete the crime;

3) *Conspiracy*: Intent to have the crime completed;

4) *First degree premeditated murder* (where so defined by statute): Premeditated intent to kill; ∧it's noted a common law murder = 2nd degree malice crime / of murder / on exame, if no specific degree accompanying the word murder, then

★ 5) *Assault*: Intent to commit a battery;

6) *Larceny and robbery*: Intent to permanently deprive another of his interest in the property taken;

7) *Burglary*: Intent at the time of entry to commit a felony in the dwelling of another;

8) *Forgery*: Intent to defraud;

9) *False pretenses*: Intent to defraud; and

10) *Embezzlement*: Intent to defraud.

3. **Malice—Common Law Murder and Arson** = the only 2 malice crimes
Although the intents required for the "malice" crimes—common law murder and arson—sound similar to specific intent (*e.g.*, the "intent to kill" for murder), these crimes are ***not*** open to the specific intent defenses. The common law created this special mental state category especially to deny to murder and arson the specific intent defenses. To establish malice in these cases, the prosecution need only show that the defendant recklessly disregarded an obvious or high risk that the particular harmful result would occur.

4. **General Intent—Awareness of Factors Constituting Crime** ex: rape & battery
Generally, all crimes require "general intent," which is an awareness of all factors constituting the crime; *i.e.*, the defendant must be aware that she is acting in the proscribed way and that any attendant circumstances required by the crime are present. (Note that the defendant need not be certain that these attendant circumstances exist; it is sufficient that she is aware of a high likelihood that they exist.)

catch all

Example: To commit the crime of false imprisonment (*see* VII.D., *infra*), the defendant must be aware that she is confining a person, and that the confinement has not been specifically authorized by law or validly consented to by the person confined.

a. **Inference of Intent from Act**
A jury can infer the required general intent merely from the doing of the act. It is not necessary that evidence specifically proving the general intent be offered by the prosecution.

b. **Transferred Intent**
If a defendant intended a harmful result to a particular person or object and, in trying to carry out that intent, caused a similar harmful result to another person or object, her intent will be transferred from the intended person or object to the one actually harmed. Any defenses or mitigating circumstances that the defendant could have asserted against the intended victim (*e.g.*, self-defense, provocation) will also be transferred in

never any crimes that have 2 different victims

most cases. The doctrine of transferred intent most commonly applies to homicide, battery, and arson. It does *not* apply to *attempt*.

Example: A shoots at B, intending to kill him. Because of bad aim, she hits C, killing him. Is A guilty of C's murder? *Held:* Yes. Her intent to kill B will be transferred to C. Note that A may also be guilty of the attempted murder of B.

Compare: A shoots at B, intending to kill him. She hits C, only wounding him. While A may be guilty of attempted murder of B, is she also guilty of attempted murder of C? *Held:* No. Transferred intent does not apply to attempt.

c. Motive Distinguished

The motive for a crime is distinct from the intent to commit it. A motive is the reason or explanation underlying the offense. It is generally held that *motive is immaterial* to substantive criminal law. A good motive will not excuse a criminal act. On the other hand, a lawful act done with bad motive will not be punished.

Example: An impoverished woman steals so that her hungry children may eat. Despite her noble *motive*—feeding her children—the woman could be held criminally liable for her acts because her *intent* was to steal.

5. Strict Liability Offenses   *no-intent crime*

A strict liability offense is one that does not require awareness of all of the factors constituting the crime. Generally, the requirement of a state of mind is not abandoned with respect to all elements of the offense, but only with regard to one or some of the elements. The major significance of a strict liability offense is that *certain defenses*, such as mistake of fact, are *not available*. *any defense to negate intent is no defense*

if crime in administrative, morality, regulatory areas, and no adverbs knowingly, intentionally, willfully → no intent crime strict liability

a. Identification of Strict Liability Offenses

Strict liability offenses, also known as public welfare offenses, are generally "regulatory" offenses, *i.e.*, offenses that are part of a regulatory scheme. They generally involve a relatively low penalty and are not regarded by the community as involving significant moral impropriety. Note that the mere fact that a statute is silent on the question of mental state does not necessarily mean that the offense is a strict liability offense. If no mental state is expressly required by the statute, the courts may still interpret the statute as requiring some mens rea, especially if the statute appears to be a codification of a traditional common law offense or if the statute imposes a severe penalty.

Example: Federal legislation prohibits the transfer of firearms not registered under federal law. Is it a defense that the defendant was ignorant of the fact that a firearm was not registered? *Held:* No, because this is a strict liability offense. Awareness of the fact of nonregistration is not necessary, although it is necessary that the defendant have been aware of the fact that she was possessing a firearm.

Compare: Federal legislation requires registration of any fully automatic machine-gun. The statute is silent on the question of mental state and provides a penalty of up to 10 years' imprisonment. *Held:* Defendant may assert as a defense that he was not aware that the weapon in his possession was automatic. The type of statute and the harsh penalty indicate that Congress did not intend to dispense with the mens rea requirement. [Staples v. United States, 511 U.S. 600 (1994)]

b. Constitutionality

The majority view is that strict liability offenses are constitutional. *Exception:* The Supreme Court struck down as a violation of due process a Los Angeles municipal ordinance imposing strict liability for failure to register as a felon. The key factor in the court's decision was the absence of "circumstances which might move one to inquire as to the necessity of registration." *Note:* The scope of this holding is limited to statutes making criminal the failure to register.

6. Model Penal Code Analysis of Fault

The M.P.C. advocates the elimination of the ambiguous common law distinction between general and specific intent. Instead, the M.P.C. proposes four categories into which the mental component of a criminal offense (*i.e.,* the element of fault) can be characterized. Because consistent use of these categories leads to analytical clarity, they have been incorporated into several state criminal codes. They likewise provide a convenient way of analyzing problems on the exam that incorporate statutes.

a. Purposely, Knowingly, or Recklessly
When a statute requires that the defendant act purposely ("intentionally"), knowingly, or recklessly, a subjective standard is being used, *i.e.,* the question is what was actually going on in the defendant's mind.

1) Purposely
A person acts purposely with respect to his conduct when it is his conscious object to engage in certain conduct or cause a certain result, *e.g.,* burglary.

2) Knowingly
A person acts knowingly with respect to the nature of his conduct when he is aware that his conduct is of that nature or that certain circumstances exist. He acts knowingly with respect to the result of his conduct when he knows that his conduct will necessarily or very likely cause such a result. Conduct performed knowingly also satisfies the mental state of a statute that requires willful conduct.

3) Recklessly
A person acts recklessly when he ***consciously disregards a substantial or unjustifiable risk*** that circumstances exist or that a prohibited result will follow, and this disregard constitutes a ***gross deviation from the standard of care*** that a reasonable person would exercise in the situation. An act performed recklessly is also performed wantonly. Recklessness requires that the actor take an unjustifiable risk and that he know of and consciously disregard the risk. Mere realization of the risk is not enough. He must know that injury might result (if he knows that it is ***certain*** to result, he acts ***knowingly***). Thus, recklessness involves both objective ("unjustifiable risk") and subjective ("awareness") elements.

b. Negligence
A person acts negligently when he ***fails to be aware of a substantial and unjustifiable risk*** that circumstances exist or a result will follow, and such failure constitutes a ***substantial deviation from the standard of care*** that a reasonable person would exercise under the circumstances. To determine whether a person acted negligently, an ***objective standard*** is used. However, it is not merely the reasonable person standard that is used in torts; the defendant must have taken a ***very unreasonable risk*** in light of the usefulness of his conduct, his knowledge of the facts, and the nature and extent of the harm that may be caused.
Example: D held himself out to the public as a doctor even though he was not a licensed physician. He treated a sick woman by wrapping her in kerosene-soaked flannels for three days. The woman died. *Held:* D is guilty of manslaughter. His good intentions were irrelevant. By objective standards, he took an unjustifiable risk.

1) Violation of Statute or Ordinance as Evidence of Negligence
Violation of a state statute, municipal ordinance, or administrative regulation may—as in tort law—be evidence of liability.
Example: A, driving in excess of the speed limit, hits and kills B, a pedestrian. A's speeding violation may be admissible as evidence of his negligence in a prosecution for manslaughter.

c. Analysis of Statutes Using Fault Standards

1) State of Mind Applies to All Material Elements of Offense
Often a statute will establish a culpable state of mind without indicating whether it is required for all the material elements of the offense. In that case, the specified state of mind applies to all material elements of the offense unless a contrary purpose appears in the statute.
Example: Under a statute imposing criminal liability on anyone who "knowingly makes a sale of an intoxicating beverage to a minor," the M.P.C. would require knowledge for each material element of the offense. Thus, if the defendant can show that she did not know that

a sale took place, that the beverage was intoxicating, or that the purchaser was a minor, she will be able to avoid liability.

2) General State of Mind Requirement—Recklessness
If the statute defining the offense (other than a strict liability offense) does not include a state of mind requirement, the defendant must have acted with at least recklessness with regard to each material element of the offense.

a) Higher Degree of Fault Suffices
Under the M.P.C.'s hierarchy of fault levels, a showing of a higher state of mind automatically satisfies a lower mental state requirement of a statute. Thus, a showing that the defendant acted purposely or knowingly will satisfy the general requirement of recklessness.

b) Other Levels of Fault Must Be Specified
Because a standard of recklessness is assumed where the state of mind is not specified, if a lower standard of negligence will satisfy liability, or if a higher standard of knowledge or purpose is required, those standards must be indicated in the language of the statute.

Example: Under a statute creating criminal liability for anyone who "sells intoxicating beverages to one whom he should know to be a minor," the material elements include the act of selling and the attendant circumstances that the beverage be intoxicating and that the purchaser be a minor. Under the M.P.C. formula, a minimum standard for recklessness is required as the state of mind for the first two elements, while the third element of the statute specifies that only a negligence level of fault is required.

7. Vicarious Liability Offenses
A vicarious liability offense is one in which a person without personal fault may nevertheless be held vicariously liable for the criminal conduct of another (usually an employee). The criminal law doctrine of vicarious liability is analogous to the tort doctrine of respondeat superior. *Note:* Unlike strict liability, which dispenses with the mens rea requirement but retains the requirement that the defendant have personally engaged in the necessary acts or omissions, vicarious liability dispenses with the personal actus reus requirement but retains the need for **mental fault on the part of the employee**.

a. Limitation on Punishment
Because the imposition of criminal liability for faultless conduct is contrary to the basic premise of criminal justice that crime requires fault on the part of the accused, at least one state court has held that imprisonment in such cases violates the due process guarantees of the state constitution. The current trend in the legislatures is to limit vicarious liability to **regulatory crimes** and to limit punishment to **fines**.

b. Implying Vicarious Liability from Underlying Strict Liability Offense
Despite some decisions to the contrary, the mere fact that the underlying offense is clearly a strict liability offense should **not** imply a legislative intent to impose vicarious liability.

Example: A statute makes it a crime "for anyone to serve an alcoholic beverage to a minor." Although a bartender may be strictly liable under this statute regardless of her belief that the customer was legally old enough to drink, this statute should not be construed to impose liability on the tavern owner who neither was present at the time the minor was served nor authorized the actions of the bartender.

8. Enterprise Liability—Liability of Corporations and Associations

a. Common Law—No Criminal Liability
At common law, a corporation could not commit a crime because it was unable to form the necessary criminal intent.

b. Modern Statutes—Vicarious Criminal Liability
Modern statutes often provide for the liability of corporations and sometimes even unincorporated associations (*e.g.,* partnerships). This liability is, by necessity, vicarious. Under such provisions, corporations may be held liable under the following conditions:

1) Act Within Scope of Office
Except where the law specifically provides otherwise, the conduct giving rise to corporate liability must be performed by an agent of the corporation acting on behalf of the corporation and within the scope of his office or employment.

2) "Superior Agent Rule"
Some jurisdictions limit corporate criminal liability to situations in which the conduct is performed or participated in by agents sufficiently high in the corporate hierarchy to presume that their acts reflect corporate policy.

c. Model Penal Code
Under the M.P.C., a corporation may be guilty of a criminal offense provided:

1) The offense consists of the *failure to discharge a specific duty* imposed by law on the corporation;

2) The offense is defined by a statute in which a *legislative purpose to impose liability* on corporations plainly appears; or

3) The commission of the offense was "authorized, requested, commanded, performed, or recklessly *tolerated by the board of directors* or by a high managerial agent acting on behalf of the corporation within the scope of his office or employment."

d. Individual Liability Independent of Enterprise Liability
Even though the corporation cannot be convicted of a particular offense and cannot be imprisoned, the person who, in the name of the corporation, performs (or causes to be performed) the conduct that is an element of the offense is legally accountable and subject to punishment to the same extent as if the conduct were performed in his name or on his own behalf. Similarly, the fact that the corporation is liable does not prevent the conviction of the individual who committed the offense.

D. CONCURRENCE OF MENTAL FAULT WITH PHYSICAL ACT REQUIRED
The defendant must have had the intent necessary for the crime at the time he committed the act constituting the crime. In addition, the intent must have prompted the act.

Example: A decides to kill B. While driving to the store to purchase a gun for this purpose, A negligently runs over B and kills him. Is A guilty of murder? No, because although at the time A caused B's death he had the intent to do so, this intent did not prompt the act resulting in B's death (*i.e.,* A's poor driving).

E. CAUSATION
Some crimes (*e.g.,* homicide) require a harmful result and causation. For a full discussion of causation, *see* VII.C.5., *infra*.

III. ACCOMPLICE LIABILITY

A. PARTIES TO A CRIME

1. Common Law
liable for the crime itself & all other foreseeable crimes
need to be actively in on the crime
presence is not by itself sufficient

The common law distinguished four types of parties to a felony: *principals in the first degree* (persons who actually engage in the act or omission that constitutes the criminal offense); *principals in the second degree* (persons who aid, command, or encourage the principal and are present at the crime); *accessories before the fact* (persons who aid, abet, or encourage the principal but are *not* present at the crime); and *accessories after the fact* (persons who assist the principal after the crime).

a. Significance of Common Law Distinctions
At common law, the distinctions between the parties had a great deal of procedural significance. For example, an accessory could not be convicted unless the principal had already been convicted, although both could be convicted in a joint trial if the jury determined the principal's guilt first. Most modern jurisdictions have abandoned this requirement, and an accessory can be convicted even if the principal has evaded apprehension or has been tried and acquitted.

2. Modern Statutes
Most jurisdictions have abolished the distinctions between principals in the first degree, principals in the second degree, and accessories before the fact (accessories after the fact are still treated separately). Under the modern approach, all "parties to the crime" can be found

guilty of the criminal offense. For convenience, this section will designate the actual perpetrator of the criminal act as the principal and the other parties to the crime as accomplices.

a. Principal

A principal is one who, with the requisite mental state, ***actually engages in the act or omission*** that causes the criminal result. Also, anyone who acts through an innocent, irresponsible, or unwilling agent is classified as a principal.

Example: A gives a poisonous drink to B to give to C. B does so; C drinks it and dies. If B did not know that the drink was poisonous, or if B was mentally ill or under duress, A, not B, is the principal. Note that the principal need not be present when the harm results.

b. Accomplice

An accomplice is one who, with the intent that the crime be committed, aids, counsels, or encourages the principal before or during the commission of the crime.

c. Accessory After the Fact

An accessory after the fact is one who receives, relieves, comforts, or assists another, knowing that he has committed a felony, in order to ***help the felon escape arrest, trial, or conviction.*** The crime committed by the principal must be a *felony* and it must be *completed* at the time the aid is rendered. Today, the crime is usually called "harboring a fugitive," "aiding escape," or "obstructing justice."

1) Penalty

Typically the punishment for this crime bears no relationship to the principal offense; five years is the most common maximum sentence. Exemptions are usually provided for close relatives of the principal offender (the common law exempted only the spouse).

B. MENTAL STATE—INTENT REQUIRED

To be convicted as an accomplice under the prevailing common law rule, a person must have given aid, counsel, or encouragement with the ***intent*** to aid or encourage the principal in the commission of the crime charged. In the absence of a statute, most courts would hold that mere ***knowledge*** that a crime would result from the aid provided is insufficient for accomplice liability, at least where the aid involves the sale of ordinary goods at ordinary prices. However, procuring an illegal item or selling at a higher price because of the buyer's purpose may constitute a sufficient "stake in the venture" for a court to find intent to aid.

Example: A tells B that he wants to buy a can of gasoline from B to burn a house down. B sells A the gasoline and A burns down the house. B is not liable as an accomplice to arson (unless it was illegal to sell gasoline in cans or B charged A twice his usual price because of what A was using the gasoline for).

C. SCOPE OF LIABILITY

An accomplice is responsible for the crimes he did or counseled ***and*** for any other crimes committed in the course of committing the crime contemplated, as long as the other crimes were ***probable or foreseeable.***

Example: A commands B to burn C's house, and B does so. The fire spreads to X's house, and it was foreseeable that it would do so. A is an accomplice to the burning of X's house.

1. Inability to Be Principal No Bar to Liability as Accomplice

One who may not be convicted of being a principal may be convicted of being an accomplice.

Example: At common law, a woman may not be convicted of rape as a principal, but may be convicted of that crime as an accomplice.

2. Exclusions from Liability

Under some circumstances, a person who would otherwise be liable as an accomplice is not subject to conviction, either because of a legislative intent to exempt him or because he has a special defense.

a. Members of the Protected Class

If the statute is intended to protect members of a limited class from exploitation or overbearing, members of that class are presumed to be immune from liability, even if they participate in the crime in a manner that would otherwise make them liable.

Example: A is charged with transporting B, a woman, in interstate commerce for immoral purposes; B is charged as an accomplice, on the ground that she encouraged and assisted A. Is B guilty? *Held:* No. The statute was intended to protect women, and thus the woman transported cannot be convicted.

b. Necessary Parties Not Provided For

If a statute defines a crime in a way that necessarily involves more than one participant and provides for the liability of only one participant, it is presumed that the legislative intent was to immunize the other participant from liability as an accomplice. The rule is most often applied to statutes making the sale of certain items a criminal offense.

Example: A asked B to sell her some heroin. B did so. Both were apprehended. B was charged as a principal for the sale of narcotics; A was charged as an accomplice. Is A subject to conviction? *Held:* No. Since the statute prohibiting sale does not mention the liability of the buyer, the presumed legislative intent is to exempt her.

c. Withdrawal

One who has rendered encouragement or aid to another may avoid liability as an accomplice if he withdraws from the crime before it is actually committed by the principal. What is necessary for an effective withdrawal *depends upon what the person initially did*.

(i) If the person merely *encouraged* the commission of the crime, withdrawal requires that he *repudiate* this encouragement.

(ii) If the person assisted by *providing some material* to the principal, withdrawal requires at least that the person attempt to *neutralize this assistance*, *e.g.*, by doing everything possible to retrieve the material provided.

If it is impossible to withdraw by these methods, an alternative means of withdrawing is to *notify authorities* or take some other action to prevent the commission of the offense. In any case, the withdrawal must occur *before* the chain of events leading to the commission of the crime becomes unstoppable.

Example: B expresses a desire to kill C. A encourages him to do so, and provides him with a gun. Later, A changes his mind. He seeks B out, and tells B that his earlier position was wrong and that B should not kill C. He also gets his gun back. Nevertheless, B obtains another gun and kills C. Is A liable as an accomplice? *Held:* No, since he did all that was possible to render his encouragement and assistance ineffective before B's plan to kill C became unstoppable.

IV. INCHOATE OFFENSES

A. IN GENERAL

The inchoate offenses are solicitation, attempt, and conspiracy. They are quite frequently considered felonies. An inchoate offense is committed prior to and in preparation for what may be a more serious offense. It is a complete offense in itself, even though the act to be done may not have been completed. At common law under the doctrine of merger, inchoate offenses were regarded as misdemeanors; if the principal offense was carried out, they were considered felonies. The doctrine of merger has been abandoned in many jurisdictions in cases involving a conspiracy, allowing an accused to be convicted of *both* conspiracy and the principal offense. However, an accused *cannot* be convicted of either attempt or solicitation *and* the principal offense.

B. SOLICITATION

At common law it was a misdemeanor to solicit another to commit a felony or an act that would breach the peace or obstruct justice. Modern statutes often retain the crime of solicitation, but some restrict it to the solicitation of certain serious felonies.

1. Elements

Solicitation consists of inciting, counseling, advising, inducing, urging, or commanding another to commit a felony with the specific ***intent that the person solicited commit the crime*** (general approval or agreement is insufficient). The offense is complete at the time the solicitation is made. It is not necessary that the person solicited agree to commit the crime or do anything in response. (If the person solicited committed the crime, the solicitor would be liable for the crime as a party; if the person solicited proceeded far enough to be liable for attempt, the solicitor would be a party to that attempt.)

2. Attempt Distinguished

Mere solicitation is not an attempt to commit the crime solicited. This distinction is important in jurisdictions where there is no crime of solicitation or where the crime of solicitation does not extend to as many offenses as does the crime of attempt.

3. Defenses and Potential Defenses

    a. Impossibility No Defense

    It is not a defense that the solicitation could not have been successful, as where the person solicited was a police undercover agent. The culpability of the solicitor is measured by the circumstances as she believed them to be.

    b. Withdrawal or Renunciation No Defense

    Once the solicitation has been made, it is generally no defense that the solicitor changed her mind or countermanded her advice or urging.

    c. Exemption from Intended Crime Is Defense

    If the solicitor could not be guilty of the intended crime because of a legislative intent to exempt her, she would have a defense. For example, a minor female could not be found guilty of solicitation of statutory rape by urging a man to have intercourse with her, because she could not be guilty of the completed crime.

C. CONSPIRACY *the people must be pursuing an unlawful objective*

1. Introduction

At common law, a conspiracy was defined as a combination or agreement between two or more persons to accomplish some criminal or unlawful purpose, or to accomplish a lawful purpose by unlawful means. *objective*

Recent state codifications require that the object of the conspiracy be a specifically proscribed offense. Yet many states essentially codify the expansive common law notion by making it a crime to conspire to commit acts injurious to the public welfare. The Supreme Court has indicated that such statutes are unconstitutionally vague unless construed narrowly.

    a. No Merger—Conviction for Conspiracy and Completed Crime

    Under the old rule, if the conspirators were successful and completed their crime, the crime of conspiracy "merged" into the completed crime. While the members of the agreement could be convicted of the completed crime, they could not be convicted of the conspiracy. This is no longer the law in most jurisdictions. (*See* the discussion of merger in I.H., *supra*.) Now, if the conspirators are successful, they can be convicted of both criminal conspiracy and the crime they committed pursuant to the conspiracy.

    b. Liability of One Conspirator for Crimes Committed by Other Conspirators

    One conspirator may, by virtue of his participation in the scheme, meet the requirements for "aiding and abetting" the commission of crimes by his co-conspirators and therefore be liable for those crimes as an accomplice. Even if the conspirator did not have the sufficient mental state for accomplice liability, a separate doctrine provides that each conspirator may be liable for the crimes of all other conspirators if ***two requirements*** are met: *each is liable for all crime if =*

        (i) The ***crimes were committed in furtherance*** of the objectives of the conspiracy; and

        (ii) The crimes were "a natural and probable consequence" of the conspiracy, *i.e.*, ***foreseeable***.

    This doctrine applies only if the conspirator has not made a legally effective withdrawal from the conspiracy before the commission of the crime by the co-conspirator. (*See* 4.b., *infra*.)

c.   **Attempt Distinguished**
In attempt cases, the law requires that there be a ***substantial step*** toward commission of the crime. In conspiracy cases, at least at common law, the agreement itself is normally sufficient to constitute the crime. Hence, in common law conspiracy cases the law intervenes at an earlier stage than the planning of the crime. The reason for this is that the secret activity is potentially more dangerous to society and, since a group is involved, it is more difficult for one person to stop the activity once the agreement has been made.

✓ 2.   **Elements**
The elements of conspiracy at common law are as follows:

(i)   An ***agreement between two or more*** persons;

(ii)   An ***intent to enter into an agreement***; and   *intent to agree*

(iii)   An ***intent to achieve the objective*** of the agreement.   *intent to pursue*

Under the traditional definition of conspiracy, the agreement itself was the culpable act (the actus reus). Today, a majority of states require an ***overt act*** in furtherance of the conspiracy, but mere preparation will usually suffice.

[margin handwritten: conspiracy doesn't merge into the substantive offense — thus a person can be charged with both the crime]

a.   **Agreement Requirement**
The parties must agree to accomplish the same objective by mutual action. The agreement need not be express. The existence of an agreement may be shown by a concert of action on the part of the conspirators over a period of time under circumstances showing that they were aware of the purpose and existence of the conspiracy and agreed to participate in the common purpose. Where multiple crimes and multiple parties are involved, there are often problems in deciding whether there is a single conspiracy or several smaller conspiracies.

[handwritten: doesn't have to be express — passive understanding is sufficient]

1)   **Object of the Agreement**
At common law, it was not necessary that there be an agreement to commit a crime in order to find a criminal conspiracy. It was only necessary that the object of the agreement was something "unlawful" or that the parties intended to accomplish something lawful by "unlawful" means. "Unlawful" in this context covered a variety of noncriminal matters that were regarded as contrary to the public welfare. But the modern trend is to limit criminal conspiracies to agreements to ***commit crimes***.

2)   **Multiple Crimes**
Where the same parties perform a number of crimes over an extended period of time, is each individual crime the subject of a separate conspiracy or are all the crimes to be treated as arising out of one overriding conspiracy? If there is an initial agreement among the parties to engage in a ***course of criminal conduct*** constituting all the crimes, then there is only ***one conspiracy***.
Example: A and B agree to commit one bank robbery each month for one year. Even though they plan to rob 12 banks, they are guilty of only one conspiracy.

3)   **Number of Conspiracies in Multiple Party Situations**
In complex situations involving numerous parties, it is sometimes important to determine how many conspiracies existed and who conspired with whom. There are two general ways to characterize situations of this sort.

a)   **"Chain" Relationship—One Large Conspiracy**
If there is a series of agreements, all of which are regarded as part of a single large scheme in which all of the parties to the subagreements are interested, the situation will be regarded as one large conspiracy involving all of the participants. The subagreements will be characterized as "links" in the overall "chain" relationship.

b)   **"Hub-and-Spoke" Relationships—Multiple Conspiracies**
One participant may enter into a number of subagreements, each involving ***different persons***. All of the agreements are similar in that they have ***one common member***. However, if it is established that the ***subagreements are***

reasonably independent of each other—if, for example, the members of each agreement (other than the common member) have little or no interest in whether the other agreements succeed—the situation will be regarded as involving numerous different and independent conspiracies. The common member can be characterized as the "hub" (as of a wheel) and each sub-agreement as a "spoke." The common member is, of course, a member of each conspiracy. But the members of each "spoke" conspiracy are not members of the other "spoke" conspiracies and have not conspired with the members of those conspiracies.

Examples: 1) In a large narcotics ring, a smuggler brings heroin into the country and sells it to a wholesaler. The wholesaler sells it to numerous retailers. How many conspiracies? One, because this is a "chain" situation. Because the smuggler-wholesaler agreement and the wholesaler-retailers agreements were all part of a scheme in which all participants were interested, there is only one conspiracy.

2) Brown agreed with A, B, and C to help each of them make fraudulent loan applications. Each application was to be an independent action and the applicants in one situation had no interest in whether the other fraudulent applications were successful. How many conspiracies? Three: Brown with A, Brown with B, and Brown with C. Since the subagreements were not part of an overall scheme in which A, B, and C all were interested, this is a "hub-and-spoke" situation. A has not conspired with B and C, but only with Brown.

4)   Implications of Requirement of Two or More Parties

A conspiracy must involve a "meeting of the minds" between at least two independent persons. Moreover, at common law there must be a meeting of at least two "guilty minds," *i.e.,* between two persons who are actually committing themselves to the scheme. If one person in a two-party conspiracy is only feigning agreement (*e.g.,* an undercover police officer), the other person cannot be convicted of conspiracy (unless the M.P.C. unilateral approach, discussed below, is followed). This requirement of two guilty parties gives rise to a number of problems.

a)   Husband and Wife

At common law, a husband and wife could not conspire together because the law viewed them as one person. They could, however, be guilty of conspiracy with a third person. This distinction has been abandoned in virtually all states today.

b)   Corporation and Agent

Since a corporation can act only through an agent, it has been held that there can be no conspiracy between the corporation and a single agent acting on behalf of the corporation. There is a split of authority as to whether the agents can be deemed co-conspirators. Note that a corporation may be a party to a conspiracy with other corporations or individuals who are not agents of the corporation.

c)   Wharton-Type Problems

(1)   Wharton Rule

Where two or more people are necessary for the commission of the substantive offense (*e.g.,* adultery, dueling, sale of contraband), the "Wharton rule" (named after its author) states that there is *no crime of conspiracy unless more parties participate in the agreement than are necessary for the crime.* Some courts hold that if the Wharton rule applies, there can never be a conviction for conspiracy. Others hold that if the rule applies, it prohibits conviction for both conspiracy and the crime that the parties agreed to commit.

Example: A and B agree to meet at dawn to engage in a duel. They are apprehended before daybreak, however. Dueling is a crime in the jurisdiction, and A is charged with conspiracy to commit dueling. Does A have a defense? Yes. The Wharton rule applies and prevents liability.

Compare: The Wharton rule does not apply to agreements with "***necessary parties not provided for***" (*see* III.C.2.b., *supra*). Thus, where a state statute prohibiting the sale of narcotics imposes criminal liability only on the seller and not on the buyer, both the buyer and seller may be guilty of conspiracy to sell narcotics (even though both parties are necessary for commission of the substantive offense).

(2) Agreement with Person in "Protected Class"

If members of a conspiracy agree to commit an act that violates a statute that was designed to protect persons within a given class, *a person within that class* cannot be guilty of the crime itself. (*See* III.C.2.a., *supra*.) Moreover, she ***cannot be guilty of a conspiracy*** to commit that crime. It follows, then, that between two people, the person ***not*** in the protected class cannot be guilty of criminal conspiracy on the basis of an agreement with the person in the protected class.

Example: A, a woman, and B, a man, agreed on a scheme in which A would be transported over state lines for purposes of prostitution. Is B guilty of criminal conspiracy? No. The act of transporting women over state lines for immoral purposes violates a statute (the Mann Act) that was designed to protect women; thus, A could not be guilty of a violation of the Act and cannot be guilty of conspiracy to violate the Act. Therefore, B cannot be guilty of criminal conspiracy because there were not two guilty parties to the agreement.

d) Effect of Acquittal of Other Conspirators

A conspiracy requires two guilty parties at common law. Thus, in most courts, the acquittal of ***all*** persons with whom a defendant is alleged to have conspired precludes conviction of the remaining defendant. This rule does ***not*** apply where the other parties are not apprehended, are charged with lesser offenses, or are no longer being prosecuted (*nolle prosequi*).

e) Compare Unilateral (Model Penal Code) Approach

Under the M.P.C.'s unilateral approach, conspiracy is established by showing that the defendant "agreed" with another to commit the crime (regardless of whether the other person shared in that commitment); it is not necessary to show an actual agreement between two or more persons. Thus, the fact that all the other parties to the conspiracy have been acquitted or were only feigning agreement will ***not*** prevent the defendant's conviction.

b. Mental State—Specific Intent

Conspiracy is a ***specific intent*** crime. There are two different intents that are necessary: intent to agree and intent to achieve the objective of the conspiracy.

1) Intent to Agree

It is very difficult to separate the intent to agree from the act of agreement. Hence, most courts do not even try. For bar exam purposes, the only thing that is important to remember is that the intent to agree can be ***inferred*** from conduct.

2) Intent to Achieve Objective

The defendant must intend to achieve the objective of the conspiracy. This intent must be established as to ***each*** individual defendant. Under the common law approach, a minimum of two persons must intend to achieve the same purpose; *i.e.,* there must be a "meeting of guilty minds."

Example: A, B, and C agree to steal D's car, but only A and B intend to keep it permanently; C intends to return it to D. Only A and B are guilty of conspiracy to commit larceny, because only they had the intent to permanently deprive D of his car. If only A so intended, and both B and C intended to return the car, then A could not be liable for conspiracy to commit larceny.

3)   Intent to Facilitate a Conspiracy

A person who acts with the intent to facilitate a conspiracy may thereby become a member of the conspiracy. However, ***intent cannot be inferred from mere knowledge***. Therefore, a merchant who sells a good in the ordinary course of business that he knows will be used to further a conspiracy does not thereby join the conspiracy. On the other hand, a merchant may be held to have joined the conspiracy if the good sold is a specialty item that cannot easily be obtained elsewhere or if the merchant otherwise has a stake in the criminal venture (*e.g.,* by raising the price of the good because of the buyer's purpose).

4)   "Corrupt Motive" Not Required

The majority rule is that the parties to a conspiracy need not have been aware that their plan was an illegal one. A minority of courts have held to the contrary, however, reasoning that a requirement of evil motive flows implicitly from the word conspiracy. According to the "corrupt motive" doctrine, which operates as an exception to the general rule that ignorance of the law will not excuse criminal liability, the parties to a conspiracy must have known that their objective was criminal. The corrupt motive doctrine is usually limited to offenses that are malum prohibitum (*see* I.D.2., *supra*).

5)   Conspiracy to Commit "Strict Liability" Crimes

Conspiracy is a specific intent crime. Therefore, a conspiracy to commit a "strict liability" crime (for which intent is not required) requires intent.

Example: A and B agree on a scheme to persuade C, a 12-year-old girl, to have intercourse with them. They believe she is 21, but this would not be a defense to the completed crime of statutory rape. Can they be convicted of conspiracy to commit statutory rape? No, because conspiracy requires knowledge of the victim's age even though the completed crime does not.

c.   Overt Act   majority rule,   [handwritten: Common law & minority rule doesn't require overt act, agreement sufficient.]

Traditionally, the conspiracy was complete when the agreement with the requisite intent was reached. This is still the law in some states. Most states, however, require that an act in furtherance of the conspiracy be performed. Any act in pursuit of the conspiracy will suffice, even an act of mere preparation. The act may be performed by any one of the conspirators.

Example: A, B, and C agreed to rob a bank. A, unbeknownst to B and C, rents a car to be used in the getaway. If an overt act is required, the renting of a car is sufficient.

3.   Termination of Conspiracy

Since acts or declarations of co-conspirators are admissible only if made in furtherance of the conspiracy, it becomes critically important to determine when the conspiracy ends. This is also important for statute of limitations purposes. The main problem is in determining whether acts of concealment after commission of the substantive offense are part of the conspiracy. Since most criminals attempt to conceal the fact that they have committed a crime, courts have generally taken the view that ***evidence of overt acts of concealment is not sufficient to make the act of concealment part of the conspiracy***. In other words, there must be direct evidence that the parties specifically agreed, prior to commission of the crime, that they would act in a certain way to conceal the fact that they had committed the crime.

Example: Suppose the statute of limitations for tax evasion is six years. If A and B conspire to commit tax evasion, does their conspiracy end at the time of the commission of the fraud, or does it extend for the six years during which time A and B presumably endeavor to keep their crime a secret? The answer depends upon whether at the time of the agreement to commit tax evasion there was also a specific subsidiary agreement to conceal the crime until the statute of limitations had run. If there was no such specific agreement, as, for example, if A and B were not aware of the statute of limitations, then the conspiracy does not extend beyond the completion of the act of evasion.

4.   Defenses

a.   Impossibility—No Defense

Impossibility is ***not a defense*** to a charge of conspiracy.

Example: A and B agree to rape a woman whom they believe is asleep. In fact, she is dead. A and B may be convicted of conspiracy to rape.

b.   Withdrawal—No Defense to Conspiracy Charge *even if it's adequate for the viability of conspiracy itself*
The general rule is that withdrawal from a conspiracy is *not a defense* to a charge of conspiracy, because the conspiracy is complete as soon as the agreement is made and an overt act is committed. The M.P.C. recognizes voluntary withdrawal as a defense if the defendant thwarts the success of the conspiracy (*e.g.,* by informing the police).

but is a defense for other's conspirator's subsequent crimes

1)   Defense to Subsequent Crimes of Co-Conspirators
A person may limit his liability for subsequent acts of the other members of the conspiracy, including the target crime for which the conspiracy was formed, if he withdraws. To withdraw, he must perform an affirmative act that *notifies all members* of the conspiracy, and such notice must be given in time for them to have the opportunity to abandon their plans. (Note that if he has also provided material assistance so as to be liable as an accomplice, he must attempt to neutralize the assistance (*see* III.C.2.c., *supra*).)

attempt = specific intent + substantial step beyond preparation in the direction of the commission of the crime. mere preparation is not by itself sufficient.

5.   Punishment
Because a defendant may be convicted of both conspiracy and the completed crime, most jurisdictions have enacted express penalty provisions for conspiracies. Some statutes make conspiracy a misdemeanor regardless of its objective; some provide a permissible maximum sentence regardless of the objective; and still others provide different maximums depending upon the objective. Note that because the punishment for conspiracy usually is not expressed as a fraction of the punishment for the completed crime, the punishment for conspiracy may be more severe than the punishment for the completed crime.

D.)   ATTEMPT
A criminal attempt is an act that, although done with the intention of committing a crime, falls short of completing the crime. An attempt therefore consists of two elements: (i) a specific intent to commit the crime, and (ii) an overt act in furtherance of that intent.

1.   Intent
The defendant must have the intent to perform an act and obtain a result that, if achieved, would constitute a crime.

Model Penal Code position and possibly impossibly to change of attempt exception: Dangers of possession when possession is not needed I will not be charged with attempted receipt of possession on a forged possession

a.   Attempt Requires Specific Intent
Regardless of the intent required for a completed offense, an attempt always requires a *specific intent*. For example, attempted murder requires the specific *intent to kill* another person, even though the mens rea for murder itself does not necessarily require a specific intent to kill (*see* VII.C.2.a.1), *infra*).

b.   Attempt to Commit Negligent Crimes Is Logically Impossible
A crime defined as the negligent production of a result cannot be attempted, because if there were an intent to cause such a result, the appropriate offense would be attempt to intentionally commit the crime rather than attempt to negligently cause the harm.

c.   Attempt to Commit Strict Liability Crimes Requires Intent
Although a strict liability crime does not require criminal intent, to attempt a strict liability crime the defendant must act with the intent to bring about the proscribed result.

2.   Overt Act
The defendant must have committed an act *beyond mere preparation* for the offense. Several tests have been used to determine whether the act requirement for attempt liability has been satisfied:

a.   Proximity Test
Most courts have used a proximity approach; *i.e.,* they have evaluated the act based on how close the defendant came to completing the offense. Under the typical proximity test, attempt requires an act that is dangerously close to success.
Example: Pointing a loaded gun at an intended victim and pulling the trigger is sufficient under the proximity test, but going to the store to purchase bullets or even driving to the intended victim's house is insufficient. [*See* People v. Rizzo, 246 N.Y. 334 (1927)]

b. **Equivocality Test**
Under the equivocality test followed by a few courts, the act by itself must demonstrate that the defendant had an unequivocal intent to commit the crime.

c. **Model Penal Code Test**
The M.P.C. requires that the act or omission constitute a "substantial step in a course of conduct planned to culminate in the commission of the crime." In addition, an act will not qualify as a substantial step unless it is strong corroboration of the actor's criminal purpose.

3. **Defenses to Liability for Attempt**

a. **Impossibility of Success**
Traditionally, the law distinguished between factual and legal impossibility. The modern view reflected in the M.P.C., which reaches the same result, is that impossibility should not be a defense when the defendant's actual intent is to do an act or bring about a result proscribed by law. For exam purposes, however, you should understand and be able to apply the traditional classifications of impossibility.

1) **Factual Impossibility Is No Defense**
It is no defense to attempt that it would have been impossible for the defendant to complete her plan, *i.e.,* do all of those things that she intended to do. This is factual impossibility.
Example: A stops B on the street, points a gun at her, and asks her to hand over her money. Unbeknownst to A, B has no money. Is A guilty of attempted robbery? Yes.

a) **Includes Impossibility Due to Attendant Circumstances**
Impossibility is also no defense when the defendant engages in conduct while mistaken about certain attendant circumstances: Had the circumstances been as she believed they were, what she set out to do would be a crime. However, because the circumstances were otherwise, what she has set out to do will not be a crime. Courts traditionally have split on whether this is legal or factual impossibility, but the better view is that it is factual impossibility and not a defense.
Example: Goods are stolen from A by B. B is apprehended and the goods are recovered. Police secure A's permission to use the goods to trap C, a suspected fence. On police orders, B takes the goods to C and offers to sell them, telling C that they are stolen. C buys them. Since the goods are no longer stolen (they are being used with the owner's permission), C is not guilty of receipt of stolen goods. Is C guilty of attempt to receive stolen goods? In most states and under the M.P.C., yes, because C, with the requisite culpability, has engaged in conduct that would constitute receipt of stolen property if the circumstances were as he believed them to be.

2) **Legal Impossibility Is a Defense**
If those things that the defendant does or intends to do would not actually be a crime, this is legal impossibility. All courts recognize this as a defense. This rule covers only those situations in which defendants set out to do things they mistakenly believe constitute crimes. Note that legal impossibility defined in this way would also be a defense under the M.P.C. because the result is not proscribed by law.
Example: B goes fishing, believing that fishing is prohibited in the lake in which she is fishing. In fact, there is no prohibition against fishing in that lake; thus, B cannot be charged with the completed crime of prohibited fishing. Is B guilty of attempted violation of the criminal law making it a crime to fish where fishing is prohibited? No, this is legal impossibility.

b. **Abandonment**
If a defendant has, with the required intent, gone beyond preparation, may she escape liability by abandoning her plans? The general rule is that abandonment is *never a defense*. The M.P.C. approach is that *withdrawal will be a defense but only if:*

1) It is *fully voluntary* and not made because of the difficulty of completing the crime or because of an increased risk of apprehension; and

2) It is a *complete abandonment* of the plan made under circumstances manifesting a renunciation of criminal purpose, not just a decision to postpone committing it or to find another victim.

4. Prosecution for Attempt
A defendant charged with a completed crime may be found guilty of either the completed crime or an attempt to commit the crime as long as the evidence presented supports such a verdict. The reverse is not true. A defendant charged only with attempt may not be convicted of the completed crime.

5. Punishment for Attempt
Most states punish attempt less severely than the crime attempted. The most common statutory scheme permits a penalty up to one-half the maximum penalty for the completed crime, with a specific maximum set for attempts to commit crimes punishable by death or life imprisonment. Under the M.P.C. and some state statutes, an attempt may be punished to the same extent as the completed crime, except for capital crimes and the most serious felonies.

V. RESPONSIBILITY AND CRIMINAL CAPACITY

A. INSANITY
The insanity defense exempts certain defendants because of the existence of an abnormal mental condition at the time of the crime. The various formulations differ significantly on what effects a mental illness must have had to entitle the defendant to an acquittal. Note that insanity is a *legal term* rather than a psychiatric one. Furthermore, insanity is a generic term comprising many possible mental abnormalities, all of which have only one thing in common: they are recognized by law as dictating certain legal consequences. Usually, the cause of a defendant's mental illness or insanity is irrelevant in determining the legal consequences.

1. Formulations of Insanity Defense

a. *M'Naghten* **Rule**

1) **Elements**
The traditional *M'Naghten* rule provides that a defendant is entitled to an acquittal if the proof establishes that:

a) A *disease* of the mind

b) *Caused a defect* of reason

c) Such that the defendant *lacked the ability at the time* of his actions to either:

(1) Know the *wrongfulness* of his actions; or

(2) Understand the *nature and quality* of his actions.

2) **Application**

a) **Defendant with Delusions**
If the defendant suffered from delusions (false beliefs), it is necessary to determine whether his actions would have been criminal if the facts had been as he believed them to be.
Example: A, because of a mental illness, believed B wanted to kill him. A killed B. Is A entitled to an acquittal on insanity grounds under the *M'Naghten* rule? *Held:* No. Even if A's delusion had been accurate, he would not have been legally entitled to kill B simply because B wanted to kill him.

b) **Belief that Acts Are Morally Right**
A defendant is not entitled to an acquittal merely because he believes his acts are morally right, unless he has lost the capacity to recognize that they are regarded by society as wrong.

trigger words

c) **Inability to Control Oneself**
Under the traditional interpretation given to the *M'Naghten* rule, it is irrelevant that the defendant may have been unable to control himself and avoid committing the crime. Loss of control because of mental illness is ***no defense***.

3) **Evidence Admissible**
In practice, the *M'Naghten* rule does not unduly restrict the evidence heard by juries. Most jurisdictions admit any evidence that reasonably tends to show the mental condition of the defendant at the time of the crime.

b. **Irresistible Impulse Test**
Under the irresistible impulse test, a defendant is entitled to an acquittal if the proof establishes that because of mental illness he was ***unable to control his actions or to conform his conduct to the law***. Contrary to what the name irresistible impulse might imply, this inability need not come upon the defendant suddenly. A number of jurisdictions apply both *M'Naghten* and the irresistible impulse test. Thus, a person is entitled to an acquittal if he meets either test.

lack
self control
a free choice

c. ***Durham* (or New Hampshire) Test**
Under the *Durham* rule, a defendant is entitled to an acquittal if the proof establishes that his crime was the "***product of mental disease or defect***." A crime is a "product of" the disease if it would not have been committed ***but for*** the disease. In this way, the *Durham* test is broader than either the *M'Naghten* or irresistible impulse tests; it was intended primarily to give psychiatrists greater liberty to testify concerning the defendant's mental condition.

Although severely criticized for being unduly vague, the *Durham* rule was followed in the District of Columbia from 1954 until 1972, at which time the court of appeals replaced it with the A.L.I. test. (*See* below.) It remains the law in a few jurisdictions.

d. **American Law Institute ("A.L.I.") or Model Penal Code Test**
Under this test, the defendant is entitled to an acquittal if the proof shows that he suffered from a ***mental disease*** or defect and as a result ***lacked substantial capacity*** to either:

lack
capacity to
conform
to requirement
of the law

(i) ***Appreciate the criminality*** (wrongfulness) of his conduct; or

(ii) ***Conform his conduct*** to the requirements of law.

This test combines the *M'Naghten* and the irresistible impulse tests by allowing for the impairment of both cognitive and volitional capacity. Highly praised, the A.L.I. test is rapidly becoming the most popular formulation, and the prevailing trend is toward its use.

2. **Exclusion of "Psychopaths"**
Many formulations (including the A.L.I. test) expressly exclude the psychopathic criminal—the person who repeatedly commits crimes without experiencing guilt. This is usually accomplished by defining "mental illness" so as to exclude any abnormality evidenced only by repeated antisocial conduct. "Sociopathic" and "psychopathic" are synonymous.

3. **Refusal to Participate in Psychiatric Examination**
If the defendant does not put his mental state in issue and does not plan to use an insanity defense, he may refuse to participate in a court-ordered psychiatric examination to determine competency to stand trial. If he does not refuse, he is entitled to the *Miranda* warnings prior to such an examination.

4. **Procedural Issues Related to Insanity Defense**
Several important procedural matters are raised by the insanity defense.

a. **Burdens of Proof**

1) **Presumption of Sanity and Burden of Producing Evidence**
All defendants are presumed sane. The insanity issue is not raised, then, until the defendant comes forward with some evidence tending to show that he was insane under the applicable test. Depending upon the jurisdiction, this burden is carried either by a mere shred (or scintilla) of evidence, or by evidence sufficient to raise a reasonable doubt as to sanity.

2) Burden of Persuasion
In some jurisdictions and under the M.P.C., once the issue has been raised, the prosecution must prove the defendant was sane beyond a reasonable doubt. In others, the defendant must prove his insanity, generally by a preponderance of the evidence. Federal courts require the defendant to prove insanity by clear and convincing evidence.

b. When Defense May Be Raised and Who May Raise It

1) Defense May Be Raised After Arraignment
The insanity defense may be raised at the arraignment when the plea is taken, but the defendant need not raise it then. A simple "not guilty" at that time does not waive the right to raise the defense at some future time. A minority of jurisdictions, however, require that the defendant give reasonable notice to the prosecution of an intent to raise the defense at trial.

2) Neither Prosecutor Nor Judge May Raise Defense for Competent Defendant
Neither a prosecutor nor a judge can assert the insanity defense when a competent defendant, who is adequately represented, has elected not to do so.

c. Pretrial Psychiatric Examination

1) Right to Support Services for Defense
Where a defendant has made a preliminary showing that it is likely he will be able to use the insanity defense, the state must provide a psychiatrist for the preparation of the defense. Where the state presents evidence that the defendant is likely to be dangerous in the future, the defendant is entitled to psychiatric examination and testimony in the sentencing proceeding. [Ake v. Oklahoma, 470 U.S. 68 (1985)]

2) No Privilege Against Self-Incrimination
At the present time, a defendant has no right to refuse to be examined by a psychiatrist appointed to aid the court in the resolution of his insanity plea. However, a defendant who does not put his mental state in issue is entitled to the *Miranda* warnings before he may be compelled to undergo a court-ordered competency examination; the defendant may then refuse to be examined.

5. Post-Acquittal Commitment to Mental Institution

a. Committed Until Cured
In most jurisdictions, acquittal by reason of insanity puts into operation a procedure by which the acquitted defendant may be committed to a mental institution until cured. In some jurisdictions, such commitment is possible only if it is proven that the defendant is presently mentally ill and dangerous. In others, commitment follows automatically.

b. Confinement May Exceed Maximum Period of Incarceration Carried by Offense
The confinement of an insanity acquittee in a mental hospital, based solely on the trial court's finding of insanity by a preponderance of the evidence, may last until he has regained his sanity or is no longer dangerous. This *does not deny due process* even if the result is confinement for a period longer than the maximum period of incarceration carried by his offense. Nor is the insanity acquittee entitled, at the end of the statutory maximum incarceration period, to a civil commitment hearing at which proof of his insanity would have to be established by clear and convincing evidence. [Jones v. United States, 463 U.S. 354 (1983)]

6. Mental Condition During Criminal Proceedings
In addition to being a defense to criminal liability, the abnormal mental condition of a defendant is relevant at two other stages of the legal proceeding.

a. Incompetency to Stand Trial
Under the Due Process Clause of the United States Constitution, a defendant may not be tried, convicted, or sentenced if, as a result of a mental disease or defect, he is *unable*:

(i) *To understand the nature of the proceedings* being brought against him; or

(ii) *To assist his lawyer* in the preparation of his defense.

The Due Process Clause prevents a defendant from being declared incompetent without notice and a hearing. Many jurisdictions grant a right to a jury determination of competence. A finding of incompetence will suspend the criminal proceedings and invariably **result in commitment** until such time as the defendant regains competence. The Constitution may demand that the defendant's hospitalization be limited to a reasonable period of time necessary to decide whether there is a likelihood of recovery in the near future.

b. Incompetency at Time of Execution
A defendant may not be executed if he is incapable of understanding the nature and purpose of the punishment. Modern statutes often permit only the warden to raise this issue. Some expressly provide for a jury determination.

7. Limits on Testimony Regarding Sanity Issue
About half the states limit evidence on the issue of insanity to expert psychiatric testimony. The M.P.C. rejects this approach, and would allow any type of evidence relevant to the issue of whether the defendant had the mental state required for the particular crime charged.

8. Diminished Capacity
Some states recognize the defense of "diminished capacity," under which the defendant may assert that as a result of a mental defect (*e.g.*, neurosis, obsessive compulsiveness, or dependent personality) short of insanity, he did not have the particular mental state (purpose, knowledge, recklessness, or negligence) required for the crime charged. Most states recognizing this defense limit it to specific intent crimes.

9. Bifurcated Trial
Some states, such as California, employ a two-stage trial process whenever the defense of insanity is raised. The first stage determines **guilt** (did the defendant actually perform the criminal act?); the second stage (which may be tried before a new jury at the judge's discretion) determines **insanity** (was the defendant legally insane at the time he performed the act?).

B. INTOXICATION
Intoxication may be caused by **any substance**. Alcohol, drugs, and medicine are the most frequent. Evidence of intoxication may be raised whenever the intoxication negates the existence of an element of a crime. The law generally distinguishes between voluntary and involuntary intoxication.

1. Voluntary Intoxication
[handwritten: is a defense only to specific intent crime only but not to general intent or any other]

Intoxication is voluntary (self-induced) if it is the result of the intentional taking without duress of a substance known to be intoxicating. The person need not have intended to become intoxicated.

a. Defense to Specific Intent Crimes
Voluntary intoxication evidence may be offered, when the defendant is charged with a crime that requires **purpose (intent) or knowledge**, to establish that the intoxication prevented the defendant from formulating the requisite intent. Thus, it may be a good defense to **specific intent** crimes, but usually will not be a sufficient defense to general intent crimes. The defense is not available if the defendant purposely becomes intoxicated in order to establish the defense.

b. No Defense to Crimes Requiring Malice or Recklessness
Voluntary intoxication is not a defense to crimes requiring malice, recklessness, or negligence, or crimes of strict liability. Thus, voluntary intoxication is not a defense to common law murder, which requires a mens rea of "malice aforethought" (*see* VII.C.2.a.1), *infra*).

Example: After drinking heavily, A breaks into a house, wrongly thinking it is her own. When surprised by B, the owner, A reacts with force, beating B with her fists. While driving home A is cited for speeding. Will A have a defense of intoxication: (i) to burglary? (Yes, if as a result she did not know that the house belonged to B or did not have the intent to commit a felony therein); (ii) to battery? (No, because as defined battery may be the result of recklessness); or (iii) to speeding? (No, because speeding is a strict liability offense).

of insanity are defense to all crimes

✓ **2. Involuntary Intoxication**
Intoxication is involuntary only if it results from the taking of an intoxicating substance (i) *without knowledge* of its nature, (ii) *under direct duress* imposed by another, or (iii) *pursuant to medical advice* while unaware of the substance's intoxicating effect.

Involuntary intoxication may be *treated as mental illness,* in which case a defendant is entitled to acquittal if, because of the intoxication, she meets whatever test the jurisdiction has adopted for insanity.

3. Relationship to Insanity
Intoxication and insanity are two separate defenses. However, continuous, excessive drinking or drug use may bring on actual insanity (*e.g.,* delirium tremens). Thus, a defendant may be able to claim both an intoxication defense and an insanity defense.

C. INFANCY

1. Common Law
At common law, the defense of lack of capacity to commit a crime by reason of infancy gave rise to three presumptions. *Physical age* (not mental age) *at the time of the crime* (not at the time of the trial) governs.

    a. Under Seven—No Criminal Liability
    Under the age of seven, a child could not be held responsible for any crime (conclusive presumption of incapability of knowing wrongfulness of acts).

    b. Under Fourteen—Rebuttable Presumption of No Criminal Liability
    Children between the ages of seven and 14 were presumed incapable of knowing the wrongfulness of their acts, but this presumption was rebuttable by clear proof that the defendant appreciated the nature and quality of his act (*e.g.,* conduct undertaken to conceal the crime). Note, however, that children under 14 were *conclusively* presumed incapable of committing *rape*.

    c. Over Fourteen—Adult
    Children age 14 or older were treated as adults.

2. Modern Statutes

    a. Some Have Abolished Presumptions
    A number of modern statutes have abolished the presumptions of the common law and have provided that no child can be convicted of a crime until a stated age is reached, usually 13 or 14. Other states, however, retain the common law presumptions.

    b. Juvenile Delinquency
    All states have enacted some type of juvenile delinquency laws or have set up special juvenile or family courts. These laws ordinarily provide that with respect to conduct that would be deemed criminal if committed by an adult, the juvenile court has exclusive jurisdiction over children under a certain age, and concurrent jurisdiction (with the criminal courts) over older children. In the "concurrent jurisdiction" situation, the child must be "charged" with delinquency in juvenile court unless the juvenile court waives jurisdiction and authorizes the trial of the child as an adult in criminal court. In most jurisdictions, the common law immunity rules for infants do not apply in juvenile court because the primary goal is rehabilitation rather than punishment.

VI. PRINCIPLES OF EXCULPATION

A. JUSTIFICATION
Under certain circumstances, the commission of a proscribed act is viewed by society as justified and hence not appropriate for criminal punishment. Generally, the defendant must raise the issue of justifiable use of force by introducing *some* evidence ("more than a scintilla") tending to show justification as an affirmative defense. Once she has done this, the state may require the prosecution to prove that the use of force was not justified, or it may impose on the defendant the burden of proving this affirmative defense by a preponderance of the evidence.

1. **Self-Defense**

    a. **Nondeadly Force**

    As a general rule, an individual who is without fault may use *such force as reasonably appears necessary* to protect herself from the imminent use of unlawful force upon herself. (*See* discussion *infra* on reasonableness and unlawful force.) There is *no duty to retreat* before using nondeadly force, even if retreat would result in no further harm to either party.

    b. **Deadly Force**

    A person may use deadly force in self-defense if (i) she is without fault, (ii) she is confronted with unlawful force, and (iii) she is threatened with imminent death or great bodily harm. *→ reasonably believe that deadly force is about to use on them ∋→ majority rule, retreat is not required.*

    1) **Without Fault**

    A person who has initiated an assault or provoked the other party will be considered the aggressor. (*See* discussion *infra.*)

    2) **Unlawful Force**

    The attacker must be using unlawful force (*i.e.*, force that constitutes a crime or a tort).

    3) **Threat of Imminent Death or Great Bodily Harm**

    The defendant must *reasonably* believe that she is faced with imminent death or great bodily harm if she does not respond with deadly force. The danger of harm must be a present one. There is no right to use deadly force if harm is merely threatened at a future time or the "attacker" has no present ability to carry out the threat.

    Example: A, who has his arms tied behind his back, says to D, "I am going to kill you." D pulls out a gun and shoots A. No self-defense.

    4) **Retreat**

    Must a person retreat as far as possible before using deadly force, if such retreat is possible without the person endangering himself? For purposes of the examination, the *majority rule* is that there is *no duty to retreat*. A person (other than the initial aggressor) may use deadly force in self-defense even if this could be avoided by retreating. Even in the minority of courts that disagree with this rule, retreat is only sometimes necessary. First, no retreat is necessary unless it can be made in complete safety. Second, no retreat is necessary in several special situations: (i) where the attack occurs in the victim's home; (ii) where the attack occurs while the victim is making a lawful arrest; and (iii) where the assailant is in the process of robbing the victim.

    exception to duty to retreat
    — in own home
    — victim of rape or robbery
    — police officer

    Example: A is standing in a public park feeding the birds. B walks up to A, pulls a knife from his pocket, and—as he comes closer to A—says, "I am going to kill you." A pulls a gun from her pocket and shoots B, killing him. Does A have a defense of self-defense? Under the majority rule the answer would be yes, because A had no duty to retreat before using deadly force, as long as the force was necessary to defend herself against imminent attack. Even under the minority approach the answer might be yes, because even if A was under a general duty to retreat before using deadly force, here it did not appear that such retreat could have been done in complete safety.

    c. **Right of Aggressor to Use Self-Defense**

    Generally, one who begins a fight has no right to use force in her own defense during that fight. But an aggressor can "regain" her right to use self-defense in two ways:

    1) **Withdrawal**

    withdraw
    An aggressor who, in good faith, effectively removes herself from the fight, and communicates to the other person her desire to remove herself, regains her right to use self-defense. *q. 26   p. 480*

    2) **Sudden Escalation**

    If the victim of the initial aggression suddenly escalates a "minor" fight into one involving deadly force and does so without giving the aggressor the chance to withdraw, the aggressor may use force in her own defense.

2.   Defense of Others
There are two issues in determining whether a person who has used force to defend another person is criminally liable for her acts.

a.   Relationship with Person Aided
Must there be some special relationship between the defendant and the person in whose defense she acted? The majority rule is no. One may use force in defense of any other person if the other requirements of the defense are met. A few jurisdictions require that the person whom the defendant aided must either have been a member of the defendant's family or the defendant's servant or employer.

b.   Status of Person Aided
A defendant has the defense of defense of others only if she reasonably believed that the person she assisted had the legal right to use force in his own defense. If in fact that person had no such legal right, does the defendant still have a defense? The better view is yes, because all that is necessary for the defense is the *reasonable appearance of the right to use force*. In a minority of jurisdictions, however, the answer is no, because the defendant "steps into the shoes of the person she defends" and therefore has no defense if that person had no legal right to use force in self-defense.

3.   Defense of a Dwelling

a.   Nondeadly Force *may never use deadly force to defense property*
A person is justified in the use of nondeadly force in defense of her dwelling when, and to the extent that, she reasonably believes that such conduct is necessary to prevent or terminate another's unlawful entry into or attack upon her dwelling.

b.   Deadly Force
One is generally justified in the use of deadly force in two situations.

1)   Tumultuous Entry Plus Personal Danger
Use of deadly force is justifiable where the entry was made or attempted in a riotous, violent, or tumultuous manner *and* the person reasonably believes that the use of force is necessary to prevent a personal attack upon herself or another in the dwelling.

2)   Felony
Use of deadly force is also justifiable where the person reasonably believes that such force is necessary to prevent the entry into the dwelling by a person who intends to commit a felony in the dwelling.

4.   Defense of Other Property

a.   Nondeadly Force
Nondeadly force may be used to defend property in one's possession from unlawful interference. In the case of real property, this means entry or trespass; in the case of personal property, this means removal or damage. The need to use force must reasonably appear imminent. Thus, force may not be used if a request to desist or refrain from the activity would suffice. In addition, the right is limited to property in one's possession. Force cannot be used to regain possession of property wrongfully taken, unless the person using it is in "immediate pursuit" of the taker.

b.   Deadly Force May Not Be Used
Defense of property alone can never justify the use of deadly force. A person may use deadly force in the defense of property generally only in conjunction with another privileged use of force, *e.g.*, self-defense, defense of others, or to effectuate an arrest.

5.   Crime Prevention

a.   Nondeadly Force
Generally, one is privileged to use force to the extent that it reasonably appears necessary to prevent a felony, riot, or other serious breach of the peace, although some states (*e.g.*, California) have extended this to the prevention of any crime.

b.   Deadly Force
The traditional rule was that deadly force could be used to prevent the commission of

any felony, but the modern view is that deadly force may be used only if the crime is a "dangerous felony" involving risk to human life. This would include robbery, arson, burglary of a dwelling, etc.

6. Use of Force to Effectuate Arrest

a. By Police Officer
The use of deadly force to apprehend a fleeing felon constitutes a seizure. The force used to effect a seizure must be reasonable. Deadly force is reasonable only when the felon threatens death or serious bodily harm and deadly force is necessary to prevent his escape. [Tennessee v. Garner, 471 U.S. 1 (1985)] Thus, a police officer cannot use deadly force to apprehend an unarmed, nondangerous felon; but an officer may use deadly force to prevent a felon from escaping if the felon poses a threat of serious bodily harm to the officer or others.

b. By Private Person
A private person has the same right to use force to make an arrest as a police officer or one acting at the direction of a police officer, except that the private person has a defense to the use of *deadly force only if* the person harmed was *actually guilty* of the offense (*i.e.,* felony) for which the arrest was made. It is not enough that it reasonably appeared that the person was guilty. A private person has a privilege to use *nondeadly force* to make an arrest if a crime was in fact committed and the private person has *reasonable grounds to believe* the person arrested has in fact committed the crime.

7. Resisting Arrest

a. Right to Resist Person Not Known to Be Police Officer
An individual may lawfully repel, with deadly force if necessary, an attack made by a police officer trying to arrest her if the individual does not know that the person is a police officer.

b. Right to Resist Known Police Officer
May a person resist arrest if the person attempting to make the arrest is known to be a police officer? The majority rule is that *nondeadly force* may be used to resist an improper arrest even if a known officer is making that arrest. A minority of courts and the M.P.C. take the position that force may not be used to resist one known to be a police officer.

8. Necessity
Conduct otherwise criminal is justifiable if, as a result of pressure from natural forces, the defendant reasonably believed that the conduct was necessary to avoid some harm to society that would exceed the harm caused by the conduct. The *test is objective*; a good faith belief in the necessity of one's conduct is insufficient. Causing the death of another person to protect property is never justified. The defense of necessity is not available if the defendant is at fault in creating a situation which requires that she choose between two evils.

Example: Throwing cargo overboard during a violent storm, if necessary to save the lives of the crew and other people on board a ship, would not constitute criminal damage to property. On the other hand, throwing some members of the crew overboard to save the cargo would never be justifiable.

a. Duress Distinguished
While duress (discussed below) involves a human threat, necessity involves pressure from physical or natural forces.

Example: A points a gun at B and threatens to kill B if she does not break into C's house and steal food. B does as she is told. B may raise the defense of duress. If, however, B is a starving victim of a plane crash in a desolate area and commits the same act, she has the defense of necessity.

9. Public Policy
A police officer (or one assisting her) is justified in using reasonable force against another, or taking property, provided the officer acts pursuant to a law, court order, or process requiring or authorizing her to so act.

Example: The public executioner is not guilty of murder when she carries out a lawfully imposed sentence of execution. If the sentence was not lawful, the executioner is still immunized from criminal liability by a reasonable belief that her conduct was required by law.

10. Domestic Authority

The parents of a minor child, or any person "in loco parentis" with respect to that child, may lawfully use reasonable force upon the child for the purpose of promoting the child's welfare. Whether or not the force is "reasonable" is judged by the totality of the circumstances, including the age, sex, and health of the child.

B. THE EXCUSE OF DURESS (ALSO CALLED COMPULSION OR COERCION)

A person is not guilty of an offense, *other than homicide*, if he performs an otherwise criminal act under the threat of imminent infliction of death or great bodily harm, provided that he reasonably believes death or great bodily harm will be inflicted on himself or on a member of his immediate family if he does not perform such conduct. Threats to harm any third person may also suffice to establish the defense of duress. Note that an act committed under duress is termed excusable rather than justifiable. The subtle distinction stems from the fact that criminal acts performed under duress are condoned by society rather than encouraged.

C. OTHER DEFENSES

1. Mistake or Ignorance of Fact

a. Mistake Must Negate State of Mind

Ignorance or mistake as to a matter of fact will affect criminal guilt only if it shows that the defendant did not have the state of mind required for the crime.

Example: A, hunting in the woods, shoots at what he reasonably believes to be a deer. In fact, it is B, who is killed. A's mistake of fact establishes that he did not have the state of mind required for murder.

Compare: A, hunting in the woods, shoots through the trees at a figure he believes to be his enemy B, intending to kill him. In fact, the figure is C, who is killed. A is guilty of murdering C despite his mistake of fact as to C's identity, because A's mistake does not negate his intent to kill a person.

b. Requirement that Mistake Be Reasonable

1) Malice and General Intent Crimes—Reasonableness Required

If the mistake or ignorance is offered to negate the existence of general intent or malice, it must be a reasonable mistake or ignorance, *i.e.,* the type of mistake or ignorance that a reasonable person would have made under the circumstances.

2) Specific Intent Crimes—Reasonableness Not Required

Any mistake of fact, reasonable or unreasonable, is a defense to a specific intent crime.

Example: A, leaving a restaurant, takes an umbrella, believing that it was the one she had left there a week ago. In fact, it belongs to B. Is A guilty of larceny? *Held:* No; since A believed the umbrella was hers, she could not have intended to deprive B of his right to it. Therefore, she lacked the state of mind necessary for larceny. Since her mistake negates a specific intent, it is not material whether it was a reasonable mistake or not.

c. Strict Liability Crimes—Mistake No Defense

Since strict liability crimes require no state of mind, mistake or ignorance of fact is no defense to them.

2. Mistake or Ignorance of Law

a. General Rule—No Defense

It is not a defense to a crime that the defendant was unaware that her acts were prohibited by the criminal law or that she mistakenly believed that her acts were not prohibited. This is true even if her ignorance or mistake was reasonable.

b. Mistake or Ignorance of Law May Negate Intent

If the mental state for a crime requires a certain belief concerning a collateral aspect of the law, ignorance or mistake as to that aspect of the law *will negate the requisite state of mind*. This situation involves ignorance of some aspect of the law *other than* the existence of the statute making the act criminal.

Examples: 1) A is charged with violating a statute prohibiting the sale of a pistol to one known to be a convicted felon. A was unaware of the statute prohibiting this, but was aware that the person to whom the pistol was sold had been convicted of assault. A mistakenly believed, however, that assault was a misdemeanor; in fact, it was a felony. Is A guilty? *Held:* No. A's ignorance of the statute prohibiting the sale does not affect her liability, but the statute requires awareness that the buyer was a convicted felon. Since A believed the buyer to be only a convicted misdemeanant, she lacked the state of mind required for the crime.

2) B, who has had her car repossessed by a loan company, honestly believes she is still the lawful owner of the vehicle and is lawfully entitled to possession of it. She sees it sitting in a parking space in front of the loan company office and takes it. Even if B is wrong about her right to take the automobile, she is not guilty of larceny because she lacks the requisite specific intent.

c. Exceptions

1) Statute Not Reasonably Available
The defendant has a defense if the statute proscribing her conduct was not published or made reasonably available prior to the conduct.

2) Reasonable Reliance on Statute or Judicial Decision
The defendant has a defense if she acted in reasonable reliance on a statute or judicial decision, even though the statute is later declared unconstitutional or the decision is overruled. The defense is strongest when the decision relied on was rendered by the highest court in the jurisdiction.

3) Reasonable Reliance on Official Interpretation or Advice
At common law, it was no defense that the defendant relied on an erroneous official statement of the law contained in an administrative order or grant, or in an official interpretation by the public officer or body responsible for the interpretation, administration, or enforcement of the law. The emerging rule, advocated by the M.P.C., provides a defense when the statement is obtained from one "charged by law with responsibility for the interpretation, administration, or enforcement of the law."

4) Compare—Reasonable Reliance on Advice of Private Counsel
Unlike reasonable reliance on an official interpretation of the law (*e.g.,* an opinion of the Attorney General), relying on the advice of one's own counsel is normally not allowed as a true affirmative defense to a crime. If, however, the reliance on the attorney negates an otherwise necessary mental state element (*e.g.,* knowingly violating the law), such reliance can demonstrate that the government has not proved its case beyond a reasonable doubt.

✓ 3. Consent   *consent of victim is never a defense to crime*

a. May Negate Element of Offense
Consent of the victim is generally no defense. However, if it negates an element of the offense, consent is a complete defense.

Examples: 1) Showing that the victim consented to intercourse is a defense to a charge of forcible rape.

2) Showing that an adult person consented to traveling with the defendant is a defense to kidnapping.

For some crimes, the consent of the victim is of no relevance (*e.g.,* consent of a victim of statutory rape has no legal significance). For other offenses, consent may be of limited effect (*e.g.,* within limits, victim may consent to infliction of physical violence, and one inflicting it will therefore not be guilty of assault or battery).

b. Requirements of Consent as Defense
Whenever consent may be a defense, it must be established that:

1) The consent was voluntarily and *freely given* (without compulsion or duress);

2) The party was *legally capable* of consenting; and

3) *No fraud* was involved in obtaining the consent.

4. Condonation by Injured Party No Defense

Forgiveness by the injured party after the crime has been committed ordinarily does not operate as a defense to the commission of a crime, unless a statute establishes such a defense.

Example: Some statutes provide that marriage of the parties will bar a prosecution for seduction.

5. Criminality of Victim No Defense

The nearly universal rule is that illegal conduct by the victim of a crime is no defense.

Example: A, knowing that B has amassed a fortune through illegal gambling, defrauds B in a real estate deal. Does B's unlawful gambling activity provide A with a defense to fraud? No.

✓ **6. Entrapment** *very narrow atmost not available becuz*

Entrapment occurs if the intent to commit the crime originated not with the defendant, but rather with the creative activities of law enforcement officers. If this is the case, it is presumed that the legislature did not intend to cover the conduct and so it is not criminal. The defense of entrapment consists of two elements; *↳ predisposition on A to commit the crime negate*

(i) The *criminal design* must have *originated with law enforcement* officers; and

(ii) The defendant must *not* have been *predisposed* to commit the crime prior to the initial contact by the government.

If the defendant offers credible evidence on these two elements, in most jurisdictions the government must then show predisposition beyond a reasonable doubt.

a. Offering Opportunity to Commit Crime Distinguished

It is not entrapment if the police officer merely provides the opportunity for the commission of a crime by one otherwise ready and willing to commit it.

Example: A, an undercover police agent, poses as a narcotics addict in need of a fix. B sells narcotics to A. Does B have the defense of entrapment? No. By posing as an addict, A merely provided an opportunity for B to commit the criminal sale.

b. Inapplicable to Private Inducements

A person cannot be entrapped by a private citizen. Inducement constitutes entrapment only if performed by an officer of the government or one working for him or under his control or direction.

c. Availability If Offense Denied

If a defendant denies her participation in the offense, she has elected not to pursue entrapment and is not entitled to raise the issue, even if the facts would otherwise permit her to do so. Under the modern trend, however, a defendant may raise the defense of entrapment even while denying participation in the offense. The Supreme Court has adopted this rule for federal offenses. [Mathews v. United States, 485 U.S. 58 (1988)]

d. Practical Difficulties of Entrapment

1) Putting Predisposition in Issue

In cases where there is extended inducement by the government, the issue becomes whether the defendant was predisposed to commit the offense or whether the intent to commit it was instilled by the officers. Predisposition must exist prior to the government's initial contact with the defendant. A mere "inclination" to engage in the illegal activity is not adequate proof of predisposition. [Jacobson v. United States, 503 U.S. 540 (1992)] However, even if predisposition is not proved, the introduction by the prosecution of potentially damaging evidence on the issue of the defendant's predisposition may cause a jury to convict on the basis of the extensive evidence of the defendant's culpable state of mind.

2) Jury Hostility

Under the general approach, since entrapment is an issue of guilt, it is decided by the jury. Some fear that juries are hostile to the defense and do not adequately evaluate whether entrapment has been established.

e.   **Minority Rule—Objective Test**
The minority rule would replace the entrapment elements set out above with a test based entirely on the nature of the police activity. Under this test, a defendant would be entitled to acquittal if the police activity was reasonably likely to cause an innocent (*i.e.,* unpredisposed) person to commit the crime. The defendant's innocence or predisposition is irrelevant. Under this approach, the issue is decided by the judge rather than the jury.

f.   **Provision of Material for Crime by Government Agent Not Entrapment**
The Supreme Court has held that under federal law an entrapment defense cannot be based upon the fact that a government agent provided material for commission of the crime, even if the material provided was contraband. [United States v. Russell, 411 U.S. 423 (1973); Hampton v. United States, 425 U.S. 484 (1976)] A few states, however, make the provision of essential material—such as ingredients for drugs or the drugs themselves—entrapment.

VII.   OFFENSES AGAINST THE PERSON

A.   ASSAULT AND BATTERY

1.   **Battery**   is a completed assault
Battery is an unlawful application of force to the person of another resulting in either bodily injury or an offensive touching. Simple battery is a misdemeanor.

a.   **State of Mind—Intent Not Required**
A battery need not be intentional. It is sufficient that the defendant caused the application of force with criminal negligence.

b.   **Indirect Application of Force Sufficient**
The force need not be applied directly. Thus, it is sufficient if the force is applied by a force or substance put in motion by the defendant. For example, battery may be committed by causing a dog to attack the victim or by causing the victim to take a poisonous substance.

c.   **Aggravated Battery**
Most statutes define certain acts as aggravated batteries and punish them as felonies. Among the most common are batteries in which:

1)   A *deadly weapon* is used (any ordinary object may become a deadly weapon depending upon how it is used);

2)   *Serious bodily injury* is caused; or

3)   The *victim is a child, woman, or police officer*.

d.   **Consent as a Defense**
Contrary to the general rule that consent of the victim is not a valid defense, some jurisdictions recognize consent as a defense to simple battery and/or certain specified batteries, *e.g.,* a medical operation, or reasonable injuries incurred in consensual athletic contests.

2.   **Assault**
In a majority of jurisdictions, an assault is either:

(i)   An *attempt to commit a battery*; or   Specific intent crime

(ii)   The *intentional creation*—other than by mere words—of a *reasonable apprehension* in the mind of the victim of imminent bodily harm.
assault as a threat is a general intent crime

A minority of jurisdictions limit assault to an attempt to commit a battery. Simple assault is a misdemeanor.   q, 31 & 32   p. 482

a.   **Present Ability to Succeed**
Some statutes define assault as an unlawful attempt to commit a battery coupled with a

present ability to succeed. Lack of an ability to succeed precludes liability under such statutes.

Example: A points an unloaded gun at B. A pulls the trigger, thereby frightening B. Is A guilty of assault under a statute defining assault as "an attempt to commit a battery, coupled with the present ability to succeed"? No. Because the gun was unloaded, A could not have succeeded in committing a battery.

b. Battery Distinguished

If there has been an actual touching of the victim, the crime can only be battery. If there has been no such touching, the act may or may not constitute an assault, depending on the circumstances.

c. Statutory Aggravated Assault

All jurisdictions treat certain "aggravated assaults" more severely than simple assault. Such aggravated assaults include, but are not limited to, assaults:

1) With a *dangerous (or deadly) weapon*;

2) With *intent to rape, maim, or murder*.

B. MAYHEM

1. Common Law

At common law, the felony of mayhem required either dismemberment (the removal of some bodily part) or disablement of a bodily part. The crime was enforced to preserve the King's right to his subject's military services.

2. Modern Statutes

Most states retain the crime of mayhem in some form, although the recent trend is to abolish mayhem as a separate offense and to treat it instead as a form of aggravated battery. Modern statutes have expanded the scope of mayhem to include permanent disfigurement. A few states require a specific intent to maim or disfigure.

C. HOMICIDE   *victim must be dead & human*

1. Classifications of Homicides

At common law, homicides were divided into three classifications:

a. *Justifiable* homicides (those commanded or authorized by law);

b. *Excusable* homicides (those for which there was a defense to criminal liability); and

c. *Criminal* homicides.

2. Common Law Criminal Homicides

At common law, criminal homicides were subdivided into three different offenses.

a. Murder   *= general intent crime – malice*

Murder is the unlawful killing of a human being with malice aforethought. Malice aforethought may be express or implied.

1) Malice Aforethought

In the absence of facts excusing the homicide or reducing it to voluntary manslaughter, malice aforethought exists if the defendant has any of the following states of mind:

(i) Intent to kill (express malice);

(ii) Intent to inflict great bodily injury;

(iii) Reckless indifference to an unjustifiably high risk to human life ("abandoned and malignant heart"); or   *brave heart murder – ex playing russian roulet*

(iv) Intent to commit a felony (felony murder; *see infra*).

In the case of (ii), (iii), or (iv), the malice is "implied."

2) Deadly Weapon Rule

Intentional use of a deadly weapon authorizes a permissive inference of intent to kill. A deadly weapon is any instrument—or in some limited circumstances, any part of the body—used in a manner calculated or likely to produce death or serious bodily injury.

Example: The following persons may be held guilty of murder under the deadly weapon rule: (i) one who pilots a speedboat through a group of bathers; (ii) one who fires a bullet into a crowded room; and (iii) a professional boxer who beats up and kills a belligerent tavern owner.

b. Voluntary Manslaughter *never attach this label unless passion involved*

Voluntary manslaughter is an intentional killing distinguishable from murder by the existence of adequate provocation; *i.e.,* a killing in the heat of passion.

1) Elements of Adequate Provocation

At common law, provocation would reduce a killing to voluntary manslaughter only if it met four tests:

a) The provocation must have been one that would arouse **sudden and intense passion** in the mind of an **ordinary person** such as to cause him to lose his self-control;

b) The defendant must have **in fact** been **provoked**;

c) There **must not have been a sufficient time** between the provocation and the killing for the passions of a reasonable person to cool. (This is a factual question that depends upon the nature of the provocation and the attendant circumstances, including any earlier altercations between the defendant and the victim); and

d) The defendant **in fact** did not cool off between the provocation and the killing.

2) When Provocation Is Adequate

Adequate provocation is most frequently recognized in cases of:

a) Being subjected to a **serious battery** or a threat of **deadly force**; and

b) Discovering one's **spouse in bed with another person**.

3) Provocation Inadequate as a Matter of Law

At common law, some provocations were defined as inadequate as a matter of law. The most significant was "**mere words**." Modern courts tend to be more reluctant to take such cases from juries and are more likely to submit to the jury the question of whether "mere words" or similar matters constitute adequate provocation.

4) Recent Expansion—Imperfect Self-Defense

Some states recognize an "imperfect self-defense" doctrine under which a murder may be reduced to manslaughter even though:

a) The **defendant was at fault** in starting the altercation; or

b) The defendant **unreasonably but honestly believed** in the necessity of responding with deadly force.

c. Involuntary Manslaughter

Involuntary manslaughter is of two types.

1) Criminal Negligence *killing from criminal negligence*

If death is caused by criminal negligence, the killing is involuntary manslaughter. Criminal negligence requires a greater deviation from the "reasonable person" standard than is required for civil liability. (Some states require that the defendant have had a subjective awareness of the risk.)

misdemeanor or unenumerated felonies

2) "Unlawful Act" Manslaughter
A killing caused by an unlawful act is involuntary manslaughter. There are two subcategories of such acts:

a) "Misdemeanor-Manslaughter" Rule
A killing in the course of the commission of a misdemeanor is manslaughter, although most courts would require either that the misdemeanor be malum in se (*i.e.,* an inherently wrongful act), or if malum prohibitum, that the death be the foreseeable or natural consequence of the unlawful conduct.

b) Felonies Not Included in Felony Murder
If a killing was caused during the commission of a felony but does not qualify as a felony murder case, the killing will be involuntary manslaughter.

3. Statutory Modification of Common Law Classification
Modern statutes often divide murder into degrees, and the bar examination often contains questions based on statutes similar to them. Under such schemes, all murders are *second degree* murders unless the prosecution proves any of the following, which would make the murder *first degree* murder:

On exam, indication of 1st degree murder:
- by label or
- statute defines it

a. Deliberate and Premeditated Killing
"Deliberate" means that the defendant made the decision to kill in a cool and dispassionate manner. "Premeditated" means that the defendant actually reflected on the idea of killing, if only for a very brief period.

b. First Degree Felony Murder
A number of statutes list specific felonies and provide that if a felony murder is committed during the perpetration of an enumerated felony, the killing is first degree murder. The prosecution need not show that the killing was either deliberate or premeditated. The felonies most commonly listed include arson, robbery, burglary, rape, mayhem, and kidnapping. Under these statutes, other felony murders are second degree murder rather than involuntary manslaughter.

c. Others
Some statutes make killings performed in certain ways first degree murder. Thus, killing by lying in wait, poison, or torture may be first degree murder.

4. Felony Murder (and Related Matters)
As the definition of malice aforethought above makes clear, a killing—even an accidental one—committed during the course of a felony is murder. Malice is implied from the intent to commit the underlying felony.

a. What Felonies Are Included?
Under the common law, there were only a handful of felonies (*see* I.D.1., *supra*); today, the criminal codes of most states have added many more. However, most courts limit the felony murder doctrine to felonies that are inherently dangerous.

b. Scope of the Doctrine
When the felony murder doctrine is combined with conspiracy law, the scope of liability becomes very broad. If, in the course of a conspiracy to commit a felony, a death is caused, all members of the conspiracy are liable for murder if the death was caused in furtherance of the conspiracy and was a foreseeable consequence of the conspiracy.

c. Limitations on Liability
There are some limitations on liability under the broad felony murder doctrine.

1) Guilty of Underlying Felony
The defendant must be guilty of the underlying felony. If he has a defense to the felony, he also has a defense to felony murder.

2) Felony Must Be Independent of Killing
The felony murder rule can be applied only where the underlying felony is independent of the killing. Thus, a felony such as manslaughter or aggravated battery will not qualify as the underlying felony for purposes of felony murder liability.

3) Foreseeability of Death

The majority rule is that death must have been a foreseeable result of the commission of the felony. However, it is important to note that *courts have been willing to find most deaths foreseeable.* A minority of courts do not apply a foreseeability requirement, requiring only that the felony be malum in se.

Example: A intentionally sets fire to a dwelling. B, a firefighter, dies in an effort to extinguish the blaze. C, the owner of the dwelling, dies of a heart attack while watching his largest possession being destroyed. Is A guilty of felony murder? Of B, yes. The death of a firefighter is a foreseeable consequence of setting a fire. Of C, no. The heart attack was unforeseeable.

4) During the Commission of a Felony—Termination of Felony

The death must have been "caused during" the commission or attempted commission of the felony, but the fact that the felony was technically completed before death was caused does not prevent the killing from being felony murder. Deaths caused while fleeing from the crime are felony murder. But once the felon has reached a *place of "temporary safety,"* the impact of the felony murder rule ceases and deaths subsequently caused are not felony murder.

5) Killing of Co-Felon by Victims of Felonies or Pursuing Police Officers

Is the defendant liable for a co-felon's death caused by resistance of the victim or police? The majority view is no. The so-called *Redline* view (the majority position) is that *liability for murder cannot be based upon the death of a co-felon* from resistance by the victim or police pursuit. Note that even under this view, the defendant can be liable for felony murder in many states when resistance by the victim or police results in the death of a third-party bystander who is not a co-felon.

d. Related Limits on Misdemeanor Manslaughter

Limits similar to those placed on felony murder are placed on involuntary misdemeanor manslaughter. If the misdemeanor involved is not malum in se, *i.e.,* one that involves conduct that is inherently wrong, a death caused during the commission of a misdemeanor is manslaughter only if death was a foreseeable result of the commission of the misdemeanor. A minority of courts limit the doctrine to malum in se misdemeanors.

Example: K is driving on a good road in excellent weather, but is slightly exceeding the posted speed limit. V dashes from behind a bush into the street and is struck by K's car. V dies. Is K guilty of involuntary manslaughter, assuming that speeding is a misdemeanor? The best answer is no, because the misdemeanor was not malum in se and death was not a foreseeable result of its commission.

5. Causation

a. General Requirement—Must Be Cause-in-Fact and Proximate Cause

When a crime is defined to require not merely conduct but also a specified result of that conduct, the defendant's conduct must be both the cause-in-fact and the proximate cause of the specified result.

1) Cause-in-Fact

The defendant's conduct must be the cause-in-fact of the result; *i.e.,* the result would not have occurred "*but for*" the defendant's conduct.

2) Common Law Requirement—"Year and a Day" Rule

The death of the victim must occur within one year and one day from the infliction of the injury or wound. If it does not occur within this period of time, there can be no prosecution for homicide, even if it can be shown that "but for" the defendant's actions, the victim would not have died as and when he did. A number of states have abolished this rule.

3) "Proximate" Causation

Problems of proximate causation arise only when the victim's death occurs because of the defendant's acts, but in a manner not intended or anticipated by the defendant. The question in such cases is whether the difference in the way death was intended or anticipated and the way in which it actually occurred breaks the chain of "proximate cause" causation.

a) All "Natural and Probable" Results Are Proximately Caused
The general rule is that a defendant is responsible for all results that occur as a "natural and probable" consequence of his conduct, even if he did not anticipate the precise manner in which they would occur. All such results are "proximately caused" by the defendant's act. This chain of proximate causation is broken only by the intervention of a "superseding factor."

b. Rules of Causation

1) Hastening Inevitable Result
An act that hastens an inevitable result is nevertheless a legal cause of that result.

Example: A terminates the life support system of B, resulting in B's death. B had only 24 hours to live. Can A be held liable for B's death? Yes. Note that society may not wish to condemn such an "act of mercy." Nevertheless, for purposes of causation analysis, A's act caused B's death.

2) Simultaneous Acts
Simultaneous acts by two or more persons may be considered independently sufficient causes of a single result.

3) Preexisting Condition
A victim's preexisting condition that makes him more susceptible to death does not break the chain of causation; *i.e.,* the defendant "takes the victim as he finds him."

Example: A, with malice aforethought, shoots B in the leg. B bleeds to death before he can receive medical attention because he is a hemophiliac. A is liable for murder despite the fact that a person without hemophilia would not have died from the shooting.

c. Intervening Acts
As a general rule, an intervening act will shield the defendant from liability if the act is a mere coincidence or is outside the foreseeable sphere of risk created by the defendant's act.

Examples: 1) *Act of Nature:* A is driving negligently. To avoid A's swerving car, B takes an unaccustomed route home. B's car is struck by lightning, and B dies. Can A be charged with manslaughter? No. The fact that lightning struck B was a mere coincidence.

2) *Act by Third Party:* A, intending to kill B, merely wounds him. B receives negligent medical treatment at a nearby hospital. B dies. Can A be held liable for B's death? Yes. Despite improvements in medical care, negligent care remains a *foreseeable risk.* A contrary result would follow if B died due to gross negligence or intentional mistreatment.

3) *Acts by the Victim:* A, intending to kill B, merely wounds him. B refuses medical treatment for religious reasons and dies. If modern medical knowledge could have saved B, can A be held liable for B's death? Most jurisdictions have held yes, because A's act directly created the risk of death and because the refusal of medical care may be found to be foreseeable. This rule may apply even if the victim acts affirmatively to harm himself. Suppose B, in unbearable pain, commits suicide. The suicide may be found to be a foreseeable consequence of A's actions. Thus, A would be liable for B's death.

6. Summary—Analytical Approach
In analyzing any homicide situation, the following questions must be asked and answered:

a. Did the defendant have any of the *states of mind* sufficient to constitute malice aforethought?

b. If the answer to a. is yes, is there proof of anything that will, under any applicable statute, raise the homicide to *first degree murder*?

c. If the answer to a. is yes, is there evidence to reduce the killing to *voluntary manslaughter*, *i.e.,* adequate provocation?

d.   If the answer to a. is no, is there a sufficient basis for holding the crime to be *involuntary manslaughter, i.e.,* criminal negligence or misdemeanor manslaughter?

e.   Is there *adequate causation* between the defendant's acts and the victim's death? Did the victim *die within a year and one day*? Was the defendant's act the *factual cause* of death? Is there anything to break the chain of *proximate causation* between the defendant's act and the victim's death?

Example: A came upon B, who was letting the air out of a tire on A's car. When A shouted at B, B picked up a rock and threw it at A, shouting obscenities. B ran off, but A went to his car, pulled a gun out, and shot at B, hitting him in the leg. B was taken to a hospital where he underwent surgery; the wrong gas was used as an anesthetic, and B died. Generally, wounds of this sort are not deadly. A testifies under oath that he merely intended to wound B as revenge for causing A the inconvenience of the flat tire. What is A's liability?

1)   Even if A intended only to wound B with a bullet, this is intent to inflict great bodily injury and is sufficient for malice aforethought.

2)   If the statute makes premeditated killings first degree murder, A almost certainly did not premeditate.

3)   While B's shouted obscenities might not be adequate provocation, a jury could certainly find that throwing the rock was such provocation.

4)   If the answer to inquiry a. had been no, A's actions would have constituted criminal negligence.

5)   There is causation. B died within a year and one day. But for A's shot, B would not have died. Negligent medical care is not a superseding intervening factor that will break the chain of proximate causation, unless it is "gross" negligence or intentional malpractice.

D.   FALSE IMPRISONMENT
The common law misdemeanor of false imprisonment consisted of:

(i)   Unlawful

(ii)   Confinement of a person

(iii)   Without his valid consent.

1.   Confinement
Confinement requires that the victim be compelled either to go where he does not wish to go or to remain where he does not wish to remain. It is not confinement to simply prevent a person from going where he desires to go, as long as alternative routes are available to him. The confinement may be accomplished by actual force, by threats, or by a show of force.

2.   "Unlawfulness"
Confinement is unlawful unless it is specifically authorized by law or by the consent of the person.

3.   Lack of Consent
Consent to the confinement precludes it from constituting false imprisonment, but the consent must be *freely given* by one with *capacity* to give such consent. Thus, consent is invalidated by coercion, threats, deception, or incapacity due to mental illness, retardation, or youth.

E.   KIDNAPPING
At common law, the misdemeanor of kidnapping was the forcible abduction or stealing away of a person from his own country and sending him into another. Modern statutes generally expand the definition of kidnapping far beyond the common law definition, although it usually remains a form of aggravated false imprisonment.

1. **General Pattern**
   Kidnapping is often defined as confinement of a person that involves either:

   a. Some *movement* (*i.e.,* "asportation") of the victim; *or*

   b. *Concealment* of the victim in a "secret" place.

2. **Aggravated Kidnapping**
   Modern statutes often contain as a separate offense an aggravated kidnapping crime. Among the more common forms of this offense are:

   a. **Kidnapping for Ransom**
      The abduction or secretion of a person for the purpose of obtaining anything of value for the return of the person is often defined as aggravated kidnapping.

   b. **Kidnapping for Purpose of Commission of Other Crimes**
      Abduction or secretion for the purpose of committing other offenses, such as robbery, is sometimes defined as aggravated kidnapping.

   c. **Kidnapping for Offensive Purpose**
      Abduction or secretion with the intent of harming the person or of committing some sexual crime with him is sometimes defined as aggravated kidnapping.

   d. **Child Stealing**
      Leading, taking, enticing, or detaining a child with the intent to keep or conceal the child from a guardian or parent is often defined as aggravated kidnapping. Use of "enticement" covers the situation in which a child is persuaded by promises or rewards to come with the defendant or remain. The consent of a child to his detention or movement is not of importance, because the child is incapacitated by age from giving valid consent.

3. **Required Movement**
   Although at common law extreme movement was required, most modern statutes require only some movement of the person; if such movement occurs, the extent of the movement is not material. Other statutes require no movement, making confinement (as used in false imprisonment) sufficient.

4. **Secrecy**
   Generally, it is not necessary that kidnapping involve secrecy. Some statutes, however, require secrecy when the kidnapping is based on confinement rather than movement of the victim.

5. **Consent**
   As with false imprisonment, free consent given by a person competent to give it precludes the confinement or movement of a person from being kidnapping. But a person may be incompetent to give such consent by reason of age (*see* above) or mental condition.

6. **Relationship to Other Offenses**
   Statutes that define kidnapping as detention involving movement of the victim mean that it is arguable that kidnapping often occurs incident to the commission of other crimes, such as robbery or rape. Some courts—but not all—have held that in such situations kidnapping (in addition to the robbery or rape) is committed only if the movement of the victim substantially increases the risk to the victim over and above that necessarily involved in the other crime. If no such increased risk is involved, the defendant will be held to have committed only the robbery or rape.

VIII. SEX OFFENSES

A. RAPE ~~slightest penetration complete the crime of rape~~
Rape, a felony, is the unlawful carnal knowledge of a woman by a man, not her husband, without her effective consent.

1. **Penetration Sufficient**
   Rape requires only the penetration of the female sex organ by the male sex organ. Emission is not necessary to complete the crime.

2.   Absence of Marital Relationship

At common law, the woman must not have been married to the man who committed the act. Today, however, most states have either dropped this requirement where the parties are estranged or separated, or abolished it entirely.

3.   Lack of Effective Consent

The intercourse must be without the victim's effective consent. Consent, even if given, may be ineffective in several situations.

a.   Intercourse Accomplished by Force

If the intercourse is accomplished by actual force, no question concerning consent is raised.

b.   Intercourse Accomplished by Threats

If intercourse is accomplished by placing the victim in fear of great and immediate bodily harm, it constitutes rape. Any consent obtained by such threats is ineffective. The failure of the victim to "resist to the utmost" does not prevent the intercourse from being rape if resistance is prevented by such threats.

c.   Woman Incapable of Consenting

If the victim is incapable of consenting, the intercourse is rape. Inability to consent may be caused by unconsciousness, by the effect of drugs or intoxicating substances, or by the victim's mental condition. If the victim is so insane or retarded as to be incapable of giving consent, intercourse with her constitutes rape.

d.   Consent Obtained by Fraud

Only in limited circumstances will intercourse with consent obtained by fraud constitute rape.

1)   Fraud as to Whether Act Constitutes Sexual Intercourse

If the victim is fraudulently caused to believe that the act is not sexual intercourse, the act of intercourse constitutes rape.

Example: D persuaded V that what was actually an act of intercourse was medical treatment accomplished by surgical instruments. Was D guilty of rape? Yes.

2)   Fraud as to Whether Defendant Is Victim's Husband

If the defendant fraudulently persuades the victim that he is her husband, is the intercourse rape? The best answer is no.

Example: D arranges for X to pretend to marry D and V. In fact, X has no authority to marry persons and there is no marriage. After the sham marriage, D has intercourse with V. Is D guilty of rape? The best answer is no because there was consent.

3)   Other Fraud

Other kinds of fraud will not make the intercourse rape.

Example: D promises to marry V at a later time and thereby induces V to consent to intercourse. D never intended to marry V. Is D guilty of rape? No. (But D may be guilty of seduction (*see* F., below).)

B.   STATUTORY RAPE   *strict liability — consent of a victim is no defense also mistake of fact no defense*

1.   Victim Below Age of Consent

Statutory rape is the crime of carnal knowledge of a female under the age of consent. Even if the female willingly participated, the offense is nevertheless committed because consent is irrelevant. The age of consent varies from state to state, generally from 16 to 18.

2.   Mistake as to Age

Will a defendant's reasonable mistake as to the victim's age prevent liability for statutory rape? For purposes of the examination, the best answer is no, since statutory rape is a ***strict liability crime***. A second best answer, to be used only if no alternative making use of the best position is presented, is that a reasonable mistake as to age will prevent conviction if the defendant reasonably believed the victim was old enough to give an effective consent.

C.   CRIME AGAINST NATURE

An early (1533) English statute made sodomy a felony, so that it became part of the American common law of crime. Sodomy is a generic term encompassing a number of different acts.

1. **Bestiality**
   Bestiality is carnal copulation with an animal by a human being (male or female).

2. **Buggery**
   Buggery is anal intercourse by a man with either another man or woman. (It was referred to as "pederasty" when committed between a man and a young boy.)

3. **Fellatio**
   Fellatio is oral stimulation of the male sex organ.

4. **Cunnilingus**
   Cunnilingus is oral stimulation of the female sex organ.

D. ADULTERY AND FORNICATION

Adultery and fornication were not common law crimes in England, but were punished by the church as ecclesiastical offenses. They are made misdemeanor offenses by statute in some states.

1. **Adultery**
   Under modern statutes, any person who cohabits or has sexual intercourse with another not his spouse commits the misdemeanor offense of adultery if:

   a. The behavior is *open and notorious; and*

   b. The person is *married* and the other person involved in such intercourse is not his spouse; or

   c. The person is not married and knows the *other person* in such intercourse is *married*.

2. **Fornication**
   Fornication is open and notorious sexual intercourse between or cohabitation by unmarried persons.

E. INCEST

Incest is a statutory offense, usually a felony, that consists of either marriage or a sexual act (intercourse or deviate sexual conduct) between persons who are too closely related.

1. **Degree of Relationship**
   No uniformity exists among the states. A majority restricts the crime to blood relations, although a significant number of states include some nonblood relatives.

2. **Degree of Responsibility**
   Some states make a distinction in penalties depending on the parties involved.

F. SEDUCTION OR CARNAL KNOWLEDGE

A statutory felony in many states, the crime of seduction is committed when a male person induces an unmarried female of previously chaste character to engage in an act of intercourse on promise of marriage. The M.P.C. includes a section on seduction; it requires only that there be a false promise of marriage and does not require chastity or that the female be unmarried.

In many states, subsequent marriage of the parties is a defense, but there is no uniformity as to whether the marriage must be entered into before indictment, after sentence, or anywhere in between.

G. BIGAMY

Bigamy is a traditional strict liability offense that consists of marrying someone while having another living spouse. At common law, a defendant is guilty of bigamy even if she reasonably believes that a purported divorce is valid or that her spouse is dead.

IX. PROPERTY OFFENSES

This section deals with a number of property offenses. But for purposes of the examination, the greatest challenge is in distinguishing among three of these: larceny, embezzlement, and false pretenses. There is no difference among the intents required for the three crimes. The major differences among these crimes are in the kind of misappropriation of the property. They are discussed in detail below and can be summarized as follows:

	activity	_method_	_intent_	_title_
larceny	taking and asportation of property from possession of another person	without consent or with consent obtained by fraud	with intent to steal	title does not pass
embezzlement	conversion of property held pursuant to a trust agreement	use of property in a way inconsistent with terms of trust	with intent to defraud	title does not pass
false pretenses	obtaining title to property	by consent induced by fraudulent mis-representation	with intent to defraud	title passes

A. LARCENY

[handwritten: specific intent crime.]

[handwritten: mistake of law is not a defense, mistake of fact is a defense]

Larceny was the basic common law property offense. It has been significantly modified by statute in many American jurisdictions. Larceny consists of:

(i)   A taking (caption); *[handwritten: wrongful, by trespass, stealing]*

(ii) And carrying away (asportation); *[handwritten: can be every slight]*

(iii) Of tangible personal property; *[handwritten: without consent]* *[handwritten circled: 9.34]*

(iv) Of another;

(v)   By trespass;

(vi) With intent to permanently (or for an unreasonable time) deprive the person of his interest in the property. *[handwritten: must exist at time of the taking or it's not common law larceny.]* *[handwritten: Taking prop on belief that it's yours or you have some right to it is not common law larceny]*

1. Property that May Be the Subject of Larceny

Larceny can be committed only by the acquisition of **personal property** capable of being possessed and of some value.

a. Realty and Severed Material

Realty and its fixtures are **not** subjects of larceny. If something is severed from the realty and taken before it comes into possession of the landowner as personal property, larceny is not committed. If, however, the landowner gains possession of the severed material as personalty, a subsequent taking of it is larceny.

Example: A went onto land owned by B and cut down 15 trees. She loaded 10 into her truck and drove off. B came onto the land, found the remaining five trees, and placed them in his shed. A returned and took them. Is A guilty of larceny of 15, 10, five, or no trees? *Held:* A is guilty of larceny of the five trees that came into B's possession after their severance from the realty.

b. Services

Obtaining services wrongfully cannot give rise to larceny.

c. Intangibles

Intangibles cannot give rise to larceny.

Example: A wrongfully obtains entrance to B's theater and observes a performance of a play. Has A committed larceny of that performance? *Held:* No. The right or ability to observe a play is intangible.

Note that gas and electricity are considered tangible goods.

d. Documents and Instruments

Documents and instruments were, at common law, regarded as merged with the matter they represented. Thus, unless they had monetary value in themselves they could not be the subject of larceny.

Example: A takes a deed to certain realty and a contract for the sale of cattle from B's desk. Is A guilty of larceny? *Held:* No. The deed "merged" with the realty and the contract merged with the intangible contract right; thus, there was no larceny.

Modern statutes have expanded larceny to include written instruments embodying intangible rights.

2. Property "Of Another"

Larceny is a crime against possession. Therefore, all that is necessary is that the property be taken from someone who has a possessory interest superior to that of the defendant.

a. Requirement that Taking Be from One with "Possession"

The property must be taken from someone with possession other than the defendant. If the defendant had possession at the time of the taking (*e.g.,* defendant is a bailee of the property), the resulting offense is not larceny, although it may be embezzlement. However, if the defendant has "custody" rather than "possession," her misappropriation of the property is larceny.

1) Custody vs. Possession

Possession involves much greater scope of authority to deal with the property than does custody.

Example: A, while in a store, asks B, the clerk, if she may take a certain suit of clothing home on approval. B consents. A then asks to see a watch to examine it; B gives it to her. A then absconds with both items. Have either of them been taken from B's possession? *Held:* The watch was taken from B's possession, because A had only the authority to look at it. The suit, on the other hand, was in A's possession at the time it was misappropriated, because of the extent of control B had given A over it.

2) Employees

Low level employees generally have only custody of their employers' property. They have possession, however, if the employer gives them especially broad powers over it or if the property is given directly to them by a third person, without the employer having intermediate possession.

3) Bailee and "Breaking Bulk"

Generally, a *bailee has possession*. If, however, she opens closed containers in which the property has been placed by the bailor (*i.e.,* she "breaks bulk"), the possession is regarded by use of a fiction as returning to the bailor. If a bailee misappropriates property *after breaking bulk*, she takes it from the possession of the bailor and is guilty of *larceny* if she has the intent to steal.

b. Possession Is All that Is Needed

The person from whom the property is taken only needs to have possession. Thus, it is larceny if property is taken from a thief, as he has a possessory interest superior to the person who takes the property from him.

Example: A takes her car to be repaired in B's garage. B does the repairs and as a result has a mechanic's lien on the car. A takes the car without paying for the repairs. Has A taken the property of another from the other's possession? *Held:* Yes. B had a possessory interest in the car and it was in his possession. It is not material that A had title to the car.

c. Joint Property

At common law, larceny could not be committed by the taking of jointly held property by one of the joint owners.

d. Lost, Mislaid, and Abandoned Property

Lost or mislaid property is regarded as constructively in the possession of the owner, and thus if it is found and taken, it is taken from his possession and larceny might be committed. Abandoned property, however, has no owner and larceny cannot be committed by appropriating it.

3. Taking

It is essential that the defendant actually obtain control of the property.

a. Destruction or Movement Is Not Sufficient

Mere destruction or movement of the property is not sufficient to constitute a taking.

Example: D knocked a glass from X's hand. It fell and broke. Is D guilty of larceny? No. Although X may have lost possession, D never obtained control. The damage to the item is irrelevant.

b. Sufficient If Caused to Occur by Innocent Agent
Even if a defendant obtains control of the property through the act of an innocent agent, it is a taking.
Example: D, pointing out a cow in a nearby field, offers to sell it to X for $10. X gives D the money and then takes the cow. In fact, the cow belonged to Y. Is D guilty of larceny of the cow? Yes. She obtained control of it by virtue of X, an innocent agent of hers.

4. Asportation
Larceny requires asportation, *i.e.,* that all parts or portions of the property be moved and that this movement—which need only be slight—be part of the carrying away process.
Example: A came upon two upside-down wheelbarrows in B's yard. She turned them both right side up, and moved one six inches toward the gate. Was she guilty of larceny of one, two, or no wheelbarrows? *Held:* Guilty of larceny of one. Merely turning the wheelbarrows over is not part of the carrying away movement; thus, it is not asportation. But merely moving the other wheelbarrow a short distance is enough, because that movement is part of carrying it away.

5. Taking Must Be "Trespassory"
The defendant must take the property from the possession of another in a trespassory manner, *i.e.,* without the consent of the person in possession of the property.

a. Taking by Consent Induced by Misrepresentations—"Larceny by Trick"
If the victim consents to the defendant's taking possession of the property but this consent has been induced by a misrepresentation, the consent is not valid. The resulting larceny is often called "larceny by trick." A major difficulty is in distinguishing larceny by trick from false pretenses. (*See* C.1., *infra.*)

6. State of Mind Required—Intent to Permanently Deprive
Generally, larceny requires that at the time of the taking the defendant must have the intent to permanently deprive the person from whom the property is taken of his interest in the property. The intent has to exist at the moment of the taking of the property.

a. Sufficient Intent

1) Intent to Create Substantial Risk of Loss
If the defendant intends to deal with the property in a manner that involves a substantial risk of loss, this is sufficient for larceny.

2) Intent to Pledge Goods or Sell Them to Owner
It is larceny to take goods with the intent to sell them back to the owner or to pledge them, because this involves the substantial equivalent of permanent loss or the high risk of permanent loss.

b. Insufficient Intent

1) Intent to Borrow
If the defendant intends to return the property within a reasonable time and at the time of the taking has a substantial ability to do so, the unauthorized borrowing does not constitute larceny. Note that many states make it a crime to borrow a motor vehicle, even when the borrower fully intends to return it ("joyriding").

2) Intent to Obtain Repayment of Debt
It is not larceny to take money or goods of another if the defendant honestly believes that she is entitled to them as repayment for a debt of the other (although the goods must not be worth more than the amount of the debt). In these situations, the defendant believes the property is "hers" and therefore lacks an intent to deprive someone else of "his" property.

c. Possibly Sufficient

1) Intent to Pay for Property
If the property taken is not for sale, the fact that the defendant intends to pay the other for it does not negate the larceny. If the property is for sale and the defendant has a specific and realistic intent to repay the person, the taking is not larceny.

2) Intent to Claim Reward

If the defendant takes goods, intending to return them and hoping for a reward, this is not larceny. However, if she takes them not intending to return them unless she is assured of a reward, this is larceny because it creates a substantial risk of loss.

7. Specialized Application of Larceny Doctrine

There are several situations in which the application of the requirements for larceny is highly technical.

a. Abandoned or Lost Property

Property abandoned by its owner, *i.e.,* discarded with the intent of giving up all rights in it, cannot be the subject of larceny. One who finds property that has merely been lost by its owner can, however, commit larceny of it. Two requirements exist:

(i) The finder must know or have reason to believe she *can find* out the *identity of the owner*; and

(ii) The finder must, at the moment she takes possession of the lost property, have the *intent* necessary for larceny.

If the finder takes possession of the lost property without the intent to steal but later formulates this intent, she has not committed larceny. Nor has she committed embezzlement, since no trust relationship between the finder and the owner has been created. (*See* below.)

b. Misdelivered Property

One to whom property is delivered by mistake may, by accepting the property, commit larceny of it. Two requirements must be met:

1) The recipient must, at the time of the misdelivery, *realize the mistake* that is being made; and

2) The recipient must, at the time she accepts the delivery, have the *intent* required for larceny.

c. "Container" Situations

1) Issue Is Whether Defendant Already Has Possession

One subcategory of "misdelivery" cases presents special problems: The "container" cases, in which the defendant is charged with larceny of an item that she discovers within another item after she has legitimately taken possession of the larger item—or the container—from the victim. The difficult question is whether, at the time she appropriates the item, does she already have possession? If so, larceny is not committed because the property is not taken from the possession of another.

2) Larceny May Depend on Whether Parties Intended to Transfer Container

One solution to this problem is to distinguish among cases according to whether or not the parties intended the original transfer to be the transfer of a container, *i.e.,* an item containing other items. If the parties intended to transfer a container, the recipient is regarded as taking immediate possession of both the container and its contents. Her later misappropriation of the contents is not larceny, because it occurs at a time when she already has possession. If, however, both parties did not intend to transfer a container but rather regarded the items transferred as empty (or otherwise not involving a transfer of contained items), the recipient does not obtain possession of the contents until she discovers them. If at the time she discovers and appropriates them she has the intent to steal, she is guilty of larceny.

d. "Continuing Trespass" Situations

A trespassory taking of property without the intent required for larceny is not, of course, larceny. However, if a defendant takes property with a wrongful state of mind but without the intent to steal, and later, while still in possession of it, forms the intent to steal it, the trespass involved in the initial wrongful taking is regarded as "continuing" and the defendant is guilty of larceny. This doctrine has no application if the defendant's initial taking of the property, although trespassory, was not motivated by a wrongful state of mind.

> *Example:*   A took X's umbrella from X's possession without X's permission, intending to use the umbrella and return it the next day. The next morning when A awoke, she examined the umbrella carefully and decided to keep it. Is A guilty of larceny of the umbrella? Yes. The larceny took place when A formed the intent to steal it. Since her initial possession was wrongful, the trespass continued until she formed the intent to steal. On the other hand, if A had taken X's umbrella by mistake, and later decided to keep it after discovering her mistake, the doctrine would not apply because her initial taking was done with an innocent state of mind.

B. EMBEZZLEMENT

Embezzlement was not originally a common law crime. Intended to plug the gaps in the law of larceny, it was made a misdemeanor by statute in 1799 and is regarded as part of American common law. Modern statutes often distinguish between grand embezzlement (a felony) and petit embezzlement (a misdemeanor) based upon the value of the property embezzled. Although variously defined in different jurisdictions, embezzlement generally requires:

always has lawful possession

(i)   The fraudulent;

(ii) Conversion;

(iii) Of property;

(iv) Of another;

(v)   By a person in lawful possession of that property.

1. Distinguished from Larceny

possession only not title

a. Manner of Obtaining Property

In embezzlement, the misappropriation of the property occurs while the defendant has lawful possession of it. In larceny, it occurs generally at the time the defendant obtains wrongful possession of the property.

> *Example:*   A was foreman of a construction crew. One day, he took a tool used by the crew to his home. The next day, he was fired. On his way out, he took another tool. Was he guilty of embezzlement of one, two, or no tools? *Held:* Only of the first tool, which he converted while it was in his possession by virtue of his employment. He had no right to possession of tools at the time he took the second.

b. Manner of Misappropriation

Larceny requires caption and asportation with the intent to permanently deprive. Embezzlement requires intentional conversion. (*See* below.)

2. Conversion

The conversion required by embezzlement requires only that the defendant deal with the property in a manner inconsistent with the trust arrangement pursuant to which he holds it. No movement or carrying away of the property is required. The conversion need not result in direct personal gain to the defendant.

> *Example:*   A trustee who siphons off trust fund money in order to donate to a favorite charity is as guilty of embezzlement as the trustee who uses the converted funds to pay his overdue gambling debts.

3. Property

Embezzlement statutes are often worded in terms of "property that may be subject to larceny"; *i.e.,* real property and services may not be embezzled. Some relatively expansive statutes, however, make embezzlement of real property a crime.

> *Example:*   A, an agent with apparent authority to sell B's real estate, fraudulently transfers the title to a bona fide purchaser. Is A guilty of embezzlement? No, under the traditional embezzlement statute. Yes, under the more expansive statute.

4. Requirement that Property Be that "Of Another"

Embezzlement requires that the property converted be that of someone other than the converter. Therefore, a person who borrows money, converts the sum to his own use, and subsequently fails to repay it is not guilty of embezzlement.

5. Fraudulent Intent

A defendant must intend to defraud for a conversion to become embezzlement. This appears to be the functional equivalent of larceny's specific intent to permanently deprive.

a. Intent to Restore

If the defendant intended to restore the *exact* property taken, it is not embezzlement. But if he intended to restore *similar or substantially identical* property, it is embezzlement, even if it was money that was initially taken and other money—of identical value—that he intended to return.

b. Claim of Right

As in larceny, embezzlement is not committed if the conversion is pursuant to a claim of right to the property, as where it is retained for payment of a debt honestly believed to be owed. The fact that the defendant retained the property openly tends to establish a claim of right.

6. Necessity for Demand for Return

If it is clear that there has been a conversion of the property, the victim need not make a demand that it be returned. If, however, there is doubt as to the existence of a conversion, a demand by the owner for return and a refusal to return by the defendant may be necessary.

7. Limitation to Property Entrusted

Some states limit embezzlement to the fraudulent conversion of property "entrusted" or "delivered" to the embezzler. These states would not punish one who finds lost property and, while in lawful possession of it, fraudulently converts it.

C. FALSE PRETENSES /false representation

The offense of false pretenses was created by English statute in 1757, and consequently is part of the common law in those American states that use 1776 as the determining date. Like larceny and embezzlement, most jurisdictions distinguish grand false pretenses (a felony) from petit false pretenses (a misdemeanor). The offense of false pretenses generally consists of:

(i) Obtaining title; *conveyance of title*

(ii) To the property of another; *false promise to do something in future is not ground for false pretense*

(iii) By an intentional (or knowing) false statement of past or existing fact;

(iv) With intent to defraud the other.

1. "Larceny by Trick" Distinguished

False pretenses differs from larceny by trick in what is obtained. If only *possession* of the property is obtained by the defendant, the offense is larceny by trick. If *title* is obtained, the offense is false pretenses. What is obtained depends upon what the victim intended to convey to the defendant.

Example: D asked X if X would sell a car and offered as payment what was purported to be a demand note signed by Y. D falsely represented that the note was one executed by Y; in fact, D himself had forged it. X agreed to sell the car but told D that the sale would not be final until she had collected the amount of the note from Y. X then permitted D to use the car until Y could be located. D drove off in the car. Has he committed larceny or false pretenses? Larceny, because X did not intend to transfer title to D. X intended only to transfer possession pending collection on the note.

Compare: Same facts as above, except the note purportedly signed by Y is due in 30 days rather than on demand. Based on Y's good credit, X agreed to convey full title to the car in exchange for the note. D drove off in the car. D has committed false pretenses rather than larceny.

2. Misrepresentation Required

There are several limits upon the misrepresentations required for false pretenses. (These also apply to larceny by trick.)

a. **False Representation Concerning Matter of Fact**
The defendant must have created a false impression as to the matter of fact. If his statements reasonably construed constitute only an opinion or a "puffing," they are not representations. It is not misrepresentation to fail to correct what is known to be a mistake that the victim holds, *if* the defendant was not responsible for creating that mistake, or the defendant has no fiduciary duty to the aggrieved party.

b. **Misrepresentation Must Relate to Present or Past Facts**
The misrepresentation must concern past facts or the present situation. A misrepresentation as to what will occur in the future is not sufficient. A false promise, even if made without the present intent to perform, is also not sufficient.

3. **Requirement that Representation Be the "Cause" of Obtaining Property**
The victim must actually be deceived by, or act in reliance on, the misrepresentation, and this must be a major factor (or the sole cause) of the victim passing title to the defendant.

4. **Intent to Defraud**
Depending on the statute involved, the defendant must either have known the statement to be false or have intended that the victim rely upon the misrepresentation. Subjecting the victim to a risk of loss will suffice.
Example:　　A obtained money from B by representing that he was securing it by a first mortgage on certain property. He intended to pay back the loan. The mortgage actually given was, as A knew, only a second mortgage. Is A guilty of false pretenses? *Held:* Yes. He knowingly subjected B to a substantially greater risk of loss of the money than B was aware of. This was a sufficient intent to defraud.

5. **Related Crimes**
Many states have enacted specific legislation covering certain conduct that resembles the crime of false pretenses but is sufficiently different to warrant separate consideration.

a. **Bad Check Legislation**
Almost all jurisdictions have created a new and separate statutory crime prohibiting the giving of a no-account or insufficient funds check with the intent to defraud.

b. **Abuse or Misuse of Credit Card**
Most jurisdictions have enacted legislation making it a misdemeanor to knowingly obtain property by means of a stolen, forged, canceled, revoked, or otherwise unauthorized credit card.

D. **ROBBERY**　= larceny + assault
Robbery, a felony in all jurisdictions, consists of the following:

(i)　A taking;

(ii)　Of personal property of another;

robbery = threat must be of immovement harm
Threat of future harm = extortion

(iii)　From the other's person or presence; ≠ will

(iv)　By force or intimidation;

picking pocket is larceny
yanking necklace is robbery

(v)　With the intent to permanently deprive him of it.

Thus, robbery is basically an aggravated form of larceny in which the taking is accomplished by force or threats of force.

1. **Force or Threats Necessary**
If force is used, it obviously must be sufficient to overcome the victim's resistance. If threats are used, they must be threats of immediate death or serious physical injury to the victim, a member of her family, a relative, or a person in her presence at the time. A threat to do damage to property will not suffice, with the exception of a threat to destroy the victim's dwelling house.

2. **Property Must Be Taken from Person or Presence of Victim**
The property must be taken from some location reasonably close to the victim, but it need not be taken from her person. Property is in the victim's presence if it is in her vicinity. Property in other rooms of the house in which the victim is located is in her presence.

3. Force or Threats Must Be Used to Obtain Property or Immediately Retain It

The force or threats must be used either to gain possession of the property or to retain possession *immediately* after such possession has been accomplished.

Example: A reached into B's pocket without B's knowledge and removed B's wallet. B felt the wallet slip out, turned around, and grabbed A as he moved away. A struck B, rendering her unconscious, and ran. Is A guilty of robbery? *Held:* Yes. The force was used to prevent the victim from immediately apprehending A and regaining the property. Thus, it is sufficiently related to the taking.

4. Aggravated Robbery

Statutes often create a form of aggravated robbery, usually defined as robbery accomplished with a deadly weapon.

E. EXTORTION *is black mail*

Extortion is an offense that generally has been expanded by modern statutes far beyond its initial common law definition.

1. Common Law Definition—Collection of Unlawful Fee

The common law misdemeanor of extortion consisted of the corrupt collection of an unlawful fee by an officer under color of his office.

2. Modern Definition—Blackmail

distinguish btw robbery & Extortion
✓ no need to take anything
✓ threat of future harm another
✓ immanent

In many modern statutes, extortion (or blackmail) is defined as obtaining property from another by means of certain oral or written threats. The prohibited threats often include threats to do physical harm to the victim or others, or threats to damage the victim's property. Under some statutes, the crime is completed when the threats are made with the intent to obtain money or something of value; the threat is the essence of the offense. Under other statutes, the money or property must actually be obtained by means of the threats.

a. Threats Need Not Involve Immediate or Physical Harm

Extortion may be committed by threats that are not sufficient for robbery. To constitute extortion, the threats do not need to involve immediate or physical harm.

b. Property Need Not Be in Victim's Presence

To constitute extortion, it is generally not necessary that the property be obtained from the victim's person or presence (as is necessary for robbery).

F. RECEIPT OF STOLEN PROPERTY

The common law misdemeanor of receipt of stolen property is substantially identical to the modern offense. The elements of the crime are:

(i) Receiving possession and control;

(ii) Of "stolen" personal property;

(iii) Known to have been obtained in a manner constituting a criminal offense;

(iv) By another person;

(v) With the intent to permanently deprive the owner of his interest in the property.

1. Possession

Manual possession of the property, while sufficient for "receiving," is not necessary. It is also receiving if: (i) the thief places the stolen property in a place that the defendant has designated; or (ii) for profit, the defendant arranges for a sale of the property by the thief to a third person.

2. "Stolen" Property

Most jurisdictions define "stolen" property broadly to include property obtained by commission of any of the property offenses. However, the property must have "stolen" status at the time it is received by the defendant. Thus, if stolen goods have been recovered by the police and are used in an undercover operation with the owner's permission, the goods are not stolen and the defendant cannot be guilty of receipt of stolen property; however, the defendant may be guilty of attempt to receive stolen goods (*see* IV.D.3.a.1)a), *supra*).

G. STATUTORY CHANGES IN PROPERTY ACQUISITION OFFENSES

Modern criminal codes have substantially altered the common law in many jurisdictions. Among the major changes are the following:

1. **Consolidation of Offenses into Theft**
   There is a growing tendency to consolidate larceny, embezzlement, false pretenses, and receipt of stolen goods under the single heading: Theft. It is important to note that theft is a modern statutory crime, not a traditional common law offense.

2. **Expansion of Property Subject to Larceny (and Other Offenses)**
   The things subject to the offenses have often been expanded to cover services, documents, and intangibles, as well as joint property.

3. **Rejection of Asportation for Larceny**
   Some jurisdictions have rejected the requirement of asportation and require only that "control" of property be obtained.

4. **Rejection of Technicalities of Trespass Requirement**
   A number of jurisdictions have replaced the detailed technicalities of the trespass requirement by a simplified requirement that the defendant have obtained unauthorized "control" over the property.

H. FORGERY

At common law, forgery and uttering a forged instrument are separate offenses.

1. **Forgery**
   Forgery consists of the following:

   a. Making or altering;

   b. Of a false writing;

   c. With intent to defraud.

2. **Uttering a Forged Instrument**
   Uttering consists of:

   a. Offering as genuine;

   b. An instrument that may be the subject of forgery and is false;

   c. With intent to defraud.

3. **Writings that Are Possible Subjects of Forgery**
   Any writing that has *apparent legal significance* is a potential subject of forgery. Writing includes typewritten, printed, engraved, and similar material.
   Example: A drafts and signs what purports to be a letter of introduction from a local physician and a letter of recommendation from a firm represented as a former employer. Both are false. Has A committed one, two, or no forgeries? *Held:* One forgery. The recommendation has apparent legal significance, because one who recommends another may incur legal liability if his recommendation is false. Thus, it can be the subject of forgery. But the letter of introduction has only social significance, and cannot be the subject of forgery.

   Writings that derive their value from the mere fact of their existence—historical or artistic value—cannot be the subject of forgery.
   Example: A painted a picture and signed it Rembrandt. She then sold it to X, representing it as an original Rembrandt. Is A guilty of forgery? No, because the picture and signature derive their value from the fact of their existence. (*Note:* A did commit false pretenses by the sale.)

4. **Required Falsity—Writing Itself Must "Be a Lie"**
   It is not sufficient that the writing contains a false statement. The writing must represent itself to be something that it is not.
   Examples: 1) A, in charge of a warehouse, issues a warehouse receipt that represents that the warehouse has received certain grain. It has not. Is this forgery? *Held:* No. The warehouse receipt contains a misrepresentation. But it is what it purports to be, *i.e.,* a warehouse receipt issued by one with authority to issue it.

2) B obtains blank receipts from A's warehouse, fills them in so they represent that certain grain has been received, and signs A's name. Is this forgery? *Held:* Yes. The instruments purport to be what they are not, *i.e.,* warehouse receipts issued by one with authority to do so.

5. Required "Making"

a. Entire Instrument or Material Alteration

Forgery can be committed by the "making" of an entire instrument. It can also, however, be committed by altering an existing instrument, if the alteration is "material," that is, if it affects a legal right. Alteration may be in the form of changing some of the writing, adding to the existing writing, removing some of the existing writing, or improperly filling in blanks left by the signer.

b. Fraudulently Obtaining Signature of Another

If the defendant fraudulently causes a third person to sign a document that the third person does not realize he is signing, forgery has been committed. But if the third person realizes he is signing the document, forgery has not been committed even if the third person was induced by fraud to sign it.

6. Required Intent—Intent to Defraud

The defendant must have had the intent to defraud, although no one need actually have been defrauded. It is not necessary that she intended to do pecuniary harm; it is sufficient if she intended to harm another in any way.

I. MALICIOUS MISCHIEF

The common law misdemeanor of malicious mischief consists of:

(i) Malicious;

(ii) Destruction of, or damage to;

(iii) Property of another.

1. Damage Required

Destruction of the property is not required for malicious mischief. All that is necessary is that some physical damage be done that impairs the utility of the property or materially diminishes its value.

2. State of Mind Required—Malice

Malice requires no ill will or hatred. It does, however, require that the damage or destruction have been intended or contemplated by the defendant.

X. OFFENSES AGAINST THE HABITATION

A. BURGLARY

At common law, the elements of burglary are:

(i) A breaking; *you can break an interior door – constructive breaking.*

(ii) And entry;

(iii) Of the dwelling; *can't be commercial structure*

(iv) Of another;

(v) At nighttime;

(vi) With the intent of committing a felony *inside* therein. *must exist @ time of breaking and entering*

1. Breaking Required

a. Actual Breaking—Minimal Force Sufficient

Actual breaking requires some use of force to gain entry, but minimal force is sufficient; opening a closed but unlocked door constitutes a breaking. If force is used to enlarge an opening so that entry can be made, the traditional rule was that this did not constitute a breaking. Under the better view, however, a breaking has occurred because force was used to gain entry.

Example: D, intending to steal a valuable painting inside V's house, approaches V's door. The door is open about six inches. D pushes it fully open and enters. Is D guilty of burglary? The best answer is yes, since force—although only minor force—was used to gain entry.

b. Constructive Breaking
Constructive breaking consists of gaining entry by means of fraud, threat, or intimidation, or by use of the chimney.

Example: P wants to get into V's apartment to commit a felonious assault on V, but V's door is securely locked. P knocks and when V asks who it is, P responds, "I am a friend of your brother and he asked me to deliver this message to you." V then unlocks the door and invites P in. P enters. P has never met V's brother. Is P guilty of burglary? Yes. Since entry was obtained by fraud, this is constructive breaking.

c. Requirement of Trespass—Consent to Enter
A breaking requires a trespass, so that if the defendant had the consent of the resident to enter, his use of force to gain entry is not a breaking. The existence of consent to enter during limited periods, however, will not prevent entry by force at other times from being a breaking. Moreover, if the consent was procured by fraud or threats, this is a constructive breaking.

d. Requirement that Breaking Be "Of the House"
The breaking must be to effect entry into the structure or some separately secured subportion of it. Thus, it is sufficient that the defendant broke to enter a closed closet or wall safe within a dwelling, but it is not enough if he merely breaks open a box or trunk within the dwelling.

e. Breaking to Exit Insufficient
The breaking *must be to gain entry*. It is not burglary to hide in a dwelling, with the intent to commit a felony, and then break to get out of the dwelling.

2. Entry Required
Entry is made by placing any portion of the body inside the structure, even momentarily. Insertion of a tool or inanimate object into the structure is entry if it is inserted for the purpose of accomplishing the felony. It is not sufficient if it is inserted for purposes of gaining entry.

Examples: 1) A approached B's dwelling and shot a bullet through his window, intending to kill B. Has A committed burglary? *Held:* Yes. He has inserted an inanimate object into the dwelling by breaking for the purpose of committing the felony.

               2) Z intends to go into V's house and steal valuable jewels from a safe. He carefully cuts out a small portion of glass from a window and reaches in with his hand to unlock the window. At that point he is apprehended. Is Z guilty of burglary? Yes. His hand had "entered" the dwelling.

3. "Dwelling"—Used for Sleeping Purposes
A structure is a dwelling if it is used with regularity for sleeping purposes.

a. Used for Other Purposes—Still a Dwelling
A structure remains a dwelling even if it is also used for other purposes, such as conducting a business.

b. Temporary Absence of Inhabitants—Still a Dwelling
Temporary absence of those dwelling in a structure will not deprive it of its character as a dwelling. It is not a dwelling, however, before anyone has moved in, even if it was built for use as a dwelling, nor does it remain a dwelling after the last dweller has moved out with no intent to return.

4. "Of Another"—Occupancy Is Determinative
The requirement is that the structure be used as a dwelling by someone other than the defendant. Occupancy rather than ownership is material. An owner can commit burglary of his own structure if it is rented and used as a dwelling by others.

5. Requirement of Nighttime
Burglary could be committed only during the nighttime, defined as that period during which the countenance of a person could not be discerned by natural light.

6. Required Intent—Intent to Commit a Felony at Time of Entry
The defendant must have intended to commit a felony. It is not necessary that this be carried out. It is, however, essential that the intent exist at the time of entry; if the intent is formed after entry is completed, burglary is not committed.

7. Modern Statutory Changes
Modern statutes have modified the common law definition of burglary in a variety of ways that differ among jurisdictions. Some of the most common are as follows:

    a. Abandonment of Requirement of Breaking
    In many jurisdictions, it is sufficient that the defendant entered the structure, even if he did not break to gain entry.

    b. Remaining in a Structure
    It is often made burglary to remain concealed in a structure with the intent to commit an offense.

    c. Broadening Structures that Can Be Burglarized
    The description of structures that can be burglarized is often expanded beyond dwellings and sometimes beyond structures to include yards and cars.

    d. Elimination of Nighttime Requirement
    The requirement that entry be at nighttime is often abandoned, although burglary at nighttime is often assigned a more severe penalty than other burglaries. Nighttime is often defined by statute in terms of sunset and sunrise.

    e. Intent to Commit Misdemeanor Theft
    The intent necessary is often expanded to make it sufficient that the defendant intended to commit any theft, even if it was misdemeanor theft.

B. ARSON *is malicious burning*
At common law, arson consisted of:

(i)   The malicious;

(ii) Burning; *not explosion, not smoke damage, water damage*

(iii) Of the dwelling; *can't be a disco or bar*

(iv) Of another.

1. Requirement of a "Burning"

    a. Necessity of Fire
    The required damage (*see* below) must be caused by fire. Damage caused by an explosion does not constitute arson.

    b. Damage Required—"Scorching" (Insufficient) vs. "Charring" (Sufficient)
material wasting   Destruction of the structure or even significant damage to it is not required to complete the crime of arson. But mere blackening by smoke or discoloration by heat (scorching) is not sufficient. There must be some damage to the fiber of the wood or other combustible material; this is generally stated as the rule that "mere charring is sufficient."

2. "Dwelling"
At common law, dwelling was defined for arson as it was for burglary. (*See* above.) Most states by statute extend arson to structures other than dwellings. (*Note:* Questions on the Multistate Exam that are testing on other arson issues (*e.g.,* malice) will often assume without saying that the jurisdiction's arson law applies to structures other than dwellings.)

3. "Of Another"—Ownership Immaterial
Arson, like burglary, is a crime against the habitation. Thus, the structure had to be used as a dwelling by another; ownership was not material, even if the defendant himself was the

owner. (*Note:* At common law, the burning of one's house was the misdemeanor of "house-burning" if other dwellings were nearby.)

4. State of Mind Required—Malice
The burning does not have to be with ill will or for any particular motive. No specific intent is required. On the other hand, it is not sufficient that the burning was accidental, even if the defendant was negligent. All that malice requires is that the defendant have acted with the intent or knowledge that the structure would burn, or with *reckless disregard* of an obvious risk that the structure would burn.

5. Related Offenses

a. Houseburning
The common law misdemeanor of houseburning consisted of:

1) Malicious (as defined in arson);

2) Burning;

3) Of one's own dwelling;

4) If the structure is situated either:

    a) In a city or town; or

    b) So near to other houses as to create a danger to them.

b. Arson with Intent to Defraud an Insurer
At common law, it was not arson to burn one's own dwelling for purposes of fraudulently collecting the insurance on it. But this is often made an offense by modern statutes.

XI. OFFENSES INVOLVING JUDICIAL PROCEDURE

A. PERJURY
A misdemeanor at common law, perjury consisted of the willful and corrupt taking of a false oath in regard to a material matter in a judicial proceeding.

1. Materiality
Materiality is an element of this offense, which must be alleged in the indictment and proved by the prosecution. The statement is material if it might affect some phase or detail of the trial, hearing, declaration, etc.

2. Contradictory Statements
If a witness has made two contradictory statements at the same proceeding and admits, before the end of the proceeding, that one of the statements is false, he cannot be prosecuted for having made the false statement. This is to encourage witnesses to correct any false statements they may have made before substantial damage is caused.

3. Civil Liability
In litigation brought under 42 U.S.C. section 1983 (Civil Rights Act), all witnesses—including police officers—are absolutely immune from civil liability based on their testimony (*i.e.*, alleged perjury) in judicial proceedings. [Briscoe v. LaHue, 460 U.S. 325 (1983)]

B. SUBORNATION OF PERJURY
A separate offense at common law, subornation of perjury consists of procuring or inducing another to commit perjury. In some states, this is not part of the perjury statute.

C. BRIBERY
The common law misdemeanor of bribery consisted of the corrupt payment or receipt of anything of value in return for official action. Under modern statutes, it can be a felony, and it may be extended to classes of persons who are not public officials (*e.g.*, athletes). Either the offering of a bribe or the taking of a bribe may constitute the crime.

1. **Mutual Criminal Intent Unnecessary**

   It is not necessary that there be mutual criminal intent on the part of both the person tendering the bribe and the recipient.

2. **Failure to Report a Bribe**

   Some statutes also make it a misdemeanor offense to fail to report a bribe.

D. COMPOUNDING A CRIME

At common law, the misdemeanor of compounding a crime consisted of entering into an agreement *for valuable consideration* to not prosecute another for a felony or to conceal the commission of a felony or whereabouts of a felon.

Under modern statutes, the definition remains essentially the same, except that it refers to *any crime* (not only felonies). A few states make it a felony offense.

E. MISPRISION OF A FELONY

At common law, the misdemeanor of misprision of a felony consisted of the failure—by someone other than a principal or accessory before the fact—to disclose or report knowledge of the commission of a felony. Misprision was distinguished from compounding a crime in that no passage of consideration was required for the former. Today most jurisdictions do not recognize the crime of misprision of a felony. In these jurisdictions, therefore, a person is under *no obligation to report a crime*.

---

hot topics

   mental state

      specific intent — 2 additional defenses =
      voluntary toxication
      mistake of fact

   transfer of intent

   accomplice liability

   solicitation
   conspiracy

hot defenses
- intoxication
- infancy
- self defense
- mistake of facts

     homicide — 5 defenses to felony murder
     larceny, embezzlement & false pretence distinctions
     robbery, burglary, arson

BAR REVIEW

Criminal Procedure

celebrating
35 *YEARS*
of preparing law students for the bar exam

CRIMINAL PROCEDURE

TABLE OF CONTENTS

I. CONSTITUTIONAL RESTRAINTS ON CRIMINAL PROCEDURE

A. INTRODUCTION

The development of numerous constitutional limitations upon the manner in which a criminal suspect may be arrested, convicted, and punished has rendered much of criminal procedure an inquiry into constitutional law.

B. INCORPORATION OF BILL OF RIGHTS INTO DUE PROCESS

The first eight amendments to the United States Constitution apply by their terms only to the federal government. However, the Supreme Court has incorporated many of these rights into the due process requirement binding on the states by virtue of the Fourteenth Amendment. Those portions of the Bill of Rights "fundamental to our concept of ordered liberty" have been so incorporated. [Duncan v. Louisiana, 391 U.S. 145 (1968)]

C. CONSTITUTIONAL REQUIREMENTS BINDING ON STATES

The following rights have been held binding on the states under the due process provisions of the Fourteenth Amendment:

1. The Fourth Amendment *prohibition against unreasonable searches and seizures* [Wolf v. Colorado, 338 U.S. 25 (1949)], and the *exclusionary rule* requiring that the result of a violation of this prohibition not be used as evidence against the defendant [Mapp v. Ohio, 367 U.S. 643 (1961)];

2. The Fifth Amendment *privilege against compulsory self-incrimination* [Malloy v. Hogan, 378 U.S. 1 (1964)];

3. The Fifth Amendment *prohibition against double jeopardy* [Benton v. Maryland, 395 U.S. 784 (1969)];

4. The Sixth Amendment right to a *speedy trial* [Klopfer v. North Carolina, 386 U.S. 213 (1967)];

5. The Sixth Amendment right to a *public trial* [*In re* Oliver, 333 U.S. 257 (1948)];

6. The Sixth Amendment right to *trial by jury* [Duncan v. Louisiana, 391 U.S. 145 (1968)];

7. The Sixth Amendment right to *confront witnesses* [Pointer v. Texas, 380 U.S. 400 (1965)];

8. The Sixth Amendment right to *compulsory process* for obtaining witnesses [Washington v. Texas, 388 U.S. 14 (1967)];

9. The Sixth Amendment right to *assistance of counsel* in felony cases [Gideon v. Wainwright, 372 U.S. 335 (1963)], and in misdemeanor cases in which imprisonment is imposed [Argersinger v. Hamlin, 407 U.S. 25 (1972)]; and

10. The Eighth Amendment *prohibition against cruel and unusual punishment* [Robinson v. California, 370 U.S. 660 (1962)].

D. CONSTITUTIONAL RIGHTS NOT BINDING ON STATES

Two provisions of the Bill of Rights have not been held binding on the states.

1. Right to Indictment

The right to indictment by a grand jury for capital and infamous crimes has been held not to be binding on the states. [Hurtado v. California, 110 U.S. 516 (1884)]

2. Prohibition Against Excessive Bail

It has not yet been determined whether the Eighth Amendment prohibition against excessive bail creates a right to bail (or whether it simply prohibits excessive bail where the right to bail exists) and whether it is binding on the states. However, most state constitutions create a right to bail and prohibit excessive bail.

II. EXCLUSIONARY RULE

A. IN GENERAL

The exclusionary rule is a judge-made doctrine that prohibits the introduction, at a criminal trial, of evidence obtained in violation of a defendant's Fourth, Fifth, or Sixth Amendment rights.

1. **Rationale**
    The main purpose of the exclusionary rule is to deter the government (primarily the police) from violating a person's constitutional rights: If the government cannot use evidence obtained in violation of a person's rights, it will be less likely to act in contravention of those rights. The rule also serves as one remedy for deprivation of constitutional rights (other remedies include civil suits, injunctions, etc.).

2. **Scope of the Rule**

    a. **Fruit of the Poisonous Tree**
        Generally, not only must *illegally obtained evidence* be excluded, but also *all evidence obtained or derived* from exploitation of that evidence. The courts deem such evidence the tainted fruit of the poisonous tree. [Nardone v. United States, 308 U.S. 338 (1939); Wong Sun v. United States, 371 U.S. 471 (1963)]

        Example: D was arrested *without probable cause* and brought to the police station. The police read D his *Miranda* warnings three times and permitted D to see two friends. After being at the station for six hours, D confessed. The confession must be excluded because it is the direct result of the unlawful arrest—if D had not been arrested illegally, he would not have been in custody and would not have confessed. [Taylor v. Alabama, 457 U.S. 687 (1982)]

        Compare: Police *have probable cause* to arrest D. They go to D's home and improperly arrest him without a warrant, in violation of the Fourth Amendment (*see* III.B.2.b.3), *infra*). D confesses at home, and the police then take him to the station. D confesses again at the station. The home confession must be excluded from evidence since it is the fruit of the illegal arrest, but the station house confession is admissible because it is not a fruit of the unlawful arrest. Because the police had probable cause to arrest D, they did not gain anything from the unlawful arrest—they could have lawfully arrested D the moment he stepped outside of his home and then brought him to the station for his confession. Thus, the station house confession was not an exploitation of the police misconduct; *i.e.,* it was not a fruit of the fact that D was arrested at home as opposed to somewhere else. [New York v. Harris, 495 U.S. 14 (1990)]

    b. **Exception—Breaking the Causal Chain**
        Under the fruit of the poisonous tree doctrine, the exclusionary rule can be very broadly applied. Recently, however, the Court has begun to narrow the scope of the rule by balancing its purpose (deterrence of government misconduct) against its costs (exclusion of probative evidence). The Court generally will not apply the rule when it will not likely deter government misconduct. Thus, if there is a weak link between the government misconduct and the evidence (*i.e.,* it is not likely that the misconduct caused the evidence to be obtained), the Court will probably not exclude the evidence.

        1) **Independent Source** of the illegally search evidence
            Evidence is admissible if the prosecution can show that it was obtained from a source independent of the original illegality.
            Example: Police illegally search a warehouse and discover marijuana, but do not seize it. The police later return to the warehouse with a valid warrant based on information totally unrelated to the illegal search. If police seize the marijuana pursuant to the warrant, the marijuana is admissible. [Murray v. United States, 487 U.S. 533 (1988)]

        2) **Intervening Act of Free Will**
            An intervening act of free will by the defendant will break the causal chain between the evidence and the original illegality and thus remove the taint. [Wong Sun v. United States, *supra*]
            Example: The defendant was released on his own recognizance after an illegal arrest but later returned to the station to confess. This voluntary act of free will removed any taint from the confession. [Wong Sun v. United States, *supra*]

            Compare: The reading of *Miranda* warnings, even when coupled with the passage of six hours and consultation with friends, was not sufficient to break the causal chain under the facts of *Taylor v. Alabama* (*see* 2.a., above).

3) Inevitable Discovery
If the prosecution can show that the police would have discovered the evidence whether or not they had acted unconstitutionally, the evidence will be admissible. [Nix v. Williams, 467 U.S. 431 (1984)]

4) Live Witness Testimony
It is difficult for a defendant to have live witness testimony excluded as the fruit of illegal police conduct, because a more direct link between the unconstitutional police conduct and the testimony is required than for exclusion of other evidence. The factors a court must consider in determining whether a sufficiently direct link exists include the extent to which the witness is freely willing to testify and the extent to which excluding the witness's testimony would deter future illegal conduct. [United States v. Ceccolini, 435 U.S. 268 (1978)]

5) In-Court Identification
The defendant *may not exclude* the witness's in-court identification on the ground that it is the fruit of an unlawful detention. [United States v. Crews, 445 U.S. 463 (1980)]

B. LIMITATIONS ON THE RULE

1. Inapplicable to Grand Juries
A grand jury witness may not refuse to answer questions on the ground that they are based on evidence obtained from an unlawful search and seizure [United States v. Calandra, 414 U.S. 338 (1974)], unless the evidence was obtained in violation of the federal wiretapping statute [Gelbard v. United States, 408 U.S. 41 (1972)].

2. Inapplicable to Civil Proceedings
The exclusionary rule does not forbid one sovereign from using in civil proceedings evidence that was illegally seized by the agent of another sovereign. [United States v. Janis, 428 U.S. 433 (1976)] Moreover, the Supreme Court would probably allow the sovereign that illegally obtained evidence to use it in a civil proceeding. The exclusionary rule does apply, however, to a proceeding for forfeiture of an article used in violation of the criminal law, when forfeiture is clearly a penalty for the criminal offense. [One 1958 Plymouth Sedan v. Pennsylvania, 380 U.S. 693 (1965)]

Example: Evidence that is inadmissible in a state criminal trial because it was illegally seized by the police may be used by the IRS. [United States v. Janis, *supra*]

3. Inapplicable to Internal Agency Rules
The exclusionary rule applies only if there is a violation of the Constitution or federal law; it does not apply to a violation of only internal agency rules. [United States v. Caceres, 440 U.S. 741 (1979)]

4. Inapplicable in Parole Revocation Proceedings
The exclusionary rule does not apply in parole revocation proceedings. [Pennsylvania v. Scott, 524 U.S. 357 (1998)]

5. Good Faith Reliance on Existing Law, Defective Search Warrant, or Clerical Error
The exclusionary rule does not apply when the police act in good faith based on case law later changed by another judicial opinion [United States v. Peltier, 422 U.S. 531 (1975)] or on a facially valid statute or ordinance as it then exists, even if the law is declared unconstitutional or the law is changed by court decision [Michigan v. DeFillippo, 443 U.S. 31 (1979); Illinois v. Krull, 480 U.S. 340 (1987)]; or when they act in reliance in good faith on a defective search warrant [United States v. Leon, 468 U.S. 897 (1984); Massachusetts v. Sheppard, 468 U.S. 981 (1984)]. Similarly, the exclusionary rule does not apply to evidence obtained during an arrest made on the basis of a computer report that, due to clerical errors not made by the police, indicated that there was an arrest warrant outstanding against the defendant. [Arizona v. Evans, 514 U.S. 1 (1995)] *Rationale:* One of the main purposes of the exclusionary rule is to deter improper police conduct, and this purpose cannot be served where police are acting in good faith.

a. Exceptions to Good Faith Reliance on Search Warrant
The Court in *Leon* and *Sheppard* suggested four exceptions to the good faith defense for

reliance on a defective search warrant. A police officer cannot rely on a defective search warrant in good faith if:

   ✓ 1)   The affidavit underlying the warrant is so lacking in probable cause that no reasonable police officer would have relied on it;

   ✓ 2)   The warrant is defective on its face (*e.g.,* it fails to state with particularity the place to be searched or the things to be seized);

   ✓ 3)   The police officer or government official obtaining the warrant lied to or misled the magistrate; or

   ✓ 4)   The magistrate has "wholly abandoned his judicial role."

6.   Use of Excluded Evidence for Impeachment Purposes
Some illegally obtained evidence that is inadmissible in the state's case in chief may nevertheless be used to impeach the defendant's credibility if he takes the stand at trial.

   a.   Voluntary Confessions in Violation of *Miranda*
   An otherwise voluntary confession taken in violation of the *Miranda v. Arizona* requirements is admissible at trial for impeachment purposes. [Harris v. New York, 401 U.S. 222 (1971); Oregon v. Hass, 420 U.S. 714 (1975)] However, a truly involuntary confession is not admissible for any purpose. [Mincey v. Arizona, 437 U.S. 385 (1978)]
   all illegally seized evidence may be admitted to impeach Δ's trial testimony.

   b.   Fruit of Illegal Searches
   The prosecution may use evidence obtained from an illegal search that is inadmissible in its direct case to impeach the defendant's statements made in response to proper cross-examination reasonably suggested by the defendant's direct examination [United States v. Havens, 446 U.S. 620 (1980)], but such illegally obtained evidence cannot be used to impeach the trial testimony of witnesses other than the defendant [James v. Illinois, 493 U.S. 307 (1990)].

7.   *Miranda* Violations
The Supreme Court has suggested that fruits derived from statements obtained in violation of *Miranda* (*see* IV.D.1., *infra*) might be admissible despite the exclusionary rule. [Oregon v. Elstad, *infra,* IV.D.4.b.]

C.   HARMLESS ERROR TEST
A conviction will not necessarily be overturned merely because improperly obtained evidence was admitted at trial; the harmless error test applies, so a conviction can be upheld if the conviction would have resulted despite the improper evidence. On appeal, the government bears the burden of showing ***beyond a reasonable doubt*** that the admission was harmless. [Chapman v. California, 386 U.S. 18 (1967); Milton v. Wainwright, 407 U.S. 371 (1972)] In a habeas corpus proceeding, if a petitioner claims a constitutional error, the petitioner must be released if the error had ***substantial and injurious effect or influence*** in determining the jury's verdict. [Brecht v. Abrahamson, 507 U.S. 619 (1993)] If the judge is in "grave doubt" as to the harm (*e.g.,* where the record is evenly balanced as to harmlessness), the petition must be granted. [O'Neal v. McAninch, 513 U.S. 432 (1995)]

D.   ENFORCING THE EXCLUSIONARY RULE

1.   Right to Hearing on Motion to Suppress
The defendant is entitled to have the admissibility of evidence or a confession decided as a matter of law by a judge out of the hearing of the jury. [Jackson v. Denno, 378 U.S. 368 (1964)] It is permissible to let the jury reconsider the "admissibility" of the evidence if the judge finds it admissible, but there is no constitutional right to such a dual evaluation. [Lego v. Twomey, 404 U.S. 477 (1972)] And the defendant is not constitutionally entitled to have a specific finding of fact on each factual question. [LaValee v. Delle Rose, 410 U.S. 690 (1973)]

2.   Burden of Proof
The government bears the burden of establishing admissibility by a preponderance of the evidence. [Lego v. Twomey, *supra*]

3. Defendant's Right to Testify

The defendant has the right to testify at the suppression hearing without his testimony being admitted against him at trial on the issue of guilt. [Simmons v. United States, 390 U.S. 377 (1968)]

III. FOURTH AMENDMENT

A. IN GENERAL

arrest warrant is not generally required in public Place

The Fourth Amendment provides that people should be free in their persons from **unreasonable** searches and seizures.

1. Search

A search can be defined as a governmental intrusion into an area where a person has a reasonable and justifiable expectation of privacy.

2. Seizure

A seizure can be defined as the exercise of control by the government over a person or thing.

3. Reasonableness

What is reasonable under the Fourth Amendment depends on the circumstances. For example, certain searches and seizures are considered to be reasonable only if the government has first obtained a warrant authorizing the action, while other searches and seizures are reasonable without a warrant. The material that follows specifically outlines the requirements for searches and seizures under the Fourth Amendment.

B. ARRESTS AND OTHER DETENTIONS

Governmental detentions of persons, including arrests, certainly constitute seizures of the person, so they must be reasonable to comply with the Fourth Amendment. Whether a seizure of the person is reasonable depends on the scope of the seizure (*e.g.,* is it an arrest or merely an investigatory stop?) and the strength of the suspicion prompting the seizure (*e.g.,* an arrest requires probable cause while an investigatory detention can be based on reasonable suspicion).

1. What Constitutes a Seizure of the Person?

Generally, it is obvious when police arrest or seize a person. When it is not readily apparent, the Supreme Court has indicated that a seizure occurs only when a reasonable person would believe that she is not free to leave. [Michigan v. Chesternut, 486 U.S. 567 (1988)—police pursuit of suspect generally not a seizure] This requires a **physical application of force** by the officer or a **submission** to the officer's show of force. It is not enough that the officer merely ordered the person to stop. [California v. Hodari D., 499 U.S. 621 (1991)]

Example: Officers boarded a bus shortly before its departure and asked individuals for identification and consent to search their luggage. The mere fact that people felt they were not free to leave because they feared that the bus would depart does not make this a seizure of the person. The test is whether under the totality of the circumstances, a reasonable person would feel that he was not free to decline the officers' requests or otherwise terminate the encounter. [Florida v. Bostick, 501 U.S. 429 (1991)]

2. Arrests

An arrest occurs when the police take a person into custody against her will for purposes of criminal prosecution or interrogation.

a. Probable Cause Requirement

An arrest must be based on probable cause. Probable cause to arrest is present when at the time of arrest, the officer has within her knowledge reasonably trustworthy facts and circumstances sufficient to warrant a reasonably prudent person to believe that the suspect has committed or is committing a crime. [Beck v. Ohio, 379 U.S. 89 (1964)]

b. Warrant Generally Not Required

In contrast to the rule for searches, police generally need not obtain a warrant before arresting a person in a **public place**, even if they have time to get a warrant. [United States v. Watson, 423 U.S. 411 (1976)]

1) Felony
A police officer may arrest a person without a warrant when she has **reasonable grounds to believe** that a felony has been committed and that the person before her committed it.

2) Misdemeanor
An officer may make a warrantless arrest for a misdemeanor **committed in her presence**. A crime is committed in the officer's "presence" if she is aware of it through any of her senses.

Note: The police may make a warrantless misdemeanor arrest even if the crime for which the arrest is made cannot be punished by incarceration. [Atwater v. Lago Vista, 532 U.S. 318 (2001)]

3) Exception—Home Arrests Require Warrant
The police must have an arrest warrant to effect a nonemergency arrest of an individual in her own home. [Payton v. New York, 445 U.S. 573 (1980)] All warrantless searches of homes are presumed unreasonable. The burden is on the government to demonstrate sufficient exigent circumstances to overcome this presumption. [Welsh v. Wisconsin, 466 U.S. 740 (1984)]

a) Homes of Third Parties
Absent exigent circumstances, the police executing an arrest warrant may not search for the subject of the warrant in the home of a third party without first obtaining a separate search warrant for the home. [Steagald v. United States, 451 U.S. 204 (1981)]

c. Effect of Invalid Arrest
An unlawful arrest, **by itself**, has no impact on a subsequent criminal prosecution. Thus, if the police improperly arrest a person (*e.g.,* at his home without a warrant), they may detain him if they have probable cause to do so [*see* New York v. Harris, 495 U.S. 14 (1990)], and the invalid arrest is not a defense to the offense charged [Frisbie v. Collins, 342 U.S. 519 (1952)]. Of course, evidence that is a fruit of the unlawful arrest may not be used against the defendant at trial because of the exclusionary rule.

3. Other Detentions

a. Investigatory Detentions (Stop and Frisk)
Police have the authority to briefly detain a person for investigative purposes even if they lack probable cause to arrest. To make such a stop, police must have a **reasonable suspicion** supported by **articulable facts** of criminal activity or involvement in a completed crime. [Terry v. Ohio, 392 U.S. 1 (1968)] *Note:* If the police also have reasonable suspicion to believe that the detainee is armed and dangerous, they may also conduct a frisk (a limited search) to ensure that the detainee has no weapons (*see* C.5.e., *infra*).

1) Reasonable Suspicion Defined
The Court has not specifically defined "reasonable suspicion." It requires something more than a vague suspicion (*e.g.,* it is not enough that the detainee was in a crime-filled area [Brown v. Texas, 443 U.S. 47 (1979)]), but full probable cause is not required. Whether the standard is met is judged under the totality of the circumstances. [United States v. Sokolow, 490 U.S. 1 (1989)]

Examples: 1) Reasonable suspicion justifying a stop is present when: (i) a suspect who is standing on a corner in a high crime area (ii) flees after noticing the presence of the police. Neither factor standing alone is enough to justify a stop, but together they are sufficiently suspicious. [Illinois v. Wardlow, 528 U.S. 119 (2000)]

2) Police had reasonable suspicion—and therefore there was no Fourth Amendment violation—where they detained Defendant at an airport while dogs sniffed his bags for drugs based on the following facts known by the police: (i) Defendant paid for airline tickets in cash with small bills; (ii) Defendant traveled under a name that did not match the name for the phone number he gave; (iii) Defendant traveled to a drug source city (Miami) and stayed

for only 48 hours, while his flight time was 20 hours; (iv) Defendant appeared nervous; and (v) Defendant refused to check his bags. [United States v. Sokolow, *supra*] *Note:* The fact that these suspicious circumstances are part of a drug courier profile used by the police neither helps nor hurts the totality of the circumstances inquiry.

2) Source of Suspicion

Like probable cause, reasonable suspicion need not arise from a police officer's personal knowledge. The suspicion can be based on a flyer, a police bulletin, or a report from an informant. [United States v. Hensley, 469 U.S. 221 (1985)]

a) Informant's Tips

Where the source of suspicion of criminal activity is an informant's tip, the tip must be accompanied by indicia of reliability sufficient to make the officer's suspicion reasonable.

Example: Police received an anonymous tip asserting that a woman was carrying cocaine and predicting that she would leave a specified apartment at a specified time, get into a specified car, and drive to a specified motel. After observing that the informant had accurately predicted the suspect's movements, it was reasonable for the police to think that the informant had inside knowledge that the suspect indeed had cocaine, thus justifying a *Terry* stop. [Alabama v. White, 496 U.S. 325 (1990)]

Compare: Police received an anonymous tip that a young black man in a plaid shirt standing at a particular bus stop was carrying a gun. When police arrived at the bus stop, they found a young black man there wearing a plaid shirt. They searched the man and found an illegal gun. Here there was not sufficient indicia of reliability in the tip to provide reasonable suspicion. The fact that the informant knows a person is standing at a bus stop does not show knowledge of any inside information; any passerby could observe the suspect's presence. Unlike the tip in *White,* the tip here did not provide predictive information and left police with no way to test the informant's knowledge and credibility. [Florida v. J.L., 529 U.S. 266 (2000)]

3) Duration and Scope

To be valid under *Terry,* the investigatory stop must be relatively brief and in any event no longer than is necessary to conduct a limited investigation to verify the officer's suspicions.

4) Development of Probable Cause

If during an investigatory detention, the officer develops probable cause, the detention becomes an arrest, and the officer can proceed on that basis. He can, for example, conduct a full search incident to that arrest.

5) What Constitutes a Stop?

If an officer merely approaches a person but does not detain her, no arrest or investigatory detention occurs. Not even reasonable suspicion is necessary in such cases. A seizure or stop occurs only if a reasonable person would believe she is not free to leave. (*See* B.1., *supra.*)

6) Property Seizures on Reasonable Suspicion

Police may briefly seize items upon reasonable suspicion that they are or contain contraband or evidence, but such seizures must be limited. [United States v. Place, 462 U.S. 696 (1983)—90-minute detention of luggage reasonably suspected to contain drugs unconstitutional]

b. Automobile Stops

Stopping a car is a seizure for Fourth Amendment purposes. Thus, generally, police may not stop a car unless they have at least reasonable suspicion to believe that a law has been violated. However, in certain cases where special law enforcement needs are involved, the Court allows police to set up roadblocks to stop cars without individualized suspicion that the driver has violated some law. To be valid, it appears that such roadblocks must: (i) stop cars on the basis of some neutral, articulable standard (*e.g.,* every car or every third car); and (ii) be designed to serve purposes closely related to a particular problem related to automobiles and their mobility. [*See* Delaware v. Prouse, 440 U.S. 648 (1979); *and see* Indianapolis v. Edmond, 531 U.S. 32 (2000)]

Examples: 1) Because of the gravity of the drunk driving problem and the magnitude of the states' interest in getting drunk drivers off the roads, police may set up roadblocks to check the sobriety of all drivers passing by. [Michigan Department of State Police v. Sitz, 496 U.S. 444 (1990)]

2) Because of the difficulty of discerning whether an automobile is transporting illegal aliens, police may set up roadblocks near the border to stop every car to check the citizenship of its occupants. [United States v. Martinez-Fuerte, 428 U.S. 543 (1976); *and see* United States v. Villamonte-Marquez, 462 U.S. 579 (1983)—suspicionless boarding of boat in channel leading to open sea justified on similar grounds]

Compare: The police may not set up roadblocks to check cars for illegal drugs. The nature of such a checkpoint is to detect evidence of ordinary criminal wrongdoing unrelated to use of cars or highway safety. If suspicionless stops were allowed under these circumstances, all suspicionless seizures would be justified. [Indianapolis v. Edmond, *supra*]

1) Police May Order Occupants Out
Provided that a police officer has lawfully stopped a vehicle, in the interest of officer safety, the officer may order the occupants (*i.e.,* the vehicle's driver *and* passengers) to get out. [Pennsylvania v. Mimms, 434 U.S. 106 (1978); Maryland v. Wilson, 519 U.S. 408 (1997)]

2) Pretextual Stops
If an officer has probable cause to believe that a traffic law has been violated, the officer may stop the suspect's car, even if the officer's ulterior motive is to investigate whether some *other law*—for which the officer lacks reasonable suspicion— is being violated. [Whren v. United States, 517 U.S. 806 (1996)—police in a high drug area stopped D's car after observing D wait a long time at an intersection, abruptly turn without signaling, and speed off at an unreasonable speed; *and see* Arkansas v. Sullivan, 532 U.S. 769 (2001)]

c. Detention to Obtain a Warrant
If the police have probable cause to believe that a suspect has hidden drugs in his house, they may, for a reasonable time, prohibit him from going into the house unaccompanied so that they can prevent him from destroying the drugs while they obtain a search warrant. [Illinois v. McArthur, 531 U.S. 326 (2001)—police kept suspect from reentering his trailer alone for two hours while an officer obtained a warrant]

d. Occupants of Premises Being Searched May Be Detained
Pursuant to the execution of a *valid warrant* to search for contraband, the police may detain occupants of the premises while a proper search is conducted. [Michigan v. Summers, 452 U.S. 692 (1981)]

e. Station House Detention
Police officers must have *full probable cause* for arrest to bring a suspect to the station for questioning [Dunaway v. New York, 442 U.S. 200 (1969)] or for fingerprinting [Hayes v. Florida, 470 U.S. 811 (1985)]. The Supreme Court has suggested that under some limited circumstances it might be permissible to require a person to go to the police station for investigatory purposes without probable cause for arrest [Davis v. Mississippi, 394 U.S. 721 (1969)], but the Court has never found such circumstances to exist.

4. Stop and Identify Statutes
A criminal statute requiring persons who loiter or wander on the streets to provide a "credible and reliable" identification when stopped by police is *unconstitutionally vague* for failure to clarify what will satisfy the identification requirement. [Kolender v. Lawson, 461 U.S. 352 (1983)]

5. Grand Jury Appearance
For all practical purposes, seizure of a person (by subpoena) for a grand jury appearance is

not within the Fourth Amendment's protection. Even if, in addition to testifying, the person is to be asked to give handwriting or voice exemplars, there is no need for the subpoena to be based on probable cause or even objective suspicion. In other words, a person compelled to appear cannot assert that it was unreasonable to compel the appearance. However, the Supreme Court has suggested that it is conceivable that such a subpoena could be unreasonable if it was extremely broad and sweeping or if it was being used for harassment purposes. [United States v. Dionisio, 410 U.S. 1 (1973); United States v. Mara, 410 U.S. 19 (1973)]

6. Deadly Force

There is a Fourth Amendment "seizure" when a police officer uses deadly force to apprehend a suspect. An officer may not use deadly force unless the officer has *probable cause* to believe that the suspect poses a significant threat of death or serious physical injury to the officer or others. [Tennessee v. Garner, 471 U.S. 1 (1985)] On the other hand, a mere *attempt to arrest* that results in the death of a suspect is not necessarily a seizure governed by the Fourth Amendment. For example, the Court has held that there was no seizure where an officer in a car pursued two suspects riding a motorcycle at high speeds and ran over and killed one of the suspects who had fallen. [Sacramento v. Lewis, 523 U.S. 833 (1998)—the Due Process Clause (not the Fourth Amendment) is applicable and would be violated only if the chase "shocked the conscience" of the Court; *see* D., *infra*]

C. EVIDENTIARY SEARCH AND SEIZURE ~highly tested area~ ~p. 5 convoiser has good flow chart~

Like arrests, evidentiary searches and seizures must be reasonable to be valid under the Fourth Amendment. Reasonableness here usually means that the police must have obtained a warrant before conducting the search, but there are six circumstances where a warrant is not required (*see* 5., *infra*).

1. General Approach

A useful analytical model of the law of search and seizure requires answers to the following questions:

a. Does the defendant have a *Fourth Amendment right*?

1) Was there *governmental conduct*?

2) Did the defendant have a *reasonable expectation of privacy*?

~4th A. might exist~
b. If so, did the police have a *valid warrant*?

c. If the police did not have a valid warrant, did they make a *valid warrantless search* and seizure?
~good →~
~no good → good faith defense applies?~
~any six exception applies?~

2. Governmental Conduct Required

The Fourth Amendment generally protects only against governmental conduct and not against searches by private persons. Government agents here include only the *publicly paid police* and those *citizens acting at their direction* or behest; private security guards are not government agents unless deputized as officers of the public police. ~deputized w power to arrest~

Example: A private freight carrier opened a package and resealed it; police later reopened the package. The Supreme Court found that this was not a "search" under the Fourth Amendment because the police found nothing more than the private carrier had found. Moreover, the warrantless field test of a substance found in the package to determine whether it was cocaine was not a Fourth Amendment "seizure," even though the testing went beyond the scope of the original private search. [United States v. Jacobsen, 466 U.S. 109 (1984)]

3. Reasonable Expectation of Privacy

To have a Fourth Amendment right, a person must have a reasonable expectation of privacy with respect to the place searched or the item seized.

a. **Standing** ~to object the legality of the search/seizure~

It is not enough merely that *someone* has an expectation of privacy in the place searched or the item seized. The Supreme Court has imposed a standing requirement so that a person can complain about an evidentiary search or seizure only if it violates his *own* reasonable expectations of privacy. [Rakas v. Illinois, 439 U.S. 128 (1978)] Whether a person has a legitimate expectation of privacy generally is based on the *totality of the circumstances*, considering factors such as ownership of the place searched and location of the item seized. [Rawlings v. Kentucky, 448 U.S. 98 (1980)] The Court has held that a person has a legitimate expectation of privacy anytime:

automatic category of standing =

✓ (i)   She owned or had a right to possession of the place searched;

✓ (ii) The place searched was in fact her home, whether or not she owned or had a right to possession of it; or

✓ (iii) She was an overnight guest of the owner of the place searched [Minnesota v. Olson, 495 U.S. 91 (1990)].

sometimes has standing to legitimately present place when the search take place

1) **Search of Third-Party Premises**
   Standing does not exist merely because a person will be harmed by introduction of evidence seized during an illegal search of a third person's property.
   Example: A police officer peered through the closed window blind of Lessee's apartment and observed Lessee and defendants bagging cocaine. When defendants left the apartment, the officer followed them to their car and arrested them. The car and apartment were searched, and cocaine and a weapon were found. At trial, defendants moved to suppress all evidence, claiming that the officer's peeking through the window blind constituted an illegal search. It was determined that defendants had spent little time in Lessee's apartment and had come there solely to conduct a business transaction (*i.e.*, bagging the cocaine). *Held:* The defendants did not have a sufficient expectation of privacy in the apartment. They were there only for a few hours and were not overnight guests. Moreover, they were there for business purposes rather than social purposes, and there is a lesser expectation of privacy in commercial settings. Therefore, the defendants had no Fourth Amendment protections in the apartment and cannot challenge the search. [Minnesota v. Carter, 525 U.S. 83 (1999)]

passenger in car doesn't have standing (who doesn't claim ownership of the car or of item seized)

individual briefly on prop of someone else solely for business purpose of cutting up drugs do not have standing to object the search

2) **No Automatic Standing to Object to Seizure of Evidence in Possessory Offense**
   Formerly, a defendant had automatic standing to object to the legality of a search and seizure anytime the evidence obtained was introduced against her in a possessory offense. (This allowed a defendant to challenge the search without specifically admitting possession of the items.) Because a defendant at a suppression hearing may now assert a legitimate expectation of privacy in the items without his testimony being used against him at trial [*see* Simmons v. United States, *supra*, II.D.3.], the automatic standing rule has been abolished as unnecessary [United States v. Salvucci, 448 U.S. 83 (1980)].

3) **No Automatic Standing for Co-Conspirator**
   That a co-conspirator may be aggrieved by the introduction of damaging evidence does not give the co-conspirator automatic standing to challenge the seizure of the evidence; the co-conspirator must show that her own expectation of privacy was violated. [United States v. Padilla, 508 U.S. 77 (1993)]

b.   **Things Held Out to the Public**

1) **Generally—No Expectation of Privacy**
   A person does not have a reasonable expectation of privacy in objects held out to the public, such as the sound of one's voice [United States v. Dionisio, *supra*, B.5.]; one's handwriting [United States v. Mara, *supra*, B.5.]; paint on the outside of a car [Cardwell v. Lewis, 417 U.S. 583 (1974)]; the smell of one's luggage (*e.g.*, drug sniffs by narcotics dogs) [United States v. Place, 462 U.S. 696 (1983)]; account records held by the bank [United States v. Miller, 425 U.S. 435 (1976)]; an automobile's movement on public roads and arrival at a private residence, even if detection of such movement requires the use of an electronic beeper placed on the automobile by the police [United States v. Knotts, 460 U.S. 276 (1983)]; or magazines offered for sale [Maryland v. Macon, 472 U.S. 463 (1985)].

- voice
- style of hand writing
- point outside of car
- account records held by bank
- monitoring location of car in public or driveway
- anything that can be see across the open field
- things that can be seen from flying over public air space
- odor emitting from luggage
- garbage left out on curb for collection

   a) **Compare—Feel of Luggage**
      Although the Supreme Court has held that one does not have a reasonable

expectation of privacy in the smell of one's luggage, one does have a reasonable expectation of privacy in luggage against physically invasive inspections. Squeezing luggage to discern its contents constitutes a search. [Bond v. United States, 529 U.S. 334 (2000)]

Example: After completing an immigration status check of passengers on a bus, Officer began walking toward the front of the bus and squeezing soft-sided luggage in the overhead compartment. Upon feeling what felt like a brick in Defendant's bag, Officer searched the bag and found a "brick" of methamphetamine. The Court held that while travelers might expect their luggage to be lightly touched or moved from time-to-time, they do not expect their luggage to be subjected to an exploratory squeeze. Therefore, Officer's conduct constitutes a search under the Fourth Amendment. [Bond v. United States, *supra*]

2) "Open Fields" Doctrine

Furthermore, under the "open fields" doctrine, areas outside the "curtilage" (dwelling house and outbuildings) are subject to police entry and search—these areas are "held out to the public" and are unprotected by the Fourth Amendment. (The court will consider the building's proximity to the dwelling, whether it is within the same enclosure—such as a fence—that surrounds the house, whether the building is used for activities of the home, and the steps taken by the resident to protect the building from the view of passersby.) [Oliver v. United States, 466 U.S. 170 (1984)] Even a building such as a barn may be considered to be outside the curtilage and therefore outside the protection of the Fourth Amendment. [United States v. Dunn, 480 U.S. 294 (1987)] In addition, the Fourth Amendment does not prohibit the warrantless search and seizure of garbage left for collection outside the curtilage of a home. [California v. Greenwood, 486 U.S. 35 (1988)]

3) Fly-Overs

The police may, within the Fourth Amendment, fly over a field to observe with the naked eye things therein. [California v. Ciraolo, 476 U.S. 207 (1986)] Even a low (400 feet) fly-over by a helicopter to view inside a partially covered greenhouse is permissible. [Florida v. Riley, 488 U.S. 445 (1989)—plurality decision based on flight being permissible under FAA regulations] The police may also take aerial photographs of a particular site. [Dow Chemical Co. v. United States, 476 U.S. 227 (1986)]

a) Compare—Technologically Enhanced Searches of Homes

The Supreme Court has held that because of the strong expectation of privacy within one's home, obtaining by sense enhancing technology any information regarding the interior of a home that could not otherwise have been obtained without physical intrusion constitutes a search, at least where the technology in question is not in general public use. [Kyllo v. United States, 533 U.S. 27 (2001)—use of thermal imager on defendant's home from outside the curtilage to detect the presence of high intensity lamps commonly used to grow marijuana constitutes a search]

4) Vehicle Identification Numbers

A police officer may constitutionally reach into an automobile to move papers to observe the auto's vehicle identification number. [New York v. Class, 475 U.S. 106 (1986)]

4. Searches Conducted Pursuant to a Warrant

To be reasonable under the Fourth Amendment, most searches must be pursuant to a warrant. The warrant requirement serves as a check against unfettered police discretion by requiring police to apply to a neutral magistrate for permission to conduct a search. A search conducted without a warrant will be invalid (and evidence discovered during the search must be excluded from evidence) unless it is within one of the six categories of permissible warrantless searches (*see* 5., *infra*).

a. Requirements of a Warrant

To be valid, a warrant must:

1) Be issued by a *neutral and detached magistrate*;

2) Be *based on probable cause* established from facts submitted to the magistrate by a government agent upon oath or affirmation; and

3) *Particularly describe* the place to be searched and the items to be seized.

b. Showing of Probable Cause
A warrant will be issued only if there is probable cause to believe that seizable evidence will be found on the premises or person to be searched. [Carroll v. United States, 267 U.S. 132 (1925)] The officers requesting the warrant must submit to the magistrate an affidavit containing sufficient facts and circumstances to enable the magistrate to make an independent evaluation of probable cause (*i.e.,* the officers cannot merely present their conclusion that probable cause exists). [United States v. Ventresca, 380 U.S. 102 (1965)]

1) Use of Informers—Totality of Circumstances Test
If the officers' affidavit of probable cause is based on information obtained from informers, its sufficiency is determined by the *totality of the circumstances*. [Illinois v. Gates, 462 U.S. 213 (1983)] The affidavit need not contain any particular fact about the informer, as long as it includes enough information to allow the magistrate to make a common sense evaluation of probable cause (*i.e.,* that the information is trustworthy).

a) Reliability, Credibility, and Basis of Knowledge
Formerly, the affidavit had to include information regarding the reliability and credibility of the informer (*e.g.,* she has given information five times in the past and it has been accurate) and her basis for the knowledge (*e.g.,* she purchased cocaine from the house to be searched). These are still relevant factors, but are no longer prerequisites.

b) Informer's Identity
Generally, the informer's identity need *not* be revealed to obtain a search warrant [McCray v. Illinois, 386 U.S. 300 (1967)] (although if the informer is a material witness to the crime, her identity may have to be revealed at or before trial).

c) Going "Behind the Face" of the Affidavit
When a defendant attacks the validity of a search warrant, the Fourth Amendment permits her to contest the validity of some of the assertions in the affidavit upon which the warrant was issued. The defendant may go "behind the face" of the affidavit.

(1) Three Requirements to Invalidate Search Warrant
A search warrant issued on the basis of an affidavit that, on its face, is sufficient to establish probable cause will be invalid if the defendant establishes *all three* of the following:

(i) A *false statement* was included in the affidavit by the affiant (*i.e.,* the police officer applying for the warrant);

(ii) The affiant *intentionally or recklessly* included that false statement (*i.e.,* the officer either knew it was false or included it knowing that there was a substantial risk that it was false); and

(iii) The false statement was *material* to the finding of probable cause (*i.e.,* without the false statement, the remainder of the affidavit could not support a finding of probable cause). Thus, the mere fact that an affiant intentionally included a false statement in the affidavit apparently will not automatically render the warrant invalid under Fourth Amendment standards.

[Franks v. Delaware, 438 U.S. 154 (1978)]

(2) Evidence May Be Admissible Even Though Warrant Not Supported by Probable Cause
A finding that the warrant was invalid because it was not supported by probable cause will not entitle a defendant to exclude the evidence

obtained under the warrant. Evidence obtained by police in **reasonable reliance** on a facially valid warrant may be used by the prosecution, despite an ultimate finding that the warrant was not supported by probable cause. [United States v. Leon, 468 U.S. 897 (1984); *and see* Massachusetts v. Sheppard, 468 U.S. 981 (1984)—technical defect in warrant insufficient basis for overturning murder conviction]

c. **Warrant Must Be Precise on Its Face**
The warrant must describe with reasonable precision the place to be searched and the items to be seized. This requirement will be strictly enforced where the warrant authorizes the seizure of books and similar items potentially protected by the First Amendment. [Stanford v. Texas, 379 U.S. 476 (1965)]

Examples: 1) A warrant authorizes the search of premises at 416 Oak Street for heroin. The structure at 416 Oak Street is a duplex. Is the warrant sufficiently precise? No. In a multi-unit dwelling, the warrant must specify which unit is to be searched. *But note:* If police reasonably believe there is only one apartment on the floor of a building, the warrant is not invalid if they discover, during the course of their search, that there are in fact two apartments on the floor. Indeed, any evidence police seize from the wrong apartment prior to the discovery of the error will be admissible. [Maryland v. Garrison, 480 U.S. 79 (1987)]

2) A was believed to have committed criminal fraud in regard to certain complex land transactions. A search warrant was issued authorizing the search for and seizure of numerous described documents and "other fruit, instrumentalities and evidence of the crime at this time unknown." Was the warrant sufficiently precise? Yes, given the complex nature of the crime and the difficulty of predicting precisely what form evidence of guilt would take. [Andresen v. Maryland, 427 U.S. 463 (1976)]

d. **Search of Third-Party Premises Permissible**
The Fourth Amendment does not bar searches of premises belonging to persons not suspected of crime, as long as there is **probable cause** to believe evidence of someone's guilt (or something else subject to seizure) will be found. Thus, a warrant can issue for the search of the offices of a newspaper if there is probable cause to believe evidence of someone's guilt of an offense will be found. [Zurcher v. Stanford Daily, 436 U.S. 547 (1978)]

e. **Neutral and Detached Magistrate Requirement**
The magistrate who issues the warrant must be neutral and detached from the often competitive business of law enforcement.

Examples: 1) The state attorney general is not neutral and detached. [Coolidge v. New Hampshire, 403 U.S. 443 (1971)]

2) A clerk of court may issue warrants for violations of city ordinances. [Shadwick v. City of Tampa, 407 U.S. 345 (1972)]

3) A magistrate who receives no salary other than compensation for each warrant issued is not neutral and detached. [Connally v. Georgia, 429 U.S. 245 (1977)]

4) A magistrate who participates in the search to determine its scope is not neutral and detached. [Lo-Ji Sales, Inc. v. New York, 442 U.S. 319 (1979)]

f. **Execution of a Warrant**

1) **Must Be Executed by the Police**
Only the police (and not private citizens) may execute a warrant. Moreover, when executing a warrant **in a home**, the police may not be accompanied by a member of the media or any other third party unless the third party is there to aid in executing the warrant (*e.g.*, to identify stolen property that might be found in the home). [Wilson v. Layne, 526 U.S. 603 (1999)—unreasonable to allow newspaper reporter and photographer to accompany police during execution of an arrest warrant in plaintiff's home] *Rationale:* To be reasonable, police action pursuant to a warrant must be related to the objectives of the warrant. The presence of reporters or other third parties not aiding in the execution of the warrant renders the

search unreasonable. Note that while the First Amendment prohibition against abridging freedom of the press is an important right, it does not supersede the very important Fourth Amendment right of persons to be free of unreasonable searches.

2) Execution Without Unreasonable Delay
The warrant should be executed without unreasonable delay because probable cause may disappear.

3) Announcement Requirement
Generally, an officer executing a search warrant must knock and announce her authority and purpose and be refused admittance before using force to enter the place to be searched. However, no announcement need be made if the officer has reasonable suspicion, based on facts, that knocking and announcing would be *dangerous or futile* or that it would *inhibit the investigation*, e.g., because it would lead to the destruction of evidence. [Richards v. Wisconsin, 520 U.S. 385 (1997)] Whether a "no knock" entry is justified must be made on a case-by-case basis; a blanket exception for warrants involving drug investigations is impermissible. [Richards v. Wisconsin, *supra*] *Note:* The fact that property damage will result from a no knock entry does not require a different standard—reasonable suspicion is sufficient. [United States v. Ramirez, 523 U.S. 65 (1998)]

4) Seizure of Unspecified Property
When executing a warrant, the police generally may seize any contraband or fruits or instrumentalities of crime that they discover, whether or not specified in the warrant.

5) Search of Persons Found on the Premises
A search warrant does not authorize the police to search persons found on the premises who are not named in the warrant. [Ybarra v. Illinois, 444 U.S. 85 (1979)] If the police have probable cause to arrest a person discovered on the premises to be searched, however, they may search her *incident to the arrest*.

6) Detention of the Occupants
A warrant to search for contraband founded on probable cause implicitly carries with it the limited authority to detain occupants of the premises while a proper search is conducted. [Michigan v. Summers, *supra*, B.3.d.]

5. Exceptions to Warrant Requirement
There are *six exceptions* to the warrant requirement; *i.e.,* six circumstances where a warrantless search is reasonable and therefore is valid under the Fourth Amendment. To be valid, a warrantless search must meet all the requirements of at least one exception.

a. Search Incident to a Lawful Arrest
The police may conduct a warrantless search incident to a lawful arrest.

1) Lawful Arrest Requirement
If an arrest is unlawful, then any search incident to that arrest is also unlawful.

2) Any Arrest Sufficient
The police may conduct a search incident to arrest whenever they arrest a person. Although the rationale for the search is to protect the arresting officer and to preserve evidence, the police need not actually fear for their safety or believe that they will find evidence of a crime as long as the suspect is placed under arrest. [United States v. Robinson, 414 U.S. 218 (1973)]

a) Issuance of Traffic Citation—Insufficient Basis
For traffic violations, if the suspect is not arrested, there can be no search incident to arrest, even if state law gives the officer the option of arresting a suspect or issuing a citation. [Knowles v. Iowa, 525 U.S. 113 (1999)—a nonconsensual automobile search conducted after the suspect was issued a citation for driving 43 m.p.h. in a 25 m.p.h. zone was illegal, and contraband found during the search was excluded from evidence] *Rationale:* When a citation is issued, there is less of a threat to the officer's safety than there is during an arrest, and the only evidence that needs to be preserved in such a case (*e.g.,* evidence of the suspect's speeding or other illegal conduct) has already been found.

3) **Geographic Scope**

Incident to a lawful arrest, the police may search the person and areas into which he might reach to obtain weapons or destroy evidence (his *"wingspan"*). [Chimel v. California, 395 U.S. 752 (1969)] The arrestee's wingspan follows him as he moves. Thus, if the arrestee is allowed to enter his home, police may follow and search areas within the arrestee's wingspan in the home. [Washington v. Chrisman, 455 U.S. 1 (1982)] The police may also make a *protective sweep* of the area beyond the defendant's wingspan if they believe accomplices may be present. [Maryland v. Buie, 494 U.S. 325 (1990)]

a) **Automobiles**

A police officer may conduct a warrantless search of the *passenger compartment* of an automobile (including containers) after arresting the occupants. The entire passenger compartment is within the arrestee's "wingspan," but not the trunk. [New York v. Belton, 453 U.S. 454 (1981)]

4) **Contemporaneousness Requirement**

A search incident to an arrest must be contemporaneous in time and place with the arrest. [Preston v. United States, 376 U.S. 364 (1964); United States v. Chadwick, 433 U.S. 1 (1977)]

5) **Search Incident to Incarceration**

The police may search an arrestee's personal belongings before incarcerating him after a valid arrest. [Illinois v. Lafayette, 459 U.S. 986 (1983)] Similarly, the police may search an entire vehicle—including closed containers within the vehicle—that has been impounded. [Colorado v. Bertine, 479 U.S. 367 (1987)]

b. **"Automobile" Exception** *[handwritten: if has probable cause → can search entire car / any place the probable item may be in/at]*

If the police have probable cause to believe that a vehicle such as an automobile contains contraband or fruits, instrumentalities, or evidence of a crime, they may search the vehicle without a warrant. [Carroll v. United States, 267 U.S. 132 (1925)] *Rationale:* Automobiles and similar vehicles are mobile and so will not likely be available for search by the time an officer returns with a warrant. Moreover, the Supreme Court has declared that people have a lesser expectation of privacy in their vehicles than in their homes.

Note: Similarly, if the police have probable cause to believe that the car itself is contraband, it may be seized from a public place without a warrant. [Florida v. White, 526 U.S. 559 (1999)]

[handwritten: probable cause can arise after vehicle is stop & before anything/body is searched]

Example: On three occasions, the police observed Defendant selling cocaine from his car, giving the police probable cause to believe that Defendant's car was used to transport cocaine. Under state law, a car used to transport cocaine is considered to be contraband subject to forfeiture. Several months later, the police arrested Defendant on unrelated drug charges while he was at work and seized his car from the parking lot without a warrant based on their prior observations. While inventorying the contents of the car, the police found cocaine and brought the present drug charges against Defendant. The cocaine was admissible into evidence. Even though the police did not have probable cause to believe that the car contained cocaine when it was seized, they did have probable cause to believe that it was contraband and therefore seizable, and inventory searches of seized items are proper (*see* 6.b., *infra*). [Florida v. White, *supra*]

1) **Scope of Search**

If the police have full probable cause to search a vehicle, they can search the *entire vehicle* (including the trunk) and all containers within the vehicle that *might contain the object* for which they are searching. [United States v. Ross, 456 U.S. 798 (1982)] Thus, if the police have probable cause to believe that drugs are within the vehicle, they can search almost any container, but if they have probable cause to believe that an illegal alien is hiding inside the vehicle, they must limit their search to areas where a person could hide.

a) **Passenger's Belongings**

The search is not limited to the driver's belongings and may extend to packages belonging to a passenger. [Wyoming v. Houghten, 526 U.S. 295 (1999)—

search of passenger's purse upheld where officer noticed driver had syringe in his pocket] *Rationale:* Like a driver, a passenger has a reduced expectation of privacy in a car.

b) Limited Probable Cause—Containers Placed in Vehicle
If the police only have probable cause to search a container (recently) placed in a vehicle, they may search that container, but the search may not extend to other parts of the car. [California v. Acevedo, 500 U.S. 565 (1991)]

Example: Assume police have probable cause to believe that a briefcase that D is carrying contains illegal drugs. Unless they arrest D, they may not make a warrantless search of the briefcase because no exception to the warrant requirement applies. They follow D, and he places the briefcase in a car. They may then approach D and search the briefcase even though they could not search it before it was placed in the car. They may not search the rest of the car, however, because D has not had an opportunity to move the drugs elsewhere in the car. Presumably, if some time passes and D has an opportunity to move the drugs, the police will have probable cause to search the entire car.

2) Motor Homes
The automobile exception extends to any vehicle that has the attributes of mobility and a lesser expectation of privacy similar to a car. For example, the Supreme Court has held that it extends to motor homes if they are not at a fixed site. [California v. Carney, 471 U.S. 386 (1985)]

3) Contemporaneousness Not Required
If the police are justified in making a warrantless search of a vehicle under this exception at the time of stopping, they may tow the vehicle to the station and search it later. [Chambers v. Maroney, 399 U.S. 42 (1970)]

Example: A vehicle search, based on probable cause, conducted three days after the vehicle was impounded is permissible. [United States v. Johns, 469 U.S. 478 (1985)]

c. Plain View
The police may make a warrantless seizure when they:

(i) Are *legitimately* present *on the premises*;

(ii) Discover *evidence, fruits or instrumentalities* of crime, or *contraband*;

(iii) See such evidence *in plain view*; and

(iv) *Have probable cause* to believe (*i.e.,* it must be immediately apparent) that the item *is* evidence, contraband, or a fruit or instrumentality of crime.

[Coolidge v. New Hampshire, *supra,* 4.e.; Arizona v. Hicks, 480 U.S. 321 (1987)]

Examples: 1) Police may seize *unspecified property* while executing a search warrant.

2) Police may seize from a lawfully stopped automobile an opaque balloon that, based on knowledge and experience, the police have probable cause to believe contains narcotics, even though the connection with the contraband would not be obvious to the average person. [Texas v. Brown, 460 U.S. 730 (1983)]

Compare: While investigating a shooting in an apartment, Officer spotted two sets of expensive stereo equipment which he had reasonable suspicion (but not probable cause) to believe were stolen. Officer moved some of the components to check their serial numbers. Such movement constituted an invalid search because of the lack of probable cause. [Arizona v. Hicks, *supra*]

1) Inadvertence Not Required
Formerly, the plain view exception applied only if the evidence was inadvertently

discovered, but inadvertence is no longer a requirement. [Horton v. California, 496 U.S. 128 (1990)]

Example: Police have probable cause to believe that the weapons and proceeds from an armed robbery are at D's home. If they obtain a warrant only to search for the proceeds, they still may seize the weapons if they are found in plain view during the search.

d. Consent *saying that they have a warrant negates consent*

The police may conduct a valid warrantless search if they have a ***voluntary and intelligent*** consent to do so. Knowledge of the right to withhold consent, while a factor to be considered, is not a prerequisite to establishing a voluntary and intelligent consent. [Schneckloth v. Bustamonte, 412 U.S. 218 (1973)]

fact specific

police do not have to warn that person has right not to give consent

Example: After Deputy stopped Defendant for speeding, gave him a verbal warning, and returned his license, Deputy asked Defendant if he was carrying any drugs in the car. Defendant answered "no" and consented to a search of his car, which uncovered drugs. Defendant argued that his consent was invalid because he had not been told that he was free to go after his license was returned. The Supreme Court, applying the principles of *Schneckloth*, found that no such warning was necessary. Voluntariness is to be determined from all of the circumstances, and knowledge of the right to refuse consent is just one factor to be considered in determining voluntariness. [Ohio v. Robinette, 519 U.S. 33 (1996)]

Note: An officer's false announcement that she has a warrant negates the possibility of consent. [Bumper v. North Carolina, 391 U.S. 543 (1968)]

1) Authority to Consent

Any person with an ***apparent equal right to use or occupy*** the property may consent to a search, and any evidence found may be used against the other owners or occupants. [Frazier v. Cupp, 394 U.S. 731 (1969); United States v. Matlock, 415 U.S. 164 (1973)] The search is valid even if it turns out that the person consenting to the search did not actually have such right, as long as the police reasonably believed that the person had authority to consent. [Illinois v. Rodriguez, 497 U.S. 177 (1990)]

2) Scope of Search

The scope of the search is limited by the ***scope of the consent***. However, consent extends to all areas to which a reasonable person under the circumstances would believe it extends.

Example: Police stopped D for a traffic violation, told him that they suspected him of carrying drugs, and asked for permission to search the car. D consented. The officers found a bag containing cocaine. At trial, D argued that his consent did not extend to any closed container (the bag). The Supreme Court held that since D knew the police were searching for drugs and did not place any restriction on his consent, it was reasonable for the police to believe that the consent extended to all areas where drugs might be found. [Florida v. Jimeno, 500 U.S. 248 (1991)]

e. Stop and Frisk

1) Standards

less than probable cause

As noted above (*see* B.3.a., *supra*), a police officer may ***stop*** a person without probable cause for arrest if she has an articulable and ***reasonable suspicion*** of criminal activity. In such circumstances, if the officer also ***reasonably believes*** that the person may be ***armed and presently dangerous***, she may conduct a protective ***frisk***. [Terry v. Ohio, 392 U.S. 1 (1968); United States v. Cortez, 449 U.S. 411 (1981)]

weapon are always admissable so long as the stop was reasonable

2) Scope of the Intrusion

a) Patdown of Outer Clothing

The scope of the frisk is generally limited to a patdown of the outer clothing for concealed instruments of assault. [Terry v. Ohio, *supra*] However, an

[handwritten margin note: evi of crim but not weapons ☑]

[handwritten margin note: how much like a weapon or contraband from the outside looking]

officer may reach directly into an area of the suspect's clothing, such as his belt, without a preliminary frisk, when she has specific information that a weapon is hidden there, even if the information comes from an informant's tip lacking sufficient reliability to support a warrant. [Adams v. Williams, 407 U.S. 143 (1972)]

b) Passenger Compartment of Automobile
The Supreme Court has expanded *Terry v. Ohio, supra,* to include the warrantless search of the passenger compartment of an automobile by police officers who have **detained** but **not arrested** the occupant, provided the search is **limited to those areas in which a weapon may be placed** or hidden and the officers possess a reasonable belief that the occupant is dangerous. [Michigan v. Long, 463 U.S. 1032 (1983)]

c) Time Limit
There is no rigid time limit for the length of an investigative stop. The Court will consider the purpose of the stop, the reasonableness of the time in effectuating the purpose, and the reasonableness of the means of investigation to determine whether a stop was too long. [United States v. Sharpe, 470 U.S. 675 (1985)]

3) Admissibility of Evidence
If a police officer conducts a patdown within the bounds of *Terry*, the officer may reach into the suspect's clothing and seize any item that the officer reasonably believes, based on its "**plain feel**," is a **weapon or contraband**. [Terry v. Ohio, *supra*; Minnesota v. Dickerson, 508 U.S. 366 (1993)—excluding from evidence cocaine that officer found during valid patdown because officer had to manipulate package to discern that it likely was drugs] Properly seized items are admissible as evidence against the suspect.

4) Ordering a Driver Out of the Car Permissible
Once a vehicle has been properly stopped for a traffic violation, a police officer may order the driver out of the automobile even without a suspicion of criminal activity. If the officer then reasonably believes that the driver may be armed and dangerous, she may conduct a frisk. [Pennsylvania v. Mimms, 434 U.S. 106 (1978)]

5) Stop and Identify Statutes
The Supreme Court has suggested, and state courts have held, that the failure to identify oneself when stopped and asked for identification by a police officer does not create probable cause for arrest. [Brown v. Texas, 443 U.S. 47 (1979); Michigan v. DeFillippo, *supra,* II.B.5.]

f. Hot Pursuit, Evanescent Evidence, and Other Emergencies

[handwritten note: for evi that might go away if we take time to get warrant. ex: scraping of fingernail]

1) No General Emergency Exception
The Supreme Court has made clear that there is no general "emergency" exception, as the need to check occupational safety violations [Marshall v. Barlow's, Inc., 436 U.S. 307 (1978)], the need to investigate a fire after it has been extinguished and its cause determined [Michigan v. Tyler, 436 U.S. 499 (1978)], and the need to search a murder scene [Mincey v. Arizona, *supra,* II.B.6.a.] do not justify warrantless searches.

2) Hot Pursuit Exception
[handwritten note: 15 minutes behind is not hot pursuit]
Police officers in hot pursuit of a **fleeing felon** may make a warrantless search and seizure. The scope of the search may be as broad as may reasonably be necessary to prevent the suspect from resisting or escaping. [Warden v. Hayden, 387 U.S. 294 (1967)] When the police have probable cause and attempt to make a warrantless arrest in a "public place," they may pursue the suspect into private dwellings. [United States v. Santana, 427 U.S. 38 (1976)]

3) Evanescent Evidence Exception
The police may seize without a warrant evidence likely to disappear before a warrant can be obtained, such as a blood sample containing alcohol [Schmerber v. California, 384 U.S. 757 (1966)] or fingernail scrapings [Cupp v. Murphy, 412 U.S. 291 (1973)].

4)   Other Emergencies Where Warrant Not Required
Certain other emergencies, such as *contaminated food or drugs* [North American Cold Storage v. City of Chicago, 211 U.S. 306 (1908)], *children in trouble* [State v. Hunt, 406 P.2d 208 (Ariz. 1965)], and *burning fires* [Michigan v. Tyler, *supra*] may justify warrantless searches and seizures.

6.   Administrative Inspections and Searches

a.   Warrant Required for Searches of Private Residences and Businesses
Inspectors must have a warrant for searches of private residences and commercial buildings. [Camara v. Municipal Court, 387 U.S. 523 (1967); Michigan v. Clifford, 464 U.S. 287 (1984)—warrantless administrative search of fire-damaged residence by officials seeking to determine origin of fire violated owners' Fourth Amendment rights; owners retained reasonable expectation of privacy in the damaged structure, and the warrantless search was unconstitutional] However, the same standard of probable cause as is required for other searches is not required for a valid administrative inspection warrant. A showing of a general and *neutral enforcement plan* will justify issuance of the warrant, which is designed to guard against selective enforcement. [Marshall v. Barlow's, Inc., *supra*]

1)   Exceptions Permitting Warrantless Searches

a)   Contaminated Food
A warrant is not required for the seizure of spoiled or contaminated food. [North American Cold Storage v. City of Chicago, *supra*]

b)   Highly Regulated Industries
A warrant is not required for searches of businesses in highly regulated industries, because of the urgent public interest and the theory that the business has impliedly consented to warrantless searches by entering into a highly regulated industry. Such industries include liquor [Colonnade Catering Corp. v. United States, 397 U.S. 72 (1970)], guns [United States v. Biswell, 406 U.S. 311 (1972)], strip mining [Donovan v. Dewey, 452 U.S. 594 (1981)], and automobile junkyards [New York v. Burger, 479 U.S. 812 (1987)], but not car leasing [G.M. Leasing Corp. v. United States, 429 U.S. 338 (1977)] or general manufacturing [Marshall v. Barlow's, Inc., *supra*].

b.   Inventory Searches
The police may search an arrestee's personal belongings in order to inventory them before incarcerating the arrestee. [Illinois v. Lafayette, *supra*, 5.a.5)] Similarly, the police may search an entire vehicle—including closed containers within the vehicle—that has been impounded. [Colorado v. Bertine, *supra*, 5.a.5)]

c.   Search of Airline Passengers
Courts have generally upheld searches of airline passengers prior to boarding. This seems to be regarded as somewhat akin to a consent or administrative search. One court, however, has held that a passenger must be permitted to avoid such a search by agreeing not to board the aircraft.

d.   Public School Searches
A warrant or probable cause is not required for searches conducted by public school officials; only *reasonable grounds* for the search are necessary. This exception is justified due to the nature of the school environment. [New Jersey v. T.L.O., 469 U.S. 325 (1985)] The Court has also upheld a school district rule that required students participating in *any extracurricular activity* to submit to random urinalysis drug testing monitored by an adult of the same sex. [School Board v. Earls, 122 S. Ct. 2559 (2002)]

e.   Probationers' Homes
The Fourth Amendment is not violated by a statute authorizing warrantless searches of a probationer's home when there are reasonable grounds to believe contraband is present. Probation systems present "special needs" that justify departures from the usual Fourth Amendment warrant requirement. [Griffin v. Wisconsin, 479 U.S. 1053 (1987)]

f. Government Employees' Desks and Files

A warrantless search of a government employee's desk and file cabinets is permissible under the Fourth Amendment if it is reasonable in scope and if it is justified at its inception by a noninvestigatory, work-related need or a reasonable suspicion of work-related misconduct. [O'Connor v. Ortega, 480 U.S. 709 (1987)]

g. Drug Testing

Although government-required drug testing constitutes a search, the Supreme Court has upheld such testing without a warrant, probable cause, or even individualized suspicion when justified by *"special needs"* beyond the general interest of law enforcement.

Examples:　　1) The government can require railroad employees who are involved in accidents to be tested for drugs after the accidents. [Skinner v. Railway Labor Executives' Association, 489 U.S. 602 (1989)]

2) The government can require persons seeking Customs positions connected to drug interdiction to be tested for drugs. There is a special need for such testing because persons so employed will have ready access to large quantities of drugs. [National Treasury Employees Union v. Von Raab, 489 U.S. 656 (1989)]

3) The government can require public school students who participate in *any extracurricular activities* to submit to random drug tests because of the special interest schools have in the safety of their students. [School Board v. Earls, *supra*]

Compare:　　1) Special needs do not justify a warrantless and nonconsensual urinalysis test to determine whether a pregnant woman has been using cocaine, where the main purpose of the testing is to generate evidence that may be used by law enforcement personnel to coerce women into drug programs. [Ferguson v. Charleston, 532 U.S. 67 (2001)]

2) The government may not require candidates for state offices to certify that they have taken a drug test within 30 days prior to qualifying for nomination or election—there is no special need for such testing. [Chandler v. Miller, 520 U.S. 305 (1997)]

7. Searches in Foreign Countries and at the Border

a. Searches in Foreign Countries

The Fourth Amendment does *not* apply to searches and seizures by United States officials in foreign countries and involving an alien, at least where the alien does not have a substantial connection to the United States. Thus, for example, the Fourth Amendment was held not to bar the use of evidence obtained in a warrantless search of an alien's home in Mexico. [United States v. Verdugo-Urquidez, 494 U.S. 259 (1990)]

b. Searches at the Border or Its Functional Equivalent

Neither citizens nor noncitizens have any Fourth Amendment rights at the border or its functional equivalent as part of the concept of national sovereignty. A functional equivalent of the border might be a point near the border where several routes all leading to the border merge.

c. Roving Patrols

1) Stops

Roving patrols inside the United States border may stop an automobile for questioning of the occupants if the officer *reasonably suspects* that the automobile may contain illegal aliens, but the apparent Mexican ancestry of the occupants alone cannot create a reasonable suspicion. [United States v. Brignoni-Ponce, 422 U.S. 873 (1975)]

2) Searches

A roving patrol inside the border may not conduct a warrantless search unless the requirements of one of the *exceptions* to the warrant requirement, such as the "automobile" exception (probable cause) or consent, are met. [Almeida-Sanchez v. United States, 413 U.S. 266 (1973)]

d. **Fixed Checkpoints**
Border officials may stop an automobile at a fixed checkpoint inside the border for questioning of the occupants even *without a reasonable suspicion* that the automobile contains illegal aliens, but they must have probable cause or consent for a search. [United States v. Martinez-Fuerte, *supra*, B.3.b.]

e. **Opening International Mail**
Permissible border searches include the opening of international mail, which postal regulations authorize when postal authorities have *reasonable cause* to suspect that the mail contains *contraband*, although the regulations prohibit the authorities from reading any correspondence inside. [United States v. Ramsey, 431 U.S. 606 (1977)]

   1) **Reopening**
   Once customs agents lawfully open a container and identify its contents as illegal, their *subsequent reopening* of the container after it has been resealed and delivered to defendant is not a search within the meaning of the Fourth Amendment, unless there is a substantial likelihood that the container's contents have been changed during any gap in surveillance. [Illinois v. Andreas, 463 U.S. 765 (1983)]

f. **I.N.S. Enforcement Actions**
The I.N.S. may do a "factory survey" of the entire work force in a factory, to determine citizenship of each employee, without raising Fourth Amendment issues. The "factory survey" is not "detention" or a "seizure" under the Fourth Amendment. [Immigration & Naturalization Service v. Delgado, 466 U.S. 210 (1984)] Furthermore, evidence illegally obtained, in violation of the Fourth Amendment, may be used in a civil deportation hearing. [Immigration & Naturalization Service v. Lopez-Mendoza, 468 U.S. 1032 (1984)]

g. **Detentions**
If the officials have a "reasonable suspicion" that a traveler is smuggling contraband in her stomach, they may detain her for a time reasonable under the circumstances. *Rationale:* Stopping such smuggling is important, yet very difficult; stomach smuggling gives no external signs that would enable officials to meet a "probable cause" standard in order to conduct a search. [United States v. Montoya de Hernandez, 473 U.S. 531 (1985)— 16-hour detention upheld until traveler, who refused an X-ray, had a bowel movement]

8. **Wiretapping and Eavesdropping** require warrant

   a. **Fourth Amendment Requirements**
   Wiretapping and any other form of electronic surveillance that violates a reasonable expectation of privacy constitute a search under the Fourth Amendment. [Katz v. United States, 389 U.S. 347 (1967)] In *Berger v. New York*, 388 U.S. 41 (1967), the Supreme Court indicated that for a valid *warrant* authorizing a wiretap to be issued, the following *requirements* must be met:

      1) A showing of *probable cause* to believe that a *specific crime* has been or is being committed must be made;

      2) The *suspected persons* whose conversations are to be overheard must be *named*;

      3) The warrant must *describe with particularity* the conversations that can be overheard;

      4) The wiretap must be limited to a *short period of time* (although extensions may be obtained upon an adequate showing);

      5) *Provisions* must be made for the *termination* of the wiretap when the desired information has been obtained; and

      6) A *return* must be made to the court, showing what conversations have been intercepted.

   b. **Exceptions**

      1) **"Unreliable Ear"**
      A speaker assumes the risk that the person to whom she is talking is unreliable. If

the person turns out to be an informer wired for sound or taping the conversation, the speaker has no basis in the Fourth Amendment to object to the transmitting or recording of the conversation as a warrantless search. [United States v. White, 401 U.S. 745 (1971)]

2) "Uninvited Ear"
A speaker has no Fourth Amendment claim if she makes no attempt to keep the conversation private. [Katz v. United States, *supra*]

c. Judicial Approval Required for Domestic Security Surveillance
A neutral and detached magistrate must make the determination that a warrant should issue authorizing electronic surveillance, including internal security surveillance of domestic organizations. The President may not authorize such surveillance without prior judicial approval. [United States v. United States District Court, 407 U.S. 297 (1972)]

d. Federal Statute
Title III of the Omnibus Crime Control and Safe Streets Act regulates interception of private "wire, oral or electronic communications." [18 U.S.C. §§2510-2520] All electronic communication surveillance (*e.g.,* phone taps, bugs, etc.) must comply with the requirements of this federal statute, which exhibits a legislative decision to require more than the constitutional minimum in this especially sensitive area.

e. Pen Registers
A pen register records only the numbers dialed from a certain phone. The Fourth Amendment does not require prior judicial approval for installation and use of pen registers. [Smith v. Maryland, 442 U.S. 735 (1979)] Neither does Title III govern pen registers, since Title III applies only when the *contents* of electronic communications are intercepted. However, by statute [18 U.S.C. §§3121 *et seq.*], police must obtain a court order finding pen register information to be relevant to an ongoing criminal investigation before utilizing a pen register. Note, however, that information obtained in violation of the statute would not necessarily be excluded from evidence in a criminal trial; the statute merely provides a criminal penalty.

f. Covert Entry to Install a Bug Permissible
Law enforcement officers do not need prior express judicial authorization for a covert entry to install equipment for electronic surveillance, which has been approved in compliance with Title III. [Dalia v. United States, 441 U.S. 238 (1979)]

D. METHODS OF OBTAINING EVIDENCE THAT SHOCK THE CONSCIENCE
Due process of law requires that state criminal prosecutions be conducted in a manner that does not offend the "sense of justice" inherent in due process. Evidence obtained in a manner offending that sense is *inadmissible*, even if it does not run afoul of one of the specific prohibitions against particular types of misconduct.

1. Searches of the Body
Intrusions into the human body implicate a person's most deep-rooted expectations of privacy. Thus, Fourth Amendment requirements apply. Ultimately, the "reasonableness" of searches into the body depends on weighing society's need for the evidence against the magnitude of the intrusion on the individual (including the threat to health, safety, and dignitary interests). [Winston v. Lee, 470 U.S. 753 (1985)]

a. Blood Tests
Taking a blood sample (*e.g.,* from a person suspected of drunk driving) by commonplace medical procedures "involves virtually no risk, trauma, or pain" and is thus a *reasonable* intrusion. [Schmerber v. California, *supra,* C.5.f.3)]

b. Compare—Surgery
But a surgical procedure under a general anesthetic (to remove a bullet needed as evidence) involves significant risks to health and a severe intrusion on privacy, and thus is *unreasonable*—at least when there is substantial other evidence. [Winston v. Lee, *supra*]

2. Shocking Inducement
If a crime is induced by official actions that themselves shock the conscience, any conviction therefrom offends due process.

Example: D appears before a state legislative commission. Members of the commission clearly indicate that the privilege against self-incrimination is available to D, although in fact D could be convicted for failure to answer. Can D's conviction for refusal to answer be upheld? No, because the crime was induced by methods that shock the conscience. [Raley v. Ohio, 360 U.S. 423 (1959)]

IV. CONFESSIONS

A. INTRODUCTION

The admissibility of a defendant's confession or incriminating admission involves analysis under the Fourth, Fifth, Sixth, and Fourteenth Amendments. We have already discussed Fourth Amendment search and seizure limitations. The Fifth Amendment gives defendants rights against testimonial self-incrimination. The Sixth Amendment gives defendants rights regarding the assistance of counsel. The Fourteenth Amendment protects against involuntary confessions.

B. FOURTEENTH AMENDMENT—VOLUNTARINESS

For confessions to be admissible, the Due Process Clause of the Fourteenth Amendment requires that they be voluntary. Voluntariness is assessed by looking at the totality of the circumstances, including the suspect's age, education, and mental and physical condition, along with the setting, duration, and manner of police interrogation. [Spano v. New York, 360 U.S. 315 (1959)]

Examples: 1) A confession will be involuntary where it was obtained by physically beating the defendant. [Brown v. Mississippi, 297 U.S. 278 (1936)]

2) D was being held for questioning. O, a young officer who was a friend of D, told D that if he did not obtain a confession, he would lose his job, which would be disastrous to his wife and children. D confessed, but the Court found the confession involuntary. [Leyra v. Denno, 347 U.S. 556 (1954)]

1. Must Be Official Compulsion

Only official compulsion will render a confession involuntary for purposes of the Fourteenth Amendment. A confession is not involuntary merely because it is the product of mental disease that prevents the confession from being of the defendant's free will. [Colorado v. Connelly, 479 U.S. 157 (1986)]

2. Harmless Error Test Applies

A conviction will not necessarily be overturned if an involuntary confession was erroneously admitted into evidence. The harmless error test applies, and the conviction will not be overturned if the government can show that there was other overwhelming evidence of guilt. [Arizona v. Fulminante, 499 U.S. 279 (1991)]

3. Can "Appeal" to Jury

A finding of voluntariness by the trial court does not preclude the defendant from introducing evidence to the jury of the circumstances of the confession in order to cast doubt on its credibility. [Crane v. Kentucky, 476 U.S. 683 (1986)]

C. SIXTH AMENDMENT RIGHT TO COUNSEL APPROACH

The Sixth Amendment provides that in all criminal prosecutions, the defendant has a right to the assistance of counsel. The right protects defendants from having to face a complicated legal system without competent help. It applies at all ***critical stages*** of a criminal prosecution (*see* VII.C.1., *infra*) and is violated when the police obtain a confession from a defendant without first obtaining a waiver of the defendant's right to have counsel present. Since *Miranda,* below, the Sixth Amendment right has been limited to cases where ***adversary judicial proceedings*** have begun (*e.g.,* formal charges have been filed). [Massiah v. United States, 377 U.S. 201 (1964)] Thus, the right does not apply in precharge custodial interrogations.

Examples: 1) The Sixth Amendment right to counsel is violated when an undisclosed, paid government informant is placed in the defendant's cell, after defendant has been indicted, and deliberately elicits statements from the defendant regarding the crime for which the defendant was indicted. [United States v. Henry, 447 U.S. 264 (1980)] However, it is not a violation merely to place an informant in a defendant's cell— the informant must take some action, beyond mere listening, designed deliberately to elicit incriminating remarks. [Kuhlman v. Wilson, 477 U.S. 436 (1986)]

2) The right to counsel is violated when police arrange to record conversations between an indicted defendant and his co-defendant. [Maine v. Moulton, 474 U.S. 159 (1985)]

1. Offense Specific

The Sixth Amendment right to counsel is "offense specific." Thus, if a defendant makes a Sixth Amendment request for counsel for one charge, he must make another request if he is subsequently charged with a separate, unrelated crime if he desires counsel for the second charge. Similarly, even though a defendant's Sixth Amendment right to counsel has attached regarding one charge, he may be questioned without counsel concerning an unrelated charge. [Illinois v. Perkins, 496 U.S. 292 (1990)]

Example: D was in jail on a battery charge. Because the police suspected D of an unrelated murder, they placed an undercover officer in D's cell. The officer elicited damaging confessions from D regarding the murder. The interrogation did not violate the Sixth Amendment since D had not been charged with the murder. [Illinois v. Perkins, *supra*] Neither did the interrogation violate D's Fifth Amendment right to counsel under *Miranda*. (*See* D.2.a., *infra*.)

a. Test for "Different Offenses"

The test for determining whether offenses are different under the Sixth Amendment is the *Blockburger* test (*see* XIII.C.1., *infra*). Under the test, two crimes are considered different offenses if each requires proof of an additional element that the other crime does not require. [Texas v. Cobb, 532 U.S. 162 (2001)]

[handwritten: favorite bar topic]

D. FIFTH AMENDMENT PRIVILEGE AGAINST COMPELLED SELF-INCRIMINA-TION—*MIRANDA*

The Fifth Amendment, applicable to the states through the Fourteenth Amendment, provides that no person "shall be compelled to be a witness against himself . . . ." This has been interpreted to mean that a person shall not be compelled to give self-incriminating testimony. The scope of what is considered to be "testimony" under the amendment will be discussed later (*see* XIV., *infra*). This section explains the applicability of the amendment to confessions.

1. The Warnings

In *Miranda v. Arizona*, 384 U.S. 436 (1966), the Fifth Amendment privilege against compelled self-incrimination became the basis for ruling upon the admissibility of a confession. The *Miranda* warnings and a valid waiver are ***prerequisites to the admissibility*** of any statement made by the accused during custodial interrogation. A person in custody must, prior to interrogation, be clearly informed that:

(i)   He has the right to remain silent;

(ii) Anything he says can be used against him in court;

(iii) He has the right to the presence of an attorney; and

(iv) If he cannot afford an attorney, one will be appointed for him if he so desires.

Note: The Supreme Court has held that the holding of *Miranda* was based on the ***requirements*** of the Fifth Amendment as made applicable to the states through the Fourteenth Amendment, and therefore Congress cannot eliminate the *Miranda* requirements by statute. [Dickerson v. United States, 530 U.S. 428 (2000)—invalidating a statute that purportedly eliminated *Miranda*'s requirements that persons in custody and being interrogated be informed of the right to remain silent and the right to counsel]

a. Need Not Be Verbatim

Miranda requires that all suspects be informed of their rights without considering any prior awareness of those rights. The warnings need not be given verbatim, as long as the substance of the warning is there. [Duckworth v. Eagan, 492 U.S. 195 (1989)—upholding warning that included statement, "We [the police] have no way of giving you a lawyer, but one will be appointed for you, if you wish, if and when you go to court"] The failure to advise a suspect of his right to appointed counsel may be found to be harmless error. [Michigan v. Tucker, 417 U.S. 433 (1974); California v. Prysock, 453 U.S. 355 (1981)]

b. Rewarning Not Needed After Break

There is generally no need to repeat the warnings merely because of a break in the interrogation, ***unless*** the time lapse has been so long that a failure to do so would seem like an attempt to take advantage of the suspect's ignorance of his rights.

2. When Required

Anyone in police custody and accused of a crime, no matter how minor a crime, must be given *Miranda* warnings ***prior to interrogation*** by the police. [Berkemer v. McCarty, 468 U.S. 420 (1984)]

a. Governmental Conduct

Miranda generally applies only to interrogation by the publicly paid police. It does not apply where interrogation is by an informant who the defendant does not know is working for the police. [Illinois v. Perkins, *supra*—*Miranda* warnings need not be given before questioning by a cellmate covertly working for the police] *Rationale:* The warnings are intended to offset the coercive nature of police-dominated interrogation, and if the defendant does not know that he is being interrogated by the police, there is no coercive atmosphere to offset.

b. Custody Requirement

Whether a person is in custody depends on whether the person's freedom of action is denied in a significant way. The more a setting resembles a traditional arrest (*i.e.,* the more constrained the defendant feels), the more likely the Court will consider it to be custody. If the detention is voluntary, it does not constitute custody. [*See* Berkemer v. McCarty, *supra*; Oregon v. Mathiason, 429 U.S. 492 (1977)] If the detention is long and is involuntary (*e.g.,* defendant is in jail on another charge), it will likely be held to constitute custody. [*See* Mathas v. United States, 391 U.S. 1 (1968)]

Example: D is in custody when he is awakened in his own room in the middle of the night by four officers surrounding his bed, who then begin to question him. [Orozco v. Texas, 394 U.S. 324 (1969)]

[handwritten margin note: probation interview & routine traffic stops are not custodial]

1) Test Is Objective

The initial determination of whether a person is in custody depends on the ***objective*** circumstances of the interrogation, not on the subjective views harbored by either the interrogating officers or the person being interrogated. Thus, for example, an officer's belief that the person being questioned is not a suspect cannot bear on the custody issue unless that view is somehow manifested. [Stansbury v. California, 511 U.S. 318 (1994)]

2) Traffic Stops Generally Not Custodial

Although a routine traffic stop curtails a motorist's freedom of movement, such a stop is presumptively temporary and brief, and the motorist knows that he typically will soon be on his way; therefore, the motorist should not feel unduly coerced. Thus, *Miranda* warnings normally need not be given during a traffic stop.

Example: Officer stopped Defendant for weaving in and out of traffic. When Officer noticed Defendant had trouble standing, he performed a field sobriety test, which Defendant failed. Without giving *Miranda* warnings, Officer then asked Defendant if he had been drinking, and Defendant admitted to recent drinking and drug use. The admission is admissible. [Berkemer v. McCarty, *supra*]

c. Interrogation Requirement

"Interrogation" refers not only to express questioning, but also to any words or actions on the part of the police that the police should know are reasonably likely to elicit an incriminating response from the suspect. [Rhode Island v. Innis, 446 U.S. 291 (1980)] However, *Miranda* does not apply to ***spontaneous statements*** not made in response to interrogation, although officers must give the warnings before any follow-up questioning. Neither does *Miranda* apply to routine booking questions (*e.g.,* name, address, age, etc.), even when the booking process is being taped and may be used as evidence. [Pennsylvania v. Muniz, 496 U.S. 582 (1990)—defendant failed sobriety test and had trouble answering booking questions]

Examples: 1) Police comments about the danger a gun would present to handicapped children, which resulted in a robbery suspect's leading them to a weapon, did not constitute interrogation when the officers were not aware that the suspect was peculiarly susceptible to an appeal to his conscience. [Rhode Island v. Innis, *supra*]

[handwritten margin note: any conduct where police do or should have known they would get an incriminating response]

2) Allowing a suspect's wife to talk to the suspect in the presence of an officer who is taping the conversation with the spouses' knowledge does not constitute interrogation. [Arizona v. Mauro, 481 U.S. 520 (1987)]

1) Break in Interrogation—Questioning by Different Police Agencies

When a second police agency continues to question a suspect at a point when the first police department terminates its questioning, the impact of an earlier denial of rights by the first department carries over into the questioning by the second agency. [Westover v. United States, 384 U.S. 436 (1966)]

d. Waiver

A suspect may waive his *Miranda* rights. To be valid, the government must show, by a preponderance of the evidence, that the waiver was **_knowing, voluntary, and intelligent_**. The Court will look to the totality of the circumstances. Note that the suspect need not be informed of all subjects of an interrogation to effect a valid waiver. [Colorado v. Spring, 479 U.S. 564 (1987)]

1) Silence *or shoulder shrugging is not a valid waiver*

Waiver will not be presumed from the mere silence of the accused after the warnings are given or from the fact that a confession was eventually obtained. Again, the court will look at the totality of the circumstances. [*See* Fare v. Michael C., 442 U.S. 707 (1979)] The accused's refusal to sign a written waiver when requested to do so is not conclusive as to the absence of a waiver. [North Carolina v. Butler, 441 U.S. 369 (1979)]

2) Request for Attorney

A request for an attorney must be specific; a request by the accused to see his probation officer, for example, is not tantamount to a request for an attorney, so that waiver of the right to counsel may still be found. [Fare v. Michael C., *supra*] In addition, a limited request for counsel accompanied by a willingness to speak without counsel is a valid waiver of the right to have counsel present during interrogation. [Connecticut v. Barrett, 479 U.S. 523 (1987)]

3) Police Deception of Defendant's Lawyer

If the *Miranda* warnings are given, a voluntary confession will be admissible even if the police lie to the defendant's lawyer about their intent to question the defendant or fail to inform the defendant that his lawyer is attempting to see him, as long as adversary judicial proceedings have not commenced. [Moran v. Burbine, 475 U.S. 412 (1986)]

e. Types of Statements

Miranda applies to both inculpatory statements and statements alleged to be merely "exculpatory."

Example: The suspect's "exculpatory" statement, when confronted with another suspect, that "I didn't shoot Manuel, you did it," led to the first suspect's conviction for murder. [Escobedo v. Illinois, 378 U.S. 478 (1964)]

f. State-Ordered Psychiatric Examination

The Fifth Amendment privilege against self-incrimination forbids admission of evidence based on a psychiatric interview of defendant who was not warned of his right to remain silent. [Estelle v. Smith, 451 U.S. 454 (1981)] The admission of such evidence may, however, constitute harmless error. [Satterwhite v. Texas, 486 U.S. 249 (1988)]

g. Limits on *Miranda*

Miranda suggested that every encounter between police and citizen was inherently coercive. Hence, interrogation would result in compelled testimony for Fifth Amendment purposes. However, the Supreme Court has been narrowing the scope of *Miranda's* application.

Example: Admission of rape and murder by a probationer to his probation officer was not compelled or involuntary, despite the probationer's obligation to periodically report and be "truthful in all matters." [Minnesota v. Murphy, 465 U.S. 420 (1984)]

h. Inapplicable at Grand Jury Hearing

The *Miranda* requirements **_do not apply_** to a witness testifying before a grand jury, even if the witness is under the compulsion of a subpoena. Such a witness who has not been charged or indicted does not have the right to have counsel present during the questioning, but he may consult with an attorney outside the grand jury room. A witness who gives false testimony before a grand jury may be convicted of perjury even though he was not given the *Miranda* warnings. [United States v. Mandujano, 425 U.S. 564 (1976); United States v. Wong, 431 U.S. 174 (1977)]

3. Right to Terminate Interrogation
The accused may terminate police interrogation by invoking either the right to remain silent or the right to counsel. The effect of each differs.

a. Right to Remain Silent
At any time prior to or during interrogation, the accused may indicate that he wishes to remain silent. If the accused so indicates, all *questioning related to the particular crime must stop*.

1) Police May Resume Questioning If They "Scrupulously Honor" Request
The police may reinitiate questioning after the defendant has invoked the right to remain silent, as long as they "scrupulously honor" the defendant's request. This means, at the very least, that the police may not badger the defendant into talking and must wait a significant time before reinitiating questioning.
Example: In the Supreme Court's only opinion directly on point, it allowed police to reinitiate questioning where: (i) the police *immediately ceased questioning* upon Defendant's request and did not resume questioning for several hours; (ii) Defendant was *rewarned* of his rights; and (iii) questioning was *limited to a crime that was not the subject of the earlier questioning*. [Michigan v. Mosely, 423 U.S. 96 (1975)]

b. Right to Counsel 5th A,
At any time prior to or during interrogation, the accused may also invoke a *Miranda* (*i.e.,* "Fifth Amendment") right to counsel. If the accused invokes this right, *all questioning must cease* until the accused is provided with an attorney or initiates further questioning himself. [Edwards v. Arizona, 451 U.S. 477 (1981)]

1) Police May Not Resume Questioning About Any Crime
Once the accused invokes his right to counsel under *Miranda,* all questioning must cease; the police may not even question the accused about a totally unrelated crime, as they can where the accused merely invokes the right to remain silent. [*See* Arizona v. Roberson, 486 U.S. 675 (1988)] *Rationale:* The right to counsel under *Miranda* is a prophylactic right designed by the Court to prevent the police from badgering an accused into talking without the aid of counsel, and this purpose can be accomplished only if *all* questioning ceases. [*See* McNeil v. Wisconsin, 501 U.S. 171 (1991)]

a) Compare—Accused May Initiate Resumption of Questioning
The accused may waive his right to counsel (*see* D.2.d.2), *supra*) after invoking the right, and thus initiate resumption of questioning.
Example: Accused cut off interrogation by asking for an attorney, but then asked the interrogating officer, "What is going to happen to me now?" The officer explained that the accused did not have to talk, and the accused said he understood. The officer then described the charge against the accused and gave him fresh *Miranda* warnings. The accused then confessed after taking a polygraph test. The Court upheld admission of the confession into evidence, finding that the accused had validly waived his rights. [Oregon v. Bradshaw, 462 U.S. 1039 (1983)]

b) Scope of Right—Custodial Interrogation
The Fifth Amendment right to counsel under *Miranda* applies whenever there is custodial interrogation.

c) Compare—Sixth Amendment Right "Offense Specific"
Recall that the Sixth Amendment right to counsel (*see* C., *supra*) attaches only after formal proceedings have begun. Moreover, whereas invocation of the Fifth Amendment right prevents all questioning, the Sixth Amendment right is "offense specific." (*See* C.1., *supra*.)

2) Request Must Be Unambiguous and Specific

A Fifth Amendment request for counsel can be invoked only by an *unambiguous* request for counsel *in dealing with the custodial interrogation*. [McNeil v. Wisconsin, *supra*; Davis v. United States, 512 U.S. 452 (1994)] The request must be sufficiently clear that a reasonable police officer in the same situation would understand the statement to be a request for counsel.

Examples: 1) The statement by the suspect being interrogated "Maybe I should talk to a lawyer" is not an unambiguous request for counsel under the Fifth Amendment, and so does not prevent further questioning.

2) D was arrested and charged with robbery. At his initial appearance, he requested the aid of counsel. After D's appearance, the police came to D's cell, gave him *Miranda* warnings, and questioned D about a crime unrelated to the robbery. D made incriminating statements. D's Fifth Amendment right to counsel was not violated because D did not request counsel in dealing with the interrogation. His post-charge request for counsel at his initial appearance was a *Sixth Amendment* request for counsel, which is offense specific (*see* C.1., *supra*).

3) Ambiguities Relevant Only If Part of Request

Once the accused has expressed an unequivocal desire to receive counsel, no subsequent questions or responses may be used to cast doubt on the request and all questioning of the accused must cease. Where the request is ambiguous, police may ask clarifying questions, but are not required to do so; rather, they may continue to interrogate the suspect until an unambiguous request is received. [Davis v. United States, *supra*] Note that if the defendant agrees to answer questions orally, but requests the presence of counsel before making any written statements, the defendant's oral statements are admissible. The defendant's agreement to talk constitutes a voluntary and knowing waiver of the right to counsel. [Connecticut v. Barrett, *supra*, 2.d.2)]

4) Counsel Must Be Present at Interrogation

Mere consultation with counsel prior to questioning does not satisfy the right to counsel—the police cannot resume questioning the accused in the absence of counsel. [Minnick v. Mississippi, 498 U.S. 146 (1991)] Of course, counsel need not be present if the defendant waives the right to counsel by initiating the exchange. (*See* 3.b.1)a), *supra*.)

Example: The accused answered a few questions during interrogation, but then requested an attorney. He was allowed to meet with his attorney three times. Subsequently, in the absence of counsel, police resumed interrogating the accused, and he made incriminating statements. The Court held that the statements must be excluded from evidence. [Minnick v. Mississippi, *supra*]

5) Statements Obtained in Violation May Be Used to Impeach

As indicated above, if the accused requests counsel, all questioning must cease unless counsel is present or the accused initiates a resumption of questioning. If *the police* initiate further questioning, the defendant's statements cannot be used by the prosecution in its case in chief, but they can be used to *impeach the defendant's* trial testimony, as long as the court finds that the defendant voluntarily and intelligently waived his right to counsel. [Michigan v. Harvey, 494 U.S. 344 (1990)] Note, however, that such illegally obtained evidence cannot be used to impeach trial testimony of witnesses other than the defendant. [James v. Illinois, 493 U.S. 307 (1990)]

4. Effect of Violation

Generally, evidence obtained in violation of *Miranda* is inadmissible at trial.

a. Use of Confession for Impeachment

A confession obtained in violation of the defendant's *Miranda* rights, but otherwise voluntary, may be used to *impeach the defendant's testimony* if he takes the stand at trial, even though such a confession is inadmissible in the state's case in chief as evidence of guilt. [Harris v. New York, 401 U.S. 222 (1971); Oregon v. Hass, 420 U.S.

714 (1975)] However, a truly involuntary confession is *inadmissible* for any purpose. [Mincey v. Arizona, *supra,* III.C.5.f.1)]

1) Silence

The prosecutor may not use the defendant's silence after receiving *Miranda* warnings to counter the defendant's insanity defense. [Wainwright v. Greenfield, 474 U.S. 284 (1986)]

2) May Be Harmless Error

A single question by the prosecutor about the defendant's silence may constitute harmless error when followed by an objection sustained by the judge and an instruction to jurors to disregard the question. [Greer v. Miller, 483 U.S. 756 (1987)]

b. Subsequent Valid Confession Admissible

An invalid confession obtained while the suspect was in custody but before the *Miranda* warnings were given will not render inadmissible a *subsequent valid confession* obtained after the warnings were given. The subsequent confession will be admissible evidence. [Oregon v. Elstad, 470 U.S. 298 (1985)] The Court in *Elstad* also suggested—but did *not* clearly hold—that "fruits" derived from statements obtained in violation of *Miranda* (physical evidence such as contraband, weapons, etc.) may be admissible, reasoning that failure to give the *Miranda* warnings is a prophylaxis and not itself a violation of the Fifth Amendment.

5. Public Safety Exception to *Miranda*

If *police interrogation* is reasonably prompted by *concern for public safety*, responses to the questions may be used in court, even though the accused is in custody and *Miranda* warnings are not given. The scope of this exception is unclear, but may be limited to the facts of the case in which the Supreme Court announced the new rule. In that case, the suspect was handcuffed, then asked where he had hidden his gun. The arrest and questioning were virtually contemporaneous, and police were reasonably concerned that the gun might be found and cause injury to an innocent person. [New York v. Quarles, 467 U.S. 649 (1984)]

V. PRETRIAL IDENTIFICATION

A. IN GENERAL

The purpose of all the rules concerning pretrial identification is to ensure that when the witness identifies the person at trial, she is identifying the person who committed the crime and not merely the person whom she has previously seen at the police station.

B. SUBSTANTIVE BASES FOR ATTACK

1. Sixth Amendment Right to Counsel

a. When Right Exists

A suspect has a right to the presence of an attorney at any *post-charge lineup or showup*. [Moore v. Illinois, 434 U.S. 220 (1977); United States v. Wade, 388 U.S. 218 (1967)] At a lineup, the witness is asked to pick the perpetrator of the crime from a group of persons, while a showup is a one-to-one confrontation between the witness and the suspect for the purpose of identification.

no right to counsel at showing of photograph

b. Role of Counsel at a Lineup

The right is simply to have an attorney present during the lineup so that the lawyer can observe any suggestive aspects of the lineup and bring them out on cross-examination of the witness. There is no right to have the lawyer help set up the lineup, to demand changes in the way it is conducted, etc.

c. Photo Identification

The accused does *not* have the right to counsel at photo identifications. [United States v. Ash, 413 U.S. 300 (1973)] However, as in the case of lineups, the accused may have a due process claim regarding the photo identification. (*See* 2., *infra.*)

d. Physical Evidence
The accused does *not* have the right to counsel when the police take physical evidence such as handwriting exemplars or fingerprints from her.

2. Due Process Standard
A defendant can attack an identification as denying due process when the identification is *unnecessarily suggestive* and there is a *substantial likelihood of misidentification*. It is clear that both parts of this standard must be met for the defendant to win, and that to meet this difficult test, the identification must be shown to have been extremely suggestive.

Examples: 1) A showup at a hospital did not deny the defendant due process when such a procedure was necessary due to the need of an immediate identification, the inability of the identifying victim to come to the police station, and the possibility that the victim might die. [Stovall v. Denno, 388 U.S. 293 (1967)]

2) A photo identification with only six snapshots did not violate due process where the procedure was necessary because perpetrators of a serious felony (robbery) were at large, and the police had to determine if they were on the right track, and the Court found little danger of misidentification. [Simmons v. United States, 390 U.S. 377 (1968)]

3) No substantial likelihood of misidentification was found in the showing of a single photograph to a police officer two days after the crime. [Manson v. Brathwaite, 432 U.S. 98 (1977)]

4) A fundamentally unfair procedure, such as when the perpetrator of the crime is known to be black and the suspect is the only black in the lineup, would violate the due process standard.

C. THE REMEDY
The remedy for an unconstitutional identification is *exclusion* of the in-court identification (unless it has an independent source). This remedy is so severe that relief is rarely granted.

1. Independent Source
A witness may make an in-court identification despite the existence of an unconstitutional pretrial identification if the in-court identification has an independent source. The factors a court will weigh in determining an independent source include the opportunity to observe the defendant at the time of the crime, the ease with which the witness can identify the defendant, and the existence or absence of prior misidentifications.

ample opportunity to observe the Δ at time of the crime

2. Hearing
The admissibility of identification evidence should be determined at a suppression hearing in the absence of the jury, but exclusion of the jury is not constitutionally required. [Watkins v. Sowders, 449 U.S. 341 (1981)] The government bears the burden of proof as to the presence of counsel or a waiver by the accused, or as to an independent source for the in-court identification, while the defendant must prove an alleged due process violation.

D. NO RIGHT TO LINEUP
The defendant is not entitled to any particular kind of identification procedure. The defendant may not demand a lineup.

E. NO SELF-INCRIMINATION ISSUE
Since a lineup does not involve compulsion to give evidence *"testimonial"* in nature, a suspect has no basis in the Fifth Amendment privilege against compelled self-incrimination to refuse to participate in one. [United States v. Wade, *supra*, B.1.a.]

VI. PRETRIAL PROCEDURES

A. PRELIMINARY HEARING TO DETERMINE PROBABLE CAUSE TO DETAIN (*"GERSTEIN* HEARINGS*"*)
A defendant has a Fourth Amendment right to be released from detention if there is no probable cause to hold him. Thus, a defendant has a right to a determination of probable cause. A preliminary hearing is a hearing held after arrest but before trial to determine whether probable cause for detention exists. The hearing is an informal, ex parte, nonadversarial proceeding.

1. **When Right Applies**
   If probable cause has already been determined (*e.g.,* the arrest is pursuant to a grand jury indictment or an arrest warrant), a preliminary hearing need not be held. If no probable cause determination has been made, a defendant has a right to a preliminary hearing to determine probable cause if "*significant pretrial constraints on the defendant's liberty*" exist. Thus, the right applies if the defendant is released only upon the posting of bail or if he is held in jail in lieu of bail. It does not apply if the defendant is released merely upon the condition that he appear for trial.

   Note: The fact that the defendant has been released does not preclude a finding of a significant constraint on liberty, since many conditions can be attached to liberty.

2. **Timing**
   The hearing must be held within a reasonable time, and the Court has determined that 48 hours is presumptively reasonable. [Riverside County v. McLaughlin, 500 U.S. 44 (1991)]

3. **Remedy**
   There is *no real remedy* for the defendant for the mere denial of this hearing, because an unlawful detention, without more, has no effect on the subsequent prosecution. However, if evidence is discovered as a result of the unlawful detention, it will be suppressed under the exclusionary rule.

B. PRETRIAL DETENTION

1. **Initial Appearance**
   Soon after the defendant is arrested, she must be brought before a magistrate who will advise her of her rights, set bail, and appoint counsel if necessary. The initial appearance may be combined with the *Gerstein* hearing, but will be held whether or not a *Gerstein* hearing is necessary. For misdemeanors, this appearance will be the trial.

2. **Bail**   *bail issue is immediately appealable*
   Most state constitutions or statutes create a right to be released on appropriate bail (either on personal recognizance or on a cash bond).

   a. **Due Process Concerns**
      Since denial of release on bail deprives a person of liberty, such denials must comply with the Due Process Clause. In upholding the Federal Bail Reform Act (which permits a court to detain an arrestee if the judge determines that no condition of release would ensure the arrestee's appearance or the safety of any person or the community), the Court held that denial of bail does not violate substantive due process (by imposing punishment before a defendant is found guilty), because the denial of bail is not punishment but a regulatory solution to the problem of persons committing crimes while out on bail. The Court also held that the federal act does not violate procedural due process because it provides detainees with a right to a hearing on the issue, expedited review, etc. [United States v. Salerno, 479 U.S. 1026 (1987)] Similar state statutes would likely be upheld, but a state statute that arbitrarily denies bail (*e.g.,* by not allowing the detainee to present evidence or denying release to a whole class of detainees) would probably violate the Due Process Clause.

   b. **Right to Be Free from Excessive Bail**
      Where the right to release exists, state constitutions and state statutes—and perhaps the Eighth Amendment as well—prohibit "excessive" bail. This has traditionally been interpreted to require that bail be set no higher than is necessary to ensure the defendant's appearance at trial.

   c. **Bail Issues Are Immediately Appealable**
      In most jurisdictions and under federal law, a refusal to grant bail or the setting of excessive bail may be appealed immediately, as an exception to the final judgment rule for appeals. If not immediately appealable, the denial of bail can be reached by an immediate petition for a writ of habeas corpus. Once the defendant is convicted, an appeal of a pretrial bail decision is moot. [Murphy v. Hunt, 455 U.S. 478 (1982)]

   d. **Defendant Incompetent to Stand Trial**
      As to deprivation of pretrial liberty by commitment of one who is not competent to stand trial, the standards for commitment and subsequent release must be essentially

identical with those for the commitment of persons not charged with crime; otherwise, there is a denial of equal protection. [Jackson v. Indiana, 406 U.S. 715 (1972)]

3. Pretrial Detention Practices

Pretrial detention practices that are reasonably related to the interest of maintaining jail security, such as double-bunking, prohibiting inmates from receiving from the outside food and personal items or books not mailed directly from the publisher, routine inspections while the detainees remain outside their rooms, and body cavity searches following contact visits, do not violate due process or the Fourth Amendment and without more do not constitute punishment. [Bell v. Wolfish, 441 U.S. 520 (1979)]

C. PRELIMINARY HEARING TO DETERMINE PROBABLE CAUSE TO PROSECUTE

A later preliminary hearing may be held to determine whether probable cause to prosecute exists. The accused has the *right to counsel* at this hearing [Coleman v. Alabama, 399 U.S. 1 (1970)], and both the prosecutor and the accused may present evidence for the record. The accused may waive the hearing. Either side may use this hearing to preserve testimony of a witness unavailable at trial (*e.g.,* the witness testifies at the preliminary hearing and dies before trial) provided there was some opportunity to cross-examine the witness at the preliminary hearing. [Ohio v. Roberts, 448 U.S. 56 (1980)]

D. GRAND JURIES   *states do not use grand jury as regulation of their charge process*

The Fifth Amendment right to indictment by grand jury has not been incorporated into the Fourteenth Amendment, but some state constitutions require grand jury indictment.
exclusion doesn't apply to conduct of grand jury

1. Charging Grand Juries

Most states east of the Mississippi and the federal system use the grand jury as a regular part of the charging process. The charging grand jury *determines probable cause to prosecute* by returning the bill of indictment submitted by the prosecutor as a "true bill." Western states generally charge by filing an information, a written accusation of crime prepared and presented by the prosecutor. Informations also are used when the defendant waives her right to grand jury indictment.

2. Special or Investigative Grand Juries

Special or investigative grand juries are used almost everywhere. This type of grand jury investigates, on its own motion, crime in the particular jurisdiction, and can initiate a criminal case by bringing an indictment.

3. Grand Jury Proceedings   *are secret, Δ has no right to appear or send witness*

a. Secrecy and Defendant's Lack of Access

Grand jury proceedings are conducted in secret. In most jurisdictions, a defendant has no right to notice that a grand jury is considering an indictment against her, to be present and confront witnesses at the proceeding, or to introduce evidence before the grand jury.

b. Particularized Need Required for Prosecutor's Access to Grand Jury Materials

The "particularized need" standard generally required under Rule 6(e) of the Federal Rules of Criminal Procedure in order to obtain access to grand jury materials must be shown by state attorneys general [Illinois v. Abbott, 460 U.S. 557 (1983)], as well as Justice Department attorneys [United States v. Sells Engineering, Inc., 463 U.S. 418 (1983)]. The disclosure of such materials to the Internal Revenue Service for the purpose of assessing tax liability, rather than for litigation, is not permitted. [United States v. Baggot, 463 U.S. 476 (1983)]

c. Subpoena Powers of Grand Jury

The grand jury may use its subpoena power to investigate the matters before it or to initiate criminal investigations of its own. Rather than returning an indictment, grand juries sometimes issue a report.

1) Government Need Not Prove Relevance

A grand jury subpoena may be quashed only if the opposing party can prove that there is no reasonable possibility that the material sought will be relevant to the grand jury investigation. The government has no initial burden of proving that the material is relevant. [United States v. R. Enterprises, Inc., 498 U.S. 292 (1991)]

2) Defamatory Reports
If the defendant or any other person believes that she has been defamed by a grand jury report, she may make a motion to seal the report.

d. No Right to Counsel or *Miranda* Warnings
A witness subpoenaed to testify before a grand jury does not have the right to receive the *Miranda* warnings, and the witness may be convicted of perjury despite the lack of warnings if she testifies falsely. A grand jury witness does not have the right to have an attorney present, but she may consult with an attorney outside the grand jury room. [United States v. Mandujano, *supra*, IV.D.2.h.; United States v. Wong, *supra*, IV.D.2.h.]

e. No Right to "Potential Defendant" Warnings
A witness who is under investigation and may well become a defendant is not entitled to a warning that she is a "potential defendant" when called to testify before the grand jury. [United States v. Washington, 431 U.S. 181 (1977)]

f. No Right to Have Evidence Excluded
A grand jury may base its indictment on evidence that would not be admissible at trial [Costello v. United States, 350 U.S. 359 (1956)], and a grand jury witness may not refuse to answer questions on the grounds that they are based upon unconstitutionally obtained evidence [United States v. Calandra, 414 U.S. 338 (1974)]. Nor may an indicted defendant have the indictment quashed on the grounds that it is based upon illegally obtained evidence.

g. No Right to Challenge Subpoena on Fourth Amendment Grounds
A suspect-witness (or any witness, for that matter) subpoenaed before a grand jury cannot attack the subpoena on the ground that the grand jury lacked "probable cause"—or any reason at all—to call her for questioning. No such attack can be made even if the subpoena also requires the witness to provide a handwriting exemplar, a voice sample, or otherwise cooperate with law enforcement officials in a manner not violating the self-incrimination privilege.

h. Exclusion of Minorities
Minorities may not be excluded from grand jury service. A conviction resulting from an indictment issued by a grand jury from which members of a minority group have been excluded will be reversed without regard to the harmlessness of the error. [Vasquez v. Hillery, 474 U.S. 254 (1986)] Note that the defendant and the excluded members need not be of the same race. [Campbell v. Louisiana, 423 U.S. 392 (1998)]

i. Dismissal Seldom Required for Procedural Defect
An indicted defendant is seldom entitled to dismissal of an indictment upon a showing that procedural error occurred during the grand jury proceedings. Generally, she is entitled to dismissal only upon a showing that the error substantially influenced the grand jury's decision to indict. [Bank of Nova Scotia v. United States, 487 U.S. 250 (1988)—defendant failed to show that prosecutorial misconduct before grand jury substantially influenced its decision to indict]

j. Exculpatory Evidence
An indictment may not be dismissed by a federal court for a prosecutor's failure to present exculpatory evidence to the grand jury unless the prosecutor's conduct violates a preexisting constitutional, legislative, or procedural rule. [United States v. Williams, 504 U.S. 36 (1992)]

E. SPEEDY TRIAL

1. Societal Interest
The Sixth Amendment right to a speedy trial is an unusual one in that the interests of society and the defendant coincide.

2. Constitutional Standard
A determination of whether the defendant's right to a speedy trial has been violated will be made by an evaluation of the totality of the circumstances. The following factors should be considered:

(i) Length of the delay;

(ii)   Reason for the delay;

(iii) Whether the defendant asserted his right; and

(iv)   Prejudice to the defendant.

[Barker v. Wingo, 407 U.S. 514 (1972)]
Example: A defendant who was arrested 8½ years after his federal indictment due solely to the government's neglect and who promptly asserted his right to a speedy trial claim was ***presumptively prejudiced*** so that an actual showing of prejudice was not necessary. [Doggett v. United States, 505 U.S. 647 (1992)]

3.   Remedy—Dismissal
The remedy for a violation of the constitutional right to a speedy trial is dismissal with prejudice. [Strunk v. United States, 412 U.S. 434 (1973)]

4.   When Right Attaches
The right to a speedy trial does not attach until the defendant has been ***arrested or charged***. It is very difficult to get relief for a pre-arrest delay under this standard, because the defendant must show prejudice from a delay, and good faith investigative delays do not violate due process. [United States v. Lovasco, 431 U.S. 783 (1977)]

A defendant is not entitled to speedy trial relief for the period between the dismissal of charges and later refiling. [United States v. MacDonald, 456 U.S. 1 (1982)] The only limitation on pre-arrest delay (other than general due process requirements) seems to be the statute of limitations for the particular crime.

a.   Knowledge of Charges Unnecessary
The Speedy Trial Clause attaches even if the defendant does not know about the charges against him and is thus not restrained in any way. [Doggett v. United States, *supra*]

5.   Special Problems
Two situations create special speedy trial problems:

a.   Detainees
A defendant incarcerated in one jurisdiction who has a charge pending in another jurisdiction has a right to have the second jurisdiction exert reasonable efforts to obtain his presence for trial of these pending charges. Failure to exert such efforts violates his right to speedy trial. [Smith v. Hooey, 393 U.S. 374 (1969)]

b.   Indefinite Suspension of Charges
It is a violation of the right to speedy trial to permit the prosecution to indefinitely suspend charges, such as permitting the government to dismiss "without prejudice," which permits reinstatement of the prosecution ***at any time***. [Klopfer v. North Carolina, 386 U.S. 213 (1967)—nolle prosequi that indefinitely suspended the statute of limitations violated speedy trial requirements]

F.   PROSECUTORIAL DUTY TO DISCLOSE EXCULPATORY INFORMATION AND NOTICE OF DEFENSES

1.   Prosecutor's Duty to Disclose Exculpatory Evidence
The government has a duty to disclose material, exculpatory evidence to the defendant. [Brady v. Maryland, 373 U.S. 83 (1963)] Failure to disclose such evidence—whether willful ***or inadvertent***—violates the Due Process Clause and is grounds for reversing a conviction if the defendant can prove that:

(i)   The evidence at issue is ***favorable to the defendant*** because it impeaches or is exculpatory; and

(ii)   ***Prejudice has resulted*** (*i.e.*, there is a ***reasonable probability*** that the result of the case would have been different if the undisclosed evidence had been presented at trial).

[Strickler v. Green, 527 U.S. 263 (1999); United States v. Bagley, 473 U.S. 667 (1985)]
Note: If the prosecution can show that the verdict is strongly supported by other evidence, sufficient prejudice will not be found.

a. **Exception—Reports on Sexually Abused Minors**
A defendant may not automatically obtain investigative reports made by a state agency in charge of investigating sexually abused minors because of the confidentiality of the minors' records. Such reports can be obtained only if they are *favorable* to the defendant and are *material* to guilt or punishment. [Pennsylvania v. Ritchie, 480 U.S. 39 (1987)]

b. **Probably Must Be Relevant to Merits**
The duty to disclose appears to extend only to evidence relevant to the prosecution's case in chief. Material going to a defense not on the merits probably need not be disclosed. [*See* United States v. Armstrong, 517 U.S. 456 (1996)—material relevant to defendant's claim that he was selected for prosecution because of his race need not be disclosed]

2. **Notice of Alibi and Intent to Present Insanity Defense**

a. **Reciprocity Required**
The prosecution may demand to know whether the defendant is going to plead insanity or raise an alibi as a defense. If the defendant is going to raise an alibi, he must list his witnesses. In return, the prosecution is required to list the witnesses it will call to rebut the defendant's defense. [Williams v. Florida, 399 U.S. 78 (1970); Wardius v. Oregon, 412 U.S. 470 (1973)]

b. **Commenting on Failure to Present the Alibi**
The prosecutor may not comment at trial on the defendant's failure to produce a witness named as supporting the alibi or on the failure to present the alibi itself. But the prosecutor may use the notice of an alibi to *impeach* a defendant who takes the stand and testifies to a different alibi.

G. COMPETENCY TO STAND TRIAL

1. **Competency and Insanity Distinguished**
Competency to stand trial must be carefully distinguished from the insanity defense, although both rest on a defendant's abnormality. Insanity is a defense to the criminal charge; a defendant acquitted by reason of insanity may not be retried and convicted, although she may be hospitalized under some circumstances. *Incompetency* to stand trial depends on a defendant's mental condition at the *time of trial*, unlike *insanity*, which turns upon a defendant's mental condition at the *time of the crime*. Incompetency is not a defense but rather a bar to trial. A defendant who is incompetent to stand trial cannot be tried. But if she later regains her competency, she can then be tried and—unless she has a defense—convicted. Note that a defendant who is competent to stand trial is competent to plead guilty.

2. **Due Process Standard**
Due process of law, as well as the state law of most jurisdictions, prohibits the trial of a defendant who is incompetent to stand trial. A defendant is incompetent to stand trial under the due process standard if, because of her present mental condition, she either:

(i) Lacks a rational as well as a factual *understanding of the charges and proceedings*; or

(ii) Lacks sufficient present *ability to consult with her lawyer* with a reasonable degree of understanding.

[Dusky v. United States, 362 U.S. 402 (1960)]

3. **Trial Judge's Duty to Raise Competency Issue**
If evidence of a defendant's incompetency appears to the trial judge, the judge has a constitutional obligation to conduct further inquiry and determine whether in fact the defendant is incompetent. If a defendant is tried and convicted but it later appears she was incompetent to stand trial, the judge's failure to raise the issue or to request a determination of competency does not constitute a "waiver." [Pate v. Robinson, 383 U.S. 375 (1966)]
Example: During preliminary proceedings at X's trial for robbery, X, while in open court, speaks irrationally and repeatedly interrupts the proceedings by shouting to a nonexistent dog in the courtroom. What, if anything, must the trial judge do before proceeding to trial? The facts here clearly require the trial

judge to investigate and determine X's competency to stand trial. The judge must hold a hearing and determine whether X is mentally ill and, if so, whether she can consult with her lawyer and understand the charges and proceedings. This must be done even if neither X nor her lawyer raises the issue.

4. Burden Can Be Placed on Defendant

A state can require a criminal defendant to prove that he is not competent to stand trial by a preponderance of the evidence; this does not violate due process. [Medina v. California, 505 U.S. 437 (1992)] However, requiring a defendant to prove incompetence by *clear and convincing evidence* violates due process. [Cooper v. Oklahoma, 517 U.S. 348 (1996)]

5. Detention of Defendant

a. Based on Incompetency

A defendant who has been found incompetent may be detained in a mental hospital for a brief period of time for evaluation and treatment. But she cannot be hospitalized indefinitely or for a long period of time simply because she has been found incompetent. This can be done only if independent "civil commitment" proceedings are begun and result in her commitment. [Jackson v. Indiana, 406 U.S. 715 (1972)]

b. Based on Insanity

A defendant who has made a successful insanity defense can be confined in a mental hospital for a term longer than the maximum period of incarceration for the offense. The insanity acquittee is not entitled to any separate civil commitment hearing at the expiration of the maximum sentence. [Jones v. United States, 463 U.S. 354 (1983)] However, a defendant acquitted by reason of insanity who is determined to have recovered sanity cannot be indefinitely committed in a mental facility merely because he is unable to prove himself not dangerous to others. [Foucha v. Louisiana, 504 U.S. 71 (1992)]

H. PRETRIAL PUBLICITY AND THE RIGHT TO A FAIR TRIAL

Excessive pretrial publicity prejudicial to the defendant may require change of venue or retrial.

Examples: 1) Defendant sought and was improperly denied a change of venue on the ground of local prejudice. His trial by a jury that was familiar with the material facts and had formed an opinion as to his guilt before the trial began (on the basis of unfavorable newspaper publicity) denied him due process. [Irvin v. Dowd, 366 U.S. 717 (1961)] However, due process will be satisfied if the judge asks the venire-persons whether they were exposed to pretrial publicity, and if so, whether it would affect their impartiality and ability to hear the case with an open mind. The judge does not have to ask about the specific source or content of the pretrial information. [Mu'Min v. Virginia, 500 U.S. 415 (1991)]

2) A new trial is required where defendant sought and was denied a change of venue after a televised interview in which defendant admitted that he had perpetrated the crimes with which he was charged, and the jury was drawn from the people who had seen the interview. [Rideau v. Louisiana, 373 U.S. 723 (1963)—jurors' claims that they could be neutral were inherently implausible]

3) Defendant's request for a change of venue because of pretrial publicity was denied because state law did not permit a change of venue in misdemeanor cases. *Held:* The law violates the right to trial by an impartial jury; a defendant must be given the opportunity to show that a change of venue is required in his case. [Groppi v. Wisconsin, 400 U.S. 505 (1971)]

VII. TRIAL

A. BASIC RIGHT TO A FAIR TRIAL

1. Right to Public Trial

The Sixth and Fourteenth Amendments guarantee the right to a public trial. [*In re* Oliver, 333 U.S. 257 (1948); Herring v. New York, 422 U.S. 853 (1975)] However, the extent of this right varies according to the stage of the proceeding involved.

a.   **Preliminary Probable Cause Hearing**
Preliminary hearings to determine whether there is probable cause on which to prosecute are presumptively open to the public and the press. [Press Enterprise Co. v. Superior Court, 478 U.S. 1 (1986)]

b.   **Suppression Hearings**
The Sixth Amendment right to a public trial extends to *pretrial suppression hearings*. Such hearings may not be closed to the public unless:

   (i)   The party seeking closure shows an *overriding interest* likely to be prejudiced by a public hearing;

   (ii)   The closure is *no broader than necessary* to protect such an interest;

   (iii)   *Reasonable alternatives* to closure have been considered; and

   (iv)   *Adequate findings* to support closure are entered by the trial court.

   [Waller v. Georgia, 467 U.S. 39 (1984)]

c.   **Trial**
The press and the public have a right under the First Amendment to attend the trial itself, even when the defense and prosecution agree to close it. A judge may not exclude the press and the public from a criminal trial without first finding that closure is necessary for a fair trial. [Richmond Newspapers, Inc. v. Virginia, 448 U.S. 555 (1980)]

   1)   **Televising Permissible**
   The state may constitutionally permit televising criminal proceedings over the defendant's objection. [Chandler v. Florida, 449 U.S. 560 (1981)]

2.   **Right to an Unbiased Judge**   *bias = either financial interest or actual malice ≠ Δ*
Due process is violated if the judge is shown to have **actual malice** against the defendant or to have had a *financial interest* in having the trial result in a verdict of guilty.
Example: D is tried before a "mayor's court" presided over by a judge who is also the mayor of the town. Half of the town's income comes from fines imposed in the court after convictions. Is the trial permissible? No. The judge has too great a financial interest in the outcome to meet due process standards. [Ward v. City of Monroeville, 409 U.S. 57 (1972)]

3.   **Must Judge Be a Lawyer?**
A defendant in a minor misdemeanor prosecution has no right to have the trial judge be a lawyer, if upon conviction he has a right to trial de novo in a court with a lawyer-judge. [North v. Russell, 427 U.S. 328 (1976)] It is likely, however, that in serious crime cases the Supreme Court will require that the judge be law-trained.

4.   **Right to Be Free of Trial Disruption**
Due process is violated if the trial is conducted in a manner or atmosphere making it unlikely that the jury gave the evidence reasonable consideration. Televising and broadcasting parts of a trial, for example, may interfere with courtroom proceedings and influence the jury by emphasizing the notoriety of the trial to such an extent that it infringes the defendant's right to a fair trial. [Estes v. Texas, 381 U.S. 532 (1965)]

5.   **Trial in Prison Clothing**
It is unconstitutional for the state to *compel* the defendant to stand trial in prison clothing. If the defendant does not wish to be tried in prison clothing, he must make a timely objection. [Estelle v. Williams, 425 U.S. 501 (1976)]

6.   **Right to Have Jury Free from Unfair Influences**
If the jury is exposed to influences favorable to the prosecution, due process is violated.
Example: During X's trial, two sheriffs, who were also prosecution witnesses, were in constant and intimate association with the jurors, eating with them, running errands for them, etc. Did the trial violate due process standards? Yes, since this association must have influenced the jurors' assessment of the credibility of the witnesses. [Turner v. Louisiana, 379 U.S. 466 (1965)]

7. No Right to Preservation of Potentially Exculpatory Evidence

Defendants have no right to have the police preserve all evidence for trial, at least where it is not certain that the evidence would have been exculpatory. Due process is violated, however, if the police *in bad faith* destroy evidence potentially useful to the defense at trial. [Arizona v. Youngblood, 488 U.S. 51 (1988)—no due process violation where police failed to preserve seminal fluid on sodomy victim's clothing; California v. Trombetta, 467 U.S. 479 (1984)—same result where police failed to preserve samples of defendant's breath]

B. RIGHT TO TRIAL BY JURY

The Sixth Amendment right to trial by jury applies to the states. [Duncan v. Louisiana, 391 U.S. 145 (1968)] The cases after *Duncan,* while zealously guarding the jury trial right, have permitted the states great latitude in the details of jury use and conduct because of (i) the view that many of the details of the jury were historical accidents, (ii) the belief that the jury will act rationally, and (iii) the cost. *if max authorized sentence exceeds 6 month*
if upto or including 6 monthes → no right to jury trial

1. Right to Jury Trial Only for "Serious" Offenses

There is no constitutional right to jury trial for petty offenses, but only for serious offenses. Also, there is no right to jury trial in juvenile delinquency proceedings. [McKeiver v. Pennsylvania, 403 U.S. 528 (1971)] *contempt—if sum of sentences exceed 6 monthes →*

a. What Constitutes a Serious Offense?

For purposes of the right to jury trial, an offense is serious if *imprisonment for more than six months* is authorized. If imprisonment of less than six months is authorized, the offense is presumptively petty, and there is no right to a jury trial. [Blanton v. City of North Las Vegas, 489 U.S. 538 (1989)] The presumption may be overcome by showing additional penalties, but a possibility of a $5,000 fine and five years' probation is not sufficient to overcome the presumption that the crime is petty. [United States v. Nachtigal, 507 U.S. 1 (1993)]

1) Aggregation of Petty Offenses

The right to a jury trial does not arise when in a single proceeding, sentences for multiple petty offenses are imposed which result in an aggregate prison sentence of more than six months. [Lewis v. United States, 518 U.S. 322 (1996)]

b. Contempt

1) Civil Contempt—No Jury Trial Right

If a penalty is imposed for purposes of compelling future compliance with a court order and the witness can avoid further penalty by complying with the order (*e.g.,* judge sentences witness to prison until she is willing to testify), the proceeding is one of "civil" contempt and no jury trial is required.

2) Criminal Contempt—Six Months Rule

When there is no statutorily authorized penalty for a crime, such as criminal contempt, the actual sentence governs the right to jury trial. Cumulative penalties totaling more than six months cannot be imposed in a *post-verdict contempt adjudication* without affording the defendant the right to a jury trial. [Codispoti v. Pennsylvania, 418 U.S. 506 (1974)]

3) Summary Contempt Punishment During Trial

If the judge summarily imposes punishment for contempt during trial, the penalties may aggregate more than six months without a jury trial. [Codispoti v. Pennsylvania, *supra*]

4) Appellate Modification Sufficient

An appellate court may reduce the sentence imposed for contempt to six months or less and thereby protect the conviction and sentence imposed without a jury from constitutional attack. [Taylor v. Hayes, 418 U.S. 488 (1974)]

5) Probation

A judge may place a contemnor on probation for a term of up to five years without affording him the right to jury trial as long as revocation of probation would not result in imprisonment for more than six months. [Frank v. United States, 395 U.S. 147 (1969)]

2. Number and Unanimity of Jurors

a. No Right to Jury of Twelve
There is no constitutional right to a jury of 12, but there must be *at least six* jurors to satisfy the right to jury trial under the Sixth and Fourteenth Amendments. [Ballew v. Georgia, 435 U.S. 223 (1978)]

b. No Absolute Right to Unanimity
There is no right to a unanimous verdict. The Supreme Court has upheld convictions based upon 11-1, 10-2, and 9-3 votes [Apodaca v. Oregon, 406 U.S. 404 (1972); Johnson v. Louisiana, 406 U.S. 356 (1972)], but probably would not approve an 8-4 vote for conviction. Six-person juries must be unanimous. [Burch v. Louisiana, 441 U.S. 130 (1979); Brown v. Louisiana, 447 U.S. 323 (1980)]

3. Right to Venire Selected from Representative Cross-Section of Community
A defendant has a right to have the venire from which the jury is selected be from a representative cross-section of the community. A defendant can complain of an exclusion of a significant segment of the community from the venire, even if he is not a member of that excluded segment. [Taylor v. Louisiana, 419 U.S. 522 (1975); Holland v. Illinois, 493 U.S. 474 (1990)] *right to cross section jury pool lent* / *no right that own jury reflect*

a. Showing of Exclusion of Significant Group Sufficient
To make out a case for exclusion, the defendant need only show the underrepresentation of a distinct and numerically significant group. [Taylor v. Louisiana, *supra*]

b. No Right to Proportional Representation on Particular Jury
The cross-sectional requirement applies only to the venire from which the jury is selected. A defendant does not have the right to proportional representation of all groups on his particular jury. [Holland v. Illinois, *supra*]

c. Use of Peremptory Challenges for Racial and Gender-Based Discrimination
In contrast to striking potential jurors for cause, a prosecutor generally may exercise peremptory challenges for any rational *or irrational* reason. However, the Equal Protection Clause forbids the use of peremptory challenges to exclude potential jurors solely on account of their race or gender. [Batson v. Kentucky, 476 U.S. 79 (1989); J.E.B. v. Alabama, 511 U.S. 127 (1994)]

1) Proving Strike Improper
An equal protection-based attack on peremptory strikes involves three steps: (i) The defendant must show *facts or circumstances that raise an inference* that the exclusion of potential jurors was based on race or gender. (ii) If such a showing is made, the prosecutor must then come forward with a *race-neutral explanation* for the strike. The reason for the strike need not be reasonable, as long as it is race-neutral. [Purkett v. Elem, 514 U.S. 765 (1995)—explanation that potential jurors were struck because of their long hair and beards was sufficient] (iii) The judge then determines whether the prosecutor's explanation was the genuine reason for striking the juror, or merely a pretext for purposeful discrimination. If the judge believes that the *prosecutor was sincere*, the strike may be upheld. [Purkett v. Elem, *supra*] *race, gender selection unconstitutional for counsel to exercise*

Note that the defendant need not be a member of the group excluded. [Powers v. Ohio, 499 U.S. 400 (1991)]

2) Defendants
It is also unconstitutional for a criminal *defendant* or the defendant's attorney to use peremptory challenges in a racially discriminatory manner. [Georgia v. McCollum, 505 U.S. 42 (1992)] The same rule probably applies to a defendant's peremptory strike based on gender.

d. Distinct and Significant Groups
A fair cross-section of the community must include minorities and women, and possibly other distinct and significant groups. A state may neither exclude women from jury duty nor automatically exempt them upon request. [Duren v. Missouri, 439 U.S. 357 (1979)]

4. Right to Impartial Jury

a. Right to Questioning on Racial Bias

A defendant is entitled to questioning on voir dire specifically directed to racial prejudice whenever race is inextricably bound up in the case. [Ham v. South Carolina, 409 U.S. 524 (1973)] In *noncapital* cases, the mere fact that the victim is white and the defendant is black is not enough to permit such questioning. [Ristaino v. Ross, 424 U.S. 589 (1976); Rosales-Lopez v. United States, 451 U.S. 182 (1982)] However, a *capital* defendant accused of an interracial crime is entitled to have prospective jurors informed of the victim's race and is entitled to voir dire questioning regarding the issue of racial prejudice. [Turner v. Murray, 476 U.S. 28 (1986)]

b. Juror Opposition to Death Penalty

In cases involving capital punishment, a state may not automatically exclude for cause all prospective jurors who express a doubt or scruple about the death penalty. [Witherspoon v. Illinois, 391 U.S. 510 (1968); Adams v. Texas, 448 U.S. 38 (1980)]

1) Standard—Impair or Prevent Performance

The standard for determining when a prospective juror should be excluded for cause is whether the juror's views would *prevent or substantially impair* the performance of his duties in accordance with his instructions and oath. [Wainwright v. Witt, 469 U.S. 412 (1985)] Thus, if a juror's doubts or scruples about the death penalty prevent or substantially impair the performance of his duties, he may be excluded from the jury, and the fact that this may result in a "death qualified" jury does not infringe on a defendant's constitutional rights. [Lockhart v. McCree, 476 U.S. 162 (1986)] However, if a juror has scruples about the death penalty, but could perform her duties and follow instructions, it is error to exclude the juror.

2) Improper Exclusion May Result in Reversal

A death sentence imposed by a jury from which a juror was improperly excluded is subject to automatic reversal. [Gray v. Mississippi, 481 U.S. 648 (1987)]

c. Juror Favoring Death Penalty

If a jury is to decide whether a defendant in a capital case is to be sentenced to death, the defendant must be allowed to ask potential jurors at voir dire if they would automatically give the death penalty upon a guilty verdict. A juror who answers affirmatively should be excluded for cause because such a juror has indicated the same type of inability to follow jury instructions (as to mitigating circumstances) as a juror who has indicated an inability to impose the death penalty under any circumstances (*see supra*). [Morgan v. Illinois, 504 U.S. 719 (1992)]

d. Use of Peremptory Challenge to Maintain Impartial Jury

Peremptory challenges are not constitutionally required. Therefore, if a trial court refuses to exclude a juror for cause whom the court should have excluded, and the defendant uses a peremptory challenge to remove the juror, there is no constitutional violation. [Ross v. Oklahoma, 487 U.S. 81 (1988); United States v. Martinez-Salazar, 528 U.S. 304 (2000)]

5. Inconsistent Verdicts

Inconsistent jury verdicts (*e.g.,* finding defendant guilty of some counts but not guilty on related counts or one defendant guilty and a co-defendant innocent on the same evidence) are not reviewable. A challenge to an inconsistent verdict would be based upon pure speculation because it is impossible to tell on which decision the jury erred. [United States v. Powell, 469 U.S. 57 (1984)]

6. Sentence Enhancement

If substantive law provides that a sentence may be increased beyond the statutory maximum for a crime if additional facts (other than prior conviction) are proved, proof of the facts must be submitted to the jury and proved beyond reasonable doubt; the defendant's right to jury trial is violated if the judge makes the determination. [Apprendi v. New Jersey, 530 U.S. 466 (2000)]

Examples: 1) The right to jury trial was violated where a statute allowed a defendant's sentence to be increased by 10 years if the sentencing judge found by a preponderance of the evidence that the crime was motivated by hate. [Apprendi v. New Jersey, *supra*]

2) Following a jury adjudication of a defendant's guilt of first degree murder, a trial judge is prohibited by the Sixth Amendment from determining whether aggravating factors justify imposition of the death penalty. The jury must make such a determination. [Ring v. Arizona, 122 S. Ct. 2428 (2002)]

a. Distinguish—Sentencing Factors

Statutory sentencing schemes can allow judges to determine the presence of sentencing factors (*i.e.*, facts) to determine whether the defendant should receive the minimum or maximum penalty available under the sentencing scheme. [Harris v. United States, 122 S. Ct. 2406 (2002)]

C. RIGHT TO COUNSEL

A defendant has a right to counsel under the Fifth and Sixth Amendments. The Fifth Amendment right applies at all custodial interrogations (*see* IV.D., *supra*). The Sixth Amendment right applies at all *critical stages* of a prosecution after formal proceedings have begun. If the right to counsel is denied *at trial*, a conviction will automatically be reversed. For nontrial denials, the harmless error test is applied.

1. Stages at Which Applicable

The defendant has the right to be represented by privately retained counsel, or to have counsel appointed for him by the state if he is indigent, at the following stages:

(i) Custodial police interrogation [Miranda v. Arizona, *supra*, IV.D.1.];

(ii) Post-indictment interrogation whether custodial or not [Massiah v. United States, *supra*, IV.C.];

(iii) Preliminary hearings to determine probable cause to prosecute [Coleman v. Alabama, *supra*, VI.C.];

(iv) Arraignment [Hamilton v. Alabama, 368 U.S. 52 (1961)];

(v) Post-charge lineups [Moore v. Illinois, *supra*, V.B.1.a.];

(vi) Guilty plea and sentencing [Mempa v. Rhay, 389 U.S. 128 (1967); Moore v. Michigan, 355 U.S. 155 (1957); Townsend v. Burke, 334 U.S. 736 (1948)];

(vii) Felony trials [Gideon v. Wainwright, 372 U.S. 335 (1963)];

(viii) Misdemeanor trials when imprisonment is actually imposed or a suspended jail sentence is imposed [Scott v. Illinois, 440 U.S. 367 (1979); Alabama v. Shelton, 122 S. Ct. 1764 (2002)]

(ix) Overnight recesses during trial [Geders v. United States, 425 U.S. 80 (1976)]; and

(x) Appeals as a matter of right [Douglas v. California, 372 U.S. 353 (1963)].

Note: The Fifth Amendment right to counsel is involved at (i) and (ii), above; the Sixth Amendment right is also involved at (ii) and at all the remaining stages.

2. Stages at Which Not Applicable

The defendant does not have a constitutional right to be represented by counsel at the following stages:

a. Blood sampling [Schmerber v. California, *supra*, III.D.1.a.];

b. Taking of handwriting or voice exemplars [Gilbert v. California, 388 U.S. 263 (1967)];

c. Pre-charge or investigative lineups [Kirby v. Illinois, 406 U.S. 682 (1972)];

d. Photo identifications [United States v. Ash, *supra*, V.B.1.c.];

e. Preliminary hearings to determine probable cause to detain [Gerstein v. Pugh, 420 U.S. 103 (1975)];

f. Brief recesses during the defendant's testimony at trial [Perry v. Leeke, 488 U.S. 272 (1989)];

g. Discretionary appeals [Ross v. Moffitt, 417 U.S. 600 (1974)];

h. Parole and probation revocation proceedings [Gagnon v. Scarpelli, 411 U.S. 778 (1973)]; and

i. Post-conviction proceeding (*e.g.,* habeas corpus) [Pennsylvania v. Finley, 481 U.S. 551 (1987)] including petitions by death-row inmates [Murray v. Giarratano, 492 U.S. 1 (1989)].

3. Waiver of Right to Counsel and Right to Defend Oneself
A defendant has the absolute right to represent himself *at trial* as long as his waiver of the right to counsel is knowing and intelligent. The court must carefully scrutinize the waiver to ensure that the defendant has a rational and factual understanding of the proceeding against him. However, the defendant need not be found capable of representing himself—the defendant's ability to represent himself has no bearing on his competence to choose self-representation. [Faretta v. California, 422 U.S. 806 (1975); Godinez v. Moran, 509 U.S. 389 (1993)] A back-up attorney may be appointed and may intervene to a limited extent, as long as the impression of self-representation is not destroyed. [McKaskle v. Wiggins, 465 U.S. 168 (1984)]

Note: On appeal, a defendant has no right to represent himself. [Martinez v. Court of Appeal, 528 U.S. 152 (2000)]

4. Indigence and Recoupment of Cost
As indicated above, if the defendant is indigent, the state will provide an attorney. Indigence involves the present financial inability to hire counsel, but none of the right to counsel cases defines indigence precisely. In any case, judges generally are reluctant to refuse to appoint counsel because of the risk of reversal should the defendant be determined indigent. The state generally provides counsel in close cases of indigence, but it may then seek reimbursement from those convicted defendants who later become able to pay. [Fuller v. Oregon, 417 U.S. 40 (1974)]

5. Effective Assistance of Counsel essay type question
The Sixth Amendment right to counsel includes the right to effective counsel. The ineffective assistance claim is the most commonly raised constitutional claim. With this claim, the defendant seeks to secure not malpractice damages, but rather a reversal of his conviction and a new trial.

a. **Effective Assistance Presumed**
Effective assistance of counsel is *presumed* unless the adversarial process is so undermined by counsel's conduct that the trial cannot be relied upon to have produced a just result. [Strickland v. Washington, 466 U.S. 668 (1984)]

b. **Right Extends to First Appeal**
Effective assistance of counsel is also guaranteed on a first appeal as of right. [Evitts v. Lucey, 469 U.S. 387 (1985)]

c. **Circumstances Constituting Ineffective Assistance**
An ineffective assistance claimant must show:

(i) *Deficient performance* by counsel; and that

(ii) But for such deficiency, the *result of the proceeding would have been different* (*e.g.,* defendant would not have been convicted or his sentence would have been shorter).

[Strickland v. Washington, *supra*] Typically, such a claim can be made out only by specifying particular errors of trial counsel, and cannot be based on mere inexperience, lack of time to prepare, gravity of the charges, complexity of defenses, or accessibility of witnesses to counsel. [United States v. Cronic, 466 U.S. 648 (1984)]

Example: Defendant pleaded guilty, was convicted, and was given 60 days to appeal. His attorney neither asked him whether he wanted to appeal nor filed an appeal. Defendant subsequently challenged his conviction, claiming ineffective assistance of counsel. The appellate court held that failure to ask a client whether he wants to appeal is per se ineffective assistance. But the Supreme Court held that the *Strickland* two-pronged test applies. The Court noted that it is not always deficient to fail to ask a client whether he wants to appeal, especially where the client has pleaded guilty. Also, even where the failure is deficient, it does not necessarily affect the ultimate outcome. The defendant must show that but for counsel's deficiency, defendant would have appealed. If the defendant cannot show that he had any valid defenses, this tends to show that the outcome would not have been affected because he probably would not have appealed. [Roe v. Flores-Ortega, 528 U.S. 470 (2000)]

d. Circumstances Not Constituting Ineffective Assistance
Circumstances not constituting ineffective assistance include:

1) Trial Tactics
Courts will not grant relief for any acts or omissions by counsel that they view as trial tactics.

2) Failure to Argue Nonfrivolous Issues
An indigent criminal defendant has no constitutional right to compel his appointed lawyer to argue nonfrivolous issues that the counsel decides, in the exercise of her professional judgment, not to present. [Jones v. Barnes, 463 U.S. 745 (1983)]

3) Rejection of Defendant's Request for a Continuance
The right to counsel is not violated by a trial court's denial of an indigent defendant's request for a continuance in order to permit further investigation when his appointed counsel asserts that she is sufficiently prepared, nor by the court's denial of the indigent defendant's request for a continuance so that he may be represented by the counsel originally assigned to the case, but who was hospitalized at the time of trial. [Morris v. Slappy, 461 U.S. 1 (1983)]

4) Failure to Raise Constitutional Claim that Is Later Invalidated
The failure of a defendant's counsel to raise a federal constitutional claim that was the law at the time of the proceeding but that was later overruled does not prejudice the defendant within the meaning of the Sixth Amendment and does not constitute ineffective assistance of counsel. [Lockhart v. Fretwell, 506 U.S. 364 (1993)]

6. Conflicts of Interest
Joint representation (*i.e.,* a single attorney representing co-defendants) is not per se invalid. However, if an attorney advises the trial court of a resulting conflict of interest at or before trial, and the court refuses to appoint separate counsel, the defendant is entitled to *automatic reversal*. [Holloway v. Arkansas, 435 U.S. 475 (1978); Cuyler v. Sullivan, 446 U.S. 335 (1980)] If the defendant does not object to joint representation in a timely manner, to obtain reversal the defendant must show that the attorney *actively* represented conflicting interests and thereby prejudiced the defendant. [Burger v. Kemp, 483 U.S. 776 (1987)]

a. Conflict with Attorney Is Rarely Ground for Relief
A defendant can rarely obtain relief by claiming a conflict of interest between himself and counsel. Conflicts between a defendant and his attorney are best analyzed as claims of ineffective assistance of counsel. To be successful, the defendant must demonstrate that the conflict with his attorney was so severe that the attorney could not effectively investigate or present the defendant's claims.

b. No Right to Joint Representation
While a defendant ordinarily has the right to counsel of her own choosing, a defendant has no right to be jointly represented with her co-defendants. Trial courts have the authority to limit joint representation to avoid potential and actual conflicts of interest. Even when all of the defendants waive any claim to conflicts of interest, the trial court can still prohibit the joint representation. [Wheat v. United States, 486 U.S. 153 (1988)]

7. Right to Support Services for Defense
Where a defendant has made a preliminary showing that he is likely to be able to use the insanity defense, the state must provide a psychiatrist for the preparation of the defense. Where a state presents evidence that the defendant is likely to be dangerous in the future, the defendant is entitled to psychiatric examination and testimony in the sentencing proceeding. [Ake v. Oklahoma, 470 U.S. 68 (1985)]

8. Seizure of Funds Constitutional
The right to counsel does not forbid the seizure—under the federal drug forfeiture statute [21 U.S.C. §853]—of drug money and property obtained with drug money, even when such

money and property were going to be used by the defendant to pay his attorney of choice. [Caplin & Drysdale, Chartered v. United States, 491 U.S. 617 (1989)]

9. **Right Limited While Testifying**
A defendant has a general right to consult with his attorney during the course of trial; however, he has no right to consult with his attorney while he is testifying. Whether a defendant has a right to consult with his attorney during breaks in his testimony depends on the character of the break. Generally, the longer the break, the more likely the Court will find the right. [*Compare* Geders v. United States, *supra*, C.1.—defendant must be allowed to talk with attorney during overnight break in defendant's testimony because ordinary trial tactics can be, and usually are, discussed during such breaks—*with* Perry v. Leeke, 488 U.S. 272 (1989)—sequestration during 15-minute break between defendant's direct testimony and cross-examination permissible because cross-examination of uncounseled witness more likely to lead to truth]

D. RIGHT TO CONFRONT WITNESSES

The Sixth Amendment grants to the defendant in a criminal prosecution the right to confront adverse witnesses. This right, held applicable to the states in *Pointer v. Texas*, 380 U.S. 400 (1965), seeks to ensure that:

(i) The fact finder and the defendant *observe the demeanor* of the testifying witness; and

(ii) The defendant has the opportunity to *cross-examine* any witness testifying against him.

The defendant is entitled to a face-to-face encounter with the witness, but absence of face-to-face confrontation between the defendant and the accuser does not violate the Sixth Amendment when preventing such confrontation serves an important public purpose (such as insulating a child witness from trauma) and the reliability of the witness's testimony is otherwise assured. [Maryland v. Craig, 497 U.S. 836 (1990)]

1. **Right Not Absolute**

   a. **Disruptive Defendant**
   A defendant has no absolute right to confront witnesses, as a judge may remove a disruptive defendant. [Illinois v. Allen, 397 U.S. 337 (1970)]

   b. **Voluntarily Leaving Courtroom**
   A defendant has not been deprived of his right of confrontation if he voluntarily leaves the courtroom during the trial, and the trial continues in his absence. [Taylor v. United States, 414 U.S. 17 (1974)]

   c. **Government May Discourage Attendance**
   Government action that has an effect of discouraging a defendant's attendance at trial will not necessarily violate the right to attend and confront witnesses.
   Example: Defendant attended his trial and testified in his own defense as the last witness. On summation, the prosecutor commented to the jury that they should consider that by choosing to testify last, defendant had an opportunity to listen to all of the other witnesses and adjust his testimony accordingly. After he was convicted, defendant claimed that the prosecutor's summation was unconstitutional because it used defendant's constitutionally protected right to attend trial as a tool to impeach his credibility and so would have the effect of discouraging attendance. The Supreme Court held that the right to attend may be burdened and upheld the conviction. [Portuondo v. Agard, 529 U.S. 61 (2000)]

2. **Introduction of Co-Defendant's Confession**
A right of confrontation problem develops with the introduction of a co-defendant's confession because of the inability of the nonconfessing defendant to compel the confessing co-defendant to take the stand for cross-examination at their joint trial.

   a. **General Rule—Confession Implicating Co-Defendant Prohibited**
   If two persons are tried together and one has given a confession that implicates the other, the right of confrontation prohibits the use of that statement, even with instructions to the jury to consider it only as going to the guilt of the "confessing" defendant. [Bruton v. United States, 391 U.S. 123 (1968)] A co-defendant's confession is inadmissible even when it interlocks with the defendant's own confession, which is admitted. [Cruz v. New York, 481 U.S. 186 (1987)]

b. Exceptions
Such a statement may be admitted if:

1) All portions referring to the other defendant can be eliminated. *Note:* It is not sufficient merely to insert a blank or some other substitution for the name of the other defendant; the redaction must not indicate the defendant's involvement. [*Compare* Richardson v. Marsh, 481 U.S. 200 (1987)—after redaction, confession indicated that defendant and a third party (who was not a co-defendant) participated in the crime and contained no indication of co-defendant's involvement, *with* Gray v. Maryland, 523 U.S. 185 (1998)—redaction "me, deleted, deleted, and a few other guys killed" the victim held to clearly refer to co-defendant];

2) The confessing defendant takes the stand and subjects himself to cross-examination with respect to the truth or falsity of what the statement asserts. This rule applies even if he denies having ever made the confession. [Nelson v. O'Neil, 402 U.S. 622 (1973)] In effect, an opportunity at trial to cross-examine the hearsay declarant with respect to the underlying facts makes the declaration nonhearsay for purposes of the Confrontation Clause; or

3) The confession of the nontestifying co-defendant is being used to rebut the defendant's claim that his confession was obtained coercively. The jury must be instructed as to the purpose of the admission. [Tennessee v. Street, 471 U.S. 409 (1985)]

3. Use of Prior Judicial Proceeding Hearsay
"Hearsay" (evidence of a person's statements other than those made at the trial) may be admissible despite the Confrontation Clause. However, if the hearsay consists of *statements made at a prior judicial proceeding,* two facts must be shown before the hearsay statement will be admitted [Ohio v. Roberts, 448 U.S. 56 (1980), *as modified by* United States v. Inadi, 475 U.S. 387 (1986)]:

(i) The prosecution has made a *good faith effort* to obtain the in-court testimony of the witness and has failed (*i.e.,* the witness is unavailable); and

(ii) The defendant has had an *opportunity to cross-examine* the person as to the testimony or has otherwise had an opportunity to test its accuracy.

[Barber v. Page, 390 U.S. 719 (1968)]
Example: Witness against D testified at a preliminary hearing that D sold him drugs. D was represented by counsel at the time. At trial, witness took the stand and testified that he could no longer remember—because of drugs—what had happened. Prosecution then offered testimony of witness at the preliminary hearing. Did admission of this violate D's right of confrontation? No. Prosecution had tried and failed to produce in-court testimony. D had adequate opportunity to test accuracy of evidence at either of two points: cross-examination at the preliminary hearing or cross-examination of witness at trial. [California v. Green, 399 U.S. 149 (1970)]

a. Limited to Prior Judicial Proceedings
The unavailability analysis of *Ohio v. Roberts, supra,* is a necessary part of the Confrontation Clause inquiry only when the challenged out-of-court statements were made in a prior judicial proceeding. The Confrontation Clause does not require a declarant to be produced at trial or shown to be "unavailable" as a prerequisite to introduction of out-of-court statements that qualify under the hearsay exceptions for "spontaneous statements" or statements made in the course of securing medical treatment. [White v. Illinois, 502 U.S. 346 (1992)]

E. BURDEN OF PROOF AND SUFFICIENCY OF EVIDENCE

1. Burden of Proof

a. Proof Beyond a Reasonable Doubt
The Due Process Clause requires in all criminal cases that the state prove guilt beyond a reasonable doubt. [*In re* Winship, 397 U.S. 358 (1970)] The prosecution must have the burden of proving the elements of the crime charged. Thus, the Supreme Court has

held that if "malice aforethought" is an element of murder, the state may not require the defendant to prove that he committed the homicide in the heat of passion, on the rationale that this would require the defendant to disprove the element of malice aforethought. [Mullaney v. Wilbur, 421 U.S. 684 (1975)] However, a state may impose the burden of proof upon the defendant in regard to an *affirmative defense* such as insanity [Leland v. Oregon, 343 U.S. 790 (1952)] or self-defense [Martin v. Ohio, 480 U.S. 228 (1987)].

Example: Under state law, in a prosecution for second degree murder, the state must prove intentional causing of death. A defendant is entitled to acquittal of second degree murder and conviction of manslaughter if he proves by a preponderance of the evidence that he acted under the influence of "an extreme emotional disturbance." May the burden of proving that be placed on the defendant? Yes, because it does not affect the state's obligation to prove all elements of the crime of second degree murder. [Patterson v. New York, 432 U.S. 197 (1977)]

b. Presumption of Innocence

Although not mentioned in the Constitution, the presumption of innocence is a basic component of a fair trial. A defendant does not have an absolute right to a jury instruction on the presumption of innocence, but the trial judge should evaluate the totality of the circumstances, including (i) the other jury instructions, (ii) the arguments of counsel, and (iii) whether the weight of the evidence was overwhelming, to determine whether such an instruction is necessary for a fair trial. [Kentucky v. Whorton, 441 U.S. 786 (1979)]

2. Presumptions

A permissive presumption allows, but does not require, the jury to infer an element of an offense from proof by the prosecutor of the basic fact, while the jury must accept a mandatory presumption even if it is the sole evidence of the elemental fact.

a. Permissive Presumptions—Rational Relation Standard

A permissive presumption must comport with the standard that there be a rational connection between the basic facts that the prosecution proved and the ultimate fact presumed, and that the latter is more likely than not to flow from the former. [Ulster County Court v. Allen, 442 U.S. 140 (1979)]

b. Mandatory Presumptions Unconstitutional

A mandatory presumption or a presumption that shifts the burden of proof to the defendant violates the Fourteenth Amendment's requirement that the state prove every element of a crime beyond a reasonable doubt. [Sandstrom v. Montana, 442 U.S. 510 (1979)]

Examples: 1) A mandatory presumption was created by jury instructions in a "malice murder" trial which stated that the "acts of a person of sound mind and discretion are presumed to be the product of a person's will, but the presumption may be rebutted," and a "person of sound mind and discretion is presumed to intend the natural and probable consequences of his acts, but the presumption may be rebutted." These instructions are unconstitutional because they would lead a reasonable juror to conclude that the state's burden of proof on intent to kill may be inferred from proof of the defendant's acts unless the defendant proves otherwise. [Francis v. Franklin, 471 U.S. 307 (1985)]

2) In a criminal contempt proceeding for failure to pay child support, the state may not presume that the defendant was able to pay the amount due. One of the elements of contempt is the ability to comply with the court's order. Thus, the state may not presume ability to pay, but rather ability to pay must be proved beyond a reasonable doubt. [Hicks v. Feiock, 485 U.S. 624 (1988)]

3. Sufficiency of Evidence

The requirement of proof beyond a reasonable doubt in the Due Process Clause means that the sufficiency of the evidence supporting a criminal conviction in state court is, to some extent, a federal constitutional issue. Due process is violated if, viewing all the evidence in the light most favorable to the prosecution, no rational judge or jury would have found the defendant guilty of the crime of which he was convicted. [Jackson v. Virginia, 443 U.S. 307 (1979)]

4. **Prior Act Evidence**

Under the Due Process Clause, as a general constitutional rule, prior act evidence is admissible for various purposes if it is probative and relevant. Thus in a criminal trial evidence of prior bodily injury was admissible to show that a child victim had sustained repeated and/or serious injuries by nonaccidental means (the "battered child syndrome") to infer that the victim's death was not accidental, even though there was no direct evidence linking the prior injuries to the defendant. [Estelle v. McGuire, 502 U.S. 62 (1991)]

5. **Right to Present Defensive Evidence**

Due process requires an opportunity to establish innocence.

Example: The arbitrary exclusion of a class of defense witnesses violates both due process and the right to compel the production of witnesses on one's own behalf.

a. **Application—Exclusionary Rules of Evidence**

Even exclusionary rules of evidence that are valid on their face may combine to deprive a defendant of a fair opportunity to rebut the prosecution's case.

Examples: 1) Given the right to an acquittal if there is reasonable doubt on any element of a criminal charge, a defendant is denied a fair trial when the state's hearsay rule prevents him from showing that another person has confessed to the crime for which he is being tried, and where the state's rule against impeaching one's own witness prevents the defendant from even using the prior confession to cast doubt on the credibility of the confessor's unexpectedly damning testimony. [Chambers v. Mississippi, 410 U.S. 284 (1973)]

2) A state's per se rule excluding hypnotically refreshed testimony unconstitutionally infringes on a defendant's right to present testimony on his own behalf. A per se rule excludes even testimony that may be reliable. [Rock v. Arkansas, 479 U.S. 1079 (1987)]

b. **Exclusion as Sanction**

A trial court may, however, exclude defense evidence as a sanction for the defendant's violation of discovery rules or procedures. For example, if the defendant's attorney fails to give advance notice that a witness will testify, the trial court may prohibit that witness from testifying. [Taylor v. Illinois, 484 U.S. 400 (1988)]

VIII.   GUILTY PLEAS AND PLEA BARGAINING

A. **GUILTY PLEA WAIVES RIGHT TO JURY TRIAL**

A guilty plea is a waiver of the Sixth Amendment right to jury trial. Between 70% and 95% of all criminal cases are settled by guilty pleas.

B. **BASIC TRENDS**

sup ct – will not disturb guilty pleas after sentencing
– treats it as contract

1. **Intelligent Choice Among Alternatives**

The Court from 1970 to the present has indicated an unwillingness to disturb a guilty plea it views as an intelligent choice among the defendant's alternatives on the advice of counsel.

2. **Contract View**

There is a trend toward the contract view of plea negotiation and bargaining. In this view, the plea agreement should be revealed in the record of the taking of the plea and its terms enforced against both the prosecutor and the defendant. [Ricketts v. Adamson, 483 U.S. 1 (1987)]

C. **TAKING THE PLEA**

1. **Advising the Defendant of the Charge, the Potential Penalty, and Her Rights**

The judge must advise the defendant personally (not the defense counsel) [McCarthy v. United States, 394 U.S. 459 (1969)], informing her:

a. Of the nature of the charge to which the plea is offered (the judge need not touch upon all elements of the offense, but the record must show that he explained to the defendant the crucial elements, such as the intent element of murder) [Henderson v. Morgan, 426 U.S. 637 (1976)];

must be on records = — nature of
— max of authorized sentence
— right not to plead guilty & demand trial
— by pleading, go directly to sentencing

     b.   Of the maximum possible penalty and of any mandatory minimum, but the failure to explain a special parole term is not fatal [United States v. Timmreck, 441 U.S. 780 (1979)]; and

     c.   That she has a right not to plead guilty, and that if she does, she waives her right to trial.

2. Requirement of Adequate Record
Boykin v. Alabama, 395 U.S. 238 (1969), requires that a record be made of the taking of all guilty pleas. The record must show that the above information was explained to the defendant, indicating that the plea was ***voluntary and intelligent***.

    a. Unfairly Informed Defendant Not Bound
    If counsel makes unfair representations to the defendant concerning the result of the defendant's pleading guilty, and the defendant can prove this, the defendant is not bound by her record answer, obtained at the plea taking, that her counsel made no such representations. [Blackledge v. Allison, 431 U.S. 63 (1977)]

    b. Not Applicable in Some Recidivist Proceedings
    The requirement of a record and transcript to show that a guilty plea was voluntary and intelligent is not applicable to recidivist proceedings where the state introduces prior guilty pleas without having transcripts of those earlier guilty plea proceedings. [Parke v. Raley, 506 U.S. 20 (1993)]

3. Remedy
The remedy for a failure to meet the standards for taking a plea is withdrawal of the plea and ***pleading anew***.

4. Factual Basis for Plea Not Constitutionally Required
There is no general requirement that the record contain evidence of the defendant's guilt or other factual basis for the plea. (*But see* D.1., below.)

D. COLLATERAL ATTACKS ON GUILTY PLEAS AFTER SENTENCE

Those pleas that are seen as an intelligent choice among the defendant's alternatives are immune from collateral attack.

Examples: 1) A plea is not involuntary merely because it was induced by a fear of the death penalty, which could be imposed only after a jury trial. Fear of the death penalty is like fear of any other penalty, which is the reason defendants plead guilty. [Brady v. United States, 397 U.S. 742 (1970)]

                2) Fear of a coerced confession in the hands of the state will not support a collateral attack, and the defendant will be bound to his choice to plead guilty. If the defendant thought the confession was coerced, he should have made a motion to suppress; if he did not, the court will think it was because he believed he could not win. [McMann v. Richardson, 397 U.S. 759 (1970)]

                3) Unconstitutional, systematic, racial exclusion in the indicting grand jury will not entitle the defendant to collateral relief. Here, also the Court views the choice not to object and to plead guilty as the result of the defendant's informed decision as to what course would be in his best interest. [Tollett v. Henderson, 411 U.S. 258 (1973)]

1. Plea Offered by Defendant Who Denies Guilt
When a defendant pleads guilty despite protesting his innocence, the plea will be seen as an intelligent choice by the defendant, and withdrawal of the plea will not be permitted when there is other strong evidence of guilt in the record. Admission of guilt is not a constitutional requisite to imposition of criminal penalty. [North Carolina v. Alford, 400 U.S. 25 (1970)]

2. Bases for an Attack on a Guilty Plea After Sentence

    a. Plea Involuntary
    Failure to meet the constitutional standards for taking a guilty plea will support a post-sentence attack on the plea.

    ✓ **b.**   **Lack of Jurisdiction**

The defendant may withdraw his plea if the court lacked jurisdiction to take the plea, or if prosecution for the offense for which the plea was offered is barred by double jeopardy. [Menna v. New York, 423 U.S. 61 (1975)]

    ✓ **c.**   **Ineffective Assistance of Counsel**

Ineffective assistance of counsel undercuts the assumption of an intelligent choice among the defendant's alternatives on the advice of counsel. Therefore, a defendant may successfully attack a guilty plea on the ground that he received ineffective assistance of counsel if, ***but for counsel's errors, the defendant probably would not have pleaded guilty*** and instead would have insisted on going to trial. [Hill v. Lockhart, 474 U.S. 52 (1985)]

    ✓ **d.**   **Failure to Keep the Plea Bargain**   *failure of prosecutor*
See E.1., below.

E.   PLEA BARGAINING

1.   **Enforcement of the Bargain**

A defendant who enters into a plea bargain has a right to have that bargain kept. The plea bargain will be ***enforced against the prosecutor and the defendant***, ***but not against the judge***, who does not have to accept the plea.

    a.   **Prosecution**

If the prosecution does not keep the bargain, the court should decide whether the circumstances require specific performance of the plea agreement or whether the defendant should be granted an opportunity to withdraw her guilty plea. [Santobello v. New York, 404 U.S. 257 (1971)] However, if the prosecutor withdraws a proposed plea bargain and the accused subsequently pleads guilty on other terms, the original offer cannot be specifically enforced despite the accused's attempt to "accept" the offer. [Mabry v. Johnson, 467 U.S. 504 (1984)]

    b.   **Defendant**

If the defendant does not live up to the plea agreement, his plea and sentence can be vacated.

    Example: D agrees to testify against a co-defendant in exchange for a reduction in charges from first to second degree murder. If D fails to testify, the prosecution can have D's plea and sentence vacated and reinstate the first degree murder charge. [Ricketts v. Adamson, B.2., *supra*]

2.   **Power of the State to Threaten More Serious Charge**

Consistent with the contract theory of plea negotiation, the state has the power to drive a hard bargain. A guilty plea is not involuntary merely because it was entered in response to the prosecution's threat to charge the defendant with a more serious crime if she does not plead guilty. [Bordenkircher v. Hayes, 434 U.S. 357 (1978)]

3.   **Power to Charge More Serious Offense**

The Supreme Court has held that there is no prosecutorial vindictiveness in charging a more serious offense when defendant demands a jury trial. [United States v. Goodwin, 457 U.S. 368 (1982)]

4.   **Admission of Statements Made in Connection with Plea Bargaining**

Under the Federal Rules of Evidence and of Criminal Procedure, statements made by a defendant in the course of unsuccessful plea negotiations are inadmissible at trial. However, such statements can be admitted *if* the defendant has knowingly and voluntarily waived the Federal Rules' exclusionary provisions. [United States v. Mezzanatto, 513 U.S. 196 (1995)]

5.   **No Right to Impeachment or Affirmative Defense Evidence**

Defendants are ***not*** entitled either to impeachment evidence or to evidence relevant to affirmative defenses prior to entering a plea agreement. Failure to provide such evidence does not make a plea involuntary. [United States v. Ruiz, 122 S. Ct. 2450 (2002)]

F.   COLLATERAL EFFECTS OF GUILTY PLEAS

1.   **Conviction May Be Used in Other Proceedings**

The Supreme Court has held that evidence of a defendant's conviction, based on a guilty plea in one state, may be introduced at trial in a second state for the purpose of proving a "specification" allowing imposition of the death penalty [Marshall v. Lonberger, 459 U.S. 422 (1983)], and a defendant is "convicted" within the meaning of the firearms disabilities provisions of the 1968 Gun Control Act when the defendant pleads guilty to a state charge punishable by more than one year, even if no formal judgment is entered and the record has been expunged. [Dickerson v. New Banner Institute, 460 U.S. 103 (1983)]

2. Does Not Admit Legality of Search
The Court has decided that a defendant's guilty plea neither admits the legality of the incriminating search nor waives Fourth Amendment claims in a subsequent civil damages action challenging the constitutionality of the incriminating search. [Haring v. Prosise, 462 U.S. 306 (1983)]

IX. CONSTITUTIONAL RIGHTS IN RELATION TO SENTENCING AND PUNISHMENT

A. PROCEDURAL RIGHTS IN SENTENCING

1. Right to Counsel
Sentencing is usually a "critical stage" of a criminal proceeding, thus requiring the assistance of counsel, as substantial rights of the defendant may be affected.

Examples: 1) The absence of counsel during sentencing after a plea of guilty, coupled with the judge's materially untrue assumptions concerning a defendant's criminal record, deprived the defendant of due process. [Townsend v. Burke, 334 U.S. 736 (1984)]

2) The absence of counsel at the time of sentencing where no sentence of imprisonment was imposed, but the defendant was put on probation, deprived the defendant of due process because certain legal rights (*i.e.,* the right to appeal) might be lost by failing to assert them at this time. [Mempa v. Rhay, *supra,* VII.C.1.]

2. Right to Confrontation and Cross-Examination
The *usual* sentence may be based on hearsay and uncross-examined reports. [Williams v. New York, 337 U.S. 241 (1949)]

a. "New" Proceeding
Where a magnified sentence is based on a statute (*e.g.,* one permitting indeterminate sentence) that requires new findings of fact to be made (*e.g.,* that defendant is a habitual criminal, mentally ill, or deficient, etc.), those facts must be found in a context that grants the right to confrontation and cross-examination. [Specht v. Patterson, 386 U.S. 605 (1966)]

b. Capital Sentencing Procedures
It is clear that a defendant in a death penalty case must have more opportunity for confrontation than need be given a defendant in other sentencing proceedings. [Gardner v. Florida, 430 U.S. 349 (1977)—sentence of death based in part upon report not disclosed to defendant invalid]

B. RESENTENCING AFTER SUCCESSFUL APPEAL AND RECONVICTION

1. General Rule—Record Must Show Reasons for Harsher Sentence
If a judge imposes a greater punishment than at the first trial after the defendant has successfully appealed and then is reconvicted, she must set forth in the record the reasons for the harsher sentence based on "objective information concerning identifiable conduct on the part of the defendant occurring after the time of the original sentencing proceedings." [North Carolina v. Pearce, 395 U.S. 711 (1969)] The purpose of this requirement is to ensure that the defendant is not vindictively penalized for exercising his right to appeal.

Note: When a defendant successfully appeals, an exception to the Double Jeopardy Clause permits retrial. (*See* XIII.B.3., *infra.*)

2. Exceptions

a. **Reconviction upon Trial De Novo**
Some jurisdictions grant the defendant the right to a trial de novo as a matter of course after a trial in an inferior court. A trial de novo involves a fresh determination of guilt or innocence without reference to the lower conviction or fact of appeal. The rationale of *Pearce* does not apply when the defendant receives a greater sentence upon a trial de novo, because the new judge reduces the likelihood of vindictiveness. [Colten v. Kentucky, 407 U.S. 104 (1972)]

b. **Jury Sentencing**
Pearce does not apply to states that use jury sentencing, unless the second jury was told of the first jury's sentence. [Chaffin v. Stynchcombe, 412 U.S. 17 (1973)]

3. **Recharging in a Trial De Novo**
The prosecutor may not obtain an indictment for a more serious charge in a trial de novo, because of the possibility of prosecutorial vindictiveness and retaliation for exercising the statutory right to a trial de novo. [Blackledge v. Perry, 417 U.S. 21 (1974)]

C. SUBSTANTIVE RIGHTS IN REGARD TO PUNISHMENT

1. **Criminal Penalties Constituting "Cruel and Unusual Punishment"**
The Eighth Amendment prohibition against cruel and unusual punishment places several limitations upon criminal punishments.

a. **Punishment Grossly Disproportionate to Offense**
A penalty that is grossly disproportionate to the seriousness of the offense committed is cruel and unusual.
Examples: 1) D, convicted of falsifying a public record, received a sentence of 20 years' imprisonment at hard labor. Did this violate the Eighth Amendment? Yes, since the penalty was so disproportionate to the offense. [Weems v. United States, 217 U.S. 349 (1910)]

    2) A sentence of life imprisonment without the possibility of parole imposed upon a recidivist following conviction of his seventh nonviolent felony, the uttering of a bad check, is significantly disproportionate to the crime and is thus a violation of the Eighth Amendment. The unconstitutional taint is not eliminated by the possibility of commutation which, unlike parole, is granted on an ad hoc, standardless basis. [Solem v. Helm, 463 U.S. 277 (1983)]

Compare: A mandatory life sentence for possession of a certain quantity of cocaine (650 grams—indicating that the defendant was a dealer) is *not* cruel and unusual, even though the statute did not allow consideration of mitigating factors (*compare* death penalty cases, below). [Harmelin v. Michigan, 501 U.S. 957 (1991)]

b. **Proportionality—No Right to Comparison of Penalties in Similar Cases**
The Eighth Amendment does not require state appellate courts to compare the death sentence imposed in a case under appeal with other penalties imposed in similar cases. [Pulley v. Harris, 465 U.S. 37 (1984)]

c. **Death Penalty**

1) **For Murder**
The death penalty is not inherently cruel and unusual punishment, but the Eighth Amendment requires that it be imposed only under a *statutory scheme* that gives the judge or jury reasonable *discretion,* full *information* concerning defendants, and *guidance* in making the decision. [Furman v. Georgia, 408 U.S. 238 (1972); Gregg v. Georgia, 428 U.S. 153 (1976)]

a) **Discretion**
A jury must be allowed discretion to consider mitigating circumstances in death penalty cases. Thus, a statute cannot make the death penalty mandatory upon conviction of first degree murder [Woodson v. North Carolina, 428 U.S. 280 (1976)], or for the killing of a police officer or firefighter [Roberts

v. Louisiana, 431 U.S. 633 (1977)], or for a killing by an inmate who is serving a life sentence [Sumner v. Shuman, 483 U.S. 66 (1987)]. Moreover, it is not sufficient to allow the jury to consider only some mitigating circumstances; they must be allowed to consider any aspect of the defendant's character or any circumstance of his crime as a factor in mitigation. [Penry v. Lynaugh, 492 U.S. 302 (1989)—death sentence reversed because jury was not allowed to consider defendant's mental retardation and abused childhood in mitigation] In addition, a death sentence must be reversed if the jurors may have been confused by jury instructions regarding their right to consider mitigating circumstances. [Mills v. Maryland, 486 U.S. 367 (1988)]

Examples: 1) A statute requires the jury to impose the death penalty if a defendant is convicted of specific crimes with aggravation, but also requires the trial judge to hear evidence of aggravating and mitigating circumstances before sentencing the defendant. The statute is constitutional. [Baldwin v. Alabama, 472 U.S. 372 (1985)]

2) A statute that instructs jurors to impose the death penalty if they find it probable that the defendant would commit criminal acts in the future, considering all aggravating or mitigating evidence presented at trial, was upheld against an argument that the instruction foreclosed consideration of the defendant's youth. The court found that consideration of future dangerousness leaves open ample room for considering youth as a mitigating factor since "the signature qualities of youth are transient." [Johnson v. Texas, 509 U.S. 350 (1993)]

(1)   Judge May Impose Death Against Advisory Jury Opinion
A trial judge may impose the death penalty even though an advisory jury has recommended a life sentence. [Spaziano v. Florida, 468 U.S. 447 (1984)] Moreover, a state is not required to define the weight that the judge must accord to an advisory jury's recommendation. [Harris v. Alabama, 513 U.S. 504 (1995)]

(2)   Evidence Required for Mitigation Instruction
Nothing in the Constitution requires state courts to give mitigating circumstance instructions where the jury has heard no evidence on mitigating circumstances. [Delo v. Lashley, 507 U.S. 272 (1993)]

b)   **Information**

(1)   Instructions on Lesser Included Offenses
A defendant is not entitled to a jury instruction on every possible lesser included offense supported by the facts in a capital case [Schad v. Arizona, 501 U.S. 624 (1991)], but a statute cannot prohibit instructions on *all* lesser included offenses [Beck v. Alabama, 447 U.S. 625 (1980)]. *Rationale:* If the jurors are not instructed on any lesser included offense and believe that the defendant is guilty of a crime other than murder, they might impose the death penalty rather than let the defendant go unpunished. But if the jury is given instructions on a lesser included offense (*e.g.*, second degree murder), they will not have to make an all or nothing choice, and so a resulting death penalty will stand.

(2)   Victim Impact Statements
A "victim impact statement" (*i.e.*, an assessment of how the crime affected the victim's family) may be considered during the sentencing phase of a capital case. *Rationale:* The defendant has long been allowed to present mitigating factors, so the jury must be allowed to counterbalance the impact on the victim's family in order to "assess meaningfully the defendant's moral culpability and blameworthiness." [Payne v. Tennessee, 501 U.S. 808 (1991)]

c)   **Guidance**
A statute providing for the death penalty may not be vague.

Example: A statute that permits imposition of the death penalty when a murder is "outrageously or wantonly vile, horrible, or inhuman in that it involved torture, depravity of mind, or an aggravated battery to the victim" is unconstitutionally vague. [Godfrey v. Georgia, 446 U.S. 420 (1980); Maynard v. Cartwright, 486 U.S. 356 (1988)]

Compare: A statute that imposes the death penalty where the murderer displayed "utter disregard for human life" provides sufficiently clear and objective standards for imposition of the death penalty where the state supreme court had construed the statute to apply only where the killing was committed by a "cold-blooded, pitiless slayer." [Arave v. Creech, 507 U.S. 463 (1993)]

d) Prior Crimes

Most states provide that prior crimes by the defendant, particularly those involving force or violence, are aggravating factors that either make the defendant eligible for the death penalty or are weighed by the jurors in reaching their decision on whether to impose the death penalty. If a death sentence is based in any part on a defendant's prior conviction, the sentence must be reversed if the prior conviction is invalidated. [Johnson v. Mississippi, 486 U.S. 578 (1988)]

e) Standard of Review

Where a death sentence has been affected by a vague or otherwise unconstitutional factor, the death sentence can still be upheld, but only if all aggravating and mitigating factors involved are reweighed by all of the judges to whom the sentence is appealed and death is still found to be appropriate. [Richmond v. Lewis, 506 U.S. 40 (1993)]

2) For Rape

The Eighth Amendment prohibits imposition of the death penalty for the crime of raping an adult woman, because the penalty is disproportionate to the offense. [Coker v. Georgia, 433 U.S. 584 (1977)]

3) For Felony Murder

The death penalty may not be imposed for felony murder where the defendant, as an accomplice, "did not take or attempt or intend to take life, or intend that lethal force be employed." [Enmund v. Florida, 458 U.S. 782 (1982)] However, the death penalty may be imposed on a felony murderer who neither killed nor intended to kill where he participated in a major way in a felony that resulted in murder, and acted with *reckless indifference to the value of human life*. [Tison v. Arizona, 481 U.S. 137 (1987)—defendants helped prisoner escape and provided him with weapons]

4) Jury Responsibility for Verdict

It is unconstitutional to diminish the jury's sense of responsibility of its role in determining a death sentence. [Caldwell v. Mississippi, 527 U.S. 373 (1985)—prosecutor's comment to the jury that its verdict is reviewable and that the verdict is not the final decision is sufficient to diminish the jury's sense of responsibility; Ring v. Arizona, VII.B.6., *supra*—unconstitutional for judge to determine after jury verdict of guilt whether aggravating factors justify imposition of the death penalty]

a) Compare—Instruction Regarding Failure to Agree

Even at the defendant's request, the court need not instruct the jury of the consequences of its failure to agree on a verdict. [Jones v. United States, 527 U.S. 373 (1999)—Eighth Amendment was not violated where court denied defendant's request that jury be instructed that judge would impose sentence if jury could not unanimously agree]

5) Racial Discrimination

Statistical evidence that black defendants who kill white victims are more likely to receive the death penalty does not establish that the penalty was imposed as a result of unconstitutional discrimination. [McCleskey v. Kemp, 481 U.S. 279 (1987)]

6) Sanity Requirement
The Eighth Amendment prohibits states from inflicting the death penalty upon a prisoner who is insane (*i.e.*, one who was sane at the time the crime was committed and was properly sentenced to death, but is insane at the time of execution) [Ford v. Wainwright, 477 U.S. 399 (1986)], but the Court has indicated that the Eighth Amendment does not prohibit execution of a murderer who is mentally retarded but competent to stand trial and not insane [Penry v. Lynaugh, *supra*, 1)a)—death penalty reversed on other grounds].

7) Mental Retardation
It is cruel and unusual punishment to impose the death penalty on a person who is mentally retarded. [Atkins v. Virginia, 122 S. Ct. 2242 (2002)]

8) For Minors
It is not cruel and unusual to impose the death penalty on murderers who were 16 or older at the time they committed murder because there is no national consensus forbidding such executions. [Stanford v. Kentucky, 492 U.S. 361 (1989)] However, execution of murderers who were younger than 16 at the time of their crime might be forbidden. [Thompson v. Oklahoma, 487 U.S. 815 (1988)—four Justices finding it cruel and unusual, one Justice finding it necessary to have a statute specifically authorizing such executions]

d. "Status" Crimes
A statute that makes it a crime to have a given "status" violates the Eighth Amendment because it punishes a mere propensity to engage in dangerous behavior. But it is no violation of the amendment to make specific activity related to a certain status criminal.

Example: A statute makes it criminal to "be a common drunkard" and to appear in public in an intoxicated condition. May a chronic alcoholic be convicted of both of these? No. He may not be convicted of being a common drunkard, because this is a prohibited status crime. But he may be convicted of appearing in public while intoxicated, because this crime prohibits the act of "appearing." [Powell v. Texas, 392 U.S. 514 (1968)]

2. Recidivist Statutes
A mandatory life sentence imposed pursuant to a recidivist statute does *not* constitute cruel and unusual punishment, even though the three felonies that formed the predicate for the sentence were nonviolent, property-related offenses. [Rummel v. Estelle, 445 U.S. 263 (1980)] (There is an apparent conflict with *Solem v. Helm, supra*, C.1.a. While *Solem* is inconsistent with *Rummel*, the Supreme Court declined to distinguish *Rummel* in reaching its holding in *Solem*.)

3. Punishing the Exercise of Constitutional Rights
A punishment of greater length or severity cannot constitutionally be reserved by statute for those who assert their right to plead innocent and to demand trial by jury. [United States v. Jackson, 390 U.S. 570 (1968)—death penalty available only for federal kidnapping defendants who insist on jury trial; penalty of death in such circumstances cannot be carried out, but guilty pleas induced by such a scheme are not automatically involuntary]

4. Consideration of Defendant's Perjury at Trial
In determining sentence, a trial judge may take into account a belief that the defendant, while testifying at trial on his own behalf, committed perjury. This is important in evaluating the defendant's prospects for rehabilitation and does not impose an improper burden upon a defendant's right to testify. [United States v. Grayson, 438 U.S. 41 (1978)]

5. Imprisonment of Indigents for Nonpayment of Fines Violates Equal Protection Clause
Where the aggregate imprisonment exceeds the maximum period fixed by statute and results directly from an involuntary nonpayment of a fine or court costs, there is an impermissible discrimination and a violation of the Equal Protection Clause. [Williams v. Illinois, 399 U.S. 235 (1970)] It is also a violation of equal protection to limit punishment to payment

of a fine for those who are able to pay it, but to convert the fine to imprisonment for those who are unable to pay it. [Tate v. Short, 401 U.S. 395 (1971)—30 days or $30]

a. Imprisonment of Parolee for Nonpayment of Fine
A trial court may not revoke a defendant's probation and imprison him for the remainder of the probation term for failure to pay a fine and make restitution without showing that the defendant actually was capable of payment or that there were no alternative forms of punishment available to meet the state's interest in punishment and deterrence. [Bearden v. Georgia, 461 U.S. 660 (1983)]

X. CONSTITUTIONAL PROBLEMS ON APPEAL

A. NO RIGHT TO APPEAL
There is apparently no federal constitutional right to an appeal. Several Supreme Court opinions suggest that all appeals could constitutionally be abolished.

B. EQUAL PROTECTION AND RIGHT TO COUNSEL ON APPEAL

1. First Appeal
If an avenue of post-conviction review (appellate or collateral) is provided, conditions that make the review less accessible to the poor than to the rich violate equal protection. [Griffin v. Illinois, 351 U.S. 12 (1956)—indigent entitled to free transcript on appeal]

Examples: 1) The Equal Protection Clause was violated where a statute requiring the payment of fees for a transcript of a preliminary hearing was applied to deny a free transcript to an indigent. [Roberts v. LaValle, 389 U.S. 40 (1968)]

2) Requiring reimbursement for costs of a trial transcription only of those incarcerated (not from those fined, given suspended sentence, or placed on probation) violates equal protection. [Rinaldi v. Yaeger, 384 U.S. 305 (1966)] But a state can distinguish between convicted and acquitted defendants in this context and require reimbursement only from those convicted. [Fuller v. Oregon, 417 U.S. 40 (1974)]

3) Illinois rule providing for trial transcript on appeal only in felony cases is an unreasonable distinction in violation of equal protection. Even in misdemeanor cases punishable by fine only, a defendant must be afforded as effective an appeal as a defendant who can pay, and where the grounds of the appeal make out a colorable need for a complete transcript, the burden is on the state to show that something less will suffice. [Mayer v. City of Chicago, 404 U.S. 189 (1971)]

a. Right to Appointed Counsel
Indigents must be given counsel at state expense during a first appeal granted to all as a matter of right. [Douglas v. California, *supra*, VII.C.1.] Mere failure to request appointment of counsel does not constitute waiver of the right to assistance of counsel on appeal.

b. Attorney May Withdraw If Appeal Frivolous
An appellate court can permit withdrawal of counsel who concludes that appeal would be frivolous. However, before doing so, the state must take steps to ***ensure that the defendant's right to counsel is not being denied.***

Examples: 1) It is sufficient to (i) require counsel to file a brief referring to anything in the record that might arguably support an appeal (an *Anders* brief) and (ii) require the appellate court to determine that counsel has correctly concluded that appeal is frivolous. [Anders v. California, 386 U.S. 738 (1967)—striking California procedure that allowed counsel to withdraw upon filing a conclusory letter that simply stated the appeal had no merit]

2) It is sufficient to require counsel to (i) summarize the procedural and factual history of the case but (ii) remain silent on the merits of the case

unless the appellate court directs otherwise. [Smith v. Robbins, 528 U.S. 259 (2000)—reasoning that this procedure ensures that a "trained legal eye" will search the record and provide some assistance to the reviewing court]

2. Discretionary Appeals

In a jurisdiction using a two-tier system of appellate courts with discretionary review by the highest court, an indigent defendant need not be provided with counsel during the second, discretionary appeal. Representation also need not be provided for an indigent seeking to invoke the United States Supreme Court's discretionary authority to review criminal convictions. [Ross v. Moffit, 417 U.S. 600 (1974)]

C. NO RIGHT TO SELF-REPRESENTATION

On appeal, a defendant has no right to represent himself. [Martinez v. Court of Appeal, 528 U.S. 152 (2000)]

D. RETRIAL AFTER REVERSAL ON APPEAL

Due process prohibits retrying a defendant whose conviction has been reversed on appeal for any offense more serious than that for which she was convicted at the first trial. This right is violated by *retrial for the more serious offense*, even if at the second trial the defendant is convicted only of an offense no more than that for which she was convicted at the first trial. [Price v. Georgia, 398 U.S. 323 (1970)]

Example: X is charged with murder. She is convicted of manslaughter and her conviction is reversed on appeal. She is again tried for murder and again convicted of manslaughter. May this conviction stand? No, because she could not be retried for anything more serious than manslaughter. This is not harmless error, because the charge of murder in the second trial may have influenced the jury toward conviction of manslaughter.

E. RETROACTIVITY

If the Court announces a new rule of criminal procedure (*i.e.*, one not dictated by precedent) in a case on direct review, the rule must be applied to *all other cases on direct review*. [Griffith v. Kentucky, 479 U.S. 314 (1987)] *Rationale:* It would be unfair to allow the one defendant whose case the Supreme Court happened to choose to hear to benefit from the new rule, while denying the benefit to other similarly situated defendants simply because they were not lucky enough to have their case chosen.

XI. COLLATERAL ATTACK UPON CONVICTIONS

A. AVAILABILITY OF COLLATERAL ATTACK

After appeal is no longer available or has proven unsuccessful, defendants may generally still attack their convictions collaterally, usually by beginning a new and separate civil proceeding involving an application for a writ of habeas corpus. This proceeding focuses on the lawfulness of a detention, naming the person having custody as the respondent.

B. HABEAS CORPUS PROCEEDING

1. No Right to Appointed Counsel

An indigent does not have the right to appointed counsel to perfect her petition for a writ of habeas corpus.

2. Burden of Proof

Because the proceeding for a writ of habeas corpus is civil in nature, the petitioner has the burden of proof by a *preponderance of the evidence* to show an unlawful detention.

3. State May Appeal

The state may appeal the granting of a writ of habeas corpus, and double jeopardy bars neither the appeal nor retrial after the granting of the writ.

4. Requirement of Custody

The state defendant must be "in custody," but it is sufficient if he is out on bail, probation, or parole. [Hensley v. Municipal Court, 411 U.S. 345 (1973)] Generally, the "in custody" requirement is *not* met by a petitioner whose sentence has expired, even if his prior conviction is used to enhance a later one [Maleng v. Cook, 490 U.S. 488 (1989)], but a petitioner who remains in jail on a *consecutive sentence* is in custody, even if the jail time for the crime being challenged has expired [Garlotte v. Fordice, 515 U.S. 39 (1995)].

XII. RIGHTS DURING PUNISHMENT—PROBATION, IMPRISONMENT, PAROLE

A. RIGHT TO COUNSEL AT PAROLE AND PROBATION REVOCATIONS

1. Probation Revocation Involving Resentencing
If revocation of probation also involves the imposition of a new sentence, the defendant is entitled to representation by counsel in all cases in which she is entitled to counsel at trial. [Mempa v. Rhay, *supra*, IX.A.1.]

2. Other Situations
If, after probation revocation, an already imposed sentence of imprisonment springs into application, *or* the case involves parole revocation, the right to counsel is much more limited.

There is a right to be represented by counsel only if, on the facts of the case, such representation is *necessary to a fair hearing*. Generally, it will be necessary if the defendant denies commission of the acts alleged or asserts an argument as to why revocation should not occur that is "complex or otherwise difficult to develop or present." In addition, each defendant must be told of her right to request appointment of counsel, and if a request is refused, the record must contain a succinct statement of the basis for the refusal. [Gagnon v. Scarpelli, 411 U.S. 778 (1973)]

B. PRISONERS' RIGHTS

1. Due Process Rights
Prison regulations and operations may create liberty interests protected by the Due Process Clause, but due process is violated only where the regulations and operations *impose "atypical and significant hardship"* in relation to the ordinary incidents of prison life. [Sandin v. Conner, 515 U.S. 472 (1995)]

2. No Fourth Amendment Protections in Search of Cells
Prisoners have no reasonable expectation of privacy in their cells, or in personal property in their cells, and hence no Fourth Amendment protection therein. [Hudson v. Palmer, 468 U.S. 517 (1984)] Additionally, prisoners have no right to be present when prison officials search their cells. [Block v. Rutherford, 468 U.S. 576 (1984)]

3. Right of Access to Courts
Prison inmates must have reasonable access to courts, and no unreasonable limitations may be put upon their ability to develop and present arguments. Inmates may not be prevented from consulting with other inmates, unless a reasonable substitute (such as a law library) is provided. [Bounds v. Smith, 430 U.S. 817 (1977); Johnson v. Avery, 393 U.S. 483 (1969)] No absolute bar against law students and other paraprofessionals interviewing inmates for lawyers may be imposed. [Procunier v. Martinez, 416 U.S. 396 (1974)]

Note: A prisoner's *Bounds* claim of inadequate prison legal resources must include a showing that the alleged deficiencies in the legal resources have resulted in a hindrance of access to court. [Lewis v. Casey, 518 U.S. 343 (1996)]

4. First Amendment Rights
Prison officials need some discretion to limit prisoners' First Amendment activities (*e.g.*, speech and assembly) in order to run a safe and secure prison. Therefore, prison regulations *reasonably related to penological interests* will be upheld even though they burden First Amendment rights. [Turner v. Safley, 482 U.S. 78 (1987)] For example, prison officials have broad discretion to regulate incoming mail to prevent contraband and even sexually explicit materials from entering the prison. Officials may even open letters from a prisoner's attorney, as long as they do so in the prisoner's presence and the letters are not read. [*See* Thornburgh v. Abbott, 490 U.S. 401 (1989); Wolff v. McDonnell, 418 U.S. 539 (1974)]

However, prison officials have less discretion to regulate outgoing mail, since it usually does not have an effect on prison safety. [Procunier v. Martinez, *supra*]

5. **Right to Adequate Medical Care**
"Deliberate indifference to serious medical needs of prisoners" constitutes cruel and unusual punishment in violation of the Eighth Amendment. However, simple negligent failure to provide care—"medical malpractice"—does not violate the amendment. [Estelle v. Gamble, 429 U.S. 97 (1976)] And while prisoners have a liberty interest in refusing medication, they can be forced to take antipsychotic drugs if an unbiased and qualified decisionmaker finds it necessary to protect the prisoner or others. [Washington v. Harper, 494 U.S. 210 (1990)] However, the forced administration of anti-psychotic medication during a defendant's murder trial absent a showing that (i) an essential state interest outweighed possible trial prejudice from the drug's side effects, and (ii) the drug was medically appropriate, was held to violate rights guaranteed by the Sixth and Fourteenth Amendments. [Riggins v. Nevada, 504 U.S. 127 (1992)]

C. NO RIGHT TO BE FREE FROM DISABILITIES UPON COMPLETION OF SENTENCE
There is no right to be free from state disenfranchisement upon conviction of a felony, even if this continues after completion of the sentence imposed. [Richardson v. Ramirez, 418 U.S. 24 (1974)]

XIII. DOUBLE JEOPARDY

A. WHEN JEOPARDY ATTACHES
The Fifth Amendment right to be free of double jeopardy for the same offense has been incorporated into the Fourteenth Amendment. [Benton v. Maryland, 395 U.S. 784 (1969)] The general rule is that once jeopardy attaches, the defendant may not be retried for the same offense.

1. **Jury Trials**
Jeopardy attaches in a jury trial at the *empaneling and swearing* of the jury. [Crist v. Bretz, 437 U.S. 28 (1978)]

2. **Bench Trials**
In bench trials, jeopardy attaches when the *first witness is sworn*.

3. **Juvenile Proceedings**
The *commencement* of a juvenile proceeding bars a subsequent criminal trial for the same offense. [Breed v. Jones, 421 U.S. 519 (1975)]

4. **Not in Civil Proceedings**
Jeopardy generally does not attach in civil proceedings other than juvenile proceedings. [One Lot Emerald Cut Stones & One Ring v. United States, 409 U.S. 232 (1972)]
Example: After the defendant is acquitted of criminal charges of smuggling, the government may still seek forfeiture of the items that the defendant allegedly smuggled into the country. [One Lot Emerald Cut Stones & One Ring v. United States, *supra*]

B. EXCEPTIONS PERMITTING RETRIAL
Certain exceptions permit retrial of a defendant even if jeopardy has attached.

1. **Hung Jury**
The state may retry a defendant whose first trial ends in a hung jury.

2. **Mistrial for Manifest Necessity**
A trial may be discontinued and the defendant reprosecuted for the same offense when there is a manifest necessity to abort the original trial [United States v. Perez, 22 U.S. 579 (1824); Illinois v. Somerville, 410 U.S. 458 (1973)] or when the termination occurs at the behest of the defendant on any grounds not constituting an acquittal on the merits [United States v. Scott, 437 U.S. 82 (1978)]. Thus, double jeopardy does not bar two trials but only a retrial after a determination on the merits.

3. **Retrial After Successful Appeal**

The state may retry a defendant who has successfully appealed a conviction, unless the ground for the reversal was insufficient evidence to support the guilty verdict. [Burks v. United States, 437 U.S. 1 (1978)] On the other hand, retrial is permitted when reversal is based on the *weight*, rather than *sufficiency*, of the evidence [Tibbs v. Florida, 457 U.S. 31 (1982)], or where a case is reversed because of erroneously admitted evidence [Lockhart v. Nelson, 488 U.S. 33 (1988)].

   a. **Charging and Sentencing on Retrial**

   Under both the Due Process Clause (*supra*, X.D.) and the Double Jeopardy Clause [*see* Green v. United States, 355 U.S. 184 (1957)], a defendant who successfully appeals a conviction cannot be *tried for a greater offense* than that of which he was convicted. However, the Double Jeopardy Clause generally does *not* prohibit imposition of a *harsher sentence* on conviction after retrial, and such a sentence is valid provided it does not run afoul of the vindictiveness concerns discussed at IX.B.1., *supra*.

      1) **Death Penalty Cases**

      Where there is a formalized, separate process for imposing the death penalty (*e.g.*, where guilt is first determined and then the jury is presented with evidence on whether to impose death), if the death penalty was not imposed at the first trial, it cannot be imposed at a second trial. [Bullington v. Missouri, 451 U.S. 430 (1981)] This rule applies only to capital sentencing proceedings. [Monge v. California, 524 U.S. 721 (1998)]

4. **Breach of Plea Bargaining**

When a defendant breaches a plea bargain agreement, his plea and sentence can be vacated and the original charges can be reinstated. [Ricketts v. Adamson, VIII.E.1.b., *supra*]

C. **SAME OFFENSE**

1. **General Rule—When Two Crimes Do Not Constitute Same Offense**

Two crimes do not constitute the same offense if *each crime requires proof of an additional element* that the other crime does not require, even though some of the same facts may be necessary to prove both crimes. [Blockburger v. United States, 284 U.S. 299 (1932)]

Example: D is arrested after the car he is driving strikes and kills a pedestrian. D is tried on the charges of reckless homicide and driving while intoxicated. D can receive separate punishments for both of the offenses because each crime requires proof of an additional element not required by the other: the homicide charge requires proof of a death but not proof of intoxication, while the driving while intoxicated charge requires proof of intoxication but not proof of a death.

   a. **Application of *Blockburger***

   Under *Blockburger*, the following do *not* constitute the same offenses:

      1) Manslaughter with an automobile and hit-and-run;

      2) Reckless driving and drunk driving;

      3) Reckless driving and failure to yield the right of way; and

      4) Uttering a forged check and obtaining money by false pretenses by using the forged check.

2. **Cumulative Punishments for Offenses Constituting Same Crime**

Imposition of cumulative punishments for two or more statutorily defined offenses, *specifically intended by the legislature to carry separate punishments*, even though constituting the "same" crime under the *Blockburger* test, *supra*, does not violate the prohibition of multiple punishments for the same offense of the Double Jeopardy Clause, when the punishments are *imposed at a single trial*. [Missouri v. Hunter, 459 U.S. 359 (1983)]

Example: D robs a store at gunpoint. D can be sentenced to cumulative punishments for both the robbery and under a "Use a gun, go to jail" statute.

Note: Absent a clear intention, it will be presumed that multiple punishments are not intended for offenses constituting the same crime under *Blockburger*. Also, imposition of multiple punishments is prohibited even if the sentences for the two crimes run concurrently. [Rutledge v. United States, 517 U.S. 292 (1996)]

3. Lesser Included Offenses

a. Retrial for Lesser Included Offense Barred
Attachment of jeopardy for the greater offense bars retrial for lesser included offenses. [Harris v. Oklahoma, 433 U.S. 682 (1977)]

Example: D is convicted of felony murder based on proof that he and an accomplice shot and killed a store clerk during an armed robbery. D cannot then be tried for the armed robbery because it is a lesser included offense of the felony murder. [Harris v. Oklahoma, *supra*]

b. Retrial for Greater Offense
Attachment of jeopardy for a lesser included offense bars retrial for the greater offense [Brown v. Ohio, 432 U.S. 161 (1977)], except that retrial for murder is permitted if the victim dies after attachment of jeopardy for battery [Diaz v. United States, 223 U.S. 442 (1912)]. However, a state may continue to prosecute a charged offense, despite the defendant's guilty plea to lesser included or "allied" offenses stemming from the same incident. [Ohio v. Johnson, 467 U.S. 493 (1984)—defendant charged with murder and manslaughter, and robbery and theft, arising from the same incident, can be prosecuted for murder and robbery after pleading guilty to manslaughter and theft over state's objection]

1) Exception—New Evidence
An exception to the double jeopardy bar exists if unlawful conduct that is subsequently used to prove the greater offense (i) has not occurred at the time of the prosecution for the lesser offense, or (ii) has not been discovered despite due diligence. [Garrett v. United States, 471 U.S. 773 (1985)]

4. Conspiracy and Substantive Offense
A prosecution for *conspiracy* is not barred merely because some of the alleged *overt acts* of that conspiracy have already been prosecuted. [United States v. Felix, 503 U.S. 378 (1992)]

5. Prior Act Evidence
The introduction of evidence of a substantive offense as prior act evidence is not equivalent to *prosecution* for that substantive offense, and therefore subsequent prosecution for that conduct is not barred. [United States v. Felix, *supra*]

6. Conduct Used as a Sentence Enhancer
The Double Jeopardy Clause is not violated when a person is indicted for a crime the conduct of which was already used to enhance the defendant's sentence for another crime. [Witte v. United States, 515 U.S. 389 (1995)—defendant indicted for conspiring to import cocaine after the conduct of the conspiracy was used to enhance his earlier sentence when he pleaded guilty to possession of marijuana]

7. Civil Actions
The Double Jeopardy Clause prohibits only repetitive *criminal* prosecutions. Thus, a state generally is free to bring a civil action against a defendant even if the defendant has already been criminally tried for the conduct out of which the civil action arises. Similarly, the government may bring a criminal action even though the defendant has already faced civil trial for the same conduct. However, if there is clear proof from the face of the statutory scheme that its purpose or effect is to impose a criminal penalty, the Double Jeopardy Clause applies. [Hudson v. United States, 522 U.S. 93 (1998)—finding no clear proof of such purpose or effect where a civil statute allowed a government agency to impose a fine and bar defendants from working in banking industry for improperly approving loans]

D. SEPARATE SOVEREIGNS
The constitutional prohibition against double jeopardy *does not apply* to trials by separate sovereigns. Thus, a person may be tried for the same conduct by both a state and the federal government [United States v. Lanza, 260 U.S. 377 (1922)] or by two states [Heath v. Alabama, 474 U.S. 82 (1986)], but not by a state and its municipalities [Waller v. Florida, 397 U.S. 387 (1970)].

E. APPEALS BY PROSECUTION
Even after jeopardy has attached, the prosecution *may appeal any dismissal* on the defendant's

motion *not constituting an acquittal on the merits*. [United States v. Scott, 437 U.S. 82 (1978)] Also, the Double Jeopardy Clause does not bar appeals by the prosecution if a *successful appeal would not require a retrial*, such as when the trial judge granted a motion to set aside the jury verdict. [United States v. Wilson, 420 U.S. 332 (1975)]

1. Appeal of Sentence
Government appeal of a sentence, *pursuant* to a congressionally enacted *statute* permitting such review, does not constitute multiple punishment in violation of the Double Jeopardy Clause. [United States v. DiFrancesco, 449 U.S. 117 (1980)]

F. COLLATERAL ESTOPPEL
The notion of collateral estoppel is embodied in the guarantee against double jeopardy. A defendant may not be tried or convicted of a crime if a prior prosecution by that sovereignty resulted in a *factual determination inconsistent with one required for conviction*. However, this doctrine has limited utility because of the general verdict in criminal trials.

Examples: 1) Where three or four armed men robbed six poker players in the home of one of the victims and the defendant was charged in separate counts with robbery of each of the six players and was tried on one count and was acquitted for insufficient evidence in a prosecution in which identity was the single rationally conceivable issue in dispute, he may not thereafter be prosecuted for robbery of a different player. [Ashe v. Swenson, 397 U.S. 436 (1970)] A second trial would not have been barred if there had been dispute at the first trial whether the alleged victim was robbed. The court did not adopt the "same transaction" test proposed by some justices, under which a defendant could not be more than once put in jeopardy for offenses arising out of the "same transactions."

2) Where the ultimate issue of identity of the person who mailed a package with a bomb that killed two persons was decided at the first trial at which defendant was acquitted, the defendant may not thereafter be convicted of the second murder, even if the jury in the first trial (for the first murder) did not have all the relevant evidence before it and the state acted in good faith. [Harris v. Washington, 404 U.S. 55 (1971)]

XIV. PRIVILEGE AGAINST COMPELLED SELF-INCRIMINATION

A. APPLICABLE TO THE STATES
As discussed above (*see* IV.D., *supra*), the Fifth Amendment prohibits the government from compelling self-incriminating testimony. The Fifth Amendment prohibition against compelled self-incrimination was made applicable to the states through the Fourteenth Amendment in *Malloy v. Hogan*, 378 U.S. 1 (1964).

[handwritten: any person under oath in any case, in any proceedings]

B. WHO MAY ASSERT THE PRIVILEGE
Only *natural persons* may assert the privilege, not corporations or partnerships. [Bellis v. United States, 417 U.S. 85 (1974)] The privilege is personal, and so may be asserted by a defendant, witness, or party only if the answer to the question might tend to incriminate him.

C. WHEN PRIVILEGE MAY BE ASSERTED
A person may refuse to answer a question whenever his response might furnish a link in the chain of evidence needed to prosecute him.

1. Proceedings Where Potentially Incriminating Testimony Sought
A person may assert the privilege in *any* proceeding in which testimony that could tend to incriminate is sought. The privilege must be claimed in civil proceedings to prevent the privilege from being waived for a later criminal prosecution. If the individual responds to the questions instead of claiming the privilege during a civil proceeding, he cannot later bar that evidence from a criminal prosecution on compelled self-incrimination grounds. [United States v. Kordel, 397 U.S. 1 (1970)]

2. Privilege Not a Defense to Civil Records Requirements
The government may require that certain records be kept and reported on where the records are relevant to an *administrative purpose*, unrelated to enforcement of criminal laws. Such records acquire a public aspect and are not protected by the Fifth Amendment.

Examples: 1) The government may require people to keep tax records and to report their income on tax forms, since this serves a legitimate administrative purpose.

Thus, a person may be prosecuted for failure to file a tax form. However, there is a Fifth Amendment privilege to refuse to answer specific questions on such forms that might be incriminating (*e.g.*, source of income). [United States v. Sullivan, 274 U.S. 259 (1927)] Therefore, if a person chooses to answer incriminating questions on such forms, the answers may be used against him in court, since they were not compelled. [Garner v. United States, 424 U.S. 648 (1976)]

2) A person charged with being an unfit parent in a proceeding to determine whether she should maintain custody of her child may be compelled to produce the child in court. Even though the production might be testimonial in nature (admits control), the state's interest here is civil (protecting the child) rather than punitive in nature. [Baltimore City Department of Social Services v. Bouknight, 493 U.S. 549 (1990)] Note, however, that the state might have to grant immunity to the parent for the production. (*See* H.1., *infra*.)

3) A person may not claim the privilege and fail to comply with a law requiring motorists to stop at the scene of an accident and leave their name and address. [California v. Byers, 402 U.S. 424 (1971)]

a. Limitation—Criminal Law Enforcement Purpose
If the registration requirement is directed not at the general public but at a *select group inherently suspect of criminal activities* and the inquiry is in an area permeated with criminal statutes, the person may assert the privilege to avoid prosecution for failure to comply with the requirement. [Albertson v. Subversive Activities Control Board, 382 U.S. 70 (1965)]

Example: The government may not require registration of a sawed-off shotgun [Haynes v. United States, 390 U.S. 85 (1968)], payment of a wagering excise tax [Grosso v. United States, 390 U.S. 62 (1968)], payment of an occupational tax for engaging in the business of accepting wagers [Marchetti v. United States, 390 U.S. 39 (1968)], individual registration as a member of the Communist Party [Albertson v. Subversive Activities Control Board, *supra*], or the registration of transfer of marijuana [Leary v. United States, 395 U.S. 6 (1969)] if compliance would require self-incrimination.

Note: Such cases as *Marchetti* and *Grosso* do not bar conviction for making false statements on the registration form; to avoid incriminating himself, the individual must instead claim the privilege. [United States v. Knox, 396 U.S. 77 (1969)]

D. METHOD FOR INVOKING THE PRIVILEGE
How the privilege may be invoked depends upon whether the person seeking to invoke it is a criminal defendant or simply a witness.

1. Privilege of a Defendant
A criminal defendant has a right not to take the witness stand at trial and not to be asked to do so. It is even impermissible to call the jury's attention to the fact that he has chosen not to testify. (*See* G.1., *infra*.)

2. Privilege of a Witness
In any other situation, the privilege does not permit a person to avoid being sworn as a witness or being asked questions. Rather, the person must listen to the questions and specifically invoke the privilege rather than answer the questions.

E. SCOPE OF PROTECTION

1. Testimonial but Not Physical Evidence
The Fifth Amendment privilege protects only testimonial or communicative evidence and not real or physical evidence. Thus, the state may require a person to produce *blood samples* [Schmerber v. California, *supra*, VII.C.2.], *handwriting exemplars* [Gilbert v. California, *supra*, VII.C.2.], or *voice samples* [United States v. Wade, *supra*, V.E.] without violating the Fifth Amendment, even though such evidence may be incriminating. In addition, a court may order a suspect to authorize foreign banks to disclose records of any accounts he may possess. Merely signing an authorization form is not testimonial if it does not require the suspect to acknowledge the existence of any account. For a suspect's communication to be

considered testimonial, it must explicitly or implicitly relate a factual assertion or disclose information. [Doe v. United States, 487 U.S. 201 (1988)]

Likewise, admission into evidence of a defendant's *refusal to submit to a blood-alcohol test* does not offend the right against self-incrimination even though he was not warned that his refusal might be introduced against him. [South Dakota v. Neville, 459 U.S. 553 (1983)]

2. **Compulsory Production of Documents**
A person served with a subpoena requiring the production of documents tending to incriminate him generally has no basis in the privilege to refuse to comply, because the act of producing the documents *does not involve testimonial self-incrimination*. Note, however, that if the document *is* within the privilege but in the hands of an attorney, the attorney-client privilege would permit the attorney to refuse to comply with the subpoena. [Fisher v. United States, 425 U.S. 391 (1976)]

   a. **Corporate Records**
   A custodian of corporate records may not resist a subpoena for such records on the ground that the production would incriminate him in violation of the Fifth Amendment. The production of the records by the custodian is not considered a personal act, but rather an act of the corporation, which possesses no Fifth Amendment privilege. [Braswell v. United States, 487 U.S. 99 (1988)]

3. **Seizure and Use of Incriminating Documents**
The Fifth Amendment does not prohibit law enforcement officers from searching for and seizing documents tending to incriminate a person. The privilege protects only against being compelled to communicate information, not against disclosure of communications made in the past. [Andresen v. Maryland, *supra*, III.C.4.c.]

F. **RIGHT TO ADVICE CONCERNING PRIVILEGE**
A lawyer may not be held in contempt of court for her good faith advice to her client to invoke the privilege and refuse to produce materials demanded by a court order. Because a witness may require the advice of counsel in deciding how to respond to a demand for testimony or evidence, subjecting the lawyer to potential contempt citation for her advice would infringe upon the protection accorded the witness by the Fifth Amendment. [Maness v. Meyers, 419 U.S. 449 (1975)]

G. **PROHIBITION AGAINST BURDENS ON ASSERTION OF THE PRIVILEGE**

1. **Comments on Defendant's Silence**
A prosecutor may not comment on a defendant's silence after being arrested and receiving *Miranda* warnings. The warnings carry an implicit assurance that silence will carry no penalty. [Greer v. Miller, 483 U.S. 756 (1987)] Neither may the prosecutor ordinarily comment on the defendant's failure to testify at trial. [Griffin v. California, 380 U.S. 609 (1965)] However, where the defendant does not testify at trial, upon timely motion she is constitutionally entitled to have the trial judge instruct the jury that they are to draw no adverse inference from the defendant's failure to testify. [Carter v. Kentucky, 450 U.S. 288 (1981)] Moreover, a judge may warn the jury not to draw an adverse inference from the defendant's failure to testify, without violating the Fifth Amendment privilege, even where the defendant objects to such an instruction. [Lakeside v. Oregon, 435 U.S. 333 (1978)]

   a. **Exception**
   The prosecutor can comment on the defendant's failure to take the stand when the comment is in response to defense counsel's assertion that the defendant was not allowed to explain his side of the story. [United States v. Robinson, 485 U.S. 25 (1988)]

   b. **Harmless Error Test Applies**
   When a prosecutor impermissibly comments on a defendant's silence, the harmless error test applies. Thus, the error is not fatal where the judge instructs the jury to disregard a question on the defendant's post-arrest silence. [Greer v. Miller, *supra*] Similarly, the error is not fatal where there is overwhelming evidence against the defendant and the prosecutor comments on the defendant's failure to proffer evidence rebutting the victim's testimony. [United States v. Hasting, 461 U.S. 499 (1987)]

2. **Penalties for Failure to Testify Prohibited**
The state may not chill the exercise of the Fifth Amendment privilege against compelled self-incrimination by imposing penalties for the failure to testify or cooperate with authorities.

Example: The state may not fire a police officer [Garrity v. New Jersey, 385 U.S. 493 (1967)], take away state contracts [Lefkowitz v. Turley, 414 U.S. 70 (1973)], or prohibit a person from holding party office [Lefkowitz v. Cunningham, 431 U.S. 801 (1977)] for failure to cooperate with investigating authorities.

Compare: There was no Fifth Amendment violation where a prisoner was required to disclose all prior sexual activities, including activities that constitute un- charged criminal offenses, in order to gain entry into a sexual abuse treat- ment program, even though refusal resulted in transfer from a medium security facility to a maximum security facility and curtailment of visitation rights, prison work and earnings opportunities, and other prison privileges. [McKune v. Lile, 122 S. Ct. 2017 (2002)]

H. ELIMINATION OF THE PRIVILEGE

1. Grant of Immunity
A witness may be compelled to answer questions if granted adequate immunity from pros- ecution.

a. "Use and Derivative Use" Immunity Sufficient
The Supreme Court has held that a grant of "use and derivative use" immunity is sufficient to extinguish the privilege. [Kastigar v. United States, 406 U.S. 441 (1972)] This type of immunity guarantees that the testimony obtained and evidence located by means of the testimony will not be used against the witness. This type of immunity is not as broad as "transactional" immunity, which guarantees immunity from prosecution for any crimes related to the transaction about which the witness testifies, because the witness may still be prosecuted if the prosecutor can show that her evidence was derived from a *source independent* of the immunized testimony.

b. Immunized Testimony Involuntary
Testimony obtained by a *promise of immunity* is, by definition, coerced and therefore involuntary. Thus, immunized testimony may not be used for impeachment of the defendant's testimony at trial. [New Jersey v. Portash, 440 U.S. 450 (1979)] Immu- nized testimony may be introduced to supply the context for a perjury prosecution. Any immunized statements, whether true or untrue, can be used in a trial for making false statements. [United States v. Apfelbaum, 445 U.S. 115 (1980)]

c. Use of Testimony by Another Sovereign Prohibited
The privilege against self-incrimination prohibits a state from compelling incriminating testimony under a grant of immunity unless the testimony and its fruits cannot be used by the prosecution in a federal prosecution. Therefore, federal prosecutors may not use evidence obtained as a result of a state grant of immunity, and vice versa. [Murphy v. Waterfront Commission, 378 U.S. 52 (1964)]

2. No Possibility of Incrimination   *statute of limitation*
A person has no privilege against compelled self-incrimination if there is no possibility of incrimination, as, for example, when the statute of limitations has run.

3. Scope of Immunity
Immunity extends only to the offenses to which the question relates and does not protect against perjury committed during the immunized testimony. [United States v. Apfelbaum, 445 U.S. 115 (1980)]

I. WAIVER OF PRIVILEGE
The nature and scope of a waiver depends upon the situation.

1. Waiver by Criminal Defendant
A criminal defendant, by taking the witness stand, waives the privilege to the extent neces- sary to subject her to any cross-examination proper under the rules of evidence.

2. Waiver by Witness
A witness waives the privilege only if she discloses incriminating information. Once such disclosure has been made, she can be compelled to disclose any additional information as long as such further disclosure does not increase the risk of conviction or create a risk of conviction on a different offense.

XV.   JUVENILE COURT PROCEEDINGS

A.   IN GENERAL
Some—but not all—of the rights developed for defendants in criminal prosecutions have also been held applicable to children who are the subjects of proceedings to have them declared "delinquents" and possibly institutionalized.

B.   RIGHTS THAT MUST BE AFFORDED
The following rights must be given to a child during the trial of a delinquency proceeding:

(i)   Written *notice* of the charges with sufficient time to prepare a defense;

(ii)   The *assistance of counsel* (court-appointed if the child is indigent);

(iii)   The *opportunity to confront* and cross-examine witnesses;

(iv)   The *right not to testify* (and other aspects of the privilege against self-incrimination); and

(v)   The right to have *"guilt"* (the commission of acts making the child delinquent) established by proof *beyond a reasonable doubt*.

[*In re* Gault, 387 U.S. 1 (1967); *In re* Winship, 397 U.S. 358 (1970)]

C.   RIGHTS NOT APPLICABLE

1.   Jury Trial
The Supreme Court has held inapplicable to delinquency proceedings the right to trial by jury. In the juvenile court context, jury trial is not necessary to assure "fundamental fairness." [McKeiver v. Pennsylvania, 403 U.S. 528 (1971)]

2.   Pretrial Detention Allowable
A finding that a juvenile is a "serious risk" to society and likely to commit a crime before trial is adequate to support pretrial detention of the juvenile, and does not violate the Due Process Clause as long as the detention is for a strictly limited time before trial may be held. [Schall v. Martin, 467 U.S. 253 (1984)]

D.   DOUBLE JEOPARDY AND "TRANSFER" OF JUVENILE TO ADULT COURT
In many jurisdictions, a juvenile court may, after inquiry, determine that a child is not an appropriate subject for juvenile court processing and "transfer" the child to adult court for trial as an adult on criminal charges. If the juvenile court adjudicates the child a delinquent, however, jeopardy has attached and the prohibition against double jeopardy prevents him from being tried as an adult for the same behavior. [Breed v. Jones, 421 U.S. 519 (1975)] The transfer issue must be *resolved before the adjudication of delinquency*.

XVI.   FORFEITURE ACTIONS

A.   INTRODUCTION
State and federal statutes often provide for the forfeiture of property such as automobiles used in the commission of a crime. Actions for forfeiture are brought directly against the property and are generally regarded as quasi-criminal in nature. Certain constitutional rights may exist for those persons whose interest in the property would be lost by forfeiture.

B.   RIGHT TO PRE-SEIZURE NOTICE AND HEARING
The owner of *personal* property (and others with interests in it) is not constitutionally entitled to notice and hearing before the property is seized for purposes of a forfeiture proceeding. [Calero-Toledo v. Pearson Yacht Leasing Co., 416 U.S. 663 (1974)] A hearing is, however, required before final forfeiture of the property. Where *real property* is seized, notice and an opportunity to be heard is required before the seizure unless the government can prove that exigent circumstances justify immediate seizure. [United States v. James Daniel Good Real Property, 510 U.S. 43 (1994)]

C.   FORFEITURES MAY BE SUBJECT TO EIGHTH AMENDMENT
The Eighth Amendment provides that excessive fines shall not be imposed. The Supreme Court

has held that this Excessive Fines Clause applies only to fines imposed as punishment, *i.e.*, penal fines. The Clause does not apply to civil fines. Thus forfeitures that are penal are subject to the Clause, but forfeitures that are civil are not.

1. Penal Forfeitures

Generally, a forfeiture will be considered penal only if it is provided for in a criminal statute. If it is penal and the Clause applies, a forfeiture will be found to be excessive only if it is ***grossly disproportionate to the gravity of the offense.*** [United States v. Bajakajian, 524 U.S. 321 (1998)]

Example: The Court held that forfeiture of $357,144 for the crime of merely failing to report that that sum was being transported out of the country was grossly disproportionate since the crime caused little harm (it would have been legal to take the money out of the country; the only harm was that the government was deprived of a piece of information). [United States v. Bajakajian, *supra*]

2. Compare—Nonpenal Forfeitures

a. Civil In Rem Forfeitures

Civil in rem forfeitures treat the property forfeited as a "wrongdoer" under a legal fiction; the action is against the property and not against an individual, and therefore this type of forfeiture is ***not*** subject to the Excessive Fines Clause.

b. Monetary Forfeitures

Monetary forfeitures (*e.g.*, forfeiture of twice the value of illegally imported goods) have also been found to be remedial in nature where they are brought in civil actions. They are seen as a form of liquidated damages to reimburse the government for losses resulting from the offense. Therefore, they are not subject to the Eighth Amendment. [*See* United States v. Bajakajian, *supra*]

D. PROTECTION FOR "INNOCENT OWNER" NOT REQUIRED

The Due Process Clause does ***not*** require forfeiture statutes to provide an "innocent owner" defense, *e.g.*, a defense that the owner took all reasonable steps to avoid having the property used by another for illegal purposes, at least where the innocent owner ***voluntarily entrusted*** the property to the wrongdoer. [Bennis v. Michigan, 517 U.S. 292 (1996)—due process not violated by forfeiture of wife's car that husband used while engaging in sexual acts with a prostitute even though wife did not know of use] In justifying its holding in *Bennis*, the Court also noted that the statute was not absolute, since the trial judge had discretion to prevent inequitable application of the statute.

hot topics := + exclusion, its limitations, fruit of poisoneous tree do
+ search & seizure (review model & flow chart in conviser
+ miranda
+ pretrial identification
+ right to jury trial & guilty plead

ineffective assistance of counsel for essay

double jeopardy
5th A privilege & compelled

BAR REVIEW

Evidence

celebrating
35 YEARS
*of preparing
law students
for the bar exam*

EVIDENCE

TABLE OF CONTENTS

I. GENERAL CONSIDERATIONS

A. DEFINING EVIDENCE LAW

The law of evidence is a system of rules and standards by which the admission of proof at the trial of a lawsuit is regulated. The material facts in the controversy are determined by proof that is filtered through the applicable rules of evidence. This proof includes testimony, writings, physical objects, and anything else presented to the senses of the jury.

B. SOURCES OF EVIDENCE LAW

In some states, evidence law is derived from a blend of common law rules and miscellaneous statutes. However, today, most jurisdictions have enacted modern evidence codes, which form a comprehensive set of statutes or rules covering all major areas of evidence law. The most important codification is the Federal Rules of Evidence, which became effective July 1, 1975. The Federal Rules govern on the Multistate Bar Examination.

C. FEDERAL RULES OF EVIDENCE

The Federal Rules of Evidence are applicable in all *civil and criminal* cases in the United States courts of appeal, district courts, Court of Claims, and in proceedings before United States magistrates. [Fed. R. Evid. 101 and 1101] For the most part, the Federal Rules have codified well-established principles of evidence law. Where the Federal Rules depart from the traditional rules of evidence, the adopted Federal Rule is likely to represent an important modern trend, which the states are likely to follow as they revise and codify existing law.

D. THRESHOLD ADMISSIBILITY ISSUES

A shorthand summary of evidence law might be stated in one sentence: *Material* and *relevant* evidence is admissible if *competent*.

1. Materiality: The Proposition to Be Proved

Materiality exists when the proffered evidence relates to one of the substantive legal issues in the case. The key questions to ask regarding materiality are: What issue is the evidence offered to prove? Is that legal issue material to the substantive cause of action or defense in the case? The answer to these questions and the determination of materiality depend upon the substantive legal issues framed by the pleadings. Thus, evidence is immaterial if the proposition for which it is offered as proof is not a legal issue in the case.

Example: In a workers' compensation proceeding, evidence of the claimant's contributory negligence would be immaterial since the workers' compensation statute abrogates it as a defense.

2. Relevance: Probativeness—The Link Between Proof and Proposition

Probativeness embraces the test of materiality and something more. Probative evidence *contributes to proving or disproving* a material issue. Assuming that the issue the evidence is offered to prove is a material one, is the evidence logically probative of that issue? Does the evidence tend to prove that issue? Does the evidence tend to make the material proposition (issue) more probably true or untrue than it would be without the evidence?

Example: Evidence that the defendant drove recklessly on a prior occasion is material because it speaks to the question of his negligence. However, it is not sufficiently probative of the issue of negligence on this particular occasion, and is therefore not relevant.

3. Federal Rules—Materiality and Probativeness Combined

In the Federal Rules of Evidence, as in most modern codes, the requirements of materiality and probativeness are combined into a single definition of relevance. Thus, Federal Rule 401 provides that "relevant evidence" means evidence tending to prove (probativeness) any fact of consequence to the action (materiality). You should watch for both aspects of the relevance problem. Ask yourself (i) whether the fact sought to be proved is itself in issue under the pleadings and the substantive law, and also (ii) whether the evidence helps to prove the fact for which it is offered.

4. Competence

As mentioned above, material and relevant evidence is admissible if competent. Evidence is competent if it *does not violate an exclusionary rule*. Basically, then, if evidence is material and relevant, the only reason such evidence would not be admitted is if it is prohibited by a special exclusionary rule of evidence. Exclusionary rules that prevent admissibility of relevant and material evidence are founded upon one or more of the following:

        a. Policies Related to Truth-Seeking
The need to ensure the reliability and authenticity of evidence is a truth-seeking policy. Examples of exclusionary rules that perform this truth-seeking function are the hearsay rule, the best evidence rule, and Dead Man statutes.

        b. Policies External to Litigation
The need to protect extrajudicial interests of society is an external policy goal. Rules granting testimonial privileges, for example, admittedly hamper the in-court search for truth.

E. EVIDENCE CLASSIFICATIONS

1. Direct or Circumstantial

        a. Direct Evidence Relies on Actual Knowledge
Direct evidence goes directly to a material issue without intervention of an inferential process. Evidence is direct when the very facts in dispute are communicated by those who have actual knowledge by means of their senses.
Example: On the issue of whether anyone had recently crossed a snow-covered bridge, the testimony of a witness that he saw a man crossing would be direct evidence.

        b. Circumstantial Evidence Relies on Inference
Circumstantial evidence is indirect and relies on inference. It is evidence of a subsidiary or collateral fact from which, alone or in conjunction with a cluster of other facts, the existence of the material issue can be inferred.
Example: On the issue of whether anyone had recently crossed a snow-covered bridge, the testimony of a witness that he saw human footprints in the snow on the bridge would be circumstantial evidence.

2. Testimonial, Documentary, or Real

        a.   *Testimonial* evidence is oral evidence given under oath. The witness responds to the questions of the attorneys.

        b.   *Documentary* evidence is evidence in the form of a writing, such as a contract or a confession.

        c.   *Real* evidence is the term applied to evidence consisting of things as distinguished from assertions of witnesses about things. Real evidence includes anything conveying a firsthand sense impression to the trier of fact, such as knives, jewelry, maps, or tape recordings.

F. LIMITED ADMISSIBILITY

1. Admissible for One Purpose but Not Another
The use of admissible evidence is a frequently encountered problem. It often happens that evidence is admissible for one purpose but is not admissible for another purpose.
Example: At the trial of the accused for assault, defendant's prior conviction for robbery may be shown by the prosecution to impeach the credibility of testimony given by the accused as a witness. The prior conviction is not admissible on the issue of defendant's guilt on the assault charge.

2. Admissible Against One Party but Not Another
It is also possible that the evidence is admissible against one party but is not admissible against another party.
Example: A post-accident admission of a negligent employee truck driver may be admissible against the truck driver in an action for negligence. However, under certain circumstances it may not be admissible against a defendant employer who owned the truck.

3. Jury Must Be Properly Instructed
As a general rule, if evidence is admissible for one purpose, it is not excluded merely because of the danger that the jury may also consider it for another incompetent purpose. When evidence that is admissible as to one party or for one purpose but is not admissible as

to another party or for another purpose is admitted, the court must, upon request, restrict the evidence to its proper scope and instruct the jury accordingly. [Fed. R. Evid. 105]

II. RELEVANCE

A. INTRODUCTION

Relevance, in the sense of probativeness, has to do with the tendency of evidence to *prove or disprove a material issue*, to render it more probably true, or untrue, than it would have been without the particular evidence. Relevance is concerned with the *substance or content* of the evidence, not with the form or manner in which it is offered (*e.g.*, hearsay rule, best evidence rule). It can be stated, as a general proposition, that all relevant evidence is admissible if it is offered in an unobjectionable form and manner. (As usual, there are some exceptions to this generalization, since some perfectly relevant evidence that is in the proper form is excluded for policy reasons.)

B. DETERMINING RELEVANCE

Relevant evidence is evidence having any tendency to make the existence of any fact that is of consequence to the determination of an action more probable than it would be without the evidence. [Fed. R. Evid. 401] Note that this definition of relevance includes materiality since it requires that the disputed fact be of consequence to the determination of the action. The basic questions to ask regarding relevancy are: "What proposition is the evidence being used to prove? Is this a material issue in the case? Is the evidence probative of that proposition?" This type of relevance is sometimes called "logical relevance."

1.   **General Rule—Must Relate to Time, Event, or Person in Controversy**

Whenever testimony or exhibit evidence that relates to a time, event, or person other than the time, event, or person directly involved in the controversy being litigated is offered, the relevance of that evidence is suspect and should be examined more carefully. In most cases, a previous similar occurrence proves little or nothing about the one in issue. In addition, the risk of confusion and unfair prejudice usually outweighs the helpfulness of this type of evidence (*see* C., *infra*). Note that when considering the relevance of such evidence, one of the important factors to consider is its proximity in time to the current events. A circumstance that would be relevant had it occurred in close time proximity to the event in question is irrelevant if instead it was very remote.

Examples: 1) Defendant is alleged to have run a red light and hit a pedestrian in the crosswalk. Proof that defendant ran other red lights in the past has little probative value in proving the occurrence in question. The probative value of such proof is outweighed by the confusion and unfair prejudice that would result from its admission.

2) On the issue of the fair market value of property in a condemnation action, the relevance of the sale price of other property depends on how comparable the other property is to the property being condemned, how close it is geographically, and how recent that sale was. Sale of a neighbor's comparable property six months ago is probably relevant, but the sale of the same property five years ago probably is not relevant.

3) In a murder prosecution, evidence that the accused had threatened the alleged victim the day before the killing may be very relevant. But compare a threat a week before; a month before; a year before; 10 years before.

2.   **Exceptions—Certain Similar Occurrences Are Relevant**

Despite the above rule, previous similar happenings and transactions of the parties and others similarly situated may be relevant if they are probative of the material issue involved, and if that probative value outweighs the risk that the evidence will confuse the jury or result in unfair prejudice. Of course, whenever a similar occurrence is offered to establish an inference about the subject occurrence, the quality of the inference depends on the similarity between the other happening and the one in issue. The following are examples of relevant similar occurrences.

a.   **Causation**

Complicated issues of causation may often be established by evidence that concerns other times, events, or persons. For example, evidence that other homes in the same area were damaged by defendant's blasting operations is some evidence that the damage to plaintiff's home was caused by defendant's activities.

b. Prior False Claims or Same Bodily Injury
Evidence that a person has previously filed similar *tort claims* or has been involved in *prior accidents* is *generally inadmissible* to show the invalidity of the present claim. At best, such evidence indicates plaintiff's tendency toward litigation or accident-proneness. In either case, the probative value is outweighed by the risk of confusion of issues and undue prejudice.

But if evidence is introduced that the party has made previous similar *false* claims, such evidence is usually relevant, under a common scheme or plan theory, to prove that the present claim is likely to be false. Likewise, where the prior claim was for an injury to the *same portion of plaintiff's body* that she claims was injured in the present case, evidence of the prior claim or injury may be relevant to prove that her present claim is false or exaggerated.

c. Similar Accidents or Injuries Caused by Same Event or Condition
Where similar accidents or injuries were caused by the same event or condition, evidence of those prior accidents or injuries is *admissible to prove*:

(i) That a defect or dangerous *condition existed*;

(ii) That the defendant had *knowledge* of the defect or dangerous condition; and

(iii) That the defect or dangerous condition was the *cause* of the present injury.

Example: In an action for dust damage from a mill, it may be proper to introduce evidence that plaintiff's neighbors have previously suffered similar dust damage, in order to prove that the mill created dust, that the mill owners knew of the dust, and that the dust caused plaintiff's damage.

1) Absence of Similar Accidents
Many courts are reluctant to admit evidence of the absence of similar accidents to show absence of negligence or lack of a defect. However, where a structural condition is involved and that condition is unchanged, the court has discretion to admit evidence of absence of other complaints to show lack of a defect. Evidence of prior safety history and absence of complaints is admissible to show *defendant's lack of knowledge* of any danger.

d. Previous Similar Acts Admissible to Prove Intent
Similar conduct previously committed by a party may be introduced to prove the party's present motive or intent when such elements are relevant.
Example: In an action against a school board for excluding a black child from school, similar exclusions of black children will be admissible into evidence to show intent.

e. Rebutting Claim of Impossibility
The requirement that prior occurrences be similar to the litigated act may be relaxed when used to rebut a claim or defense of impossibility. For example, if defendant denies negligent speeding on the ground that his automobile could never go above 50 m.p.h., plaintiff may rebut by showing that on other occasions, even under different circumstances, the vehicle was traveling at 75 m.p.h.

f. Sales of Similar Property
Evidence of sales of similar personal or real property that are not too remote in time is *admissible to prove value*. However, unlike commonly sold items of personal property, each parcel of real property is considered unique. Thus, the problem of producing evidence of other transactions requires a preliminary finding that the character, usage, proximity, date of sale, etc., are sufficiently similar to the property in issue. Evidence of prices quoted in mere *offers* is *not admissible* because to determine the sincerity of these offers would lead to collateral disputes. However, offers by a party to the present action to buy or sell the property may be admissible as admissions.

g. Habit
Habit describes one's regular response to a specific set of circumstances (*e.g.,* "she always takes a staircase two steps at a time"). In contrast, character describes one's disposition in respect to general traits (*e.g.,* "she's always in a hurry"). Since habits are more specific and particularized, evidence of habit is relevant and can be introduced in circumstances when it is not permissible to introduce evidence of character. Thus, under Federal Rule 406, "evidence of the habit of a person . . . is relevant to prove that the conduct of the person . . . on a particular occasion was in conformity with the habit . . . ."

Example: Evidence could be introduced to show that a driver habitually failed to stop at a certain stop sign as circumstantial evidence that she failed to stop at the time in question. In contrast, evidence cannot be introduced to show that a person is a careless driver since that is closer to character than habit.

Many states either do not admit evidence of habit to show that a particular act occurred, or else limit admissibility to those cases where there are no eyewitnesses. Federal Rule 406 admits habit evidence freely and abandons the "no eyewitness" requirement. Even where admissible, however, the habit must be shown to be a regular response to a repeated specific situation.

h. Industrial or Business Routine
Just as evidence of personal habit is relevant to show conduct, evidence that a business or firm had an established business routine is relevant as tending to show that a particular event occurred.

Example: Evidence of a regular mailing procedure, such as a custom of picking up letters from a certain table and mailing them, would be relevant as evidence to show that a particular letter left on the table was duly mailed.

i. Industrial Custom as Evidence of Standard of Care

1) Industrial Custom Distinguished from Business Routine
Custom of the industry should be distinguished from business routine. In the latter case, the particular conduct and habit of a party are being offered to show that the party acted in the same manner on the occasion in question. Custom of the industry is offered to prove the actions of other persons in the same industry in an attempt to show adherence to or deviance from an industry-wide standard of care.

2) Relevant to Standard of Care but Not Conclusive
When one of the issues in dispute is negligence arising out of inadequate safety devices or precautions, evidence of general custom or usage in the same kind of business under the same circumstances may be introduced by either party as tending to establish a standard by which reasonable or ordinary care may be judged. Although custom of the trade or business is admissible on the standard of care to be exercised, it is not conclusive.

C. DISCRETIONARY EXCLUSION OF RELEVANT EVIDENCE (PRAGMATIC RELEVANCE)
A trial judge has broad discretion to exclude relevant evidence if its probative value is substantially outweighed by the danger of *unfair prejudice*, *confusion of the issues*, or *misleading the jury*, or by considerations of *undue delay*, waste of time, or needless presentation of cumulative evidence. [Fed. R. Evid. 403] "*Unfair surprise*" is listed as an additional basis for exclusion under some state rules, but it was omitted under the Federal Rules on the theory that surprise can be prevented by discovery and pretrial conference or mitigated by granting a continuance.

Certain items of evidence may be directed to a material issue in the case and may be very probative of that issue, but they are excluded because of predictable policies designed to ensure an orderly and efficient proceeding and to encourage certain public policy solutions to legal problems. For example, inflammatory matter, which may be very probative of the issues, will not be admitted because of the potential prejudicial effect on the jury.

D. EXCLUSION OF RELEVANT EVIDENCE FOR PUBLIC POLICY REASONS (POLICY-BASED RELEVANCE)
Certain evidence of questionable relevance is excluded by the Federal Rules because public

policy favors the behavior involved. For example, the law encourages the repair of defective premises that cause injury, and consequently, evidence of the subsequent repair may not be admitted to prove antecedent negligence, even though it may be probative of the issue. Evidence excluded for public policy reasons is set forth below.

1. Liability Insurance

a. Inadmissible to Show Negligence or Ability to Pay

Evidence that a person was or was not insured against liability is **not admissible** upon the issue of whether she **acted negligently** or otherwise wrongfully. Nor is it admissible to show **ability to pay** a substantial judgment. [Fed. R. Evid. 411]

b. When Admissible

Proof that a person carried liability insurance may be admissible and relevant for other purposes. Issue identification is important in these cases, since proof of the fact that the defendant maintained insurance **may be used**:

1) To Prove Ownership or Control

Evidence that the defendant maintained insurance may be admitted for the limited purpose of proving the defendant's ownership or control when ownership or control is disputed.

Example: P sues D and alleges that D owned the building in which P fell on a defective staircase, further alleging a cause of action for negligence. D denies all allegations, and thereby puts in issue the question of ownership of the premises. P may show that D had insured the premises as evidence of ownership, but the evidence will only be used for the limited purpose of proving that issue.

2) For Purposes of Impeachment

Evidence that the defendant is insured may be used for the limited purpose of impeaching a witness.

Example: An investigator testifies on behalf of defendant. Plaintiff may demonstrate the bias or interest of this witness by showing that she is employed by defendant's liability insurance company.

3) As Part of Admission

An admission of liability may be so coupled with a reference to insurance coverage that the reference to insurance cannot be severed without lessening its value as an admission of liability.

Example: "Don't worry; my insurance company will pay off."

2. Subsequent Remedial Measures

a. Inadmissible to Prove Negligence or Culpable Conduct

Evidence of repairs or other precautionary measures made following an injury is inadmissible to prove negligence, culpable conduct, a defect in a product or its design, or a need for a warning or instruction. [Fed. R. Evid. 407] The purpose of the rule is to encourage people to make such repairs.

b. When Admissible

Although evidence of subsequent repairs is not admissible to prove negligence, etc., this evidence may still be admissible for other purposes. Some of these purposes are:

1) To Prove Ownership or Control

Evidence of subsequent repairs performed by the defendant may be introduced to prove ownership or control, since a stranger would hardly make repairs.

2) To Rebut Claim that Precaution Was Not Feasible

Evidence of repairs or other precautionary measures made following an accident is admissible to establish the feasibility of precautionary measures when such feasibility is controverted.

3) To Prove Destruction of Evidence

Evidence of subsequent remedial measures may be admitted to prove that the opposing party has destroyed evidence; *e.g.,* repainting a fender to cover up evidence of a collision (spoliation).

3. Settlement Offers—Negotiations Not Admissible

Evidence of compromises or offers to compromise is inadmissible to prove liability for or invalidity of a claim that is disputed as to validity or amount. [Fed. R. Evid. 408] *Rationale:* Public policy favors the settlement of disputes without litigation, and settlement would be discouraged if either side were deterred from making offers by the fear that they would be admitted in evidence.

The Federal Rules also exclude "any conduct or statement" made in the course of negotiating a compromise, as well as the offer to compromise itself; therefore, admissions of fact made during compromise negotiations are inadmissible. This position encourages settlements by allowing complete candor between the parties in negotiations. [Fed. R. Evid. 408] *But note:* Rule 408 does not exclude evidence that would ***otherwise be discoverable*** because it was presented during compromise negotiations. Thus, if defendant presents a document to plaintiff during compromise negotiations to facilitate a compromise and the document was discoverable by plaintiff, it will be admissible in evidence notwithstanding that it was presented during compromise negotiations.

a. Must Be a Claim

Although the filing of a suit is not a prerequisite for this exclusionary rule, there must be some indication, express or implied, that a party is going to make some kind of claim. Thus, a party's volunteered admission of fact accompanying an offer to settle immediately following the incident is usually admissible because there has not been time for the other party to indicate an intent to make a claim.

b. Claim Must Be Disputed as to Liability or Amount

To trigger the exclusionary feature of Rule 408, the claim must be disputed as to liability or amount. Thus, if a party admits liability and the amount of liability but offers to settle (rather than litigate) for a lesser amount, every statement made in connection with that offer is admissible.

4. Withdrawn Guilty Pleas and Offers to Plead Guilty Not Admissible

Under the Federal Rules neither withdrawn guilty pleas, pleas of nolo contendere, offers to plead guilty, nor evidence of statements made in negotiating such pleas are admissible in any proceeding. [Fed. R. Evid. 410] Most jurisdictions concur. The ***evidentiary value*** of a withdrawn plea of guilty as an admission is deemed ***offset by the prejudicial effect*** of the evidence. Moreover, it is felt that the judge who permitted the withdrawal of the guilty plea must have decided that there was a good reason to withdraw it and, under these circumstances, the significance of the initial plea is minimal. Most courts exclude offers to plead guilty on reasoning similar to that advanced for not admitting offers to compromise as proof of liability in civil cases.

a. Waiver

The protection of Rule 410 for plea negotiations may be validly waived unless there is an affirmative indication that the defendant entered the waiver agreement unknowingly or involuntarily. [United States v. Mezzanatto, 513 U.S. 196 (1995)]

Example: Defendant, who was charged with a drug offense, wished to arrange a deal with the government in exchange for his cooperation. As a prerequisite to this discussion, Prosecutor required that Defendant (i) be completely truthful and (ii) agree that any statements made by him in the course of the plea negotiations could be used to impeach him if he testified in a contrary fashion at trial. Defendant agreed. If at some point thereafter the discussion breaks off and Defendant is tried on the charges, Prosecutor may use statements made in the plea negotiations to impeach Defendant. [United States v. Mezzanatto, *supra*]

5. Payment of Medical Expenses Not Admissible

Similarly, evidence that a party paid (or offered to pay) the injured party's medical expenses is ***not admissible to prove liability*** for the injury. [Fed. R. Evid. 409] This rule is based upon the concern that such payment might be prompted solely by "humanitarian motives." However, unlike the situation with compromise negotiation (3., *supra*), ***admissions of fact*** accompanying offers to pay medical expenses ***are admissible.***

E. CHARACTER EVIDENCE—A SPECIAL RELEVANCE PROBLEM

The rules regarding use of character evidence are affected by three major concerns. These are: (i) the purpose for which evidence of character is offered; (ii) the method to be used to prove character; and (iii) the kind of case, civil or criminal.

1. **Purposes for Offer of Character Evidence**

   a. **To Prove Character When Character Itself Is Ultimate Issue in Case**
   When a person's character itself is the ultimate issue in the case, character evidence must be admitted. Cases where character is itself one of the material propositions in issue are confined mostly to civil litigation and are rare even among civil actions.

   b. **To Serve as Circumstantial Evidence of How a Person Probably Acted**
   It is the use of character as circumstantial evidence of how a person probably acted that raises the most difficult problems of relevance, especially in criminal cases.

   c. **To Impeach Credibility of Witness**
   The discussion of the use of character evidence to impeach the credibility of a witness is postponed for later discussion under the heading of "Credibility—Impeachment." (*See* VI.E., *infra.*)

2. **Means of Proving Character**
   Depending upon the jurisdiction, the purpose of the offer, and the nature of the case, the following types of evidence may be used to prove character:

   a. **Evidence of Specific Acts as Demonstrating Character**
   Evidence of specific acts of the person in question as demonstrating that person's character is permitted only in a few instances, such as where character is itself one of the ultimate issues in the case.

   b. **Opinion Testimony**
   Witnesses who know the person may testify regarding their opinions about the person's character.

   c. **Testimony as to Person's General Reputation in Community**
   Testimony by witnesses as to a person's general reputation in the community is in some sense hearsay since reputation is really what people say about a person. On the other hand, because reputation is a general indication of character, and because it involves fewer side issues than either of the above methods, it is the most common means of showing character.

3. **Generally Not Admissible in Civil Cases**
   Evidence of character to prove the conduct of a person in the litigated event is generally not admissible in a civil case. The reasons given are that the slight probative value of character is outweighed by the danger of prejudice, the possible distraction of the jury from the main question in issue, and the possible waste of time required by examination of collateral issues.
   Examples: 1) Defendant may not introduce evidence that she is generally a cautious driver to prove that she was not negligent on the day in question.

                    2) Plaintiff may not introduce evidence that the defendant is usually a reckless driver to prove that she was negligent on the day in question.

   Such circumstantial use of prior behavior patterns for the purpose of drawing the inference that, at the time and place in question, the actor probably acted in accord with her prior behavior pattern is not permitted. A person's *general behavior patterns* (as distinguished from her habits and business routines) are *irrelevant* and inadmissible in evidence.

   a. **Exception—When Character Is Directly in Issue**
   When a person's character itself is one of the issues in the case, character evidence is not only admissible, but indeed is the best method of proving the issue.
   Examples: 1) In a defamation action, when D is being sued for calling P a thief and pleads as an affirmative defense that she spoke the truth (*i.e.*, that P is indeed a thief), P's character is clearly in issue.

                    2) When an employer is charged with negligently retaining an employee "of unstable and violent disposition," the character of the employee is also in issue.

   When character is directly in issue, almost all courts will admit evidence of specific acts that show this character (*e.g.*, in Example 1) above, D may offer evidence that on different occasions P has stolen things to show that he is a thief). Under the Federal Rules, any of the types of evidence (*reputation*, *opinion*, *or specific acts*) may be used to prove character when character is directly in issue. [Fed. R. Evid. 405(b)]

4. Accused in a Criminal Case—Prosecution Cannot Initiate, but Accused Can
The general rule is that the prosecution cannot initiate evidence of the bad character of the defendant merely to show that she is more likely to have committed the crime of which she is accused. However, the accused may introduce evidence of her good character to show her innocence of the alleged crime.

The rationale is that even though the evidence is of some relevance, the prosecution should not be permitted to show that the defendant is a bad person, since the jury might then decide to convict her regardless of her guilt of the crime charged. However, since the life or liberty of the defendant is at stake, she should be allowed to introduce evidence of her good character since it may have a tendency to show that she did not commit the crime charged.

a. How Defendant Proves Character

1) Reputation and Personal Opinion Testimony
A defendant puts her character in issue by calling a qualified witness to testify to the defendant's good reputation (or that he has heard nothing bad) *for the trait involved* in the case. Under Federal Rule 405, the witness may also give his personal opinion concerning that trait of the defendant. However, the witness may *not* testify to *specific acts of conduct* of the defendant to prove the trait in issue.

2) Testifying Places Defendant's Credibility—Not Character—in Issue
A defendant does not put her character in issue merely by taking the stand and giving testimony on the facts of the controversy. However, if the defendant takes the stand, she puts her credibility in issue and is subject to impeachment. (*See* "Credibility—Impeachment," VI.E., *infra*.)

b. How Prosecution Rebuts Defendant's Character Evidence
If the defendant puts her character in issue by having a character witness testify as to his opinion of the defendant or the defendant's reputation, the prosecution may rebut in the following manner:

1) Cross-Examination
The prosecution may test the character witness by cross-examination regarding the basis for his opinion or knowledge of the reputation that he has testified about. In most jurisdictions, one is allowed to inquire on cross-examination whether the reputation witness has *heard* of particular instances of the defendant's misconduct pertinent to the trait in question. The rationale is that since the reputation witness relates what he has heard, the inquiry tests the accuracy of his hearing and reporting. Since the character witness may now testify in the form of opinion as well as by reputation, it follows that the basis of the opinion can be exposed. Thus, under Federal Rule 405(a), cross-examination inquiry is allowable as to whether the opinion witness *knows* of, as well as whether he has *heard* of, specific instances of misconduct. The distinction in form between "Have you heard" and "Do you know" is eliminated by the statement in Rule 405(a), which provides that "on cross-examination, inquiry is allowable into relevant specific instances of conduct." Note that if the witness denies knowledge of these specific instances of conduct, the prosecutor *may not* prove them by extrinsic evidence; he is limited to inquiry on cross-examination.

2) Testimony of Other Witnesses as to Defendant's Bad Reputation
The prosecution may rebut the defendant's character evidence by calling qualified witnesses to testify to the defendant's bad reputation or their opinion of the defendant's character for the particular trait involved.

5. Victim in Criminal Case

a. Defendant's Initiative
The defendant may introduce reputation or opinion evidence of a bad character trait of the alleged crime victim when it is relevant to show the defendant's innocence. However, by specific exception, this rule does not extend to showing the bad character of rape victims.

Example: In an assault or murder prosecution where the defendant claims self-defense, she may introduce evidence of the victim's violent character as tending to show that the victim was the aggressor.

b. Prosecution Rebuttal

Once the defendant has introduced evidence of a bad character trait of the alleged victim, the prosecution may counter with reputation or opinion evidence of (i) the *victim's good character*, or (ii) the ***defendant's bad character*** for the ***same trait***. [Fed. R. Evid. 404(a)]

Example: Defendant is charged with the murder of Victim. Defendant pleads self-defense and offers evidence that Victim was a violent person. Prosecutor can rebut such evidence with evidence that Victim was a nonviolent person and/or with evidence that Defendant is a violent person.

c. Rape Cases—Victim's Past Behavior Inadmissible

In any civil or criminal proceeding involving alleged sexual misconduct, evidence offered to prove the sexual behavior or sexual disposition of the alleged victim is generally inadmissible. [Fed. R. Evid. 412(a)]

1) Exceptions in Criminal Cases

In a criminal case, evidence of sexual behavior by the victim offered to prove that a person other than the accused was the ***source of semen, injury, or other physical evidence*** is admissible. Also, specific instances of sexual behavior between the victim and the accused are admissible by the prosecution, or by the defense to prove ***consent***. Evidence of a victim's sexual behavior is also admissible when its exclusion would violate the defendant's constitutional rights. [Fed. R. Evid. 412(b)(1)]

2) Exceptions in Civil Cases

In civil cases, evidence offered to prove the sexual disposition or behavior of the alleged victim is admissible if it is otherwise admissible under the Federal Rules and its probative value substantially outweighs the danger of harm to the victim and of unfair prejudice to any party. Evidence of an alleged victim's reputation is admissible only if it has been placed in controversy by the victim. [Fed. R. Evid. 412(b)(2)]

3) Procedure

To offer evidence under the above exceptions, the party must file a motion 14 days before trial describing the evidence and its purpose, and must serve the motion on all parties and notify the victim. Before admitting the evidence, the court must conduct an in camera hearing and afford the victim and the parties a right to be heard. [Fed. R. Evid. 412(c)]

6. Specific Acts of Misconduct Generally Inadmissible

The basic rule is that when a person is charged with one crime, extrinsic evidence of her other crimes or misconduct is inadmissible if such evidence is offered solely to establish a criminal disposition. Thus, this statement of Federal Rule 404(b) is merely another way of saying that the prosecution may not show the accused's bad character to imply criminal disposition. The danger again is that the jury may convict the defendant because of past crimes rather than because of her guilt of the offense charged.

a. Admissible If Independently Relevant

Evidence of other crimes or misconduct is admissible if these acts are relevant to some issue other than the defendant's character or disposition to commit the crime charged. While acknowledging that prior acts or crimes are not admissible to show conformity or to imply bad character, Federal Rule 404(b) goes on to say that such prior acts or crimes may be admissible for other purposes (*e.g.*, to show motive, opportunity, intent, preparation, plan, knowledge, identity, or absence of mistake) whenever these issues are relevant in either a ***criminal or a civil case***. Upon request by the accused, the prosecution in a criminal case must provide reasonable notice prior to trial (or during trial if pretrial notice is excused for good cause shown) of the general nature of any of this type of evidence the prosecution intends to introduce at trial.

Example: Husband is on trial for the alleged shooting murder of Wife. Husband claims an accident occurred as he was cleaning the gun. Prosecution may prove that six months ago Husband tried to stab Wife. This evidence is not offered to show that the defendant is the kind of violent man likely to have murdered his wife (*i.e.*, general bad character or violent disposition); rather, it is offered to show absence of mistake, that the killing was probably not an accident.

1) Examples of Relevant Misconduct

a) Motive
The commission of a prior crime may be evidence of a motive to commit the crime for which the defendant is accused.

b) Intent
In many crimes, such as forgery, passing counterfeit money, larceny by trick, and receiving stolen property, intent is the gravamen of the crime. Evidence that defendant committed prior similar wrongful acts is admissible to establish guilty knowledge and to negate good faith.

c) Absence of Mistake or Accident
There are cases in which the defense of accident or mistake may be anticipated. In these situations prosecution evidence of similar misconduct by the defendant is admissible to negate the possibility of mistake or accident. (*See* example above.)

d) Identity
Evidence, including misconduct, that connects this defendant to the crime (*e.g.,* theft of gun used in later crime) is admissible. Similarly, evidence that the accused committed prior criminal acts that are so distinctive as to operate as a "signature" may be introduced to prove that the accused committed the act in question (modus operandi).

e) Common Plan or Scheme—Preparation
Evidence that the defendant recently stole some burglar tools is probative of the fact that she committed the burglary for which she is accused.

f) Other
Similar acts or related misconduct may be used to prove opportunity, knowledge, or any relevant fact other than the accused's general bad character or criminal disposition.

2) Quantum of Proof for Independently Relevant Acts of Misconduct
Under Federal Rule 404(b), independently relevant uncharged misconduct by the defendant will be admissible, without a preliminary ruling, as long as (i) there is *sufficient evidence to support a jury finding* that the defendant committed the prior act (*i.e.,* the standard of Federal Rule 104); and (ii) its probative value on the issue of motive, intent, identity, or other independently relevant proposition is not substantially outweighed by the danger of unfair prejudice (*i.e.,* the test of Federal Rule 403). [Huddleston v. United States, 485 U.S. 681 (1988)]

b. Prior Acts of Sexual Assault or Child Molestation
Evidence of a defendant's prior acts of sexual assault or child molestation is admissible in a civil or criminal case where the defendant is accused of committing an act of sexual assault or child molestation. The party who intends to offer this evidence must disclose the evidence to the defendant 15 days before trial (or later with good cause). [Fed. R. Evid. 413-415]

III. JUDICIAL NOTICE

A. JUDICIAL NOTICE OF FACT
Judicial notice is the *recognition of a fact as true without formal presentation of evidence*. In most instances the costly, time-consuming, and cumbersome process of formal proof is required to ensure fact-finding accuracy. However, self-evident propositions need not be subjected to this

process, but instead may be judicially noticed. Judicial notice, like the presumption, is a judicial shortcut, a substitute for proof. The underlying policy considerations include expediting the trial and avoiding judicial disrepute where the lack of evidence might result in a conclusion contrary to well-known facts. For example, requiring proof that Washington, D.C., is the capital of the United States would require unnecessary time in a situation where a contrary conclusion would be ridiculous.

1. Facts Appropriate for Judicial Notice

The Federal Rule conforms to the existing state rules governing judicial notice. Federal Rule 201(b) defines a fact that may be noticed as "one not subject to reasonable dispute in that it is either (i) generally known within the territorial jurisdiction of the trial court" (notorious facts), or (ii) "capable of accurate and ready determination by resort to sources whose accuracy cannot reasonably be questioned" (manifest facts). Judicial notice may be taken of such facts *at any time*, whether or not requested, and such notice is mandatory if a party requests and supplies the court with the necessary information. A party is entitled to be heard on the propriety of taking judicial notice and the tenor of the matter noted.

a. Matters of Common Knowledge in the Community—Notorious Facts

Judicial notice will be taken of the body of facts that well-informed persons generally know and accept. Though usually facts of common knowledge are known everywhere, it is sufficient for judicial notice if they are known in the community where the court is sitting.

Examples: A court sitting in New York City will take judicial notice that:

1) The streets in Manhattan are numbered east and west from Fifth Avenue and that the odd numbers are on the north side of the street.

2) Many people are subject to low blood pressure and poor circulation.

3) The ordinary period of human gestation is 280 days.

b. Facts Capable of Certain Verification—Manifest Facts

Some facts, while not generally known and accepted, are easily verified by resorting to easily accessible, well-established sources.

Examples: 1) Judicial notice will be taken of the time of the rising or setting of the sun and moon on a particular day since this fact, although not commonly known, can be estimated quickly and accurately by reference to an almanac.

2) The court will accept without proof that February 14, 1999, was a Sunday by reference to a calendar.

c. Judicial Notice of Scientific Principles

1) Judicial Notice of Scientific Basis of Test Results

Trial courts have increasingly taken judicial notice of scientific principles as a type of manifest fact. Once a particular scientific test or principle has become sufficiently well-established (*i.e.*, generally accepted among the scientific community), courts no longer require proof (expert testimony) of the underlying basis of the test. The results of such a test are therefore admissible into evidence.

Example: A trial court will take judicial notice of the reliability of radar speed tests, ballistics tests, and paternity blood tests, and will admit the results of these tests into evidence upon a showing that the tests were properly conducted.

2) Conclusiveness of Test Results

Some scientific tests have achieved such universal acceptance that not only are the test results admissible into evidence, but the results are binding on the finder of fact in civil cases.

Example: Where a blood test indicates that the accused father could not have been the parent of the child, that result is conclusive on the issue of paternity, and other evidence on that issue will be excluded.

    d. **Judge's Personal Knowledge**
What a judge knows personally is not the same as what he may judicially notice. A judge may have to ignore facts that he knows as a private person if those facts are neither commonly known in the community nor capable of certain verification by resort to easily accessible sources of indisputable accuracy.

2. Procedural Aspects of Judicial Notice

    a. **Requirement of a Request**
The general rule is that a party must formally request that notice be taken of a particular fact.

    b. **Judicial Notice by Appellate Court**
Judicial notice may be taken for the first time on appeal. A reviewing court is required to take judicial notice of any matter that the trial court properly noticed or was obliged to notice.

    c. **Conclusiveness of Judicial Notice**
Federal Rule 201(g) provides that a judicially noticed fact is conclusive in a civil case but not in a criminal case. The Federal Rule states that in a civil case, the court shall instruct the jury to accept as conclusive any fact judicially noticed; in a criminal case, on the other hand, the jury is instructed that it may, but is not required to, accept as conclusive any fact judicially noticed.

3. "Adjudicative" and "Legislative" Facts
The Federal Rules govern *only judicial notice of "adjudicative" facts* (*i.e.*, facts that relate to the parties in a particular case) not "legislative" facts (*i.e.*, policy facts that relate to legal reasoning and the lawmaking process). The drafters of Federal Rule 201 reasoned that "legislative" facts are a necessary part of the judicial reasoning process, so that a rule imposing a requirement of indisputability and a formal procedure for taking judicial notice of these matters would destroy the concept of judge-made law. [Advisory Committee Note to Rule 201] Therefore, "legislative" facts need not meet the requirements of Rule 201 that facts must be either of common knowledge or capable of indisputable verification to be judicially noticed.

B. JUDICIAL NOTICE OF LAW—MANDATORY OR PERMISSIVE
The judge's task of finding applicable law is accomplished by informal investigation of legal source materials. This process, unmentioned in the Federal Rules of Evidence, has been traditionally described in terms of the judge taking judicial notice of the law applicable to the case.

1. Classification Depends on Accessibility of Source Materials
Judicial notice of law is mandatory in some instances and permissive in others. This mandatory-permissive classification is explainable in terms of the likely accessibility of source materials for different types of laws. State public law is easily available in reported volumes and, therefore, it is reasonable to require the court to be aware of and to notice it. Descriptions of foreign law or private acts are usually less available and, therefore, the court is permitted—but not required—to judicially notice such laws. In some cases, the contents of such laws may have to be established by proof to the satisfaction of the judge.

2. Mandatory Judicial Notice
Most courts must take judicial notice without request of:

    a. *Federal public law*—the United States Constitution, federal treaties, public acts of Congress, and federal case law.

    b. *State public law*—the constitution, public statutes, and common law of the states.

    c. *Official regulations*—the official compilation of codes and rules and regulations of the forum state and the federal government, except those relating to internal organization or management of a state agency.

3. Permissive Judicial Notice
Most courts may, upon being supplied with sufficient information, take judicial notice of municipal ordinances and private acts or resolutions of Congress and of the local state legislature. Similarly, the laws of foreign countries may be judicially noticed.

IV. REAL EVIDENCE

A. IN GENERAL

1. Addressed Directly to Trier of Fact
Real or demonstrative evidence is addressed directly to the trier of fact. The object in issue is presented for *inspection by the trier of fact*. Ordinarily the evidence is addressed to the sense of sight (*e.g.*, exhibition of injured arm to jury to demonstrate extent of injury), but it may be directed to other senses as well (*e.g.*, sound recording of factory noise played during a nuisance trial).

2. Special Problems
This form of proof, which allows the triers of fact to reach conclusions based upon their own perceptions rather than relying upon those of witnesses, frequently involves special problems. Often there is concern regarding *proper authentication* of the "object." Additionally, the possibility exists that physical production of the thing may be too *burdensome* or may inspire *prejudicial emotions* outweighing its probative value to the litigation.

B. TYPES OF REAL EVIDENCE

1. Direct
Real evidence may be direct evidence; *i.e.*, it may be offered to prove the facts about the object as an end in itself. For example, in a personal injury case, evidence of a permanent injury could be introduced by an exhibition of the injury itself to the trier of fact.

2. Circumstantial
Real evidence may also be circumstantial; *i.e.*, facts about the object are proved as a basis for an inference that other facts are true. For example, in a paternity case, the trier of fact may be shown the baby for the purpose of comparing its appearance and the appearance of the alleged father. In this case, the trier of fact is being asked to draw an inference that, since the child and alleged father look alike, the paternal relationship exists.

3. Original
Real evidence may be original; *i.e.*, it may have had some connection with the transaction that is in question at the trial. An example of this kind of evidence would be an alleged murder weapon.

4. Prepared
Real evidence may also be prepared; *e.g.*, sketches or models may be made to be shown to the trier of fact. This category of real evidence is called *"demonstrative evidence."*

C. GENERAL CONDITIONS OF ADMISSIBILITY
Real evidence, like all other forms of evidence, must be *relevant* to the proposition in issue. The admissibility of real proof also depends on additional legal requirements, such as those that follow.

1. Authentication
The object must first be identified as being what the proponent claims it to be. Real evidence is commonly authenticated by recognition testimony or by establishing a chain of custody.

a. Recognition Testimony
If the object has significant features that make it identifiable upon inspection, a witness may authenticate the object by testifying that the object is what the proponent claims it is.

Examples: 1) If a prosecutor offers a knife into evidence and claims that the knife is the very weapon used in the murder, the object may be authenticated by a witness who testifies that he can identify the knife as the one found next to the deceased.

2) If a prosecutor offers a knife into evidence and claims that it is *similar* to the knife used in the murder, it may be authenticated by a witness who testifies that the offered knife is indeed similar to the one found next to the deceased.

3) A witness can testify that a photograph is a fair and accurate representation of that which it is purported to depict.

b. Chain of Custody

If the evidence is of a type that is likely to be confused or can be easily tampered with, the proponent of the object must present evidence of chain of custody. The proponent of the evidence must show that the object has been held in a substantially **unbroken chain of possession.** The proponent need not negate all possibilities of substitution or tampering, but must show adherence to some system of identification and custody.

Example: A custodial chain—from the taking, to the testing, to the exhibiting of the sample—must be established before evidence of a blood alcohol test will be admitted.

2. Condition of Object; Useful Probativeness

If the condition of the object is significant, it must be shown to be in substantially the **same condition at the trial.** Moreover, the object must be logically helpful or reliable in tending to prove the proposition in issue.

Example: Would it be helpful in a paternity proceeding to present the baby so that the trier of fact can ascertain physical resemblance to the alleged father?

3. Legal Relevance

Assuming the object has been properly identified and is probative, the discretion of the trial judge is called upon to decide whether some auxiliary policy or principle outweighs the need to admit the real evidence. Such policies limiting the use of real evidence frequently concern:

a. **Physical inconvenience** of bringing the object into the courtroom;

b. **Indecency or impropriety**; or

c. **Undue prejudice** where the probative value of the object or exhibit is outweighed by the danger of unfair prejudice.

D. PARTICULAR TYPES OF REAL PROOF

1. Reproductions and Explanatory Real Evidence

When properly authenticated, relevant photographs, movies, diagrams, maps, sketches, or other **reproductions are admissible** if their value is not outweighed by the danger of unfair prejudice. On the other hand, items used entirely for **explanatory purposes** (such as skeletons, anatomy charts, etc.) are permitted at a trial, but are usually **not admitted into evidence** and are not given to the jury during its deliberations. These items are not represented to be reproductions of the real thing, but are merely used as aids to testimony.

Example: A doctor may use a model of an average male skeleton to explain his testimony. The skeleton may be marked for identification in order to preserve the record, but it is not admitted into evidence.

Compare: If the skeleton was offered as a reproduction of the bone structure of the deceased, assuming there is no undue prejudice, it may be admitted into evidence on a showing that it accurately represents the bone structure of the deceased.

2. Maps, Charts, Models, Etc.

Maps, charts, models, etc., are usually admissible for the purpose of illustrating testimony. Since these are all reproductions, they must be authenticated by testimonial evidence showing that they are **faithful reproductions** of the object or thing depicted. As with other real evidence, introduction of these items is within the discretion of the court, and they may be excluded where they would be wasteful of time or where they would unduly impress the trier of fact with the importance of the material.

3. Exhibition of Child in Paternity Suits

Almost all courts permit exhibition of the child for the purpose of showing whether it is of the race of the putative father. The courts are divided with respect to the propriety of exhibiting the child in order to prove physical resemblance to the putative father, but a growing majority of courts refuse to permit exhibition of the child.

4. Exhibition of Injuries

The exhibition of injuries in a personal injury or criminal case is generally permitted, but the court has discretion to exclude this evidence if the exhibition would result in unfair prejudice.

5. Jury View of the Scene

Closely related to real and demonstrative evidence is the matter of jury views of premises and places at issue in the case. In the trial court's discretion, they are permitted, sparingly, in both civil and criminal cases. The importance of information that could be obtained by a view, and the ease with which photographs, diagrams, or maps could be substituted for such a view, will be pivotal considerations to the trial judge. Any significant changes of condition in the premises that are to be viewed will also affect the decision. The trial judge usually need not be present during a jury view. The parties and their attorneys are usually permitted to attend, but the view will be conducted by a disinterested court attaché and neither counsel nor the parties will be permitted to engage in any commentary.

6. Demonstrations

The court, in its discretion, may permit experiments or demonstrations to be performed in the courtroom.

a. Demonstrations Showing Effect of Bodily Injury

Demonstrations to show the effect of bodily injury are usually excluded where the exhibition would reveal hideous wounds, elicit cries of pain, or otherwise unduly dramatize the injury and inflame the minds of the jurors.

b. Demonstrations Under Sole Control of Witness Are Excluded

Demonstrations may also be excluded where they are under the sole control of the witness and thus not subject to effective cross-examination. For example, an injured plaintiff might attempt to demonstrate lack of locomotion by showing that he cannot move a limb. The demonstration itself cannot be effectively cross-examined. However, if testimony is given to the same effect, it may be impeached by contradictory evidence.

c. Scientific Experiments

The judge may permit scientific experiments to be performed in the courtroom provided:

1) The conditions are *substantially similar* to those that attended the original event, and

2) The experiment will *not result in undue waste of time or confusion* of the issues.

V. DOCUMENTARY EVIDENCE

A. IN GENERAL

Documentary evidence, like other kinds of evidence, *must be relevant* in order to be admissible. In the case of writings, the authenticity of the document is one aspect of its relevancy. Of course, documentary evidence, even if fully authenticated and relevant, *may be excluded if it violates a rule of competency* such as the best evidence or hearsay rule. Whenever any problem or question concerns a document, you should consider three separate and distinct possible barriers to admissibility (authentication, best evidence, and hearsay).

B. AUTHENTICATION

Before a writing or any secondary evidence of its content may be received in evidence, the writing must be authenticated by proof showing that the writing is what the proponent claims it is. The writing is usually not self-authenticating. It needs a testimonial sponsor or shepherding angel to prove that the writing was made, signed, or adopted by the particular relevant person. [Fed. R. Evid. 901-903]

1. Quantum of Proof of Authenticity

Authentication of documentary or, for that matter, real evidence requires only enough evidence to support a finding that the matter is what its proponent claims it is. It is not required that the proponent establish its genuineness by a preponderance of the evidence as a condition to admissibility. All that is necessary under Federal Rules 104(b) and 901 is proof *sufficient to support a jury finding* of genuineness.

2. **Authentication by Pleadings or Stipulation**

The genuineness of a document may be admitted through the discovery process, through stipulation at pretrial conference, or by a failure to deny an allegation in a pleading.

3. **Evidence of Authenticity**

In general, a writing may be authenticated by any evidence that serves to establish its authenticity. The Federal Rules do not limit the methods of authentication, but rather list several examples of proper authentication. [Fed. R. Evid. 901]

a. **Admissions**

A writing may be authenticated by evidence that the party against whom the writing is offered has either *admitted* its authenticity or *acted upon* the writing as authentic.

b. **Testimony of Eyewitness**

A writing may be authenticated by testimony of one who *sees it executed* or *hears it acknowledged*. Modern statutes eliminate the common law necessity of producing a subscribing witness, unless specifically required by statute. [Fed. R. Evid. 903] If testimony of a subscribing witness is required (*e.g.*, in authenticating a will), his denial or failure to recollect the execution of the writing does not preclude authentication by other evidence.

c. **Handwriting Verifications**

A writing may also be authenticated by evidence of the genuineness of the handwriting of the maker.

1) **Nonexpert Opinion**

A lay witness who has personal knowledge of the handwriting of the supposed writer may state his opinion as to whether the document is in that person's handwriting. (This is an exception to the opinion rule, *see* VI.C.1., *infra*.) Note, however, that a nonexpert cannot become familiar with the handwriting merely for the purpose of testifying.

2) **Comparison of Writings**

An expert witness or the trier of fact (*e.g.*, jury) can determine the genuineness of a writing by comparing the questioned writing with another writing proved to be genuine. (Note that authentication by comparison is not limited to handwriting. Fingerprints, blood, hair, clothing fibers, and numerous other things can be authenticated by comparison with authenticated specimens.)

d. **Ancient Documents**

Under the Federal Rules, a document may be authenticated by evidence that it:

(i) Is at least *20 years old*;

(ii) Is in such condition as to be *free from suspicion* concerning its authenticity; and

(iii) Was *found in a place* where such writing, if authentic, would likely be kept.

1) **Federal Rules Distinguished from Majority of Jurisdictions**

The Federal Rules apply to *all writings*. However, most jurisdictions limit the ancient documents rule to *dispositive instruments* (*e.g.*, deeds, wills, etc.). In addition, most courts require that such documents be over *30 years old*.

e. **Reply Letter Doctrine**

A writing may be authenticated by evidence that it was written in response to a communication sent to the claimed author. The content of the letter must make it unlikely that it was written by anyone other than the claimed author of the writing.

f. **Circumstantial Evidence in General**

The rules for ancient documents and reply letters, above, involve authentication by circumstantial evidence. A complete list of ways to authenticate by circumstantial evidence would be impossible. Any proof tending in reason to *establish genuineness* is sufficient. For example, authentication may be established by the content of the writing and a showing that it contains information known only to the purported author. Alternatively it may be demonstrated that the author had the disputed writing in his custody at a prior time under circumstances evidencing his belief in its genuineness.

g. Photographs

1) Accurate Representation of Facts

As a general rule, photographs are admissible only if identified by a witness as a portrayal of certain facts relevant to the issue and verified by the witness as a correct representation of those facts. It suffices if the witness who identifies the photograph is familiar with the scene or object that is depicted. In general, it is *not necessary to call the photographer* to authenticate the photograph.

2) Unattended Camera—Proper Operation of Camera

In some situations, a photograph will portray an event that was observed by the camera. For example, an unmanned surveillance camera may produce a photograph of a burglar taken at a time when no other person was on the premises. Such a photograph may be admitted upon a showing that the camera was properly operating at the relevant time and that the photograph was developed from film obtained from that camera.

h. X-Ray Pictures, Electrocardiograms, Etc.

Unlike photographs, an X-ray picture cannot be authenticated by testimony of a witness that it is a correct representation of the facts. Therefore, a different procedure of authentication is necessary. First, it must be shown that the *process used is accurate* (as to X-rays, the court will usually take judicial notice of this). Then it must be shown that the *machine itself was in working order* and the *operator was qualified* to operate it. Finally, a *custodial chain* must be established to forestall the danger that the evidence has been substituted or tampered with.

4. Compare—Authentication of Oral Statements

Oral statements often require authentication as to the *identity of the speaker*. Although this is technically a "relevance" topic, the rules are the same as those that apply to the authenticity of documents.

a. When Necessary

Not all oral statements need to be authenticated; only where the identity of the speaker is important (*e.g.,* admission by a party) is authentication required.

b. Methods of Authentication

1) Voice Identification

A voice, whether heard firsthand or through a device (*e.g.,* a tape recording) may be identified by the opinion of anyone who has heard the voice at *any time*. Thus, in contrast to the rule for handwriting verification, a person can become familiar with a voice after litigation has begun and for the sole purpose of testifying.

2) Telephone Conversations

Statements made during a telephone conversation may be authenticated by one of the parties to the call who testifies to one of the following:

a) He recognized the other party's voice.

b) The speaker has knowledge of certain facts that only a particular person would have.

c) He called, for example, Mr. A's telephone number, and a voice answered, "This is Mr. A" or "This is the A residence." This authenticates the conversation as being with Mr. A or his agent.

d) He called the person's business establishment and talked with the person answering the phone about matters relevant to the business. This is sufficient to show that the person answering the phone held a position in the business.

5. Self-Authenticating Documents

Contrary to the general rule, which requires testimonial sponsorship, there are certain writings that are said to "prove themselves" or to be "self-identifying" on their face. Federal

Rule 902 specifically provides that extrinsic evidence of authenticity as a condition to admissibility is not required as to the following:

a. Certified copies of *public records*;

b. *Official publications* (*i.e.,* books, pamphlets, or other publications purporting to be issued by a public authority);

c. Printed materials purporting to be *newspapers or periodicals*;

d. *Trade inscriptions,* signs, tags, or labels purporting to have been affixed in the course of business and indicating ownership, control, or origin;

e. *Documents accompanied by a certificate of acknowledgment* executed in the manner provided by law by a notary public or other officer authorized by law to take acknowledgments;

f. *Commercial paper,* signatures thereon, and documents relating thereto, to the extent provided by general commercial law; and

g. *Business records* certified as such by a custodian or other qualified person.

C. BEST EVIDENCE RULE

The best evidence rule is more accurately called the *"original document rule."* It may be stated as follows: In proving the terms of a writing (recording, photograph, or X-ray), where the terms are material, the original writing must be produced. Secondary evidence of the writing, such as oral testimony regarding the writing's contents, is permitted only after it has been shown that the original is unavailable for some reason other than the serious misconduct of the proponent. [Fed. R. Evid. 1002]

1. Rule Expresses Preference for Originals

Simply stated, the rule applies to writings and expresses a preference for originals. It reflects the belief that the exact words of a writing, particularly in the case of operative or dispositive instruments such as contracts, deeds, or wills, should be presented to the court; that there is a hazard of inaccuracy in common methods of approximating the contents of a writing; and that oral testimony based on memory of the terms of the writing presents greater risk of error than oral testimony concerning other situations.

2. Applicability of the Rule

For the most part, the rule applies to two classes of situations: (i) where the writing is a *legally operative or dispositive instrument* such as a contract, deed, will, or divorce decree; or (ii) where the *knowledge of a witness* concerning a fact results from having *read* it in the document.

Examples: 1) Witness may not testify about the content of a written deed unless sufficient reason is given for not producing the original deed.

2) Witness who memorized mileage recorded on car sticker for a certain date, and who had no other source of knowledge on this significant litigated issue, may not testify as to the mileage without establishing a reason for the unavailability of the writing.

3. Nonapplicability of the Rule

a. Fact to Be Proved Exists Independently of Any Writing

Where the fact to be proved has an existence independent of any writing, the best evidence rule does not apply. Therefore, the rule does not apply to all events that happen to have been memorialized by documents. There are many writings that the substantive law does not regard as essential repositories of the facts recorded. These writings happen to record details of essentially nonwritten transactions. As to these, oral testimony may be given without production of, or explanation for the absence of, the original writings.

Examples: 1) Witness may testify orally that he paid for goods received without producing the receipt that was given.

2) Facts such as birth, marriage, age, and death may be proved orally, although certificates evidencing these facts are in existence. However, since a divorce is effective only by a judicial decree, the best evidence rule requires that the fact of divorce be proved by the decree itself.

3) Testimony heard at a prior trial may be testified to in another case without production of the stenographic transcript of the prior testimony. One who heard the prior testimony can repeat it.

4) Admissions or confessions of a party may be testified to orally by anyone who heard them, even though the admissions or confessions were later reduced to writing.

The above examples are in contrast to those writings that are considered as essential repositories of the facts recorded. Written contracts, deeds, wills, and judgments are viewed as such repositories—they are considered written transactions—and as such are within the rule.

b.   Writing Is Collateral to Litigated Issue
Any narration by a witness is likely to include references to transactions consisting partly of written communications. The best evidence rule does not apply to writings of minor importance (*i.e.*, ones that are collateral) to the matter in controversy. [Fed. R. Evid. 1004(4)] For example, an expert witness testifying on the value of a car is allowed to establish his status as a car dealer without production of his dealer's license. The test of "collateralness" is likely to take into account:

1)   *Centrality* of the writing to the major issues of a litigation;

2)   *Complexity* of the relevant features of the writing; and

3)   Existence of a *genuine dispute* as to the contents of the writing.

c.   Summaries of Voluminous Records
When it would be inconvenient to examine a voluminous collection of writings, recordings, or photographs in court, the proponent may present their contents in the form of a chart, summary, or calculation. [Fed. R. Evid. 1006] However, the originals or duplicates (*see* 4.c., *infra*) must be made available for examination and copying, and the judge may order them to be produced in court.

d.   Public Records
The best evidence rule is modified so that a proponent may offer into evidence a copy of an official record or a copy of a document that has been recorded and filed. Such a copy must be *certified as correct* by the custodian of the document or other person authorized to do so, or *testified to be correct* by a person who compared it to the original. [Fed. R. Evid. 1005] The purpose of this exception is to prevent the loss or absence of public documents due to litigation.

4.   Definitions of "Writings," "Original," and "Duplicate"

a.   Writings, Recordings, and Photographs
The Federal Rules govern writings, recordings, and photographs. Writings and recordings are defined broadly as "letters, words, or numbers, or their equivalent; set down by handwriting, typewriting, printing, photostating, photographing, magnetic impulse, mechanical or electronic recording, or other form of data compilation." Photographs are more narrowly defined as "still photographs, X-ray films, and motion pictures." [Fed. R. Evid. 1001]

b.   "Original"
An original is the writing or recording itself or any duplicate intended by the person executing it to have the same effect as an original.

Example: D types a ribbon and one carbon of a letter that is defamatory to P. D sends a ribbon copy to P himself and the carbon to the newspaper. In P's defamation action, the document legally operative to create tort liability was the "published" carbon, not the ribbon copy.

c. **Admissibility of Duplicates**
The Federal Rules define a duplicate as "a counterpart produced by the same impression as the original, or from the same matrix, or by means of photography . . . or by mechanical or electronic re-recording, or by chemical reproduction, or by other equivalent techniques which accurately reproduce the original." [Fed. R. Evid. 1001(4)] A duplicate is thus an *exact copy of an original*, *e.g.,* a carbon copy or photocopy. Duplicates are *admissible* the same as originals in federal courts, *unless* (i) the authenticity of the original is challenged, or (ii) under the circumstances, it would be unfair to admit the duplicate in place of the original. [Fed. R. Evid. 1003] The rationale for admitting duplicates under such a relaxed standard is that by definition these documents are exact copies of the original, and therefore their introduction into evidence would be objectionable only if some question existed as to the genuineness of the original.

5. **Admissibility of Secondary Evidence of Contents**
If the proponent cannot produce the original writing or recording in court, he may offer secondary evidence of its contents in the form of copies (*e.g.*, handwritten copies, which would not be considered duplicates because they are not exact copies), notes, or oral testimony about the contents of the original if a satisfactory explanation is given for the nonproduction of the original.

a. **Satisfactory Foundation**
A valid excuse justifying the admissibility of secondary evidence would include:

1) **Loss or Destruction of Original**
A proper foundation for the admissibility of secondary evidence is laid by a showing that the original has been lost and cannot be found despite diligent search, or was destroyed in good faith.

2) **Original Outside Jurisdiction and Unobtainable**
If the document is within the jurisdiction, it must be subpoenaed. If not, some reasonable effort or request to the third party for production must be shown before secondary evidence will be admitted. A proper foundation is laid, however, if it is shown that the original is (i) in the possession of a third party, (ii) outside the jurisdiction, and (iii) unobtainable.

3) **Original in Possession of Adversary Who, After Notice, Fails to Produce**
If the opponent has custody of the original, a showing of his custody, service of a timely notice to produce, and his failure to produce it in court will justify the admissibility of secondary evidence. Where the pleadings give notice to the opposite party that he will be charged with possession of the writing, service of the notice to produce is unnecessary.

b. **No Degrees of Secondary Evidence**
The Federal Rules recognize no degrees of secondary evidence. Once a satisfactory explanation for nonproduction of the original is established, the party seeking to prove the contents of a writing, photograph, or recording may do so by any kind of secondary evidence ranging from handwritten copies to oral testimony. This abolition of degrees of secondary evidence is a departure from the rule existing in most American jurisdictions. [Fed. R. Evid. 1004]

c. **Testimony or Written Admission of Party**
A proponent may prove the contents of a writing, recording, or photograph through the testimony, deposition, or written admission of the party against whom it is offered, and need not account for the nonproduction of the original. [Fed. R. Evid. 1007] However, it is also generally held that the *contents* of a writing, photograph, etc., *cannot be proved simply by out-of-court oral admissions* of the party against whom such evidence is offered (unless of course the original is otherwise accounted for).
Example: Witness testifies, "I heard D say that the telegram he received stated . . . ." D's oral admissions outside court are inadmissible to prove the contents of the telegram. [Fed. R. Evid. 1007]

6. **Functions of Court and Jury**
Ordinarily, it is for the court to make the determinations of fact that determine the admissibility of duplicates, other copies, and oral testimony as to the contents of an original. However, the Federal Rules specifically reserve three questions of *preliminary fact for the jury*:

    (i)   Whether the original ever existed;

    (ii)   Whether a writing, recording, or photograph produced at trial is an original; and

    (iii)   Whether the evidence offered correctly reflects the contents of the original.

    [Fed. R. Evid. 1008]

D. PAROL EVIDENCE RULE

The essence of the parol evidence rule is as follows: If an agreement is reduced to writing, that writing is the agreement and hence constitutes the only evidence of it. All *prior or contemporaneous negotiations* or agreements *are merged* into the written agreement. Parol (extrinsic) evidence is not admissible to add to, detract from, or alter the agreement as written.

1. Substantive and Evidentiary Aspects

This rule, although actually a part of the substantive law of contracts, is also important as an evidentiary principle because of its *impact on materiality*. Prior and contemporary oral agreements are not material when offered to vary the terms of an apparently complete written contract.

2. Nonapplicability of Parol Evidence Rule

From an evidentiary standpoint, counsel invoking the rule is saying, "Here is the agreement. Its terms, having been reduced to writing by the parties, are indisputable; they cannot be put in issue. It follows that no evidence can be received in respect to those terms." This approach helps to explain why the parol evidence rule does not apply to exclude evidence of prior or contemporaneous agreements on the following issues:

a. Completion of Incomplete or Ambiguous Contract

In some situations, the written instrument may be valid but still incomplete or ambiguous. In these cases, parol evidence is admitted not to contradict or vary the writing but to complete the entire agreement of which the writing was only part. In these situations, parol evidence will be admitted if the contract does not appear on its face to be the entire agreement between the parties and the parol evidence is consistent with, and not contradictory of, the written instrument. If there is uncertainty, ambiguity, or reasonable dispute as to the meaning of contract terms, parol evidence is admissible to explain the ambiguity.

b. Reformation of Contract

Where a party alleges facts, such as mistake, entitling him to reformation of the written agreement, the parol evidence rule is inapplicable. This is so because the party is asserting that, despite the apparently unambiguous contract, its terms do not in fact constitute the agreement intended.

c. Challenge to Validity of Contract

The parol evidence rule does not bar admission of parol evidence to show that what appears to be a contractual obligation is, in fact, no obligation at all. Thus, evidence is admissible to show that the *contract was void or voidable* and has been avoided, or was made subject to a valid *condition precedent* that has not been satisfied. Specifically, parol evidence is admissible to establish or disprove a contract attacked on grounds of:

    1)   Fraud, duress, or undue influence inducing consent;

    2)   Lack of consideration;

    3)   Illegality of subject matter;

    4)   Material alteration;

    5)   Nondelivery, if the agreement required delivery for the instrument to be effective; or

    6)   Execution or delivery upon a condition precedent, as long as the parol condition does not contradict the writing. However, proof of an oral condition subsequent allegedly made at or before the time of the written contract would be barred by the rule.

3. Subsequent Modifications of Written Contract
The rule applies only to negotiations or agreements made ***prior to, or at the time of,*** the execution of the written contract. Parol evidence is admissible to show subsequent modification or discharge of the written contract.

VI. TESTIMONIAL EVIDENCE

A. COMPETENCY OF WITNESSES
Witnesses are not "authenticated" in the same sense as real or documentary evidence. However, they too must pass tests of basic reliability to establish their competence to give testimony. Unlike the authentication situation pertaining to real or documentary proof, witnesses are generally ***presumed to be competent*** until the contrary is demonstrated.

1. Basic Testimonial Qualifications
There are four basic testimonial attributes that every witness must have to some degree. These are the capacity to observe, to recollect, to communicate, and to appreciate the obligation to speak truthfully. These, along with sincerity, are the qualities at which the cross-examiner directs his skill.

A diminution of any of these capacities usually goes only to the weight of the testimony and serves to make the witness less persuasive. However, a witness can be so deficient in one or more of these basic qualifications that she will be deemed incompetent to testify at all. The problem of infancy is a good example for all aspects of the basic qualifications. A witness may be too young ***at the time of the event*** to be able to accurately perceive what happened or to be able to remember at the time of the trial. The witness may also be too young ***at the time of the trial*** to effectively relate or communicate or appreciate the obligation to tell the truth.

a. Ability to Observe—Perception
The issue of a witness's ability to observe may arise in the following manner: W testifies on direct to details of how an intersection automobile collision occurred. On cross-examination, W admits that her attention was directed to the intersection by the sound of the crash. The direct testimony regarding details of the accident occurring before the collision will be stricken.

b. Ability to Remember—Memory
An example of a witness incompetent for this reason would be one who is suffering from senility or amnesia.

c. Ability to Relate—Communication
The ability to relate concerns the ability of the witness to communicate effectively with the trier of fact.

d. Appreciation of Oath Obligation
The witness must have sufficient intelligence and character to know and desire to tell the truth. The witness may be sworn by oath or affirmation. However, unsworn testimony may be permissible if the witness (*e.g.*, a child) appreciates the obligation to tell the truth.

2. Federal Rules of Competency

a. Personal Knowledge and Oath Required
Federal Rule 601 provides that "Every person is competent to be a witness except as otherwise provided in these rules." The rules do not specify any mental or moral qualifications for witness testimony beyond these two limitations:

1) ***The witness must have personal knowledge*** of the matter he is to testify about. The requirement of "personal knowledge" means that the witness must have observed the matter and must have a present recollection of his observation. [Fed. R. Evid. 602]

2) ***The witness must declare he will testify truthfully***, by oath or affirmation. [Fed. R. Evid. 603]

b. **Use of Interpreter**
If a witness requires an interpreter, the interpreter must be qualified and take an oath to make a true translation. [Fed. R. Evid. 604]

c. **Applicability of State Rules in Diversity Cases**
Federal Rule 601 provides that the competency of a witness shall be determined by state law in civil actions "with respect to an element of a claim or defense as to which state law supplies the rules of decision."

3. **Modern Modifications of Common Law Disqualifications**
At common law there were several grounds upon which a person could be disqualified from giving testimony. Persons were incompetent to testify if they had a financial interest in the suit, if they were the spouse of a party, if they lacked religious belief, if they had been convicted of a crime, or if they lacked mental capacity. These common law disqualifications have been almost entirely removed under the Federal Rules and in the vast majority of American jurisdictions.

a. **Lack of Religious Belief**
Lack of religious belief is no longer a basis for excluding a witness. Not only are a person's religious convictions irrelevant in determining the competence of a witness, but they may also not be shown or commented upon for the purpose of affecting the credibility of a witness.

b. **Infancy**
There is *no precise age* at which an infant is deemed competent or incompetent to testify under oath. The competence of an infant depends on the capacity and intelligence of the particular child. This test is an individual one, to be determined by the trial judge upon preliminary examination.

c. **Insanity**
An insane person, even one who has been adjudicated incompetent, *may testify*, provided he understands the obligation to speak truthfully and possesses the capacity to give a correct account of what he has perceived in reference to the issue in dispute.

d. **Conviction of Crime**
The common law disqualification of felons has been removed by statute in most states. However, conviction of a crime may be shown to *affect the credibility* of the competent witness.

e. **Interest**
The common law disqualification of parties or interested persons has been abolished in most states. The only remaining vestiges of this disqualification are the so-called Dead Man Acts, discussed later.

f. **Judge as Witness**
Federal Rule 605 provides that the presiding judge *may not testify as a witness*, and that no objection need be made to preserve the point. The basis for this disqualification is that when the judge is called as a witness, her role as a witness is inconsistent with her role as presiding judge which requires her to maintain impartiality.

g. **Juror as Witness**
Under Federal Rule 606, jurors are *incompetent to testify* before the jury in which they are sitting. The rationale is that a juror-witness cannot impartially weigh his own testimony and cannot be thoroughly cross-examined for fear of creating antagonism.

The Federal Rule also prevents a juror from testifying in post-verdict proceedings as to matters or statements occurring during the course of jury deliberations, except that a juror may testify as to whether "extraneous prejudicial information" or any "outside influence" was brought to bear on any juror.

4. **Dead Man Acts**
The last remaining vestige of true incompetency of a witness appears in Dead Man Acts. These statutes exist in most jurisdictions and their provisions vary from state to state. Although there is *no Dead Man Act in the Federal Rules of Evidence*, state Dead Man Acts operate to disqualify witnesses in federal cases where state law provides the rule of

decision (most diversity cases). For bar examination purposes, only generalized comments are appropriate, and there are common provisions to most Dead Man Acts that could appear in a multistate bar exam question.

a. Rationale

The Dead Man Acts generally provide that a party or person interested in the event, or his predecessor in interest, is incompetent to testify to a ***personal transaction or communication with a deceased***, when such testimony is offered against the representative or successors in interest of the deceased. The rationale of the statute is to ***protect estates from perjured claims***. The assumption is that the survivor claimant may lie since the deceased cannot talk back. Because death has silenced one party, the statute closes the mouth of the living person who, being interested in the litigation's outcome, wishes to testify on her own behalf against someone who is suing or defending in a representative capacity (*e.g.*, executor, administrator, heir, legatee, devisee).

b. Common Elements

Most Dead Man Acts have the following common elements and applications:

1) Applicable to Civil Cases Only

The bar to competency created by a Dead Man Act applies only to civil cases and has no application in criminal cases.

2) Protected Parties

The statute is designed to protect those who claim directly under the decedent. They usually include an executor, administrator, heir, legatee, and devisee. If a protected party is on either side of the lawsuit (suing or defending), the statute applies to prevent an interested person from testifying on his own behalf.

Examples: 1) Plaintiff sues the executor of the estate for a debt owed by the decedent. The executor is a protected party and the act applies.

2) Executor sues defendant for negligence in causing the death of the decedent. Executor is a protected party and the act applies.

3) Heir sues executor, legatees, and devisees in a will contest. Heir is a protected party, as are the adverse parties. The act applies.

3) Interested Person

A person is "interested in the event" if he stands to gain or lose by the direct and immediate operation of the judgment, or if the judgment may be used for or against him in a subsequent action. Thus, in states where a spouse has an inchoate right in the other spouse's property, both spouses may be interested and incompetent to testify. Similarly, a shareholder of a corporation and the co-maker of a note may be disqualified under the rule.

a) Predecessor in Interest

Most Dead Man Acts disqualify not only the person interested but also the predecessor in interest.

Example: If A assigns to B a claim against Decedent, and B sues the estate, both A and B are incompetent. B is interested in the event; A is the person from, through, or under whom B derived his interest.

b) Party Adverse to Protected Party

As a short rule of thumb, a party adverse to the protected party is always an interested person who will be rendered incompetent by the Dead Man Act. For other nonparty witnesses, ask whether the witness has a ***pecuniary interest in the outcome of the case*** or is a predecessor in interest with the adverse party.

4) Exceptions and Waiver of the Act

There are numerous situations where the Dead Man Act either will not apply against an interested person or the protected party may waive its effect. Of course, if an exception applies or the statute is waived, the interested person is competent to testify. The following are common to most jurisdictions:

a) Facts Occurring After Death

An interested person may always testify to facts that occurred *after* the death of the deceased, since the protection of the rule is not needed.

b) "Door Openers"

The estate representatives and those claiming under the decedent may *waive the protection* of the statute. Common provisions for waiver include:

(1) If the protected party calls the interested person to testify about the transaction, the interested person may explain all matters about which he is examined.

(2) Where the testimony of the deceased given at a former trial or at a deposition is read in evidence, the interested person may explain all matters about which he is examined.

(3) Where there is a failure to make timely and proper objection. Objection is to the incompetency of the witness, not to the incompetency of the testimony.

(4) If the protected party or an agent of the deceased testifies to a transaction with an interested person, the interested person may testify about the same transaction.

B. FORM OF EXAMINATION OF WITNESS

The judge may exercise reasonable control over the examination of witnesses in order to aid the effective ascertainment of truth, to avoid wasting time, and to protect witnesses from harassment or undue embarrassment. Questions that frequently arise concerning the form of examination of witnesses are: when may leading questions be used, what other types of questions are objectionable, and when and how may a witness use memoranda.

1. Leading Questions

a. Generally Objectionable

A question is leading and generally objectionable on direct examination when it suggests to the witness the fact that the examiner expects and wants to have confirmed. Questions calling for "yes" or "no" answers and questions *framed to suggest the answer desired* are usually leading.

Example: On direct examination plaintiff is asked, "Is it true or not that at the time in question, you were driving well within the speed limit?" The question is leading.

b. When Permitted

Leading questions are permitted on *cross-examination*. Trial judges will usually allow leading questions on *direct examination* in noncrucial areas *if no objection is made:*

(i) If used to elicit *preliminary or introductory matter*;

(ii) When the witness *needs aid to respond* because of loss of memory, immaturity, or physical or mental weakness; or

(iii) When the witness is *hostile* and improperly uncooperative, an *adverse* party, or a person *identified with an adverse party*.

[Fed. R. Evid. 611(c)]

2. Improper Questions

The following types of questions are improper and are not permitted:

a. Misleading

A question is misleading and thus is not permitted if it is one that cannot be answered without making an unintended admission.

Example: "Do you still beat your wife?"

b. Compound

Questions that require a single answer to more than one question are not permitted.

Example: "Did you see and hear the intruder?"

c. Argumentative

Argumentative questions, which are leading questions that reflect the examiner's interpretation of the facts, are improper.

Example: "Why were you driving so recklessly?"

d. Conclusionary

A question that calls for an opinion or conclusion that the witness is not qualified or permitted to make is improper.

Example: "What did your friend think about that?" The witness could not know his friend's thoughts, and is not permitted to give his opinion as to his friend's thoughts.

e. Assuming Facts Not in Evidence

An attorney is not allowed to ask a question that assumes a disputed fact is true when it has not been established in the case.

Example: In a case where there is no evidence that Defendant had been drinking, the following question is improper: "After Defendant finished his fifth beer, he got up and went to his car, didn't he?"

f. Cumulative

An attorney is generally not permitted to ask a question that has already been asked and answered. More repetition is allowed on cross-examination than on direct, but if it is apparent that the cross-examiner is not moving forward, the judge may disallow the question.

g. Harassing or Embarrassing

The trial judge, in her discretion, may disallow cross-examination that is unduly harassing or embarrassing.

3. Use of Memoranda by Witness

A witness cannot read her testimony from a prepared memorandum. However, a memorandum may be used in certain circumstances to refresh the recollection of the witness, to substitute for the witness's forgotten testimony upon authentication of the memorandum, or in cross-examination of the witness.

a. Present Recollection Revived—Refreshing Recollection

A witness may use any writing or thing for the purpose of refreshing her present recollection. She usually may not read from the writing while she actually testifies, since the writing is *not authenticated*, is *not in evidence*, and may be used solely to refresh her recollection. The writing is intended to help her to recall by jogging her memory. The sworn testimony must demonstrate a *present* recollection.

b. Past Recollection Recorded—Recorded Recollection

Where a witness states that she has insufficient recollection of an event to enable her to testify fully and accurately, even after she has consulted a writing given to her on the stand, the *writing itself may be read into evidence* if a proper foundation is laid for its admissibility. This use of a memorandum as evidence of a past recollection is frequently classified as an *exception to the hearsay rule*. The foundation for receipt of the writing into evidence must include proof that:

(i) The witness at one time had *personal knowledge* of the facts recited in the writing;

(ii) The writing was *made by the witness* or made *under her direction* or that it was *adopted by the witness*;

(iii) The writing was *timely made* when the matter was fresh in the mind of the witness;

(iv) The writing is *accurate* (*i.e.,* witness must vouch for the accuracy of the writing); and

(v) The witness has *insufficient recollection* to testify fully and accurately.

Remember that, under the Federal Rule, if admitted, the writing may be read into evidence and heard by the jury, but *the document itself is not received* as an exhibit unless offered by the adverse party. [Fed. R. Evid. 803(5)]

c. **Inspection and Use in Cross-Examination**
Under Federal Rule 612, whenever a witness has used a writing to refresh her memory on the stand, an adverse party is entitled to have the writing produced at trial, to inspect it, to cross-examine the witness thereon, and to introduce into evidence those portions that relate to the witness's testimony. If the witness has refreshed her memory before trial by looking at the writing, it is within the court's discretion to require production of the document and to permit inspection, cross-examination, and introduction of pertinent excerpts.

As noted above, under Federal Rule 803(5), an adverse party may introduce into evidence a writing that the proponent has read into evidence as past recollection recorded.

C. OPINION TESTIMONY
The word opinion used in this context includes all opinions, inferences, conclusions, and other subjective statements made by a witness. A basic premise of our legal system is that, in general, witnesses should testify as to facts within their personal knowledge and that the trier of fact should draw any conclusions therefrom. Therefore, the general policy of the law is to restrict the admissibility of opinion evidence, except in cases where the courts are sure that it will be necessary or at least helpful. Of course, the difference between "fact" and "opinion" is a matter of degree. Therefore, there cannot be any clear-cut opinion rule.

1. **Opinion Testimony by Lay Witnesses**

   a. **General Rule of Inadmissibility**
   Opinions by lay witnesses are generally inadmissible. However, there are many cases where, from the nature of the subject matter, no better evidence can be obtained. In these cases, where the event is likely to be perceived as a whole impression (*e.g.*, intoxication, speed) rather than as more specific components, opinions by lay witnesses are generally admitted.

   b. **When Admissible**
   In most jurisdictions and under the Federal Rules, opinion testimony by lay witnesses is admissible when:

   (i) It is rationally *based on the perception of the witness;*

   (ii) It is *helpful to a clear understanding* of her testimony or to the determination of a fact in issue; and

   (iii) It is *not based on scientific, technical, or other specialized knowledge* (if so based, the witness's testimony would need to meet the requirements for expert testimony stated in Rule 702, *see* 2.a., *infra*).

   [Fed. R. Evid. 701]
   Example: Think how much easier and clearer it is for a witness to say someone looked "drunk" than it is to describe her gait, speech, eyes, diction, breath, and manner. All these things can also be brought out, but the term "drunk" may be more meaningful than any of them.

   Some jurisdictions are stricter and allow lay opinion testimony only in cases of "necessity" when it is difficult for the witness to express her perception in any form other than opinion.

   c. **Procedure**
   Unless waived by a failure to object, a proper foundation must be laid by showing that the witness had the opportunity to observe the event that forms the basis of her opinion. Additionally, the court in its discretion may require a witness to state the facts observed before stating her opinion.

d. Situations Where Opinions of Lay Witnesses Are Admissible

1) General Appearance or Condition of a Person
Testimony that a person was "elderly," "about 60 years old," "strong," "weak," or "ill" would be admissible, but testimony that a person is suffering from specific diseases or specific injuries usually requiring knowledge of an expert would not.

2) State of Emotion
A witness would be permitted to testify that a person appeared "angry" or "was joking" but probably not that two persons were "in love" or appeared to have a strong affection for each other.

3) Matters Involving Sense Recognition
A witness would be permitted to testify that an object was "heavy," "red," "bulky," or that a certain beverage tasted like whiskey.

4) Voice or Handwriting Identification
Lay opinion is permissible and often essential to identify telephone voices and handwriting. In these instances a foundation must first be laid to show familiarity with the voice or handwriting.

5) Speed of Moving Object
A witness may estimate in miles per hour the speed of a moving object but must first show some experience in observing the rate of speed of moving objects. Characterization that a vehicle was going "fast" or "very fast" has been permitted.

6) Value of Own Services
A witness may give her opinion as to the value of her own services.

7) Rational or Irrational Nature of Another's Conduct (Sanity)
In many jurisdictions, a witness is permitted to state her opinion as to the sanity of another person. Some states limit these opinions to testimony describing the acts of a person whose sanity is in question and allow the witness to state only whether those acts impressed her at the time as rational or irrational (*e.g.*, "She acted like a madwoman").

8) Intoxication
A witness who has seen a person and is able to describe that person's actions, words, or conduct, may express an opinion as to whether that person was or was not intoxicated. In many states, the details of the person's appearance must be given as a foundation for the opinion.
Example: In Defendant's trial on a charge of driving while intoxicated, Witness testifies for the prosecution that Defendant "smelled of alcohol, his speech was incoherent, his eyes glassy and bloodshot, he could not stand or walk without assistance, he was slumped over the wheel of his vehicle," and, finally, that he "was intoxicated."

e. Situations Where Opinions of Lay Witnesses Are Not Admissible

1) Agency or Authorization
When agency or authorization is in issue, the witness generally may not state a conclusion as to her authorization. Rather she must be asked by whom she was employed and the nature, terms, and surrounding circumstances of her employment.

2) Contract or Agreement
When the existence of an express contract is in issue, a witness generally may not state her opinion that an agreement was made. Rather she must be asked about the facts, the existence or nonexistence of which establish whether a contract existed.

2. Opinion Testimony by Expert Witnesses

a. Requirements of Expert Testimony
The expert may state an opinion or conclusion, provided the following conditions are satisfied:

1) **Subject Matter Must Be Appropriate for Expert Testimony**
Under Federal Rule 702, expert opinion testimony is admissible if the subject matter is one where scientific, technical, or other specialized knowledge would assist the trier of fact in understanding the evidence or determining a fact in issue. This test of assistance to the trier of fact subdivides into two requirements:

(i) The opinion must be *relevant* (*i.e.*, it must "fit" the facts of the case); and

(ii) The methodology underlying the opinion must be *reliable* (*i.e.*, the proponent of the expert testimony must satisfy the trial judge by a preponderance of the evidence that (a) the opinion is based on sufficient facts or data; (b) the opinion is the product of reliable principles and methods; and (c) the expert has reliably applied the principles and methods to the facts of the case).

[Fed. R. Evid. 702; *and see* Kumho Tire Co. v. Carmichael, 526 U.S. 137 (1999); Daubert v. Merrell Dow Pharmaceuticals, Inc., 509 U.S. 579 (1993)]

2) **Witness Must Be Qualified as an Expert**
To testify as an expert, a person must have special knowledge, skill, experience, training, or education sufficient to qualify him as an expert on the subject to which his testimony relates. [Fed. R. Evid. 702]

3) **Expert Must Possess Reasonable Probability Regarding His Opinion**
The expert must possess reasonable certainty or probability regarding his opinion. If the opinion of the expert is a mere guess or speculation, it is inadmissible.
Example: It would be error to permit plaintiff's medical expert to testify that plaintiff's symptoms "suggested" diabetes and "indicated" that the disease was caused by the accident.

4) **Opinion Must Be Supported by Proper Factual Basis**
The expert's opinion may be based upon one or more of these three possible sources of information: (i) facts that the expert knows from his own observation; (ii) facts presented in evidence at the trial and submitted to the expert, usually by hypothetical question; or (iii) facts not in evidence that were supplied to the expert out of court, and which are of a type reasonably relied upon by experts in the particular field in forming opinions on the subject. Note that the expert may give opinion testimony on direct examination without disclosing the basis of the opinion, unless the court orders otherwise. However, the expert may be required to disclose such information on cross-examination. [Fed. R. Evid. 705]

a) **Personal Observation**
If the expert has examined the person or thing about which he is testifying, he may relate those facts observed by him and upon which he bases his opinion. [Fed. R. Evid. 703]
Example: An expert may testify that he examined plaintiff's leg following the accident, and in his opinion the plaintiff sustained a compound fracture.

b) **Facts Made Known to Expert at Trial**
The expert's opinion may be based upon the evidence introduced at the trial and related to the expert by counsel in the form of a *hypothetical question*. The hypothetical question may be based on facts derived from any of the three sources of information noted above. Federal Rule 705 adopts the modern trend in providing that the hypothetical question need not be asked.

c) **Facts Made Known to Expert Outside Court**
Under Federal Rule 703, the expert may base an opinion upon facts not known personally but supplied to him outside the courtroom (*e.g.*, reports of nurses, technicians, or consultants). The Federal Rule further provides that such facts *need not be in evidence or even of a type admissible* in evidence, as long as the facts are of a kind *reasonably relied upon* by experts in the particular field. However, if the facts are of a type inadmissible in evidence, the proponent of the expert opinion must *not* disclose those facts to the jury unless the court determines that their probative value in assisting the jury to evaluate the expert's opinion *substantially* outweighs their prejudicial effect.

Example: A physician bases his expert opinion upon (i) a personal examination of the patient, (ii) statements by the patient as to her medical history, and (iii) medically germane statements by the patient's relatives. The results of the personal examination are admissible and may therefore be relied upon by the physician because they are relevant, material, based on personal knowledge, and not subject to any exclusionary rule. The statements of the patient are admissible through an exception to the hearsay rule. The statements by the relatives, though inadmissible hearsay, may properly form a basis for a physician's expert opinion testimony because they are the facts reasonably relied upon by physicians in making a diagnosis; however, these statements should not be disclosed to the jury without the court first finding that their probative value substantially outweighs prejudice.

b. Opinion May Embrace Ultimate Issue

Federal Rule 704(a) and the modern trend repudiate the traditional prohibition on opinions embracing the ultimate issue in the case. The rule provides: "Testimony in the form of an opinion or inference otherwise admissible is not objectionable because it embraces the ultimate issue to be decided by the trier of fact." Note, however, that to be admissible under the Federal Rules, the expert opinion must "assist the trier of fact" to understand the evidence or determine a fact in issue. Thus, an expert's conclusion that "X had testamentary capacity" is still inadmissible because it is not helpful to the jury.

1) Exception—Criminal Defendant's Mental State

The Federal Rules *prohibit* ultimate issue testimony in one situation: In a criminal case in which the defendant's mental state constitutes an element of the crime or defense, an expert may not state an opinion as to whether the accused did or did not have the mental state in issue. [Fed. R. Evid. 704(b)]

c. Authoritative Texts and Treatises

An expert may be cross-examined concerning statements contained in any scientific publication, as long as the publication is established as reliable authority. For example, the witness may be asked, "Doesn't Dr. Killum, in his book on diseases of the pancreas, disagree with your conclusion here?" A publication may be established as reliable by: (i) the direct testimony or cross-examination admission of the expert, (ii) the testimony of another expert, or (iii) judicial notice. Thus, even if the expert refuses to recognize the text as authoritative, it can be used on cross-examination if its reliability is established by one of the other methods.

The Federal Rules have expanded the admissibility of learned texts and treatises beyond impeachment of experts. Statements from an established treatise may be read into the record as substantive evidence, and may even be introduced on direct examination of a party's own expert. [Fed. R. Evid. 803(18)—exception to hearsay rule] There are two important limitations: (i) an expert must be on the stand when a statement from a treatise is read into evidence; and (ii) the relevant portion is read into evidence but is not received as an exhibit (*i.e.,* the jury never sees it).

D. CROSS-EXAMINATION

1. Necessity for Cross-Examination

Cross-examination of adverse witnesses is a matter of right in every trial of a disputed issue of fact. It is recognized as the *most efficacious truth-discovering device*. The principal basis for excluding hearsay is that the declarant whose testimony is offered cannot be subjected to the test of cross-examination. If adequate cross-examination is prevented by the death, illness, or refusal of a witness to testify on cross-examination, the direct examination is rendered incompetent and will be stricken.

2. Scope of Cross-Examination

Although a party is entitled as of right to some cross-examination, the extent or scope of cross-examination, like the order of calling witnesses, is frequently a matter of judicial discretion. Cross-examination is hedged about by far fewer rules than is direct examination.

On cross-examination, leading questions are permissible, as are, obviously, efforts at impeachment. The most significant restriction is that the scope of cross-examination cannot range beyond the subject matter of the direct examination. This restriction does not apply to inquiries directed toward impeachment of the witness.

a. Restrictions on Scope
Under Federal Rule 611(b) and in the majority of American jurisdictions, *cross-examination is limited to*: (i) matters brought out on *direct examination* and the inferences naturally drawn from those matters, and (ii) matters affecting the *credibility of the witness*.

b. Significance of Restrictions
The question of the proper scope of cross-examination is important since it affects the *right to use leading questions*. And, in jurisdictions that do not allow a party to impeach his own witness, going beyond the scope of direct examination means that you have made the witness "your own witness" and therefore cannot impeach his testimony. Further, if the party placing a witness on the stand is the holder of a privilege, the court may hold it waived to the extent that the other party may engage in cross-examination; therefore, the scope of cross-examination permitted may determine to what extent the cross-examining party may inquire into privileged material.

c. Collateral Matters
The general rule is that the cross-examiner is *bound by the answers of the witness* to questions concerning collateral matters. Thus the cross-examiner cannot refute the response of the witness by producing extrinsic evidence. Indeed some federal courts resolve the matter under Rule 403 by treating the evidence on the collateral matter as being substantially outweighed by time considerations and the danger of confusion of the issues. Certain matters of impeachment, however, are recognized as sufficiently important to merit development by extrinsic evidence (*e.g.*, bias or interest of the witness may be shown by other evidence even if denied by the witness on cross-examination). Other matters of impeachment are limited solely to inquiry on cross-examination (*e.g.*, prior misconduct of the witness not resulting in conviction but affecting the witness's credibility). Once beyond recognized impeachment techniques, the test as to what is "collateral" is sufficiently vague to permit a wide exercise of discretion by the trial judge.

E. CREDIBILITY—IMPEACHMENT
Impeachment means the casting of an adverse reflection on the veracity of the witness. The primary method of impeachment is by cross-examination of the witness under attack, although witnesses are often impeached by extrinsic proof that casts doubt on credibility. In terms of relevance, any matter that tends to prove or disprove the credibility of the witness should be admitted here.

1. Accrediting or Bolstering

a. General Rule—No Bolstering Until Witness Impeached
A party may not bolster or accredit the testimony of his witness until the witness has been impeached.

Example: A prior statement made by W at the time of the event that is consistent with W's in-court testimony would not be admissible to show that W's memory of the event is excellent or that he told the same story twice and therefore is especially worthy of belief.

b. Exceptions
The rule against accrediting is subject to exception where timeliness may raise an inference on the substantive issues of the case.

1) Timely Complaint
In certain cases a party may prove that the witness made a timely complaint, in order to bolster the party's credibility.

Examples: 1) Evidence of a prompt complaint of a rape victim is admissible to bolster the complainant's credibility in a subsequent criminal prosecution.

2) Where a defendant in a criminal trial claims that a confession offered against him was obtained by coercion, he may show that he complained of mistreatment at the first suitable opportunity.

2) Prior Identification

Evidence of any prior statement of identification made by a witness is admissible not only to bolster the witness's testimony but also as substantive evidence that the identification was correct. [Fed. R. Evid. 801(d)(1)(C); *and see* VII.B.1., *infra*]

2. Any Party May Impeach

Contrary to the traditional rule, under which a party could not impeach his own witness, the Federal Rules provide that the credibility of a witness may be attacked by any party, ***including the party calling him***. [Fed. R. Evid. 607] Even under the traditional rule, however, a party could impeach his own witness if the witness: (i) was an adverse party, (ii) was hostile, (iii) was one required to be called by law, or (iv) gave damaging surprise testimony.

3. Impeachment Methods—Cross-Examination and Extrinsic Evidence

A witness may be impeached either by cross-examination (by eliciting facts from the witness that discredit his own testimony) or by extrinsic evidence (by putting other witnesses on the stand who will introduce facts discrediting his testimony).

There are certain well-recognized, often-used impeachment methods. These traditional impeachment devices include: the use of prior inconsistent statements; a showing of bias or interest in the litigation; an attack on the character of the witness by showing convictions of crime, prior acts of misconduct, or poor reputation for veracity; and a showing of sensory deficiencies. The basic questions for each of these methods are: Is the examiner limited to impeachment by cross-examination alone or may he produce extrinsic evidence? If extrinsic evidence is permissible, must a foundation first be laid by inquiry on cross-examination?

a. Prior Inconsistent Statements

For the purpose of impeaching the credibility of a witness, a party may show that the witness has, on another occasion, made statements that are inconsistent with some material part of his present testimony. Under the Federal Rules, an inconsistent statement may be proved by either cross-examination or extrinsic evidence. To prove the statement by extrinsic evidence, certain requirements must first be met: (i) a ***proper foundation*** must be laid; and (ii) the statement must be ***relevant*** to some issue in the case, *i.e.*, it cannot be a "collateral matter."

1) Laying a Foundation

Extrinsic evidence of the witness's prior inconsistent statement is admissible only if the witness is, at some point, given an ***opportunity to explain or deny*** the allegedly inconsistent statement. (The opportunity need not come before introduction of the statement under the Federal Rules.) This foundation requirement may be dispensed with, however, where "the interests of justice otherwise require" (as where the witness has left the stand and is not available when his prior inconsistent statement is discovered). [Fed. R. Evid. 613(b)] The courts generally agree that inconsistent statements by a hearsay declarant may be used to impeach the declarant despite the lack of a foundation (obviously, where the declarant is not a witness no foundation could be laid anyway). [Fed. R. Evid. 806]

2) Evidentiary Effect of Prior Inconsistent Statements

In most cases, prior inconsistent statements are hearsay, admissible only to impeach the witness. However, where the statement was made ***under oath at a prior trial, hearing, or other proceeding, or in a deposition, it is admissible non-hearsay*** (*i.e.*, it may be considered as substantive proof of the facts stated!). (*See* VII.B.1., *infra*.)

b. Bias or Interest

Evidence that a witness is biased or has an interest in the outcome of a suit tends to show that the witness has a ***motive to lie***. A witness may always be impeached by extrinsic evidence of bias or interest, provided a proper foundation is laid. Note that evidence that is substantively inadmissible may be admitted for impeachment purposes if relevant to show bias or interest.

Examples: 1) It may be shown that a witness is being paid to testify, that a witness is financing the case, or that he otherwise has a financial interest in the outcome of the litigation.

2) Inferences of bias may be shown by evidence of family or other relationship, business relationship, or by conduct or expressions of the witness demonstrating a friendship toward a party.

3) In a criminal case, it is proper for the defense to ask a prosecution witness whether he has been promised immunity from punishment for testifying, whether an indictment is pending against him, or whether he is on parole. This evidence may show a motive for the witness to curry the favor of the state.

4) Hostility toward a party may be shown by adverse statements against the party, or by the fact that the witness had a fight or quarrel with him or has a lawsuit pending against him.

1) Foundation

Most courts require that before a witness can be impeached by extrinsic evidence of bias or interest, he must first be asked about the facts that show bias or interest on cross-examination. If the witness on cross-examination admits the facts claimed to show bias or interest, it is within the trial judge's discretion to decide whether extrinsic evidence may be introduced as further proof of bias or interest.

2) Justification for Bias

Even though it is shown that a witness is biased, no evidence may be admitted to show that he was justified in his bias. This might make him look more reasonable, but is not very relevant to whether his bias might make him less credible.

c. Conviction of Crime

Under certain circumstances, a witness may be impeached by proof of conviction of a crime. [Fed. R. Evid. 609] The fact that the witness (including a defendant who testifies in a criminal case) has been convicted of a crime may usually be proved by either eliciting an admission on cross-examination or by the record of conviction.

1) Actual Conviction Required

This type of impeachment requires an actual conviction of a crime. The fact that the witness has been arrested or indicted may not be elicited here.

2) Type of Crime

a) Crime Involving Dishonesty

Under the Federal Rules, a witness may be impeached by *any crime* (felony or misdemeanor) *involving dishonesty* (deceit) *or a false statement*. The trial court has no discretion—not even under Federal Rule 403—to disallow impeachment by such crimes.

b) Felony Not Involving Dishonesty

A witness may also be impeached, under the Federal Rules, by *any felony* whether or not it involves dishonesty or a false statement. However, if the felony is one that does not involve dishonesty or false statement, the trial court may exercise discretion to exclude it under one of the following standards.

(1) Accused in Criminal Case

If, in a criminal case, the witness being impeached is the accused, the felony conviction will be admitted only if the government shows that its probative value as impeachment evidence outweighs its prejudicial effect.

(2) Witness Other than Accused in Criminal Case

In the case of any witness other than the accused in a criminal case, any felony conviction is admissible, but the court retains discretion under Rule 403 to exclude it if its probative value as impeachment evidence is *substantially outweighed* by the danger of unfair prejudice.

(3) Compare the Balancing Tests

Note that under Federal Rule 609, different balancing tests apply for the exercise of discretion. If the felony conviction is offered to impeach the accused in a criminal case, the discretionary standard (*supra*) favors exclusion since the probative value of the felony (not involving dishonesty or false statement) must outweigh prejudice. In the case of *all* other witnesses, the balancing test favors admission since the conviction will be excluded only if the danger of prejudice substantially outweighs its probative value.

3) Must Not Be Too Remote
Under the *Federal Rules*, a conviction is usually too remote and inadmissible if *more than 10 years* have elapsed since the date of *conviction* or the date of *release* from the confinement imposed for the conviction, whichever is the later date. In extraordinary circumstances, such convictions can be admitted, but only if the trial judge determines that the probative value of the conviction substantially outweighs its prejudicial effect, and the adverse party is given notice that the conviction is to be used as impeachment. [Fed. R. Evid. 609(b)]

4) Juvenile Adjudication Generally Not Admissible
Juvenile offenses are generally not admissible for impeachment purposes. However, under the Federal Rules, a judge has the discretion in a criminal case to admit evidence of a juvenile offense committed by a witness other than the accused if the evidence would be admissible to attack the credibility of an adult and if the evidence is necessary to a determination of the accused's guilt or innocence. [Fed. R. Evid. 609(d); Davis v. Alaska, 415 U.S. 308 (1974)]

5) Effect of Pardon Depends on Basis
In most states, a conviction may be shown even though the witness has subsequently been pardoned. Under the Federal Rules, however, the conviction may not be shown if the pardon was based on innocence or if the person pardoned has not been convicted of a subsequent crime punishable by death or imprisonment in excess of one year. [Fed. R. Evid. 609(c)]

6) Pending Appeal Does Not Affect Admissibility
In most jurisdictions and under the Federal Rules, a conviction may be used to impeach even though an appeal is pending, though the pendency of the appeal may also be shown. [Fed. R. Evid. 609(e)]

7) Constitutionally Defective Conviction Invalid for All Purposes
Where the prior felony conviction was obtained in violation of the defendant's Sixth Amendment rights (*e.g.*, to have counsel, to confront witness, etc.), the conviction is generally invalid for all purposes—including impeachment.

8) Means of Proof—Extrinsic Evidence Permitted
A prior conviction may be shown either by the *cross-examination* of the witness or by *introducing a record* of the judgment. *No foundation need be laid*. Note, however, that when a witness is being cross-examined about previous convictions, the questions must be asked in good faith (*i.e.*, with a reasonable belief as to the existence of the conviction). Improper questioning may be grounds for a mistrial.

d. Specific Instances of Misconduct—Bad Acts

1) General Rule—Interrogation Permitted
The traditional majority view is that, subject to discretionary control of the trial judge, a witness may be interrogated upon cross-examination with respect to any immoral, vicious, or criminal act of his life that may *affect his character* and show him to be *unworthy of belief*. Inquiry into "bad acts" is permitted even though the witness was never convicted. Federal Rule 608 permits such inquiry, in the discretion of the court, only if the act of misconduct is *probative of truthfulness* (*i.e.,* is an act of deceit or lying).

2) Counsel Must Inquire in Good Faith
The cross-examiner must act in good faith with some reasonable basis for believing that the witness may have committed the "bad act" inquired about.
Example: It would be error for the prosecution to inquire about an act when the prosecutor knows that the witness has been tried for the act and acquitted.

3) Extrinsic Evidence Not Permitted

Extrinsic evidence of "bad acts" is not permitted. A specific act of misconduct relevant to impair credibility can be elicited *only on cross-examination* of the witness. If the witness denies the act, the cross-examiner cannot refute the answer by calling other witnesses or producing other evidence. It is not usually improper for the cross-examiner, acting in good faith, to continue the cross-examination after a denial in the hope that the witness will change his answer.

e. Opinion or Reputation Evidence for Truth

1) By Proof of Reputation

A witness may be impeached by showing that she has a poor reputation for truthfulness. The usual method of impeachment is to ask other witnesses about her general reputation for truth and veracity in the community in which she lives. The modern view is to allow evidence of reputation in business circles as well as in the community in which the witness resides.

2) By Opinion Evidence

Most states do not allow the impeaching witness to state her opinion as to the character of a witness for truth and veracity. However, the *Federal Rules allow* an impeaching witness to state her personal opinions, based upon acquaintance, as to the truthfulness of the witness sought to be impeached. [Fed. R. Evid. 608(a)]

f. Sensory Deficiencies

A witness may be impeached by showing that he had no knowledge of the facts to which he testified, or that his faculties of perception and recollection were so impaired as to make it doubtful that he could have perceived those facts. Such a showing can be made either *on cross-examination or by the use of extrinsic evidence*.

1) Defects of Capacity

a) Perceptive Disabilities

It is, of course, proper to show deficiencies of the senses, such as deafness or color blindness, that would have substantially impaired the witness's ability to perceive the facts to which he testifies. It may also be shown that at the time the witness observed the events his perception was temporarily diminished (*e.g.*, that he was sleepy or under the influence of alcohol or drugs).

b) Lack of Memory

A witness can be impeached by showing that he has a poor memory of the events about which he testifies. This is usually done on cross-examination by asking the witness about other related matters to suggest the inference that if his memory of related matters is poor, his recollection of the events to which he is testifying is doubtful.

c) Mental Disorders

Psychiatric evidence of a mental disorder that would affect a witness's credibility has been admitted by some courts (particularly in sex offense cases).

2) Lack of Knowledge

a) Expert Witnesses

The credibility of an expert witness may be attacked by cross-examining him as to (i) his general knowledge of the field in which he is claiming to be an expert, and (ii) his particular knowledge of the facts upon which his opinion is based.

b) Opinion Witnesses

The credibility of an opinion witness may be attacked by showing lack of knowledge. For example, a witness who gives opinion evidence on the value of land may be cross-examined regarding her knowledge of land values and may be asked about sales of other land.

c) Character Witnesses

As discussed earlier, when a character witness testifies to the good character of another (*e.g.*, a defendant), the witness may be cross-examined regarding the basis of his statement that the defendant's character is good. In other words, the testimony of the character witness may be discredited by asking him about specific criminal or immoral acts committed by the defendant, on the theory that if the witness has no knowledge of these acts, he does not really know the defendant's character. [Fed. R. Evid. 405(a)]

In most courts, a character witness may testify only as to *reputation*. Therefore, on cross-examination, the only acceptable form of question is: "Have you *heard* that the defendant . . . ?" However, under the Federal Rules and in modern jurisdictions that permit character witnesses to testify as to their *opinions* of character, questions in the form, "Do you *know* . . . ?" would be proper.

4. Impeachment on Collateral Matter

Where a witness makes a statement not directly relevant to the issues in the case, the rule against impeachment (other than by cross-examination) on a collateral matter applies to bar the opponent from proving the statement untrue either by extrinsic contradictory facts or by a prior inconsistent statement. The purpose of the rule is to avoid the possibility of unfair surprise, confusion of issues, and undue consumption of time resulting from the attempt to prove and disprove facts that are not directly relevant.

Example: Plaintiff's witness testifies, "I saw the accident on the way home from church." If it is conceded that the witness saw the accident, it would be a collateral matter for the defendant to show that the witness was on his way home from a pool hall rather than church. It would not be "collateral" to show that the witness was on his way home from a dinner at the plaintiff's house, because that suggests *bias*, which is a separate basis for impeachment (*see* 3.b., *supra*).

5. Impeachment of Hearsay Declarant

There are many occasions in which out-of-court statements are admitted into evidence by means of exceptions and limitations to the general rule excluding hearsay. These statements are frequently admitted into evidence even though the person who made the statement (the declarant) does not testify at the trial. The party against whom the statement has been admitted may wish to impeach the credibility of the declarant so that the jury will discount or assign less probative value to the statement. Under Federal Rule 806, the credibility of a declarant may be attacked (and if attacked, may be supported) by evidence that would be admissible if the declarant had testified as a witness. Of course, the declarant need not be given the opportunity to explain or deny prior inconsistent statements. In addition, the party against whom the out-of-court statement was offered may call the declarant as a witness and cross-examine him about the statement.

6. Rehabilitation

A witness who has been impeached may be rehabilitated on redirect examination or by extrinsic evidence.

a. Explanation on Redirect

For purposes of rehabilitation, the witness on redirect examination may explain or clarify facts brought out on cross-examination.

Example: A witness testifying for the prosecution in an organized crime murder trial admitted to making a prior inconsistent statement. On redirect, the witness is permitted to explain that he gave a prior untruthful statement favoring the defendant out of fear of being killed by the defendant's gang.

b. Good Reputation for Truth

When the witness's general character for truth and veracity has been attacked, the party for whom the impeached witness has testified may call other witnesses to testify to the good reputation for truth of the impeached witness or to give their opinion as to the truthfulness of the impeached witness.

c. Prior Consistent Statement

1) Generally Not Permitted

A party may not ordinarily rehabilitate a witness by showing a prior consistent statement. As a general rule this is true even when the witness has been impeached by showing a prior inconsistent statement. The inconsistency is not removed by the fact that the witness made more than one consistent statement.

2) Exceptions

Where the opposing counsel has impeached the credibility of a witness by making an express or an implied charge that the witness is lying or exaggerating because of some motive, counsel may introduce into evidence a prior consistent statement made by the witness before the time of the alleged motive to lie or exaggerate. Under Federal Rule 801(d)(1)(B), this statement not only is used to bolster the witness's testimony, but also is substantive evidence of the truth of its contents. (*See* VII.B.1., *infra*.)

Example: Defense attorney intimated on cross-examination that the prosecution witness was biased against his client because of a fight they recently had. The prosecutor may introduce evidence of a statement the witness made, consistent with his testimony, before the fight occurred.

F. OBJECTIONS, EXCEPTIONS, OFFERS OF PROOF

1. Objections

Unless an objection is made by opposing counsel, almost any kind of evidence will be admitted. Failure to object is deemed a *waiver* of any ground for objection. The trial judge need not raise grounds for objection on her own, but may take notice of plain errors affecting substantial rights (*e.g.,* admission of coerced confession not objected to by defense).

a. Objections to Trial Testimony

Objections should be made after the question, but before the answer, if it is apparent that the question calls for inadmissible matter (*e.g.,* hearsay) or that the question is in improper form (*e.g.,* leading). Otherwise, a motion to strike must be made as soon as the witness's answer emerges as inadmissible (*e.g.,* "Q: What color was the automobile? A: My sister told me it was gray").

b. Objections to Deposition Testimony

Objections to the *form* of a question (*e.g.,* leading) are waived unless made during the deposition, thereby affording counsel an opportunity to correct the form of his question. An objection based on a *testimonial privilege* should also be made then, lest it be deemed waived. However, objections going to the substance of a question or answer (*e.g.,* relevance, hearsay) can be postponed until the deposition is offered in evidence.

c. Specificity of Objections

An objection may be either *general* ("I object") or *specific* ("Object, hearsay"). The importance of whether an objection is general or specific lies in the extent to which each type preserves the evidentiary issue on appeal. The following rules apply:

1) General Objection Sustained

If a general objection is sustained and the evidence excluded, the ruling will be upheld on appeal if there was *any ground* for the objection. In the absence of specificity in the trial court, it will be assumed that the ruling was placed upon the right ground.

2) General Objection Overruled

If a general objection is overruled and the evidence admitted, the objection is not available on appeal unless the evidence was *not admissible under any circumstances* for any purpose.

3) Specific Objection Sustained

If a specific objection is sustained and the evidence is excluded, the ruling will be upheld on appeal only if the ground stated was the correct one, unless the evidence excluded was not competent and could not be made so.

d. "Opening the Door"

One who introduces evidence on a particular subject thereby asserts its relevance and cannot complain, except on grounds other than relevance, if his adversary thereafter offers evidence on the same subject. And counsel need not "stand" on his overruled relevance objection; he can offer counterevidence without thereby abandoning his relevance objection.

e. Effect of Introducing Part of Transaction
Where part of a conversation, act, or writing, etc., is introduced into evidence, the adverse party may require the proponent of the evidence to introduce any other part that ought, in fairness, to be considered contemporaneously with it. [Fed. R. Evid. 106] The party who introduced the original part of the transaction cannot object to the introduction of other parts on the ground of lack of competency or hearsay, etc. The theory is that the party has *waived any objections by introducing the part.*

f. Motion to Strike—Unresponsive Answers
Unresponsive answers are subject to a motion to strike by examining counsel, but not by opposing counsel. Examining counsel, in other words, can "adopt" an unresponsive answer if it is not objectionable on some other ground.

2. Exceptions
The common law rule requiring a party to "except" from an adverse trial court ruling in order to preserve the issue for appeal has been abolished in most jurisdictions. In some states, however, a written motion for a new trial, specifying the grounds, may be required.

3. Offers of Proof
On some occasions, error cannot be based on exclusion of evidence unless there has been an "offer of proof" that discloses the nature, purpose, and admissibility of the rejected evidence. There are three types of "offers of proof."

a. Witness Offer
Subsequent to a sustained objection by opposing counsel, the examining counsel proceeds with his examination of a witness on the stand, out of the jury's hearing, thus making his record by the question-and-answer method.

b. Lawyer Offer
Counsel himself states, in narrative form, what the witness would have testified had he been permitted to do so. The "witness offer" is generally preferred to the "lawyer offer" and can be required by the trial court, especially if opposing counsel denies that the witness would testify as narrated.

c. Tangible Offer
A marked, authenticated, and offered item of tangible evidence is its own offer of proof.

G. TESTIMONIAL PRIVILEGES
Testimonial privileges, which permit one to refuse to disclose and prohibit others from disclosing certain sorts of confidential information in judicial proceedings, have two basic reasons for their existence: (i) *practicality*, and (ii) society's desire to *encourage certain relationships* by ensuring their confidentiality, even at the high price of losing valuable information.

Some of the testimonial privileges are frankly grounded on hardheaded practicality. The particular kind of disclosure could not be obtained, as a practical matter, even if there were no privilege. No priest, even when confronted by a contempt of court citation, would breach the priest-penitent relationship. Society values some relationships sufficiently that it is willing to protect their confidential nature even at the expense of the loss of information relevant to the issues of a lawsuit. These relationships will be encouraged if confidentiality, when desired, is assured. To put it more concretely, persons might forgo needed medical attention or be less than candid with legal counsel were there no guarantee that communications made during the physician-patient and attorney-client relationships would be accorded confidential status in legal proceedings.

1. Federal Rules—No Specific Privilege Provisions
The Federal Rules have no specific privilege provisions. Federal Rule 501 provides that the privilege of a witness or person shall be governed by the principles of the common law as they may be interpreted by the courts of the United States in the light of reason and experience. The federal courts currently recognize the attorney-client privilege, the privilege for spousal communications, and the psychotherapist/social worker-client privilege. In civil actions when state law supplies the rule of decision as to an element of a claim or defense, the state law applies with respect to testimonial privileges as well. Thus, in *diversity* cases, the state law of privilege applies.

2. General Considerations

a. Persons Who May Assert a Privilege

A privilege is personal, and may be asserted only by the party whose interest is sought to be protected or by someone authorized to assert it on the holder's behalf (*e.g.,* guardian of incompetent holder). If the privilege is held by more than one person, each of them can claim the privilege. In certain cases, the person with whom the confidence was shared may claim it on the holder's behalf. For example, an attorney may assert his client's privilege in the client's absence.

b. Confidentiality

To be privileged, a communication must be shown to have been made in confidence. Many states, however, recognize a presumption that any disclosures made in the course of a relationship for which a privilege exists were made in confidence.

c. Comment on Privilege Forbidden

No inference should be drawn from the fact that a witness has claimed a privilege. Thus, counsel for the parties and the judge are not permitted to make any comment or argument based on a claim of privilege.

d. Waiver

All types of privileges are waived by the following:

(i) *Failure to claim the privilege* by the holder herself or failure to object when privileged testimony is offered;

(ii) *Voluntary disclosure* of the privileged matter by the holder (or someone else with the holder's consent) unless the disclosure is also privileged; or

(iii) A *contractual provision* waiving in advance the right to claim a privilege.

A privilege is not waived where someone wrongfully disclosed information without the holder's consent. Similarly, a waiver of the privilege by one joint holder does not affect the right of another joint holder to claim the privilege.

e. Eavesdroppers

A privilege based on confidential communications is not abrogated because the communication is overheard by someone whose presence is unknown to the parties; *i.e.,* the privilege still applies to the parties to the confidential communication. There is some question, however, as to whether the eavesdropper may testify. The traditional view is that the eavesdropper may testify to what he has overheard. But a significant number of modern cases and statutes assert that as long as the holder of the privilege was not negligent, there is no waiver of the privilege, and the eavesdropper is also prohibited from testifying.

3. Attorney-Client Privilege

The first testimonial privilege ever established was the attorney-client privilege. It is a common law privilege, although in some jurisdictions it has now been codified by statute. It carries with it fewer exceptions than any other privilege.

Essentially, communications between an attorney and client, made during professional consultation, are privileged from disclosure. In other words, a client has a privilege to refuse to disclose, and to prevent others from disclosing, confidential communications between herself (or her representative) and her attorney (or her attorney's representative). Objects and preexisting documents are not protected.

a. Attorney-Client Relationship

The attorney-client privilege requires that the attorney-client relationship exist at the time of the communications. The client, or his representative, must be seeking the professional services of the attorney at the crucial time. Retainer negotiations, involving disclosures made before the attorney has decided to accept or decline the case, are covered if the other requirements of the privilege are present.

1) Client

A "client," in the context of the typical formulation of the attorney-client privilege, can be an individual private citizen, a public officer, a corporation, or any other organization or entity, public or private, seeking professional legal services.

2) Representative of Client

A "representative of a client" is one having the **authority to obtain legal services or to act on advice** rendered by an attorney, on behalf of the client.

3) Attorney

An "attorney" is any person who is authorized or, in many jurisdictions, who is **reasonably believed** by the client to be authorized, to practice law in any state or nation.

4) Representative of Attorney

A "representative of an attorney" is one employed by the attorney to assist in the rendition of professional services, *e.g.*, a clerk or secretary.

5) Corporation as Client

A corporation, as indicated above, can be a "client" within the meaning of the attorney-client privilege. The statements of **any corporate officials or employees** made to the attorney are protected if they were authorized or directed by the corporation to make such statements.

b. Confidential Communication

A communication is "confidential" if it was not intended to be disclosed to third persons, other than those to whom disclosure would be in furtherance of the rendition of legal services to the client or those who are necessary for the transmission of the communication. Communications made in the known presence and hearing of a stranger are not privileged.

1) Communications Through Agents

Communications made to third persons are confidential, and thus covered by the attorney-client privilege, if necessary to transmit information between the attorney and client. Examples include: communications by the client to the attorney's secretary or messenger; information (not documents) given to the attorney by the client's accountant; communications between the client's liability insurer and the attorney; and communications through an interpreter.

a) Examination by Doctor

When a client is examined by a doctor at the attorney's request, the communications involved between the client and doctor (and the doctor and attorney) are not covered by the physician-patient privilege because no treatment is contemplated. These communications are, however, covered by the attorney-client privilege because the examination is necessary to help the client communicate her condition to the attorney. Note that this privilege would be waived if the doctor were later called as an expert witness by the same client.

Example: P, a pedestrian, was struck by a car driven by D. P employs Attorney to bring a negligence suit against D to recover for the physical injuries P suffered in the accident. Attorney sends P to Dr. Z for an evaluation of the extent and permanence of P's injuries. Attorney does not intend to call Dr. Z as an expert witness at trial. At trial, D's attorney, believing that P may have admitted to some negligence of his own when describing his injury, calls Dr. Z to testify to his examination of P. If P objects claiming attorney-client privilege, he may prevent Dr. Z from testifying.

2) No Privilege Where Attorney Acts for Both Parties

Where an attorney acts for both parties to a transaction, no privilege can be invoked in a lawsuit between the two parties (they obviously did not desire and could not expect confidentiality as between themselves in a joint consultation), but the **privilege can be claimed** in a suit between either or both of the two parties and **third persons** (multiple parties can desire and expect confidentiality as against the outside world).

c. Client as Holder of Privilege

The privilege, if it exists, can be claimed by the client, her guardian or conservator, the personal representative of a deceased client, or the successor, trustee, or similar representative of a corporation, association, etc. The person who was the attorney at the time of the communication can claim the privilege, but only on behalf of the client. The attorney's authority to do this is presumed in the absence of any evidence to the contrary.

d. Duration of Privilege
The attorney-client privilege applies indefinitely. Termination of the attorney-client *relationship* does not terminate the privilege. The privilege even continues to apply after the client's death. *Rationale:* Knowing that communications will remain confidential even after death encourages the client to communicate fully and frankly with her attorney. [Swidler & Berlin v. United States, 524 U.S. 399 (1998)]

e. Nonapplicability of the Privilege
There are three significant exceptions to the application of the attorney-client privilege:

1) Legal Advice in Aid of Future Wrongdoing
There is no privilege if the services of the attorney were sought or obtained as an aid in the planning or actual commission of something that the *client knew, or should have known, was a crime or a fraud*.

2) Claimants Through Same Deceased Client
There is no privilege regarding a communication relevant to an issue between parties, all of whom claim through the same deceased client—regardless of whether the claims are by testate or intestate succession or by inter vivos transaction.

3) Dispute Between Attorney and Client
There is no privilege for a communication that is relevant to an issue of *breach of duty* by the attorney to his client (malpractice) or by the client to her attorney (*e.g.*, client's failure to pay her attorney's fee for professional services).

f. Waiver of the Privilege
The privilege belongs solely to the client and she alone can waive it. If the client chooses to waive the privilege, her attorney may be compelled to testify.

g. Attorney's Work Product
Documents prepared by an attorney for his *own use* in prosecuting his client's case are not protected by the attorney-client privilege. However, they may be protected by the attorney's "work product" rule. In *Hickman v. Taylor*, 329 U.S. 495 (1947), the United States Supreme Court held that the work product of a lawyer—in that case, statements of interviews with potential witnesses—is not subject to discovery except in cases of necessity.

4. Physician-Patient Privilege
The physician-patient privilege is a statutory privilege, which has not been adopted in all jurisdictions. However, in a substantial number of jurisdictions, a physician (and, in some jurisdictions, a dentist or nurse) is foreclosed from divulging in judicial proceedings information that he acquired while attending a patient in a professional capacity, which information was necessary to enable the physician to act in his professional capacity.

a. Elements of Physician-Patient Privilege

1) Professional Member of Relationship Must Be Present
If the professional member of the relationship is not present for purposes of treatment, and that fact is known to the patient, the relationship does not exist and no privilege attaches.

2) Information Must Be Acquired While Attending Patient
The information must be acquired while attending the patient in the course of treatment; the privilege does not apply to information obtained by the professional in some other way.

3) Information Must Be Necessary for Treatment
If information given by the patient deals with a nonmedical matter (*e.g.*, details of an accident), the information is not privileged. Physicians have also been held competent to testify regarding facts that a lay witness might observe which are not induced by the professional relationship, such as the observable fact that the patient was ill, dates of treatment, or description of clothing worn by the patient.

> *Example:* A treating physician who removed clothing of unconscious accident victim will be permitted to testify that a heroin packet fell out of the patient's right sock.

b. Nonapplicability of the Privilege
There are many exceptions and implied waivers of the physician-patient privilege, and the privilege is of little importance as a result. The privilege does not apply (or is impliedly waived) in the following situations:

1) Patient Puts Physical Condition in Issue
The physician-patient privilege is not applicable in those situations creating the largest number of litigated cases, since a person cannot invoke the privilege where he himself has put his physical condition in issue, *e.g.*, where he sues for personal injuries.

2) In Aid of Wrongdoing
Like the attorney-client privilege, there is no privilege if the physician's services were sought or obtained in aid of the planning or commission of a crime or tort, or to escape detection or apprehension after the commission of a crime or tort.

3) Dispute Between Physician and Patient
There is no privilege regarding a communication relevant to an issue of breach, by the physician or by the patient, of a duty arising out of the physician-patient relationship, *e.g.*, malpractice, failure to pay one's bill.

4) Agreement to Waive the Privilege
The patient may agree by contract (*e.g.*, life insurance policy) to waive the privilege.

5) Federal Cases Applying Federal Law of Privilege
In cases where state law does not supply the rule of privilege (*i.e.,* most federal question cases), the federal courts do not recognize any physician-patient privilege. They do, however, recognize a psychotherapist-client privilege (*see* below).

c. Criminal Proceedings
There is a split of authority as to the applicability of the physician-patient privilege in criminal proceedings. In some states, the privilege applies in both civil and criminal cases. In a number of others, it cannot be invoked in criminal cases generally. In still other states, the privilege is denied in felony cases, and in a few states, it is denied only in homicide cases. Note that where a psychiatrist is involved, however, the applicable privilege is the psychotherapist-client privilege (below), which is more widely accepted in all proceedings than the physician-patient privilege.

d. Patient Holds the Privilege
The privilege belongs to the patient, and he may decide to claim or waive it.

5. Psychotherapist/Social Worker-Client Privilege
The United States Supreme Court recognizes a federal privilege for communications between a psychotherapist (psychiatrist or psychologist) or licensed social worker and his client. [Jaffee v. Redmond, 518 U.S. 1 (1996)—confidential communications between police officer and licensed social worker following a shooting were privileged] Thus, the federal courts and virtually all of the states recognize a privilege for this type of confidential communication. In most particulars, this privilege operates in the same manner as the attorney-client privilege (*supra*).

6. Husband-Wife Privilege
Under the early rule, spouses were absolutely incompetent to testify for or against each other during the period of marriage, and this incompetency had the same effect as the Dead Man Acts—neither spouse could speak out in court if the other spouse was a party. The prohibition against spousal testimony in favor of the party-spouse has been abandoned. However, there remains in many states a rule that permits an accused in a criminal case to prevent his spouse from testifying against him. Apart from this rule of spousal immunity, a modern separate privilege exists in most jurisdictions that protects confidential communications during marriage. Thus, there are two separate privileges as follows: (i) the privilege not to testify against a spouse in a criminal case—spousal immunity, and (ii) the privilege for confidential marital communications.

a. Spousal Immunity

1) Privilege Not to Testify in Criminal Cases
In many jurisdictions, a married person whose spouse is the defendant in a criminal case *may not be called as a witness by the prosecution*, and a married person *may not be compelled to testify* against his spouse in *any* criminal proceeding. (This second part of the privilege exists even where the spouse is not a defendant, such as in grand jury proceedings.) The purpose of this immunity is to protect the marital relationship from the disruption that would follow from allowing one spouse to testify against the other.

a) Federal Courts—Privilege Belongs to Witness-Spouse
In federal courts, one spouse *may* testify against the other in criminal cases, with or without the consent of the party-spouse. Thus, the witness-spouse may not be compelled to testify, nor may she be foreclosed from testifying (except as to confidential communications, *infra*). [*See* Trammel v. United States, 445 U.S. 40 (1980)] Some states (*e.g.,* California) follow the federal view.

b) State Courts—Privilege Belongs to Party-Spouse
In most state courts, the privilege belongs to the party-spouse. Thus the witness-spouse may not be compelled to testify, and she may be foreclosed from testifying if the party-spouse asserts the privilege.

2) Valid Marriage Required
There must be a valid marriage for the privilege to exist. No privilege exists if the marriage is void (*e.g.,* because it is incestuous, bigamous, or a sham).

3) Immunity May Be Asserted Only During Marriage
The privilege lasts only during the marriage and terminates upon divorce or annulment. If a marriage exists, the privilege can be asserted even as to matters that took place *before* the marriage. Remember, however, that in federal court the privilege belongs to the witness. Therefore, an accused cannot use marriage to silence a federal court witness.

b. Privilege for Confidential Marital Communications
In any civil or criminal case, either spouse, whether or not a party, has a privilege to refuse to disclose, and to prevent another from disclosing, a confidential communication made between the spouses while they were husband and wife. The rationale is to encourage open communication and trust and confidence between husband and wife.

1) Both Spouses Hold Privilege
Both spouses jointly hold this privilege, and either can refuse to disclose the communication or prevent any other person from disclosing the confidential communication.

2) Elements of the Privilege

a) Marital Relationship
The communication must be made during a valid marriage. Divorce will *not* terminate the privilege retroactively, but communications after divorce are not privileged.

b) Reliance upon Intimacy
The communication must be made in reliance upon the intimacy of the marital relationship. Routine exchanges of a business nature, abusive language, and misconduct directed to the spouse are not privileged. If the communication was made in the *known* presence of a stranger, it is not privileged. The confidential communication may be by conduct and need not be spoken.

c. Nonapplicability of Privileges
Neither the spousal immunity nor the confidential marital communications privilege applies in actions between the spouses or in cases involving crimes against the testifying spouse or either spouse's children (*e.g.,* assault and battery, incest, bigamy, child abuse, etc.).

7. Privilege Against Self-Incrimination
Under the Fifth Amendment of the United States Constitution, a witness cannot be compelled to testify against himself. (For full discussion, *see* Criminal Procedure outline.) Thus, any witness may refuse to answer any question whose answer might incriminate him, and a criminal defendant may use the privilege to refuse to take the witness stand at all. The privilege belongs to the witness; a party cannot assert it on the witness's behalf.

a. "Incriminating" Defined
Testimony is incriminating if it ties the witness to the commission of a *crime* or would furnish a lead to evidence tying the witness to a crime; the testimony need not prove guilt. [Hoffman v. United States, 341 U.S. 479 (1951)] A witness cannot refuse to answer because of exposure to civil liability; it must be to avoid *criminal* liability.

b. When Privilege Applies
The privilege can be claimed at any state or federal proceeding, whether civil or criminal, at which the witness's appearance and testimony are compelled (*e.g.,* by subpoena). The privilege can be invoked only by natural persons, not corporations or associations.

8. Clergy-Penitent Privilege
A person has a privilege to refuse to disclose, and to prevent others from disclosing, a confidential communication by the person to a member of the clergy in the clergy member's capacity as a spiritual adviser. A member of the clergy can be a minister, priest, rabbi, or other similar functionary of a religious organization, or reasonably believed to be so by the person consulting him. This common law privilege is very similar in its operation to the attorney-client privilege, *supra.*

9. Accountant-Client Privilege
This is a statutory privilege, found in a number of jurisdictions, which is similar to the attorney-client privilege, *supra.*

10. Professional Journalist Privilege
Whether a journalist may be forced to divulge her sources of information has been a much litigated question and the subject of a trend of statutory authority. The Supreme Court has held that there is no constitutional protection for a journalist's source of information, so the existence of the privilege is *limited to individual state statutes* which have been recently growing in number.

Less than half of the states have enacted statutes protecting the journalist's source of information, and the protection ranges from an absolute privilege to one qualified by the need for disclosure in the public interest.

11. Governmental Privileges

a. Identity of Informer
The federal government, or a state or subdivision of a state, generally has a privilege to refuse to disclose the identity of a person who has furnished to a law enforcement officer information purporting to reveal the commission of a crime.

1) Privilege Claimed by Government
The privilege can be claimed by an appropriate representative of the government, such as a prosecutor.

2) No Privilege If Identity Otherwise Voluntarily Disclosed
No privilege exists if the identity of the informer or his interest in the subject matter of his communication has been voluntarily disclosed by a holder of the privilege, such as a prosecutor, or if the informer appears as a witness in the case.

3) Judge May Dismiss If Informer's Testimony Crucial
If the government elects not to disclose the identity of an informer and there is a reasonable probability that the informer could provide testimony necessary to the fair determination of guilt or innocence, the judge on his own motion or that of the accused shall dismiss the proceedings.

b. Official Information
This is a general catch-all privilege that attaches to certain communications made *by or*

to public officials. Official information has been defined as information not open to the public, relating to the internal affairs of the government or its subdivisions. It applies to some fairly low-level communications made by or to officials (*e.g.*, a judge's communications to his law clerk).

H. EXCLUSION AND SEQUESTRATION OF WITNESSES

Upon a party's request, the trial judge will order witnesses excluded from the courtroom so they cannot listen to the testimony of other witnesses. [Fed. R. Evid. 615] The trial judge may also do this on his own motion. However, Federal Rule 615 prohibits the exclusion of: (i) a *party* or a designated officer or employee of a party, (ii) a person whose *presence is essential* to the presentation of a party's case, or (iii) a person *statutorily authorized* to be present.

VII. THE HEARSAY RULE

A. STATEMENT OF THE RULE

The Federal Rules define hearsay as "a statement, other than one made by the declarant while testifying at the trial or hearing, offered in evidence to prove the truth of the matter asserted." [Fed. R. Evid. 801(c)] The rule against hearsay is probably the most important exclusionary rule of evidence. If a statement is hearsay, and no exception to the rule is applicable, the evidence must be excluded upon appropriate objection to its admission. [Fed. R. Evid. 802] An out-of-court statement that incorporates other hearsay is known as "hearsay on hearsay." This type of statement is admissible only if each part of the statement falls within an exception to the hearsay rule. If one part of the statement is inadmissible, the entire statement is inadmissible.

1. Reason for Excluding Hearsay

The reason for excluding hearsay is that the adverse party was *denied the opportunity to cross-examine the declarant*; *i.e.*, the party had no chance to test the declarant's perception (how well did she observe the event she purported to describe), her memory (did she really remember the details she related), her sincerity (was she deliberately falsifying), and her ability to relate (did she really mean to say what now appears to be the thrust of her statement).

a. Cross-Examination of Declarant

Note that it is the declarant who made the statement that the adverse party was not able to cross-examine. Of course, the adverse party can cross-examine the witness who repeats the statement, but this does not help much where all the witness does is repeat a statement as to which the party needs to cross-examine the original declarant.

If W (witness on the stand) testifies as to what D (declarant making out-of-court statement) said about an event, and D's statement is *offered for its truth*, then the opportunity to cross-examine W is not enough. The party against whom W testifies has *no opportunity to test* the perception, the memory, the articulateness, or the veracity of D, the very witness whose account of the event the jury is being asked to believe. Of course, W is available for cross-examination, but W is only repeating what D said, and W is of little help in the attempt to question the accuracy of D's version.

b. Cross-Examination at Time Statement Made

Note too that the *declarant and witness can be the same person*. For example, a witness might state, "I don't remember anything about the accident but I do remember that later that day I said to my wife, 'the black car went through the red light.' " Since the adverse party could not cross-examine the witness-declarant as to his perception, memory, sincerity, or ability to relate at the time the statement was made, the statement is hearsay. It is *contemporaneous* cross-examination that is required.

2. "Statement"

For purposes of the hearsay rule, a "statement" is (i) an oral or written assertion, or (ii) nonverbal conduct intended as an assertion. [Fed. R. Evid. 801(a)]

a. Oral Statements

"Statement" includes oral statements (*i.e.,* where the witness testifies that somebody said " . . . ").

b. **Writings**
Any written document that is offered in evidence constitutes a "statement" for hearsay purposes.

c. **Assertive Conduct**
Conduct intended by the actor to be a substitute for words (*e.g.*, the nod of the declarant's head indicating yes) is a "statement" within the meaning of the hearsay rule.

d. **Nonassertive Conduct**
Under the traditional common law definition of hearsay, "statement" included non-assertive conduct—sometimes called "Morgan hearsay." Nonassertive conduct is conduct the declarant *did not intend as an assertion* but which is being offered as an assertion. However, under modern codes and the Federal Rules, evidence of non-assertive conduct is not hearsay. The rationale is that the likelihood of fabrication is less with nonassertive conduct than with assertive or verbal conduct.

Examples: 1) Consider the conduct of a deceased sea captain who, after examining every part of a ship, embarked in it with his family, when his conduct is being introduced on the question of the seaworthiness of the vessel. Although the sea captain did not intend his embarking on the vessel to serve as an assertion of anything, his conduct can be used to imply that he thought the ship was seaworthy and, since he knew his business, that the ship was in fact seaworthy.

2) Similarly, the fact that a doctor treated a person for plague is non-assertive conduct by the doctor that could be used to show that the person had plague.

3. **"Offered to Prove the Truth of the Matter"**
This is the most crucial component of the hearsay rule. The basic reason for rejecting hearsay evidence is that a statement offered to prove that which it asserts is true may not be trustworthy without the guarantees of cross-examination. However, where the out-of-court statement is introduced for any purpose other than to prove the truth of the matter asserted, there is no need to cross-examine the declarant, and so the statement is not hearsay.

Example: The witness on the stand testifies, "On April 2, Decla said to me, 'Yesterday I was in Buffalo.'" If the issue is whether Decla was in Buffalo on April 1, the testimony is hearsay. It is *not* hearsay if the issue is whether on April 2, Decla was capable of talking. On the latter issue, it is enough to cross-examine W.

The following are other examples of out-of-court statements that are not hearsay.

a. **Verbal Acts or Legally Operative Facts**
There are certain utterances to which the law attaches legal significance (*e.g.,* words of contract, defamation, bribery, cancellation, permission). Evidence of such statements (sometimes called "legally operative facts") is not hearsay because the issue is simply whether the statements were made.

Examples: 1) In an action on a *contract*, words that constitute the offer, acceptance, rejection, etc., are not hearsay because they are offered only to prove what was said, and not that it was true.

2) Similarly, in a *defamation* action, the statement alleged to be a slander or libel may be admissible as nonhearsay. Thus if D said, "X is a thief," X will introduce D's statement not to show its truth—that he himself is a thief—but merely to show that the actionable statement was made.

b. **Statements Offered to Show Effect on Hearer or Reader**
A statement that is inadmissible hearsay to prove the truth of the statement may nevertheless be admitted to show the statement's effect on the hearer or reader.

Examples: 1) In a *negligence case* where knowledge of a danger is the issue, a third person's statement of warning is admissible for the limited purpose of showing *knowledge or notice* on the part of a listener. Thus, a statement to the defendant driver, "Your tire is about to burst," is admissible to show that the defendant had notice of the possible danger. Of course, it is inadmissible hearsay to show that the statement was true—*i.e.,* that there was in fact a defect or dangerous condition.

2) H is on trial for the stabbing murder of W. H claims the killing was done by a bushy-haired, one-armed man whom H saw fleeing the scene. Policeman, P, testifies for the prosecution that H was arrested immediately after the killing and that a letter was found in H's possession. The letter states, "Your wife has been having an affair with your neighbor, Mr. Gigolo, for the last five years. Wise up!" The letter was signed, "A friend." Prosecutor offers this letter to establish H's motive for killing W. Is the letter hearsay? No! True, the letter is an out-of-court statement of "friend." But it is not offered to prove the truth of its contents. The letter is relevant to the issue of *motive* and would still be relevant to motive if, in fact, W had been faithful. The letter, true or not, is offered to show the probable effect it had on H when he read it.

c. **Statements Offered as Circumstantial Evidence of Declarant's State of Mind**
Statements by a declarant that serve as circumstantial evidence of the declarant's state of mind are not hearsay. Such statements are not offered to prove the truth of the matters asserted but only that the declarant *believed* them to be true. The most common examples of this type of nonhearsay are evidence of *insanity* and evidence of *knowledge*.

Examples: 1) In a proceeding where the declarant's sanity is in issue, evidence is offered to show that the declarant had stated out of court, "I am John the Baptist." This statement would not be introduced as proof of its truth, but rather as circumstantial evidence of the declarant's insanity.

2) Evidence that before an accident an automobile driver stated, "My brakes are defective," is not admissible to prove that the brakes were defective, but is admissible to show that the declarant believed the brakes were defective but drove the car anyway.

1) **Compare—State of Mind Exception**
Statements that reflect directly (rather than circumstantially) on the declarant's state of mind are *hearsay but are admissible* under an exception to the hearsay rule (*see* D.1., *infra*). Many courts have used this "state of mind exception" to admit all declarations that reflect on the declarant's state of mind without regard to the fact that many could simply be admitted as nonhearsay. Although the ability to distinguish the two may be helpful for exam purposes, as a practical matter, the distinction makes little difference because the result (admissibility of the statements) is the same.

4. **Nonhuman Declarations**
There is no such thing as animal or machine hearsay. Hearsay involves an out-of-court statement by a *person*. Therefore, a witness who testifies to the time of day (what the clock says) or to radar readings (what the machine says) is not testifying to hearsay. Similarly, the behavior of a drug-sniffing dog in identifying a suspect is not hearsay. The issues presented by these examples are ones of relevance or reliability of the mechanism or animal. For example, a witness may testify to the actions of a drug-sniffing dog in identifying a suspect if there is a foundation showing that the dog was properly trained and is reliable in identifying drug carriers.

5. **Illustrations of Hearsay and Nonhearsay**
The following are specific examples of the application of the hearsay definition.

a. **Hearsay**

1) On the issue of whether the traffic light was red or green, the witness testifies that he was told by Decla that the light was green. (*Oral* hearsay.)

2) On the issue of whether a glassine envelope contained heroin, the prosecution offers a crime laboratory report that the envelope contained heroin. (*Written* hearsay.)

3) On the issue of whether Spano had been a resident of New York for one year prior to commencing his lawsuit, Spano offers the affidavit of Decla that Spano had lived in Buffalo for 10 years. (**Written** hearsay; under oath, but hearsay nonetheless.)

4) On the issue of whether Yuckl was the child molester, a police officer testifies that when he asked the child-victim whether the perpetrator had a beard, the child nodded his head. (Hearsay by **assertive conduct**; nodding, which translates, "Yes, the man had a beard.")

5) On the issue of whether the painting sold to Harvey was actually a genuine Picasso, there is offered a dealer's bill of sale describing the painting as a Picasso. (**Written** hearsay.)

b. Nonhearsay

1) In a contract action, the written, executed contract is offered. (Although an extrajudicial writing, it is not offered to prove the truth of matters asserted in it; **legally operative fact**.)

2) In an action for fraud, on the issue of defendant's good faith in representing to plaintiff that a painting was a genuine Picasso, defendant offers a bill of sale from his art dealer describing the painting as a Picasso. (Offered to prove **defendant's good faith** in repeating a representation; not offered to prove that the painting was in fact a Picasso. The evidence, in other words, was offered to show the impact of the dealer's representation on the defendant's state of mind, *i.e.,* his belief.)

3) On the issue of whether landlord knew about a defective stair, a witness testifies that he heard Decla say to the landlord, "The stair is broken." (Offered to prove **notice**, not that the stair was in fact broken.)

4) On the issue of whether the complaining witness had a venereal disease, Grutz testifies for the prosecution that the complaining witness had not been placed in the venereal disease ward upon her admission to the girls' reformatory. (Nonhearsay under the Federal Rules, since it is **nonassertive conduct**.)

5) On the issue of whether a transfer of a share of stock from Decla to Bushmat was a sale or a gift, Bushmat testifies that Decla made a statement at the time of the transfer: "I'm giving you this share of stock as a birthday present." (**Legally operative** words of gift.)

6) Action for personal injuries by a guest in an automobile against its owner. On the issues of contributory negligence and assumption of risk, a witness testifies that an hour before the accident a mechanic said to the owner in the presence of the guest, "The tread on that left front tire is paper thin. You're likely to have a blowout." (**Notice, knowledge**; not offered to establish that in truth the tread was thin.)

7) Action of P against D. Witness No. 1 testifies for P that D's car was going "over 70 miles an hour." To impeach Witness No. 1, D offers the testimony of Witness No. 2 that Witness No. 1 said a day after the accident that D was going "slowly." (Used solely to cast **doubt on credibility**; not offered to establish the truth of the assertion.)

B. STATEMENTS THAT ARE NONHEARSAY UNDER THE FEDERAL RULES
Federal Rule 801(d) removes from the definition of hearsay certain statements that would be hearsay under the common law definition. Since the following types of statements are not hearsay, when relevant, they are admissible as substantive evidence.

1. Prior Statements by Witness
Certain statements by a person who testifies at the trial or hearing, and is *subject to cross-examination* about the statements, are not hearsay.

a. Prior Inconsistent Statement
A witness's prior inconsistent statement is not hearsay if it was made **under oath** at a prior proceeding or deposition. [Fed. R. Evid. 801(d)(1)(A)] For example, a statement made by the witness during grand jury testimony, if inconsistent with her in-court

testimony, would be admissible not only to impeach her credibility (VI.E.3.a., *supra*) but also as substantive proof.

b.   Prior Consistent Statement

A prior consistent statement, regardless of whether made under oath, is not hearsay if it is offered to rebut an express or implied charge that the witness is lying or exaggerating because of some motive. [Fed. R. Evid. 801(d)(1)(B); *see* VI.E.6.c., *supra*] Note that a consistent statement offered for this purpose is admissible only when made *before* the alleged motive to lie or exaggerate came into being; *i.e.,* a prior consistent statement made after the motive to lie arose is not admissible. [Tome v. United States, 513 U.S. 150 (1995)]

c.   Prior Statement of Identification

A witness's prior statement identifying a person after perceiving him is not hearsay. [Fed. R. Evid. 801(d)(1)(C)] Photo identifications are within the scope of this rule. Note that the prior identification need not have been made at a formal proceeding or under oath, and its admissibility is not limited to rehabilitation of the witness.

2.   Admissions by Party-Opponent

Although traditionally an exception to the hearsay rule, an admission by a party-opponent is not hearsay at all under the Federal Rules. [Fed. R. Evid. 801(d)(2)] An admission is a statement made or act done that amounts to a *prior acknowledgment* by one of the parties to an action of one of the relevant facts. If the party said or did something that now turns out to be inconsistent with his contentions at trial, the law simply regards him as *estopped* from preventing its admission into evidence. The party who made the prior statement can hardly complain about not having had the opportunity to cross-examine himself. He said it. He is stuck with it. Let him explain it if he can.

a.   In General

To be an admission, the statement need not have been against interest at the time it was made (compare the statement against interest exception, C.3., *infra*). The statement may even be in the form of an opinion.

1)   Personal Knowledge Not Required

Lack of personal knowledge *does not necessarily exclude* a party's admission (*e.g.*, president of defendant company said, "My company has investigated the matter thoroughly and the reports indicate that we were negligent"). In fact, an admission may be predicated on hearsay.

2)   Judicial and Extrajudicial Admissions

Formal judicial admissions (in pleadings, responses to requests to admit, stipulations) are *conclusive*; informal judicial admissions made during testimony *can be explained*; extrajudicial (evidentiary) admissions are *not conclusive and can be explained*. A formal judicial admission in one proceeding may become an extrajudicial or evidentiary admission in another proceeding. (Plea of guilty to traffic infraction admissible in civil action on same facts.) A formal judicial admission that is withdrawn may in that same action become an informal admission (statements in original answer admissible though superseded by amendment). A withdrawn plea of guilty in a criminal case is not, however, admissible against a defendant in any civil or criminal proceeding. [Fed. R. Evid. 410]

3)   Adoptive Admissions

A party may expressly or impliedly adopt someone else's statement as his own, thus giving rise to an "adoptive admission." [Fed. R. Evid. 801(d)(2)(B)]

Example: Where Plaintiff claims an orthopedic abnormality in a suit against Defendant, Defendant may properly offer against Plaintiff, Plaintiff's prior application for a chauffeur's license which included a doctor's certificate stating that Plaintiff had "no orthopedic abnormality."

a)   Silence

If a party fails to respond to accusatory statements where a reasonable person would have spoken up, his silence may be considered an implied admission. For silence to be an admission the following requirements must be met:

(i) The party must have **heard and understood** the statement;

(ii) The party must have been **physically and mentally capable of denying** the statement; and

(iii) A **reasonable person would have denied** the accusation under the same circumstances.

Note that failure to reply to an accusation or statement made by the police in a criminal case can **almost never** be used as an implied admission of a criminal act.

b. Vicarious Admissions

An admission is frequently not the statement or act of the party against whom the admission is offered at trial. The question that remains is—what relationship must exist between the declarant and the party to make the former's statement admissible against the latter?

1) Co-Parties

Admissions of a party are **not receivable against her co-plaintiffs or co-defendants** merely because they happen to be joined as parties to the action. If there are two or more parties, the admission of one is receivable against her but, in the absence of authority, not against her co-party.

2) Principal-Agent

Under the Federal Rules, statements by an agent concerning any matter within the scope of her agency, made **during the existence of the employment relationship**, are not hearsay and are admissible against the principal. [Fed. R. Evid. 801(d)(2)(D)] Therefore, under the Federal Rule, if a truck driver-employee has an accident while on the job and admits that she was negligent, this admission may be introduced against her employer. Under the traditional admission exception to the hearsay rule, an agent's statements were admissible against the principal only if making such statements was within the scope of her authority.

3) Partners

After a partnership is shown to exist, an admission of one partner, relating to matters **within the scope of the partnership business**, is binding upon her co-partners since, as to such matters, each partner is deemed the agent of the others.

4) Co-Conspirators

Admissions of one conspirator, made to a third party **in furtherance of a conspiracy to commit a crime or a civil wrong**, at a time when the declarant was participating in the conspiracy, are admissible against co-conspirators. The thought is that a conspiracy is analogous to a partnership: "partners in crime." The government need not demonstrate the unavailability of a nontestifying co-conspirator as a prerequisite to admission of the co-conspirator's out-of-court statements under Rule 801(d)(2)(E). [United States v. Inadi, 475 U.S. 387 (1986)]

5) Privies in Title and Joint Tenants—State Courts Only

Where one person succeeds to the same property rights formerly enjoyed by another, there is often such privity that the rights of the present owner may be affected by admissions of the former owner made before the owner parted with her interest. In most state courts, admissions of each joint owner are admissible against the other, and admissions of a former owner of real property made at the time she held title are **admissible against those claiming under** her (grantees, heirs, devisees, or otherwise). These statements are not considered admissions under the Federal Rules, although they may be admissible under one of the hearsay exceptions (*e.g.*, as a statement against interest).

6) Preliminary Determination of Agency or Conspiracy—Court Must Consider Contents of Hearsay Statement

Before a hearsay statement is admissible as a vicarious admission, the court must make a preliminary determination of the declarant's relationship with the party against whom the statement is being offered. When making a determination of (i) the declarant's authority to make the statement, (ii) the existence and scope of an agency relationship, or (iii) the existence of a conspiracy and participation by the declarant and the party, the ***court must consider the contents of the offered statement***, but the statement alone is not sufficient to establish the required relationship or authority. [Fed. R. Evid. 801(d)(2)]

C. HEARSAY EXCEPTIONS—DECLARANT UNAVAILABLE

Certain kinds of hearsay are considered to have special guarantees of trustworthiness and are recognized exceptions to the hearsay exclusion. The Federal Rules treat the exceptions in two groups—those that require the declarant be unavailable, and those under which the declarant's availability is immaterial. This section covers the five important exceptions requiring the declarant's unavailability: (i) former testimony, (ii) statements against interest, (iii) dying declarations, (iv) statements of personal or family history, and (v) statements offered against party procuring declarant's unavailability.

1. "Unavailability" Defined

A declarant is unavailable if:

(i) He is exempted from testifying by court ruling on the ground of ***privilege***;

(ii) He persists, despite a court order, in ***refusing to testify*** concerning the statement;

(iii) He testifies to ***lack of memory*** of the subject matter of the statement;

(iv) He is unable to be present or testify because of ***death or physical or mental illness***; or

(v) He is absent (*e.g.,* beyond the reach of the trial court's subpoena) and the statement's ***proponent*** has been ***unable to procure*** his ***attendance or testimony*** by process or other reasonable means.

[Fed. R. Evid. 804(a)(1)-(5)] Note that a declarant is not unavailable if his "unavailability" was procured by the proponent of the statement.

2. Former Testimony

The testimony of a now unavailable witness given at another hearing or in a deposition taken in accordance with law is admissible in a subsequent trial as long as there is a sufficient similarity of parties and issues so that the opportunity to develop testimony or cross-examine at the prior hearing was meaningful. [Fed. R. Evid. 804(b)(1)] This exception is the clearest example of hearsay with special guarantees of trustworthiness, since the former testimony was given during formal proceedings and under oath by a witness subject to cross-examination.

a. Identity of Parties

The requirement of identity of parties does not mean that parties on both sides of the controversies must be identical. It requires only that the party ***against whom*** the testimony is offered must have been a party, or in privity with a party, in the former action. (Privity includes grantor-grantee, testator-executor, life tenant-remainderman, joint tenants.) The requirement of identity of parties is intended merely to ensure that the party against whom the testimony is offered (or a party in privity with him) had an adequate opportunity and motive to cross-examine the witness.

b. Identity of Subject Matter

The former testimony is admissible upon any trial in the same or another action of the same subject matter. Again, the sole purpose of this requirement is to ensure that the party against whom the transcript of testimony is offered had an adequate opportunity to cross-examine the unavailable witness on the relevant issue. Obviously, the "cause of action" in both proceedings need not be identical. It is enough if the "subject matter" of the testimony is the same. In other words, the party against whom the testimony is offered must have had an opportunity and similar motive to develop declarant's testimony at the prior hearing.

c. Opportunity to Develop Testimony at Prior Hearing

The party against whom the former testimony is offered (or a predecessor in civil cases) must have had the opportunity to develop the testimony at the prior proceeding by direct, cross, or redirect examination of the declarant. Thus, the ***grand jury testimony*** of an unavailable declarant is ***not admissible*** as former testimony against the accused at trial. This is because grand jury proceedings do not provide the opportunity for cross-examination.

d. Under Oath
The former testimony must have been given under oath or sworn affirmation.

e. Use in Criminal Proceedings
It has been argued that the use in a criminal proceeding of former testimony from some prior trial violates the defendant's constitutional ***right to confront and cross-examine*** all adverse witnesses. However, the Supreme Court has rejected this argument, holding that there is ***no violation*** of an accused's right of confrontation, as long as:

1) The accused or his attorney was present and ***had the opportunity to cross-examine*** at the time the testimony was given (*e.g.*, at a preliminary examination or a former trial for the same offense); ***and***

2) The witness, whose former testimony is sought to be used, is now ***unavailable***, despite bona fide efforts by the prosecution to produce him. [California v. Green, 399 U.S. 149 (1970)] *Note:* A greater showing of "unavailability" is required in criminal cases than in civil cases. For example, a mere showing that a witness is incarcerated in a prison outside the state has been held insufficient to establish "unavailability" (because no showing that he could not be produced by prosecution). [Barber v. Page, 390 U.S. 719 (1968)]

3. Statements Against Interest
A statement of a person, now unavailable as a witness, against that person's pecuniary, proprietary, or penal interest when made, as well as collateral facts contained in the statement, is admissible under the statement against interest exception to the hearsay rule. [Fed. R. Evid. 804(b)(3)]

The reason for this exception lies in the exigency of the declarant being unavailable and the circumstantial probability of trustworthiness (declarant is unlikely to knowingly make a statement against her interest unless the statement is true). The statement against interest differs most significantly from an admission in that under the statement against interest exception the statement ***must be against interest when made*** and the declarant whose statement is admitted may be a stranger to the litigation rather than a party.

a. Requirements of the Statement
To qualify as an exception to the hearsay rule, a statement against interest must meet the following requirements:

1) The statement must have been ***against pecuniary, proprietary, or penal interest when made***.

2) Declarant must have had ***personal knowledge of the facts***.

3) Declarant must have been ***aware that the statement is against her interest*** and she must have had ***no motive to misrepresent*** when she made the statement.

4) Declarant must be ***unavailable as a witness***.

b. Collateral Facts
In addition to the fact against interest, the statement often contains collateral facts not against interest. These connected collateral facts are also admissible.
Example: A written receipt acknowledging payment and specifying date of payment, the person who made payment, and the nature of the claim paid is admissible in its entirety.

c. Risk of Civil Liability
Under the Federal Rules, statements subjecting the declarant to civil liability are specifically admissible. [Fed. R. Evid. 804(b)(3)]

d. Risk of Criminal Liability
Many courts have been reluctant to admit evidence of statements that subject the

declarant to penal liability for fear of opening a door to a flood of perjured testimony. The modern trend and the Federal Rules permit statements against penal interest. However, where a criminal defendant wishes to show her own innocence by introducing statements by another admitting the crime, the Federal Rules require that there be *corroborating circumstances* indicating the trustworthiness of such statements. [Fed. R. Evid. 804(b)(3)]

1) Third-Party Confession Allowed
States that do not allow statements against penal interest may not exclude the confession of a third party where to do so would deprive the accused of a *fair trial*. [Chambers v. Mississippi, 410 U.S. 284 (1973)]

2) Co-Defendant's Confession May Not Be Admissible
The confession of a co-defendant *implicating herself and the accused* may not be admissible because of *confrontation* problems.

e. "Statement" Means Single Remark
A "statement" against interest for purposes of the exception means a single self-inculpatory remark, not an extended declaration. Thus, if a person makes a declaration containing statements that are against his interest and statements that are not, the statements that are not against interest are not admissible, even though they are part of a broader narrative that is on the whole against the declarant's interest. [Williamson v. United States, 512 U.S. 594 (1994)]

Example: X confessed to receiving and transporting drugs, but in so doing implicated Y as the owner of the drugs. The statements implicating Y did not contain any information against X's interest, although the confession as a whole was clearly against X's penal interest. X refused to testify at Y's trial. X's statements implicating Y are not within the scope of the hearsay exception for statements against interest and are thus inadmissible. The exception covers only those remarks that inculpate the declarant, not the extended declaration. [*See* Williamson v. United States, *supra*]

4. Dying Declarations—Statements Under Belief of Impending Death
In a prosecution for *homicide or a civil action*, a declaration made by the now unavailable declarant while *believing his death was imminent* that concerns the *cause or circumstances* of what he believed to be his impending death is admissible. [Fed. R. Evid. 804(b)(2)] The declarant need not actually die, but he must be unavailable (*see* 1., *supra*) at the time the declaration is offered.

Note that under the traditional view, still followed by some states, the declaration was admissible only in homicide prosecutions (not civil actions) and then only if the declarant actually died.

5. Statements of Personal or Family History
Statements concerning birth, marriage, divorce, death, relationship, etc., are admissible under an exception to the hearsay rule. Hearsay statements concerning family history are often necessary to prove the facts of people's everyday lives. For example, most people rely on the hearsay statements of others for the knowledge of where they were born, who their relatives are, etc.

a. Statement Need Not Have Been Made Before Controversy
In most jurisdictions, the statement must have been made at a time when no controversy existed as to the matters stated—to ensure their reliability. However, the Federal Rules have dropped this requirement on the theory that the time at which the statement was made affects its weight rather than its admissibility. [Fed. R. Evid. 804(b)(4)]

b. Usually Declarant Must Be a Family Member
The now unavailable declarant must be a member of the family in question or otherwise intimately associated with the family. Most jurisdictions require that the declarant be related by blood or marriage to the family whose history is involved. Some jurisdictions, and the Federal Rules, have extended this requirement to admit statements by declarants who are so intimately associated with the family that they are likely to have accurate information concerning the matters declared (*e.g.*, the family doctor). [Fed. R. Evid. 804(b)(4)]

c. **Personal Knowledge Required**
The declarant's statements may be based either on her own personal knowledge of the facts involved or on her knowledge of family reputation.

d. **Other Ways to Prove Pedigree**
Personal and family history may be proven by use of other exceptions to the hearsay rule. For example, it may be proven by: vital statistics [Fed. R. Evid. 803(9)]; records of religious organizations [Fed. R. Evid. 803(11)]; marriage certificates and other certificates [Fed. R. Evid. 803(12)]; family records [Fed. R. Evid. 803(13)]; statements in property documents [Fed. R. Evid. 803(15)]; reputation [Fed. R. Evid. 803(19)]; and judgments [Fed. R. Evid. 803(23)]. For these exceptions, the declarant's availability is immaterial.

6. **Statements Offered Against Party Procuring Declarant's Unavailability**
The statements of a person (now unavailable as a witness) *are admissible* when offered against a party who has engaged or acquiesced in wrongdoing that intentionally procured the declarant's unavailability. [Fed. R. Evid. 804(b)(6)] In effect, a party forfeits his right to object on hearsay grounds to the admission of an unavailable declarant's statements when the party's deliberate wrongdoing procured the unavailability of the declarant as a witness.

D. **HEARSAY EXCEPTIONS—DECLARANT'S AVAILABILITY IMMATERIAL**
The following exceptions do not require that the declarant be unavailable. The admissibility of these declarations proceeds upon the theory that the out-of-court declarations were made under circumstances that make them more reliable and therefore preferable to the actual in-court testimony of the declarant. Included in this group of exceptions are the following:

1. **Present State of Mind**
A statement of a declarant's then-existing state of mind, emotion, sensation, or physical condition is admissible. [Fed. R. Evid. 803(3)] The exception is based on the need to obtain evidence as to the declarant's internal state of mind or emotion. It must usually be made under circumstances of apparent sincerity. The statement is often offered to establish the *intent* of a person, either as a direct fact to be proved as such (domicile, criminal intent) or as a basis for a circumstantial inference that the intent was probably carried out.

a. **Rationale**
The rationale is that (i) insofar as the declarant knows her own state of mind, there is no need to check her perception; (ii) since the statement is of present state of mind, there is no need to check her memory; and (iii) since state of mind is in issue, it must be shown some way—and very often, the declarant's own statement is the only way.

b. **When Admissible**

1) **State of Mind Directly in Issue and Material to the Controversy**
Declarations of existing state of mind are admissible when the declarant's state of mind is directly in issue and material to the controversy.
Example: In a case where the domicile of Edwina is material, Edwina's statement that "I love living in Colorado" is admissible.

2) **Offered to Show Subsequent Acts of Declarant**
Declarations of existing state of mind are also admissible when the declarant's state of mind is not directly in issue—if they are declarations of intent offered to show subsequent acts of the declarant; *i.e.,* a declaration of intent to do something in the future is admitted as circumstantial evidence tending to show that the intent was carried out. In *Mutual Life Insurance Co. v. Hillmon*, 145 U.S. 285 (1892), a hearsay written statement was admitted into evidence to prove the declarant did what he said he intended to do.
Examples: 1) The location of X on May 15 is relevant. W may testify that she heard X say on May 8 that "I intend to go to Denver next week."

2) In a prosecution of a husband for murder of his wife, the wife's prior statements that she intended to commit suicide are admissible.

c. **Statements of Memory or Belief Generally Not Admissible**
The hearsay statement is *not admissible* if it expresses a memory or belief of the

declarant, and the statement is offered for the purpose of proving the ***truth of the fact remembered or believed.***

Example: Declarant's out-of-court statement, "I think I left the keys in the car," may not be introduced for the purpose of proving that he left the keys in the car.

Statements of memory or belief are ***admissible***, however, to prove facts remembered or believed concerning the execution, revocation, identification, or terms of ***declarant's will***.

2.   Excited Utterances

A declaration made by a declarant during or soon after a startling event is admissible. The declaration must be made under the stress of excitement produced by the startling event. The declaration must concern the immediate facts of the startling occurrence. [Fed. R. Evid. 803(2)] The spontaneousness of such a declaration and the consequent lack of opportunity for reflection and deliberate fabrication provide an adequate guarantee of its trustworthiness.

a.   Startling Event Required

There must have been some occurrence startling enough to produce a nervous excitement and thus render the declaration an unreflective and sincere expression of the declarant's impression. The declaration ***must relate to the startling event***.

b.   Declaration Must Be Made While Under Stress of Excitement

The declaration must have been made while the declarant was under the stress of the excitement (*i.e.*, ***before the declarant had time to reflect*** upon it). The time element is the most important factor in determining whether the declaration was made under the stress of the excitement. If a declaration is made while the event is still in progress, it is easy to find that the excitement prompted the utterance. Declarations made shortly after the event have sometimes been excluded as mere narrative of past events. But when the declaration is made so near to the time of the occurrence as to negate any probability of fabrication, it is usually admissible.

3.   Present Sense Impressions

A present sense impression is admissible as an exception to the hearsay rule.

a.   Comment Made Concurrently with Sense Impression

If a person perceives some event that is not particularly shocking or exciting, and it does not in fact produce excitement in the observer, that person may nevertheless be moved to comment on what she perceived at the time of receipt of the sense impression or immediately thereafter. [Fed. R. Evid. 803(1)]

b.   Safeguards

Such a comment regarding a situation then before the declarant, *i.e.*, the statement of a present sense impression, does not have the supposed safeguards of impulse, emotion, or excitement, but there are other safeguards of reliability. Statements of present sense impression are ***safe from defects in memory***. There is usually little or ***no time for calculated misstatement***. The statement will usually have been made to another person—the very witness who reports it—who would have ***equal opportunity to observe*** and to contradict or correct a misstatement.

Example: Decla said to N, "Look at that car go." W may testify that Decla made the statement in order to prove that the car was speeding.

4.   Declarations of Physical Condition

a.   Present Bodily Condition—Admissible

Generally, declarations of present bodily condition are admissible as an exception to the hearsay rule, even though they are not made to a physician. They may be made to a spouse, relative, friend, or any other person. Of course, declarations made to a physician are admissible. [Fed. R. Evid. 803(3)] Such declarations relate to symptoms, including the existence of pain. Because they are contemporaneous with the symptoms, they are more reliable than present testimony based upon recollection.

Example: Victim tells friend, "My ankle hurts so much it must be broken." The statement is admissible as a declaration of present pain, although it is not to be used to prove the ankle was in fact broken.

b. **Past Bodily Condition—Admissible If to Assist Diagnosis or Treatment**
As a general rule, declarations of past physical condition are excluded, since there is no way to check the memory of the declarant by cross-examination and there is a greater likelihood of falsification where the declarant is describing a past condition. However, the Federal Rules, recognizing that a patient has a strong motive to tell the truth when seeking medical treatment, admit declarations of past physical condition *if made to medical personnel to assist in diagnosing or treating the condition*. [Fed. R. Evid. 803(4)] Furthermore, the Federal Rule allows declarations not only of past symptoms and medical history, but also of the *cause or source of the condition* insofar as reasonably pertinent to diagnosis or treatment. Moreover, contrary to the majority state view, Rule 803(4) permits such declarations even when made to a doctor employed to testify.

5. **Business Records**
Any writing or record, whether in the form of an entry in a book or otherwise, made as a memorandum or record of any act, transaction, occurrence, or event is admissible in evidence as proof of that act, transaction, occurrence, or event, if made in the regular course of any business; and if it was the regular course of such business to make it at the time of the act, transaction, occurrence, or event or within a reasonable time thereafter.

a. **Rationale**
The rationale for this exception lies in the belief that special reliability is provided by the *regularity* with which business records are kept, their *use and importance* in the business, and the *incentive* of employees *to keep accurate records* or risk employment penalties. If a record qualifies as a business record, it may be admitted without calling the author of the record or the employee with personal knowledge of the recorded event. It makes no difference that the record is self-serving and offered in evidence by the party whose business made the record.

b. **Elements of Business Records Exception**
Under the Federal Rules and modern statutes, the main requirements for admissibility of a business record are as follows:

1) **"Business"**
Under the Federal Rules, "business" includes every "association, profession, occupation, and calling of every kind, whether or not conducted for profit." Thus, the definition would include records made by churches, hospitals, schools, etc. [Fed. R. Evid. 803(6)]

2) **Entry Made in Regular Course of Business**
It must also appear that the record was made in the course of a regularly conducted business activity, and that it was customary to make the type of entry involved (*i.e.*, that the entrant had a duty to make the entry).

a) **Business Activity**
The record must have been maintained in conjunction with a business activity.

(1) **Example—Hospital Records**
Entries in hospital records are generally admissible to the extent that they are *related to the medical diagnosis or treatment* of the patient (the primary business of the hospital). For example, a patient's statement that she was injured on X's property would probably be inadmissible because whether she was injured on X's property or someone else's is unrelated to her medical treatment.

(2) **The Rule of *Palmer v. Hoffman*—Records Prepared for Litigation**
A similar aspect of the "business activity" requirement was raised in the case of *Palmer v. Hoffman*, 318 U.S. 109 (1943). In that case, railroad personnel, in accordance with their regular practice, prepared a report concerning an accident in which the railroad was involved. The United States Supreme Court held that the report was not admissible at trial because it was prepared in anticipation of litigation, and railroading, not litigating, was the railroad's primary business.

(a) Narrow Interpretation

Many courts have interpreted the rule of *Palmer v. Hoffman* narrowly. These courts have generally ***excluded*** such a self-serving employee accident report only when the report was prepared ***primarily*** for litigation and the author of the report had a strong motive to misrepresent.

(b) Federal Rules—Court's Discretion

The Federal Rules have dealt with the problem of *Palmer v. Hoffman* by granting the trial court discretion to exclude any business record if the ***source of information*** or other circumstances indicate the record lacks trustworthiness. [Fed. R. Evid. 803(6)]

b) Entrant Under Duty to Record

For a record to have been made in the regular course of a business activity, the entrant must have had some duty to make the entry as part of her employment (*i.e.*, records kept as a hobby do not qualify). This duty may be either public (statutory, etc.) or private (contractual—including duties imposed by an employer).

3) Personal Knowledge

The business record must consist of matters within the personal knowledge of the entrant *or* within the personal knowledge of someone with a business duty to transmit such matters to the entrant.

a) Recorder Need Not Have Personal Knowledge of Event

Most business records statutes do not require that the person making the entries have personal knowledge of the event. Indeed, where the one who has personal knowledge of the transaction (informant) and the one making the record (recorder) are both employees of the business, there is no problem. Once established as a business record, it is admissible without calling either the informant or the recorder, even though the recorder lacked personal knowledge. The integrity of the special reliability assumption is maintained because the informant was under a ***business duty to report*** accurately and the recorder was under a ***business duty to properly record*** the information.

b) Informant Must Be Under Business Duty to Convey Information

A problem arises, however, when the informant with personal knowledge is an outsider, having little or no connection with the business whose records are being offered in evidence. The well-known case of *Johnson v. Lutz*, 253 N.Y. 124 (1930), engrafted a limitation on the business records exception. It holds that an entry is admissible as a business record only when the record was made by the employee recorder on information obtained directly by him or imparted to him by an informant who was under a business duty to convey such information. Thus, a police report entry by a police officer was held inadmissible where the informant was a third person who was under no "business" duty to convey information (the "business" being law enforcement). The statutory business records exception, in other words, was not intended to permit receipt in evidence of hearsay statements made by third persons not engaged in the business in question or under any duty in connection with it. Thus, the rationale is that the assumed reliability justifying the hearsay exception cannot be maintained if the information in the record was supplied by an outsider who had no business incentive to report accurately.

c) Recorded Statement May Be Admissible Under Other Exceptions

If, as in *Johnson v. Lutz*, the record-maker and the informant are not business related, the recorded statement of the informant may nonetheless be receivable with the help of some other exceptions to the hearsay rule. This involves a two-phase process. The business records exception serves as a vehicle for demonstrating the bare fact that the ***statement was made*** (*i.e.*, it allows the paper record to substitute for the in-court testimony of the employees who received the information); the second phase involves reference to some ***independent ground of admissibility*** of the statement to establish the ***truth*** of assertions contained in it. A police report entry is receivable where the informant was a party and his statement constituted an ***admission***. Note too that certain police reports may be admissible under the public records exception (*see* 7.a., *infra*).

4) Entry Made Near Time of Event
The entry must have been made at or near the time of the transaction while the entrant's knowledge of the facts was still fresh.

5) Authentication
The authenticity of the record must be established. The usual method of authentication is to have the custodian or other qualified witness testify to the identity of the record and the mode of its preparation. However, a foundation witness is not necessary to authenticate the record (*i.e.,* the record will be self-authenticating) if the custodian or other qualified person certifies in writing that the record meets the requirements of the business records exception. [Fed. R. Evid. 803(6), 902(11)]

Normally, the original or first permanent record of the transaction must be introduced, but where the records to be introduced are voluminous, summaries or compilations may be admitted.

6) Entrant Need Not Be Unavailable
For the business record to be admissible, the person who made the entry need not be unavailable as a witness.

7) Trustworthiness
The court may exclude an otherwise qualifying business record if the source of information or the method or circumstances of preparation indicate lack of trustworthiness.

c. Use of Business Records as Evidence of No Transaction
At common law, business records were admitted only to prove the facts contained therein. They were not admissible for negative purposes—*i.e.*, to show that no transaction had taken place. However, the modern trend allows business records to be used to prove the nonoccurrence or the nonexistence of a matter if it was the regular practice of the business to record all such matters. [Fed. R. Evid. 803(7)] For example, the lack of any entry showing payment in a business record may be evidence that in fact no payment was made.

6. Past Recollection Recorded
Witnesses are permitted to refresh their memories by looking at almost anything—either before or while testifying. This is called ***present recollection revived*** (*see* VI.B.3.a., *supra*). However, if the witness's memory cannot be revived, a party may wish to introduce a memorandum that the witness made at or near the time of the event. Use of the writing to prove the facts contained therein raises a hearsay problem; but if a proper foundation can be laid, the contents of the memorandum may be introduced into evidence under the ***past recollection recorded*** exception to the hearsay rule. The rationale is that a writing made by an observer when the facts were still fresh in her mind is probably more reliable than her testimony on the stand—despite the fact that cross-examination is curtailed. For admissibility requirements, *see* VI.B.3.b., *supra*.

7. Official Records and Other Official Writings

a. Public Records and Reports
The exception for public records and reports is necessary to avoid having public officers leave their jobs constantly to appear in court and testify to acts done in their official capacity, especially since the entrant could probably add nothing to the record. Also, such records are presumed to be trustworthy because officials are under a duty to record properly that which they do.

1) What May Be Admitted
Records, reports, statements, or data compilations, in any form, of a public office or agency are admissible to the extent that they set forth:

(i) The activities of the office or agency;

(ii) Matters observed pursuant to a duty imposed by law (excluding police observations in criminal cases); or

(iii) In civil actions and proceedings and against the government in criminal cases, factual findings (including opinions and conclusions) resulting from an investigation made pursuant to authority granted by law, unless the sources of information or other circumstances indicate lack of trustworthiness.

[Fed. R. Evid. 803(8); Beech Aircraft Corp. v. Rainey, 488 U.S. 153 (1989)]

Examples:　　1) A manual prepared by the office that processes Medicare claims explaining which claims are properly payable under Medicare is admissible against the defendant in a Medicare fraud case under Federal Rule 803(8)(A).

2) A police officer arrives at the scene of the accident. Several witnesses tell him that Dan drove through a stop sign and hit Vic, who was riding a bicycle. The police officer has had many years' experience in evaluating accident scenes. From the tire marks, he decides that Dan did indeed run the stop sign. In his report he includes the statements of the witnesses and his evaluation of the scene, including his conclusion that Dan ran the stop sign. Everything except the witnesses' statements can be admitted under Federal Rule 803(8)(C), including the officer's conclusion. The witnesses' statements can be admitted only if they fall within some other exception. Remember that the investigative report is admissible only in civil cases and only *against the government* in criminal cases. The report could not be offered against Dan in a criminal prosecution.

3) An Equal Employment Opportunity Commission investigator's report would be admissible in an action against an employer alleging discriminatory employment practices. As with the officer's report above, any hearsay statements will be excised unless they fall within an exception, but the investigator's conclusions and opinions are admissible.

2)　Requirements for Admissibility

a)　Duty to Record
The writing must have been made by, and within the scope of duty of, the public employee.

b)　Entry Near Time of Event
The writing must have been made at or near the time of the act, condition, or event.

c)　Trustworthiness
The sources of information and other circumstances must be such as to indicate its trustworthiness.

b.　Records of Vital Statistics
Records of births, deaths, and marriages are admissible if the report was made to a public office pursuant to requirements of law. [Fed. R. Evid. 803(9)]

c.　Statement of Absence of Public Record
A certificate from the custodian of public records that she has diligently searched and failed to find a record is admissible to prove that the matter was not recorded, or, inferentially, that the matter did not occur. [Fed. R. Evid. 803(10)]

d.　Judgments
A certified copy of a judgment is always admissible proof that such judgment has been entered. The problem is to what extent the facts adjudicated in the former proceeding can be introduced to prove facts in the present case.

1) Prior Criminal Conviction—Felony Conviction Admissible
The traditional view, still followed by most state courts, is that a judgment of conviction is inadmissible. First, it is merely the "opinion" of the jury, and second, it is hearsay as proof of the fact asserted, *i.e.*, the guilt of the defendant. Of course, under certain circumstances the conviction may be used for impeachment. The Federal Rules, however, specifically provide that judgments of felony convictions are *admissible in both criminal and civil actions to prove any fact essential to the judgment*. In the Rules, felony convictions are defined as crimes punishable by death or imprisonment in excess of one year. [Fed. R. Evid. 803(22)] The convictions that may be used are limited to felonies because persons may choose not to defend misdemeanor charges (*e.g.*, traffic violations).

a) Admissible to Prove Fact Only Against Accused
In a criminal case, the government may use a prior conviction for this purpose only against the accused. Against persons *other than the accused*, the government may use prior convictions *only for impeachment*.

2) Prior Criminal Acquittal—Excluded
The exclusionary rule is still applied to records of prior acquittals. The reason is that a criminal acquittal may establish only that the state did not prove the defendant guilty beyond a reasonable doubt, whereas the evidentiary standard is lower in civil cases.

3) Judgment in Former Civil Case

a) Inadmissible in Criminal Proceeding
A civil judgment is clearly inadmissible in a subsequent criminal proceeding because of the differing standards of proof.

b) Generally Inadmissible in Civil Proceeding
The general rule is that civil judgments are also inadmissible in subsequent civil proceedings. However, there are certain statutory *exceptions* to the rule of inadmissibility. For example, under the Federal Rules, a prior civil judgment is admissible as proof of matters of personal, family, or general history, or boundaries of land, if it would be provable by reputation evidence (*e.g.*, X may prove her citizenship by a judgment establishing that X's parents were citizens). [Fed. R. Evid. 803(23)]

8. Ancient Documents and Documents Affecting Property Interests
Under the Federal Rules, statements in *any* authenticated document *20 years old or more* are admissible. [Fed. R. Evid. 803(16)] Moreover, in contrast to the traditional view that only ancient property-disposing documents qualified for the exception, statements in a document affecting an interest in property (*e.g.*, deed, will, etc.) are admissible regardless of the age of the document. [Fed. R. Evid. 803(15)]

9. Learned Treatises
Many courts do not admit statements from standard scientific treatises or authoritative works as substantive proof, limiting admissibility to use as impeachment of the qualifications of the expert witness. The Federal Rules recognize an exception to the hearsay rule for learned treatises. Federal Rule 803(18) provides for the substantive admissibility of a learned treatise if the treatise is:

(i) Called to the attention of the expert witness upon cross-examination or relied upon by her during direct examination; and

(ii) Established as reliable authority by the testimony or admission of the witness, by other expert testimony, or by judicial notice.

Even under the Federal Rules, however, the relevant portion of the treatise is not actually shown to the jury; it is admissible by being read into the record.

10. Reputation
In addition to reputation testimony concerning a person's character [Fed. R. Evid. 803(21)], reputation evidence concerning someone's personal or family history [Fed. R. Evid. 803(19)] or concerning land boundaries or the community's general history [Fed. R. Evid. 803(20)] is admissible hearsay.

11. Family Records
Statements of fact concerning personal or family history contained in family Bibles, genealogies, jewelry engravings, engravings on urns, crypts, or tombstones, or the like are admissible hearsay. [Fed. R. Evid. 803(13)]

12. Market Reports
Market reports and other published compilations (lists, directories, etc.) are admissible if generally used and relied upon by the public or by persons in a particular occupation. [Fed. R. Evid. 803(17)]

E. RESIDUAL "CATCH-ALL" EXCEPTION OF FEDERAL RULES
The Federal Rules provide a general catch-all exception for hearsay statements not covered by specific exceptions. [Fed. R. Evid. 807] There are three requirements for a statement to be admitted under the catch-all exception:

1. "Trustworthiness" Factor
First of all, the statement must have "circumstantial guarantees of trustworthiness" that are equivalent to those of statements admitted under other hearsay exceptions.

2. "Necessity" Factor
The statement must be offered on a *material fact*, and must be *more probative* as to that fact than any other evidence which the proponent can reasonably produce so that the *"interests of justice"* will be served by its admission.

3. Notice to Adversary
Finally, the proponent must give notice in advance of trial to the adverse party as to the nature of the statement (including the name and address of the declarant) so that the adversary has an opportunity to prepare to meet it.

F. CONSTITUTIONAL ISSUES

1. The Confrontation Clause
In criminal cases, it may be argued that the use of hearsay evidence violates the accused's *right to "confront" and cross-examine* the witnesses against him. Supreme Court decisions have veered away from reading the hearsay rule into the Constitution; *i.e.*, the Court has indicated that the requirements of the Confrontation Clause may be met where circumstances indicate the reliability of the hearsay statement. [Dutton v. Evans, 400 U.S. 74 (1970)]

a. Two-Step Analysis for Former Testimony
In a case concerning the admission of a statement given by the declarant at a defendant's preliminary hearing, the United States Supreme Court formulated a two-step analysis for Confrontation Clause issues. [Ohio v. Roberts, 448 U.S. 56 (1980)]

1) Unavailability
First, the prosecution must produce the declarant or demonstrate that the declarant is unavailable.

2) Reliability
If the declarant is unavailable, the prosecution must then show that the hearsay it is offering is reliable. The prosecution may do this by showing either that: (i) the hearsay falls within a firmly rooted hearsay exception; or (ii) there are particularized guarantees of trustworthiness, *i.e.*, that the hearsay statement was made under circumstances that are likely to produce a trustworthy statement.

b. One-Step Analysis for Other Hearsay Exceptions

1) No Unavailability Requirement
Unavailability will not be required when it serves no useful purpose (*i.e.*, a more reliable statement is not possible). For example, in *United States v. Inadi*, 475 U.S. 387 (1986), the Court held that the Confrontation Clause did not require the prosecution either to produce the declarant or to demonstrate her unavailability if the hearsay statement offered was an admission by a co-conspirator. The Court reasoned that such a statement, having been made during and in furtherance of a conspiracy, would be more reliable than the in-court testimony of the declarant. Subsequently, the Court has held that hearsay may be offered under the excited

utterance and statements for medical diagnosis or treatment exceptions without having first to produce the declarant or demonstrate unavailability. [White v. Illinois, 502 U.S. 346 (1992)]

2) **Reliability**
When the hearsay falls within a firmly rooted hearsay exception, the Confrontation Clause is satisfied. The Court has held admissions by co-conspirators fall within a firmly rooted exception, as co-conspirators' statements have traditionally been admissible. [Bourjaily v. United States, 483 U.S. 171 (1987)] In *White v. Illinois, supra*, the Court found that the excited utterance and statements for medical diagnosis or treatment exceptions were also firmly rooted. However, in *Idaho v. Wright*, 497 U.S. 805 (1990), the Court held that Idaho's residual hearsay exception was not firmly rooted. Therefore, the Court examined the admitted hearsay—an out-of-court accusation of sexual abuse made by a three-year-old to a doctor—to see if there were particularized guarantees of trustworthiness. The Court found that the statements were not made under circumstances that would likely produce trustworthy statements and held that the admission of these statements violated the Confrontation Clause.

c. **The Right to Physically Face Witnesses**
The Sixth Amendment guarantee of confrontation includes not only the right to cross-examine witnesses, but also the right to physically face them at trial. The Supreme Court held that right to be violated at a child sex abuse trial because a screen was erected in court between the defendant and two youthful complainants so they could not see the defendant as they testified. [Coy v. Iowa, 487 U.S. 1012 (1988)] However, the Court has also held that the right of confrontation is not absolute. A child witness in a sexual abuse case may testify via one-way closed circuit television without violating the defendant's confrontation rights *if the trial judge makes individual findings of probable trauma to the child* from testifying in the defendant's presence. [Maryland v. Craig, 497 U.S. 836 (1990)]

2. **The Right to a Fair Trial**
In addition, the Court has held that state hearsay rules and other exclusionary rules cannot be applied where the effect would be to deprive an accused of her Fourteenth Amendment due process right to a *fair trial* [Chambers v. Mississippi, 410 U.S. 284 (1973)], or deny her right to compulsory process [Rock v. Arkansas, 483 U.S. 44 (1987)].

VIII. PROCEDURAL CONSIDERATIONS

A. **BURDENS OF PROOF**
The term "burden of proof" as used by judges and lawyers at trial encompasses two separate meanings or burdens. Thus, burden of proof can mean:

1. **Burden of Producing or Going Forward with Evidence**

   a. **Produce Sufficient Evidence to Raise Fact Question for Jury**
   This defines the burden of one party to introduce sufficient evidence to avoid judgment against her as a matter of law. It is the burden of producing sufficient evidence to create a fact question of the issue involved, so that the issue may appropriately reach the jury. The burden of producing evidence is a critical mechanism for judicial control of the trial. Although the burden is usually cast upon the party who has pleaded the existence of the fact, the burden as to this fact may shift to the adversary when the pleader has discharged her initial duty.

   b. **Prima Facie Case May Shift Burden of Production**
   Consider *Plaintiff v. Defendant* in a negligence action. Plaintiff offers evidence in her case-in-chief of Defendant's negligence. Defendant's motion for a nonsuit made at the conclusion of Plaintiff's case is denied. This denial reflects a judicial ruling that Plaintiff has made out a prima facie case of Defendant's negligence. Put another way, it means that Plaintiff has met her burden of going forward with evidence on the negligence issue.

   Now assume that Defendant rests immediately after Plaintiff's case-in-chief without producing any rebuttal evidence. Plaintiff then moves for a directed verdict in her favor, claiming that Defendant was negligent as a matter of law. If this motion were granted, it would mean that (i) Plaintiff's evidence was sufficiently persuasive, (ii) the burden shifted to Defendant, and (iii) Defendant failed to meet his newly imposed burden of producing evidence of no negligence. If Plaintiff's motion were denied, it would mean only that Plaintiff met her initial burden but that it did not shift to Defendant; and, therefore, the burden of production having dropped out of the case, the matter is now for the jury. Once in the hands of the jury, the question is whether Plaintiff has met her burden of persuasion.

2. Burden of Persuasion (Proof)

a. Determined by Jury After All Evidence Is In
This is what is usually meant when the term "burden of proof" is used. This burden becomes a crucial factor only if the parties have sustained their burdens of production and only when all the evidence is in. When the time of decision comes, the jury must be instructed how to decide the issue if their minds remain in doubt. There are no tie games in the litigation process. Either the plaintiff or the defendant must win. If, after all the proof is in, the issue is equally balanced in the minds of the jury, then the party with the burden of persuasion must lose.

b. Jury Instructed as to Which Party Has Burden of Persuasion
The burden of persuasion does not shift from party to party during the course of the trial simply because it need not be allocated until it is time for a decision by the trier of fact. The jury will be told which party has the burden of persuasion and what the quantum of proof should be. The jury is never told anything about the burden of going forward with evidence because that burden is a matter for the judge alone.

c. Quantum or Measure of Proof
The trier of fact must be persuaded of the truth of disputed facts by one of the following standards, depending upon the nature of the action:

1) Preponderance of the Evidence
The preponderance of the evidence standard applies in most civil cases. This standard has been defined as meaning that the fact finder must be persuaded by the party to whom the burden on the issue has been allocated that the fact is *more probably true than not true.*

2) Clear and Convincing Proof
Some civil cases (an oral contract to make a will or issues of fraud) often require proof by "clear and convincing evidence." This standard requires the trier of fact to be persuaded that there is a *high probability* that the fact in question exists.

3) Beyond a Reasonable Doubt
This is the *highest standard* and applies to criminal cases. In a criminal prosecution, the guilt of the defendant must be established beyond a reasonable doubt.

B. PRESUMPTIONS
A presumption is a rule that requires that a particular inference be drawn from an ascertained set of facts. It is a form of substitute proof or evidentiary shortcut in that proof of the presumed fact is rendered unnecessary once evidence has been introduced of the basic fact that gives rise to the presumption. Presumptions are established for a wide variety of overlapping policy reasons. In some cases, the presumption serves to correct an imbalance resulting from one party's superior access to the proof on a particular issue. In others, the presumption was created as a time saver to eliminate the need for proof of a fact that is highly probable in any event. In other words, the inference from the basic fact to the presumed fact is so probable and logical that it is sensible to assume the presumed fact upon proof of the basic fact. In still other situations, the presumption serves as a social or economic policy device. It operates to favor one contention by giving it the benefit of a presumption and to correspondingly handicap the disfavored adversary.

Example: A common presumption is that the driver of a vehicle is the owner's agent. When plaintiff has been injured by the negligent operation of a vehicle, the nondriving, owner-defendant will be liable for the negligence of the driver if the driver is the owner's agent. Plaintiff's burden of proving that the driver was the agent of the owner is aided by a presumption of agency that arises upon proof of ownership. The justification of this presumption of agency from ownership may be explained in terms of *fairness* in light of defendant's superior access to the evidence; in terms of *probability* since it is unlikely that defendant's car was stolen by the driver; or in terms of a *social policy* of promoting safety or increasing available compensation for traffic victims by widening the responsibility of owners.

1. Effect—Shift Burden of Production

Federal Rule 301 provides that a presumption imposes on the party against whom it is directed the burden of going forward with evidence to rebut or meet the presumption. A presumption does not, however, shift to such party the burden of proof in the sense of the risk of nonpersuasion, which remains throughout the trial upon the party on whom it was originally cast.

Example: Plaintiff has the burden of going forward and the burden of persuasion on the issue of Edwina's death. Plaintiff introduces evidence sufficient to support the fact that Edwina has been absent without tidings for a period of seven years. The proof of this basic fact causes a presumption of the presumed fact, Edwina's death. Plaintiff has made out a prima facie case on Edwina's death. More than that, if the defendant is silent and fails to offer proof in rebuttal (either of the presumed fact of death, or the basic fact of absence for a period of seven years), the jury will be instructed that they *must* find Edwina is dead if they believe the absence for seven years.

2. Rebutting a Presumption

A presumption is overcome or destroyed when the adversary produces some evidence contradicting the presumed fact. In other words, the *presumption is of no force or effect* when sufficient contrary evidence is admitted. This is the federal view adopted by Federal Rule 301 except where state law provides the rule of decision (*see* 6., *infra*).

Example: Plaintiff-victim of automobile driver's negligence sues owner. Plaintiff proves ownership, thus giving rise to the presumption that the driver was the agent of the owner. Defendant-owner testifies that the driver was not his agent, and his evidence could justify a jury finding that the driver was without authority from the owner. At this point, plaintiff's presumption is gone. He will have to sustain the burden of proving by a preponderance of the evidence that the driver was the agent of the owner or his case will fail.

a. Amount of Contrary Evidence Necessary

The amount of contrary evidence that must be introduced to overcome the presumption has never been clearly articulated. Some cases require "enough evidence to support a finding of the nonexistence of the presumed fact." Others simply require "substantial evidence."

3. Distinguish True Presumptions from Inferences and Substantive Law

The true presumption with its mandatory rebuttable inference should not be confused with inferences and rules of substantive law.

a. Permissible Inferences

The permissible inference (prima facie case or sometimes erroneously called "presumption of fact") will allow a party to meet the burden of production but *will not shift the burden* to the adversary. Examples of situations giving rise to permissible inferences are:

1) Res Ipsa Loquitur

A permissible inference of negligence arises where the instrumentality causing injury was under the exclusive control of the defendant and the accident would not ordinarily occur without negligence.

2) Spoliation or Withholding Evidence

The intentional destruction or mutilation of relevant evidence may give rise to an inference that the destroyed evidence is unfavorable to the spoliator. An unfavorable inference may also arise when a party fails to produce evidence or witnesses within his control which he is naturally expected to produce.

3) Undue Influence

Where the attorney who drafted a will is its principal beneficiary to the exclusion of the natural objects of the testator's bounty, an inference of undue influence may be found.

b. "Presumptions" in Criminal Cases

1) Accused Is Presumptively Innocent
The accused in a criminal case is presumptively innocent until the prosecution proves every element of the offense beyond a reasonable doubt. Accordingly, it is clear that in criminal cases "presumptions" do not shift to the accused the burden of producing evidence, nor of persuading the fact finder. A "presumption" in a criminal case is truly nothing more than a *permissible inference.*

2) Judge's Instructions on Presumed Facts Against Accused
The trial judge in a criminal case is not free to charge the jury that it *must* find a "presumed" fact against the accused. When the existence of a presumed fact is submitted to the jury, the judge shall instruct the jury that it *may* regard the basic facts as sufficient evidence of the presumed fact but that it is not required by law to do so. If the presumed fact establishes guilt, is an element of the offense, or negates a defense, its existence must be found (proved) beyond a reasonable doubt.

c. Conclusive Presumptions
This form of inference goes beyond the true presumption since it *cannot be rebutted* by contrary evidence. A "conclusive" presumption is really a rule of substantive law.

Example: In some states, it is conclusively presumed that a child under a certain age (*e.g.,* seven years old) cannot commit a crime. No evidence to the contrary can rebut this presumption, and part of the proof of the case requires a showing that the accused is over the minimum age.

4. Specific Presumptions
The following are common rebuttable presumptions:

a. Presumption of Legitimacy
The law presumes that every person is legitimate. The presumption applies to all cases where legitimacy is in dispute. The mere fact of birth gives rise to the presumption. The presumption is destroyed by evidence of illegitimacy that is "clear and convincing." For example, the presumption is overcome by proof of a husband's impotency, proof of lack of access, or the negative result of a properly conducted blood grouping test.

b. Presumption Against Suicide
When the cause of death is in dispute, a presumption arises in *civil* (not criminal) cases that the death was not a suicide.

c. Presumption of Sanity
Every person is presumed sane until the contrary is shown. The presumption of sanity applies in *criminal as well as civil* cases.

d. Presumption of Death from Absence
A person is presumed dead in any action involving the property of such person, the contractual or property right contingent upon his death, or the administration of his estate, if:

1) The person is unexplainably absent for a continuous period of *seven years* (death is deemed to have occurred on the last day of the seven-year period); and

2) He *has not been heard from,* or of, by those with whom he would normally be expected to communicate.

e. Presumption from Ownership of Car—Agent Driver
Proof of ownership of a motor vehicle gives rise to the presumption that the owner was the driver or that the driver was the owner's agent.

f. Presumption of Chastity
There is a presumption that every person is chaste and virtuous.

g. Presumption of Regularity
The general presumption is that no official or person acting under an oath of office will

do anything contrary to his official duty, or omit anything that his official duty requires to be done.

h. Presumption of Continuance
Proof of the existence of a person, an object, a condition, or a tendency at a given time raises a presumption that it continued for as long as is usual with things of that nature.

i. Presumption of Mail Delivery
A letter shown to have been properly addressed, stamped, and mailed is presumed to have been delivered in the due course of mail. The presumption is said to be based upon the probability that officers of the government will perform their duty.

j. Presumption of Solvency
A person is presumed solvent, and every debt is presumed collectible.

k. Presumption of Bailee's Negligence
Upon proof of delivery of goods in good condition to a bailee and failure of the bailee to return the goods in the same condition, there is a presumption that the bailee was negligent.

l. Presumption of Marriage
Upon proof that a marriage ceremony was performed, it is presumed to have been legally performed and that the marriage is valid. A presumption of marriage also arises from cohabitation.

5. Conflicting Presumptions
If two or more conflicting presumptions arise, the judge shall apply the presumption that is founded on the weightier considerations of policy and logic. For example, where the validity of a later marriage is attacked by evidence of a prior valid marriage, the presumption of the validity of the later marriage is deemed to prevail over the presumption of the continuance of the first marriage.

6. Choice of Law Regarding Presumptions in Civil Actions
Under the Federal Rules, the effect of a presumption respecting a fact that is an element of a claim or defense as to which the rule of decision is supplied by state law is also governed by state law.

C. RELATIONSHIP OF PARTIES, JUDGE, AND JURY

1. Party Responsibility
Ours is an adversarial adjudicative process and so, the focus is on party responsibility or, perhaps what is more to the point, on lawyer responsibility. Very little happens in the litigation process unless some lawyer makes it happen by filing pleadings and motions, by initiating discovery, by entering into stipulations, by calling witnesses and offering exhibits at trial, or by interposing objections to the admission of evidence. In other words, the parties, through their lawyers, frame the issues in a litigation by making allegations, admissions, and denials in their pleadings, and by entering into binding stipulations. They assume the burden of proving the issues they have raised. And then, by deciding which witnesses to call to the stand and what tangible exhibits to introduce (and by deciding to what they will object), they control the flow of evidence. But the parties and their lawyers are not the only ones to be allocated important responsibilities in the adversary trial process.

2. Court-Jury Responsibility
Under our system, the trial court is more umpire than advocate. The trial judge's primary responsibility is to fairly superintend the trial; the judge is not permitted to become a partisan in it. As a general rule, questions of law are for the trial court to deal with, and questions of fact determination are for the jury, although trial judges frequently encounter the necessity of making preliminary fact determinations in connection with such matters as the admission or exclusion of evidence. (Of course, both types of questions—legal and factual—are for the trial court in a nonjury case.)

3. Preliminary Determination of Admissibility
In most cases, the existence of some preliminary or foundational fact is an essential condition to the admissibility of proffered evidence. Thus, before a written contract may be received in evidence, it must be shown that the contract is genuine; and before testimony as

to an alleged dying declaration may be admitted into evidence, it must be shown that the declaration was made under a sense of impending death. In some cases, the existence or nonexistence of the preliminary fact is determined by the jury with the judge merely deciding whether the evidence of the foundational fact is sufficient to allow the jury to find its existence. In other cases, the question of the preliminary fact must be decided by the judge alone—in which case the evidence will not even be heard by the jury unless the judge first finds the preliminary or foundational fact.

a. Preliminary Facts Decided by Jury

The Federal Rules of Evidence distinguish preliminary facts to be decided by the jury from those to be decided by the judge, on the ground that the former questions involve the *relevancy* of the proffered evidence, while the latter questions involve the *competency* of evidence that is relevant. Rule 104(b) of the Federal Rules of Evidence defines preliminary facts to be decided by the jury as those where the answer to the preliminary question determines whether the proffered evidence is relevant at all. For example, if a statement is proffered to show notice to X, the jury must decide whether X heard it. If X did not, the statement is irrelevant for that purpose; but the decision is left ultimately to the jury because if the jury does not believe X heard it, they will not use it anyway.

1) Role of the Judge

Before the judge allows the proffered evidence to go to the jury, she must find that the proponent of the proffered evidence has introduced evidence sufficient to sustain a finding of the existence of the preliminary fact. The court may *instruct the jury* to determine whether the preliminary fact exists and to disregard the proffered evidence if the jury finds that the preliminary fact does not exist. Such an instruction may be desirable if the trier of fact would otherwise be confused, but with most questions of conditional relevancy the instruction will be unnecessary, since a rational jury will disregard these types of evidence anyway unless they believe in the existence of the foundational fact. If the judge allows the introduction of evidence and then subsequently determines that a jury could not reasonably find that the preliminary fact exists, she must instruct the jury to disregard that evidence.

2) Examples of Preliminary Facts Decided by Jury

a) Agency

If plaintiff sues defendant upon an alleged contract, evidence of negotiations with a third party is inadmissible because it is irrelevant unless the third party is shown to be defendant's agent. However, the evidence of the negotiations with the third party is admissible if there is evidence sufficient to sustain a finding of the agency.

b) Authenticity of a Document

If there is a dispute about whether a note was signed by the defendant (as opposed to a forger), the authenticity of the document is to be left for the jury. In a sense this is merely an issue of relevancy, since the note, if forged, is irrelevant to the liability of the defendant.

c) Credibility

When a conviction of a crime is offered to attack the credibility of a witness, the judge must admit the evidence and allow the jury to determine the witness's credibility if there is evidence sufficient to identify the witness as the person convicted.

d) Personal Knowledge

The question of whether a witness had personal knowledge can go to the jury if there is sufficient evidence to sustain a finding that the witness had personal knowledge.

b. Preliminary Facts Decided by Judge

1) Facts Affecting Competency of Evidence

The question of the existence or nonexistence of all preliminary facts other than those of conditional relevance must be determined by the court. In most cases, the questions which must be decided by the judge involve the competency of the evidence or the existence of a privilege. These questions are withheld from the jury because it is felt that once the jury hears the disputed evidence, the damage will have been done and the instruction to disregard the evidence, if the preliminary fact is not found, will be ineffective.

2) Requirements for Privilege

Preliminary facts to establish the existence of a privilege must be determined by the court. This must be so or else a privilege might be ignored merely because there was sufficient evidence (and this might not be a great deal) for a jury to find it did not exist. Whether or not the jury believed that the facts giving rise to the privilege existed, they would still have heard the privileged evidence, subject only perhaps to a most unrealistic instruction to disregard it if they found the privilege to exist.

3) Requirements for Hearsay Exceptions

All preliminary fact questions involving the standards of trustworthiness of alleged exceptions to the hearsay rule must also be determined by the court. For example, the court must decide whether a statement offered as a dying declaration was made under a sense of impending death, or whether a purported business record was made in the regular course of business. The reason for this is that otherwise the jury will hear the hearsay evidence where the judge's finding is not that it fell within an exception to the hearsay rule, but only that there was enough evidence for the jury to so find. The jurors, however, once they have heard the hearsay evidence, might ignore the judge's instruction to disregard it unless they found the preliminary fact.

4) Others

The above two cases are the most important where the judge must first determine the existence of a foundational fact. However, there are several other major categories.

a) The judge must determine whether a witness is disqualified for *lack of mental capacity.*

b) The judge must rule on the qualifications of a witness as *an expert.*

c) If a conviction of a crime is offered to attack credibility and the disputed preliminary fact is whether a *pardon* has been granted to the witness so convicted (the pardon rendering the impeaching conviction inadmissible), the judge must make the determination.

d) The judge must determine whether a witness is sufficiently acquainted with a person whose sanity is in question in order for him to be *qualified to express an opinion* as to that person's sanity.

e) The judge is required to determine the preliminary facts necessary to warrant reception of *secondary evidence of a writing* (*e.g.,* whether original writing was lost or destroyed).

f) The judge is required to determine the *voluntariness of a confession* before he allows the jury to hear it. This is a rule of constitutional law. The theory is that otherwise the jury might hear involuntary confessions but rely on them anyway because the jury felt that they were nonetheless trustworthy.

5) Procedure for Preliminary Fact Determinations by Judge

a) What Evidence May Be Considered

Federal Rule 104(a) permits the trial judge to consider any (nonprivileged) *relevant evidence,* even though not otherwise admissible under the rules of evidence. Thus, the trial judge may consider affidavits or hearsay in ruling on preliminary fact questions. Most state courts, however, hold that the rules of evidence apply in preliminary fact determinations as much as in any other phase of the trial; thus, only admissible evidence may be considered.

b) Presence of Jury

Whether the jury should be excused during the preliminary fact determination is generally within the discretion of the trial judge. However, because of the potential for prejudice to the accused in a criminal trial, the jury *must* be excused during hearings on the "voluntariness" of the accused's confession, or whenever the accused testifies during the preliminary fact hearing and requests that the jury be excused. [Fed. R. Evid. 104(c)]

c. Testimony by Accused Does Not Waive Privilege Against Self-Incrimination

An accused may testify as to any preliminary matter (*e.g.,* circumstances surrounding allegedly illegal search) without subjecting herself to having to testify generally at the trial. Furthermore, while testifying upon a preliminary matter, an accused is not subject to cross-examination on other issues in the case. [Fed. R. Evid. 104(d)]

d. Judicial Power to Comment upon Evidence

The trial judge is expected to marshal or summarize the evidence when necessary. However, in most state courts, the trial judge may not comment upon the weight of the evidence or the credibility of witnesses. In federal court, the trial judge has traditionally been permitted to comment on the weight of the evidence and the credibility of witnesses.

e. Power to Call Witnesses

The judge may call witnesses upon her own initiative and may interrogate any witnesses who testify but may not demonstrate partisanship for one side of the controversy.

f. Rulings

A trial judge has an obligation to rule promptly on counsel's evidentiary objections and, when requested to do so by counsel, to state the grounds for her rulings.

g. Instructions on Limited Admissibility of Evidence

When evidence that is admissible as to one party or for one purpose, but inadmissible as to another party or for another purpose, is admitted, the trial judge, on request, shall restrict the evidence to its proper scope and instruct the jury accordingly, *e.g.,* "Ladies and gentlemen of the jury, the testimony that you have just heard is receivable against the defendant Bushmat only and will in no way be considered by you as bearing on the guilt or innocence of the co-defendant Lishniss." [Fed. R. Evid. 105]

BAR REVIEW

Real Property

celebrating **35** **YEARS** *of preparing law students for the bar exam*

REAL PROPERTY

TABLE OF CONTENTS

I. ESTATES IN LAND

A. IN GENERAL

"Estates in land" are *possessory interests* in land. These interests may be *presently* possessory (present estates), or they may become possessory in the *future* (future interests). They may be "freeholds," which give possession under some legal title or right to hold (*e.g.,* fees or life estates), or they may be "nonfreeholds," which give mere possession (*i.e.,* leases). Estates in land may be of potentially infinite duration, as in the case of a fee simple, or they may be of limited duration, as in the case of an estate for years. But whatever their characteristics, "estates in land" must be distinguished from *nonpossessory* interests such as easements, profits, covenants, and servitudes.

This section of the outline will examine various estates in land. It divides the interests into two classes: present interests and future interests. However, some future interests (those following defeasible fees) will be considered with the present interests to which they are attached.

B. PRESENT POSSESSORY ESTATES

1. Fee Simple Absolute

An estate in fee simple absolute is the largest estate permitted by law. It invests the holder of the fee with full possessory rights, now and in the future. The holder can sell it, divide it, or devise it; and if she dies intestate, her heirs will inherit it. The fee simple has an indefinite and potentially infinite duration. The common law rule requiring technical words of inheritance ("and his heirs") has been abolished by statute in nearly all jurisdictions. Typically, such statutes provide: "A fee simple title is presumed to be intended to pass by a grant of real property unless it appears from the grant that a lesser estate was intended."

Example: A conveyance from "A to B" is presumed to pass a fee simple interest if A owned one. At common law, absent the words of inheritance, even a conveyance "to B in fee simple" would convey only a life estate to B.

2. Defeasible Fees

Defeasible fees are fee simple estates of *potentially* infinite duration that can be terminated by the happening of a specified event. Because defeasible fees can result in forfeitures, courts will construe, where possible, a purported limitation as a mere declaration of the grantor's purpose or motive for making the grant (*i.e.,* as precatory language).

a. Fee Simple Determinable (and Possibility of Reverter)

A fee simple determinable, also called a determinable fee, is an estate that *automatically terminates* on the happening of a stated event and goes back to the grantor. (It must be distinguished from the fee simple subject to a condition subsequent, where the grantor must take affirmative steps to terminate the estate of the grantee if the stated event occurs.) It is created by the use of durational, adverbial language, such as "for so long as," "while," "during," or "until." A fee simple determinable can be conveyed by the owner thereof, but his grantee takes the land subject to the termination of the estate by the happening of the event.

Example: O conveys land "to A for so long as no alcoholic beverages are consumed on the premises." This gives A a fee simple, because the estate may last forever if no one ever quaffs a brew. If A conveys his fee simple determinable estate to B, B will own the "for so long as" estate. If A does not convey his estate, on A's death it will pass by will or intestacy to his successors, and so on. If, however, someone ever consumes an alcoholic beverage on the premises, the estate will automatically come to an end according to its own terms; and O will immediately and automatically become the owner of the fee simple, without taking any steps to terminate A's interest.

1) Correlative Future Interest in Grantor—Possibility of Reverter

Since the grantee's estate may end upon the happening of the stated event, there is a possibility that the land may revert back to the grantor. The interest that is left in a grantor who conveys an estate in fee simple determinable is called a "possibility of reverter." It is a future interest, because it becomes possessory only upon the occurrence of the stated event.

a) Possibility of Reverter Need Not Be Expressly Retained

At common law and in nearly all states today, the grantor does not have to expressly retain a possibility of reverter. It arises **automatically** in the grantor as a consequence of his conveying a fee simple determinable estate, with its built-in time limitation.

b) Transferability of Possibility of Reverter

At early common law, the possibility of reverter could not be transferred inter vivos or devised by will. An attempted transfer of the interest was invalid; but the possibility of reverter was not extinguished by the attempted transfer and would still descend to the heirs of the owner. Today, in most jurisdictions, the possibility of reverter can be transferred inter vivos or devised by will, and descends to the owner's heirs if she dies intestate.

2) Correlative Future Interest in Third Party—Executory Interest

A possibility of reverter arises only in the grantor, not in a third party. If a comparable interest is created in a third party, it is an executory interest. (*See* C.3., *infra*.)

b. Fee Simple Subject to Condition Subsequent (and Right of Entry)

A fee simple subject to a condition subsequent is created when the grantor retains the power to terminate the estate of the grantee upon the happening of a specified event. Upon the happening of the event stated in the conveyance, the estate of the grantee **continues until the grantor exercises her power** of termination (right of entry) by bringing suit or making reentry. The following words are usually held to create conditions subsequent: "upon condition that," "provided that," "but if," and "if it happens that."

Example: A, owning Blackacre in fee simple, conveys it "to B and his heirs, on the express condition that the premises are never to be used by B for the sale of liquor and in the event that they are so used, then A or her heirs may enter and terminate the estate hereby conveyed." B has a fee simple subject to a condition subsequent. A has a right of entry. If the condition is broken, A has a power to terminate the estate of B by asserting her **right of entry**.

1) Correlative Future Interest in Grantor—Right of Entry

A right of entry (also known as "right of reentry" or "power of termination") is the future interest retained by the transferor who conveys an estate on condition subsequent. It is necessary to **expressly** reserve the right of entry in the grantor; this retained interest does not automatically arise as in the case of a fee simple determinable and possibility of reverter.

a) Waiver of Right of Entry

Since the grantor can elect whether or not to terminate the grantee's estate, she may waive her right or power to enforce a forfeiture by express agreement or by her conduct. (Such is not the case with a fee simple determinable, where the forfeiture is automatic.)

(1) Inaction by Itself Not a Waiver

The general rule is that when there is a breach of the condition and the grantor simply does nothing about it, the power of termination is not waived. However, where there is any element of **detrimental reliance** by the fee holder, many courts treat inaction as a waiver on an estoppel or laches theory.

b) Transferability of Right of Entry

At common law, a right of entry was **not devisable or transferable inter vivos** to a third person. The right of entry did, however, descend to the heirs of the grantor on her death. Today, in most jurisdictions, a right of entry is still **not** alienable inter vivos. (Indeed, in a handful of states, an attempted transfer destroys it.) But in most states, rights of entry are devisable; and in all states, they descend to the owner's heirs.

2) Correlative Future Interest in Third Party—Executory Interest

A right of entry can be created only in favor of the grantor and her heirs. If a similar interest is created in favor of a third party, the interest is called an executory interest (*e.g.,* "if the property is ever used for other than church purposes, then to C and his heirs"). Unlike a right of entry, an executory interest is subject to the *Rule Against Perpetuities*.

3) Compare—Fee Simple Determinable
This estate is distinguished from a determinable fee in that the breach of the condition does *not* itself terminate the estate and immediately revest the fee in the grantor or her successor. The estate continues in the grantee or his successor unless or until the grantor or her successor affirmatively elects to terminate it.

c. Fee Simple Subject to an Executory Interest
A fee simple subject to an executory interest is an estate that, upon the happening of a stated event, is *automatically divested in favor of a third person* rather than the grantor.

Examples: 1) O conveys land "to A Church; provided, however, that if the premises shall ever cease to be used for church purposes, title shall pass to the American Heart Association." A Church has a fee simple subject to an executory interest in favor of the Heart Association. O does not have a right of entry because no such interest was reserved in the conveyance. The Heart Association's interest is not a right of entry because that future interest can be reserved only in favor of a grantor. The Heart Association's future interest is not a remainder because it divests a fee simple. Therefore, it is an executory interest.

Note: Executory interests are subject to the Rule Against Perpetuities, but the Heart Association's interest is valid because of the "charity-to-charity" exception to the Rule. (*See* E.1.e.1), *infra.*)

2) O conveys land "to A Church for so long as the premises are used for church purposes, and if they shall ever cease to be so used, then and in that event to the American Red Cross." A Church has a fee simple determinable subject to an executory interest in favor of the American Red Cross. O has no possibility of reverter because he has not retained any interest; he has conveyed away his entire estate in the property. The future interest in the Red Cross cannot be a possibility of reverter because that interest arises only in a grantor, and the Red Cross is a grantee. It is an executory interest and not a remainder because it divests a fee simple. (Further discussion of these points will come later.)

Note: Were it not for the "charity-to-charity" exception to the Rule Against Perpetuities, the executory interest in favor of the American Red Cross would violate the Rule.

d. Limitations on Possibilities of Reverter and Rights of Entry
In a few states, statutes limit the permissible duration of possibilities of reverter and rights of entry to a certain number of years (usually 30) in order to foster marketability of title. Other statutes (usually called "marketable title acts") require the rerecording of various future interests (including possibilities of reverter and rights of entry) every 20 to 40 years or they become unenforceable.

3. Fee Tail
The fee tail, typically created by the words "to B and the heirs of his body," limited inheritance to *lineal descendants* of the grantee. If no lineal descendants survived at the grantee's death, the property either reverted to the grantor or her successors or passed to a designated remainderman. Today, most United States jurisdictions have abolished the fee tail and have enacted statutes under which any attempt to create a fee tail results in the creation of a fee simple.

4. Life Estate
An estate for life is an estate that is not terminable at any fixed or computable period of time, but cannot last longer than the life or lives of one or more persons. It may arise by operation of law or may be created by an act or agreement of the parties.

a. Life Estates by Marital Right (Legal Life Estates)
Such estates arise under *dower* and *curtesy*, the common law interests of wife and husband, respectively, in real property of which the other spouse was seised during marriage (including property acquired before marriage). At common law, a surviving

wife's dower right entitled her to a life estate in an undivided one-third of her husband's lands. A surviving husband's right of curtesy gave him a life estate in all his wife's lands if issue were born. For exam purposes, it is important to remember that a conveyance by a husband to a bona fide purchaser does not defeat dower unless the wife joins in the conveyance. Likewise, a husband's creditors cannot defeat a wife's dower rights. Most states have abolished both dower and curtesy and have instead given the surviving spouse a statutory right to take a portion of the deceased spouse's estate. Community property states do not recognize either dower or curtesy.

b. Conventional Life Estate

1) For Life of Grantee
The usual life estate is measured by the life of the grantee and is called simply a life estate. It may be indefeasible (so that it will end *only* when the life tenant dies), or it may be made defeasible in the same ways that fee estates can be defeasible (*e.g.,* determinable, subject to a condition subsequent, subject to an executory interest). In such a case, the estate may end *before* the life tenant dies if the limiting condition occurs. (*See* Example 5), below.)

Examples: 1) A conveys "to B for life." In this case, B has an estate in the land for as long as he lives. On his death, the land reverts to A, the grantor.

2) "To A for life, then to B." This is a life estate because it is measured by the life of A and is not terminable at a fixed period of time.

3) "To A for life, but in no event for more than 10 years." This is an estate for years and not a life estate since the estate in A will end in 10 years (*i.e.,* a fixed time period).

4) "To A for 10 years if he lives so long." This is also an estate for years and not a life estate since the estate in A will end in 10 years.

5) "To A for life or until she remarries." This is a life estate subject to a limitation, but nevertheless a life estate. The estate in A will not end at any fixed or computable time period. It can be termed a "life estate determinable," and is analogous to the fee simple determinable discussed above.

6) "To B and C after the life of A." A has an implied life estate.

2) Life Estate Pur Autre Vie (Life of Another)
A life estate pur autre vie is a life estate measured by the life of someone other than the life tenant. Such an estate can be created *directly* by the grantor, *e.g.,* "to A for the life of B." A's estate ends when B dies. It can also be created *indirectly*, as where the grantor conveys "to B for life," and B later conveys his interest to A. A owns an estate measured by B's life; it ends when B dies.

a) Inheritability
At common law, if A died before B, the property was regarded as without an owner until B died. Today, statutes provide that such estates are devisable and inheritable if no special occupant is named in the original grant. (A "special occupant" is a person named by the grantor to take the balance of the term, if any.)

c. Rights and Duties of Life Tenant—Doctrine of Waste
A tenant for life is entitled to all the ordinary uses and profits of the land; but he cannot lawfully do any act that would injure the interests of the person who owns the remainder or the reversion. If he does, the future interest holder may sue for *damages and/or to enjoin* such acts.

1) Affirmative (Voluntary) Waste—Natural Resources
As a general rule, a life tenant may not consume or exploit natural resources on the property (timber, minerals, oil, etc.). *Exceptions* to this rule allow exploitation in the following circumstances:

(i) In reasonable amounts where necessary *for repair and maintenance* of the land;

(ii) Where the life tenant is *expressly given the right to exploit* such resources in the grant;

(iii) Where *prior to the grant, the land was used in exploitation* of such natural resources, so that in granting the life estate the grantor most likely intended the life tenant to have the right to exploit (*but see* "open mines doctrine," below); and

(iv) In many states, where the *land is suitable only for such exploitation* (a mine, etc.).

Note: There is a vague "reasonableness" limit on the amount of oil or coal a life tenant can remove from the property.

a) Open Mines Doctrine

If mining (extraction of minerals) was done on the land before the life estate began, the life tenant may continue to mine the property—but is limited to the mines *already open.* The life tenant may not open any new mines. There is a trend away from this limitation, applying instead the rule in (iii), above, to all natural resources, including minerals.

2) Permissive Waste

Permissive waste occurs when the life tenant allows the land to fall into disrepair or fails to take reasonable measures to protect the land.

a) Obligation to Repair

A life tenant is obligated to preserve the land and structures in a *reasonable state of repair,* to the extent of the income or profits derived from the land (or if the life tenant is using the property himself and receiving no rent, then to the extent of the reasonable rental value of the land). But the tenant is under no obligation to make permanent improvements on the land, no matter how wise it might seem to do so.

b) Obligation to Pay Interest on Encumbrances

A life tenant is obligated to pay interest on any encumbrances on the land to the extent of the income or profits from the land (or in their absence to the extent of the reasonable rental value of the land). However, he does not have to pay anything on the principal of the debt; reversioners or remaindermen must pay the principal in order to protect their interests.

The foregoing applies to encumbrances on the entire fee simple estate. Of course, a life tenant could place a mortgage on the life estate alone, and would then be liable for both principal and interest payments.

c) Obligation to Pay Taxes

The life tenant is obligated to pay *all ordinary taxes* on the land to the extent of the income or profits from the land (or in their absence to the extent of the reasonable rental value of the land).

d) Special Assessments for Public Improvements

If the life of a public improvement on the land is shorter than the expected duration of the life estate, the life tenant is obligated to pay all of the assessment. However, if the improvement is likely to outlast the life estate (*e.g.,* curbing, sewers, water mains, a change in grade of a street), taxes and assessments are *apportioned* equitably between the life tenant and the holders of all future interests.

(1) Apportionment of Costs

Costs are usually apportioned by using the ratio produced by market value of the life estate over the market value of the property.

e) No Obligation to Insure Premises

The life tenant is under no obligation to insure the premises for the benefit of a remainderman. However, both the life tenant and the remainderman have an insurable interest.

f)   No Liability for Third Party's Torts
Under the modern view, life tenants are not responsible to remaindermen (as they were at common law) for damages caused by third-party tortfeasors. The life tenant's action against such third parties is limited to the damages to the life estate.

3)   Ameliorative Waste
Ameliorative waste consists of acts that economically benefit the property. Ameliorative waste occurs when the use of the property is substantially changed, but the change increases the value of the property. At common law, any change to existing buildings or other improvements was always actionable waste, even if it improved the value of the property. Under modern authorities, however, a life tenant can substantially alter or even demolish existing buildings if:

(i)   The market value of the future (or other nonpossessory) interests is not diminished; and *either*

(ii)   The remaindermen do not object; *or*

(iii) A substantial and permanent change in the neighborhood conditions has deprived the property in its current form of reasonable productivity or usefulness.

Example: A holds a life estate in Blackacre, and B holds the remainder. The premises consist of an old and somewhat shabby apartment building that is nearly fully rented and produces a consistent income. The surrounding neighborhood includes many similar buildings. A proposes to demolish the building and construct a new shopping center on the land, which will produce much higher income. B objects to the change and brings an action to enjoin the demolition. B will prevail even though A's proposed changes would increase the value of the property. Since the existing building is economically productive and consistent with the neighborhood, A's commission of waste would not be justified.

a)   Compare—Leasehold Tenant
Leasehold tenants are treated differently from life tenants. Most leasehold tenants remain liable for ameliorative waste even if the neighborhood has changed and the market value of the premises is increased. (*See* II.C.1.a.3), *infra*.)

b)   Compare—Worthless Property
Under modern authority, a life tenant may ask for a judicial sale in a partition proceeding if it appears that the land is practically worthless in its present state. The proceeds are put in trust with income to the life tenant.

d.   Renunciation of Life Estates
A life tenant who receives the estate by will or intestacy may renounce it, perhaps because owning it would be burdensome. If this occurs, the courts generally *accelerate* the future interest that follows the life estate, allowing it to become possessory immediately.

5.   Estates for Years, Periodic Estates, Estates at Will, Tenancies at Sufferance
These nonfreehold present estates in land are considered in the Landlord and Tenant section of this outline (*see* II.A., *infra*).

C.   FUTURE INTERESTS
A future interest is an estate that does not entitle the owner thereof to possession immediately, but will or may give the owner possession in the future. A future interest is a *present*, legally protected right in property; it is not an expectancy.
Examples: 1) O conveys land "to A for life, and on A's death to B in fee simple." A has a present possessory life estate. B has a future interest. (B's future interest is an indefeasibly vested remainder.) Upon the termination of A's possessory life estate, B's remainder in fee simple will become a present possessory estate in fee simple.

2) O conveys land "to A for life, and on A's death to B in fee simple if B survives A." A has a present possessory life estate. B has a future interest. (It is a contingent remainder.) Upon the termination of A's life estate, B's remainder in fee simple *may* become a present possessory estate in fee simple. B must survive A in order to take. (In this example, O also has a future interest. He has not conveyed away the interest represented by the contingency that B may predecease A. If B does predecease A, on the termination of A's life estate title to the land will *revert* to O. O's retained future interest is called a reversion.)

3) After the conveyance "to A for life, and on A's death to B," B can transfer his remainder interest to another person. If B dies during A's lifetime, his vested remainder will pass to the devisees under his will or (if B left no will) to his intestate heirs.

1.   Reversionary Interests—Future Interests in Transferor

a.   Possibilities of Reverter and Rights of Entry
These future interests are discussed above in connection with the present estates to which they are attached.

b.   Reversions
A person owning an estate in real property can create and transfer a lesser estate (in the durational sense). The residue left in the grantor, which *arises by operation of law*, is a reversion.

Examples: 1) O, owning land in fee simple, conveys it (i) "to A for life," or (ii) "to A for 99 years." In each case, O has a reversion in fee simple. She (or her successors) will be entitled to present possession of the land when the granted estate terminates.

2) O, owning a life estate in land, leases it "to B for 20 years." O has a reversion in a life estate. If O is still alive when B's lease expires, title will revert to O for life. What happens if, 10 years after this transfer, O dies? B's lease will come to an end, for he was given a lease by one holding only a life estate. O cannot convey a greater interest than she has.

3) O, owning land in fee simple, conveys it "to B for life, and on B's death to C if C survives B." B has a life estate, C has a contingent remainder, and O has a reversion that will take in present possession at B's death if C predeceases B.

Reversions are transferable, devisable by will, and descendible by inheritance. The holder of a reversion may sue a possessory owner for waste and may recover against third-party wrongdoers for damages to the property (to the extent of the injury to the reversion).

c.   All Reversionary Interests Are "Vested"
Although a reversionary interest becomes possessory in the future, it is a vested interest, not a contingent interest, because both the owner and the event upon which it will become possessory are certain. This is true even if the reversionary interest is determinable or defeasible. Because it is a vested interest, a reversionary interest is *not subject to the Rule Against Perpetuities*.

2.   Remainders
A remainder is a future interest created in a transferee that is *capable of taking* in present possession and enjoyment (*i.e.,* capable of becoming a present interest) *upon the natural termination of the preceding estates* created in the same disposition. Unlike a reversion, which arises by operation of law from the fact that the transferor has not made a complete disposition of his interest, a remainder *must be expressly created in the instrument creating the intermediate possessory estate*. At common law, the only preceding estates that could support a remainder were life estates and fee tails. Since nearly all American jurisdictions have abolished the fee tail estate, a safe rule of thumb is that remainders *always follow life estates*. (*Note:* According to the Restatement of Property, under modern law, a remainder can also follow a term of years. However, there is very little case law on the point, and it is so rare that it is extremely unlikely to be tested.)

Examples: 1) "To A for life, and on A's death to B and his heirs." A has a present possessory life estate. B has a remainder in fee simple. It is a remainder because upon the expiration of A's life estate (natural termination of the preceding estate), B will be entitled to present possession and enjoyment of the property. The term "remainder" derives from the consequence that when A's life estate comes to an end, title "remains away" from the transferor instead of reverting back to him.

2) On Monday, O conveys Blackacre "to A for life." On Wednesday, O conveys "all of my right, title, and interest in Blackacre" to B. B holds a reversion, not a remainder. B's future interest was not created in the same disposition that gave A a life estate. The Monday conveyance gave A a life estate and raised a reversion in O. The Wednesday conveyance transferred O's reversion to B. "Once a reversion, always a reversion."

A remainder cannot "cut short" or divest a preceding estate prior to its normal expiration. Therefore, a remainder can *never follow a fee simple*, which has a potentially infinite duration. Future interests that cut short a preceding estate or follow a gap after it are called executory interests. (*See* 3., *infra.*)

a. Indefeasibly Vested Remainder
An indefeasibly vested remainder is a remainder that:

(i)   Can be created in and held only by an *ascertained person or persons* in being;

(ii) *Must be certain to become possessory on termination of the prior estates* (*i.e.,* there is no condition that may operate to prevent the remainder from someday becoming a present interest);

(iii) *Must not be subject to being defeated or divested* (compare the vested remainder subject to total divestment, below); and

(iv) *Must not be subject to being diminished in size* (compare the vested remainder subject to open, below).

Examples: 1) "To A for life, and on A's death to B." A has a life estate; B has an indefeasibly vested remainder which is certain to take in possession on the termination of A's life estate.

What if B dies in A's lifetime? There is no stated condition that B survive A in order to take, and the courts do not imply such a condition. B's indefeasibly vested remainder passes by will or intestacy to his successors, who own an indefeasibly vested remainder.

2) "To A for life, then to A's first-born son in fee." At the time of this disposition, A has no children. The state of title: life estate in A, contingent remainder in the first son to be born to A, reversion in fee simple in the transferor. (The reversion will take in present possession if A never has a son.) The remainder is not vested because it is not created in an ascertained person in being. Also, it is subject to the condition that A have a child.

Two years later A has a son, John. The state of title: life estate in A, indefeasibly vested remainder in fee simple in John.

b. Vested Remainder Subject to Open
This is a vested remainder created in a class of persons ("children," "brothers and sisters," etc.) that is certain to take on the termination of the preceding estates, but is *subject to diminution* by reason of other persons becoming entitled to share in the remainder. It is also called a "vested remainder subject to partial divestment."

Examples: 1) "To A for life, and on A's death to her children in equal shares." If at the time of this disposition A has no children, the state of title is: life estate in A; contingent remainder in the unborn children of A; reversion in fee in the transferor, which will take in possession if A never has any children.

Suppose two years later a child, Bob, is born to A. The state of title is: Life estate in A, vested remainder subject to open in Bob. Bob's remainder is vested because he is in existence and ascertained and his taking is not subject to any contingency. But it is vested subject to open because A may have more children.

Two years later another child, Ray, is born to A. Bob's remainder has been partially divested in favor of Ray, who also meets the description "children of A." Bob and Ray now hold the vested remainder as tenants in common (each with an undivided one-half share) **subject to open**— that is, their vested remainders will be partially divested if more children are born to A.

Two years later Bob dies; shortly thereafter, A dies. Bob's successors (by will or intestacy) and Ray are entitled to present possession and enjoyment of the property. Bob's share of the remainder was subject to partial divestment, but it was not subject to being totally defeated. No condition of survival was attached to Bob's interest. Bob (or his successors) was certain to take; the only question was the size of his share.

2) Gift by will "to my wife, Rowena, for life, and on her death to **my** children in equal shares." T is survived by Rowena and by three children. At first blush this looks like a vested remainder subject to open because it is a remainder to someone's children. In reality, though, it is **indefeasibly vested**. T, being dead, can have no more children. (Slight qualification of answer: If Rowena is pregnant with T's child at T's death, the posthumous child, if born alive, will share in the gift.)

1) **Divesting Interests Are Executory Interests**
Once the remainder vests in one existing member of the class, the divesting interest in the unborn members of the class is called an executory interest.

2) **Effect on Marketability of Title**
Note that where there are outstanding interests in the unborn children, the vested remainderman and the life tenant cannot jointly convey good title.
Example: A "to B for life, remainder to C's children." D wants to buy the land, and desires to know if he can get good title if he purchases from B and all of C's living children. The answer is no, as long as C is alive, because it is possible for C to have more children (no matter what C's age). Thus, there would be outstanding interests in the unborn children of C, and D would not get good title.

c. **Vested Remainder Subject to Total Divestment**
A vested remainder subject to total divestment arises when the remainderman is in existence and ascertained and his interest is not subject to any condition precedent, but his right to possession and enjoyment is subject to being defeated by the happening of some **condition subsequent**.
Examples: 1) "To X for life, remainder to A and his heirs, but if at A's death he is not survived by issue, to B and his heirs." Here A has a vested remainder in fee simple, but his fee simple interest is subject to being divested if at his death he is not survived by issue. (B has a shifting executory interest.)

2) "To A for life, then to B for life." A has a life estate. B has a vested remainder in a life estate subject to total divestment. The transferor has a reversion in fee. B's remainder is vested even though (as a practical matter) he must survive A in order to take. But this practical requirement does not make B's remainder contingent. The only condition to B's taking is the natural termination of A's life estate, and this "condition" is inherent in any remainder life estate. There is no other condition precedent. However, B's remainder life estate is not indefeasibly vested, for it will be **defeated if he dies in A's lifetime**. Therefore, it is a vested remainder subject to total divestment.

3) "To A for life, and on A's death to B; but if B predeceases A, on A's death to C." A has a life estate. B has a vested remainder subject to total divestment. Although B's taking is **contingent on his surviving A**, that

contingency is expressed as a condition subsequent—meaning that B's remainder is vested subject to total divestment. (C has a shifting executory interest.)

d. Contingent Remainder

There are two ways to create a contingent remainder.

1) Subject to Condition Precedent

A remainder will be classified as contingent if its taking in possession is subject to a condition precedent ("contingent as to *event*").

Examples: 1) "To A for life, and on A's death to B if B survives A." A has a life estate; B has a contingent remainder in fee simple. The transferor has a reversion, which will become a possessory estate on the termination of A's life estate if B predeceases A. Here B's taking is subject to a contingency, stated as a condition precedent, that he must survive A in order to take.

Compare this with Example 3) in the preceding section. In that example, B's taking is also subject to a contingency; he must survive A in order to take. Thus in substance, this example and Example 3) are quite similar. But in classifying future interests, the general rule is that *it is form and not substance that counts*. In Example 3), the contingency of survival is expressed as a condition subsequent; therefore, B's remainder is vested subject to total divestment. But in this example the contingency of survival is expressed as a condition precedent; therefore, B's remainder is a contingent remainder.

2) "To A for life, and on A's death to B if B marries C." Here B is an ascertained person, but there is a condition precedent to B's taking: he must marry C. If B marries C in A's lifetime, his remainder will become indefeasibly vested.

3) A conveys "to B for life, then to C and his heirs if C survives B; if C does not survive B, then to D and his heirs." Each remainder is contingent since each is subject to a condition precedent. They are mutually exclusive and exhaustive; *i.e.,* only one can come into possession, and when it does the other can never do so. These are called alternative contingent remainders.

Compare: A conveys "to B for life, then to C and his heirs, but if C marries D, then to E and his heirs." Here C, an ascertained person, takes a vested remainder because it is not limited on a condition precedent. C's remainder is ready to come into possession whenever B dies. But the marriage condition is subsequent—C's marriage to D will forfeit his estate. E's interest is called an executory interest.

2) Unborn or Unascertained Persons

A remainder is contingent if it is created in favor of unborn or unascertained persons ("contingent as to *person*"), because until the remainderman is ascertained, there is no one ready to take possession should the preceding estate come to an end.

Examples: 1) "To A for life, and on A's death, per stirpes to such of A's descendants as survive her." At the time of this disposition, A is in poor health and she has two adult children (B and C) who are very healthy. State of title: A has a life estate; there is a contingent remainder in such of A's descendants as survive A; the transferor has a reversion (for A may not be survived by any descendants).

While the odds are in B and C's favor that they will take the remainder upon A's death, they are not named as the remaindermen. The remainder is in such of A's descendants as survive A, and we will not be able to identify the remaindermen until A dies and we can see which of A's descendants survived her.

2) O transfers securities in trust "to pay the income to A for life, and on A's death to distribute the trust corpus to A's heirs." There is a contingent remainder in A's heirs. It is true that A's heirs will be determined the moment A dies and A's life estate terminates. But at the time O makes the transfer, the remaindermen are not ascertained, for "*nemo est haeres viventis*" (no one is heir of the living). The persons who turn out to be A's heirs will not be ascertained until A dies.

3) Destructibility of Contingent Remainders

At common law, a contingent remainder had to vest prior to or upon termination of the preceding freehold estate or it was destroyed.

Examples: 1) A conveyed "to B for life, and then to the heirs of C." If B predeceased C, there were no heirs of C to take possession so the remainder was destroyed and A or his estate retook possession.

2) A conveyed "to B for life, then to C if she reaches age 21." If B died before C reached 21, the remainder was destroyed. (Note that whenever a grantor created a contingent remainder, he retained a reversion, which was normally defeasible.)

Analysis: Why are the interests in the above examples remainders and not executory interests? In each instance it is possible that the future interest will take effect at the natural expiration of B's life estate (as remainders do), or that it will take effect following a gap after B's estate (as executory interests do). The rule is that if an interest may operate as either a remainder or an executory interest (depending on the circumstances at B's death), it is a remainder. Thus, at common law, if such a remainder was then called upon to act as an executory interest, it could not do so and was destroyed.

a) Rule Abolished

Today, the rule of destructibility has been abolished in all but a few states. Thus, in the two examples given above, on B's death, A's *reversion* would take over, and would then give way to a springing executory interest on C's death in the first example, and on C's attaining age 21 in the second. (Note that the contingent remainders are not destroyed when the preceding estate ends, but instead become executory interests, since they will divest the transferor's estate.)

b) Related Doctrine of Merger

Whenever the same person acquires all of the existing interests in land, present and future, a merger occurs. That person then holds a fee simple absolute. For example, suppose A conveys by deed "to B for life." A now has a reversion. Subsequently, by a later deed, A conveys his reversion interest to B. B will have a fee simple absolute by merger. (A similar result would follow if B conveyed her life estate to A.) What's more, the common law held (as an aspect of the destructibility doctrine) that if a person acquired all of the interests in land *except* a contingent remainder, the merger would occur anyway, and the contingent remainder would be destroyed! Contingent remainders were considered to be such flimsy, ephemeral interests that they would not keep the merger from occurring. Note that this is still the rule in those few states retaining the common law rule of destructibility.

Example: In the first example above (A "to B for life, then to the heirs of C"), title stands as a life estate in B, a contingent remainder in the as yet unascertained heirs of C, and a reversion (if C is still alive at the death of B) in A. If A then purchased B's interest, A would hold an estate pur autre vie (for the life of B) and a reversion. At common law, A's two interests on either side of the contingent remainder *merged*, wiping out the contingent remainder and giving A a fee simple.

(1) Compare—Interests Created Simultaneously

If a life estate and the next vested interest were created simultaneously (by the same instrument), there would be no merger at that time because that would defeat the grantor's obvious intent to create a contingent remainder. However, if the life tenant subsequently conveyed his interest to the holder of the next vested estate, the contingent remainder would then be destroyed.

e. **Rule in Shelley's Case (Rule Against Remainders in Grantee's Heirs)**
At common law, where a freehold estate (usually a life estate) was given to A (by will or inter vivos transfer), and in the same instrument a *remainder was limited to the "heirs" or to the "heirs of the body" of A*, and the freehold estate and the remainder were both legal or both equitable, the purported remainder in the heirs was not recognized, and A took both the freehold estate and the remainder. The Rule operated (regardless of the grantor's intent) to convert what would otherwise have been a contingent remainder in the heirs into a remainder in the ancestor.

Examples: 1) A grants or devises land "to B for life, and then to the heirs of B." Apart from the Rule in Shelley's Case, the title would be: Life estate in B, contingent remainder in fee simple in B's heirs. But by virtue of the Rule, the title is: Life estate in B, vested remainder in B in fee simple. (Here the law of merger causes B's life estate to merge with his remainder so that B gets a present estate in fee simple.)

2) A "to B for life, then to C for life, then to the heirs of B." B has a life estate, and the Rule in Shelley's Case transforms the contingent remainder in the heirs of B into a vested remainder in fee simple in B. But merger does not occur because of the intervening *vested* remainder limited to C.

3) A "to B for life, then to C for life, then to the heirs of C." The Rule in Shelley's Case operates, as does merger, and C has a vested remainder in fee simple.

4) A "to B for life, then one day after B's death to the heirs of B." The Rule in Shelley's Case does not operate because the interest limited to the heirs of B is not a remainder (it can never take over immediately at the termination of the prior freehold estate), but rather is an executory interest.

Compare: O conveys land "to A and his heirs." A takes a fee simple—not by operation of the Rule in Shelley's Case, but because the words "and his heirs" are words of limitation denoting that a fee simple estate has been conveyed. (*See* I.B.1., *supra.*) (It is a common student error to conclude, in this case, that "A takes a fee simple because of the Rule in Shelley's Case." This rule is triggered *only* by the attempted creation of a remainder in the grantee's heirs.)

Note: This Rule has been *abolished in most states today*, but arises occasionally where a conveyance was executed prior to abolition of the Rule.

f. **Doctrine of Worthier Title (Rule Against Remainders in Grantor's Heirs)**
Under the Doctrine of Worthier Title ("DOWT"), a remainder limited to the grantor's heirs is invalid, and the grantor retains a reversion in the property. This doctrine is still applied to inter vivos transfers in a majority of states, but most states treat it only as a rule of construction (*i.e.,* it does not apply if the grantor has clearly manifested an intent to create a future interest in his heirs).

Example: O deeds property "to A for life, and on A's death to my heirs at law," or ". . . and on A's death to my next of kin." In most states, the disposition gives A a life estate and presumptively leaves a reversion in fee simple in O. The burden of establishing that O really intended to create a remainder in his heirs (or next of kin) would be on the parties so contending. The litigation would arise after O's death, and would be between (i) the persons designated as O's heirs under the state's intestacy laws, claiming that they take on A's death by remainder, and (ii) the devisees under O's will, contending that O died owning a reversion.

In a state that has abolished the doctrine, the state of title is: Life estate in A; contingent remainder in O's heirs; reversion in O.

Compare: 1) O deeds property "to A for life, and on A's death to my children in equal shares." On O's death, his children, X and Y, are O's sole heirs. DOWT does not apply. The doctrine applies only when there is a disposition, following a life estate, to the transferor's "***heirs***" or "***next of kin***," or words of like effect.

2) O deeds property "to A for life, and on A's death to the heirs born to my wife Martha and me." DOWT does not apply; the disposition creates a life estate in A and a vested remainder subject to open in the children of O and Martha. Although O used the term "heirs," it is clear from the context that he was not using the term in its technical sense, but was referring to his children by his wife Martha.

3. Executory Interests

Here is a good shorthand rule for classifying executory interests. Remember that there are two and only two future interests that can be created in a transferee: remainders and executory interests. ***If it is not a remainder because the preceding estate is not a life estate, then it must be an executory interest.*** Thus, an executory interest is any future interest in a transferee that does not have the characteristics of a remainder, *i.e.,* it is not capable of taking on the natural termination of the preceding life estate. More specifically, an executory interest is an interest that divests the interest of another.

a. Shifting Executory Interest—Divests a Transferee

A shifting executory interest is one that divests the interest of another transferee; *i.e.,* it cuts short a prior estate created by the same conveyance.

Examples: 1) "To A and her heirs; but if B returns from Canada, then and in that event to B and his heirs." A has a fee simple subject to an executory interest. Since the future interest is created in a transferee, it has to be either a remainder or an executory interest. B's future interest is not a remainder because it does not follow the natural termination of the preceding estate (here, A's fee simple estate). If B's interest does take in present possession, it will divest A's fee simple, and title will *shift* to B.

2) A conveys "to B for life, remainder to C and his heirs, ***but if C predeceases B***, to D and his heirs." D's interest does not await the expiration of C's vested remainder, but instead may cut it short.

b. Springing Executory Interest—"Follows a Gap" or Divests a Transferor

A springing executory interest is an interest that follows a gap in possession or divests the estate of the transferor.

Examples: 1) O conveys property "to A when and if A marries B." State of title: Fee simple subject to an executory interest in O; springing executory interest in fee simple in A. A's interest is not a remainder because if A's future interest becomes a present interest (if A marries B), it will divest O's fee simple. Since it ***divests the estate of a transferor***, it is a springing executory interest.

2) O conveys property "to A for life, and one year after A's death to B." A has a life estate. O has a reversion. B has a springing executory interest in fee simple. B's interest cannot be a remainder because of the one-year gap; it is not capable of taking on the natural termination of the preceding estate (A's life estate). It is therefore an executory interest. It is a springing executory interest because it ***springs out of the transferor's reversion***.

c. Executory Interest Follows a Fee

A ***remainder cannot follow a fee simple interest*** of any kind. Therefore, any interest that follows a fee and is held by a third person is an executory interest.

Examples: 1) O conveys land "to Church for so long as the premises are used for church purposes, and if they shall ever cease to be so used, then and in that event to the American Red Cross." Church has a fee simple determinable subject to an executory interest; the Red Cross has an executory interest that is valid under the charity-to-charity exception to the Rule Against Perpetuities.

2) O conveys "to Church; provided, however, that if the premises shall ever cease to be used for church purposes, then and in that event to the American Red Cross." Church has a fee simple subject to an executory interest; the Red Cross has an executory interest that is valid under the charity-to-charity exception to the Rule Against Perpetuities.

d. Differences Between Executory Interests and Remainders

It is important to be able to distinguish between executory interests and remainders for the following reasons: (i) executory interests are not destructible, while contingent remainders are still destructible in a few jurisdictions; (ii) executory interests are not considered vested, whereas contingent remainders can become vested; (iii) the Rule in Shelley's Case does not apply to executory interests, but it does apply to remainders limited to the heirs of the grantee for life.

4. Importance of Classifying Interests "In Order"

Future interests are classified clause by clause—which will often mean that the label appended to the first future interest created in a disposition will determine the label to be appended to a second future interest created in the same disposition. For instance, if the first future interest is a contingent remainder, subsequent future interests must also be contingent remainders. Similarly, if the first future interest is a vested remainder subject to divestment, the following future interests will be executory interests.

Examples: 1) O conveys land "to A for life, and on A's death to B if B survives A; but if B does not survive A, on A's death to C." A has a life estate. B has a contingent remainder since B's taking is subject to a contingency (expressed in condition precedent form) that B must survive A in order to take. C has an alternate contingent remainder.

Since the contingency of B's survival is expressed both as a condition precedent and (in the next clause) as a condition subsequent, why is B's remainder classified as contingent rather than as vested subject to total divestment? The explanation is that interests are classified "in order." Looking first at the clause giving an interest to B, here the contingency is expressed as a condition precedent; therefore, B's remainder is contingent. Then, having classified B's interest, we turn to C's interest. But since B's interest has already been determined to be a contingent remainder, C's interest is necessarily an alternate contingent remainder.

2) O conveys land "to A for life, and on A's death to B. But if B predeceases A, on A's death to C." Watch this one carefully, for the answer turns on the principle that we classify interests "in order." First of all, A has a life estate. Next we classify B's interest. It is a remainder, for it is capable of taking on the natural termination of the preceding estate (A's life estate). It is a vested remainder in fee simple because B is an ascertained person and there is *no condition precedent* to B's taking other than the termination of A's life estate. Having classified it as a vested remainder, we read on ("but if") and see that B's estate will be defeated if he predeceases A. Therefore, it is a vested remainder subject to total divestment upon the happening of this condition, which is expressed in *condition subsequent* form.

Having classified B's remainder as vested subject to total divestment, we turn to C's interest. It cannot be a remainder, for a remainder follows the natural termination of the preceding estate—B's estate, which is a vested remainder in fee simple. But *no remainder can follow a fee simple*, for a fee simple is an estate of potentially infinite duration. If C does take, it will cut short B's vested remainder in fee simple some time short of infinity. Therefore, C's interest is an executory interest—a *shifting executory interest*, since it divests a transferee.

But isn't C's interest capable of taking on the natural termination of A's life estate (if B predeceases A)? Yes, but that does not affect our classification. A remainder is a future interest capable of taking on the termination of the *preceding* estate, and here the preceding estate is B's.

Suppose, some years after this disposition, B dies during A's lifetime. What is the state of title? The answer: Life estate in A, indefeasibly vested *remainder* in C. Now that B's estate is out of the way, the preceding estate is A's life estate, and so now we can change the label and call C's interest a remainder.

5.   **Transferability of Remainders and Executory Interests**

a.   **Vested Remainders Are Transferable, Devisable, and Descendible**
At common law and in all jurisdictions today, vested remainders are fully transferable during life, devisable by will, and descendible by inheritance. This is true of all types of vested remainders: indefeasibly vested, vested subject to open, and vested subject to total divestment.

b.   **Contingent Remainders and Executory Interests Are Transferable Inter Vivos**
At common law, contingent remainders and executory interests were not assignable. While this is still the rule in a few states, most American courts hold that these interests are freely transferable.

c.   **Contingent Remainders and Executory Interests Are Usually Devisable and Descendible**
Whereas the rule at common law was that contingent remainders and executory interests were not transferable inter vivos, it has always been held that these interests are devisable and descendible—*unless,* of course, the holder's *survival is a condition* to the interest's taking.
Example: "To A for life, and on A's death to B; but if B does not survive A, on A's death to C." State of title: Life estate in A, vested remainder subject to total divestment in B, and shifting executory interest in C. Suppose B dies in A's lifetime, leaving a will that devises "all my property" to Mrs. B. B's remainder interest does not pass under his will because, by the terms of the disposition, that interest failed when B died in A's lifetime.

d.   **Any Transferable Future Interest Is Reachable by Creditors**
The rule followed in nearly all states is this: If a future interest can, under the laws of the state, be transferred voluntarily by its owner, it is also subject to involuntary transfer; that is, it can be reached by the owner's creditors by appropriate process.

e.   **Practical Ability to Transfer Marketable Title**
Technically, most states consider all types of future interests transferable, but in practice those interests held by unborn or unascertained persons are not transferable because courts will not appoint a guardian for purposes of conveying land. (*See* VI.A.3.a.1)b), *infra.*)

6.   **Class Gifts**
A "class" is a group of persons having a common characteristic. Typically, they stand in the same relation to each other or to some other person (*e.g.,* children, grandchildren, descendants, nephews and nieces, etc.). In a gift to a class, the share of each member of the class is determined by the number of persons in the class.

a.   **Definitional Problems**

1)   **Dispositions to "Children"**
A gift to a person's "children" generally includes that person's children from all marriages as well as adopted children. That person's stepchildren, grandchildren, and nonmarital children are generally not included in the class.

2)   **Dispositions to "Heirs"**
A disposition to the "heirs" of someone presumptively includes those persons who would take the named person's estate according to the laws of descent and distribution if she were to die without a will.

3)   **Dispositions to "Issue" or "Descendants"**
The terms "issue" and "descendants" refer to the lineal offspring of the designated person, whatever the degree of relationship (children, grandchildren, great-grandchildren, etc.). As a general principle, the issue or descendants take per stirpes.

4)   **Class Members in Gestation**
Persons in gestation at the time set for distribution are included in a class. The common law presumption is that a child born within 10 lunar months or 280 calendar days after the necessary point in time was in gestation at that time.

b. **When the Class Closes—The Rule of Convenience**
When a gift is made to a group of persons generically described as a class, such as to someone's "children," there is the possibility that other persons may be born who meet the class description. This raises the question, when does the class "close"? That is, when is the maximum membership of the class determined, such that persons born thereafter are excluded from sharing in the gift? In resolving this problem, the common law courts developed the rule of convenience. This is a rule of construction, not a rule of law. It is applicable in the absence of an expression of intent to include all persons who meet the class description regardless of when they are born. Under the rule, a *class closes when some member of the class can call for a distribution of her share of the class gift*. It is presumed that the ordinary transferor intends to include all members of the class, whenever born, *provided* that this would *not cause any undue inconvenience*. Thus, the rule of convenience is based on a policy of including as many persons in the class as possible, consistent with permitting a distribution of the property at the first opportunity without the necessity of a future rebate.

1) **Outright Gift—Class Closes at Time Gift Is Made**
When a *will* makes an outright gift to a class, if any class members are alive at the testator's death, the class closes as of the *date of the testator's death.*
Example: T's will devises property "to the children of my good friend, John Brown." John has three children (A, B, and C) at the time of T's death; another child (D) is born two years later. The class closes at T's death; A, B, and C share the gift. D is excluded by the rule of convenience.

Here, additional members of the class are included up to the time of T's death because there is no inconvenience in doing so. But we close the class at T's death because it is assumed that T would want an immediate distribution, rather than postponing distribution until John Brown's death, which is the only time we will be sure that John Brown will have no more children. If we were to include D, we would also have to include E, F, and G, who might be born later. Moreover, if we distributed one-third shares to A, B, and C at T's death, but required them to make rebates if more children should be born later to their father, John, all sorts of practical problems would arise. To avoid these problems, there is a strong constructional preference to close the class at T's death.

a) **No Class Members Alive at Testator's Death—Class Stays Open**
If there are no members of the class living at the testator's death, all after-born persons who come within the class designation are included. Thus, if T had bequeathed $100,000 "to the children of John," and John had no children living at T's death or born within the period of gestation thereafter, then all John's children, whenever born, are included, regardless of any possible inconvenience in keeping the class open this long.

2) **Postponed Gift—Class Closes at Time Fixed for Distribution**
When possession and enjoyment of a gift are postponed, as where the gift follows a life estate, the class remains open until the time fixed for distribution (*e.g.,* death of life tenant).
Example: T's will creates a trust to pay the income to W for life, and on W's death to pay the principal to the children of John. At the time T executes his will John has two children (A and B). After the will is executed but before T dies, another child (C) is born to John. After T's death but during W's lifetime, another child (D) is born to John. W dies; two years later John has another child (E).

The class closes at W's death; A, B, C, and D each take a one-fourth share. E is excluded by the rule of convenience. There was no inconvenience in leaving the class open until W's death, for the time had not yet come to distribute the corpus. But when W dies, it is time to make a distribution; the class is closed in order to determine the minimum shares going to each class member.

3) Dispositions Subject to Condition of Reaching Given Age

When there is a gift to a class conditioned upon the members attaining a certain age, the class closes when (i) the preceding estate, if any, terminates, and (ii) the first class member reaches the specified age. That class member's minimum share should be determined and distributed to her when she reaches the specified age.

Examples: 1) T's will devises his residuary estate "to the children of John who live to attain the age of 21." At T's death, John has three children: A (age 22), B (age 16), and C (age 10). The class closes at T's death. A is entitled to immediate distribution of her share, and the minimum size of that share must be fixed as of T's death, at one-third. If B lives to attain age 21, but C dies before attaining that age, on C's death, A and B's shares will be increased to one-half.

Two years after T's death, another child (D) is born to John. D is excluded by the rule of convenience. The class was closed at T's death in order to determine the minimum size of A's share so that this share could be distributed to her.

Suppose none of John's children is 21 at T's death. The class remains open until a child of John reaches the designated age, at which time the class closes.

2) T's will devises his residuary estate "to Wanda for life, and on Wanda's death to such of John's children as live to attain the age of 21." Here the class will close, and the remaindermen who share in the disposition will be determined, when two things occur: (i) Wanda dies; **and** (ii) a child of John reaches age 21. If at T's death one of John's children is over age 21, it does not matter; the class remains open until Wanda's life estate terminates. Likewise, if at Wanda's death no child of John has attained age 21, the class remains open until one of John's children reaches that age. If at Wanda's death a child has attained age 21, the class will close at that time.

4) Rule of Convenience Is a Rule of Construction Only

The rule of convenience is a rule of construction only. If the transferor explicitly sets forth the time when membership of the class is to be determined, or if he provides that all members of the class, whenever born, are to share in the gift, then his directions will govern. However, courts have a strong preference for application of the rule of convenience unless there is a fairly clear indication that it is not to govern.

7. Survival

As a general rule, all future interests can pass at death by will or inheritance; *i.e.,* they are descendible and devisable. This is true **unless** the interest's taking is subject to an expressed or implied contingency of survival.

Examples: 1) "To my sister Sue for life, and on Sue's death to her children in equal shares." At the time of T's death, Sue has three children: A, B, and C. C dies, then Sue dies survived by A and B. The remainder is shared by A, B, and the estate of C (*i.e.,* the estate takes under C's will or by intestacy), each with one-third shares. *Analysis:* A, B, and C had vested remainders subject to open, but their interests were not in terms conditioned on surviving the life beneficiary—and the law does not imply such a condition of survival. On C's death his vested remainder subject to open passes via his will or by intestacy. (*Note:* This example does **not** invoke the lapsed gift doctrine of Wills law, for C was alive at the testator's death.)

2) "To A for life, and on A's death to B if B is then living; but if B is not then living, to C." C dies, then B dies, then A dies. Who takes? Answer: The takers under C's will or by intestacy. B and C were given alternative contingent remainders. B's remainder was contingent on his surviving A, and B did not meet the condition; his estate was defeated. C's remainder was contingent on B's not surviving A; it was not in terms contingent on C's surviving A, and the law does not imply such a condition.

a. Express Words of Survival

In each of the following examples, the italicized language imposes a condition precedent that the remaindermen must survive the life tenant in order to take.

Examples: 1) "To A for life, remainder to his ***surviving children.***"

2) "To A for life, and should he ***die leaving children,*** to such children."

3) "To A for life, and after the death of A, remainder to the children of A ***then living.***"

b. Implied Contingency of Survival—Gifts to "Issue," "Descendants," or "Heirs"

Gifts to a person's "issue," "descendants," or "heirs" imply a condition of surviving the named ancestor.

D. TRUSTS

An express trust involves the holding of title to property by a trustee, who has an equitable fiduciary duty to deal with it for the benefit of other persons (the beneficiaries).

1. Private Trust Concepts and Parties

a. Settlor

The settlor is the person who ***creates the trust*** by manifesting an intent to do so. While a trust of personal property may be expressed orally, the Statute of Frauds requires a writing to create a trust of real property. The settlor must own the property at the time the trust is created and must intend to make the trust effective immediately.

b. Trustee

The trustee ***holds legal title to the property***, but must act under the instructions of the settlor who created the trust. The trustee has a fiduciary duty to use the highest care and skill for the beneficiaries. If the trustee has no duties at all, the trust will fail, and legal title will vest immediately in the beneficiaries. However, if the trustee dies, resigns, or refuses to serve, the trust will not fail; a court of equity will appoint a substitute trustee.

c. Beneficiaries

The beneficiaries are the ***persons for whose benefit the trust is created and held***; they hold equitable title to the property. Every private trust must have at least one beneficiary, and the beneficiaries must be definitely identifiable by the time their interest comes into enjoyment and, in all events, within the period of the Rule Against Perpetuities. Acceptance of the benefits of the trust is normally presumed, but a beneficiary may renounce his rights under the trust within a reasonable time after learning of its creation. A trust may be for a class of beneficiaries (*e.g.*, all the living descendants of Mary Jones), provided that the class is small enough to be "reasonably definite."

d. Res

The res is ***the property that is the subject of the trust***. If there is no res, the trust fails. The res may be real property or personal property (tangible or intangible), and it may be either a present interest or a future interest (vested or contingent). The trust res must be segregated from other property of the settlor, but this does not preclude a trust of a fractional share interest, such as a trust of "an undivided one-half interest in Blackacre," where the settlor owns all of Blackacre.

e. Application of Rule Against Perpetuities

The Rule Against Perpetuities (*see* E., *infra*) applies to the equitable future interests of the beneficiaries in a private trust just as it does to "legal" future interests.

Example: O conveys land to T "in trust for the benefit of A so long as the existing house on the land remains standing, and then for the benefit of the then-living descendants of A." The equitable interest of the descendants of A is void because it is not certain to vest or fail within 21 years after the life of any person living at the time the trust is created.

2. Creation of Trusts

a. Inter Vivos Conveyance

An inter vivos trust can be created by the settlor's conveyance of the trust res to the trustee while the settlor is alive. For real property, this must be done by a writing to satisfy the Statute of Frauds; this is usually accomplished by delivery of a deed.

b. Inter Vivos Declaration

The settlor may declare that he is now holding certain property (previously held outright by the settlor) in trust for certain beneficiaries. No deed or delivery is necessary, but if the res is real property, the declaration must be in writing and signed by the settlor.

c. Testamentary Conveyance

The settlor may create the trust by language in his will, and may also transfer the res to the trustee by a devise in the will. The trust will come into existence only upon the death of the settlor.

d. Pour-Over into Existing Trust

The settlor may create an inter vivos trust before death. The settlor's will may then bequeath property to the trust—"pouring it over" into the trust.

3. Charitable Trusts

a. Beneficiaries

A charitable trust, unlike the private trusts described above, must have an ***indefinite*** group of beneficiaries. The beneficiaries must be reasonably numerous and not individually identified. The trust may be for the benefit of an established charity (*e.g.*, the American Red Cross) or for a group of persons (*e.g.*, the victims of Hurricane Andrew).

b. Application of Rule Against Perpetuities

The Rule Against Perpetuities does not apply to trusts that are ***entirely charitable***. Such trusts may have infinite life. This is true even if the trust benefits two charities, one with a present interest and the other with a future interest that would normally violate the Rule Against Perpetuities. Note, however, that if either the first or second interest is noncharitable, the exemption from the Rule Against Perpetuities does not apply and the second gift is void.

Examples: 1) O conveys land to T in trust "for the benefit of the victims of Hurricane Andrew, and when all houses destroyed by the hurricane have been rebuilt, then for the benefit of the American Red Cross." The interest of the Red Cross may not vest until more than 21 years after the death of any person living when the trust is created, but it is still a valid interest.

2) O conveys land to T in trust "for the benefit of my son John, whose house was destroyed by Hurricane Andrew, and when his house has been rebuilt, then for the benefit of the American Red Cross." The interest of the Red Cross may not vest until more than 21 years after the death of any person living when the trust is created, and it is void.

c. Cy Pres Doctrine

If the purposes of a charitable trust are impossible to fulfill, are illegal, or have been completely fulfilled, a court may redirect the trust to a different purpose that is "as near as may be" (a translation of the Latin "cy pres") to the settlor's original intent.

d. Enforcement of Charitable Trusts

Neither the settlor nor the beneficiaries may bring an action to enforce a charitable trust. (This is contrary to the rule for private trusts, in which either party may bring such an action.) However, charitable trusts may be enforced by an action of the attorney general of the state.

E. THE RULE AGAINST PERPETUITIES

The Rule Against Perpetuities may be stated as follows: "No interest in property is valid unless it must vest, if at all, not later than 21 years after one or more lives in being at the creation of the interest." The Rule might be more easily understood if it had been expressed as an affirmative proposition: "An interest is void if there is any possibility, however remote, that the interest may vest more than 21 years after some life in being at the creation of the interest." This paraphrase of the Rule properly places the emphasis on the ***possibility*** of remote vesting, the test by which the invalidity of an interest is shown. If a situation can be imagined in which the interest might not vest within the perpetuities period, the interest is void. This is the result even though the circumstances that might bring about the remote vesting are unlikely to occur or are unrealistic. (All kinds of unlikely things are considered capable of happening under the Rule.) The Rule applies to the following legal and equitable future interests in personal or real property:

(i) Contingent remainders;

(ii) Executory interests;

(iii) Class gifts (even if vested remainders);

(iv) Options and rights of first refusal; and

(v) Powers of appointment.

1. Analysis of the Rule

a. When the Perpetuities Period Begins to Run
The validity of interests under the Rule is determined ***at the time the interests are created,*** taking into account the facts then existing. The "lives in being plus 21 years" period begins to run, and the measuring lives used to show the validity of an interest must be in existence, at that time.

1) Wills—Date of Testator's Death
The perpetuities period in the case of a will begins to run on the date of the testator's death.

2) Revocable Trusts—Date Trust Becomes Irrevocable
In the case of revocable trusts, the perpetuities period begins to run on the date the trust becomes irrevocable. This will be at the settlor's death unless the settlor amends the trust, making it irrevocable, during his lifetime.

3) Irrevocable Trusts—Date Trust Is Created
The perpetuities period for irrevocable trusts begins to run on the date the trust is created.

4) Deeds—Date Deed Is Delivered with Intent to Pass Title
In the case of a deed, the perpetuities period begins to run on the date the deed is delivered with the intent to pass title.

b. "Must Vest"
To be valid under the Rule, it must be shown that the interest created in the transferee must vest, regardless of what might happen, within lives in being plus 21 years. An interest becomes "vested" for purposes of the Rule when: (i) it becomes a present possessory estate; or (ii) it becomes an indefeasibly vested remainder or a vested remainder subject to total divestment. Remember that the Rule is applicable only to future interests created in third persons; consequently, the Rule generally applies only to contingent remainders, executory interests, and vested remainders subject to open.

Examples: 1) "To A for life, then to A's children for their lives, and on the death of the last survivor of A's children, to B in fee simple." At the time of this disposition A has two very young children and is quite capable of having more children in the future. (i) A has a present possessory life estate. A's present children have vested remainders in life estates that are subject to open in favor of any future children born to A. There is a contingent remainder in a life estate in A's unborn children—but this interest is valid under the Rule because the children's life estates will vest at their birth, which will be in A's lifetime. B has an indefeasibly vested remainder in fee simple. (ii) B's interest is valid under the Rule even though it may be years before B (or her successors) is entitled to present possession and enjoyment of the property, and even though B (or her successors) may not succeed to present possession and enjoyment until the death of some person not now in being (*i.e.,* a future-born child of A may be the last survivor of A's children). Despite all this, B's interest is valid under the Rule because it is an ***indefeasibly vested remainder from the time of its creation.***

2) "To A for life, then to B; but if at B's death she is not survived by children, then in that event to C." (i) A has a present possessory life estate. B has a vested remainder subject to total divestment in fee simple. C has a shifting executory interest in fee simple. (ii) C's interest is valid under the Rule. B's is the relevant life that can be used to show

that C's interest will vest within the perpetuities period. If B dies in A's lifetime not survived by children, C's interest will become an indefeasibly vested remainder. If B survives A and thereafter dies not survived by children, C's executory interest will become a present possessory estate. Of course, B may die in A's lifetime (or after A's death) leaving children surviving her, in which case C's interest is extinguished. But that does not matter; the Rule requires that an interest must vest, *if it does vest* ("if at all"), within lives in being plus 21 years.

3) "To A for life, and on her death to such of her children as attain the age of 35." At the time this disposition takes effect, A is a 60-year-old woman who has had a hysterectomy. She has two children, ages 30 and 25. Under the common law Rule, here is what might happen: A *might* give birth to a child (defying medical science in the process). Then A's other two children might die before attaining age 35; then A might die before the afterborn attained his 14th birthday. (Key: 35 minus 21 is 14.) The afterborn child lives on to attain age 35. If these events were to occur, the remainder to such of A's children as attain age 35 would vest remotely. Since these events *might* occur, the remainder violates the Rule; it is stricken.

c.   **"If at All"**
This simply means that the interest does not have to vest within the perpetuities period in order to be valid; after all, many contingent remainders never vest because the condition precedent to their taking is not satisfied.
Examples: 1) "To A for life, and on A's death to B if B is then living." A has a life estate, B has a contingent remainder, and the transferor has a reversion. B may never take, for she may predecease A. But if B does take ("if at all"), her interest will vest—here, will become a possessory estate—on A's death, when we will know whether B has survived A. In this case, B is "her own life in being," for the condition precedent to B's taking must occur, if it does occur, within B's lifetime. B's interest is valid under the Rule.

2) "To A in fee, but on the express condition that if marijuana is ever smoked on the premises during B's lifetime or within 21 years after B's death, then and in that event to B in fee." A has a fee simple subject to an executory interest; B has an executory interest in fee simple. B's interest might not take, for marijuana might not be smoked on the premises during B's lifetime or within 21 years thereafter. But if B's interest does take, by the terms of the disposition it must take during B's lifetime or within 21 years thereafter. B's interest is valid under the Rule.

d.   **"Lives in Being"**
The law allows any lives to be used to show the validity or invalidity of an interest, but no lives are of any help unless they are somehow connected with the vesting of an interest. The measuring lives need not be given a beneficial interest in the property, and they need not even be expressly referred to in the instrument, but there must be some connection that insures vesting or failure of the interest within the perpetuities period.
Examples: 1) "To A for life, then to such of A's children as attain the age of 21." Here the relevant measuring life is A. All of A's children are going to attain age 21, *if at all,* within 21 years after A's death. (This includes a child in the mother's womb at A's death, for the perpetuities period includes any period of gestation actually involved.)

2) Outright disposition of residue by will, "to such of my nephews and nieces as attain the age of 21." At the time of T's death she has two brothers and six nephews and nieces, all of whom are under age 21. Is the gift valid under the Rule? The answer: It depends. Specifically, it depends on whether T's parents are living. The *relevant measuring lives* are T's brothers and sisters, because all of T's nephews and nieces will attain 21, if at all, within 21 years after their parents' deaths. If T's parents are dead, her two brothers are all the brothers she is ever going

to have; and T's nephews and nieces will be the children of these brothers. The disposition is valid.

But if T's parents are alive, they *might* have another child (call him Excelsior), a brother or sister of T not alive at T's death. Then T's two brothers and six nephews and nieces who were alive at T's death might die. Then Excelsior might have a child who lives to attain age 21—more than 21 years after any life in being. Since this might happen, the disposition is invalid under the Rule.

1) Who Can Be Used as Measuring Lives

In all the examples in this chapter, the measuring lives used to show the validity or invalidity of interests are referred to or are indirectly involved in the disposition itself. It is a common drafting practice to use a *"perpetuities saving clause"* (i) to make sure that the Rule has not been accidentally violated, for the Rule is difficult to master; and (ii) sometimes to extend the duration of trusts to the maximum extent permitted under the Rule. The clause reads something like this: "Notwithstanding anything herein to the contrary, any trust created hereunder shall terminate, if it has not previously terminated, 21 years after the death of the survivor of the following named persons: _____; and the remaining principal and undistributed income of such trusts shall be distributed to. . . ."

In the blanks are inserted the names of the persons to be used as "artificial" measuring lives. Most commonly, the descendants then living of the transferor are specifically named. Alternatively, the clause might provide: "after the death of the survivor of all my descendants who shall be living at the time of my death"—this clause works in a will but does not work in an irrevocable trust. A few more aggressive draftsmen will name 10 healthy babies born in some local hospital on the day the instrument is executed—the probability is that this will permit the trust to run for 100 years.

2) Reasonable Number of Human Lives Can Be Used

Animals and organizations cannot be used as measuring lives; only humans can be used as measuring lives. Also, the number of measuring lives must be reasonable.

Examples: 1) "The trust will terminate 21 years after the death of the survivor of all persons listed in the Manhattan telephone directory." Clearly impermissible.

2) "The trust will terminate 21 years after the death of the survivor of all the descendants of Queen Victoria who are alive at the time of my death." This "royal lives" clause was widely used in England shortly after the turn of the century, and the English courts grudgingly sustained it. If the name of some currently famous person were used in this fashion, it is highly questionable whether American courts would sustain the disposition.

e. Interests Exempt from Rule

1) Gift Over to Second Charity

A charitable trust may last forever (*i.e.,* neither the Rule Against Perpetuities nor any analogous rule applies). However, like any other gift, a gift for charitable purposes is void for remoteness if it is contingent upon the happening of an event that may not occur within the perpetuity period. The only exception to this rule is that if there is a gift to Charity A, followed by a gift over to Charity B upon a possibly remote event, the gift over is valid. Remember, this is the charity-to-charity exception. The Rule Against Perpetuities applies to dispositions over from a *charity to an individual* on a remote condition, *and* to dispositions over from an *individual to a charity* on a remote condition.

Examples: 1) "To the Georgetown YMCA for so long as the premises are used for YMCA purposes; and when they shall cease to be so used, then and in that event to the American Cancer Society." The YMCA has a fee simple subject to an executory interest; the Cancer Society has a shifting executory interest. The gift over to the Cancer Society is valid under the charity-to-charity exception to the Rule.

2) "To the Georgetown YMCA for so long as the premises are used for YMCA purposes; and when they shall cease to be so used, then and in that event to John Hancock, his heirs, successors and assigns." Classifying the interests without regard to the Rule, the YMCA would have a fee simple subject to an executory interest; John Hancock would have a shifting executory interest—which is stricken because it violates the Rule. The YMCA has a fee simple determinable, and the transferor has a possibility of reverter.

3) "To John Hancock, his heirs, successors and assigns, provided that no marijuana is ever smoked on the premises; and if marijuana is ever smoked on the premises, to the Georgetown YMCA." Classifying interests without regard to the Rule, Hancock would have a fee simple subject to an executory interest; the YMCA would have a shifting executory interest—which is stricken because it violates the Rule; thus Hancock has a fee simple absolute.

2) Vested Interests

A vested remainder in an individual is not subject to the Rule. Thus, a devise "to A for life, then to A's children for life, then to B in fee simple" is wholly valid. B has a presently vested remainder. It may vest in *possession* long after lives in being if A leaves some surviving children born after the testator's death, but the remainder to B is presently vested in interest, and that is what counts.

a) Compare—Class Gifts Are Subject to Rule

Vested remainders in a class, however, are subject to the Rule *so long as the class remains open*.

3) Reversionary Interests

Reversions, possibilities of reverter, and rights of entry are all vested in interest and hence are not subject to the Rule Against Perpetuities. (Even so, in many states, there are statutes expressly limiting the duration of possibilities of reverter or rights of entry.)

a) Compare—Executory Interests Are Subject to Rule

Possibilities of reverter and rights of entry, which are exempt from the Rule, must be carefully distinguished from executory interests, which are subject to the Rule. Remember that executory interests are created in *transferees*; possibilities of reverter and rights of entry are created only in the *grantor* (or the *testator's heirs* if a will is involved). An understanding of this distinction has frequently been tested by the bar examiners.

Example: O conveys Blackacre "to School so long as it is used for educational purposes, and when it is no longer so used, to A." A has an executory interest that violates the Rule because it may vest in possession many years after all lives in being are dead. Since any interest that violates the Rule is void and is stricken from the instrument, this leaves a determinable fee in the school and a possibility of reverter in O. O can now, by a second deed, transfer her possibility of reverter to A (if possibilities of reverter have been made transferable by statute in the jurisdiction). To get a possibility of reverter in A, two pieces of paper are required: one creating the possibility of reverter in O; the second transferring it to A.

f. Consequence of Violating the Rule—Interest Is Stricken

An interest that violates the Rule is void and is stricken (subject to the possible application of a perpetuities reform statute). However, all other interests created in the instrument of transfer that are valid under the Rule are given effect.

1) Exception—"Infectious Invalidity"

There is an important exception to the preceding statement. Under the principle of "infectious invalidity," if the invalid gift is an essential part of the transferor's dispositive scheme, such that to strike this interest and give effect to the remaining interests would be to subvert the transferor's intent—if it is determined that the transferor would prefer that the entire disposition fail—then the entire disposition is void.

2.   The Rule in Operation—Common Pitfall Cases

a.   Executory Interest Following Defeasible Fee Violates the Rule

An executory interest that follows a defeasible fee, with no limit on the time within which it must vest, violates the Rule Against Perpetuities and is stricken. The effect on the remaining fee estate depends on whether the estate is determinable or subject to a condition subsequent. If the defeasible fee is phrased in durational terms (*e.g.,* "for so long as," "until"), the estate will still terminate upon the happening of the stated event and the grantor will have a possibility of reverter. In contrast, if the fee is subject to a condition subsequent, the condition is also stricken and the estate becomes a fee simple absolute.

Examples: 1) "To John Brown for so long as no marijuana is smoked on the premises; and if marijuana is ever smoked on the premises, then to Candy Barr." (i) John Brown has a fee simple subject to an executory interest; Candy Barr has an executory interest in fee simple. (ii) Candy's interest violates the Rule. Things may stay quiet for generations, long beyond 21 years after the deaths of John and Candy (the only relevant lives in this case). Then someone might light up, triggering the executory interest. Since this *might* happen, the executory interest might vest (*i.e.,* might become a possessory estate) long after lives in being plus 21 years. Candy's interest violates the Rule, and it is stricken. This leaves a fee simple determinable in John Brown, and a possibility of reverter in the transferor. The possibility of reverter is valid; retained interests in the transferor are not subject to the Rule.

What if marijuana is smoked on the premises within five years after the transfer, well within lives in being plus 21 years, meaning that in actuality there was no remote vesting? It does not matter. Under the Rule we do not "wait and see." It is *what might happen* that counts, viewing the facts as they exist *at the time the interest is created.* What actually happens is irrelevant.

2) "To John Brown; provided, however, that if marijuana is ever smoked on the premises, then to Candy Barr." (i) John Brown has a fee simple subject to an executory interest; Candy Barr has an executory interest in fee simple. (ii) Candy's interest violates the Rule, under the analysis given in Example 1). Again we strike Candy's interest—leaving John Brown with a fee simple absolute. (Contrast this with the result in Example 1), where the transferor had a possibility of reverter. This is the result of two different forms of expressing the gift to John Brown. Whenever a fee simple determinable is created ("so long as"), the transferor automatically has a possibility of reverter. But when a fee on a condition subsequent is created, the transferor does not have a right of entry unless the right of entry is expressly raised.)

b.   Age Contingency Beyond Age Twenty-One in Open Class

A gift to an open class conditioned upon the members surviving to an age beyond 21 violates the Rule Against Perpetuities.

Example: "To A for life, then to such of A's children as live to attain the age of 25." At the time of this disposition, A has two children: X (age 12) and Y (age nine). (i) A has a life estate; there is a contingent remainder in A's children who live to attain age 25, and a reversion in the transferor (for none of A's children may ever reach age 25). (ii) The remainder to A's children violates the Rule. After this transfer, A *might have another child* (Z); before this afterborn child (who cannot be used as a life in being) attains age four, A, X, and Y might die; then Z might live on to age 25, at which time the remainder to A's children would vest in Z. But if this were to happen (and it might), the remainder would vest beyond lives in being plus 21 years. Since the interest might vest remotely, it is stricken.

c.   The Fertile Octogenarian

A woman is *conclusively presumed* to be capable of bearing children regardless of her age or medical condition.

Example: Suppose, in the preceding example, X and Y were age 24 and 22, respectively, and A was a 60-year-old woman who has undergone a hysterectomy. Under the "remote possibilities" test, it is *possible* for a woman, of whatever age and medical condition, to bear children. Thus, A might have another child, Z. The remainder to A's children violates the Rule.

d. The Unborn Widow or Widower

The problem is that the term "widow" (and "widower"), like "heir," is a technical word with a technical meaning: You do not know who a person's widow (or widower) is until he dies and you can determine to whom he was married at his death.

Example: "To A for life, then to his widow for life; and on the death of A's widow, to such of A's descendants as are then living." (i) A has a life estate; there is a contingent remainder in a life estate in his widow; there is a contingent remainder in fee simple in A's descendants; and the transferor has a reversion. (ii) The remainder in the descendants violates the Rule. Although A is now happily married, he might divorce his wife (or she might die), and A might marry someone who was not alive at the time the interest was created. A might have a child by this widow; then everyone now on the scene might die; the *widow might live for more than 21 years after the death of all lives in being,* then die—leaving the afterborn child or children as "A's descendants then living."

e. The Administrative Contingency

A gift that is conditioned on an administrative contingency (*e.g.,* admission to probate) violates the Rule. The key question is "under the facts as they existed at the time of the gift, what might happen?"

Example: Disposition of residuary estate "per stirpes to such of my descendants as are living at the time my will is admitted to probate." Alternatively, a will of a German national written during World War II: "to such of my relations in Germany as are living at the time World War II is officially declared at an end." Under the "what might happen" approach of the common law Rule, wills are not probated, wars do not come to an end, decrees of distribution are never entered, etc. Moreover, since no person's lifetime is connected to the condition attached to this type of gift, we cannot use a life in being; we must use the "period in gross" of 21 years. And since the will "might not" be probated within 21 years, the gift is void.

The fact that the testator's will is in fact probated three weeks after her death does not matter. We do not wait and see. Rather, looking from the time of the testator's death, and taking into account facts as they existed at that time, the question is what might happen.

f. Options and Rights of First Refusal

The right of a purchaser under an option or a right of first refusal (*see* F.4.e., *infra*) is treated as a contingent future interest (*e.g.,* an executory interest). If the option is structured so that it *might* be exercised later than the end of the Rule's period, it is usually held void.

Example: A is a subdivision developer and gives B an option to purchase a lot in the subdivision "to be exercised within 60 days after the City Council grants approval for the filing of a subdivision plat." While the parties may expect this to occur soon, it is *possible* that it will not occur within 21 years after any life in being at the creation of the option. Hence, the option may be held void.

1) Reasonable Time Limit May Be Inferred

A significant minority of courts, in applying the Rule to these interests, will construe the option as lasting only for a reasonable time, which is invariably less than 21 years, and thus will uphold it. Under this view, the option in the example above would be sustained on the ground that the parties intended it to expire if the City Council failed to act within a reasonable time, less than 21 years. Similarly, if the parties to the option are natural persons, some courts construe the option as lasting only for their lifetimes; hence, it is valid under the Rule.

2) Options Connected to Leaseholds

If a tenant under a lease has an option to purchase the leased premises during the lease term, the Rule is not applied, no matter how long the term. However, a tenant may attempt to transfer the option to some other party, thereby separating it from the leasehold estate. While some courts do not permit the option to be transferred separately, most courts hold that the transferability of the option depends on the original parties' intent when they entered into the lease and option agreement. If the court finds that the option has been separated from the leasehold estate, so that it is no longer exercisable by the tenant, the option becomes subject to the Rule Against Perpetuities.

3. Application of the Rule to Class Gifts

a. "Bad-as-to-One, Bad-as-to-All" Rule

The general principle that the Rule does not invalidate interests that "vest" within the perpetuities period *does not apply to vested remainders subject to open.* The class gift rule, sometimes called the "all-or-nothing" rule, requires that:

(i) The class must close within the perpetuities period; and

(ii) All conditions precedent for *every* member of the class must be satisfied, if at all, within the perpetuities period.

If it is possible that a disposition might vest remotely with respect to any member of the class, the *entire class gift is invalid.*

Examples: 1) "To A for life, then to such of A's children as live to attain the age of 35." At the time of this disposition, A has two children: X (age 38) and Y (age 33). (i) A has a life estate. X has a vested remainder subject to open. There is a contingent remainder in such of A's other children as live to attain the age of 35. (ii) The remainder to A's children violates the Rule; the transferor has a reversion in fee. While X's remainder is vested subject to open, it is not vested for purposes of the Rule. Here is what might happen: A might have another child (Z); before Z attains age 14, A, X, and Y might die, etc. The *gift with respect to any afterborn child of A clearly violates the Rule;* under the "bad-as-to-one, bad-as-to-all" class gift rule, *the entire class gift is void*.

Why does the "class closing" rule not save the gift? Since X is already age 35, doesn't this mean that the class will close on the life tenant's death? The answer is: yes it does, but this does not help. Although we will close the class at that point, the class as closed might include the afterborn Z, who might be under age 14 at that time; and it still might be more than lives in being plus 21 years before Z's interest might vest.

2) "To A for life, then to A's children for their lives, and on the death of the last survivor of A's children, to A's grandchildren in fee." At the time this disposition takes effect, A is alive and has two children and three grandchildren. A has a life estate, the two children have vested remainders subject to open in a life estate, and the three grandchildren have vested remainders subject to open in fee. The remainder to A's grandchildren is void because every member of the class will not be ascertained until the death of the survivor of A's children; and that surviving child might be born to A after the date of this disposition. Then all of A's children and grandchildren who are lives in being might die and 21 years after their deaths, this afterborn child might give birth to a child (GC-4); although GC-4's interest would vest at birth, under the hypothesized facts it would vest remotely.

b. Class Closing Rules May Save Disposition

In some cases the "rule of convenience" applicable to class gifts can be relied on to save a gift from the Rule.

Example: "To A for life, and on her death to A's grandchildren in fee." At the time of this disposition, A has two children and three grandchildren. A has a life estate and the grandchildren have vested remainders subject to open. As in the preceding example, A might have an afterborn child who might produce afterborn grandchildren—but there is one difference. Under the "rule of convenience" the *class will be closed at the time any member of the class can demand a distribution*—here the death of A, a life in being. Consequently, all members of the class who will be permitted to share in the remainder will be determined on A's death.

c. "Gift to Subclass" Exception

Separate gifts vest at different times. Each gift to a subclass may be treated as a separate gift under the Rule.

Example: "To pay the income to A for life, then to A's children for their lives, and as each child of A dies, to distribute the corpus to such child's issue then living, per stirpes." A has two children at the time of this disposition. In this case, the remainder to issue has been made by a gift to subclasses; as each child dies his issue are to take the share on which he was receiving income. With respect to A's two children now alive, the class of "issue then living" will be determined on their deaths; the gift is good. If A should have another child after the date of this disposition, the *remainder to such afterborn child's issue is void* since it might vest beyond the lives in being plus 21 years.

d. Per Capita Gift Exception

Where there is a separate gift of a fixed sum to each class member, each gift is tested separately under the Rule.

Example: T's will bequeaths "$1,000 each to such of A's grandchildren as live to attain the age of 21, whether alive at my death or born thereafter." At T's death A has two children and five grandchildren. Here we have a per capita gift to each member of the class; there is no problem of knowing within the perpetuities period the number of class members who share in an aggregate gift, and thus the size of each share. Here the amount to be received by each member is ascertainable without reference to the number of persons in the class. The bequest is valid for all grandchildren by A's two children who were alive at T's death. (This includes all future-born grandchildren as well as the five now on the scene, for all such grandchildren will reach 21, if at all, within 21 years after their parent's death.)

However, the *bequest is void for any grandchildren by a child born to A after T's death.* Such an afterborn child cannot be used as a life in being.

4. Perpetuities Reform Legislation

Most states have enacted one of the following types of statutes designed to eliminate some of the harsh results of the common law Rule Against Perpetuities:

a. A *"wait and see"* statute, under which the validity of an interest following one or more life estates is determined on the basis of facts existing at the end of the life estate rather than at the creation of the interest;

b. A *cy pres* approach, borrowed from Trusts law, under which an invalid interest is reformed to comply with the Rule and carry out the grantor's intent as nearly as possible;

c. A statute dealing with *specific perpetuities problems* (*e.g.,* age contingencies reduced to age 21, women over age 55 presumed incapable of childbearing, gift to widow presumed to mean the person who was the spouse on the date the gift was created); or

d. The *Uniform Statutory Rule Against Perpetuities*, which provides an alternative 90-year vesting period. The Uniform Rule takes a "wait and see" approach in determining whether an interest actually vests within 90 years.

5. Technique for Analysis of Perpetuities Problems

In applying the Rule Against Perpetuities, these three steps should be followed:

a. Determine What Interests Are Created

First, determine what interests are created, applying the proper future interests labels, as though there were no Rule Against Perpetuities.

b. Apply the Rule

Determine the measuring life or lives that can be used to show either that the interest must vest within lives in being plus 21 years *or* that the interest might not vest within that period. At this step, assume that there is no such thing as a perpetuities reform statute, for the statute is not brought into play unless there is a perpetuities problem.

    c.   **Apply Reform Statute**
If the particular jurisdiction has a perpetuities reform statute that is triggered by the perpetuities violation, apply the statute to reform or save the gift.

F.   THE RULE AGAINST RESTRAINTS ON ALIENATION

As a general rule, any restriction on the transferability of a legal (as distinguished from an equitable) interest in property is void: The restriction violates the common law Rule Against Restraints on Alienation. "Restraint on alienation" means an express restriction on the transferability of property. Like the Rule Against Perpetuities, this is a rule of public policy that is designed to prevent property from being tied up and taken out of commerce.

1.   **Types of Restraints on Alienation**
There are three types of restraints on alienation: (i) *disabling* restraints, under which any attempted transfer is ineffective; (ii) *forfeiture* restraints, under which an attempted transfer results in a forfeiture of the interest; and (iii) *promissory* restraints, under which an attempted transfer breaches a covenant.

Examples: 1) Property is transferred to A in fee simple, with the added proviso that "neither A nor any of her children shall have the right to transfer the land or any interest therein." Under this restriction, if given effect (*it is not*), any attempted transfer would simply be ineffective. This is a disabling restraint.

                    2) Property is transferred to A in fee simple, with the added proviso that "if A shall attempt to transfer the land or any interest therein during her lifetime, her estate shall cease, and title therein shall vest in B." This is a forfeiture restraint.

                    3) Property is transferred to A in fee simple, with the added proviso that "A hereby covenants that she will not transfer the land or any interest therein without [the transferor's] prior written consent." Under this promissory restraint, if given effect, the remedy is injunction or damages for breach of contract.

2.   **All Disabling Restraints on Legal Interests Are Void**
All disabling restraints on legal interests of whatever type (fee simple, life estate) are void. Disabling restraints are seen as particularly offensive because (i) unlike the other types of restraints, transfers are totally prohibited, (ii) they enable a person to deny the validity of his own conveyance, and (iii) they exempt the property from the person's creditors even while he is enjoying the property.

3.   **All Restraints (of Whatever Type) on Fee Simple Are Void**
All restraints on fee simple estates are void even if transferability is restricted for a short period of time (*e.g.,* for 10 years, or for life).

4.   **Valid Restraints on Alienation**

    a.   **Forfeiture and Promissory Restraints on Life Estates**
Forfeiture and promissory restraints on life estates are valid. A life estate is inalienable as a practical matter since few would be willing to pay full value for an estate of uncertain duration; thus, little is lost by giving effect to the transferor's intention to restrict the estate's transferability. (However, *disabling* restraints on legal life estates are void.)

    b.   **Forfeiture Restraint on Transferability of a Future Interest**
A forfeiture restraint on the transferability of a future interest, during the period when the interest is a future interest, is valid.

    c.   **Restraint on Partition by Co-Tenants (If Limited to a Reasonable Time)**
In general, any co-tenant has the right to demand a partition by judicial sale at any time. However, the courts give effect to a provision prohibiting partition by any one co-tenant, provided that the restriction is to last for only a reasonable time. They reason that the restriction does not make the land inalienable because (i) any co-tenant can transfer her interest to a third person at any time, and (ii) the restraint can be eliminated if the co-tenants join in a deed to a third person, thereby terminating the co-tenancy relationship.

d. Reasonable Restrictions in Commercial Transactions
The courts tend to uphold restrictions on transferability that arise in the context of a commercial transaction on the theory that the restriction appears in an agreement entered into by the parties, it is a product of their bargaining, and presumably serves a useful purpose in facilitating the parties' objectives. Thus, restrictions on transferability that are part of a bargained-for agreement, as distinguished from a donative transaction, are valid.

Examples: 1) O borrows money from M Bank and gives the bank a mortgage on land. The mortgage provides that the land shall not be transferable by O without M's consent, and that if the land is transferred without consent, the entire indebtedness shall be accelerated and shall become immediately due and payable. This "due on sale" restriction on transferability is reasonable because M has an interest in approving who shall be the transferee of the land in which it has a security interest.

2) A, B, C, and D each own 25% of the stock in a closely held corporation. The articles of incorporation provide that no shareholder shall transfer her stock without the consent of a majority of the other shareholders. This restriction on transferability is valid since, because of the closely held nature of the business, the shareholders have a legitimate concern over the identity of their associates.

e. Right of First Refusal
The right to have the first opportunity to purchase real estate when it becomes available, or the right to meet any offer, is valid if reasonable (*e.g.,* by specifying fair market value or other reasonable price). [Restatement (Second) of Property §4.4]

f. Restrictions on Transferability of Leaseholds
A provision in a lease prohibiting the lessee's assignment or subletting of her leasehold interest without the consent of the landlord is given effect in all jurisdictions.

g. Restraints on Alienation of Equitable Interest (Spendthrift Clauses) Are Valid
The rule applicable to restrictions on equitable interests (*i.e.,* those held in trust) is the exact opposite of the rule applicable to legal interests. Spendthrift clauses, which are true disabling restraints, are given effect in the great majority of American jurisdictions. (*See* Trusts outline.)

G. CONCURRENT ESTATES
Any of the estates in land previously discussed can be held concurrently by several persons. These persons all have the right to the enjoyment and possession of the land at the same time. Three of the chief forms of concurrent ownership in land are discussed here: joint tenancy, tenancy by the entirety, and tenancy in common.

1. Joint Tenancy
A joint tenancy can be created between two or more co-tenants. Its distinguishing feature is the *right of survivorship*. Conceptually, when one joint tenant dies, the property is freed from his concurrent interest; the survivor or survivors retain an undivided right in the property, which is no longer subject to the interest of the deceased co-tenant. The survivors do not succeed to the decedent's interest; they hold free of it.

a. Creation

1) Four Unities Required
At common law, four unities are required to create a joint tenancy:

a)   Unity of *time* (interests vested at the same time);

b)   Unity of *title* (interests acquired by the same instrument);

c)   Unity of *interest* (interests of the same *type* and *duration*); and

d)   Unity of *possession* (interests give identical rights to enjoyment).

2) Modern Law
The above requirements have been eroded in some jurisdictions; *e.g.,* by statute in

some states, an owner can create a joint tenancy in herself and another by a single deed (she need not use a strawman conveyance), even though the unities of "time" and "title" are not satisfied. Similarly, as indicated below, a number of transactions are no longer found to sever a joint tenancy despite the seeming absence of continued unities.

3) Express Language Required
Under modern law, *joint tenancies are disfavored*. Hence, there must be a clear expression of intent to create this estate, or it will not be recognized. The usual language required is "to A and B as *joint tenants with right of survivorship*." Today, when two or more persons take property by a single conveyance, a tenancy in common, not a joint tenancy, is presumed. A joint tenancy results only when an intention to create a right of survivorship is clearly expressed.

b. Severance
A joint tenancy can be terminated by a suit for *partition*, which can be brought by any joint tenant. It may also be terminated by various acts by any joint tenant.

1) Inter Vivos Conveyance by One Joint Tenant
An inter vivos conveyance by one joint tenant of her undivided interest destroys the joint tenancy so that the transferee takes the interest as a tenant in common and not as a joint tenant. This rule applies to both *voluntary and involuntary* conveyances (even secret conveyances).

a) Where More than Two Joint Tenants
Where property is held in joint tenancy by three or more joint tenants, a conveyance by one of them destroys the joint tenancy *only as to the conveyor's interest*. The other joint tenants continue to hold in joint tenancy as between themselves, while the grantee holds her interest as a tenant in common with them.

b) Conveyances that May Not Result in Severance
Where a joint tenant makes a conveyance but retains some interest in the property, the transfer may not effect a severance.

(1) Judgment Liens
In most jurisdictions, when a plaintiff obtains a money judgment against a defendant, that judgment becomes a lien on the defendant's real estate in the county where the judgment is docketed. (This is automatic in some states; in others, the lien must be recorded in the real estate records.) The lien then "runs with the land," burdening it until the judgment is paid or until the lien expires under a statute of limitations (*e.g.,* 10 years). Suppose such a lien is obtained against one of several joint tenants but not against the others. Does it sever the joint tenancy, converting it into a tenancy in common? The majority view is that it does not; a lien is not considered a sufficiently substantial "conveyance" to destroy the unities of time and title. However, if the plaintiff who obtained the judgment then proceeds to enforce it by *foreclosure* (often termed a "judgment sale"), the sheriff's deed issued to the buyer at that sale *will sever* the joint tenancy. That follows from the fact that the sheriff's deed conveys the defendant's full title.

Example: A and B own land as joint tenants with right of survivorship. P sues A on a tort claim, and obtains and records a judgment. If A dies at that point, B owns the entire land (by virtue of the right of survivorship), and P has a lien on nothing. However, assume that P has a judgment sale, and a sheriff's deed is issued to Q, who buys at the sale. Then A dies. B and Q each own a one-half interest in the land as tenants in common.

(2) Mortgages
In the majority of states, a mortgage is regarded as a lien on title, and one joint tenant's execution of a mortgage on her interest does not by itself cause a severance. (Rather, the severance occurs only if the mortgage is foreclosed and the property sold.) But in the minority of states,

which regard a mortgage as a transfer of title, the transfer destroys unity of title and severs the joint tenancy.

Example: A, B, and C are joint tenants. A mortgages her interest to Lender, who records. Thereafter, A dies and Lender seeks to enforce her mortgage on an undivided one-third interest in the property. In a state following the "lien theory" of mortgages, Lender loses. A's mortgage did not sever the joint tenancy. Lender's rights were lost when A died prior to foreclosure. A's interest evaporated, and with it Lender's security interest.

(3) Leases

Theoretically, when one joint tenant leases her interest in jointly held property, the lease destroys the unity of interest and thereby should effect a severance (which is the view taken by some states). But other states hold that the joint tenancy is not destroyed but is merely temporarily suspended (for the length of the lease).

(a) Death of Lessor

There is a split among the states following the latter view, on what happens if the lessor/joint tenant dies before the end of the lease. Some courts hold that since the lessor's own right to possession would cease on her death, so must the right of any lessee (*i.e.,* lessor could not convey more than she had). Others hold that the lease operates as a "temporary severance," and the remaining joint tenant's survivorship rights are therefore postponed until the end of the lease.

2) Contract to Convey by One Joint Tenant

In most states, a severance also results where one joint tenant executes a valid contract to convey her interest to another, even though no actual transfer of title has yet been made. The contract to convey is enforceable in equity, and hence is treated as an effective transfer of an equitable interest. Thus, if the vendor dies before the title is transferred, the purchaser is entitled to a deed from the vendor's estate and becomes a tenant in common with the original joint tenant or tenants.

a) Compare—Executory Contract by All Joint Tenants

There is a split as to whether an executory contract to sell, entered into by all the joint tenants, will terminate the joint tenancy. Suppose that on January 1, A and B, joint tenants, contract with X to sell and deliver title to Blackacre to X on February 1. A dies on January 15. Two questions arise: (i) On February 1, is B entitled to the full sales proceeds as surviving joint tenant, or is A's estate entitled to one-half (on the theory that the January 1 contract worked an equitable conversion, which created in the vendors a contract right to receive money that was held in tenancy in common)? And, (ii) will X have to obtain a deed not only from B but also from A's administrator on the theory that the retained legal title (for security purposes) was held in tenancy in common?

(1) Common Law View—Joint Tenancy Continues

The common law view, still followed by many courts, is that a joint tenancy continues in both the right to the proceeds and the retained legal title, meaning that B gets the full sales proceeds and can give good title.

(2) Other Courts—Tenancy in Common

Other jurisdictions, however, proceed on the doctrine of equitable conversion and hold that the executory contract converts A and B's land ownership rights to a mere contract right to receive the purchase price (which they hold as tenants in common because of the statutory presumption favoring such tenancies). Further, the legal title to the land, retained for security purposes, is also held to be in tenancy in common.

3) Testamentary Disposition by One Joint Tenant Has No Effect

A joint tenancy is not terminated where a joint tenant executes a will devising her interest to another or dies with such a will in effect. The reason is that a will is ambulatory (effective only at death) and hence is inoperative as to joint tenancy property, because at the instant of death the decedent's rights in the property evaporate. (The result would be contra if all joint tenants had agreed that the decedent could devise her interest; but in such a case, the agreement itself would cause the severance.)

a) Compare—"Secret" Deeds
As indicated above, an inter vivos conveyance severs a joint tenancy. This is true even though the deed is kept "secret" and the interest transferred is to take effect only upon the death of the grantor. However, if the grantee does not know about the deed, the grantee's acceptance *after* the death of the grantor does not relate back to defeat the right of survivorship. (*See* VI.C.4.b., *infra*.)

4) Effect of One Joint Tenant's Murdering Another
Some states have passed statutes under which the felonious and intentional killing of one joint tenant by another joint tenant operates as a severance. In other states, the surviving joint tenant holds the ill-gained portion on a constructive trust for the decedent's estate. Thus, the homicidal survivor keeps her original share but does not profit from her felony.

2. Tenancy by the Entirety
A tenancy by the entirety is a marital estate akin to a joint tenancy between husband and wife. It is not recognized in community property states, but in about 21 common law jurisdictions, it arises presumptively in any conveyance made to husband and wife.

a. Right of Survivorship
The estate carries a right of survivorship, which operates in the same manner as the right of survivorship incident to a joint tenancy.

b. Severance Limited
The major distinction between a joint tenancy and a tenancy by the entirety concerns severance. A tenancy by the entirety cannot be terminated by involuntary partition. It can be terminated only by: (i) the death of either spouse (leaving the survivor sole owner of the fee); (ii) divorce (leaving the parties as tenants in common with no right of survivorship); (iii) mutual agreement; or (iv) execution by a joint creditor of *both* husband and wife (a creditor of one or the other cannot execute).

c. Individual Spouse Cannot Convey or Encumber
In most states, an individual spouse may not convey or encumber tenancy by the entirety property. A deed or mortgage executed by only one spouse is ineffective.

3. Tenancy in Common
A tenancy in common is a concurrent estate with no right of survivorship. Each owner has a distinct, proportionate, undivided interest in the property. This interest is freely alienable by inter vivos and testamentary transfer, is inheritable, and is subject to claims of the tenant's creditors. The only "unity" involved is possession: Each tenant is entitled to possession of the whole estate. Today, by statute, multiple grantees are presumed to take as tenants in common. The same is true where multiple transferees take by descent.

4. Incidents of Co-Ownership

a. Possession
Each co-tenant has the right to possess all portions of the property; no co-tenant has the right to exclusive possession of any part. A co-tenant out of possession cannot bring a possessory action unless there has been an "ouster" by the tenant in possession. A claim of right to exclusive possession can constitute an ouster.

b. Rents and Profits
In most jurisdictions (but not all), a co-tenant in possession has the right to retain profits gained by her use of the property. A co-tenant in possession need not share such profits with co-tenants out of possession, nor reimburse them for the rental value of her use of the land, unless there has been an ouster or an agreement to the contrary. However, a co-tenant out of possession has a right to share in *rents from third parties* and in *profits* derived from a use of the land that reduces its value (*e.g.,* removal of minerals, etc.).

c. **Effect of One Concurrent Owner's Encumbering the Property**
A joint tenant or tenant in common may place a mortgage on her interest, but may not, of course, encumber the other co-tenant's interest. If a tenancy in common is involved, the mortgagee can foreclose only on the mortgaging co-tenant's interest. Likewise, if a joint tenancy is involved and the mortgage itself does not sever the joint tenancy (*see* 1.b.1)b)(2), *supra*), the mortgagee can foreclose on the mortgagor/co-tenant's interest and the foreclosure sale itself will cause a severance. But in the case of a joint tenancy, the mortgagee runs the risk that the mortgaging co-tenant will die before foreclosure, extinguishing the mortgagee's interest. The same principles apply to judgment liens obtained against an individual co-tenant.

Example: A and B are joint tenants with right of survivorship. A injures C in an accident, and C sues A, obtaining a personal injury judgment against A for $1,000. This judgment is, by statute, a lien on A's one-half interest in the land, but it does not cause a severance. If A dies before the lien is foreclosed and is survived by B, B owns the land free and clear of the lien. But if C forecloses the lien before A's death, the foreclosure sale will cause a severance, and the buyer at the sale will own a one-half interest in the land as a tenant in common with B.

d. **Ouster**
Under the unity of possession, each co-tenant is entitled to possess and enjoy the whole of the property subject to the equal right of her co-tenant. If one tenant *wrongfully excludes* another co-tenant from possession of the whole or any part of the whole of the premises, there is an ouster. The ousted co-tenant is entitled to receive his share of the fair rental value of the property for the time he was wrongfully deprived of possession.

e. **Remedy of Partition**
A joint tenant or tenant in common has a right to judicial partition, either in kind (division of the tract into parcels) or by sale and division of the proceeds (in accordance with the ownership interests as modified by permitted recoupments for improvements, repairs, taxes, and the like).

f. **Expenses for Preservation of Property—Contribution**
Under certain circumstances, equity courts will compel contribution between concurrent owners.

1) **Repairs—Contribution May Be Compelled for Necessary Repairs**
A co-tenant who pays more than her pro rata share of the cost of necessary repairs is entitled to contribution from the other co-tenants in actions for accounting or partition. Although the courts are split on whether a co-tenant who makes necessary repairs can maintain an independent action for contribution against the other co-tenants, the majority view is that she can compel contribution, provided she has notified the other co-tenants of the need for repairs. Moreover, several recent decisions authorize contribution even without such notice.

The common law view was that since no co-tenant has a duty to make necessary repairs, a co-tenant who makes such repairs cannot bring an action to compel contribution from the other co-tenants. This is now the minority view.

2) **Improvements—No Contribution or Setoff**
Generally, there is no right of contribution for the cost of improvements, nor can they be set off in an action for accounting. Only in an action for partition can the value of improvements be recouped.

3) **Taxes and Mortgages—Contribution Can Be Compelled**
Each co-tenant has a duty to pay her share of taxes and payments due on mortgages on the entire property. A tenant who is not in sole possession can pay the taxes and mortgage payments and then compel contribution from the other co-tenants. However, a co-tenant in sole possession will receive reimbursement only for the amount that exceeds the rental value of the property.

g. **Duty of Fair Dealing Among Co-Tenants**
A confidential relationship exists among co-tenants. Accordingly, the acquisition by

one co-tenant of any outstanding title or lien that might affect the estate held by all the co-tenants is deemed to be an acquisition on behalf of all the other co-tenants as well. Thus, when one co-tenant purchases or otherwise acquires a lienholder's (mortgagee's) claim against the co-tenancy property, she must give the other co-tenants a reasonable time to pay their share and acquire a proportionate interest. Courts carefully scrutinize the fairness of transactions between co-tenants. Lastly, it is difficult for one co-tenant to *adversely possess* against other co-tenants. (*See* V.B.5.b., *infra*.)

Example: A and B own land as co-tenants. Neither pays the annual property taxes. The county conducts a tax sale and A buys the property for $500. If B is willing to pay A $250, many courts will compel A to put the property in co-tenancy again.

II. LANDLORD AND TENANT

A. NATURE OF LEASEHOLD
A leasehold is an estate in land. The tenant has a present possessory interest in the leased premises, and the landlord has a future interest (reversion). Certain rights and liabilities flow from this property relationship between landlord and tenant. The three major types of leasehold estates are *tenancies for years*, *periodic tenancies*, and *tenancies at will*. There is a fourth category called *tenancies at sufferance*.

1. Tenancies for Years

a. Fixed Period of Time
A tenancy for years is one that is to continue for a fixed period of time. It may be for *more or less* than a year (*e.g.,* 10 days or 10 years); it may be determinable (similar to a fee simple determinable) or on condition subsequent. The termination date of a tenancy for years is usually certain. As a result, the tenancy expires at the end of the stated period *without either party giving notice to the other*. Even if the date of termination is uncertain (*e.g.,* L leases the premises to T "until the end of the war"), *most courts* hold that if the parties have attempted to state some period of duration, the lease creates a tenancy for years.

b. Creation
Tenancies for years are normally created by written leases. In most states, the Statute of Frauds requires that a lease creating a tenancy for more than one year be in writing. In addition, most states have statutes that restrict the number of years for which a leasehold estate may be created (*e.g.,* 51 years for farm property and 99 years for urban property). When the lease term exceeds the statutory maximum, most courts hold that the lease is *entirely* void. Likewise, where the lease contains an *option to renew* for a period beyond the permitted maximum, most courts hold the entire lease void.

c. Termination
A tenancy for years ends *automatically* on its termination date.

1) Breach of Covenants
In most tenancy for years leases, the landlord reserves the right to terminate if the tenant breaches any of the leasehold covenants. This reserved power is called the landlord's *right of entry*.

####### a) Failure to Pay Rent
In many jurisdictions, if the tenant fails to pay the promised rent, the landlord has the right to terminate the lease *even in the absence of a reserved right of entry*.

2) Surrender
A tenancy for years also terminates upon surrender. Surrender consists of the tenant giving up his leasehold interest to the landlord and the landlord accepting. Usually the same *formalities* are required for the surrender of a leasehold as are necessary for its creation. Thus, a writing is necessary for the surrender of a leasehold if the unexpired term is more than one year.

2.   Periodic Tenancies

A periodic tenancy is a tenancy that continues from year to year or for successive fractions of a year (*e.g.,* weekly or monthly) until terminated by proper notice by either party. The beginning date must be certain, but the *termination date is always uncertain* until notice is given.

All conditions and terms of the tenancy are carried over from one period to the next unless there is a lease provision to the contrary. Periodic tenancies do not violate the rules limiting the length of leaseholds since each party retains the power to terminate upon giving notice.

a.   Creation

Periodic tenancies can be created in three ways:

1)   By Express Agreement

Periodic tenancies can be created by express agreement (*e.g.,* "Landlord leases to Tenant from month to month").

2)   By Implication

A periodic tenancy will be implied if the lease has no set termination but does provide for the payment of rent at specific periods.

Example: "Landlord leases to Tenant at a rent of $100 *payable monthly* in advance." The reservation of monthly rent will give rise to a periodic tenancy from *month to month*.

Note: If the lease reserves an annual rent, payable monthly (*e.g.,* "$6,000 per annum, payable $500 on the first day of every month commencing January 1"), the majority view is that the periodic tenancy is from *year to year*.

3)   By Operation of Law

A periodic tenancy may arise even without an express or implied agreement between the parties.

a)   Tenant Holds Over

If a tenant for years remains in possession after the termination of his tenancy period, the landlord may elect to treat the tenant as a periodic tenant on the same terms as the original lease. (*See* 5.b., *infra.*)

b)   Lease Invalid

If a lease is invalid (*e.g.,* because of failure to satisfy the Statute of Frauds) and the tenant nonetheless goes into possession, the tenant's periodic payment of rent will convert what would otherwise be a tenancy at will into a periodic tenancy. The period of the tenancy coincides with the period for which the rent is paid.

b.   Termination—Notice Required

A periodic tenancy is *automatically renewed*, from period to period, until proper notice of termination is given by either party. Many jurisdictions have statutorily prescribed the notice required to terminate a periodic tenancy. In general, the guidelines are as follows:

(i)   The tenancy must end at the *end of a "natural" lease period*.

(ii)   For a tenancy from year to year, *six months' notice* is required.

(iii) For tenancies less than one year in duration, a *full period in advance* of the period in question is required by way of notice (*e.g.,* for a month-to-month periodic tenancy, one full month's notice is required).

In general, the notice required to terminate a periodic tenancy must be in *writing* and must actually be *delivered* to the party in question or deposited at his residence in a manner similar to that required for service of process.

3.   Tenancies at Will

A tenancy at will is an estate in land that is terminable at the will of either the landlord or the tenant. To be a tenancy at will, both the landlord and the tenant must have the right to terminate the lease at will.

(i) If the lease gives *only the landlord* the right to terminate at will, a *similar right* will generally be *implied in favor of the tenant* so that the lease creates a tenancy at will.

(ii) If the lease is only at the will of the *tenant* (*e.g.,* "for so long as the tenant wishes"), courts usually *do not imply a right to terminate in favor of the landlord*. Rather, most courts interpret the conveyance as creating a life estate or fee simple, either of which is terminable by the tenant. (If the Statute of Frauds is not satisfied, the conveyance is a tenancy at will.)

a. Creation
A tenancy at will generally arises from a specific understanding between the parties that *either party may terminate* the tenancy at any time. Note that unless the parties *expressly agree* to a tenancy at will, the payment of regular rent (*e.g.,* monthly, quarterly, etc.) will cause a court to treat the tenancy as a periodic tenancy. Thus, tenancies at will are quite rare. Although a tenancy at will can also arise when the lease is for an indefinite period (one that does not satisfy the requirements for creating a tenancy for years), or when a tenant goes into possession under a lease that does not satisfy the requisite formalities (usually the Statute of Frauds), rent payments will usually convert it to a periodic tenancy.

b. Termination
A tenancy at will may be terminated by *either party without notice*. However, a reasonable demand to quit the premises is required. A tenancy at will terminates by *operation of law* if:

1) Either party *dies*;

2) The tenant commits *waste*;

3) The tenant attempts to *assign* his tenancy;

4) The *landlord transfers his interest* in the property; or

5) The *landlord executes a term lease* to a third person.

4. Tenancies at Sufferance
A tenancy at sufferance (sometimes called "occupancy at sufferance") arises when a tenant *wrongfully* remains in possession after the expiration of a lawful tenancy (*e.g.,* after the stipulated date for the termination of a tenancy for years; or after the landlord has exercised a power of termination). Such a tenant is a wrongdoer and is *liable for rent*. The tenancy at sufferance lasts only until the landlord takes steps to evict the tenant. No notice is required to end the tenancy, and authorities are divided as to whether this is even an estate in land.

5. The Hold-Over Doctrine
When a tenant continues in possession after the termination of his right to possession, the landlord has two choices of action:

a. Eviction
The landlord may treat the hold-over tenant as a trespasser and evict him under an unlawful detainer statute.

b. Creation of Periodic Tenancy
The landlord may, in his sole discretion, bind the tenant to a new periodic tenancy.

1) Terms
The terms and conditions of the expired tenancy (*e.g.,* rent, covenants, etc.) apply to the new tenancy. If the original lease term was for one year or more, a year-to-year tenancy results from holding over. (In residential leases, however, most courts would look instead to the period of the rental payment, and make that the period of the new periodic tenancy.) If the original term was for less than one year, the periodic term is determined by the manner in which the rent was due and payable under the prior tenancy.
Example: A tenant was holding under a six-month term tenancy with rent payable monthly. The tenant holds over and the landlord binds him to a new tenancy. The new periodic tenancy is a month-to-month tenancy.

2) Altered Terms

If the landlord notifies the tenant before termination of the tenancy that occupancy after termination will be at an increased rent, the tenant will be held to have acquiesced to the new terms if he does not surrender. The tenant will be held to the new terms *even if he objects* to the increased rent, provided that the rent increase is reasonable.

c. What Does Not Constitute Holding Over

The landlord cannot bind the tenant to a new tenancy under the hold-over doctrine if: (i) the tenant remains in possession for only a *few hours* after termination of the lease, or leaves a few articles of personal property on the premises; (ii) the delay is *not the tenant's fault* (*e.g.,* because of severe illness); or (iii) it is a *seasonal lease* (*e.g.,* summer cottage).

d. Double Rent Jeopardy

Many state statutes provide that if a tenant *willfully* remains in possession after his term expires and after the landlord makes a *written demand for possession*, the landlord may collect double rent for the time the tenant in fact remains in possession.

e. Forcible Entry Statutes

Most states by statute prohibit forcible entry, *i.e.,* entry against the will of the possessor. Under such statutes, a landlord must not use force or self-help to remove a hold-over tenant. Some states also bar the landlord from more subtle methods of regaining possession, *e.g.,* changing the locks and locking out the tenant.

The statutes allow the landlord to *evict* a tenant who has remained in possession after his right to possession has terminated. The sole issue is "who has the right to possession"; questions of title must be litigated in ejectment actions rather than in eviction actions.

B. LEASES

A lease is a contract containing the promises of the parties. It governs the relationship between the landlord and tenant over the term of the lease. In general, covenants in a lease are independent of each other; *i.e.,* one party's performance of his promise does not depend on the other party's performance of his promise. Thus, if one party breaches a covenant, the other party can recover *damages*, but must still perform his promises and *cannot terminate* the landlord-tenant relationship.

Example: L leases an office space to T for five years. T covenants to pay $750 per month, and L covenants to paint the office once each year. At the beginning of the second year, L refuses to paint the office. T may recover damages from L (the decrease in fair rental value or the cost of painting), but T may not terminate the lease or refuse to pay his rent because of L's breach.

Note that the doctrines of actual and constructive eviction (D.2., *infra*) and implied warranty of habitability (D.3., *infra*) are exceptions to this rule of independence of covenants. An exception also exists in nearly all states for nonpayment of rent; under these statutes, if a tenant fails to pay, the landlord may terminate the lease.

C. TENANT DUTIES AND LANDLORD REMEDIES

1. Tenant's Duty to Repair (Doctrine of Waste)

A tenant cannot damage—commit waste on—the leased premises. The rules governing waste in the leasehold context are very much like those governing waste in the context of the life estate.

a. Types of Waste

1) Voluntary (Affirmative) Waste

A tenant is liable to the landlord for voluntary waste. Voluntary waste results when the tenant intentionally or negligently damages the premises. It also includes exploiting minerals on the property unless the property was previously so used, or unless the lease provides that the tenant may do so.

2) Permissive Waste

Unless the lease provides otherwise, the tenant has no duty to the landlord to make any substantial repairs (*i.e.,* to keep the premises in good repair). However, it is the tenant's duty to repair broken windows or a leaking roof and to take such other steps as are needed to prevent damage from the elements (*i.e.,* keep the premises "wind and water tight"). If the tenant fails to do so, he is liable to the landlord for any resulting damage, but not for the cost of repair. By statute in a growing minority of states, residential tenants have additional duties: (i) not to cause housing code violations; (ii) to keep the premises clean and free of vermin; and (iii) to use plumbing, appliances, etc., in a reasonable manner. Note that even when the burden of repair is on the landlord, the tenant does have a duty to report deficiencies promptly to the landlord.

3) Ameliorative Waste
A tenant is under an obligation to return the premises in the same nature and character as received. Therefore, a tenant is not permitted to make substantial alterations to leased structures even if the alteration increased the value of the property.

a) Liability—Cost of Restoration
The tenant is liable for the cost of restoration should he commit ameliorative waste.

b) Modern Exception—Value of Premises Decreasing
Where, through the passage of time, the demised premises have been significantly reduced in value, courts will permit a change in the character of the premises as long as:

(1) The change *increases the value* of the premises;

(2) The change *is performed by a long-term tenant* (*e.g.,* 25 years); and

(3) The change *reflects a change* in the nature and character of the neighborhood.

b. Destruction of the Premises Without Fault
If the leased premises are destroyed (*e.g.,* by fire) without the fault of either the landlord or the tenant, no waste is involved. In this situation, the common law held that the lease continues in effect. In the absence of lease language, neither party has a duty to restore the premises, but the tenant has a duty to continue paying the rent.

1) Majority View—Tenant Can Terminate Lease
In most states, statutes or case law now give the tenant an option to terminate the lease if the premises are destroyed without the tenant's fault, even in the presence of an explicit covenant to repair (*see* below).

c. Tenant's Liability for Covenants to Repair
Where the tenant covenants to keep the premises in good repair, the condition of the premises at the beginning and end of the tenancy must be compared in order to determine whether there has been a breach.

1) Ordinary Wear and Tear
If the tenant covenants to repair the premises, he has a duty to repair even ordinary wear and tear unless the covenant *expressly excludes* such wear and tear. However, there is no duty to repair structural failures or damage resulting from fire or other casualty unless such repairs are *expressly included* in the covenant.

2) Acts of Third Parties
Under the common law, the tenant is liable under such a covenant for all other defects regardless of their cause (*e.g.,* third persons, acts of God, etc.).

3) Reconstruction
At common law, if the tenant has covenanted to repair and the premises are completely destroyed, the tenant is liable for reconstruction.

2. Duty to Not Use Premises for Illegal Purpose

If the tenant uses the premises for an illegal purpose, and the landlord is not a party to the illegal use, the landlord may terminate the lease or obtain damages and injunctive relief.

a. Occasional Unlawful Conduct Does Not Breach Duty

Occasional unlawful conduct of the tenant does not breach this duty. The duty is breached only when the illegal conduct is continuous (*e.g.,* if the tenant operates a gambling ring out of the leased premises).

b. Landlord Remedies—Terminate Lease, Recover Damages

If the conduct is continuous, the landlord may terminate the lease and recover the damages. If the conduct has first been stopped by a public authority, the landlord may terminate and recover damages, but only if she acts within a reasonable time after the use has been stopped. Alternatively, the landlord faced with unlawful tenant conduct may keep the lease in force and seek injunctive or monetary relief.

3. Duty to Pay Rent

At common law, rent is due at the end of the leasehold term. However, leases usually contain a provision making the rent payable at some other time (*e.g.,* "monthly in advance").

a. When Rent Accrues

At common law, rent is not apportionable; *i.e.,* it does not accrue from day to day, but rather accrues all at once at the end of the term. However, most states today have statutes that provide that if a leasehold terminates before the term originally agreed on, the tenant must pay a *proportionate amount* of the agreed rent.

b. Rent Deposits

Landlords often require a deposit by the tenant at the outset of the lease. If the money is considered a *security deposit*, the landlord will not be permitted to retain it beyond the extent of his recoverable damages. But if the deposit is denominated a *"bonus"* or a future rent payment (*e.g.,* the last month's rent), then most courts permit the landlord to retain it after the tenant has been evicted.

c. Termination of Rent Liability—Surrender

If a tenant effectively conveys back (surrenders) his leasehold to the landlord, the tenant's liability for future rent ends. Normally, this occurs when there is an agreement between the landlord and tenant that the tenant's interest in the demised premises will end. If the unexpired term of the lease is more than one year, the surrender must be in writing to satisfy the Statute of Frauds.

4. Landlord Remedies

a. Tenant on Premises But Fails to Pay Rent—Evict or Sue for Rent

At common law, a breach, such as failure to pay rent, resulted only in a cause of action for money damages; a breach by either party did not give rise to a right to terminate the lease. Most leases, however, grant the nonbreaching party the right to terminate. Furthermore, nearly all states have enacted an *unlawful detainer statute*, which permits the landlord to evict a defaulting tenant. These statutes provide for a quick hearing, but severely limit the issues that may be raised. Under most statutes, the only issue properly before the court is the landlord's right to rent and possession. The tenant cannot raise counterclaims.

b. Tenant Abandons—Do Nothing or Repossess

If the tenant *unjustifiably* abandons the property, the landlord has two options: she may do nothing, or she may repossess.

1) Landlord Does Nothing—Tenant Remains Liable

By the traditional view, the landlord may let the premises lie idle and collect the rent from the abandoning tenant, unless the tenant tenders an acceptable substituting tenant. However, the majority view requires the landlord to make reasonable efforts to *mitigate* his damages by reletting to a new tenant. Under this view, if he could have done so but does not attempt to relet, his recovery against the tenant will be reduced accordingly.

2) Landlord Repossesses—Tenant's Liability Depends on Surrender
If the landlord repossesses and/or relets the premises, the tenant's liability will depend on whether the landlord has accepted a surrender of the premises. If surrender is not found, the tenant remains liable for the difference between the promised rent and the fair rental value of the property (or, in the case of reletting, between the promised rent and the rent received from the reletting). However, if the landlord's reletting or use of the premises for her own profit constitutes acceptance of surrender, the abandoning tenant is free from any rent liability accruing after abandonment.

a) Acts that Constitute Acceptance of Surrender
If the landlord resumes possession of the demised premises for himself, this conduct usually constitutes acceptance of the surrender, and the tenant will be relieved of any further liability.

b) Acts that Do Not Constitute Acceptance of Surrender
The fact that the landlord enters the premises after abandonment to make repairs, receives back the keys, or offers to attempt to relet the premises on behalf of the tenant, does not by itself constitute an acceptance of the offered surrender.

D. LANDLORD DUTIES AND TENANT REMEDIES

Subject to modification by the lease, a statute, or the implied warranty of habitability, the general rule is that a landlord has *no duty to repair or maintain* the premises. Leases, however, commonly prescribe landlord liability to tenant in several areas. If a lease does not expressly prescribe landlord duties, some duties will be implied.

1. Duty to Deliver Possession of Premises

a. Landlord Duty—Must Deliver Actual Possession
Statutes in most states require the landlord to put the tenant in actual possession of the premises at the beginning of the leasehold term. In a minority of states, the landlord's obligation is merely to give the tenant the legal right to possession. The difference can be important if the leased premises are occupied by a prior, hold-over tenant who has not moved out. Under the majority view, the landlord is in breach if she has not evicted the hold-over tenant by the beginning of the new tenant's term. Under the minority view, it is up to the new tenant to bring eviction proceedings against the hold-over tenant.

b. Tenant Remedy—Damages
In states following the majority rule, a tenant is entitled to damages against a landlord in breach of the duty to deliver possession. If, for example, the tenant had to find more expensive housing during the interim or suffered business losses as a consequence of the landlord's breach, he may recover for these items.

2. Quiet Enjoyment

There is implied in every lease a covenant that neither the landlord nor someone with paramount title (*e.g.,* a prior mortgagee of the landlord who forecloses) will interfere with the tenant's quiet enjoyment and possession of the premises. The covenant of quiet enjoyment may be breached in any one of three ways: actual eviction, partial actual eviction, or constructive eviction.

a. Actual Eviction
Actual eviction occurs when the landlord or paramount title holder excludes the tenant from the *entire* leased premises. Actual eviction *terminates* the tenant's obligation to pay rent.

b. Partial Actual Eviction
Partial actual eviction occurs when the tenant is physically excluded from only *part* of the leased premises. (The part from which the tenant is excluded need not be a substantial part of the premises for breach to occur.) The tenant's remedies for breach will differ depending on whether the partial eviction was caused by the landlord or by one with paramount title.

1) Partial Eviction by Landlord—Entire Rent Obligation Relieved
Partial eviction by the landlord relieves the tenant of the obligation to pay rent for

the *entire* premises, even though the tenant continues in possession of the remainder of the premises.

2) Partial Eviction by Third Person—Rent Apportioned

Partial eviction by a third person with paramount title results in an apportionment of rent; *i.e.,* the tenant is liable for the reasonable rental value of the portion that he continues to possess.

c. Constructive Eviction

If the landlord does an act or fails to provide some service that he has a legal duty to provide, and thereby makes the property uninhabitable, the tenant may *terminate the lease* and may also seek *damages*. The following conditions must be met:

1) The acts that cause the injury must be by the *landlord* or by persons acting for him. Acts of neighbors or strangers will not suffice.

2) The resulting conditions must be very bad, so that the court can conclude that the *premises are uninhabitable*. Typical examples are flooding, absence of heat in winter, loss of elevator service in a warehouse, etc.

3) The tenant must move out, thereby showing that the premises were uninhabitable. If he does not *vacate within a reasonable time*, he has waived the right to do so.

3. Implied Warranty of Habitability

More than half of the states have now adopted by court decision or statute the implied warranty of habitability for residential tenancies; it is clearly a growing trend. (It is rarely applied to nonresidential cases, unlike constructive eviction.) The standards are more favorable to tenants than in constructive eviction, and the range of remedies is much broader.

a. Standard—Reasonably Suitable for Human Residence

The standard usually applied is the local housing code if one exists; if there is none, the court asks whether the conditions are reasonably suitable for human residence.

b. Remedies

The following remedies have been adopted by various courts for violation of the implied warranty (although few courts have adopted all):

1) Tenant may move out and *terminate lease* (as in a constructive eviction).

2) Tenant may *make repairs* directly, and *offset the cost* against future rent obligations. (Some states limit this remedy by statute to a fixed amount, such as one month's rent, or to only one occasion each year.)

3) Tenant may reduce or *abate rent* to an amount equal to the fair rental value in view of the defects in the property. (In many jurisdictions, the tenant may withhold all rent until the court determines the amount of this fair rental value, and may then pay it without risk of the landlord's terminating the lease for rent delinquency.)

4) Tenant may remain in possession, pay full rent, and seek *damages* against the landlord.

4. Retaliatory Eviction

If a tenant exercises the legal right to report housing or building code violations or other rights provided by statute (*e.g.,* a residential landlord-tenant act), the landlord is not permitted to terminate the tenant's lease in retaliation. The landlord is also barred from penalizing the tenant in other ways, such as raising the rent or reducing tenant services. This protection is recognized by residential landlord-tenant acts in nearly half the states. These statutes usually *presume* a retaliatory motive if the landlord acts within, say, 90 to 180 days after the tenant exercises his or her rights. In other states, the same conclusion is reached by judicial construction of the eviction and code statutes. The protection generally applies to tenants under both periodic leases when the landlord gives notice to terminate and fixed-term leases when the landlord refuses to renew. To overcome the presumption, the landlord must show a valid, nonretaliatory reason for his actions.

E. ASSIGNMENTS AND SUBLEASES

Absent an express restriction in the lease, a tenant may freely transfer his leasehold interest, in whole or in part. If he makes a *complete transfer of the entire remaining term*, he has made an *assignment*. If he *retains any part* of the remaining term, the transfer is a *sublease*.

Example: L leases property to T for a 10-year term. One month later, T transfers his interest to T1 for nine years, retaining the right to retake the premises (reversion) after nine years. The effect of his transfer is to create a sublease between T (sublessor) and T1 (sublessee).

If, on the other hand, T had transferred to T1 for the remaining period of the lease, reserving no rights, the transfer would constitute an assignment of the lease from T (assignor) to T1 (assignee). (*Note:* It is not controlling that the parties denominate the transfer an "assignment" or "sublease." The court still examines what interest, if any, is retained by T to determine the nature of the transaction.)

1. Consequences of Assignment

The label given to a transfer—an assignment or sublease—determines whether the landlord can proceed directly against the transferee or only against the transferor. To be an assignment, the transfer must be on the same terms as the original lease *except that the tenant may reserve a right of termination (reentry) for breach of the terms of the original lease* that has been assigned; *e.g.,* "to A for the balance of the leasehold term. However, should A fail to make the rental payments to the landlord, the right to reenter and reclaim the premises is reserved." If the transfer is an assignment, the assignee stands in the shoes of the original tenant in a direct relationship with the landlord. The assignee and the landlord are in *"privity of estate,"* and each is liable to the other on all covenants in the lease that "run with the land."

a. Covenants that Run with the Land

A covenant "runs" if the original parties to the lease so intend, and if the covenant *"touches and concerns"* the leased land; *i.e.,* it benefits the landlord and burdens the tenant (or vice versa) with respect to their interests in the property. (These requirements are discussed in detail at IV.D., *infra.*) Covenants held to run with the land (unless the parties specify otherwise) include: covenants to *do or not do a physical act* (*e.g.,* to repair, to conduct a business on the land in a specified manner, to supply heat); covenants to *pay money* (*e.g.,* rent, taxes, etc.); and covenants regarding the *duration* of the lease (*e.g.,* termination clauses).

b. Rent Covenant Runs with the Land

Since the covenant to pay rent runs with the land, an assignee owes the rent *directly* to the landlord. He does not owe rent for the period before the assignment, but only for the time that he is in "privity of estate," *i.e.,* from the time of assignment until the end of the lease or until the assignee himself reassigns.

1) Reassignment by Assignee—Privity of Estate with Landlord Ends

If the assignee reassigns the leasehold interest, his privity of estate with the landlord ends, and he is not liable for the subsequent assignee's failure to pay rent. However, if the first assignee specifically promised the landlord that he would be liable for the rent for the remainder of the lease term, he may be obligated to pay based on *privity of contract*, even though his reassignment ended the privity of estate.

a) Effect of Assignee Assuming Rent Obligation

If the assignee made no promise to the landlord but did promise the original tenant that he would pay all future rent, the landlord may be able to sue the assignee as a *third-party beneficiary* of the contract between the original tenant and the assignee.

2) Original Tenant Remains Liable

After assignment, the original tenant is no longer in privity of estate with the landlord. However, if (as is likely) the tenant promised to pay rent in his lease with the landlord, he can still be held liable on his original contractual obligation to pay, *i.e.,* on privity of contract. This allows the landlord to sue the original tenant where the assignee has disappeared, is judgment-proof, etc.

Example: L rents to T for three years at $2,400 per year. After one year, T assigns to T1. T1 pays the rent for one year, and then assigns to T2. T2 fails to pay rent. L can collect from T or T2 but not from T1 (unless T1 made some *promise* on the basis of which L can sue him).

2. **Consequences of Sublease**

In a sublease, the sublessee is considered the tenant of the original lessee, and usually pays rent directly to the original lessee, who in turn pays rent to the landlord under the main lease.

a. **Liability of Sublessee for Rent and Other Covenants**

The sublessee is liable to the original lessee for whatever rent the two of them agreed to in the sublease. However, the sublessee is *not personally liable to the landlord* for rent or for the performance of any other covenants made by the original lessee in the main lease. The reason is that the sublessee has no contractual relationship with the landlord (no privity of contract), and does not hold the tenant's full estate in the land (no privity of estate); therefore, the covenants in the main lease do not "run with the land" and bind the sublessee.

1) **Termination for Breach of Covenants**

Even though the sublessee is not personally liable to the landlord, the landlord can still terminate the main lease for nonpayment of rent or, if so stated in the lease, breach of other tenant covenants. If this occurs, the sublease will automatically terminate at the same time.

2) **Distress—Landlord's Lien**

In many states (especially in nonresidential leases), the landlord who does not receive rent when due can assert a lien on the personal property found on the leased premises. This applies to property owned by sublessees as well as that owned by the original tenant.

b. **Assumption by Sublessee**

It is possible for the sublessee to assume the rent covenant and other covenants in the main lease. An assumption is not implied, but must be expressed. If this occurs, the sublessee is bound by the assumption agreement and becomes personally liable to the landlord on the covenants assumed. The landlord is considered a third-party beneficiary of the assumption agreement.

c. **Rights of Sublessee**

The sublessee can enforce all covenants made by the original lessee in the sublease, but has no direct right to enforce any covenants made by the landlord in the main lease. However, it is likely (though there is very little case law on point) that a sublessee in a residential lease would be permitted to enforce the implied warranty of habitability against the landlord.

3. **Covenants Against Assignment or Sublease**

a. **Strictly Construed Against Landlord**

Many leases contain covenants on the part of the tenant not to assign or sublease without the consent of the landlord. These are strictly construed against the landlord. Thus, a covenant prohibiting assignment does not prohibit subleasing and vice versa.

b. **Waiver of Covenant**

Even if the lease has a valid covenant against assignment, the covenant may be held waived if the landlord knows of the assignment and does not object. This often occurs when the landlord knowingly accepts rent from the assignee.

c. **Continuing Waiver**

If the landlord grants consent to one transfer, he waives his right to avoid future transfers unless he expressly reserves the right to do so. Reservation of right must take place at the time of granting consent.

d. **Transfer in Violation of Lease Not Void**

If a tenant transfers (assigns or sublets) in violation of a prohibition in the lease against transfers, the transfer is not void. However, the landlord usually may terminate the lease under either the lease terms or a statute. Alternatively, he may sue for damages if he can prove any.

e. **Reasonableness**

In a minority of states, the landlord may not unreasonably withhold consent to transfers by the tenant. The majority imposes no such limitation.

4. Assignments by Landlords

a. Right to Assign
A landlord may assign the rents and reversion interest that he owns. This is usually done by an ordinary deed from the landlord to the new owner of the building. Unless required by the lease (which is very unlikely), the consent of the tenants is not required.

b. Rights of Assignee Against Tenants
Once the tenants are given reasonable evidence that the assignment has occurred, they are legally obligated to recognize and pay rent to the new owner as their landlord. This is called *attornment*. The benefits of all other tenant covenants (*e.g.,* to repair, to pay taxes) also run with the landlord's estate and benefit the new landlord, provided that they touch and concern the land.

c. Liabilities of Assignee to Tenants
The assignee is liable to the tenants for performance of all covenants made by the original landlord in the lease, provided that those covenants touch and concern the land. The burdens of those covenants run with the landlord's estate and become the burdens of the new landlord. The *original landlord also remains liable* on all of the covenants he made in the lease.

Example: L leases to T, and in the lease covenants to repair and maintain the premises. L then sells the building to L2, subject to the lease. Because a covenant to repair and maintain touches and concerns the land, L2 is personally liable to T if L2 fails to perform the covenant. L also remains liable.

F. CONDEMNATION OF LEASEHOLDS

1. Entire Leasehold Taken by Eminent Domain—Rent Liability Extinguished
If all the leased land is condemned for the full balance of the lease term, the tenant's liability for rent is extinguished because both the leasehold and the reversion have merged in the condemnor and there is no longer a leasehold estate. Absent a lease provision to the contrary, the lessee is entitled to compensation for the taking of the leasehold estate (*i.e.,* fair market value of the lease).

2. Temporary or Partial Taking—Tenant Entitled to Compensation Only
If the taking is temporary (*i.e.,* for a period less than the remaining term), or if only a portion of the leased property is condemned, the tenant is *not* discharged from the rent obligation but is entitled to compensation (*i.e.,* a share of the condemnation award) for the taking.

G. TORT LIABILITY OF LANDLORD AND TENANT

1. Landlord's Liability
At common law, subject to a few exceptions, a landlord had no duty to make the premises safe. Today there are many significant exceptions to this rule.

a. Concealed Dangerous Condition (Latent Defect)
If, at the time the lease is entered into, the landlord knows (or should know) of a dangerous condition that the tenant could not discover upon reasonable inspection, the landlord has a *duty to disclose* the dangerous condition. Failure to disclose results in liability for any injury resulting from the condition.

Once disclosure is made, if the tenant accepts the premises, she is considered to have assumed the risk of injuries to herself or her guests (*e.g.,* family members, invitees, licensees); the landlord is no longer liable.

b. Public Use
A landlord is liable for injuries to members of the public if, at the time of the lease, he: (i) knows or should know of a dangerous condition, (ii) has reason to believe that the tenant may admit the public before repairing the condition (*e.g.,* because of short lease term), and (iii) fails to repair the condition. The landlord's liability extends only to people who enter the premises for the purpose for which the public is invited. Note that the tenant's promise to repair does not relieve the landlord of liability if the landlord has reason to suspect the tenant will admit the public before making the repair.

c. **Defects Arising After Tenant Takes Possession**
Generally, a landlord is *not liable* for injuries resulting from dangerous conditions that arise after the tenant takes possession. However, if the landlord voluntarily undertakes repairs that he is not obligated to make, he owes a duty of reasonable care. If the repairs are done negligently, the landlord is liable to those who do not know of the negligence and are injured.

d. **Landlord Contracts to Repair**
If a landlord covenants to repair, most courts hold that he is liable in tort for an injury to the tenant or the tenant's guests resulting from his failure to repair or negligent repair.

e. **Legal Duty to Repair**
If the landlord has a statutory duty to repair (*e.g.*, under the housing code), he may be liable to the tenant or the tenant's guests for injuries resulting from his failure to repair. Some courts hold that violation of the housing code (or similar statute) is negligence per se, but most courts hold that it is merely *evidence of negligence*, which the jury may or may not find conclusive. The same analysis probably applies to a violation of the implied warranty of habitability, but there are very few cases on point.

f. **Common Areas**
The landlord has a duty to exercise *reasonable care* over common areas, such as halls, walks, elevators, etc., that remain under his control. The landlord is liable for any injury resulting from a dangerous condition that could reasonably have been discovered and made safe. This duty is the same as the duty an owner-occupier owes his guests (*see* Torts outline).

g. **Furnished Short-Term Residence**
Where a furnished house or apartment is leased for a short term (*i.e.*, three months or less) for immediate occupancy, many jurisdictions hold that the landlord is liable if the premises are defective and cause injury to a tenant.

h. **Modern Trend—General Duty of Reasonable Care**
Increasingly, the courts are simply holding that landlords have a *general duty of reasonable care* with respect to residential tenants, and that they will be held liable for personal injuries of tenants and their guests resulting from the landlord's *ordinary negligence*, without regard to the exceptions discussed above. This duty is ordinarily not imposed until the landlord has *notice* of a particular defect and a reasonable opportunity to repair it.

1) **Security**
Some recent cases have held landlords liable for injuries inflicted on tenants by third-party criminals, where the landlord failed to comply with *housing code* provisions dealing with security, or failed to maintain *ordinary security* measures (*e.g.*, working locks on apartment doors), or where he *advertised extraordinary security* measures (television surveillance, doormen, security patrols, etc.) and then failed to provide them.

2. **Tenant's Liability**
The tenant, as occupier of the premises, may be liable in tort to third persons for dangerous conditions or activities on the leased property. The duty of care owed by the tenant as an occupier of land is discussed in the Torts outline.

III. FIXTURES

A. **IN GENERAL**
A "fixture" is a chattel that has been so affixed to land that it has ceased being personal property and has become part of the realty. For example, S and B contract to sell and buy a house. Before vacating, S removes a "built-in" refrigerator. B claims that the item was "part of the house." Is the refrigerator a "fixture"? If so, B is entitled to its return or appropriate compensation.

It is important in dealing with "fixture" problems to distinguish between *common ownership* cases and *divided ownership* cases. Courts treat them differently even though they often purport to apply the same tests. "Common ownership" cases are those in which the person who brings the chattel onto the land owns both the chattel and the realty (*e.g.*, X installs a furnace in her own home). "Divided ownership" cases are either ones where the person who owns and installs the chattel does not own the land (*e.g.*, T installs a furnace in her rented home, which belongs to L); or the person owns the land but does not own the chattel (*e.g.*, it is subject to a security interest held by the seller). In addition, there are cases involving more than two persons (*e.g.*, conflicting claims are made by the person having a security interest in the chattel and the mortgagee of the land).

B. CHATTELS INCORPORATED INTO STRUCTURE ALWAYS BECOME FIXTURES

In both common ownership and divided ownership cases, where the items become incorporated into the realty so that they lose their identity, they become part of the realty. Examples include bricks built into a building or concrete poured into a foundation. Similarly, where identification is possible, but removal would occasion considerable loss or destruction, the items are considered fixtures, *e.g.*, heating pipes embedded in the wall or floor of a house.

C. COMMON OWNERSHIP CASES

1. Annexor's Intent Controls in Common Ownership Cases

In all common ownership cases where a chattel is not incorporated into a structure, whether an item is a "fixture" (*i.e.*, part of the realty) depends upon the objective intention of the party who made the "annexation." This intention is determined by considering: (i) the nature of the article (*i.e.*, how essential the item is to normal use of the premises); (ii) the manner in which it is attached to the realty (the more substantially attached, the more likely it was intended to be permanent); (iii) the amount of damage that would be caused by its removal; and (iv) the adaptation of the item to the use of the realty (*e.g.*, custom window treatments, wall-to-wall carpet).

a. Constructive Annexation

In some cases an article of personal property is considered a fixture even though it is not physically annexed to the real estate at all. This is because it is so *uniquely adapted* to the real estate that it makes no sense to separate it. Examples include the keys to the doors of a house; curtain rods that have been cut and sized to the brackets on the walls of a house, even if the rods themselves are not presently installed; and a carpet that has been cut to fit an unusually shaped room, even if the carpet is not nailed or glued in place.

b. Vendor-Purchaser Cases

The typical situation is where the owner of land affixes chattels to the land and subsequently conveys the land without expressly providing whether the chattels are to pass with the realty. The intention test works fairly well. The question boils down to whether an owner bringing the disputed chattel to the realty would intend that it become part of the realty. Or to put it another way, *whether a reasonable purchaser would expect* that the disputed item was part of the realty.

c. Mortgagor-Mortgagee Cases

The intention test is universally applied to determine whether the owner (mortgagor) intended the chattels to become "part of the realty." Where the mortgagor has made the annexation *prior* to the giving of the mortgage, the question is what the "reasonably objective" lender expects to come within the security of her lien. However, where the annexation is made *after* the giving of the mortgage, the same considerations arguably should *not* apply because each item that is "added" to the lien of the mortgage represents a *windfall* to the mortgagee should foreclosure occur. Nevertheless, courts universally apply the same intention test regardless of when the annexation was made. (Courts also usually apply the intention test where items are annexed by one in possession of land under an *executory contract* to purchase.)

2. Effect of Fixture Classification

a. Conveyance

If a chattel has been categorized as a fixture, it is part of the real estate. A conveyance of the real estate, in the absence of any specific agreement to the contrary, passes the fixture with it. The fixture, as part of the realty, passes to the new owner of the real estate.

b. Mortgage

To the extent that the owner of the real estate mortgages the realty, in the absence of an agreement to the contrary, the mortgage attaches to all fixtures on the real estate.

c. Agreement to Contrary

Even though the concept of fixtures may apply and a chattel becomes a fixture, an agreement between a buyer and seller (similarly, between a mortgagor and mortgagee) can cause a severance of title. For example, a buyer and seller may agree that the seller will retain the right to remove fixtures. Similarly, a mortgagor and mortgagee can agree that the mortgage lien shall not attach to specified fixtures. The effect of such an agreement is to de-annex, so far as relevant, the chattel from the realty and reconvert the fixture into a chattel.

D. DIVIDED OWNERSHIP CASES

In divided ownership cases, unlike the ones just discussed, the chattel is owned and brought to the realty by someone who is not the landowner (*e.g.*, a tenant, a licensee, or a trespasser). The question is whether the ownership of the chattel has passed to the landowner. Courts often say that the intention test (C.1., *supra*) is to be applied in these cases too. But the exceptions disprove the rule.

1. Landlord-Tenant

Early English law favored the landlord. However, American law created a trade fixtures exception under which tradesmen-tenants could remove an item that otherwise would have been a "fixture." Later, this exception was expanded to include all tenants generally. Some courts have treated the trade fixtures exception as consistent with the annexor's-intention test; *i.e.*, a tenant's annexations are removable because "it was not the intention of the tenant to make them permanent annexations to the freehold and thereby donations to the owner of it."

a. Agreement

An agreement between the landlord and tenant is controlling on whether the chattel annexed to the premises was intended to become a fixture. To the extent that the landlord and tenant specifically agree that such annexation is not to be deemed a fixture, the agreement controls.

b. No Intent If Removal Does Not Cause Damage

In the absence of an express agreement to the contrary, a tenant may remove a chattel that he has attached to the demised premises as long as the removal does not cause substantial damage to the demised premises or the virtual destruction of the chattel. In other words, the tenant will *not* have manifested an intention to permanently improve the freehold (and the concept of fixtures will be inapplicable) as long as the removal of the chattel does not cause substantial damage to the premises or the destruction of the chattel.

c. Removal Must Occur Before End of Lease Term

Generally, a tenant must remove his annexed chattels before the termination of his tenancy or they become the property of the landlord. If the duration of the tenancy is indefinite (*e.g.*, tenancy at will), the removal must occur within a reasonable time after the tenancy terminates. Similarly, a tenant has a reasonable time for removal if he holds over during unsuccessful negotiations for a new lease.

d. Tenant Has Duty to Repair Damages Resulting from Removal

Tenants are responsible for repairing damages caused by removal of "fixtures."

2. Life Tenant and Remainderman

The same rules should apply here as in the landlord-tenant cases. Historically, however, results have been more favorable to the remaindermen (or reversioners). Apart from statute, the removal privilege has been unrealistically limited to the duration of the term.

3. Licensee and Landowner

Licenses to bring items onto land usually contain agreements respecting removal. In the absence of agreement, licensees are permitted to remove the items subject to a duty to repair damages caused thereby.

4. Trespasser and Landowner

Trespassers (*e.g.*, adverse possessors before the running of the statute of limitations) normally lose their annexations whether installed in good faith or not. This follows from the intention test: The good faith trespasser, believing the land to be her own, normally intends annexation of an item to be permanent.

E. THIRD-PARTY CASES
Any of the foregoing cases is complicated by the addition of third-person claimants. The situations can be classified under two headings.

1. Third Person Claims Lien on Land to Which Chattels Affixed
Suppose Landowner mortgages her land to Mortgagee. Landowner then leases the land to Tenant, who annexes an item (*e.g.*, a machine) that is a "trade fixture" and thus removable at the end of the term. Landowner defaults before the end of the term, and Mortgagee forecloses. Is the item subject to the lien of the mortgage?

(i) Generally, no. In this situation, the mortgagee has no greater rights than the mortgagor, provided only that the original sufficiency of the security is not impaired (*e.g.*, removal would not substantially damage a building in existence when the mortgage was given).

(ii) The same result obtains where a buyer under an installment land contract leases to a tenant, the tenant makes annexations, and the buyer then defaults. The seller is treated in the same manner as the mortgagee in the first example.

If, in the above example, the land mortgage is made *after* the lease and after the tenant has annexed an item that is a "trade fixture" as against the landlord-mortgagor, and, as is usual, the land mortgagee has *notice* of the tenant's rights, the mortgagee is in no better position than the landlord-mortgagor. If the mortgagee does not have notice, he wins if the item would have been considered a fixture as between the mortgagee and the mortgagor. (The same result pertains in cases where the landlord *sells* the property after the making of a lease.)

2. Third Person Claims Lien on Chattel Affixed to Land
Suppose Landowner purchases a furnace from Seller and installs it in her house. She owes a balance on the purchase price of the furnace, and therefore grants Seller a *security interest* in the furnace (in accordance with Article 9 of the Uniform Commercial Code). Suppose further that Landowner also executes a *mortgage* on her house, to Mortgagee. If Landowner subsequently defaults on her payments, both on the furnace and the house, is Seller or Mortgagee entitled to priority? (Same issue where Landowner *sells* the house without mentioning the security interest.)

a. U.C.C. Rules
Normally, the rule is that whichever interest is *first recorded* in the local *real estate records* wins. (Thus, if the chattel security interest was recorded first, it constitutes "constructive notice" to all subsequent lenders or purchasers.) However, an *exception* allows a *"purchase money security interest"* in an affixed chattel (here, the interest given Seller to secure payment on the furnace) to prevail even over a *prior recorded* mortgage on the land, as long as the chattel interest is recorded *within 20 days* after the chattel is affixed to the land. [U.C.C. §9-334]

The document used to record the chattel security interest is known as a *"fixture filing."* (This is a separate instrument from the "financing statement," which is required to be filed to perfect the chattel security interest in the first place.)

b. Liability for Damages Caused by Removal
In the above example, if Seller were entitled to priority, she would be entitled to remove the furnace. However, she would have to reimburse Mortgagee for any *damages or repair* necessitated by the removal (but *not* for diminution in value of the property due to the lack of a furnace).

IV. RIGHTS IN THE LAND OF ANOTHER—EASEMENTS, PROFITS, COVENANTS, AND SERVITUDES

A. IN GENERAL
Easements, profits, covenants, and servitudes are *nonpossessory* interests in land. They create a right to *use land possessed by someone else*. For example, A, the owner of Blackacre, grants to

B, the owner of an adjacent parcel, Whiteacre, the right to use a path over Blackacre connecting Whiteacre to a public road. An easement has been created, giving B the right to use—but *not* to possess—the pathway over Blackacre. Easements, profits, covenants, and servitudes have many similarities in operation, coverage, creation, and termination. They also have important differences, mainly in the requirements that must be met for their enforcement.

B. EASEMENTS

1. Introduction

The holder of an easement has the *right to use* a tract of land (called the servient tenement) for a special purpose, but has *no right to possess and enjoy* the tract of land. The owner of the servient tenement continues to have the right of full possession and enjoyment subject only to the limitation that he cannot interfere with the right of special use created in the easement holder. Typically, easements are created in order to give their holder the right of access across a tract of land, *e.g.,* the privilege of laying utility lines, or installing sewer pipes and the like. Easements are either affirmative or negative, appurtenant or in gross.

a. Types of Easements

1) Affirmative Easements

Affirmative easements entitle the holder *to enter upon the servient tenement and make an affirmative use of it* for such purposes as laying and maintaining utility lines, draining waters, and polluting the air over the servient estate. The *right-of-way* easement is another instance of an affirmative easement. Thus, an affirmative easement privileges the holder of the benefit to make a use of the servient estate that, absent the easement, would be an unlawful trespass or nuisance.

2) Negative Easements

A negative easement does not grant to its owner the right to enter upon the servient tenement. It does, however, entitle the privilege holder to compel the possessor of the servient tenement to *refrain from engaging in activity* upon the servient tenement that, were it not for the existence of the easement, he would be privileged to do. In reality, a negative easement is simply a restrictive covenant. (*See* D.1.e.1), *infra.*)

Example: A owns Lot 6. By written instrument, he stipulates to B that he will not build any structure upon Lot 6 within 35 feet of the lot line. B has acquired a negative easement in Lot 6.

Courts hesitate to recognize new forms of negative easements and generally have confined them to a traditional handful: easements for *light, air, subjacent or lateral support,* and for the *flow of an artificial stream*.

b. Easement Appurtenant

An easement is deemed appurtenant when the right of special use benefits the holder of the easement in his physical use or enjoyment of another tract of land. For an easement appurtenant to exist, there must be *two tracts* of land. One is called the dominant tenement, which has the benefit of the easement. The second tract is the servient tenement, which is subject to the easement right. One consequence of appurtenance is that the benefit passes with transfers of the benefited land, regardless of whether the easement is mentioned in the conveyance.

Example: A owns Lot 6 and B owns Lot 7, which are adjoining tracts of land. By a written instrument, B grants to A the right to cross B's tract (Lot 7). A's use and enjoyment of Lot 6 is benefited by virtue of the acquisition of the right to use Lot 7 for this special purpose. The right is an easement appurtenant. B remains the owner of Lot 7. A has only a right to use Lot 7 for a special purpose, *i.e.,* the right to cross the tract.

1) Use and Enjoyment

In an easement appurtenant, the benefits to be realized by the easement must be directly beneficial to the possessor of the *dominant tenement* in his physical use and enjoyment of that tract of land. It is not sufficient that the easement makes use of the land more profitable.

Example: A owns Lot 6 and B owns adjacent Lot 7. A grants to B the right to use part of Lot 6 to mine coal. The right is not an easement appurtenant since the benefit granted is not related to B's physical use and enjoyment of Lot 7.

2) **Benefit Attached to Possession**

The benefit of an easement appurtenant becomes an incident of the possession of the dominant tenement. All who possess or subsequently succeed to title to the dominant tenement become, by virtue of the fact of possession, entitled to the benefit of the easement. There can be no conveyance of the easement right apart from possession of the dominant tenement, except that the easement holder may convey the easement to the owner of the servient tenement in order to extinguish the easement.

3) **Transfer of Dominant and Servient Estates**

Both the dominant and servient parcels can be transferred. As discussed above, if the dominant parcel is transferred, the benefit of the easement goes with it automatically—even if it is not mentioned in the deed—and becomes the property of the new owner. If the servient parcel is transferred, its new owner takes it subject to the burden of the easement, unless she is a bona fide purchaser (*see* VI.E.3., *infra*) with no notice of the easement. There are three ways the person who acquires the servient land might have notice of the easement: (i) actual knowledge; (ii) notice from the visible appearance of the easement on the land; and (iii) notice from the fact that the document creating the easement is recorded in the public records. Everyone who buys land is expected to inspect the land physically and to examine the public records.

Example: A owns Lot 6 and grants B (the owner of Lot 7) an easement for a driveway across Lot 6 to benefit adjacent Lot 7. The easement is not recorded. Then A sells Lot 6 to X. The tire tracks of the driveway are plainly visible at the time of the sale. X is therefore not a bona fide purchaser, and takes Lot 6 subject to the easement.

c. **Easement in Gross**

An easement in gross is created where the holder of the easement interest acquires a right of special use in the servient tenement independent of his ownership or possession of another tract of land. In an easement in gross, the easement holder is not benefited in his use and enjoyment of a possessory estate by virtue of the acquisition of that privilege. There is no dominant tenement. An easement in gross passes entirely apart from any transfer of land.

Example: A owns Lot 6. By a written instrument, she grants to B the right to build a pipeline across Lot 6. B receives the privilege independent of his ownership or possession of a separate tract of land. B has acquired an easement in gross.

Easements in gross can be either personal (*e.g.*, O gives friend right to swim and boat on lake) or commercial (*e.g.*, utility or railroad track easements). Generally, an easement in gross is transferable only if the easement is for a commercial or economic purpose.

d. **Judicial Preference for Easements Appurtenant**

If an easement interest is created and its owner holds a corporeal (possessory) estate that is or could be benefited in physical use or enjoyment by the acquisition of the privilege, the easement will be deemed appurtenant. This is true even though the deed creating the easement makes no reference to a dominant tenement.

Example: A conveys to "B, her heirs, successors and assigns, the right to use a strip 20 feet wide on the north edge of Blackacre for ingress and egress to Whiteacre." Because there is ambiguity as to whether the benefit was intended to attach to B's land, Whiteacre, or to B personally, a court will apply the constructional preference and hold that the benefit was intended to be appurtenant, with the consequence that any conveyance of Whiteacre by B will carry with it the right to use the strip across Blackacre.

2. **Creation of Easements**

The basic methods of creating an easement are: express grant or reservation, implication, and prescription.

a. **Express Grant**

Since an easement is an interest in land, the Statute of Frauds applies. Therefore, any easement must be in writing and signed by the grantor (the holder of the servient tenement) unless its duration is brief enough (commonly one year or less) to be outside a particular state's Statute of Frauds' coverage. An easement can be created by conveyance. A grant of an easement must comply with all the formal requisites of a deed. An easement is presumed to be of perpetual duration unless the grant specifically limits the interest (*e.g.,* for life, for 10 years, etc.).

b. Express Reservation

An easement by reservation arises when the owner (of a present possessory interest) of a tract of land conveys title but reserves the right to continue to use the tract for a special purpose after the conveyance. In effect, the grantor passes title to the land but reserves unto himself an easement interest. Note that, under the majority view, the easement can be reserved *only for the grantor*; an attempt by the grantor to reserve an easement for anyone else is void. (There is a growing trend to permit reservations in third parties, but it remains a minority view.)

Example: G owns Lot 6 and Lot 7, which are adjacent. G sells Lot 7 to B. Later, when G is about to sell Lot 6 to A, B asks G to reserve an easement over Lot 6 in favor of B. G agrees to do so, and executes a deed of Lot 6 to A that contains the following language: "Reserving an easement for a driveway in favor of Lot 7, which is owned by B." The reservation clause is void and no easement is created.

c. Implication

An easement by implication is created by *operation of law* rather than by written instrument. It is an exception to the Statute of Frauds. There are only two types of implied easements: (i) an intended easement based on a use that existed when the dominant and servient estates were severed, and (ii) an easement by necessity.

1) Easement Implied from Existing Use ("Quasi-Easement")

An easement may be implied if, prior to the time the tract is divided, a use exists on the "servient part" that is reasonably necessary for the enjoyment of the "dominant part" and a court determines that the parties intended the use to continue after division of the property. It is sometimes called a "quasi-easement" before the tract is divided because an owner cannot hold an easement on his own land.

a) Existing Use at Time Tract Divided

For a use to give rise to an easement, it must be apparent and continuous at the time the tract is divided. "Apparent" means that a grantee could discover the existence of the use upon reasonable inspection. A nonvisible use may still be "apparent" if surface connections or the like would put a reasonable person on notice of its existence.

b) Reasonable Necessity

Whether a use is reasonably necessary to the enjoyment of the dominant parcel depends on many factors, including the cost and difficulty of the alternatives and whether the price paid reflects the expected continued use of the servient portion of the tract.

c) Grant or Reservation

An easement implied in favor of the grantee is said to be created by implied grant, while an easement implied in favor of the grantor is said to be created by implied reservation.

2) Easements Implied Without Any Existing Use

In two limited situations, easements are implied in a conveyance even though there is no preexisting use.

a) Subdivision Plat

Where lots are sold in a subdivision with reference to a recorded plat or map that also shows streets leading to the lots, buyers of the lots have implied easements to use the streets in order to gain access to their lots. These easements continue to exist even if the *public* easements held by the city or county in the streets are later vacated.

b) Profit a Prendre

Where a landowner grants a profit a prendre to a person to remove a valuable product of the soil (*e.g.,* grass, asphalt, ore, etc.), the holder of the profit also has an implied easement to pass over the surface of the land and to use it as reasonably necessary to extract the product.

3) Easement by Necessity

When the owner of a tract of land sells a part of the tract and by this division deprives one lot of access to a public road, a right-of-way by absolute necessity is created by implied grant or reservation over the lot with access to the public road. The owner of the servient parcel has the right to locate the easement, provided the location is reasonably convenient. An easement by necessity terminates when the necessity ceases.

d. Prescription

Acquiring an easement by prescription is analogous to acquiring property by adverse possession. (*See* V., *infra.*) Many of the requirements are the same: To acquire a prescriptive easement, the use must be ***open and notorious***; ***adverse and under claim of right***; ***and continuous and uninterrupted for the statutory period***. Note that the public at large can acquire an easement in private land if members of the public use the land in a way that meets the requirements for prescription.

1) Open and Notorious

The user must not attempt to conceal his use. Underground or other nonvisible uses, such as pipes and electric lines, are considered open and notorious if the use could be discovered (*e.g.,* through surface connections) upon inspection.

2) Adverse

The use must not be with the owner's permission. Unlike adverse possession, the use need not be exclusive. The user of a common driveway, for example, may acquire a prescriptive easement even though the owner uses it too.

3) Continuous Use

Continuous adverse use does not mean constant use. A continuous claim of right with periodic acts that put the owner on notice of the claimed easement fulfills the requirement. Note that tacking is permitted for prescriptive easements, just as for adverse possession (*see* V.B.4.b., *infra*).

4) When Prescriptive Easements Cannot Be Acquired

Negative easements cannot arise by prescription, nor generally may easements in public lands. An easement by necessity cannot give rise to an easement by prescription. However, if the necessity ends, so does the easement, and the use is adverse from that point forward.

3. Scope

Courts enforcing easements are often called upon to interpret the arrangement in order to determine the ***scope*** and ***intended beneficiaries*** of the interest. The key to interpretation employed in all these cases is the ***reasonable intent of the original parties***. What would the parties reasonably have provided had they contemplated the situation now before the court? What result would reasonably serve the purposes of the arrangement?

a. General Rules of Construction

If, as typically happens, the language used is general (*e.g.,* "a right-of-way over Blackacre"), the following rules of construction usually apply: (i) ambiguities are resolved in favor of the grantee (unless the conveyance is gratuitous); (ii) subsequent conduct of the parties respecting the arrangement is relevant; (iii) the parties are assumed to have intended a scope that would reasonably serve the purposes of the grant and to have foreseen reasonable changes in the use of the dominant estate. The rule of reasonableness will be applied only to the extent that the governing language is general. If the location or scope of the permitted use is spelled out in detail, the specifics will govern, and reasonable interpretation will be excluded.

Examples: 1) In 1890, A, the owner of Blackacre, granted to B, the owner of Whiteacre, a "right-of-way" over Blackacre for purposes of ingress and egress to Whiteacre from the public highway running along the western boundary of Blackacre. At the time of the grant, there were only horses and buggies, no automobiles. Applying a "rule of reasonableness" to the general language creating the right-of-way, a court would probably find that the right-of-way could today be used for cars. If, however, the use of cars would impose a ***substantially*** greater burden on Blackacre, the court would probably find against this use on grounds that it was outside the scope reasonably contemplated by A and B.

2) If, in the example just given, the right-of-way was specifically dedicated ("only to the use of horses and carriages"), automobile use would be excluded. Similarly, if the right-of-way was specifically located (*e.g.,* "over the southern 10 feet of Blackacre"), the rule of reasonableness could not be invoked to change or enlarge the location.

b. Absence of Location
If an easement is created but not specifically located on the servient tenement, an easement of sufficient width, height, and direction to make the intended use reasonably convenient will be implied. The owner of the servient tenement may select the location of the easement so long as her selection is reasonable.

c. Changes in Use
In the absence of specific limitations in the deed creating an easement, the courts will assume that the easement is intended by the parties to meet both present and future reasonable needs of the dominant tenement.

Examples: 1) A roadway easement of unspecified width was created in 1920, when cars were only six feet wide. In the 1970s, however, cars were considerably wider. Since the original roadway easement was not specifically limited in width, the easement will expand in size to accommodate the changing and expanding needs of the owner of the dominant tenement.

2) But a basic change in the nature of the use is not allowed. Thus, a telephone or power line may not be added on the roadway. (Many courts are more liberal in allowing such additions if the roadway easement is public rather than private.)

d. Easements by Necessity or Implication
In the case of easements by necessity, the *extent of the necessity determines the scope* of the easement. Since there is no underlying written instrument to interpret, courts will look instead to the circumstances giving rise to the easement. Similarly, with other implied easements, the *quasi-easement* will provide the starting point for the court's construction of the scope of the easement. Modifications in the easement will be enforced to the extent that they are necessary for reasonably foreseeable changes in the use of the dominant parcel.

e. Use of Servient Estate
Absent an express restriction in the original agreement, the owner of the servient estate may use her land in any way she wishes so long as her conduct does not interfere with performance of the easement, profit, covenant, or servitude.

Example: A grants to B Water Company the right to lay water pipes in a specified five-foot right-of-way. A is not by this grant necessarily precluded from granting similar rights in the same right-of-way to a competing company, so long as the second grant does not interfere with the use made by B, the original grantee. A may also build over the right-of-way so long as the structure does not unreasonably interfere with B's use.

The holder of the benefit has a duty to make repairs (*e.g.,* fill in potholes on a right-of-way) and, absent a special agreement, the servient owner has no duty to do so.

f. Intended Beneficiaries—Subdivision of Dominant Parcel
When an easement is created for the benefit of a landowner, and the landowner later subdivides the parcel, there is a question whether each subdivision grantee will succeed to the original benefit. The answer will turn on whether the extension of the benefit to each of the subdivided parcels will burden the servient estate to a greater extent than was contemplated by the original parties. Absent any other evidence on intent, a court will not find an intent to allow an extension if extending the benefit to each parcel in the subdivision will unreasonably overburden the servient estate. Weighing all the circumstances, a court could find subdivision into four lots reasonable, but subdivision into 50 lots unreasonable; it is determined on a case-by-case basis.

Example: A, owner of Blackacre, grants to B, owner of Whiteacre, a right-of-way easement of ingress and egress over Blackacre. B then subdivides

Whiteacre into 150 lots. If A and B had not contemplated the subdivision of Whiteacre, and if use of the right-of-way by all 150 lot owners would substantially interfere with A's use of Blackacre (in a way that B's use alone would not), a court would probably not find an intent that the benefit of the right-of-way easement attach to each of the 150 parcels.

g. Effect of Use Outside Scope of Easement

When the owner of an easement uses it in a way that exceeds its legal scope, the easement is said to be *surcharged*. The remedy of the servient landowner is an *injunction* of the excess use, and possibly damages if the servient land has been harmed. However, the excess use *does not terminate* the easement or give the servient landowner a power of termination.

4. Termination of Easements

An easement, like any other property interest, may be created to last in perpetuity or for a limited period of time. To the extent the parties to its original creation provide for the natural termination of the interest, such limitations will control.

a. Stated Conditions

If the parties to the original creation of an easement set forth specific conditions upon the happening of which the easement right will terminate, the conditions will be recognized. On this basis, the following conditions are valid: an easement granted "so long as repairs are maintained," an easement granted "so long as X is the holder of the dominant tenement," an easement granted "until the dominant tenement is used for commercial purposes," etc.

b. Unity of Ownership

By definition, an easement is the right to use the lands of another for a special purpose. On this basis, the ownership of the easement and of the servient tenement must be in different persons. If ownership of the two comes together in one person, the easement is extinguished.

1) Complete Unity Required

For an easement to be extinguished, there must be complete unity of ownership as between the interest held in the easement and that held in the servient tenement. In other words, if the holder of an easement acquires an interest in the servient tenement, the easement is extinguished only if he acquires an interest in the servient tenement of *equal or greater duration* than the duration of the easement privilege. Conversely, if the holder of the servient tenement acquires the easement interests, the title acquired must be *equal to or greater than her interest* or estate in the servient tenement. If there is incomplete acquisition of title, the easement will not be extinguished.

Example: A is the owner of the servient tenement in fee simple. B has an access easement across the servient tenement and the duration of the easement is in fee simple. A conveys a 10-year term tenancy in the servient tenement to B. There is no complete unity of ownership. The easement right is of longer duration than is the estate acquired by B in the servient tenement. Therefore, the easement is not extinguished.

2) No Revival

If complete unity of title is acquired, the easement is extinguished. Even though there may be later separation, the easement will not be automatically revived.

Example: A owns Lot 6, the servient tenement. B owns adjacent Lot 7. A grants to B the privilege of crossing Lot 6, *i.e.,* grants an easement appurtenant to B. Assume A conveys Lot 6 to B in fee simple. The easement would be extinguished since B then holds both the easement and title to the servient tenement. If, thereafter, B conveys Lot 6 to C, the easement is not revived. Of course, it could be created anew.

c. Release

An easement may be terminated by a release given by the owner of the easement interest to the owner of the servient tenement. A release requires the *concurrence of both owners* and is, in effect, a conveyance. The release must be executed with all the formalities that are required for the valid creation of an easement.

1) Easement Appurtenant

The basic characteristic of an easement appurtenant is that it becomes, for the purpose of succession, an incident of possession of the dominant tenement. This basic characteristic requires that the easement interest not be conveyed independently of a conveyance of the dominant tenement. However, an easement appurtenant may be conveyed to the owner of the servient tenement without a conveyance (to the same grantee) of the dominant tenement. This is an exception to the general alienability characteristics of an easement appurtenant (*see* B.1.b., *supra*).

2) Easement in Gross

The basic characteristic of an easement in gross is that unless it is for a commercial purpose, it is inalienable. However, an easement in gross can be released; *i.e.,* can be conveyed to the owner of the servient tenement. This is an exception to the general characteristics of an easement in gross.

3) Statute of Frauds

The Statute of Frauds requires that every conveyance of an interest in land that has a duration long enough to bring into play a particular state's Statute of Frauds (typically one year) must be evidenced by a writing. This writing requirement is also applicable to a release of an easement interest. If the easement interest that is being conveyed has a duration of greater than one year, it must be in writing in order to satisfy the Statute of Frauds. An oral release is ineffective, although it may become effective by estoppel.

d. Abandonment

It has become an established rule that an easement can be extinguished without conveyance where the owner of the privilege demonstrates by physical action an intention to ***permanently*** abandon the easement. To work as an abandonment, the owner must have manifested an intention never to make use of the easement again.

Example: A owns Lot 6 and B owns Lot 7, which are immediately adjacent. A grants to B an easement across Lot 6. This easement is specifically located on the servient tenement and is a walkway. Subsequently, B constructs a house on Lot 7 that completely blocks his access to the walkway. By the physical action of constructing the house in such a way that access to the walkway (*i.e.,* the easement) is denied, B has physically indicated an intent not to use the easement again. The easement is extinguished by abandonment.

1) Physical Act Required

An abandonment of an easement occurs when the easement holder physically manifests an intention to permanently abandon the easement. Such physical action brings about a termination of the easement by operation of law and therefore no writing is required; *i.e.,* the Statute of Frauds need not be complied with.

2) Mere Words Insufficient

The oral expressions of the owner of the easement that he does not intend to use the easement again (*i.e.,* wishes to abandon) are insufficient to constitute an abandonment of the easement. For words to operate as a termination, such expression will only be effective if it qualifies as a release. In other words, the Statute of Frauds must be complied with.

3) Mere Nonuse Insufficient

An easement is not terminated merely because it is not used for a long period by its owner. To terminate the easement, the nonuse must be combined with other evidence of intent to abandon it. Nonuse itself is not considered sufficient evidence of that intent.

e. Estoppel

While the assertions of the holder of the easement are insufficient to work a termination unless there is valid compliance with the requirements of a release, an easement may be extinguished by virtue of the reasonable reliance and change of position of the owner of the servient tenement, based on assertions or conduct of the easement holder.

Example: The owner of a right-of-way tells the owner of the servient tenement that the owner of the servient tenement may build a building on the servient tenement in such a way as to make the right-of-way no longer usable, and the servient owner does in fact build the building. There will be an extinguishment of the easement by estoppel.

For an easement to be extinguished by estoppel, three requirements must be satisfied. Namely, there must be (i) some *conduct or assertion* by the owner of the easement, (ii) a *reasonable reliance* by the owner of the servient tenement, (iii) coupled with a *change of position*. Even though there is an assertion by the easement holder, if the owner of the servient tenement does not change her position based upon the assertion, the easement will not be terminated.

f. Prescription
An easement may be extinguished, as well as created, by prescription. Long continued possession and enjoyment of the servient tenement in a way that would indicate to the public that no easement right existed will end the easement right. Such long continued use works as a statute of limitations precluding the whole world, including the easement holder, from asserting that his privilege exists.

The termination of an easement by prescription is fixed by analogy to the creation of an easement by prescription. The owner of the servient tenement must so *interfere with the easement* as to create a cause of action in favor of the easement holder. The interference must be open, notorious, continuous, and nonpermissive for the period of 20 years.

g. Necessity
Easements created by necessity *expire as soon as the necessity ends*.
Example: A, the owner of a tract of land, sells a portion of it that has no access to a highway except over the remaining lands of A. B, the purchaser, acquires by necessity a right-of-way over the remaining lands of A. Some years later, a highway is built so that B no longer needs the right-of-way across A's property. The easement ends since the necessity has disappeared.

h. Condemnation
Condemnation of the servient estate will extinguish the nonpossessory interest. Courts are split, however, on whether the holder of the benefit is entitled to compensation for the value lost.

i. Destruction of Servient Estate
If the easement is in a structure (*e.g.,* a staircase), involuntary destruction of the structure (*e.g.,* by fire or flood) will extinguish the easement. Voluntary destruction (*e.g.,* tearing down a building to erect a new one) will not, however, terminate the easement.

5. Compare—Licenses
Licenses, like affirmative easements, privilege their holder to go upon the land of another (the licensor). Unlike an affirmative easement, the license is *not an interest in land*. It is merely a *privilege*, revocable at the will of the licensor. (Although licenses may acquire some of the characteristics of easements through estoppel or by being coupled with an interest.) The Statute of Frauds does not apply to licenses, and licensees are not entitled to compensation if the land is taken by eminent domain. Licenses are quite common; examples of licensees include delivery persons, plumbers, party guests, etc.

a. Assignability
An essential characteristic of a license is that it is *personal to the licensee* and therefore *not alienable*. The holder of a license privilege cannot convey such right. In fact, most courts have held that the license privilege is so closely tied to the individual parties that it is revoked, by operation of law, upon an attempted transfer by the licensee.

b. Revocation and Termination
Another essential characteristic of a license is that it is revocable by nature. It may be revoked at any time by a manifestation of the licensor's intent to end it. This manifestation may be by a formal notice of revocation or it may consist of conduct that obstructs

the licensee's continued use. Similarly, the licensee can surrender the privilege whenever he desires to do so. A license ends by operation of law upon the death of the licensor. In addition, a conveyance of the servient tenement by the licensor terminates the licensee's privilege.

1) Public Amusement Cases

Tickets issued by theaters, race courses, and other places of amusement have given rise to some controversy. The traditional rule is that such tickets create a license. Once describing the tickets as granting a license, the essential characteristic of a license applies; *i.e.,* it is revocable by nature. On this basis, the licensor may terminate the licensee's privilege at will.

2) Breach of Contract

A license may be granted pursuant to an express or implied contract between the licensor and licensee. On this basis, the termination of the licensee's privilege may constitute a breach of contract. While many courts may grant a cause of action for money damages for a revocation of a license in breach of contract, they continue to sustain the licensor's right to terminate the licensee's privilege to continue to remain on the servient tenement.

Example: A pays a $70 greens fee to play 18 holes of golf on B's property. After A has played only nine holes, B terminates A's right to be on B's property. Since A acquired a license and it is revocable by its very nature, B's action is not, in property terms, wrongful. However, A may have a cause of action against B to recoup part or all of A's $70.

c. Failure to Create an Easement

The Statute of Frauds requires that any conveyance of an interest in land (including an easement interest) of duration greater than one year must be in writing to be enforceable. If a party attempts to create an easement orally, the result is the creation of a license, *i.e.,* a revocable privilege. Note, however, that if an oral attempt to create an easement is subsequently "executed," to the extent that it would be inequitable to permit its revocation (*e.g.,* the licensee has expended substantial funds in reliance on the license), the licensor may be estopped to revoke the license.

d. Irrevocable Licenses

1) Estoppel Theory

If a licensee invests substantial amounts of money or labor in reliance on a license, the licensor may be estopped to revoke the license, and the license will thus become the equivalent of an affirmative easement.

Example: A orally licenses B to come onto Blackacre to excavate a drainage ditch connected to B's parcel, Whiteacre. B does so at substantial expense. A will probably be estopped to revoke the license and prevent B from using the ditch.

Under the majority view, such irrevocable licenses or easements by estoppel last until the owner receives sufficient benefit to reimburse himself for the expenditures made in reliance on the license. A minority of courts treat easements by estoppel like any other affirmative easements and give them a potentially infinite duration.

2) License Coupled with an Interest

If a license is coupled with an interest, it will be irrevocable as long as the interest lasts.

a) Vendee of a Chattel

The purchaser of a chattel located upon the seller's land is, in the absence of an express stipulation to the contrary, given the privilege to enter upon the seller's land for the purpose of removing the chattel. The purchaser's right is irrevocable. He must, however, enter at reasonable times and in a reasonable manner.

Example: A, the owner of Blackacre, sells 100 crates of oranges stored in a shed on Blackacre and at the same time licenses B to come onto Blackacre to remove the crates of oranges. B has an irrevocable license to enter Blackacre and remove the crates within a reasonable time.

b) Termination of Tenancy
If a tenant's right to possess land has been lawfully terminated, the tenant may still reenter the land at reasonable times and in a reasonable manner for the purpose of removing his chattels. This is an irrevocable privilege.

c) Inspection for Waste
The owner of a future interest in land (*e.g.,* a landlord, holder of a reversionary interest, or a remainderman) is privileged to enter upon the land, at reasonable times and in a reasonable manner, for the purpose of determining whether waste is being committed by the holder of the present possessory estate.

C. PROFITS
Like an easement, a profit (profit a prendre) is a *nonpossessory* interest in land. The holder of the profit is entitled to enter upon the servient tenement and take the soil or a substance of the soil (*e.g.,* minerals, timber, oil, or game). Also, like an easement, a profit may be appurtenant or in gross. In contrast to easements, however, there is a constructional preference for profits in gross rather than appurtenant.

1. Creation
Profits are created in the same way as easements.

2. Alienability
A profit appurtenant follows the ownership of the dominant tenement. A profit in gross may be assigned or transferred by the holder.

3. Exclusive and Nonexclusive Profits Distinguished
When an owner grants the *sole right* to take a resource from her land, the grantee takes an exclusive profit and is solely entitled to the resources, even to the exclusion of the owner of the servient estate. By contrast, when a profit is nonexclusive, the owner of the servient estate may grant similar rights to others or may take the resources herself. Ordinarily, profits (like easements) are construed as nonexclusive.

4. Scope
The extent and nature of the profit is determined by the words of the *express grant* (if there was a grant), or by *the nature of the use* (if the profit was acquired by prescription). Note that implied in every profit is an easement entitling the profit holder to enter the servient estate to remove the resource.

Example: A, the owner of Blackacre, grants B the right to come onto Blackacre to carry off gravel from a pit on Blackacre. B has a profit with respect to the gravel and also the benefit of an implied affirmative easement to go onto Blackacre by reasonable means to remove the gravel.

a. Apportionment of Profits Appurtenant
Courts treat the subdivision of land with a profit appurtenant just as they treat the subdivision of land with an easement appurtenant. The *benefit of the profit* will attach to each parcel in a subdivision *only* if the burden on the servient estate is not as a result *overly increased*.

Example: A, owner of Blackacre, grants B, owner of adjacent Whiteacre, the right to take water from a pond situated on Blackacre. If the profit was to take water for purposes of household consumption on Whiteacre, then an increase in use from 1 to 150 households when Whiteacre is subdivided will probably be viewed as overburdensome to Blackacre.

If, however, the profit was to take water for purposes of irrigating Whiteacre, apportionment would be allowed because subdivision would not increase the number of acres to be irrigated and consequently would not impose a greater burden on Blackacre.

b. Apportionment of Profits in Gross
Since profits are freely alienable, a question frequently arises as to whether the holder

of a profit can convey it to several people. If a profit is exclusive, the holder may transfer the profit to as many transferees as he likes. Likewise, if the grant of the profit specifies a limit on the profit (less than all), the right can be transferred to multiple transferees. If, however, the profit is nonexclusive and not limited as to amount, it is generally not divisible. Undue burden to the servient estate is again the benchmark, however, and a nonexclusive profit may be assigned to a single person or to several persons jointly if the multiple assignees work together and take no more resources than would have been taken by the original benefit holder.

5. Termination

Profits are terminated in the same way as easements. In addition, *misuse* of a profit, unduly increasing the burden (typically through an improper apportionment), will be held to *surcharge* the servient estate. The result of surcharge in this case is to extinguish the profit. (Contrast this with the result when the benefit of an *affirmative easement* is misused: improper or excessive use increasing the burden on the servient estate is *enjoinable* but, in most jurisdictions, does not extinguish the easement.)

D. COVENANTS RUNNING WITH THE LAND AT LAW (REAL COVENANTS)

A real covenant, normally found in deeds, is a *written promise* to do something on the land (*e.g.,* maintain a fence) or a promise not to do something on the land (*e.g.,* conduct commercial business). Real covenants run with the land at law, which means that subsequent owners of the land may enforce or be burdened by the covenant. To run with the land, however, the benefit and burden of the covenant must be analyzed separately to determine whether they meet the requirements for running.

1. Requirements for Burden to Run

If all requirements are met for the burden to run, the successor in interest to the burdened estate will be bound by the arrangement entered into by her predecessor as effectively as if she had herself expressly agreed to be bound.

a. Intent

The covenanting parties must have intended that successors in interest to the covenantor be bound by the terms of the covenant. The requisite intent may be inferred from circumstances surrounding creation of the covenant, or it may be evidenced by language in the conveyance creating the covenant (*e.g.,* "this covenant runs with the land," or "grantee covenants for herself, her heirs, successors and assigns").

b. Notice

Under the common law, a subsequent purchaser of land that was subject to a covenant took the land burdened by the covenant, whether or not she had notice. However, under American recording statutes (*see* VI.E., *infra*), if the covenant is not recorded, a bona fide purchaser who has no notice of the covenant and who records her own deed *will take free* of the covenant. Hence as a practical matter, if the subsequent purchaser pays value and records (as will nearly always be true), she is not bound by covenants of which she has no actual or constructive notice.

c. Horizontal Privity

This requirement rests on the relationship between the *original covenanting parties*. Specifically, horizontal privity requires that, at the time the promisor entered into the covenant with the promisee, the two shared *some interest in the land independent of the covenant* (*e.g.,* grantor-grantee, landlord-tenant, mortgagor-mortgagee).

Examples: 1) A and B are neighboring landowners, neither having any rights in the other's land. For good consideration, A promises B, "for herself, her heirs, successors and assigns," that A's parcel "will never be used for other than residential purposes." The horizontal privity requirement is *not* met, and successors in interest to A will *not* be bound because at the time A made this covenant, she and B shared no interest in land independent of the covenant.

2) The horizontal privity requirement will be met if, at the time the covenant was entered into, the covenanting parties shared an interest in the burdened land; *e.g.,* if A were B's landlord or if A were B's mortgagee or if A owned the parcel in fee and B held the benefit of an easement in it. Assume, for example, that A, owner of Blackacre in fee,

promised B, holder of a right-of-way easement over Blackacre, "always to keep the right-of-way free of snow or other impediment to B's use of the right-of-way." Horizontal privity is met by the existence of an affirmative easement in Blackacre at the time the covenant was made.

3) The requisite shared interest in land would also be found if the covenant were made in a grantor-grantee deed between the covenanting parties. Assume, for example, that A, the owner of Blackacre and Whiteacre, deeds Whiteacre to B, promising "not to use Blackacre for other than residential purposes." Horizontal privity exists here by virtue of the grantor-grantee relationship between A and B.

d. Vertical Privity

To be bound, the successor in interest to the covenanting party must hold the *entire durational interest* held by the covenantor at the time she made the covenant.

Example: A, who owns Blackacre and Whiteacre in fee simple absolute, sells Whiteacre to B and, in the deed, covenants for herself, her heirs, successors and assigns, to contribute one-half the expense of maintaining a common driveway between Blackacre and Whiteacre. A then transfers Blackacre to C "for life," retaining a reversionary interest for herself. B *cannot* enforce the covenant against C because C does not possess the entire interest (fee simple absolute) held by her predecessor in interest, A, at the time A made the promise.

e. Touch and Concern

The covenant must be of the type that "touches and concerns" the land. The phrase "touch and concern the land" is not susceptible to easy definition. It generally means that the effect of the covenant is to make the land itself more useful or valuable to the benefited party. The covenant must affect the legal relationship of the parties as landowners and not merely as members of the community at large. Therefore, as a general matter, for the burden of a covenant to run, performance of the burden must diminish the landowner's right, privileges, and powers in connection with her enjoyment of the land.

1) Negative Covenants

For the burden of a negative covenant to touch and concern the land, the covenant must restrict the holder of the servient estate in his *use of that parcel* of land.

Examples: 1) A, who owned Blackacre and Whiteacre, covenanted with B, the grantee of Whiteacre, that she would not erect a building of over two stories on Blackacre. The burden of the covenant touches and concerns Blackacre because it diminishes A's rights in connection with her enjoyment of Blackacre.

2) A, who owned Blackacre and Whiteacre, covenanted with B, the grantee of Whiteacre, that she would never operate a shoe store within a radius of one mile of Whiteacre. The covenant does not touch and concern Blackacre because its performance is unconnected to the enjoyment of Blackacre.

Note the similarity of negative covenants and negative easements. The primary difference between them is that negative easements are limited to a few traditional categories, but there are no limits on negative covenants.

2) Affirmative Covenants

For the burden of an affirmative covenant to touch and concern the land, the covenant must require the holder of the servient estate *to do something*, increasing her obligations in connection with enjoyment of the land.

Examples: 1) A, who owned Blackacre and Whiteacre, covenanted with B, the grantee of Whiteacre, to keep the building on Blackacre in good repair. The covenant touches and concerns Blackacre because it increases A's obligations in connection with her enjoyment of Blackacre.

2) A owned Blackacre and Whiteacre, which were several miles apart. A covenanted with B, the grantee of Whiteacre, to keep the

building on Whiteacre in good repair. The covenant does not touch and concern Blackacre because its performance is unconnected to the use and enjoyment of Blackacre.

3) A, the grantee of a parcel in a residential subdivision, covenants to pay an annual fee to a homeowners' association for the maintenance of common ways, parks, and other facilities in the subdivision. At one time, it was thought that such covenants, because physically unconnected to the land, do not touch and concern. The prevailing view today is that the burden will run because the fees are a charge on the land, increasing A's obligations in connection with the use and enjoyment of it.

3)   Relation Between Benefit and Burden

The Restatement of Property imposes as an additional requirement that for the burden of a covenant to run, both the benefit and the burden of the covenant must meet the touch and concern test. Thus, under the Restatement view, if the benefit is personal to the covenantee, the burden will not run; *i.e.,* for the burden to run, the benefit of the promise must benefit the promisee in the physical use or enjoyment of the land possessed by her. No clear majority of states has lined up behind the Restatement approach, and the most that can be said is that a conflict exists on the point.

2.   Requirements for Benefit to Run

If all requirements for the benefit to run are met, the successor in interest to the promisee will be allowed to enjoy the benefit (*i.e.,* enforce the covenant).

a.   Intent

The covenanting parties must have intended that the successors in interest to the covenantee be able to enforce the covenant. Surrounding evidence of intent, as well as language in the instrument of conveyance, is admissible.

b.   Vertical Privity

The benefit of a covenant runs to the assignees of the original estate or of any lesser estate (*e.g.,* a life estate). The owner of *any* succeeding possessory estate can enforce the benefit at law. In the majority of states today, horizontal privity is not required for the benefit to run. As a consequence, if horizontal privity is missing, the benefit may run to the successor in interest to the covenantee even though the burden is not enforceable against the successor in interest of the covenantor.

Example: A, who owns Blackacre, covenants with her neighbor, B, who owns Whiteacre, that "A, her successors and assigns will keep the building on Blackacre in good repair." Horizontal privity is missing. B then conveys Whiteacre, the dominant estate, to C. C can enforce the benefit of the affirmative covenant against A because horizontal privity is not needed for the benefit to run. If, however, A conveys Blackacre to D, neither B nor C could enforce the covenant against D, for horizontal privity is required for the burden to run.

c.   Touch and Concern

For the benefit of a covenant to touch and concern the land, the promised performance must benefit the covenantee and her successors *in their use and enjoyment of the benefited land*.

Examples: 1) A, who owned Blackacre and Whiteacre, covenanted with B, the grantee of Whiteacre, not to erect a building over two stories on Blackacre. The benefit of the covenant touches and concerns Whiteacre because, by securing B's view, it increases his enjoyment of Whiteacre.

2) A, who owned Blackacre, covenanted with B, a supermarket operator owning no adjacent land, not to run a supermarket on Blackacre. The benefit of the covenant does *not* touch and concern because it is not connected to and does not operate to increase B's enjoyment of any piece of land.

3) A, who owned Blackacre and Whiteacre, covenanted with B, the grantee of Whiteacre, to keep the building on Blackacre freshly painted and in good repair. The benefit of the covenant touches and concerns

Whiteacre because, by assuring the view of an attractive house, it increases the value of Whiteacre.

4) A, who owned Blackacre, covenanted with B, a supermarket operator owning no adjacent land, to erect and maintain on Blackacre a billboard advertising B's supermarkets. The benefit of the covenant does not touch and concern because it is not connected to and does not operate to increase B's enjoyment of any piece of land.

3. Specific Situations Involving Real Covenants

a. Promises to Pay Money
The majority rule is that if the money is to be used in a way connected with the land, the burden will run with the land. The most common example is a covenant to pay a homeowners' association an annual fee for maintenance of common ways, parks, etc., in a subdivision.

b. Covenants Not to Compete
Covenants not to compete have created several problems. Clearly, the burden of the covenant—restricting the use to which the land may be put—"touches and concerns" the land. However, the benefited land, while "commercially enhanced," is not affected in its physical use. Thus, some courts have refused to permit the benefit of such covenants to run with the land.

The Restatement of Property, somewhat inconsistently, permits the benefit but not the burden of such covenants to run. Most courts seem willing to overlook these technical distinctions and permit both the benefit and the burden of covenants not to compete to run with the land.

c. Racially Restrictive Covenants
If a covenant purports to prohibit an owner from transferring land to persons of a given race, no court (state or federal) is permitted to enforce the covenant. To do so would involve the court in a violation of the Equal Protection Clause of the Fourteenth Amendment.

4. Remedies—Damages Only
A breach of a real covenant is remedied by an award of money damages, not an injunction. If equitable relief, such as an injunction, is sought, the promise must be enforced as an equitable servitude rather than a real covenant (*see* below). Note that a real covenant gives rise to personal liability only. The damages are collectible out of the defendant's general assets.

5. Termination
As with all other nonpossessory interests in land, a real covenant may be terminated by: (i) the holder of the benefit executing a *release in writing*; (ii) *merger* (fee simple title to both the benefited and burdened land comes into the hands of a single owner); and (iii) *condemnation* of the burdened property.

E. EQUITABLE SERVITUDES
If a plaintiff wants an injunction or specific performance, he must show that the covenant qualifies as an equitable servitude. An equitable servitude is a covenant that, regardless of whether it runs with the land at law, equity will enforce against the assignees of the burdened land who have *notice* of the covenant. The usual remedy is an injunction against violation of the covenant.

1. Creation
Generally, equitable servitudes are created by covenants contained in a writing that satisfies the Statute of Frauds. As with real covenants, acceptance of a deed signed only by the grantor is sufficient to bind the grantee as promisor. There is one exception to the writing requirement: Negative equitable servitudes may be implied from a common scheme for development of a residential subdivision.

a. Servitudes Implied from Common Scheme
When a developer subdivides land into several parcels and some of the deeds contain negative covenants but some do not, negative covenants or equitable servitudes binding *all* the parcels in the subdivision may be implied under the doctrine of "reciprocal negative servitudes." The doctrine applies only to negative covenants and equitable

servitudes and not to affirmative covenants. Two requirements must be met before reciprocal negative covenants and servitudes will be implied: (i) a common scheme for development and (ii) notice of the covenants.

Example: A subdivides her parcel into lots 1 through 50. She conveys lots 1 through 45 by deeds containing express covenants by the respective grantees that they will use their lots only for residential purposes. A orally assures the 45 grantees that *all* 50 lots will be used for residential purposes. Some time later, after the 45 lots have been developed as residences, A conveys lot 46 to an oil company, which plans to operate a service station on it. The deed to lot 46 contains no express residential restriction. A court will nonetheless imply a negative covenant, prohibiting use for other than residential purposes on lot 46 because both requirements have been met for an implied reciprocal negative servitude. First, there was a *common scheme*, here evidenced by A's statements to the first 45 buyers. Second, the oil company was on *inquiry notice* of the negative covenant because of the uniform residential character of the other lots in the subdivision development.

1) Common Scheme

Reciprocal negative covenants will be implied only if at the time that sales of parcels in the subdivision began, the developer had a plan that all parcels in the subdivision be developed within the terms of the negative covenant. If the scheme arises after some lots are sold, it cannot impose burdens on the lots previously sold without the express covenants. The developer's common scheme may be evidenced by a *recorded plat*, by a *general pattern* of prior restrictions, or by *oral representations*, typically in the form of statements to early buyers that all parcels in the development will be restricted by the same covenants that appear in their deeds. On the basis of this scheme, it is inferred that purchasers bought their lots relying on the fact that they would be able to enforce subsequently created equitable servitudes similar to the restrictions imposed in their deeds.

2) Notice

To be bound by the terms of a covenant that does not appear in his deed, a grantee must, at the time he acquired his parcel, have had notice of the covenants contained in the deeds of other buyers in the subdivision. The requisite notice may be acquired through *actual notice* (direct knowledge of the covenants in the prior deeds); *inquiry notice* (the neighborhood appears to conform to common restrictions); or *record notice* (if the prior deeds are in the grantee's chain of title he will, under the recording acts, have constructive notice of their contents).

2. Enforcement

For successors of the original promisee and promisor to enforce an equitable servitude, certain requirements must be met.

a. Requirements for Burden to Run

1) Intent

The covenanting parties must have intended that the servitude be enforceable by and against assignees. No technical words are required to express this intent. In fact, the intent may be ascertained from the purpose of the covenant and the surrounding circumstances.

2) Notice

A subsequent purchaser of land burdened by a covenant is not bound by it in equity unless she had actual or constructive notice of it when she acquired the land. This rule is part of the law of equitable servitudes, and exists apart from the recording acts.

3) Touch and Concern

This is the same requirement as applies to real covenants (*see* D.1.e., *supra*).

b. Requirements for Benefit to Run

The benefit of the equitable servitude will run with the land (and thus to successors in interest of the original parties) if the original parties so *intended* and the servitude *touches and concerns* the benefited property.

c. Privity Not Required

The majority of courts enforce the servitude not as an in personam right against the owner of the servient tenement, but as an equitable property interest in the land itself. There is, therefore, no need for privity of estate.

Examples: 1) A acquires title to Blackacre by adverse possession. Even though he is not in privity of estate with the original owner, he is subject to the equitable servitude since the servitude is an interest in the land.

2) A and B are neighboring landowners, neither having any rights in the other's land. A promises B, "for herself, her heirs, successors, and assigns," that A's parcel "will never be used for other than residential purposes." B records the agreement. A sells Blackacre to C. The burden created by this promise would *not run at law* as a negative covenant because horizontal privity is missing. However, under an equitable servitude theory, the burden *will run*, and an injunction will issue against other than residential uses.

3) Same as above, but A transfers only a life estate to C. Again, the burden would not run at law because of the absence of vertical privity. The burden would, however, be enforceable as an equitable servitude.

d. Implied Beneficiaries of Covenants—General Scheme

If a covenant in a subdivision deed is silent as to who holds its benefit, any neighbor in the subdivision will be entitled to enforce the covenant if a general scheme or plan is found to have existed at the time he purchased his lot.

Example: A subdivides her parcel into Lots 1 through 10. She conveys Lot 1 to B, who covenants to use the lot for residential purposes only. A then conveys Lot 2 to C, who makes a similar covenant. Thereafter, A conveys the balance of the lots to other grantees by deeds containing the residential restriction. Can C enforce the restrictions against B? Can B enforce against C?

Subsequent purchaser versus prior purchaser (C v. B): In most jurisdictions, C (the later grantee) can enforce the restriction against B if the court finds a common plan of residential restrictions at the very outset of A's sales. (Evidence would be the similar covenant restrictions in all the deeds.) The rationale is that B's promise was made for the benefit of the land at that time retained by A, the grantor. Such land, Lots 2 through 10, became the dominant estate. When A thereafter conveyed Lot 2 to C, the benefit of B's promise passed to C with the land.

Prior purchaser versus subsequent purchaser (B v. C): In most jurisdictions, B could likewise enforce the restriction against C, even though A made no covenant in her deed to B that A's retained land would be subject to the residential restrictions.

There are two theories on which a prior purchaser can enforce a restriction in a subsequent deed from a common grantor. One theory is that B is a third-party beneficiary of C's promise to A. The other theory is that an implied reciprocal servitude attached to A's retained land at the moment she deeded Lot 1 to B. Under this theory, B is enforcing an *implied* servitude on Lot 2 and *not* the express covenant later made by C.

3. Equitable Defenses to Enforcement

A court in equity is not bound to enforce a servitude if it cannot in good conscience do so.

a. Unclean Hands

A court will not enforce a servitude if the person seeking enforcement is violating a similar restriction on his own land. This defense will apply even if the violation on the complainant's land is less serious, as long as it is of the same general nature.

b. Acquiescence

If a benefited party acquiesces in a violation of the servitude by one burdened party, he may be deemed to have abandoned the servitude as to other burdened parties. (Equitable servitudes, like easements, may be abandoned.) Note that this defense will not apply if the prior violation occurred in a location so distant from the complainant that it did not really affect his property.

c. **Estoppel**
If the benefited party has acted in such a way that a reasonable person would believe that the covenant was abandoned, and the burdened party acts in reliance thereon, the benefited party will be estopped to enforce the covenant. Similarly, if the benefited party fails to bring suit against a violator within a reasonable time, the action may be barred by *laches*.

d. **Changed Neighborhood Conditions**
Changed neighborhood conditions may also operate to end an equitable servitude. If the neighborhood has changed significantly since the time the servitude was created, with the result that it would be inequitable to enforce the restriction, injunctive relief will be withheld. (Many courts, however, will allow the holder of the benefit to bring an action at law for damages.)

Example: A, the owner of Blackacre and Whiteacre, adjacent parcels in an undeveloped area, sells Blackacre to B, extracting a promise that Blackacre "will always be used only for residential purposes." Fifteen years later, the neighborhood has developed as a commercial and industrial center. If B or her successors in interest to Blackacre now wish to use the parcel for a store, an injunction will probably *not* issue. A may, however, recover from B or her successors any damages that she may suffer from termination of the residential restriction.

1) **Zoning**
Zoning plays an important role in determining whether changed conditions will be allowed as a defense to enforcement of an equitable servitude. Zoning that is inconsistent with the private restriction imposed by the equitable servitude will not of itself bar the injunction, but it will provide good evidence that neighborhood conditions have changed sufficiently to make the injunction unjust. Thus, in the example above, the position of B or her successors would be fortified by a showing that the area in which Blackacre is situated is presently zoned for commercial uses.

2) **Concept of the "Entering Wedge"**
The concept of the "entering wedge" also plays an important role in changed condition cases. If the equitable servitude is part of a general plan of restrictions in a subdivision, and if the parcel in question is located somewhere at the outer edge of the subdivision, changed conditions outside of the subdivision will not bar the injunction if it is shown that lifting the restriction on one parcel will produce changed conditions for surrounding parcels, requiring that their restrictions also be lifted, and so on (the "domino effect"). Thus, in the example above, if removing the restriction and allowing commercial development of Blackacre would produce changed conditions for the neighboring, similarly restricted parcel—Whiteacre—with the consequence that its servitude could not be equitably enforced, the injunction against commercial use on Blackacre will probably be allowed, notwithstanding the changed conditions. Note that injunctive relief may be granted if the substantial change occurs within the subdivision.

4. **Termination**
Like other nonpossessory interests in land, an equitable servitude may be terminated by a *written release* from the benefit holder(s), *merger* of the benefited and burdened estates, or *condemnation* of the burdened property. (*See* B.4.b., c., h., *supra.*)

F. **RELATIONSHIP OF COVENANTS TO ZONING ORDINANCES**
Both restrictive covenants and zoning ordinances (*see* IX.C., *infra*) may affect legally permissible uses of land. Both must be complied with, and neither provides any excuse for violating the other. For example, if the zoning permits both residential and commercial use but an applicable covenant allows only residential use, the covenant will control.

These two forms of land use restrictions are enforced differently. As discussed above, covenants (if they meet the relevant requirements) can be enforced by nearby property owners at law or in equity. Zoning, on the other hand, is not subject to enforcement by private suit, but can be enforced only by local governmental officials.

G. PARTY WALLS AND COMMON DRIVEWAYS

Often, a single wall or driveway will be built partly on the property of each of two adjoining landowners. Absent an agreement between the owners to the contrary, courts will treat the wall as belonging to each owner to the extent that it rests upon her land. Courts will also imply mutual cross-easements of support, with the result that each party has the right to use the wall or driveway, and neither party can unilaterally destroy it.

1. Creation

While a *written agreement* is required by the Statute of Frauds for the express creation of a party wall or common driveway agreement, an "irrevocable license" can arise if there has been detrimental reliance on a parol agreement. Party walls and common driveways can also result from *implication* or *prescription*.

2. Running of Covenants

If party wall or common driveway owners agree to be mutually responsible for maintaining the wall or driveway, the burdens and benefits of these covenants will run to successive owners of each parcel. The cross-easements for support satisfy the requirement of horizontal privity because they are mutual interests in the same property. And each promise touches and concerns the adjoining parcels.

V. ADVERSE POSSESSION

A. IN GENERAL

Title to real property may be acquired by adverse possession. (Easements may also be acquired by prescription.) Gaining title by adverse possession results from the operation of the statute of limitations for trespass to real property. If an owner does not, within the statutory period, take legal action to eject a possessor who claims adversely to the owner, the owner is thereafter barred from bringing suit for ejectment. Moreover, title to the property vests in the possessor.

B. REQUIREMENTS

1. Running of Statute

The statute of limitations begins to run when the claimant goes adversely into possession of the true owner's land (*i.e.*, the point at which the true owner could first bring suit). The filing of suit by the true owner is not sufficient to stop the period from running; the suit must be pursued to judgment. However, if the true owner files suit before the statutory period (*e.g.*, 20 years) runs out and the judgment is rendered after the statutory period, the judgment will relate back to the time that the complaint was filed.

2. Open and Notorious Possession

Possession is open and notorious when it is the kind of use the usual owner would make of the land. The adverse possessor's occupation must be *sufficiently apparent* to put the true owner on *notice* that a trespass is occurring. If, for example, Water Company ran a pipe under Owner's land and there was no indication of the pipe's existence from the surface of the land, Water Company could not gain title by adverse possession because there was nothing to put Owner on notice of the trespass.

Example: A's use of B's farmland for an occasional family picnic will not satisfy the open and notorious requirement because picnicking is not necessarily an act consistent with the ownership of farmland.

3. Actual and Exclusive Possession

a. Actual Possession Gives Notice

Like the open and notorious requirement, the requirement of actual possession is designed to give the true owner notice that a trespass is occurring. It is also designed to give her notice of the *extent* of the adverse possessor's claim. As a general rule, the adverse possessor will gain title only to the land that she actually occupies.

1) Constructive Possession of Part

Actual possession of a portion of a unitary tract of land is sufficient adverse possession as to give title to the whole of the tract of land after the statutory period, as long as there is a *reasonable proportion* between the portion actually possessed and the whole of the unitary tract, and the possessor has color of title (*i.e.,* a document purporting to give him title) to the whole tract. Usually, the proportion will be held reasonable if possession of the portion was sufficient to put the owner or community on notice of the fact of possession.

b.   **Exclusive Possession—No Sharing with Owner**
"Exclusive" merely means that the possessor is not sharing with the true owner or the public at large. This requirement does not prevent two or more individuals from working *together* to obtain title by adverse possession. If they do so, they will obtain the title as tenants in common.

Example: A and B are next door neighbors. They decide to plant a vegetable garden on the vacant lot behind both of their homes. A and B share expenses and profits from the garden. If all other elements for adverse possession are present, at the end of the statutory period, A and B will own the lot as tenants in common.

4.   **Continuous Possession**
The adverse claimant's possession must be continuous throughout the statutory period. Continuous possession requires only the degree of occupancy and use that the average owner would make of the property.

a.   **Intermittent Periods of Occupancy Not Sufficient**
Intermittent periods of occupancy generally are not sufficient. However, constant use by the claimant is not required so long as the possession is of the type that the usual owner would make of the property. For example, the fact that the adverse possessor is using the land for the intermittent grazing of cattle will probably not defeat continuity if the land is *normally* used in this manner.

b.   **Tacking Permitted**
There need not be continuous possession by the same person. Ordinarily, an adverse possessor can take advantage of the periods of adverse possession by her predecessor. Separate periods of adverse possession may be "tacked" together to make up the full statutory period with the result that the final adverse possessor gets title, provided there is privity between the successive adverse holders.

1)   **"Privity"**
Privity is satisfied if the subsequent possessor takes by descent, by devise, or by deed purporting to convey title. Tacking is not permitted where one adverse claimant ousts a preceding adverse claimant or where one adverse claimant abandons and a new adverse claimant then goes into possession.

2)   **Formalities on Transfer**
Even an oral transfer of possession is sufficient to satisfy the privity requirement.

Example: A received a deed describing Blackacre, but by mistake built a house on an adjacent parcel, Whiteacre. A, after pointing the house out to B and orally agreeing to sell the house and land to her, conveyed to B, by a deed copied from her own deed, describing the property as Blackacre. The true owner of Whiteacre argues that there was no privity between A and B because the deed made no reference to Whiteacre, the land actually possessed. Nonetheless, the agreed oral transfer of actual possession is sufficient to permit tacking.

5.   **Hostile**
The possessor's occupation of the property must be hostile (adverse). This means merely that the possessor does *not have the true owner's permission* to be on the land. It does not mean anger or animosity. The state of mind of the adverse possessor is irrelevant. By the large majority view, it does not matter whether the possessor believes she is on her own land, knows she is trespassing on someone else's land, or has no idea of who owns the land.

a.   **If Possession Starts Permissively—Must Communicate Hostility**
If the possessor enters with permission of the true owner (*e.g.,* under a lease or license), the possession does not become adverse until the possessor makes clear to the true owner the fact that she is claiming "hostilely." This can be done by explicit notification, by refusing to permit the true owner to come onto the land, or by other acts inconsistent with the original permission.

b. **Co-Tenants—Ouster Required**
Possession by one co-tenant is not ordinarily adverse to her co-tenants, since each co-tenant has a right to the possession of all the property. Thus, sole possession or use by one co-tenant is not adverse, unless there is a clear repudiation of the co-tenancy; *e.g.,* one co-tenant ousts the others or makes an explicit declaration that he is claiming exclusive dominion over the property.

c. **If Grantor Stays in Possession—Permission Presumed**
If a grantor remains in possession of land after her conveyance, she is presumed to be there with the permission of her grantee. Only the grantor's open repudiation of the conveyance will start the limitation period running against the grantee. Likewise, if the tenant remains in possession after the expiration of her lease, she is presumed to have the permission of the landlord.

d. **Compare—Boundary Line Agreements**
There is a separate but related doctrine that may be helpful here. It operates where a boundary line (usually a fence) is fixed by agreement of the adjoining landowners, but later turns out not to be the "true" line. Most courts will fix ownership *as per the agreed line*, provided it is shown that (i) there was original *uncertainty* as to the true line; (ii) the agreed line was *established* (*i.e.,* agreed upon); and (iii) there has been *lengthy acquiescence* in the agreed line by the adjoining owners and/or their successors.

1) **Establishment Requirement**
The establishment requirement can be implied by acquiescence. A past dispute is not necessary to show uncertainty, although it can be good evidence of it. But a showing of original uncertainty is required; otherwise, in a court's view, a parol transfer of land would result.

C. DISABILITY

1. **Effect of Disabilities—Statute Tolled**
The statute of limitations does not begin to run for adverse possession (or easements by prescription) if the true owner was under some disability to sue *when the cause of action first accrued* (*i.e.,* the inception of the adverse possession). Typical disabilities are: minority, imprisonment, and insanity.
Examples: 1) O, the true owner, is five years old when A goes into adverse possession. The statute will not begin to run until O reaches the age of majority.

2) O, the true owner, is declared insane six months after A begins using a pathway adversely. The statute is *not* tolled, since O's disability arose *after* the statute began to run.

2. **No Tacking of Disabilities**
Only a disability of the *owner* existing at the time the cause of action arose is considered. Thus, disabilities of successors in interest or subsequent additional disabilities of the owner have no effect on the statute.
Examples: 1) O is a minor at the time A goes into adverse possession of O's land. One year before O reaches the age of majority, O is declared insane. The statute is not tolled by reason of O's insanity (a subsequent disability). Thus, the statute begins to run from the date O reaches the age of majority, whether she is then sane or insane.

2) O, the true owner, is insane when A begins an adverse use. Ten years later, O dies intestate and the land goes to her heir, H, who is then 10 years old. The statute of limitations begins to run upon O's death and is not tolled by H's minority. H's minority is a "supervening" disability and cannot be tacked to O's.

3. **Maximum Tolling Periods**
In some states, the maximum tolling period is 20 years; thus, the maximum period of the statute of limitations would be the regular statute of limitations period plus the maximum 20-year tolling period.

D. ADVERSE POSSESSION AND FUTURE INTERESTS
The statute of limitations does not run against the holder of a future interest (*e.g.,* a remainder)

until that interest becomes possessory. Until the prior present estate terminates, the holder of the future interest has no right to possession, and thus, no cause of action against a wrongful possessor.

Examples: 1) A devises Blackacre to B for life and then to C. Thereafter, X goes into possession and possesses adversely for the statutory period. X has acquired B's life estate by adverse possession, but has not acquired any interests against C. Of course, if following B's death, X or her successor stays in possession for the statutory period, X will have acquired C's rights also.

2) X enters into adverse possession of Blackacre. Four years later, A devises Blackacre to B for life and then to C. X continues her adverse possession for seven more years. The statute of limitations is 10 years. In this case, X has acquired the whole title by adverse possession. An adverse possession begun against the owner of the fee simple absolute cannot be interrupted by a subsequent division of the estate.

1. **Possibility of Reverter—Statute of Limitations Runs on Happening of Event**
   In a conveyance "to A for so long as" some event occurs or fails to occur, on the happening of the event the fee simple determinable automatically comes to an end and the grantor (or his successors) is entitled to present possession. At that point, the grantor has a cause of action to recover possession of the property. If he does not bring the action within the period specified by the applicable statute of limitations (and if A or her successors have the requisite open, notorious, continuous, and adverse possession), his action will be barred.

2. **Right of Entry—Happening of Event *Does Not* Trigger Statute of Limitations**
   In the case of a right of entry, on the happening of the stated event the grantor (or his successors) has only a right to reenter the property, a power to terminate the grantee's estate. Until the grantor asserts his right of entry, no cause of action arises because the grantee's continued possession of the land is proper: her fee simple estate has not been terminated. Thus (in most states) the statute of limitations does not operate to bar assertion of a right of entry even though the condition triggering the right of entry has been breached.

   a. **Grantor Must Act Within Reasonable Time to Avoid Laches**
      However, to avoid the title problems that might otherwise be presented, most courts hold that the holder of the right of entry must bring his action within a reasonable time after the event occurs. If he fails to do so, his action is barred by laches. As for what constitutes a reasonable time, many courts look to the statute of limitations governing actions for possession of real property.

E. **EFFECT OF COVENANTS IN TRUE OWNER'S DEED**
   The exact nature of the title obtained depends on the possessor's activities on the land. For example, assume there is a recorded restrictive covenant limiting use of the land to a single-family residence. If the possessor uses the land in violation of that covenant for the limitations period, she takes title free of the covenant. But if she complies with the covenant, she takes title subject to it, and it remains enforceable against her (at least in an equitable action).

F. **LAND THAT CANNOT BE ADVERSELY POSSESSED**
   The statute of limitations does not run against government-owned land (federal, state, or local) or land registered under a Torrens system.

VI. CONVEYANCING

A. **LAND SALE CONTRACTS**
   Most transfers of land are preceded by contracts of sale. These normally contemplate escrows (delivery of deed to a third person to be held until purchase price paid) before closing (exchange of purchase price and deed).

1. **Statute of Frauds Applicable**
   To be enforceable, a land contract must be in writing and signed by the party to be charged. The writing need not be a formal contract; a memorandum suffices—*e.g.,* escrow instructions can be the contract of sale. The Statute of Frauds requires that the writing contain all "essential terms" of the contract. These are: (i) a ***description*** of the property (*see* B.3., *infra*), (ii) identification of ***the parties*** to the contract, and (iii) the ***price*** and manner of

payment (if agreed upon). Incidental matters (*e.g.,* prorating of taxes, furnishing of deeds, title insurance, etc.) can be determined by custom; they need not appear in the writing nor even have been agreed upon.

a. Doctrine of Part Performance
A court may give specific performance of a contract (though not damages) despite the absence of a writing if additional facts are present.

1) Theories to Support the Doctrine

a) Evidentiary Theory
Courts state that if acts done by a party can be explained only by reference to an agreement, these acts unequivocally establish the existence of an oral contract.

b) Hardship or Estoppel Theory
If acts done by a party in reliance on the contract would result in hardship to such an extent that it would be a fraud on that party were the contract not specifically enforced, the other party will be estopped from asserting the Statute of Frauds as a defense.

2) Acts of Part Performance
In most states, two of the following are required:

(i) *Possession* of the land by the purchaser;

(ii) Making of substantial *improvements*; and/or

(iii) *Payment* of all or part of the purchase price by the purchaser.

Some state courts will go beyond this list and will accept as "part performance" other types of detrimental reliance by the purchaser, such as performance of services or sale of other land.

3) Can Seller Obtain Specific Performance Based on Buyer's Acts?

a) Evidentiary Theory
Under the evidentiary theory, it is immaterial who performed the acts constituting the part performance. Since they refer unequivocally to a contract, the seller may obtain specific performance based on the buyer's acts.

b) Hardship or Estoppel Theory
Under the hardship or estoppel theory, however, the *plaintiff* must be the one whose action would result in hardship if the Statute of Frauds were invoked. Consequently, the seller normally *cannot* rely on the buyer's acts. Even so, make sure that you ascertain whether the *seller* has done anything that would cause him a hardship if the Statute of Frauds were successfully asserted by the buyer.

2. Doctrine of Equitable Conversion
Under the doctrine of equitable conversion, once a contract is signed and each party is entitled to specific performance, equity regards the purchaser as the owner of the real property. The seller's interest, which consists of the right to the proceeds of sale, is considered to be personal property. The bare legal title that remains in the seller is considered to be held in trust for the purchaser as security for the debt owed the seller. But note that possession follows the legal title; so even though the buyer is regarded as owning the property, the seller is entitled to possession until the closing.

a. Risk of Loss
Where the property is destroyed (without fault of either party) before the date set for closing, the majority rule is that, since the buyer is deemed the owner of the property, the *risk of loss is on the buyer*. Thus, the buyer must pay the contract price despite a loss due to fire or other casualty, unless the contract provides otherwise. Some states, however, have adopted the Uniform Vendor and Purchaser Risk Act, which places the risk on the seller unless the buyer has either legal title or possession of the property at the time of the loss.

1) Casualty Insurance

Suppose the buyer has the risk of loss, as is true under the majority view, but the seller has fire or casualty insurance that covers the loss. In the event of loss, allowing the seller to recover the full purchase price on the contract and to collect the insurance proceeds would be unjust enrichment. Hence, the courts require the seller to give the buyer credit, against the purchase price, in the amount of the insurance proceeds.

b. Passage of Title upon Death

The doctrine of equitable conversion also affects the passage of title when a party to a contract of sale dies before the contract has been completed. In general, it holds that a deceased seller's interest passes as personal property and a deceased buyer's interest as real property.

1) Death of Seller

If the seller dies, the "bare" legal title passes to the takers of his real property, but they must give up the title to the buyer when the contract closes. When the purchase price is paid, the money passes as personal property to those who take the seller's personal property. Note that if the property is *specifically* devised, the specific devisee will probably take the proceeds of the sale. (*See* F.1.b., *infra.*)

2) Death of Buyer

If the buyer dies, the takers of his real property can demand a conveyance of the land at the closing of the contract. Moreover, they are entitled to exoneration out of the personal property estate; thus, the takers of his personal property will have to pay the purchase price out of their share of the buyer's estate.

3. Marketable Title

There is an implied warranty in *every* land sale contract that at closing the seller will provide the buyer with a title that is "marketable."

a. "Marketability" Defined—Title Reasonably Free from Doubt

Marketable title is title reasonably free from doubt, *i.e.,* title that a reasonably prudent buyer would be willing to accept. It need not be a "perfect" title, but the title must be free from questions that might present an unreasonable risk of litigation. Generally, this means an unencumbered fee simple with good record title.

1) Defects in Record Chain of Title

Title may be unmarketable because of a defect in the chain of title. Examples include: a significant *variation in the description* of the land from one deed to the next, a deed in the chain that was *defectively executed* and thus fails to meet the requirements for recordation, and evidence that a prior grantor *lacked capacity* to convey the property. Many courts hold that an ancient lien or mortgage on the record will not render title unmarketable if the seller has proof of its satisfaction or the statute of limitations on the claim would have run under any possible circumstance, including tolling for disabilities.

a) Adverse Possession

Historically, a title acquired by adverse possession was not considered marketable since the purchaser might be later forced to defend in court the facts that gave rise to the adverse possession against the record owner. On the bar exam, *title acquired by adverse possession is unmarketable*, despite the fact that most recent cases are contra. Most of the recent cases hold adverse possession titles to be marketable if: (i) the possession has been for a very lengthy period; (ii) the risk that the record owner will sue appears to be very remote; and (iii) the probability of the record owner's success in such a suit appears to be minimal. Since the bar examiners have yet to recognize this line of cases, the modern view should be considered only as a fallback position on the bar exam.

b) Future Interest Held by Unborn or Unascertained Parties

Even though most states consider all types of future interests to be transferable, it is often impossible for the owners of the present and future interests, acting together, to transfer a marketable fee simple absolute title. This is because the future interests are often held by persons who are unborn or unascertainable.

> *Example:*   "To A for life, and upon A's death to A's eldest surviving daughter." Assume that at the time of this conveyance A has one daughter, B. State of title: A has a life estate, and B has a contingent remainder. A and B together can transfer the land to a purchaser, such as C, but the title is not marketable. It may turn out that, upon A's death, B will have predeceased A, and some other daughter (perhaps not even yet born when A and B transferred to C) will be "A's eldest surviving daughter." Since that daughter did not join in the conveyance to C, she is not bound by it, and she owns the land. On the other hand, if B does turn out to be A's eldest surviving daughter (which cannot be determined until A's death), then C's title will become a marketable fee simple at that time.

While most courts will appoint a guardian ad litem to represent unborn or unascertained persons in *litigation*, the majority will not appoint such a guardian for purposes of *conveying* the land.

2) Encumbrances
Generally, mortgages, liens, easements, and covenants render title unmarketable unless the buyer waives them.

a) Mortgages and Liens
A seller has the right to satisfy a mortgage or lien at the closing, with the proceeds from the sale. Therefore, as long as the purchase price is sufficient and this is accomplished simultaneously with the transfer of title (usually through the use of escrows), the buyer cannot claim that the title is unmarketable; the closing will result in a marketable title.

b) Easements
An easement that reduces the value of the property (*e.g.,* an easement of way for the benefit of a neighbor) renders title unmarketable. The majority of courts, however, have held that a beneficial easement (*e.g.,* utility easement to service property) that was visible or known to the buyer does not constitute an encumbrance. Some courts go so far as to hold that the buyer is deemed to have agreed to take subject to any easement that was notorious or known to the buyer when she entered into the contract.

c) Covenants
Restrictive covenants render title unmarketable.

d) Encroachments
A significant encroachment constitutes a title defect, regardless of whether an adjacent landowner is encroaching on the seller's land or vice versa. However, the encroachment will not render title unmarketable if: (i) it is very slight (only a few inches) and does not inconvenience the owner on whose land it encroaches; (ii) the owner encroached upon has indicated that he will not sue on it; or (iii) it has existed for so long (many decades) that it has become legal by adverse possession, provided that the state recognizes adverse possession titles as being marketable (*see* 1)a), *supra*).

3) Zoning Restrictions
Generally, zoning restrictions do not affect the marketability of title; they are not considered encumbrances. An *existing violation* of a zoning ordinance, however, does render title unmarketable.

4) Waiver
Any of the above-mentioned title defects can be waived in the contract of sale.

b. Quitclaim Deed—No Effect
The fact that a contract calls for a quitclaim deed, which does not contain any covenants for title, does not affect the warranty to provide marketable title (unless so provided in the contract).

c. Time of Marketability
If, as is usual, the seller has agreed to furnish title "at date of closing," the buyer cannot rescind prior to that date on grounds that the seller's title is not marketable.

1) Installment Land Contract

Similarly, where an installment land contract is used, the seller's obligation is to furnish marketable title *when delivery is to occur*, *e.g.*, when the buyer has made his final payment. Therefore, a buyer cannot withhold payments or seek other remedies (*e.g.*, rescission) on grounds that the seller's title is unmarketable prior to the date of promised delivery. The buyer might get rescissionary relief before the date of delivery by showing that the seller cannot possibly cure the defects in time. Or, under compelling circumstances, a court might require the seller to quiet title during the contract period.

d. Remedy If Title Not Marketable

If the buyer determines that the seller's title is unmarketable, he must notify the seller and give a reasonable time to cure the defects, even if this requires extension of the closing date. The notice must specify the nature of the defects. If the seller fails to cure the defects, the buyer may pursue several remedies.

1) Rescission, Damages, Specific Performance

In the absence of a contractual stipulation to the contrary, if title is not marketable, the buyer can rescind, sue for damages for breach, get specific performance with an abatement of the purchase price, or, in some jurisdictions, require the seller to quiet title. The seller cannot sue successfully for damages or specific performance.

2) Merger

If the buyer permits the closing to occur, the contract is said to merge with the deed and, in the absence of fraud, the seller is no longer liable on the implied contractual warranty of marketable title. (However, the buyer may have an action for violation of promises made in the deed; *see* D., *infra*.)

4. Time of Performance

a. Presumption—Time Not of the Essence

In general, the courts assume that time is not "of the essence" in real estate contracts. This means that the closing date stated in the contract is not absolutely binding in equity, and that a party, even though late in tendering her own performance, can still enforce the contract if she tenders within a reasonable time after the date. (A month or two is typically considered a reasonable time.)

b. When Presumption Overcome

Time will be considered "of the essence" if:

1) The *contract* so states; or

2) The *circumstances* indicate it was the parties' intention; *e.g.*, the land is rapidly fluctuating in value or a party must move from out of town and has no other place to go; or

3) One party gives the other *notice* that she desires to make time of the essence, and does so within a reasonable time prior to the date designated for closing.

c. Effect of Time of the Essence Construction

If time is of the essence, a party who fails to tender performance on the date set for closing is in total breach and loses her right to enforce the contract.

d. Liability When Time Not of the Essence

Even if time is not of the essence, a party who is late in tendering performance is liable in damages for the incidental losses she has caused, such as additional mortgage interest, taxes, etc.

5. Tender of Performance

In general, the buyer's obligation to pay the purchase price and the seller's obligation to convey the title are deemed to be *concurrent conditions*. This means that neither party is in breach of the contract until the other party tenders her performance, even if the date designated for the closing has passed.

a. When Party's Tender Excused
A party's tender is unnecessary and is excused if the party has repudiated the contract, or if it is impossible for the other party to perform (*e.g.,* if the seller does not have marketable title and cannot get it).

b. Neither Party Tenders Performance
If neither party tenders performance, the closing date is automatically extended indefinitely until one of them does so.

c. Buyer Finds Seller's Title Unmarketable
If the buyer determines that the seller's title is unmarketable, the buyer must give the seller a reasonable time to cure title defects.

6. Remedies for Breach of the Sales Contract

a. Damages
The usual measure of damages is the difference between the contract price and the market value of the land on the date of the breach. Incidental damages, such as title examination and moving or storage costs, can also be recovered.

1) Liquidated Damages
Sales contracts usually require the buyer to deposit "earnest money" with the seller, and provide that if the buyer defaults in performance, the seller may retain this money as liquidated damages. The courts routinely uphold the seller's retention of the deposit if the amount appears to be reasonable in light of the seller's anticipated and actual damages. Many courts will uphold a retention of a deposit of up to 10% of the sales price without further inquiry into its reasonableness. Even without a liquidated damages clause, many courts will uphold retention of the deposit, on the ground that giving restitution of the funds to the buyer would unjustly reward a party in breach.

b. Specific Performance

1) Buyer's Remedy
A court of equity will order a seller to convey the title if the buyer tenders the purchase price. The remedy at law (damages) is deemed inadequate, since the buyer is getting land and land is unique.

If the seller cannot give marketable title, but the buyer wishes to proceed with the transaction, she can usually get specific performance with an *abatement of the purchase price* in an amount reflecting the title defect.

2) Seller's Remedy
Somewhat illogically, the courts also generally will give a specific performance decree for the seller if the buyer is in breach. This is sometimes explained as necessary to have "mutuality of remedy." A few courts in recent years have refused to award specific performance to sellers if the property is not unique (*e.g.,* if a developer is selling a house in a large subdivision of similar houses).

c. Special Rules for Unmarketable Title
If the seller's title is unmarketable for reasons that do not indicate the seller's bad faith (*i.e.,* he did not realize that his title was defective when he signed the contract), about half of the courts limit the buyer's recovery of damages to incidental out-of-pocket costs (title examination, etc.) and return of the buyer's earnest money deposit. The other half of the courts give the buyer the standard measure of contract damages mentioned above.

7. Seller's Liability for Defects on Property

a. Warranty of Fitness or Quality—New Construction Only
The common law rule is that contracts of sale and deeds of real property, unlike conveyances of personal property, carry no implied warranties of quality or fitness for the purpose intended. One exception is a contract for the sale of a building under construction or to be constructed, on the ground that the buyer has no opportunity to inspect. A majority of courts have now extended the implied warranty of fitness or quality to the sale of any *new house* by the builder. The warranty implied is that the new house is

designed and constructed in a reasonably workmanlike manner and suitable for human habitation. A few courts have gone further, allowing a later owner of the house to recover from the original builder despite lack of privity.

b. Negligence of Builder

A person who contracts for construction may always sue a builder for negligence in performing a building contract. Moreover, many courts now permit the ultimate vendee (*e.g.,* a subdivision buyer) to sue the builder despite the fact that the seller hired the builder and the buyer thus lacks "privity."

c. Liability for Sale of Existing Land and Buildings

A seller of existing land and buildings (not new construction) may be liable to the purchaser for defects in the improvements (*e.g.,* a leaky roof or basement, termite infestation, a nonfunctioning septic system) on any of several different theories.

1) Misrepresentation (Fraud)

This theory requires proof that the seller made a *false statement of fact* (oral or written) to the buyer, that the buyer *relied* on the statement, and that it *materially affected* the value of the property. The seller must either have known that the statement was false, or have made it negligently (without taking reasonable care to determine its truth).

2) Active Concealment

The seller is liable as above, even without making any statement, if the seller took steps to conceal a defect in the property (*e.g.,* paneling over a wall to conceal cracks).

3) Failure to Disclose

A majority of states now hold sellers liable for failure to disclose defects if the following factors are present:

(i) The seller *knows* or has reason to know of the defect;

(ii) The defect is *not obvious* or apparent, and the seller realizes that the buyer is unlikely to discover it by ordinary inspection; *and*

(iii) The defect is *serious*, and would probably cause the buyer to reconsider the purchase if it were known.

These decisions are more likely to impose liability on the seller if the property is a personal residence, if the defect is dangerous, and if the seller personally created the defect or previously attempted to repair it and failed to do so.

d. Disclaimers of Liability

Sellers sometimes attempt to avoid liability for property defects by inserting clauses in sales contracts exculpating the seller.

1) "As Is" Clauses

A general clause, such as "property sold as is" or "with all defects," is *not* sufficient to overcome a seller's liability for fraud, concealment, or (in the states that recognize it) failure to disclose.

2) Specific Disclaimers

If the exculpatory clause identifies and disclaims liability for specific types of defects (*e.g.,* "seller is not liable for leaks in the roof"), it is likely to be upheld.

8. Real Estate Brokers

Most real estate sales contracts are negotiated by real estate brokers. The broker who obtains the "listing" from the seller is the *seller's agent*. Other agents who participate in the sale (*e.g.,* through a multiple listing service) are also the seller's agents, unless they specifically agree to serve as the buyer's agent. While these agents owe a fiduciary duty to the seller, they also have a duty to the buyer to disclose material information about the property if they have actual knowledge of it. Traditionally, the agent's commission was earned when he or she found a buyer who was "ready, willing, and able" to purchase the property, even if the buyer later backed out of the contract. But the growing trend of the cases is to award the commission only if the sale actually closes, or if it fails to close because of the seller's fault.

B. DEEDS—FORM AND CONTENT

Transfer of title to an interest in real property occasionally occurs through operation of law; but in most circumstances transfer can be accomplished only by a deed that satisfies various formalities required by statute.

1. Formalities

a. Statute of Frauds

The Statute of Frauds requires that a deed be in *writing*, signed by the grantor.

b. Description of Land and Parties

A deed must identify the land. The description need not be formal, and it may incorporate extrinsic information, but it *must be unambiguous*. The parties (grantor and grantee) must also be identified. This may be done by name, or by describing them in some other way (*e.g.,* "I grant this land to my eldest daughter," or "I convey this land to the present members of the law review at State University"). If the deed is delivered with the identity of the grantee left blank, the courts will presume that the person taking delivery has authority to fill in the name of the grantee, and if she does so, the deed is valid. But if the land description is left blank, no such authority is presumed, and the deed is void unless the grantee was explicitly given authority to fill in the description, and did so. The grantee must actually exist; hence, a deed delivered to a grantee who is in fact dead at the time of the delivery is void.

c. Words of Intent

The deed must evidence an intention to transfer realty, but technical words are unnecessary. The word "grant" by itself is sufficient in many states.

d. Consideration Not Required

The deed need not recite any consideration, nor must any consideration pass in order to make a deed valid.

e. Seal Is Unnecessary

A seal is unnecessary.

f. Attestation and Acknowledgment Generally Unnecessary

Attestation by witnesses is generally unnecessary, as is an acknowledgment. *But note:* Either or both might be required for the deed to be recorded.

g. Signature

A deed must be signed by the grantor. The grantor may designate an agent to sign on the grantor's behalf, but if the signing is not done in the grantor's presence, the Statute of Frauds generally requires that the agent's authority be written. In the case of deeds by corporations, statutes usually provide for execution by two officers of the corporation and the affixing of the corporation's seal. If the deed represents a conveyance of all or a substantial part of the corporation's assets, a resolution of the board of directors approving the transfer may be necessary. (The *grantee's signature is not necessary* even if the deed contains covenants on her part. Her acceptance of the deed is sufficient to make the covenants enforceable.)

2. Defective Deeds and Fraudulent Conveyances

a. Void and Voidable Deeds

A deed that is defective may be either void or voidable. "Void" implies that the deed will be set aside by the court even if the property has passed to a bona fide purchaser. "Voidable" implies that the deed will be set aside only if the property has *not* passed to a bona fide purchaser.

1) Void Deeds

Deeds considered void include those that are forged, were never delivered, or were obtained by fraud in the factum (*i.e.,* the grantor was deceived and did not realize that he was executing a deed).

2) Voidable Deeds

Deeds considered voidable include those executed by persons younger than the age of majority or who otherwise lack capacity (*e.g.,* because of insanity), and deeds obtained through fraud in the inducement, duress, undue influence, mistake, and breach of fiduciary duty.

b. **Fraudulent Conveyances**

Even when a deed complies with the required formalities mentioned above, it may be set aside by the grantor's creditors if it is a fraudulent conveyance. Under the Uniform Fraudulent Transfers Act, which nearly all states have adopted, a conveyance is fraudulent if it was made: (i) with actual intent to hinder, delay, or defraud any creditor of the grantor; or (ii) without receiving a reasonably equivalent value in exchange for the transfer, and the debtor was insolvent or became insolvent as a result of the transfer. However, the deed will not be set aside as against any grantee who took in good faith and paid reasonably equivalent value.

3. **Description of Land Conveyed**

In *land contracts and deeds*, property may be described in various ways; *i.e.,* by reference to a government survey, by metes and bounds, by courses and angles, by references to a recorded plat, by reference to adjacent properties, by the name of the property, or by a street and number system.

a. **Sufficient Description Provides a Good Lead**

A description is sufficient if it provides a good lead as to the identity of the property sought to be conveyed.

Example: A conveyance of "all my land," or "all my land in Alameda County," provides a sufficient lead. The intention of the grantor is clear and the meaning of this intention can be proved without difficulty (by checking the land records of Alameda County).

b. **Insufficient Description—Title Remains in Grantor**

If the description is too indefinite, title remains in the grantor, subject to the possibility of a suit for reformation of the deed.

Example: A conveyance of "one acre off the western end of my 30-acre tract" (the 30-acre tract being adequately described) would probably fail for uncertainty. "Off the western end" is too vague to ascertain *which* acre, and the admission of parol evidence here would be considered a violation of the Statute of Frauds.

c. **Parol Evidence Admissible to Clear Up Ambiguity**

The general rule is that parol evidence is admissible to explain or supplement a written description or to clear up an ambiguity. If there is a *patent ambiguity*—one appearing on the face of the deed—parol evidence is normally admissible to ascertain the parties' intent. For example, one part of the deed states that it is conveying "Blackacre" but later it purports to convey an interest in "Whiteacre." Parol evidence is admissible to show which property the grantor intended to convey. Where the ambiguity is *latent*—not apparent on the face of the deed—parol evidence is generally admissible. For example, if A grants to B "my house in San Francisco," parol evidence is admissible to show which house A owns.

1) **Compare—Inadequate Description**

If, however, A grants to B "my house in San Francisco," and it turns out that A owns *three* houses in that city, the conveyance would probably fail for lack of adequate description. (*But note:* If there is an underlying original agreement in which there was no mistake or ambiguity, and the only mistake was in the *writing* of the instrument, relief might be available by way of *reformation* of the deed.)

d. **Rules of Construction**

Where there is a mistake or inconsistency in the description (as where the deed leaves in doubt the exact location of a property line, or measurements give two different locations for the line), the following rules of construction are applied to carry out the parties' probable intent. (These are not "rules of law" and will not be applied where there is clear evidence showing a contrary intent.)

1) Natural monuments prevail over other methods of description; *i.e.,* artificial monuments, courses and distances, surfaces, acreage, or general descriptions (*e.g.,* a call from "Point X to the old oak tree," prevails over a call from "Point X south 100 feet").

2) Artificial monuments (*e.g.,* stakes, buildings, etc.) prevail over all but natural monuments.

3) Courses (*e.g.,* angles) prevail over distances (*e.g.,* "west 90 degrees to Main St." prevails over "west 100 feet to Main St.").

4) All the foregoing prevail over general descriptions such as name (*e.g.,* "Walker's Island") or quantity (*e.g.,* "being 300 acres").

e. Land Bounded by Right-of-Way

1) Title Presumed to Extend to Center of Right-of-Way
If land is described as being bounded by a street, highway, or other right-of-way, or if the land conveyed is otherwise described but actually is bounded by such, there is a rebuttable presumption that the title of the grantee extends to the center of the right-of-way (assuming that the grantor owns to the center), or to the full width of it if the grantor retains no adjoining land. This presumption accords with (i) the presumed intention of the parties, and (ii) the public policy that disfavors a grantor's retention of thin strips of land.

a) Evidence to Rebut Presumption
In many jurisdictions, a description such as "running *along* the street" has been held sufficient to rebut the presumption that the grantee took title to the center. (This is to be distinguished from the language "*bounded* on the west by the highway" to which the presumption applies.)

But where the monument involved is a *body of water*, more definite language is necessary to rebut the presumption that the grantee takes title to the center. This is because, unlike streets, there are no public rights in most bodies of water abutting on land (except possible navigation easements), and because a grantee of land adjoining water normally expects a right of access to the water.

b) Measuring from Monument
Notwithstanding the general rule, and unless a contrary intention is expressed, measurements *from* a right-of-way are presumed to start from the side and not the center. Again, this is based on the parties' presumed intent.

2) Variable Boundary Line Cases

a) Slow Change in Course Changes Property Rights
The *slow and imperceptible* change in course of a river or stream serving as a boundary operates to change the legal boundary. Where land is described as abutting upon a body of water, any slow and imperceptible deposit of soil ("accretion") belongs to the owner of the abutting land (the riparian owner). Where accretion builds up in an irregular pattern over the lands of several adjacent property owners, courts determine title to it in a "just and equitable manner," either by (i) merely extending the property lines out into the water with each landowner getting the property that falls within the lines as extended; or (ii) dividing up the newly formed land in proportion to the owners' interests in the adjoining lands. Similarly, slow erosion of a stream's bank results in the owner losing title to the affected area.

b) Avulsion Does Not Change Property Rights
A sudden, perceptible change of a watercourse ("avulsion") does not change property rights. Thus, if a river changes course suddenly, boundaries remain where they were, even if someone who formerly had river access now finds himself landlocked.

c) Encroachment of Water Does Not Change Fixed Boundary Lines
According to the majority view, where property is encroached upon by a body of water (*e.g.,* lake enlarges), previously fixed boundary lines do not change and ownership rights are not affected. Indeed, the boundary lines can still be proven even though the land is completely under water.

f. Reformation of Deeds

Reformation is an equitable action in which the court rewrites the deed to make it conform to the intention of the parties. It will be granted if the deed does not express what the parties agreed to, either because of their *mutual mistake* or a *scrivener's* (drafter's) *error*. It will also be granted for *unilateral mistake*, but only if the party who is not mistaken induced the mistake by *misrepresentation* or some other inequitable conduct. If the property has passed to a bona fide purchaser who relied on the original language of the deed, the court will not reform it.

C. DELIVERY AND ACCEPTANCE

1. Delivery—In General

A deed is not effective to transfer an interest in realty unless it has been delivered. Physical transfer of a deed is not necessary for a valid delivery. Nor does physical transfer alone establish delivery (although it might raise a presumption thereof). Rather, "delivery" refers to the *grantor's intent*; it is satisfied by *words or conduct* evidencing the grantor's intention that the deed have *some present operative effect*; *i.e.,* that *title* pass immediately and irrevocably, even though the right of possession may be postponed until some future time.

Examples: 1) A draws an instrument conveying Blackacre to B and hands the instrument to B "for safekeeping." Although handed to the named grantee, this is not a valid delivery. There is no evidence that A intended the instrument to have any *present* operative effect.

2) A draws an instrument conveying Blackacre to B. A attempts to give the instrument to B personally but is unable to find B; nevertheless, A quits possession of Blackacre and thereafter treats B as the owner thereof. Nearly all courts would hold that there has been a sufficient delivery.

Under some circumstances (*i.e.,* when a third party is involved), conditional delivery is permissible. This type of delivery becomes effective only upon the occurrence of a condition, but the transfer then *relates back* to the time of the conditional delivery. The grantor has only limited rights to revoke prior to the occurrence of the condition. (*See* further discussion of conditional deliveries, 3., *infra.*)

a. Manual Delivery

The delivery requirement will be satisfied where the grantor physically or manually delivers the deed to the grantee. Manual delivery may be accomplished by means of the mails, by the grantor's agent or messenger, or by physical transfer by the grantor's attorney in the grantor's presence.

b. Presumptions Relating to Delivery

As a matter of theory, a deed may be delivered by words without an act of physical transfer. Delivery is presumed if the deed is: (i) *handed* to the grantee, (ii) *acknowledged* by the grantor before a notary, or (iii) *recorded*. Unless there is some clear expression of intent that the grantor envisioned the passage of title to the grantee without physical delivery, the continued possession of the deed by the grantor raises a presumption of nondelivery and therefore no passage of title. Conversely, possession by a grantee of a properly executed deed raises a presumption that the delivery requirement has been satisfied. Note, however, that the presumptions involved are rebuttable.

c. Delivery Cannot Be Canceled

Title passes to the grantee upon effective delivery. Therefore, returning the deed to the grantor has no effect; it constitutes neither a cancellation nor a reconveyance.

d. Parol Evidence

1) Admissible to Prove Grantor's Intent

The *majority rule* is that any type of parol evidence, including conduct or statements made by the grantor *before or after* the alleged delivery, is admissible to prove her intent.

2) Not Admissible to Show Delivery to Grantee Was Conditional

If a deed is *unconditional on its face* and is given *directly to the grantee*, in most jurisdictions parol evidence is not admissible to show that the delivery was subject to a condition.

Example: A delivers an absolute deed of Blackacre to B, but **tells** B that the deed is effective only if B pays off the encumbrance on the property, or only if A does not return from the hospital. Under the above rule, even if B never pays off the encumbrance or if A returns from the hospital, B is the owner of Blackacre and A cannot claim there was no valid delivery. *Rationale:* The rule is designed to avoid unsettling of land titles which appear to be in the grantee's name, and to protect both innocent third parties and grantees from testimony fabricated by grantors.

3) Admissible to Show No Delivery Intended
But while parol evidence is not admitted to prove that a delivery was subject to a condition, parol evidence *is* admissible to prove that the grantor did not intend the deed to have any present effect at all.

Example: A tells B, "I want you to have Blackacre when I die, and I'm giving you this deed to Blackacre so that you can have it **at that time**." Most courts would hold that A's statements are admissible, and that despite the unconditional nature of the deed itself, they show that A did not intend the deed to have any present effect.

a) Deed Intended as Mortgage
Parol evidence is *always* admissible to show that a deed absolute on its face was intended by the parties to be a mortgage; *i.e.,* there was no intent to convey title outright.

b) Transfer of Deed to Bona Fide Purchaser ("BFP")
Suppose A gives B a deed for examination by B's attorney (deed not intended to be effective at this point). B wrongfully records it and sells to C, a BFP. On these facts, A would prevail against C unless estopped to assert lack of delivery (*see* below). In other words, absent estoppel, a subsequent BFP is not protected; if there was no delivery, the BFP's grantor had no power to convey.

(1) Estoppel in Favor of Innocent Purchaser
Even though the grantor is allowed to show that no delivery at all was intended as against the grantee, he often is estopped to assert lack of delivery against an innocent purchaser. For example, A gives B a deed but does not intend the deed to be presently effective. B shows the deed to an innocent purchaser, P, who buys the land in reliance thereon. P will prevail in litigation with A, the original grantor, if it appears that A **negligently permitted** B to have possession of the deed. The rationale is that as between two innocent parties, the one who contributed most directly to the loss must bear the burden of it, and that in many cases A must be deemed responsible for entrusting B with a deed absolute on its face. The same result obtains where the grantee records the deed and an innocent purchaser relies on the recordation.

4) Comment
Obviously, the above rules give the courts flexibility to find either delivery or nondelivery in many situations. It is also evident that there exists a theoretical inconsistency in admitting parol evidence to show that no delivery was intended, but not to show that delivery was "conditional." This inconsistency has been criticized by numerous commentators.

2. Retention of Interest by Grantor or Conditional Delivery
Problems arise when the grantor attempts to retain an interest in the property (*e.g.,* a life estate) or when he attempts to make the passage of title dependent upon the happening of a condition or event other than delivery.

a. No Delivery—Title Does Not Pass
If the grantor executes a deed but fails to deliver it during his lifetime, no conveyance of title takes place. Without adequate delivery, the title does not pass to the intended grantee.

b. No Recording—Title Passes
If the grantor executes and delivers a deed but fails to have it recorded, title passes

even though the parties thought the deed would be ineffective until recording. Therefore, an agreement between the grantor and grantee to the effect that the deed will not be recorded until some event takes place in the future does not affect the passage of title.

c. **Express Condition of Death of Grantor Creates Future Interest**
Where a deed, otherwise properly executed and delivered, contains an express provision that the title will not pass until the grantor's death, the effect is to create a present possessory life estate in the grantor and a future estate in the grantee. Note, however, that this result follows only when the deed expressly contains such a provision.

d. **Conditions Not Contained in Deed**
If a deed is absolute on its face, but is delivered to the grantee with an oral condition (*e.g.,* "title is not to pass until I return from the Orient"), the traditional view was that the condition dropped out and the delivery became absolute. A growing minority of cases enforces the condition. Where the condition is the grantor's death, the deed is usually held "testamentary" and therefore void (unless executed with testamentary formalities). .

e. **Test—Relinquishment of Control**
To make an effective delivery, the grantor must relinquish absolute and unconditional control.

3. **Where Grantor Gives Deed to Third Party**
In this situation, the rules are quite different; *conditional delivery is permissible*. Three situations should be distinguished: (i) where the grantor gives the deed to a third party, there being *no conditions* appended; (ii) where the grantor in a *commercial* context gives such a deed to a third party, there being conditions appended; and (iii) where the situation is the same as in (ii), but the transaction is *donative*.

a. **Transfer to Third Party with No Conditions**
Where A (the grantor) gives C a deed naming B as grantee and instructs C to give the deed to B, has a delivery occurred? Most courts say yes. Since A indicated an intent to make the deed presently operative, B has a right to the deed and A should not be able to get it back. However, if A told C to retain the deed and give it to B upon A's later instructions, no delivery would have occurred.

Where there are no specific instructions regarding delivery, the question is one of A's intent. If C is B's attorney, delivery seems clear. But if C is A's attorney, a court might infer that C was merely A's agent and that A thus retained the power to recall the deed. (A few courts hold that C is to be treated as A's agent *in all circumstances*, even if A manifests a clear intention of present effectiveness, and consequently no delivery occurs.)

b. **Transfer to Third Party with Conditions (Commercial Transaction)**
Suppose that A gives C a deed naming B as grantee and tells C to transfer the deed to B when B has paid $5,000 on A's account on or before September 1. This is the *true escrow* situation—the true conditional delivery. Under the circumstances outlined below, a valid conditional delivery has occurred. The deed has a present operative effect in that title will transfer automatically upon the occurrence of the condition. A will retain title only if the condition does not occur.

1) **Parol Evidence Admissible to Show Conditions**
Even though a deed is unconditional, the general rule is that parol evidence is admissible to show the conditions and terms upon which a deed was deposited with the escrow. (This is contrary to the rule excluding parol evidence where transfer is directly to the grantee.) If the escrow custodian has violated parol conditions, there will be no valid delivery. Once the condition occurs, whether parol or not, title automatically vests in the grantee and the escrow holds the deed as the grantee's agent.

2) **Grantor's Right to Recover Deed**

a) **Majority View—Can Recover Only If No Written Contract**
Under the majority view, if the grantor seeks to recover the deed prior to the occurrence of the condition, the grantee can object only if there is an enforceable

written contract to convey. (On the other hand, once the condition occurs, title passes even in the absence of an enforceable contract.)

(1) The requirement of a written contract is based on the Statute of Frauds' consideration that oral contracts to convey realty should not become enforceable simply because the deed has been deposited with a third party.

(2) Ordinarily, the contract to convey will be a buy-sell land contract. However, written escrow instructions are often a sufficient memorandum of the contract to satisfy the Statute of Frauds.

b) Minority View—No Right to Recover
A strong minority prohibits revocation even in the absence of an enforceable underlying contract. Deposit of the deed with a third party on stated conditions is seen to obviate most possibilities of fraud.

3) Breach of Escrow Conditions—Title Does Not Pass
Where the grantee wrongfully acquires the deed from the escrow holder prior to performance of the conditions of the escrow, title does not pass. Therefore, even though the grantee is in possession of the deed, she cannot convey any interest in the land to a subsequent transferee, even a bona fide purchaser.

a) Estoppel Cases
A *few* cases have held that where the escrow holder was chosen by the grantor, the grantor is bound by the escrow holder's acts and is estopped to deny a valid delivery and passage of title to the grantee. Thus, an innocent purchaser ("BFP") from the grantee may acquire good title. An important factor is whether the grantor has allowed the grantee to take possession of the property prior to completion of the conditions of the escrow. If the grantor has remained in possession, the purchaser may be held to have notice of the grantor's interest and cannot be a BFP.

4) "Relation Back" Doctrine
In an escrow transaction, title does not pass to the grantee until performance of the named conditions. However, where justice requires, the title of the grantee will "relate back" to the *time of the deposit of the deed in escrow*. Generally, the relation back doctrine will be applied if:

(i) The *grantor dies* (doctrine applied to avoid the rule that title must pass before death if instrument is not a will);

(ii) The grantor *becomes incompetent* (doctrine applied to avoid the rule that an incompetent cannot convey title); or

(iii) A *creditor* of the grantor (who is not a bona fide purchaser or mortgagee) *attaches the grantor's title* (doctrine applied to cut off the creditor's claim).

a) Not Applied If Intervening Party Is Bona Fide Purchaser or Mortgagee
The relation back doctrine is not applied where the intervening third party is a bona fide purchaser or mortgagee. However, if the sales contract is recorded, there can be no intervening bona fide purchasers since its recordation gives constructive notice.

b) Not Applied in Favor of Escrow Grantee with Knowledge
The relation back doctrine will not be applied in favor of an escrow grantee who, at the time she performs the terms and conditions of the escrow, has actual or constructive knowledge of prior equities of other persons (*e.g.,* that the grantor conveyed to another). But if the escrow grantee has performed part of the conditions when she acquires such knowledge, she will be protected against all but bona fide purchasers or mortgagees.

c. Transfer to Third Party with Conditions (Donative Transactions)
If the grantor gives a deed to a third party with instructions to turn it over to the named donee only when certain conditions occur, is there a valid delivery or can the grantor change her mind and demand the deed back before the conditions occur?

1) **Condition Unrelated to Grantor's Death—Delivery Irrevocable**
Where A gives to C a deed naming B as grantee, and instructs C to give it to B "when B marries," etc., many courts find a valid conditional delivery despite the absence of any enforceable contract to convey. In such cases, the courts have held that A's intent at *the time of the transfer to C* was to create a "springing future interest" in B. Such a finding makes the delivery irrevocable.

2) **Where Condition Is Grantor's Death**
Where A executes a deed to B and hands the deed to C with instructions to give it to B upon the death of A, most courts hold that the grantor *cannot* get her deed back since her intent was to presently convey a future interest to the grantee (either a remainder, with a life estate reserved in the grantor, or an executory limitation). Note that this analysis also makes the gift inter vivos, not testamentary, and thus not in conflict with the Statute of Wills. *Caution:* In dealing with death cases, make sure that it was the grantor's intent that the deed be operative immediately to convey a future interest.

   a) **Limitation—No Delivery If Conditioned on Survival**
   Where A's instructions to C are to deliver the deed to B only if B survives A, it is generally held that there is no valid delivery because it was A's intent to retain title and possession until her death.

4. **Acceptance**

   a. **Usually Presumed**
   There must be an acceptance by the grantee in order to complete a conveyance. In most states, acceptance is presumed if the conveyance is beneficial to the grantee (whether or not the grantee knows of it). In other states, acceptance is presumed only where the grantee is shown to have knowledge of the grant and fails to indicate rejection of it. Acceptance is presumed in all states if the grantee is an infant or an incompetent.

   b. **Usually "Relates Back"**
   Acceptance (presumed or otherwise) usually "relates back" to the date of "delivery" of the deed in escrow. However, many courts refuse to "relate back" an acceptance where it would defeat the rights of *intervening third parties* such as BFPs, attaching creditors of the grantor, or surviving joint tenants. A few states will not even "relate back" an acceptance if doing so defeats the devisees of the grantor.

5. **Dedication**
Land may be transferred to a public body (*e.g.,* a city or county) by dedication. An *offer* of dedication may be made by written or oral statement, submission of a map or plat showing the dedication, or opening the land to public use. An *acceptance* by the public agency is necessary. This may be accomplished by a formal resolution, approval of the map or plat, or actual assumption of maintenance or construction of improvements by the agency.

D. **COVENANTS FOR TITLE AND ESTOPPEL BY DEED**
There are three types of deeds characteristically used to convey property interests other than leaseholds: the *general warranty* deed, the *special warranty* deed (usually statutory), and the *quitclaim* deed. The major difference between these deeds is the scope of assurances (covenants for title) they give to the grantee and the grantee's successors regarding the title being conveyed. The general warranty deed normally contains five covenants for title (*see* 1.a.1)-5), *infra*). The special warranty deed contains fewer and more limited assurances. The quitclaim deed usually contains no assurances; it releases to the grantee whatever interest the grantor happens to own. Covenants for title must be distinguished from covenants for other than title (*i.e.,* covenants running with the land used for private land regulation). "Covenants for title" is a self-contained topic.

1. **Covenants for Title in a General Warranty Deed**
In this day of recording acts and title insurance, covenants for title are not much relied upon for title assurance. A general warranty deed is one in which the grantor covenants against title defects created both by himself and by *all prior titleholders*. In a special warranty deed, however, the grantor covenants only that he himself did not create title defects; he represents nothing about what prior owners might have done. General warranty deeds are a rarity in a number of states where many conveyances are made with statutory form special warranty deeds.

a. Usual Covenants

A grantor may give any or all of the following covenants, which are classified as the "usual covenants for title." A deed containing such covenants is called a "general warranty deed."

1) Covenant of Seisin

The covenant of seisin is a covenant that the grantor has the estate or interest that she purports to convey. Both title and possession at the time of the grant are necessary to satisfy the covenant.

2) Covenant of Right to Convey

The covenant of the right to convey is a covenant that the grantor has the power and authority to make the grant. Title alone will ordinarily satisfy this covenant, as will proof that the grantor was acting as the authorized agent of the titleholder.

3) Covenant Against Encumbrances

The covenant against encumbrances is a covenant assuring that there are neither visible encumbrances (easements, profits, etc.) nor invisible encumbrances (mortgages, etc.) against the title or interest conveyed.

4) Covenant for Quiet Enjoyment

The covenant for quiet enjoyment is a covenant that the grantee will not be disturbed in her possession or enjoyment of the property by a third party's *lawful* claim of title.

5) Covenant of Warranty

The covenant of warranty is a covenant wherein the grantor agrees to defend on behalf of the grantee any lawful or reasonable claims of title by a third party, and to compensate the grantee for any loss sustained by the claim of superior title. This covenant and the covenant for quiet enjoyment are generally considered to be identical.

6) Covenant for Further Assurances

The covenant for further assurances is a covenant to perform whatever acts are reasonably necessary to perfect the title conveyed if it turns out to be imperfect. This is not one of the "usual covenants" but is frequently given in addition thereto.

7) No Implied Warranties or Covenants

In the absence of statute, no covenants of title are implied in deeds. Moreover, the implied (or express) covenant of marketable title found in contracts of sale of real estate is no longer assertable once a deed has been delivered, unless fraud or mistake is shown.

b. Breach of Covenants

Three of the covenants (seisin, right to convey, encumbrances) are *present covenants* and are breached, if at all, at the time of conveyance. Quiet enjoyment, warranty, and further assurances are *future covenants* and are breached only upon interference with the possession of the grantee or her successors. This distinction is important in that it determines when the statute of limitations begins running and whether a remote grantee of the covenantor can sue.

1) Covenants of Seisin and Right to Convey

The covenants of seisin and right to convey are breached at the time of conveyance *if the grantor is not the owner* of the interest she purports to convey (or has not been authorized to so convey). If there is a breach, the grantee has a cause of action against which the statute of limitations begins to run at the time of conveyance. If the grantee reconveys, the general rule is that the subsequent grantee has no right of action against the covenantor. In a few jurisdictions, it is implied that the original grantee assigned the cause of action to the subsequent grantee, thus permitting suit against the original grantor-covenantor. (The latter is probably the better rule since the subsequent grantee most likely paid the original grantee the market value.)

Example: A conveys Blackacre to B by a deed containing a covenant of seisin. A purports to convey a fee simple, but in fact X was the owner of Blackacre. Soon thereafter, B conveys to C. Under the usual view, B, but not C, may recover from A. In a few jurisdictions, it is implied that B assigned her cause of action to C.

2) Covenant Against Encumbrances
The covenant against encumbrances is breached and a cause of action arises at the time of conveyance if the property is encumbered. Most jurisdictions hold that the covenant is breached even if the grantee knew of the encumbrance, whether it be an encumbrance on title (*e.g.,* a mortgage) or a physical encumbrance (*e.g.,* an easement or servitude), but others hold there is no breach if the grantee knew of a physical encumbrance.

These jurisdictions charge grantees with constructive notice of visible physical encumbrances (*e.g.,* right-of-way). Several cases go so far as to hold that a covenant against encumbrances is not breached where the encumbrance ("visible" or not) is a benefit to the land involved (*e.g.,* an easement for a sewer or for an adjacent street).

3) Covenants for Quiet Enjoyment, Warranty, and Further Assurances
Covenants for quiet enjoyment, warranty, and further assurances are not breached until a ***third party interferes with the possession*** of the grantee or her successors. (*But note:* A covenant for quiet enjoyment or of warranty is not breached by the covenantor's refusal to defend title against a ***wrongful*** claim or eviction by a third party.)

a) Covenant Runs to Successive Grantees
These covenants are viewed as "continuous"; *i.e.,* they can be breached a number of times. Their benefit "runs" with the grantee's estate (unlike covenants of seisin and against encumbrances).
Example: A conveys to B by a deed containing a covenant of warranty. B thereafter conveys to C and C to D, and then D is evicted by a third party with title that was paramount when A conveyed to B. D can successfully sue A.

b) Requirement of Notice
The covenantor is not liable on her covenant of warranty or of further assurances, unless the party seeking to hold her liable gives her notice of the claim against the title she conveyed.

c) Any Disturbance of Possession
Most courts hold that any disturbance of possession suffices to constitute a breach. Thus, if the covenantee cannot obtain complete possession or pays off an adverse, paramount claim in order to retain possession, this is a sufficient disturbance of possession. *Compare:* A disturbance of the covenantee's possession is not required as a prerequisite to recovery for breach of covenants of seisin, right to convey, or against encumbrances.

c. Damages and Remote Grantees
Suppose successive conveyances from A to B to C to D, each conveyance containing full covenants. D is evicted by X, who was the true owner when A conveyed to B. D may sue A, B, or C, since each gave a covenant of warranty the benefit of which "ran" with the land. But what is the measure of D's recovery? Is it the consideration the defendant (*i.e.,* A, B, or C) received? Is it the consideration D paid (an indemnity theory) so that if D was a donee, she gets nothing?

Many states permit D to recover to the extent of the ***consideration received*** by the defendant-covenantor (even though it exceeds the consideration paid by D). Under this view, defendant-shopping is advisable (to sue whomever received most). The defendant who is held liable then has a cause of action against any prior covenantor, until ultimately A is held liable. In other states, D can recover only the ***actual consideration she paid*** (but not to exceed the amount received by the defendant-covenantor).

2. Statutory Special Warranty Deed
Statutes in many states provide that (unless expressly negated) the use of the word "grant" in a conveyance creates ***by implication*** the following two limited assurances against ***acts of***

the grantor (not her predecessors): (i) that prior to the time of the execution of such conveyance, the *grantor has not conveyed the same estate* or any interest therein to any person other than the grantee; and (ii) that the estate conveyed is free from encumbrances made *by the grantor*.

3. Quitclaim Deeds

A quitclaim deed is basically a *release of whatever interest*, if any, the grantor has in the property. Hence, the use of covenants warranting the grantor's title is basically inconsistent with this type of deed; *i.e.,* if the deed contains warranties, it is not a quitclaim deed.

4. Estoppel by Deed

If a grantor purports to convey an estate in property that she does not then own, her *subsequent acquisition of title to the property will inure to the benefit of the grantee*. In other words, the grantor impliedly covenants that she will convey title immediately upon its acquisition.

Example: In a leading case, the grantor warranted the property as being "free and clear," even though the deed elsewhere recited that it was subject to a mortgage. When the grantor later acquired the mortgage, the court held that it inured to the benefit of the grantee, even though the latter was at no time misled.

a. Applies to Warranty Deeds

The doctrine is most frequently applied where the conveyance is by warranty deed. Regardless of covenants for title, many courts hold that if the deed expressly purports to convey a fee simple or other *particular estate*, the grantee is entitled to that estate if later acquired by the grantor. In most states, however, the doctrine will not be applied where the conveyance is by a quitclaim deed.

b. Rights of Subsequent Purchasers

The majority of courts hold that title inures to the benefit of the grantee only *as against the grantor* (who is estopped to deny that she acquired title on behalf of the grantee). This is a personal estoppel only. Consequently, if the grantor transfers her after-acquired title to an innocent purchaser for value, the BFP gets good title. (There is no basis for invoking an estoppel against an innocent purchaser without notice.)

1) Effect of Recordation by Original Grantee

If the original grantee records the deed she receives from the grantor, the question arises as to whether this recordation imparts sufficient notice of the grantee's interest, so as to prevent a subsequent purchaser from being a BFP. This depends on the subsequent grantee's *burden of searching the title*. (*See* discussion, E.4., *infra*.)

c. Remedies of Grantee

In jurisdictions following the estoppel rationale, the original grantee, at her election, may *accept title* to the land *or sue for damages for breach of covenants* for title. However, if an innocent purchaser of the after-acquired title is involved, the grantee has no rights against the BFP.

E. RECORDING

At common law, in nearly all cases priority was given to the grantee *first in time*. Thus, if A conveyed Blackacre to B and then made an identical conveyance to C, B prevailed over C on the theory that after the first conveyance A had no interest left to convey.

1. Recording Acts—In General

Statutes, known as "recording acts," require a grantee to make some sort of recordation so as to give "notice to the world" that title to certain property has already been conveyed, and thus to put subsequent purchasers on guard. These statutes are in effect in some form in every state. Basically, recording acts set up a system by which any instrument affecting title to property located in a certain county can be recorded in that county. These acts seek to protect all subsequent BFPs from secret, unrecorded interests of others.

a. Purpose of Recordation—Notice

Recordation is not essential to the validity of a deed, as between the grantor and grantee. However, if a grantee does not record her instrument, she may lose out against a subsequent BFP. By recording, the grantee gives constructive (or "record") *notice to everyone*. Hence, as stated earlier, proper recording prevents anyone from becoming a subsequent BFP.

b. Requirements for Recordation

    1) What Can Be Recorded—Instrument Affecting an Interest in Land
Practically every kind of ***deed, mortgage, contract to convey***, or other instrument creating or affecting an interest in land can be recorded. *Note:* A judgment or decree affecting title to property can also be recorded. And, even before judgment, where a ***lawsuit is pending that may affect title*** to property, any party to the action can record a ***lis pendens*** (notice of pending action), which will effectively put third parties on notice of all claims pending in the lawsuit.

    2) Grantor Must Acknowledge Deed
Most recording statutes provide that, in order to be recorded, a deed must be acknowledged by the grantor before a notary public. This requirement offers some protection against forgery. Problems may arise if the recorder records a deed that has not been acknowledged or has been improperly acknowledged.

c. Mechanics of Recording

    1) Filing Copy
The grantee or her agent normally presents the deed to the County Recorder, who photographs it and files the copy in the official records. These records are kept chronologically.

    2) Indexing
The recorder also indexes the deed to permit title searches. The usual indexes are the grantor-grantee and grantee-grantor indexes, which are arranged by reference to the parties to the conveyance. Tract indexes, which index the property by location, exist in some urban localities.

2. Types of Recording Acts
There are three major types of recording acts, classified as "notice," "race-notice," and "race" statutes. Note that the burden is on the subsequent taker to prove that he qualifies for protection under the statute.

a. Notice Statutes
Under a notice statute, a subsequent BFP (*i.e.,* a person who gives valuable consideration and has no actual notice of the prior instrument) prevails over a prior grantee who failed to record. The important fact under a notice statute is that the subsequent purchaser ***had no actual or constructive notice*** at the time of the conveyance. Constructive notice includes both record notice and inquiry notice (*see* 3.b.3), *infra*). A typical notice statute provides:

> "A conveyance of an interest in land (other than a lease for less
> than one year) shall not be valid against any subsequent purchaser
> for value, without notice thereof, unless the conveyance is re-
> corded."

Note also that the subsequent bona fide purchaser is protected, regardless of whether she records at all.

Example: On January 1, O conveys Blackacre to A. A does not record. On January 15, O conveys Blackacre to B, who gives valuable consideration and has no notice of the deed from O to A. B prevails over A.

> ***What if A records before B?*** Suppose in the example above that A recorded on January 18, and B never recorded. This is ***irrelevant*** under a "notice" statute, because B had no notice ***at the time of her conveyance*** from O. B is protected against a ***prior*** purchaser even though B does not record her deed (this is the difference between "notice" and "race-notice" statutes). Of course, if B does not record, she runs the risk that a subsequent purchaser will prevail over her, just as she prevailed over A.

b. Race-Notice Statutes
Under a race-notice statute, a subsequent BFP is protected only if she records ***before***

the prior grantee. *Rationale:* The best evidence of which deed was **delivered** first is to determine who recorded first. To obviate questions about the time of delivery and to add an inducement to record promptly, race-notice statutes impose on the BFP the additional requirement that she record first. A typical race-notice statute provides:

> "Any conveyance of an interest in land, other than a lease for less than one year, shall not be valid against any subsequent purchaser for value, without notice thereof, whose conveyance is **first recorded**."

Example: On January 1, O conveys Blackacre to A. A does not record. On January 15, O conveys Blackacre to B. On January 18, A records. On January 20, B records. A prevails over B because B did not record first.

c. Race Statutes
Under a pure race statute, whoever records first wins. Actual notice is irrelevant. The rationale is that actual notice depends upon extrinsic evidence, which may be unreliable. **Very few states** have race statutes.

Example: On January 1, O conveys Blackacre to A. A does not record. On January 15, O conveys Blackacre to B. B **knows** of the deed to A. B records. Then A records. B prevails over A because she recorded first. It is immaterial that she had actual notice of A's interest; she is still deemed a BFP because there was no "record" notice of A's interest.

3. Who Is Protected by Recording Acts
Only **bona fide purchasers** ("BFPs") are entitled to prevail against a prior transferee under "notice" and "race-notice" statutes. To attain this status, a person must satisfy three requirements (each of which is discussed in detail below). The person must:

(i) Be a **purchaser** (or mortgagee or creditor if the statute so allows; *see* below);

(ii) Take **without notice** (actual, constructive, or inquiry) of the prior instrument; and

(iii) Pay **valuable consideration**.

Note: If these requirements are not met, the person is not protected by the recording acts, so that the common law rule of first in time prevails.

Example: A, the owner of Blackacre, executes a contract of sale of the land to B on Monday. B immediately **records the contract**. On Tuesday, A deeds the land to C. C pays valuable consideration for the land, but is not a BFP because C is held to have constructive notice of B's rights. *Result:* B is entitled to enforce the contract against C, paying C the rest of the price and compelling C to deliver a deed to B. (If B had failed to record the contract, and C had no other notice of it, C would have taken free of B's contract rights. B would have an action in damages against A for breach of contract, but would not have a claim for specific performance against C.)

a. Purchasers
All recording acts protect purchasers (of the fee or any lesser estate).

1) Donees, Heirs, and Devisees Not Protected
Donees, heirs, and devisees are not protected because they do not give value for their interests.

Example: A, the owner of Blackacre, conveys it to B on Monday. B fails to record. A dies on Tuesday and his heirs/devisees succeed to his property interests. Even though A's heirs/devisees may be unaware of the prior conveyance of Blackacre to B, B prevails. But if the heirs/devisees convey to C, a bona fide purchaser, C prevails if he records first (or, without recording, under a pure notice statute). The heirs/devisees were cloaked with the indicia of ownership.

2) Mortgagees
Mortgagees for value are treated as "purchasers," either expressly by the recording act or by judicial classification.

Example: A, the owner of a parcel in State X known as Blackacre, deeds the parcel to B on Monday, but B fails to record the deed. On Tuesday,

A executes a mortgage to Bank. State X has a race-notice recording statute. Bank is a good faith purchaser for value, and immediately records its mortgage. *Result:* Bank has a valid mortgage on the land, while the title to the land is held by B. (If Bank had not been a BFP, or had failed to record, B would hold the title free of Bank's mortgage.)

3) Judgment Creditors

In nearly all states, a plaintiff who obtains a money judgment can obtain, by statute, a judgment lien on the defendant's real estate. A typical statute reads as follows:

> Any judgment properly filed shall, for 10 years from filing, be a lien on the real property then owned or subsequently acquired by any person against whom the judgment is rendered.

Is a plaintiff who obtains a judgment lien under such a statute protected by the recording acts from a prior unrecorded conveyance made by the defendant? The cases are split, but the majority holds that the judgment lienor is not protected. These courts usually reason either (i) the plaintiff is not a BFP, since he did not pay value for the judgment, or (ii) the judgment attaches only to property "owned" by the defendant, and not to property the defendant has previously conveyed away, even if that conveyance was not recorded.

Example: On January 1, O grants a mortgage on Blackacre to A. A does not record the mortgage. On January 15, B, who had previously sued O on a tort claim, obtains and properly files a judgment against O. B has no knowledge of the mortgage from O to A. Which lien has priority, A's mortgage or B's judgment lien? By the majority view, A has priority despite A's failure to record the mortgage. B is not protected by the recording act.

4) Purchaser from Heir

A person who buys land from the heir or devisee of the record owner (now deceased) is protected against a prior unrecorded conveyance from the record owner.

Example: O conveys Blackacre to A, who does not record. O dies, leaving H as her heir. (H does not prevail over A because he is not a purchaser.) H conveys to B, a BFP, who records. B prevails over A in nearly all jurisdictions.

An heir who purchases the interests of her co-heirs, without notice of the prior unrecorded conveyance, is entitled to the same protection as any other purchaser to the extent of her purchase.

5) Transferees from Bona Fide Purchaser—Shelter Rule

A person who takes from a BFP will prevail against any interest that the transferor-BFP would have prevailed against. This is true even where the transferee had *actual knowledge* of the prior unrecorded interest.

Example: O conveys to A, who fails to record. O then conveys to B, a BFP, who records. B then conveys to C, who has actual knowledge of the O to A deed. C prevails over A. (And this is true whether C is a donee or purchaser.)

a) Rationale

If the rule were otherwise, a BFP might not be able to convey an interest in the land. The transferee is not protected for her own sake, but rather for the sake of the BFP from whom she received title.

b) Exception—No "Shipping Through"

This rule will not help someone who *previously* held title and had notice of the unrecorded interest. In the example above, if O repurchased from B, O would have notice of A's interest and could not claim the benefit of the "shelter rule."

b. Without Notice

"Without notice" means the purchaser had no actual, record, or inquiry notice of the prior conveyance at the time she paid the consideration and received her interest in the land. The fact that the purchaser obtains knowledge of the adverse claim after the conveyance but before she records it is immaterial; she only has to be "without notice" *at the time of the conveyance*.

1) Actual Notice

The subsequent purchaser must show that she did not actually know of any prior unrecorded conveyance. Actual notice includes knowledge obtained from any source (*e.g.,* newspaper, word-of-mouth, etc.).

2) Record Notice—Chain of Title

The fact that a deed has been recorded does not necessarily mean that a purchaser is entitled to the protection of the recording system. A subsequent purchaser will only be charged with notice of all conveyances that are recorded and appear in the chain of title.

a) "Wild Deeds"

A "wild deed" is a recorded deed that is not connected to the chain of title. It does not give constructive notice because the subsequent bona fide purchaser cannot feasibly find it.

Example: Presume that A owns Blackacre, which she contracts to sell to B. The contract is not recorded, and A remains in possession. B thereupon conveys Blackacre by deed to C, and C records. A then conveys Blackacre by deed to D. Did C's recordation charge D with constructive notice of C's claim to equitable title to Blackacre derived through B? *No.* D is not charged with notice because there was no way for him to find the B-C deed. Nothing related it to A. It was not in A's chain of title; it was a "wild deed."

Compare: If the jurisdiction maintained a tract index, it would not be hard to find that B-C deed. It would be indexed under Blackacre's block and lot number. But it is impossible to find in a grantor-grantee index without looking at the descriptions of all the recorded properties.

b) Deeds Recorded Late

A deed recorded after the grantor therein is shown by the record to have parted with title through another (subsequent) instrument is not constructive notice in most states.

Example: A conveys to B on May 1. A conveys to C, a donee, on May 15. C records on June 1. B records on June 15. C conveys to D on July 1. D has no actual notice of the A-B deed.

C v. B: As between B and C, B would win because C (a donee) was not a bona fide purchaser.

D v. B: In *notice* statute jurisdictions, most courts hold that D will prevail over B because the A-B deed was recorded "late" and is not in D's chain of title; *i.e.,* the search burden is too great if D is required to search "down" the grantor index to the present time for each grantor in the chain.

In several *race-notice* jurisdictions, however, B's recordation is treated as giving constructive notice to any purchaser *subsequent to* such recordation. In these states, the title searcher must search to the present date under the name of each person who ever owned the property in order to pick up deeds recorded late.

(1) Shelter Doctrine

If C in the example above were a BFP, D would win in any event, for she would "shelter" under C. This result would be the same even if D had actual knowledge of the A-B deed; otherwise C's power to transfer would be restricted.

(2) Lis Pendens Protection

What can B do to protect herself when she records her deed and finds the A-C deed on record? She can bring suit against C to expunge C's deed and file a lis pendens (litigation pending) notice under C's name, so any purchaser from C will have notice of B's claim.

c) Deeds Recorded Before Grantor Obtained Title

There is a split of authority on whether a recorded deed, obtained from a grantor who had no title at that time but who afterwards obtains title, is constructive notice to a subsequent purchaser from the same grantor.

Example: Suppose that on June 1, O owns Blackacre, but on that same day, A conveys Blackacre by warranty deed to B who promptly records. On July 2, O conveys Blackacre to A, and this deed is also promptly recorded. On August 3, A conveys Blackacre to C, a bona fide purchaser who has no actual notice of the prior A to B deed.

Majority view: Most courts protect C over B on the theory that a deed from A that was recorded prior to the time title came to A is not in the chain of title and so does not give C constructive notice of B's claim to Blackacre. *Rationale:* It would put an excessive burden on the title searcher to have to search the index under each grantor's name *prior* to the date the grantor acquired title.

Minority view: However, a minority of courts protect B over C on the basis that as soon as A acquired title from O, it transferred automatically to B by virtue of A's earlier deed to B. Therefore, A had nothing to transfer to C. (*Criticism:* The minority view sharply increases the costs of title search.)

d) Deed in Chain Referring to Instrument Outside Chain

Where a recorded document in the chain of title refers to another instrument, such reference may be sufficient to impart constructive notice of the other instrument, even if it is unrecorded or is not itself in the chain of title.

Example: O mortgages Blackacre to A, who does not record. Later, O sells Blackacre to B by deed which recites that title is subject to A's mortgage. This deed is recorded. B then sells to C. C takes subject to A's mortgage, even though it was never recorded, because of the reference to it in the O to B deed.

e) Restrictive Covenants—Deeds from Common Grantor

(1) Subdivision Restrictions

Suppose that O, a subdivider, is developing a residential subdivision. She sells lot #1 to A, and the deed provides that lot #1 is restricted to residential use. The deed also provides that "O on behalf of herself, her heirs and assigns, promises to use her remaining lots (#2, #3, etc.) for residential purposes only." A records the deed. O then sells lot #2 to B. The deed to B contains no restrictions. B wishes to erect a gas station. Is B bound by the restrictions in the O to A deed of which he had no actual notice? The courts are split.

(a) Some charge B with reading *all* deeds given by a common grantor, not just the deeds to his particular tract. Hence, B has constructive notice and is bound by the restriction.

(b) However, the *better view* is contra; *i.e.,* because the burden of title search would be excessive, deeds to other lots given by a common grantor are not in B's chain of title.

(2) Adjacent Lots

Suppose that O owns lot #1 and lot #2. She grants lot #2 to A with an easement of way over lot #1. The deed to A is indexed as a deed to lot #2; no mention is made of lot #1. Subsequently, O conveys lot #1 to B without mentioning the easement. As with subdivision restrictions, the courts are split as to whether B is required to read O's deeds of adjoining lots.

f) Merchantable Title Act

In about 15 states, a *search cut-off date* is established by statute; *e.g.,* defects of title reaching back further than 40 years are barred (a title searcher need only check the chain of title back 40 years). The exact cut-off point varies from state to state.

3) Inquiry Notice

Inquiry notice means that if the subsequent grantee is bound to make reasonable inquiry, she will be held to have knowledge of any facts that such inquiry *would have revealed* (even though she made none).

a) Generally No Inquiry from Quitclaim Deed

In a *majority* of states, quitclaim grantees are treated under the recording system the same as warranty deed grantees; *i.e.,* they are not charged with inquiry notice from the mere fact that a quitclaim deed was used.

b) Inquiry from References in Recorded Instruments

If a recorded instrument makes reference to an unrecorded transaction, the grantee is bound to make inquiry to discover the nature and character of the unrecorded transaction.

Example: A grants an easement in Blackacre to B, who does not record. A thereafter conveys the fee to C and in the deed states that the property is "subject to an easement." C records. D purchases Blackacre from C without any knowledge of the easement. The reference to the easement in the A to C deed creates a *duty to inquire* concerning the easement. If a reasonable inquiry would have informed D of the easement, she has notice of it even though the deed of the easement was never recorded. (Remember the grantee is charged with constructive knowledge of the fruits of a reasonable inquiry even though she made no inquiry.) Thus, D will take subject to B's unrecorded interest in Blackacre.

c) Inquiry from Unrecorded Instruments in Chain of Title

Suppose A, the record owner, conveys a life estate to B by a deed that is not recorded. Thereafter, B purports to convey a fee simple to C, a purchaser for valuable consideration, without actual notice that B merely has a life estate. A would prevail over C with respect to the remainder interest because C is "required" (at her peril) to demand a viewing of B's title documents at the time of the purchase when they are unrecorded.

d) Inquiry from Possession

A title search is not complete without an examination of possession. If the possession is unexplained by the record, the subsequent purchaser is obligated to make inquiry. The subsequent purchaser is charged with knowledge of whatever an inspection of the property would have disclosed *and* anything that would have been disclosed by inquiring of the possessor.

Example: A, the owner of Blackacre, conveys it to B, who fails to record. However, B goes into possession of Blackacre. Thereafter, A executes an identical conveyance of Blackacre to C, who purchases for valuable consideration and without actual notice of the prior unrecorded conveyance to B. A majority of states hold that C is placed on constructive notice of B's interest. An examination of possession would have revealed B's presence, and B's possession is inconsistent with A's ownership.

Similarly, the physical appearance of the land may give notice of an adverse interest. For example, tire tracks passing over the land to an adjacent parcel may give notice of an easement.

c. Valuable Consideration

A person is protected by the recording statute only from the time that valuable consideration was given. Thus, if a deed was delivered before the consideration was paid, the purchaser will not prevail over deeds recorded before the consideration was given. Valuable consideration must be more than merely nominal. A person who claims to be a BFP must prove that *real* consideration was paid.

1) Test—Substantial Pecuniary Value

The test is different from that of contract law, where any consideration suffices to support a contract. Here, the claimant must show that he is not a donee but a purchaser. The consideration need not be adequate, nor the market value of the property, but it must be of substantial pecuniary value. ("Love and affection" is not valuable consideration.)

2) Property Received as Security for Antecedent Debts Is Insufficient

One who receives a deed or mortgage only as security for a preexisting debt has not given valuable consideration.

Example: O becomes indebted to A. O conveys Blackacre to B, who does not record. O then gives A a mortgage on Blackacre to secure the indebtedness, and A records. A did not give valuable consideration, and B prevails over A.

4. Title Search

Suppose X has contracted to sell Blackacre to Y. Prior to closing, Y, the buyer, will have a title search performed to assure herself that X really owns Blackacre and to determine if there are any encumbrances on X's title. How will Y's title searcher(s) proceed?

a. Tract Index Search

In a tract index jurisdiction, the job is comparatively easy. The searcher looks at the page indexed by block and/or lot describing Blackacre and at a glance can see prior recorded instruments conveying, mortgaging, or otherwise dealing with Blackacre.

b. Grantor and Grantee Index Search

The search is much more complicated in a grantor and grantee index jurisdiction.

Examples: 1) V owned Blackacre in 1900. In 1930, V conveyed Blackacre to W. In 1955, W conveyed Blackacre to X. In 1960, X gave B Bank a mortgage on the property. In 1970, X conveyed Blackacre to O. O contracts to sell the land to A. A's title searcher will look in the *grantee* index under O's name from the present back to 1970, when she finds the deed from X, then under X's name from 1970 to 1955, when she finds the deed from W to X, then under W's name from 1955 to 1930, then under V's name from 1930 backward. The searcher will then look in the *grantor* index under V's name from 1900 to 1930, under W's name from 1930 to 1955, under X's name from 1955 to 1970, and under O's name from 1970 to the present. In this manner, she will pick up the mortgage to B Bank, which was recorded in 1960 in the grantor index under X's name.

2)

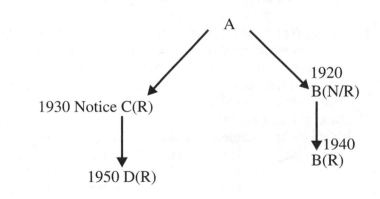

1920   A conveys to B.

1930   A executes an identical conveyance of Blackacre to C. C pays valuable consideration, but C has actual knowledge of the prior unrecorded conveyance to B. C records.

1940   B records.

1950   C conveys his interest in Blackacre to D, who purchases without notice of the conveyance to B and who pays valuable consideration.

In searching the title, D will first look in the grantee index under C's name to discover if his seller, C, ever acquired title. He will find that C acquired title in 1930 from A. Next, he will look in the grantor index under C's name to discover if C made any prior conveyances, and then will look in the grantee index once again, this time under A's name, to discover if A ever acquired title. D will find that A acquired title in 1910. Then he will look in the grantor index under A's name to discover if A made a conveyance prior to his conveyance to C. Under the majority rule, D is required to look under A's name in the grantor index only through 1930. D will find no conveyances. In 1930, D will find the recorded conveyance to C and he need look no further. On this basis, D will not find the recorded conveyance to B since B recorded after 1930. B's recording is "out of the chain of title," and therefore D is not charged with notice.

Under a *pure notice or race-notice statute,* as between B and C, B will prevail since C, having knowledge of B's unrecorded conveyance, is not a protected party. However, as between B and D, many courts hold that D should prevail since B's recording is out of the chain of title. The cases are split. Since notice is irrelevant under *pure race* statutes, C would prevail over B since C recorded first. Once it is established that C prevails over B, D obviously takes good title.

c. Other Instruments and Events Affecting Title
The title searcher's job may be complicated by marriages and divorces (*e.g.,* a woman's name may have changed between her appearance as grantee and her reappearance as grantor) and by the fact that a number of interests in the land may be filed and indexed elsewhere than in the Recording Office (*e.g.,* judgment liens may appear in the trial court's judgment docket, and tax liens may be filed only in the Tax Assessor's Office). Similarly, discovering whether land has passed by will or intestacy rather than by conveyance may require a search of probate records.

5. Effect of Recordation
Proper recordation gives all prospective subsequent grantees constructive notice of the existence and contents of the recorded instruments; *i.e.,* there can be no subsequent bona fide purchasers. Recordation also raises *presumptions* that the instrument has been validly delivered and that it is authentic. These presumptions are rebuttable, not conclusive.

a. Does Not Validate Invalid Deed
As stated earlier, recordation is not necessary for a valid conveyance. Nor does recordation validate an invalid conveyance, such as a forged or undelivered deed.

b. Does Not Protect Against Interests Arising by Operation of Law
Furthermore, recordation does not protect a subsequent purchaser against interests that arise by operation of law, rather than from a recordable document (*e.g.,* dower rights; prescriptive and implied easements; title by adverse possession). Since there is no instrument to record in order to perfect such interests, the recording acts do not apply, and subsequent purchasers take subject to the interests. (*Remember:* If the recording act is inapplicable, the common law priority rules apply.)

Example: O is the record owner of Blackacre. X adversely possesses Blackacre for the period of the statute of limitations. O then conveys Blackacre to A, a bona fide purchaser. Even though X's interest has never been recorded, X prevails against A.

1) Exception
A court *may* protect a subsequent bona fide purchaser from an unrecorded *implied easement* that is *not visible* upon inspection of the premises (*e.g.,* an underground sewer).

c. **Recorder's Mistakes**
An instrument is considered recorded from and after the time it is filed at the recorder's office, irrespective of whether it is actually listed on the indexes. If the recorder's office has made an error in recording, the subsequent purchaser has an action against the recorder's office. There is a strong minority view that protects the searcher.

d. **Effect of Recording Unacknowledged Instrument**
As discussed above, the recording acts require that before an instrument can be recorded, it must be acknowledged by the grantor before a notary. What happens if the recorder, by oversight, records a deed that has not been acknowledged or has been defectively acknowledged?

1) **No Acknowledgment—No Constructive Notice**
Since an unacknowledged deed does not qualify for recordation, it does not give constructive notice to subsequent purchasers. Hence, unless the subsequent purchaser has other notice of the earlier deed, the subsequent purchaser will prevail.
Example: O conveys Blackacre to A by deed that is not acknowledged, but the recorder nevertheless records it. Later, O conveys to B by an acknowledged deed, which B records. B prevails over A unless B had *actual* notice of the deed from O to A (which she might have if she searched the title records) or *inquiry* notice (as she would have if A was in possession of Blackacre).

2) **Compare—Defective Acknowledgment**
Where a recorded instrument has been acknowledged, but the acknowledgment is defective for some reason *not apparent on the face* of the instrument, the better view is that the recordation does impart constructive notice. *Rationale:* A hidden defect in the acknowledgment should not be allowed to destroy the constructive notice that the document otherwise clearly imparts. Purchasers should be entitled to rely on what *appears* to be a perfectly recorded document.
Example: A deed bears what appears to be a valid acknowledgment but is in fact invalid because the notary was disqualified to act or because the grantor did not appear personally in front of the notary to acknowledge her signature, as required by law.

F. CONVEYANCE BY WILL

A will is a conveyance that is prepared and executed by the property owner during life, but which does not "speak" or operate until the date of the owner's death. Thus, a will is "ambulatory," meaning that it can be revoked or modified so long as the testator is alive. Some special situations arise when there is a change in the status of the property or beneficiaries between the time the will is executed and the testator's death.

1. **Ademption**
If property is specifically devised or bequeathed in the testator's will, but the testator no longer owns that property at the time of death, the gift is adeemed. This means that the gift fails and is not replaced by other property. The reason the property is no longer owned by the testator generally does not matter; *i.e.*, it does not matter whether the testator sold the property or it was accidentally destroyed.
Example: T owns Blackacre and executes a will devising "Blackacre to my daughter Mary." Prior to his death, T sells Blackacre to A and deposits the proceeds of the sale in a bank account. Upon T's death, Mary is not entitled to Blackacre or to its proceeds. Note that if the will had provided for T's executor to sell Blackacre and distribute the proceeds to Mary, she would be entitled to the proceeds even though the sale occurred before T's death.

a. **Not Applicable to General Devises**
Ademption does not apply unless the gift mentioned specific property. A specific devise or legacy is one that can be satisfied only by the delivery of a particular item; it cannot be satisfied by money. Thus, a bequest of "$10,000," or even of "$10,000 to be paid out of the sale of my IBM stock" cannot be adeemed.

b. **Not Applicable to Land Under Executory Contract**
If the testator enters into an enforceable contract of sale of property after making a specific devise of it by will, the doctrine of equitable conversion holds that the testator's

interest is converted into personal property. Logically, an ademption has occurred, and the proceeds of sale when the closing occurs should not pass to the specific devisee of the property. The traditional case law agrees, but the statutes of most states have reversed this result.

Example: T owns Blackacre and executes a will devising "Blackacre to my daughter Mary." Prior to his death, T enters into a contract to sell Blackacre to A. After T's death the contract is completed, and A pays the purchase price for the land. Mary is entitled to the purchase price in substitution of the land itself.

1) No Ademption Under Uniform Probate Code and Most Statutes

The Uniform Probate Code and the statutes in most states provide that when property subject to a specific devise is placed under contract of sale before the decedent's death, the proceeds of the sale will pass to the specific devisee.

2) No Ademption If Decedent Incompetent When Contract Formed

If the decedent is unable to enter into the contract, and instead it is entered into by a guardian, attorney in fact, or other representative, courts usually do not apply the equitable doctrine, and they allow the proceeds of the sale to pass to the specific devisee.

c. Other Proceeds Not Subject to Ademption

When property is damaged or destroyed before the testator's death but the casualty insurance proceeds are not paid until after the testator's death, ademption does not usually apply. The beneficiary of the specific bequest takes the insurance proceeds. Similarly, ademption usually does not apply to property condemned by the government when the taking was before death but the condemnation award was paid after death.

d. Partial Ademption

If the testator specifically devises property and then sells or gives away a part of that property, only that portion is adeemed; the remainder passes to the devisee.

2. Exoneration

If a testator makes a specific devise of real estate that is subject to a mortgage or other lien, the devisee is entitled to have the land "exonerated" by the payment of the lien from the testator's residuary estate. Thus, the property will pass to the devisee free of encumbrances. There is a growing trend toward abolition of the exoneration doctrine, although it is still the majority view. In states that have abolished it, the property will pass to the devisee subject to a preexisting mortgage or other lien unless the will expressly provides for a payoff of the lien.

3. Lapse and Anti-Lapse Statutes

A lapse occurs when the beneficiary of a gift in a will *dies before the testator*. Under the common law, if a lapse occurred, the gift was void. However, nearly all states now have statutes that prevent lapse by permitting the gift to pass to the predeceasing beneficiary's living descendants under certain circumstances. These statutes vary as to the scope of beneficiaries covered.

a. Degree of Relationship to Testator

Many of the anti-lapse statutes apply only when the named beneficiary is a descendant of the testator. Others apply if the beneficiary is more remotely related, such as a descendant of the testator's grandparent. Others apply to any relative, and still others apply to any beneficiary at all.

1) Descendants Are Substituted

The anti-lapse statute does not save the gift for the predeceasing beneficiary's estate; rather it substitutes the beneficiary's descendants for the beneficiary. Thus, property will never pass under the anti-lapse statute to a predeceasing beneficiary's spouse. The property passes to the beneficiary's descendants under the method of distribution (*e.g.,* per stirpes, per capita) used by the state's intestate succession (inheritance) statute.

b. Inapplicable If Beneficiary Dead When Will Executed

If the beneficiary is already dead when the will is executed, the anti-lapse statute usually does not apply, and the gift will lapse and fail.

c. **Application to Class Gifts**

Ordinarily, if a gift is made by will to a class (*e.g.*, "to my children," or "to the descendants of my brother Bob"), and some members of the class die before the testator, the gift is simply given to the surviving members of the class. However, if class members within the coverage of an anti-lapse statute predecease the testator leaving surviving issue, the statute will apply, and the issue will take the deceased class member's share of the gift.

d. **Anti-Lapse Statute Does Not Apply If Contrary Will Provision**

The anti-lapse statute does not apply if there is a contrary will provision—*i.e.*, if the gift is contingent on the beneficiary's surviving the testator.

G. CROPS (EMBLEMENTS)

The law recognizes two types of crops: *Fructus naturales* are crops that grow spontaneously on the land; *i.e.*, they are produced by nature alone and are perennial (they do not require planting). *Fructus industriales (emblements)* are annual crops produced through cultivation. Fructus naturales are real property and title to them passes automatically with the land. Fructus industriales are personalty.

1. **Conveyance of Land Includes Crops**

Generally, the owner of the land is presumed to be the owner of both types of crops, and a conveyance of land carries with it all the crops growing on it. This presumption is based on the presumed intent of the parties, and a contrary intent may be shown.

2. **Exception—Harvested Crops**

An exception to the general rule is recognized for crops that have already been harvested or severed from the land. Such crops do not pass with the conveyance of the land, and the former owner has the right to reenter the land to remove them.

a. **Ripened But Unharvested Crops**

Some jurisdictions hold that ripened fructus industriales (annual crops) likewise do not pass with a conveyance of the land. These courts treat the ripened crops as having been "constructively severed" upon ripening, because they no longer need to draw sustenance from the soil.

3. **Exception—Crops Planted by Tenant**

Under the doctrine of emblements, title to crops planted by a tenant during the term of his tenancy remains in the tenant unless there is a contrary provision in the lease. A conveyance of the land by the landlord does not pass title to the tenant's crops. The tenant retains his right to enter upon the property to cultivate, harvest, and remove crops planted prior to the termination of his estate. For this doctrine to apply, the tenancy must have: (i) been for an *uncertain duration* and (ii) terminated *without fault* on the part of the tenant.

a. **Compare—Trespasser**

The doctrine of emblements is limited to tenants. One who planted crops while on the land as a trespasser has no title to the crops and has no right of entry to remove them. Crops planted by an adverse possessor acting under a *claim of right*, however, are generally held to belong to him.

VII. SECURITY INTERESTS IN REAL ESTATE

A. TYPES OF SECURITY INTERESTS

A security interest in real estate operates to secure some other obligation, usually a promise to repay a loan, which is represented by a promissory note. If the loan is not paid when due, the holder of the security interest can either take title to the real estate or have it sold and use the proceeds to pay the debt with accrued interest and any legal and court costs. Of the five types of security interests, the first three are most important.

1. **Mortgage**

The debtor/notemaker is the mortgagor; he gives the mortgage (along with the note) to the lender, who is the mortgagee. Most states require that a lender realize on the real estate to satisfy the debt only by having a judicial (court-ordered) foreclosure sale conducted by the sheriff.

2. Deed of Trust

The debtor/notemaker is the trustor. The trustor gives the deed of trust to a third-party trustee, who is usually closely connected with the lender (*e.g.,* the lender's lawyer, affiliated corporation, or officer). In the event of default, the lender (termed the beneficiary) instructs the trustee to proceed with foreclosing the deed of trust by sale. Many states allow the sale to be either judicial (as with a mortgage) or nonjudicial, under a "power of sale" clause which authorizes the trustee to advertise, give appropriate notices, and conduct the sale personally.

3. Installment Land Contract

In an installment land contract, the debtor is the purchaser of the land who signs a contract with the vendor, agreeing to make regular installment payments until the full contract price (including accruing interest) has been paid. Only at that time will the vendor give a deed transferring legal title to the purchaser. In case of default, the contract usually contains a forfeiture clause providing that the vendor may cancel the contract, retain all money paid to date, and retake possession of the land.

4. Absolute Deed—Equitable Mortgage

A landowner needing to raise money may "sell" the land to a person who will pay cash and may give the "buyer" an absolute deed rather than a mortgage. This may seem to be safer than a mortgage loan to the creditor and may seem to have tax advantages. However, if the court concludes, by clear and convincing evidence, that the deed was really given for security purposes, they will treat it as an "equitable" mortgage and require that the creditor foreclose it by judicial action, like any other mortgage. This result will be indicated by the following factors: (i) the existence of a debt or promise of payment by the deed's grantor; (ii) the grantee's promise to return the land if the debt is paid; (iii) the fact that the amount advanced to the grantor/debtor was much lower than the value of the property; (iv) the degree of the grantor's financial distress; and (v) the parties' prior negotiations.

5. Sale-Leaseback

A landowner needing to raise money may sell her land to another for cash and may then lease the land back for a long period of time. As in the case of the absolute deed, the grantor/lessee may attack such a transaction later as a disguised mortgage. Factors that will lead the court to such a result are: (i) the fact that the regular rent payments on the lease are virtually identical to payments that would be due on a mortgage loan; (ii) the existence of an option to repurchase by the grantor/lessee; and (iii) the fact that the repurchase option could be exercised for much less than the probable value of the property at that time, so that the repurchase would be very likely to occur.

B. TRANSFERS BY MORTGAGEE AND MORTGAGOR

All parties to a mortgage or deed of trust can transfer their interests. Ordinarily, the mortgagor transfers by deeding the property, while the mortgagee usually transfers by endorsing the note and executing a separate assignment of the mortgage. The note and mortgage must pass to *the same person* for the transfer to be complete.

1. Transfer by Mortgagee

a. Transfer of Mortgage Without Note

The case law is divided, with some states holding that the transfer of the mortgage automatically transfers the note as well, unless the mortgagee-transferor expressly reserves the rights to the note (which there would rarely be any reason for the mortgagee to do). In these states, the transferee of the mortgage can then file an equitable action and compel a transfer of the note as well. Other states hold that, since the note is the principal evidence of the debt, a transfer of the mortgage without the note is a nullity and is void.

b. Transfer of Note Without Mortgage

The *note can be transferred without the mortgage*, but the mortgage will automatically follow the properly transferred note, unless the mortgagee-transferee expressly reserves the rights to the mortgage (which there would rarely be any reason for the mortgagee to do). No separate written assignment of the mortgage is necessary, although it is customary for the transferee to obtain and record an assignment of the mortgage.

1) Methods of Transferring the Note

The note may be transferred either by endorsing it and delivering it to the transferee, or by a separate document of assignment. Only if the former method is used can the transferee become a holder in due course under U.C.C. Article 3.

a) Holder in Due Course Status
To be a holder in due course of the note, the following requirements must be met:

(1) The note must be *negotiable in form*, which means that it must be payable to "bearer" or "to the order of" the named payee. It must contain a promise to pay a fixed amount of money (although an adjustable interest rate is permitted), and no other promises, except that it may contain an acceleration clause and an attorneys' fee clause.

(2) The original note must be *endorsed* (*i.e.*, signed) by the named payee. Endorsement on a photocopy or some other document is not acceptable.

(3) The original note must be *delivered* to the transferee. Delivery of a photocopy is not acceptable.

(4) The transferee must take the note in *good faith* and must pay *value* for it. ("Value" implies an amount that is more than nominal, although it need not be as great as the note's fair market value.) The transferee *must not have any notice* that the note is overdue or has been dishonored, or that the maker has any defense to the duty to pay it.

b) Benefits of Holder in Due Course Status
A holder in due course will take the note free of any personal defenses that the maker might raise. "Personal defenses" include failure of consideration, fraud in the inducement, waiver, estoppel, and payment. The holder in due course is, however, still subject to "real" defenses that the maker might raise. These include infancy, other incapacity, duress, illegality, fraud in the execution, forgery, discharge in insolvency, and any other insolvency.

2) Payment to One Without Note Does Not Count
A mortgagor is expected to demand to see the promissory note before making payment. The note is considered to embody the obligation. If possession of the note has been transferred by the original mortgagee, a payment to the mortgagee will not count, and the holder of the note can still demand payment. This is so even if the mortgagor had no notice that the note had been transferred.

Example: A borrows $50,000 from B and gives B a note for that amount, secured by a mortgage on Blackacre. One year later, B assigns the note and mortgage to C, transferring actual possession of the note to C. Two years thereafter A, who does not realize that B no longer holds the note, pays $50,000 plus interest to B. This payment is ineffective against C, and C can sue A on the note or foreclose the mortgage on Blackacre.

2. Transfer by Mortgagor—Grantee Takes Subject to Mortgage
If the mortgagor sells the property and conveys a deed, the grantee takes subject to the mortgage, which remains on the land. Unless there is a specific clause in the mortgage, the mortgagee has no power to object to the transfer.

a. Assumption
Often the grantee signs an assumption agreement, promising to pay the mortgage loan. If she does so, she becomes primarily liable to the lender (usually considered a third-party beneficiary), while the original mortgagor becomes secondarily liable as a surety. If the mortgagee and grantee modify the obligation, the original mortgagor is completely discharged of liability.

b. Nonassuming Grantee
A grantee who does not sign an assumption agreement does not become personally liable on the loan. Instead, the original mortgagor remains primarily and personally liable. However, if the grantee does not pay, the mortgage may be foreclosed, thus wiping out the grantee's investment in the land.

c. **Due-on-Sale Clauses**

Most modern mortgages contain "due-on-sale" clauses, which purport to allow the lender to demand full payment of the loan if the mortgagor transfers any interest in the property without the lender's consent. Such clauses are designed to both: (i) protect the lender from sale by the mortgagor to a poor credit risk or to a person likely to commit waste; and (ii) allow the lender to raise the interest rate or charge an "assumption fee" when the property is sold.

1) **Enforceability**

The Garn-St. Germain Depository Institutions Act of 1982 preempts state law and makes due-on-sale clauses enforceable for all types of mortgage lenders on all types of real estate for transfers occurring after October 15, 1982, regardless of whether the loan was made before or after that date. However, on one- to four-family residential loans, a due-on-sale clause cannot be triggered by certain types of "nonsubstantive" transfers, *e.g.*, transfers to a spouse, transfers at the death of a joint tenant, etc.

C. POSSESSION BEFORE FORECLOSURE

When a mortgagor defaults on his debt, the mortgagee can sue on the debt or foreclose on the mortgage. A mortgagee may wish to take possession of the property, or begin receiving the rents from the property, before foreclosure. This is especially important in states where foreclosure is a lengthy process.

1. **Theories of Title**

The mortgagee may have a right to take possession before foreclosure, depending on the theory the state follows.

a. **The Lien Theory**

According to the lien theory, the mortgagee is considered the holder of a *security interest only* and the mortgagor is deemed the owner of the land until foreclosure. About half of the states follow this theory, which provides that the mortgagee may not have possession before foreclosure.

b. **The Title Theory**

Under the title theory, legal *title is in the mortgagee* until the mortgage has been satisfied or foreclosed. About 20 states follow this theory, which provides that the mortgagee is entitled to possession upon demand at any time. In practice, this means that as soon as a default occurs, the mortgagee can take possession.

c. **The Intermediate Theory**

The intermediate theory is a compromise position in which legal *title is in the mortgagor until default*, and upon default, legal title is in the mortgagee. Only a handful of states follow this theory, which provides that the mortgagee may demand possession when a default occurs. There is little practical difference between this theory and the title theory.

2. **Mortgagor Consent and Abandonment**

All states agree that the mortgagee may take possession if the mortgagor gives consent to do so, or if the mortgagor abandons the property.

3. **Risks of Mortgagee in Possession**

The mortgagee who takes possession prior to foreclosure can intercept the rents, prevent waste, make repairs, and lease out vacant space. However, despite these advantages, most mortgagees do not wish to take possession because of the liability risks it presents. These risks include a very strict duty to account for all rents received, a duty to manage the property in a careful and prudent manner, and potential liability in tort to anyone injured on the property.

4. **Receiverships**

Instead of becoming a "mortgagee in possession," most mortgagees attempt to intercept the rents before foreclosure by getting a receiver appointed by the court to manage the property. Courts will generally appoint receivers for rental property upon a showing of some combination of three factors: (i) that waste is occurring; (ii) that the value of the property is inadequate to secure the debt; and (iii) that the mortgagor is insolvent.

D. FORECLOSURE

Foreclosure is a process by which the mortgagor's interest in the property is terminated. The property is generally sold to satisfy the debt in whole or in part (foreclosure by sale). Almost all states *require* foreclosure by sale. All states allow *judicial sale*, while about one-half also allow nonjudicial sale under a *power of sale*. The nonjudicial sale is often permitted with deeds of trust but not with mortgages. Foreclosure sales are conducted by auction, with the highest bidder taking the property. The lender may bid at the sale, and in many cases the lender is the sole bidder. (*Note:* For convenience, the discussion below speaks of mortgagors and mortgagees, but the same principles apply to deed-of-trust trustors and beneficiaries.)

1. **Redemption**

    a. **Redemption in Equity**
        At any time *prior to the foreclosure sale,* the mortgagor has the right to redeem the land or free it of the mortgage by paying off the amount due, together with any accrued interest. If the mortgagor has defaulted on a mortgage or note that contains an "acceleration clause" permitting the mortgagee to declare the full balance due in the event of default, the full balance must be paid in order to redeem. A mortgagor's right to redeem her own mortgage cannot be waived in the mortgage itself; this is known as "clogging the equity of redemption" and is prohibited. However, the right can be waived later for consideration.

    b. **Statutory Redemption**
        About half the states give the mortgagor (and sometimes junior lienors) a statutory right to redeem for some fixed period after the foreclosure sale has occurred; this period is usually six months or one year. The amount to be paid is usually the foreclosure sale price, rather than the amount of the original debt. Be careful to distinguish equitable redemption, which is universally recognized (but only up to the date of the sale), from statutory redemption, which is only recognized by about half of the states and applies only *after* foreclosure has occurred.

2. **Priorities**
    Generally, the priority of a mortgage is determined by the time it was placed on the property. When a mortgage is foreclosed, the buyer at the sale will take title as it existed when the mortgage was placed on the property. Thus, foreclosure will terminate interests junior to the mortgage being foreclosed but will not affect senior interests.

    a. **Effect of Foreclosure on Various Interests**

        1) **Junior Interests Destroyed by Foreclosure**
            Foreclosure destroys all interests junior to the mortgage being foreclosed. In other words, junior mortgages, liens, leases, easements, and all other types of interests will be wiped out. If a lien senior to that of the mortgagee is in default, the junior mortgagee has the right to pay it off (*i.e.,* redeem it) in order to avoid being wiped out by its foreclosure. Thus, those with interests subordinate to those of the foreclosing party are necessary parties to the foreclosure action. Failure to include a necessary party results in the preservation of that party's interest despite foreclosure and sale.

        2) **Senior Interests Not Affected**
            Foreclosure does not affect any interest senior to the mortgage being foreclosed. *The buyer at the sale takes subject to such interest.* She does not become personally liable on such senior interests, but she will be forced to pay them in order to prevent their foreclosure in the future.

    b. **Modification of Priority**
        As noted above, priorities among mortgages on the same real estate are normally determined simply by chronology: the earliest mortgage placed on the property is first in priority, the next mortgage is second, and so on. However, the chronological priority may be changed in the following ways:

        1) **Failure to Record**
            If the first mortgagee fails to record, and the second mortgagee records, gives value, and takes without notice of the first, the second mortgagee will have priority over the first by virtue of the normal operation of the recording acts.

        2) **Subordination Agreement**
            A first mortgagee may enter into an agreement with a junior mortgagee, subordinating its priority to the junior mortgagee. Such agreements are generally enforced. However, a broad promise to subordinate to any mortgage (or a vaguely described

mortgage) to be placed on the property in the future may be considered too inequitable to enforce.

3) Purchase Money Mortgages

A purchase money mortgage ("PMM"), given when the mortgagor buys the property, is considered to have priority over non-PMM mortgages executed at about the same time, even if the other mortgages are recorded first. A PMM is:

(i) A mortgage given to the vendor of the property as a part of the purchase price; or

(ii) A mortgage given to a third-party lender, who is lending the funds to allow the buyer to purchase the property.

As between two PMMs, one to the vendor and one to a third-party lender, the vendor's mortgage is usually given priority over the third-party lender's. If two PMMs are given to two third-party lenders, their priority is determined by the chronological order in which the mortgages were placed on the property, the recording act, and a subordination agreement (if any). Note that in these cases, the recording acts are often of no use because two purchase-money mortgagees will almost always know of each other's existence and, thus, have notice.

4) Modification of Senior Mortgage

Suppose there are two mortgages on the land. The landowner enters into a modification agreement with the senior mortgagee, raising its interest rate or otherwise making it more burdensome. The junior mortgage will be given *priority over the modification*. For example, if the first mortgage debt is larger because of the modification, the second mortgage gains priority over the increase in the debt.

5) Optional Future Advances

In general, a mortgage may obligate the lender to make further advances of funds after the mortgage is executed, and such advances will have the same priority as the original mortgage. However, if a junior mortgage is placed on the property and the senior lender later makes an "optional" advance while having notice of the junior lien, the advance will lose priority to the junior lien. An optional advance is one that the senior lender is not contractually bound to make. Numerous states have reversed this rule by statute, but it remains the majority view.

3. Proceeds of Sale

The proceeds of the foreclosure sale are used first to pay expenses of the sale, attorneys' fees, and court costs; then to pay the principal and accrued interest on the loan that was foreclosed; next to pay off any junior liens or other junior interests in the order of their priority; and finally, any remaining proceeds are distributed to the mortgagor. In many cases, there is no surplus remaining after the principal debt is paid off.

4. Deficiency Judgments

Where the proceeds of the sale are insufficient to satisfy the mortgage debt, the mortgagee can bring a personal action against the mortgagor/debtor for the deficiency. However, a number of states limit the deficiency that can be recovered to the difference between the debt and the property's fair market value when the fair market value is higher than the foreclosure price. Other states prohibit deficiency judgments entirely on purchase-money mortgages and on deeds of trust that are foreclosed by power of sale.

Examples: 1) Assume that land has a fair market value of $50,000 and is subject to three mortgages executed by its owner, whose name is MR. The mortgages have priorities and secure outstanding debts in the amounts shown below, which are owed to three different creditors, ME1, ME2, and ME3:

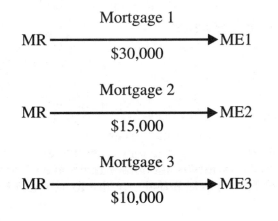

Mortgage 1

MR ──────────► ME1
$30,000

Mortgage 2

MR ──────────► ME2
$15,000

Mortgage 3

MR ──────────► ME3
$10,000

Assume that Mortgage 1 is foreclosed, and the bid at the sale is $50,000 (the fair value of the land). How will the funds be distributed?

In an actual case, the funds would first be used to pay any attorneys' fees and expenses of the foreclosure, and then to any accrued interest on Mortgage 1. However, we will assume that these items are zero.

The $50,000 in funds from the sale will then be used to pay off the mortgages in the order of their priority. Thus, $30,000 is applied to fully pay off Mortgage 1. Then, $15,000 is applied to fully pay off Mortgage 2. There is a remaining balance from the foreclosure sale of $5,000, which is applied toward payment of Mortgage 3. Since this is not enough to discharge Mortgage 3 fully, ME3 is left with a deficiency of $5,000, and may sue MR for a personal judgment in this amount unless state antideficiency statutes prohibit it.

2) Assume the same facts as above, except that the bid at the sale is $60,000 rather than $50,000. This will allow full payment of Mortgage 1 ($30,000), Mortgage 2 ($15,000), and Mortgage 3 ($10,000), and will leave a surplus of $5,000. Assuming there are no further liens or encumbrances on the property, this $5,000 will be paid over to MR, the mortgagor.

3) Now assume the same facts as in the original problem, except that it is Mortgage 2 that is being foreclosed. Mortgage 1 exists, but it is either not in default or its holder has not yet taken action to foreclose it.

Recall from the outline above that foreclosure does not affect any interest senior to the mortgage being foreclosed. Thus, foreclosure of Mortgage 2 will not affect Mortgage 1, which will continue to exist on the property in the hands of the foreclosure sale purchaser. Such a purchaser will not be personally liable to pay Mortgage 1 off, but as a practical matter, if Mortgage 1 is not paid, sooner or later ME1 will foreclose it. Hence, the buyer at the foreclosure sale of Mortgage 2 will have a strong economic incentive to pay Mortgage 1; otherwise, she will be subjected to the foreclosure action of ME1, and may well lose much or all of her investment in the property.

What will a wise bidder at the foreclosure sale on Mortgage 2 bid? The maximum is $20,000, which is the fair value of the land ($50,000) minus the amount the successful bidder will subsequently have to pay to discharge Mortgage 1 ($30,000).

If the bid at the foreclosure sale of Mortgage 2 is $20,000, how will the money be distributed? None of it will go to ME1, since he still has his mortgage on the property. $15,000 of the funds will be applied to fully pay off Mortgage 2, and $5,000 will remain to be applied against the $10,000 balance owed on Mortgage 3 (which is, of course, wiped out by the foreclosure of Mortgage 2). ME3 will still have a $5,000 deficiency, as in the first example above.

E. INSTALLMENT LAND CONTRACTS

Installment contracts usually provide for forfeiture rather than foreclosure as the vendor's remedy in the event of default. However, since forfeiture is often a harsh remedy, the courts have tended to resist enforcing forfeiture clauses and in doing so have developed the following theories:

1. Equity of Redemption

Several states allow the contract purchaser who is in default to pay off the accelerated full balance of the contract and to keep the land. In other words, they grant the purchaser a grace period. This is roughly analogous to the equity of redemption in mortgage law. A few states have statutory schedules of grace periods, which often provide for a longer time if a greater percentage of the total price has been paid.

2. Restitution

A number of decisions allow actions by the vendor for forfeiture of the land but require her to refund to the purchaser any amount by which his payments exceed the vendor's damages.

The court may measure these damages by the property's fair rental value while the purchaser was in possession or by any drop in market value since the contract was executed.

3. Treat as a Mortgage
A few states, by statute or case law, now treat installment contracts like mortgages, at least for purposes of the vendor's remedies. In effect, the vendor must foreclose the contract by judicial sale in order to realize on the real estate, and she cannot simply reclaim the land.

4. Waiver
Many cases hold that where a vendor has established a pattern of accepting late payments from the purchaser, she cannot suddenly insist on strict on-time payment and declare a forfeiture if such payment is not forthcoming. Such a pattern is said to constitute a waiver of strict performance. To reinstate strict performance, the vendor must send the purchaser a notice of her intention to do so and must allow a reasonable time for the purchaser to make up any late payments and to get back "on stream."

5. Election of Remedies
It is commonly held that the vendor who elects to pursue a forfeiture cannot also bring an action for damages or for specific performance. The vendor must choose only one remedy and forgo all others.

VIII. RIGHTS INCIDENTAL TO OWNERSHIP OF LAND (NATURAL RIGHTS)

A. IN GENERAL
The owner of real property has the exclusive right to use and possess the surface, the airspace, and the soil of the property. This right is subject to restrictions in the chain of title (*e.g.*, easements and covenants), to the law of nuisance, and to any valid laws or regulations that restrict the use of the land (*e.g.*, zoning ordinances).

B. RIGHT TO LATERAL AND SUBJACENT SUPPORT OF LAND

1. Right to Lateral Support
Ownership of land carries with it the right to have the land supported in its *natural state* by adjoining land. This normally means a right to have one's land undisturbed by withdrawal of support (*e.g.*, by excavations on adjoining land).

a. Support of Land in Natural State
A landowner is *strictly liable* if his excavation causes adjacent land to subside (*i.e.*, slip or cave in). Thus, he will be liable even if he used the utmost care.

b. Support of Buildings on Land
If land is improved by buildings and an adjacent landowner's excavation causes subsidence, the adjacent landowner will be *strictly liable* for damages to the buildings caused by the excavation only if it is shown that the land would have collapsed in its natural state (*i.e.*, that it would have collapsed in the absence of the buildings and improvements). Even if the land would not have collapsed in its natural state (*i.e.*, the collapse would not have occurred except for the weight of the buildings), the excavating landowner is liable for loss or damage to the buildings if his excavation is found to have been done *negligently*. (Tort rules apply here.)

2. Right to Subjacent Support
When a landowner conveys to a grantee the right to take minerals from beneath the land, the grantor retains the right to have the surface supported unless the conveyance expressly includes authority to destroy the surface if "reasonably necessary" to extract the mineral.

a. Support of Land and Buildings
This right of support extends not only to the land in its natural state but also to all buildings existing on the date when the subjacent estate is severed from the surface. However, the underground occupant is liable for damages to subsequently erected buildings only if he was *negligent*.

b. Interference with Underground Waters
Note that an underground occupant is liable for negligently damaging springs and

wells, whereas an adjoining landowner is not liable for interfering with underground percolating waters.

C.   WATER RIGHTS
Different rules apply depending on whether the water rights claimed involve (i) water in watercourses (*e.g.*, streams, rivers, and lakes, including underground watercourses); (ii) ground or percolating water (*e.g.*, water normally pumped or drawn from wells); or (iii) surface water (*e.g.*, rainfall, seepage). Exam questions normally concern who has priority to use the water from watercourses and from the ground, and to what extent a landowner may obstruct or divert the flow of surface water.

1.   Watercourses
There are two major systems for allocation of water in watercourses: (i) the *riparian doctrine* (generally applied in the eastern states where water is or was relatively abundant), and (ii) the *prior appropriation doctrine* (generally used in the 17 western states where water is relatively scarce).

a.   Riparian Doctrine
Under the riparian doctrine, water does not belong to the public generally or to the state (with certain exceptions) but rather to the "riparian" proprietors who own land bordering on the watercourse. All of these landowners have "riparian rights" and none can use the water so as to deprive the others of these rights.

1)   What Land Is Riparian
Under the *majority rule*, all tracts held under unity of ownership are riparian if the tracts are contiguous and *any* of them front on the water. Thus, if a riparian owner purchases a parcel which is contiguous to the riparian parcel, riparian rights attach to the newly acquired parcel. The *minority rule* limits riparian rights to the smallest tract of land ever owned abutting the water. Under this view, if a back portion of a riparian tract is sold, it becomes nonriparian and can never regain riparian rights.

a)   Riparian Owner
Riparian owners include the fee owner of the abutting land and, to the extent of their title, lessees and easement owners of such land.

b)   Doctrine Applies Only to Riparian Parcel
The riparian doctrine permits use of water only in connection with activities carried out on the riparian parcel. Riparian rights cannot be conveyed for the use of nonriparian land nor can they be lost by nonuse.

2)   Nature of Riparian Right

a)   Natural Flow Theory
Under the "natural flow" theory, a riparian owner is entitled to the water in the bordering stream or lake subject to the limitation that *he may not substantially or materially diminish its quantity, quality, or velocity*. Thus, a downstream owner can enjoin an upstream owner's use even though the downstream owner has plenty of water for his own use. No state appears to adhere strictly to this theory because it operates to limit beneficial upstream use and leads to "waste" of the resource.

b)   Reasonable Use Theory
Under the more common theory, all riparian owners share the right of "reasonable use." The general idea is that the right of each riparian owner to use the stream (*e.g.,* to divert for irrigation, to pollute, etc.) is subject to a like reasonable right in other riparian owners. *Each riparian owner must submit to reasonable use* by other riparian owners, and cannot enjoin such use unless it substantially interferes with the needs of those who have a like right (*i.e.*, unless actual damage is shown).

####### (1)   Factors to Consider
In determining whether an owner's use of water is "reasonable," courts generally balance the utility of the use against the gravity of the harm. (Note the analogy to nuisance law.) Six factors are helpful in this balancing process: (i) the *purpose* of the questioned use; (ii) the *destination*

to which the water is taken for use; (iii) the *extent* of the use; (iv) the *pollution* of water by use; (v) whether the use involves an *alteration* in the manner of flow; and (vi) *miscellaneous* types of conduct which may give rise to litigation. (These factors may be remembered more easily by using the acronym MAPPED.)

c) Natural vs. Artificial Use

Under either of the above theories, water use is categorized as "natural" or "artificial." Natural uses include those necessary for the daily sustenance of human beings (household consumption, gardening, minimal number of livestock, etc.). All other uses, including irrigation and manufacturing, are artificial. *Natural uses prevail over artificial.* Upper riparians can take all that they need for natural uses. However, they cannot take for artificial purposes unless there is enough water for the domestic wants of all.

b. Prior Appropriation Doctrine

Under the prior appropriation doctrine, the water belongs initially to the state, but the right to divert and use it can be acquired by an individual whether or not he is a riparian owner. Initially, individual rights were established by actual use; thus, each appropriator acquired a vested property right "to divert a given quantity of water, at given times from a given place, to use at a given place for a given purpose."

1) Factors to Note for Bar Exam

Present day acquisition and governance of rights under this doctrine are largely dealt with under complex state-administered permit systems that are too detailed for coverage here. However, it is sufficient for bar examination purposes to note that: (i) appropriative rights were originally determined simply by priority of beneficial use; (ii) if there is a decrease in stream flow, priority is accorded in terms of time of appropriation (*i.e.*, the junior appropriators in descending order of priority must suffer); (iii) in many states, an appropriative right can be severed from the land it serviced when acquired and transferred (*i.e.*, can be sold to another for use on other land), provided no injury is caused to existing uses; and (iv) an appropriative right (unlike a riparian one) can be lost by abandonment (intent and nonuse).

2. Ground Water

If water comes from an underground watercourse (*e.g.*, a defined stream or river), the riparian or prior appropriation doctrines apply. However, the presumption is that underground water is percolating (*i.e.*, the water moves through the ground diffusely and is usually withdrawn by wells from the underground water table). There are four different rules for determining rights in underground water.

a. Absolute Ownership Doctrine

The absolute ownership doctrine is followed by approximately 12 eastern states. The owner of the land overlying the source basin may extract as much water as she wishes and use it for whatever purpose she desires (including export). There is no firmly established system for allocation among overlying owners.

b. Reasonable Use Doctrine

The majority view, followed by about 25 states, allows the surface owner to make "reasonable use" of the ground water. This rule differs from the absolute ownership rule mainly with respect to exporting water off site: Exporting is allowed only to the extent that it does not harm other owners who have rights in the same aquifer. On the other hand, virtually all beneficial uses of water *on the land* are considered reasonable and are allowed.

c. Correlative Rights Doctrine

In California, the owners of overlying land own the underground water basin as joint tenants, and each is allowed a reasonable amount for her own use.

d. Appropriative Rights Doctrine

In some western states, the prior appropriation doctrine applies to ground water as well as water courses. Priority of use determines appropriative rights. In most western states, rights to percolating water are now determined by a state water board which controls annual yield, prohibits water waste, etc.

3. **Surface Waters**

Diffused surface waters are those that have no channel but pass over the surface of the land. The source may be rainfall, melting snow, seepage, etc. A landowner can use surface waters within her boundaries for any purpose she desires. Problems concern the right of a lower owner to restrict a flow that would naturally cross his land (*e.g.*, by dikes) and the right of an upper owner to alter or divert a natural flow onto other lands (*e.g.*, by drains, channels, or sloughs). The acting landowner's liability to other landowners depends upon which doctrine the state follows.

a. **Natural Flow Theory**

Under the natural flow theory, followed by about half the states, a landowner cannot refuse to take natural drainage, cannot divert surface water onto the land of another, and cannot alter the rate or manner of natural flow where such actions would injure others above or below him. Since this theory imposes substantial impediments on development (*e.g.*, no paving, large roofs, culverts, etc.), most states have "softened" the rule to permit *reasonable* changes in natural flow. And a few states have held the doctrine inapplicable to urban property (since development would otherwise be retarded).

b. **Common Enemy Theory**

Under the common enemy theory, followed by half of the states, surface water is a common enemy and any owner can build dikes or change drainage to get rid of it. However, many courts have modified the doctrine and have held landowners to a standard of ordinary care to avoid unnecessary and negligent injury to the land of others.

c. **Reasonable Use Theory**

The growing trend is to apply the reasonable use doctrine which, as in nuisance and watercourse cases, requires balancing the utility of the use against the gravity of the harm. Judicial mitigation of both the natural flow and common enemy doctrines often results in an approximation of the reasonable use theory.

d. **Compare—Capture of Surface Water**

A landowner can capture (*e.g.*, by dam, rain barrels) as much surface water as he wishes. It can be diverted to any purpose on or off the land. Owners below have no cause of action unless the diversion is malicious.

D. **RIGHTS IN AIRSPACE**

The right to the airspace above a parcel is not exclusive, but the owner is entitled to freedom from excessive noise and transit by aircraft. If flights are so low as to be unreasonably disturbing, they constitute a trespass or (if the airport is government-owned) a taking by inverse condemnation.

E. **RIGHT TO EXCLUDE—REMEDIES OF POSSESSOR**

1. **Trespass**

If the land is invaded by a *tangible* physical object that interferes with the right of exclusive possession, there is a trespass.

2. **Private Nuisance**

If the land is invaded by *intangibles*, *e.g.*, odors or noises, that substantially and unreasonably interfere with use and possession, the possessor may bring an action for private nuisance.

3. **Continuing Trespass**

If the land is repeatedly invaded by a trespasser, *e.g.*, the invader repeatedly swings a crane over the property, the possessor may sue for either trespass or nuisance.

4. **Law or Equity**

If the possessor wants to force the invader to stop the invasion of the property, the remedy is an injunction in equity. If the possessor wants damages, the remedy is an action at law.

a. **Ejectment**

The remedy at common law to remove a trespasser from the property is ejectment.

b. Unlawful Detainer
In the landlord-tenant situation, the landlord may force the tenant to vacate the premises by the statutory remedy of unlawful detainer. (In some states, the term used to describe this action is forcible detainer or summary ejectment.) The action may be joined with a demand for money damages in rent due.

IX. COOPERATIVES, CONDOMINIUMS, AND ZONING

A. COOPERATIVES
In the most common form of housing cooperative, title to the land and buildings is held by a corporation that leases the individual apartments to its shareholders. Thus, the residents in a cooperative are both tenants of the cooperative (by virtue of their occupancy leases) and owners of the cooperative (by virtue of their stock interests). Stock interests in the cooperative are not transferable apart from the occupancy lease to which they are attached.

1. Restriction on Transfer of Interests
Because the members of a cooperative are tenants, the cooperative may retain the same controls over assignment and sublease of the apartments as may be exercised by any other landlord.

2. Mortgages
Permanent financing is provided through a blanket mortgage on the entire property owned by the cooperative corporation (land and buildings). This mortgage has priority over the occupancy leases. Failure to meet the payments on the blanket mortgage may result in the termination of the leases through foreclosure of the mortgage. Thus, each cooperative tenant is vitally concerned that the other tenants pay their shares of the blanket mortgage.

3. Maintenance Expenses
Ordinarily, cooperative tenants are not personally liable on the note or bond of the blanket mortgage. However, under their occupancy leases, each tenant is liable for her proportionate share of all of the expenses of the cooperative (including payments on the mortgage as well as other operating expenses).

B. CONDOMINIUMS
In a condominium, each owner owns the interior of her individual unit plus an undivided interest in the exterior and common elements.

1. Restriction on Transfer of Interests
Since condominium unit ownership is treated as fee ownership, the ordinary rules against restraints on alienation apply. A few jurisdictions (*e.g.*, New York) by statute allow reasonable restraints on transfer of condominium units.

2. Mortgages
Each unit owner finances the purchase of her unit by a separate mortgage on her unit. Consequently, unit owners need not be as concerned about defaults by others as they must be in a cooperative.

3. Maintenance Expenses
Each unit owner is personally liable on her own mortgage and each pays her own taxes (unlike the cooperative situation, but like any other homeowner). In addition, each unit owner is liable to contribute her proportionate share to the common expenses of maintaining the common elements, including insurance thereon.

C. ZONING
The state may enact statutes to reasonably control the use of land for the protection of the *health, safety, morals, and welfare* of its citizens. Zoning is the division of a jurisdiction into districts in which certain uses and developments are permitted or prohibited. The zoning power is based on the state's police power and is limited by the Due Process Clause of the Fourteenth Amendment. Other limitations are imposed by the Equal Protection Clause of the Fourteenth Amendment and the "no taking without just compensation" clause of the Fifth Amendment. (*See* Constitutional Law outline.) Cities and counties can exercise zoning power only if authorized to do so by state enabling acts. Ordinances that do not conform to such acts are "ultra vires" (beyond the authority of the local body) and void.

1. **Nonconforming Use**
A use that exists at the time of passage of a zoning act and that does not conform to the statute cannot be eliminated at once. Some statutes provide for the gradual elimination of such nonconforming uses (*e.g.*, the use must end in 10 years).

2. **Special Use Permits**
Some unusual uses (*e.g.*, hospitals, funeral homes, etc.) require issuance of a special permit even though the zoning of the particular district (*e.g.*, commercial) allows that type of use.

3. **Variance**
A variance from the literal restrictions of a zoning ordinance may be granted by administrative action. The property owner must show that the ordinance imposes a unique hardship on him and that the variance will not be contrary to the public welfare.

4. **Unconstitutional Takings and Exactions**
A zoning ordinance may so reduce the value of real property that it constitutes a taking under the Fifth and Fourteenth Amendments. If an ordinance constitutes a taking, the local government must pay damages to the landowner equal to the value reduction. If the ordinance regulates activity that would be considered a nuisance under common law principles, it will not be a taking even if it leaves the land with no economic value.

   a. **Denial of *All* Economic Value of Land—Taking**
   If a government regulation denies a landowner *all* economic use of his land, the regulation is equivalent to a physical appropriation and is thus a taking (unless the use was prohibited by nuisance or property law when the owner acquired the land). [Lucas v. South Carolina Coastal Council, 505 U.S. 1003 (1992)—state's zoning ordinance, adopted after owner purchased lots, was a taking because it prohibited owner from erecting any permanent structures on the lots]

   b. **Denial of *Nearly All* Economic Value—Balancing Test**
   If a regulation so decreases the value of the property that there is very little economic value, the court will balance the following factors to determine whether there has been a taking:

      (i) The *social goals* sought to be promoted;

      (ii) The *diminution* in value to the owner; and

      (iii) The owner's *reasonable expectations* regarding use of the property.

   Generally, the regulation will be found to be a taking only if it *unjustly* reduces the economic value of the property (*e.g.*, greatly reduces the property value and only slightly promotes the public welfare). [Pennsylvania Coal Co. v. Mahon, 260 U.S. 393 (1922); Keystone Bituminous Coal Association v. DeBenedictis, 480 U.S. 470 (1987)]

   c. **Unconstitutional Exactions**
   Local governments often demand, in exchange for zoning approval for a new project, that the landowner give up some land for a public purpose, such as street widening. However, such demands are unconstitutional under the Fifth and Fourteenth Amendments unless they meet the tests set out below. [Nolan v. California Coastal Commission, 483 U.S. 825 (1987); Dolan v. City of Tigard, 512 U.S. 374 (1994)]

      1) **Essential Nexus**
      The local government's demand must be *rationally connected* to some additional burden that the proposed project will place on public facilities or rights. Thus, a city could demand land for a street widening upon a showing that the proposed project would otherwise increase traffic congestion and pollution along the street in question.

      2) **Rough Proportionality**
      Even if the "essential nexus" test above is met, the local government must not demand too much. The required dedication must be *reasonably related*, both in *nature* (the essential nexus) and *extent* (the amount of the exaction), to the impact of the proposed development.

3) Burden of Proof
The local government has the burden of showing that both the essential nexus and rough proportionality tests are met.

d. Remedy
If a property owner challenges a regulation and the court determines that there was a taking, the government will be required to either (i) compensate the owner for the taking or (ii) terminate the regulation and pay the owner for any damages that occurred while the regulation was in effect. [First Evangelical Church v. County of Los Angeles, 482 U.S. 304 (1987)]

BAR REVIEW

Torts

celebrating
35 **YEARS**
*of preparing
law students
for the bar exam*

TORTS

TABLE OF CONTENTS

I. INTENTIONAL TORTS

A. PRIMA FACIE CASE

To establish a prima facie case for intentional tort liability, it is generally necessary that plaintiff prove the following:

(i) *Act* by defendant;

(ii) *Intent*; and

(iii) *Causation*.

1. Act by Defendant

The "act" requirement for intentional tort liability refers to a *volitional movement* on defendant's part.

Examples: 1) Chauncey tripped and was falling. To break the fall, Chauncey stretched out his hand, which struck Darby. Even though the movement was reflexive, it nonetheless was one dictated by the mind, and hence will be characterized as volitional.

2) Lulu suffered an epileptic attack. During the course of it, she struck Darby. This is not a volitional act.

3) Chauncey pushed Lulu into Darby. Chauncey has committed a volitional act; Lulu has not.

2. Intent

The requisite intent for this type of tort liability may be either specific or general.

a. Specific Intent

An actor "intends" the consequences of his conduct if his *goal* in acting is to bring about these consequences.

b. General Intent

An actor "intends" the consequences of his conduct if he *knows with substantial certainty* that these consequences will result.

Example: D, five years old, pulls a chair out from under P as she is sitting down. Even if D did not desire that she hit the ground, if he knew with substantial certainty that she was trying to sit and would hit the ground, he will have the intent necessary for battery. [Garratt v. Dailey, 279 P.2d 1091 (Wash. 1955)]

c. Actor Need Not Intend Injury

The intent of the actor that is relevant for purposes of intentional torts is the intent to bring about the consequences that are the basis of the tort. Thus, a person may be liable even for an unintended injury if he intended to bring about such "basis of the tort" consequences.

Example: A intends to push B and does so. B falls and breaks his arm. This conduct gives rise to a cause of action for battery. The "consequences" that are the basis of this tort are harmful or offensive contact to the plaintiff's person. In this case, the actor intended to bring about harmful or offensive contact to B. Hence, he will be liable even though it was not intended that B break his arm.

d. Transferred Intent

1) General Rule

The transferred intent doctrine applies where the defendant intends to commit a tort against one person but instead (i) commits a different tort against that person, (ii) commits the same tort as intended but against a different person, or (iii) commits a different tort against a different person. In such cases, the *intent to commit a tort against one person is transferred to the other tort or to the injured person* for purposes of establishing a prima facie case.

Example: A swings at B, intending only to frighten him. A's blow lands on C. A's intent to commit assault on B is transferred to C, and A's act constitutes a battery on C.

2) Limitations on Use of Transferred Intent
Transferred intent may be invoked only where the tort intended and the tort that results are both within the following list:

a) Assault;

b) Battery;

c) False imprisonment;

d) Trespass to land; and

e) Trespass to chattels.

e. Motive Distinguished
Motive impels a person to act to achieve a result. *Intent* denotes the purpose to use a particular means to effect that result. ***Only the intent is relevant*** for purposes of establishing the prima facie case. Thus, for example, even though defendant acts without a hostile motive or desire to do any harm, or even where he is seeking to aid the plaintiff, he may be liable.

Note: Evil motive is not an essential element of most torts, but *malice* or ulterior purpose is an essential element of some (*e.g.,* malicious prosecution, abuse of process). Further, malice may sometimes negate a privilege that defendant might have, and it may permit the recovery of *punitive damages*.

f. Minors and Incompetents Can Have Requisite Intent
Under the majority view, both minors and incompetents will be *liable* for their intentional torts; *i.e.,* they are held to possess the requisite intent.

3. Causation
The result giving rise to liability must have been legally caused by the defendant's act or something set in motion thereby. The causation requirement will be satisfied where the ***conduct of defendant is a substantial factor*** in bringing about the injury.

B. PRIMA FACIE CASE—INTENTIONAL TORTS TO THE PERSON

1. Battery

a. Prima Facie Case
To establish a prima facie case for battery, the following elements must be proved:

1) An act by the defendant which brings about *harmful* or *offensive contact* to the plaintiff's person;

2) *Intent* on the part of the defendant to bring about harmful or offensive contact to the plaintiff's person; and

3) *Causation*.

b. Harmful or Offensive Contact
Whether any given contact is to be construed as harmful or offensive is judged by whether it would be considered harmful or offensive by *a reasonable person* of ordinary sensibilities. Contact is deemed "offensive" if the plaintiff has not expressly or impliedly consented to it (*see* D.1., *infra*).

c. Meaning of "Plaintiff's Person"
For purposes of a battery, anything *connected* to the plaintiff's person is viewed as part of the plaintiff's person.
Example: Chauncey grabbed Lulu's purse, which was hanging from her shoulder. He may be liable for a battery. (He would also be liable if he had grabbed an article of clothing she was wearing, a cane she was holding, etc.)

d. Causation
The defendant is liable not only for "direct" contact, but also for "indirect" contact; *i.e.,* it will be sufficient if he ***sets in motion a force*** that brings about harmful or offensive contact to the plaintiff's person.

Examples: 1) Chauncey, intending to set a trap, dug a hole in the road upon which Lulu was going to walk. Lulu fell in. Causation exists.

2) Horace struck a glass door so that the breaking glass cut Bowater. Causation exists.

e. **Apprehension Not Necessary**
A person may recover for battery even though he is not conscious of the harmful or offensive contact when it occurs (*e.g.,* unauthorized surgery performed on unconscious patient).

f. **Transferred Intent**
The doctrine of transferred intent *applies* in battery cases.

g. **Actual Damages Not Required**
It is not necessary to sustain a prima facie case for battery that plaintiff prove actual damages. Plaintiff can recover at least *nominal damages* even though he suffered no severe actual damage. In a majority of jurisdictions, *punitive damages* may be recovered where defendant acted with *malice*.

2. **Assault**

a. **Prima Facie Case**
To establish a prima facie case for assault, the following elements must be proved:

1) An act by the defendant creating a *reasonable apprehension* in plaintiff of *immediate harmful* or *offensive contact* to plaintiff's person;

2) *Intent* on the part of the defendant to bring about in the plaintiff apprehension of immediate harmful or offensive contact with the plaintiff's person; and

3) *Causation*.

b. **Construction of "Apprehension"**

1) **Requirement of Reasonableness**
The apprehension of harmful or offensive contact must be a reasonable one. Courts generally will not protect a plaintiff against exaggerated fears of contact (unless defendant knows of the unreasonable fear and uses it to put plaintiff in apprehension). In determining whether the apprehension in a given case is reasonable, the courts will usually apply *a reasonable person test*.

a) **Fear, Intimidation, etc., Distinguished**
Apprehension is not the same as fear or intimidation. Note that "apprehension" here is used in the sense of *expectation*. Thus, one may reasonably apprehend an immediate contact although he believes he can defend himself or otherwise avoid it.

b) **Knowledge of Act Required**
Obviously, for there to be an apprehension, the plaintiff must have been aware of the defendant's act. Contrast this with battery (above), in which the plaintiff need not be aware of the contact at the time thereof.

c) **Knowledge of Defendant's Identity Not Required**
In contrast, it is not necessary that the plaintiff know who the defendant is at the time of the act; *i.e.,* one only need apprehend an immediate harmful or offensive contact, not the identity of the person who is directing this unpermitted force at him.

d) **Defendant's Apparent Ability to Act Is Sufficient**
A person may be placed in reasonable apprehension of immediate harmful or offensive contact even though the defendant is *not actually capable* of causing injury to the plaintiff's person. For such apprehension to be reasonable, however, it is necessary that the defendant have the apparent ability to bring about such contact.

Example: Jan points an unloaded gun at Myron. Myron does not know that the gun is not loaded. Myron's apprehension of immediate harmful or offensive contact is reasonable.

e) Effect of Words

(1) Overt Act Required

Some overt act is necessary. Words alone, however violent, generally do not constitute an assault because they cannot create a reasonable apprehension of immediate harmful or offensive contact. A different result might occur when such words are accompanied by some overt act, *e.g.,* a clenching of the fist. Moreover, *words may negate an assault* by making unreasonable any apprehension of immediate contact, even though the defendant commits a hostile act.

Example: James shakes a clenched fist while talking to Myron, and says, "If I weren't such a good guy, I'd hit you." There is no reasonable apprehension of harmful or offensive contact.

(2) Conditional Threat Is Sufficient

Note that if the words and act combine to form a conditional threat, an assault will result.

Example: Robber points a gun at Plaintiff and says, "Your money or your life." Robber is liable for an assault.

2) Requirement of Immediacy

The apprehension must be of immediate harmful or offensive contact. Threats of future contact are insufficient. Similarly, there is no assault if the defendant is too far away to do any harm or is merely preparing for a future harmful act.

c. Causation

Plaintiff's apprehension must have been legally caused by the defendant's act or something set in motion thereby, either directly or indirectly.

d. Transferred Intent

The doctrine of transferred intent *applies* to assault cases.

e. No Requirement of Damages

It is not necessary to prove actual damages to sustain a prima facie case for assault. If the case is otherwise made out, plaintiff can recover *nominal damages*. Most states allow *punitive damages* to be awarded where defendant's actions have been malicious.

3. False Imprisonment

a. Prima Facie Case

To establish a prima facie case for false imprisonment, the following elements must be proved:

1) An act or omission to act on the part of the defendant that *confines* or *restrains* the plaintiff to a *bounded* area;

2) *Intent* on the part of the defendant to confine or restrain the plaintiff to a bounded area; and

3) *Causation*.

b. Sufficient Methods of Confinement or Restraint

Actionable confinement or restraint may result in a variety of ways. The following should be noted:

1) Physical Barriers

Defendant may falsely imprison plaintiff by confining him through the use of physical barriers.

2) Physical Force

False imprisonment will result where plaintiff is restrained by the use of physical force directed at *him* or a member of his *immediate family*. An action may also lie if the force is directed against *plaintiff's property*.

Example: Lulu remained in a building because her purse had been confiscated by Chauncey. She could have left the building but that would have necessitated leaving the purse behind. False imprisonment could result if the purse was wrongfully withheld.

3)   Direct Threats of Force
Direct threats of force by the defendant to the plaintiff's person or property or against persons of the plaintiff's immediate family can constitute false imprisonment.

4)   Indirect Threats of Force
False imprisonment can also arise from indirect threats of force, *i.e.,* acts or words that *reasonably* imply that the defendant will use force against plaintiff's person or property or persons of plaintiff's immediate family.

5)   Failure to Provide Means of Escape
Where plaintiff has lawfully come under defendant's control and it would be impossible to leave without defendant's assistance (and it was understood between the parties that such assistance would be forthcoming), the withholding of such assistance with the intent to detain plaintiff will make defendant liable. In short, the courts impose an *affirmative duty* on the defendant to take steps to release the plaintiff. If defendant intentionally breaches this duty, this is sufficient for false imprisonment. But, of course, it must first be established that defendant owes such a duty.

Examples: 1) Jailor refused to release a prisoner at the end of his jail sentence. Jailor may be liable for false imprisonment.

2) Plaintiff is imprisoned for failing to produce corporate records. Defendant has the records but is under no legal duty to produce them and refuses to do so. There is no false imprisonment.

6)   Invalid Use of Legal Authority
The invalid use of legal authority amounts to false imprisonment if it results in a confinement of plaintiff.

   a)   False Arrests
An action for false imprisonment does *not* lie for an arrest or a detention made by virtue of legal process duly issued by a court or official having jurisdiction to issue it. However, where an arrest by a police officer or private citizen for a criminal offense *without a warrant* is unlawful (*i.e.,* not privileged), it may constitute false imprisonment.

      (1)   When Arrests Are Privileged

         (a)   Felony Arrests Without Warrant
A felony arrest without a warrant by a *police officer* (or a private citizen acting at the officer's direction) is valid if the officer has *reasonable grounds* to believe that a felony has been committed and that the person arrested has committed it. Such an arrest by a *private person* will be privileged only if a felony has *in fact* been committed and the private person has reasonable grounds for believing that the person arrested has committed it.

         (b)   Misdemeanor Arrests Without Warrant
Both police officers and private citizens are privileged for misdemeanor arrests without a warrant if the misdemeanor was a *breach of the peace* and was committed in the presence of the arresting party.

         (c)   Arrests to Prevent a Crime Without a Warrant
Where a felony or breach of the peace is in the process of being, or reasonably appears about to be, committed, both police officers and private citizens are privileged to make an arrest.

(2) Amount of Force Allowable

(a) Felony Arrest
For felony arrests, both police officers and private citizens may use that degree of force reasonably necessary to make the arrest; however, deadly force is permissible only when the suspect poses a threat of serious harm to the arresting party or others.

(b) Misdemeanor Arrest
For misdemeanor arrests, both police officers and private citizens are privileged to use only that degree of force necessary to effect the arrest, but never deadly force.

b) "Shoplifting" Detentions Are Privileged
What if a shopkeeper suspects someone of shoplifting and detains that individual to ascertain whether this is the case? He may be liable for false imprisonment. But if he does nothing and permits the suspect to simply leave the premises, the merchandise and all possibilities of proving theft will be lost. Hence, by statute in some states and case law in others, shopkeepers have been given a privilege to detain for investigation. For the privilege to apply, the following conditions must be satisfied:

(1) There must be a *reasonable belief* as to the fact of theft;

(2) The detention must be conducted in a *reasonable manner* and only nondeadly force can be used; and

(3) The detention must be only for a *reasonable period of time* and only for the purpose of making an investigation.

c. Insufficient Forms of Confinement or Restraint
As stated above, restraints or confinements produced by requiring the plaintiff to choose between injury to his person or property and his freedom of motion are generally actionable. However, a cause of action will not be sustained for all forms of restraint or confinement.

1) Moral Pressure
A cause of action will not be sustained if a person remains in the area merely because he is responding to the exertion of moral pressure.

2) Future Threats
Similarly, a cause of action will not be sustained if a person remains in the area in response to future threats against person or property.

d. No Need to Resist
Plaintiff is not under any obligation to resist physical force that is being applied to confine him. Similarly, where there is a threat of force, he is not obligated to test the threat where the defendant has the apparent ability to carry it out.

e. Time of Confinement
It is *immaterial*, except as to the extent of damages, how short the time period of the confinement is.

f. Awareness of Imprisonment
Most American cases hold that awareness of confinement is a necessary element of the tort. The Restatement provides an exception to this requirement where the person confined is actually injured by the confinement (*e.g.,* an infant locked in a bank vault for several days).

g. What Is a Bounded Area?
For an area to be "bounded," the plaintiff's freedom of movement in *all directions* must be limited; *e.g.,* merely blocking plaintiff's access to a portion of a park does not constitute false imprisonment. The area will *not* be characterized as "bounded" if there is a *reasonable means of escape* of which plaintiff is aware.

h. Causation
Plaintiff's confinement must have been legally caused by the defendant's act or something set in motion thereby, either directly or indirectly.

i. Transferred Intent
The doctrine of transferred intent *applies* to false imprisonment.

j. No Requirement of Damages
It is not necessary to prove actual damages to sustain a prima facie case for false imprisonment. Again, if defendant's conduct was motivated by malice, plaintiff may also be entitled to punitive damages.

k. False Imprisonment and Malicious Prosecution Distinguished
One who participates in, procures, or instigates an unlawful arrest without proper authority may be liable for false arrest. Note that merely giving information to the police about the commission of a crime, leaving to the police the decision whether to make an arrest, does not constitute false imprisonment, as long as one stops short of instigating the arrest. Whether the defendant instigated the arrest or merely furnished information to the police is a question for the trier of fact. Where information only is given, there may be liability for malicious prosecution (*see* II.D.1., *infra*), if not for false imprisonment.

4. Intentional Infliction of Emotional Distress

a. Prima Facie Case
To establish a prima facie case for intentional infliction of emotional distress, the following elements must be proved:

1) An act by defendant amounting to *extreme* and *outrageous conduct*;

2) Intent on part of defendant to cause plaintiff to suffer *severe* emotional distress, or *recklessness* as to the effect of defendant's conduct;

3) *Causation*; and

4) *Damages*—*severe* emotional distress.

b. Extreme and Outrageous Conduct

1) Some Courts Reluctant to Recognize Tort
This tort covers those situations where the defendant intentionally "shocks" the plaintiff but there is *no physical injury* or threat thereof. Some states have been reluctant to recognize this as a cause of action because of the difficulty of proving "shock" (and the ease with which it could be falsified), the speculative nature of the damage, and fear of a flood of litigation.

2) Liability Limited by Requiring Proof of Outrageous Conduct
To protect against potential abuses, the courts will limit liability for this tort to those situations where "outrageous conduct" on the part of the defendant is proved. "Outrageous conduct" is *conduct that transcends all bounds of decency* tolerated by society. In the absence of such conduct by the defendant, it is generally held that an average person of ordinary sensibilities would not suffer the kind of severe mental injury that is contemplated by the tort.

3) Examples of Outrageous Conduct

a) Extreme Business Conduct
Certain extreme methods of business conduct may be construed as outrageous conduct, *e.g.,* use of extreme methods of collection, if repeated, may be actionable.

b) Misuse of Authority
Misuse of authority in some circumstances may be actionable, *e.g.,* school authorities threatening and bullying pupils.

      c)   **Offensive or Insulting Language**
Generally, offensive or insulting language will ***not*** be characterized as "outrageous conduct." This result could change if there is a ***special relationship*** between plaintiff and defendant or a ***sensitivity*** on plaintiff's part of which defendant is aware. (*See* below.)

4)   Special Relationship Situations
Common carriers and ***innkeepers*** owe special duties to their patrons that will be a basis for liability even when the act is something less than outrageous, *e.g.,* bus driver making insulting remarks to passenger.

5)   Known Sensitivity
If defendant knows that plaintiff is more sensitive and thus more susceptible to emotional distress than the average person, liability will follow if the defendant uses extreme and outrageous conduct intentionally to cause such distress and succeeds. These rules may also apply where defendant's conduct is directed at individuals in certain groups such as children, pregnant women, and elderly people.

c.   Intent
Defendant will be liable not only for intentional conduct but also for ***reckless*** conduct, *i.e.,* acting in reckless disregard of a high probability that emotional distress will result.

d.   Causation
The defendant's conduct must have proximately caused the plaintiff's emotional distress.

1)   Intent/Causation Requirements in Bystander Cases
When the defendant intentionally causes severe, ***physical*** harm to a third person and the plaintiff suffers severe ***emotional*** distress because of her relationship to the injured person, the elements of intent and causation may be harder to prove. To establish these elements in such cases, the plaintiff is generally required to show the following:

    (i)   The plaintiff was ***present*** when the injury occurred to the other person;

    (ii)   The plaintiff was a ***close relative*** of the injured person; and

    (iii)   The ***defendant knew*** that the plaintiff was present and a close relative of the injured person.

Note: The plaintiff does not need to establish presence or a family relationship if she shows that the defendant had a ***design or purpose*** to cause severe distress to plaintiff.

Example: Defendant called Susan and threatened to kill Mike, with whom Defendant knew Susan was living. Defendant then made good his threat. Liability will attach when Susan suffers severe emotional distress by showing that Defendant's ***purpose*** was to cause her severe distress, even though she was not a relative of Mike and was not present when he was murdered.

2)   Special Liability for Mishandling Corpses
In an analogous situation, many courts have allowed recovery where the mental distress resulted from the intentional or reckless mishandling of a relative's corpse. Although this cause of action is almost always for emotional distress arising from action directed toward another (the corpse), the courts have created a special category of liability for such conduct.

e.   Actual Damages Required
Actual damages are required (nominal damages will not suffice). But it is ***not*** necessary to prove ***physical injuries*** to recover. It is, however, necessary to establish ***severe*** emotional distress (*i.e.,* more than a reasonable person could be expected to endure). Punitive damages are allowable where defendant's conduct was improperly motivated.

C. PRIMA FACIE CASE—INTENTIONAL TORTS TO PROPERTY

1. Trespass to Land

a. Prima Facie Case
To establish a prima facie case for trespass to land, the following elements must be proved:

1) An act of *physical invasion* of plaintiff's real property by defendant;

2) *Intent* on defendant's part to bring about a physical invasion of plaintiff's real property; and

3) *Causation*.

b. Physical Invasion of Plaintiff's Land

1) What Constitutes "Physical Invasion"?
The interest protected by this tort is the interest in exclusive possession of realty. Hence, all that is necessary to satisfy this element is that there be a physical invasion of plaintiff's land.

a) Defendant Need Not Enter onto Land
It is not necessary that the defendant personally come onto the land; *e.g.,* trespass exists where defendant floods plaintiff's land, throws rocks onto it, or chases third persons upon it.

b) Lawful Right of Entry Expires
A trespass to land may also exist where defendant remains on plaintiff's land after an otherwise lawful right of entry has lapsed.

2) If No Physical Object Enters Land
If no physical object has entered onto plaintiff's land, *e.g.,* damage resulted from blasting concussions, the courts generally do not treat the controversy as a trespass case. Rather, they treat it as a *nuisance* case or as a case of *strict liability* if ultrahazardous activities are involved.

3) What Constitutes "Land"?
The trespass may occur on the surface of the land, below the surface, or above it.

Courts generally construe plaintiff's "land" to include air space and subsurface space to the height or depth plaintiff can make beneficial use of such space. Thus, for example, one could commit a trespass by stringing wires over the land, flying an airplane at low altitudes over it, tunneling under it, etc.

c. Intent Required
Mistake as to the lawfulness of the entry is *no defense* as long as defendant intended the entry upon that particular piece of land. Intent to trespass is not required—*intent to enter on the land* is sufficient.

Example: Relying on boundary markers fixed by a reputable surveyor, Farmer clears land for cultivation that he believes to be his. In fact, the survey was in error and Farmer cleared a portion of Neighbor's land. Farmer is liable to Neighbor for trespass to land.

d. Who May Bring Action?
An action for trespass may be maintained by *anyone in actual or constructive possession* of the land. This is so even if that possession is without title. If no one is in possession, the *true owner* is presumed in possession and may maintain the action.

If the action is maintained by a *lessee*, some decisions allow him to recover only to the extent that the trespass damages the leasehold interest. Other cases allow a full recovery for all damage done to the property, but require the lessee to account to the lessor for excess over damages to the leasehold.

e. Causation
The physical invasion of plaintiff's property must have been legally caused by the defendant's act or something set in motion thereby.

f.   Transferred Intent
The doctrine of transferred intent *applies* to trespass to land.

g.   No Requirement of Damages
As with most other intentional torts, damage is presumed; *i.e.,* actual injury to the land is *not* an essential element of the cause of action.

Example: Tom intentionally bounced a tennis ball against the side of a building owned by Owen. Although no damage was done to Owen's building, Tom is liable for trespass. In contrast, if Tom had accidentally but negligently hit Owen's building with the ball, Tom would not be liable unless Owen established damages as part of the negligence prima facie case.

2.   Trespass to Chattels

a.   Prima Facie Case
To establish a prima facie case of trespass to chattels, the following elements must be proved:

1)   An act of defendant that *interferes with plaintiff's right of possession* in the chattel;

2)   *Intent to perform the act* bringing about the interference with plaintiff's right of possession;

3)   *Causation*; and

4)   *Damages*.

b.   Act by Defendant
Trespass to chattels is designed to protect a person against interferences with his *right to possess* his chattels. Hence, any act of interference will suffice. These generally take two forms:

1)   **Intermeddling**
An intermeddling is conduct by defendant that in some way serves to directly damage plaintiff's chattels, *e.g.,* denting plaintiff's car, striking plaintiff's dog.

2)   **Dispossession**
A dispossession is conduct on defendant's part serving to dispossess plaintiff of his lawful right of possession.

c.   Intent Required
Mistake as to the lawfulness of defendant's actions (*e.g.,* a mistaken belief that defendant owns the chattel) is *no defense* to an action for trespass to chattels. Again, as with trespass to land, the intent to trespass is not required—*intent to do the act of interference* with the chattel is sufficient.

d.   Who May Bring Trespass to Chattels Action?
Anyone with possession or the immediate *right to possession* may maintain an action for trespass to chattels.

e.   Causation
The interference with plaintiff's possessory interests in the chattel must have been caused by defendant's act or something set in motion thereby.

f.   Actual Damages Required
As a general rule, nominal damages will not be awarded for trespass to chattels; *i.e.,* in the absence of any actual damages, an action will not lie. However, if the trespass amounts to a dispossession, the loss of possession itself is deemed to be an actual harm.

g.   Transferred Intent
The doctrine of transferred intent *applies* to trespass to chattels.

h.   Trespass to Chattels and Conversion Distinguished
As discussed below, conversion grants relief for interferences with a chattel so serious

in nature, or so serious in consequences, as to warrant requiring the defendant to pay its full value in damages. For those interferences not so serious in nature or consequences, trespass to chattels is the appropriate action.

3. Conversion

a. Prima Facie Case
To establish a prima facie case for conversion, the following elements must be proved:

1) An act by defendant *interfering* with plaintiff's right of possession in the chattel that is *serious enough* in nature or consequence to warrant that the defendant *pay the full value* of the chattel;

2) *Intent* to perform the act bringing about the interference with plaintiff's right of possession; and

3) *Causation*.

b. Acts of Conversion
One can act in such a way as to seriously invade another's chattel interest in a variety of ways. These include:

1) Wrongful acquisition, *e.g.,* theft, embezzlement.

2) Wrongful transfer, *e.g.,* selling, misdelivering, pledging.

3) Wrongful detention, *e.g.,* refusing to return to owner.

4) Substantially changing.

5) Severely damaging or destroying.

6) Misusing the chattel.

c. Mere Intent to Perform Act Required
The only intent required is the intent to perform the act that interferes with the plaintiff's right of possession. Even if the conduct is wholly innocent, liability may attach where the interference is serious in nature.

1) Bona Fide Purchaser May Be Liable
Under this principle, even a bona fide purchaser of chattel may become a converter if the chattel had been stolen from the true owner.

2) Accidental Conduct Insufficient
Accidentally causing damage to or loss of another's chattel does not amount to conversion unless the actor was using the chattel without permission when the accident occurred. (Note that the actor may be liable in negligence for accidental damage.)

d. Seriousness of Interference or Consequence
Usually, where the interference with possessory rights is insubstantial (*e.g.,* where a person momentarily takes another person's property or merely moves it for her own convenience), the actor is not viewed as asserting sufficient interference for conversion (although it may suffice for trespass to chattels). However, such interference with the possessory rights of another in the chattel, if serious enough, may amount to conversion. Thus, for example, if this person *refuses to return* the chattel when asked, or *alters* it, she may be liable for conversion because her action so seriously interferes with another's chattel rights that it amounts to a claim of dominion and control on the actor's part. No specific rule can be stated for these situations; however, the *longer the withholding period* and the *more extensive the use* of the chattel during this time, the more likely it is that conversion has resulted.

e. Special Situation of Bailees Receiving Stolen Property
A bailee receiving goods from a thief without notice of the improper taking may return the goods to the thief without liability to the real owner. However, if the bailee has

notice and the real owner makes a demand for his goods, the bailee is liable for conversion if she returns the goods to the thief.

f. Subject Matter of Conversion
Property subject to conversion is limited to tangible *personal property* and *intangibles* that have been *reduced to physical form* (*e.g.,* a promissory note), and documents in which title to a chattel is merged (*e.g.,* a bill of lading or a warehouse receipt). Intangibles such as a bakery route, customer lists, or the goodwill of a business may not be the subject of conversion. Neither may real property be converted.

g. Who May Bring Action for Conversion?
Anyone with *possession* or the *immediate right to possession* may maintain an action for conversion. Possession is viewed as sufficient title against a wrongdoer. However, if the person in possession is not the true owner, she is accountable to the true owner for any recovery to the extent of the owner's interest.

h. Causation
The interference with plaintiff's chattel interests must have been legally caused by the defendant's act or something set in motion thereby.

i. Remedies
The basic conversion remedies are:

1) Damages
The plaintiff is entitled to damages for the *fair market value* of the chattel. This value is generally computed as of the *time and place of conversion*. The defendant is given title upon satisfaction of the judgment so that, in effect, there is a forced sale of the chattel. Note that even if the defendant wishes to return the item, the plaintiff is not obligated to take it back once it has been converted.

2) Replevin
If the plaintiff wishes to have the chattel returned, he may get it by availing himself of the remedy of replevin.

D. DEFENSES TO THE INTENTIONAL TORTS

1. Consent
A defendant is not liable for an otherwise tortious act if the plaintiff consented to the defendant's act. Consent may be given expressly; it may also be implied from custom, conduct, or words, or by law.

a. Express (Actual) Consent
Express (actual) consent exists where the plaintiff has expressly shown a willingness to submit to defendant's conduct.

1) Consent by Mistake
Where a plaintiff expressly consents by mistake, the consent is still a valid defense unless the defendant caused the mistake or knows of the mistake and takes advantage of it.

2) Consent Induced by Fraud
If the expressly given consent has been induced by fraud, the consent generally is *not a defense*. The fraud must, however, go to an essential matter; if it is only with respect to a collateral matter, the consent remains effective.

Examples: 1) Charles expressly consents to balance an apple on his head for Roberta to attempt to shoot it off from 50 yards. She told him she was a professional trick-shot artist, which was not true. Fraud goes to an essential matter; consent is ineffective.

2) Same as above, except that Roberta was in fact a professional trick-shot artist. However, she gave him a $10 bill she knew to be counterfeit. This is a collateral matter; consent is effective.

3) Consent Obtained by Duress
Consent obtained by duress may be held *invalid*. Note, however, that threats of

future action or of some future economic deprivation do not constitute legal duress sufficient to invalidate the express consent.

b.   Implied Consent
Plaintiff's consent may also be implied in a given case. There are two basic kinds of implied consent, apparent consent and consent implied by law.

1)   Apparent Consent
Apparent consent is that which a *reasonable person would infer* from plaintiff's conduct. Thus, for example, somebody who voluntarily engages in a body contact sport impliedly consents to the normal contacts inherent in playing it.

a)   Inferred from Usage and Custom
Such consent may also be inferred as a matter of usage or custom. Thus, for example, a person is presumed to consent to the ordinary contacts of daily life, *e.g.,* minor bumping in a crowd.

2)   Consent Implied by Law
In some situations, consent may be implied by law where action is necessary to save a person's life or some other important interest in person or property. Thus, for example, consent will be implied in an *emergency* situation where the plaintiff is incapable of consenting and a reasonable person would conclude that some contact is necessary to prevent death or serious bodily harm, *e.g.,* surgical operation where a person is unconscious after an automobile accident.

c.   Capacity Required
Incompetents, drunken persons, and very young children are deemed incapable of consent to tortious conduct. Consent of parent or guardian is necessary to constitute a defense in such a case.

d.   Criminal Acts
For purposes of tort liability, the *majority* view is that a person *cannot consent* to a criminal act. A minority and the Restatement of Torts take the contrary position and view consent to a criminal act as a valid defense in a civil action for an intentional tort.

1)   Modern Trend
The modern tendency has been to differentiate between illegal acts that are *breaches of the peace*, *e.g.,* a street fight (consent ineffective), and those that are not a breach of the peace, *e.g.,* an act of prostitution (consent effective).

2)   Consent Invalid Where Law Seeks to Protect Members of Victim's Class
Where the act is made criminal to protect a limited class against its own lack of judgment (*e.g.,* statutory rape), consent is not a good defense in an action by a member of that class.

e.   Exceeding Consent Given
If the defendant goes beyond the act consented to and does something substantially different, he is *liable*; *e.g.,* consent to perform a tonsillectomy is not consent to perform an appendectomy (unless, of course, an emergency situation is present).

2.   Self-Defense
When a person has reasonable grounds to believe that he is being, or is about to be, attacked, he may use such force as is reasonably necessary for protection against the potential injury.

a.   When Is Defense Available?

1)   Reasonable Belief
The actor need only have a reasonable belief as to the other party's actions; *i.e.,* apparent necessity, not actual necessity, is sufficient. Hence, reasonable mistake as to the existence of the danger does not vitiate the defense.

2)   Retaliation Not Allowed
Self-defense is limited to the right to use force to prevent the commission of a tort. Thus, one may never use force in retaliation (where there is no longer any threat of injury).

3)   Retreat Not Necessary
A substantial majority of the courts hold that one need not attempt to escape, but may stand his ground (and even use deadly force when necessary to prevent death or serious bodily harm to himself). A growing modern trend would impose a duty to retreat before using deadly force where this can be done safely *unless* the actor is in his own home.

4)   Not Available to Aggressor
The initial aggressor is not privileged to defend himself against the other party's reasonable use of force in self-defense. However, if the other uses deadly force against an aggressor who had only used nondeadly force, the aggressor may defend himself with deadly force.

b.   How Much Force May Be Used?
One may use only that force that *reasonably* appears to be *necessary to prevent the harm*. One may not use force likely to cause death or serious bodily injury unless he reasonably believes that he is in danger of serious bodily injury. If more force than necessary is used, the actor loses the privilege of self-defense.

c.   Extends to Third-Party Injuries
If, in the course of reasonably defending himself, one *accidentally* injures a bystander, he is nevertheless protected by the defense. (He might, however, be liable to the by-stander on a negligence theory if his conduct warranted it.) If the actor *deliberately* injures a bystander in trying to protect himself, he probably cannot raise the privilege of self-defense.

3.   Defense of Others

a.   When Is Defense Available?
The actor need only have a *reasonable belief* that the person being aided would have the right of self-defense. Thus, even if the person aided has no defense (*e.g.*, if he were the initial aggressor), his defender is not liable as long as he reasonably believed that the person aided could have used force to protect himself.

b.   How Much Force May Be Used?
The defender, assuming he is justified, may use as much force as he could have used in self-defense if the injury were threatened to him (*see* above).

4.   Defense of Property

a.   When Is Defense Available?
Generally, one may use reasonable force to prevent the commission of a tort against her property.

1)   Request to Desist Usually Required
A request to desist must precede the use of force, unless the circumstances make it clear that the request would be futile or dangerous.

2)   Effect of Mistake
Reasonable mistake is allowed as to the property owner's right to use force in defense of property where the mistake involves whether an intrusion has occurred or whether a request to desist is required. However, mistake is not allowed where the entrant has a privilege to enter the property that supersedes the defense of property right (*see* 4), below). In such a case the property owner is liable for mistakenly using force against a privileged entrant unless the entrant himself intentionally or negligently caused the mistake (*e.g.,* by refusing to tell the prop-erty owner the reason for the intrusion).

3)   Limited to Preventing Commission of Tort
Defense of property is limited to *preventing the commission of a tort* against the defendant's property. Thus, once the defendant has been permanently dispos-sessed of the property and the commission of the tort is complete, she may not use force to recapture it. However, where one is in *"hot pursuit"* of someone who wrongfully dispossessed her of her property, the defense still operates because the other is viewed as still in the process of committing the tort against the property.

4) **Superseded by Other Privileges**
Whenever an actor has a privilege to enter upon the land of another because of necessity, right of reentry, right to enter upon another's land to recapture chattels, etc. (discussed below), that privilege supersedes the privilege of the land possessor to defend her property.

b. **How Much Force May Be Used?**
One may use *reasonable* force to defend property. However, she may *not* use force that will cause death or serious bodily harm. (Of course, if the invasion of property also entails a serious threat of bodily harm to the owner, she may then invoke the defense of self-defense and use deadly force.) Further, one may not use indirect deadly force such as a trap, spring gun, or vicious dog when such force could not lawfully be directly used, *e.g.,* against a mere trespasser.

5. Reentry onto Land

a. **Common Law Privilege**
In former years, it was held that a person who had been *tortiously dispossessed* from her land (by fraud or force) could use *reasonable force* to regain possession if she acted promptly upon discovering the dispossession. (Note that this did not apply to a tenant merely overstaying her lease.)

b. **No Such Privilege Under Modern Law**
However, in most states today there are *summary procedures* for recovering possession of real property. Hence, resort to "self-help" is no longer allowed; the owner who uses force to retake possession is thus liable for whatever injury she inflicts.

6. Recapture of Chattels

a. **When Is Defense Available?**
The basic rule is the same as that for land: where another's possession began lawfully (*e.g.,* a conditional sale), one may use only peaceful means to recover the chattel. *Force* may be used to recapture a chattel only when in *"hot pursuit"* of one who has obtained possession wrongfully, *e.g.,* by theft.

1) **Timely Demand Required**
A demand to return the chattel must precede the use of force, unless the circumstances make it clear that the demand would be futile or dangerous.

2) **Recovery Only from Wrongdoer**
The recapture may only be from a tortfeasor or some third person who knows or should know that the chattels were tortiously obtained. If the chattels have come to rest in the hands of an innocent party, this will cut off the actor's privilege to use force to effect recapture.

b. **How Much Force May Be Used?**
Reasonable force, *not* including force sufficient to cause death or serious bodily harm, may be used to recapture chattels.

c. **Entry upon Land to Remove Chattel**

1) **On Wrongdoer's Land**
Where chattels are located on the land of the wrongdoer, the owner is privileged to enter upon the land and reclaim them at a *reasonable time* and in a *reasonable manner*. It is generally required that there be a demand for the return of the chattels before any such entry.

2) **On Land of Innocent Party**
Similarly, when the chattels are on the land of an innocent party, the owner may enter and reclaim her chattel at a *reasonable time* and in a *peaceful manner* when the landowner has been given *notice* of the presence of the chattel and refuses to return it. In this case, the chattel owner will be liable for any actual damage caused by entry.

3) **On Land Through Owner's Fault**
If the chattels are on the land of another through the owner's fault, there is *no*

> > *privilege* to enter upon the land. They may be recovered only through legal process.

> **d. Shopkeeper's Privilege**
> Shopkeepers may have a privilege to reasonably detain individuals whom they reasonably believe to be in possession of "shoplifted" goods. (*See* B.3.b.6)b), *supra.*)

7. Privilege of Arrest
Depending on the facts of the particular case, one may have a privilege to make an arrest of a third person.

> **a. Invasion of Land**
> The privilege of arrest carries with it the privilege to enter another's land for the purpose of effecting the arrest.

> **b. Subsequent Misconduct**
> Although the arrest itself may be privileged, the actor may still be liable for subsequent misconduct, *e.g.,* failing to bring the arrested party before a magistrate, unduly detaining the party in jail, etc.

> **c. Mistake**
> One who makes an arrest under the mistaken belief that it is privileged may be liable for false imprisonment. (*See* B.3.b.6)a)(1), *supra.*)

8. Necessity
A person may interfere with the real or personal property of another where the interference is reasonably and apparently necessary to avoid threatened injury from a natural or other force and where the threatened injury is substantially more serious than the invasion that is undertaken to avert it.

> **a. Public Necessity**
> Where the act is for the public good (*e.g.,* shooting a rabid dog), the defense is absolute.

> **b. Private Necessity**
> Where the act is solely to benefit *any person* (the actor, the owner of the land, or some other third person) or to protect *any property* from destruction or serious injury (*e.g.,* tying up to a dock in a storm), the defense is qualified; *i.e.,* the actor must pay for any injury he causes.

9. Discipline
A parent or teacher may use reasonable force in disciplining children, taking into account the age and sex of the child and the seriousness of the behavior.

II. HARM TO ECONOMIC AND DIGNITARY INTERESTS

In contrast to the intentional torts, the torts in this section involve less tangible harms to a person's relational interests with other persons in society.

Depending on the tort involved, the level of fault required for the prima facie case may range from intent to strict liability.

A. DEFAMATION

1. Prima Facie Case
To establish a prima facie case for defamation, the following elements must be proved:

> (i) *Defamatory language* on the part of the defendant;

> (ii) The defamatory language must be *"of or concerning" the plaintiff*—i.e., it must identify the plaintiff to a reasonable reader, listener, or viewer;

> (iii) *Publication* of the defamatory language by the defendant to a third person; and

> (iv) *Damage to the reputation* of the plaintiff.

Where the defamation refers to a public figure or involves a matter of public concern, two additional elements must be proved as part of the prima facie case:

(v) *Falsity* of the defamatory language; and

(vi) *Fault* on defendant's part.

2. **Defamatory Language**

Defamatory language is language that tends to adversely affect one's reputation. This may result from impeaching the individual's honesty, integrity, virtue, sanity, or the like.

a. **Inducement and Innuendo**

If the statement standing alone is defamatory, it is defamatory "on its face." However, a statement is also actionable if the defamatory meaning becomes apparent only by adding extrinsic facts. The plaintiff pleads and proves such additional facts as inducement and establishes the defamatory meaning by innuendo. Inducement and innuendo identify to the courts and the parties that extrinsic facts are being introduced to the court by the plaintiff to establish the first element of a prima facie case.

Example: Defendant publishes an erroneous report that Plaintiff has given birth to twins. This is defamatory because Plaintiff pleads and establishes that she had been married only one month.

b. **Methods of Defamation**

Not all defamation consists of direct remarks. Pictures, satire, drama, etc., may convey an actionable defamatory meaning.

c. **Statements of Opinion**

While a statement of fact may always be defamatory, a statement of opinion is actionable only if it appears to be based on specific facts, *and* an express allegation of those facts would be defamatory.

Example: The statement "I don't think Robert can be trusted with a key to the cash register" implies personal knowledge of dishonest conduct by Robert, and thus may be actionable.

1) **Distinguishing Fact and Opinion**

Whether a published statement is one of "fact" or "opinion" depends on the circumstances surrounding the publication and the nature of the words used. Generally, the broader the language used, the less likely that it will be reasonably interpreted as a statement of fact or an opinion based on specific facts.

d. **Who May Be Defamed?**

1) **Individual**

Any *living* person may be defamed. Defamation of a deceased person is not actionable.

2) **Corporation, Unincorporated Association, and Partnership**

In a limited sense, a corporation, unincorporated association, or partnership may also be defamed, *e.g.,* by remarks as to its financial condition, honesty, integrity, etc.

3. **"Of or Concerning" the Plaintiff**

The plaintiff must establish that a *reasonable* reader, listener, or viewer would understand that the defamatory statement referred to the plaintiff.

a. **Colloquium**

A statement may be actionable even though no clear reference to the plaintiff is contained on the face of the statement. In such a case, however, the plaintiff is required to introduce additional extrinsic facts that would lead a reasonable reader, listener, or viewer to perceive the defamatory statement as referring to the plaintiff. Pleading and proving such extrinsic facts to show that the plaintiff was, in fact, intended is called "colloquium."

b. **Group Defamation**

A significant issue is presented in respect to this prima facie case element when the defamatory language refers to a group without identifying any particular individual within that group. In such cases, the following rules operate:

1) **All Members of Small Group**
   Where the defamatory language refers to all members of a small group, each member may establish that the defamatory statement was made of and concerning him by alleging that he is a member of the group.

2) **All Members of Large Group**
   If, however, the defamatory statement refers to all members of a large group, no member of that group may establish this element of the cause of action.

3) **Some Members of Small Group**
   Where the defamatory language refers to some members of a small group, plaintiff can recover if a reasonable person would view the statement as referring to the plaintiff.

4. Publication
A statement is not actionable until there has been a "publication." The publication requirement is satisfied when there is a *communication to a third person who understood it.*
Example: Libby saw a defamatory statement about Jeffrey printed in Russian. The publication requirement is not met unless it is shown that Libby understood the foreign words.

The communication to the third person may be made either *intentionally or negligently.*

a. **Only Intent to Publish Required**
   Once publication is established, it is no defense that defendant had no idea that she was defaming plaintiff because she neither knew nor had reason to know that plaintiff existed (use of fictional name), nor knew that the publication was defamatory. It is the intent to publish, not the intent to defame, that is the requisite intent.
   Example: Defendant published a false statement that Plaintiff had given birth to twins. If Defendant neither knew nor had reason to know that Plaintiff had been married only one month, Defendant is nonetheless liable.

b. **Repetition**
   Each repetition of the defamatory statement is a separate publication for which the plaintiff may recover damages.

c. **"Single Publication" Rule—Statute of Limitations**
   However, as to publication of a defamatory statement in a number of copies of the same newspaper, magazine, or book, most American courts have adopted the "single publication" rule. Under this rule, all copies of a newspaper, magazine, or book edition are treated as only one publication. The publication is deemed to occur when the finished product is released by the publisher for sale (a matter which is, obviously, most important for the running of the statute of limitations). Damages are still calculated on the total effect of the story on all of the readers.

d. **Who May Be Liable?**

1) **Primary Publisher**
   Each individual who takes part in making the publication is charged with the publication as a primary publisher; *e.g.,* a newspaper or TV station carrying a defamatory message would be viewed as a primary publisher and held responsible for that message to the same extent as the author or speaker.

2) **Republisher**
   A republisher (*i.e.,* one who repeats a defamatory statement) will be held *liable* on the same general basis as a primary publisher. This is so even if the repeater states the source or makes it clear that she does not believe the defamation.

   Note: Where there has been a republication, the original defamer's liability may be increased to encompass any new harm caused by the repetition if the republication was either (i) intended by the original defamer or (ii) reasonably foreseeable to her.

3) Secondary Publishers

One who is responsible only for disseminating materials that might contain defamatory matter (*e.g.,* a vendor of newspapers, a player of a tape) is viewed as a secondary publisher. Such individuals are liable only *if they know or should know* of the defamatory content.

5. Damage to Plaintiff's Reputation

In ascertaining whether this element of the plaintiff's prima facie case has been satisfied, it may be necessary to distinguish between libel and slander. As will be seen below, the burden of proof as to damages (to plaintiff's reputation) may depend on this distinction.

a. General and Special Damages

1) General or Presumed Damages

General damages are presumed by law and need not be proved by the plaintiff. They are intended to compensate the plaintiff for the general injury to her reputation caused by the defamation.

Note: Constitutional free speech and press considerations may restrict an award of presumed damages when the defamation involves matters of "public concern." [Dun & Bradstreet, Inc. v. Greenmoss Builders, Inc., 472 U.S. 749 (1985)] (*See* 7.d.3), *infra.*)

2) Special Damages

Special damages in a defamation law context means that the plaintiff must specifically prove that she suffered *pecuniary loss* as a result of the defamatory statement's effect on her reputation, and are not proved merely by evidence of actual injury—such as the loss of friends, humiliation, or wounded feelings. The loss of a job, a prospective gift or inheritance, an advantageous business relationship, or customers are pecuniary losses such as those contemplated by the special damages requirement.

b. Libel

1) Definition

Libel is a defamatory statement recorded in *writing or* some *other permanent form*. A libel may also be recorded by radio or television in some circumstances. (*See* below.)

2) Damages Rules for Libel

a) General Damages Presumed

In most jurisdictions, general damages are *presumed by law* for all libels; *i.e.,* special damages need not be established.

b) Libel Distinction—Minority Position

A substantial minority of courts distinguish between libel per se and libel per quod in determining whether a libel is actionable without proof of special damages.

(1) Libel Per Se—Presumed Damages

These courts take the position that injury to the reputation of the plaintiff is presumed by law only if the statement is libelous and defamatory on its face (called libel per se). Thus, such libels are actionable without pleading or proving special damages.

(2) Libel Per Quod—Special Damages Usually Required

The libelous statement that is not defamatory on its face, but that requires reference to extrinsic facts to establish its defamatory content, is characterized as libel per quod by these courts. These courts generally require special damages to be pleaded and proved for such libels.

c. Slander

1) Definition

Slander is *spoken defamation*. It is to be distinguished from libel in that the defamation is in less permanent and less physical form.

a)   **Characterization of Repetitions**
Where the original defamation is libel, any repetition, even if oral, is also libel. On the other hand, the written repetition of a slander will be characterized as libel.

b)   **Distinguishing Between Libel and Slander**
In some cases, it is difficult to determine whether the defamation should be characterized as libel or slander, *e.g.,* defamation made on a radio or television program, or on a recording. The courts consider several factors in making the characterization:

(1)   How *permanent* is the form? The more permanent the form, the more likely it will be held to be libel.

(2)   How *broad* is the *area of dissemination*? The broader the area of dissemination, the more likely it will be characterized as libel.

(3)   How *premeditated* is the character of the defamation? The more premeditated it is, the more likely it will be characterized as libel.

c)   **Radio and Television—Scripted Material Is Libel**
Note that if the defamation in a radio or television program is in a script, it is already in libel form, so that any repetition will also be libel. If the defamation is ad-libbed, the courts are split; the modern trend treats it as libel. However, if the defamation is ad-libbed by a guest speaker rather than the broadcaster's employee, the broadcaster is liable only if it was *negligent* in not preventing the utterance.

2)   **Damages Rules for Slander**

a)   **Special Damages Usually Required**
In slander, injury to reputation is *not presumed*. Thus, ordinary slander is not actionable in the absence of pleading and proof of special damages.

b)   **Slander Per Se—Injury Presumed**
If, however, the spoken defamation falls within one of four categories, characterized as slander per se, an injury to reputation is presumed without proof of special damages. These four categories are:

(1)   **Business or Profession**
A defamatory statement adversely reflecting on plaintiff's abilities in his business, trade, or profession is actionable without pleading or proof of special damages. Statements that the plaintiff is dishonest or lacks the basic skill to perform his profession or carry out his office are examples of this slander per se category. The statement must, however, directly relate to plaintiff's profession, trade, or business.
Example: Statement about an engineer stating "he is a Communist" is not directly related to his trade.

(2)   **Loathsome Disease**
A defamatory statement that the plaintiff is presently suffering from a foul and loathsome disease is actionable without pleading or proof of special damages. Historically, this slander per se category has been limited to venereal disease and leprosy.

(3)   **Crime Involving Moral Turpitude**
A defamatory statement that the plaintiff is or was guilty of a crime involving moral turpitude is actionable without pleading or proof of special damages. Because common law crimes generally are deemed to involve moral turpitude (*e.g.,* assault, larceny, perjury), this category of slander per se incorporates a large number of statements. Thus, the allegation that a married man has a mistress implies that he is guilty of the crimes of fornication and adultery.

(4) Unchastity of a Woman
A defamatory statement imputing unchaste behavior to a woman is actionable without pleading or proof of special damages.

d. "Per Se"
"Per se" means defamatory on its face when used in libel actions and means slander within one of the four categories when used in slander actions.

6. Falsity
At common law, a defamatory statement was presumed to be false. The Supreme Court, however, has rejected this presumption in all cases in which the plaintiff is constitutionally required to prove some type of fault (*see* below). In these cases, the plaintiff must prove as an element of the prima facie case that the statement was false. [Philadelphia Newspapers, Inc. v. Hepps, 475 U.S. 767 (1986)]

a. Exam Approach
Even where the statement is true, it may nonetheless give rise to liability if it is uttered under circumstances sufficient to constitute intentional infliction of severe emotional distress or invasion of right to privacy; hence, consider these torts as well when your exam question presents potentially defamatory statements. However, where plaintiff is a public figure who would be barred on First Amendment grounds from recovering for defamation, he will not be allowed to rely on these other tort theories. [Hustler Magazine, Inc. v. Falwell, 485 U.S. 46 (1988)]

7. Fault on Defendant's Part
Although at common law defamation liability could be strict, a number of Supreme Court decisions based on the First Amendment now impose a fault requirement in cases involving public figures or matters of public concern. The degree of fault to be established depends on the type of plaintiff, *i.e.,* whether he is a public official or public figure as compared with a private person plaintiff involved in a matter of public concern.

a. Public Officials—Malice Required
A public official may not recover for defamatory words relating to his official conduct in the absence of "clear and convincing" proof that the statement was made with "malice." (*See* below.) [New York Times v. Sullivan, 376 U.S. 254 (1964)]

b. Public Figures—Malice Required
The rule of *New York Times v. Sullivan* has been extended to cover litigation where the plaintiff is a public figure. [Associated Press v. Walker, 388 U.S. 130 (1967); Curtis Publishing Co. v. Butts, 388 U.S. 130 (1967)]

1) What Constitutes a Public Figure?
A person may be deemed a "public figure" on one of two grounds: (i) where he has achieved *such pervasive fame or notoriety* that he becomes a public figure for all purposes and contexts (*e.g.,* celebrity sports figure); or (ii) where he voluntarily assumes a *central role* in a particular *public controversy* (*e.g.,* prominent community activist) and thereby becomes a "public figure" for that limited range of issues. [Gertz v. Robert Welch, Inc., 418 U.S. 323 (1974)]

In *Gertz,* the Court indicated that it might be possible for a person to become a public figure through no purposeful action of his own, but considered such instances to be "exceedingly rare." Subsequent cases support this interpretation. [Time, Inc. v. Firestone, 424 U.S. 448 (1976); Hutchinson v. Proxmire, 443 U.S. 111 (1979); Wolston v. Reader's Digest Association, 443 U.S. 157 (1979)]

c. What Is Malice?

1) Test
Malice was defined by the Supreme Court in *New York Times v. Sullivan* as:

a) *Knowledge* that the statement was false, *or*

b) *Reckless disregard* as to its truth or falsity.

2) What Constitutes "Knowledge or Reckless Falsity"?
It must be shown that the defendant was subjectively aware that the statement he

published was false or that he was subjectively reckless in making the statement. [New York Times v. Sullivan, *supra*]

a) Reckless Conduct—Subjective Standard
"Reckless" conduct is *not* measured by a reasonable person standard or by whether a reasonable person would have investigated before publishing. There must be a showing that the defendant in fact (subjectively) *entertained serious doubts* as to the truthfulness of his publication.

b) Spite, etc., Not Enough
It is not enough that the defendant is shown to have acted with spite, hatred, ill will, or intent to injure the plaintiff.

3) Alteration of Quotation as Malice
A journalist deliberately altering a quotation attributed to a public figure can be found to have "knowledge of falsity" if it can be established that the alteration results in a *material change in the meaning conveyed by the statement*. [Masson v. New Yorker Magazine, 501 U.S. 496 (1991)]

d. Private Persons Need Not Prove Malice
Where the defamatory statement relates to a *nonpublic* personage, there is less concern for freedom of speech and press. In addition, private individuals are more vulnerable to injury from defamation because they usually do not have as effective opportunities for rebuttal as public personages. Accordingly, defamation actions brought by private individuals are subject to constitutional limitations only when the defamatory statement involves a matter of "public concern." And even in those cases, the limitations are not as great as those established for public officials and public figures. [Gertz v. Robert Welch, Inc., *supra*]

1) Matters of Public Concern—At Least Negligence Required
When the defamatory statement involves a matter of public concern, *Gertz* imposes two restrictions on private plaintiffs: (i) it prohibits liability without fault, and (ii) it restricts the recovery of presumed or punitive damages.

a) No Liability Without Fault
Where the statement published is such that its defamatory potential was *apparent* to a reasonably prudent person, the plaintiff must show that the defendant permitted the false statement to appear, if not through malice, at least through *negligence* as to its truth or falsity.

(1) The Supreme Court has left open the question of what the fault standard would be where the statement published involved *no* apparent defamatory potential (*i.e.,* factual misstatements that are innocent on their face and require proof of extrinsic facts to be defamatory, such as libel per quod).

b) Damages Limited to "Actual Injury"
Assuming the defendant was in fact negligent in ascertaining the truth of what it published—but still it had no actual knowledge of the falsity, nor was it guilty of reckless disregard for the truth—damages can be recovered but are limited to the *"actual injury"* sustained by the plaintiff; *i.e.,* presumed damages are prohibited.

(1) **"Actual Injury"**
The Supreme Court has deliberately chosen not to define this term, but has stated that it is *not limited to out-of-pocket loss*. It may include impairment of reputation and standing in the community, personal humiliation, and mental anguish and suffering (*i.e.,* an injury to reputation not resulting in special damages may still be actionable). The important point is that there must be *competent evidence* of "actual" injury (no presumed damages), although there need be no evidence that assigns an actual dollar value to the injury.

(2) **Presumed Damages or Punitive Damages Allowable Where Malice Found**
It follows that if the plaintiff cannot prove "actual injury," he cannot

recover any damages, ***unless*** he can show that the publication was made with knowledge of its falsity or with reckless disregard for the truth. There is no constitutional protection for publications made with "knowledge or reckless falsity," and hence, the plaintiff is entitled to whatever recovery is permitted under state law in such cases (*i.e.,* "presumed" or general damages and even punitive damages in appropriate cases). Note that this approach is simply a restatement of the general rule in torts that damages must be proved in negligence actions (*see infra,* III.E.) but usually are not required where the defendant is more culpable, such as for intentional torts.

2) Matters of Purely Private Concern—No Constitutional Limitations
When the defamatory statement involves a matter of purely private concern, the constitutional limitations established by *Gertz* do ***not*** apply; only the four elements of the common law prima facie case are required. Thus, presumed and punitive damages might be recoverable even if malice is not established.

3) What Is a Matter of Public Concern?
To determine whether the matter is a public or private concern, the courts will look to the content, form, and context of the publication. [Dun & Bradstreet, Inc. v. Greenmoss Builders, Inc., *supra*]

Example: In *Dun & Bradstreet,* the Court determined that a credit agency's erroneous report of plaintiff's bankruptcy, distributed to five subscribers, was speech solely in the private interest of the speaker and its specific business audience. The content (the bankruptcy of a small business), the form (a credit agency report), and the context (a communication to only five subscribers) established that a matter of public concern was not involved.

8. Defenses to Defamation

a. Consent
As with all torts, consent is a complete defense to a defamation action. (The rules relating to consent discussed under intentional torts, *supra,* also apply here.)

b. Truth
In cases of purely private concern where plaintiff is not required to prove falsity (*see* A.6., *supra*), defendant may establish the truth of the statement as a complete defense.

c. Absolute Privilege
Under certain circumstances, the speaker is not liable for defamatory statements because he enjoys an absolute privilege. Such absolute privileges are ***not*** affected by a showing of malice, abuse, or excessive provocation, as in the case of qualified privileges (*see* below). Absolute privilege exists in the following cases:

1) Judicial Proceedings
All statements made by the judge, jurors, counsel, witnesses, or parties in judicial proceedings are absolutely privileged. The privilege attaches to ***all*** aspects of the proceedings, *e.g.,* statements made in open court, pretrial hearing, deposition, or in any of the pleadings or other papers in the case.

There is a requirement that the statement bear some ***reasonable relationship*** to the proceedings.

2) Legislative Proceedings
All remarks made by either federal or state legislators in their official capacity in hearings or floor debates are likewise absolutely privileged.

There is ***no requirement of a reasonable relationship*** to any matter at hand.

3) Executive Proceedings
A governmental executive official is absolutely privileged with respect to any statement made by her while exercising the functions of her office.

There is a requirement that the statement have some ***reasonable relationship*** to the executive matter or proceeding in which she is acting.

4) "Compelled" Broadcast or Publication
A radio or TV station compelled to allow a speaker the use of the air, a newspaper compelled to print public notices, etc., is absolutely privileged in an action based on the content of the compelled publication. [Farmers Educational Cooperative v. WDAY, 360 U.S. 525 (1959)]
Example: Radio station gave time to one candidate for public office and hence came under obligation to extend similar treatment to other candidates for the same office. Station had no right to censor these later speeches. Thus, no liability attaches for defamation they might contain.

5) Communications Between Spouses
Communications from one spouse to another are generally treated as being absolutely privileged.

Note: Some states have dealt with communications between spouses on the basis that there is no publication. This is not the preferred view.

d.   Qualified Privilege
In certain situations, a speaker may say something defamatory without being liable because of the existence of a qualified privilege.

1)   Qualified Privilege Situations
Included within the category of qualified privilege situations are the following:

a)   Reports of Public Proceedings
There is a qualified privilege for reports of public hearings or meetings. This includes judicial, legislative, or executive proceedings as well as other proceedings of sufficient public interest, *e.g.,* political convention, trade association meeting, etc.

The privilege *excuses accurate reports* of statements that were false when made, but it *does not excuse inaccuracies* in the reporting of statements.

b)   Public Interest

(1)   Publication to One Acting in Public Interest
Statements made to those who are to take official action of some kind are qualifiedly privileged.
Example: Statements made to a parole board about a prisoner by one who opposed the grant of parole are privileged.

(2)   Fair Comment and Criticism
One is permitted to make remarks that disparage another's acts in the course of a critique of public interest, *e.g.,* book reviews, articles on public institutions, etc. The matter commented upon must be of *general public interest*.

Note: Obviously, the "qualified privilege" areas of subsections a) and b) have generally been preempted by the constitutional requirements imposed by *New York Times v. Sullivan* and its progeny, *supra*.

c)   Interest of Publisher
Where defendant's statement is made to defend her own actions, property, or reputation, it may be privileged.
Example: A statement by a debtor explaining to a collection agency her reason for not paying a bill is qualifiedly privileged even if defamatory statements are contained therein.

d)   Interest of Recipient
A qualified privilege is recognized when the recipient has an interest in the information and it is reasonable for the defendant to make the publication, *i.e.,* when she is not a mere intermeddler.
Examples: 1) A statement by a credit bureau to a customer is qualifiedly privileged.

2) A statement made by a former employer to a prospective employer about a job applicant is qualifiedly privileged.

e) Common Interest of Publisher and Recipient
Where there is a common interest between the publisher and the recipient, there is a qualified privilege.

Example: A statement by one board member of a charitable foundation, relating to the foundation's business, to another board member is qualifiedly privileged.

2) Loss of Qualified Privilege Through Abuse
A qualified privilege exists only if exercised in a reasonable manner and for a proper purpose. Thus, even though the facts might otherwise give rise to a qualified privilege situation, the actor may have lost this privilege by virtue of his conduct. There are two basic ways in which this generally occurs:

a) Statement Not Within Scope of Privilege
The allegedly protected statement must fall within the scope of the privilege. Hence, the privilege does not encompass the publication of irrelevant defamatory matter unconnected with the public or private interest entitled to protection.

Similarly, the privilege does not cover publication to any person whose hearing or reading of the statement could not reasonably be believed to be necessary for the furtherance of that interest.

b) Malice
A qualified privilege will be lost if it is shown that the speaker acted with malice. "Malice" here means that the statement was made with (i) *knowledge* that it was untrue or (ii) a *reckless disregard* as to its truth or falsity.

Note: At common law, many courts held that malice in the sense of ill will of defendant toward plaintiff would result in loss of the qualified privilege. Most courts no longer define malice in this way, however. As long as defendant is using a proper occasion for a qualified privilege in a proper way, she will not lose this privilege simply because she bears ill will toward plaintiff.

3) Qualified Privilege—Burden of Proof
The *defendant bears the burden* of proving that a privilege exists. If the privilege is qualified, the plaintiff then bears the burden of proving that the privilege has been lost through excessive publication or malice.

9. Mitigating Factors
Several matters, while not defenses to an action, may be considered by the trier of fact on the issue of damages. These include:

a. No Actual Malice
Malice may be inferred from some statements, but if the jury is shown that there was no actual malice, such evidence is admissible to mitigate damages. To this end, defendant may prove the source of her information and grounds for her belief.

b. Retraction
Unless made immediately after publication so as to negate the defamatory effect of a statement, retraction does not undo the wrong. But the court may consider it to show *lack of actual malice* in mitigation of damages. A failure to retract after a request to do so is often allowed as evidence to the opposite effect.

c. Anger
Anger of the speaker may be a mitigating circumstance *if provoked* by the plaintiff.

B. INVASION OF RIGHT TO PRIVACY
The right to protection against unreasonable interferences with an individual's solitude is well recognized. The tort of invasion of privacy as it has developed, however, includes protection of "personality" as well as protection against interference with solitude. In all, the tort includes the following four kinds of wrongs:

(i) ***Appropriation*** by defendant of plaintiff's picture or name for defendant's ***commercial advantage***;

(ii) ***Intrusion*** by the defendant upon plaintiff's ***affairs*** or ***seclusion***;

(iii) Publication by the defendant of facts placing the plaintiff in a ***false light***; and

(iv) Public disclosures of ***private facts*** about the plaintiff by the defendant.

1. Appropriation of Plaintiff's Picture or Name

a. Prima Facie Case
To establish a prima facie case for invasion of privacy—appropriation of plaintiff's picture or name—only one element need be proved:

1) ***Unauthorized use*** by defendant of plaintiff's picture or name for defendant's ***commercial advantage***.

b. Limited to Advertisement or Promotion of Product or Services
Liability is generally limited to the use of plaintiff's picture or name in connection with the promotion or advertisement of a product or service, *e.g.,* use of plaintiff's picture to advertise an automobile.

The mere fact that defendant is using plaintiff's picture or name for his own personal profit may not, by itself, be sufficient. Thus, for example, the use of a personality's name in a magazine story, even if motivated by profit, may not be actionable.

2. Intrusion on Plaintiff's Affairs or Seclusion

a. Prima Facie Case
To establish a prima facie case for invasion of privacy—intrusion on the plaintiff's affairs or seclusion—the following elements must be proved:

1) ***Act of prying or intruding*** on the affairs or seclusion of the plaintiff by the defendant;

2) The intrusion is something that would be ***objectionable to a reasonable person***; and

3) The thing to which there is an intrusion or prying is ***"private."***

b. Invasion of Plaintiff's Private Affairs or Seclusion
For liability to attach, there must be an invasion of the plaintiff's private affairs or seclusion; *e.g.,* defendant puts a microphone in plaintiff's bedroom.

c. Intrusion Objectionable to a Reasonable Person
For liability to attach, the intrusion by defendant must be something that would be objectionable to a reasonable person.

d. Intrusion Must Be into Something "Private"
For liability to attach, the intrusion by defendant must be into something within the plaintiff's own private domain. Thus, for example, taking pictures of a person in a public place is not actionable.

3. Publication of Facts Placing Plaintiff in False Light

a. Prima Facie Case
To establish a prima facie case for invasion of privacy—publication by defendant of facts placing plaintiff in a false light—the following elements must be proved:

1) Publication of ***facts*** about plaintiff by defendant placing plaintiff in a ***false light*** in the public eye;

2) The "false light" is something that would be ***objectionable to a reasonable person*** under the circumstances; and

3) ***Malice*** on the part of defendant where the published matter is in the ***public interest***.

b. **Publication or Public Disclosure**
For liability to attach, there must be *publicity* concerning the "false light" facts; this requires *more* than "publication" in the defamation sense.

c. **What Is "False Light"?**
A fact will be deemed to present plaintiff in a false light if it attributes to him:

(i) Views that he does not hold, or

(ii) Actions that he did not take.

Note: This element involves falsity and, as such, may also involve defamation if the falsity affects reputation.

d. **Objectionable to Reasonable Person**
To be actionable, this "false light" must be something that would be objectionable to a reasonable person under the circumstances.

e. **Malice Necessary Where in Public Interest**
In *Time, Inc. v. Hill*, 385 U.S. 374 (1967), a case involving this particular invasion of privacy branch, the Supreme Court held that the First Amendment prohibits recovery for invasion of privacy in cases where the published matter is in the public interest, unless the plaintiff establishes that the defendant acted with malice. Malice here, as in *New York Times v. Sullivan*, goes to knowledge of falsity or reckless disregard for the truth.

After *Gertz* and *Dun & Bradstreet* (discussed *supra* under Defamation), the Supreme Court may be expected to give the states a slightly larger scope in which to protect privacy where a public figure is not involved. Thus, where the public interest in the information is not overriding and where the risks to the privacy interests of the private person are clear on the face of the material to a reasonably prudent publisher, the Supreme Court may choose in the future to permit an action in privacy without proof of malice in the *New York Times* sense. However, at least in public figure cases, the *Time, Inc. v. Hill* requirement of malice still holds. [*See* Hustler Magazine, Inc. v. Falwell, 485 U.S. 46 (1988)]

4. **Public Disclosure of Private Facts About Plaintiff**

a. **Prima Facie Case**
To establish a prima facie case for invasion of privacy—public disclosure of private facts about plaintiff—the following elements must be proved:

1) Publication or public disclosure by defendant of *private* information about the plaintiff; and

2) The matter made public is such that a *reasonable person would object* to having it made public.

b. **Publication or Public Disclosure**
For liability to attach, there must be publicity concerning a private fact; *i.e.,* the disclosure must be a public disclosure, not a private one.

c. **Facts Must Be Private**
The facts disclosed must be "private." For example, there is no liability for matters of public record, since these facts are not private.

d. **Disclosure Objectionable to Reasonable Person**
To be actionable, the disclosure of private facts must be such that a reasonable person would find it objectionable.
Example: Barbara showed, in a public exhibition, a movie of Sandy's cesarean operation. This may be actionable.

e. **Facts May Be True**
Liability may attach under this privacy branch if the elements of a prima facie case are satisfied even though the factual statement about the plaintiff is true.

f. Constitutional Privilege

The rationale of *Time, Inc. v. Hill* appears to encompass this branch of the invasion of privacy tort as well. In other words, if the matter is one of **legitimate public interest**, the publication is privileged if made without malice.

1) Effect of Passage of Time

The mere passage of time does not preclude the "public interest" characterization of a publication. Hence, it has frequently been held that the life of one **formerly** in the public eye has become public property, even though that person is no longer in the public eye.

Example: A magazine published the life history of a former child prodigy. This may be construed to be a matter in the public interest.

2) Absolute Privilege with Regard to Matters of Public Record

Where the matters republished are taken from official public records, there is an absolute constitutional privilege (*e.g.,* rape victim's name obtained from police records or court proceedings used in newspaper article).

5. Causation

The invasion of plaintiff's interest in privacy must have been **proximately caused** by defendant's conduct.

6. Proof of Special Damages Unnecessary

In an action for invasion of right to privacy, the plaintiff need not plead and prove special damages, provided the elements of a prima facie case are present. In other words, emotional distress and mental anguish **are** sufficient damages.

7. Basis of Liability

The basis for liability in a privacy action may rest upon an **intentional** or **negligent** invasion. It also appears that **strict liability** may be a sufficient basis (as in defamation).

8. Defenses to Invasions of Privacy

a. Consent

Consent is a defense to an action for invasion of the right to privacy. Some states, by statute, require that the consent be in writing. Here, as in all consent defense situations, the defendant may nonetheless be liable if the consent granted has been exceeded.

Example: Plaintiff consents to be interviewed, and a picture taken during the interview is used in conjunction with an advertisement for a product. Liability may attach.

Note that mistake, even if reasonable, as to whether consent was given (which in fact was not) is **not** a valid defense.

b. Defamation Defenses

Those defenses to actions for defamation that are based on **absolute and qualified privileges** appear applicable to those invasion of right to privacy actions predicated on publication grounds, *i.e.,* "false light" and "public disclosure of private facts" actions. Thus, for example, one may have an absolute privilege to comment as a participant in judicial proceedings or a qualified privilege to report public proceedings.

Note: Truth is **not** a good defense to most invasion of privacy actions. Similarly, inadvertence, good faith, and lack of malice generally are **not** good defenses.

9. Right of Privacy—Miscellaneous

a. Right Is Personal

The right of privacy is a personal right and does not extend to members of a family. The right of privacy does not survive the death of plaintiff and is not assignable.

b. Not Applicable to Corporations

Only individuals may avail themselves of a right to privacy action; it does not apply to corporations.

C. MISREPRESENTATION

1. Intentional Misrepresentation (Fraud, Deceit)

a. Prima Facie Case
To establish a prima facie case of intentional misrepresentation, fraud, or deceit, the following elements must be proved:

1) *Misrepresentation* made by defendant;

2) *Scienter*;

3) An *intent to induce* plaintiff's *reliance* on the misrepresentation;

4) *Causation* (*i.e.,* actual reliance on the misrepresentation);

5) *Justifiable reliance* by plaintiff on the misrepresentation; and

6) *Damages*.

b. The Misrepresentation
Usually, there is a requirement that the false representation be of a *material past or present fact*. In certain cases, however, a misrepresentation of opinion may be actionable. (This is really a justifiable reliance question. *See* below.)

1) No General Duty to Disclose
No general duty to disclose a material fact or opinion to one is imposed upon another. Thus, simple failure to disclose a material fact or opinion does not generally satisfy the first element of this cause of action. A few general *exceptions* exist, however:

a) Defendant stands in such a *fiduciary relationship* to plaintiff as would call for a duty of disclosure.

b) Defendant selling real property knows that plaintiff is unaware of, and cannot reasonably discover, material information about the transaction (*e.g.,* builder does not tell buyer that the house was built on a landfill).

c) Where defendant speaks and her *utterance deceives plaintiff,* she will be under a duty to inform plaintiff of the true facts.

2) Active Concealment Actionable
Where a person actively conceals a material fact, she is under a duty to disclose this fact, and failure to do so satisfies the first element of a prima facie case (*e.g.,* salesperson turns back odometer on an automobile).

c. Scienter
To establish a prima facie case, plaintiff must prove that defendant made the representation knowing it to be false or, alternatively, that it was made with reckless disregard as to its truth or falsity. This element of the prima facie case is often given the technical name of "scienter."

Example: A corporation's president stated falsely that last year's profits were $100,000 without having looked at a profit and loss statement. Scienter is present.

Note: If scienter is not present, defendant may still be liable for negligent misrepresentation (discussed below).

d. Intent to Induce Reliance
The defendant must have intended to induce plaintiff or a class of persons to which plaintiff belongs to act or refrain from acting in reliance on the misrepresentation.

1) Continuous Deception Exception
An exception exists where the misrepresentation is a "continuous deception," *e.g.,* mislabeling of product by manufacturer, misrepresentation in negotiable instrument. In such cases, it is not necessary that the reliance of a particular plaintiff be

intended. Anyone into whose possession the product or instrument has come may bring an action.

2) Third-Party Reliance Problem

One recurring problem is where the defendant communicates directly to one person and another relies upon the misrepresentation. In such cases, the defendant is viewed as intending to deceive the person who relies upon the misrepresentation *if the defendant could reasonably foresee that the plaintiff will have such reliance*.

Example: Chauncey sends an intentionally false profit statement to a stockbroker, and a customer of the stockbroker relies on this statement to his detriment. Liability exists.

e. Causation

Plaintiff must prove that the misrepresentation played a substantial part in inducing him to act as he did. In short, plaintiff must prove "actual reliance."

f. Justifiable Reliance

1) Reliance on Fact Almost Always Justified

Even though it may have been intended by defendant that plaintiff rely on the representation, plaintiff must nonetheless prove that such reliance was "justified." As a practical matter, the reliance of plaintiff on representations of fact is almost always justified. Only where the facts are obviously false is such reliance not justified.

a) No Duty to Investigate

Courts do not impose a duty on plaintiff to investigate the veracity of defendant's representation of fact. This is so even though it would be easy for plaintiff to do this. If, however, plaintiff does in fact investigate, he may not rely on representations by defendant inconsistent with the facts reasonably ascertainable from such investigation.

2) Reliance on Opinion Usually Not Justifiable

As a general matter, reliance on false statements of opinion, value, or quality will be viewed as unjustified. Some exceptions to this general rule do exist, however.

a) Superior Knowledge of Defendant

If the defendant making a false representation of opinion has a superior knowledge of the subject matter, then reliance by a person without such knowledge may be viewed as justified.

b) Statements of Law

Statements of law are viewed as statements of opinion and normally may not be justifiably relied upon. An exception exists where a statement is made by a lawyer to a layperson, in which case the "superior knowledge" rule operates. A further exception exists where the statement of law implies the existence of facts that are false.

Example: Defendant falsely states that the house she is offering for sale conforms to the city plumbing and electrical requirements. Liability exists.

c) Statements of Future Events

Statements of future events are viewed as statements of opinion and may not be justifiably relied upon. An exception exists if the statement of future events may be characterized as a statement of "present intent," which is viewed as a statement of fact.

Example: Defendant promises to pay plaintiff $50 per month installments for the next two years. This may be viewed as a statement of "fact." (Characterization of statements of future events as "present intent" statements is generally limited to those cases where the defendant has control over the future event, as in this example.)

g. Damages

In an action for intentional misrepresentation, plaintiff may recover *only* if he has suffered *actual pecuniary loss* as a result of the reliance on the false statement. Most courts use a contract measure of damages—plaintiff may recover the "benefit of the bargain," *i.e.,* the value of the property as represented less the value of the property as it actually is.

2. Negligent Misrepresentation

a. Prima Facie Case
The prima facie case for negligent misrepresentation is similar to that for intentional misrepresentation. The following elements must be proved:

1) *Misrepresentation* made by defendant in *business or professional capacity*;

2) *Breach of duty* toward *particular plaintiff*;

3) *Causation*;

4) *Justifiable reliance* by plaintiff upon the misrepresentation; and

5) *Damages*.

b. Liability Confined to Commercial Transactions
The ambit of liability for negligent misrepresentation is much more confined than that for deceit. Generally, the action is confined to only those misrepresentations made in a commercial setting, *i.e.,* made by the defendant in a business or professional capacity.

c. Duty Owed Only to Particular Plaintiff Whose Reliance Contemplated
Liability attaches for a negligent misrepresentation only if reliance by the particular plaintiff could be contemplated. In other words, defendant is under a duty of care only to those persons to whom the representation was made or to specific persons who defendant *knew* would rely on it. Foreseeability that the statement will be communicated to third persons may be sufficient to impose liability for deceit (above), but it does *not* suffice for negligent misrepresentation in most states.
Example: Chauncey sends a negligently prepared profit statement to a stockbroker, and a customer of the stockbroker relies upon this statement to her detriment. Liability does not exist. (*Compare* example in section 1.d.2), above.)

d. Other Elements
The elements of causation, justifiable reliance, and damages are analyzed the same as under intentional misrepresentation.

D. WRONGFUL INSTITUTION OF LEGAL PROCEEDINGS

1. Malicious Prosecution

a. Prima Facie Case
To establish a prima facie case for malicious prosecution, the following elements must be proved:

1) *Institution of criminal proceedings* against plaintiff;

2) Termination *favorable to plaintiff*;

3) *Absence of probable cause* for prosecution;

4) *Improper purpose* of defendant; and

5) *Damages*.

b. Institution of Criminal Proceedings
For liability to attach for malicious prosecution, the defendant must have initiated a *criminal* proceeding against plaintiff. The "initiation" of the proceeding can be by warrant, arrest, indictment, etc.

1) Defendant Must Initiate Proceedings

Remember, the defendant must have initiated the proceedings himself. Simply giving the full story to the prosecutor, whereupon the prosecutor decides to prosecute, is not sufficient for a later malicious prosecution action against the informer in most states.

2) Prosecuting Attorneys Privileged

Prosecuting attorneys are absolutely privileged and cannot be sued for malicious prosecution (even when they act in bad faith and without probable cause).

c. Termination of Proceedings in Plaintiff's Favor

The plaintiff may bring such an action only if the prior proceedings were terminated in her favor; *e.g.,* she was acquitted, the case was dismissed, charges were dropped, etc. The termination must demonstrate the *innocence* of the accused.

d. Absence of Probable Cause for Prior Proceedings

To recover, the plaintiff must establish that the defendant initiated the prior proceedings without probable cause. She may do so by showing *either* (i) that there were insufficient facts for a reasonable person to believe that plaintiff was guilty; *or* (ii) that the defendant did not actually believe the plaintiff to be guilty.

1) Effect of Indictment

Note that indictment by a grand jury is prima facie evidence of probable cause. However, failure of a grand jury to indict is *not* evidence that there was no probable cause.

2) Prior Action Based on Advice

If defendant instituted the prior proceedings on advice of counsel after full disclosure of the facts, this establishes probable cause.

e. Improper Purpose in Bringing Suit

For purposes of malicious prosecution, the malice or improper purpose element of the prima facie case is satisfied when it is shown that defendant's primary purpose in instituting the prior action was something other than bringing a person to justice.

f. Damages

Damages must be *proved*. Plaintiff may recover damages for all harms that are the proximate result of defendant's wrong, *e.g.,* expenses in defending criminal suit, embarrassment, etc. Punitive damages are often awarded, since defendant's improper purpose is, of course, already proved to establish the case.

g. False Arrest Distinguished

In a false arrest situation, the false arrest itself is illegal, *e.g.,* made without a valid warrant. In a malicious prosecution situation, the arrest itself is carried out in a lawful manner, but is pursuant to a maliciously instituted prosecution.

2. Wrongful Civil Proceedings

Most jurisdictions have extended the malicious prosecution action to encompass wrongfully instituted civil cases. The same general rules govern as apply in malicious prosecution. However, lack of probable cause is harder to show in civil actions because reasonable people would more readily file a doubtful case where the only consequences to the person sued are civil.

3. Abuse of Process

It is a tort to use any form of process—civil or criminal—to bring about a result other than that for which the form of process was intended; *e.g.,* defendant garnished an account to force plaintiff to sign a lease. The prima facie elements of the action are (i) the wrongful use of the process for an ulterior purpose, and (ii) some definite act or threat against plaintiff to accomplish the ulterior purpose.

a. Malicious Prosecution Distinguished

If the defendant uses the particular machinery of the law for the immediate purpose for which it was designed, he is not liable for abuse of process notwithstanding any malicious intent. Abuse of process is not the wrongful institution of the action or proceeding, but rather the improper use of process in connection therewith. Hence, the merits of the action itself are of no relevance. In contrast to malicious prosecution, therefore, neither want of probable cause nor favorable termination are elements of the tort.

E. INTERFERENCE WITH BUSINESS RELATIONS

To establish a prima facie case for interference with contract or prospective economic advantage, the following elements must be proved:

(i) Existence of a *valid contractual relationship* between plaintiff and a third party or a *valid business expectancy* of plaintiff;

(ii) *Defendant's knowledge* of the relationship or expectancy;

(iii) *Intentional interference* by defendant that induces a breach or termination of the relationship or expectancy; and

(iv) *Damage* to plaintiff.

1. Not Limited to Existing Contracts

Plaintiff has a cause of action not only for interference with existing contracts but also for interference with probable future business relationships for which plaintiff has a reasonable expectation of financial benefit.

Example: A real estate broker may have a cause of action against one who improperly diverts potential buyers of the property that the broker was selling.

2. Intent Required

Defendant must have *intended* to interfere with the existing or prospective contractual relationships of plaintiff. Most courts do not permit recovery for negligent interference with contract in the absence of some independent tort, such as negligent misrepresentation (*supra*).

3. Damages

Plaintiff must prove actual damage from the interference, but may also recover mental distress damages and punitive damages in appropriate cases.

4. Privileges

An interferor's conduct may be privileged where it is a proper attempt to obtain business for the interferor or protect its interests, particularly if the interference is only with plaintiff's prospective advantage rather than with an existing contract. What is proper depends on both the interests that the interferor is advancing and the means used to interfere.

Example: A bank collecting on an existing promissory note is privileged to induce the debtor to pay it off, even if that will cause the debtor to fail to satisfy obligations owing to other parties.

III. NEGLIGENCE

A. PRIMA FACIE CASE

To establish a prima facie case for negligence, the following elements must be proved:

1. The existence of a *duty* on the part of the defendant *to conform to a specific standard of conduct* for the protection of the plaintiff against an unreasonable risk of injury;

2. *Breach* of that duty by the defendant;

3. That the breach of duty by the defendant was the *actual and proximate cause* of the plaintiff's injury; and

4. *Damage* to the plaintiff's person or property.

B. THE DUTY OF CARE

1. Introduction—General Duty of Care

A general duty of care is imposed on all human activity. When a person engages in an activity, he is under a legal duty to act as an *ordinary, prudent, reasonable person*. It is presumed that an ordinary, prudent, reasonable person will take precautions against creating unreasonable risks of injury to other persons. Thus, if the defendant's conduct creates an unreasonable risk of injury to persons in the position of the plaintiff, the general duty of care extends from the defendant to the plaintiff. No duty is imposed on a person to take precautions against events that cannot reasonably be foreseen. Therefore, if at the time of the negligent conduct, no foreseeable risk of injury to a person in the position of the plaintiff is created by the defendant's act, the general duty of care does not extend from the defendant to the plaintiff.

In addition, certain other factors such as the status of the parties (*e.g.,* owners or occupiers of land) or statutes may limit or extend this general duty.

2. To Whom Is the Duty of Care Owed?

a. General Rule—Foreseeable Plaintiffs
A duty of care is owed only to foreseeable plaintiffs.

b. The "Unforeseeable" Plaintiff Problem

1) The Problem
The "unforeseeable" plaintiff problem arises when defendant breaches a duty to one plaintiff (P1) and also causes injury thereby to a second plaintiff (P2) to whom a foreseeable risk of injury might or might not have been created at the time of the original negligent act.

Example: An employee of Defendant negligently aided a passenger boarding the train, causing the passenger to drop a package. The package exploded, causing a scale a substantial distance away to fall upon a second passenger. Is the second passenger a foreseeable plaintiff?

2) The Solution(s)
Defendant's liability to P2 will depend upon whether the Andrews or Cardozo view in *Palsgraf* is adopted. [Palsgraf v. Long Island Railroad, 248 N.Y. 339 (1928)] Most courts considering this issue have followed the Cardozo view.

a) Andrews View
According to the Andrews view in *Palsgraf,* the second plaintiff (P2) may establish the existence of a duty extending from the defendant to her by showing that the defendant has breached a duty he owed P1. In short, defendant owes a duty of care to **anyone** who suffers injuries as a proximate result of his breach of duty to **someone**.

b) Cardozo View
According to the Cardozo view in *Palsgraf,* the second plaintiff (P2) can recover only if she can establish that a reasonable person would have foreseen a risk of injury to her in the circumstances, *i.e.,* that she was located in a foreseeable *"zone of danger."*

c. Specific Situations

1) Rescuers
A rescuer is a foreseeable plaintiff as long as the rescue is not wanton; hence, defendant is liable if he negligently puts himself or a third person in peril and plaintiff is injured in attempting a rescue.

2) Prenatal Injuries
Prenatal injuries are actionable; *i.e.,* a duty of care is owed toward a fetus. The fetus must have been *viable* at the time of injury. (Most states also permit a wrongful death action (VII.C.2., *infra*) if the fetus dies from the injuries.)

a) "Wrongful Life" Action Not Recognized
In most states, the failure to diagnose a congenital defect of the fetus or to properly perform a contraceptive procedure does *not* permit the unwanted child to recover damages for "wrongful life," even if the child is born handicapped.

b) Compare—"Wrongful Birth" and "Wrongful Pregnancy"
The child's parents, however, *do* have an action: either for failure to diagnose

the defect ("wrongful birth") or for failure to properly perform a contraceptive procedure ("wrongful pregnancy"). The mother can recover damages for the unwanted labor (medical expenses and pain and suffering). If the child has a defect, parents may recover the additional medical expenses to care for the child and, in some states, damages for emotional distress. If the child is born healthy in a wrongful pregnancy case, most cases do *not* permit the parents to recover child-rearing expenses, just damages for the unwanted labor.

3) Intended Beneficiaries of Economic Transactions

A third party for whose economic benefit a legal or business transaction is made (*e.g.*, the beneficiary of a will) is owed a duty of care if the defendant could reasonably foresee harm to that party if the transaction is done negligently.

3. What Is Applicable Standard of Care?

a. Basic Standard—The Reasonable Person

Defendant's conduct is measured against the reasonable, ordinary, prudent person. This reasonable person has the following characteristics, measured by an *objective* standard:

1) Physical Characteristics—Same as Defendant's

Notwithstanding application of the objective standard, the "reasonable person" is considered to have the *same physical characteristics as the defendant*. However, a person is expected to know his physical handicaps and is under a duty to exercise the care of a person with such knowledge; *e.g.*, it may be negligent for an epileptic to drive a car.

2) Average Mental Ability

Defendant must act as would a person with average mental ability. Unlike the rule as to physical characteristics, *individual mental handicaps are not considered*; *i.e.*, low IQ is no excuse. Likewise, insanity is no defense, and the defendant is held to the standard of a reasonable person under the circumstances.

3) Same Knowledge as Average Member of Community

Defendant is deemed to have knowledge of things known by the average member of the community, *e.g.*, that fire is hot. Again, the individual shortcomings of the particular defendant are *not* considered. On the other hand, a defendant with knowledge superior to that of the average person is required to use that knowledge.

b. Particular Standards of Conduct

Some persons are held to a standard of conduct different from that of the ordinary person.

1) Professionals

A person who is a professional or has special skills (*e.g.*, doctor, lawyer, airplane mechanic, etc.) is required to possess and exercise the knowledge and skill of a member of the profession or occupation in good standing in similar communities.

The professional must also use such superior judgment, skill, and knowledge as he actually possesses. Thus, a specialist might be held liable where a general practitioner would not.

a) Duty to Disclose Risks of Treatment

A doctor proposing a course of treatment or a surgical procedure has a duty to provide the patient with enough information about its risks to enable the patient to make an *informed consent* to the treatment. If an undisclosed risk was serious enough that a reasonable person in the patient's position would have withheld consent to the treatment, the doctor has breached this duty.

Example: Patient consents to an operation not necessary to save his life. Patient is not informed that there is a 40% probability of paralysis in such operations, and paralysis results. Since a reasonable person would not have consented to the operation had the risks been disclosed, Doctor has breached his duty of disclosure.

2) Children

A majority of courts take the view that a child is required to conform to the standard of care of a child of *like age, education, intelligence, and experience*. This permits a *subjective* evaluation of these factors.

a) Minimum Age for Capacity to Be Negligent

There is a minimum age for which it is meaningful to speak of a child being capable of conforming his conduct to a standard of care. Most courts, however, do not fix this age at any arbitrary figure. Each case is dealt with in terms of whether there is evidence that the individual child—plaintiff or defendant—has the experience, intelligence, maturity, training, or capacity to conform his conduct to a standard of care. It is unlikely, nonetheless, that a court would view a child *below the age of four* as having the capacity to be negligent. Or, to put it another way, it is unlikely that a court would impose a legal duty to avoid injuries to others or himself upon a child who is under four.

b) Children Engaged in Adult Activities

Where a child engages in an activity that is normally one that only adults engage in, most cases hold that he will be required to conform to the same standard of care as an adult in such an activity, *e.g.,* driving an automobile, flying an airplane, driving a motorboat.

3) Common Carriers and Innkeepers

Common carriers and innkeepers are required to exercise a very high degree of care toward their passengers and guests; *i.e.,* they are *liable for slight negligence*.

4) Automobile Driver to Guest

In most jurisdictions today, the duty owed by the driver of an automobile to a rider is one of ordinary care.

a) Guest Statutes

A few states have guest statutes. Under these statutes, the driver's only duty to a nonpaying rider is to *refrain from gross or wanton and willful misconduct*. Note that guest statutes do not apply to "passengers," *i.e.,* riders who contribute toward the expense of the ride; they are owed a duty of ordinary care.

5) Bailment Duties

a) Duties Owed by Bailor

(1) Gratuitous Bailments

Where the bailment is for the sole benefit of the bailee, the bailor need only inform the bailee of *known* dangerous defects in the chattel. There is no duty with regard to unknown defects.

(2) Bailments for Hire

Where the bailment is for hire, the bailor owes a duty to inform the bailee of *defects known* to him, *or* of which he *would have known* by the exercise of reasonable diligence.

b) Duties Owed by Bailee

(1) Sole Benefit of Bailor Bailment

Where the bailment is for the sole benefit of the bailor (bailee is uncompensated), only *slight diligence* is required, and liability will exist only where there is gross negligence.

(2) Sole Benefit of Bailee Bailment

Where the bailment is for the sole benefit of the bailee (*e.g.,* bailor gratuitously loans his property), *great diligence* is required, and liability will result from slight negligence.

(3) Mutual Benefit Bailments

Bailments for hire and pledges are for the mutual benefit of bailor and bailee, and *ordinary due care* is required.

c) Modern Trend

Today the trend is away from such classifications and toward a rule that considers whether the bailee exercised ordinary care under all the circumstances. These circumstances include, *e.g.,* value of the goods, type of bailment, custom of a trade, etc.

c. Standard of Care in Emergency Situations

The existence of an emergency, presenting little time for reflection, may be considered as among the circumstances under which the defendant acted; *i.e.,* he must act as the reasonable person would under the same emergency. The emergency may *not* be considered, however, if it is of the defendant's own making.

d. Standard of Care Owed by Owners and/or Occupiers of Land

In this section, duty problems are resolved by application of special rules that have been developed imposing duties on individuals because of their relationship to property. In some cases, the duty of the owner or occupier depends on whether the injury occurred on or off his premises; in others it depends on the legal status of the plaintiff in regard to the property, *i.e.,* trespasser, licensee, or invitee.

1) Duty of Possessor to Those Off the Premises

a) Natural Conditions

The general rule is that a landowner owes *no duty* to protect one outside the premises from natural conditions on the land.

Example: One is not liable for bugs that live in trees on one's land but that "visit" the neighbors from time to time.

Note: An exception exists for decaying trees next to sidewalks or streets in urban areas.

b) Artificial Conditions

As a general rule, there is also *no duty* owing for artificial conditions. Two major *exceptions* exist, however.

(1) Unreasonably Dangerous Conditions

A landowner is liable for damage caused by unreasonably dangerous artificial conditions or structures abutting adjacent land.

Example: While one would not be liable for natural collections of ice on the sidewalk, he might be liable for negligently permitting water to drain off his roof and form ice on the sidewalk.

(2) Duty to Protect Passersby

A landowner also has a duty to *take due precautions* to protect persons passing by from dangerous conditions, *e.g.,* by erecting a barricade to keep people from falling into an excavation at the edge of the property.

c) Conduct of Persons on Property

An owner of land has a duty to exercise reasonable care with respect to his own activities on the land and to control the conduct of others on his property so as to avoid unreasonable risk of harm to others outside the property.

2) Duties of Possessor to Those on the Premises

In most jurisdictions, the nature of a duty of an owner or occupier of land to those on the premises depends on the legal status of the plaintiff in regard to the property, *i.e.,* trespasser, licensee, or invitee.

a) Duty Owed to a Trespasser

(1) Definition of Trespasser

A trespasser is one who comes onto the land without permission or privilege.

(2) Duty Owed Undiscovered Trespassers

A landowner owes *no duty* to an undiscovered trespasser. He has no duty to inspect in order to ascertain whether persons are coming onto his property.

(3) Duty Owed Discovered Trespassers

Once a landowner discovers the presence of a trespasser, he is under a duty to exercise ordinary care to **warn** the trespasser of, or to **make safe**, **artificial conditions** known to the landowner that involve a **risk of death or serious bodily harm** and that the trespasser is unlikely to discover. There is no duty owed for natural conditions and less dangerous artificial conditions.

The owner or occupier also has a duty to exercise reasonable care in the exercise of *"active operations"* on the property.

(a) When Is a Trespasser "Discovered"?

A trespasser is discovered, of course, when she is actually noticed on the property by the owner or occupier. But in addition, a trespasser is viewed as discovered if the owner or occupier is notified by information sufficient for a reasonable person to conclude that someone is on the property.

(4) Duty Owed Anticipated Trespassers

The majority of states now treat anticipated trespassers on generally the same basis as discovered trespassers in terms of the duty owed them by the landowner.

(a) When Is a Trespasser "Anticipated"?

An "anticipated trespasser" situation arises where the landowner knows or should reasonably know of the presence of trespassers who constantly cross over a section of his land. (Although note that if the owner has posted "no trespassing" signs, this might serve to convert these "anticipated" trespassers into "undiscovered" trespassers.)

(5) Infant Trespassers—"Attractive Nuisance" Doctrine

Most courts impose upon a landowner the duty to exercise *ordinary care* to avoid reasonably foreseeable risk of harm to children caused by artificial conditions on his property. Under the general rule, to assess this special duty upon the owner or occupier of land in regard to children on his property, the plaintiff must show the following:

(i) There is a dangerous condition present on the land of which the owner is or should be aware;

(ii) The owner knows or should know that young persons frequent the vicinity of this dangerous condition;

(iii) The condition is likely to cause injury, *i.e.,* is dangerous, because of the child's inability to appreciate the risk; and

(iv) The expense of remedying the situation is slight compared with the magnitude of the risk.

(a) What Is a Dangerous Condition?

As noted above, a dangerous condition exists where something on the land is likely to cause injury to children because of their inability to appreciate the risk. This usually is an artificial condition, but in some circumstances a natural condition might suffice.

1] Where Applied

The attractive nuisance doctrine has been applied to abandoned automobiles, lumber piles, sand bins, and elevators. Bodies of water are generally not dangerous conditions because the dangers are viewed as obvious and well-known. If, however, a body of water contains elements of unusual danger to children, it may be characterized as a dangerous

condition, *e.g.,* logs or plants floating in water, or a thick
scum that appears to be a path on the water.

(b) Foreseeability of Harm Is True Basis of Liability
Under the traditional "attractive nuisance" doctrine, it was necessary for the child/plaintiff to establish that she was lured onto the
property by the attractive nuisance/dangerous condition. This no
longer is the case. Most jurisdictions have substantially revised
their attractive nuisance doctrines to bring them within general
negligence concepts. Foreseeability of harm to a child is the true
basis of liability and the element of attraction is important only
insofar as it indicates that the trespass should have been anticipated
by the landowner.

(6) Duty of Easement and License Holders to Trespassers
While employees and independent contractors acting on behalf of the
landowner have the status of the landowner, persons with an easement
or license to use the land do not; they must exercise reasonable care to
protect the trespasser.
Example: Power Company obtains an easement from Leonard to
run high-tension wires across Leonard's land. Because of
Power Company's negligent failure to maintain the
wires, one of them falls and injures Plaintiff, an undiscovered trespasser on Leonard's land. Power Company is
liable to Plaintiff.

b) Duty Owed to a Licensee

(1) Definition of Licensee
A licensee is one who enters on the land with the landowner's permission, express or implied, for her *own purpose or business* rather than
for the landowner's benefit.

(2) Duty Owed
The owner or occupier has a *duty to warn* the licensee of a dangerous
condition *known* to the owner or occupier that creates an unreasonable
risk of harm to the licensee and that the licensee is unlikely to discover.

(a) No Duty to Inspect
The owner or occupier has *no duty* to a licensee *to inspect* for
defects *nor to repair* known defects.

(b) Duty of Care for Active Operations
The owner or occupier also has a duty to *exercise reasonable care*
in the conduct of "active operations" for the protection of the
licensee whom he knows to be on the property.

(3) Social Guests Are Licensees
The social guest is a licensee. Performance of minor services for the
host does not make the guest an invitee.

c) Duty Owed to an Invitee

(1) Definition of Invitee
An invitee is a person who enters onto the premises in response to an
express or implied invitation of the landowner. Basically, there are two
classes of invitees:

(a) Those who enter as members of the public for a purpose for which
the land is *held open to the public,* *e.g.,* museums, churches,
airports; and

(b) Those who enter for a purpose *connected with the business* or
other interests of the landowner or occupier, *e.g.,* store customers
and persons accompanying them, employees, persons making
deliveries, etc.

(2) Characterization of Privileged Entrants

There may be a problem of characterization regarding persons entering the premises in exercise of a privilege, *e.g.,* police, firefighters, census takers, etc. In some situations, they are characterized as licensees, in others as invitees. The following rules should be noted:

(a) An entrant serving some ***purpose of the possessor*** generally is treated as an invitee, *e.g.,* garbage collectors, mail carriers, etc.

(b) One who comes ***under normal circumstances during working hours*** generally is treated as an invitee, *e.g.,* census takers, health inspectors, etc.

(c) Under the *"firefighter's rule,"* police officers and firefighters are generally treated like licensees rather than invitees, based on public policy or assumption of risk grounds. They cannot recover for a landowner's failure to inspect or repair dangerous conditions that are an inherent risk of their law enforcement or firefighting activity.

(3) Scope of Invitation

A person loses her status as an invitee if she exceeds the scope of the invitation—if she goes into a portion of the premises where her invitation cannot reasonably be said to extend. (Note that the invitation normally does extend to the entrance and steps of a building.)

Example: Gas station customer, buying gas, loses status as invitee when she leaves pumps and falls in grease pit inside station. (Reversion to licensee, perhaps even trespasser, status.)

(4) Duty Owed

The landowner owes an invitee a general duty to use reasonable and ordinary care in keeping the property reasonably safe for the benefit of the invitee. This general duty includes the ***duties owed to licensees*** (to warn of nonobvious, dangerous conditions known to the landowner and to use ordinary care in active operations on the property) ***plus*** a ***duty to make reasonable inspections*** to discover dangerous conditions and, thereafter, make them safe.

(a) Warning May Suffice

The requirement to "make safe" dangerous conditions usually is satisfied if a reasonable warning has been given.

(b) Obviousness of Danger

A duty to warn usually does not exist where the dangerous condition is so obvious that the invitee should reasonably have been aware of it. "Obviousness" is determined by all of the surrounding circumstances.

Example: A banana peel visible on the floor of a supermarket might not be considered obvious if a shopper's attention would likely be diverted by shelf displays.

d) Users of Recreational Land

In almost all states, a different standard applies by statute to users of recreational land. If an owner or occupier of open land permits the public to use the land for recreational purposes ***without charging a fee***, the landowner is not liable for injuries suffered by a recreational user unless the landowner ***willfully and maliciously*** failed to guard against or warn of a dangerous condition or activity.

Example: The owner of a large tract of undeveloped rural land who permits the general public to use a pond on the land for swimming and fishing would be covered by this type of statute, whereas the owner of a swimming pool who permits his house guests to swim whenever they visit would not be covered by the statute (he would owe his guests the usual duties owed to licensees).

e) Modern Trend—Rejection of Rules Based on Entrant's Legal Status
A strong minority of states have abolished the distinction between licensees and invitees and simply apply a reasonable person standard to dangerous conditions on the land. A few of these states have gone even further and abolished the trespasser distinction as well.

3) Duties of a Lessor of Realty

a) General Duty Rule
Ordinarily, tort liability in regard to conditions on the property is an *incident of occupation and control*. Thus, when the owner leases the entire premises to another, the lessee, coming into occupation and control, becomes burdened with the duty to maintain the premises in such a way as to avoid unreasonable risk of harm to others. Similarly, where the owner leases *portions* of the premises to tenants, the owner continues to be subject to liability for unreasonably dangerous conditions in those portions of the premises such as corridors, entry lobby, elevators, etc., used in common by all tenants, or by third persons, and over which the owner has retained occupation and control.

b) Exceptions
This basic duty, however, is subject to certain exceptions and extensions, as set forth below.

(1) Duty of Lessor to Lessee
The lessor is obligated to give *warning* to the lessee of *existing defects* in the premises of which the lessor is aware, or has reason to know, and which he knows the lessee is not likely to discover on reasonable inspection.

(2) Effect of Lessor's Covenant to Repair
If the lessor has covenanted to make repairs and reserves the right to enter the leased premises for the purpose of inspecting for defects and repairing them, he is subject to *liability for unreasonably dangerous conditions*.

(3) Effect of Voluntary Repairs by Lessor
If the lessor, though under no obligation to make repairs, does so, he is subject to liability if he does so *negligently*, failing to cure the defect; it is not necessary that his negligent repairs make the condition worse.

(4) Effect of Admission of the Public
If the lessor leases the premises knowing that the lessee intends to admit the public, the lessor is subject to *liability for unreasonably dangerous conditions existing at the time he transfers possession* where the nature of the defect and length and nature of the lease indicate that the tenant will not repair (*e.g.,* lessor rents convention hall to tenant for three-day period). This liability continues until the defect is actually remedied. A mere warning to the lessee concerning the defect is *not* sufficient.

(The duty of care of tenants and lessors is also covered in the Real Property outline.)

c) Tenant Remains Liable to Invitees and Licensees
Keep in mind that the potential liability of the lessor for dangerous conditions on the premises does not relieve the tenant, as occupier of the land, of liability for injuries to third persons from the dangerous conditions within the tenant's control.

4) Duties of Vendor of Realty
The vendor, at the time of transfer of possession to the vendee, has the *duty to disclose* concealed, unreasonably dangerous conditions of which the vendor knows or has reason to know, and of which he knows the vendee is ignorant and is not likely to discover on reasonable inspection. The vendor's responsibility

continues until the vendee should have, in the exercise of reasonable care in inspection and maintenance, discovered and remedied the defect.

e. Statutory Standards of Care

1) When Statutory Standard Applicable
The precise standard of care in a common law negligence case may be established by proving the applicability to that case of a statute providing for a *criminal* penalty. If this is done, the statute's specific duty will replace the more general common law duty of due care. In proving the availability of the statutory standard, plaintiff must show the following:

a) Plaintiff Within Protected Class
The plaintiff must show that she is in the class intended to be protected by the statute.
Example: A statute requiring a landowner to keep a building in safe condition is meant to protect only those rightfully on the premises and not trespassers.

b) Particular Harm to Be Avoided
The plaintiff must show that the statute was designed to prevent the type of harm that the plaintiff suffered.
Example: Violation of a Sunday closing law is not evidence of negligence in the case of an accident in a store on Sunday.

c) Standards Clearly Defined
The statute must be clear as to what standard of conduct is expected, where and when it is expected, and of whom it is expected.

2) Excuse for Violation
Violation of some statutes may be excused:

a) Where *compliance would cause more danger* than violation; *e.g.,* defendant drives onto wrong side of road to avoid hitting children who dart into his path; or

b) Where *compliance would be beyond defendant's control*; *e.g.,* blind pedestrian crosses against light.

3) Effect of Establishing Violation of Statute
Most courts still adhere to the rule that violation of a statute is "negligence per se." This means that plaintiff will have established a *conclusive presumption of duty and breach of duty.* (Plaintiff still must establish causation and damages to complete the prima facie case for negligence.)

A significant *minority* of courts, however, are unwilling to go this far. They hold either that (i) a rebuttable presumption as to duty and breach thereof arises, or (ii) the statutory violation is only prima facie evidence of negligence.

4) Effect of Compliance with Statute
Even though the violation of an applicable criminal statute may be negligence, compliance with it will *not necessarily establish due care*. If there are unusual circumstances or increased danger beyond the minimum that the statute was designed to meet, it may be found that there is negligence in not doing more.

5) Violation of a Civil Remedy Statute
Where the statute in question provides for a civil remedy, plaintiff will sue directly under the statute; *i.e.,* it is not a common law negligence case.

f. Duty Regarding Negligent Infliction of Emotional Distress
The duty to avoid negligent infliction of emotional distress is breached when defendant creates a foreseeable risk of physical injury to plaintiff, either by (i) causing a threat of physical impact that leads to emotional distress or (ii) directly causing severe emotional distress that by itself is likely to result in physical symptoms.
Examples: 1) Driver negligently ran a red light and skidded to a stop inches away from Pedestrian, who was properly crossing the street in a crosswalk.

Pedestrian's shock from nearly being run over caused her to suffer a heart attack. Pedestrian can recover for negligent infliction of emotional distress.

2) Doctor negligently confused Patient's file with another and told Patient he had a terminal illness. Patient, who in fact did not have the illness, was shocked and suffered a heart attack as a result. Patient can recover for negligent infliction of emotional distress. Although there was no threat of physical impact from Doctor's negligence, negligently providing a false diagnosis of a terminal illness creates a foreseeable risk of physical injury solely from the severe emotional distress that is caused.

1) Requirements
Two requirements must be satisfied for plaintiff to prevail:

a) Plaintiff Must Suffer Physical Injury from the Distress
For plaintiff to recover damages, defendant's conduct must cause plaintiff emotional distress that results in some *physical injury*. Emotional distress without physical injury is insufficient in most jurisdictions (but note that severe shock to the nervous system that causes physical symptoms is considered a physical injury).

(1) Special Situations Where Physical Injury Not Required
Several cases have permitted plaintiff to recover in the absence of physical injury in special situations where defendant's negligence creates a great likelihood of severe emotional distress, such as the erroneous report of a relative's death or the mishandling of a relative's corpse.

b) Plaintiff Must Be Within the "Target Zone" or "Zone of Danger"
If plaintiff's distress is caused by threat of physical impact, the threat must be directed at plaintiff or someone in her immediate presence. A bystander outside the "zone of danger" of physical injury who sees defendant negligently injuring another cannot recover damages for her own distress.

(1) Modern Trend Rejects "Target Zone" Requirement
A strong modern trend allows recovery based on foreseeability even if plaintiff is outside the "target zone" as long as (i) plaintiff and the person injured by defendant are *closely related*, (ii) *plaintiff was present* at the scene of the injury, and (iii) plaintiff *personally observed or perceived* the event.
Example: Mother sees her child struck by negligently driven automobile on the other side of the street and goes into shock. While the majority view would not allow recovery because Mother was not within the "target zone," the modern trend would allow recovery.

2) Compare—Emotional Distress Damages as Parasitic Element of Damages from Other Tort
The tort of negligent infliction of emotional distress is not the only way to recover damages for emotional distress. If plaintiff is the victim of another tort that causes physical injury, plaintiff can "tack on" damages for emotional distress as a "parasitic" element of his physical injury damages.
Example: Plaintiff was struck by a piece of metal when the engine blew on a defectively manufactured lawn mower. The piece of metal lodged in his spine at an inoperable location, significantly increasing his risk of future paralysis. In plaintiff's products liability action against the manufacturer of the lawn mower, plaintiff can recover damages not only for his physical injury but also for the emotional distress he suffers from his knowledge of the risk of paralysis, because it arose out of the physical injury caused by the defective product.

g. Affirmative Duties to Act

1) General Rule—No Duty to Act
As a general matter, no legal duty is imposed on any person to affirmatively act for the benefit of others. This general rule is, however, subject to exception, as indicated below.

2) Assumption of Duty to Act by Acting
One who gratuitously acts for the benefit of another, although under no duty to do so in the first instance, is then under a duty to act like an ordinary, prudent, reasonable person and continue the assistance.
Example: Defendant, under no duty to aid Plaintiff who has been injured, picks her up and carries her into a room. He then leaves her there unattended for seven hours and Plaintiff's condition is worsened. Defendant, having acted, may be considered to have breached his duty to act reasonably.

    a) "Good Samaritan" Statutes
A number of states have enacted statutes exempting licensed doctors, nurses, etc., who voluntarily and gratuitously render emergency treatment, from liability for ordinary negligence. Liability still exists, however, for gross negligence.

3) Peril Due to Defendant's Negligence
One whose negligence places another in a position of peril is under a duty to use reasonable care to aid or assist that person.

4) Special Relationship Between Parties
A defendant having a special relationship to the plaintiff (*e.g.,* parent-child, employer-employee) may be liable for failure to act if the plaintiff is in peril.

    a) Duty of Common Carriers
Common carriers are under a duty to use reasonable care to aid or assist passengers.

    b) Duty of Places of Public Accommodation
Innkeepers, restaurateurs, shopkeepers, and others who gather the public for profit have a duty to use reasonable care to aid or assist their patrons and to prevent injury to them from third persons.

5) Role of Contract in Creating Duty

    a) Nonfeasance—No Duty
In general, for mere nonfeasance, there is no tort duty of care, regardless of whether the defendant promises to undertake action gratuitously or for consideration. Liability for breach of contract extends only to parties in privity.

    b) Misfeasance—Due Care Required
However, for misfeasance, failure to perform with due care contractual obligations owed to one may give rise to violation of a legal duty.
Example: Pursuant to a contract with the building owner, Defendant inspected and repaired the elevator, and did so carelessly. The elevator operator is injured as a result. Defendant is liable to the operator.

6) Duty to Control Third Persons
Generally, there is no duty to prevent a third person from injuring another. In some situations, however, such an affirmative duty might be imposed. In such cases, it must appear that the defendant had the *actual ability* and *authority* to control the third person's action. Thus, for example, bailors may be liable for the acts of their bailees, parents may be liable for the acts of their children, employers may be liable for the acts of their employees, etc.

It is generally required for imposition of such a duty that the defendant *knows* or *should know* that the third person is likely to commit such acts as would require the exercise of control by the defendant.

C. BREACH OF DUTY

Where the defendant's conduct falls short of that level required by the applicable standard of care owed to the plaintiff, she has breached her duty. Whether the duty of care is breached in an individual case is a question for the trier of fact.

Proof of breach is twofold: *First*, it must be shown what in fact happened. *Second*, it must be shown from these facts that the defendant acted unreasonably. Proof of what happened may be established by either direct or circumstantial evidence. Other matters may also be offered into evidence to establish the standard by which defendant's conduct is to be measured, *e.g.,* custom or usage, applicability of a statute, etc.

1. Custom or Usage

Custom or usage may be introduced to establish the standard of care in a given case. However, customary methods of conduct do not furnish a test that is conclusive for controlling the question of whether certain conduct amounted to negligence.

2. Violation of Statute

As we have seen above, the existence of a duty owed to plaintiff and breach thereof may be established by proof that defendant violated an applicable statute.

3. Res Ipsa Loquitur

The circumstantial evidence doctrine of res ipsa loquitur ("the thing speaks for itself") deals with those situations where the fact that a particular injury occurred may itself establish or tend to establish a breach of duty owed. Where the facts are such as to strongly indicate that plaintiff's injuries resulted from defendant's negligence, the trier of fact may be permitted to infer defendant's liability. Res ipsa loquitur requires the plaintiff to show the following:

a. Inference of Negligence

Plaintiff must establish that the accident causing his injury is the type that would not normally occur unless someone was negligent.

Example: A windowpane fell from a second story window in Defendant's building, landing on Plaintiff. Res ipsa loquitur may apply.

b. Negligence Attributable to Defendant

Plaintiff must establish evidence connecting defendant with the negligence in order to support a finding of liability. Usually, this requirement is satisfied by showing that the instrumentality that caused the injury was in the *sole control* of defendant. To satisfy this requirement, it is enough to show that the power of control and opportunity to exercise that power are with defendant; actual possession of the instrumentality is not necessary.

1) Multiple Defendants Problem

Where more than one person may have been in control of the instrumentality, res ipsa loquitur generally may *not* be used to establish a prima facie case of negligence against any individual party.

Example: Plaintiff left the operating room with an injury to part of her body that was healthy prior to entering the operating room. The injury was not in the zone of the original operation. Res ipsa loquitur may not be available to establish that any individual in that room was negligent. This is so despite the fact that, clearly, someone was negligent. (A substantial *minority* of courts in such cases where defendants have control of the evidence require each defendant to establish that his negligence did not cause the injury. [*See, e.g.,* Ybarra v. Spangard, 25 Cal. 2d 486 (1944)])

Compare: The doctrine would be available where a particular defendant had the power of control over the site of the injury. For example, Plaintiff sues Surgeon after a sponge was left in his body at the site of the surgery. Even though Surgeon left it to her assistants to remove the sponges and close up the wound, her responsibility and power of control over the surgery itself allows Plaintiff to use res ipsa loquitur against her.

c. Plaintiff's Freedom from Negligence

Plaintiff must also establish that the injury was not attributable to him, but may do so by his own testimony.

d. Effect of Res Ipsa Loquitur

1) No Directed Verdict for Defendant
The doctrine, where applicable, does not change the burden of proof, nor does it create a presumption of negligence. Where the res ipsa element has been proved, the plaintiff has made a prima facie case and no directed verdict may be given for the defendant.

2) Effect of Defendant's Evidence of Due Care
However, the effect of defendant's evidence that due care was exercised has the same effect in a res ipsa case as in all other cases. If the jury rejects the defendant's evidence and draws the permissible inference of negligence, it will find for the plaintiff. If defendant's evidence overcomes the permissible inference that may be drawn from the res ipsa proof, the jury may find for the defendant. Such a finding for the defendant may result even where defendant rests without offering evidence on the issue if the jury elects not to infer negligence.

D. CAUSATION

1. Actual Cause (Causation in Fact)
Before the defendant's conduct can be considered a proximate cause of plaintiff's injury, it must first be a *cause in fact* of the injury. Several tests exist:

a. "But For" Test
An act or omission to act is the cause in fact of an injury when the injury would not have occurred **but for** the act.
Example: Failure to provide a fire escape is a cause of death of one who is thereby unable to flee a fire, but it is not a cause of death of one who suffocated in bed.

1) Concurrent Causes
The "but for" test applies where several acts combine to cause the injury, but none of the acts standing alone would have been sufficient (*e.g.,* two negligently driven cars collide, injuring a passenger). But for any of the acts, the injury would not have occurred.

b. Additional Tests
Under certain circumstances, the "but for" test is inadequate to determine causation in fact. The courts must rely upon other tests.

1) Joint Causes—Substantial Factor Test
Where several causes concur to bring about an injury—and any one alone would have been sufficient to cause the injury—it is sufficient if defendant's conduct was a "substantial factor" in causing the injury.
Example: Two fires meet and burn a farm. Either fire alone would have done the damage without the other. Under the "but for" test, neither was the "cause," since, looking at either fire alone, the loss would have occurred without it. Rather than reach this result, the courts consider as causes all those things that were a "substantial factor" in causing injury.

2) Alternative Causes Approach

a) Burden of Proof Shifts to Defendants
A problem of causation exists where two or more persons have been negligent, but uncertainty exists as to which one caused plaintiff's injury. Under the alternative causes approach, plaintiff must prove that harm has been caused to him by one of them (with uncertainty as to which one). The burden of proof then shifts to defendants, and each must show that his negligence is not the actual cause.
Example: Alex and Basil both negligently fire shotguns in Clara's direction. Clara is hit by one pellet, but she cannot tell which gun fired the shot. Under the alternative causes approach, Alex and Basil will have to prove that the pellet was not theirs. If unable to do this, they may both be liable. [Summers v. Tice, 33 Cal. 2d 80 (1948)]

b) Applied in Enterprise Liability Cases
This concept has been extended in some cases to encompass industry groups.

Example: Daughters of women who took the anti-miscarriage drug diethylstilbestrol ("DES") contracted cancer as a result of the drug manufacturer's negligence. However, because the cancer appeared many years after the DES was ingested, it was usually impossible to determine which manufacturer of DES had supplied the drug taken by any particular plaintiff. Several courts have required all producers of DES unable to prove their noninvolvement to pay in proportion to their percentage of the market share. [*See* Sindell v. Abbott Laboratories, 26 Cal. 3d 588, *cert. denied,* 449 U.S. 912 (1980)]

2. Proximate Cause (Legal Causation)
In addition to being a cause in fact, the defendant's conduct must also be a proximate cause of the injury. Not all injuries "actually" caused by defendant will be deemed to have been proximately caused by his acts. Thus, the doctrine of proximate causation is a *limitation of liability* and deals with liability or nonliability for unforeseeable or unusual consequences of one's acts.

a. General Rule of Liability
The general rule of proximate cause is that the defendant is liable for all harmful results that are *the normal incidents of and within the increased risk caused by* his acts. In other words, if one of the reasons that make defendant's act negligent is a greater risk of a particular harmful result occurring, and that harmful result does occur, defendant generally is liable. This test is based on *foreseeability*.

b. Direct Cause Cases
A direct cause case is one where the facts present an *uninterrupted chain* of events from the time of the defendant's negligent act to the time of plaintiff's injury. In short, there is no external intervening force of any kind.

1) Foreseeable Harmful Results—Defendant Liable
If a particular harmful result was at all foreseeable from defendant's negligent conduct, the unusual manner in which the injury occurred or the unusual timing of cause and effect is irrelevant to defendant's liability.

Example: D is driving her sports car down a busy street at a high rate of speed when a pedestrian steps out into the crosswalk in front of her. D has no time to stop, so she swerves to one side. Her car hits a parked truck and bounces to the other side of the street, where it hits another parked vehicle, propelling it into the street and breaking the pedestrian's leg. D is liable despite the unusual way in which she caused the injury to the pedestrian.

2) Unforeseeable Harmful Results—Defendant Not Liable
In the rare case where defendant's negligent conduct creates a risk of a harmful result, but an entirely different and totally unforeseeable type of harmful result occurs, most courts hold that defendant is not liable for that harm.

Example: D, a cabdriver, is driving too fast on a busy elevated highway, threatening P, his passenger, with injury. Without warning, the section of highway that D is on collapses because its support beams had deteriorated with age. P is seriously injured. Even if D's negligent conduct was an actual cause of P's injury (because the cab would not have been on that section of the highway but for D's speeding), courts would not hold D liable for the injury to P.

c. Indirect Cause Cases
An indirect cause case is one where the facts indicate that a force came into motion *after* the time of defendant's negligent act and combined with the negligent act to cause injury to plaintiff. In short, indirect cause cases are those where *intervening forces* are present. Whether an intervening force will cut off defendant's liability for plaintiff's injury is determined by foreseeability.

1) Foreseeable Results Caused by Foreseeable Intervening Forces—Defendant Liable
Where defendant's negligence caused a foreseeable harmful response or reaction

from an intervening force or created a foreseeable risk that an intervening force would harm plaintiff, defendant is liable for the harm caused.

a) Dependent Intervening Forces

Dependent intervening forces are normal responses or reactions to the situation created by defendant's negligent act. ***Dependent intervening forces are almost always foreseeable***.

The following are common dependent intervening forces:

(1) Subsequent Medical Malpractice

The original tortfeasor is usually liable for the aggravation of plaintiff's condition caused by the malpractice of plaintiff's treating physician.

(2) Negligence of Rescuers

Generally, rescuers are viewed as foreseeable intervening forces, and the original tortfeasor is liable for their negligence.

(3) Efforts to Protect Person or Property

Defendant is liable for negligent efforts on the part of persons to protect life or property of themselves or third persons endangered by defendant's negligence.

(4) "Reaction" Forces

Where defendant's actions cause another to "react" (*e.g.,* negligently firing a gun at another's feet), liability attaches for any harm inflicted by the "reacting" person on another.

(5) Subsequent Disease

The original tortfeasor is liable for diseases caused in part by the weakened condition in which defendant has placed the plaintiff by negligently injuring her; *e.g.,* injury caused by defendant weakens plaintiff, making her susceptible to pneumonia.

(6) Subsequent Accident

Where the plaintiff suffers a subsequent injury following her original injury, and the original injury was a substantial factor in causing the second accident, the original tortfeasor is usually liable for damages arising from the second accident. For example, as a result of defendant's negligence, plaintiff's leg is broken. Walking on crutches, plaintiff falls and breaks her other leg.

b) Independent Intervening Forces

Independent intervening forces also operate on the situation created by defendant's negligence but are independent actions rather than natural responses or reactions to the situation. Independent intervening forces may be foreseeable where ***defendant's negligence increased the risk that these forces would cause harm*** to the plaintiff.

The following are common fact situations involving independent intervening forces:

(1) Negligent Acts of Third Persons

Defendant is liable for harm caused by the negligence of third persons where such negligence was a foreseeable risk created by defendant's conduct.
Example: D negligently blocked a sidewalk, forcing P to walk in the roadway, where he is struck by a negligently driven car. D is liable to P.

(2) Criminal Acts and Intentional Torts of Third Persons

If defendant's negligence created a foreseeable risk that a third person would commit a crime or intentional tort, defendant's liability will not be cut off by the crime or tort.
Example: D, a parking lot attendant, negligently left the keys in P's car and the doors unlocked when he parked it, allowing a thief to steal it. D is liable to P.

(3) Acts of God

Acts of God will not cut off defendant's liability if they are foreseeable.

Example: D, a roofer, negligently left a hammer on P's roof at the end of the day. P is struck by the hammer when a strong wind blows it off the roof. D is liable to P.

2) Foreseeable Results Caused by Unforeseeable Intervening Forces—Defendant Usually Liable

The problem: Defendant is negligent because his conduct threatens a result of a particular kind that will injure plaintiff. This result is ultimately produced by an *unforeseeable* intervening force. Most courts would generally find liability here because they give greater weight to foreseeability of result than to foreseeability of the intervening force. An exception exists, however, where the intervening force is an unforeseeable *crime* or *intentional tort* of a third party; it will be deemed a "superseding force" that cuts off defendant's liability (*see* discussion below).

Examples: 1) Defendant failed to clean residue out of an oil barge, leaving it full of explosive gas. Negligence, of course, exists since an explosion resulting in harm to any person in the vicinity was foreseeable from any one of several possible sources. An unforeseeable bolt of lightning struck the barge, exploding the gas and injuring workers on the premises. Defendant is liable.

2) Same facts as above example, except that an arsonist caused the explosion. Most courts would not hold Defendant liable here. They think it unfair to make him responsible for such malevolent conduct. The important point here is that an unforeseeable intervening force may still relieve the defendant of liability if it is an unforeseeable crime or intentional tort of a third party.

3) Unforeseeable Results Caused by Foreseeable Intervening Forces—Defendant Not Liable

Most intervening forces that produce unforeseeable results are considered to be unforeseeable intervening forces (*see* below). Similarly, most results caused by foreseeable intervening forces are treated as foreseeable results. In the rare case where a foreseeable intervening force causes a totally unforeseeable result, most courts would not hold the defendant liable.

Example: D, a cabdriver, was driving recklessly during a violent windstorm that was blowing large branches and other debris onto the road, creating a risk to P, his passenger, that D would not be able to stop the cab in time to avoid an accident. D slammed on his brakes to avoid a large branch in the road, causing his cab to swerve sideways onto the shoulder of the road. Before he could proceed, another branch crashed onto the roof of the cab, breaking a window and causing P to be cut by flying glass. D is not liable to P even though his negligent driving was the actual (but for) cause of P's injury and the wind that was blowing the branches down was a foreseeable intervening force.

4) Unforeseeable Results Caused by Unforeseeable Intervening Forces—Defendant Not Liable

As a general rule, intervening forces that produce unforeseeable results (*i.e.,* results that were not within the increased risk created by defendant's negligence) will be deemed to be unforeseeable and *superseding*. A superseding force is one that serves to **break the causal connection** between defendant's initial negligent act and the ultimate injury, and itself becomes a direct, immediate cause of the injury. Thus, defendant will be relieved of liability for the consequences of his antecedent conduct.

Example: D negligently blocks a road, forcing P to take an alternate road. Another driver negligently collides with P on this road, injuring him. Even though D is an actual (but for) cause of P's injury, the other driver's conduct is an unforeseeable intervening force because D's negligence did not increase the risk of its occurrence. Thus, the other driver is a superseding force that cuts off D's liability for his original negligent act.

d. Unforeseeable Extent or Severity of Harm—Defendant Liable
In both direct cause and indirect cause cases, the fact that the extent or severity of the harm was not foreseeable does not relieve defendant of liability; *i.e.,* the tortfeasor takes his victim as he finds him. Thus, where defendant's negligence causes an aggravation of plaintiff's existing physical or mental illness, defendant is liable for the damages caused by the aggravation.

Example: A car negligently driven by D collides with a car driven by P. P suffers a slight concussion, which was foreseeable, and also suffers a relapse of an existing mental illness, which was not foreseeable. D is liable for all of P's damages.

E. DAMAGES

Damage is an essential element of plaintiff's prima facie case for negligence. This means *actual* harm or injury. Unlike for some of the intentional torts, damage will not be presumed. Thus, nominal damages are not available in an action in negligence; some proof of harm must be offered.

1. Damages Recoverable in the Action

a. Personal Injury
Plaintiff is to be compensated for *all* his damages (past, present, and prospective), both special and general. This includes fair and adequate compensation for medical expenses and lost earnings plus amounts for pain and suffering (including emotional distress), together with compensation for impaired future earning capacity. The latter will be discounted to present value so as to avoid an excess award; *i.e.,* plaintiff receives an amount that, if securely invested, would produce the income that the jury wishes him to have.

1) Foreseeability Irrelevant
As noted above in the proximate cause section, it is generally not necessary to foresee the extent of the harm. In other words, a tortfeasor takes the victim as he finds him.

b. Property Damage
The measure of damages for property damage is the reasonable *cost of repair*, or, if the property has been almost or completely destroyed, its *fair market value* at the time of the accident.

c. Punitive Damages
In addition to the various types of compensatory damages discussed above, plaintiff may also be able to recover punitive damages in most jurisdictions if defendant's conduct was "wanton and willful," reckless, or malicious.

d. Nonrecoverable Items
Certain items are not recoverable as damages in negligence actions. These include:

1) Interest from date of damage in personal injury action; and

2) Attorneys' fees.

2. Duty to Mitigate Damages
As in all cases, the plaintiff has a duty to take reasonable steps to mitigate damages—in property damage cases to preserve and safeguard the property, and in personal injury cases to seek appropriate treatment to effect a cure or healing and to prevent aggravation. Failure to mitigate precludes recovery of any additional damages caused by aggravation of the injury.

3. Collateral Source Rule
As a general rule, damages are not reduced or mitigated by reason of benefits received by plaintiff from other sources, *e.g.,* health insurance, sick pay from employer. Hence, at trial, defendants may not introduce evidence relating to any such financial aid from other sources. A growing number of states have made exceptions to this rule in certain types of actions (*e.g.,* medical malpractice actions), allowing defendants to introduce evidence of insurance awards or disability benefits.

Note: These damages rules also are generally applicable to actions based on intentional torts.

F. DEFENSES TO NEGLIGENCE

1. Contributory Negligence

a. Standard of Care for Contributory Negligence

1) General Rule
The standard of care required is the same as that for ordinary negligence.

2) Rescuers
It is not contributorily negligent to attempt to rescue a person or property from danger unless the attempt is completely reckless under the circumstances.

3) Remaining in Danger
It may be contributorily negligent to fail to remove oneself from danger, *e.g.,* remaining in a car with a drunk driver.

4) Violation of Statute by Plaintiff
Plaintiff's contributory negligence may be established by his violation of a statute under the same rules that govern whether a statute can establish defendant's negligence (*see* B.3.e., *supra*).

5) As Defense to Violation of Statute by Defendant
Contributory negligence is ordinarily a defense to negligence proved by defendant's violation of an applicable statute. But where the defendant's negligence arose from violation of a statute designed to protect this particular class of plaintiffs from their own incapacity and lack of judgment, then plaintiff's contributory negligence is *not* a defense.

Example: D is exceeding the speed limit in a school zone when a child on his way to school darts into the street without looking. Because of her speed, D is unable to stop and hits the child. Any contributory negligence on the child's part is not a defense to D's violation of the statute, because the statute was designed to protect children on their way to school.

b. Avoidable Consequences Distinguished
As we have seen, plaintiff owes a duty to mitigate damages to person or property after the damage is inflicted. If he does not properly do this, then damages will be mitigated. Failure to do this, however, is an avoidable consequence, not contributory negligence.

c. No Defense to Intentional Torts
Contributory negligence is never a defense to an action for an intentional tort or for willful or wanton misconduct.

d. Effect of Contributory Negligence
At common law, plaintiff's contributory negligence completely barred his right to recover. This was so even though the degree of defendant's negligence was much greater than that of plaintiff.

The severe consequences of strict application of contributory negligence rules initially caused courts to develop "escape" doctrines, such as *last clear chance* (below). More recently, however, most jurisdictions have rejected entirely the "all or nothing" approach of contributory negligence in favor of a *comparative negligence* system (discussed *infra*).

e. Last Clear Chance
The doctrine of last clear chance, sometimes called "the humanitarian doctrine," permits the plaintiff to recover *despite* his own contributory negligence. Under this rule, the person with the last clear chance to avoid an accident who fails to do so is liable for negligence. (In effect, last clear chance is plaintiff's rebuttal against the defense of contributory negligence.)

Example: Bowater negligently parked his car on the railroad tracks. The train engineer saw him in time to stop but failed to do so. The engineer had the last clear chance, and thus the railroad will be liable for the accident.

1) "Helpless" vs. "Inattentive" Peril
Many cases distinguish between "helpless" and "inattentive" peril situations in applying last clear chance rules.

a) Helpless Peril
Helpless peril exists where plaintiff, through his contributory negligence, puts himself in a position of actual peril from which he cannot extricate himself. In many states, defendant is liable under these circumstances if she had either *actual* knowledge of plaintiff's predicament or if she *should have known* of plaintiff's predicament. Other states require actual knowledge.

b) Inattentive Peril
Inattentive peril exists where plaintiff, through his own negligence, is in a position of actual peril from which he could extricate himself if he were attentive. Almost all courts require *actual* knowledge of plaintiff's predicament on defendant's part.

2) Prior Negligence Cases
For last clear chance to operate, defendant must have been able to avoid harming plaintiff *at the time of the accident*. In short, defendant must have had the "last clear chance" to avoid the accident. Hence, if defendant's only negligence had occurred earlier, *e.g.,* she negligently failed to have the steering wheel fixed, the courts will not apply last clear chance.

f. Imputed Contributory Negligence
Driver and Passenger are involved in an automobile accident with Cyclist. Driver is negligent; Cyclist is also negligent. Passenger, who is injured, brings an action against Cyclist. Cyclist argues that liability should be denied because of Driver's negligence to the same extent as if Passenger had been negligent himself. This is the concept of "imputed contributory negligence."

1) General Rule—Plaintiff May Proceed Against Both Negligent Parties
As a general rule, a plaintiff's action for his damages is *not* barred by imputed contributory negligence. He may proceed against both negligent parties as joint tortfeasors to the extent that each is a legal cause of the harm.

2) When Contributory Negligence Is Imputed
Contributory negligence will be imputed *only* where the plaintiff and the negligent person stand in such a relationship to each other that the courts find it proper to charge plaintiff with that person's negligence, *i.e.,* where plaintiff would be found *vicariously* liable for the negligent person's conduct if a third party had brought the action. (*See also* Vicarious Liability, VII.A., *infra.*)

3) Common Fact Situations
The following situations should be noted for bar examination purposes:

a) Master and Servant
The contributory negligence of the servant (employee, agent) acting within the scope of employment will be imputed to the master (employer, principal) when the latter is a plaintiff suing a third person.

b) Partners and Joint Venturers
The contributory negligence of one partner or joint venturer will be imputed to the other when the other is a plaintiff suing a third person.

c) Husband and Wife
The contributory negligence of one spouse will *not* be imputed to the other when the other is a plaintiff suing a third person.

d) Parent and Child
The contributory negligence of the parent or guardian is *not* imputed to the child, nor is the contributory negligence of the child imputed to the parent in actions against a third party.

Note: As to sections c) and d) above, note that in a spouse's action for loss of the other spouse's services, or a parent's action for loss of a child's services or recovery of his medical expenses, the contributory negligence of the injured spouse or child **will** bar recovery by the other spouse or by the parent. This is not because negligence is imputed, but because the loss of services action is derivative and cannot succeed unless the main action succeeds (*see* VII.D.3., *infra*). This result would also be obtained in a wrongful death action.

e) Automobile Owner and Driver
Unless the automobile owner would be vicariously liable for the driver's negligence (because, *e.g.,* the driver was a servant within the scope of employment), the contributory negligence of the driver will **not** be imputed to her. (Remember, in situations where the owner is a passenger, she may be liable for her **own negligence** in not preventing the accident.)

2. Assumption of Risk
The plaintiff may be denied recovery if he assumed the risk of any damage caused by the defendant's acts. This assumption may be expressed or implied. To have assumed risk, either expressly or impliedly, the plaintiff must have **known of the risk** and **voluntarily** assumed it. It is irrelevant that plaintiff's choice is unreasonable.

a. Implied Assumption of Risk
Implied assumption of risk situations are harder to resolve as, of course, the fact issues are difficult to prove.

1) Knowledge of Risk
Plaintiff must have known of the risk. Knowledge may be implied where the risk is one that the average person would clearly appreciate, *e.g.,* risk of being hit by a foul ball in a baseball game.

2) Voluntary Assumption
The plaintiff must voluntarily go ahead in the face of the risk. However, plaintiff may not be said to have assumed the risk where there is no available alternative to proceeding in the face of the risk, *e.g.,* the only exit from a building is unsafe.

3) Certain Risks May Not Be Assumed
Because of public policy considerations, the courts uniformly hold that some risks may not be assumed. These include:

a) Common carriers and public utilities are not permitted to limit their liability for personal injury by a disclaimer on, *e.g.,* a ticket, a posted sign, etc.

b) When a statute is enacted to protect a class, members of that class will not be deemed to have assumed any risk.
Example: When a statute imposes safety regulations on an employer, the employee is held not to have assumed the risk where the statute is violated.

c) Risks will not be assumed in situations involving fraud, force, or an emergency. Thus, for example, one could take action to save his person or property without assuming a risk unless his actions involve an unreasonable risk out of proportion to the value of those rights.

b. Express Assumption of Risk
The risk may be assumed by express agreement. Such exculpatory clauses in a contract, intended to insulate one of the parties from liability resulting from his own negligence, are closely scrutinized but are generally enforceable. (Note that it is more difficult to uphold such an exculpatory clause in an adhesion contract.)

c. No Defense to Intentional Torts
Assumption of risk is not a defense to intentional torts. It is, however, a defense to wanton or reckless conduct.

3. Comparative Negligence
A substantial **majority** of states now permit a contributorily negligent plaintiff to recover a percentage of his damages under some type of **comparative negligence** system. In every

case where contributory negligence is shown, the trier of fact weighs plaintiff's negligence against that of defendant and reduces plaintiff's damages accordingly.

Example: Defendant negligently drove through a stop sign and collided with Plaintiff, who was contributorily negligent by driving inattentively. Plaintiff suffers damages of $100,000. If a jury finds that Plaintiff was 30% negligent and Defendant was 70% negligent, Plaintiff will recover $70,000.

a. Types of Comparative Negligence

1) "Partial" Comparative Negligence
Most comparative negligence jurisdictions will still bar plaintiff's recovery if his negligence passes a threshold level. In some of these states, a plaintiff may recover if his negligence was *less serious* than that of defendant (*i.e.,* plaintiff may recover only if he was 49% or less at fault). In the other jurisdictions, a plaintiff may recover if his negligence was *no more serious* than that of defendant (*i.e.,* plaintiff may recover only if he was 50% or less at fault).

a) Multiple Defendants
If several defendants have contributed to plaintiff's injury, most of these states use a "combined comparison" approach to determine the threshold level (*i.e.,* plaintiff's negligence is compared with the total negligence of all the defendants combined).

2) "Pure" Comparative Negligence
The "pure" variety of comparative negligence, adopted in a third of the comparative negligence states, allows recovery no matter how great plaintiff's negligence is (*e.g.,* if plaintiff is 90% at fault and defendant 10%, plaintiff may still recover 10% of his damages).

b. Comparative Negligence Illustrations

1) Partial Comparative Negligence Jurisdiction—Single Defendant
Plaintiff is 30% negligent and Defendant is 70% negligent in causing the accident. Each party suffers $100,000 in damages. Plaintiff will recover $70,000 from Defendant—$100,000 minus 30% ($30,000). Defendant will recover nothing from Plaintiff because Defendant was more than 50% at fault.

2) Partial Comparative Negligence Jurisdiction—Multiple Defendants
Plaintiff is 40% negligent in causing the accident and suffers $100,000 in damages. D1 is 35% negligent and D2 is 25% negligent. Plaintiff can recover $60,000 from either D1 or D2 under joint and several liability rules (*infra,* VII.B.1.). (The paying defendant can then go against the nonpaying defendant for contribution, discussed *infra* at VII.B.3.) Note that if D1 or D2 also suffered damages, each of them would have a claim against the other two negligent parties because each one's negligence is less than the total negligence of the other two.

3) Pure Comparative Negligence Jurisdiction
Same facts as in illustration 1). Plaintiff has a right to recover $70,000 from Defendant, and Defendant has a right to recover $30,000 from Plaintiff. Defendant's damages will be offset against Plaintiff's damages, and Plaintiff will have a net recovery of $40,000.

c. Effect on Other Doctrines

1) Last Clear Chance
Last clear chance is *not* used in most comparative negligence jurisdictions.

2) Assumption of Risk

a) Implied Assumption of Risk
Most comparative negligence jurisdictions have abolished entirely the defense of implied assumption of risk. In these jurisdictions, traditional assumption of risk situations must be broken down into two categories:

(1) When the defendant has only a *limited duty* to the plaintiff because of plaintiff's knowledge of the risks (*e.g.,* being hit by a foul ball at a

baseball game), a court may protect the defendant simply by holding that the defendant did not breach his limited duty of care.

(2) More common is the situation that is a *variant of contributory negligence,* in that defendant's initial breach of duty to plaintiff is superseded by plaintiff's assumption of a risk (*e.g.,* builder is negligent in not barricading torn-up sidewalk, but pedestrian chooses to use it despite availability of reasonable alternate route). Here, the *reasonableness* of plaintiff's conduct is relevant: If the plaintiff has behaved unreasonably, plaintiff is contributorily negligent and damages will be apportioned under the state's comparative negligence statute.

b) Express Assumption of Risk
Most comparative negligence jurisdictions retain the defense of express assumption of risk.

3) Wanton and Willful Conduct
In most comparative negligence jurisdictions, plaintiff's negligence *will* be taken into account even though the defendant's conduct was "wanton and willful" or "reckless." However, plaintiff's negligence is still not a defense to intentional tortious conduct by the defendant.

IV. LIABILITY WITHOUT FAULT
(STRICT LIABILITY)

A. PRIMA FACIE CASE
To establish a prima facie case for strict liability, the following elements must be shown:

1. The existence of an *absolute duty* on the part of defendant to *make safe*;

2. *Breach* of that duty;

3. The breach of the duty was the *actual* and *proximate cause* of plaintiff's injury; and

4. *Damage* to the plaintiff's person or property.

B. LIABILITY FOR ANIMALS

1. Trespassing Animals
The owner is strictly liable for the damage done by the trespass of his animals (other than household pets) as long as it was *reasonably foreseeable*.

2. Personal Injuries

a. Wild (Dangerous) Animals—Strict Liability
The owner is strictly liable for injuries caused by wild animals (*e.g.,* lion, bear, or any other animal that can never be fully tamed), as long as the person injured did nothing, voluntarily or consciously, to bring about the injury.

b. Domestic (Nondangerous) Animals—Knowledge Required
The owner of a domestic or inherently nondangerous animal (*e.g.,* a dog or cat) is *not* strictly liable for injuries it causes. Such liability does, however, attach if the owner has knowledge of that particular animal's dangerous propensities (*i.e.,* propensities more dangerous than normal for that species). This rule applies even if the animal has never actually injured anyone. Some states have "dog bite" statutes, applicable only to dogs, which impose strict liability in personal injury actions even without prior knowledge of dangerous characteristics.

c. Persons Protected

1) Licensees and Invitees—Landowner Strictly Liable
Strict liability for injuries inflicted by wild animals or abnormally dangerous domestic animals kept by the landowner on his land will usually be imposed where the person injured came onto the land as an invitee or licensee.

a) **Public Duty Exception**
An exception is recognized where the landowner is under a *public duty to keep the animals* (*e.g.*, as a public zookeeper); in such cases, negligence must be shown.

2) **Trespassers Must Prove Negligence**
Strict liability in such cases generally is *not* imposed in favor of undiscovered trespassers against landowners. Trespassers cannot recover for injuries inflicted by the landowner's wild animals or abnormally dangerous domestic animals in the absence of *negligence*, *e.g.*, as where the landowner knows that trespassers are on the land and fails to warn them of the animal.

a) **Compare—Intentional Use of Vicious Watchdogs**
A landowner who protects his property from intruders by keeping a vicious watchdog that he knows is likely to cause *serious bodily harm* may be liable even to trespassers for injuries caused by the animal. This liability is based on intentional tort principles: Because the landowner is not entitled to use deadly force in person to protect only property, he also may not use such force indirectly. (*See* I.D.4.b., *supra*.)

C. ULTRAHAZARDOUS OR ABNORMALLY DANGEROUS ACTIVITIES

1. **Definition**
An activity may be characterized as ultrahazardous or abnormally dangerous if it involves a substantial risk of serious harm to person or property no matter how much care is exercised. Whether an activity is ultrahazardous is a question of law that the court can decide on a motion for directed verdict.

2. **Test**
The courts generally impose three requirements in finding an activity to be ultrahazardous:

(i) The activity must *involve a risk of serious harm* to persons or property;

(ii) The activity must be one that *cannot be performed without risk of serious harm* no matter how much care is taken; and

(iii) It must *not be a commonly engaged-in activity* by persons in the community.
Example: In *Rylands v. Fletcher*, 3 H.L. 330 (1868), the House of Lords held a mill owner strictly liable when a neighbor's mines were flooded by water escaping from the mill owner's reservoir. This was considered an abnormal use in "mining country." (Other examples of ultrahazardous activities include blasting, manufacturing explosives, crop dusting, and fumigating.)

The minority of courts that follow the approach of the Restatement (Second) also take into account the value of the activity and its appropriateness to the location.

3. **Products Liability**
There may be strict liability imposed for damage caused by products, depending on the theory used by a court in resolving such problems. (*See* V.D., *infra*.)

D. EXTENT OF LIABILITY

1. **Scope of Duty Owed**
As contrasted with negligence, the duty owed is an *absolute duty to make safe* the animal, activity, or condition that is classified as "ultrahazardous," and liability is imposed for any injuries to persons or property resulting therefrom.

a. **To Whom Is the Duty Owed?**
In most states, the duty is owed only to *"foreseeable plaintiffs"*—persons to whom a reasonable person would have foreseen a risk of harm under the circumstances. (Generally, strict liability is not imposed on a defendant's blasting that hurled rock onto a person so far away that no reasonable person would have foreseen a danger. Note, however, that some courts find liability for all blasting harm because of the intrinsic danger of defendant's activity.)

b. **Duty Limited to "Normally Dangerous Propensity"**
The harm must result from the kind of danger to be anticipated from the dangerous animal or ultrahazardous activity; *i.e.,* it must flow from the "normally dangerous propensity" of the condition or thing involved.

Example: D's toothless pet leopard escapes from its cage without fault on D's part and wanders into a park, causing P to break her arm while trying to flee. D is strictly liable to P.

Compare: D's dynamite truck blows a tire without warning and hits Pedestrian. D is not strictly liable to Pedestrian. However, if the truck then crashed and exploded, and the explosion injured Bystander, D would be strictly liable to Bystander.

2. **Proximate Cause**
The majority view is that the same rules of direct and indirect causation govern in strict liability as they do in negligence—defendant's liability can be cut off by unforeseeable intervening forces. In fact, the courts tend to hold more intervening forces "unforeseeable."

3. **Defenses**

a. **Contributory Negligence States**
In contributory negligence states, plaintiff's contributory negligence is **no** defense if the plaintiff simply failed to realize the danger or guard against its existence (unknowing contributory negligence). It **is** a defense, however, if plaintiff **knew** of the danger and his unreasonable conduct was the very cause of the ultrahazardous activity miscarrying. Courts call this conduct "knowing" contributory negligence or a type of assumption of risk. Furthermore, assumption of risk of any type is a good defense to strict liability in contributory negligence states.

Example: P knowingly and unreasonably tries to pass D's dynamite truck on a sharp curve, causing it to turn over and explode. Regardless of whether P's conduct is called contributory negligence or assumption of risk, P cannot recover.

b. **Comparative Negligence States**
Most comparative negligence states will now simply apply the same comparative negligence rules that they apply to negligence cases.

V. PRODUCTS LIABILITY

A. **BASIC PRINCIPLES**
In this context, "products liability" is the generic phrase used to describe the liability of a supplier of a product to one injured by the product.

1. **Theories of Liability**
Plaintiffs in products liability cases may have one of five possible theories of liability available to them:

(i) *Intent*;

(ii) *Negligence*;

(iii) *Strict liability*;

(iv) *Implied warranties of merchantability and fitness for a particular purpose*; and

(v) *Representation theories (express warranty and misrepresentation)*.

In an exam question, always consider a defendant's potential liability under each of the theories unless the call of the question indicates the theory that the plaintiff is using.

2. **Existence of a Defect**
To find liability under any products liability theory, plaintiff must show that the product was "defective" when the product left defendant's control.

a. **Types of Defects**

1) **Manufacturing Defects**
When a product emerges from a manufacturing process not only different from the other products, but also more dangerous than if it had been made the way it should have been, the product may be so "unreasonably dangerous" as to be defective because of the manufacturing process.

2) **Design Defects**
When all the products of a line are made identically according to manufacturing specifications, but have dangerous propensities because of their mechanical features or packaging, the entire line may be found to be defective because of poor design.

a) **Inadequate Warnings**
Inadequate warnings can be analyzed as a type of design defect. A product must have clear and complete warnings of any dangers that may not be apparent to users.

b. **What Is a "Defective Product"?**
In most jurisdictions, a product can be the basis for a products liability action if it is in a "defective condition unreasonably dangerous" to users.

1) **Manufacturing Defects**
For a manufacturing defect, the plaintiff will prevail if the product was *dangerous beyond the expectation of the ordinary consumer* because of a departure from its intended design.

a) **Defective Food Products**
Defects in food products are treated the same as manufacturing defects—the "consumer expectation" approach is used.

2) **Design Defects**
For design defects, the plaintiff usually must show a reasonable alternative design, *i.e.*, that a *less dangerous modification or alternative was economically feasible.*

The factors that the courts consider under the "feasible alternative" approach are the following:

(i)   Usefulness and desirability of the product;

(ii) Availability of safer alternative products;

(iii) The dangers of the product that have been identified by the time of trial;

(iv) Likelihood and probable seriousness of injury;

(v)   Obviousness of the danger;

(vi) Normal public expectation of danger (especially for established products);

(vii) Avoidability of injury by care in use of product (including role of instructions and warnings); and

(viii) Feasibility of eliminating the danger without seriously impairing the product's function or making it unduly expensive.

Examples: 1) Although people often cut themselves on sharp knives, knives are of great utility. Since there is no way to avoid the harm without destroying the utility of the product, and the danger is apparent to users, the product is not *unreasonably* dangerous and the supplier would not be liable for injuries.

2) A power lawn mower that is marketed with no guard over the opening from which cut grass is blown may be unreasonably dangerous even though the product carries several warnings that

hands and feet should be kept away from the opening and that rocks may be ejected from the opening. While the product's danger is within the expectations of the user, a court will **compare the harm caused** by the product with what it would *cost* to put a guard on the opening and consider whether the guard would impair the machine's operation in order to determine whether the product is "defective."

a) Effect of Government Safety Standards
A product is deemed to be defective in design or warnings if it fails to comply with applicable government safety standards. On the other hand, a product's *compliance* with applicable government safety standards is evidence—but not conclusive—that the product is *not* defective. [Restatement (Third) of Torts—Products Liability §4]

c. Common Defect Problems

1) Misuse
Some products may be safe if used as intended, but may involve serious dangers if used in other ways. Courts have required suppliers to **anticipate reasonably foreseeable uses** even if they are "misuses" of the product.

Examples: 1) Although a screwdriver is intended only for turning screws, a manufacturer must anticipate that screwdrivers are commonly used to pry up lids of tins and must make screwdrivers reasonably safe for that use as well as for their intended use.

2) Liquid furniture polish provided for home use may be fit for its intended use, but the manufacturer must anticipate that it will be used around small children who may play with the bottle and spill or drink its contents. Thus, the manufacturer may have to design a product that is either safe when drunk or that has a child-proof top. A simple warning of danger may not suffice in most states under the "feasible alternative" approach if a child-proof top would cost little to install.

2) Scientifically Unknowable Risks
Occasionally, totally unpredictable hazards of a product do not become apparent until after the product has been marketed. This situation arises most frequently with new drugs that yield unpredictable side effects. Even though these drugs might be dangerous beyond consumer expectations, courts have generally refused to find the drugs unreasonably dangerous where it was impossible to anticipate the problem and make the product safer or provide warnings.

3) Allergies
Some products affect different users differently—the problem of allergic reaction. If the allergic group is significant in number, the product is defective unless adequate warnings are conveyed. The modern trend requires such **warnings** whenever the manufacturer knows that there is a danger of allergic reaction, even though the number affected may be very small.

3. No Requirement of Contractual Privity Between Plaintiff and Defendant
Whether the parties to the suit are in privity with each other is generally irrelevant under current law except for some of the warranty theories of liability.

a. Defined
The parties are in privity when a contractual relationship exists between them, such as a *direct sale* by the defendant retailer to the plaintiff buyer or the buyer's agent.

b. Vertical Privity Absent
Privity does not exist where the injured plaintiff, usually the buyer, is in the direct distribution chain but is suing a remote party—the wholesaler or the manufacturer—rather than the retailer who sold the product to the plaintiff.

c. Horizontal Privity Absent
Privity is also absent where the defendant, usually the retailer, is in the direct distribution

chain with the buyer, but the plaintiff injured by the product is not the buyer, but rather the buyer's friend, neighbor, or a complete stranger.

B. LIABILITY BASED ON INTENT
A defendant will be liable to anyone injured by an unsafe product if the defendant intended the consequences or knew that they were substantially certain to occur. Liability based on an intentional tort is not very common in products liability cases.

1. Tort Involved
If the requisite intent on the part of the defendant is established, the intentional tort on which the cause of action most likely will be based is *battery*.

2. Privity Not Required
The presence or absence of privity is irrelevant where liability is based on an intentional tort.

3. Damages
In addition to compensatory damages, punitive damages are available in a products liability case based on intent, to the same extent as with intentional torts in general.

4. Defenses
The usual defenses available in intentional torts cases, such as consent, would be applicable. Negligence defenses, such as contributory negligence and assumption of risk, are not applicable.

C. LIABILITY BASED ON NEGLIGENCE

1. Prima Facie Case
To establish a prima facie case for negligence in a products liability case, the following elements must be proved:

    a.   The existence of a *legal duty* owed by the defendant to that particular plaintiff;

    b.   *Breach* of that duty;

    c.   *Actual* and *proximate cause*; and

    d.   *Damages*.

2. Defendant with Duty of Care to Plaintiff

a. Commercial Suppliers
In the usual case, the duty of due care arises when the defendant engages in the affirmative conduct associated with being a commercial supplier of products. "Suppliers" include: the manufacturer of a chattel or a component part thereof, assembler, wholesaler, retailer, or even a used car dealer who sells reconditioned or rebuilt cars. Those who repair a product owe a general duty of care, but are not usually "suppliers" for purposes of products liability cases.

1) Labeling Another's Product
A retailer who *labels* a product as the retailer's own or assembles a product from components manufactured by others is liable for the negligence of the actual manufacturer, even though the retailer is not personally negligent.

b. Privity Not Required
Since the case of *MacPherson v. Buick,* 217 N.Y. 382 (1916), and its extensions, absence of privity is *not* a defense. The duty of due care is owed to *any foreseeable plaintiff*—user, consumer, or bystander (such as a pedestrian injured when struck by an automobile with defective brakes).

3. Breach of Duty
To prove breach of duty, the plaintiff must show (i) *negligent conduct* by the defendant leading to (ii) the supplying of a *"defective product"* by the defendant.

a. Negligence
The defendant's conduct must fall below the standard of care expected of a reasonable

person under like circumstances, considering such superior skill or training as defendant has or purports to have.

1) Proof of Negligence in Manufacturing Defect Case

a) Liability of Manufacturer
To show negligence in a manufacturing defect case, the plaintiff may invoke *res ipsa loquitur* against the manufacturer if the error is usually something that does not occur without the negligence of the manufacturer.

b) Liability of Dealer
Retailers and wholesalers owe a duty of due care to their customers and foreseeable victims. But the majority view is that a dealer who buys from a reputable supplier or manufacturer with no reason to anticipate that the product is dangerous need make only a cursory inspection of the goods to avoid liability for manufacturing defects.

2) Proof of Negligence in Design Defect Case
To establish that a manufacturer's negligence has resulted in a design defect, the plaintiff must show that those designing the product *knew or should have known* of enough facts to put a reasonable manufacturer on notice about the dangers of marketing the product as designed. Negligence is *not* shown if the danger of the product becomes apparent to the reasonable manufacturer only after the product has reached the public.

b. Defective Product
The analysis of whether a product is so "unreasonably dangerous" as to be defective, discussed *supra,* applies equally to products liability actions based on negligence and to those based on strict tort liability.

4. Causation
The standard negligence analysis for both actual causation and proximate cause applies to products liability cases based on negligence.

a. Intermediary's Negligence
An intermediary's negligent failure to discover a defect is *not* a superseding cause, and the defendant whose original negligence created the defect will be held liable along with the intermediary. But when the intermediary's conduct becomes something more than ordinary foreseeable negligence, it becomes a superseding cause.

Example: P buys a defective product from Retailer who bought it from D. D would still be liable to P if Retailer had negligently failed to notice a serious defect attributable to D. But if Retailer had in fact discovered the defect but failed to warn P of it, D would not be liable.

5. Nature of Damages Recoverable
A plaintiff may recover for personal injury and property damages as under the usual negligence analysis. However, if the plaintiff suffers *only* economic loss (the product does not work as well as expected or requires repairs), most courts do not permit recovery under a negligence theory, requiring the plaintiff to bring an action for breach of warranty to recover such damages.

6. Defenses
The standard negligence defenses are applicable to any products liability case predicated on negligence. Thus, in comparative negligence states, plaintiff's contributory negligence may be used to reduce his recovery in an action against a negligent supplier of defective chattels.

D. LIABILITY BASED ON STRICT TORT LIABILITY
For those products liability cases where negligence on the part of the supplier would be difficult to prove, plaintiffs formerly attempted to bring their claims under traditional breach of warranty law as an alternative to using a negligence theory. Gradually, courts began to discard the privity requirement in warranty cases so that an increasing number of victims could recover without proof of negligence. This development has led to an openly announced strict liability in tort for products liability cases.

1. **Prima Facie Case**
   To establish a prima facie case in products liability based on strict liability in tort, the following elements must be proved:

   a. Strict duty owed by a *commercial supplier*;

   b. *Breach* of that duty;

   c. *Actual* and *proximate cause*; and

   d. *Damages*.

2. **Defendant Must Be "Commercial Supplier"**
   Plaintiff must prove that defendant is a *commercial* supplier of the product in question, as distinguished from a casual seller (*e.g.,* a homemaker who sells a jar of jam to a neighbor). Thus, strict liability applies when the defendant is a manufacturer (including the manufacturer of a defective component part), retailer, assembler, or wholesaler.

   Examples: 1) A theater may be held strictly liable for selling rotten candy. Even though the theater is not in the primary business of selling candy and similar products, it is a retail supplier of those products.

   2) If the boiler in use on a shoe manufacturer's land explodes, the shoe manufacturer's liability is *not* analyzed in terms of products liability because the manufacturer is not a commercial supplier of boilers.

   Most courts have expanded strict liability to include mass producers of new homes, commercial lessors, and sellers of used products that have been reconditioned or rebuilt.

   a. **Distinction Between Product and Service**
      Strict liability is imposed only on one who supplies a product, as opposed to one primarily performing a service. Restaurants are treated as suppliers of products, while most courts treat a transfusion of infected blood (*e.g.,* that gives the recipient hepatitis) as the rendition of a service.

      Example: If an airplane crashes due to defective piloting of the plane, a passenger must prove negligence in order to sue the airline company. However, if the passenger sues the manufacturer for a defect in the plane itself, strict liability in tort may be used.

3. **Product Not Substantially Altered**
   To hold the commercial supplier strictly liable for a product defect, the product must be expected to, and must in fact, reach the user or consumer without substantial change in the condition in which it is supplied.

4. **Privity Not Required**
   As with liability based on negligence, a majority of courts extend this strict duty *to any supplier in the chain of distribution* and extend the protection not only to buyers, but also to members of the buyer's family, guests, friends, and employees of the buyer, and foreseeable bystanders.

5. **Breach of Duty**
   To establish breach of duty for a strict liability action, the plaintiff need not prove that the defendant was at fault in selling or producing a defective product—only that the product in fact is so defective as to be "unreasonably dangerous" (*see* A.2.b., *supra*). As with products liability based on negligence, the two main categories of defects are manufacturing defects and design defects. The only difference in analysis is that the element of *negligence need not be proved* in a strict liability case. Thus, in contrast to a negligence action, a retailer in a strict liability action may be liable for a manufacturing or design defect simply because it was a commercial supplier of a defective product—*even if it had no opportunity to inspect the manufacturer's product before selling it*.

6. **Causation**

   a. **Actual Cause**
      To prove actual cause, the plaintiff must trace the harm suffered to a defect in the product that existed when the product left the defendant's control. If the plaintiff claims that one of the defective conditions was the lack of an adequate warning, plaintiff is entitled to a presumption that an adequate warning would have been read and heeded.

b. Proximate Cause

The same concepts of proximate cause governing general negligence and strict liability actions are applicable to strict liability actions for defective products. As with products liability cases based on negligence, the negligent failure of an intermediary to discover the defect does not void the supplier's strict liability.

7. Nature of Damages Recoverable

The types of damages recoverable in strict liability actions for defective products are the same as those recoverable in negligence actions, namely personal injury and property damages. Once again, most states *deny* recovery under strict liability when the sole claim is for *economic loss*.

8. Defenses

a. Contributory Negligence States

According to Restatement (Second) section 402A, ordinary contributory negligence is not a defense in a strict products liability action where the plaintiff merely *failed to discover the defect or guard against its existence*, or where plaintiff's misuse was reasonably foreseeable (*supra*, A.2.c.1)). On the other hand, other types of unreasonable conduct, such as voluntarily and unreasonably encountering a known risk (*i.e.,* assumption of risk), are defenses.

b. Comparative Negligence States

As with other strict liability actions, most comparative negligence states apply their comparative negligence rules to strict products liability actions. [*See* Restatement (Third) of Torts—Products Liability §17]

c. Disclaimers of Liability Ineffective

Disclaimers of liability are *irrelevant* in negligence or strict liability cases if personal injury or property damage has occurred.

E. IMPLIED WARRANTIES OF MERCHANTABILITY AND FITNESS

1. Proof of Fault Unnecessary

If a product fails to live up to the standards imposed by an implied warranty, the warranty is breached and the defendant will be liable. Plaintiff need not prove any fault on defendant's part.

2. Scope of Coverage

Although the Uniform Commercial Code ("U.C.C.") provisions apply only to the *sale of goods*, the modern trend is to apply implied warranties to *bailment* and *lease* cases by analogizing to the sales provisions.

3. Implied Warranty of Merchantability

When a merchant who deals in a certain kind of goods sells such goods, there is an implied warranty that they are *merchantable*. [U.C.C. §2-314] "Merchantable" means that the goods are of a quality equal to that *generally acceptable* among those who deal in similar goods and are *generally fit for the ordinary purposes* for which such goods are used.

4. Implied Warranty of Fitness for Particular Purpose

An implied warranty of fitness for a particular purpose arises when the seller knows or has reason to know:

(i) The particular purpose for which the goods are required; *and*

(ii) That the buyer is relying on the seller's skill or judgment to select or furnish suitable goods.

[U.C.C. §2-315] Usually the seller will be a merchant of the type of goods in question, but this is not essential.

5. Privity

a. Vertical Privity No Longer Required

Although in the early period of warranty law, courts held strictly to the requirement of complete privity between the plaintiff and defendant, a trend developed with courts finding the needed privity between remote parties on various fictions and theories—*e.g.,* the warranty ran with the goods, or the retailer was the manufacturer's agent. As a result, most courts no longer require vertical privity between the buyer and the manufacturer in implied warranty actions.

b.   U.C.C. Alternatives on Horizontal Privity
Although U.C.C. section 2-318 is silent on the issue of vertical privity, it offers the states three alternative versions on the issue of horizontal privity: Alternative A extends implied warranty protection to a *buyer's family*, *household*, *and guests* who suffer personal injury; Alternative B extends protection to any natural person who suffers personal injury; and Alternative C covers any person who suffers any injury. *Most states have adopted Alternative A*, the narrowest modification of the privity requirement.

6.   Effect of Disclaimers
Disclaimers of liability for breach of implied warranty *must be specific* and are narrowly construed. [U.C.C. §2-316] Contractual limitations on *personal injury* damages resulting from a breach of warranty for consumer goods are prima facie *unconscionable*. [U.C.C. §2-719]

7.   Causation
Issues of actual cause and proximate cause are treated as in an ordinary negligence case.

8.   Damages
In addition to personal injury and property damages, purely *economic losses* are recoverable in implied warranty actions.

9.   Defenses

a.   Assumption of Risk
U.C.C. section 2-715 indicates that when the plaintiff assumes the risk by using a product while knowing of the breach of warranty, any resulting injuries are not proximately caused by the breach.

b.   Contributory Negligence
Courts in contributory negligence jurisdictions have adopted an approach similar to that used in strict liability in tort—that unreasonable failure to discover the defect does not bar recovery but that unreasonable conduct *after* discovery does bar recovery.

c.   Comparative Negligence
So also, courts in comparative negligence jurisdictions use comparative fault notions in warranty cases to reduce the damage award in the same way as in strict liability cases.

d.   Notice of Breach
U.C.C. section 2-607 requires the buyer to give the seller notice *within a reasonable time* after the buyer discovers or should have discovered the breach. Most courts have held that the requirement applies even in personal injury cases and where there is no privity between the parties.

F.   REPRESENTATION THEORIES (EXPRESS WARRANTY AND MISREPRESENTATION OF FACT)
The two theories discussed in this section differ from those previously discussed because they involve some affirmative representation by the defendant beyond the act of distributing a product. When the product does not live up to the representation, both contract and tort problems are created.

1.   Express Warranty
An express warranty arises where a seller or supplier makes any affirmation of fact or promise to the buyer relating to the goods that becomes part of the "basis of the bargain." [U.C.C. §2-313]

a.   Scope of Coverage
As with implied warranties, the trend is to extend express warranties to bailments and other nonsales transactions by analogy.

b.   Privity Not Required
Although U.C.C. section 2-318 declares that its privity alternatives apply to express as

well as implied warranties, most courts have held privity to be irrelevant in express warranty cases.

c. **"Basis of the Bargain"**
If the buyer is suing, the warranty must have been "part of the basis of the bargain." This is probably less difficult to show than a buyer's subjective "reliance" on the representation. If someone not in privity is permitted to sue, this remote person need *not* have known about the affirmation as long as it became part of the basis of the bargain for someone else in the chain of distribution.

d. **Basis of Liability—Breach of Warranty**
As with implied warranties, the plaintiff need *not* show that the breach occurred through the fault of the defendant, but only that a breach of the warranty did in fact occur.

Example: The defendant advertises its hand lotion as "completely safe" and "harmless." Even if there is nothing wrong with the product itself, a buyer who suffers an allergic reaction may bring a successful warranty action.

e. **Effect of Disclaimers**
U.C.C. section 2-316 provides that a disclaimer will be effective only to the extent that it can be read consistently with any express warranties made. This has the effect of making it practically impossible to disclaim an express warranty.

f. **Causation, Damages, and Defenses**
These elements are analyzed the same as under implied warranties, *supra*.

2. **Misrepresentation of Fact**
Liability for misrepresentation may arise when a representation by the seller about a product induces reliance by the buyer. In products cases, liability for misrepresentation is usually based on strict liability, but may also arise for intentional and negligent misrepresentations.

a. **Defendant's State of Mind**

1) **Strict Liability**
As long as the defendant is a seller engaged in the business of selling such products, there is no need to show fault on the defendant's part. The plaintiff need only show that the representation proved false, without regard to the defendant's state of mind.

2) **Intentional Misrepresentation**
For intentional misrepresentations, the plaintiff must show that the misrepresentation was made *knowingly* or with *reckless* disregard for the facts.

3) **Negligent Misrepresentation**
For negligence liability, knowledge of the misrepresentation on the part of the defendant need not be proved. The plaintiff need only show that a reasonable person should have known such representations to be false when making them.

b. **Material Fact Required**
The misrepresentation must be of a material fact, *i.e.,* a fact concerning the quality, nature, or appropriate use of the product on which a normal buyer may be expected to rely. "Puffing" and statements of opinion are not sufficient.

c. **Intent to Induce Reliance of Particular Buyer**
The defendant must have intended to induce the reliance of the buyer, or a class of persons to which the buyer belongs, in a particular transaction. Evidence of a representation made to the public by label, advertisement, or otherwise is sufficient to show an intent to induce reliance by anyone into whose hands the product may come.

d. **Justifiable Reliance**
There is no liability if the misrepresentation is not known or does not influence the transaction. Reliance may be found if the representation was a *substantial factor* in inducing the purchase, even though not the sole inducement.

1) Reliance Need Not Be Victim's

As with express warranties, *privity is irrelevant* for misrepresentation and the required reliance may be shown to be that of a prior purchaser who passed the product on to the victim.

Example: D, a manufacturer of automobiles, advertises that its cars contain "shatterproof" glass. H reads this advertisement and, partly in reliance on it, buys one of D's cars. While H's friend, F, is driving the car, a stone is thrown through the windshield, shattering the glass. F, hurt by flying glass, has a strict liability action against D for misrepresentation even though F is not in privity with D and knows nothing of the "shatterproof" representation.

e. Actual Cause

Reliance by the purchaser serves to show actual cause.

f. Proximate Cause and Damages

Both elements are analyzed in the same manner as for products liability cases based on negligence or strict liability, *supra*. If the plaintiff can show that the misrepresentation was intentional, some courts will allow punitive damages to be claimed.

g. Defenses

1) Assumption of Risk

If the plaintiff is entitled to rely on the representation, a defense of assumption of risk does not apply.

Example: D markets a mace pen to be used against attackers. The product's label says that it instantly renders attackers helpless when sprayed in their faces. When holdup men demanded money from P, P shot his mace pen in their faces but it had no effect—except that the attackers got angry and shot P. D's claim that P assumed the risk of injury by not complying with the attacker's demands fails, since P reasonably relied on the product to achieve its stated results.

2) Contributory Negligence (Fault)

Whether contributory negligence is a defense depends on the type of misrepresentation. For negligent misrepresentations, contributory negligence is a valid defense. In strict liability actions, the plaintiff's unreasonable behavior is analyzed as in other strict liability actions for defective products, *supra*. If the plaintiff can show that the defendant's misrepresentation was intentional, contributory negligence would be no defense.

VI. NUISANCE

A. BASIS OF LIABILITY

Nuisance is *not* a separate tort in itself, subject to rules of its own. Nuisances are types of harm—the invasion of either private property rights or public rights by conduct that is tortious because it falls into the usual categories of tort liability. In other words, the defendant's conduct may have been intentional or negligent or subjected to liability on a strict liability basis. As a practical matter, nuisances generally are *intentional* interferences because defendant has been made aware that his conduct is interfering with plaintiff's use of her land. (If strict liability is the basis for redressing a nuisance, courts sometimes refer to this as an "absolute" nuisance or "nuisance per se.")

B. PRIVATE NUISANCE

Private nuisance is a *substantial, unreasonable interference* with another private individual's *use or enjoyment* of property he actually possesses or to which he has a right of immediate possession.

1. Substantial Interference

The interference with plaintiff's right in his land must be substantial. This means that it must be *offensive, inconvenient, or annoying to an average person in the community*. It will not be characterized as substantial if it is merely the result of plaintiff's hypersensitivity or specialized use of his own property.

2. **Unreasonable Interference**

For a nuisance based on intent or negligence, the interference with plaintiff's use of his land must be unreasonable. To be characterized as unreasonable, the severity of the inflicted *injury must outweigh the utility* of defendant's conduct. In balancing these respective interests, courts take into account that every person is entitled to use his own land in a reasonable way, considering the neighborhood, land values, and existence of any alternative courses of conduct open to defendant.

3. **Trespass to Land Distinguished**

Trespass to land is to be distinguished from private nuisance. In the former, there is an interference with the landowner's *exclusive possession* by a physical invasion of the land; in the latter, there is an interference with *use or enjoyment*.

C. PUBLIC NUISANCE

Public nuisance is an act that unreasonably interferes with the *health, safety, or property rights of the community*, *e.g.*, blocking a highway or using a building to commit criminal activities such as prostitution, bookmaking, etc. Recovery is available for public nuisance only if a private party has suffered some unique damage not suffered by the public at large.

Example: Pedestrians generally are inconvenienced by having to walk around an obstruction maintained by defendant on the sidewalk. Plaintiff, however, has tripped and fallen. This unique damage permits plaintiff to recover for the public nuisance.

D. REMEDIES

1. **Damages**

For a private nuisance, or for a public nuisance where plaintiff has suffered some unique damage, the usual remedy is damages.

2. **Injunctive Relief**

Where the *legal remedy* of damages is *unavailable or inadequate*, injunctive relief may be granted. The legal remedy may be inadequate for a variety of reasons, *e.g.*, the nuisance is a continuing wrong, the nuisance is of the kind that will cause irreparable injury, etc. In deciding whether an injunction should issue, the courts take into consideration the relative hardships that will result to the parties from the grant or denial of the injunction. Hardships will not be balanced, however, where defendant's conduct was either willful or against an assertion of right by plaintiff.

3. **Abatement by Self-Help**

   a. **Abatement of Private Nuisance**

   One has the privilege to enter upon defendant's land and personally abate the nuisance after notice to defendant and defendant's refusal to act. The force used may be only that necessary to accomplish the abatement, and the plaintiff is liable for additional harm done.

   b. **Abatement of Public Nuisance**

   One who has suffered some unique damage has a similar privilege to abate a public nuisance by self-help. In the absence of such unique damage, however, a public nuisance may be abated or enjoined only by public authority.

E. DEFENSES

1. **Legislative Authority**

Conduct consistent with what a zoning ordinance or other legislative license permits is highly persuasive, but not necessarily conclusive proof that the use is not a nuisance.

2. **Conduct of Others**

No one actor is liable for all the damage caused by the concurrence of his acts and others.

   Example: Ten steel mills are polluting a stream. Each steel mill is responsible only for the pollution it causes.

3. **Contributory Negligence**

Contributory negligence is not ordinarily a defense to the tort of nuisance. However, when a nuisance is based on a negligence theory, one may not avert the consequences of his own contributory negligence by affixing to the negligence of the wrongdoer the label of a nuisance. In such a case, a plaintiff, though pleading nuisance, may have to show his freedom from contributory negligence.

4. "Coming to the Nuisance"

The problem: Has plaintiff assumed the risk, thereby being barred from recovery by the fact that he has "come to the nuisance," by purchasing land and moving in next to the nuisance after it is already in existence or operation? The prevailing rule is that, in the absence of a prescriptive right, the defendant may not condemn surrounding premises to endure the nuisance; *i.e.,* the *purchaser is entitled to reasonable use or enjoyment of his land* to the same extent as any other owner as long as he buys in good faith and not for the sole purpose of a harassing lawsuit.

VII. GENERAL CONSIDERATIONS FOR ALL TORT CASES

A. VICARIOUS LIABILITY

Vicarious liability is liability that is derivatively imposed. In short, this means that one person commits a tortious act against a third party, and another person is liable to the third party for this act. This may be so even though the other person has played no part in it, has done nothing whatever to aid or encourage it, or indeed has done everything possible to prevent it. This liability rests upon a special relationship between the tortfeasor and the person to whom his tortious conduct is ultimately imputed.

The basic situations that you should note for bar examination purposes are set out below.

1. Doctrine of Respondeat Superior

A master/employer will be vicariously liable for tortious acts committed by her servant/employee if the tortious acts occur *within the scope of the employment relationship*.

a. Frolic and Detour

An employee on a delivery or on a business trip for his employer may commit a tort while deviating from the employer's business to run a personal errand. If the deviation was minor in time and geographic area, the employee will still be considered to be acting within the scope of employment rather than on a "frolic" of his own (for which the employer would not be liable).

b. Intentional Torts

It is usually held that intentional tortious conduct by servants is *not* within the scope of employment. In some circumstances, however, courts find intentional tortious conduct to be within the ambit of this relationship. Essentially, this finding exists where:

1) Force is authorized in the employment, *e.g.,* bouncer.

2) Friction is generated by employment, *e.g.,* bill collector.

3) Servant is furthering business of master, *e.g.,* removing customers from premises because rowdy.

2. Independent Contractor Situations

In general, a principal will *not* be liable for tortious acts of her agent if the latter is an independent contractor. Two broad *exceptions* exist, however:

(i) The independent contractor is engaged in *inherently dangerous activities*, *e.g.,* blasting.

(ii) The duty, because of *public policy* considerations, is simply nondelegable, *e.g.,* the duty of a business to keep its premises safe for customers; the duty of a motorist to keep his car in safe working order.

a. Liability for Negligent Selection

Both in respondeat superior and independent contractor cases, the employer may be liable for her *own negligence* in selecting the servant or independent contractor (*e.g.,* hospital liable for contracting with physician who negligently treats hospital's patient). (This is **not** vicarious liability.)

3. **Partners and Joint Venturers**

Each member of a partnership or joint venture is vicariously liable for the tortious conduct of another member committed in the scope and course of the affairs of the partnership or joint venture.

   a. **What Is a Joint Venture?**

   A joint venture, although similar to a partnership, is for a more limited time period and more limited purpose. It is generally an undertaking to execute a small number of acts or objectives. A joint venture exists when two or more people enter into an activity if two elements are present:

   1) **Common Purpose**

   The test is not precise, but it would appear that the majority of courts would now look for a "business purpose." The sharing of expenses between individuals is often highly persuasive.

   Examples: 1) Two roommates were driving to a store to get decorating materials for their apartment when an accident occurred. *Held:* Joint venture.

   2) Two parents were driving child to hospital. *Held:* No joint venture.

   2) **Mutual Right of Control**

   It is not crucial that the party does or does not give directions; it is sufficient if there is an understanding between the parties that each has a right to have her desires respected on the same basis as the others.

4. **Automobile Owner for Driver**

The general rule is that an automobile owner is **not vicariously liable** for the tortious conduct of another driving his automobile. However, many states by statute or judicial precedent have adopted the "*family car*" doctrine, by which the owner is liable for tortious conduct of **immediate family or household members** who are driving with the owner's express or implied permission. A number of states have now gone further by enacting "*permissive use*" statutes imposing liability for damage caused by **anyone** driving with such consent.

   a. **Liability for Owner's Negligence**

   Remember that the owner may be liable for her **own negligence** in entrusting the car to a driver. Some states have also imposed liability upon the owner if she was present in the car at the time of the accident, upon the theory that she could have prevented the negligent driving, and hence was negligent herself in not doing so. (This is not vicarious liability.)

5. **Bailor for Bailee**

Under the general rule, the bailor is **not vicariously liable** for the tortious conduct of his bailee. As above, the bailor may be liable for her **own negligence** in entrusting the bailed object. (This is not vicarious liability.)

6. **Parent for Child**

A parent is **not vicariously liable** for the tortious conduct of the child at common law. Note, however, that most states, by statute, make parents liable for the willful and intentional torts of their minor children up to a certain dollar amount (*e.g.,* $5,000).

   a. **Child Acting as Agent for Parents**

   Courts may impose vicarious liability if the child commits a tort while acting as the agent for the parents.

   Example: Parent vicariously liable if child is in an accident while running an errand for his mother, or driving his sister to school, but not while on a date.

   b. **Parent Liable for Own Negligence**

   The parent may be held liable for her **own negligence** in allowing the child to do something, *e.g.,* use a dangerous object without proper instruction. Further, if the parent is apprised of the child's conduct on past occasions showing a tendency to injure another's person or property, she may be liable for not using due care in exercising control to mitigate such conduct, *e.g.,* by allowing the child to play with other children he has a history of attacking.

7. Tavernkeepers

At common law, no liability was imposed on vendors of intoxicating beverages for injuries resulting from the vendee's intoxication, whether the injuries were sustained by the vendee or by a third person as a result of the vendee's conduct. Many states, to avoid this common law rule, have enacted *"Dramshop Acts."* Such acts usually create a *cause of action in favor of any third person injured* by the intoxicated vendee. Several courts have imposed liability on tavernkeepers even in the absence of a Dramshop Act. This liability is based on ordinary negligence principles (the foreseeable risk of serving a minor or obviously intoxicated adult) rather than vicarious liability.

B. PARTIES—MULTIPLE DEFENDANT ISSUES

1. Joint and Several Liability

When two or more tortious acts combine to proximately cause an *indivisible* injury to a plaintiff, each tortfeasor is jointly and severally liable for that injury. This means that *each is liable* to the plaintiff for the *entire damage* incurred. Joint and several liability applies even though each tortfeasor acted entirely independently. However, if the actions are independent, plaintiff's injury is divisible, and it is possible to identify the portion of injuries caused by each defendant (*e.g.,* Car 1 breaks plaintiff's leg, and Car 2 breaks plaintiff's arm), then each will only be liable for the identifiable portion.

a. Tortfeasors Acting in Concert

When two or more tortfeasors act in concert (*i.e.,* by agreement) and injure plaintiff, then each will be jointly and severally liable for the entire injury. This is so even though the injury is divisible and one could identify what each tortfeasor has done alone.

b. Statutory Limitations

Many states have limited the joint liability doctrine by statute. Two of the most common types of statutes abolish joint liability either (i) for those tortfeasors judged to be less at fault than the plaintiff, or (ii) for all tortfeasors with regard to noneconomic damages (*e.g.,* pain and suffering). The liability of a tortfeasor in these situations is proportional to his fault.

2. Satisfaction and Release

a. Satisfaction

If plaintiff recovers full payment from one tortfeasor, either by settlement or payment of a judgment, there is a "satisfaction." She may not recover further against any other joint tortfeasor. Until there is a satisfaction, however, she may proceed against other jointly liable parties.

b. Release

A release is a surrender of plaintiff's cause of action against the party to whom the release is given. Such a release to one of two tortfeasors at common law necessarily released the other. A majority of the states have now rejected the common law rule and provide that a release of one tortfeasor does *not* discharge other tortfeasors unless expressly provided in the release agreement. Rather, the claim against the others is reduced to the extent of the amount stipulated in the agreement or the amount of consideration paid, whichever is greater.

3. Contribution and Indemnity

a. Contribution

As stated above, where joint and several tort liability exists, it permits plaintiff to recover the entire judgment amount from any tortfeasor. The rule of contribution, adopted in some form in most states, allows any tortfeasor required to pay more than his share of damages to have a claim against the other jointly liable parties for the excess. Thus, contribution is a device whereby responsibility is *apportioned* among those who are at fault.

1) **Methods of Apportionment**

    a) **Comparative Contribution**
        Most states have a comparative contribution system (discussed below), whereby contribution is imposed *in proportion to the relative fault* of the various tortfeasors.

    b) **Equal Shares**
        A minority of states require all tortfeasors to pay *equal shares* regardless of their respective degrees of fault.

2) **Contribution Tortfeasor Must Have Liability**
The tortfeasor from whom contribution is sought must be originally liable to the plaintiff. If the contribution tortfeasor has a defense that would bar liability, such as intra-family tort immunity, he is not liable for contribution.

3) **Not Applicable to Intentional Torts**
Contribution is not allowed in favor of those who committed intentional torts. This is so even though each of the tortfeasors was equally culpable.

b. **Indemnity**
Indemnity involves *shifting the entire loss* between or among tortfeasors, in contrast to apportioning it as in contribution. Indemnity is available in the following circumstances:

1) **Right to Indemnity by Contract**
Contracts in which one person promises to indemnify another against consequences of his own negligence are generally upheld. The right to indemnification will not be read into an agreement unless there is evidence that the right was clearly intended.

2) **Vicarious Liability**
When one is held for damages caused by another simply because of his relationship to that person (*e.g.,* master for servant's torts, landowner with nondelegable duty breached by an independent contractor, etc.), this party may seek indemnification from the person whose conduct actually caused the damage.

3) **Indemnity Under Strict Products Liability**
Each supplier of a defective product, where strict liability rules apply, is liable to an injured customer, but each supplier has a right of indemnification against all previous suppliers in the distribution chain. The manufacturer is ultimately liable if the product was defective when it left its hands.

4) **Identifiable Difference in Degree of Fault**
A number of jurisdictions extend the principle of indemnity to allow one joint tortfeasor to recover against a co-joint tortfeasor where there is a considerable difference in degree of fault. In other words, he who is least at fault may be able to recover indemnification from the "more wrongful" tortfeasor.

    a) **Examples**
        The most common examples of such indemnification are:

        (1) **Retailers Who Negligently Rely on Product's Condition**
            Retailers who negligently fail to discover a product's defect may receive indemnification from the manufacturer who negligently manufactured it.

        (2) **Where Liability Imposed Under Secondary Duty**
            One whose liability is based on a secondary duty may recover indemnification from the person who had a primary duty.
            Example: Municipal corporation under duty to keep streets safe may recover from a person who creates the unsafe condition causing an accident.

        (3) **Active/Passive Negligence Doctrine**
            Some jurisdictions allow a joint tortfeasor who is passively negligent to

recover indemnification from a joint tortfeasor who is actively negligent.

Example: Charles parked his car in a no-parking zone, blocking the view of drivers approaching the intersection. Bowater, driving at 70 m.p.h., hits a pedestrian who could not be seen until it was too late to stop. If the pedestrian sues Charles and recovers, Charles may seek full reimbursement from Bowater by way of indemnification.

b) Effect of Comparative Negligence System

Most states with comparative negligence systems *reject* indemnity in degree of fault situations, instead applying a general comparative contribution system and apportioning damages based upon relative fault (*see* discussion below). These states continue to permit indemnity where indemnity rules are not based on differences in degree of fault, *e.g.,* vicarious liability cases.

c. Comparative Contribution

A *majority* of states have now adopted a comparative contribution system based on the *relative fault* of the various tortfeasors. Comparative contribution changes the traditional method of apportionment in contribution cases (*supra*) and supplants indemnification rules based on identifiable differences in degree of fault. In both situations, nonpaying tortfeasors are required to contribute only in proportion to their relative fault.

C. SURVIVAL AND WRONGFUL DEATH

1. Survival of Tort Actions

At common law, a tort action abated at the death of either the tortfeasor or the victim. Most states have changed this by statute, *i.e.,* the "survival acts." Thus, a victim's cause of action will survive to permit recovery of all damages from the time of injury to the time of death. In the majority of states, these acts apply to both torts to *property* and torts resulting in *personal injury*.

a. Torts that Expire on Victim's Death

Exceptions exist in most jurisdictions for those torts that invade an *intangible personal interest,* e.g., defamation, malicious prosecution, etc. These torts are felt to be so personal as to expire upon the victim's death.

2. Wrongful Death

Every state has now enacted some form of wrongful death act.

a. Who May Bring Action?

In some jurisdictions, the personal representative is the proper party to bring the action; in others, the surviving spouse or next of kin herself might be the proper party.

b. Measure of Recovery

The measure of recovery in wrongful death actions under most statutes is for the pecuniary injury resulting to the spouse and next of kin. Basically, this allows recovery for loss of support, loss of consortium, etc. It does *not* allow any recovery for decedent's pain and suffering; those damages would be an element of a personal injury survival action (*see* above) brought on behalf of the decedent.

1) Deaths of Children, Elderly People

Even though the actual loss of support may be very small where decedent is a child or elderly person, most states, nonetheless, allow recovery. Usually, the judgment is quite modest.

2) Rights of Creditors

Creditors of the decedent have no claim against the amount awarded.

c. Effect of Defenses

1) Defenses Against Deceased

Recovery is allowed *only* to the extent that the deceased could have recovered in the action if he had lived. Thus, for example, his contributory negligence would reduce a wrongful death recovery in comparative negligence states.

2) Defenses Against Beneficiary
Defenses against potential beneficiaries do not bar the action. However, that particular beneficiary recovers nothing and his damages are not to be included by the jury in the total damages assessed.

D. TORTIOUS INTERFERENCES WITH FAMILY RELATIONSHIPS

1. Husband-Wife
In most jurisdictions, both husbands and wives may recover damages for loss of their spouse's consortium or services because of injuries to the spouse from defendant's tortious conduct, whether intentional, negligent, or based on strict liability.
Example: Chauncey hits Husband on the head with a lead pipe, leaving him in a coma for several months and permanently disabled. Wife can recover from Chauncey for loss of consortium and services.

2. Parent-Child

a. Parent's Actions
A parent may maintain an action for loss of the child's services when the child is injured as a result of defendant's tortious conduct, whether such conduct is intentional, negligent, or based on strict liability.

b. Child's Action
A child has *no* action in most jurisdictions against one who tortiously injures his parent.

3. Nature of Action for Family Relationship Interference
The action for interference with family relationships is *derivative.* Recovery in the derivative action depends on the potential success of the injured family member's own action. Thus, any defense that would prevent recovery by the injured family member, *e.g.,* her own contributory negligence, will also prevent recovery in the derivative action for interference with family relationships.

Further, a defense against a family member seeking such a derivative recovery may also defeat the action.
Example: Husband and Wife, while driving, collide with Chauncey's car. Wife is severely injured; Husband and Chauncey are both negligent. Husband's derivative action for loss of Wife's consortium and services will be defeated by his own contributory negligence.

E. TORT IMMUNITIES

1. Intra-Family Tort Immunities

a. Injury to Person
Under the traditional view, one member of a family unit (*i.e.,* husband, wife, or unemancipated child) could *not* sue another in tort for personal injury. This view has undergone substantial change in most states.

1) Husband-Wife Immunity Abolished
Most states have abolished interspousal immunity. Either spouse may now maintain a tort action against the other.

2) Parent-Child Immunity Limited
A slight majority of states have abolished parent-child immunity; however, these states generally grant parents broad discretion in the parent's exercise of parental authority or supervision. The remaining states retain parent-child immunity but do not apply it in cases of *intentional* tortious conduct and, in many of these states, in *automobile accident* cases (at least to the extent of insurance coverage).

b. Injury to Property
A suit for property damage may usually be maintained by any family member against any other family member. In short, to the extent that intra-family tort immunity exists, it applies to personal, not property, injuries.

2. **Governmental Tort Immunity**

Under the doctrine of sovereign immunity, governmental units were traditionally not subject to tort actions unless they had consented to the suit. Now, by statute and judicial decision, that immunity is considerably limited. Note, however, that a waiver of sovereign immunity does not create any new tort duties; it only waives immunity for existing statutory or common law duties of care.

a. **Federal Government**

By virtue of the Federal Tort Claims Act, Title 28 U.S.C., the United States has *waived immunity* for tortious acts. Under its provisions, the federal government may now be held liable to the same extent as a private individual. However, the Act spells out several situations where this immunity will still attach:

1) **United States Still Immune for Certain Enumerated Torts**

Immunity still attaches for (i) assault, (ii) battery, (iii) false imprisonment, (iv) false arrest, (v) malicious prosecution, (vi) abuse of process, (vii) libel and slander, (viii) misrepresentation and deceit, and (ix) interference with contract rights.

2) **Discretionary Acts Distinguished from Ministerial Acts**

The immunity is not waived for acts characterized as "discretionary," as distinguished from those acts termed "ministerial." In general, discretionary activity is that which takes place at the *planning or decisionmaking level*, while ministerial acts are performed at the *operational level* of government (*e.g.*, repairing traffic signals, driving a vehicle).

3) **Government Contractors**

A government contractor may assert the federal government's immunity defense in a products liability case if the contractor conformed to reasonable, precise specifications approved by the government and warned the government about any known dangers in the product.

b. **State Governments**

Most states have substantially waived their immunity from tort actions to the same extent as the federal government. Thus, immunity still attaches for discretionary acts and for legislative and judicial decisionmaking.

Note: Where federal or state sovereign immunity still attaches, it also, as a general rule, covers not only "the government" but the various federal and state agencies as well, *e.g.*, schools, hospitals, etc.

c. **Municipalities**

About half of the states have abolished municipal tort immunity by statute or judicial decision to the same extent that they have waived their own immunity. Hence, immunity is abolished for everything but discretionary acts and policy decisions.

1) **Immunity Abolished—Public Duty Rule Limitation**

Where municipal immunity has been abolished, many courts apply the "public duty" doctrine to limit the scope of government liability. A duty that is owed to the public at large, such as the duty of police to protect citizens, is not owed to any particular citizen, and no liability exists for failure to provide police protection in the absence of a *special relationship* between the municipality and the citizen that gives rise to a special duty. A special relationship can be shown by: (i) an assumption by the municipality, through promises or actions, of an affirmative duty to act on behalf of the party who was injured; (ii) knowledge on the part of the municipality's agents that inaction could lead to harm; (iii) some form of direct contact between the municipality's agents and the injured party; and (iv) that party's justifiable reliance on the municipality's affirmative undertaking.

2) **Immunity Retained—Limited to Governmental Functions**

Where municipal immunity still exists in its traditional form, the courts have sought in many instances to avoid its consequences. This has primarily been accomplished by differentiating between "governmental" and "proprietary" functions of the municipality. Immunity attaches to the former but not to the latter.

a) **Governmental Functions**

Certain functions historically have been construed such that they could only be performed adequately by the government, and thus they are held to be "governmental" in character, *e.g.,* police, fire, courts, etc. As stated above, ***tort immunity attaches*** to those functions.

b) Proprietary Functions
If the municipality is performing a function that might as well have been provided by a private corporation, the function is construed as a "proprietary" one (*e.g.,* utility companies, maintaining airport parking lot, etc.). ***No tort immunity*** attaches here.

The inference that a function is "proprietary" is strengthened where the city collects ***revenues*** by virtue of providing the service.

d. Immunity of Public Officials
In addition to the immunity conferred on the government entity, government officials may also have immunity from tort liability. Immunity applies to a public officer carrying out his official duties where they involve ***discretionary*** acts (*supra*) done without malice or improper purpose. On the other hand, for acts that are construed as ***ministerial*** (which generally involve lower-level officials), no tort immunity applies.

3. Charitable Immunity
The majority of jurisdictions have abrogated the common law rule of charitable immunity either by statute or decision. Even where such immunity still exists, it is riddled with exceptions.